Financial Aid
for Native Americans
2009-2011

RSP FINANCIAL AID DIRECTORIES OF INTEREST TO MINORITIES

College Student's Guide to Merit and Other No-Need Funding, 2008-2010
Selected as one of the "Outstanding Titles of the Year" by *Choice,* this directory describes 1,300 no-need funding opportunities for college students. 498 pages. ISBN 1-58841-166-4. $32.50, plus $7 shipping.

Directory of Financial Aids for Women, 2009-2011
Nearly 1,500 funding programs set aside for women are described in this biennial directory, which has been called "the cream of the crop" by *School Library Journal* and the "best available reference source" by *Guide to Reference.* 574 pages. ISBN 1-58841-194-X. $45, plus $7 shipping.

Financial Aid for African Americans, 2009-2011
More than 1,250 scholarships, fellowships, grants, and internships open to African Americans are described in this award-winning directory. 500 pages. ISBN 1-58841-177-X. $42.50, plus $7 shipping.

Financial Aid for Asian Americans, 2009-2011
This is the source to use if you are looking for financial aid for Asian Americans; more than 1,000 sources of free money are described and thoroughly indexed. 406 pages. ISBN 1-58841-178-8. $40, plus $7 shipping.

Financial Aid for Hispanic Americans, 2009-2011
Nearly 1,200 funding programs open to Americans of Mexican, Puerto Rican, Central American, or other Latin American heritage are described here. 474 pages. ISBN 1-58841-179-6. $42.50, plus $7 shipping.

Financial Aid for Native Americans, 2009-2011
Detailed information is provided on 1,350 funding opportunities open to American Indians, Native Alaskans, and Native Pacific Islanders. 510 pages. ISBN 1-58841-180-X. $45, plus $7 shipping.

Financial Aid for Research and Creative Activities Abroad, 2008-2010
Described here are nearly 1,100 scholarships, fellowships, grants, etc. available to support research, professional, or creative activities abroad. 412 pages. ISBN 1-58841-188-5. $45, plus $7 shipping.

Financial Aid for Study and Training Abroad, 2008-2010
This directory, which *Children's Bookwatch* calls "invaluable," describes nearly 1,000 financial aid opportunities available to support study abroad. 362 pages. ISBN 1-58841-189-3. $40, plus $7 shipping.

Financial Aid for the Disabled and Their Families, 2008-2010
Named one of the "Best Reference Books of the Year" by *Library Journal,* this directory describes in detail more than 1,300 funding opportunities. 520 pages. ISBN 1-58841-183-4. $40, plus $7 shipping.

Financial Aid for Veterans, Military Personnel, and Their Dependents, 2008-2010
According to *Reference Book Review,* this directory (with its 1,300 entries) is "the most comprehensive guide available on the subject." 478 pages. ISBN 1-58841-182-6. $40, plus $7 shipping.

High School Senior's Guide to Merit and Other No-Need Funding, 2008-2010
Here's your guide to 1,100 funding programs that *never* look at income level when making awards to college-bound high school seniors. 416 pages. ISBN 1-58841-165-6. $29.95, plus $7 shipping.

How to Pay for Your Degree in Education & Related Fields, 2009-2011
This directory identifies 900+ sources of free money open to undergraduate and graduate students working on a degree in education. 302 pages. ISBN 1-58841-190-7. $30, plus $7 shipping.

How to Pay for Your Degree in Journalism & Related Fields, 2008-2010
Use this directory to identify more than 650 scholarships, fellowships, grants, and awards available to support undergraduate and graduate students working on a degree in journalism, broadcasting, communications, public relations, and other related fields. 236 pages. ISBN 1-58841-064-155-9. $30, plus $7 shipping.

How to Pay for Your Law Degree, 2008-2010
Here's information on 625 fellowships, loans, grants, and awards open to students working on a law degree (J.D., LL.M., etc.). There's no other guide like this one. 238 pages. ISBN 1-58841-185-0. $30, plus $7 shipping.

Money for Christian College Students, 2009-2011
This is the only directory to describe more than 800 funding opportunities for Christian students working on a college or graduate degree (secular or religious). 248 pages. ISBN 1-58841-196-6. $30, plus $7 shipping.

Financial Aid for Native Americans 2009-2011

Gail Ann Schlachter
R. David Weber

A Listing of Scholarships, Fellowships, Grants, Internships, and Awards Open Primarily or Exclusively to Native Americans and a Set of Six Indexes (Program Title, Sponsoring Organization, Residency, Tenability, Subject, and Deadline Date)

Reference Service Press
El Dorado Hills, California
2009

© 2009 Gail Ann Schlachter

All rights reserved. No part of this publication may be reproduced, stored in a retrieval system, or transmitted, in any form or by any means, electronic, mechanical, photocopying, recording, or otherwise, except for the inclusion of brief quotations in a review, without the prior permission in writing from the publisher. Reference Service Press vigorously defends its copyright protection.

ISBN 10: 158841180X
ISBN 13: 9781588411808

10 9 8 7 6 5 4 3 2 1

Reference Service Press (RSP) began in 1977 with a single financial aid publication *(The Directory of Financial Aids for Women)* and now specializes in the development of financial aid resources in multiple formats, including books, large print books, disks, CD-ROMs, print-on-demand reports, eBooks, and online sources. Long recognized as a leader in the field, RSP has been called by the *Samba Report on Directory Publishing* "a true success in the world of independent directory publishers." Both Kaplan Educational Centers and Military.com have hailed RSP as "the leading authority on scholarships."

Reference Service Press
El Dorado Hills Business Park
5000 Wind play Drive, Suite 4
El Dorado Hills, CA 95762-9319
    (916) 939-9620
    Fax: (916) 939-9626
    E-mail: info@rspfunding.com
Visit our web site: www.rspfunding.com

Manufactured in the United States of America
Price: $45, plus $7 shipping.

ACADEMIC INSTITUTIONS, LIBRARIES, ORGANIZATIONS AND OTHER QUANTITY BUYERS:
Discounts on this book are available for bulk purchases. Write or call for information on our discount programs.

Contents

Introduction 3
- Why This Directory Is Needed 3
- What's Updated 3
- What Makes This Directory Unique 4
- What's Excluded 4
- How the Directory Is Organized 5
- Sample Entry 7
- How to Use the Directory 8
- Plans to Update the Directory 9
- Other Related Publications 9
- Acknowledgements 9

About the Authors 11

Financial Aid Programs Open to Native Americans 13
- **Scholarships:** Money for Undergraduate Study 15
- **Fellowships:** Money for Graduate Study 169
- **Grants:** Money for Research, Projects, and Creative Activities ... 281
- **Awards:** Money for Achievement and Recognition 373
- **Internships:** Money for Work Experience 385

Indexes 451
- Program Title Index 453
- Sponsoring Organization Index 477
- Residency Index 487
- Tenability Index 491
- Subject Index 497
- Calendar Index 509

Introduction

WHY THIS DIRECTORY IS NEEDED

Despite our country's ongoing economic problems and increased college costs, the financial aid picture for minorities has never looked brighter. Currently, billions of dollars are set aside each year specifically for Native Americans, African Americans, Asian Americans, and Hispanic Americans. This funding is open to minorities at any level (high school through postdoctoral and professional) for a variety of activities, including study, research, travel, training, career development, and creative projects.

While numerous print or online listings have been prepared to identify and describe general financial aid opportunities (those open to all segments of society), those resources have never covered more than a small portion of the programs designed primarily or exclusively for minorities. As a result, many advisors, librarians, scholars, researchers, and students were often unaware of the extensive funding available to Native Americans and other minorities. But, with the ongoing publication of *Financial Aid for Native Americans* that has all changed. Here, in just one place, Native American students, professionals, and postdoctorates now have current and detailed information about the special resources set aside specifically for them.

Financial Aid for Native Americans is prepared biennially as part of Reference Service Press' four-volume *Minority Funding Set* (the other volumes in the set cover funding for Asian Americans, African Americans, and Hispanic Americans). Each of the volumes in this set is sold separately, or the complete set can be purchased at a discounted price (for more information, contact Reference Service Press's marketing department).

No other source, in print or online, offers the extensive coverage provided by these titles. That's why the Grantsmanship Center labeled the set "a must for every organization serving minorities," *Reference Sources for Small and Medium-Sized Libraries* called the titles "the absolute best guides for finding funding," and *Reference Books Bulletin* selected each of the volumes in the *Minority Funding Set* as their "Editor's Choice." *Financial Aid for Native Americans,* itself, has also received rave reviews. According to *Choice,* "This is a unique and valuable resource" which is "highly recommended." *Reference Books Bulletin* calls it a "landmark resource" and *EMIE Bulletin* concluded that the directory was "definitely designed to ease what can be a very stressful process." Perhaps *American Reference Books Annual* sums up the critical reaction best: "extraordinarily useful...absolutely essential."

WHAT'S UPDATED?

The preparation of each new edition of *Financial Aid for Native Americans* involves extensive updating and revision. To make sure that the information included in the 2009-2011 edition of the directory is both reliable and current, the editors at Reference Service Press 1) reviewed and updated all relevant programs covered in the previous edition of the directory, 2) collected information on all programs open to Native Americans that were added to Reference Service Press' funding database since the last edition of the directory, and then 3) searched extensively for new program leads in a variety of sources, including printed directories, news reports, journals, newsletters, house organs, annual reports, and sites on the Internet. Since all program descriptions included in the directory are written directly from information supplied by the sponsoring organizations in printed announcements or online (no information is ever taken from secondary sources), we contacted all sponsoring organizations identified in this process up to four times in writing and, if necessary, up to 3 times by telephone. Despite our best efforts, however, some sponsoring organizations still failed to respond and, as a result, their programs are not included in this edition of the directory.

The 2009-2011 edition of *Financial Aid for Native Americans* completely revises and updates the previous edition. Programs that have ceased operations have been dropped from the listing. Profiles of continuing programs have been rewritten to reflect operations in 2009-2011; more than 85 percent of the continuing programs reported substantive changes in their locations, requirements (particularly application deadline), benefits, or eligibility requirements since the 2006-2008 edition. In addition, more than 500 new entries have been added to the program section of the directory. The resulting listing describes the 1,350+ biggest and best sources of free money available to Native Americans, including scholarships, fellowships, grants, awards, and internships.

WHAT MAKES THIS DIRECTORY UNIQUE?

The 2009-2011 edition of *Financial Aid for Native Americans* will help American Indians, Native Alaskans (including Eskimos and Aleuts), and Native Hawaiians tap into the billions of dollars available to them, as minorities, for study, research, creative activities, past accomplishments, future projects, professional development, work experience, and many other activities. The listings cover every major subject area, are sponsored by nearly 900 different private and public agencies and organizations, and are open to Native Americans at any level, from college-bound high school students through professionals and postdoctorates.

Not only does *Financial Aid for Native Americans* provide the most comprehensive coverage of available funding (1,356 entries), but it also displays the most informative program descriptions (on the average, up to three time the detail found in any other listing). In addition to this extensive and focused coverage, *Financial Aid for Native Americans* also offers several other unique features. First of all, hundreds of funding opportunities listed here have never been covered in any other source. So, even if you have checked elsewhere, you will want to look at *Financial Aid for Native Americans* for additional leads. And, here's another plus: all of the funding programs in this edition of the directory offer "free" money; not one of the programs will ever require you to pay anything back (provided, of course, that you meet the program requirements).

Further, unlike other funding directories, which generally follow a straight alphabetical arrangement, *Financial Aid for Native Americans* groups entries by type of funding (scholarships, grants, awards, etc.), to make it easy for you to search for appropriate programs. This same convenience is offered in the indexes, where title, sponsoring organization, geographic, subject, and deadline date entries are each subdivided by type of funding.

Finally, we have tried to anticipate all the ways you might wish to search for funding. The volume is organized so you can identify programs not only by type, but by subject focus, sponsoring organization, program title, residency requirements, where the money can be spent, and even deadline date. Plus, we've included all the information you'll need to decide if a program is right for you: purpose, eligibility requirements, financial data, duration, special features, limitations, number awarded, and application date. You even get fax numbers, toll-free numbers, e-mail addresses, and web sites (when available), along with complete contact information.

WHAT'S EXCLUDED?

While this book is intended to be the most comprehensive source of information on funding available to Native Americans, there are some programs we've specifically excluded from the directory:

- *Programs that do not accept applications from U.S. citizens or residents.* If a program is open only to foreign nationals or excludes Americans from applying, it is not covered.

INTRODUCTION

- *Programs that are open equally to all segments of the population.* Only funding opportunities set aside primarily or exclusively for American Indians, Native Alaskans, and/or Native Hawaiians are included here.

- *Money for study or research outside the United States.* Since there are comprehensive and up-to-date directories that describe the available funding for study and research abroad (see the list of Reference Service Press titles opposite the directory's title page), only programs that fund activities in the United States are covered here.

- *Programs that offer small monetary awards.* The emphasis here is on programs that offer significant compensation. If the maximum a programs offers is less than $1,000 per year, it is not included in this listing.

- *Programs administered by individual academic institutions solely for their own students.* The directory identifies "portable" programs—ones that can be used at any number of schools. Financial aid administered by individual schools specifically for their own students is not covered. Write directly to the schools you are considering to get information on their offerings.

- *Money that must be repaid.* Only "free money" is identified here. If a program requires repayment or charges interest, it's not listed. Now you can find out about billions of dollars in aid and know (if you meet the program requirements) that not one dollar of that will ever need to be repaid.

HOW THE DIRECTORY IS ORGANIZED

Financial Aid for Native Americans is divided into two sections: 1) a descriptive list of funding opportunities open to Native Americans and 2) a set of six indexes to help you pinpoint appropriate funding programs.

Financial Aid Programs Open to Native Americans. The first section of the directory describes more than 1,350 sources of free money available to American Indians, Native Alaskans, and/or Native Hawaiians. The focus is on financial aid available to American citizens or permanent residents and tenable in the United States. The programs described here are sponsored by nearly 900 different government agencies, professional organizations, corporations, sororities and fraternities, foundations, religious groups, educational associations, and military/veterans organizations. All areas of the sciences, social sciences, and humanities are covered.

Entries in this section are grouped into the following five categories, to help you in your search for a specific kind of financial assistance (e.g., a scholarship for undergraduate study, a grant for independent research, an award for outstanding literary achievement):

Scholarships: Programs that support studies at the undergraduate level in the United States. Usually no return of service or repayment is required. For information on funding for research on the undergraduate level, see the Grants category below.

Fellowships: Programs that support studies at the graduate level in the United States, including work on a master's degree, doctorate, professional degree (e.g., law, medicine), or specialist's certificate. Usually no return of service or repayment is required. For information on funding for research on the graduate level, see the Grants category below.

Grants: Programs that provide funds to support Native Americans' innovative efforts, travel, projects, creative activities, or research on any level (from undergraduate to postdoctorates, professional, or other).

Awards: Competitions, prizes, and honoraria offered in recognition of Native Americans' personal accomplishments, professional contributions, or public service. Prizes received solely as the result of entering contests are excluded.

Internships: Work experience programs for Native American undergraduates, graduate students, and recent graduates. Only salaried positions are described.

Programs that supply more than one type of assistance are listed in all relevant subsections. For example, both undergraduate and graduate Native American students may apply for the Council of Energy Resource Tribes Scholarship, so the program is described in both the scholarship and the fellowship subsections.

Entries in each subsection are arranged alphabetically by program title and have been written to give you a concise but clear picture of the available funding. In addition, information (when available) is provided on organization address and telephone numbers (including fax and toll-free), e-mail address, web site, purpose, eligibility, money awarded, duration, special features, limitations, number of awards, and application deadline. The sample entry on page 7 illustrates and explains the program entry structure.

The information reported for each of the programs in this section was obtained as a result of research inquiries sent or searches conducted during the first quarter of 2009. While *Financial Aid for Native Americans* is intended to be as comprehensive as possible, some sponsoring organizations did not respond to our research requests and, consequently, are not included in this edition of the directory.

Indexes. To help you find the aid you need, we have constructed six indexes; these will let you access the listings by program title, sponsoring organization, residency, tenability, subject focus, and deadline date. These indexes use a word-by-word alphabetical arrangement. Note: numbers in the index refer to entry numbers, not to page numbers in the book.

Program Title Index. If you know the name of a particular funding program and want to find out where it is covered in the directory, use the Program Title Index. To assist you in your search, every program is listed by all its known names, former names, and abbreviations. Since one program can be included in several subsections (e.g., a program providing assistance to both undergraduate and graduate students is described in both the scholarships and the fellowships subsections), each entry number in the index has been coded to indicate program type (for example, "F" = Fellowships; "G" = Grants). By using this coding system, you can avoid duplicate entries and turn directly to the programs that match your financial interests.

Sponsoring Organization Index. This index makes it easy to identify agencies that offer funding primarily or exclusively to Native Americans. Nearly 900 organizations are indexed here. As in the Program Title Index, we've used a code to help you determine which organizations offer scholarships, fellowships, grants, awards, and/or internships.

Residency Index. Some programs listed in this book are restricted to Native Americans in a particular state or region. Others are open to Native Americans wherever they live. This index helps you identify programs available only to residents in your area as well as programs that have no residency requirements. Further, to assist you in your search, we've also indicated the type of funding offered to residents in each of the areas listed in the index.

Tenability Index. This index identifies the geographic locations where the funding described in *Financial Aid for Native Americans* may be used. Index entries (city, county, state, province, region, country, continent) are arranged alphabetically (word by word) and subdivided by program type. Use this index when you are looking for money to support your activities in a particular geographic area.

Subject Index. This index allows you to identify the subject focus of each of the financial aid opportunities described in *Financial Aid for Native Americans*. More than 250 different subject terms are listed. Extensive "see" and "see also" references, as well as type-of-program subdivisions, will help you locate appropriate funding opportunities.

Calendar Index. Since most financial aid programs have specific deadline dates, some may have closed by the time you begin to look for funding. You can use the Calendar Index to determine which programs are still open. This index is arranged by program type (e.g., scholarship, loan, internship) and subdivided by month during which the deadline falls. Filing dates can and quite

INTRODUCTION

SAMPLE ENTRY

(1) **[350]**

(2) **COCA-COLA FIRST GENERATION SCHOLARSHIP**

(3) American Indian College Fund
Attn: Scholarship Department
8333 Greenwood Boulevard
Denver, CO 80221
(303) 426-8900
Toll-free: (800) 776-FUND   Fax: (303) 426-1200
E-mail: info@collegefund.org
Web: www.collegefund.org

(4) **Purpose** To provide financial assistance to Native Americans who are attending a Tribal College or University (TCU) and are the first in their family to attend college.

(5) **Eligibility** This program is open to American Indians or Alaska Natives who are enrolled full time in their first or second semester at an eligible TCU. Applicants must have a GPA of 3.0 or higher and be able to demonstrate financial need. They must be the first in their immediate family to attend college. Along with their application, they must submit 1) short essays (up to 500 words each) on how they perceive themselves as leaders in their school or community and how their education will help the Native American community; and 2) a personal statement of 1,000 words that includes their personal background, their academic background, their educational and career goals, and how this scholarship will help them achieve those goals.

(6) **Financial data** The stipend is $5,000 per year.

(7) **Duration** 1 year; may be renewed, provided the recipient maintains a GPA of 3.0 or higher and participates actively in campus and community life.

(8) **Additional information** This program is sponsored by the Coca-Cola Company in partnership with the American Indian College Fund.

(9) **Number awarded** 1 or more each year.

(10) **Deadline** May of each year.

DEFINITION

(1) **Entry number:** Consecutive number assigned to the funding profiles and used to index the entry.

(2) **Program title:** Title of scholarship, fellowship, grant, award, or internship.

(3) **Sponsoring organization:** Name, address, and telephone number, toll-free number, fax number, e-mail address, and/or web site (when information was available) for organization sponsoring the program.

(4) **Purpose:** Identifies the major program requirements; read the rest of the entry for additional detail.

(5) **Eligibility:** Qualifications required of applicants, plus information on application procedure and selection process.

(6) **Financial data:** Financial details of the program, including fixed sum, average amount, or range of funds offered, expenses for which funds may and may not be applied, and cash-related benefits supplied (e.g., room and board).

(7) **Duration:** Period for which support is provided; renewal prospects.

(8) **Additional information:** Any unusual (generally nonmonetary) benefits, features, restrictions, or limitations associated with the program.

(9) **Number awarded:** Total number of recipients each year or other specified period.

(10) **Deadline:** The month by which applications must be submitted.

often do vary from year to year; consequently, this index should be used only as a guide for deadlines beyond 2011.

HOW TO USE THE DIRECTORY

Here are some tips to help you get the most out the funding opportunities listed in *Financial Aid for Native Americans*.

To Locate Programs Offering a Particular Type of Assistance. If you are looking for programs offering a particular type of financial aid (e.g., a scholarship for undergraduate courses, a grant for independent research, an award for outstanding literary achievement), turn first to the definitions of the various program types on pages 5 and 6 in the Introduction and then browse through the entries in each of the appropriate categories in the first section of the directory (scholarships, fellowships, grants, awards, or internships). Keep in mind that more than one of these subsections may contain funding leads for you. For example, if you are a graduate student looking for money to help you pay for the educational and research costs associated with your master's degree, you will not want to overlook the opportunities described in the fellowships, loans, grants, and even awards subsections. Note: since programs with multiple purposes are listed in every appropriate location, each of these subsections functions as a self-contained entity. As a result, you can browse through any of the subsections in the directory without first consulting an index.

To Find Information on a Particular Financial Aid Program. If you know the name of a particular financial aid program, and the type of assistance offered by the program (scholarship, fellowship, grant, etc.), then go directly to the appropriate category in the first section of the directory, where you will find the program profiles arranged alphabetically by title. But be careful: program titles can be misleading. For example, the John Shurr Journalism Award is a really a scholarship, the Holly A. Cornell Scholarship is actually a fellowship, and the Mickey Leland Energy Fellowship is, in fact, an internship. So, if you are looking for a specific program and do not find it in the subsection you have checked, be sure to refer to the Program Title Index to see if it is covered elsewhere in the directory. To save time, always check the Program Title Index first if you know the name of a specific award but are not sure under which subsection it has been listed. Since we index each program by all its known names and abbreviations, you'll also be able to track down a program there when you only know the popular rather than official name.

To Locate Programs Sponsored by a Particular Organization. The Sponsoring Organization Index makes it easy to identify agencies that provide financial assistance to Native Americans or to identify specific financial aid programs offered by a particular organization. Each entry number in the index is coded to identify program type, so that you can easily target appropriate entries.

To Browse Quickly Through the Listings. Turn to the type of funding that interests you (scholarships, fellowships, awards, etc.) and read the "Purpose" paragraph in each entry. In seconds, you'll know if this is an opportunity that you might want to pursue. If it is, be sure to read the rest of the information in the entry, to make sure you meet all of the program requirements before writing or going on the Internet for an application form. Please, save your time and energy. Don't apply if you don't qualify!

To Locate Funding Available to Native Americans from or Tenable in a Particular City, County, or State. The Residency Index identifies financial aid programs open to Native Americans in a specific state, region, etc. The Tenability Index shows where the money can be spent. In both indexes, "see" and "see also" references are used liberally, and index entries for a particular geographic area are subdivided by type of program (scholarships, fellowships, grants, awards, internships) to help you identify the funding that's right for you. When using these indexes, always check the listings under the term "United States," since the programs indexed there have no geographic restrictions and can be used in any area.

To Locate Financial Aid Programs Open to Native Americans in a Particular Subject Area. Turn to the Subject Index first if you are interested in identifying financial aid programs for Native Americans in a particular subject area (more than 250 different subject fields are listed there).

INTRODUCTION

To facilitate your search, the type of funding available (scholarships, fellowships, grants, awards, internships) is clearly labeled. Extensive cross-references are provided. As part of your search, be sure to check the listings in the index under the heading "General Programs;" those programs provide funding in any subject area (although they may be restricted in other ways).

To Locate Financial Aid Programs for Native Americans by Deadline Date. If you are working with specific time constraints and want to weed out the financial aid programs whose filing dates you won't be able to meet, turn first to the Calendar Index and check the program references listed under the appropriate program type and month. Keep in mind: not all sponsoring organizations supplied deadline information, so not all programs are indexed in this section. To identify every relevant financial aid program, regardless of filing date, read through all the entries in each of the program categories (scholarships, fellowships, etc.) that apply.

To Locate Financial Aid Programs Open to All Segments of the Population. Only programs available to Native Americans are listed in this publication. However, there are thousands of other programs that are open equally to all segments of the population. To identify these programs, talk to your local librarian, check with your financial aid office on campus, use a computerized scholarship or grant search service, look at the list of RSP resources on the page opposite the title page in this directory, or go online to: www.rspfunding.com/prod_prodalpha.html.

PLANS TO UPDATE THE DIRECTORY

This volume, covering 2009-2011, is the sixth edition of *Financial Aid for Native Americans*. The next biennial edition will cover the years 2011-2013 and will be issued in mid-2011.

OTHER RELATED PUBLICATIONS

In addition to *Financial Aid for Native Americans,* Reference Service Press publishes several other titles dealing with fundseeking, including the award-winning *Directory of Financial Aids for Women; Financial Aid for the Disabled and Their Families;* and *Financial Aid for Veterans, Military Personnel, and Their Dependents.* Since each of these titles focuses on a separate population group, there is very little duplication in the listings. For more information on Reference Service Press' award-winning publications, write to the company at 5000 Windplay Drive, Suite 4, El Dorado Hills, CA 95762, give us a call at (916) 939-9620, fax us at (916) 939-9626, send us an e-mail at info@rspfunding.com, or visit our expanded web site: www.rspfunding.com.

ACKNOWLEDGEMENTS

A debt of gratitude is owed all the organizations that contributed information to the 2009-2011 edition of *Financial Aid for Native Americans*. Their generous cooperation has helped to make this publication a current and comprehensive survey of awards.

ABOUT THE AUTHORS

Dr. Gail Ann Schlachter has worked for more than three decades as a library manager, a library educator, and an administrator of library-related publishing companies. Among the reference books to her credit are the biennially-issued *Directory of Financial Aids for Women* and two award-winning bibliographic guides: *Minorities and Women: A Guide to Reference Literature in the Social Sciences* (which was chosen as an "outstanding reference book of the year" by *Choice)* and *Reference Sources in Library and Information Services* (which won the first Knowledge Industry Publications "Award for Library Literature"). She was the reference book review editor for *RQ* (now *Reference and User Services Quarterly)* for 10 years, is a past president of the American Library Association's Reference and User Services Association, is the former editor-in-chief of the *Reference and User Services Association Quarterly,* and is currently serving her fourth term on the American Library Association's governing council. In recognition of her outstanding contributions to reference service, Dr. Schlachter has been named the University of Wisconsin School of Library and Information Studies "Alumna of the Year" and has been awarded both the Isadore Gilbert Mudge Citation and the Louis Shores/Oryx Press Award.

Dr. R. David Weber teaches economics and history at East Los Angeles College (Wilmington, California), where he directed the Honors Program for many years. He has written a number of critically-acclaimed reference works, including *Dissertations in Urban History* and the three-volume *Energy Information Guide.* With Gail Schlachter, he is the author of Reference Service Press' *Financial Aid for the Disabled and Their Families,* which was selected by *Library Journal* as one of the "best reference books of the year," and a number of other financial aid titles, including the *College Student's Guide to Merit and Other No-Need Funding,* which was chosen as one of the "outstanding reference books of the year" by *Choice.*

Financial Aid Programs
Open to Native Americans

- *Scholarships*
- *Fellowships*
- *Grants*
- *Awards*
- *Internships*

Scholarships

Described here are 539 funding programs open to Native Americans that are available to support studies on the undergraduate level in the United States. Usually no return of service or repayment is required. Note: other funding opportunities for Native American undergraduates are also described in the Grants, Awards, and Internships sections. So, if you are looking for a particular program and don't find it in this section, be sure to check the Program Title Index to see if it is covered elsewhere in the directory.

SCHOLARSHIPS

[1]
AAAE FOUNDATION SCHOLARSHIPS FOR NATIVE AMERICANS
American Association of Airport Executives Foundation
Attn: AAAE Foundation Scholarship Program
601 Madison Street, Suite 400
Alexandria, VA 22314
(703) 824-0500   Fax: (703) 820-1395
E-mail: cindy.dewitt@aaae.org
Web: www.aaae.org

Purpose To provide financial assistance to Native American upper-division college students who are majoring in aviation.
Eligibility This program is open to full-time Native American college juniors or seniors who are enrolled in an aviation program and have a GPA of 3.0 or higher. Each college or university may nominate only 1 student for this scholarship. Selection is based on academic record, financial need, participation in school and community activities, work experience, and a personal statement.
Financial data The stipend is $1,000.
Duration 1 year.
Number awarded 1 or more each year.
Deadline May of each year.

[2]
ACCENTURE UNDERGRADUATE SCHOLARSHIPS
American Indian Graduate Center
Attn: Executive Director
4520 Montgomery Boulevard, N.E., Suite 1-B
Albuquerque, NM 87109-1291
(505) 881-4584   Toll-free: (800) 628-1920
Fax: (505) 884-0427   E-mail: aigc@aigc.com
Web: www.aigc.com

Purpose To provide financial assistance for college to Native American high school seniors interested in majoring in selected fields.
Eligibility This program is open to enrolled members of U.S. federally-recognized American Indian tribes and Alaska Native groups and other students who can document one-fourth degree federally-recognized Indian blood. They must be nominated by a school official. Nominees must be planning to enter a 4-year college or university to work full time on a professional, teaching, social services, high technology, or business degree. They must be able to demonstrate financial need, academic achievement (GPA of 3.0 or higher), and leadership in school, civic, and extracurricular activities. Along with their application, they must submit a 500-word essay on their most outstanding intellectual endeavor.
Financial data Stipends are $20,000 or $2,000 per year.
Duration 1 year for the $20,000 awards; 4 years for the $2,000 awards.
Additional information This program, established in 2005, is supported by Accenture.
Number awarded 5 each year: 3 at $20,000 and 2 at $2,000.
Deadline April of each year.

[3]
ADOLPH VAN PELT SCHOLARSHIPS
Association on American Indian Affairs, Inc.
Attn: Director of Scholarship Programs
966 Hungerford Drive, Suite 12-B
Rockville, MD 20850
(240) 314-7155   Fax: (240) 314-7159
E-mail: lw.aaia@verizon.net
Web: www.indian-affairs.org

Purpose To provide financial assistance to Native American undergraduate students.
Eligibility This program is open to Native American students interested in working on an undergraduate degree on a full-time basis. Applicants must submit documentation of financial need, a Certificate of Indian Blood showing at least one-quarter Indian blood, proof of tribal enrollment, an essay on their educational goals, 2 letters of recommendation, and their most recent transcript. Selection is based on merit and need.
Financial data The stipend is $1,500.
Duration 1 year; recipients may reapply.
Number awarded 1 or more each year.
Deadline June of each year.

[4]
ADULT VOCATIONAL TRAINING PROGRAM OF THE WYANDOTTE NATION
Wyandotte Nation of Oklahoma
Attn: Department of Education
64790 East Highway 60
Wyandotte, OK 74370
(918) 678-2297, ext. 230
Toll-free: (800) 256-2539, ext. 230
E-mail: info@wyandotte-nation.org
Web: www.wyandotte-nation.org

Purpose To provide financial assistance for vocational training to members of the Wyandotte Nation of Oklahoma.
Eligibility This program is open to Wyandotte tribal members who are attending or will be attending a vocational training program. Applicants must be able to demonstrate financial need.
Financial data A stipend is awarded (amount not specified).
Duration Up to 2 years.
Number awarded Varies each year.

[5]
AFOGNAK CAREER ENHANCEMENT OPPORTUNITIES PROGRAM
Afognak Native Corporation
215 Mission Road, Suite 212
Kodiak, AK 99615
(907) 486-6014   Toll-free: (800) 770-6014
Fax: (907) 486-2514
E-mail: scholarships@afognak.com
Web: afognak.com/scholarships.php

Purpose To provide financial assistance to members of the Afognak Native Corporation in Alaska who are interested in pursuing higher education other than in a traditional college, university, or vocational school program.

Eligibility This program is open to Alaska Natives who are original Afognak Native Corporation enrollees and their lineal descendants. Applicants must be seeking more education to increase their career opportunities through means other than full-time traditional college or university attendance. Along with their application, they must submit a letter that describes their future educational and career goals and explains how this training will help them achieve those goals. Financial need is considered in the selection process.
Financial data The stipend is $2,000 per calendar year.
Duration 1 year; may be renewed.
Number awarded Varies each year.
Deadline Applications may be submitted at any time.

[6]
AFOGNAK HIGHER EDUCATION PROGRAM

Afognak Native Corporation
215 Mission Road, Suite 212
Kodiak, AK 99615
(907) 486-6014   Toll-free: (800) 770-6014
Fax: (907) 486-2514
E-mail: scholarships@afognak.com
Web: afognak.com/scholarships.php

Purpose To provide financial assistance to members of the Afognak Native Corporation in Alaska who are interested in enrolling in a traditional college, university, graduate school, or vocational program.
Eligibility This program is open to Alaska Natives who are original Afognak Native Corporation enrollees and their lineal descendants. Applicants must be high school graduates or GED recipients who have been accepted to or are enrolled at an accredited college, university, or vocational school to work on an associate, bachelor's, master's, or doctoral degree. Along with their application, they must submit a letter that provides a personal history (information about their family and their special talents and abilities, community involvement, plans for the future, philosophy of life), future plans for education, and how their education may benefit the Alutiiq people and their commitment to the Alutiiq community. Financial need is considered in the selection process.
Financial data A stipend is awarded (amount not specified).
Duration 1 year; may be renewed if the recipient maintains a GPA of 2.0 or higher.
Number awarded Varies each year.
Deadline April of each year.

[7]
AISES GOOGLE SCHOLARSHIP

American Indian Science and Engineering Society
Attn: Scholarship Coordinator
2305 Renard, S.E., Suite 200
P.O. Box 9828
Albuquerque, NM 87119-9828
(505) 765-1052, ext. 106   Fax: (505) 765-5608
E-mail: shirley@aises.org
Web: www.aises.org

Purpose To provide financial assistance to members of the American Indian Science and Engineering Society (AISES) who are working on an undergraduate or graduate degree in a computer-related field.
Eligibility This program is open to AISES members who are full-time undergraduate or graduate students at a 4-year college or university or a full-time student at a 2-year college enrolled in a program leading to a 4-year degree. Applicants must be majoring in computer science, computer engineering, or management information systems. They must have a GPA of 3.5 or higher and be able to document ancestry as an American Indian, Alaskan Native, or Native Hawaiian. Along with their application, they must submit a 500-word essay on their educational and/or career goals, interest in and motivation to continue higher education, understanding of the importance of college and commitment to completion, commitment to learning, and giving back to the community. Financial need is not considered in the selection process. U.S. citizenship is required.
Financial data The total award is $10,000, disbursed equally over the recipient's course of study.
Duration Until completion of a degree.
Additional information This program, established in 2008, is funded by Google Inc.
Number awarded 20 each year.
Deadline June of each year.

[8]
ALAN COMPTON AND BOB STANLEY MINORITY AND INTERNATIONAL SCHOLARSHIP

Baptist Communicators Association
Attn: Scholarship Committee
1715-K South Rutherford Boulevard, Suite 295
Murfreesboro, TN 37130
(615) 904-0152   E-mail: bca.office@comcast.net
Web: www.baptistcommunicators.org

Purpose To provide financial assistance to minority and international students who are working on an undergraduate degree to prepare for a career in Baptist communications.
Eligibility This program is open to undergraduate students of minority or international origin. Applicants must be majoring in communications, English, journalism, or public relations with a GPA of 2.5 or higher. Their vocational objective must be in Baptist communications. Along with their application, they must submit a statement explaining why they want to receive this scholarship.
Financial data The stipend is $1,000.
Duration 1 year; recipients may reapply.
Additional information This program was established in 1996.
Number awarded 1 each year.
Deadline December of each year.

[9]
ALASKA NATIVE TRIBAL HEALTH CONSORTIUM SCHOLARSHIPS

Alaska Native Tribal Health Consortium
Attn: Native Development Coordinator
4000 Ambassador Drive, Suite 114
Anchorage, AK 99508
(907) 729-1348   Toll-free: (800) 684-8361
Fax: (907) 729-1335   E-mail: kruesch@anthc.org
Web: www.anthc.org/jt/int

Purpose To provide financial assistance for college or graduate school to Natives and American Indians who are residents of Alaska and interested in a career in health care.

Eligibility This program is open to Alaska Natives and American Indians who are undergraduates or graduate students interested in preparing for a career in the field of health care. Applicants must be residents of Alaska enrolled full time. Along with their application, they must submit a resume, 3 letters of recommendation, documentation of financial need, and a 1-page personal statement that covers their personal and educational history, accomplishments, educational and career goals, involvement in the Native community, and how this scholarship and degree program contribute to their career goals.

Financial data The stipend is $5,000 per year.

Duration 1 year; may be renewed if they maintain a minimum GPA of 2.0 for undergraduates or 3.0 for graduate students.

Number awarded 10 each year: 5 for undergraduate students and 5 for graduate students.

Deadline February of each year.

[10]
ALEUT FOUNDATION PART-TIME SCHOLARSHIPS

The Aleut Corporation
Attn: Aleut Foundation
703 West Tudor Road, Suite 102
Anchorage, AK 99503-6650
(907) 646-1929   Toll-free: (800) 232-4882
Fax: (907) 646-1949
E-mail: taf@thealeutfoundation.org
Web: www.thealeutfoundation.org

Purpose To provide financial assistance for college or graduate school to Native Alaskans with ties to the Aleutian Islands who are enrolled part time.

Eligibility This program is open to residents of Alaska who are 1) an original enrollee or descendant of an original enrollee of The Aleut Corporation (TAC); 2) a beneficiary or a descendant of a beneficiary of the Aleutian Pribilof Islands Restitution Trust; or 3) an original enrollee or descendant of an original enrollee of the Isanotski Corporation (IC). Applicants must be enrolled in an associate, bachelor's, or higher degree program as a part-time student (at least 3 credit hours). They must have a GPA of 2.0 or higher. Along with their application, they must include a letter of intent, up to 500 words in length, that covers their educational goals and how they intend to use their education in the Aleut community.

Financial data The stipend depends on the number of credit hours in the undergraduate or graduate program, to a maximum of $1,200 per year.

Duration 1 year.

Additional information The foundation began awarding scholarships in 1987.

Number awarded Varies each year; recently, 2 of these scholarships were awarded.

Deadline June of each year for annual scholarships; November of each year for spring scholarships.

[11]
ALEUT FOUNDATION SCHOLARSHIP PROGRAM

The Aleut Corporation
Attn: Aleut Foundation
703 West Tudor Road, Suite 102
Anchorage, AK 99503-6650
(907) 646-1929   Toll-free: (800) 232-4882
Fax: (907) 646-1949
E-mail: taf@thealeutfoundation.org
Web: www.thealeutfoundation.org

Purpose To provide financial assistance to Native Alaskans with ties to the Aleutian Islands who plan to attend college in any state.

Eligibility This program is open to residents of Alaska who are 1) an original enrollee or descendant of an original enrollee of The Aleut Corporation (TAC); 2) a beneficiary or a descendant of a beneficiary of the Aleutian Pribilof Islands Restitution Trust; or 3) an original enrollee or descendant of an original enrollee of the Isanotski Corporation (IC). Applicants must have earned a GPA of 3.5 or higher for the Honors Scholarship, 3.0 or higher for the Exceptional Scholarship, 2.5 or higher for the Achievement Scholarship, or 2.0 or higher for the Merit Scholarship. They must be enrolled or planning to enroll full time at a college or university in any state to work on an undergraduate degree. Along with their application, they must include a letter of intent, up to 500 words in length, that covers their educational goals and how they intend to use their education in the Aleut community.

Financial data Annual stipends are $3,000 for Honors Scholarships, $2,500 for Exceptional Scholarships, $2,000 for Achievement Scholarships, or $1,500 for Merit Scholarships.

Duration 1 year; may be renewed.

Additional information The foundation began awarding scholarships in 1987.

Number awarded Varies each year; recently, 80 of these scholarships were awarded, including 20 Honors Scholarships, 37 Exceptional Scholarships, 14 Achievement Scholarships, and 9 Merit Scholarships.

Deadline June of each year for annual scholarships; November of each year for spring scholarships.

[12]
ALEUT FOUNDATION VOCATIONAL SCHOLARSHIPS

The Aleut Corporation
Attn: Aleut Foundation
703 West Tudor Road, Suite 102
Anchorage, AK 99503-6650
(907) 646-1929   Toll-free: (800) 232-4882
Fax: (907) 646-1949
E-mail: taf@thealeutfoundation.org
Web: www.thealeutfoundation.org

Purpose To provide financial assistance for vocational school to Native Alaskans with ties to the Aleutian Islands.

Eligibility This program is open to residents of Alaska who are 1) an original enrollee or descendant of an original enrollee of The Aleut Corporation (TAC); 2) a beneficiary or a descendant of a beneficiary of the Aleutian Pribilof Islands Restitution Trust; or 3) an original enrollee or descendant of an original enrollee of the Isanotski Corporation (IC). Applicants must be enrolled in or accepted to a vocational program on a full-time basis. Along with their application, they must include a letter of intent, up to 500 words in length, that covers their educational goals and how they intend to use their education in the Aleut community.

Financial data The stipend is $1,700 per year.

Duration 1 semester (at least 6 weeks); may be renewed.

Additional information The foundation began awarding scholarships in 1987.

Number awarded Varies each year; recently, 4 of these scholarships were awarded.

Deadline June of each year for annual scholarships; November of each year for spring scholarships.

[13]
ALEUTIAN/PRIBILOF ISLANDS ASSOCIATION EDUCATION AND TRAINING PROGRAM

Aleutian/Pribilof Islands Association, Inc.
Attn: Human Services
201 East Third Avenue
Anchorage, AK 99501-2544
(907) 276-2700   Fax: (907) 279-4351
E-mail: apiai@apiai.com
Web: www.apiai.com/HmnSvcDesc.asp?page=ET

Purpose To provide financial assistance for college or other training to Alaska Native students with ties to the Aleutian/Pribilof Islands region.

Eligibility This program is open to Alaska Natives or American Indians who are either members of a federally-recognized tribe in the Aleutian/Pribilof Islands region or residents of the region. Applicants must be attending or planning to attend higher education, vocational training, certification training, short-term training, or other training. They must be able to demonstrate financial need and that their proposed study will assist them in obtaining and retaining long-term self-sustaining employment.

Financial data Recipients are entitled to 1) a tuition stipend for tuition, books, and fees, or 2) a monthly stipend for essential basic needs (food, clothing, shelter, and transportation to school).

Duration Up to 1 year.

Number awarded Varies each year.

[14]
ALEUTIAN/PRIBILOF ISLANDS ASSOCIATION VOCATIONAL REHABILITATION ASSISTANCE

Aleutian/Pribilof Islands Association, Inc.
Attn: Human Services
201 East Third Avenue
Anchorage, AK 99501-2544
(907) 276-2700   Fax: (907) 279-4351
E-mail: apiai@apiai.com
Web: www.apiai.com/HmnSvcDesc.asp?page=VR

Purpose To provide financial assistance to Alaska Natives from the Aleutian/Pribilof Islands region who have a disability and are interested in vocational training.

Eligibility This program is open to Alaska Natives/American Indians who have a tribal card or Certificate of Indian Blood and are living in the Aleutian/Pribilof Islands Association service area. Applicants must have 1) a documented disability; and 2) a reasonable and necessary unmet need for supportive services while attending training or seeking long-term self-sustaining employment.

Financial data The amount of the assistance depends on the need of the recipient.

Duration Up to 1 year.

Number awarded Varies each year.

[15]
ALFRED J. DURAN SR. TRUST SCHOLARSHIP

Northern Arapaho Tribe
Attn: Sky People Higher Education
P.O. Box 8480
Ethete, WY 82520
(307) 332-5286   Toll-free: (800) 815-6795
Fax: (307) 332-9104
E-mail: assistant@skypeopleed.org
Web: www.skypeopleed.org

Purpose To provide financial assistance to members of the Northern Arapaho Tribe who are working on an undergraduate or graduate degree in any field.

Eligibility This program is open to full-time undergraduate and graduate students who have an undergraduate GPA of 2.0 or higher or the graduate GPA required by their school. Applicants must be of one-fourth Northern Arapaho descent (enrolled or non-enrolled) and must submit a Certificate of Indian Blood or other verification of Northern Arapaho blood with at least one-fourth degree. They may be working on a degree in any field. Along with their application, they must submit a 1-page personal statement that includes a brief history of their background, academic ability and achievement, work or leadership experience, participation in community-related activities, and career goals. Selection is based on that statement, potential to contribute to the community upon graduation, academic ability and achievement, and a letter of recommendation.

Financial data The stipend is $1,000 per year.

Duration 1 year; may be renewed.

Additional information Recipients are expected to apply for employment with the Northern Arapaho Tribe after graduation.

Number awarded 2 each year.

Deadline June of each year.

SCHOLARSHIPS

[16]
ALL NATIVE AMERICAN HIGH SCHOOL ACADEMIC TEAM SCHOLARSHIPS
American Indian Graduate Center
Attn: Executive Director
4520 Montgomery Boulevard, N.E., Suite 1-B
Albuquerque, NM 87109-1291
(505) 881-4584 Toll-free: (800) 628-1920
Fax: (505) 884-0427 E-mail: aigc@aigc.com
Web: www.aigc.com

Purpose To provide financial assistance for college to Native American high school students.

Eligibility This program is open to enrolled members of U.S. federally-recognized American Indian tribes and Alaska Native groups and other students who can document one-fourth degree federally-recognized Indian blood. A teacher or community member must nominate students. Nominees must be high school juniors or seniors planning to enroll full time at an accredited college or university. Along with their application, they must submit a 500-word essay on their most outstanding intellectual endeavor. Selection is based on the student's academic, artistic, or leadership endeavor. Financial need is also considered.

Financial data A stipend is awarded (amount not specified).

Duration 1 year.

Additional information This program is supported by the Tommy Hilfiger Corporate Foundation.

Number awarded 10 each year.

Deadline April of each year.

[17]
ALLOGAN SLAGLE MEMORIAL SCHOLARSHIP
Association on American Indian Affairs, Inc.
Attn: Director of Scholarship Programs
966 Hungerford Drive, Suite 12-B
Rockville, MD 20850
(240) 314-7155 Fax: (240) 314-7159
E-mail: lw.aaia@verizon.net
Web: www.indian-affairs.org

Purpose To provide financial assistance for college to Native American students whose tribe is not federally-recognized.

Eligibility This program is open to American Indian and Native Alaskan full-time undergraduate students. Applicants must be members of tribes that are either state-recognized or that are not federally-recognized but are seeking federal recognition. Along with their application, they must submit documentation of financial need, a Certificate of Indian Blood showing at least one-quarter Indian blood (if available), proof of tribal enrollment, an essay on their educational goals, 2 letters of recommendation, and their most recent transcript. Selection is based on need.

Financial data The stipend is $1,500.

Duration 1 year; recipients may reapply.

Number awarded 1 or more each year.

Deadline July of each year.

[18]
ALYESKA MATCH SCHOLARSHIPS
Cook Inlet Tribal Council, Inc.
Attn: Tribal Scholarships and Grants Program
3600 San Jeronimo Drive, Suite 286
Anchorage, AK 99508
(907) 793-3578 Toll-free: (877) 985-5900
Fax: (907) 793-3589 E-mail: scholarships@citci.com
Web: www.citci.com//page/44

Purpose To provide financial assistance to Alaska Natives who are working on an undergraduate degree or certificate at a school in any state in fields that will prepare them for employment on the Trans-Alaska Pipeline System (TAPS).

Eligibility This program is open to Alaska Natives who are enrolled in college or a vocational training program in any state. Applicants must be studying a field specified by Alyeska Pipeline Service Company that relates to future employment on the TAPS. Recently, those included engineering (civil, electrical, mechanical, safety, engineering technology); safety (occupational safety and health, chemistry, certified safety professional (CSP), associate safety professional (ASP), certified industrial hygienist); information technology (including marketing and graphic design); and process technology. Applicants must be able to demonstrate unmet financial need even though they are receiving other funding. Awards are granted on a first-come, first-served basis.

Financial data The maximum stipend is $5,000. Awards are intended to be applied to tuition, fees, course-required books and supplies, and on-campus housing and meal plans only.

Duration 1 year; may be renewed up to 4 additional years if the recipient maintains a GPA of 2.0 or higher.

Additional information Funding for this program is provided by Alyeska Pipeline Service Company.

Number awarded Varies each year.

Deadline June or each year for fall; November of each year for spring.

[19]
AMELIA KEMP MEMORIAL SCHOLARSHIP
Women of the Evangelical Lutheran Church in America
Attn: Scholarships
8765 West Higgins Road
Chicago, IL 60631-4101
(773) 380-2736 Toll-free: (800) 638-3522, ext. 2736
Fax: (773) 380-2419 E-mail: emily.hansen@elca.org
Web: www.elca.org

Purpose To provide financial assistance to lay women of color who are members of Evangelical Lutheran Church of America (ELCA) congregations and who wish to study on the undergraduate, graduate, professional, or vocational school level.

Eligibility This program is open to ELCA lay women of color who are at least 21 years of age and have experienced an interruption of at least 2 years in their education since high school. Applicants must have been admitted to an educational institution to prepare for a career in other than a church-certified profession. U.S. citizenship is required.

Financial data The maximum stipend is $1,000.

Duration Up to 2 years.

Number awarded Varies each year, depending upon the funds available.
Deadline February of each year.

[20]
AMERICAN ASSOCIATION OF BLACKS IN ENERGY NATIONAL SCHOLARSHIPS

American Association of Blacks in Energy
Attn: Scholarship Committee
1625 K Street, N.W., Suite 405
Washington, DC 20006
(202) 371-9530   Fax: (202) 371-9218
E-mail: info@aabe.org
Web: aabe.org/node/1403

Purpose To provide financial assistance to Native American and other underrepresented minority high school seniors who are interested in majoring in engineering, mathematics, or physical science in college.
Eligibility This program is open to members of minority groups underrepresented in energy-related fields (African Americans, Hispanics, and Native Americans) who are graduating high school seniors. Applicants must have a "B" academic average overall and a "B" average in mathematics and science courses. They must be planning to attend an accredited college or university to major in business, engineering, mathematics, or the sciences. Along with their application, they must submit a transcript, 2 letters of reference, and documentation of financial need. The applicant who demonstrates the most outstanding achievement and promise is presented with the Premier Award. All applications must be submitted to the local office of the sponsoring organization in the student's state. For a list of local offices, contact the scholarship committee at the national office.
Financial data The stipends are $3,000. The Premier Award is an additional $5,000. All funds are paid directly to the students upon proof of enrollment at an accredited college or university.
Duration 1 year; nonrenewable.
Number awarded 6 each year (1 in each of the organization's regions); of those 6 winners, 1 is chosen to receive the Premier Award.
Deadline March of each year.

[21]
AMERICAN CHEMICAL SOCIETY SCHOLARS PROGRAM

American Chemical Society
Attn: Department of Diversity Programs
1155 16th Street, N.W.
Washington, DC 20036
(202) 872-6250   Toll-free: (800) 227-5558, ext. 6250
Fax: (202) 872-4361   E-mail: scholars@acs.org
Web: portal.acs.org

Purpose To provide financial assistance to Native American and other underrepresented minority students who have a strong interest in chemistry and a desire to prepare for a career in a chemically-related science.
Eligibility This program is open to 1) college-bound high school seniors; 2) college freshmen, sophomores, and juniors enrolled full time at an accredited college or university; 3) community college graduates and transfer students who plan to study for a bachelor's degree; and 4) community college freshmen. Applicants must be African American, Hispanic/Latino, or American Indian. They must be majoring or planning to major in chemistry, biochemistry, chemical engineering, or other chemically-related fields, such as environmental science, materials science, or toxicology, and planning to prepare for a career in the chemical sciences or chemical technology. Students planning careers in medicine or pharmacy are not eligible. U.S. citizenship or permanent resident status is required. Selection is based on academic merit (GPA of 3.0 or higher) and financial need.
Financial data Stipends range up to $3,000 per year.
Duration 1 year; may be renewed.
Additional information This program was established in 1994.
Number awarded Approximately 100 new awards are granted each year.
Deadline March of each year.

[22]
AMERICAN INDIAN ARTS COUNCIL SCHOLARSHIP PROGRAM

American Indian Arts Council, Inc.
Attn: Scholarship Committee
725 Preston Forest Shopping Center, Suite B
Dallas, TX 75230
(214) 891-9640   Fax: (214) 891-0221
E-mail: aiac@flash.net

Purpose To provide financial assistance to American Indian undergraduates or graduate students planning a career in the arts or arts administration.
Eligibility This program is open to American Indian undergraduate and graduate students who are preparing for a career in fine arts, visual and performing arts, communication arts, creative writing, or arts administration or management. Applicants must be currently enrolled in and attending a fully-accredited college or university. They must provide official tribal documentation verifying American Indian heritage and have a GPA of 2.5 or higher. Applicants majoring in the visual or performing arts (including writing) must submit slides, photographs, videotapes, audio tapes, or other examples of their work. Letters of recommendation are required. Awards are based on either merit or merit and financial need. If the applicants wish to be considered for a need-based award, a letter from their financial aid office is required to verify financial need.
Financial data Stipends range from $250 to $1,000 per semester.
Duration 1 semester; may be renewed if the recipient maintains a GPA of 2.5 or higher.
Additional information This program was established in 1993.
Number awarded Varies each year.
Deadline September of each year for the fall semester; February of each year for the spring semester.

SCHOLARSHIPS

[23]
AMERICAN INDIAN CHAMBER OF COMMERCE OF CALIFORNIA SCHOLARSHIP

American Indian Chamber of Commerce of California
Attn: AICC Scholarship
555 West Fifth Street, 31st Floor
Los Angeles, CA 90017
E-mail: stateadmin@aicccal.org
Web: www.aicccal.org/scholarship.html

Purpose To provide financial assistance for college or graduate school to American Indians who live or attend school in California.
Eligibility This program is open to American Indians who 1) are on a federal- or state-recognized tribal roll and identified by a tribal enrollment card; or 2) have an official letter from a federal- or state-recognized tribe or agency verifying tribal membership or Indian blood. Applicants must be full-time degree candidates at an accredited institution of higher learning (junior college, trade/vocational school, 4-year university, graduate school) in California or residents of California attending an institution of higher learning elsewhere in the United States. Along with their application, they must submit an educational commitment essay describing their chosen field of study, educational goals, career goals, involvement in the Indian community, and how this scholarship will help in furthering their education. Selection is based on transcripts (30 points), a letter of recommendation (20 points), the educational commitment essay (50 points), and major chosen (bonus 10 points if majoring in business).
Financial data Stipends are $2,500 or $1,500.
Duration 1 year.
Additional information This program, which began in 1999, includes the Darlene Dyer Stanhoff Memorial Scholarship.
Number awarded 6 each year: 1 at $2,500 and 5 at $1,500.
Deadline October of each year.

[24]
AMERICAN INDIAN CHAMBER OF COMMERCE OF WISCONSIN SCHOLARSHIPS

American Indian Chamber of Commerce of Wisconsin, Inc.
Attn: Scholarship Program
10809 West Lincoln Avenue, Suite 102
West Allis, WI 53227
(414) 604-2044   Toll-free: (877) 603-2044
Fax: (414) 604-2070   E-mail: marie@aiccw.org
Web: www.aiccw.org/scholarship.php

Purpose To provide financial assistance for college or graduate school to American Indian students from Wisconsin.
Eligibility This program is open to residents of Wisconsin who can provide proof of enrollment in an American Indian tribe by at least 1 parent. Applicants must be enrolled full time in a vocational/technical school, 2-year or 4-year college or university, tribal college, or graduate school. Preference is given to students majoring in business administration or a related field at a 4-year college or university. Along with their application, they must submit a 1-page statement explaining their educational goals and any obstacles they may have to overcome to achieve those goals.
Financial data The stipend is $1,000.
Duration 1 year.
Additional information The program also provides a $2,000 scholarship to a student majoring in business at the University of Wisconsin at Oshkosh.
Number awarded 1 or more each year.
Deadline April of each year.

[25]
AMERICAN INDIAN COMMUNITY COLLEGE SCHOLARSHIP

Scholarship Administrative Services, Inc.
Attn: MEFUSA Program
457 Ives Terrace
Sunnyvale, CA 94087

Purpose To provide financial assistance to American Indian high school seniors who are interested in attending a community college.
Eligibility This program is open to American Indian seniors graduating from high schools anywhere in the United States. Applicants must be enrolled members of a federally-recognized tribal organization and planning to attend a community college on a full-time basis. Along with their application, they must submit a 1,000-word essay on their educational and career goals, how a community college education will help them to achieve those goals, and how they plan to serve the American Indian community after completing their education. Selection is based on the essay, high school GPA (2.5 or higher), SAT or ACT scores, involvement in the American Indian community, and financial need.
Financial data The stipend is $5,000 per year.
Duration 1 year; may be renewed 1 additional year if the recipient maintains full-time enrollment and a GPA of 2.5 or higher.
Additional information This program is sponsored by the Minority Educational Foundation of the United States of America (MEFUSA) and administered by Scholarship Administrative Services, Inc. MEFUSA was established in 2001 to meet the needs of minority students who "show a determination to get a college degree," but who, for financial or other personal reasons, are not able to attend a 4-year college or university. Requests for applications should be accompanied by a self-addressed stamped envelope, the student's e-mail address, and the source where they found the scholarship information.
Number awarded Up to 100 each year.
Deadline April of each year.

[26]
AMERICAN INDIAN EDUCATION FOUNDATION SCHOLARSHIP PROGRAM

American Indian Education Foundation
P.O. Box 27491
Albuquerque, NM 87125-9847
Toll-free: (800) 881-8694
E-mail: info@aiefprograms.org
Web: www.nrcprograms.org

Purpose To provide financial assistance for college to American Indian and Alaskan Native students.
Eligibility This program is open to full-time students of Native American or Alaskan Native descent who are cur-

rently attending or planning to attend a 2-year college, a 4-year college or university, or a vocational/technical school. Applicants may be either graduating high school seniors or undergraduates who are entering, continuing, or returning to college. Along with their application, they must submit a 4-page essay in which they describe themselves as a student, their ultimate career goals, their plans for working in or with the Indian community, and their participation in leadership and/or community service activities. A GPA of 2.0 to 3.4 is desirable, but all current or future undergraduate students are encouraged to apply. An ACT score of 14 or higher is desirable. Financial need is considered in the selection process. All finalists are considered for the Paul Francis Memorial Scholarship and the Josephine Nipper Memorial Scholarship; priority for those awards is given to applicants who demonstrate true commitment to bettering their community.
Financial data The stipend is $2,000 per year.
Duration 1 year; may be renewed.
Number awarded More than 100 each year.
Deadline April of each year.

[27]
AMERICAN INDIAN FELLOWSHIP IN BUSINESS SCHOLARSHIP

National Center for American Indian Enterprise
   Development
Attn: Scholarship Committee
953 East Juanita Avenue
Mesa, AZ 85204
(480) 545-1298, ext. 243
Toll-free: (800) 4-NCAIED, ext. 243
Fax: (480) 545-4208   E-mail: events@ncaied.org
Web: www.ncaied.org/scholarships.php

Purpose To provide financial assistance to American Indian upper-division and graduate students working on a business degree.
Eligibility This program is open to American Indians who are currently enrolled full time in college at the upper-division or graduate school level and working on a business degree. Applicants must submit a letter on their reasons for pursuing higher education and their plans following completion of their degree. Selection is based on grades (30%), an essay on their community involvement (30%), an essay on personal challenges they have faced (25%), an essay on their paid or volunteer business experience (10%), and the quality of those essays (5%).
Financial data A stipend is awarded (amount not specified).
Duration 1 year.
Number awarded Up to 5 each year.
Deadline July of each year.

[28]
AMERICAN INDIAN SERVICES SCHOLARSHIP PROGRAM

American Indian Services
1902 North Canyon Road, Suite 100
Provo, UT 84604
(801) 375-1777   Toll-free: (888) 227-4120
Fax: (801) 375-1643
Web: www.americanindianservices.org/students.html

Purpose To provide financial assistance for college to Native Americans who demonstrate financial need.
Eligibility This program is open to undergraduate students who have completed no more than 150 semester credits at a university, college, junior college, or technical school with a GPA of 2.25 or higher. Applicants must be able to document their Indian heritage with a Certificate of Indian Blood (CIB), other official document, or an official document for their parent or grandparent. They must be at least one-quarter North American Native Indian blood. Along with their application, they must submit a 1-page letter about themselves, including their tribe, where they are from, the school they are attending, their area of study, their educational goals and future plans, and why they feel they need this scholarship. Selection is based on financial need, academic status, and availability of funds.
Financial data Students are expected to arrange for payment of half their tuition. This program pays the other half, from $200 to $1,500.
Duration 1 semester; may be renewed if the recipient maintains a GPA of 2.25 or higher.
Number awarded Recently, more than 1,500 of these scholarships were awarded.
Deadline February of each year for classes starting in April or May; May of each year for classes starting in June; August of each year for classes starting in August or September; November of each year for classes starting in January.

[29]
AMERICAN INSTITUTE OF ARCHITECTS MINORITY/DISADVANTAGED SCHOLARSHIP PROGRAM

American Institute of Architects
Attn: American Architectural Foundation
1799 New York Avenue, N.W.
Washington, DC 20006-5292
(202) 626-7511   Fax: (202) 626-7420
E-mail: info@archfoundation.org
Web: www.archfoundation.org

Purpose To provide financial assistance to high school and college students from minority and/or disadvantaged backgrounds who are interested in studying architecture in college.
Eligibility This program is open to students from minority and/or disadvantaged backgrounds who are high school seniors, students in a community college or technical school transferring to an accredited architectural program, or college freshmen entering a professional degree program at an accredited program of architecture. Students who have completed 1 or more years of a 4-year college curriculum are not eligible. Initially, candidates must be nominated by 1 of the following organizations or persons: an individual

architect or firm, a chapter of the American Institute of Architects (AIA), a community design center, a guidance counselor or teacher, the dean or professor at an accredited school of architecture, or the director of a community or civic organization. Nominees are reviewed and eligible candidates are invited to complete an application form in which they write an essay describing the reasons they are interested in becoming an architect and provide documentation of academic excellence and financial need. Selection is based primarily on financial need.
Financial data Stipends range from $500 to $2,500 per year, depending upon individual need. Students must apply for supplementary funds from other sources.
Duration 9 months; may be renewed for up to 2 additional years.
Additional information This program, established in 1970, is offered jointly by the American Architectural Foundation (AAF) and the AIA.
Number awarded Up to 20 each year.
Deadline Nominations are due by December of each year; final applications must be submitted in January.

[30]
AMERICAN PHYSICAL SOCIETY SCHOLARSHIPS FOR MINORITY UNDERGRADUATE PHYSICS MAJORS

American Physical Society
Attn: Committee on Minorities
One Physics Ellipse
College Park, MD 20740-3844
(301) 209-3232   Fax: (301) 209-0865
Web: www.aps.org

Purpose To provide financial assistance to Native American and other underrepresented minority students interested in studying physics on the undergraduate level.
Eligibility Any African American, Hispanic American, or Native American who plans to major in physics and who is a high school senior or college freshman or sophomore may apply. U.S. citizenship or permanent resident status is required. The selection committee especially encourages applications from students who are attending or planning to attend institutions with historically or predominantly Black, Hispanic, or Native American enrollment. Selection is based on commitment to the study of physics and plans to work on a physics baccalaureate degree.
Financial data Stipends are $2,000 per year in the first year or $3,000 in the second year; funds must be used for tuition, room, and board. In addition, $500 is awarded to the host department.
Duration 1 year; renewable for 1 additional year with the approval of the APS selection committee.
Additional information APS conducts this program, which began in 1980 as the Corporate-Sponsored Scholarships for Minority Undergraduate Students Who Major in Physics, in conjunction with the Corporate Associates of the American Institute of Physics. Each scholarship is sponsored by a corporation, which is normally designated as the sponsor. A corporation generally sponsors from 1 to 10 scholarships, depending upon its size and utilization of physics in the business.
Number awarded Varies each year; recently, 26 of these scholarships were awarded.

Deadline February of each year.

[31]
AMS UNDERGRADUATE SCHOLARSHIPS

American Meteorological Society
Attn: Fellowship/Scholarship Program
45 Beacon Street
Boston, MA 02108-3693
(617) 227-2426, ext. 246   Fax: (617) 742-8718
E-mail: scholar@ametsoc.org
Web: www.ametsoc.org

Purpose To provide financial assistance to minority and other undergraduates majoring in meteorology or an aspect of atmospheric sciences.
Eligibility This program is open to full-time students entering their final year of undergraduate study and majoring in meteorology or an aspect of the atmospheric or related oceanic and hydrologic sciences. Applicants must intend to make atmospheric or related sciences their career. They must be U.S. citizens or permanent residents enrolled at a U.S. institution and have a cumulative GPA of 3.25 or higher. Along with their application, they must submit 200-word essays on 1) their most important achievements that qualify them for this scholarship, and 2) their career goals in the atmospheric or related oceanic or hydrologic fields. Selection is based on academic excellence and achievement; financial need is not considered. The sponsor specifically encourages applications from women, minorities, and students with disabilities who are traditionally underrepresented in the atmospheric and related oceanic sciences.
Financial data Stipends range from $700 to $5,000 per year.
Duration 1 year.
Additional information Requests for an application must be accompanied by a self-addressed stamped envelope.
Number awarded Varies each year; recently, 15 of these scholarships were awarded.
Deadline February of each year.

[32]
AMY LOUISE HUNTER-WILSON, M.D. MEMORIAL SCHOLARSHIP

Wisconsin Medical Society
Attn: Executive Director, Wisconsin Medical Society
    Foundation
330 East Lakeside Street
P.O. Box 1109
Madison, WI 53701-1109
(608) 442-3722   Toll-free: (866) 442-3800, ext. 3722
Fax: (608) 442-3851   E-mail: eileenw@wismed.org
Web: www.wisconsinmedicalsociety.org/foundation

Purpose To provide financial assistance to American Indians (especially those from Wisconsin) interested in working on a degree in medicine, nursing, or allied health care.
Eligibility This program is open to members of federally-recognized American Indian tribes who are 1) full-time students enrolled in a health career program at an accredited institution, 2) adults returning to school in an allied health field, and 3) adults working in a non-professional health-related field returning for a professional license or degree.

Applicants must be working on a degree or advanced training as a doctor of medicine, nurse, physician assistant, technician, or other health-related professional. Preference is given to residents of Wisconsin who are students at educational institutions in the state. U.S. citizenship is required. Selection is based on financial need, academic achievement, personal qualities and strengths, and letters of recommendation.
Financial data Stipends range from $1,000 to $4,000.
Duration 1 year.
Number awarded Varies each year. Recently 7 of these scholarships were awarded: 3 at $1,000, 2 at $1,500, 1 at $2,000, and 1 at $4,000.
Deadline January of each year.

[33]
ANAC STUDENT DIVERSITY MENTORSHIP SCHOLARSHIP
Association of Nurses in AIDS Care
3538 Ridgewood Road
Akron, OH 44333-3122
(330) 670-0101   Toll-free: (800) 260-6780
Fax: (330) 670-0109   E-mail: anac@anacnet.org
Web: www.anacnet.org

Purpose To provide financial assistance to student nurses from Native American and other minority groups who are interested in HIV/AIDS nursing and in attending the national conference of the Association of Nurses in AIDS Care (ANAC).
Eligibility This program is open to student nurses from a diverse racial or ethnic background, defined to include African Americans, Hispanics/Latinos, Asians/Pacific Islanders, and American Indians/Alaskan Natives. Candidates must have a genuine interest in HIV/AIDS nursing, be interested in attending the ANAC national conference, and desire to develop a mentorship relationship with a member of the ANAC Diversity Specialty Committee. They must be currently enrolled in an accredited nursing program at any level (e.g., L.P.N., A.D.N., diploma, B.S.N., or graduate nursing). Nominees may be recommended by themselves, nursing faculty members, or ANAC members, but their nomination must be supported by an ANAC member. Along with their nomination form, they must submit a 500-word personal statement describing their interest or experience in HIV/AIDS care and why they want to attend the ANAC conference.
Financial data Recipients are awarded a $1,000 scholarship (paid directly to the school), up to $599 in reimbursement of travel expenses to attend the ANAC annual conference, free conference registration, an award plaque, a free ticket to the awards ceremony at the conference, and a 1-year ANAC membership.
Duration 1 year.
Additional information The mentor will be assigned at the conference and will maintain contact during the period of study.
Number awarded 1 each year.
Deadline May of each year.

[34]
ANNE H. MYERS SCHOLARSHIP
Ke Ali'i Pauahi Foundation
Attn: Financial Aid & Scholarship Services
567 South King Street, Suite 160
Honolulu, HI 96813
(808) 534-3966   Toll-free: (800) 842-4682, ext. 43966
Fax: (808) 534-3890   E-mail: scholarships@pauahi.org
Web: www.pauahi.org

Purpose To provide financial assistance to undergraduate students from Hawaii, especially those of Hawaiian descent.
Eligibility This program is open to residents of Hawaii who are enrolled full time at an accredited college or university in any state and working on an undergraduate degree. Applicants must be able to demonstrate financial need and a record of academic achievement. Preference is given to Native Hawaiians (descendants of the aboriginal inhabitants of the Hawaiian Islands prior to 1778).
Financial data A stipend is awarded (amount not specified).
Duration 1 year.
Number awarded 1 or more each year.
Deadline April of each year.

[35]
APICDA HIGHER EDUCATION SCHOLARSHIPS
Aleutian Pribilof Island Community Development Association
Attn: Human Resources Director
509 West Third Avenue, Suite 101
Anchorage, AK 99501
(907) 929-5273   Toll-free: (800) 927-4232
Fax: (907) 929-5275   E-mail: ldelgado@apicda.com
Web: www.apicda.com

Purpose To provide financial assistance to Alaska residents who have ties to member communities of the Aleutian Pribilof Island Community Development Association (APICDA) and are planning to attend college or graduate school in any state.
Eligibility This program is open to residents of Alaska who have an affiliation with APICDA either through an historical relationship (Natives and non-Natives who have an historical relationship with 1 or more of the following communities: Akutan, Atka, False Pass, Nelson Lagoon, Nikolski, St. George, and Unalaska) or a residency relationship (full-time residents of those communities for at least the past 5 years). Applicants must intend to return to (or work for the benefit of) the APIDCA region upon completion of school. They must be working on or planning to work on an associate, bachelor's, master's, or doctoral degree. Along with their application, they must submit a personal statement that includes their educational and professional development goals, why they wish to attend school, what they plan to do after receiving their degree, and the contributions they believe they will be able to make to the communities of the APICDA region or to Alaska in general after achieving their goals.
Financial data The stipend is $2,500 per semester. Funds may be used for registration, tuition, books, room, board, and other reasonable educational expenses.

Duration 1 year; may be renewed as long as the recipient maintains full-time enrollment and a GPA of 2.0 or higher.
Number awarded Varies each year; recently 87 of these scholarships were awarded.
Deadline June of each year for full-year scholarships; November of each year for winter or spring terms.

[36]
APICDA SUPPLEMENTAL EDUCATION GRANTS
Aleutian Pribilof Island Community Development Association
Attn: Human Resources Director
509 West Third Avenue, Suite 101
Anchorage, AK 99501
(907) 929-5273   Toll-free: (800) 927-4232
Fax: (907) 929-5275   E-mail: ldelgado@apicda.com
Web: www.apicda.com

Purpose To provide financial assistance for vocational or related training to Alaska residents with ties to member communities of the Aleutian Pribilof Island Community Development Association (APICDA).
Eligibility This program is open to residents of the following communities in Alaska: Akutan, Atka, False Pass, Nelson Lagoon, Nikolski, St. George, and Unalaska. Applicants must be interested in a program of vocational education, training, or correspondence study. Along with their application, they must submit a brief statement on their educational and professional development goals, why they wish to attend school, what they plan to do after receiving their training, and the contribution they will make to the APICDA region after achieving their educational goals.
Financial data The stipend depends on the need of the recipient, to a maximum of $3,000 per year. Funds may be used for registration, tuition, books, transportation, or other reasonable educational expenses.
Duration 1 term; may be renewed.
Number awarded Varies each year; recently, 30 of these scholarships were awarded.
Deadline Applications may be submitted at any time, but they must be received at least 10 days prior to the start date of the training or education course.

[37]
APPRAISAL INSTITUTE MINORITIES AND WOMEN EDUCATIONAL SCHOLARSHIP PROGRAM
Appraisal Institute
Attn: Minorities and Women Scholarship Fund
550 West Van Buren Street, Suite 1000
Chicago, IL 60607
(312) 335-4191   Fax: (312) 335-4196
E-mail: hrichmond@appraisalinstitute.org
Web: www.appraisalinstitute.org

Purpose To provide financial assistance to women and minority undergraduate students majoring in real estate or allied fields.
Eligibility This program is open to members of groups underrepresented in the real estate appraisal profession. Those groups include women, American Indians, Alaska Natives, Asians and Pacific Islanders, Blacks or African Americans, and Hispanics. Applicants must be full- or part-time students enrolled in real estate courses within a degree-granting college, university, or junior college. They must have a GPA of 2.5 or higher and be able to demonstrate financial need. U.S. citizenship is required.
Financial data The stipend is $1,000 per year. Funds are paid directly to the recipient's institution to be used for tuition and fees.
Duration 1 year.
Number awarded At least 1 each year.
Deadline April of each year.

[38]
AQQALUK TRUST SCHOLARSHIPS
Robert Aqqaluk Newlin, Sr. Memorial Trust
Attn: Education Director
P.O. Box 509
Kotzebue, AK 99752
(907) 442-1607   Toll-free: (866) 442-1607
Fax: (907) 442-2289   E-mail: erica.nelson@nana.com
Web: www.aqqaluktrust.com/scholar.html

Purpose To provide financial assistance for college to Alaska Natives who are associated with the Northwest Alaska Native Association (NANA) Regional Corporation.
Eligibility This program is open to NANA shareholders, descendants of NANA shareholders, and dependents of NANA shareholders and their descendants. Applicants must have a GED or high school diploma with a cumulative GPA of 2.0 or higher and be enrolled or accepted for enrollment at an accredited or authorized college, university, or vocational technical skills program for which a certificate of completion is issued at the conclusion of studies. Along with their application, they must submit a statement that explains how they intend to use their education to enhance Inupiaq values and culture, summarizes their accomplishments, and describes their educational and career goals.
Financial data Stipends are $2,000 per semester for full-time students or $1,000 per semester for part-time students. Funds must be used for tuition, fees, books, course-related supplies, room, board, and similar expenses.
Duration 1 semester; recipients may reapply by providing a letter updating their educational and career goals, explaining how they are moving toward their goals, and reporting how the previous funds were spend.
Additional information The NANA Regional Corporation previously administered its scholarship program, but it recently transferred its education department to the Robert Aqqaluk Newlin, Sr. Memorial Trust. Sponsors of the program include the NANA Regional Corporation, Teck Cominco Limited, and Qivliq, LLC.
Number awarded Varies each year, depending upon the availability of funds and qualified applicants.
Deadline College and university students must apply by July of each year for fall semester or quarter, October of each year for winter quarter, January of each year for spring semester, February of each year for spring quarter, or May of each year for summer school. Vocational/technical students must apply before the start of training.

[39]
ARAPAHO EDUCATIONAL TRUST SCHOLARSHIP

Northern Arapaho Tribe
Attn: Sky People Higher Education
P.O. Box 8480
Ethete, WY 82520
(307) 332-5286   Toll-free: (800) 815-6795
Fax: (307) 332-9104
E-mail: assistant@skypeopleed.org
Web: www.skypeopleed.org

Purpose To provide financial assistance to members of the Northern Arapaho Tribe who are working on an undergraduate or graduate degree in engineering, law, or the sciences.

Eligibility This program is open to full-time undergraduate and graduate students who have an undergraduate GPA of 2.0 or higher or the graduate GPA required by their school. Applicants must be of one-fourth Northern Arapaho descent (enrolled or non-enrolled) and must submit a Certificate of Indian Blood or other verification of Northern Arapaho blood with at least one-fourth degree. They must be working on a degree in engineering, law, or the sciences. Along with their application, they must submit a 1-page personal statement that includes a brief history of their background, academic ability and achievement, work or leadership experience, participation in community-related activities, and career goals. Selection is based on that statement, potential to contribute to the community upon graduation, academic ability and achievement, and a letter of recommendation.

Financial data The stipend is $1,500 per year.
Duration 1 year; may be renewed.
Additional information The recipient is expected to apply for employment with the Northern Arapaho Tribe after graduation.
Number awarded 1 each year.
Deadline June of each year.

[40]
ARAPAHO RANCH EDUCATIONAL TRUST SCHOLARSHIP

Northern Arapaho Tribe
Attn: Sky People Higher Education
P.O. Box 8480
Ethete, WY 82520
(307) 332-5286   Toll-free: (800) 815-6795
Fax: (307) 332-9104
E-mail: assistant@skypeopleed.org
Web: www.skypeopleed.org

Purpose To provide financial assistance to members of the Northern Arapaho Tribe who are working on an undergraduate or graduate degree in conservation-related fields.

Eligibility This program is open to full-time undergraduate and graduate students who have an undergraduate GPA of 2.0 or higher or the graduate GPA required by their school. Applicants must be of one-fourth Northern Arapaho descent (enrolled or non-enrolled) and must submit a Certificate of Indian Blood or other verification of Northern Arapaho blood with at least one-fourth degree. They must be working on a degree in range conservation, forestry, animal sciences, or ranch and range management. Along with their application, they must submit a 1-page personal statement that includes a brief history of their background, academic ability and achievement, work or leadership experience, participation in community-related activities, and career goals. Selection is based on that statement, potential to contribute to the community upon graduation, academic ability and achievement, and a letter of recommendation.

Financial data The stipend is $2,000 per year.
Duration 1 year; may be renewed.
Number awarded 1 each year.
Deadline June of each year.

[41]
ARCTIC EDUCATION FOUNDATION SCHOLARSHIPS

Arctic Education Foundation
P.O. Box 129
Barrow, AK 99723
(907) 852-8633   Toll-free: (800) 770-2772
Fax: (907) 852-2774   E-mail: swilliams@asrc.com
Web: www.arcticed.com

Purpose To provide financial assistance Inupiat Natives who have ties to the Arctic Slope region of Alaska and plan to attend a college or graduate school in any state.

Eligibility This program is open to U.S. citizens who are 1) a northern Alaskan Inupiat Native currently residing in the Arctic Slope region of Alaska; 2) an original shareholder of the Arctic Slope Regional Corporation (ASRC); or 3) a direct lineal descendant of an original ASRC shareholder. Applicants must be attending or planning to attend a college, university, or vocational/technical school in any state as a full- or part-time undergraduate or graduate student. Along with their application, they must submit documentation of financial need and a short paragraph on their personal plans upon completion of study.

Financial data The stipend depends on the need of the recipient.
Duration 1 year; may be renewed.
Number awarded Varies each year.
Deadline February of each year for spring quarter or early summer; May of each year for summer school; July of each year for fall semester or quarter; or November of each year for spring semester or winter quarter.

[42]
ARTHUR C. PARKER SCHOLARSHIPS

Society for American Archaeology
900 Second Street, N.E., Suite 12
Washington, DC 20002-3560
(202) 789-8200   Fax: (202) 789-0284
E-mail: headquarters@saa.org
Web: ecommerce.saa.org

Purpose To provide financial assistance to Native American students and professionals interested in additional training in archaeological methods.

Eligibility This program is open to high school seniors, college undergraduates, graduate students, and personnel of tribal or other Native cultural preservation programs. Applicants must be Native Americans or Pacific Islanders from the United States, including U.S. Trust Territories, or indigenous people from Canada. Documentation of Native identity is required, but applicants do not have to be enrolled in a Native group, of certified Indian status, or a member of a group formally recognized by the U.S. or Canadian government to be eligible. Applicants must be interested in attending a training program in archaeological methods offered by an accredited college or university, including field work, analytical techniques, and curation. Other types of archaeological methods training programs are considered on a case-by-case basis. Individuals may apply themselves, or they may be nominated by a high school teacher, current professor, or cultural preservation program supervisor. Along with the application, they must submit 1) a letter of nomination or recommendation; 2) a personal statement describing why they are interested in attending the archaeological methods training program and how the training will benefit them as well as their Native community; 3) a brief description of the training program; 4) an itemized budget; and 5) documentation of Native identity.

Financial data The stipend is $4,000.
Additional information Half of 1 of these scholarships is funded by the Society for American Archaeology. The other half of that scholarship and all of the other scholarships, designated as NSF Scholarships for Archaeological Training for Native Americans and Native Hawaiians, are funded by the National Science Foundation (NSF).
Number awarded 4 each year.
Deadline December of each year.

[43]
ASSE DIVERSITY COMMITTEE SCHOLARSHIP
American Society of Safety Engineers
Attn: ASSE Foundation
1800 East Oakton Street
Des Plaines, IL 60018
(847) 768-3435   Fax: (847) 768-3434
E-mail: agabanski@asse.org
Web: www.asse.org

Purpose To provide financial assistance to upper-division and graduate student members of the American Society of Safety Engineers (ASSE) who come from diverse groups.
Eligibility This program is open to ASSE student members who are majoring in occupational safety, health, and environment or a closely-related field (e.g., industrial or environmental engineering, environmental science, industrial hygiene, occupational health nursing). Undergraduates must be full-time students who have completed at least 60 semester hours with a GPA of 3.0 or higher. Graduate students must also be enrolled full time, have completed at least 9 semester hours with a GPA of 3.5 or higher, and have had a GPA of 3.0 or higher as an undergraduate. Along with their application, they must submit 2 essays of 300 words or less: 1) why they are seeking a degree in occupational safety and health or a closely-related field, a brief description of their current activities, and how those relate to their career goals and objectives; and 2) why they should be awarded this scholarship (including career goals and financial need). A goal of this program is to support individuals regardless of race, ethnicity, gender, religion, personal beliefs, age, sexual orientation, physical challenges, geographic location, university, or specific area of study. U.S. citizenship is not required.
Financial data The stipend is $1,000 per year.
Duration 1 year; recipients may reapply.
Number awarded 1 each year.
Deadline November of each year.

[44]
ASSE UPS DIVERSITY SCHOLARSHIPS
American Society of Safety Engineers
Attn: ASSE Foundation
1800 East Oakton Street
Des Plaines, IL 60018
(847) 768-3435   Fax: (847) 768-3434
E-mail: agabanski@asse.org
Web: www.asse.org

Purpose To provide financial assistance to Native American and other minority upper-division student members of the American Society of Safety Engineers (ASSE).
Eligibility This program is open to ASSE student members who are U.S. citizens and members of minority ethnic or racial groups. Applicants must be majoring in occupational safety, health, and environment or a closely-related field (e.g., industrial or environmental engineering, environmental science, industrial hygiene, occupational health nursing). They must be full-time students who have completed at least 60 semester hours with a GPA of 3.0 or higher. Along with their application, they must submit 2 essays of 300 words or less: 1) why they are seeking a degree in occupational safety and health or a closely-related field, a brief description of their current activities, and how those relate to their career goals and objectives; and 2) why they should be awarded this scholarship (including career goals and financial need).
Financial data The stipend is $5,250 per year.
Duration 1 year; recipients may reapply.
Additional information Funding for this program is provided by the UPS Foundation.
Number awarded 2 each year.
Deadline November of each year.

[45]
ASSOCIATION FOR WOMEN GEOSCIENTISTS MINORITY SCHOLARSHIP
Association for Women Geoscientists
Attn: AWG Foundation
P.O. Box 30645
Lincoln, NE 68503-0645
E-mail: awgscholarship@yahoo.com
Web: www.awg.org/eas/minority.html

Purpose To provide financial assistance to Native American and other underrepresented minority women who are interested in working on an undergraduate degree in the geosciences.
Eligibility This program is open to women who are African American, Hispanic, or Native American (including Eskimo, Hawaiian, Samoan, or American Indian). Applicants must be full-time students working on, or planning to work on, an undergraduate degree in the geosciences (including geology, geophysics, geochemistry, hydrology, meteorology, physical oceanography, planetary geology, or earth science education). They must submit a 500-word essay on why they have chosen to major in the geosciences and their career goals, 2 letters of recommendation, high school

and/or college transcripts, and SAT or ACT scores. Financial need is not considered in the selection process.
Financial data A total of $5,000 is available for this program each year.
Duration 1 year; may be renewed.
Additional information This program, first offered in 2004, is supported by ExxonMobil Foundation.
Number awarded 1 or more each year.
Deadline June of each year.

[46]
ASSOCIATION ON AMERICAN INDIAN AFFAIRS DISPLACED HOMEMAKER SCHOLARSHIPS
Association on American Indian Affairs, Inc.
Attn: Director of Scholarship Programs
966 Hungerford Drive, Suite 12-B
Rockville, MD 20850
(240) 314-7155   Fax: (240) 314-7159
E-mail: lw.aaia@verizon.net
Web: www.indian-affairs.org

Purpose To provide financial assistance to Native American displaced homemakers who are trying to complete their college education.
Eligibility This program is open to full-time college students who are Native Americans and have special needs because of family responsibilities. Examples of displaced homemakers include students who are attending college for the first time at the age of 40 because they have put off higher education to raise their children, students who are entering or returning to college after their children enter elementary school, and men or women who have been divorced and had to leave college to care for children and are now returning. Applicants must submit documentation of financial need, a Certificate of Indian Blood showing at least one-quarter Indian blood, proof of tribal enrollment, an essay on their educational goals and family responsibilities, 2 letters of recommendation, and their most recent transcript.
Financial data The stipend is $1,500. Awards are intended to assist recipients with child care, transportation, and some basic living expenses as well as educational costs.
Duration Up to 3 years.
Number awarded Varies each year.
Deadline June of each year.

[47]
A.T. ANDERSON MEMORIAL SCHOLARSHIP PROGRAM
American Indian Science and Engineering Society
Attn: Scholarship Coordinator
2305 Renard, S.E., Suite 200
P.O. Box 9828
Albuquerque, NM 87119-9828
(505) 765-1052, ext. 106   Fax: (505) 765-5608
E-mail: shirley@aises.org
Web: www.aises.org

Purpose To provide financial assistance to members of the American Indian Science and Engineering Society who are majoring in designated fields as undergraduate or graduate students.
Eligibility This program is open to members of the society who can furnish a Certificate of Indian Blood or proof of enrollment in an American Indian tribe or Alaskan Native group. Applicants must be full-time students at the undergraduate or graduate level attending an accredited 4-year college or university or a 2-year college leading to an academic degree in engineering, mathematics, medicine, natural resources, physical science, the sciences, or technology. They must submit a 500-word essay on their educational and career goals, including their interest in and motivation to continue higher education, an understanding of the importance of college and completing their educational and/or career goals, and a commitment to learning and giving back to the community. Selection is based on the essay, academic achievement (GPA of 3.0 or higher), leadership potential, and commitment to helping other American Indians. Financial need is not considered.
Financial data The annual stipend is $1,000 for undergraduates or $2,000 for graduate students.
Duration 1 year; nonrenewable.
Additional information This program was launched in 1983 in memory of A.T. Anderson, a Mohawk and a chemical engineer who worked with Albert Einstein. Anderson was 1 of the society's founders and was the society's first executive director. The program includes the following named awards: the Al Qöyawayma Award for an applicant who is majoring in science or engineering and also has a strong interest in the arts, the Norbert S. Hill, Jr. Leadership Award, the Polingaysi Qöyawayma Award for an applicant who is working on a teaching degree in order to teach mathematics or science in a Native community or an advanced degree for personal improvement or teaching at the college level, and the Robert W. Brocksbank Scholarship.
Number awarded Varies; generally, 200 or more each year, depending upon the availability of funds from corporate and other sponsors.
Deadline June of each year.

[48]
BAKER HUGHES SCHOLARSHIPS
Society of Women Engineers
Attn: Scholarship Selection Committee
230 East Ohio Street, Suite 400
Chicago, IL 60611-3265
(312) 596-5223   Toll-free: (877) SWE-INFO
Fax: (312) 644-8557
E-mail: scholarshipapplication@swe.org
Web: societyofwomenengineers.swe.org

Purpose To provide financial assistance to minority and other women working on an undergraduate or graduate degree in designated engineering specialties.
Eligibility This program is open to women who are sophomores, juniors, seniors, or graduate students at 4-year ABET-accredited colleges and universities. Applicants must be working on a degree in computer science or chemical, electrical, mechanical, or petroleum engineering and have a GPA of 3.0 or higher. Preference is given to members of groups underrepresented in engineering or computer science. Selection is based on merit.
Financial data The stipend is $5,000.
Duration 1 year.

Additional information This program is sponsored by Baker Hughes Incorporated.
Number awarded 3 each year.
Deadline May of each year.

[49]
BANK2 BANKING SCHOLARSHIP
Chickasaw Foundation
110 West 12th Street
P.O. Box 1726
Ada, OK 74821-1726
(580) 421-9030 Fax: (580) 421-9031
E-mail: ChickasawFoundation@chickasaw.net
Web: www.chickasaw.net

Purpose To provide financial assistance to members of the Chickasaw Nation who are preparing for a career in banking.
Eligibility This program is open to Chickasaw students who are currently enrolled at a 4-year college or university as a full-time undergraduate student. Applicants must be majoring in finance, business, or accounting and preparing for a career in banking. Along with their application, they must submit high school or college transcripts, 2 letters of recommendation, a copy of their Chickasaw Nation citizenship card, and a 1-page essay on their long-term goals and plans for achieving them. Financial need is not considered in the selection process.
Financial data The stipend is $4,000 per year.
Duration 1 year.
Additional information This program is supported by Bank2, headquartered in Oklahoma City and owned by the Chickasaw Nation.
Number awarded 1 each year.
Deadline June of each year.

[50]
BANK2 TA-OSSAA-ASHA' SCHOLARSHIPS
Chickasaw Foundation
110 West 12th Street
P.O. Box 1726
Ada, OK 74821-1726
(580) 421-9030 Fax: (580) 421-9031
E-mail: ChickasawFoundation@chickasaw.net
Web: www.chickasaw.net

Purpose To provide financial assistance to members of the Chickasaw Nation who are preparing for a career in banking.
Eligibility This program is open to Chickasaw students who are currently enrolled at an accredited institution of higher education as a full-time undergraduate student. Applicants must be majoring in finance, business, or accounting and preparing for a career in banking. Along with their application, they must submit high school or college transcripts, 2 letters of recommendation, a copy of their Chickasaw Nation citizenship card, and a 1-page essay on their long-term goals and plans for achieving them. Financial need is not considered in the selection process.
Financial data The stipend is $1,000 per year.
Duration 1 year.
Additional information This program is supported by Bank2, headquartered in Oklahoma City and owned by the Chickasaw Nation.
Number awarded 4 each year.
Deadline June of each year.

[51]
BERING STRAITS FOUNDATION HIGHER EDUCATION AND VOCATIONAL TRAINING SCHOLARSHIPS
Bering Straits Native Corporation
Attn: Bering Straits Foundation
110 Front Street, Suite 300
P.O. Box 1008
Nome, AK 99762-1008
(907) 443-4305 Toll-free: (800) 478-5079 (within AK)
Fax: (907) 443-2985
E-mail: foundation@beringstraits.com
Web: www.beringstraits.com

Purpose To provide supplemental financial assistance to Alaska Natives with ties to the Bering Straits area who are entering or enrolled in an undergraduate or graduate program in any state.
Eligibility This program is open to Native Alaskans enrolled to the Bering Straits Native Corporation and lineal descendants (natural or adopted children) of persons enrolled to the Bering Straits Native Corporation. Applicants for higher education scholarships must be graduating or have graduated from high school with a GPA of 3.0 or higher (or have earned a GED); applicants for vocational training scholarships must be high school seniors with a GPA of 2.5 or higher. All applicants must be accepted or currently enrolled (as an undergraduate or graduate student) at an accredited college, university, or vocational school in any state as a full-time student and be able to demonstrate financial need. Along with their application, they must submit a personal statement outlining their educational goals and objectives.
Financial data Stipends range from $500 to $1,000 per semester for students who have a GPA of 3.0 or higher, up to $400 per semester for students who have a GPA less than 3.0, or up to $500 per semester for vocational students. Funds are paid directly to the recipient's school.
Duration 1 semester; may be renewed if the recipient maintains a GPA of 2.0 or higher during the first semester and 2.5 or higher in succeeding semesters.
Number awarded Varies each year.
Deadline June of each year for the fall semester; December of each year for the spring semester.

FINANCIAL AID PROGRAMS

[52]
BERNARD BOUSCHOR HONORARY SCHOLARSHIP PROGRAM

Sault Tribe of Chippewa Indians
Attn: Higher Education Department
Two Ice Circle
Sault Ste. Marie, MI 49783
(906) 635-7784 Toll-free: (800) 793-0660
Fax: (906) 635-7785 E-mail: jlewton@saulttribe.net
Web: www.saulttribe.com

Purpose To provide financial assistance for college to members of the Sault Tribe of Chippewa Indians.

Eligibility This program is open to enrolled members of the Sault Tribe who have been accepted at or are attending a 2-year or 4-year college or university in the United States or Canada as a full-time student. Applicants must submit an essay of 300 to 500 words on how their education will benefit them and why they should receive the scholarship.

Financial data The stipend is $1,000 per year.
Duration 1 year.
Number awarded 20 each year.
Deadline May of each year.

[53]
BHP BILLITON SCHOLARSHIP PROGRAM

BHP Billiton-New Mexico Coal
Attn: Scholarship Program
P.O. Box 561
Waterflow, NM 87421
(505) 598-2169 Fax: (505) 598-2102
E-mail: bhpnmscholarship@bhpbilliton.com
Web: www.bhpbilliton.com

Purpose To provide financial assistance to enrolled members of the Navajo Nation or Ute Mountain Ute Tribe majoring in selected fields.

Eligibility This program is open to registered members of the Navajo Nation and the Ute Mountain Ute Tribe who are graduating high school seniors or undergraduates enrolled full time at a 4-year college or university. Applicants must have an ACT score of 22 or higher, have a GPA of 3.0 or higher, and be interested in majoring in engineering (mining, civil, environmental, mechanical, or electrical), accounting, labor or industrial relations, human resources, information systems, or occupational safety. They must submit a Certificate of Indian Blood, transcripts, an acceptance letter from an institution, and a cover letter indicating their career goals and objectives for earning their degree.

Financial data Stipends range from $500 to $1,000 per year. Funds are paid in 2 equal installments.
Duration 1 year; may be renewed.
Number awarded Varies each year; recently, 109 of these scholarships were awarded.
Deadline June of each year.

[54]
BIA HIGHER EDUCATION GRANT PROGRAM

Bureau of Indian Affairs
Attn: Office of Indian Education Programs
1849 C Street, N.W.
MS 3512-MIB
Washington, DC 20240-0001
(202) 208-6123 Fax: (202) 208-3312
Web: www.oiep.bia.edu

Purpose To provide financial assistance to undergraduate students who belong to or are affiliated with federally-recognized Indian tribes.

Eligibility This program is open to 1) members of American Indian tribes who are eligible for the special programs and services provided through the Bureau of Indian Affairs (BIA) because of their status as Indians, and 2) individuals who are at least one-quarter degree Indian blood descendants of those members. Applicants must be 1) enrolled or planning to enroll at an accredited college or university in a course of study leading to an associate of arts or bachelor's degree and 2) able to demonstrate financial need. Most tribes administer the grant program directly for their members, but other tribal members may contact the BIA Office of Indian Education Programs to learn the name and address of the nearest Education Line Officer who can provide an application and assistance in completing it.

Financial data Individual awards depend on the financial need of the recipient; they range from $300 to $5,000 and average $2,800 per year. Recently, a total of $20,290,000 was available for this program.
Duration 1 year; may be renewed for up to 4 additional years.
Additional information Funds may be used for either part-time or full-time study. This program was authorized by the Snyder Act of 1921.
Number awarded Approximately 9,500 students receive assistance through this program annually.
Deadline June of each year for fall term; October of each year for spring term; April of each year for summer school.

[55]
BILL DICKEY GOLF SCHOLARSHIPS

Bill Dickey Scholarship Association.
Attn: Scholarship Committee
1140 East Washington Street, Suite 103
Phoenix, AZ 85034
(602) 258-7851 Fax: (602) 258-3412
E-mail: andrea@bdscholar.org
Web: www.nmjgsa.org/bdsa_scholarships.htm

Purpose To provide financial assistance to Native American and other minority high school seniors and undergraduate students who excel at golf.

Eligibility This program is open to graduating high school seniors and current undergraduate students who are members of minority groups (African American, Asian/Pacific Islander, Hispanic, or American Indian/Alaskan Native). Applicants must submit a 500-word essay on this question: "One of the principal goals of education and golf is fostering ways for people to respect and get along with individuals who think, dress, look, and act differently. How might you make this goal a reality?" Selection is based on academic

achievement; personal recommendations; participation in golf, school, and community activities; and financial need.
Financial data Stipends range from 1-time awards of $1,000 to 4-year awards of $6,000 per year. Funds are paid directly to the recipient's college.
Duration 1 year or longer.
Additional information This program was established in 1984 as the National Minority Junior Golf Association Scholarship and given its current name in 2006. Support is provided by the Jackie Robinson Foundation, PGA of America, Anheuser-Busch, the Tiger Woods Foundation, and other cooperating organizations.
Number awarded Varies; generally 80 or more each year.
Deadline April of each year.

[56]
BILL FRYREAR MEMORIAL SCHOLARSHIPS

Chickasaw Foundation
110 West 12th Street
P.O. Box 1726
Ada, OK 74821-1726
(580) 421-9030 Fax: (580) 421-9031
E-mail: ChickasawFoundation@chickasaw.net
Web: www.chickasaw.net

Purpose To provide financial assistance to members of the Chickasaw Nation who are working on an undergraduate degree in art or history.
Eligibility This program is open to Chickasaw students who are currently enrolled at an accredited institution of higher education as a full-time undergraduate student. Applicants must be majoring in art or history. Along with their application, they must submit high school or college transcripts, 2 letters of recommendation, a copy of their Chickasaw Nation citizenship card, and a 1-page essay on their long-term goals and plans for achieving them. Financial need is not considered in the selection process.
Financial data The stipend is $1,000 per year.
Duration 1 year.
Number awarded 1 each year.
Deadline June of each year.

[57]
BILL TAYLOR SCHOLARSHIP ENDOWMENT

North Carolina Community Foundation
Attn: Grant and Scholarship Administrator
4601 Six Forks Road, Suite 524
Raleigh, NC 27609
(919) 828-4387 Toll-free: (800) 201-9533
Fax: (919) 828-5495
E-mail: khinton@nccommunityfoundation.org
Web: www.nccommunityfoundation.org

Purpose To provide financial assistance to enrolled members of the Eastern Band of Cherokees who interested in working on a business administration or business-related degree.
Eligibility Eligible to apply are students working on a degree in business administration or a business-related program. Applicants must be enrolled members of the Eastern Band of Cherokees.
Financial data A stipend is awarded (amount not specified).
Duration 1 year.
Additional information This program was established by the Tribal Casino Gaming Enterprise/Harrah's' Cherokee Smokey Mountain Casino.
Number awarded 1 or more each year.
Deadline May of each year.

[58]
BILL THUNDER, JR./ARAPAHO RANCH TRUST SCHOLARSHIP

Northern Arapaho Tribe
Attn: Sky People Higher Education
P.O. Box 8480
Ethete, WY 82520
(307) 332-5286 Toll-free: (800) 815-6795
Fax: (307) 332-9104
E-mail: assistant@skypeopleed.org
Web: www.skypeopleed.org

Purpose To provide financial assistance to members of the Northern Arapaho Tribe who are working on an undergraduate or graduate degree in agriculture or a related field.
Eligibility This program is open to full-time undergraduate and graduate students who have an undergraduate GPA of 2.0 or higher or the graduate GPA required by their school. Applicants must be of one-fourth Northern Arapaho descent (enrolled or non-enrolled) and must submit a Certificate of Indian Blood or other verification of Northern Arapaho blood with at least one-fourth degree. They must be working on a degree in agriculture or a related field (agribusiness, veterinary studies, animal science, horticulture, resource economics, rangeland ecosystem science, or agronomy). Along with their application, they must submit a 1-page personal statement that includes a brief history of their background, academic ability and achievement, work or leadership experience, participation in community-related activities, and career goals. Selection is based on that statement, potential to contribute to the community upon graduation, academic ability and achievement, and a letter of recommendation.
Financial data The stipend is $2,500 per year.
Duration 1 year; may be renewed.
Additional information The recipient is expected to apply for employment with the Northern Arapaho Tribe after graduation.
Number awarded 1 each year.
Deadline June of each year.

[59]
BILLY L. CYPRESS SCHOLARSHIP

Seminole Tribe of Florida
Attn: Higher Education Advisor
3100 North 63 Avenue
Hollywood, FL 33024
(954) 989-6840, ext. 1311 Toll-free: (877) 592-6573
Fax: (954) 893-8856
Web: www.seminoletribe.com

Purpose To provide financial assistance to members of the Seminole Tribe of Florida who plan to attend college in any state.
Eligibility This program is open to Seminole tribal members who are applying to or currently enrolled in a program

of higher education at a college, university, or vocational school in any state.
Financial data The amount of the award depends on the availability of funds and the need of the recipient.
Duration 1 year; may be renewed.
Number awarded Varies each year.
Deadline June of each year for fall term; October of each year for spring term; March of each year for summer term.

[60]
BLACKFEET ADULT VOCATIONAL TRAINING GRANTS
Blackfeet Nation
Attn: Higher Education Program
P.O. Box 850
Browning, MT 59417
(406) 338-7539   Fax: (406) 338-7530
E-mail: bhep@3rivers.net
Web: www.blackfeetnation.com

Purpose To provide financial assistance for vocational training to members of the Blackfeet and other tribes.
Eligibility This program is open to enrolled members of a federally-recognized tribe between 18 and 35 years of age in need of training to obtain reasonable and satisfactory employment. Applicants must be willing to accept full-time employment as soon as possible after completion of training. Along with their application they must submit high school or GED transcripts, college transcripts (if they have ever attended college), a copy of the admission letter from the school they plan to attend, a financial needs analysis, a Certificate of Indian Blood, a copy of marriage license (if a spouse is claimed as financially dependent), a copy of birth certificates for any family members claimed as financially dependent, and military discharge papers (if applicable). Grants are awarded according to the following priorities: 1) Blackfeet tribal members residing on or near the Blackfeet Reservation; 2) Blackfeet tribal members residing off the Blackfeet Reservation; 3) members of other federally-recognized tribes (as funding permits); and 4) second training grant applicants (as funding permits).
Financial data The amount awarded varies, depending upon the recipient's educational requirements and financial needs. The maximum for an unmarried student with no dependents is $3,200 per year; for a student with 3 or more dependents; the maximum stipend is $3,800 per year. Funds are sent to the school's financial aid officer.
Duration Up to 24 months (36 months for registered nursing students) of full-time training.
Number awarded Varies each year.
Deadline February of each year.

[61]
BLACKFEET HIGHER EDUCATION GRANTS
Blackfeet Nation
Attn: Higher Education Program
P.O. Box 850
Browning, MT 59417
(406) 338-7539   Fax: (406) 338-7530
E-mail: bhep@3rivers.net
Web: www.blackfeetnation.com

Purpose To provide financial assistance to members of the Blackfeet Tribe who are interested in working on an undergraduate degree at a college or university in any state.
Eligibility Applicants must be enrolled members of the Blackfeet Tribe and be enrolled or accepted for enrollment as an undergraduate at an academically recognized college or university in any state. They must submit a 1-page letter describing their career goals and academic plans, high school or GED transcripts, college transcripts (if they have previously attended college), a copy of the admission letter from the college or university they plan to attend, a financial needs analysis, and a Certificate of Indian Blood. Scholarships are awarded according to the following priorities: 1) renewal of grants to students currently funded who are in good academic and financial aid standing and submit the application packet on time; 2) college seniors not currently funded who can graduate within the current academic year; 3) 2-year degree graduates who apply within 1 year of earning their associate degree; 4) high school seniors who apply within 1 year of earning their high school diploma; 5) applicants previously funded who are in good academic and financial aid standing and submit the application packet in a timely manner; and 6) candidates who submit late applications (supported only if funding permits).
Financial data The amount awarded varies, depending upon the recipient's educational requirements and financial needs. The maximum for an unmarried student with no dependents is $3,200 per year; for a student with 3 or more dependents; the maximum stipend is $3,800 per year. Funds are sent to the school's financial aid officer.
Duration 1 year; may be renewed up to a total of 10 semesters or 15 quarters.
Additional information Recipients must enroll as full-time students and earn no less than 12 credit hours per term with a GPA of 2.0 or higher as freshmen, 13 credits and 2.2 as sophomores, 14 credits and 2.4 as juniors, and 15 credits and 2.6 as seniors. Students who attend private schools or institutions outside of Montana must pay the difference in tuition, unless no comparable program exists at Montana public institutions.
Number awarded Varies each year.
Deadline February of each year; March of each year for summer term.

SCHOLARSHIPS

[62]
BLOSSOM KALAMA EVANS MEMORIAL SCHOLARSHIPS

Hawai'i Community Foundation
Attn: Scholarship Department
1164 Bishop Street, Suite 800
Honolulu, HI 96813
(808) 566-5570　　　　　Toll-free: (888) 731-3863
Fax: (808) 521-6286
E-mail: scholarships@hcf-hawaii.org
Web: www.hawaiicommunityfoundation.org

Purpose To provide financial assistance to residents of Hawaii of native ancestry who are interested in working on an undergraduate or graduate degree at a school in any state.

Eligibility This program is open to residents of Hawaii who are of Hawaiian ancestry and enrolled as full-time juniors, seniors, or graduate students at a college or university in any state. Applicants must be able to demonstrate financial need and academic achievement (GPA of 2.7 or higher). Along with their application, they must submit an essay indicating their reasons for attending college, their planned course of study, their career goals, and how they plan to use their knowledge to serve the needs of the Native Hawaiian community.

Financial data The amounts of the awards depend on the availability of funds and the need of the recipient; recently, stipends averaged $1,166.

Duration 1 year.

Number awarded Varies each year; recently, 9 of these scholarships were awarded.

Deadline February of each year.

[63]
BOIS FORTE HIGHER EDUCATION PROGRAM

Bois Forte Band of Chippewa
Attn: Department of Education and Training
5344 Lake Shore Drive
P.O. Box 16
Nett Lake, MN 55772
(218) 757-3261　　　　　Toll-free: (800) 221-8129
Fax: (218) 757-3312
E-mail: bmason@educ.boisforte.gov
Web: www.boisforte.com/divisions/education.htm

Purpose To provide financial assistance for undergraduate or graduate study to enrolled members of the Bois Forte Band of Chippewa Indians.

Eligibility Eligible to apply for this assistance are enrolled members of the Bois Forte Band of Chippewa Indians. Applicants must have been accepted at an institution of higher education and had their financial need determined by that institution based on the Free Application for Federal Student Aid (FAFSA). Minnesota residents must apply to the Indian Scholarship Assistance Program of the Minnesota Indian Scholarship Program. Applicants wishing to attend school outside of Minnesota must complete an out-of-state application form. Applicants must also apply for financial assistance from all other available sources, including but not limited to public and private grants and scholarships. They must not be in default of any tribal, federal, or state student education loan or in noncompliance with child support payments. Applicants are interviewed. Financial assistance is awarded on a first-come, first-served basis.

Financial data The maximum amount awarded is $5,000 per year for undergraduates or $6,250 per year for graduate students.

Duration 1 year; may be renewed for a total of 10 semesters of full-time enrollment or part-time equivalent provided recipients maintain a GPA of 2.0 or higher.

Additional information Students may receive financial assistance for summer school.

Number awarded Varies each year.

Deadline Applications may be submitted any time after January 1 but should be received no later than 8 weeks prior to the first day of school.

[64]
BOOKER T. WASHINGTON SCHOLARSHIPS

National FFA Organization
Attn: Scholarship Office
6060 FFA Drive
P.O. Box 68960
Indianapolis, IN 46268-0960
(317) 802-4419　　　　　Fax: (317) 802-5419
E-mail: scholarships@ffa.org
Web: www.ffa.org

Purpose To provide financial assistance to Native American and other minority FFA members who are interested in studying agriculture in college.

Eligibility This program is open to members who are graduating high school seniors planning to enroll full time in college. Applicants must be members of a minority ethnic group (African American, Asian American, Pacific Islander, Hispanic, Alaska Native, or American Indian) planning to work on a 4-year degree in agriculture. Selection is based on academic achievement (10 points for GPA, 10 points for SAT or ACT score, 10 points for class rank), leadership in FFA activities (30 points), leadership in community activities (10 points), and participation in the Supervised Agricultural Experience (SAE) program (30 points). U.S. citizenship is required.

Financial data Scholarships are either $10,000 or $5,000. Funds are paid directly to the recipient.

Duration 1 year; nonrenewable.

Number awarded 4 each year: 1 at $10,000 and 3 at $5,000.

Deadline February of each year.

[65]
BREAKTHROUGH TO NURSING SCHOLARSHIPS FOR RACIAL/ETHNIC MINORITIES

National Student Nurses' Association
Attn: NSNA Foundation
45 Main Street, Suite 606
Brooklyn, NY 11201
(718) 210-0705　　　　　Fax: (718) 210-0710
E-mail: nsna@nsna.org
Web: www.nsna.org

Purpose To provide financial assistance to Native American and other disadvantaged minority undergraduate and graduate students who wish to prepare for careers in nursing.

Eligibility This program is open to students currently enrolled in state-approved schools of nursing or pre-nursing associate degree, baccalaureate, diploma, generic master's, or generic doctoral programs. Graduating high school seniors are not eligible. Support for graduate education is provided only for a first degree in nursing. Applicants must be able to demonstrate that they are from a disadvantaged background, including membership in a racial or ethnic minority underrepresented among registered nurses (American Indian or Alaska Native, Hispanic or Latino, Native Hawaiian or other Pacific Islander, Black or African American, or Asian). Selection is based on academic achievement, financial need, and involvement in student nursing organizations and community health activities.
Financial data Stipends range from $1,000 to $5,000. A total of approximately $155,000 is awarded each year by the foundation for all its scholarship programs.
Duration 1 year.
Additional information Applications must be accompanied by a $10 processing fee.
Number awarded Varies each year. Recently, 5 of these scholarships were awarded: 2 sponsored by the American Association of Critical-Care Nurses and 3 sponsored by the Mayo Clinic.
Deadline January of each year.

[66]
BRISTOL BAY NATIVE CORPORATION EDUCATION FOUNDATION HIGHER EDUCATION SCHOLARSHIPS
Bristol Bay Native Corporation
Attn: BBNC Education Foundation
111 West 16th Avenue, Suite 400
Anchorage, AK 99501
(907) 278-3602   Toll-free: (800) 426-3602
Fax: (907) 276-3924   E-mail: pelagiol@bbnc.net
Web: www.bbnc.net/education/students

Purpose To provide financial assistance to shareholders of Bristol Bay Native Corporation (BBNC) who are interested in attending college in any state.
Eligibility This program is open to BBNC shareholders who have a high school diploma or equivalent and are enrolled or planning to enroll in an accredited college or university as a full-time student. Applicants must have a GPA of 2.0 or higher and be able to demonstrate financial need. Along with their application, they must submit an essay on how they became interested in their proposed field of study, any special circumstances they want to be considered, and their desire to work in the region or for a BBNC subsidiary company. Selection is based on the essay (35%), cumulative GPA (40%), financial need (20%), and letters of recommendation (5%).
Financial data Stipends may be as high as $10,000 per year, but recently they ranged from $750 to $3,000 per year.
Duration 1 year.
Number awarded Varies each year. Recently, 100 of these scholarships were awarded.
Deadline April of each year.

[67]
BROWN AND CALDWELL MINORITY SCHOLARSHIP
Brown and Caldwell
Attn: Scholarship Program
201 North Civic Drive, Suite 115
P.O. Box 8045
Walnut Creek, CA 94596
(925) 937-9010   Fax: (925) 937-9026
E-mail: scholarships@brwncald.com
Web: www.brownandcaldwell.com

Purpose To provide financial assistance to Native American and other minority students working on an undergraduate degree in an environmental or engineering field.
Eligibility This program is open to members of minority groups (African Americans, Hispanics, Asians, Pacific Islanders, Native Americans, and Alaska Natives) who are full-time students in their junior year at an accredited 4-year college or university. Applicants must have a GPA of 3.0 or higher and a declared major in civil, chemical, or environmental engineering or an environmental science (e.g., biology, ecology, geology, hydrogeology, industrial hygiene, toxicology). Along with their application, they must submit an essay (up to 250 words) on why their future career goals are in environmental science. They must be U.S. citizens or permanent residents and available to participate in a summer internship at a Brown and Caldwell office. Financial need is not considered in the selection process.
Financial data The stipend is $3,000.
Duration 1 year.
Additional information As part of the paid summer internship at a Brown and Caldwell office at 1 of more than 40 cities in the country, the program provides a mentor to guide the intern through the company's information and communications resources.
Number awarded 1 each year.
Deadline February of each year.

[68]
BROWN FOUNDATION ACADEMIC SCHOLARSHIPS
Brown Foundation for Educational Equity, Excellence and Research
Attn: Scholarship Committee
1515 S.E. Monroe
P.O. Box 4862
Topeka, KS 66604
(785) 235-3939   Fax: (785) 235-1001
E-mail: brownfound@juno.com
Web: brownvboard.org

Purpose To provide financial assistance to currently-enrolled college juniors of color who are interested in preparing for a teaching career.
Eligibility This program is open to members of minority groups entering their junior year of college in preparation for a teaching career. Applicants must be enrolled at least half time at an institution of higher education with an accredited program in education and have GPA of 3.0 or higher. Along with their application, they must submit brief essays on 1) their involvement in school, religious, community, and/or other activities; 2) why they aspire to a career in education, their goals, and the level at which they plan to teach; and 3) the impact *Brown v. the Board of Education* has had on

the field of education. Selection is based on the essays; GPA; school, community, and leisure activities; career plans and goals in education; and recommendations.
Financial data The stipend is $1,000 per year.
Duration 2 years (junior and senior years).
Additional information The first Brown Foundation Scholarships were awarded in 1989.
Number awarded Varies each year; recently, 2 of these scholarships were awarded.
Deadline March of each year.

[69]
BRUCE T. AND JACKIE MAHI ERICKSON SCHOLARSHIP

Ke Ali'i Pauahi Foundation
Attn: Financial Aid & Scholarship Services
567 South King Street, Suite 160
Honolulu, HI 96813
(808) 534-3966   Toll-free: (800) 842-4682, ext. 43966
Fax: (808) 534-3890   E-mail: scholarships@pauahi.org
Web: www.pauahi.org

Purpose To provide financial assistance to undergraduate or graduate students, especially Native Hawaiians, who are working on research or a degree related to Hawaiian arts and crafts.
Eligibility This program is open to students working full time on an undergraduate or graduate degree related to the creation of crafts, art, and photography and/or independent research relating to historical Hawaiian crafts and arts. Financial need is considered in the selection process. Residency in Hawaii is not required. Preference is given to Native Hawaiians (descendants of the aboriginal inhabitants of the Hawaiian Islands prior to 1778).
Financial data A stipend is awarded (amount not specified).
Duration 1 year.
Additional information This program was established in 2006.
Number awarded 1 or more each year.
Deadline April of each year.

[70]
BUFFALO BANDITS NATIVE AMERICAN COLLEGE FUND

Buffalo Bandits
Attn: Daniel Keem
HSBC Arena
One Seymour H. Knox III Plaza
Buffalo, NY 14203-3096
(716) 855-4287   Fax: (716) 855-4120
E-mail: dan.keem@sabres.com
Web: www.bandits.com

Purpose To provide financial assistance to Native American college students who live in New York or Ontario, Canada.
Eligibility This program is open to students of Native American descent living in western New York or southern Ontario. Applicants must be attending an accredited college or university. Along with their application, they must submit a letter of recommendation from an instructor or employer and a 1-page essay describing why they should be chosen for the award and what it would mean to them.
Financial data The stipend is $1,000.
Duration 1 year.
Number awarded 1 each year.
Deadline January of each year.

[71]
BURLINGTON NORTHERN SANTA FE FOUNDATION SCHOLARSHIP

American Indian Science and Engineering Society
Attn: Scholarship Coordinator
2305 Renard, S.E., Suite 200
P.O. Box 9828
Albuquerque, NM 87119-9828
(505) 765-1052, ext. 106   Fax: (505) 765-5608
E-mail: shirley@aises.org
Web: www.aises.org

Purpose To provide financial assistance for college to outstanding American Indian and Alaskan Native high school seniors from designated states who are members of American Indian Science and Engineering Society (AISES).
Eligibility This program is open to AISES members who are seniors graduating from high schools in the service area of the Burlington Northern and Santa Fe Corporation (Arizona, California, Colorado, Kansas, Minnesota, Montana, New Mexico, North Dakota, Oklahoma, Oregon, South Dakota, and Washington). Applicants must be planning to attend an accredited 4-year college or university in any state and major in business, education, engineering, mathematics, medicine or health administration, natural or physical sciences, or technology. They must submit 1) a Certificate of Indian Blood or proof of enrollment in an American Indian tribe or Alaskan Native group; 2) a 500-word essay on their educational and career goals, including their interest in and motivation to continue higher education, an understanding of the importance of college and a commitment to completing their educational and/or career goals, and a commitment to learning and giving back to the community; and 3) school transcripts showing a GPA of 2.0 or higher. Financial need is also considered in the selection process.
Financial data The stipend is $2,500 per year.
Duration 4 years or until completion of a baccalaureate degree, whichever occurs first.
Additional information This program is funded by the Burlington Northern Santa Fe Foundation and administered by AISES.
Number awarded 5 new awards are made each year.
Deadline April of each year.

[72]
BUSINESS REPORTING INTERN PROGRAM FOR MINORITY COLLEGE SOPHOMORES AND JUNIORS
Dow Jones Newspaper Fund
P.O. Box 300
Princeton, NJ 08543-0300
(609) 452-2820   Fax: (609) 520-5804
E-mail: newsfund@wsj.dowjones.com
Web: DJNewspaperFund.dowjones.com

Purpose To provide work experience and financial assistance to Native American and other minority college students who are interested in careers in journalism.

Eligibility This program is open to college sophomores and juniors who are U.S. citizens interested in careers in journalism and participating in a summer internship at a daily newspaper as a business reporter. Applicants must be members of a minority group (African American, Hispanic, Asian American, Pacific Islander, American Indian, or Alaskan Native) and enrolled as full-time students. They must submit a resume, 3 to 5 recently-published clips, a list of courses with grades, and a 500-word essay on why they want to spend the summer writing business news.

Financial data Interns receive a salary of at least $350 per week during the summer and a $1,000 scholarship at the successful completion of the program.

Duration 10 weeks for the summer internship; 1 year for the scholarship.

Additional information Interns attend a 1-week training seminar and then work as business reporters on a daily newspaper. Recently, the seminar was held at New York University.

Number awarded Up to 12 each year.

Deadline October of each year.

[73]
CALISTA SCHOLARSHIP FUND
Calista Corporation
Attn: Calista Scholarship Fund
301 Calista Court, Suite A
Anchorage, AK 99518-3028
(907) 279-5516   Toll-free: (800) 277-5516
Fax: (907) 644-6376
E-mail: scholarships@calistacorp.com
Web: www.calistacorp.com/scholarship/default.asp

Purpose To provide financial assistance to Alaska Natives with ties to the Calista region who are interested in working on an undergraduate or graduate degree.

Eligibility This program is open to Alaska Native shareholders and lineal descendants of Alaska Native shareholders with ties to the Calista region. Applicants must be at least a high school graduate or have earned a GED and be in good academic standing with a GPA of 2.0 or higher. Along with their application, they must submit an essay (up to 500 words) on their educational and career goals. Financial need is considered in the selection process.

Financial data The amount awarded depends upon the recipient's GPA. Recipients with a GPA of 2.0 to 2.49 are awarded $500 per semester, recipients with a GPA of 2.5 to 2.99 are awarded $750 per semester, and recipients with a GPA of 3.0 or higher are awarded $1,000 per semester. The funds are paid in 2 equal installments; the second semester check is not issued until grades from the previous semester's work are received.

Duration 1 year; recipients may reapply.

Additional information This program was established in 1994.

Number awarded Varies each year; recently, 79 of these scholarships were awarded.

Deadline June of each year.

[74]
CAP LATHROP ENDOWMENT SCHOLARSHIP FUND
Cook Inlet Region, Inc.
Attn: The CIRI Foundation
3600 San Jeronimo Drive, Suite 256
Anchorage, AK 99508-2870
(907) 793-3575   Toll-free: (800) 764-3382
Fax: (907) 793-3585 E-mail: tcf@thecirifoundation.org
Web: www.thecirifoundation.org/designated.htm

Purpose To provide financial assistance for undergraduate or graduate studies in media-related fields to Alaska Natives and their lineal descendants.

Eligibility This program is open to Alaska Native enrollees under the Alaska Native Claims Settlement Act (ANCSA) of 1971 and their lineal descendants. Proof of eligibility must be submitted. Applicants may be enrollees of any of the 13 ANCSA regional corporations, but preference is given to original enrollees/descendants of Cook Inlet Region, Inc. (CIRI) who have a GPA of 3.0 or higher. There are no Alaska residency requirements or age limitations. Applicants must be accepted or enrolled full time in a 2-year undergraduate, 4-year undergraduate, or graduate degree program. They must be majoring in a media-related field (e.g., telecommunications, broadcast, business, engineering, journalism) and planning to work in the telecommunications or broadcast industry in Alaska after graduation. Along with their application, they must submit a 500-word statement on their educational and career goals and how they are contributing, or planning to contribute, to a positive Alaska Native community. Selection is based on that statement, academic achievement, rigor of course work or degree program, student financial contribution, financial need, grade level, previous work performance, community service, and relationship of degree program to career goals.

Financial data The stipend is $3,500 per year. Funds must be used for tuition, university fees, books, required class supplies, and campus housing and meal plans for students who must live away from their permanent home to attend college. Checks are sent directly to the recipient's school.

Duration 1 year (2 semesters).

Additional information This program was established in 1997. Recipients must attend school on a full-time basis and must plan to work in the broadcast or telecommunications industry in Alaska upon completion of their academic degree.

Number awarded 1 each year.

Deadline May of each year.

SCHOLARSHIPS

[75]
CAPE FOX SCHOLARSHIPS
Sealaska Corporation
Attn: Sealaska Heritage Institute
One Sealaska Plaza, Suite 301
Juneau, AK 99801-1249
(907) 463-4844   Toll-free: (888) 311-4992
Fax: (907) 586-9293
E-mail: scholarship@sealaska.com
Web: www.sealaskaheritage.org

Purpose To provide financial assistance for undergraduate or graduate study to Native Alaskans who have a connection to the Cape Fox Corporation.

Eligibility This program is open to lineal descendants of Alaska Natives enrolled to Cape Fox Corporation, whether or not the applicant owns Cape Fox Corporation stock. Applicants must be enrolled or accepted for enrollment as full-time undergraduate or graduate students. Along with their application, they must submit 2 essays: 1) their personal history and educational goals, and 2) their expected contributions to the Alaska Native or Native American community. Financial need is also considered in the selection process.

Financial data The amount of the award depends on the availability of funds, the number of qualified applicants, class standing, and cumulative GPA.

Duration 1 year; may be renewed up to 5 years for a bachelor's degree, up to 3 years for a master's degree, up to 2 years for a doctorate, or up to 3 years for vocational study. The maximum total support is limited to 9 years. Renewal depends on recipients' maintaining full-time enrollment and a GPA of 2.5 or higher as an undergraduate or 3.0 or higher as a graduate student.

Number awarded Varies each year.

Deadline February of each year.

[76]
CAREER UPGRADE GRANTS
Cook Inlet Region, Inc.
Attn: The CIRI Foundation
3600 San Jeronimo Drive, Suite 256
Anchorage, AK 99508-2870
(907) 793-3575   Toll-free: (800) 764-3382
Fax: (907) 793-3585   E-mail: tcf@thecirifoundation.org
Web: www.thecirifoundation.org/grants.htm

Purpose To provide financial assistance for employment skills upgrades to Alaska Natives who are original enrollees to the Cook Inlet Region, Inc. (CIRI) and their lineal descendants.

Eligibility This program is open to Alaska Native enrollees to CIRI under the Alaska Native Claims Settlement Act (ANCSA) of 1971 and their lineal descendants. Applicants should have a high school diploma or GED, have a GPA of 2.5 or higher, be preparing to enter or reenter or upgrade in the job market upon completion of training, and be able to demonstrate the availability of employment. They must be accepted or enrolled part time in a course of study that directly contributes toward potential employment or employment upgrade. Alaska residency is not required. Along with their application, they must submit a 500-word statement on their educational and career goals and how they are contributing, or planning to contribute, to a positive Alaska Native community. Selection is based on that statement, academic achievement, rigor of course work or degree program, student financial contribution, financial need, grade level, previous work performance, community service, and relationship of degree program to career goals.

Financial data The maximum stipend is $4,500 per calendar year.

Duration 1 quarter; recipients may reapply.

Additional information Only part-time study is supported. Total course credits may not exceed 11 credit hours per application.

Number awarded Varies each year; recently, 70 of these grants were awarded.

Deadline March, June, September, or November of each year.

[77]
CARL H. MARRS SCHOLARSHIP FUND
Cook Inlet Region, Inc.
Attn: The CIRI Foundation
3600 San Jeronimo Drive, Suite 256
Anchorage, AK 99508-2870
(907) 793-3575   Toll-free: (800) 764-3382
Fax: (907) 793-3585   E-mail: tcf@thecirifoundation.org
Web: www.thecirifoundation.org/designated.htm

Purpose To provide financial assistance for undergraduate or graduate studies in business-related fields to Alaska Natives who are original enrollees to Cook Inlet Region, Inc. (CIRI) and their lineal descendants.

Eligibility This program is open to Alaska Native enrollees to CIRI under the Alaska Native Claims Settlement Act (ANCSA) of 1971 and their lineal descendants. There are no Alaska residency requirements or age limitations. Applicants must be accepted or enrolled full time in a 4-year undergraduate or a graduate degree program in business administration, economics, finance, organizational management, accounting, or a similar field. They must have a GPA of 3.7 or higher. Along with their application, they must submit a 500-word statement on their educational and career goals and how they are contributing, or planning to contribute, to a positive Alaska Native community. Selection is based on that statement, academic achievement, rigor of course work or degree program, student financial contribution, financial need, grade level, previous work performance, community service, and relationship of degree program to career goals.

Financial data The stipend is $20,000 per year.

Duration 1 year; may be renewed.

Additional information This program was established in 2001.

Number awarded Varies each year; recently, 2 of these scholarships were awarded.

Deadline May of each year.

[78]
CARTWRIGHT SCHOLARSHIP PROGRAM
American Indian College Fund
Attn: Scholarship Department
8333 Greenwood Boulevard
Denver, CO 80221
(303) 426-8900   Toll-free: (800) 776-FUND
Fax: (303) 426-1200   E-mail: info@collegefund.org
Web: www.collegefund.org

Purpose To provide financial assistance to Native American males who are attending or planning to attend a Tribal College or University (TCU).
Eligibility This program is open to male American Indians or Alaska Natives who are enrolled or planning to enroll full time at an eligible TCU. Applicants must have a GPA of 3.0 or higher and be able to demonstrate financial need. They must be willing to commit to mentoring other male students locally and encourage them to attend college. Along with their application, they must submit 1) short essays (up to 500 words each) on how they perceive themselves as leaders in their school or community and how their education will help the Native American community; and 2) a personal statement of 1,000 words that includes their personal background, their academic background, their educational and career goals, and how this scholarship will help them achieve those goals.
Financial data The stipend is $2,000.
Duration 1 year.
Additional information This program was established in 2004.
Number awarded 1 or more each year.
Deadline May of each year.

[79]
CATERPILLAR FFA SCHOLARSHIPS
National FFA Organization
Attn: Scholarship Office
6060 FFA Drive
P.O. Box 68960
Indianapolis, IN 46268-0960
(317) 802-4419   Fax: (317) 802-5419
E-mail: scholarships@ffa.org
Web: www.ffa.org

Purpose To provide financial assistance to Native American and other minority FFA members who are interested in studying engineering, welding, or machinery in college.
Eligibility This program is open to members who are graduating high school seniors and current college students working or planning to work full time on a 2-year or 4-year degree in engineering, welding, or machinery. Applicants must exhibit strong leadership skills and be members of a minority ethnic group (African American, Asian American, Pacific Islander, Hispanic, Alaska Native, or American Indian). They must have a GPA of 2.8 or higher. Selection is based on academic achievement (10 points for GPA, 10 points for SAT or ACT score, 10 points for class rank), leadership in FFA activities (30 points), leadership in community activities (10 points), and participation in the Supervised Agricultural Experience (SAE) program (30 points). U.S. citizenship is required.
Financial data The stipend is $2,000. Funds are paid directly to the recipient.
Duration 1 year; nonrenewable.
Additional information This program is sponsored by Caterpillar, Inc.
Number awarded 10 each year.
Deadline February of each year.

[80]
CECELIA SOMDAY EDUCATION FUND
Confederated Tribes of the Colville Reservation
Attn: Higher Education Office
P.O. Box 150
Nespelem, WA 99155-0150
(509) 634-2779   Fax: (509) 634-2790
E-mail: gloria.atkins@colvilletribes.com
Web: www.colvilletribes.com/scholarship.htm

Purpose To provide financial assistance to members of the Colville Confederated Tribes who wish to attend college in any state.
Eligibility This program is open to enrolled members of the Confederated Tribes of the Colville Reservation who have a GPA of 3.0 or higher for their past 3 years of high school and/or college study. Applicants must be interested in attending a college, university, or vocational/technical school in any state. They should be able to demonstrate strong involvement in school and community activities and a desire to have a positive future impact on the tribe.
Financial data A stipend is awarded (amount not specified).
Duration 1 year; may be renewed.
Additional information The Colville Reservation was established in 1872 as a federation of 12 tribes: Colville, Nespelem, San Poil, Lake, Palus, Wenatchee, Chelan, Entiat, Methow, southern Okanogan, Moses Columbia, and Nez Perce. The reservation is located in north central Washington, primarily in Ferry and Okanogan counties.
Number awarded Varies each year.
Deadline March of each year.

[81]
CENTRAL INTELLIGENCE AGENCY UNDERGRADUATE SCHOLARSHIP PROGRAM
Central Intelligence Agency
Attn: Human Resource Management
Recruitment and Retention Center, 4B14-034 DD1
Washington, DC 20505
(703) 371-2107
Web: https:

Purpose To provide financial aid and work experience to high school seniors and college sophomores, especially minorities and people with disabilities, who are interested in working for the Central Intelligence Agency (CIA) after graduation from college.
Eligibility This program is open to U.S. citizens who are either high school seniors or college sophomores. Seniors must be at least 18 years of age by April of the year they apply and have minimum scores of 1000 on the critical reading and mathematics SAT or 21 on the ACT. College sophomores must have a GPA of 3.0 or higher. All applicants must be able to demonstrate financial need (household income of $70,000 or less for a family of 4 or $80,000 or less for a family of 5 or more) and be able to meet the same employ-

ment standards as permanent employees of the CIA. This program was developed, in part, to assist minority and disabled students, but it is open to all students who meet the requirements.

Financial data Scholars are provided a salary and up to $18,000 per year for tuition, fees, books, and supplies. They must agree to continue employment with the CIA after college graduation for a period 1.5 times the length of their college support.

Duration 1 year; may be renewed if the student maintains a GPA of 3.0 or higher and full-time enrollment in a 4- or 5-year college program.

Additional information Scholars work each summer at a CIA facility. In addition to a salary, they receive the cost of transportation between school and the Washington, D.C. area and a housing allowance.

Number awarded Varies each year.

Deadline October of each year.

[82]
CHARLES COCKETT 'OHANA SCHOLARSHIP
Ke Ali'i Pauahi Foundation
Attn: Financial Aid & Scholarship Services
567 South King Street, Suite 160
Honolulu, HI 96813
(808) 534-3966   Toll-free: (800) 842-4682, ext. 43966
Fax: (808) 534-3890   E-mail: scholarships@pauahi.org
Web: www.pauahi.org

Purpose To provide financial assistance to undergraduate students, especially those of Hawaiian descent, who have an outstanding record of community service.

Eligibility This program is open to undergraduate students who are enrolled full time at an accredited college or university in any state. Applicants must be able to demonstrate financial need, a commitment to make a difference in the community and participate in school activities, and a GPA of 2.0. Along with their application, they must submit an essay describing their involvement in community service, including organizations, number of hours, and length of volunteer service. Residence in Hawaii is not required. Preference is given to Native Hawaiians (descendants of the aboriginal inhabitants of the Hawaiian Islands prior to 1778).

Financial data A stipend is awarded (amount not specified).

Duration 1 year.

Number awarded 1 or more each year.

Deadline April of each year.

[83]
CHEROKEE NATION PELL SCHOLARSHIPS
Cherokee Nation
Attn: Office of Higher Education
17675 South Muskogee Avenue
P.O. Box 948
Tahlequah, OK 74465
(918) 453-5465   Toll-free: (800) 256-0671 (within OK)
Fax: (918) 458-6195
E-mail: highereducation@cherokee.org
Web: www.cherokee.org

Purpose To provide financial assistance to undergraduate students who belong to the Cherokee Nation and qualify for federal Pell Grants.

Eligibility This program is open to citizens of the Cherokee Nation, regardless of their permanent residence. Applicants who qualify for federal Pell Grant funding are eligible for this additional assistance through the U.S. Bureau of Indian Affairs (BIA).

Financial data Available funding is divided equally among all Pell eligible students who complete the application process.

Duration Up to 8 semesters.

Number awarded Varies each year; nearly 1,600 students receive support from all Cherokee Nation Undergraduate Scholarship programs.

Deadline June of each year.

[84]
CHEROKEE NATION SCHOLARSHIP PROGRAM
Cherokee Nation
Attn: Office of Higher Education
17675 South Muskogee Avenue
P.O. Box 948
Tahlequah, OK 74465
(918) 453-5465   Toll-free: (800) 256-0671 (within OK)
Fax: (918) 458-6195
E-mail: highereducation@cherokee.org
Web: www.cherokee.org

Purpose To provide financial assistance for undergraduate study in any state to citizens of the Cherokee Nation who do not qualify for federal Pell Grants.

Eligibility This program is open to citizens of the Cherokee Nation who do not qualify for Pell Grant funding and are not interested in attending Haskell Indian Nations University (for which separate funding is available). Applicants must be attending or planning to attend a college or university in any state. They must be residents of the Cherokee nation area, defined as those counties within and contiguous to the Cherokee Nation boundaries; tribal citizens living outside the Cherokee Nation area are not eligible. In the selection process, first preference is given to continuing students who received funding from this program previously. Second preference is based on academic level (seniors, juniors, sophomores, freshmen, in that order). Third preference is based on academic performance (GPA, ACT/SAT score, college placement tests, GED score) and financial need.

Financial data The stipend is $1,000 per semester.

Duration Up to 8 semesters.

Additional information The Cherokee Nation area covers all or part of the following Oklahoma counties: Adair, Cherokee, Craig, Delaware, Mayes, McIntosh, Muskogee, Nowata, Ottawa, Rogers, Sequoyah, Tulsa, Wagoner, and Washington. Contiguous counties include Haskell, Le Flore, Osage, and Pittsburg counties in Oklahoma, Benton, Crawford, and Washington counties in Arkansas; Cherokee, Labette, and Montgomery counties in Kansas; and McDonald County in Missouri.

Number awarded Varies each year; nearly 1,600 students receive support from all Cherokee Nation Undergraduate Scholarship programs.

Deadline June of each year.

[85]
CHEROKEE NATION TRIBAL COUNCIL AWARD
Cherokee Nation
Attn: Cherokee Nation Education Corporation
17675 South Muskogee Avenue
P.O. Box 948
Tahlequah, OK 74465
(918) 453-5420   Toll-free: (800) 256-0671 (within OK)
Fax: (918) 458-6195   E-mail: cnec@cherokee.org
Web: www.cherokee.org

Purpose To provide financial assistance to high school senior citizens of the Cherokee Nation who are planning to attend college in any state and who reside outside the tribal jurisdictional boundaries.

Eligibility This program is open to citizens of the Cherokee Nation who are graduating from high schools outside the jurisdictional area of the tribe. Applicants must be planning to enroll at a college, university, or vocational/technical school in any state. Selection is based on GPA, ACT score, cultural and community activities, personal academic goals, commitment to work with Cherokee people in the future, and financial need.

Financial data The stipend is $1,000 per semester ($2,000 per year).

Duration 1 year. Renewal for the second semester requires the recipient to earn a GPA of 2.5 or higher in the first semester.

Additional information These scholarships were first awarded in 2008.

Number awarded Varies each year; recently, 4 of these scholarships were awarded.

Deadline March of each year.

[86]
CHEYENNE AND ARAPAHO HIGHER EDUCATION GRANTS
Cheyenne and Arapaho Tribes of Oklahoma
Attn: Higher Education Program
P.O. Box 38
Concho, OK 73022
(405) 262-7652   Toll-free: (800) 247-4612
Fax: (405) 262-5419   E-mail: mbell@c-a-tribes.org
Web: www.c-a-tribes.org/higher-education

Purpose To provide financial assistance to enrolled Cheyenne-Arapaho tribal members who are interested in working on an undergraduate or graduate degree at a college in any state.

Eligibility This program is open to Cheyenne-Arapaho Indians who are at least a high school graduate (or the equivalent), approved for admission by a college or university, and in financial need. Applicants may be enrolled or planning to enroll in a postsecondary school in any state. The vast majority of students assisted under this program are at the undergraduate level, although graduate and/or married students are eligible for consideration and assistance. Summer and part-time students may apply as well, as long as application is made well in advance of enrollment and is accompanied by an official need evaluation.

Financial data The amount of the award depends on the need of the applicant.

Duration 1 year; renewable.

Number awarded 40 to 80 each year.

Deadline May of each year for fall semester; October for spring semester; or March for summer session.

[87]
CHICKASAW FOUNDATION FINE ARTS SCHOLARSHIP
Chickasaw Foundation
110 West 12th Street
P.O. Box 1726
Ada, OK 74821-1726
(580) 421-9030   Fax: (580) 421-9031
E-mail: ChickasawFoundation@chickasaw.net
Web: www.chickasaw.net

Purpose To provide financial assistance to members of the Chickasaw Nation interested in studying fine arts in college.

Eligibility This program is open to Chickasaw students who are currently enrolled full time as a junior or senior at an accredited 4-year college. Applicants must be majoring in fine arts (dance, dramatics, arts, music) and have a GPA of 3.0 or higher. Along with their application, they must submit high school or college transcripts, 2 letters of recommendation, a copy of their Certificate of Indian Blood, a copy of their Chickasaw Nation citizenship card, and a 1-page essay on their long-term goals and plans for achieving them. Financial need is not considered in the selection process.

Financial data The stipend is $1,500.

Duration 1 year.

Number awarded 1 each year.

Deadline June of each year.

[88]
CHICKASAW NATION AGRICULTURE SCHOLASTIC PROGRAM
Oklahoma Youth Expo
Attn: Scholarship Program
431 N.E. 14th Street
Oklahoma City, OK 73104
(405) 235-0404   Fax: (405) 235-1727
Web: www.okyouthexpo.com/scholarships.htm

Purpose To provide financial assistance to members of the Chickasaw Nation who are high school seniors, exhibit at the Oklahoma Youth Expo (OYE), and plan to attend college in Oklahoma to major in any subject.

Eligibility This program is open to members of the Chickasaw Nation who are high school seniors and exhibit at the OYE (membership in an Oklahoma 4-H Club or Oklahoma FFA chapter is required to exhibit). Applicants must be planning to enroll full time at an institution of higher education in Oklahoma where they may major in any subject field. They must have a Chickasaw Nation CIB card and a Chickasaw Nation Membership Card. Along with their application, they must submit 500-word essays on 1) how the junior livestock program has contributed to their higher educational and career pursuits, and 2) their 10-year goals in life and how those pursuits will help make Oklahoma a better place. Selection is based on financial need, academics, community involvement, and junior agriculture program participation.

Financial data The stipend is $2,500.

Duration 1 year; nonrenewable.
Additional information This program is sponsored by the Chickasaw Nation.
Number awarded 3 each year.
Deadline December of each year.

[89]
CHICKASAW NATION DIVISION ON AGING SCHOLARSHIP

Chickasaw Foundation
110 West 12th Street
P.O. Box 1726
Ada, OK 74821-1726
(580) 421-9030 Fax: (580) 421-9031
E-mail: ChickasawFoundation@chickasaw.net
Web: www.chickasaw.net

Purpose To provide financial assistance to members of the Chickasaw Nation who are upper-division students in geriatrics.
Eligibility This program is open to Chickasaw students who are currently enrolled full time at an accredited institution of higher education. Applicants must be classified as juniors or seniors at a 4-year college. They must be majoring in a field related to geriatrics. Along with their application, they must submit high school or college transcripts, 2 letters of recommendation, a copy of their Chickasaw Nation citizenship card, and a 1-page essay on their long-term goals and plans for achieving them. Financial need is not considered in the selection process.
Financial data The stipend is $1,000.
Duration 1 year.
Number awarded 1 each year.
Deadline June of each year.

[90]
CHICKASAW NATION GENERAL SCHOLARSHIPS

Chickasaw Nation
Attn: Department of Education Services
122 East Main
Ada, OK 74820
(580) 421-7711 Fax: (580) 436-3733
E-mail: education.services@chickasaw.net
Web: www.chickasaweducationservices.com

Purpose To provide financial assistance to members of the Chickasaw Nation who are working on an undergraduate or graduate degree at a school in any state.
Eligibility This program is open to members of the Chickasaw Nation who are working full or part time on an undergraduate, graduate, or doctoral degree at an accredited college or university in any state. Applicants must have a GPA of 3.0 or higher.
Financial data Stipends depend on the level of academic study, the number of units the recipients are taking, and their GPA. The range is from $150 per semester (for part-time freshmen and sophomores with a GPA of 3.0 to 3.49) to $550 per semester (for full-time graduate students with a GPA of 4.0).
Duration 1 semester; recipients may reapply.
Number awarded Varies each year.
Deadline January of each year for spring semester; June of each year for summer semester; August of each year for fall semester for continuing students; March of each year for high school seniors.

[91]
CHICKASAW NATION HIGHER EDUCATION GRANTS

Chickasaw Nation
Attn: Department of Education Services
122 East Main
Ada, OK 74820
(580) 421-7711 Fax: (580) 436-3733
E-mail: education.services@chickasaw.net
Web: www.chickasaweducationservices.com

Purpose To provide financial assistance to needy members of the Chickasaw Nation who are working on an undergraduate or graduate degree at a school in any state.
Eligibility This program is open to members of the Chickasaw Nation who are working full or part time on an undergraduate, graduate, or doctoral degree at an accredited college or university in any state. Applicants must have a GPA of 2.0 or higher. They may be attending a community college, regional college or university, or research university.
Financial data For full-time undergraduates, stipends are $1,200 per semester at community colleges, $1,500 per semester at regional colleges and universities, or $2,400 per semester at research universities. For full-time graduate students, stipends are $2,400 per semester. For full-time doctoral students, stipends are $3,000 per semester. For part-time undergraduates, stipends are $100 per credit hour at community colleges, $125 per credit hour at regional colleges and universities, or $200 per credit hour at research universities. For part-time graduate students, stipends are $200 per credit hour at regional colleges and universities or $250 per credit hour at research universities. For part-time doctoral students, stipends are $250 per credit hour.
Duration 1 semester; recipients may reapply.
Number awarded Varies each year.
Deadline January of each year for spring semester; June of each year for summer semester; August of each year for fall semester for continuing students; March of each year for high school seniors.

[92]
CHICKASAW NATION LIFE-TIME SCHOLARSHIPS

Chickasaw Nation
Attn: Department of Education Services
122 East Main
Ada, OK 74820
(580) 421-7711 Fax: (580) 436-3733
E-mail: education.services@chickasaw.net
Web: www.chickasaweducationservices.com

Purpose To provide financial assistance to members of the Chickasaw Nation who are working on an undergraduate or graduate degree at a school in any state.
Eligibility This program is open to members of the Chickasaw Nation who are working full time on an undergraduate, graduate, or doctoral degree at an accredited college or university in any state. Applicants must have a GPA of 3.0 or higher, a GED score of 2800 or higher, or (for home-schooled students) an ACT score of 20 or higher. Along with their application, they must submit a 2- to 3-page essay on

their past accomplishments, future goals, tribal involvement, and community involvement. Finalists are interviewed.
Financial data A stipend is awarded (amount not specified). Funds may be used for tuition, fees, supplies, books, room, and board.
Duration 1 year; may be renewed provided the recipient maintains a GPA of 3.0 or higher.
Number awarded 5 each year.
Deadline June of each year.

[93]
CHICKASAW NATION LIGHTHORSE SCHOLARSHIP
Chickasaw Foundation
110 West 12th Street
P.O. Box 1726
Ada, OK 74821-1726
(580) 421-9030 Fax: (580) 421-9031
E-mail: ChickasawFoundation@chickasaw.net
Web: www.chickasaw.net

Purpose To provide financial assistance to members of the Chickasaw Nation who are working on an undergraduate degree in a field related to law enforcement.
Eligibility This program is open to Chickasaw students who are currently enrolled full time at a 2- or 4-year college or university and working on an undergraduate degree in criminal justice, police science, or another field related to law enforcement. Applicants must have a GPA of 3.0 or higher. Along with their application, they must submit high school or college transcripts, 2 letters of recommendation, a copy of their Chickasaw Nation citizenship card, and a 1-page essay on their long-term goals and plans for achieving them. Financial need is not considered in the selection process.
Financial data The stipend is $1,000.
Duration 1 year.
Number awarded 1 each year.
Deadline June of each year.

[94]
CHIEF FREEMAN JOHNSON SCHOLARSHIP
Rochester City School District
Attn: Native American Resource Center
494 Averill Avenue, Portable 15
Rochester, NY 14607
(585) 262-8966 Fax: (585) 262-8937

Purpose To provide financial assistance for college or graduate school to Native Americans from New York.
Eligibility This program is open to Native American students of at least one-quarter blood who are residents of New York. Applicants must be attending vocational, undergraduate, or graduate school and have applied for all other sources of financial aid.
Financial data A stipend is awarded (amount not specified).
Duration 1 year; may be renewed if the recipient maintains of GPA of 2.0 or higher.
Number awarded 1 or more each year.
Deadline July of each year.

[95]
CHIEF MANUELITO SCHOLARSHIP PROGRAM
Navajo Nation
Attn: Office of Navajo Nation Scholarship and Financial Assistance
P.O. Box 1870
Window Rock, AZ 86515-1870
(928) 871-7640 Toll-free: (800) 243-2956
Fax: (928) 871-6561
E-mail: onnsfacentral@navajo.org
Web: www.onnsfa.org

Purpose To provide financial assistance to academically superior members of the Navajo Nation who are interested in working on an undergraduate degree.
Eligibility This program is open to enrolled members of the Navajo Nation who are attending or planning to enroll as full-time students at an accredited college or university. Applicants who are graduating high school seniors must have the following minimum combinations of ACT score and GPA: 21 and 3.8, 22 and 3.7, 23 and 3.6, 24 and 3.5, 25 and 3.4, 26 and 3.3, 27 and 3.2, 28 and 3.1, or 29 and 3.0. They must have completed in high school at least 1 unit of Navajo language and at least half a unit of Navajo government. Applicants who are current undergraduate students must have completed at least 24 semester credit hours with an overall GPA of 3.0 or higher.
Financial data The stipend is $7,000 per year.
Duration 1 year; may be renewed if the recipient maintains full-time status and a GPA of 3.0 or higher.
Additional information This program was established in 1980.
Number awarded Varies each year; recently, 79 of these scholarships were awarded.
Deadline April of each year.

[96]
CHIEF PUSHMATAHA COLLEGE SCHOLARSHIP FUND
Choctaw Nation
Attn: Scholarship Advisement Program
16th and Locust
P.O. Drawer 1210
Durant, OK 74702-1210
(580) 924-8280
Toll-free: (800) 522-6170, ext. 2547 (within OK)
Fax: (580) 924-1267
E-mail: jomcdaniel@choctawnation.com
Web: www.choctawnation-sap.com/scholarships.html

Purpose To provide financial assistance to Choctaw Indian college students who can demonstrate academic excellence.
Eligibility This program is open to college students who have a Choctaw Adult Membership card. Applicants must be able to demonstrate academic excellence and high potential. They must register online with the Choctaw Honor Scholars Program.
Financial data A stipend is awarded (amount not specified).
Duration 1 year.
Number awarded Varies each year; a private donor provides $40,000 in funds for this program annually and the

Choctaw Nation matches that (so a total of $80,000 is available annually).

[97]
CHIPS QUINN SCHOLARS PROGRAM

Freedom Forum
Attn: Chips Quinn Scholars Program
555 Pennsylvania Avenue, N.W.
Washington, DC 20001
(202) 292-6271 E-mail: kcatone@freedomforum.org
Web: www.chipsquinn.org

Purpose To provide work experience, career mentoring, and scholarship support to Native American and other minority college students and recent graduates who are majoring in journalism.

Eligibility This program is open to students of color who are college juniors, seniors, or recent graduates with journalism majors or career goals in newspapers. Candidates must be nominated or endorsed by journalism faculty, campus media advisers, editors of newspapers, or leaders of minority journalism associations. Along with their application, they must submit a resume, transcripts, 2 letters of recommendation, and an essay of 200 to 500 words on why they want to be a Chips Quinn Scholar. Reporters must also submit 6 samples of published articles they have written; photographers must submit 6 samples of their work on a CD. Applicants must have a car and be available to work as a full-time intern during the spring or summer. U.S. citizenship or permanent resident status is required. Campus newspaper experience is strongly encouraged.

Financial data Students chosen for this program receive a travel stipend to attend a workshop at the Freedom Forum in Arlington, Virginia prior to reporting for their internship. Upon completion of the internship, they receive a $1,600 scholarship.

Duration Internships are for 10 to 12 weeks; the scholarship is for 1 year.

Additional information This program was established in 1991 in memory of the late John D. Quinn Jr., managing editor of the *Poughkeepsie Journal.* Funding is provided by the Freedom Forum, formerly the Gannett Foundation. After graduating from college and obtaining employment with a newspaper, alumni of this program are eligible to apply for fellowship support to attend professional journalism development activities.

Number awarded Approximately 70 each year. Since the program began, more than 1,000 scholars have been selected.

Deadline October of each year.

[98]
CHOCTAW NATION AGRICULTURE SCHOLASTIC PROGRAM

Oklahoma Youth Expo
Attn: Scholarship Program
431 N.E. 14th Street
Oklahoma City, OK 73104
(405) 235-0404 Fax: (405) 235-1727
Web: www.okyouthexpo.com/scholarships.htm

Purpose To provide financial assistance to members of the Choctaw Nation who are high school seniors, exhibit at the Oklahoma Youth Expo (OYE), and plan to attend college in Oklahoma to major in any subject.

Eligibility This program is open to members of the Choctaw Nation who are high school seniors and exhibit at the OYE (membership in an Oklahoma 4-H Club or Oklahoma FFA chapter is required to exhibit). Applicants must be planning to enroll full time at an institution of higher education in Oklahoma where they may major in any subject field. They must have a Choctaw Nation CIB card and a Choctaw Nation Membership Card. Along with their application, they must submit 500-word essays on 1) how the junior livestock program has contributed to their higher educational and career pursuits, and 2) their 10-year goals in life and how those pursuits will help make Oklahoma a better place. Selection is based on financial need, academics, community involvement, and junior agriculture program participation.

Financial data The stipend is $2,500.

Duration 1 year; nonrenewable.

Additional information This program is sponsored by the Choctaw Nation.

Number awarded 2 each year.

Deadline December of each year.

[99]
CHOCTAW NATION HIGHER EDUCATION GRANTS

Choctaw Nation
Attn: Higher Education Department
16th and Locust
P.O. Drawer 1210
Durant, OK 74702-1210
(580) 924-8280
Toll-free: (800) 522-6170, ext. 2224 (within OK)
Fax: (580) 924-1267
E-mail: lelar@choctawnation.com
Web: www.choctawnation.com

Purpose To provide financial assistance to Choctaw Indians who are interested in working on an undergraduate degree and can demonstrate financial need.

Eligibility This program is open to students who are attending or planning to attend an accredited college or university and have a Certificate of Indian Blood (CIB) and tribal membership card showing Choctaw descent. Students in vocational and technical schools or correspondence courses are not eligible. Applicants must be able to demonstrate financial need.

Financial data The stipend depends on the need, class level, and enrollment status of the recipient; maximum awards are $400 per semester for part-time students, $500 per semester for full-time freshmen, $600 per semester for full-time sophomores, $700 per semester for full-time juniors, or $800 per semester for full-time seniors.

Duration 1 year; may be renewed for up to 4 additional years as long as the recipient enrolls in at least 12 hours per semester (or at least 6 hours for part-time students) with a GPA of 2.0 or higher.

Additional information This program began in 1984 with funding from the Bureau of Indian Affairs.

Number awarded Varies each year.

Deadline September of each year for fall semester; March of each year for spring semester.

[100]
CHOCTAW NATION HIGHER EDUCATION SCHOLARSHIPS

Choctaw Nation
Attn: Higher Education Department
16th and Locust
P.O. Drawer 1210
Durant, OK 74702-1210
(580) 924-8280
Toll-free: (800) 522-6170, ext. 2224 (within OK)
Fax: (580) 924-1267
E-mail: lelar@choctawnation.com
Web: www.choctawnation.com

Purpose To provide financial assistance to Choctaw Indians who are interested in working on an undergraduate degree.

Eligibility This program is open to students who are attending or planning to attend an accredited college or university and have a Certificate of Indian Blood (CIB) and tribal membership card showing Choctaw descent. Students in vocational and technical schools or correspondence courses are not eligible. Applicants must have a GPA of 2.5 or higher. Financial need is not considered in the selection process.

Financial data The stipend depends on GPA: $600 per semester for full-time students with a GPA of 2.50 to 2.99, $800 per semester for full-time students with a GPA of 3.00 to 3.49, or $1,000 per semester for full-time students with a GPA of 3.50 to 4.00. Part-time students receive $500 per semester regardless of GPA.

Duration 1 year; may be renewed for up to 4 additional years as long as the recipient enrolls in at least 12 hours per semester (or at least 6 hours for part-time students) with a GPA of 2.5 or higher.

Additional information The Choctaw Nation established this program in 1998.

Number awarded Varies each year.

Deadline September of each year for fall semester; March of each year for spring semester.

[101]
CHOY-KEE 'OHANA SCHOLARSHIP

Ke Ali'i Pauahi Foundation
Attn: Financial Aid & Scholarship Services
567 South King Street, Suite 160
Honolulu, HI 96813
(808) 534-3966   Toll-free: (800) 842-4682, ext. 43966
Fax: (808) 534-3890   E-mail: scholarships@pauahi.org
Web: www.pauahi.org

Purpose To provide financial assistance to undergraduate students, especially those of Hawaiian descent, who are attending college in any state.

Eligibility This program is open to undergraduate students who are enrolled full time at an accredited college or university in any state. Applicants must have a GPA of 3.0 or higher and be able to demonstrate financial need. Along with their application, they must submit an essay on what they consider the biggest problem in Hawaii and potential solutions. Residence in Hawaii is not required. Preference is given to Native Hawaiians (descendants of the aboriginal inhabitants of the Hawaiian Islands prior to 1778).

Financial data A stipend is awarded (amount not specified).

Duration 1 year.

Number awarded 1 or more each year.

Deadline April of each year.

[102]
CHUGACH HERITAGE FOUNDATION SCHOLARSHIPS

Chugach Alaska Corporation
Attn: Chugach Heritage Foundation
560 East 34th Avenue, Fourth Floor
Anchorage, AK 99503
(907) 563-8866   Toll-free: (800) 858-2768
Fax: (907) 550-4147
E-mail: scholarships@chugach-ak.com
Web: www.chugachheritagefoundation.org

Purpose To provide financial assistance to undergraduate and graduate students who are original enrollees of the Chugach Alaska Corporation or their descendants and attending college in any state.

Eligibility This program is open to original enrollees and the descendants of original enrollees of the Chugach Alaska Corporation. Applicants must be enrolled or planning to enroll at an accredited college, university, or vocational program in any state as an undergraduate or graduate student. They must have a GPA of 2.0 or higher.

Financial data For full-time students, stipends are $2,400 per year for students working on an associate degree or 1- or 2-year certificate, $3,000 per year for juniors and seniors, or $6,000 per year for graduate students. Stipends for part-time students are pro-rated appropriately.

Duration 1 year; may be renewed if the recipient maintains a GPA of 2.0 or higher.

Additional information Recipients who achieve a GPA of 3.5 or higher receive a bonus of $600 per academic year.

Number awarded Varies each year.

Deadline Applications may be submitted at any time, but they must be received at least 30 days prior to the first day of class.

[103]
CHUGACH HERITAGE FOUNDATION VOCATIONAL TRAINING FUNDING

Chugach Alaska Corporation
Attn: Chugach Heritage Foundation
560 East 34th Avenue, Fourth Floor
Anchorage, AK 99503
(907) 563-8866   Toll-free: (800) 858-2768
Fax: (907) 550-4147
E-mail: scholarships@chugach-ak.com
Web: www.chugachheritagefoundation.org

Purpose To provide financial assistance to students who are original enrollees of the Chugach Alaska Corporation or their descendants and enrolled in a vocational training program in any state.

Eligibility This program is open to original enrollees and the descendants of original enrollees of the Chugach Alaska Corporation. Applicants must be registered for training that will broaden their employment opportunities or maintain

SCHOLARSHIPS

their skill level at a school in any state. They must have a GPA of 2.0 or higher.
Financial data The stipend is $2,000 per year.
Duration 1 year; may be renewed if the recipient maintains a GPA of 2.0 or higher.
Number awarded Varies each year.
Deadline Applications may be submitted at any time, but they must be received at least 30 days prior to the first day of class.

[104]
CHUGACHMIUT HIGHER EDUCATION GRANTS
Chugachmiut
Attn: Education and Training Coordinator
1840 Bragaw Street, Suite 110
Anchorage, AK 99508-3463
(907) 562-4155   Toll-free: (800) 478-4155 (within AK)
Fax: (907) 563-2891   E-mail: Info@chugachmiut.org
Web: www.chugachmiut.org

Purpose To provide financial assistance to Alaska Natives from the Chugach Region who are interested in attending college or graduate school in any state.
Eligibility This program is open to enrolled tribal members of the Chugach Region who are working, full or part time, on an undergraduate or graduate degree at a college or university in any state. Applicants must be able to demonstrate financial need. Along with their application, they must submit a statement with their personal and educational history, accomplishments, educational and career goals, and how the degree program they are planning to attend fits in with their educational and career goals.
Financial data A stipend is awarded (amount not specified).
Duration 1 year; may be renewed if the recipient maintains of GPA of 2.0 or higher.
Additional information Chugachmiut is a tribal consortium of 7 native communities in the Chugach region of Alaska.
Number awarded Varies each year.
Deadline May of each year.

[105]
CHUGACHMIUT VOCATIONAL TRAINING TUITION ASSISTANCE
Chugachmiut
Attn: Education and Training Coordinator
1840 Bragaw Street, Suite 110
Anchorage, AK 99508-3463
(907) 562-4155   Toll-free: (800) 478-4155
Fax: (907) 563-2891   E-mail: Info@chugachmiut.org
Web: www.chugachmiut.org

Purpose To provide financial assistance for vocational training to Native Alaskans and American Indians living in the Chugach region of Alaska.
Eligibility This program is open to Native Alaskans and American Indians who are residing in the Chugach region of Alaska. Applicants must be interested in an accredited program of career training, technical training, or certification that will lead to employment. They must submit documentation of financial need and a statement describing their career goals and how the proposed training will help them accomplish those goals. Priority is given to applicants who plan to work in the region.
Financial data The stipend depends on the need of the recipient.
Duration Until completion of the program, provided the recipient maintains regular attendance and satisfactory progress in all classes.
Additional information Chugachmiut is a tribal consortium of 7 native communities in the Chugach region of Alaska.
Number awarded Varies each year.
Deadline Applications may be submitted at any time, but they must be received at least 2 weeks before the start of the training program.

[106]
CIRI FOUNDATION ACHIEVEMENT SCHOLARSHIPS
Cook Inlet Region, Inc.
Attn: The CIRI Foundation
3600 San Jeronimo Drive, Suite 256
Anchorage, AK 99508-2870
(907) 793-3575   Toll-free: (800) 764-3382
Fax: (907) 793-3585   E-mail: tcf@thecirifoundation.org
Web: www.thecirifoundation.org/scholarships.htm

Purpose To provide financial assistance for undergraduate or graduate studies to Alaska Natives who are original enrollees to Cook Inlet Region, Inc. (CIRI) and their lineal descendants.
Eligibility This program is open to Alaska Native enrollees to CIRI under the Alaska Native Claims Settlement Act (ANCSA) of 1971 and their lineal descendants. There are no Alaska residency requirements or age limitations. Applicants must be accepted or enrolled full time in a 4-year or graduate degree program. They must have a GPA of 3.0 or higher. Along with their application, they must submit a 500-word statement on their educational and career goals and how they are contributing, or planning to contribute, to a positive Alaska Native community. Selection is based on that statement, academic achievement, rigor of course work or degree program, student financial contribution, financial need, grade level, previous work performance, community service, and relationship of degree program to career goals.
Financial data The stipend is $8,000 per year.
Duration 1 year (2 semesters).
Number awarded Varies each year.
Deadline May of each year.

[107]
CIRI FOUNDATION EXCELLENCE SCHOLARSHIPS
Cook Inlet Region, Inc.
Attn: The CIRI Foundation
3600 San Jeronimo Drive, Suite 256
Anchorage, AK 99508-2870
(907) 793-3575   Toll-free: (800) 764-3382
Fax: (907) 793-3585   E-mail: tcf@thecirifoundation.org
Web: www.thecirifoundation.org/scholarships.htm

Purpose To provide financial assistance for undergraduate or graduate studies to Alaska Natives who are original enrollees to Cook Inlet Region, Inc. (CIRI) and their lineal descendants.

FINANCIAL AID PROGRAMS

Eligibility This program is open to Alaska Native enrollees to CIRI under the Alaska Native Claims Settlement Act (ANCSA) of 1971 and their lineal descendants. There are no Alaska residency requirements or age limitations. Applicants must be accepted or enrolled full time in a 4-year undergraduate or a graduate degree program. They must have a GPA of 3.5 or higher. Along with their application, they must submit a 500-word statement on their educational and career goals and how they are contributing, or planning to contribute, to a positive Alaska Native community. Selection is based on that statement, academic achievement, rigor of course work or degree program, student financial contribution, financial need, grade level, previous work performance, community service, and relationship of degree program to career goals.
Financial data The stipend is $10,000 per year.
Duration 1 year (2 semesters).
Number awarded Varies each year; recently, 7 of these scholarships were awarded.
Deadline May of each year.

[108]
CIRI FOUNDATION GENERAL SEMESTER SCHOLARSHIPS
Cook Inlet Region, Inc.
Attn: The CIRI Foundation
3600 San Jeronimo Drive, Suite 256
Anchorage, AK 99508-2870
(907) 793-3575   Toll-free: (800) 764-3382
Fax: (907) 793-3585   E-mail: tcf@thecirifoundation.org
Web: www.thecirifoundation.org/scholarships.htm

Purpose To provide financial assistance for undergraduate or graduate studies to Alaska Natives who are original enrollees to Cook Inlet Region, Inc. (CIRI) and their lineal descendants.
Eligibility This program is open to Alaska Native enrollees to CIRI under the Alaska Native Claims Settlement Act (ANCSA) of 1971 and their lineal descendants. There are no Alaska residency requirements or age limitations. Applicants must be accepted or enrolled full time in a 2-year, 4-year, or graduate degree program. They must have a GPA of 2.5 or higher. Along with their application, they must submit a 500-word statement on their educational and career goals and how they are contributing, or planning to contribute, to a positive Alaska Native community. Selection is based on that statement, academic achievement, rigor of course work or degree program, student financial contribution, financial need, grade level, previous work performance, community service, and relationship of degree program to career goals.
Financial data The stipend is $2,500 per semester.
Duration 1 semester; recipients may reapply.
Number awarded Varies each year; recently, 213 of these scholarships were awarded.
Deadline May or November of each year.

[109]
CIRI FOUNDATION SPECIAL EXCELLENCE SCHOLARSHIPS
Cook Inlet Region, Inc.
Attn: The CIRI Foundation
3600 San Jeronimo Drive, Suite 256
Anchorage, AK 99508-2870
(907) 793-3575   Toll-free: (800) 764-3382
Fax: (907) 793-3585   E-mail: tcf@thecirifoundation.org
Web: www.thecirifoundation.org/scholarships.htm

Purpose To provide financial assistance for undergraduate or graduate studies in selected fields to Alaska Natives who are original enrollees to Cook Inlet Region, Inc. (CIRI) and their lineal descendants.
Eligibility This program is open to Alaska Native enrollees to CIRI under the Alaska Native Claims Settlement Act (ANCSA) of 1971 and their lineal descendants. There are no Alaska residency requirements or age limitations. Applicants must be accepted or enrolled full time in a 4-year undergraduate or a graduate degree program. They must have a GPA of 3.7 or higher. Preference is given to students working on a degree in business, education, mathematics, sciences, health services, or engineering. Along with their application, they must submit a 500-word statement on their educational and career goals and how they are contributing, or planning to contribute, to a positive Alaska Native community. Selection is based on that statement, academic achievement, rigor of course work or degree program, student financial contribution, financial need, grade level, previous work performance, community service, and relationship of degree program to career goals.
Financial data The stipend is $20,000 per year.
Duration 1 year; may be renewed.
Additional information This program was established in 1997.
Number awarded 1 or more each year.
Deadline May of each year.

[110]
CIRI FOUNDATION VOCATIONAL TRAINING GRANTS
Cook Inlet Region, Inc.
Attn: The CIRI Foundation
3600 San Jeronimo Drive, Suite 256
Anchorage, AK 99508-2870
(907) 793-3575   Toll-free: (800) 764-3382
Fax: (907) 793-3585   E-mail: tcf@thecirifoundation.org
Web: www.thecirifoundation.org/grants.htm

Purpose To provide financial assistance for professional preparation after high school to Alaska Natives who are original enrollees to the Cook Inlet Region, Inc. (CIRI) and their lineal descendants.
Eligibility This program is open to Alaska Native enrollees to CIRI under the Alaska Native Claims Settlement Act (ANCSA) of 1971 and their lineal descendants. Applicants should have a high school diploma or GED, have a GPA of 2.5 or higher, and be able to document the availability of employment upon completion of the training. They must be accepted or enrolled part or full time in a technical skills certificate or degree program, such as (but not limited to) craft/trade, automotive technology, office occupations, and computer technology. Alaska residency is not required.

Along with their application, they must submit a 500-word statement on their educational and career goals and how they are contributing, or planning to contribute, to a positive Alaska Native community. Selection is based on that statement, academic achievement, rigor of course work or degree program, student financial contribution, financial need, grade level, previous work performance, community service, and relationship of degree program to career goals.

Financial data The maximum stipend is $4,500 per calendar year.

Duration 1 quarter; recipients may reapply.

Number awarded Varies each year; recently, 42 of these grants were awarded.

Deadline March, June, September, or November of each year.

[111]
CITI FOUNDATION SCHOLARSHIP PROGRAM

American Indian College Fund
Attn: Scholarship Department
8333 Greenwood Boulevard
Denver, CO 80221
(303) 426-8900 Toll-free: (800) 776-FUND
Fax: (303) 426-1200 E-mail: info@collegefund.org
Web: www.collegefund.org

Purpose To provide financial assistance to Native American students from any state who are attending designated tribal colleges in South Dakota.

Eligibility This program is open to American Indians or Alaska Natives from any state enrolled full time at Oglala Lakota College, Sinte Gleska University, or Sisseton Wahpeton College (all in South Dakota). Applicants must have a GPA of 3.0 or higher and be able to demonstrate financial need. They must be willing to work with other scholarship recipients at their campus to organize a professional development component called the Citi Foundation Career Exploration Day. Along with their application, they must submit 1) short essays (up to 500 words each) on how they perceive themselves as leaders in their school or community and how their education will help the Native American community; and 2) a personal statement of 1,000 words that includes their personal background, their academic background, their educational and career goals, and how this scholarship will help them achieve those goals.

Financial data The stipend is $4,000.

Duration 1 year.

Additional information This scholarship is sponsored by the Citigroup Foundation in partnership with the American Indian College Fund.

Number awarded 1 or more each year.

Deadline May of each year.

[112]
CITIZEN POTAWATOMI NATION ADULT VOCATIONAL TRAINING

Citizen Potawatomi Nation
Attn: Employment and Training
1601 South Gordon Cooper Avenue
Shawnee, OK 74801-8699
(405) 275-5269 Toll-free: (800) 880-9880
Fax: (405) 878-4668
E-mail: jgardner@potawatomi.org
Web: www.potawatomi.org

Purpose To provide financial assistance for vocational training to members of the Citizen Potawatomi Nation.

Eligibility This program is open to Citizen Potawatomi Nation tribal members who are attending or planning to attend a designated vocational technical school in central Oklahoma. Also eligible are members of the Kickapoo Tribe of Oklahoma, the Sac and Fox Nation, and the Iowa Tribe of Oklahoma. Applicants must be residents of the Citizen Potawatomi Nation service area, which covers Cleveland, Lincoln, Payne, and Pottawatomie counties, as well as the eastern portion of Oklahoma County. They must be able to demonstrate financial need.

Financial data The amount awarded depends upon the recipient's financial need.

Duration 1 semester; may be renewed.

Number awarded Varies each year.

Deadline August for the fall semester or December for the spring semester.

[113]
CITIZEN POTAWATOMI NATION HIGHER EDUCATION GRANTS

Citizen Potawatomi Nation
Attn: Employment and Training
1601 South Gordon Cooper Avenue
Shawnee, OK 74801-8699
(405) 275-5269 Toll-free: (800) 880-9880
Fax: (405) 878-4668
E-mail: jgardner@potawatomi.org
Web: www.potawatomi.org

Purpose To provide financial assistance to members of the Citizen Potawatomi Nation and neighboring Indians who are working on a bachelor's degree in any state.

Eligibility This program is open to Citizen Potawatomi Nation tribal members who are working full time on a bachelor's degree at a college or university in any state. Also eligible are members of the Kickapoo Tribe of Oklahoma, the Sac and Fox Nation, and the Iowa Tribe of Oklahoma. Applicants must be residents of the Citizen Potawatomi Nation service area, which covers Cleveland, Lincoln, Payne, and Pottawatomie counties, as well as the eastern portion of Oklahoma County. They must have a GPA of 2.0 or higher, be able to demonstrate financial need, and apply for all other available financial aid (this award is intended to be supplementary).

Financial data The amount awarded depends upon the recipient's financial need.

Duration 1 year; may be renewed.

Additional information The tribe has operated this program since 1989 through a contract with the Bureau of Indian Affairs.

Number awarded Varies; generally, 70 or more each year.
Deadline July of each year for fall semester; December of each year for spring semester; May of each year for summer session.

[114]
CITIZEN POTAWATOMI NATION TRIBAL ROLLS SCHOLARSHIPS
Citizen Potawatomi Nation
Attn: Office of Tribal Rolls
1601 South Gordon Cooper Avenue
Shawnee, OK 74801-8699
(405) 275-5269　　　　Toll-free: (800) 880-9880
Fax: (405) 878-4668
E-mail: jgardner@Potawatomi.org
Web: www.potawatomi.org

Purpose To provide financial assistance for college or graduate school to members of the Citizen Potawatomi Nation.
Eligibility This program is open to enrolled members of the Citizen Potawatomi Nation who are enrolled or planning to enroll in an undergraduate or graduate degree program, vocational technical career courses, or other accredited educational program in any state. Applicants must have a GPA of 2.0 or higher and be able to demonstrate financial need.
Financial data Stipends are $1,500 per semester for full-time students or $750 per semester for part-time students.
Duration 1 semester; may be renewed, provided the recipient maintains a GPA of 2.0 or higher.
Number awarded Varies each year; recently, 125 of these scholarships were awarded, including 94 to undergraduates, 10 to vocational/technical students, and 21 to graduate students.
Deadline July of each year for the fall semester, November of each year for the spring semester, or May for summer session.

[115]
CLEM JUDD, JR. MEMORIAL SCHOLARSHIP
Hawai'i Hotel & Lodging Association
Attn: Hawaii Hotel Industry Foundation
2270 Kalakaua Avenue, Suite 1506
Honolulu, HI 96815
(808) 923-0407　　　　Fax: (808) 924-3843
E-mail: hhla@hawaiihotels.org
Web: www.hawaiihotels.org

Purpose To provide financial assistance to Native Hawaiians who are upper-division students working on a degree in hotel management at a school in any state.
Eligibility This program is open to Hawaii residents who can provide proof of their Hawaiian ancestry through birth certificates of their parents or grandparents. Applicants must be a junior or senior at an accredited college or university (in any state) and majoring in hotel management. They must have a GPA of 2.8 or higher. Financial need is not considered in the selection process.
Financial data The stipend ranges from $2,000 to $2,500.
Duration 1 year.

Additional information This program was established in 1996.
Number awarded 1 each year.
Deadline June of each year.

[116]
COCA-COLA FIRST GENERATION SCHOLARSHIP
American Indian College Fund
Attn: Scholarship Department
8333 Greenwood Boulevard
Denver, CO 80221
(303) 426-8900　　　　Toll-free: (800) 776-FUND
Fax: (303) 426-1200　　E-mail: info@collegefund.org
Web: www.collegefund.org

Purpose To provide financial assistance to Native Americans who are attending a Tribal College or University (TCU) and are the first in their family to attend college.
Eligibility This program is open to American Indians or Alaska Natives who are enrolled full time in their first or second semester at an eligible TCU. Applicants must have a GPA of 3.0 or higher and be able to demonstrate financial need. They must be the first in their immediate family to attend college. Along with their application, they must submit 1) short essays (up to 500 words each) on how they perceive themselves as leaders in their school or community and how their education will help the Native American community; and 2) a personal statement of 1,000 words that includes their personal background, their academic background, their educational and career goals, and how this scholarship will help them achieve those goals.
Financial data The stipend is $5,000 per year.
Duration 1 year; may be renewed, provided the recipient maintains a GPA of 3.0 or higher and participates actively in campus and community life.
Additional information This program is sponsored by the Coca-Cola Company in partnership with the American Indian College Fund.
Number awarded 1 or more each year.
Deadline May of each year.

[117]
COCOPAH HIGHER EDUCATION GRANTS
Cocopah Indian Tribe
Attn: Education Department
County 15th and Avenue G
Somerton, AZ 85350
(928) 627-2101　　　　Fax: (928) 627-3173
E-mail: cocopah@cocopah.com
Web: www.cocopah.com/docs/education.html

Purpose To provide financial assistance to members of the Cocopah Indian Nation who are attending or planning to attend college to work on an undergraduate degree.
Eligibility This program is open to enrolled members of the Cocopah Indian Nation who are enrolled at or accepted to an accredited college or university in the United States. Applicants with a GPA of 2.99 or lower must attend their local community college; applicants with a GPA of 3.0 or higher are allowed to attend their local community college or a university in the state in which they reside; applicants with a GPA of 3.5 or higher may attend an institution in any state. They must submit documentation of financial need,

although awards are available to students who have no unmet need. Awards are granted in the following priority order: 1) continuing undergraduates in good academic standing; 2) graduating high school seniors; 3) students returning to college after an absence of 1 or more years; and 4) non-financial need students. Part-time students may attend only a public college or university in their home state.

Financial data For full-time students at in-state public universities and colleges who can document financial need, grants are intended to cover tuition, books, room and board, transportation, personal costs, and any other expenses deemed necessary by the institution's financial aid department. For full-time students at private and out-of-state colleges and universities who can document financial need, assistance is based on average attendance costs at the institution, as determined by the tribal education department. Full-time students who cannot document financial need are eligible for assistance if funds are available; the amount of that assistance depends on the average attendance costs at their institution, as determined by the tribal education department. Part-time students receive payment of direct costs only (tuition, fees, and textbooks) for the program in which they are enrolled at an in-state public college or university.

Duration 1 year; may be renewed, provided the recipient maintains a GPA of 2.0 or higher.

Number awarded Varies each year.

Deadline April of each year for fall semester; September of each year for spring semester.

[118]
COCOPAH SUMMER TUITION ASSISTANCE
Cocopah Indian Tribe
Attn: Education Department
County 15th and Avenue G
Somerton, AZ 85350
(928) 627-2101 Fax: (928) 627-3173
E-mail: cocopah@cocopah.com
Web: www.cocopah.com/docs/education.html

Purpose To provide financial assistance to members of the Cocopah Indian Nation who are interested in working during the summer on an undergraduate or graduate degree.

Eligibility This program is open to enrolled members of the Cocopah Indian Nation who are enrolled at or accepted by an accredited college or university in the United States. Undergraduates should have a GPA of 2.0 or higher; graduate students should have a GPA of 3.0 or higher. Applicants must be interested in attending school during the summer. They must be able to document financial need.

Financial data Maximum grants are $2,500 for graduate students or $1,000 for undergraduates. Funds may be used for payment of direct costs only (tuition, fees, and textbooks).

Duration 1 summer term.

Number awarded Varies each year.

Deadline March of each year.

[119]
COLBERT "BUD" BAKER SCHOLARSHIP
Chickasaw Foundation
110 West 12th Street
P.O. Box 1726
Ada, OK 74821-1726
(580) 421-9030 Fax: (580) 421-9031
E-mail: ChickasawFoundation@chickasaw.net
Web: www.chickasaw.net

Purpose To provide financial assistance to members of the Chickasaw Nation who are majoring or minoring in American history, education, or pre-law.

Eligibility This program is open to Chickasaw students who are currently enrolled full time at an accredited institution of higher education. Applicants must be classified as juniors or seniors at a 4-year college. They must be 1) majoring in history, or 2) majoring in education or pre-law with a minor in history. The history emphasis must be on Chickasaw tribal history or Native American studies. Along with their application, they must submit high school or college transcripts, 2 letters of recommendation, a copy of their Chickasaw Nation citizenship card, and a 1-page essay on their long-term goals and plans for achieving them. Financial need is not considered in the selection process.

Financial data The stipend is $1,200.

Duration 1 year.

Number awarded 3 each year.

Deadline June of each year.

[120]
COLGATE "BRIGHT SMILES, BRIGHT FUTURES" MINORITY SCHOLARSHIPS
American Dental Hygienists' Association
Attn: Institute for Oral Health
444 North Michigan Avenue, Suite 3400
Chicago, IL 60611
(312) 440-8918 Toll-free: (800) 735-4916
Fax: (312) 440-8929 E-mail: institute@adha.net
Web: www.adha.org/institute/Scholarship/index.htm

Purpose To provide financial assistance to minority students and males of any race enrolled in undergraduate programs in dental hygiene.

Eligibility This program is open to members of groups currently underrepresented in the dental hygiene profession (Native Americans, African Americans, Hispanics, Asians, and males) who are active members of the Student American Dental Hygienists' Association (SADHA) or the American Dental Hygienists' Association (ADHA). Applicants must have a GPA of 3.0 or higher, be able to document financial need of at least $1,500, and have completed at least 1 year of full-time enrollment in an accredited dental hygiene program in the United States. Along with their application, they must submit a statement that covers their long-term career goals, their intended contribution to the dental hygiene profession, their professional interests, and how their extracurricular activities and their degree enhance the attainment of their goals.

Financial data The stipend is $1,250.

Duration 1 year; nonrenewable.

Additional information These scholarships are sponsored by the Colgate-Palmolive Company.

Number awarded 2 each year.
Deadline April of each year.

[121]
COLLEGE STUDENT PRE-COMMISSIONING INITIATIVE

U.S. Coast Guard
Attn: Recruiting Command
2300 Wilson Boulevard, Suite 500
Arlington, VA 22201
(703) 235-1775   Toll-free: (877) NOW-USCG
Fax: (703) 235-1881
E-mail: Margaret.A.Jackson@uscg.mil
Web: www.gocoastguard.com/cspi.html

Purpose To provide financial assistance to college students at minority institutions willing to serve in the Coast Guard following graduation.
Eligibility This program is open to students enrolled as sophomores or juniors at a 4-year college or university with at least 25% minority population. Applicants must be U.S. citizens; have a GPA of 2.5 or higher; have scores of 1000 or higher on the SAT, 1100 or higher on the SAT I, 23 or higher on the ACT, or 109 or higher on the ASVAB GT; be between 21 and 26 years of age at the time of college graduation; and meet all physical requirements for a Coast Guard commission. They must agree to attend the Coast Guard Officer Candidate School following graduation and serve on active duty as an officer for at least 3 years.
Financial data Those selected to participate receive full payment of tuition, books, and fees; monthly housing and food allowances; medical and life insurance; special training in leadership, management, law enforcement, navigation, and marine science; 30 days paid vacation per year; and a monthly salary of up to $2,200.
Duration 2 years.
Number awarded Varies each year.
Deadline February of each year.

[122]
COLORADO INDIAN EDUCATION FOUNDATION SCHOLARS PROGRAM

Rocky Mountain Indian Chamber of Commerce
Attn: Colorado Indian Education Foundation
924 West Colfax Avenue, Suite 104F
P.O. Box 40749
Denver, CO 80204
(303) 629-0102   Fax: (303) 595-8880
E-mail: info@rmicc.org
Web: www.rmicc.org/foundation.html

Purpose To provide financial assistance to American Indians from Colorado who are interested in attending college in the state.
Eligibility This program is open to American Indian residents of Colorado who can verify that they 1) are on a federal or state-recognized tribal roll and are identified by a tribal enrollment card; 2) have an official letter from a federal or state recognized tribe or agency stating tribal membership or Indian blood; 3) have a family tree and officially sealed birth certificates establishing that at least 1 parent is Indian; or 4) are an enrolled official member of a terminated tribe. Applicants must be enrolled or planning to enroll at an accredited college, university, or vocational/trade school in Colorado. They must have a GPA of 2.5 or higher. Along with their application, they must submit a 500-word essay describing their chosen field of study, educational goals, career goals, involvement in the Indian community, and how this scholarship will help them in furthering their education. Financial need is not considered in the selection process.
Financial data The stipend is $1,000.
Duration 1 year.
Number awarded 8 each year.
Deadline October of each year.

[123]
COMANCHE NATION ADULT VOCATIONAL TRAINING PROGRAM

Comanche Nation
Attn: Higher Education
P.O. Box 908
Lawton, OK 73502
(580) 492-3743   Fax: (580) 492-4017
Web: www.comanchenation.com

Purpose To provide financial assistance to adult members of the Comanche Nation who are interested in vocational training.
Eligibility This program is open to adult enrolled members of the Comanche Nation who are attending full-time programs offered by state vocational schools. They must be seeking financial assistance and vocational counseling.
Financial data A stipend is awarded (amount not specified).
Duration This program supports long-term vocational training.
Number awarded Varies each year.

[124]
COMANCHE NATION COLLEGE SCHOLARSHIP PROGRAM

Comanche Nation
Attn: Higher Education
P.O. Box 908
Lawton, OK 73502
(580) 492-3743   Fax: (580) 492-4017
Web: www.comanchenation.com

Purpose To provide financial assistance to members of the Comanche Nation who are interested in working on an undergraduate or graduate degree.
Eligibility This program is open to enrolled members of the Comanche Nation who are high school graduates or GED recipients and attending or planning to attend a college or university. Applicants must intend to work on a bachelor's, master's, or doctoral degree or be enrolled in a 2-year program that will transfer to a 4-year institution. They must be able to demonstrate financial need and offer a reasonable assurance that they will be able to complete their degree program.
Financial data A stipend is awarded (amount not specified).
Duration 1 year; may be renewed.
Number awarded Varies each year.

Deadline March of each year for summer; May of each year for fall; September of each year for spring.

[125]
COMMUNITY-BASED EDUCATION PROGRAM
The Aleut Corporation
Attn: Aleut Foundation
703 West Tudor Road, Suite 102
Anchorage, AK 99503-6650
(907) 646-1929 Toll-free: (800) 232-4882
Fax: (907) 646-1949
E-mail: taf@thealeutfoundation.org
Web: www.thealeutfoundation.org/static/cbe.aspx

Purpose To provide financial assistance for job training to Native Alaskans with ties to the Aleutian Islands.

Eligibility This program is open to residents of Alaska who are original enrollees of The Aleut Corporation (TAC) or their descendants. Applicants must be interested in participating in community-based career enhancement training. They must indicate if they are currently employed and if the proposed training is required for their current position.

Financial data The program provides payment of all costs of the training.

Duration Training programs are provided as available; most are only a few weeks in length.

Number awarded Varies each year; recently, 4 communities were approved to have training.

[126]
COMPUTERCRAFT CORPORATION SCHOLARSHIP
Chickasaw Foundation
110 West 12th Street
P.O. Box 1726
Ada, OK 74821-1726
(580) 421-9030 Fax: (580) 421-9031
E-mail: ChickasawFoundation@chickasaw.net
Web: www.chickasaw.net

Purpose To provide financial assistance to members of the Chickasaw Nation who are majoring in fields of interest to ComputerCraft Corporation.

Eligibility This program is open to Chickasaw students who are currently enrolled full time as an undergraduate student. The sponsor recruits computer engineers, graphic designers, biologists, conference managers, and international trade specialists. Preference may be given to those majors, but all fields of study are eligible. Applicants must have a GPA of 2.5 or higher. Along with their application, they must submit high school or college transcripts, 2 letters of recommendation, a copy of their Chickasaw Nation citizenship card, and a 1-page essay on their long-term goals and plans for achieving them. Financial need is not considered in the selection process.

Financial data The stipend is $1,500 per year.

Duration 1 year.

Number awarded 1 each year.

Deadline June of each year.

[127]
CONAGRA FOODS FOUNDATION SCHOLARSHIPS
National FFA Organization
Attn: Scholarship Office
6060 FFA Drive
P.O. Box 68960
Indianapolis, IN 46268-0960
(317) 802-4419 Fax: (317) 802-5419
E-mail: scholarships@ffa.org
Web: www.ffa.org

Purpose To provide financial assistance to FFA members who are ethnic minorities and planning to major in selected fields related to agriculture at designated universities.

Eligibility This program is open to members who are graduating high school seniors and ethnic minorities (African Americans, Asian Americans, Pacific Islanders, Hispanics, Alaska Natives, or American Indians). Applicants must have a GPA of 3.0 or higher. They must intend to enroll full time at an approved university to work on a 4-year degree in the following agriculture-related fields: agronomy and crop science, farm and ranch management, agricultural communications, education, business management, economics, finance, sales and marketing, engineering, or food science and technology. Selection is based on academic achievement (10 points for GPA, 10 points for SAT or ACT score, 10 points for class rank), leadership in FFA activities (30 points), leadership in community activities (10 points), and participation in the Supervised Agricultural Experience (SAE) program (30 points). U.S. citizenship is required.

Financial data The stipend is $2,000 per year. Funds are paid directly to the recipient.

Duration 4 years, provided the recipients maintain a GPA of 3.0 or higher.

Additional information Funding for these scholarships is provided by the ConAgra Foods Foundation. The approved universities are University of Nebraska at Lincoln, Purdue University, Cornell University, Iowa State University, University of Iowa, Texas Tech, North Dakota State University, or University of Illinois at Urbana-Champaign.

Number awarded 4 each year.

Deadline February of each year.

[128]
CONFEDERATED SALISH AND KOOTENAI TRIBES HIGHER EDUCATION SCHOLARSHIPS
Confederated Salish and Kootenai Tribes
Attn: Tribal Education Department
P.O. Box 278
Pablo, MT 59855
(406) 675-2700, ext. 1072 Toll-free: (877) 575-0086
Fax: (406) 275-2814 E-mail: tribaled@cskt.org
Web: www.cskt.org/services/education.htm

Purpose To provide financial assistance to members of the Confederated Salish and Kootenai Tribes who are interested in attending college or graduate school in any state.

Eligibility This program is open to enrolled members of the Confederated Salish and Kootenai Tribes who are enrolled or accepted for enrollment at an accredited college, university or vocational/technical school. Applicants must be able to demonstrate financial need. Assistance is available to students in the following priority order: 1) continuing students in good standing; 2) new students who have never received tribal higher education funding; 3) returning students who have taken a break from school for 1 or more quarters or semesters; and 4) part-time students. A small fund is set aside for graduate students.

Financial data For students at public colleges and universities in Montana, stipends supplement other funding available to the student to pay for tuition and fees, room and board, books, and miscellaneous expenses related to school. For students at private or out-of-state colleges and universities, support is limited to the level at public in-state colleges. Assistance for part-time students is capped at $3,000 per year and support for graduate students is limited to $2,000 per year.

Duration 1 year; may be renewed, provided recipients maintain a GPA of 2.0 or higher and full-time enrollment.

Number awarded Varies each year. Recently, 258 of these scholarships were awarded, including 141 to students at Salish Kootenai College, 39 to students at the University of Montana, 7 to students at the Bozeman or Billings campuses of Montana State University, 71 to students at colleges and universities outside Montana, and 10 to graduate students.

Deadline April of each year.

[129]
CONFEDERATED TRIBES OF THE UMATILLA INDIAN RESERVATION HIGHER EDUCATION SCHOLARSHIPS

Confederated Tribes of the Umatilla Indian Reservation
Attn: Education and Training Department
73239 Confederated Way
P.O. Box 638
Pendleton, OR 97801
(541) 966-2248   Fax: (541) 276-6543
E-mail: LouFarrow@ctuir.com
Web: www.umatilla.nsn.us/ed.html

Purpose To provide financial assistance for college or graduate school to Indians affiliated with the Confederated Tribes of the Umatilla Indian Reservation (CTUIR).

Eligibility This program is open to tribal members enrolled or planning to enroll in a bachelor's degree program at an accredited college or university; support for a master's or doctoral degree is also available if funds are available. Applicants must submit a complete information sheet, a personal letter outlining education goals, 3 letters of recommendation, high school or college transcripts or GED test scores, a college acceptance letter, documentation of financial need, and their Certificate of Indian Blood.

Financial data A stipend is awarded (amount not specified).

Duration 1 year; may be renewed.

Additional information The CTUIR was established in 1949 when the Cayuse, Walla Walla, and Umatilla tribes entered into an agreement regarding their reservation in northeastern Oregon and southeastern Washington.

Number awarded Varies each year.

Deadline June of each year for fall quarter or semester; October of each year of winter quarter or semester; January of each year for spring quarter; April of each year for summer quarter.

[130]
CONTINENTAL SOCIETY, DAUGHTERS OF INDIAN WARS SCHOLARSHIP

Continental Society, Daughters of Indian Wars
c/o Jean Belew, Scholarship Chair
500 Mt. Pleasant Road, N.E.
Fairmount, GA 30139
E-mail: belewjean@yahoo.com

Purpose To provide financial assistance to Native American college students who are interested in preparing for a career in education or social service.

Eligibility Applicants must be certified tribal members of a federally-recognized tribe, plan to prepare for a career in education or social service, plan to work on a reservation, be a junior at an accredited college, have earned at least a 3.0 GPA, and carry at least 10 quarter hours or 8 semester hours. Selection is based primarily on academic achievement and commitment to the field of study; financial need is not necessary but is considered.

Financial data The stipend is $1,000.

Duration 1 year; may be renewed.

Number awarded 1 each year.

Deadline June of each year.

[131]
COOK INLET TRIBAL COUNCIL TRIBAL HIGHER EDUCATION PROGRAM

Cook Inlet Tribal Council, Inc.
Attn: Tribal Scholarships and Grants Program
3600 San Jeronimo Drive, Suite 286
Anchorage, AK 99508
(907) 793-3578   Toll-free: (877) 985-5900
Fax: (907) 793-3589   E-mail: scholarships@citci.com
Web: www.citci.com//page/42

Purpose To provide financial assistance to Alaska Native shareholders of the Cook Inlet Region, Inc. (CIRI) and their descendants who are working on an undergraduate or graduate degree.

Eligibility This program is open to Alaska Native shareholders of CIRI and their descendants, regardless of residence, who are enrolled or planning to enroll full time at an accredited college, university, or vocational training facility. Applicants must be working on a certificate, associate, bachelor's, or graduate degree. Along with their application they must submit a letter of reference, a 200-word statement of purpose, their Certificate of Indian Blood (CIB), a letter of acceptance from the school, transcripts, their Student Aid Report, a budget forecast, and (for males) documentation of Selective Service registration. Awards are presented on a first-come, first-served basis as long as funds are available.

Financial data This program provides supplementary matching financial aid. Awards are intended to be applied to tuition, fees, course-required books and supplies, and on-campus housing and meal plans only. Total funding over a lifetime educational career is limited to $15,000.

Duration 1 year; may be renewed up to 4 additional years if the recipient maintains a GPA of 2.0 or higher.

Additional information Students whose CIB gives their village as Tyonek, Kenai, Ninilchik, Knik, or Salamatof must apply directly to their village organization.

Number awarded Varies each year, depending on the availability of funds.
Deadline June of each year for fall; November of each year for spring.

[132]
COPPER RIVER NATIVE ASSOCIATION ADULT VOCATIONAL TRAINING SCHOLARSHIP

Copper River Native Association
Mile 104 Old Richardson Highway
P.O. Box H
Copper Center, AK 99573
(907) 822-8801   Fax: (907) 822-5241
E-mail: pbxoperator@crnative.org
Web: www.crnative.org

Purpose To provide financial assistance for vocational training to Alaska Natives enrolled in the Ahtna Region.
Eligibility Applicants must be at least one-fourth Alaska Native or Native American, must be enrolled in the Ahtna Region, must have a letter of acceptance from an appropriate postsecondary institution, must have a definite financial need, and must have at least a 2.0 GPA. They are expected to apply for other sources of financial aid (e.g., Veteran's Administration, Alaska Commission on Postsecondary Education), in addition to this program. Alaska residency is not required.
Financial data The stipend generally covers the cost of tuition and books. The money is sent directly to the recipient's school.
Duration 1 year; may be renewed if the recipient maintains a GPA of 2.0 or higher.
Additional information The association is also known as Atna'T'Aene Nene.
Number awarded Varies each year.

[133]
COPPER RIVER NATIVE ASSOCIATION HIGHER EDUCATION SCHOLARSHIP

Copper River Native Association
Mile 104 Old Richardson Highway
P.O. Box H
Copper Center, AK 99573
(907) 822-8801   Fax: (907) 822-5241
E-mail: pbxoperator@crnative.org
Web: www.crnative.org

Purpose To provide financial assistance for undergraduate or graduate studies to Alaska Natives who are enrolled in the Copper River Native Association.
Eligibility Eligible for this program are Alaska Natives who are enrolled to Ahtna Inc., are at least one-quarter blood quantum, and are lineal descendants (children, grandchildren, natural or adopted). Applicants must be enrolled or accepted as full-time students at an accredited college or university on the undergraduate (4-year program) or graduate school level. They should have at least a 2.0 GPA. Alaska residency is not required. Applicants are expected to apply for other financial aid programs. Selection is based on scholastic achievement (primary factor), previous work performance, education and community involvement, financial need, recommendations, years in school, seriousness of purpose, major field of study, practicality of education and professional goals, and completeness of the application.
Financial data The stipend is $2,000 per semester. Funds are to be used for tuition, university fees, books, and campus related/approved room and board. The money is sent directly to the recipient's school.
Duration 1 year; may be renewed if the recipient maintains a GPA of 2.0 or higher.
Additional information The association is also known as Atna'T'Aene Nene.
Number awarded Varies each year.

[134]
COQUILLE INDIAN TRIBE ADULT VOCATIONAL TRAINING GRANTS

Coquille Indian Tribe
Attn: Education Department
3050 Tremont
P.O. Box 783
North Bend, OR 97459
(541) 756-0904, ext. 243   Toll-free: (800) 622-5869
Fax: (541) 756-0847
E-mail: ebryson@coquilletribe.org
Web: www.coquilletribe.org

Purpose To provide financial assistance to members of the Coquille Indian Tribe who are attending or planning to attend vocational school in any state.
Eligibility This program is open to enrolled members of the Coquille Indian Tribe who are entering or continuing at a vocational/technical school in any state. Along with their application, they must submit a personal essay on their vocational goals and how the tribe will benefit by sending them to school.
Financial data A stipend is awarded (amount not specified).
Duration 1 year; may be renewed, provided the recipient maintains a GPA of 2.0 or higher.
Number awarded Varies each year.

[135]
COQUILLE INDIAN TRIBE COMPUTER EQUIPMENT PROGRAM

Coquille Indian Tribe
Attn: Education Department
3050 Tremont
P.O. Box 783
North Bend, OR 97459
(541) 756-0904, ext. 243   Toll-free: (800) 622-5869
Fax: (541) 756-0847
E-mail: ebryson@coquilletribe.org
Web: www.coquilletribe.org

Purpose To provide funding for purchase of computer equipment to members of the Coquille Indian Tribe who are working full time on an undergraduate or graduate degree.
Eligibility This program is open to enrolled members of the Coquille Indian Tribe who have been enrolled for at least 2 semester as full-time undergraduate or graduate students at an accredited college or university in any state. Applicants must be seeking funding for the purchase of computer equipment. Undergraduates must have a GPA of 2.0

or higher and graduate students must have a GPA of 3.0 or higher.
Financial data The grant is $1,000; funds must be used for purchase of computer equipment or programming, and not for training, shipping, and/or maintenance of equipment.
Duration This is a 1-time grant.
Number awarded Varies each year.

[136]
COQUILLE INDIAN TRIBE EDUCATION SCHOLARSHIP
Coquille Indian Tribe
Attn: Education Department
3050 Tremont
P.O. Box 783
North Bend, OR 97459
(541) 756-0904, ext. 243   Toll-free: (800) 622-5869
Fax: (541) 756-0847
E-mail: ebryson@coquilletribe.org
Web: www.coquilletribe.org

Purpose To provide financial assistance to high school senior members of the Coquille Indian Tribe who are planning to attend college in any state.
Eligibility This program is open to enrolled members of the Coquille Indian Tribe who are graduating high school seniors. Applicants must be planning to enroll full time at an accredited college, university, or vocational/technical school in any state. Along with their application, they must submit a personal essay on their career goals, why they chose their educational field, their past and present involvement with the Native American community, their past and present involvement with their school and/or community, and how they plan to use their education to benefit the Coquille Indian Tribe. Selection is based on academic achievement as well as service to the Coquille Indian Tribe or (for students who live outside the service area) other Native American groups.
Financial data The stipend is $5,000.
Duration 1 year; nonrenewable.
Number awarded 1 or more each year.
Deadline June of each year.

[137]
COQUILLE INDIAN TRIBE HIGHER EDUCATION GRANTS
Coquille Indian Tribe
Attn: Education Department
3050 Tremont
P.O. Box 783
North Bend, OR 97459
(541) 756-0904, ext. 243   Toll-free: (800) 622-5869
Fax: (541) 756-0847
E-mail: ebryson@coquilletribe.org
Web: www.coquilletribe.org

Purpose To provide financial assistance to members of the Coquille Indian Tribe who are attending or planning to attend college or graduate school in any state.
Eligibility This program is open to enrolled members of the Coquille Indian Tribe who are entering or continuing full-time undergraduate or graduate students at an accredited college or university in any state. Along with their application, they must submit 1) a personal essay on their career goals, why they chose their educational field, their past and present involvement with the Native American community, their past and present involvement with their school and/or community, and how they plan to use their education to benefit the Coquille Indian Tribe; 2) a description of their involvement with a Native American or diversity group on their campus (entering students must submit this statement after completion of their first semester); and 3) documentation of financial need.
Financial data A stipend is awarded (amount not specified).
Duration 1 year; may be renewed, provided the recipient remains enrolled full time and maintains a GPA of 2.0 or higher as an undergraduate or 3.0 or higher as a graduate student.
Number awarded Varies each year.

[138]
COUNCIL OF ENERGY RESOURCE TRIBES SCHOLARSHIPS
Council of Energy Resource Tribes
Attn: Education Program Director
695 South Colorado Boulevard, Suite 10
Denver, CO 80246-8008
(303) 282-7576, ext. 12   Fax: (303) 282-7584
E-mail: info@CERTRedEarth.com
Web: www.certredearth.com/education.php

Purpose To provide financial assistance to American Indians who are interested in studying fields related to mathematics, business, science, engineering, or other technical fields on the undergraduate or graduate school level.
Eligibility This program is open to Indian high school seniors, college students, and graduate students who have participated in a qualifying program conducted by the Council of Energy Resource Tribes (CERT). Applicants must be enrolled or planning to enroll full time at an accredited 2- or 4-year tribal, public, or private college or university and major in business, engineering, science, mathematics, computer technology, or a related field. Along with their application, they must submit official tribal affiliation documents, university or college enrollment verification, and their most recent academic transcripts. Financial need is also considered in the selection process.
Financial data The stipend is $1,000 per year.
Duration 1 year; may be renewed up to 4 additional years, provided the recipient maintains a GPA of 2.5 or higher.
Additional information From 1981 through 2005, CERT operated the Tribal Research Institute in Business, Engineering & Science (TRIBES) program for high school seniors. From 1986 through 2006 it also operated the CERT Intern Program for college students. Effective in 2006, it replaced those programs with the CERT Scholars Program. High school seniors who are accepted as CERT Scholars are eligible to apply for these scholarships. Undergraduate and graduate students who participated in the earlier programs are also eligible to apply for these scholarships.
Deadline September of each year for fall semester; February of each year for spring semester.

SCHOLARSHIPS

[139]
COW CREEK BAND ADULT VOCATIONAL TRAINING PROGRAM
Cow Creek Band of Umpqua Tribe of Indians
Attn: Education Director
2371 N.E. Stephens Street, Suite 100
Roseburg, OR 97470
(541) 677-5575   Toll-free: (800) 929-8229
Fax: (541) 677-5574
Web: www.cowcreek.com

Purpose To provide financial assistance to members of the Cow Creek Bank of Umpqua Tribe of Indians who reside in the tribal service area and are interested in vocational training.
Eligibility This program is open to Cow Creek members who reside in the 7-county service area in Oregon. Applicants must be interested in enrolling full time in a vocational training program in any state that takes 2 years or under to complete. Along with their application, they must submit a statement of their educational goals and plans, documentation of financial need, information on other financial aid received, and transcripts.
Financial data The maximum grant is $5,000 per academic year.
Duration 1 year; may be renewed 1 additional year.
Additional information The Cow County Band service area focuses on Douglas County, Oregon, but includes portions of the following adjacent counties: Coos, Curry, Jackson, Josephine, Klamath, and Lane.
Number awarded Varies each year.
Deadline February of each year for spring term, May of each year for summer term, July of each year for fall term, or November of each year for winter term.

[140]
COW CREEK BAND CONTINUING AND DISTANCE EDUCATION PROGRAM
Cow Creek Band of Umpqua Tribe of Indians
Attn: Education Director
2371 N.E. Stephens Street, Suite 100
Roseburg, OR 97470
(541) 677-5575   Toll-free: (800) 929-8229
Fax: (541) 677-5574
Web: www.cowcreek.com

Purpose To provide financial assistance to members of the Cow Creek Bank of Umpqua Tribe of Indians who plan to work on a certificate or an undergraduate or graduate degree through a continuing or distance education program.
Eligibility This program is open to Cow Creek members, regardless of where they live, who are interested in obtaining a certificate, 2-year degree, 4-year degree, master's degree, or doctoral degree through a continuing or distance education program. Applicants must submit a statement of their educational goals and plans and relevant transcripts. They are not required to apply for other financial aid.
Financial data The program provides partial payment of tuition, fees, and books, to a maximum that is adjusted annually.
Duration 1 year; may be renewed until completion of a certificate or degree.
Additional information Recipients may enroll for 1 to 7 credits each academic term.
Number awarded Varies each year.
Deadline Applications may be submitted at any time, but they must be received at least 1 month before the program begins.

[141]
COW CREEK BAND HIGHER EDUCATION PROGRAM
Cow Creek Band of Umpqua Tribe of Indians
Attn: Education Director
2371 N.E. Stephens Street, Suite 100
Roseburg, OR 97470
(541) 677-5575   Toll-free: (800) 929-8229
Fax: (541) 677-5574
Web: www.cowcreek.com

Purpose To provide financial assistance to members of the Cow Creek Bank of Umpqua Tribe of Indians who plan to attend college in any state to work on an undergraduate or graduate degree.
Eligibility This program is open to Cow Creek members, regardless of where they live, who are interested in obtaining a 4-year undergraduate degree, master's degree, or doctoral degree program at a college or university in any state. Applicants must submit a statement of their educational goals and plans and documentation of financial need. They must apply for all other financial aid for which they might be eligible. Full-time enrollment is required.
Financial data Stipends are $5,000 per academic year for students at 2-year colleges, $7,000 per academic year for students at 4-year colleges and universities, or $10,000 per academic year for graduate students.
Duration 1 year; may be renewed up to 4 additional years.
Number awarded Varies each year.
Deadline July of each year for fall quarter or semester; November of each year for winter quarter or spring semester; February of each year for spring quarter; or May of each year for summer session.

[142]
COW CREEK BAND TRIBAL EDUCATION PROGRAM
Cow Creek Band of Umpqua Tribe of Indians
Attn: Education Director
2371 N.E. Stephens Street, Suite 100
Roseburg, OR 97470
(541) 677-5575   Toll-free: (800) 929-8229
Fax: (541) 677-5574
Web: www.cowcreek.com

Purpose To provide financial assistance to members of the Cow Creek Bank of Umpqua Tribe of Indians who reside outside the tribal service area and are interested in vocational training.
Eligibility This program is open to Cow Creek members who reside outside the 7-county service area in Oregon. Applicants must be interested in enrolling full time in a vocational training program in any state that takes 2 years or under to complete. Along with their application, they must submit a statement of their educational goals and plans,

documentation of financial need, information on other financial aid received, and transcripts.
Financial data The maximum grant is $5,000 per academic year.
Duration 1 year; may be renewed 1 additional year.
Number awarded Varies each year.
Deadline February of each year for spring term, May of each year for summer term, July of each year for fall term, or November of each year for winter term.

[143]
CRAZY HORSE MEMORIAL JOURNALISM SCHOLARSHIP

South Dakota Newspaper Association
527 Main Avenue, Suite 202
P.O. Box 8100
Brookings, SD 57006-8100
Toll-free: (800) 658-3697 Fax: (605) 692-6388
E-mail: sdna@sdna.com
Web: www.sdna.com

Purpose To provide financial assistance to Native American students interested in preparing for a career in journalism.
Eligibility This program is open to Native American students enrolled or planning to enroll at a college or university. Applicants must be interested in preparing for a journalism career, although they are not required to major in journalism in college. Along with their application, they must submit a 500-word essay explaining their interest in journalism and 2 letters of reference.
Financial data The stipend is $2,000.
Duration 1 year.
Additional information This program is sponsored by the Crazy Horse Memorial Foundation.
Number awarded 1 each year.
Deadline March of each year.

[144]
CREEK NATION HIGHER EDUCATION SCHOLARSHIPS

Muscogee (Creek) Nation of Oklahoma
Attn: Higher Education Program
P.O. Box 580
Okmulgee, OK 74447
(918) 732-7689 Toll-free: (800) 482-1979, ext. 7690
E-mail: (918) 732-7694
E-mail: cdavis@muscogeenation-nsn.gov
Web: www.muscogeenation-nsn.gov

Purpose To provide financial assistance to needy Creek undergraduate students who plan to attend college in any state.
Eligibility This program is open to Creek students of any degree of Indian blood who are attending or planning to attend an accredited institution of higher learning in any state. Applicants must be eligible to receive Pell Grants. They must submit copies of their Certificate of Indian Blood (CIB) and tribal enrollment card.
Financial data Maximum stipends are $1,000 per semester for dependent students, $1,500 per semester for independent students, or $2,000 per semester for married students.
Duration 1 year; may be renewed for a maximum of 10 semesters of funding as long as the recipient enrolls in at least 15 hours per term and maintains a GPA of 2.0 or higher.
Additional information The Muscogee (Creek) Nation of Oklahoma administers the Higher Education Program. This program expends funds appropriated by Congress for the education of Indian students and administered by the Bureau of Indian Affairs.
Number awarded Varies each year.
Deadline May of each year for fall semester; December of each year for spring semester.

[145]
CREEK NATION TRIBAL FUNDS GRANT PROGRAM

Muscogee (Creek) Nation of Oklahoma
Attn: Higher Education Program
P.O. Box 580
Okmulgee, OK 74447
(918) 732-7689 Toll-free: (800) 482-1979, ext. 7690
E-mail: (918) 732-7694
E-mail: cdavis@muscogeenation-nsn.gov
Web: www.muscogeenation-nsn.gov

Purpose To provide financial assistance to enrolled citizens of the Muscogee (Creek) Nation attending an accredited college or university in any state.
Eligibility This program is open to enrolled citizens of the Muscogee (Creek) Nation (with no minimum blood quantum required) who are enrolled or planning to enroll in an accredited college or university in any state. Applicants must submit copies of their Certificate of Indian Blood (CIB) and tribal enrollment card. Financial need is not required.
Financial data The maximum stipend is $1,000 per semester for full-time students (12 credit hours or more per semester) or $500 per semester for part-time students (less than 12 hours). Support may not exceed $2,000 per year. The award may be used to supplement other financial aid sources.
Duration 1 year; may be renewed up to 3 additional years (as long as the recipient maintains at least a 2.5 GPA).
Number awarded Varies each year.
Deadline May of each year for fall semester; December of each year for spring semester.

[146]
CREEK NATION TRIBAL INCENTIVE GRANT PROGRAM

Muscogee (Creek) Nation of Oklahoma
Attn: Higher Education Program
P.O. Box 580
Okmulgee, OK 74447
(918) 732-7689 Toll-free: (800) 482-1979, ext. 7690
E-mail: (918) 732-7694
E-mail: cdavis@muscogeenation-nsn.gov
Web: www.muscogeenation-nsn.gov

Purpose To provide financial assistance to enrolled citizens of the Muscogee (Creek) Nation who have an excellent academic record and are attending an accredited college or university in any state.
Eligibility This program is open to enrolled citizens of the Muscogee (Creek) Nation (with no minimum blood quantum

required) who are enrolled or planning to enroll in an accredited college or university in any state. Applicants must have a GPA of 3.0 or higher. They must submit copies of their Certificate of Indian Blood (CIB) and tribal enrollment card.
Financial data The maximum stipend is $700 per semester for full-time students (12 credit hours or more per semester) or $350 per semester for part-time students (less than 12 hours). Support may not exceed $1,400 per year. The award may be used to supplement other financial aid sources.
Duration 1 semester; may be renewed for up to 9 additional semesters.
Number awarded Varies each year.
Deadline May of each year for fall semester; December of each year for spring semester.

[147]
C.T. LANG JOURNALISM MINORITY SCHOLARSHIP AND INTERNSHIP
Albuquerque Journal
Attn: Scholarship Committee
7777 Jefferson Street, N.E.
P.O. Drawer J
Albuquerque, NM 87103
(505) 823-7777

Purpose To provide financial assistance and work experience to Native American and other minority upper-division students in journalism programs at universities in New Mexico.
Eligibility This program is open to minority students from any state who are majoring or minoring in journalism at a New Mexico university in their junior year with a GPA of 2.5 or higher. Applicants must be enrolled full time. They must be planning a career in newswriting, photography, design, copy editing, or online. Selection is based on clips of published stories, a short autobiography that explains the applicant's interest in the field, a grade transcript, and a letter of recommendation.
Financial data The scholarship is $1,000 per semester; the recipient also receives a paid internship and moving expenses.
Duration The scholarship is for 2 semesters (fall and spring). The internship is for 1 semester.
Additional information This program is funded by the *Albuquerque Journal,* where the internship takes place.
Number awarded 1 each year.
Deadline December of each year.

[148]
CUMMINS SCHOLARSHIPS
Society of Women Engineers
Attn: Scholarship Selection Committee
230 East Ohio Street, Suite 400
Chicago, IL 60611-3265
(312) 596-5223   Toll-free: (877) SWE-INFO
Fax: (312) 644-8557
E-mail: scholarshipapplication@swe.org
Web: societyofwomenengineers.swe.org

Purpose To provide financial assistance to minority and other women working on an undergraduate or graduate degree in designated engineering specialties.
Eligibility This program is open to women who are sophomores, juniors, seniors, or graduate students at 4-year ABET-accredited colleges and universities. Applicants must be working on a degree in computer science or automotive, chemical, computer, electrical, industrial, manufacturing, materials, or mechanical engineering and have a GPA of 3.5 or higher. Preference is given to members of groups underrepresented in engineering or computer science. Selection is based on merit.
Financial data The stipend is $1,000.
Duration 1 year.
Additional information This program is sponsored by Cummins, Inc.
Number awarded 2 each year.
Deadline May of each year.

[149]
DAKOTA INDIAN FOUNDATION SCHOLARSHIP
Dakota Indian Foundation
P.O. Box 340
Chamberlain, SD 57325
(605) 234-5472   Fax: (605) 234-5858
Web: www.dakotaindianfoundation.com

Purpose To provide financial assistance to American Indians (especially those of Sioux heritage) who are currently enrolled in college.
Eligibility Eligible to apply are American Indians (priority given to those of Sioux heritage) who are currently enrolled in college as a sophomore, junior, or senior. A copy of tribal registration must be provided. Applicants must have a GPA of 2.0 or higher and may be studying in any field. Selection is based on financial need, recommendations, academic achievement, potential, and priority of selected majors.
Financial data The stipend is $1,000 per semester ($2,000 per year).
Duration 1 semester; recipients may reapply.
Number awarded Varies each year.
Deadline July of each year for the fall semester; January of each year for the spring semester.

[150]
DAN AND RACHEL MAHI EDUCATIONAL SCHOLARSHIP
Ke Ali'i Pauahi Foundation
Attn: Financial Aid & Scholarship Services
567 South King Street, Suite 160
Honolulu, HI 96813
(808) 534-3966   Toll-free: (800) 842-4682, ext. 43966
Fax: (808) 534-3890 E-mail: scholarships@pauahi.org
Web: www.pauahi.org

Purpose To provide financial assistance to undergraduate or graduate students, especially those of Hawaiian descent.
Eligibility This program is open to students working full time on an undergraduate or graduate degree who have a GPA of 2.0 or higher. Financial need is considered in the selection process. Residency in Hawaii is not required. Preference is given to Native Hawaiians (descendants of the aboriginal inhabitants of the Hawaiian Islands prior to 1778).

Financial data A stipend is awarded (amount not specified).
Duration 1 year.
Number awarded 1 each year.
Deadline April of each year.

[151]
DANIEL KAHIKINA AND MILLIE AKAKA SCHOLARSHIP

Ke Ali'i Pauahi Foundation
Attn: Financial Aid & Scholarship Services
567 South King Street, Suite 160
Honolulu, HI 96813
(808) 534-3966   Toll-free: (800) 842-4682, ext. 43966
Fax: (808) 534-3890   E-mail: scholarships@pauahi.org
Web: www.pauahi.org

Purpose To provide financial assistance to undergraduate or graduate students, especially those of Hawaiian descent.
Eligibility This program is open to students working full time on an undergraduate or graduate degree who have a GPA of 3.2 or higher. Financial need is considered in the selection process. Residency in Hawaii is not required. Preference is given to Native Hawaiians (descendants of the aboriginal inhabitants of the Hawaiian Islands prior to 1778).
Financial data A stipend is awarded (amount not specified).
Duration 1 year.
Additional information Recipients are strongly encouraged to provide at least 10 hours of community service to the Council for Native Hawaiian Advancement.
Number awarded 1 each year.
Deadline April of each year.

[152]
DANIEL KOVACH FOUNDATION MINORITY STUDENT SCHOLARSHIP

Daniel Kovach Scholarship Foundation
5506 Red Robin Road
Raleigh, NC 27613
(919) 630-4895   E-mail: danielkovach@gmail.com
Web: www.collegescholarships.org

Purpose To provide financial assistance to undergraduate and graduate students who are members of minority groups.
Eligibility This program is open to full-time undergraduate and graduate students who are Black, Hispanic, Native American, or Pacific Islander. Applicants must have a GPA of 3.0 or higher. Along with their application, they must submit a 300-word essay on how being a minority affected their pre-college education, how being a minority has positively affected their character, and where they see themselves in 10 years. U.S. citizenship is required.
Financial data The stipend is $1,000.
Duration 1 year.
Additional information This scholarship was first awarded in 2006.
Number awarded 1 each year.
Deadline November of each year.

[153]
DAVID SANKEY MINORITY SCHOLARSHIP IN METEOROLOGY

National Weather Association
Attn: Executive Director
228 West Millbrook Road
Raleigh, NC 27609-4304
(919) 845-1546   Fax: (919) 845-1546
E-mail: exdir@nwas.org
Web: www.nwas.org/dsscholarship.html

Purpose To provide financial assistance to Native Americans and other minorities working on an undergraduate or graduate degree in meteorology.
Eligibility This program is open to members of minority ethnic groups who are either entering their sophomore or higher year of undergraduate study or enrolled as graduate students. Applicants must be working on a degree in meteorology. Along with their application, they must submit a 1-page letter describing their interest and involvement in meteorology. Selection is based on that letter, college transcripts, and 2 letters of recommendation.
Financial data The stipend is $1,000.
Duration 1 year.
Additional information This program was established in 2002.
Number awarded 1 each year.
Deadline April of each year.

[154]
DENNIS WONG AND ASSOCIATES SCHOLARSHIP

Ke Ali'i Pauahi Foundation
Attn: Financial Aid & Scholarship Services
567 South King Street, Suite 160
Honolulu, HI 96813
(808) 534-3966   Toll-free: (800) 842-4682, ext. 43966
Fax: (808) 534-3890   E-mail: scholarships@pauahi.org
Web: www.pauahi.org

Purpose To provide financial assistance to undergraduate or graduate students in liberal arts or science, especially those of Hawaiian descent.
Eligibility This program is open to students working full time on an undergraduate degree in liberal arts or science or a graduate degree in a professional field. Applicants must have a well-rounded and balanced record of achievement in preparation for career objectives. Financial need is considered in the selection process. Residency in Hawaii is not required. Preference is given to Native Hawaiians (descendants of the aboriginal inhabitants of the Hawaiian Islands prior to 1778).
Financial data A stipend is awarded (amount not specified).
Duration 1 year.
Number awarded 2 each year.
Deadline April of each year.

[155]
DISTANCE DELIVERY SCHOLARSHIPS
The Aleut Corporation
Attn: Aleut Foundation
703 West Tudor Road, Suite 102
Anchorage, AK 99503-6650
(907) 646-1929   Toll-free: (800) 232-4882
Fax: (907) 646-1949
E-mail: taf@thealeutfoundation.org
Web: www.thealeutfoundation.org

Purpose To provide financial assistance to Native Alaskans with ties to the Aleutian Islands who are interested in working on a college degree through a distance delivery program.

Eligibility This program is open to residents of Alaska who do not have access to a college classroom and are 1) an original enrollee or descendant of an original enrollee of The Aleut Corporation (TAC); 2) a beneficiary or a descendant of a beneficiary of the Aleutian Pribilof Islands Restitution Trust; or 3) an original enrollee or descendant of an original enrollee of the Isanotski Corporation (IC). Applicants must have a GPA of 2.0 or higher and be enrolled in a distance delivery program. They may have been working on a college degree for some time or want to remain in their community while taking classes. Along with their application, they must include a letter of intent, up to 500 words in length, that covers their educational goals and how they intend to use their education in the Aleut community.

Financial data A stipend is awarded (amount not specified).

Duration 1 year; may be renewed.

Additional information The foundation established this program in 2008.

Number awarded Varies each year.

Deadline June of each year for annual scholarships; November of each year for spring scholarships.

[156]
DORA AMES LEE LEADERSHIP DEVELOPMENT FUND
United Methodist Church
General Board of Global Ministries
Attn: Health and Welfare Program
475 Riverside Drive, Room 330
New York, NY 10115
(212) 870-3871   Toll-free: (800) UMC-GBGM
E-mail: jyoung@gbgm-umc.org
Web: hbs.gbgm-umc.org

Purpose To provide financial assistance to Methodists and other Christians of Asian or Native American descent who are preparing for a career in a health-related field.

Eligibility This program is open to U.S. citizens who are of Asian American, Pacific Islander, or Native American descent. Applicants must be professed Christians, preferably United Methodists. They must be attending a college or university to enter or continue in a health-related field. Financial need is considered in the selection process.

Financial data The stipend is $2,000.

Duration 1 year.

Additional information This program was established in 1980.

Number awarded 6 each year.

Deadline June of each year.

[157]
DOYON FOUNDATION BASIC SCHOLARSHIPS
Doyon, Limited
Attn: Doyon Foundation
1 Doyon Place, Suite 300
Fairbanks, AK 99701-2941
(907) 459-2050   Toll-free: (888) 478-4755, ext. 2050
Fax: (907) 459-2065   E-mail: foundation@doyon.com
Web: www.doyonfoundation.com

Purpose To provide financial assistance to undergraduate and graduate students enrolled or descended from enrolled members of Doyon, Limited.

Eligibility This program is open to undergraduate or graduate students who are enrolled or the descendants of enrolled members of Doyon, Limited. Applicants must be accepted or enrolled at an accredited college, university, technical institute, or vocational school. Both part-time and full-time students are eligible, but full-time students must be accepted into a degree program.

Financial data Stipends are $800 per semester for full-time students or $400 per semester for part-time students.

Duration 1 year. Undergraduate students may reapply if they maintain a GPA of 2.0 or higher; graduate or master's degree students may reapply if they maintain a GPA of 3.0 or higher; and specialist or doctoral students may reapply if they maintain a GPA of 3.25 or higher.

Number awarded Varies each year; recently, scholarships were awarded to 228 full-time students and 40 part-time students.

Deadline March of each year for summer school, April of each year for fall semester, September of each year for winter term (vocational students only), November of each year for spring semester.

[158]
DOYON FOUNDATION COMPETITIVE SCHOLARSHIPS
Doyon, Limited
Attn: Doyon Foundation
1 Doyon Place, Suite 300
Fairbanks, AK 99701-2941
(907) 459-2050   Toll-free: (888) 478-4755, ext. 2050
Fax: (907) 459-2065   E-mail: foundation@doyon.com
Web: www.doyonfoundation.com

Purpose To provide financial assistance to undergraduate and graduate students enrolled or descended from enrolled members of Doyon, Limited.

Eligibility This program is open to undergraduate or graduate students who are enrolled or the descendants of enrolled members of Doyon, Limited. Applicants must be accepted or enrolled at an accredited college, university, or vocational/technical school in a program that lasts at least 6 weeks. Along with their application, they must submit a personal essay on their educational goals, professional goals, extracurricular and community service activities or volunteerism, and cultural awareness and contributions to a healthy Native community. Selection is based on the essay (40 points), GPA (40 points), letters of recommendation (30 points), and personal impression (10 points).

Financial data Stipends range from $2,000 to $7,000 per year.

Duration 1 year. Undergraduate students may reapply if they maintain a GPA of 2.0 or higher; graduate or master's degree students may reapply if they maintain a GPA of 3.0 or higher; and specialist or doctoral students may reapply if they maintain a GPA of 3.25 or higher. Students can receive a total of $10,000 throughout their entire undergraduate or vocational career. Students who continue in a 1- or 2-year master's degree program are eligible to receive an additional $10,000, for a total maximum of $20,000. Students who work on a 3- to 5-year graduate degree (e.g., Ph.D., M.D., J.D.) can receive an additional $10,000 for a total maximum of $30,000.

Additional information This program includes the Morris Thompson Scholarship Fund and the Rosemarie Maher Memorial Fund. Recipients must attend school on a full-time basis. Scholarship recipients of $5,000 or more are encouraged to complete at least 1 summer internship during their 4 years of study. Scholarship recipients of less than $5,000 are encouraged to do 1 of the following: serve on a local or regional board or commission, volunteer at least 20 hours, or give presentations on their field of study. A written report detailing the internship or service and lessons learned is required upon completion of the internship.

Number awarded Varies each year; recently, 52 new and renewal scholarships, with a total value of $178,352, were awarded.

Deadline April of each year.

[159]
DR. HANS AND CLARA ZIMMERMAN FOUNDATION EDUCATION SCHOLARSHIPS

Hawai'i Community Foundation
Attn: Scholarship Department
1164 Bishop Street, Suite 800
Honolulu, HI 96813
(808) 566-5570   Toll-free: (888) 731-3863
Fax: (808) 521-6286
E-mail: scholarships@hcf-hawaii.org
Web: www.hawaiicommunityfoundation.org

Purpose To provide financial assistance to Hawaii residents who are nontraditional students planning to major in education.

Eligibility This program is open to Hawaii residents who have worked for at least 2 years and are returning to school as full-time students majoring in education. Applicants must be able to demonstrate academic achievement (GPA of 2.8 or higher), good moral character, and financial need. Along with their application, they must submit a short statement describing their community service and how their college education will help them achieve their career goals. Preference is given to students of Hawaiian ancestry, students from the neighboring islands who plan to teach in Hawaii, and students with some teaching experience.

Financial data The amount of the award depends on the availability of funds and the need of the recipient; recently, stipends averaged $2,825.

Duration 1 year.

Additional information This scholarship was established in 1997.

Number awarded Varies each year; recently, 28 of these scholarships were awarded.

Deadline February of each year.

[160]
DR. PHILLIP R. LEE HEALTH CAREERS SCHOLARSHIP

California Rural Indian Health Board, Inc.
Attn: Administrative Services Department
4400 Auburn Boulevard, Second Floor
Sacramento, CA 95841
(916) 929-9761   Toll-free: (800) 274-4288
Fax: (916) 929-7246
E-mail: shelley.whitebear@crihb.net
Web: www.crihb.org/scholarship.htm

Purpose To provide financial assistance to Indians, especially those from California, working on a degree in a health-related field at a school in California.

Eligibility This program is open to American Indians and Alaska Natives who are enrolled at an accredited college or university in California. Applicants must be working on a degree in a field related to health care. They must submit certification from their tribe or the U.S. Bureau of Indian Affairs. Priority is given to applicants who are 1) employed by a California tribal health program; 2) enrolled in a nursing degree program; 3) within 1 or 2 years of graduating; and 4) from a community background that indicates the likelihood of long-term employment at a California Tribal Health Clinic. Financial need is considered in the selection process.

Financial data Stipends range up to $2,800 per semester.

Duration 1 semester; may be renewed as long as the recipient maintains a GPA of 3.0 or higher.

Additional information This program is supported by the California Wellness Foundation.

Number awarded Varies each year.

Deadline August of each year for fall; December of each year for spring.

[161]
DR. ROE B. LEWIS MEMORIAL SCHOLARSHIPS

Southwest Indian Agricultural Association
P.O. Box 93524
Phoenix, AZ 85070-3524
(520) 562-6722   Fax: (520) 562-2840
E-mail: swiaa@att.net
Web: www.swindianag.com

Purpose To provide financial assistance to American Indians working on an undergraduate or graduate degree in a field related to agriculture or natural resources.

Eligibility This program is open to American Indians enrolled in a federally-recognized band, nation, or tribe. Applicants must be working on an undergraduate or graduate degree in agriculture or natural resources at an accredited vocational school, technical school, college, or university. Along with their application, they must submit an essay explaining how they plan to use their education to promote, educate, and/or improve agriculture on southwest reservations. First-year undergraduates must have a GPA of 2.5 or

higher; all other students must have a GPA of 3.0 or higher. Financial need is not considered in the selection process.
Financial data The stipend is $1,000.
Duration 1 year.
Number awarded 3 each year: 2 to undergraduates and 1 to a graduate student.
Deadline November of each year.

[162]
DWAYNE "NAKILA" STEELE SCHOLARSHIP
Ke Ali'i Pauahi Foundation
Attn: Financial Aid & Scholarship Services
567 South King Street, Suite 160
Honolulu, HI 96813
(808) 534-3966   Toll-free: (800) 842-4682, ext. 43966
Fax: (808) 534-3890   E-mail: scholarships@pauahi.org
Web: www.pauahi.org

Purpose To provide financial assistance to undergraduate students, especially those of Hawaiian descent, working on a degree in Hawaiian language.
Eligibility This program is open to full-time undergraduate students who are attending college in any state. Applicants must be able to demonstrate financial need; interest in the Hawaiian, language, culture, and history; and commitment to contribute to the greater community. Along with their application, they must submit 2 letters of recommendation, including 1 from a teacher or counselor and 1 from a community organization or other citing how they are working toward perpetuating the Hawaiian language. Preference is given to Native Hawaiians (descendants of the aboriginal inhabitants of the Hawaiian Islands prior to 1778).
Financial data A stipend is awarded (amount not specified).
Duration 1 year.
Number awarded 1 each year.
Deadline April each year.

[163]
DWIGHT DAVID EISENHOWER TRIBAL COLLEGES AND UNIVERSITIES TRANSPORTATION FELLOWSHIPS
Department of Transportation
Federal Highway Administration
Attn: Office of Professional and Corporate
   Development, HPC-32
4600 North Fairfax Drive, Suite 800
Arlington, VA 22203-1553
(703) 235-0538   Toll-free: (877) 558-6873
Fax: (703) 235-0593
E-mail: transportationedu@dot.gov
Web: www.fhwa.dot.gov/opd/universitygrants.htm

Purpose To provide financial assistance to undergraduate students working on a degree in a transportation-related field at a Tribal College or University (TCU).
Eligibility This program is open to students enrolled at a TCU and working on a degree in a transportation-related field (i.e., engineering, accounting, business, architecture, environmental sciences). Applicants must be U.S. citizens or have an I-20 (foreign student) or I-551 (permanent resident) identification card. They must have a GPA of 3.0 or higher. Selection is based on their proposed plan of study, academic achievement (based on class standing, GPA, and transcripts), transportation work experience, and letters of recommendation.
Financial data Fellows receive payment of full tuition and fees (to a maximum of $10,000) and a monthly stipend of $1,450. They are also provided with a 1-time allowance of up to $1,500 to attend the annual Transportation Research Board (TRB) meeting.
Duration 1 year.
Additional information This program is administered by participating TCUs.
Number awarded Varies each year.
Deadline January of each year.

[164]
DWIGHT MOSLEY SCHOLARSHIPS
United States Tennis Association
Attn: USTA Serves
70 West Road Oak Lane
White Plains, NY 10604
(914) 696-7223   E-mail: eliezer@usta.com
Web: www.usta.com

Purpose To provide financial assistance for college to high school seniors from diverse ethnic backgrounds who have participated in an organized community tennis program.
Eligibility This program is open to high school seniors from diverse ethnic backgrounds who have excelled academically, demonstrated achievements in leadership, and participated extensively in an organized community tennis program. Applicants must be planning to enroll as a full-time undergraduate student at a 4-year college or university. They must have a GPA of 3.0 or higher and be able to demonstrate financial need and sportsmanship. Along with their application, they must submit 1) an essay about themselves and how their participation in a tennis program has influenced their life; and 2) documentation of a state and/or section ranking of the United States Tennis Association. Males and females are considered separately.
Financial data The stipend is $2,500 per year. Funds are paid directly to the recipient's college or university.
Duration 4 years.
Number awarded 2 each year: 1 male and 1 female.
Deadline February of each year.

[165]
EARL FRAWNER FAMILY SCHOLARSHIP
Miami Nation
Attn: Education Committee
202 South Eight Tribes Trail
P.O. Box 1326
Miami, OK 74355
(918) 542-1445   Fax: (918) 542-7260
E-mail: edu@miamination.com
Web: www.miamination.com

Purpose To provide financial assistance to upper-division college students who are enrolled members of the Miami Tribe of Oklahoma.
Eligibility This program is open to enrolled members of the Miami Tribe of Oklahoma who are entering their junior or senior year of college. Applicants must have maintained

good grades during their freshman and sophomore years. Along with their application, they must submit a high school transcript or equivalent (GED), 3 letters of recommendation, documentation of financial need, and a 1-page essay with the title, "Tell Us About Yourself."
Financial data The stipend is $2,500 per year.
Duration 1 year; students who receive the award as a junior may renew it for their senior year.
Number awarded 2 each year: 1 to a junior and 1 to a senior.
Deadline April of each year.

[166]
EATON MULTICULTURAL SCHOLARS PROGRAM
Eaton Corporation
Attn: EMSP
1111 Superior Avenue
Cleveland, OH 44114-2584
(216) 523-4354 E-mail: mildredneumann@eaton.com
Web: www.eaton.com

Purpose To provide financial assistance and work experience to Native American and other minority college students interested in a career in designated fields.
Eligibility This program is open to full-time minority students who are U.S. citizens or permanent residents. Applicants must have completed 1 year in an accredited program and have 3 remaining years of course work before completing a bachelor's degree. They must be majoring in information technology, engineering, supplier resource management, or accounting. Selection is based on academic performance, the student's school recommendation, and an expressed interest in pursuing challenging and rewarding internship assignments.
Financial data Stipends range from $500 to $3,000 per year. Funds are paid directly to the recipient's university to cover the cost of tuition, books, supplies, equipment, and fees.
Duration 3 years.
Additional information In addition to the scholarships, recipients are offered paid summer internships at company headquarters in Cleveland. The target schools participating in this program recently were Cornell, Detroit-Mercy, Florida A&M, Georgia Tech, Illinois at Chicago, Illinois at Urbana-Champaign, Lawrence Technological, Marquette, Massachusetts Institute of Technology, Michigan at Ann Arbor, Michigan at Dearborn, Michigan State, Milwaukee School of Engineering, Minnesota, Morehouse College, North Carolina A&T State, North Carolina State, Northwestern, Notre Dame, Ohio State, Purdue, Southern, Tennessee, Western Michigan, and Wisconsin at Madison. This program was established in 1994. Until 2002, it was known as the Eaton Minority Engineering Scholars Program.
Number awarded Varies each year; a total of $150,000 is available for this program annually.
Deadline December of each year.

[167]
EDITH KANAKA'OLE FOUNDATION HIGHER EDUCATION SCHOLARSHIP
Edith Kanaka'ole Foundation
Attn: Higher Education Scholarship
1500 Kalaniana'ole Avenue
Hilo, HI 96720-4814
(808) 961-5242 Fax: (808) 961-4789
Web: www.edithkanakaolefoundation.org

Purpose To provide financial assistance to Native Hawaiians who are attending or planning to attend a college or university on the island of Hawai'i.
Eligibility This program is open to students who are of Native Hawaiian ancestry in whole or in part. Applicants must be attending or planning to attend a college or university on Hawai'i island as a full-time student. They must have a GPA of 2.5 or higher and agree to complete a "give back" program. Preference is given to 1) students in a discipline that has little or no Native Hawaiian representation, very low Hawaiian enrollment, and/or low exit degree completion; 2) lessees in the Department of Hawaiian Homes or a child of a lessee; 3) students born and raised in the districts of Ka'u, Kohala, Puna, or Hilo; 4) upper-division or advanced standing students; and 5) Hawaiian cultural practitioners.
Financial data A stipend is awarded (amount not specified); funds are not intended to be the recipient's primary source of higher education funding.
Duration 1 year; may be renewed if the recipient maintains a GPA of 3.0 or higher.
Number awarded 1 each year.

[168]
EDNA P. MCCURDY SCHOLARSHIPS
Ounalashka Corporation
Attn: Edna P. McCurdy Scholarship Foundation
400 Salmon Way
P.O. Box 149
Unalaska, AK
(907) 581-1276 Fax: (907) 581-1496
E-mail: info@ounalashka.com
Web: www.ounalashka.com/EPMcC%20Guidelines

Purpose To provide financial assistance to shareholders of the Ounalashka Corporation and their descendants who are interested in attending college in any state.
Eligibility This program is open to shareholders of the Ounalashka Corporation and their dependents who are attending or planning to attend a college, university, or trade school in any state as a full-time students. Applicants must submit official grade transcripts, evidence of acceptance at the school, an estimate of expenses, 2 letters of recommendation, and a brief essay on their reasons for requesting this assistance.
Financial data Funding is intended to pay all or part of the costs of tuition, room and board (only for students living on campus), books, and laboratory fees.
Duration 1 semester; may be renewed as long as the recipient maintains a GPA of 2.0 or higher and full-time enrollment.
Number awarded Varies each year.

[169]
EDSA MINORITY SCHOLARSHIP

Landscape Architecture Foundation
Attn: Scholarship Program
818 18th Street, N.W., Suite 810
Washington, DC 20006-3520
(202) 331-7070　　　　　　　　Fax: (202) 331-7079
E-mail: scholarships@lafoundation.org
Web: www.laprofession.org

Purpose To provide financial assistance to Native American and other minority college students who are interested in studying landscape architecture.

Eligibility This program is open to African American, Hispanic, Native American, and minority college students of other cultural and ethnic backgrounds. Applicants must be entering their final 2 years of undergraduate study in landscape architecture. Along with their application, they must submit a 500-word essay on a design or research effort they plan to pursue (explaining how it will contribute to the advancement of the profession and to their ethnic heritage), work samples, and 2 letters of recommendation. Selection is based on professional experience, community involvement, extracurricular activities, and financial need.

Financial data The stipend is $3,500.

Additional information This scholarship was formerly designated the Edward D. Stone, Jr. and Associates Minority Scholarship.

Number awarded 1 each year.

Deadline February of each year.

[170]
EDUCATION AWARDS FOR HOPI TRIBAL MEMBERS

Hopi Tribe
Attn: Grants and Scholarship Program
P.O. Box 123
Kykotsmovi, AZ 86039
(928) 734-3533　　　　　Toll-free: (800) 762-9630
Fax: (928) 734-9575
E-mail: TLomakema@hopi.nsn.us
Web: www.hopi.nsn.us/education_htgsp.asp

Purpose To provide financial assistance to needy students of Hopi ancestry who are working on an undergraduate, graduate, or postgraduate degree.

Eligibility This program is open to students who are working on an associate, baccalaureate, graduate, or postgraduate degree. Applicants must be enrolled members of the Hopi Tribe. They must have a GPA of 2.5 or higher or a composite of 50% or higher on the GED and be able to demonstrate financial need.

Financial data The maximum grant is $2,500 per semester ($5,000 per year).

Duration 1 semester; may be renewed for up to 10 terms of undergraduate study or up to 5 terms of graduate study, provided the recipient maintains a GPA of 2.5 or higher as an undergraduate or 3.0 as a graduate student.

Additional information This grant is awarded as a secondary source of financial aid to eligible students who are also receiving aid from the Bureau of Indian Affairs (BIA) Higher Education program. Recipients must attend school on a full-time basis.

Number awarded Varies each year.

Deadline June of each year for fall or winter term; November of each year for spring term; March of each year for summer session.

[171]
EDWARD DAVIS SCHOLARSHIP FUND

Edward Davis Education Foundation
645 Griswold Street, Suite 1210
Detroit, MI 48226
(313) 963-2209　　　　　Toll-free: (877) 847-9060
Web: www.latinosonwheels.com/edef_foundation.php

Purpose To provide financial assistance to Native American and other minority students interested in preparing for a career in an automotive-related profession.

Eligibility This program is open to minority (African American, Asian Indian American, Asian Pacific American, Hispanic American, or Native American) high school seniors or students who are currently enrolled full time at a college, university, or technical school. Applicants must be interested in preparing for a career in the automotive industry. They must have a GPA of 2.7 or higher. Along with their application, they must submit 250-word essays on 1) what diversity in the automotive industry means to them, and 2) how their automotive profession or endeavors will have an impact on diversity. Financial need is not considered in the selection process. U.S. citizenship is required.

Financial data Stipends range from $1,000 to $2,500.

Duration 1 year.

Additional information This scholarship, established in 1998, honors the first African American to own a new car dealership.

Deadline July of each year.

[172]
EDWIN MAHIAI COPP BEAMER SCHOLARSHIP

Ke Ali'i Pauahi Foundation
Attn: Financial Aid & Scholarship Services
567 South King Street, Suite 160
Honolulu, HI 96813
(808) 534-3966　　Toll-free: (800) 842-4682, ext. 43966
Fax: (808) 534-3890　　E-mail: scholarships@pauahi.org
Web: www.pauahi.org

Purpose To provide financial assistance to undergraduate students, especially those of Hawaiian descent, preparing for a career in music.

Eligibility This program is open to undergraduate students working on a degree in music, specifically piano and/or voice, with emphasis on Hawaiian music, opera, or musical theater. Applicants must be able to demonstrate a serious commitment to music training, a career in music, and dedication to artistic excellence. Along with their application, they must submit a personal essay describing their background, musical accomplishments, and educational goals. Residency in Hawaii is not required. Finalists are asked to present an informal musical performance or (for non-Hawaii residents) to provide a video of their performance. Preference is given to Native Hawaiians (descendants of the aboriginal inhabitants of the Hawaiian Islands prior to 1778).

Financial data A stipend is awarded (amount not specified).

Duration 1 year.
Number awarded 1 or more each year.
Deadline April of each year.

[173]
EIGHT NORTHERN INDIAN PUEBLOS COUNCIL HIGHER EDUCATION GRANT PROGRAM
Eight Northern Indian Pueblos Council, Inc.
Attn: Higher Education Program
P.O. 4250
Espanola, NM 87533
(505) 747-3841, ext. 13   Fax: (505) 747-3994
E-mail: enicp_he@yahoo.com

Purpose To provide financial assistance for college to members of designated Pueblos in New Mexico.
Eligibility This program is open to enrolled members of the following Pueblos: Tesuque, San Ildefonso, Nambe, Pojoaque, and Picuris. Applicants must be enrolled or planning to enroll full time in an associate or baccalaureate degree program and have a GPA of 2.0 or higher. They may major in any subject area. Financial need is considered in determining the amount of the award.
Financial data The amount awarded varies, depending upon the recipient's financial need, up to $5,000 per year. Generally, however, scholarships range between $1,000 and $1,800 per year.
Duration 1 year; may be renewed for up to 4 additional years.
Number awarded Varies each year.
Deadline June of each year for the fall term; December of each year for the spring term; April of each year for summer school (for seniors only).

[174]
EKLUTNA, INCORPORATED SCHOLARSHIP AND GRANT PROGRAM
Cook Inlet Region, Inc.
Attn: The CIRI Foundation
3600 San Jeronimo Drive, Suite 256
Anchorage, AK 99508-2870
(907) 793-3575   Toll-free: (800) 764-3382
Fax: (907) 793-3585 E-mail: tcf@thecirifoundation.org
Web: www.thecirifoundation.org

Purpose To provide financial assistance for professional preparation after high school to Alaska Natives who are original enrollees of Eklunta, Inc. and their lineal descendants.
Eligibility This program is open to Alaska Native enrollees to Eklunta, Inc. under the Alaska Native Claims Settlement Act (ANCSA) of 1971 and their lineal descendants. Applicants must be 1) accepted or enrolled full time in an accredited or otherwise approved postsecondary college or university; or 2) enrolled part or full time in a technical skills education program. They must have a GPA of 2.5 or higher. higher. Along with their application, they must submit a 500-word statement on their educational and career goals and how they are contributing, or planning to contribute, to a positive Alaska Native community. Selection is based on that statement, academic achievement, rigor of course work or degree program, student financial contribution, financial need, grade level, and community service.
Financial data The stipend is $1,000 per year.
Duration 1 year.
Additional information This program was established in 2008. Funds are provided equally by Eklunta, Inc. and the CIRI Foundation.
Number awarded Varies each year.
Deadline Applications for scholarships (for academic study) must be submitted by May of each year. Applications for grants (for vocational or technical programs) are due by March, June, September, or November of each year.

[175]
ELIZABETH AND SHERMAN ASCHE MEMORIAL SCHOLARSHIP
Association on American Indian Affairs, Inc.
Attn: Director of Scholarship Programs
966 Hungerford Drive, Suite 12-B
Rockville, MD 20850
(240) 314-7155   Fax: (240) 314-7159
E-mail: lw.aaia@verizon.net
Web: www.indian-affairs.org

Purpose To provide financial assistance to Native Americans interested in working on an undergraduate or graduate degree in public health.
Eligibility This program is open to American Indian and Alaskan Native full-time undergraduate and graduate students working on a degree in public health. Applicants must submit documentation of financial need, a Certificate of Indian Blood showing at least one-quarter Indian blood, proof of tribal enrollment, an essay on their educational goals, 2 letters of recommendation, and their most recent transcript. Selection is based on merit and need.
Financial data The stipend is $1,500.
Duration 1 year.
Number awarded 1 or more each year.
Deadline June of each year.

[176]
ELLEN MASIN PERSINA SCHOLARSHIP
National Press Club
Attn: General Manager's Office
529 14th Street, N.W.
Washington, DC 20045
(202) 662-7532
Web: www.press.org/activities/aboutscholarship.cfm

Purpose To provide funding to Native American and other minority high school seniors interested in preparing for a journalism career in college.
Eligibility This program is open to minority high school seniors who have been accepted to college and plan to prepare for a career in journalism. Applicants must 1) demonstrate an ongoing interest in journalism through work in high school and/or other media; 2) submit a 1-page essay on why they want to prepare for a career in journalism; and 3) have a GPA of 2.75 or higher in high school. Financial need is considered in the selection process.
Financial data The stipend is $5,000 per year.
Duration 4 years.
Additional information The program began in 1991. In the past, the Press Club has drawn on the Washington Association of Black Journalists and Youth Connections (a

nationwide organization that produces free papers written by high school students).
Number awarded 1 or more each year.
Deadline February of each year.

[177]
EMILIE HESEMEYER MEMORIAL SCHOLARSHIP
Association on American Indian Affairs, Inc.
Attn: Director of Scholarship Programs
966 Hungerford Drive, Suite 12-B
Rockville, MD 20850
(240) 314-7155   Fax: (240) 314-7159
E-mail: lw.aaia@verizon.net
Web: www.indian-affairs.org

Purpose To provide financial assistance for college to Native American students, especially those interested in majoring in education.
Eligibility This program is open to American Indian and Native Alaskan full-time undergraduate students. Preference is given to students working on a degree in education. Applicants must submit documentation of financial need, a Certificate of Indian Blood showing at least one-quarter Indian blood, proof of tribal enrollment, an essay on their educational goals, 2 letters of recommendation, and their most recent transcript.
Financial data The stipend is $1,500 per year.
Duration 1 year; may be renewed up to 3 additional years or until completion of a degree, provided the recipient maintains satisfactory progress.
Number awarded 1 or more each year.
Deadline June of each year.

[178]
EMPOWER SCHOLARSHIP AWARDS
Courage Center
Attn: EMPOWER Scholarship Program
3915 Golden Valley Road
Minneapolis, MN 55422
(763) 520-0214   Toll-free: (888) 8-INTAKE
Fax: (763) 520-0562   TTY: (763) 520-0245
E-mail: empower@couragecenter.org
Web: www.couragecenter.org

Purpose To provide financial assistance to students of color interested in preparing for a career in the medical rehabilitation field.
Eligibility This program is open to ethnically diverse students accepted at or enrolled in an institution of higher learning. Applicants must be residents of Minnesota or have volunteered in a program of the Courage Center. They must be able to demonstrate a career interest in the medical rehabilitation field by completing at least 200 hours of career-related volunteer service and must have a GPA of 2.0 or higher. Selection is based on career intentions, need, and achievements, not academic rank.
Financial data The stipend is $1,500.
Duration 1 year.
Additional information This program, established in 1995, is also identified by its acronym as the EMPOWER Scholarship Award.
Number awarded 2 each year.
Deadline May of each year.

[179]
EPA GREATER RESEARCH OPPORTUNITIES (GRO) FELLOWSHIPS FOR UNDERGRADUATE ENVIRONMENTAL STUDY
Environmental Protection Agency
Attn: National Center for Environmental Research
Ariel Rios Building
1200 Pennsylvania Avenue, N.W.
Washington, DC 20460
(202) 343-9741   Toll-free: (800) 490-9194
E-mail: boddie.georgette@epa.gov
Web: es.epa.gov/ncer/rfa

Purpose To provide financial assistance and summer internships to minority and other undergraduates who are enrolled at colleges and universities that receive limited federal funding and who are interested in majoring in fields related to the environment.
Eligibility This program is open to U.S. citizens or permanent residents who are enrolled full time at a college or university in this country that receives less than $35 million in federal research and development expenditures. That includes, but is not limited to, Minority Serving Institutions, defined as Historically Black Colleges and Universities (HBCUs), Hispanic Serving Institutions (HSIs), Tribal Colleges and Universities (TCUs), Native Hawaiian Serving Institutions (NHSIs), and Alaska Native Serving Institutions (ANSIs). Applicants must have at least 2 years remaining for completion of a bachelor's degree and must be majoring in environmental science, physical sciences, natural and life sciences, mathematics and computer science, social sciences, economics, or engineering. They must be available to work as interns at an EPA facility during the summer between their junior and senior years. A goal of the program is to meet the need for scientists from diverse cultural backgrounds, so the sponsor strongly encourages women, minorities, and persons with disabilities to apply. A minimum GPA of 3.0 is required.
Financial data The fellowship provides up to $17,000 per year, including up to $10,000 for tuition and academic fees, a stipend of $4,500 ($500 per month for 9 months), and an expense allowance of up to $2,500 for items and activities for the direct benefit of the student's education, such as books, supplies, and travel to professional conferences and workshops. The summer internship grant is $7,500, including a stipend of $6,000, an allowance of $1,000 for travel to and from the site, and an allowance of $500 for travel while at the site.
Duration The final 2 years of baccalaureate study, including 12 weeks during the summer between those years.
Additional information This program began in 1982. It was formerly known as Culturally Diverse Academic Institutions Undergraduate Student Fellowships program and subsequently as Minority Academic Institutions Undergraduate Student Fellowships.
Number awarded Approximately 15 each year.
Deadline November of each year.

[180]
ETHEL AND EMERY FAST SCHOLARSHIP
Ethel and Emery Fast Scholarship Foundation, Inc.
12620 Rolling Road
Potomac, MD 20854
(301) 762-1102　　　　　　　Fax: (301) 279-0201
E-mail: qccarol@erols.com

Purpose To provide financial assistance to qualified Native Americans enrolled as undergraduates or graduate students.

Eligibility Applicants must 1) be Native Americans enrolled in a federally-recognized tribe, 2) have successfully completed 1 year of their undergraduate or graduate school program, 3) be enrolled in school full time, and 4) be able to demonstrate financial need. Along with their application, they must submit documentation of Native American eligibility, an original transcript, a letter confirming enrollment, a federal income tax return, a statement of financial need, and a personal statement (up to 2 pages) describing they current situation, their future aspirations in terms of their academic pursuits, and how this scholarship will assist them in attaining their goals.

Financial data A stipend is awarded (amount not specified). Funds are paid directly to the recipient's college or university and can only be used to pay for tuition, room, board, and fees.

Duration 1 year.

Number awarded Varies each year.

Deadline August of each year for the fall semester; January of each year for the spring semester.

[181]
ETHEL CURRY SCHOLARSHIPS
Minnesota Department of Education
Attn: Manager, Minnesota Indian Education
1500 Highway 36 West
Roseville, MN 55113-4266
(651) 582-8832　　　　　　　Toll-free: (800) 657-3927
E-mail: mde.indian-education@state.mn.us
Web: education.state.mn.us

Purpose To provide financial assistance to Native Americans in Minnesota who are interested in working on an undergraduate or graduate degree.

Eligibility This program is open to Indians who are enrolled in a Minnesota-based tribe or community. Applicants must be attending an accredited postsecondary institution in Minnesota as a junior, senior, or graduate student. They must have a GPA of 3.0 or higher. Selection is based on merit.

Financial data The stipend is $3,000 per year for undergraduates or $6,000 per year for graduate students.

Duration Up to 4 years.

Number awarded Varies each year; recently, 12 of these scholarships were awarded.

Deadline May of each year.

[182]
EYAK FOUNDATION SCHOLARSHIPS
Eyak Corporation
Attn: Eyak Foundation
901 LeFevre Street
P.O. Box 340
Cordova, AK 99574
(907) 424-7161　　　　　　　Fax: (907) 424-5161
Web: www.eyakcorporation.com

Purpose To provide financial assistance to Native Alaskans who are shareholders of the Eyak Corporation or their descendants and are interested in working on an undergraduate or graduate degree in any state.

Eligibility This program is open to Native Alaskans who are enrolled or planning to enroll in an accredited undergraduate or graduate program at a college or university, vocational education school, or continuing education program in any state. Applicants must be a shareholder of the Eyak Corporation or a lineal descendant of a Native shareholder. They must have a GPA of 2.5 or higher and be able to demonstrate financial need. Along with their application, they must submit a personal history and statement of educational goals.

Financial data The stipend is $1,000.

Duration 1 year.

Additional information The Eyak Foundation was formerly named the Cordova Native Foundation.

Number awarded 5 each year.

Deadline June of each year.

[183]
FIRST AMERICANS IN THE ARTS SCHOLARSHIPS
First Americans in the Arts
P.O. Box 17780
Beverly Hills, CA 90209-3780
(310) 270-5388　　　　　　　Fax: (310) 671-3212
E-mail: admin@firstamericans.org
Web: www.firstamericans.org

Purpose To provide financial assistance to Native American students in fields related to film and the entertainment business.

Eligibility This program is open to full-time students currently enrolled in a recognized institution of higher learning and working on a degree related to film and the entertainment business (production, directing, screen writing, production design, cinematography, or acting). Applicants must provide documentation of at least one-quarter American Indian or Alaskan Native blood. U.S. citizenship is required. Along with their application, they must submit documentation of financial need and a 500-word essay on why they are pursuing their field of study, their future plans, and their scholarship funding need.

Financial data A stipend is awarded; the amount depends on the availability of funds. Funds may be used only for costs directly related to school.

Duration 1 year; may be renewed up to 3 additional years if funds are available.

Number awarded Varies each year; recently, 3 of these scholarships were awarded.

Deadline December of each year.

[184]
FIRST PERSON JOURNALISM SCHOLARSHIP FUND

MIGIZI Communications, Inc.
Attn: Scholarship Committee
3123 East Lake Street
Minneapolis, MN 55406
(612) 721-6631 Fax: (612) 721-3936
Web: migizi.org/mig/scholarships.html

Purpose To provide financial assistance to Native American students working on an undergraduate or graduate degree in journalism.
Eligibility This program is open to Native American undergraduate and graduate students preparing for a career in journalism or mass communications. Applicants must be able to document financial need. Along with their application, they must submit a 500-word essay on 1) how and in what capacity they have been involved in journalism, 2) why journalism is important, and 3) their plans for the future and how they plan to use their studies to help the community.
Financial data The stipend is $1,000.
Duration 1 year; nonrenewable.
Number awarded 1 each year.
Deadline May of each year.

[185]
FIRST SERGEANT DOUGLAS AND CHARLOTTE DEHORSE SCHOLARSHIP

Catching the Dream
8200 Mountain Road, N.E., Suite 203
Albuquerque, NM 87110-7835
(505) 262-2351 Fax: (505) 262-0534
E-mail: NScholarsh@aol.com
Web: www.catchingthedream.org

Purpose To provide financial assistance to American Indians who have ties to the military and are working on an undergraduate or graduate degree.
Eligibility This program is open to American Indians who 1) have completed 1 year of an Army, Navy, or Air Force Junior Reserve Officer Training (JROTC) program; 2) are enrolled in an Army, Navy, or Air Force Reserve Officer Training (ROTC) program; or 3) are a veteran of the U.S. Army, Navy, Air Force, Marines, Merchant Marine, or Coast Guard. Applicants must be enrolled in an undergraduate or graduate program of study. Along with their application, they must submit a personal essay, high school transcripts, and letters of recommendation.
Financial data A stipend is awarded (amount not specified).
Duration 1 year.
Additional information This program was established in 2007.
Number awarded 1 or more each year.
Deadline April of each year for fall semester or quarter; September of each year for spring semester or winter quarter.

[186]
FLANDREAU SANTEE SIOUX ADULT VOCATIONAL TRAINING GRANTS

Flandreau Santee Sioux Tribe
Attn: Higher Education Committee
P.O. Box 283
Flandreau, SD 57028
(605) 997-2859 Fax: (605) 997-2951
E-mail: elaine.stephens@fsst.org
Web: www.fsst.org/Agnesrossedu_main.html

Purpose To provide financial assistance to members of the Flandreau Santee Sioux Tribe and other Indians who live near the reservation and are interested in attending vocational school.
Eligibility This program is open to enrolled members of the Flandreau Santee Sioux Tribe and members of other federally-recognized tribes who live within 50 miles of Tribal Headquarters. Applicants must be between 18 and 35 years of age and in need of training at a vocational/technical institute to obtain reasonable and satisfactory employment. They must apply for all available federal funding, using the Free Application for Student Aid (FAFSA). Awards are granted on a first-come, first-served basis.
Financial data Students receive a payment of $300 per month, up to the actual cost of tuition or $2,400 per year.
Duration 1 semester; may be renewed.
Additional information Funding for this program is provided by the U.S. Bureau of Indian Affairs (BIA).
Number awarded Varies each year.
Deadline July of each year for fall semester or quarter; December of each year for spring semester or winter quarter; January of each year for spring quarter; May of each year for summer session.

[187]
FLANDREAU SANTEE SIOUX BIA HIGHER EDUCATION GRANTS

Flandreau Santee Sioux Tribe
Attn: Higher Education Committee
P.O. Box 283
Flandreau, SD 57028
(605) 997-2859 Fax: (605) 997-2951
E-mail: elaine.stephens@fsst.org
Web: www.fsst.org/Agnesrossedu_main.html

Purpose To provide financial assistance to members of the Flandreau Santee Sioux Tribe who are interested in attending college in any state.
Eligibility This program is open to enrolled members of the tribe who are interested in attending a college or university in any state and working on an undergraduate degree. They must apply for all available federal funding, using the Free Application for Student Aid (FAFSA). Awards are granted on a first-come, first-served basis.
Financial data For the first semester of each year, full-time students receive $900 as freshmen, $1,000 as sophomores, $1,100 as juniors, or $1,200 as seniors. For the second semester of each year, full-time students who have a GPA of 2.0 to 3.0 during the first semester receive the same amounts; those who have less than 2.0 receive $720 as freshmen, $800 as sophomores, $880 as juniors, or $960 as seniors; those who have more than 3.0 receive $1,000 as freshmen, $1,100 as sophomores, $1,200 as juniors, or

$1,300 as seniors. Part-time students receive stipends equal to half the amount of full-time students in the same category.
Duration 1 semester; may be renewed.
Additional information Funding for this program is provided by the U.S. Bureau of Indian Affairs (BIA).
Number awarded Varies each year.
Deadline July of each year for fall semester or quarter; December of each year for spring semester or winter quarter; January of each year for spring quarter; May of each year for summer session.

[188]
FLANDREAU SANTEE SIOUX STUDENT ASSISTANCE SCHOLARSHIPS

Flandreau Santee Sioux Tribe
Attn: Higher Education Committee
P.O. Box 283
Flandreau, SD 57028
(605) 997-2859　　　　　Fax: (605) 997-2951
E-mail: elaine.stephens@fsst.org
Web: www.fsst.org/Agnesrossedu_main.html

Purpose To provide financial assistance to members of the Flandreau Santee Sioux Tribe who live on the reservation and are interested in attending college or graduate school in any state.
Eligibility This program is open to enrolled members of the tribe who live on the reservation in Moody County, South Dakota. Applicants must be interested in attending a college, university, or vocational/technical institute in any state and working on an undergraduate or graduate degree. They must apply for all available federal funding, using the Free Application for Student Aid (FAFSA). Awards are granted on a first-come, first-served basis.
Financial data For the first semester of each year, full-time undergraduates receive $800 as freshmen, $900 as sophomores, $1,000 as juniors, or $1,100 as seniors. For the second semester of each year, full-time undergraduates who have a GPA of 2.0 to 3.0 during the first semester receive the same amounts; those who have less than 2.0 receive $640 as freshmen, $720 as sophomores, $800 as juniors, or $880 as seniors; those who have more than 3.0 receive $900 as freshmen, $1,000 as sophomores, $1,100 as juniors, or $1,200 as seniors. For full-time graduate students, stipends are $2,500 for the first semester, $2,500 for the second semester if they have a GPA between 3.0 and 3.5, $2,000 for the second semester if they a GPA less than 3.0, or $2,700 for the second semester if they have a GPA greater than 3.5. Part-time undergraduates and graduate students receive stipends equal to half the amount of full-time students in the same category. Vocational training students receive $500 at the beginning of the term and then $150 per month, to a total of $2,150 per year.
Duration 1 semester; may be renewed.
Additional information Funding for this program is provided by revenue from the Tribe's gaming operations.
Number awarded Varies each year.
Deadline July of each year for fall semester or quarter; December of each year for spring semester or winter quarter; January of each year for spring quarter; May of each year for summer session.

[189]
FLINTCO SCHOLARSHIP

Choctaw Nation
Attn: Scholarship Advisement Program
16th and Locust
P.O. Drawer 1210
Durant, OK 74702-1210
(580) 924-8280
Toll-free: (800) 522-6170, ext. 2547 (within OK)
Fax: (580) 924-1267
E-mail: jomcdaniel@choctawnation.com
Web: www.choctawnation-sap.com/scholarships.html

Purpose To provide financial assistance to Choctaw Indian high school seniors who are interested in working on an undergraduate degree.
Eligibility This program is open to graduating high school seniors who have a Choctaw Adult Membership card. Applicants must be planning to enroll in a 4- or 5-year program in construction management, construction science, or a closely-related degree program. They must register online with the Choctaw Honor Scholars Program.
Financial data A stipend is awarded (amount not specified).
Duration 1 year.
Additional information This program is funded by Flintco, Inc.
Number awarded Varies each year; a total of $25,000 is available for this program annually.

[190]
FLORIDA EMPLOYMENT AND TRAINING PROGRAM

Florida Governor's Council on Indian Affairs
Attn: Employment and Training Program
1341 Cross Creek Circle
Tallahassee, FL 32301
(850) 488-0730　　　　　Toll-free: (800) 322-9186
Fax: (850) 487-1472　　　 E-mail: info@fgcia.com
Web: www.fgcia.com

Purpose To provide financial assistance to needy Native Americans in Florida or Georgia who are interested in obtaining additional education or training.
Eligibility Unemployed, underemployed, or economically disadvantaged Native Americans (Native Hawaiians, Alaskan Natives, American Indians) are eligible to apply for this support. The Florida Governor's Council on Indian Affairs provides this service for 63 of the 67 counties in Florida and all of the state of Georgia.
Financial data Tuition and other services are offered to recipients.
Duration Up to 1 year.
Additional information Funds may be used for a vocational/technical degree, an A.A. or associate degree, GED preparation, or adult education.
Number awarded Varies each year.

SCHOLARSHIPS

[191] FMMDA SCHOLARSHIPS

Ford Motor Minority Dealers Association
Attn: Executive Director
16000 West Nine Mile Road, Suite 603
Southfield, MI 48075
(248) 557-2500 Toll-free: (800) 247-0293
Fax: (248) 557-2882 E-mail: deedee0914@aol.com
Web: www.fmmda.org

Purpose To provide financial assistance for college to Native American and other minority high school seniors, especially those from a single parent family.

Eligibility This program is open to minority high school seniors who are planning to attend college. Applicants must have a GPA of 2.5 or higher, be able to document financial need, and be sponsored by a minority dealer that is a member of the association. They must submit a short essay (up to 100 words) on "Why I want to attend a college or university and what I hope to achieve by doing so." Preference is given to applicants from a single-parent family. Scholarships are awarded on a first-come, first-served basis. Applications are available only from members of the Ford Motor Minority Dealers Association (FMMDA).

Financial data The stipend is $2,500.

Duration 1 year.

Additional information This program includes 2 named scholarships: the William E. Shack, Jr. Scholarship and the G. Michael McDonald Scholarship.

Number awarded 10 each year.

Deadline November of each year.

[192] FOOL SOLDIER SCHOLARSHIP

Sioux Falls Area Community Foundation
Attn: Scholarship Coordinator
300 North Phillips Avenue, Suite 102
Sioux Falls, SD 57104-6035
(605) 336-7055, ext. 20 Fax: (605) 336-0038
E-mail: pgale@sfacf.org
Web: www.sfacf.org

Purpose To provide financial assistance to descendants of specified Indians in South Dakota who are interested in attending college in any state.

Eligibility This program is open to enrolled members of South Dakota Indian tribes who are graduating from high school. Applicants must have a GPA of 2.0 or higher and be able to demonstrate financial need. They must be planning to attend an accredited college, university, or technical school in any state. Along with their application, they must document descendancy from 1 or more of the Fool Soldiers, a group of Teton Lakota men who ransomed the freedom of 2 white women and 6 children held captive by a band of Dakota Indians in 1862.

Financial data The stipend is $500. Funds are paid in 2 equal installments and are to be used for tuition, fees, and/or books.

Duration 1 year.

Additional information This program was established in 1997.

Number awarded 1 or more each year.

Deadline March of each year.

[193] FORD MOTOR COMPANY SCHOLARSHIPS

American Indian College Fund
Attn: Scholarship Department
8333 Greenwood Boulevard
Denver, CO 80221
(303) 426-8900 Toll-free: (800) 776-FUND
Fax: (303) 426-1200 E-mail: info@collegefund.org
Web: www.collegefund.org

Purpose To provide financial assistance to Native American college students who are majoring in designated fields at mainstream colleges and universities.

Eligibility This program is open to American Indians and Alaska Natives who have proof of enrollment or descendancy and have achieved at least sophomore status as a full-time student in a bachelor's degree program at a mainstream institution. Applicants must have a GPA of 3.0 or higher and be able to demonstrate financial need. They must have declared a major in accounting, computer engineering, electrical engineering, finance, information systems, marketing, mechanical engineering, or operations management. Along with their application, they must submit 1) short essays (up to 500 words each) on how they perceive themselves as leaders in their school or community and how their education will help the Native American community; and 2) a personal statement of 1,000 words that includes their personal background, their academic background, their educational and career goals, and how this scholarship will help them achieve those goals.

Financial data The stipend is $10,000 per year.

Duration 1 year; may be renewed.

Additional information This program is funded by the Ford Motor Company in partnership with the American Indian College Fund.

Number awarded Varies each year.

Deadline May of each year.

[194] FORD MOTOR COMPANY TRIBAL COLLEGE SCHOLARSHIP

American Indian College Fund
Attn: Scholarship Department
8333 Greenwood Boulevard
Denver, CO 80221
(303) 426-8900 Toll-free: (800) 776-FUND
Fax: (303) 426-1200 E-mail: info@collegefund.org
Web: www.collegefund.org

Purpose To provide financial assistance to Native Americans who are attending a Tribal College or University (TCU) and majoring in specified fields.

Eligibility This program is open to American Indians or Alaska Natives who are enrolled full time and are at least sophomores at an eligible TCU. Applicants must have a GPA of 3.0 or higher and be able to demonstrate financial need. They must have declared a major in mathematics, science, engineering, business, teacher training, or environmental science. Along with their application, they must submit 1) short essays (up to 500 words each) on how they perceive themselves as leaders in their school or community and how their education will help the Native American community; and 2) a personal statement of 1,000 words that includes their personal background, their academic back-

ground, their educational and career goals, and how this scholarship will help them achieve those goals.
Financial data The stipend is $5,000.
Duration 1 year.
Additional information This program is funded by the Ford Motor Company in partnership with the American Indian College Fund.
Number awarded 1 or more each year.
Deadline May of each year.

[195]
FORT PECK TRIBES ADULT VOCATIONAL TRAINING PROGRAM
Fort Peck Assiniboine and Sioux Tribes
Attn: Education Department
P.O. Box 1027
Poplar, MT 59255-1027
(406) 768-5136   Toll-free: (800) 799-2926
Fax: (406) 768-3556
Web: www.fortpecktribes.org

Purpose To provide financial assistance for vocational training to Assiniboine and Sioux members of the Fort Peck Tribes in Montana.
Eligibility This program is open to enrolled members of the Fort Peck Assiniboine and Sioux Tribes between 17 and 35 years of age. Applicants must have a high school diploma or GED, be actively pursuing a certificate of completion in an adult vocational training program, and be able to demonstrate expectation of employment. Along with their application, they must submit a copy of their high school diploma or GED, a Certificate of Degree of Indian Blood, evidence of financial need, and, if relevant, a marriage license, birth certificates for all family members claimed as financial dependents, and military discharge papers. First priority is given to continuing students who are enrolled tribal members living on or near the Fort Peck Reservation, second to first-time applicants who are enrolled tribal members living on or near the reservation, third to enrolled tribal members living off the reservation, and fourth to enrolled members of other federally-recognized tribes.
Financial data Stipends depend on the need of the recipient.
Duration Up to 24 months (or 36 months for pre-nursing students).
Number awarded Varies each year.
Deadline January of each year.

[196]
FORT PECK TRIBES SCHOLARSHIP GRANT ASSISTANCE
Fort Peck Assiniboine and Sioux Tribes
Attn: Education Department
P.O. Box 1027
Poplar, MT 59255-1027
(406) 768-5136   Toll-free: (800) 799-2926
Fax: (406) 768-3556
Web: www.fortpecktribes.org

Purpose To provide financial assistance to members of the Fort Peck Assiniboine and Sioux Tribes who are interested in attending college in any state.
Eligibility This program is open to enrolled members of the Fort Peck Assiniboine and Sioux Tribes who have or will have a high school diploma or GED certificate. Applicants must be enrolled or planning to enroll at an institution of higher education in any state. They must be able to document financial need. Priority in funding is given to seniors, juniors, sophomores, and freshmen, in that order.
Financial data The maximum stipend is $3,600 per year for students who live off the reservation or $1,800 per year for students who live on the reservation. Funding is the same, regardless of whether the student attends school in Montana or another state.
Duration 1 year; may be renewed, provided the recipient maintains a GPA of 2.0 or higher.
Number awarded Varies each year.
Deadline July of each year for fall and spring semesters; April of each year for summer school.

[197]
FORUM FOR CONCERNS OF MINORITIES SCHOLARSHIPS
American Society for Clinical Laboratory Science
Attn: Forum for Concerns of Minorities
6701 Democracy Boulevard, Suite 300
Bethesda, MD 20817
(301) 657-2768   Fax: (301) 657-2909
E-mail: ascls@ascls.org
Web: www.ascls.org/leadership/awards/fcm.asp

Purpose To provide financial assistance to Native American and other minority students in clinical laboratory scientist and clinical laboratory technician programs.
Eligibility This program is open to minority students who are enrolled in a program in clinical laboratory science, including clinical laboratory science/medical technology (CLS/MT) and clinical laboratory technician/medical laboratory technician (CLT/MLT). Applicants must be able to demonstrate financial need. Membership in the American Society for Clinical Laboratory Science is encouraged but not required.
Financial data Stipends depend on the need of the recipients and the availability of funds.
Duration 1 year.
Additional information Information is also available from Ruby Howard, 5207 Griffith Road, Gaithersburg, MD 20882, E-mail: rmhowa@aol.com.
Number awarded 2 each year: 1 to a CLS/MT student and 1 to a CLT/MLT student.
Deadline March of each year.

[198]
FOUNDATION OF RESEARCH AND EDUCATION DIVERSITY SCHOLARSHIPS
American Health Information Management Association
Attn: Foundation of Research and Education
233 North Michigan Avenue, Suite 2150
Chicago, IL 60601-5806
(312) 233-1131   Fax: (312) 233-1431
E-mail: fore@ahima.org
Web: www.ahima.org/fore/student/programs.asp

Purpose To provide financial assistance to Native American and other minority members of the American Health

Information Management Association (AHIMA) who are interested in working on an undergraduate or graduate degree in health information administration or technology.
Eligibility This program is open to AHIMA members who are enrolled in a health information administration or health information technology program accredited by the Commission on Accreditation of Allied Health Education Programs. Applicants must be minorities, be working on an undergraduate or graduate degree on at least a half-time basis, and have a GPA of 3.0 or higher. U.S. citizenship is required. Selection is based (in order of importance) on GPA and academic achievement, volunteer and work experience, commitment to the health information management profession, suitability to the health information management profession, quality and suitability of references provided, and clarity of application.
Financial data Stipends range from $1,000 to $5,000.
Duration 1 year; nonrenewable.
Number awarded Varies each year. Recently, 10 of these scholarships were awarded.
Deadline April of each year.

[199]
FOUR CORNERS POWER PLANT NAVAJO SCHOLARSHIPS

Pinnacle West Capital Corporation
Attn: Four Corners Power Plant Program
P.O. Box 355
MS 4918
Fruitland, NM 87416
(505) 598-8213
Web: www.pinnaclewest.com

Purpose To provide financial assistance to members of the Navajo Nation who live near the Four Corners and are interested in attending college in any state to prepare for a career in the electric utility industry.
Eligibility This program is open to members of the Navajo Nation who live near the Four Corners and are attending or planning to attend a college or university in any state as a full-time student. Applicants must intend to major in a field that will prepare them for a career in the electric utility industry (e.g., accounting, business administration, chemistry, computer science, engineering, human resources, medical science and technology, nursing, occupational safety, vocational programs, or water treatment). They must have a cumulative GPA of 2.5 or higher. Along with their application, they must submit 3 essays of 300 words each on 1) their career plans, why they have chosen that field, and what they have done to demonstrate their interest in that field; 2) their ability to deal with others effectively; and 3) how society will benefit from their education.
Financial data The stipend ranges from $1,000 to $1,500 per year.
Duration 1 year; may be renewed, provided the recipient continues to meet eligibility requirements.
Additional information This program was established in 1995.
Number awarded Varies each year.
Deadline June of each year.

[200]
FRANCES CRAWFORD MARVIN AMERICAN INDIAN SCHOLARSHIP

National Society Daughters of the American Revolution
Attn: Committee Services Office, Scholarships
1776 D Street, N.W.
Washington, DC 20006-5303
(202) 628-1776
Web: www.dar.org/natsociety/edout_scholar.cfm

Purpose To provide financial assistance to Native American students who are working on an undergraduate degree.
Eligibility This program is open to Native Americans enrolled full time at a 2-year or 4-year college or university. Applicants must have a GPA of 3.0 or higher. Selection is based on academic achievement and financial need.
Financial data The stipend depends on the availability of funds.
Duration 1 year; nonrenewable.
Number awarded 1 each year.
Deadline January of each year.

[201]
FRANCES CRAWFORD MARVIN AMERICAN INDIAN SCHOLARSHIP

National Society Daughters of the American Revolution
Attn: Committee Services Office, Scholarships
1776 D Street, N.W.
Washington, DC 20006-5303
(202) 628-1776
Web: www.dar.org/natsociety/edout_scholar.cfm

Purpose To provide financial assistance to Native American students who are working on an undergraduate degree.
Eligibility This program is open to Native Americans enrolled full time at a 2-year or 4-year college or university. Applicants must have a GPA of 3.0 or higher. Selection is based on academic achievement and financial need.
Financial data The stipend depends on the availability of funds.
Duration 1 year; nonrenewable.
Number awarded 1 each year.
Deadline January of each year.

[202]
FRANCES JOHNSON MEMORIAL TRUST SCHOLARSHIP

Northern Arapaho Tribe
Attn: Sky People Higher Education
P.O. Box 8480
Ethete, WY 82520
(307) 332-5286   Toll-free: (800) 815-6795
Fax: (307) 332-9104
E-mail: assistant@skypeopleed.org
Web: www.skypeopleed.org

Purpose To provide financial assistance to members of the Northern Arapaho Tribe who are working on an undergraduate or graduate degree in nursing or a health-related field.
Eligibility This program is open to full-time undergraduate and graduate students who have an undergraduate GPA of 2.0 or higher or the graduate GPA required by their

school. Applicants must be at least one-fourth Northern Arapaho descent (enrolled or non-enrolled) and must submit a Certificate of Indian Blood or other verification of Northern Arapaho blood with at least one-fourth degree. They must be working on a degree in nursing or a health-related field. Along with their application, they must submit a 1-page personal statement that includes a brief history of their background, academic ability and achievement, work or leadership experience, participation in community-related activities, and career goals. Selection is based on that statement, potential to contribute to the community upon graduation, academic ability and achievement, and a letter of recommendation.

Financial data The stipend is $1,500 per year.
Duration 1 year; may be renewed.
Additional information The recipient is expected to apply for employment, after graduation, at the Tribal Health Program, Indian Health Services, at health care facilities on the Wind River Indian Reservation, or in the local communities of Lander or Riverton.
Number awarded 1 each year.
Deadline June of each year.

[203]
FRED L. HATCH MEMORIAL TEACHER EDUCATION SCHOLARSHIP

Sault Tribe of Chippewa Indians
Attn: Higher Education Department
Two Ice Circle
Sault Ste. Marie, MI 49783
(906) 635-7784   Toll-free: (800) 793-0660
Fax: (906) 635-7785   E-mail: jlewton@saulttribe.net
Web: www.saulttribe.com

Purpose To provide financial assistance to members of the Sault Tribe in Michigan who are enrolled in a teacher education program.
Eligibility This program is open to members of the Sault Tribe who are college juniors or higher and are one-quarter Indian blood quantum or more. Applicants must be attending an accredited Michigan 4-year public college or university on a full-time basis and have a cumulative GPA of 3.0 or higher. They must be enrolled in a teacher education program.
Financial data The stipend is $1,000 per year.
Duration 1 year; may be renewed.
Number awarded 1 or more each year.
Deadline May of each year.

[204]
FSNE MULTIMEDIA SCHOLARSHIP

Florida Society of Newspaper Editors
c/o Florida Press Association
2636 Mitcham Drive
Tallahassee, FL 32308
(850) 521-1161   Fax: (850) 577-3611
E-mail: info@fsne.org
Web: www.fsne.org/mmscholar.shtml

Purpose To provide financial assistance to Native American and other minority students from any state who are majoring in journalism or communications at a college or university in Florida and also complete a paid multimedia internship at a newspaper in the state.
Eligibility This program is open to full-time minority students from any state enrolled in accredited journalism or mass communication programs at 4-year colleges and universities in Florida who have a GPA of 2.5 or higher. Preference is given to students between their junior and senior year, but others are welcome to apply. They must first arrange through the normal application process for an internship at a Florida newspaper in the field of multimedia or multiplatform journalism, which includes combinations of print, online, video, and audio journalism. The internship may be at any time during the current calendar year. After their acceptance as an intern, they may apply for this scholarship. Along with their application, they must submit a 300-word autobiographical essay explaining why they want to prepare for a career in journalism and provide a standard resume, references, and clips or examples of relevant classroom work.
Financial data The scholarship stipend is $3,000. Funds are released after the designee successfully completes the internship.
Duration 1 academic year for the scholarship.
Additional information Information is also available from Pat Yack, FSNE Scholarship Committee, The Florida Times-Union, 1 Riverside Avenue, Jacksonville, FL 32202, E-mail: pat.yack@jacksonville.com. This program is sponsored by the John S. and James L. Knight Foundation.
Number awarded 1 each year.
Deadline May of each year.

[205]
GATES MILLENNIUM UNDERGRADUATE SCHOLARS PROGRAM

Bill and Melinda Gates Foundation
P.O. Box 10500
Fairfax, VA 22031-8044
Toll-free: (877) 690-GMSP   Fax: (703) 205-2079
Web: www.gmsp.org

Purpose To provide financial assistance to outstanding low-income minority students, particularly those interested in majoring in specific fields in college.
Eligibility This program is open to African Americans, Alaska Natives, American Indians, Hispanic Americans, and Asian Pacific Islander Americans who are graduating high school seniors with a GPA of 3.3 or higher. Principals, teachers, guidance counselors, tribal higher education representatives, and other professional educators are invited to nominate students with outstanding academic qualifications, particularly those likely to succeed in the fields of computer science, education, engineering, library science, mathematics, public health, or science. Nominees should have significant financial need and have demonstrated leadership abilities (through participation in community service, extracurricular, or other activities). U.S. citizenship or permanent resident status is required. Nominees must be planning to enter an accredited college or university as a full-time, degree-seeking freshman in the following fall.
Financial data The program covers the cost of tuition, fees, books, and living expenses not paid for by grants and scholarships already committed as part of the recipient's financial aid package.

SCHOLARSHIPS

Duration 4 years or the completion of the undergraduate degree, if the recipient maintains at least a 3.0 GPA.
Additional information This program, established in 1999, is funded by the Bill and Melinda Gates Foundation and administered by the United Negro College Fund with support from the American Indian Graduate Center, the Hispanic Scholarship Fund, and the Asian & Pacific Islander American Scholarship Fund.
Number awarded Under the Gates Millennium Scholars Program, a total of 4,000 students receive support each year.
Deadline January of each year.

[206]
G.C. AND RUTH WHITMORE MEMORIAL SCHOLARSHIP

Occaneechi Band of the Saponi Nation
Attn: Scholarship Chair
103 East Center Street
P.O. Box 356
Mebane, NC 27302-0356
(910) 304-3723   Fax: (910) 304-3724
E-mail: obsn@mebtel.net
Web: www.occaneechi-saponi.org

Purpose To provide financial assistance to members of the Occaneechi Band of the Saponi Nation (OBSN) who are interested in attending college in any state.
Eligibility This program is open to enrolled OBSN members who are graduating high school seniors or current college undergraduates. Applicants must be enrolled or planning to enroll full time an a 2- or 4-year college or university in any state. Applicants must submit a 1-page essay on the topic, "How can American Indians live in the modern world without losing their cultural identity?" They may also submit a brief statement of any financial hardships they are facing. Selection is based on academic achievement, American Indian activities, extracurricular activities, volunteer service and community involvement, awards and honors, references, and the essay.
Financial data A stipend is awarded (amount not specified).
Duration 1 year.
Number awarded 1 or more each year.
Deadline March of each year.

[207]
GENERAL MILLS FOUNDATION TRIBAL COLLEGE SCHOLARSHIP PROGRAM

American Indian College Fund
Attn: Scholarship Department
8333 Greenwood Boulevard
Denver, CO 80221
(303) 426-8900   Toll-free: (800) 776-FUND
Fax: (303) 426-1200   E-mail: info@collegefund.org
Web: www.collegefund.org

Purpose To provide financial assistance to Native American students from any state who are attending a Tribal College or University (TCU) in Minnesota or New Mexico.
Eligibility This program is open to American Indians and Alaska Natives from any state who are enrolled full time at an eligible TCU in Minnesota or New Mexico. Applicants must have a GPA of 2.5 or higher and be able to demonstrate financial need. Along with their application, they must submit 1) short essays (up to 500 words each) on how they perceive themselves as leaders in their school or community and how their education will help the Native American community; and 2) a personal statement of 1,000 words that includes their personal background, their academic background, their educational and career goals, and how this scholarship will help them achieve those goals.
Financial data The stipend is $2,000.
Duration 1 year.
Additional information This scholarship is sponsored by the General Mills Foundation in partnership with the American Indian College Fund.
Number awarded 25 each year.
Deadline May of each year.

[208]
GENERAL MOTORS ENGINEERING SCHOLARSHIP

American Indian Science and Engineering Society
Attn: Scholarship Coordinator
2305 Renard, S.E., Suite 200
P.O. Box 9828
Albuquerque, NM 87119-9828
(505) 765-1052, ext. 106   Fax: (505) 765-5608
E-mail: shirley@aises.org
Web: www.aises.org

Purpose To provide financial assistance to members of the American Indian Science and Engineering Society (AISES) who are working on an undergraduate or graduate degree in engineering.
Eligibility This program is open to AISES members who are full-time undergraduate or graduate students in engineering, with a preference given to electrical, industrial, or mechanical engineering majors. Applicants must have a GPA of 3.0 or higher and be members of an American Indian tribe or Alaskan Native group or otherwise considered to be an American Indian or Alaskan Native by the tribe or group with which affiliation is claimed. They must submit an essay that explains their knowledge of and experiences with American Indian tribal culture, discusses their specific interests in engineering, and states how they will contribute their knowledge or professional experience to a Native American community. Financial need is not considered in the selection process.
Financial data The stipend is $3,000.
Duration 1 year; nonrenewable.
Additional information This program, established in 2002, is funded by General Motors.
Number awarded 3 each year.
Deadline June of each year.

[209]
GENERAL MOTORS MINORITY DEALERS ASSOCIATION MINORITY SCHOLARSHIP PROGRAM

General Motors Minority Dealers Association
29433 Southfield Road, Suite 210
Southfield, MI 48076
(248) 552-9040 Toll-free: (888) 377-5233
Fax: (248) 552-9022
E-mail: scholarshipinfo@gmsac.com
Web: www.gmmda.org/main.cfm?location=15

Purpose To provide financial assistance for college to Native American and other ethnic minority high school seniors and college students.

Eligibility This program is open to ethnic minority graduating high school seniors and current college students who are enrolled or planning to enroll full time at an accredited 2-year or 4-year college or university in the United States. Applicants must be U.S. citizens with a GPA of 3.0 or higher. Along with their application, they must submit a personal statement of 500 to 750 words explaining 1) how their school experiences, including academics, extracurricular activities, outside activities, and work experiences, are shaping their educational and career goals, and 2) why they should be considered for this scholarship. Selection is based on that statement, academic excellence, leadership and participation in school and community activities, work experience, education, and career aspirations.

Financial data The stipend is $2,500.
Duration 1 year.
Additional information This program began in 2004.
Number awarded Varies each year; recently, 18 of these scholarships were awarded.
Deadline November of each year.

[210]
GENERAL MOTORS MINORITY ENGINEERING AND SCIENCE SCHOLARSHIP PROGRAM

General Motors Corporation
Attn: GM Scholarship Administration Center
700 West Fifth Avenue
Naperville, IL 60563
Toll-free: (888) 377-5233 Fax: (630) 428-2695
E-mail: scholarshipinfo@gmsac.com

Purpose To provide financial assistance to Native American and other underrepresented minority college students interested in majoring in an engineering or science program of interest to General Motors.

Eligibility This program is open to minority (African American, Hispanic, or Native American) students currently enrolled or planning to enroll full time at a 4-year college or university with sufficient credits to be classified as a sophomore or junior. Applicants must have a GPA of 3.0 or higher and plans to enroll in engineering or science; preference is given to students in chemical, electrical, industrial, manufacturing, or mechanical engineering or other closely-related fields of science or engineering. They must be U.S. citizens or have eligibility to work permanently in the United States. Along with their application, they must include a letter of recommendation from a college instructor or other representative, official transcripts from their college, and a personal statement (500 to 750 words) about how their college experiences (academics, extracurricular activities, outside activities, work experience) are shaping their educational and career goals. Selection is based on that statement, academic performance, proficiencies, and demonstrated skills in areas of interest to General Motors. Financial need is not considered.

Financial data The stipend is $5,000 per year.
Duration 1 year.
Additional information Summer internships at a General Motors facility may also be available to recipients.
Number awarded A limited number are awarded each year.
Deadline May of each year.

[211]
GEORGE GENG ON LEE MINORITIES IN LEADERSHIP SCHOLARSHIP

Capture the Dream, Inc.
Attn: Scholarship Program
484 Lake Park Avenue, Suite 15
Oakland, CA 94610
(510) 343-3635 E-mail: info@capturethedream.org
Web: www.capturethedream.org

Purpose To provide financial assistance for college to Native Americans and other minorities who can demonstrate leadership.

Eligibility This program is open to members of minority groups who are graduating high school seniors or current full-time undergraduates at 4-year colleges and universities. Applicants must submit a 1,000-word essay on why they should be selected to receive this scholarship, using their experiences within school, work, and home to display the challenges they have faced as a minority and how they overcame adversity to assume a leadership role. They should also explain how their career goals and future aspirations will build them as a future minority leader. Financial need is considered in the selection process. U.S. citizenship or permanent resident status is required.

Financial data The stipend is $1,000.
Duration 1 year.
Number awarded 1 or more each year.
Deadline July of each year.

[212]
GEORGE K. NOLAN TRIBAL JUDICIAL SCHOLARSHIP

Sault Tribe of Chippewa Indians
Attn: Higher Education Department
Two Ice Circle
Sault Ste. Marie, MI 49783
(906) 635-7784 Toll-free: (800) 793-0660
Fax: (906) 635-7785 E-mail: jlewton@saulttribe.net
Web: www.saulttribe.com

Purpose To provide financial assistance to members of the Sault Tribe of Chippewa Indians who are working on a degree in a field related to law.

Eligibility This program is open to enrolled members of the Sault Tribe who are attending a 2-year or 4-year college or university as a full-time sophomore or higher. Applicants must be majoring in law enforcement, legal studies, political science, public administration, or tribal law. They must sub-

mit documentation of financial need and an essay of 300 to 500 words on how the scholarship will help them realize their goals.
Financial data The stipend is $1,000 per year.
Duration 1 year.
Number awarded 1 each year.
Deadline May of each year.

[213]
GEORGE M. BROOKER COLLEGIATE SCHOLARSHIP FOR MINORITIES

Institute of Real Estate Management Foundation
Attn: Foundation Coordinator
430 North Michigan Avenue
Chicago, IL 60611-4090
(312) 329-6008   Toll-free: (800) 837-0706, ext. 6008
Fax: (312) 410-7908   E-mail: kholmes@irem.org
Web: www.irem.org

Purpose To provide financial assistance to Native Americans and other minorities interested in preparing (on the undergraduate or graduate school level) for a career in the real estate management industry.
Eligibility This program is open to junior, senior, and graduate minority (non-Caucasian) students majoring in real estate or, if their college has no real estate major, in a related field. Applicants must be preparing for a career in real estate, especially real estate management, after graduation. They must have completed at least 2 courses in real estate and have a GPA of 3.0 or higher in their major. Along with their application, they must submit an essay (up to 500 words) on why they want to follow a career in real estate management, what they hope to accomplish in the field, and why they believe that success in the field will come. Financial need is not considered in the selection process.
Financial data Stipends are $1,000 for undergraduates or $2,500 for graduate students. Funds are disbursed to the institution the student attends to be used only for tuition expenses.
Duration 1 year; nonrenewable.
Number awarded 3 each year: 2 for undergraduates and 1 for a graduate student.
Deadline March of each year.

[214]
GEOSCIENCE MINORITY STUDENT SCHOLARSHIPS

American Geological Institute
Attn: Minority Participation Program
4220 King Street
Alexandria, VA 22302-1502
(703) 379-2480, ext. 227   Fax: (703) 379-7563
E-mail: cmm@agiweb.org
Web: www.agiweb.org/mpp/index.html

Purpose To provide financial assistance to Native American and other underrepresented minority undergraduate and graduate students interested in working on a degree in the geosciences.
Eligibility This program is open to members of ethnic minority groups underrepresented in the geosciences (Blacks, Hispanics, American Indians, Eskimos, Hawaiians, and Samoans). U.S. citizenship or permanent resident status is required. Applicants must be full-time students enrolled in an accredited institution working on an undergraduate or graduate degree in the geosciences, including geology, geochemistry, geophysics, hydrology, meteorology, physical oceanography, planetary geology, or earth science education; students in other natural sciences, mathematics, or engineering are not eligible. Selection is based on a 250-word essay on career goals and why the applicant has chosen a geoscience as a major, work experience, recommendations, honors and awards, extracurricular activities, and financial need.
Financial data Stipends range from $500 to $3,000 per year.
Duration 1 academic year; renewable if the recipient maintains satisfactory performance.
Additional information Funding for this program is provided by ExxonMobil Corporation, ConocoPhillips, ChevronTexaco Corporation, Marathon Corporation, and the Seismological Society of America.
Number awarded Varies each year; recently, 25 of these scholarships were awarded.
Deadline February of each year.

[215]
GLADYS KAMAKAKUOKALANI AINOA BRANDT SCHOLARSHIPS

Ke Ali'i Pauahi Foundation
Attn: Financial Aid & Scholarship Services
567 South King Street, Suite 160
Honolulu, HI 96813
(808) 534-3966   Toll-free: (800) 842-4682, ext. 43966
Fax: (808) 534-3890   E-mail: scholarships@pauahi.org
Web: www.pauahi.org

Purpose To provide financial assistance to undergraduate and graduate students, especially those of Hawaiian descent, who are preparing for a career in education.
Eligibility This program is open to full-time juniors, seniors, and graduate students who are planning to enter the education profession. Applicants must have a GPA of 2.5 or higher and be able to demonstrate financial need. Preference is given to Native Hawaiians (descendants of the aboriginal inhabitants of the Hawaiian Islands prior to 1778) and current or former residents of Kaua'i.
Financial data A stipend is awarded (amount not specified).
Duration 1 year.
Number awarded Varies each year; recently, 3 of these scholarships were awarded.
Deadline April of each year.

[216]
GLENN GODFREY MEMORIAL SCHOLARSHIP

Koniag Incorporated
Attn: Koniag Education Foundation
6927 Old Seward Highway, Suite 103
Anchorage, AK 99518-2283
(907) 562-9093   Toll-free: (888) 562-9093
Fax: (907) 562-9023   E-mail: kef@alaska.com
Web: www.koniageducation.org

Purpose To provide financial assistance to Alaska

Natives with ties to the Koniag region who have demonstrated leadership and plan to attend college in any state.
Eligibility This program is open to college sophomores, juniors, and seniors who are Alaska Native shareholders of the Koniag region or descendants of those original enrollees. Applicants be enrolled in or accepted at an accredited college, university, or vocational school in any state. They must have a GPA of 2.5 or higher and be able to demonstrate leadership in school, community, athletics, church, or Native culture activities. Along with their application, they must submit an essay on what they expect to accomplish in the next 10 years, how the scholarship will help them achieve that goal, and how they plan to give back to the community.
Financial data The stipend is $5,000. Funds are sent directly to the recipient's school and may be used for tuition, fees, books, and on-campus room and meals.
Duration 1 year; may be renewed up to 2 additional years, provided the recipient maintains a GPA of 2.5 or higher and participates in school, community, or church activities.
Number awarded 1 each year.
Deadline August of each year.

[217]
GOLDMAN SACHS SCHOLARSHIP FOR EXCELLENCE
Goldman, Sachs & Company
Attn: Human Capital Management
Diversity Recruiting
180 Maiden Lane, 23rd Floor
New York, NY 10038
(212) 855-6184   E-mail: cindy.joseph@gs.com
Web: www2.goldmansachs.com
Purpose To provide financial assistance and work experience to Native American and other underrepresented minority students preparing for a career in the financial services industry.
Eligibility This program is open to undergraduate students of Black, Hispanic, and Native American heritage. Applicants must be entering their sophomore or junior year with a GPA of 3.4 or higher. Students with all majors and disciplines are encouraged to apply, but they must be able to demonstrate an interest in the financial services industry. Along with their application, they must submit 2 essays of 500 words or fewer on the following topics: 1) why they are interested in the financial services industry; and 2) their current involvement with a campus or community-based organization. Selection is based on academic achievement, interest in the financial services industry, community involvement, and demonstrated leadership and teamwork capabilities.
Financial data Sophomores receive a stipend of $5,000, a summer internship at Goldman Sachs that pays a salary of $7,500, an opportunity to receive a second award upon successful completion of the internship, and an offer to return for a second summer internship. Juniors receive a stipend of $7,500 and a summer internship at Goldman Sachs that pays a salary of $7,500.
Duration Up to 2 years.
Additional information This program was initiated in 1994 when it served only students at 4 designated Historically Black Colleges and Universities: Florida A&M University, Howard University, Morehouse College, and Spelman College. It has since been expanded to serve underrepresented minority students in all states.
Number awarded 1 or more each year.
Deadline December of each year.

[218]
GRAND PORTAGE SCHOLARSHIP PROGRAM
Grand Portage Tribal Council
Attn: Education Director
P.O. Box 428
Grand Portage, MN 55605
(218) 475-0121   Fax: (218) 475-2284
E-mail: gpeduc@boreal.org
Web: www.grandportage.com/tribal.html
Purpose To provide financial assistance for undergraduate or graduate study to Minnesota Chippewa Tribe members.
Eligibility Applicants must be an enrolled member of the Grand Portage Band of Chippewa or have a parent who is enrolled. They must be enrolled at or accepted for enrollment at an accredited training program or degree-granting college or university and have applied for all other forms of financial aid. Residents of states other than Minnesota are eligible only for college or university study, not for vocational training.
Financial data The amount of the award is based on the need of the recipient.
Duration 1 year; may be renewed for a total of 10 semesters or 15 quarters to complete a 4-year degree program if recipients maintain full-time enrollment and a GPA of 2.0 or higher. Adjustments are considered for part-time and/or graduate study.
Number awarded Varies each year.
Deadline At least 8 weeks before school starts.

[219]
GRAND TRAVERSE BAND ADULT VOCATIONAL TRAINING GRANTS
Grand Traverse Band of Ottawa and Chippewa Indians
Attn: Higher Education
845 Business Park Drive
Traverse City, MI 49686
(231) 534-7760   Toll-free: (866) 534-7760
Fax: (231) 534-7773
E-mail: joyce.wilson@gtbindians.com
Web: www.gtbindians.org/departments/index.html
Purpose To provide financial assistance to members of the Grand Traverse Band (GTB) of Ottawa and Chippewa Indians who are interested in attending a vocational/technical institute in any state.
Eligibility This program is open to enrolled GTB members who are working on or planning to work on licensing or certification in a vocational field. Applicants must be able to document financial need. Along with their application, they must submit a personal statement on how they plan to serve their Indian community after they have successfully completed their course of study.
Financial data Stipends are $5 per credit hour, to a maximum of $4,800 per year or $2,400 per year for programs less

than 480 hours. Recipients are also entitled to a grant of up to $500 per year for licensing fees, certifications, and state board fees.
Duration Students must be able to complete their programs within 3 years.
Number awarded Varies each year.

[220]
GRAND TRAVERSE BAND HIGHER EDUCATION GRANTS
Grand Traverse Band of Ottawa and Chippewa Indians
Attn: Higher Education
845 Business Park Drive
Traverse City, MI 49686
(231) 534-7760   Toll-free: (866) 534-7760
Fax: (231) 534-7773
E-mail: joyce.wilson@gtbindians.com
Web: www.gtbindians.org/departments/index.html

Purpose To provide financial assistance to members of the Grand Traverse Band (GTB) of Ottawa and Chippewa Indians who are interested in attending college or graduate school in any state.
Eligibility This program is open to enrolled GTB members who are working on or planning to work on an associate, bachelor's, master's, or doctoral degree at a college or university in any state. Applicants must be able to document financial need. Along with their application, they must submit a personal statement on how they plan to serve their Indian community after they have successfully completed their course of study.
Financial data Stipends for associate degree students are $200 per credit hour, to a maximum of $4,800 per year; stipends for bachelor's degree students are $250 per credit hour, to a maximum of $6,000 per year; stipends for graduate students are $600 per credit hour, to a maximum of $7,200 per year.
Duration 1 semester; may be renewed as long as the recipient maintains a GPA of 2.0 or higher.
Number awarded Varies each year.

[221]
HANA SCHOLARSHIPS
United Methodist Church
Attn: General Board of Higher Education and Ministry
Office of Loans and Scholarships
1001 19th Avenue South
P.O. Box 340007
Nashville, TN 37203-0007
(615) 340-7344   Fax: (615) 340-7367
E-mail: umscholar@gbhem.org
Web: www.gbhem.org/loansandscholarships

Purpose To provide financial assistance to upper-division and graduate Methodist students who are of Hispanic, Asian, Native American, Alaska Native, or Pacific Islander ancestry.
Eligibility This program is open to full-time juniors, seniors, and graduate students at accredited colleges and universities in the United States who have been active, full members of a United Methodist Church (UMC) for at least 1 year prior to applying. Applicants must have at least 1 parent who is Hispanic, Asian, Native American, Alaska Native, or Pacific Islander. They must be able to demonstrate involvement in their Hispanic, Asian, or Native American (HANA) community in the UMC. Selection is based on that involvement, academic ability (GPA of at least 2.85 for undergraduates or 3.0 for graduate students) and financial need. U.S. citizenship or permanent resident status is required.
Financial data The maximum stipend is $3,000 for undergraduates or $5,000 for graduate students.
Duration 1 year; recipients may reapply.
Number awarded 50 each year.
Deadline March of each year.

[222]
HAWAII HOTEL INDUSTRY FOUNDATION NATIVE HAWAIIAN SCHOLARSHIP
Hawai'i Hotel & Lodging Association
Attn: Hawaii Hotel Industry Foundation
2270 Kalakaua Avenue, Suite 1506
Honolulu, HI 96815
(808) 923-0407   Fax: (808) 924-3843
E-mail: hhla@hawaiihotels.org
Web: www.hawaiihotels.org

Purpose To provide financial assistance to Native Hawaiians who are high school seniors interested in working on a degree in hotel management at a college in any state.
Eligibility This program is open to Hawaii residents who can provide proof of their Hawaiian ancestry through birth certificates of their parents or grandparents. Applicants must be graduating high school seniors and planning to attend an accredited college or university (in any state) to major in hotel management. They must have a GPA of 2.8 or higher. Financial need is not considered in the selection process.
Financial data The stipend is $1,000 per year.
Duration 1 year; may be renewed up to 3 additional years, provided the recipient maintains a GPA of 2.8 or higher.
Additional information This program was established in 2007.
Number awarded 5 each year.
Deadline June of each year.

[223]
HAWAIIAN CIVIC CLUB OF HONOLULU SCHOLARSHIP
Hawaiian Civic Club of Honolulu
Attn: Scholarship Committee
P.O. Box 1513
Honolulu, HI 96806
E-mail: newmail@hotbot.com
Web: www.hcchonolulu.org/scholarship

Purpose To provide financial assistance for undergraduate or graduate studies to persons of Hawaiian descent.
Eligibility Applicants must be of Hawaiian descent (descendants of the aboriginal inhabitants of the Hawaiian Islands prior to 1778), residents of Hawaii, able to demonstrate academic achievement, and enrolled or planning to enroll full time in an accredited 2-year college, 4-year college, or graduate school. Graduating seniors and current undergraduate students must have a GPA of 2.5 or higher;

graduate students must have at least a 3.0 GPA. Along with their application, they must submit a 2-page essay on a topic that changes annually but relates to issues of concern to the Hawaiian community; a recent topic related to the leadership, cultural and governmental, of the Hawaiian community. Selection is based on the quality of the essay, academic standing, financial need, and the completeness of the application package.

Financial data The amount of the stipend varies. Scholarship checks are made payable to the recipient and the institution and are mailed to the college or university financial aid office. Funds may be used for tuition, fees, books, and other educational expenses.

Duration 1 year.

Additional information Recipients may attend school in Hawaii or on the mainland. Information on this program is also available from Ke Ali'i Pauahi Foundation, Attn: Financial Aid and Scholarship Services, 567 King Street, Suite 160, Honolulu, HI 96813, (808) 534-3966.

Number awarded Varies each year; recently, 54 of these scholarships, worth $34,800, were awarded.

Deadline May of each year.

[224]
HAWAIIAN HOMES COMMISSION SCHOLARSHIPS

Hawai'i Community Foundation
Attn: Scholarship Department
1164 Bishop Street, Suite 800
Honolulu, HI 96813
(808) 566-5570   Toll-free: (888) 731-3863
Fax: (808) 521-6286
E-mail: scholarships@hcf-hawaii.org
Web: www.hawaiicommunityfoundation.org

Purpose To provide financial assistance for undergraduate or graduate studies to persons of Hawaiian descent.

Eligibility Applicants must be 50% or more of Hawaiian descent (descendants of the aboriginal inhabitants of the Hawaiian Islands prior to 1778) or a homestead lessee (at least 25% Hawaiian ancestry). They must be U.S. citizens, enrolled in full-time study in an undergraduate or graduate degree program, and able to demonstrate financial need and academic excellence. Undergraduates must have a GPA of 2.0 or higher. Graduate students must have a GPA of 3.0 or higher. Current Hawaiian residency is not required. Special consideration is given to applicants with exceptional academic merit and proven commitment to serving the Native Hawaiian community. Along with their application, they must submit a short statement indicating their reasons for attending college, their planned course of study, and their career goals. Selection is based on academic achievement, good moral character, and financial need.

Financial data The amounts of the awards depend on the availability of funds and the need of the recipient; recently, stipends averaged $2,014.

Duration 1 year.

Additional information This program is sponsored by the state Department of Hawaiian Home Lands.

Number awarded Varies each year; recently, 111 of these scholarships were awarded.

Deadline February of each year.

[225]
HAYNES/HETTING AWARD

Philanthrofund Foundation
Attn: Scholarship Committee
1409 Willow Street, Suite 305
Minneapolis, MN 55403-3251
(612) 870-1806   Toll-free: (800) 435-1402
Fax: (612) 871-6587   E-mail: info@PfundOnline.org
Web: www.philanthrofund.org/scholarships.html

Purpose To provide funds to African American and Native American Minnesota students who are associated with gay, lesbian, bisexual, and transgender (GLBT) activities.

Eligibility This program is open to residents of Minnesota and students attending a Minnesota educational institution who are African American or Native American. Applicants must be self-identified as GLBT or from a GLBT family. They may be attending or planning to attend trade school, technical college, college, or university (as an undergraduate or graduate student). Preference is given to graduating high school seniors. Selection is based on the applicant's 1) affirmation of GLBT identity or commitment to GLBT communities; 2) evidence of experience and skills in service and leadership; and 3) evidence of service and leadership in GLBT communities, including serving as a role model, mentor, and/or adviser.

Financial data The stipend is $2,000. Funds must be used for tuition, books, fees, or dissertation expenses.

Duration 1 year.

Number awarded 1 each year.

Deadline January of each year.

[226]
HEALTH PROFESSIONS PREGRADUATE SCHOLARSHIP PROGRAM

Indian Health Service
Attn: Scholarship Program
801 Thompson Avenue, Suite 120
Rockville, MD 20852
(301) 443-6197   Fax: (301) 443-6048
E-mail: dawn.kelly@ihs.gov
Web: www.ihs.gov

Purpose To provide financial support to American Indian students interested in majoring in pre-medicine, pre-podiatry, or pre-dentistry in college.

Eligibility Applicants must be American Indians or Alaska Natives; be high school graduates or the equivalent; have the capacity to complete a health professions course of study; and be enrolled or accepted for enrollment in a baccalaureate degree program to prepare for entry into a school of medicine, podiatry, or dentistry. Priority is given to students entering their junior or senior year; support is provided to freshmen and sophomores only if remaining funds are available. Selection is based on academic performance, work experience and community background, faculty/employer recommendations, and applicant's reasons for seeking the scholarship. Recipients must intend to serve Indian people upon completion of their professional health care education.

Financial data Awards provide a payment directly to the school for tuition and required fees; a stipend for living expenses of approximately $1,250 per month for 10 months; a lump sum to cover the costs of books, laboratory

expenses, and other necessary educational expenses; a payment of $300 for travel expenses; and up to $400 for approved tutorial costs.
Duration Up to 4 years of full-time study or up to 8 years of part-time study.
Number awarded Varies each year.
Deadline April of each year.

[227]
HEALTH PROFESSIONS PREPARATORY SCHOLARSHIP PROGRAM
Indian Health Service
Attn: Scholarship Program
801 Thompson Avenue, Suite 120
Rockville, MD 20852
(301) 443-6197   Fax: (301) 443-6048
E-mail: dawn.kelly@ihs.gov
Web: www.ihs.gov

Purpose To provide financial assistance to Native American students who need compensatory or preprofessional education to qualify for enrollment in a health professions school.
Eligibility Applicants must be American Indians or Alaska Natives; be high school graduates or the equivalent; have the capacity to complete a health professions course of study; and be enrolled or accepted for enrollment in a compensatory or preprofessional general education course or curriculum. The qualifying fields of study include pre-medical technology, pre-dietetics, pre-nursing, pre-pharmacy, pre-physical therapy, pre-social work, pre-engineering, pre-sanitarian (environmental health), pre-occupational therapy, and pre-clinical psychology. Recipients must intend to serve Indian people upon completion of their professional health care education as a health care provider in the discipline for which they are enrolled at the pregraduate level.
Financial data Awards provide a payment directly to the school for tuition and required fees; a stipend for living expenses of approximately $1,250 per month for 10 months; a lump sum to cover the costs of books, laboratory expenses, and other necessary educational expenses; a payment of $300 for travel expenses; and up to $400 for approved tutorial costs.
Duration Up to 2 years of full-time study or up to 4 years of part-time study.
Number awarded Varies each year.
Deadline April of each year.

[228]
HIGHER EDUCATION SCHOLARSHIPS OF THE WYANDOTTE NATION
Wyandotte Nation of Oklahoma
Attn: Department of Education
64790 East Highway 60
Wyandotte, OK 74370
(918) 678-2297, ext. 230
Toll-free: (800) 256-2539, ext. 230
E-mail: info@wyandotte-nation.org
Web: www.wyandotte-nation.org

Purpose To provide financial assistance to members of the Wyandotte Nation of Oklahoma who are interested in attending college in any state.
Eligibility This program is open to Wyandotte tribal members who are attending or will be attending an accredited college or university in any state. Applicants must be able to demonstrate financial need.
Financial data The stipend is $500 per semester ($1,000 per year).
Duration 1 semester; may be renewed up to 7 additional semesters.
Number awarded Varies each year.

[229]
THE HILL GROUP SCHOLARSHIP
Chickasaw Foundation
110 West 12th Street
P.O. Box 1726
Ada, OK 74821-1726
(580) 421-9030   Fax: (580) 421-9031
E-mail: ChickasawFoundation@chickasaw.net
Web: www.chickasaw.net

Purpose To provide financial assistance to members of the Chickasaw Nation who are interested in working on an undergraduate degree.
Eligibility This program is open to Chickasaw students who are currently enrolled at an accredited institution of higher education as a full-time undergraduate student. Applicants may be majoring in any field, but they must have a GPA of 2.0 or higher. Along with their application, they must submit high school or college transcripts, 2 letters of recommendation, a copy of their Chickasaw Nation citizenship card, and a 1-page essay on their long-term goals and plans for achieving them. Financial need is not considered in the selection process.
Financial data The stipend is $2,000 per year.
Duration 1 year.
Number awarded 2 each year.
Deadline June of each year.

[230]
HILTON TRIBAL COLLEGE DIVERSITY SCHOLARSHIP
American Indian College Fund
Attn: Scholarship Department
8333 Greenwood Boulevard
Denver, CO 80221
(303) 426-8900   Toll-free: (800) 776-FUND
Fax: (303) 426-1200   E-mail: info@collegefund.org
Web: www.collegefund.org

Purpose To provide financial assistance to Native Americans who are entering a Tribal College or University (TCU) to prepare for a career in hospitality management.
Eligibility This program is open to American Indians or Alaska Natives who are planning to enroll full time as an entering freshman at an eligible TCU. Applicants must have a GPA of 3.0 or higher and be able to demonstrate financial need. Priority is given to students interested in preparing for a career in hospitality management. Along with their application, they must submit 1) short essays (up to 500 words each) on how they perceive themselves as leaders in their school or community and how their education will help the

Native American community; and 2) a personal statement of 1,000 words that includes their personal background, their academic background, their educational and career goals, and how this scholarship will help them achieve those goals.
Financial data The stipend is $2,500.
Duration 1 year.
Additional information This program is funded by the Hilton Hotels Corporation in partnership with the American Indian College Fund.
Number awarded 1 or more each year.
Deadline May of each year.

[231]
HO-CHUNK NATION HIGHER EDUCATION SCHOLARSHIPS
Ho-Chunk Nation
Attn: Higher Education Division
P.O. Box 667
Black River Falls, WI 54615
(715) 284-4915   Toll-free: (800) 362-4476
Fax: (715) 284-1760
E-mail: higher.education@ho-chunk.com
Web: www.ho-chunknation.com/?PageId=47

Purpose To provide financial assistance to undergraduate or graduate students who are enrolled members of the Ho-Chunk Nation.
Eligibility Applicants must be enrolled members of the Ho-Chunk Nation who have been accepted at an accredited college, university, or vocational college in the United States as an undergraduate or graduate student. Applicants must intend to attend a nonprofit institution that is accredited by a regional agency and by the U.S. Department of Education as eligible to receive student financial aid funds. If they are determined by their school's financial aid office to have no financial need, they are eligible to receive non-need grants. If their school determines that they have financial need, they are eligible for need-based grants. Funds are awarded with the expectation that graduates will return to the Ho-Chunk Nation to use their knowledge and expertise to protect and strengthen the economic self-sufficiency and sovereignty of the nation.
Financial data Non-need grants cover direct costs of tuition, required fees, and books, up to the maximum award. Need-based grants are capped at $7,000 per academic year for full-time undergraduates or $12,000 per academic year for full-time graduate students. Awards for part-time students per academic year are for direct costs (tuition, required fees, and books) not covered by another source, to a maximum of $4,500 for undergraduates or $9,000 for graduate students. Funds are paid directly to the recipient's school.
Duration 1 year. Support is limited to 10 semesters for undergraduates, 6 semesters for master's degree students, or 10 semesters for doctoral students. Undergraduates must maintain a GPA of 2.0 or higher and graduate students 3.0 or higher in order to continue receiving funds.
Number awarded Varies each year.
Deadline April of each year or 4 months before the start of the term.

[232]
HO-CHUNK NATION SUMMER TUITION ASSISTANCE
Ho-Chunk Nation
Attn: Higher Education Division
P.O. Box 667
Black River Falls, WI 54615
(715) 284-4915   Toll-free: (800) 362-4476
Fax: (715) 284-1760
E-mail: higher.education@ho-chunk.com
Web: www.ho-chunknation.com/?PageId=47

Purpose To provide financial assistance to Ho-Chunk undergraduate or graduate students who wish to continue their postsecondary studies during the summer.
Eligibility Applicants must be enrolled members of the Ho-Chunk Nation; have been accepted at an accredited public vocational or technical school, college, or university in the United States in an undergraduate or graduate program; and be interested in attending summer school on a full-time basis.
Financial data This program pays up to $2,500 to undergraduate recipients and up to $5,000 to graduate school recipients. Funds must be used for tuition, fees, or books. Funds are paid directly to the recipient's school.
Duration Summer months. May be renewed for a total of 6 summers of support.
Additional information Undergraduate recipients must earn a GPA of 2.0 or higher in the summer classes; graduate school recipients must earn 3.0 or higher.
Number awarded Varies each year.
Deadline The priority deadline is the end of April of each year.

[233]
HO-CHUNK NATION TRAINING AND EMPLOYMENT ASSISTANCE
Ho-Chunk Nation
Attn: Higher Education Division
P.O. Box 667
Black River Falls, WI 54615
(715) 284-4915   Toll-free: (800) 362-4476
Fax: (715) 284-1760
E-mail: higher.education@ho-chunk.com
Web: www.ho-chunknation.com/?PageId=47

Purpose To provide financial assistance to enrolled members of the Ho-Chunk Nation who are interested in obtaining a postsecondary diploma/certificate (1-year program) or associate of arts degree (2-year program).
Eligibility Applicants must be enrolled members of the Ho-Chunk Nation and be planning to obtain either a diploma/certificate (1-year program) or an associate of arts degree (2-year program). They must intend to attend school on a full-time basis. Both need-based and non-need applicants are considered.
Financial data The tribal grants do not exceed $5,000 per academic year. Students who receive funding under this program are considered either need-based or non-need students. Students who show financial need receive 2 equal payments each academic term; one half of their term award is sent at the beginning of the term and the second half is sent in the middle of their term after verification that they are still enrolled on a full-time basis. Students who are

determined to have "no financial need" (no-need students) may be considered for a grant to cover direct costs (tuition, fees, and books) only up to the maximum award amount, based upon the availability of funds.
Duration 1 year; may be renewed for a total of 6 semesters, provided the recipient maintains a GPA of 2.0 or higher.
Deadline April of each year or 4 months before the start of the term.

[234]
HOOPA TRIBAL EDUCATION ASSOCIATION ADULT VOCATIONAL TRAINING AWARDS
Hoopa Valley Tribe
Attn: Hoopa Tribal Education Association
P.O. Box 428
Hoopa, CA 95546-0428
(530) 625-4413   Fax: (530) 625-5444
E-mail: hoopaeducation@gmail.com
Web: www.hoopa-nsn.gov

Purpose To provide financial assistance to members of the Hoopa Tribe who are attending or planning to attend a vocational/technical institute in any state.
Eligibility This program is open to enrolled members of the Hoopa Tribe who are attending or planning to attend a vocational/technical institute in any state. Applicants must intend to work full time on a vocational certificate or license. They must be able to demonstrate financial need. Along with their application, they must submit a letter describing their vocational goals and an itemized list of expenses for the services they are requesting.
Financial data A stipend is awarded (amount not specified).
Duration 1 semester; may be renewed up to a total of 3 years.
Number awarded Varies each year.

[235]
HOOPA TRIBAL EDUCATION ASSOCIATION HIGHER EDUCATION AWARDS
Hoopa Valley Tribe
Attn: Hoopa Tribal Education Association
P.O. Box 428
Hoopa, CA 95546-0428
(530) 625-4413   Fax: (530) 625-5444
E-mail: hoopaeducation@gmail.com
Web: www.hoopa-nsn.gov

Purpose To provide financial assistance to members of the Hoopa Tribe who are attending or planning to attend college or graduate school in any state.
Eligibility This program is open to enrolled members of the Hoopa Tribe who are attending or planning to attend an accredited college or university in any state. Applicants must intend to work full time on an undergraduate or graduate degree. They must be able to demonstrate financial need. Along with their application, they must submit an educational plan that outlines the course work required for completing their degree and an estimate of the time remaining until completion.
Financial data A stipend is awarded (amount not specified).

Duration 1 semester; may be renewed up to a total of 3 years for a 2-year degree, 5 years for a 4-year, or until completion of a graduate degree.
Number awarded Varies each year.
Deadline June of each year for fall semester or academic year; November of each year for winter quarter; December of each year for spring semester; March of each year for spring quarter; May of each year for summer session.

[236]
HOPI ACADEMIC ACHIEVEMENT AWARDS
Hopi Tribe
Attn: Grants and Scholarship Program
P.O. Box 123
Kykotsmovi, AZ 86039
(928) 734-3533   Toll-free: (800) 762-9630
Fax: (928) 734-9575
E-mail: TLomakema@hopi.nsn.us
Web: www.hopi.nsn.us/education_htgsp.asp

Purpose To provide financial assistance to academically outstanding high school seniors of Hopi ancestry who are planning to attend college in any state.
Eligibility This program is open to graduating high school seniors who are enrolled members of the Hopi Tribe. Applicants must have a cumulative GPA of 3.5 or higher and minimum scores of 1040 on the combined critical reading and mathematics SAT or 22 on the ACT. They must be planning to attend a college or university in any state. Selection is based on academic merit.
Financial data The maximum stipend is $7,000 per semester ($14,000 per year).
Duration 1 semester; may be renewed up to 9 additional semesters.
Additional information Recipients must attend school on a full-time basis.
Number awarded Varies each year.
Deadline June of each year.

[237]
HOPI TRIBAL MEMBERS BIA HIGHER EDUCATION GRANTS
Hopi Tribe
Attn: Grants and Scholarship Program
P.O. Box 123
Kykotsmovi, AZ 86039
(928) 734-3533   Toll-free: (800) 762-9630
Fax: (928) 734-9575
E-mail: TLomakema@hopi.nsn.us
Web: www.hopi.nsn.us/education_htgsp.asp

Purpose To provide financial assistance to needy students of Hopi ancestry who are working on an undergraduate, graduate, or postgraduate degree.
Eligibility This program is open to students who are working on an associate, baccalaureate, graduate, or postgraduate degree. Applicants must be enrolled members of the Hopi Tribe. They must have a GPA of 2.5 or higher or a composite of 50% or higher on the GED and be able to demonstrate financial need.
Financial data The maximum grant is $2,500 per semester ($5,000 per year).

Duration 1 semester; may be renewed for up to 10 terms of undergraduate study or up to 5 terms of graduate study, provided the recipient maintains a GPA of 2.5 or higher as an undergraduate or 3.0 as a graduate student.
Additional information This grant is awarded as a secondary source of financial aid to eligible students who are also receiving aid from the Bureau of Indian Affairs (BIA) Higher Education program. Recipients must attend school on a full-time basis.
Number awarded Varies each year.
Deadline June of each year for fall or winter term; November of each year for spring term; March of each year for summer session.

[238]
HOPI TUITION/BOOK SCHOLARSHIPS

Hopi Tribe
Attn: Grants and Scholarship Program
P.O. Box 123
Kykotsmovi, AZ 86039
(928) 734-3533   Toll-free: (800) 762-9630
Fax: (928) 734-9575
E-mail: TLomakema@hopi.nsn.us
Web: www.hopi.nsn.us/education_htgsp.asp

Purpose To provide financial assistance to students of Hopi ancestry who are working on an undergraduate, graduate, or postgraduate degree.
Eligibility This program is open to students who are working on an associate, baccalaureate, graduate, or postgraduate degree. Applicants must be an enrolled member of the Hopi Tribe. They must be pursuing a postsecondary degree for at least 1 of the following reasons: personal growth, career enhancement, career change, and/or continuing education. Both full- and part-time students may apply. Financial need is not required, but students must have applied for federal aid before applying for this award.
Financial data The scholarship covers the cost of tuition, fees, and books.
Duration 1 year; may be renewed if the recipient maintains a cumulative GPA of 2.5 or higher.
Number awarded Varies each year.
Deadline June of each year for fall or winter term; November of each year for spring term; March of each year for summer session.

[239]
HOWARD KECK/WESTMIN ENDOWMENT SCHOLARSHIP FUND

Cook Inlet Region, Inc.
Attn: The CIRI Foundation
3600 San Jeronimo Drive, Suite 256
Anchorage, AK 99508-2870
(907) 793-3575   Toll-free: (800) 764-3382
Fax: (907) 793-3585 E-mail: tcf@thecirifoundation.org
Web: www.thecirifoundation.org/designated.htm

Purpose To provide financial assistance for undergraduate or graduate studies to Alaska Natives who are original enrollees to Cook Inlet Region, Inc. (CIRI) and their lineal descendants.
Eligibility This program is open to Alaska Native enrollees to CIRI under the Alaska Native Claims Settlement Act (ANCSA) of 1971 and their lineal descendants. There are no Alaska residency requirements or age limitations. Applicants must be accepted or enrolled full time in a 2-year undergraduate, 4-year undergraduate, or graduate degree program. They may be studying in any field but must have a GPA of 2.5 or higher. Along with their application, they must submit a 500-word statement on their educational and career goals and how they are contributing, or planning to contribute, to a positive Alaska Native community. Selection is based on that statement, academic achievement, rigor of course work or degree program, student financial contribution, financial need, grade level, previous work performance, community service, and relationship of degree program to career goals.
Financial data The stipend is $20,000 per year, $10,000 per year, $8,000 per year, or $2,500 per semester, depending on GPA.
Duration 1 semester or 1 year.
Additional information This fund was established in 1986.
Number awarded Varies each year; recently, 5 of these scholarships were awarded.
Deadline May of each year for annual scholarships; May or November of each year for semester scholarships.

[240]
HOWARD ROCK FOUNDATION UNDERGRADUATE SCHOLARSHIP PROGRAM

Cook Inlet Region, Inc.
Attn: The CIRI Foundation
3600 San Jeronimo Drive, Suite 256
Anchorage, AK 99508-2870
(907) 793-3575   Toll-free: (800) 764-3382
Fax: (907) 793-3585 E-mail: tcf@thecirifoundation.org
Web: www.thecirifoundation.org/designated.htm

Purpose To provide financial assistance for undergraduate study to Alaska Natives and their lineal descendants.
Eligibility This program is open to Alaska Natives who are original enrollees or lineal descendants of a regional or village corporation under the Alaska Native Claims Settlement Act (ANCSA) of 1971 or a member of a tribal organization or other Native organization. The corporation or other Native organization with which the applicant is affiliated must be a current member of Alaska Village Initiatives, Inc. Applicants must have a GPA of 2.5 or higher and must be able to demonstrate financial need. They must be accepted or enrolled full time in a 4-year undergraduate program. Preference is given to juniors and seniors. Along with their application, they must submit a 500-word statement on their educational and career goals and how they are contributing, or planning to contribute, to a positive Alaska Native community.
Financial data The stipend is $2,500 per year. Funds are to be used for tuition, university fees, books, course-required supplies, and (for students who must live away from their permanent home in order to attend college) room and board. Checks are made payable to the student and the university and are sent directly to the student's university.
Duration 1 year.
Additional information This program, established in 1986, is funded by Alaska Village Initiatives, Inc. The CIRI Foundation assumed its administration in 1999.

Number awarded Varies each year.
Deadline March of each year.

[241]
HP SCHOLAR AWARDS
Hewlett-Packard Development Company
Attn: HP Scholar Program Manager
3000 Hanover Street
Palo Alto, CA 94304-1185
(650) 857-1501   Fax: (650) 857-5581
Web: www.hp.com/scholars

Purpose To provide financial assistance to Native American and other underrepresented minority high school seniors and community college transfer students interested in studying engineering at designated universities.
Eligibility This program is open to African American, Latino, and American Indian high school seniors and community college transfer students interested in enrolling as a full-time, first-year student at a partnership university of the HP (Hewlett-Packard) Scholars program (San Jose State University, University of California at Los Angeles, North Carolina A&T University, Morgan State University, or University of Washington). Applicants must be interested in majoring in computer science, computer engineering, or electrical engineering. They should also be willing to work as a summer intern at an HP facility in California, Colorado, Idaho, Oregon, Texas, or Washington. Along with their application, they must submit a 2-page autobiographical narrative that includes their educational objectives, reasons they are applying for this scholarship, and their financial need. Selection is based on that statement, academic achievement, financial need, family educational history (preference is given to first generation students), letters of recommendation, and demonstrated interest in mathematics, science, and engineering.
Financial data The stipend is $3,000 per year. Scholars also receive an HP Productivity Package, which includes an HP laptop, printer, and PDA. The total value of the award, including the scholarship stipend, the Productivity Package, and the internships, is more than $40,000.
Duration 4 years of study, including 3 summers for internships.
Number awarded Varies each year.
Deadline March of each year.

[242]
HUALAPAI EMPLOYMENT ASSISTANCE PROGRAM
Hualapai Nation Education Office
Attn: Education and Training Department
460 Hualapai Way
P.O. Box 179
Peach Springs, AZ 86434-0179
(928) 769-2216   Fax: (928) 769-2243
Web: www.hualapai-nsn.gov

Purpose To provide financial assistance to Hualapai Tribe Indians who are interested in obtaining a diploma, certificate, or associate of arts degree at a vocational/technical/junior college.
Eligibility This program is open to enrolled members of the Hualapai Tribe who are 18 years of age or older and have graduated from high school (or earned a GED) and plan to attend a junior, technical, or community college on a full-time basis (at least 12 credit hours).
Financial data The amount of the award depends on the need of the recipient and the availability of funds.
Duration 1 year; may be renewed to a maximum of 24 months for vocational/occupation training or to a maximum of 36 months for registered nurse training.
Number awarded A limited number are awarded each year.
Deadline Applications must be submitted at least 2 weeks before each term begins.

[243]
HUALAPAI HIGHER EDUCATION GRANTS
Hualapai Nation Education Office
Attn: Education and Training Department
460 Hualapai Way
P.O. Box 179
Peach Springs, AZ 86434-0179
(928) 769-2216   Fax: (928) 769-2243
Web: www.hualapai-nsn.gov

Purpose To provide financial assistance to members of the Hualapai Tribe who are interested in working on an undergraduate degree.
Eligibility This program is open to enrolled members of the Hualapai Tribe who have graduated from high school (or earned the GED) and plan to attend college full time (at least 12 credit hours per term). Grants are awarded in the following priority order: 1) continuing students in good standing; 2) incoming freshmen; 3) adults who have previously attended or taken college classes; 4) adults never attending college; 5) repeating or probationary students.
Financial data Up to $5,000 per year.
Duration 1 year; may be renewed as long as the recipient maintains full-time academic standing and at least a 2.0 GPA.
Additional information Recipients may pursue any area of study.
Number awarded Varies each year.
Deadline June of each year for fall term; October of each year for spring term; March of each year for summer sessions.

[244]
HUNA HERITAGE FOUNDATION EDUCATION ASSISTANCE PROGRAM
Huna Heritage Foundation
Attn: Education Programs
9301 Glacier Highway, Suite 210
Juneau, AK 99801
(907) 523-3682   Toll-free: (800) 428-8298
Fax: (907) 789-1896   E-mail: kmiller@hunaheritage.org
Web: www.hunaheritage.org/education.html

Purpose To provide financial assistance to Huna Totem shareholders and their descendants who are attending or planning to attend college or graduate school in any state.
Eligibility This program is open to Huna Totem shareholders and descendants who have a high school diploma or GED certificate. Applicants must be accepted by or attending a college or university in any state as a full-time undergraduate or graduate student. Internships, appren-

ticeships, and on-the-job training may also be funded. Students must have applied to other programs before they apply for this assistance. Proof of awards or denial by other programs must be supplied.
Financial data Stipends range up to $2,000 per year. Funding is intended to help pay for whatever costs other grant programs do not cover.
Duration 1 year; recipients may reapply.
Number awarded Varies each year; recently, 19 of these scholarships were awarded for the fall semester and 29 for the spring semester.
Deadline October of each year for first or second quarter or fall semester; January of each year for third or fourth quarter or spring or summer semester.

[245]
HUNA HERITAGE FOUNDATION VOCATIONAL EDUCATION ASSISTANCE PROGRAM
Huna Heritage Foundation
Attn: Education Programs
9301 Glacier Highway, Suite 210
Juneau, AK 99801
(907) 523-3682 Toll-free: (800) 428-8298
Fax: (907) 789-1896 E-mail: kmiller@hunaheritage.org
Web: www.hunaheritage.org/education.html
Purpose To provide financial assistance to Huna Totem shareholders and their descendants who are interested in pursuing vocational education.
Eligibility This program is open to Huna Totem shareholders or descendants (as defined in accordance with the Alaska Native Claim Settlement Act Amendments of 1987) who are at least 18 years of age (high school students are eligible at 17 years of age) and either unemployed or underemployed. They must be in need of training in order to be employable. Applicants who are underemployed must show how the lack of additional training would result in hardship. All applicants must be interested in pursuing vocational education or apprenticeships that 1) are approved by the National Accreditation Association, the Alaska Department of Education's Division of Vocational Education, or the U.S. Bureau of Apprenticeship Training; 2) are enrolled full time (at least 30 hours of study per week and include shop practices as an integral component); and 3) lead to employment at the completion of training.
Financial data The amount of assistance depends on the nature of the program and the need of the recipient.
Duration 1 year. Recipients may be eligible for a second award only if they can demonstrate that they continue to be unemployed, underemployed, or unable to work in their primary occupation due to physical or other disability.
Number awarded Varies each year; recently, 7 of these awards were presented.
Deadline October of each year for first or second quarter or fall semester; January of each year for third or fourth quarter or spring or summer semester.

[246]
HYATT HOTELS FUND FOR MINORITY LODGING MANAGEMENT STUDENTS
American Hotel & Lodging Educational Foundation
Attn: Manager of Foundation Programs
1201 New York Avenue, N.W., Suite 600
Washington, DC 20005-3931
(202) 289-3181 Fax: (202) 289-3199
E-mail: ahlef@ahlef.org
Web: www.ahlef.org/content.aspx?id=19828
Purpose To provide financial assistance to Native American and other minority college students working on a degree in hotel management.
Eligibility This program is open to students majoring in hospitality management at a 4-year college or university as at least a sophomore. Applicants must be members of a minority group (African American, Hispanic, American Indian, Alaskan Native, Asian, or Pacific Islander). They must be enrolled full time. Along with their application, they must submit a 500-word personal essay on when and why they became interested in the hospitality field, the characteristics or qualifications that will allow them to succeed, and how their education will help them to achieve their career objectives and future goals. Selection is based on industry-related work experience; financial need; academic record and educational qualifications; professional, community, and extracurricular activities; personal attributes, including career goals; the essay; and neatness and completeness of the application. U.S. citizenship or permanent resident status is required.
Financial data The stipend is $2,000.
Duration 1 year.
Additional information Funding for this program, established in 1988, is provided by Hyatt Hotels & Resorts.
Number awarded Varies each year; recently, 19 of these scholarships were awarded. Since this program was established, it has awarded scholarships worth nearly $400,000 to approximately 200 minority students.
Deadline April of each year.

[247]
IDA M. POPE MEMORIAL TRUST SCHOLARSHIPS
Hawai'i Community Foundation
Attn: Scholarship Department
1164 Bishop Street, Suite 800
Honolulu, HI 96813
(808) 566-5570 Toll-free: (888) 731-3863
Fax: (808) 521-6286
E-mail: scholarships@hcf-hawaii.org
Web: www.hawaiicommunityfoundation.org
Purpose To provide financial assistance to Native Hawaiian women who are interested in working on an undergraduate or graduate degree.
Eligibility This program is open to female residents of Hawaii who are Native Hawaiian, defined as a descendant of the aboriginal inhabitants of the Hawaiian islands prior to 1778. Applicants must be enrolled in an accredited associate, bachelor's, or graduate degree program. They must be able to demonstrate academic achievement (GPA of 3.0 or higher), good moral character, and financial need. Along with their application, they must submit a short statement

indicating their reasons for attending college, their planned course of study, and their career goals.
Financial data The amounts of the awards depend on the availability of funds and the need of the recipient; recently, stipends averaged $1,000.
Duration 1 year; may be renewed.
Number awarded Varies each year; recently, 61 of these scholarships were awarded.
Deadline February of each year.

[248]
IDAHO GROW YOUR OWN TEACHER SCHOLARSHIP PROGRAM
Idaho State Board of Education
Len B. Jordan Office Building
650 West State Street, Room 307
P.O. Box 83720
Boise, ID 83720-0037
(208) 332-1574   Fax: (208) 334-2632
E-mail: board@osbe.idaho.gov
Web: www.boardofed.idaho.gov/scholarships/gyo.asp

Purpose To provide financial assistance to students at selected Idaho colleges and universities who are interested in becoming teachers of bilingual education or English as a Second Language (ESL) or to Native American education students.
Eligibility This program is open to Idaho school district employees and volunteers who are 1) interested in completing an associate and/or baccalaureate degree in education with a bilingual or ESL endorsement, or 2) Native Americans preparing to teach in Idaho school districts with a significant Native American student population. Applicants must be attending Boise State University, the College of Southern Idaho, Lewis-Clark State College, or Idaho State University.
Financial data The stipend is $3,000 per year for full-time students; the stipend for part-time students depends on the number of credit hours and the fee charged to part-time students at the participating college or university.
Duration 1 year.
Number awarded Varies each year.

[249]
INDIAN NURSE SCHOLARSHIP AWARDS
National Society of the Colonial Dames of America
c/o Dumbarton House
2715 Que Street, N.W.
Washington, DC 20007-3071
(202) 337-2288   Fax: (202) 337-0348
Web: www.nscda.org/ps/pa.htm

Purpose To provide financial assistance to American Indians interested in preparing for a career in nursing.
Eligibility This program is open to American Indians who are high school graduates (or the equivalent) and enrolled full time in a nursing program at an accredited school. Applicants must be within 2 years of completing the course for which the scholarship is being given, have maintained the scholastic average required by their school, be recommended by their counselor or school officer, not be receiving an Indian Health Service Scholarship, have a career goal directly related to the needs of the Indian people, and be in financial need.
Financial data The stipend is $1,000 per semester ($2,000 per year). Funds are to be used for tuition or fees. The money is sent directly to the recipient's school.
Duration 1 semester; those students who continue to meet the eligibility requirements and have been recommended for continuation are given priority consideration for additional periods of support.
Additional information This program was established in 1928.
Number awarded 10 to 15 each year.

[250]
INDIAN SUMMER CRIMINAL WELFARE/SOCIAL JUSTICE SCHOLARSHIP
Milwaukee Indian Education Committee
c/o American Indian Student Services
University of Wisconsin at Milwaukee
Holton G-48
P.O. Box 413
Milwaukee, WI 53201
(414) 229-5880   Fax: (414) 229-5930
E-mail: amour@uwm.edu
Web: www.indiansummer.org

Purpose To provide financial assistance to American Indians from Wisconsin who are studying or planning to study criminal justice or social welfare at a college in any state.
Eligibility This program is open to Wisconsin residents who are American Indians by tribal enrollment or descendancy (having 1 or more ancestors who are tribally enrolled). Applicants must be accepted or in good standing at an institution of higher education in any state and majoring in criminal justice or social welfare. They must submit a 1-page statement describing their educational goals, the reasons they feel they should receive the scholarship, their community service, and any special needs. Preference is given to applicants who have provided service to the Indian community and have not previously received a scholarship.
Financial data The stipend is $1,000.
Duration 1 year.
Additional information Support for this program is provided by Indian Summer Festivals, Inc.
Number awarded 1 each year.
Deadline July of each year.

[251]
INDIAN SUMMER RECENT HIGH SCHOOL GRADUATE SCHOLARSHIP
Milwaukee Indian Education Committee
c/o American Indian Student Services
University of Wisconsin at Milwaukee
Holton G-48
P.O. Box 413
Milwaukee, WI 53201
(414) 229-5880   Fax: (414) 229-5930
E-mail: amour@uwm.edu
Web: www.indiansummer.org

Purpose To provide financial assistance to American Indian high school seniors from Wisconsin who are planning to attend college in any state.
Eligibility This program is open to Wisconsin residents who are American Indians by tribal enrollment or descen-

dancy (having 1 or more ancestors who are tribally enrolled). Applicants must be accepted or in good standing at an institution of higher education in any state. They must submit a 1-page statement describing their educational goals, the reasons they feel they should receive the scholarship, their community service, and any special needs. Preference is given to applicants who have provided service to the Indian community and have not previously received a scholarship.

Financial data The stipend is $1,000.
Duration 1 year.
Additional information Support for this program is provided by Indian Summer Festivals, Inc.
Number awarded 1 each year.
Deadline July of each year.

[252]
INDUSTRY MINORITY SCHOLARSHIPS

American Meteorological Society
Attn: Fellowship/Scholarship Program
45 Beacon Street
Boston, MA 02108-3693
(617) 227-2426, ext. 246   Fax: (617) 742-8718
E-mail: scholar@ametsoc.org
Web: www.ametsoc.org

Purpose To provide financial assistance to Native American and other underrepresented minority students entering college and planning to major in meteorology or an aspect of atmospheric sciences.

Eligibility This program is open to members of minority groups traditionally underrepresented in the sciences (especially Hispanics, Native Americans, and Blacks/African Americans) who are entering their freshman year at a college or university and planning to work on a degree in the atmospheric or related oceanic and hydrologic sciences. Applicants must submit an official high school transcript showing grades from the past 3 years, a letter of recommendation from a high school teacher or guidance counselor, a copy of scores from an SAT or similar national entrance exam, and a 500-word essay on a topic that changes annually; recently, applicants were invited to write on global change and how they would use their college education in atmospheric science (or a closely-related field) to make their community a better place in which to live. Selection is based on the essay and academic performance in high school.

Financial data The stipend is $3,000 per year.
Duration 1 year; may be renewed for the second year of college study.
Additional information This program is funded by grants from industry and by donations to the American Meteorological Society (AMS) 21st Century Campaign. Requests for an application must be accompanied by a self-addressed stamped envelope.
Number awarded Varies each year; recently, 6 of these scholarships were awarded.
Deadline February of each year.

[253]
INSPIRATIONAL EDUCATOR SCHOLARSHIP

Ke Ali'i Pauahi Foundation
Attn: Financial Aid & Scholarship Services
567 South King Street, Suite 160
Honolulu, HI 96813
(808) 534-3966   Toll-free: (800) 842-4682, ext. 43966
Fax: (808) 534-3890   E-mail: scholarships@pauahi.org
Web: www.pauahi.org

Purpose To provide financial assistance to undergraduate students, especially those of Hawaiian descent, preparing for a career in education.

Eligibility This program is open to students working full or part time on an undergraduate degree in education. Applicants must submit 1) an essay on their commitment to education and how they would use the scholarship funds for educational costs; and 2) letters of recommendation, especially from their prior and prospective employers in the Hawaiian community. Residency in Hawaii is not required. Preference is given to Native Hawaiians (descendants of the aboriginal inhabitants of the Hawaiian Islands prior to 1778).

Financial data A stipend is awarded (amount not specified).
Duration 1 year.
Number awarded 1 each year.
Deadline April of each year.

[254]
INSTITUTE FOR INTERNATIONAL PUBLIC POLICY FELLOWSHIPS

United Negro College Fund Special Programs
  Corporation
2750 Prosperity Avenue, Suite 600
Fairfax, VA 22031
(703) 677-3400   Toll-free: (800) 530-6232
Fax: (703) 205-7645   E-mail: iippl@uncfsp.org
Web: www.uncfsp.org

Purpose To provide financial assistance and work experience to Native American and other minority students who are interested in preparing for a career in international affairs.

Eligibility This program is open to full-time sophomores at 4-year institutions who have a GPA of 3.2 or higher and are nominated by the president of their institution. Applicants must be African American, Hispanic/Latino American, Asian American, American Indian, Alaskan Native, Native Hawaiian, or Pacific Islander. They must be interested in participating in policy institutes, study abroad, language training, internships, and graduate education that will prepare them for a career in international service. U.S. citizenship or permanent resident status is required. Preference is given to students interested in pursuing advanced language and area studies in targeted world areas who are supported by Title VI fellowships. Targeted languages include Arabic, Azeri, Armenian, Dari, Hindi, Kazakh, Kyrgyz, Persian, Pashto, Tajik, Turkish, Turkmen, Uzbek, Urdu, and other languages spoken in central and south Asia, the Middle East, and Russia/eastern Europe.

Financial data For the sophomore summer policy institute, fellows receive student housing and meals in a university facility, books and materials, all field trips and excursions, and a $1,050 stipend. For the junior year study

abroad component, half the expenses for 1 semester are provided. For the junior summer policy institute, fellows receive student housing and meals in a university facility, books and materials, travel to and from the institute, and a $1,000 stipend. For the summer language institute, fellows receive tuition and fees, books and materials, room and board, travel to and from the institute, and a $1,000 stipend. During the internship, a stipend of up to $3,500 is paid. During the graduate school period, fellowships are funded jointly by this program and the participating graduate school. The program also provides $15,000 toward a master's degree in international affairs with the expectation that the graduate school will provide $15,000 in matching funds.
Duration 2 years of undergraduate work and 2 years of graduate work, as well as the intervening summers.
Additional information This program consists of 6 components: 1) a sophomore year summer policy institute based at Clark Atlanta University's Department of International Affairs and Development, comprised of lectures, discussions, and group assignments, complemented by guest speakers and local site visits to international agencies and organizations in Washington, D.C. and New York; the program of study includes international politics, research methods, U.S. foreign policy, international business, economics, and selected area studies; 2) a junior year study abroad program at an accredited overseas institution; 3) a junior year summer institute of intensive academic preparation for graduate school, with course work in economics, mathematics, communication skills, and policy analysis; 4) for students without established foreign language competency, a summer language institute following the senior year; 5) fellows with previously established foreign language competence participate in a post-baccalaureate internship to provide the practical experience needed for successful graduate studies in international affairs; and 6) a master's degree in international affairs (for students who are admitted to such a program). This program is administered by the United Negro College Fund Special Programs Corporation in partnership with the Hispanic Scholarship Fund Institute and the Association of Professional Schools of International Affairs; funding is provided by a grant from the U.S. Department of Education.
Number awarded 30 each year.
Deadline March of each year.

[255]
IOLA M. HENHAWK NURSING SCHOLARSHIP
Seneca Nation of Indians
Attn: Allegany Education Department
P.O. Box 231
Salamanca, NY 14779
(716) 945-1790, ext. 3103   Fax: (716) 945-7170
E-mail: dhoag@sni.org
Web: www.sni.org
Purpose To provide financial assistance to members of the Seneca Nation of Indians who are interested in studying nursing in college.
Eligibility This program is open to enrolled Seneca Indians interested in preparing for a career in nursing. Both high school seniors and students already enrolled in college are eligible. Applicants must submit a certificate of tribal affiliation, letter of acceptance from the college, transcript, and personal letter describing their need and the proposed use of the funds.
Financial data The stipend is $1,000 per year. Funds are paid directly to the college financial aid office to be used for tuition or such course-related expenses as laboratory fees or books.
Duration 1 year.
Additional information This program was established in 1993.
Number awarded 1 or more each year.
Deadline June of each year.

[256]
IOWA TRIBE HIGHER EDUCATION PROGRAM
Iowa Tribe of Oklahoma
Attn: Human Services
RR 1, Box 721
Perkins, OK 74059
(405) 547-2402   Toll-free: (888) 336-4692
Fax: (405) 547-1090
E-mail: HumanServices@iowanation.org
Web: www.iowanation.org
Purpose To provide financial assistance for college to members of the Iowa Tribe of Oklahoma.
Eligibility This program is open to Iowa tribal members who are enrolled or planning to enroll in a college or university.
Financial data The stipend is $400 per semester for single students or $530 per semester for married students.
Duration 1 semester; may be renewed.
Number awarded Varies each year.

[257]
IRENE C. HOWARD MEMORIAL SCHOLARSHIPS
Chickasaw Foundation
110 West 12th Street
P.O. Box 1726
Ada, OK 74821-1726
(580) 421-9030   Fax: (580) 421-9031
E-mail: ChickasawFoundation@chickasaw.net
Web: www.chickasaw.net
Purpose To provide financial assistance to members of the Chickasaw Nation who are working on a college degree in nutrition or other fields.
Eligibility This program is open to Chickasaw students who are currently enrolled at an accredited institution of higher education as a full-time undergraduate student. Applicants must be majoring in science, liberal arts, or nutrition science. They must have a GPA of 3.5 or higher. Along with their application, they must submit high school or college transcripts, 2 letters of recommendation, a copy of their Chickasaw Nation citizenship card, and a 1-page essay on their long-term goals and plans for achieving them. Financial need is not considered in the selection process.
Financial data The stipend is $8,000 per year.
Duration 1 year.
Number awarded 1 each year.
Deadline June of each year.

[258]
JACKIE ROBINSON SCHOLARSHIPS
Jackie Robinson Foundation
Attn: Education and Leadership Development Program
3 West 35th Street, 11th Floor
New York, NY 10001-2204
(212) 290-8600   Fax: (212) 290-8081
E-mail: general@jackierobinson.org
Web: www.jackierobinson.org

Purpose To provide financial assistance for college to Native American and other minority high school seniors.

Eligibility This program is open to members of an ethnic minority group who are high school seniors accepted at a 4-year college or university. Applicants must have a mathematics and critical reading SAT score of 1000 or higher or ACT score of 21 or higher. Selection is based on academic achievement, financial need, dedication towards community service, and leadership potential. U.S. citizenship is required.

Financial data The maximum stipend is $7,200 per year.

Duration 4 years.

Additional information The program also offers personal and career counseling on a year-round basis, a week of interaction with other scholarship students from around the country, and assistance in obtaining summer jobs and permanent employment after graduation. It was established in 1973 by a grant from Chesebrough-Pond.

Number awarded 100 or more each year.

Deadline March of each year.

[259]
JALENE KANANI BELL 'OHANA SCHOLARSHIP
Ke Ali'i Pauahi Foundation
Attn: Financial Aid & Scholarship Services
567 South King Street, Suite 160
Honolulu, HI 96813
(808) 534-3966   Toll-free: (800) 842-4682, ext. 43966
Fax: (808) 534-3890   E-mail: scholarships@pauahi.org
Web: www.pauahi.org

Purpose To provide financial assistance to undergraduate and graduate students from Hawaii, especially those of Hawaiian descent, working on a degree in Hawaiian language.

Eligibility This program is open to full- and part-time undergraduate and graduate students who are residents of Hawaii. Applicants must be able to demonstrate financial need; interest in the Hawaiian, language, culture, and history; and a GPA of 2.5 or higher. Along with their application, they must submit an essay of 1 to 2 pages on their personal, community, and volunteer experiences; future goals; and source of their inspiration and strength. Preference is given to Native Hawaiians (descendants of the aboriginal inhabitants of the Hawaiian Islands prior to 1778).

Financial data A stipend is awarded (amount not specified).

Duration 1 year.

Number awarded 1 or more each year.

Deadline April each year.

[260]
JAMES D. VOELKER FOUNDATION NATIVE AMERICAN SCHOLARSHIP
James D. Voelker Foundation
P.O. Box 15222
Lansing, MI 48901-5222
Web: www.voelkerfdn.org/Scholarships.asp

Purpose To provide financial assistance to students enrolled in Wisconsin or Michigan tribes who live in any state and are interested in pursuing a legal education.

Eligibility This program is open to students who are enrolled members of a federally-recognized Michigan or Wisconsin tribe (applicants may live in any state) and are interested in studying law and working toward a career that will benefit Native American people. Applicants do not need to be currently enrolled in law school, but if they apply as undergraduates they must ultimately intend to attend law school. Selection is based on academic achievements and financial need (preference is given to applicants with the greatest need).

Financial data The amount awarded varies annually; recently, the scholarships were at least $4,000 each.

Duration 1 year.

Additional information Recipients must provide an annual report on their progress.

Number awarded 1 or more each year.

[261]
JEWELL HILTON BONNER SCHOLARSHIP
Navy League of the United States
Attn: Scholarships
2300 Wilson Boulevard
Arlington, VA 22201-3308
(703) 528-1775   Toll-free: (800) 356-5760
Fax: (703) 528-2333   E-mail: cjarvis@navyleague.org
Web: www.navyleague.org/scholarship

Purpose To provide financial assistance for college to dependent children of sea service personnel, especially Native Americans.

Eligibility This program is open to U.S. citizens who are 1) dependents or direct descendants of an active, Reserve, retired, or honorably discharged member of the U.S. sea service (including the Navy, Marine Corps, Coast Guard, or Merchant Marines), or 2) current active members of the Naval Sea Cadet Corps. Applicants must be entering their freshman year of college. Along with their application, they must submit transcripts, 2 letters of recommendation, SAT/ACT scores, documentation of financial need, proof of qualifying sea service duty, and a 1-page personal statement on why they should be considered for this scholarship. Preference is given to applicants of Native American heritage.

Financial data The stipend is $2,500 per year.

Duration 4 years, provided the recipient maintains a GPA of 3.0 or higher.

Number awarded 1 each year.

Deadline February of each year.

[262]
JOHN AND MURIEL LANDIS SCHOLARSHIPS
American Nuclear Society
Attn: Scholarship Coordinator
555 North Kensington Avenue
La Grange Park, IL 60526-5592
(708) 352-6611   Toll-free: (800) 323-3044
Fax: (708) 352-0499   E-mail: outreach@ans.org
Web: www.ans.org/honors/scholarships

Purpose To provide financial assistance to Native American and other undergraduate or graduate students who are interested in preparing for a career in nuclear-related fields.

Eligibility This program is open to undergraduate and graduate students at colleges or universities located in the United States who are preparing for, or planning to prepare for, a career in nuclear science, nuclear engineering, or a nuclear-related field. Qualified high school seniors are also eligible. Applicants must have greater than average financial need and have experienced circumstances that render them disadvantaged. They must be sponsored by an organization (e.g., plant branch, local section, student section) within the American Nuclear Society (ANS). Along with their application, they must submit an essay on their academic and professional goals, experiences that have affected those goals, and other relevant information. Selection is based on that essay, academic achievement, letters of recommendation, and financial need. Women and members of minority groups are especially urged to apply. U.S. citizenship is not required.

Financial data The stipend is $4,000, to be used to cover tuition, books, fees, room, and board.

Duration 1 year; nonrenewable.

Number awarded Up to 8 each year.

Deadline January of each year.

[263]
JOHN BENNETT HERRINGTON SCHOLARSHIP
Chickasaw Foundation
110 West 12th Street
P.O. Box 1726
Ada, OK 74821-1726
(580) 421-9030   Fax: (580) 421-9031
E-mail: ChickasawFoundation@chickasaw.net
Web: www.chickasaw.net

Purpose To provide financial assistance to members of the Chickasaw Nation who are preparing for a career in space aeronautics.

Eligibility This program is open to Chickasaw students who are currently enrolled full time at an accredited institution of higher education. Applicants must be classified as juniors or seniors at a 4-year college and have a GPA of 2.5 or higher. They must be majoring in chemistry, engineering, geophysics, mathematics, natural science, physics, or a related field. Their career interest must relate to space aeronautics. Along with their application, they must submit high school or college transcripts, 2 letters of recommendation, a copy of their Chickasaw Nation citizenship card, and a 1-page essay on their long-term goals and plans for achieving them. Financial need is not considered in the selection process.

Financial data The stipend is $11,000 per year.

Duration Up to 2 years.

Number awarded 1 each year.

Deadline June of each year.

[264]
JOHN C. ROUILLARD AND ALICE TONEMAH MEMORIAL SCHOLARSHIPS
National Indian Education Association
Attn: Awards Committee
110 Maryland Avenue, N.E., Suite 104
Washington, DC 20002
(202) 544-7290   Fax: (202) 544-7293
E-mail: niea@niea.org
Web: www.niea.org

Purpose To provide financial assistance for college or graduate school to members of the National Indian Education Association (NIEA).

Eligibility This program is open to American Indians, Native Hawaiians, and Alaska Natives working full time on an associate, bachelor's, master's, or doctoral degree. Applicants must be members of NIEA and be nominated by a member. They must have demonstrated leadership qualities, maintained high academic achievement, served as a role model for other students, and shown creativity or commitment in the following areas: 1) promoted an understanding and an appreciation of Native American culture in an educational setting; 2) demonstrated positive, active leadership in student affairs; 3) demonstrated and/or encouraged student involvement in educational or community activities; and/or 4) achieved their educational goals and objectives.

Financial data Stipends range from $1,000 to $2,500. Funds may be used for educational expenses not covered by other sources.

Duration 1 year.

Number awarded 1 or more each year.

Deadline September of each year.

[265]
JOHN N. COLBERG ENDOWMENT SCHOLARSHIP FUND
Cook Inlet Region, Inc.
Attn: The CIRI Foundation
3600 San Jeronimo Drive, Suite 256
Anchorage, AK 99508-2870
(907) 793-3575   Toll-free: (800) 764-3382
Fax: (907) 793-3585   E-mail: tcf@thecirifoundation.org
Web: www.thecirifoundation.org/designated.htm

Purpose To provide financial assistance for undergraduate or graduate studies leading to a career in the law to Alaska Natives who are original enrollees to Cook Inlet Region, Inc. (CIRI) and their lineal descendants.

Eligibility This program is open to Alaska Native enrollees to CIRI under the Alaska Native Claims Settlement Act (ANCSA) of 1971 and their lineal descendants. There are no Alaska residency requirements or age limitations. Applicants must be accepted or enrolled full time in a 4-year undergraduate or a graduate degree program. Preference is given to students who are working on a degree leading to the study of law and have a GPA of 2.5 or higher. Along with their application, they must submit a 500-word statement on their educational and career goals and how they are contributing, or planning to contribute, to a positive

Alaska Native community. Selection is based on that statement, academic achievement, rigor of course work or degree program, student financial contribution, financial need, grade level, previous work performance, community service, and relationship of degree program to career goals.
Financial data The stipend is $10,000 per year, $8,000 per year, or $2,500 per semester, depending on GPA.
Duration 1 semester or 1 year.
Additional information This program was established in 2003.
Number awarded 1 or more each year.
Deadline May of each year for annual scholarships; May or November of each year for semester scholarships.

[266]
JOHN SHURR JOURNALISM AWARD
Cherokee Nation
Attn: Cherokee Nation Education Corporation
17675 South Muskogee Avenue
P.O. Box 948
Tahlequah, OK 74465
(918) 453-5420   Toll-free: (800) 256-0671 (within OK)
Fax: (918) 458-6195   E-mail: cnec@cherokee.org
Web: www.cherokee.org

Purpose To provide financial assistance to citizens of the Cherokee Nation who are enrolled at a college or university in any state and working on an undergraduate or graduate degree in journalism.
Eligibility This program is open to citizens of the Cherokee Nation who are currently enrolled in an undergraduate or graduate program in journalism or mass communications at a college or university in any state. Applicants must have a GPA of 3.0 or higher. They are not required to reside in the Cherokee Nation area. Along with their application, they must submit a 1-page essay on how their background and interests make them want to be a modern journalist storyteller, what they hope to learn in college about journalism, what they want to accomplish with a career in the news business, and how their Cherokee heritage will come into play for those issues. Financial need is also considered in the selection process.
Financial data The stipend is $1,000 per semester ($2,000 per year).
Duration 1 year.
Additional information Recipients are expected to apply for an 8-week paid internship with *The Cherokee Phoenix* newspaper in Tahlequah, Oklahoma during the summer following their scholarship year.
Number awarded 1 each year.
Deadline Applications are accepted until the scholarship is awarded.

[267]
JOHNNY PINEAPPLE SCHOLARSHIP FUND
Ke Ali'i Pauahi Foundation
Attn: Financial Aid & Scholarship Services
567 South King Street, Suite 160
Honolulu, HI 96813
(808) 534-3966   Toll-free: (800) 842-4682, ext. 43966
Fax: (808) 534-3890   E-mail: scholarships@pauahi.org
Web: www.pauahi.org

Purpose To provide financial assistance to undergraduate students, especially those of Hawaiian descent working on a degree in Hawaiian language or studies.
Eligibility This program is open to undergraduate students working full time on a degree in Hawaiian language or Hawaiian studies at an accredited institution of higher learning in any state. Applicants must have a GPA of 3.5 or higher. Along with their application, they must submit an essay describing their involvement in community service and how they intend to continue to benefit the Hawaiian community. Financial need is considered in the selection process. Residency in Hawaii is not required. Preference is given to Native Hawaiians (descendants of the aboriginal inhabitants of the Hawaiian Islands prior to 1778).
Financial data A stipend is awarded (amount not specified).
Duration 1 year.
Number awarded 1 or more each year.
Deadline April of each year.

[268]
JOSEPH A. SOWA SCHOLARSHIPS
Ke Ali'i Pauahi Foundation
Attn: Financial Aid & Scholarship Services
567 South King Street, Suite 160
Honolulu, HI 96813
(808) 534-3966   Toll-free: (800) 842-4682, ext. 43966
Fax: (808) 534-3890   E-mail: scholarships@pauahi.org
Web: www.pauahi.org

Purpose To provide financial assistance to undergraduate students, especially those of Hawaiian descent, who are preparing for a career in communications.
Eligibility This program is open to undergraduate students who are planning to major in communications. Applicants must have a GPA of 3.0 or higher and be able to demonstrate financial need. Along with their application, they must submit an essay describing their plan to maximize the potential of young people through communication as well as to demonstrate leadership potential in the community. Preference is given to Native Hawaiians (descendants of the aboriginal inhabitants of the Hawaiian Islands prior to 1778).
Financial data A stipend is awarded (amount not specified).
Duration 1 year.
Additional information This program began in 2008.
Number awarded 1 or more each year.
Deadline April of each year.

[269]
JOSEPH K. LUMSDEN MEMORIAL SCHOLARSHIP
Sault Tribe of Chippewa Indians
Attn: Higher Education Department
Two Ice Circle
Sault Ste. Marie, MI 49783
(906) 635-7784   Toll-free: (800) 793-0660
Fax: (906) 635-7785   E-mail: jlewton@saulttribe.net
Web: www.saulttribe.com

Purpose To provide financial assistance to members of the Sault Tribe in Michigan who are upper-division or graduate students.

Eligibility This program is open to members of the Sault Tribe who are college juniors or higher and are one-quarter Indian blood quantum or more. Applicants must be attending an accredited Michigan 4-year public college or university on a full-time basis and have a cumulative GPA of 3.0 or higher. They must be able to demonstrate financial need.

Financial data The stipend is $1,000 per year.

Duration 1 year; may be renewed.

Number awarded 1 each year.

Deadline May of each year.

[270]
JUANITA CORWIN SCHOLARSHIPS
Central Council, Tlingit and Haida Indian Tribes of Alaska
Attn: Higher Education Services
3239 Hospital Drive
Juneau, AK 99801
(907) 463-7375   Toll-free: (800) 344-1432, ext. 7375
Fax: (907) 463-7321
Web: www.hied.org

Purpose To provide financial assistance for undergraduate and graduate studies to enrolled Tlingit or Haida tribal members.

Eligibility This program is open to both undergraduate and graduate students. Applicants must be Tlingit or Haida tribal members, regardless of service area, community affiliation, origination, residence, tribal compact, or signatory status. They must have a GPA of 3.0 or higher and be attending (or planning to attend) school on a full-time basis. Selection is based on financial need, a statement of personal goals, and a list of academic, professional, and/or personal activities.

Financial data The stipend is $1,000.

Duration 1 year.

Number awarded 3 each year: 1 to a graduating high school senior, 1 to a current undergraduate student, and 1 to a current graduate student.

Deadline September of each year.

[271]
JUDITH MCMANUS PRICE SCHOLARSHIPS
American Planning Association
Attn: Leadership Affairs Associate
122 South Michigan Avenue, Suite 1600
Chicago, IL 60603-6107
(312) 431-9100   Fax: (312) 431-9985
E-mail: fellowship@planning.org
Web: www.planning.org/institutions/scholarship.htm

Purpose To provide financial assistance to women and underrepresented minority students enrolled in undergraduate or graduate degree programs at recognized planning schools.

Eligibility This program is open to undergraduate and graduate students in urban and regional planning who are women or members of the following minority groups: African American, Hispanic American, or Native American. Applicants must be citizens of the United States and able to document financial need. They must intend to work as practicing planners in the public sector. Along with their application, they must submit a 2- to 5-page personal statement describing how their education will be applied to career goals and why they chose planning as a career path. Selection is based (in order of importance) on 1) commitment to planning as reflected in the personal statement and resume; 2) academic achievement and/or improvement during the past 2 years; 3) letters of recommendation; 4) financial need; and 5) professional presentation.

Financial data Stipends range from $2,000 to $4,000 per year. The money may be applied to tuition and living expenses only. Payment is made to the recipient's university and divided by terms in the school year.

Duration 1 year; recipients may reapply.

Additional information This program was established in 2002.

Number awarded Varies each year; recently, 2 of these scholarships were awarded.

Deadline April of each year.

[272]
JUMP START AWARDS
Cook Inlet Region, Inc.
Attn: The CIRI Foundation
3600 San Jeronimo Drive, Suite 256
Anchorage, AK 99508-2870
(907) 793-3575   Toll-free: (800) 764-3382
Fax: (907) 793-3585   E-mail: tcf@thecirifoundation.org
Web: www.thecirifoundation.org/grants.htm

Purpose To provide financial assistance to Alaska Natives who are original enrollees to the Cook Inlet Region, Inc. (CIRI) or their lineal descendants and are currently enrolled in college part time while concurrently enrolled in high school.

Eligibility This program is open to Alaska Native enrollees to CIRI under the Alaska Native Claims Settlement Act (ANCSA) of 1971 and their lineal descendants. Applicants must be enrolled or accepted for enrollment at a recognized or accredited college, training program, or other authorized postsecondary training program on a part-time basis while concurrently enrolled in high school or equivalent program. There is no Alaska residency requirement. Along with the application, they must submit a 500-word statement on their

educational and career goals and how they are contributing, or planning to contribute, to a positive Alaska Native community. Selection is based on that statement, academic achievement, rigor of course work or degree program, student financial contribution, financial need, grade level, previous work performance, community service, and relationship of degree program to career goals.
Financial data Up to $2,000 may be awarded to each recipient during the calendar year.
Duration 1 quarter; recipients may reapply.
Number awarded Varies each year; recently, 7 of these awards were presented.
Deadline March, June, September, or November of each year.

[273]
KAW NATION ACADEMIC SCHOLARSHIP PROGRAM
Kaw Nation
Attn: Education and Social Services Department
P.O. Box 50
Kaw City, OK 74641
(580) 269-1186   Fax: (580) 269-2116
E-mail: khowe@kawnation.com
Web: www.kawnation.com/Programs/edsvcs.html
Purpose To provide financial assistance for college to members of the Kaw Nation who can demonstrate academic achievement.
Eligibility This program is open to Kaw tribal members who are working on or planning to work on a college degree. Applicants must have a GPA of 3.0 or higher. Financial need is not considered in the selection process.
Financial data A stipend is awarded (amount not specified).
Duration 1 year; may be renewed, provided the recipient maintains a GPA of 3.0 or higher and full-time enrollment.
Number awarded Varies each year.
Deadline June of each year.

[274]
KAW NATION ADULT EDUCATION
Kaw Nation
Attn: Education and Social Services Department
P.O. Box 50
Kaw City, OK 74641
(580) 269-1186   Fax: (580) 269-2116
E-mail: khowe@kawnation.com
Web: www.kawnation.com/Programs/edsvcs.html
Purpose To provide financial assistance for short-term vocational training to members of the Kaw Nation and other Native Americans living in the Kaw service area.
Eligibility This program is open to Kaw tribal members and other Native Americans living within the Kaw Nation service area. Applicants must be interested in taking short-term certification classes at a vocational/technical school.
Financial data A stipend is awarded (amount not specified).
Duration Classes must be short-term only.
Number awarded Varies each year.

[275]
KAW NATION ADULT VOCATIONAL TRAINING PROGRAM
Kaw Nation
Attn: Education and Social Services Department
P.O. Box 50
Kaw City, OK 74641
(580) 269-1186   Fax: (580) 269-2116
E-mail: khowe@kawnation.com
Web: www.kawnation.com/Programs/edsvcs.html
Purpose To provide financial assistance for vocational school to members of the Kaw Nation and other Native Americans living in the Kaw service area who can demonstrate need.
Eligibility This program is open to Kaw tribal members and other Native Americans living within the Kaw Nation service area. Applicants must be enrolled or planning to enroll at a vocational/technical school. They must be able to demonstrate financial need.
Financial data A stipend is awarded (amount not specified).
Duration 1 or 2 years.
Number awarded Varies each year.

[276]
KAW NATION HIGHER EDUCATION GRANT PROGRAM
Kaw Nation
Attn: Education and Social Services Department
P.O. Box 50
Kaw City, OK 74641
(580) 269-1186   Fax: (580) 269-2116
E-mail: khowe@kawnation.com
Web: www.kawnation.com/Programs/edsvcs.html
Purpose To provide financial assistance for college to members of the Kaw Nation who can demonstrate need.
Eligibility This program is open to Kaw tribal members who are working on or planning to work on a college degree. Applicants must be able to demonstrate financial need.
Financial data A stipend is awarded (amount not specified).
Duration 1 year; may be renewed.
Number awarded Varies each year.
Deadline May of each year for fall semester; October of each year for spring semester.

[277]
KAWERAK HIGHER EDUCATION SCHOLARSHIPS
Kawerak, Inc.
Attn: Education, Employment, and Training Division
P.O. Box 948
Nome, AK 99762
(907) 443-4351   Toll-free: (800) 450-4341
Fax: (907) 443-4480   E-mail: wfd.spec@kawerak.org
Web: www.kawerak.org
Purpose To provide financial assistance to Alaska Natives from the Bering Straits region who are interested in attending college in any state.
Eligibility This program is open to tribally enrolled members of Native villages in the Bering Straits region of Alaska. Applicants must be enrolled or accepted for enrollment in

a 2-year or 4-year degree program at a college or university in any state. They must submit verification of tribal membership, documentation of financial need, official transcripts, 2 letters of recommendation, and a letter of intent providing the name of the school they wish to attend, their class standing, their major area of study, their projected graduation date, and their educational and personal goals.
Financial data The stipend is $1,500 per semester.
Duration 1 semester; may be renewed if the recipient remains enrolled full time with a GPA of 2.0 or higher.
Number awarded Varies each year.
Deadline July of each year for fall semester or quarter; December of each year for spring semester or winter quarter; February of each year for spring quarter; April of each year for summer semester or quarter.

[278]
KAWERAK VOCATIONAL TRAINING SCHOLARSHIPS
Kawerak, Inc.
Attn: Education, Employment, and Training Division
P.O. Box 948
Nome, AK 99762
(907) 443-4399 Toll-free: (800) 450-4341
Fax: (907) 443-4454 E-mail: eet.intake@kawerak.org
Web: www.kawerak.org

Purpose To provide financial assistance to Alaska Natives from the Bering Straits region who are interested in vocational training.
Eligibility This program is open to tribally enrolled members of Native villages in the Bering Straits region of Alaska, but residency there is not required. Applicants must be unemployed or underemployed and interested in obtaining vocational training to gain job skills for employment. They must have been accepted into an accredited vocational or trade school for training in an occupation that is in demand in the region. Along with their application, they must submit verification of tribal membership, documentation of financial need, official transcripts, 2 letters of recommendation, and a letter of intent providing the name of the school they wish to attend, their employment and personal goals, and where they wish to seek employment.
Financial data The stipend depends on the need of the recipient. Tribal members who no longer reside in the region may receive a grant up to $1,500.
Duration Funding is provided for a single training program. Recipients may reapply, but their applications receive a lower priority.
Number awarded Varies each year.
Deadline Applications may be submitted at any time, but they must be received at least 2 weeks before the start of the training program.

[279]
KENAI NATIVES ASSOCIATION SCHOLARSHIP AND GRANT FUND
Cook Inlet Region, Inc.
Attn: The CIRI Foundation
3600 San Jeronimo Drive, Suite 256
Anchorage, AK 99508-2870
(907) 793-3575 Toll-free: (800) 764-3382
Fax: (907) 793-3585 E-mail: tcf@thecirifoundation.org
Web: www.thecirifoundation.org

Purpose To provide financial assistance for undergraduate or graduate studies to Alaska Natives who are original enrollees of the Kenai Natives Association (KNA) and their lineal descendants.
Eligibility This program is open to Alaska Native enrollees of KNA under the Alaska Native Claims Settlement Act (ANCSA) of 1971 and their lineal descendants. There are no Alaska residency requirements or age limitations. Applicants must be accepted or enrolled full time in a 2-year, 4-year, or graduate degree program or technical skills training program. They must have a GPA of 2.5 or higher. Along with their application, they must submit a 500-word statement on their educational and career goals and how they are contributing, or planning to contribute, to a positive Alaska Native community. Selection is based on that statement, academic achievement, rigor of course work or degree program, student financial contribution, financial need, grade level, previous work performance, community service, and relationship of degree program to career goals.
Financial data The stipend depends on the availability of funds.
Duration 1 semester; recipients must reapply each semester.
Additional information This program was established in 1989. Funds are provided by the KNA and the Tanaina Corporation with matching funds from the CIRI Foundation.
Number awarded 1 or more each year.
Deadline May or November of each year.

[280]
KENAITZE INDIAN TRIBE HIGHER EDUCATION SCHOLARSHIP PROGRAM
Kenaitze Indian Tribe
P.O. Box 988
Kenai, AK 99611
(907) 283-3633 Fax: (907) 283-3052
E-mail: education@kenaitze.org
Web: www.kenaitze.org/education/index.html

Purpose To provide financial assistance to members of recognized Native Alaskan Tribes who plan to attend college or graduate school in any state.
Eligibility This program is open to members of federally-recognized tribes and Native Alaskans of at least one-quarter degree blood. Applicants must be enrolled or planning to enroll full time at a college or university in any state and work on a baccalaureate degree. They are also expected to apply for federal financial aid through the FAFSA. Along with their application, they must submit a letter on their goals and educational plans, verification of Indian ancestry (CIB or tribal card), a letter of acceptance to the school they plan to attend, transcripts, a completed FAFSA application, and an Alaska driver's license. Limited

support may be provided to graduate students if funds are available.
Financial data The amount awarded varies, depending upon the available funds and the recipient's unmet needs. Funds are paid directly to the educational institution.
Duration 1 year; may be renewed if the recipient maintains a GPA of 2.5 of higher.
Additional information This program is funded by the U.S. Bureau of Indian Affairs.
Number awarded Varies each year.
Deadline May of each year for fall; November of each year for spring or winter.

[281]
KEWEENAW BAY INDIAN COMMUNITY BIA HIGHER EDUCATION GRANTS
Keweenaw Bay Indian Community-Lake Superior Band of Chippewa Indians
Attn: Education Department
16429 Bear Town Road
Baraga, MI 49908
(906) 353-4117   E-mail: amy@kbic-nsn.gov
Web: www.kbic-nsn.gov/html/education.htm

Purpose To provide financial assistance to members of the Keeweenaw Bay Indian Community (KBIC) of the Lake Superior Band of Chippewa Indians who live in Michigan and are interested in attending college in the state.
Eligibility This program is open to enrolled KBIC tribal members who are residents of Michigan. Applicants must be attending or planning to attend a 2-year or 4-year college or university in Michigan to work on an associate or bachelor's degree. They must be able to demonstrate financial need and apply for all other assistance for which they might be eligible.
Financial data A stipend is awarded (amount not specified).
Duration 1 semester; may be renewed.
Additional information This program is supported by the U.S. Bureau of Indian Affairs (BIA).
Number awarded Varies each year.
Deadline April of each year.

[282]
KEWEENAW BAY INDIAN COMMUNITY SOVEREIGN STUDENT FUND
Keweenaw Bay Indian Community-Lake Superior Band of Chippewa Indians
Attn: Education Department
16429 Bear Town Road
Baraga, MI 49908
(906) 353-4117   E-mail: amy@kbic-nsn.gov
Web: www.kbic-nsn.gov/html/education.htm

Purpose To provide financial assistance to members of the Keeweenaw Bay Indian Community (KBIC) of the Lake Superior Band of Chippewa Indians who live in designated Michigan counties and are interested in attending college in any state.
Eligibility This program is open to enrolled KBIC tribal members who have been residents of the following Michigan counties: Baraga, Houghton, Marquette, or Ontonagon.

Applicants must be attending or planning to attend a college or university in any state. Selection is based on merit.
Financial data A stipend is awarded (amount not specified).
Duration 1 semester; may be renewed, provided the recipient maintains a GPA of 2.0 or higher.
Number awarded Varies each year.

[283]
KICK START AWARDS
Cook Inlet Region, Inc.
Attn: The CIRI Foundation
3600 San Jeronimo Drive, Suite 256
Anchorage, AK 99508-2870
(907) 793-3575   Toll-free: (800) 764-3382
Fax: (907) 793-3585   E-mail: tcf@thecirifoundation.org
Web: www.thecirifoundation.org/grants.htm

Purpose To provide financial assistance to Alaska Natives who are original enrollees to the Cook Inlet Region, Inc. (CIRI) or their lineal descendants and do not currently meet the GPA requirements for other scholarships offered by the foundation.
Eligibility This program is open to Alaska Native enrollees to CIRI under the Alaska Native Claims Settlement Act (ANCSA) of 1971 and their lineal descendants. Applicants must be enrolled or accepted for enrollment in a degree or technical skills certificate program but have a GPA below the 2.5 requirement for other scholarships offered by The CIRI Foundation. They must demonstrate a commitment to meeting the 2.5 GPA requirement in 1 semester. There is no Alaska residency requirement. Along with the application, they must submit a 500-word statement on their educational and career goals and how they are contributing, or planning to contribute, to a positive Alaska Native community. Selection is based on that statement, academic achievement, rigor of course work or degree program, student financial contribution, financial need, grade level, previous work performance, community service, and relationship of degree program to career goals.
Financial data Up to $2,000 may be awarded to each recipient during the calendar year.
Duration 1 year; nonrenewable.
Number awarded Varies each year; recently, 3 of these awards were presented.
Deadline March, June, September, or November of each year.

[284]
KIKIKTAGRUK INUPIAT CORPORATION SCHOLARSHIPS
Kikiktagruk Inupiat Corporation
Attn: Selection Committee
373A Second Avenue
P.O. Box 1050
Kotzebue, AK 99752
(907) 442-3165   Fax: (907) 442-2165
E-mail: info@kicorp.org
Web: www.kicorp.org/shareholders.html

Purpose To provide financial assistance for college or vocational school in any state to shareholders of the Kikiktagruk Inupiat Corporation (KIC) and their descendants.

Eligibility This program is open to KIC shareholders and their children who are attending or planning to attend a college or vocational school in any state as a full-time student. Applicants must submit a copy of their high school transcripts, 2 letters of recommendation, and a cover letter describing themselves and their goals. Awards are presented on a first-come, first-served basis.
Financial data The stipend is $500 per semester ($1,000 per year) for full-time students or $250 per semester for part-time and short vocational program students.
Duration 1 semester; may be renewed for 1 additional semester per year if the recipient maintains a GPA of 2.0 or higher.
Additional information Kikiktagruk Inupiat Corporation was established in 1973 as a village corporation under the terms of the Alaska Native Claims Settlement Act (ANCSA) of 1971.
Number awarded Varies each semester.
Deadline Applications must be submitted at least 2 weeks before the semester starts.

[285]
KIMBALL OFFICE SCHOLARSHIP
International Interior Design Association
Attn: IIDA Foundation
222 Merchandise Mart, Suite 567
Chicago, IL 60654
(312) 467-1950   Toll-free: (888) 799-4432
Fax: (312) 467-0779 E-mail: iidahq@iida.org
Web: www.iida.org/i4a/pages/index.cfm?pageid=156

Purpose To provide financial assistance to Native American and other minority students enrolled in the senior year of an interior design program.
Eligibility This program is open to college seniors of African, Asian, Latino, or Native American heritage. Applicants must be working on a degree in interior design. Selection is based on excellence in academics and promising design talent.
Financial data The stipend is $5,000.
Duration 1 year.
Additional information This program was established in 2006 by Kimball Office, a unit of Kimball International, Inc.
Number awarded 1 each year.

[286]
KIRBY MCDONALD EDUCATION ENDOWMENT SCHOLARSHIP FUND
Cook Inlet Region, Inc.
Attn: The CIRI Foundation
3600 San Jeronimo Drive, Suite 256
Anchorage, AK 99508-2870
(907) 793-3575   Toll-free: (800) 764-3382
Fax: (907) 793-3585 E-mail: tcf@thecirifoundation.org
Web: www.thecirifoundation.org/designated.htm

Purpose To provide financial assistance for undergraduate or graduate studies to Alaska Natives who are original enrollees to Cook Inlet Region, Inc. (CIRI) and their lineal descendants.
Eligibility This program is open to Alaska Native enrollees to CIRI under the Alaska Native Claims Settlement Act (ANCSA) of 1971 and their lineal descendants. There are no Alaska residency requirements or age limitations. Applicants must be accepted or enrolled full time in a 4-year undergraduate or a graduate degree program. Preference is given to students in the culinary arts, but students in business administration and engineering are also eligible. They must have a GPA of 2.5 or higher. Along with their application, they must submit a 500-word statement on their educational and career goals and how they are contributing, or planning to contribute, to a positive Alaska Native community. Selection is based on that statement, academic achievement, rigor of course work or degree program, student financial contribution, financial need, grade level, previous work performance, community service, and relationship of degree program to career goals.
Financial data The stipend is $10,000 per year, $8,000 per year, or $2,500 per semester, depending on GPA.
Duration 1 semester or 1 year.
Additional information This program was established in 1991.
Number awarded 1 or more each year.
Deadline May of each year for annual scholarships; May or November of each year for semester scholarships.

[287]
KONIAG EDUCATION FOUNDATION ACADEMIC ACHIEVEMENT/GRADUATE SCHOLARSHIPS
Koniag Incorporated
Attn: Koniag Education Foundation
6927 Old Seward Highway, Suite 103
Anchorage, AK 99518-2283
(907) 562-9093   Toll-free: (888) 562-9093
Fax: (907) 562-9023 E-mail: kef@alaska.com
Web: www.koniageducation.org/KEFScholarship.html

Purpose To provide financial assistance to Alaska Natives with ties to the Koniag region who plan to attend college or graduate school in any state.
Eligibility This program is open to high school seniors, high school and GED graduates, college students, and graduate students who are Alaska Native shareholders of the Koniag region or descendants of those original enrollees. Applicants must supply proof of eligibility and documentation of financial need. They must have a GPA of 3.0 or higher and be enrolled or planning to enroll at a college or university in any state. Along with their application, they must submit a 300- to 600-word letter that includes their personal and family history, their schooling, and their educational and life goals.
Financial data Stipends range up to $2,500 per year. Funds are sent directly to the recipient's school and may be used for tuition, books, supplies, room, board, and transportation.
Duration 1 year; may be renewed, provided recipients maintain a GPA of 3.0 or higher.
Additional information The Koniag Education Foundation was established in 1993 by the directors of Koniag, Inc. The Koniag region covers Kodiak Island, many smaller islands, and a portion of the Alaska Peninsula.
Number awarded Varies each year.
Deadline March of each year for summer term; May of each year for fall or spring term.

[288]
KONIAG EDUCATION FOUNDATION CAREER DEVELOPMENT GRANTS

Koniag Incorporated
Attn: Koniag Education Foundation
6927 Old Seward Highway, Suite 103
Anchorage, AK 99518-2283
(907) 562-9093   Toll-free: (888) 562-9093
Fax: (907) 562-9023   E-mail: kef@alaska.com
Web: www.koniageducation.org/KEFCareerDev.html

Purpose To provide financial assistance to Alaska Natives with ties to the Koniag region who are interested in attending a short-term career development course.

Eligibility This program is open to high school seniors, high school graduates, and currently-enrolled vocational school students who are Alaska Native shareholders of the Koniag region or descendants of those original enrollees. Applicants must supply proof of eligibility and documentation of financial need. They must be interested in attending an accredited career development activity, including non-degree, part-time, short-term courses of study that will increase their opportunities for employment or job advancement. Along with their application, they must submit a letter that includes information about their talents and abilities, community involvement, plans for the future, how their education would contribute to the Alaska Native community, why they wish to attend the school they have chosen, why they have chosen the area they plan to study, and their long-range educational goals.

Financial data Stipends range up to $1,000.

Duration Up to 6 weeks. Students may obtain only 2 of these grants each year.

Additional information The Koniag Education Foundation was established in 1993 by the directors of Koniag, Inc. The Koniag region covers Kodiak Island, many smaller islands, and a portion of the Alaska Peninsula.

Number awarded Varies each year.

Deadline Applications may be submitted at any time.

[289]
KONIAG EDUCATION FOUNDATION COLLEGE/UNIVERSITY BASIC SCHOLARSHIPS

Koniag Incorporated
Attn: Koniag Education Foundation
6927 Old Seward Highway, Suite 103
Anchorage, AK 99518-2283
(907) 562-9093   Toll-free: (888) 562-9093
Fax: (907) 562-9023   E-mail: kef@alaska.com
Web: www.koniageducation.org

Purpose To provide financial assistance to Alaska Natives who have ties to the Koniag region and plan to attend college in any state.

Eligibility This program is open to high school seniors, high school and GED graduates, and college students who are Alaska Native shareholders of the Koniag region or descendants of those original enrollees. Applicants must supply proof of eligibility and documentation of financial need. They must have a GPA of 2.0 or higher and be enrolled or planning to enroll at an accredited college or university in any state. Along with their application, they must submit a 300- to 600-word letter that includes their personal and family history, their schooling or work history, and their educational and life goals.

Financial data Stipends range up to $1,000. Funds are sent directly to the recipient's school and may be used for tuition, books, supplies, room, board, and transportation.

Duration 1 year; may be renewed, provided recipients maintain a GPA of 2.0 or higher.

Additional information The Koniag Education Foundation was established in 1993 by the directors of Koniag, Inc. The Koniag region covers Kodiak Island, many smaller islands, and a portion of the Alaska Peninsula.

Number awarded Varies each year.

Deadline March of each year for summer term; May of each year for fall or spring term.

[290]
KONIAG EDUCATION FOUNDATION VOCATIONAL EDUCATION GRANTS

Koniag Incorporated
Attn: Koniag Education Foundation
6927 Old Seward Highway, Suite 103
Anchorage, AK 99518-2283
(907) 562-9093   Toll-free: (888) 562-9093
Fax: (907) 562-9023   E-mail: kef@alaska.com
Web: www.koniageducation.org/KEFVocational.html

Purpose To provide financial assistance to Alaska Natives with ties to the Koniag region who are interested in a program of vocational education.

Eligibility This program is open to high school seniors, high school graduates, and currently-enrolled vocational school students who are Alaska Native shareholders of the Koniag region or descendants of those original enrollees. Applicants must have a GPA of 2.0 or higher and be enrolled or planning to enroll in a state-accredited or municipally-recognized vocational school. They must supply proof of eligibility; a demonstration of how the training will assist them in gaining employment, job security, and/or advancement; and documentation of financial need. Along with their application, they must submit a 300- to 600-word letter that includes their personal and family history, their schooling or work history, and their educational and life goals.

Financial data Stipends range up to $2,500. Funds are sent directly to the recipient's school and may be used for tuition, books, supplies, room, board, and transportation.

Duration At least 6 weeks; may be renewed, provided the recipient maintains a GPA of 2.0 or higher.

Additional information The Koniag Education Foundation was established in 1993 by the directors of Koniag, Inc. The Koniag region covers Kodiak Island, many smaller islands, and a portion of the Alaska Peninsula.

Number awarded Varies each year.

Deadline March of each year for summer term; May of each year for fall or spring term.

[291]
KOTZEBUE I.R.A. ADULT VOCATIONAL TRAINING GRANT

Native Village of Kotzebue-Kotzebue I.R.A.
Attn: Education Coordinator
P.O. Box 296
Kotzebue, AK 99752-0296
(907) 442-3467   Fax: (907) 442-2162
E-mail: info@kotzebueira.org
Web: kotzebueira.org/education.html

Purpose To provide financial assistance to enrolled members of the Native Village of Kotzebue-Kotzebue I.R.A. who are interested in attending an accredited vocational technical institute to prepare for employment.

Eligibility Enrolled members of the Native Village of Kotzebue-Kotzebue I.R.A. currently residing in Kotzebue are eligible to apply for a grant to assist with the costs of attending an accredited vocational technical institute to gain the skills and training necessary to secure employment. Applicants must have been residents of Kotzebue for at least 31 days prior to submitting an application; must be at least 18 years of age; must be unemployed, underemployed, or in need of training to obtain reasonable employment; and must be able to document financial need. They must have a high school diploma or a GED certificate (or be in the process of earning the degree). A Certificate of Indian Blood indicating at least a quarter quantum Alaska Native or American Indian blood must be submitted. Priority is given to first-time applicants.

Financial data The amount awarded varies, depending upon the needs of the recipient and the funds available.

Duration The length of training in any field is limited to 24 months (36 months for nursing programs).

Number awarded Varies each year.

Deadline Applications may be submitted at any time, but they must be received at least 10 days before the start of the program.

[292]
KOTZEBUE I.R.A. HIGHER EDUCATION SCHOLARSHIP

Native Village of Kotzebue-Kotzebue I.R.A.
Attn: Education Coordinator
P.O. Box 296
Kotzebue, AK 99752
(907) 442-3467   Fax: (907) 442-2162
E-mail: info@kotzebueira.org
Web: kotzebueira.org/education.html

Purpose To provide financial assistance for college to eligible members of the Native Village of Kotzebue.

Eligibility Applicants must be officially enrolled members of the Kotzebue I.R.A. and must provide a copy of Certificate of Indian Blood showing at least a quarter quantum Alaska Native or American Indian blood. They must be enrolled at an accredited postsecondary school (in any state). Religious postsecondary educational institutions must be accredited and course hours must be transferable to 3 nonreligious postsecondary educational institutions. All applicants must be at least 18 years of age and able to demonstrate financial need. Both full- and part-time students are eligible, but full-time students receive priority.

Financial data The amount of the scholarship is based on the availability of funds appropriated each year by the U.S. Congress. Generally, full-time students receive $1,200 per semester and part-time students receive enough to cover the costs of books, fees, and tuition. Students on academic probation receive $600 for full time and half the costs of books, fees, and tuition for part time.

Duration 1 semester; may be renewed, provided the recipient maintains a GPA of 2.0 or higher.

Number awarded Varies each year.

Deadline July of each year for the fall semester; December of each year for the spring semester; or April of each year for the summer semester.

[293]
KURT KLUMB BUSINESS SCHOLARSHIP

Milwaukee Indian Education Committee
c/o American Indian Student Services
University of Wisconsin at Milwaukee
Holton G-48
P.O. Box 413
Milwaukee, WI 53201
(414) 229-5880   Fax: (414) 229-5930
E-mail: amour@uwm.edu
Web: www.indiansummer.org

Purpose To provide financial assistance to American Indians from Wisconsin who are studying or planning to study business in college in any state.

Eligibility This program is open to Wisconsin residents who are American Indians by tribal enrollment or descendancy (having 1 or more ancestors who are tribally enrolled). Applicants must be accepted or in good standing at an institution of higher education in any state and majoring in business. They must submit a 1-page statement describing their educational goals, the reasons they feel they should receive the scholarship, their community service, and any special needs. Preference is given to applicants who have provided service to the Indian community and have not previously received a scholarship.

Financial data The stipend is $1,000.

Duration 1 year.

Additional information Support for this program is provided by Indian Summer Festivals, Inc.

Number awarded 1 each year.

Deadline July of each year.

[294]
KUSKOKWIM EDUCATIONAL FOUNDATION GENERAL SCHOLARSHIPS

The Kuskokwim Corporation
Attn: Kuskokwim Educational Foundation, Inc.
P.O. Box 227
Aniak, AK 99557
(907) 675-4275   Toll-free: (800) 478-4275 (within AK)
Fax: (907) 675-4276   E-mail: dg@kuskokwim.com
Web: www.kuskokwim.com

Purpose To provide financial assistance for college or graduate school to Native people and their descendants with ties to The Kuskokwim Corporation (TKC) region.

Eligibility This program is open to Native people and their descendants from The Kuskokwim Corporation region in

Alaska. Applicants may be high school seniors, high school graduates, currently-enrolled college students, college graduates, or graduate students. They must be interested in attending school on a full-time basis. Along with their application, they must submit a letter or essay describing their talents, special interests, accomplishments, educational objectives, reasons for selecting those objectives, and progress toward achieving those objectives; documentation of financial need; transcripts; and 2 letters of recommendation.

Financial data Stipends range from $100 to $1,500 per year. Funds are sent to the recipient's school in 2 equal installments.

Duration 1 year; may be renewed if the recipient maintains full-time enrollment and a GPA of 2.0 or higher as an undergraduate, a GPA of 3.0 or higher as a graduate student, or satisfactory progress as a vocational student.

Additional information Recipients may use the funds for college and university courses, vocational and continuing education, student exchange programs, and other educational opportunities approved by the board.

Number awarded Varies each year; recently, 20 of these scholarships were awarded.

Deadline June of each year for fall semester; November of each year for spring semester.

[295]
LAGRANT FOUNDATION UNDERGRADUATE SCHOLARSHIPS

Lagrant Foundation
Attn: Programs Manager
626 Wilshire Boulevard, Suite 700
Los Angeles, CA 90071-2920
(323) 469-8680   Fax: (323) 469-8683
E-mail: erickaavila@lagrant.com
Web: www.lagrantfoundation.org/site/?page_id=3

Purpose To provide financial assistance to Native American and other minority college students who are interested in majoring in advertising, public relations, or marketing.

Eligibility This program is open to African Americans, Asian Pacific Americans, Hispanics, and Native Americans who are full-time students at a 4-year accredited institution. Applicants must have a GPA of 2.75 or higher and be either majoring in advertising, marketing, or public relations or minoring in communications with plans to prepare for a career in advertising, marketing, or public relations. Along with their application, they must submit 1) a 1- to 2-page essay outlining their career goals; what steps they will take to increase ethnic representation in the fields of advertising, marketing, and public relations; and the role of an advertising, marketing, or public relations practitioner; 2) a paragraph describing the college and/or community activities in which they are involved; 3) a brief paragraph describing any honors and awards they have received; 4) a letter of reference; 5) a resume; and 6) an official transcript. Applicants majoring in public relations must also submit an essay on the importance and relevance of the Arthur W. Page Society Principles. Those students must have a GPA of 3.0 or higher.

Financial data The stipend is $5,000 per year.

Duration 1 year.

Additional information Support for the public relations scholarships is provided by the Arthur W. Page Society.

Number awarded 10 each year, including 2 supported by the Arthur W. Page Society.

Deadline February of each year.

[296]
LAND O'LAKES PURINA FEED SCHOLARSHIPS

National FFA Organization
Attn: Scholarship Office
6060 FFA Drive
P.O. Box 68960
Indianapolis, IN 46268-0960
(317) 802-4419   Fax: (317) 802-5419
E-mail: scholarships@ffa.org
Web: www.ffa.org

Purpose To provide financial assistance to Native American and other minority FFA members interested in studying agriculture in college.

Eligibility This program is open to members who are currently enrolled full time at a 4-year college or university and who represent a minority ethnic group (African American, Asian American, Pacific Islander, Hispanic, Alaska Native, or American Indian). Applicants must be working on a degree in selected areas of agriculture. They must have a GPA of 3.0 or higher. Selection is based on academic achievement (10 points for GPA, 10 points for SAT or ACT score, 10 points for class rank), leadership in FFA activities (30 points), leadership in community activities (10 points), and participation in the Supervised Agricultural Experience (SAE) program (30 points). U.S. citizenship is required.

Financial data The stipend is $1,000 per year. Funds are paid directly to the recipient.

Duration 1 year; nonrenewable.

Additional information Funding for these scholarships is provided by Purina Mills, LLC.

Number awarded Varies each year, depending on the number of participating Purina dealers.

Deadline February of each year.

[297]
LARRY MATFAY SCHOLARSHIP

Koniag Incorporated
Attn: Koniag Education Foundation
6927 Old Seward Highway, Suite 103
Anchorage, AK 99518-2283
(907) 562-9093   Toll-free: (888) 562-9093
Fax: (907) 562-9023   E-mail: kef@alaska.com
Web: www.koniageducation.org

Purpose To provide financial assistance to Alaska Natives with ties to the Koniag region who are enrolled in undergraduate or graduate study in a field related to Alutiiq culture.

Eligibility This program is open to college juniors, seniors, and graduate students who are Alaska Native shareholders of the Koniag region or descendants of those original enrollees. Applicants must supply proof of eligibility and documentation of financial need. They must have a GPA of 2.5 or higher cumulatively (3.0 or higher within their major) and be majoring in anthropology, history, Alaska Native or American Indian studies, or another discipline that

involves research and learning about Alutiiq culture. Along with their application, they must submit a 300- to 600-word letter that includes their personal and family history, their schooling or work history, and their educational and life goals.
Financial data The stipend is $1,000 per year. Funds are sent directly to the recipient's school and may be used for tuition, books, supplies, room, board, and transportation.
Duration 1 year; may be renewed.
Additional information Recipients are also eligible to apply for a Koniag Education Foundation Academic Achievement/Graduate Scholarship. The Koniag Education Foundation was established in 1993 by the directors of Koniag, Inc. The Koniag region covers Kodiak Island, many smaller islands, and a portion of the Alaska Peninsula.
Number awarded 1 each year.
Deadline March of each year for summer term; May of each year for fall or spring term.

[298]
LAUNCHING LEADERS UNDERGRADUATE SCHOLARSHIP

JPMorgan Chase
Campus Recruiting
Attn: Launching Leaders
277 Park Avenue, Second Floor
New York, NY 10172
(212) 270-6000
E-mail: bronwen.x.baumgardner@jpmorgan.com
Web: launchingleaders.jpmorgan.com/01.0.ashx

Purpose To provide financial assistance and work experience to Native Americans and other underrepresented minority undergraduate students interested in a career in financial services.
Eligibility This program is open to Black, Hispanic, and Native American students enrolled as sophomores or juniors and interested in financial services. Applicants must have a GPA of 3.5 or higher. Along with their application, they must submit 500-word essays on 1) why they should be considered potential candidates for CEO of the sponsoring bank in 2020; and 2) the special background and attributes they would contribute to the sponsor's diversity agenda. They must be interested in a summer associate position in the sponsor's investment banking, sales and trading, or research divisions.
Financial data The stipend is $5,000 for recipients accepted as sophomores or $7,500 for recipients accepted as juniors. For students accepted as sophomores and whose scholarship is renewed for a second year, the stipend is $10,000. The summer associateship is a paid position.
Duration 1 year; may be renewed 1 additional year if the recipient successfully completes the 10-week summer associate program and maintains a GPA of 3.5 or higher.
Number awarded Approximately 12 each year.
Deadline November of each year.

[299]
LAWRENCE MATSON MEMORIAL ENDOWMENT FUND SCHOLARSHIPS

Cook Inlet Region, Inc.
Attn: The CIRI Foundation
3600 San Jeronimo Drive, Suite 256
Anchorage, AK 99508-2870
(907) 793-3575   Toll-free: (800) 764-3382
Fax: (907) 793-3585 E-mail: tcf@thecirifoundation.org
Web: www.thecirifoundation.org/designated.htm

Purpose To provide financial assistance for undergraduate or graduate studies in selected liberal arts to Alaska Natives who are original enrollees to Cook Inlet Region, Inc. (CIRI) and their lineal descendants.
Eligibility This program is open to Alaska Native enrollees to CIRI under the Alaska Native Claims Settlement Act (ANCSA) of 1971 and their lineal descendants. There are no Alaska residency requirements or age limitations. Applicants must be accepted or enrolled full time in a 4-year undergraduate or a graduate degree program in the following liberal arts fields: language, education, social sciences, arts, communications, or law. They must have a GPA of 2.5 or higher. Along with their application, they must submit a 500-word statement on their educational and career goals and how they are contributing, or planning to contribute, to a positive Alaska Native community. Selection is based on that statement, academic achievement, rigor of course work or degree program, student financial contribution, financial need, grade level, previous work performance, community service, and relationship of degree program to career goals.
Financial data The stipend is $10,000 per year, $8,000 per year, or $2,500 per semester, depending on GPA.
Duration 1 semester or 1 year.
Additional information This fund was established in 1989.
Number awarded Varies each year. Recently, 3 of these scholarships were awarded: 1 at $10,000 per year, 1 at $8,000 per year, and 1 at $2,500 per semester.
Deadline May of each year for annual scholarships; May or November of each year for semester scholarships.

[300]
LEADERSHIP FOR DIVERSITY SCHOLARSHIP

California School Library Association
1001 26th Street
Sacramento, CA 95816
(916) 447-2684   Fax: (916) 447-2695
E-mail: csla@pacbell.net
Web: www.csla.net/awa/scholarships.htm

Purpose To provide financial assistance to Native American and other minority students who any state interested in earning a credential as a library media teacher in California.
Eligibility This program is open to students who are members of a traditionally underrepresented group enrolled in a college or university library media teacher credential program in California. Applicants must intend to work as a library media teacher in a California school library media center for a minimum of 3 years. Along with their application, they must submit a 250-word statement on their school library media career interests and goals, why they should be considered, what they can contribute, their commitment

to serving the needs of our multicultural and multilingual students, and their financial situation.
Financial data The stipend is $1,500.
Duration 1 year.
Number awarded 1 each year.
Deadline April of each year.

[301]
LEECH LAKE POSTSECONDARY GRANT PROGRAM
Leech Lake Band of Ojibwe
Attn: Education Division
115 Sixth Street, N.W., Suite E
Cass Lake, MN 56633
(218) 335-8250   Toll-free: (800) 442-3909
Fax: (218) 335-8339
Web: www.llojibwe.com/llojibwe/Education.html

Purpose To provide financial assistance to Minnesota Chippewa Tribe high school graduates who are interested in postsecondary education.
Eligibility Applicants must be at least one-quarter Indian ancestry, residents of Minnesota for at least 1 year, high school graduates or the equivalent, and enrolled members of the Leech Lake Band of Ojibwe or eligible for enrollment. Financial need is required.
Financial data Stipends range up to $3,000 per year, depending on need.
Duration 1 year; may be renewed.
Additional information Applicants for this program must also apply for financial aid administered by their institution and any other aid for which they may be eligible (e.g., work-study, Social Security, veteran's benefits). Recipients may attend a college, university, or vocational school.
Number awarded Varies each year.
Deadline For vocational school students, at least 8 weeks before school starts; for college or university students, June of each year.

[302]
LEON C. HART MEMORIAL SCHOLARSHIP
Gravure Association of America
Attn: Gravure Education Foundation
1200-A Scottsville Road
Rochester, NY 14624
(585) 436-2150   Fax: (585) 436-7689
E-mail: bcarlson@gaa.org
Web: www.gaa.org/GEF/gef-scholarship.html

Purpose To provide financial assistance to college students, especially those from diverse ethnic backgrounds, who are interested in a career in printing.
Eligibility This program is open to students who are enrolled full time in a field related to printing at a designated Gravure Resource Center supported by the Gravure Education Foundation (GEF) of the Gravure Association of America. Applicants must have a GPA of 3.0 or higher. Along with their application, they must submit a 300-word essay on "How Involvement in my Community/School Has Made a Difference." Selection is based on the essay, financial need, transcripts, and either extracurricular involvement in school activities or community involvement. Preference is given to students of diverse ethnic backgrounds and to students who show an interest in printing education as a career path.
Financial data The stipend is $1,000.
Duration 1 year.
Additional information GEF Gravure Resource Centers are located at the following universities: Rochester Institute of Technology, Western Michigan University, California Polytechnic State University at San Luis Obispo, Arizona State University, Clemson University, Murray State University, and the University of Wisconsin at Stout. This program is named in honor of a former executive director of the GEF who began his career as a printer for the Afro-American Newspaper in Baltimore, Maryland.
Number awarded 1 each year.
Deadline May of each year.

[303]
LEONARD M. PERRYMAN COMMUNICATIONS SCHOLARSHIP FOR ETHNIC MINORITY STUDENTS
United Methodist Communications
Attn: Communications Resourcing Team
810 12th Avenue South
P.O. Box 320
Nashville, TN 37202-0320
(615) 742-5481   Toll-free: (888) CRT-4UMC
Fax: (615) 742-5485
E-mail: scholarships@umcom.org
Web: crt.umc.org/interior.asp?ptid=44&mid=10270

Purpose To provide financial assistance to Native American and other minority United Methodist college students who are interested in careers in religious communications.
Eligibility This program is open to United Methodist ethnic minority students enrolled in accredited institutions of higher education as juniors or seniors. Applicants must be interested in preparing for a career in religious communications. For the purposes of this program, "communications" is meant to cover audiovisual, electronic, and print journalism. Selection is based on Christian commitment and involvement in the life of the United Methodist church, academic achievement, journalistic experience, clarity of purpose, and professional potential as a religious journalist.
Financial data The stipend is $2,500 per year.
Duration 1 year.
Additional information The scholarship may be used at any accredited institution of higher education.
Number awarded 1 each year.
Deadline March of each year.

[304]
LIKO A'E SCHOLARSHIPS
Liko A'e Native Hawaiian Scholarship Program
c/o Maui Community College
310 West Ka'ahumanu Avenue
Kahului, HI 96732-1617
(808) 984-3366   Fax: (808) 984-3562
E-mail: lhokoana@hawaii.edu
Web: www.likoae.org/scholarship_info.asp

Purpose To provide financial assistance for college or graduate school to Native Hawaiian students.
Eligibility This program is open to U.S. citizens who are descendants of the aboriginal inhabitants of the Hawaiian

Islands prior to 1778. Applicants must be enrolled or accepted as full- or part-time students in an accredited 2- or 4-year degree-granting institution of higher education. Undergraduates must have a GPA of 2.0 or higher and graduate students must have a GPA of 3.0 or higher. Selection is based on merit (as judged by GPA and responses to essay questions) and financial need. Preference is given to students working on degrees in professions in which Native Hawaiians are underrepresented. Some of the scholarships are designated for students from smaller rural communities who are working on a degree in education.
Financial data A stipend is awarded (amount not specified). Child care assistance is also provided.
Duration 1 year.
Additional information This program was established in 2003 by a grant from the U.S. Department of Education and is administered by Maui Community College.
Number awarded Varies each year.
Deadline Deadlines are in May, August, November, and February.

[305]
LOCKHEED MARTIN TCU SCHOLARSHIP
American Indian College Fund
Attn: Scholarship Department
8333 Greenwood Boulevard
Denver, CO 80221
(303) 426-8900   Toll-free: (800) 776-FUND
Fax: (303) 426-1200   E-mail: info@collegefund.org
Web: www.collegefund.org

Purpose To provide financial assistance to Native Americans who are attending a Tribal College or University (TCU) and majoring in pre-engineering.
Eligibility This program is open to American Indians or Alaska Natives who are enrolled full time and are at least sophomores at an eligible TCU. Applicants must have a GPA of 2.9 or higher and be able to demonstrate financial need. They must have declared a major in pre-engineering (including electrical, computer, aerospace, mechanical, chemical, or material engineering or computer science) and be planning to complete a bachelor's degree in engineering at a tribal college and/or at a mainstream university. Along with their application, they must submit 1) short essays (up to 500 words each) on how they perceive themselves as leaders in their school or community and how their education will help the Native American community; and 2) a personal statement of 1,000 words that includes their personal background, their academic background, their educational and career goals, and how this scholarship will help them achieve those goals.
Financial data The stipend is $5,000.
Duration 1 year.
Additional information This program is funded by Lockheed Martin in partnership with the American Indian College Fund. Recipients are also offered a summer internship with Lockheed Martin.
Number awarded 1 or more each year.
Deadline May of each year.

[306]
LORI PIESTEWA VOCATIONAL/TECHNICAL OR 4-YEAR SCHOLARSHIP
Milwaukee Indian Education Committee
c/o American Indian Student Services
University of Wisconsin at Milwaukee
Holton G-48
P.O. Box 413
Milwaukee, WI 53201
(414) 229-5880   Fax: (414) 229-5930
E-mail: amour@uwm.edu
Web: www.indiansummer.org

Purpose To provide financial assistance to American Indians from Wisconsin who are attending or planning to attend a vocational/technical school or 4-year college or university in any state.
Eligibility This program is open to Wisconsin residents who are American Indians by tribal enrollment or descendancy (having 1 or more ancestors who are tribally enrolled). Applicants must be accepted or in good standing at a 4-year college or university or vocational/technical school in any state. They must submit a 1-page statement describing their educational goals, the reasons they feel they should receive the scholarship, their community service, and any special needs. Preference is given to applicants who have provided service to the Indian community and have not previously received a scholarship.
Financial data The stipend is $1,000.
Duration 1 year.
Additional information Support for this program is provided by Indian Summer Festivals, Inc.
Number awarded 1 each year.
Deadline July of each year.

[307]
MADELINE MOOSE SCHOLARSHIP FUND
MIGIZI Communications, Inc.
Attn: Scholarship Committee
3123 East Lake Street
Minneapolis, MN 55406
(612) 721-6631   Fax: (612) 721-3936
Web: migizi.org/mig/scholarships.html

Purpose To provide financial assistance to Native American students working on an undergraduate degree related to Ojibwe language and culture.
Eligibility This program is open to Native American undergraduate students enrolled at an accredited 4-year college or university. Applicants must be studying Ojibwe language and culture as part of a degree program. Along with their application, they must submit documentation of financial need and a 500-word essay on 1) how they are currently involved in Ojibwe language and/or revitalization, 2) why continuing Ojibwe language and culture is important to future generations, and 3) their plans for the future and how they plan to use their studies to help the community. Preference is given to students at tribal colleges and universities.
Financial data The stipend is $1,000.
Duration 1 year; nonrenewable.
Number awarded 1 each year.
Deadline May of each year.

[308]
MAE LASLEY/OSAGE SCHOLARSHIPS
Osage Scholarship Fund
c/o Roman Catholic Diocese of Tulsa
P.O. Box 690240
Tulsa, OK 74169-0240
(918) 294-1904 Fax: (918) 294-0920
E-mail: sarah.jameson@dioceseoftulsa.org
Web: www.osagetribe.com

Purpose To provide financial assistance to Osage Indians who are Roman Catholics attending college or graduate school.

Eligibility This program is open to Roman Catholics who are attending or planning to attend a college or university as an undergraduate or graduate student. Applicants must be Osage Indians on the rolls in Pawhuska, Oklahoma and have of copy of their Certificate of Indian Blood (CIB) or Osage tribal membership card. Selection is based on academic ability and financial need.

Financial data The stipend is $1,000 per year.

Duration 1 year; may be renewed if the recipient maintains full-time enrollment and a GPA of 2.5 or higher as an undergraduate or 3.0 or higher as a graduate student.

Number awarded Normally, 10 each year: 2 for students attending St. Gregory's University in Shawnee, Oklahoma as freshmen and 8 for any college or university.

Deadline April of each year.

[309]
MAJOR RIDGE AWARD
Cherokee Nation
Attn: Cherokee Nation Education Corporation
17675 South Muskogee Avenue
P.O. Box 948
Tahlequah, OK 74465
(918) 453-5420 Toll-free: (800) 256-0671 (within OK)
Fax: (918) 458-6195 E-mail: cnec@cherokee.org
Web: www.cherokee.org

Purpose To provide financial assistance to high school seniors who are citizens of the Cherokee Nation, are planning to attend college in any state, and are interested n submitting essays on Major Ridge.

Eligibility This program is open to citizens of the Cherokee Nation who are graduating from high schools within or outside the jurisdictional area of the tribe. Applicants must be planning to enroll at a college, university, or vocational/technical school in any state. Along with their application, they must submit an essay on Major Ridge, a major figure in Cherokee history. Selection is based on GPA, ACT score, cultural and community activities, personal academic goals, commitment to work with Cherokee people in the future, and financial need.

Financial data The stipend is $1,000 per semester ($2,000 per year).

Duration 1 year. Renewal for the second semester requires the recipient to earn a GPA of 2.5 or higher in the first semester.

Number awarded 1 each year.

Deadline March of each year.

[310]
MARATHON OIL CORPORATION COLLEGE SCHOLARSHIP PROGRAM OF THE HISPANIC SCHOLARSHIP FUND
Hispanic Scholarship Fund
Attn: Selection Committee
55 Second Street, Suite 1500
San Francisco, CA 94105
(415) 808-2365 Toll-free: (877) HSF-INFO
Fax: (415) 808-2302 E-mail: scholar1@hsf.net
Web: www.hsf.net/Scholarships.aspx?id=464

Purpose To provide financial assistance to Native American and other minority upper-division and graduate students working on a degree in a field related to the oil and gas industry.

Eligibility This program is open to U.S. citizens, permanent residents, and visitors with a passport stamped I-551 who are of Hispanic American, African American, Asian Pacific Islander American, or American Indian/Alaskan Native heritage. Applicants must be currently enrolled full time at an accredited 4-year college or university in the United States, Puerto Rico, Guam, or the U.S. Virgin Islands with a GPA of 3.0 or higher. They must be 1) sophomores majoring in chemical engineering, civil engineering, electrical engineering, mechanical engineering, petroleum engineering, geology, geophysics, accounting, marketing, global procurement or supply chain management, environmental health and safety, energy management or petroleum land management, transportation and logistics, or geotechnical engineering; or 2) seniors planning to work on a master's degree in geology or geophysics. Along with their application, they must submit 600-word essays on 1) their career interest in the oil and gas industry; 2) how they contribute to their community and what they have learned from their experiences; and 3) an academic challenge they have faced and how they have overcome it. Selection is based on academic achievement, personal qualities, community service, interest and commitment to a career in the oil and gas industry, and financial need.

Financial data The stipend is $10,000 per year.

Duration 2 years (the junior and senior undergraduate years or the first 2 years of a master's degree program).

Additional information This program is jointly sponsored by Marathon Oil Corporation and the Hispanic Scholarship Fund (HSF). Recipients may be offered a paid 8- to 10-week summer internship at various Marathon Oil Corporation locations.

Number awarded 1 or more each year.

Deadline October of each year.

[311]
MARTHA MILLER TRIBUTARY SCHOLARSHIP
Sault Tribe of Chippewa Indians
Attn: Higher Education Department
Two Ice Circle
Sault Ste. Marie, MI 49783
(906) 635-7784 Toll-free: (800) 793-0660
Fax: (906) 635-7785 E-mail: jlewton@saulttribe.net
Web: www.saulttribe.com

Purpose To provide financial assistance to members of the Sault Tribe of Chippewa Indians interested in attending college to work on a degree in human services or social work.

Eligibility This program is open to enrolled members of the Sault Tribe who have been accepted at or are attending a 2-year or 4-year college or university. Applicants must be working on or planning to work on an undergraduate degree in human services or social work. Along with their application, they must submit an essay of 300 to 500 words on how their education will benefit them and why they should receive the scholarship.

Financial data The stipend is $1,000 per year.
Duration 1 year.
Number awarded 1 each year.
Deadline May of each year.

[312]
MARTIN LUTHER KING JR. SCHOLARSHIP AWARDS

American Correctional Association
Attn: Scholarship Award Committee
206 North Washington Street, Suite 200
Alexandria, VA 22314
(703) 224-0000   Toll-free: (800) ACA-JOIN
E-mail: jenniferb@aca.org
Web: www.aca.org/pastpresentfuture/awards.asp

Purpose To provide financial assistance for undergraduate or graduate study to Native American and other minorities interested in a career in the criminal justice field.

Eligibility Members of the American Correctional Association (ACA) may nominate a minority person for these awards. Nominees do not need to be ACA members, but they must have been accepted to or be enrolled in an undergraduate or graduate program in criminal justice at a 4-year college or university. Along with the nomination package, they must submit a 250-word essay describing their reflections on the ideals and philosophies of Dr. Martin Luther King and how they have attempted to emulate those qualities in their lives. They must provide documentation of financial need, academic achievement, and commitment to the principles of Dr. King.

Financial data A stipend is awarded (amount not specified). Funds are paid directly to the recipient's college or university.
Number awarded 1 each year.
Deadline May of each year.

[313]
MARTIN OLSON MEMORIAL SCHOLARSHIP

Bering Straits Native Corporation
Attn: Bering Straits Foundation
110 Front Street, Suite 300
P.O. Box 1008
Nome, AK 99762-1008
(907) 443-4305   Toll-free: (800) 478-5079 (within AK)
Fax: (907) 443-2985
E-mail: foundation@beringstraits.com
Web: www.beringstraits.com

Purpose To provide supplemental financial assistance to Alaska Natives with ties to the Bering Straits area who are enrolled in an undergraduate or graduate program in any state.

Eligibility This program is open to Native Alaskans enrolled to the Bering Straits Native Corporation or as an "At Large" member. Applicants must be enrolled full time in an accredited institution or vocational school in any state as an undergraduate or graduate student. Along with their application, they must submit transcripts, 2 letters of recommendation, documentation of financial need, and a short personal statement outlining their career goals.

Financial data A stipend is awarded (amount not specified). Funds are paid directly to the recipient's school.
Duration 1 year; may be renewed if the recipient maintains a GPA of 2.0 or higher and full-time enrollment.
Number awarded 1 each year.
Deadline June of each year.

[314]
MARY K. MORELAND AND DANIEL T. JENKS SCHOLARSHIP

Chickasaw Foundation
110 West 12th Street
P.O. Box 1726
Ada, OK 74821-1726
(580) 421-9030   Fax: (580) 421-9031
E-mail: ChickasawFoundation@chickasaw.net
Web: www.chickasaw.net

Purpose To provide financial assistance to members of the Chickasaw Nation interested in studying education in college.

Eligibility This program is open to Chickasaw students who are currently enrolled full time as an undergraduate at an accredited 4-year college. Applicants must be majoring in education and have a GPA of 3.0 or higher. Along with their application, they must submit high school or college transcripts, 2 letters of recommendation, a copy of their Chickasaw Nation citizenship card, and a 1-page essay on their long-term goals and plans for achieving them. Financial need is not considered in the selection process.

Financial data The stipend is $2,000.
Duration 1 year.
Number awarded 1 each year.
Deadline June of each year.

[315]
MARY TINKER SCHOLARSHIP FUND

Osage Nation Education Department
Attn: Scholarship Coordinator
HC 66
P.O. Box 990
Hominy, OK 74035
(918) 287-5301   Toll-free: (800) 390-6724
Fax: (918) 287-5567   E-mail: jholding@osagetribe.com
Web: www.osagetribe.com/education/index.aspx

Purpose To provide financial assistance for college or graduate school to members of the Osage Tribe.

Eligibility This program is open to Osage tribal students who are enrolled or planning to enroll in a 2-year or 4-year college or university. A point system is used to rank applicants, including such factors as student status (freshman through graduate student), number of previous full-time semesters in college, GPA from previous semester, full-time

or part-time enrollment, qualification for federal Pell Grant, and Osage blood quantum.
Financial data The amount of the award depends on the number of points earned by the recipient.
Duration 1 semester; may be renewed.
Number awarded Varies each year.
Deadline June of each year for fall semester; December of each year for spring semester; April of each year for summer school.

[316]
MASSACHUSETTS INDIAN ASSOCIATION SCHOLARSHIP FUND

Massachusetts Indian Association
c/o Marjorie Findlay
245 Rockland Road
Carlisle, MA 01741
Fax: (978) 369-5828

Purpose To provide financial assistance for college or graduate school to Native Americans.
Eligibility Native American students anywhere in the United States may apply for these scholarships if they have a tribal number, are in good academic standing, and can demonstrate financial need.
Financial data The stipends range up to $750 for undergraduate students and $1,500 for graduate students. The funds are intended to supplement other aid by paying for books, lab fees, and other course-related expenses. Grants may be used for tuition, if necessary.
Duration 1 year; may be renewed.
Number awarded Varies each year.
Deadline September of each year.

[317]
MASSACHUSETTS NATIVE AMERICAN TUITION WAIVER PROGRAM

Massachusetts Office of Student Financial Assistance
454 Broadway, Suite 200
Revere, MA 02151
(617) 727-9420   Fax: (617) 727-0667
E-mail: osfa@osfa.mass.edu
Web: www.osfa.mass.edu

Purpose To provide financial assistance for college to Massachusetts residents who are Native Americans.
Eligibility Applicants for this assistance must have been permanent legal residents of Massachusetts for at least 1 year and certified by the Bureau of Indian Affairs as Native Americans. They may not be in default on any federal student loan.
Financial data Eligible students are exempt from any tuition payments for an undergraduate degree or certificate program at public colleges or universities in Massachusetts.
Duration Up to 4 academic years, for a total of 130 semester hours.
Additional information Recipients may enroll either part or full time in a Massachusetts publicly-supported institution.
Number awarded Varies each year.
Deadline April of each year.

[318]
MAUREEN L. AND HOWARD N. BLITMAN, P.E. SCHOLARSHIP TO PROMOTE DIVERSITY IN ENGINEERING

National Society of Professional Engineers
Attn: NSPE Educational Foundation
1420 King Street
Alexandria, VA 22314-2794
(703) 684-2833   Fax: (703) 836-4875
E-mail: education@nspe.org
Web: www.nspe.org

Purpose To provide financial assistance for college to members of Native Americans and other underrepresented minorities interested in preparing for a career in engineering.
Eligibility This program is open to members of underrepresented ethnic minorities (African Americans, Hispanics, or Native Americans) who are high school seniors accepted into an ABET-accredited engineering program at a 4-year college or university. Applicants must have a GPA of 3.5 or higher, verbal SAT score of 600 or higher, and math SAT score of 700 or higher (or English ACT score of 29 or higher and math ACT score of 29 or higher). They must submit brief essays on an experience they consider significant to their interest in engineering, how their study of engineering will contribute to their long-term career plans, how their ethnic background has influenced their personal development and perceptions, and anything special about them that they would like the selection committee to know. Financial need is not considered in the selection process. U.S. citizenship is required.
Financial data The stipend is $5,000 per year; funds are paid directly to the recipient's institution.
Duration 1 year; nonrenewable.
Number awarded 1 each year.
Deadline February of each year.

[319]
MENOMINEE INDIAN TRIBAL SCHOLARSHIPS

Menominee Indian Tribe of Wisconsin
Attn: Tribal Education Office
P.O. Box 910
Keshena, WI 54135
(715) 799-5110   Fax: (715) 799-5102
E-mail: vnuske@mitw.org
Web: menominee-nsn.gov

Purpose To provide financial assistance for college or graduate school to Menominee Indians.
Eligibility This program is open to enrolled members of the Menominee Indian Tribe of Wisconsin who are graduating high school seniors, undergraduates at 4-year colleges and universities, technical college students, or graduate students. Applicants must submit an essay of 1 to 2 pages on how their education will benefit them, including their community service and extracurricular activities. The essay should not discuss financial need, because the selection committee assumes that all students have financial need. Selection is based on the essay (30 points), a letter of support (5 points), and GPA (15 points if 3.5 or higher, 10 points if 3.00 to 3.49, or 5 points if 2.0 to 2.99).
Financial data The stipend is $500 per semester ($1,000 per year). Funds are sent directly to the recipient's school.

Duration Up to 10 semesters.
Number awarded 4 each year: 1 to each category of student.
Deadline March of each year.

[320]
MENOMINEE INDIAN TRIBE ADULT VOCATIONAL TRAINING PROGRAM
Menominee Indian Tribe of Wisconsin
Attn: Tribal Education Office
P.O. Box 910
Keshena, WI 54135
(715) 799-5110   Fax: (715) 799-5102
E-mail: vnuske@mitw.org
Web: menominee-nsn.gov

Purpose To provide financial assistance to Menominee Indians who are interested in a program of vocational training.
Eligibility This program is open to adult enrolled members of the Menominee Indian Tribe of Wisconsin who are working on an associate degree, certificate, or technical college diploma. Applicants must be able to demonstrate financial need.
Financial data A stipend is awarded (amount not specified).
Duration The maximum training period for Adult Vocational Training students is 24 months. Training for nursing is 36 months. Renewal awards require the student to maintain a minimum GPA of 2.0 and to carry at least 12 credits per term.
Additional information Part-time study is not supported under this program.
Deadline February of each year.

[321]
MERCER DIVERSITY SCHOLARSHIP PROGRAM
Mercer Human Resource Consulting LLC
1166 Avenue of the Americas
New York, NY 10036
(212) 345-7000   Fax: (212) 345-7414
Web: www.mercerhr.com/diversityscholarship

Purpose To provide financial assistance and work experience to Native American and other minority undergraduates working on a degree in selected business-related fields.
Eligibility This program is open to students who identify as Hispanic or Latino, Black or African American, Native Hawaiian or other Pacific Islander, American Indian, Alaska Native, or Asian. Applicants must be sophomores or juniors and either have a GPA of at least 3.25 or rank in the top 5% of their class (if their school uses a ranking system). They must be working on a degree in actuarial sciences, mathematics, statistics, business, economics, finance, or liberal arts and sciences. Along with their application, they must submit a 1-page essay on why they are interested in Mercer Human Resource Consulting and the unique skills they can contribute. If a summer internship at Mercer is available, they must be willing to accept it. Selection is based on academic achievement, campus and community involvement, and a writing sample. Finalists are interviewed.
Financial data The stipend is $5,000 per year. A paid summer internship may also be offered.
Duration 1 year; may be renewed, provided the recipients accept a summer internship if offered, maintain a GPA of at least 3.25 or rank in the top 5% of their class, and act as an ambassador for Mercer at their school.
Number awarded Up to 20 each year.
Deadline December of each year.

[322]
MESBEC PROGRAM
Catching the Dream
8200 Mountain Road, N.E., Suite 203
Albuquerque, NM 87110-7835
(505) 262-2351   Fax: (505) 262-0534
E-mail: NScholarsh@aol.com
Web: www.catchingthedream.org/Scholarship.htm

Purpose To provide financial assistance to American Indian students who are interested in working on an undergraduate or graduate degree in selected fields.
Eligibility This program is open to American Indians who can provide proof that they have at least one-quarter Indian blood and are a member of a U.S. tribe that is federally-recognized, state-recognized, or terminated. Applicants must be enrolled or planning to enroll full time and major in the 1 of the following fields: mathematics, engineering, science (including medicine), business administration, education, or computer science. They may be entering freshmen, undergraduate students, graduate students, or Ph.D. candidates. Along with their application, they must submit documentation of financial need, 3 letters of recommendation, copies of applications and responses from all other sources of funding for which they are eligible, official transcripts, standardized test scores (ACT, SAT, GRE, MCAT, LSAT, etc.), and an essay explaining their goals in life, college plans, and career plans (especially how those plans include working with and benefiting Indians). Selection is based on merit and potential for improving the lives of Indian people.
Financial data Stipends range from $500 to $5,000 per year.
Duration 1 year; may be renewed.
Additional information MESBEC is an acronym that stands for the priority areas of this program: mathematics, engineering, science, business, education, and computers. The sponsor was formerly known as the Native American Scholarship Fund.
Number awarded Varies; generally, 30 to 35 each year.
Deadline April of each year for fall term; September of each year for spring and winter terms; March of each year for summer school.

[323]
MESCALERO APACHE TRIBAL SCHOLARSHIP
Mescalero Apache Tribe
Attn: Tribal Education Department
P.O. Box 176
Mescalero, NM 88340
(505) 671-4494   Fax: (505) 671-4454

Purpose To provide financial assistance for undergraduate or graduate education to members of the Mescalero Apache Tribe.

Eligibility This program is open to enrolled members of the Mescalero Apache Tribe who are high school seniors, high school graduates, or currently-enrolled undergraduate or graduate students. Applicants must have a GPA of 2.0 or higher, Financial need is considered in the selection process.
Financial data The amount awarded varies, up to $8,000 per year.
Duration 1 year; may be renewed for up to 3 additional years.
Number awarded Varies each year.
Deadline May of each year for the fall term; October for the spring term.

[324]
MICHAEL J. BERKELEY FOUNDATION SCHOLARSHIPS

Michael J. Berkeley Foundation
Attn: Scholarship Committee
28 High Ridge Road
P.O. Box 724
Mt. Kisco, NY 10549
(914) 244-1668
E-mail: scholarships@mikebfoundation.org
Web: www.mikebfoundation.org/scholarships.html

Purpose To provide financial assistance for college to Native American and other minority students who have been involved in golf.
Eligibility This program is open to full-time undergraduate students of color who are enrolled or planning to enroll at an accredited college or university. Applicants must have been involved in the game of golf. Along with their application, they must submit 2 essays: 1 on the aspect of the life and legacy of Michael J. Berkeley that impacted them the most and 1 on their choice of other topics related to their involvement in golf. Selection is based on the essays, academic achievement, extracurricular and community involvement, leadership and team skills, commendations, honors, letters of recommendation, financial need, written communication skills, and verbal communication skills as demonstrated in a telephone interview.
Financial data The stipend is $3,000 per year.
Duration 1 year; may be renewed.
Additional information These scholarships, first awarded in 2003, are provided in memory of a victim of the September 11, 2001 attack on the World Trade Center.
Number awarded Varies each year; recently, 10 new and 10 renewal scholarships were awarded.
Deadline April of each year.

[325]
MICHIGAN INDIAN ELDERS ASSOCIATION SCHOLARSHIP

Michigan Indian Elders Association
c/o Robert S. Menard, President
1910 North Lake Drive
Ishpeming, MI 49849
(906) 485-5364   Fax: (906) 485-5364
E-mail: menard@chartermi.net
Web: www.michiganindianelders.org

Purpose To provide financial assistance to members of constituent tribes and bands of the Michigan Indian Elders Association (MIEA) who are interested in attending college in any state.
Eligibility This program is open to enrolled members of the 11 MIEA constituent tribes and bands and their direct descendants. Applicants must be 1) graduating high school seniors who have a GPA of 3.0 or higher; 2) students currently enrolled in college, university, or trade school who have a GPA of 3.0 or higher; or 3) holders of a GED certificate who passed all 5 GED equivalency tests with a minimum score of at least 40 and an average score of at least 45. They must be attending or planning to attend a public college, university, or trade school in any state as a full-time student. Financial need is not considered in the selection process.
Financial data Stipends are $1,000 or $500.
Duration 1 year.
Additional information The constituent tribes and bands are the Bay Mills Indian Community, Grand Traverse Band of Ottawa and Chippewa Indians, Hannahville Band of Potawatomi Indians, Keweenaw Bay Indian Community, Lac View Desert Band of Law Superior Chippewa Indians, Little River Band of Ottawa Indians, Little Traverse Bay Band of Odawa Indians, Match-E-Be-Nash-She-Wish Band of Potawatomi Indians, Pokagon Band of Potawatomi Indians, Saginaw Chippewa Indian Tribe, and Sault Ste. Marie Tribe of Chippewa Indians.
Number awarded Up to 8 each year, including 1 at $1,000 and at least 4 at $500.
Deadline June of each year.

[326]
MICHIGAN INDIAN TUITION WAIVER PROGRAM

Inter-Tribal Council of Michigan, Inc.
Attn: Michigan Indian Tuition Waiver
2956 Ashmun Street
Sault Ste. Marie, MI 49783-3720'
(906) 632-6896   Toll-free: (800) 562-4957
Fax: (906) 632-1810   E-mail: christin@itcmi.org
Web: www.itcmi.org/ituition.html

Purpose To exempt members of Indian tribes from tuition at Michigan postsecondary institutions.
Eligibility This program is open to Michigan residents who have lived in the state for at least 12 months and can certify at least one-quarter North American Indian blood from a federally-recognized or state historic tribe. Applicants must be attending a public college, university, or community college in Michigan. The program includes full- and part-time study, academic-year and summer school, and undergraduate and graduate work.

Financial data All qualified applicants are entitled to waiver of tuition at Michigan public institutions.
Duration Indian students are entitled to the waiver as long as they attend college in Michigan.
Additional information This program was established in 1976 as the result of an agreement between the state of Michigan and the federal government under which the state agreed to provide free tuition to North American Indians in exchange for the Mt. Pleasant Indian School, which the state acquired as a training facility for the developmentally disabled.
Number awarded Varies each year.

[327]
MICKEY WILLIAMS MINORITY STUDENT SCHOLARSHIPS

Society of Nuclear Medicine
Attn: Grants and Awards
1850 Samuel Morse Drive
Reston, VA 20190-5316
(703) 708-9000, ext. 1255   Fax: (703) 708-9020
E-mail: grantinfo@snm.org
Web: interactive.snm.org

Purpose To provide financial support to Native American and other minority students working on an associate or bachelor's degree in nuclear medicine technology.
Eligibility This program is open to students accepted or enrolled in a baccalaureate or associate degree program in nuclear medicine technology. Applicants must be members of a minority group: African American, Native American (including American Indian, Eskimo, Hawaiian, and Samoan), Hispanic American, Asian American, or Pacific Islander. They must have a cumulative GPA of 2.5 or higher and be able to demonstrate financial need. Along with their application, they must submit an essay on their reasons for entering the nuclear medicine technology field, their career goals, and their financial need. U.S. citizenship or permanent resident status is required.
Financial data The stipend is $5,000.
Duration 1 year; may be renewed for 1 additional year.
Additional information This program is supported by corporate sponsors of the Professional Development and Education Fund (PDEF) of the Society of Nuclear Medicine Technologist Section.
Number awarded Varies each year; recently, 3 of these scholarships were awarded.
Deadline October of each year.

[328]
MICROSOFT NATIONAL SCHOLARSHIPS

Microsoft Corporation
Attn: Microsoft Scholarship Program
One Microsoft Way
Redmond, WA 98052-8303
(425) 882-8080   TTY: (800) 892-9811
E-mail: scholars@microsoft.com
Web: www.microsoft.com/college/ss_overview.mspx

Purpose To provide financial assistance and summer work experience to undergraduate students, especially members of underrepresented groups, interested in preparing for a career in computer science or other related technical fields.
Eligibility This program is open to students who are enrolled full time and making satisfactory progress toward an undergraduate degree in computer science, computer engineering, or a related technical discipline (such as electrical engineering, mathematics, or physics) with a demonstrated interest in computer science. Applicants must be enrolled at a 4-year college or university in the United States, Canada, or Mexico. They must have a GPA of 3.0 or higher. Although all students who meet the eligibility criteria may apply, a large majority of scholarships are awarded to women, underrepresented minorities (African Americans, Hispanics, and Native Americans), and students with disabilities. Along with their application, students must submit an essay that describes the following 4 items: 1) how they demonstrate their passion for technology outside the classroom; 2) the toughest technical problem they have worked on, how they addressed the problem, their role in reaching the outcome if it was team-based, and the final outcome; 3) a situation that demonstrates initiative and their willingness to go above and beyond; and 4) how they are currently funding their college education.
Financial data Scholarships cover 100% of the tuition as posted by the financial aid office of the university or college the recipient designates. Scholarships are made through that school and are not transferable to other academic institutions. Funds may be used for tuition only and may not be used for other costs on the recipient's bursar bill, such as room and board.
Duration 1 year.
Additional information Selected recipients are offered a paid summer internship where they will have a chance to develop Microsoft products.
Number awarded Varies each year; a total of $540,000 is available for this program annually.
Deadline January of each year.

[329]
MILLE LACS BAND SCHOLARSHIP PROGRAM

Mille Lacs Band of Ojibwe
Attn: Higher Education Office
43408 Oodena Avenue
Onamia, MN 56359-2236
(320) 532-7508   Toll-free: (800) 532-9059
Fax: (320) 532-3785
E-mail: mlbsp@MilleLacsOjibwe.nsn.us
Web: www.millelacsojibwe.org/scholarship.asp

Purpose To provide financial assistance for college to members of the Mille Lacs Band of Ojibwe.
Eligibility This program is open to enrolled members of the band, their non-enrolled biological children, and legally adopted children of enrolled band members. Applicants may be attending a 2-year college, 4-year college, or vocational/technical school. Financial need is required. Applicants for this program must also apply for financial aid administered by their institution and any other aid for which they may be eligible (e.g., work-study, Social Security, veteran's benefits).
Financial data This program provides a stipend of up to $6,000 per year and an allowance of up to $375 per semester for books and supplies.

Duration Students at 2-year institutions are eligible for 8 quarters or 5 semesters of support; students at 4-year institutions are allowed 15 quarters or 10 semesters to complete their program.
Number awarded Varies each year.
Deadline For vocational school students, at least 8 weeks before school starts; for college or university students, June of each year.

[330]
MILLENNIUM SCHOLARSHIP PROGRAM OF THE CHICKASAW NATION

Chickasaw Nation
Attn: Department of Education Services
122 East Main
Ada, OK 74820
(580) 421-7711   Fax: (580) 436-3733
E-mail: education.services@chickasaw.net
Web: www.chickasaweducationservices.com

Purpose To provide financial assistance for college to graduating high school seniors who are members of the Chickasaw Nation.
Eligibility This program is open to members of the Chickasaw Nation who are graduating from high school with a GPA of 2.5 or higher. Applicants must submit a copy of their Chickasaw Nation citizenship card, high school transcripts, documentation of financial need, and an essay of 500 to 600 words on their past accomplishments, future goals, travel involvement, and community involvement.
Financial data The stipend is $1,000.
Duration 1 year; nonrenewable.
Number awarded Up to 50 each year.
Deadline March of each year.

[331]
MINNESOTA INDIAN SCHOLARSHIP PROGRAM

Minnesota Office of Higher Education
Attn: Manager of State Financial Aid Programs
1450 Energy Park Drive, Suite 350
St. Paul, MN 55108-5227
(651) 642-0567   Toll-free: (800) 657-3866
Fax: (651) 642-0675   TTY: (800) 627-3529
E-mail: Ginny.Dodds@state.mn.us
Web: www.ohe.state.mn.us

Purpose To provide financial assistance to Native Americans in Minnesota who are interested in working on an undergraduate or graduate degree in any field.
Eligibility Applicants must be at least one-fourth degree Indian ancestry; members of a recognized Indian tribe; at least high school graduates (or approved equivalent); accepted by an accredited college, university, or vocational school in Minnesota; and residents of Minnesota for at least 1 year. They must be attending college or graduate school at least three-fourths time.
Financial data The stipend depends on need, to a maximum of $4,000 per year for undergraduates or $6,600 per year for graduate students. Awards are paid directly to the student's school or college.
Duration 1 year; may be renewed up to 4 additional years, provided the recipient maintains a GPA of 2.0 or higher and sends official grade transcripts to the office for review after each quarter or semester.
Number awarded Approximately 700 each year.
Deadline June of each year.

[332]
MINORITIES IN GOVERNMENT FINANCE SCHOLARSHIP

Government Finance Officers Association
Attn: Scholarship Committee
203 North LaSalle Street, Suite 2700
Chicago, IL 60601-1210
(312) 977-9700   Fax: (312) 977-4806
Web: www.gfoa.org

Purpose To provide financial assistance to Native American and other minority upper-division and graduate students who are preparing for a career in state and local government finance.
Eligibility This program is open to upper-division and graduate students who are preparing for a career in public finance with a major in public administration, accounting, finance, political science, economics, or business administration (with a specific focus on government or nonprofit management). Applicants must be members of a minority group, citizens or permanent residents of the United States or Canada, and able to provide a letter of recommendation from a representative of their school. Selection is based on career plans, academic record, plan of study, letters of recommendation, and GPA. Financial need is not considered.
Financial data The stipend is $5,000.
Duration 1 year.
Additional information This program defines minorities as Black or African Americans, American Indians or Alaskan Natives, Hispanics or Latinos, Native Hawaiians or other Pacific Islanders, or Asians.
Number awarded 1 or more each year.
Deadline February of each year.

[333]
MINORITY ENTREPRENEURS SCHOLARSHIP PROGRAM

International Franchise Association
Attn: Director of Diversity Initiatives Educational Foundation
1501 K Street, N.W., Suite 350
Washington, DC 20005
(202) 662-0784   Fax: (202) 628-0812
E-mail: mbrewer@franchise.org
Web: www.franchise.org/files/Scholarships.aspx

Purpose To provide financial assistance to Native American and other minority students and adult entrepreneurs enrolled in academic or professional development programs related to franchising.
Eligibility This program is open to 1) college students enrolled at an accredited college or university, and 2) adult entrepreneurs who have at least 5 years of business ownership or managerial experience. Applicants must be members of a minority group (defined as African Americans, American Indians, Hispanic Americans, and Asian Americans). Students should be enrolled in courses or programs relating to business, finance, marketing, hospitality,

franchising, or entrepreneurship. Adult entrepreneurs should be enrolled in professional development courses related to franchising, such as those recognized by the Institute of Certified Franchise Executives (ICFE).
Financial data The stipend is $3,000.
Duration 1 year.
Additional information This award is cosponsored by the IFA Educational Foundation and Marriott International.
Number awarded 5 each year.

[334]
MINORITY NURSE MAGAZINE SCHOLARSHIP PROGRAM
Minority Nurse Magazine
Attn: Career Recruitment Media
211 West Wacker Drive, Suite 900
Chicago, IL 60606
(312) 525-3095   Fax: (312) 429-3336
E-mail: pchwedyk@alloyeducation.com
Web: www.minoritynurse.com

Purpose To provide financial assistance to Native Americans and other minorities who are working on a bachelor's or master's degree in nursing.
Eligibility This program is open to minority nursing students currently enrolled in 1) the third or fourth year of an accredited B.S.N. program; 2) an accelerated program leading to a B.S.N. degree (e.g., R.N. to B.S.N., B.A. to B.S.N.); or 3) an accelerated master's entry nursing program (e.g., R.N. to M.S.N., B.S. to M.S.N.). Along with their application, they must submit a 250-word essay on their academic and personal accomplishments, community service, and goals for their future nursing career. Selection is based on academic excellence (GPA of 3.0 or higher), demonstrated commitment of service to the student's minority community, and financial need. U.S. citizenship of permanent resident status is required.
Financial data The stipends are $1,000 or $500.
Duration 1 year.
Additional information These scholarships were first offered in 2000. Winners are announced in the fall issue of *Minority Nurse* magazine.
Number awarded 4 each year: 2 at $1,000 and 2 at $500.
Deadline June of each year.

[335]
MINORITY SCHOLARSHIP AWARD FOR ACADEMIC EXCELLENCE IN PHYSICAL THERAPY
American Physical Therapy Association
Attn: Department of Minority/International Affairs
1111 North Fairfax Street
Alexandria, VA 22314-1488
(703) 706-3143   Toll-free: (800) 999-APTA, ext. 3143
Fax: (703) 706-8519   TDD: (703) 683-6748
E-mail: min-intl@apta.org
Web: www.apta.org

Purpose To provide financial assistance to Native American and other minority students who are interested in becoming a physical therapist or physical therapy assistant.
Eligibility This program is open to U.S. citizens and permanent residents who are members of the following minority groups: African American or Black, Asian, Native Hawaiian or other Pacific Islander, American Indian or Alaska Native, or Hispanic/Latino. Applicants must be in the final year of a professional physical therapy or physical therapy assistant education program. They must submit a personal essay outlining their professional goals and minority service. U.S. citizenship or permanent resident status is required. Selection is based on 1) demonstrated evidence of contributions in the area of minority affairs and services with an emphasis on contributions made while enrolled in a physical therapy program; 2) potential to contribute to the profession of physical therapy; and 3) scholastic achievement.
Financial data The stipend varies; recently, minimum awards were $6,000 for physical therapy students or $3,000 for physical therapy assistant students.
Duration 1 year.
Number awarded Varies each year. Recently, 12 of these awards were granted: 11 to professional physical therapy students and 1 to a physical therapy assistant student.
Deadline November of each year.

[336]
MINORITY SCHOLARSHIP IN CLASSICS AND CLASSICAL ARCHAEOLOGY
American Philological Association
Attn: Executive Director
University of Pennsylvania
292 Logan Hall
249 South 36th Street
Philadelphia, PA 19104-6304
(215) 898-4975   Fax: (215) 573-7874
E-mail: apaclassics@sas.upenn.edu
Web: www.apaclassics.org

Purpose To prepare Native American and other minority undergraduates during the summer for advanced work in the classics or classical archaeology.
Eligibility Eligible to apply are minority (African American, Hispanic American, Asian American, and Native American) undergraduate students who wish to engage in summer study as preparation for graduate work in the classics or classical archaeology. Applicants may propose participation in summer programs in Italy, Greece, Egypt, or other classical centers; language training at institutions in the United States or Canada; or other relevant courses of study. Selection is based on academic qualifications, especially in classics; demonstrated ability in at least 1 classical language; quality of the proposal for study with respect to preparation for a career in classics; and financial need. Applications must be endorsed by a member of the American Philological Association (APA) or the Archaeological Institute of American (AIA).
Financial data The maximum award is $3,000.
Duration 1 summer.
Additional information This program is offered jointly by the APA and the AIA. Information is also available from the AIA, c/o Boston University, 656 Beacon Street, Sixth Floor, Boston, MA 02215-2006, (617) 358-4184, Fax: (617 353-6550, E-mail: fellowships@aia.bu.edu.
Number awarded 2 each year.
Deadline December of each year.

[337]
MISHKOSWIN (STRENGTH) SCHOLARSHIP PROGRAM

Indigenous Early Intervention Alliance
Attn: Office of American Indian Projects
411 North Central Avenue, Suite 880M
Phoenix, AZ 85004
(602) 496-0102
E-mail: mdniles@indigenous-early-intervention.com
Web: indigenous-early-intervention.com

Purpose To provide financial assistance for college or graduate school to members of American Indian tribes.

Eligibility This program is open to enrolled members of any tribe who are working on or planning to work on an undergraduate or graduate degree at a college or university. Applicants must have demonstrated "courage, bravery, and dedication to their college education." Along with their application, they must submit a short essay on their plans following graduation from college. Preference is given to students who 1) are residing on their reservation at the time of application, and 2) plan to return to their tribe following college graduation.

Financial data A stipend is awarded (amount not specified).

Duration 1 year; nonrenewable.

Number awarded 1 each year.

Deadline August of each year.

[338]
MISS INDIAN USA SCHOLARSHIP PROGRAM

American Indian Heritage Foundation
P.O. Box 750
Pigeon Forge, TN 37868
(703) 819-0979   E-mail: MissIndianUSA@indians.org
Web: www.indians.org/catalog/our_programs.php

Purpose To recognize and reward the most beautiful and talented Indian women.

Eligibility American Indian women between the ages of 18 and 26 are eligible to enter this national contest if they are high school graduates and have never been married, cohabited with the opposite sex, been pregnant, or had children. U.S. citizenship is required. Selection is based on public appearance (20%), a traditional interview (15%), a contemporary interview (15%), beauty of spirit (15%), a cultural presentation (10%), scholastic achievement (10%), a platform question (10%), and a finalist question (5%).

Financial data Awards vary each year. Recently, Miss Indian USA received an academic scholarship of $4,000 plus a cash grant of $6,500, a wardrobe allowance of $2,000, appearance fees of $3,000, a professional photo shoot worth $500, gifts worth more than $4,000, honoring gifts worth more than $2,000, promotional materials worth more than $2,000, and travel to Washington, D.C. with a value of approximately $2,000; the total value of the prize was more than $26,000. Members of her court received scholarships of $2,000 for the first runner-up, $1,500 for the second runner-up, $1,000 for the third runner-up, and $500 for the fourth runner-up.

Duration This competition is held annually.

Additional information The program involves a week-long competition in the Washington, D.C. metropolitan area that includes seminars, interviews, cultural presentations, and many public appearances. The application fee is $100 if submitted prior to mid-April or $200 if submitted later. In addition, a candidate fee of $750 is required.

Number awarded 1 winner and 4 runners-up are selected each year.

Deadline May of each year.

[339]
MOHAWK HIGHER EDUCATION PROGRAM

St. Regis Mohawk Tribe
Attn: Roderick A. Cook, Higher Education
Community Building
412 State Route 37
Hogansburg, NY 13655-3109
(518) 358-2272, ext. 215   Toll-free: (800) 800-8679
Fax: (518) 358-3203   E-mail: rcook@srmt-nsn.gov
Web: srmt-nsn.gov/pgm_03_03.htm

Purpose To provide financial assistance for college to members of the St. Regis Mohawk Tribe.

Eligibility This program is open to members of the St. Regis Mohawk Tribe who are enrolled full time in an accredited 2- or 4-year college degree program. Applicants must be able to demonstrate unmet financial need after receipt of all other financial aid (e.g., federal Pell Grants, New York TAP Awards). First priority is given to enrolled members who live on the reservation, second to enrolled members who live near the reservation, and third to one-quarter degree descendants of enrolled members. Awards are presented on a first-come, first-served basis.

Financial data The stipend depends on the need of the recipient.

Duration 1 year; may be renewed as long as the recipient maintains a GPA of 2.0 or higher as a freshman or 2.5 or higher afterwards.

Additional information This program has been in operation since 1986.

Number awarded Varies each year.

Deadline July of each year for fall or academic year; October of each year for spring.

[340]
MONTANA AMERICAN INDIAN STUDENT WAIVER

Montana Guaranteed Student Loan Program
2500 Broadway
P.O. Box 203101
Helena, MT 59620-3101
(406) 444-6570   Toll-free: (800) 537-7508
Fax: (406) 444-1869
E-mail: scholarships@mgslp.state.mt.us
Web: www.mgslp.state.mt.us

Purpose To provide financial assistance to Montana Indians interested in attending college or graduate school in the state.

Eligibility Eligible to apply are Native American students (one-quarter Indian blood or more) who have been residents of Montana for at least 1 year prior to application, have graduated from an accredited high school or federal Indian school, and can demonstrate financial need.

Financial data Students eligible for this benefit are entitled to attend any unit of the Montana University System

without payment of undergraduate or graduate registration or incidental fees.
Duration Students are eligible for continued fee waiver as long as they maintain reasonable academic progress and full-time status (12 or more credits for undergraduates, 9 or more credits for graduate students).
Number awarded Varies; more than $1 million in waivers are approved each year.

[341]
MORGAN STANLEY SCHOLARS PROGRAM
American Indian College Fund
Attn: Scholarship Department
8333 Greenwood Boulevard
Denver, CO 80221
(303) 426-8900   Toll-free: (800) 776-FUND
Fax: (303) 426-1200   E-mail: info@collegefund.org
Web: www.collegefund.org

Purpose To provide financial assistance to American Indian students at mainstream 4-year institutions who are preparing for a career in the business and financial services industry.
Eligibility Eligible to apply are American Indians or Alaska Natives who are currently enrolled full time in a 4-year degree program at a mainstream institution in the United States and are interested in preparing for a career in the financial services industry (e.g., information technology, investment banking, investment management, marketing, branch operations, financial advising, financial accounting, credit card services). Applicants must have a GPA of 3.0 or higher and be able to demonstrate financial need. Along with their application, they must submit 1) short essays (up to 500 words each) on how they perceive themselves as leaders in their school or community and how their education will help the Native American community; and 2) a personal statement of 1,000 words that includes their personal background, their academic background, their educational and career goals, and how this scholarship will help them achieve those goals.
Financial data The stipend is $10,000.
Duration 1 year.
Additional information This scholarship is sponsored by Morgan Stanley, in partnership with the American Indian College Fund. Selected students may also be considered for internship opportunities with Morgan Stanley.
Number awarded 5 each year.
Deadline May of each year.

[342]
MORGAN STANLEY TRIBAL SCHOLARS PROGRAM
American Indian College Fund
Attn: Scholarship Department
8333 Greenwood Boulevard
Denver, CO 80221
(303) 426-8900   Toll-free: (800) 776-FUND
Fax: (303) 426-1200   E-mail: info@collegefund.org
Web: www.collegefund.org

Purpose To provide financial assistance to Native American students currently enrolled full time at a Tribal College or University (TCU) to prepare for a career in business and the financial services industry.
Eligibility This program is open to American Indians and Alaska Natives who are enrolled full time at an eligible TCU. Applicants must have a GPA of 3.0 or higher and be able to demonstrate financial need. They must be interested in a career in business and the financial services industry (e.g., information technology, investment banking, investment management, marketing, branch operations, financial advising, financial accounting, credit card services). Along with their application, they must submit 1) short essays (up to 500 words each) on how they perceive themselves as leaders in their school or community and how their education will help the Native American community; and 2) a personal statement of 1,000 words that includes their personal background, their academic background, their educational and career goals, and how this scholarship will help them achieve those goals.
Financial data The stipend is $2,500.
Duration 1 year.
Additional information This scholarship is sponsored by Morgan Stanley, in partnership with the American Indian College Fund.
Number awarded 10 each year.
Deadline May of each year.

[343]
MORRIS K. UDALL SCHOLARSHIPS
Morris K. Udall Foundation
Attn: Program Manager, Scholarship Program
130 South Scott Avenue
Tucson, AZ 85701-1922
(520) 901-8562   Fax: (520) 670-5530
E-mail: millage@udall.gov
Web: www.udall.gov/udall.asp?link=200

Purpose To provide financial assistance to 1) college sophomores and juniors who intend to prepare for a career in environmental public policy and 2) Native American and Alaska Native students who intend to prepare for a career in health care or tribal public policy.
Eligibility Each 2-year and 4-year college and university in the United States and its possessions may nominate up to 6 sophomores or juniors for either or both categories of this program: 1) students who intend to prepare for a career in environmental public policy, and 2) Native American and Alaska Native students who intend to prepare for a career in health care or tribal public policy. For the first category, the program seeks future leaders across a wide spectrum of environmental fields, such as policy, engineering, science, education, urban planning and renewal, business, health, justice, and economics. For the second category, the program seeks future Native American and Alaska Native leaders in public and community health care, tribal government, and public policy affecting Native American communities, including land and resource management, economic development, and education. Nominees must be U.S. citizens, nationals, or permanent residents with a GPA of 3.0 or higher. Along with their application, they must submit an 800-word essay discussing a significant public speech, legislative act, or public policy statement by former Congressman Morris K. Udall and its impact on their field of study, interests, and career goals. Selection is based on demonstrated commitment to 1) environmental issues through substantial commitment to and participation in 1 or

more of the following: campus activities, research, community service, or public service; or 2) tribal public policy or Native American health through substantial contributions to and participation in 1 or more of the following: campus activities, tribal involvement, community or public service, or research; a course of study and proposed career likely to lead to positions where the nominee can make significant contributions to the shaping of environmental, tribal public policy, or Native American health care issues, whether through scientific advances, public or political service, or community action; and leadership, character, desire to make a difference, and general well-roundedness.
Financial data The maximum stipend for scholarship winners is $5,000 per year. Funds are to be used for tuition, fees, books, and room and board. Honorable mention stipends are $350.
Duration 1 year; recipients nominated as sophomores may be renominated in their junior year.
Number awarded Approximately 80 scholarships and 50 honorable mentions are awarded each year.
Deadline Faculty representatives must submit their nominations by early March of each year.

[344]
MUTUAL OF OMAHA ACTUARIAL SCHOLARSHIP FOR MINORITY STUDENTS
Mutual of Omaha
Attn: Strategic Staffing-Actuarial Recruitment
Mutual of Omaha Plaza
Omaha, NE 68175
(402) 351-3300
Web: www.mutualofomaha.com

Purpose To provide financial assistance and work experience to Native American and other minority undergraduate students who are preparing for an actuarial career.
Eligibility This program is open to members of minority groups (African American, Hispanic, Native American, Asian or Pacific Islander, or Alaskan Eskimo) who have completed at least 24 semester hours of full-time study. Applicants must be working on an actuarial or mathematics-related degree with the goal of preparing for an actuarial career. They must have a GPA of 3.0 or higher and have passed at least 1 actuarial examination. Prior to accepting the award, they must be available to complete a summer internship at the sponsor's home office in Omaha, Nebraska. Along with their application, they must submit a 1-page personal statement on why they are interested in becoming an actuary and how they are preparing themselves for an actuarial career.
Financial data The scholarship stipend is $2,500 per year. Funds are paid directly to the student. For the internship, students receive an hourly rate of pay, subsidized housing, and financial incentives for successful examination results received during the internship period.
Duration 1 year. Recipients may reapply if they maintain a cumulative GPA of 3.0 or higher.
Number awarded Varies each year.
Deadline January of each year.

[345]
MYAAMIA SCHOLARSHIP
Miami Nation
Attn: Education Committee
202 South Eight Tribes Trail
P.O. Box 1326
Miami, OK 74355
(918) 542-1445   Fax: (918) 542-7260
E-mail: edu@miamination.com
Web: www.miamination.com

Purpose To provide financial assistance for college to high school seniors who are enrolled members of the Miami Tribe of Oklahoma.
Eligibility This program is open to graduating high school seniors who are enrolled members of the Miami Tribe of Oklahoma. Applicants must have a GPA of 3.0 or higher and be planning to attend a college or university as a full-time student. Along with their application, they must submit a high school transcript or equivalent (GED), 3 letters of recommendation, documentation of financial need, and a 1-page essay with the title, "Tell Us About Yourself."
Financial data The stipend is $1,000 per semester.
Duration 1 semester; may be renewed up to 7 additional semesters if the recipient remains enrolled full time with a college GPA of 3.0 or higher.
Number awarded Only 10 students may be receiving this scholarship at any given time.
Deadline April of each year.

[346]
MYRON AND LAURA THOMPSON SCHOLARSHIP
Ke Ali'i Pauahi Foundation
Attn: Financial Aid & Scholarship Services
567 South King Street, Suite 160
Honolulu, HI 96813
(808) 534-3966   Toll-free: (800) 842-4682, ext. 43966
Fax: (808) 534-3890   E-mail: scholarships@pauahi.org
Web: www.pauahi.org

Purpose To provide financial assistance to undergraduate or graduate students, especially those of Hawaiian descent, working on a degree in early childhood education.
Eligibility This program is open to full-time undergraduate and graduate students working on a degree in early childhood education. Applicants must be able to demonstrate financial need; an interest in the Hawaiian language, culture, history, and values; and commitment to contribute to the greater community. Preference is given to Native Hawaiians (descendants of the aboriginal inhabitants of the Hawaiian Islands prior to 1778) and students who demonstrate an interest in working with Hawaiian children in Hawaii after completion of their education.
Financial data A stipend is awarded (amount not specified).
Duration 1 year.
Number awarded 1 each year.
Deadline April each year.

[347]
NAAJ SCHOLARSHIPS

Native American Journalists Association
c/o University of Oklahoma
Gaylord College
395 West Lindsey
Norman, OK 73019-0001
(405) 325-9008   Fax: (405) 325-7565
E-mail: info@naja.com
Web: www.naja.com

Purpose To provide financial assistance to student members of the Native American Journalists Association (NAJA) who are interested in a career in journalism or journalism education.

Eligibility This program is open to NAJA members who are high school seniors, undergraduates, or graduate students working on or planning to work on a degree in journalism. Applicants must include proof of enrollment in a federal- or state-recognized tribe; work samples; transcripts; a personal statement that demonstrates financial need, area of interest (print, broadcast, photojournalism, new media, journalism education), and the student's reasons for preparing for a career in journalism; and 3 letters of recommendation.

Financial data The stipends range from $500 to $5,000.

Duration 1 year.

Additional information Support for this program is provided by GMAC, the James M. Cox Foundation, the Samuel I. Newhouse Foundation, *The Arizona Republic*, and CNN.

Number awarded Varies each year; recently, 10 of these scholarships were awarded.

Deadline March of each year.

[348]
NACME PRE-ENGINEERING STUDENT SCHOLARSHIPS

National Action Council for Minorities in Engineering
440 Hamilton Avenue, Suite 302
White Plains, NY 10601-1813
(914) 539-4010   Fax: (914) 539-4032
Web: www.nacme.org

Purpose To provide financial assistance to Native American and other underrepresented minority high school seniors interested in studying engineering in college.

Eligibility This program is open to African American, Latino, and American Indian high school seniors planning to attend an engineering school. Applicants must have demonstrated academic excellence, leadership skills, and a commitment to science and engineering as a career.

Financial data The stipend is $1,500.

Duration 1 year.

Number awarded Varies each year; recently, 6 of these scholarships were awarded.

[349]
NAIEA/NY SCHOLARSHIP

Native American Indian Education Association of New York
c/o Monica Antone-Watson
15 Indian Territory
Oneida, NY 13421
(315) 363-9517   E-mail: ckissam@stlawu.edu

Purpose To provide financial assistance to Native American students from New York who plan to attend college in any state.

Eligibility This program is open to enrolled members and children of enrolled members from recognized tribes or nations who reside in New York. Applicants must be attending or planning to attend a postsecondary institution in any state. Along with their application, they must submit official tribal certification, a letter of acceptance from a college or university, proof of attendance, and a personal letter expressing their need and expected use of the scholarship. Selection is based on need and academic merit.

Financial data A stipend is awarded (amount not specified).

Duration 1 year.

Additional information Information is also available from Carol Kissam, (518) 229-5605.

Number awarded 1 or more each year.

Deadline September of each year.

[350]
NALE PROGRAM

Catching the Dream
8200 Mountain Road, N.E., Suite 203
Albuquerque, NM 87110-7835
(505) 262-2351   Fax: (505) 262-0534
E-mail: NScholarsh@aol.com
Web: www.catchingthedream.org/Scholarship.htm

Purpose To provide financial assistance to American Indian paraprofessionals in the education field who wish to return to college or graduate school.

Eligibility This program is open to paraprofessionals who are working in Indian schools and who plan to return to college or graduate school to complete their degree in education, counseling, or school administration. Applicants must be able to provide proof that they are at least one-quarter Indian blood and a member of a U.S. tribe that is federally-recognized, state-recognized, or terminated. Along with their application, they must submit documentation of financial need, 3 letters of recommendation, copies of applications and responses from all other sources of funding for which they are eligible, official transcripts, standardized test scores (ACT, SAT, GRE, MCAT, LSAT, etc.), and an essay explaining their goals in life, college plans, and career plans (especially how those plans include working with and benefiting Indians). Selection is based on merit and potential for improving the lives of Indian people.

Financial data Stipends range from $500 to $5,000 per year.

Duration 1 year; may be renewed.

Additional information The sponsor was formerly known as the Native American Scholarship Fund.

Number awarded Varies; generally, 15 or more each year.

Deadline April of each year for fall term; September of each year for spring and winter terms; March of each year for summer school.

[351]
NAMEPA BEGINNING FRESHMEN AWARD
National Association of Multicultural Engineering
 Program Advocates, Inc.
Attn: National Scholarship Selection Committee Chair
341 North Maitland Avenue, Suite 130
Maitland, FL 32751-4761
(407) 647-8839 Fax: (407) 629-2502
E-mail: namepa@namepa.org
Web: www.namepa.org/awards.html

Purpose To provide financial assistance to Native American and other underrepresented minority high school seniors who are planning to major in engineering.

Eligibility This program is open to African American, Hispanic, and American Indian high school seniors who have been approved for admission to an engineering program at an institution affiliated with the National Association of Multicultural Engineering Program Advocates (NAMEPA). For a list of affiliated schools, write to the sponsor. Applicants must have a GPA of 2.7 or higher and minimum cumulative scores of 25 on the ACT or 1000 on the critical reading and mathematics SAT. They must submit a copy of their high school transcript; test scores; a letter of recommendation; and a 1-page essay on why they have chosen engineering as a profession, why they think they should be selected, and an overview of their future aspirations as an engineer. Financial need is not considered in the selection process.

Financial data The stipend is $1,000, paid in 2 equal installments.

Duration 1 year; nonrenewable.

Additional information Support for this program is provided by the ALCOA Foundation. NAMEPA formerly stood for the National Association of Minority Engineering Program Administrators, Inc.

Number awarded Varies each year; recently, NAMEPA awarded a total of 20 scholarships for its Beginning Freshman Awards and its Transfer Engineering Awards.

Deadline May of each year.

[352]
NASA MOTIVATING UNDERGRADUATES IN SCIENCE AND TECHNOLOGY (MUST) SCHOLARSHIP PROGRAM
Hispanic College Fund
Attn: Scholarship Processing
1301 K Street, N.W., Suite 450-A West
Washington, D.C. 20005
(202) 296-5400 Toll-free: (800) 644-4223
Fax: (202) 296-3774
E-mail: hcf-info@hispanicfund.org
Web: www.hispanicfund.org/scholarships.php

Purpose To provide financial assistance to Native Americans and members of other underrepresented groups who are working on an undergraduate degree in a field of science, technology, engineering, or mathematics (STEM).

Eligibility This program is open to U.S. citizens from an underrepresented group, including women, African Americans, Hispanic Americans, Native Americans, and persons with disabilities. Applicants must be entering their freshman, sophomore, junior, or senior year at an accredited college or university in the 50 states or Puerto Rico as a full-time student. They must have a GPA of 3.0 or higher and a major in a STEM field of study.

Financial data Stipends provide payment of 50% of the tuition and fees at the recipient's institution, to a maximum of $10,000. The stipend for the summer research experience is $5,000.

Duration 1 year; recipients may reapply.

Additional information This program is sponsored by the National Aeronautics and Space Administration (NASA) with support from the United Negro College Fund Special Programs Corporation (UNCFSP) and the Society of Hispanic Engineers-Advancing Hispanic Excellence in Technology, Engineering, Math, and Science, Inc. (AHETEMS). Scholars are eligible to participate in a summer research experience at a NASA center. All applications must be submitted online; no paper applications are available.

Number awarded 100 each year.

Deadline May of each year.

[353]
NATIONAL CENTER FOR COOPERATIVE EDUCATION SCHOLARSHIPS
National Center for Cooperative Education
c/o Haskell Indian Nations University
Natural Resources Liaison Office
155 Indian Avenue, Box 5018
Lawrence, KS 66046
(785) 749-8414 E-mail: daeifler@fs.fed.us
Web: www.haskell.edu

Purpose To provide financial assistance and work experience to American Indian and Alaska Native students interested in preparing for a career in a natural resource field.

Eligibility This program is open to American Indian and Alaska Native students who have finished at least their freshman year at an accredited college or university. Applicants must be working on a bachelor's or higher degree in a natural resources field, including forestry, soil conservation, range management, geographic information systems (GIS), wildlife management, watershed/hydrology, fisheries management, or civil engineering. They must be interested in preparing for a career with tribes, the Bureau of Indian Affairs (BIA), or other natural resources agencies. Along with their application, they must submit a letter that includes their perception of their academic and professional strengths and a description of their academic and career potential. They must also be interested in summer employment related to their academic field of study.

Financial data The scholarship stipend is $5,000 per year. The salary for summer employment ranges from $9 to $11 per hour.

Duration 1 academic year and 1 summer; may be renewed.

Additional information The National Center for Cooperative Education (NCCE) was established in 1997 by the BIA.

Number awarded Varies each year.

Deadline March of each year.

SCHOLARSHIPS

[354]
NATIONAL NATIVE AMERICAN LAW ENFORCEMENT ASSOCIATION ACADEMIC SCHOLARSHIP PROGRAM

National Native American Law Enforcement Association
Attn: Academic Scholarship Program
P.O. Box 171
Washington, DC 20044
(202) 204-3065   Fax: (866) 506-7631
E-mail: info@nnalea.org
Web: www.nnalea.org

Purpose To provide financial assistance for college to Indian high school seniors with an interest in law enforcement.

Eligibility Applicants must be of Indian heritage with a GPA of 2.5 or higher. Along with their application, they must provide transcripts and a 200-word essay on how we can improve relations between law enforcement and people in Indian Country.

Financial data Stipends are $2,500 or $2,000.

Duration 1 year.

Additional information The highest ranked applicant is awarded the Don Leonard Memorial Academic Scholarship, named in honor of a charter member of the National Native American Law Enforcement Association (NNALEA) who was killed in the bombing of the Alfred P. Murrah Federal Building in Oklahoma City, Oklahoma on April 19, 1995.

Number awarded 5 each year: 1 at $2,500 and 4 at $2,000.

Deadline November of each year.

[355]
NATIONAL OCEANIC AND ATMOSPHERIC ADMINISTRATION EDUCATIONAL PARTNERSHIP PROGRAM WITH MINORITY SERVING INSTITUTIONS UNDERGRADUATE SCHOLARSHIPS

Oak Ridge Institute for Science and Education
Attn: Science and Engineering Education
P.O. Box 117
Oak Ridge, TN 37831-0117
(865) 241-6704   Fax: (865) 576-8293
E-mail: MCarl.Wheeler@orau.gov
Web: see.orau.org

Purpose To provide financial assistance and research experience to undergraduate students at Minority Serving Institutions who are majoring in scientific fields of interest to the National Oceanic and Atmospheric Administration (NOAA).

Eligibility This program is open to juniors at Minority Serving Institutions, including Hispanic Serving Institutions (HSIs), Historically Black Colleges and Universities (HBCUs), and Tribal Colleges and Universities (TCUs). Applicants must be majoring in atmospheric science, biology, cartography, chemistry, computer science, engineering, environmental science, geodesy, geography, marine science, mathematics, meteorology, photogrammetry, physical science, physics, or remote sensing. They must also be interested in participating in a research internship at a NOAA site. U.S. citizenship is required.

Financial data This program provides payment of tuition and fees (to a maximum of $4,000 per year) and a stipend during the internship of $650 per week.

Duration 2 academic years and 2 summer internships.

Additional information This program is funded by NOAA through an interagency agreement with the U.S. Department of Energy and administered by Oak Ridge Institute for Science and Education (ORISE).

Number awarded 15 each year.

Deadline February of each year.

[356]
NATIONAL SPACE GRANT COLLEGE AND FELLOWSHIP PROGRAM

National Aeronautics and Space Administration
Attn: Program Manager
NASA Headquarters
Washington, DC 20546-0001
(202) 358-1523   Fax: (202) 358-3048
E-mail: jdasch@hq.nasa.gov
Web: www.nasa.gov

Purpose To provide financial assistance to minority and other undergraduate and graduate students interested in preparing for a career in a space-related field at a college or university participating in the National Space Grant program.

Eligibility This program is open to undergraduate and graduate students at colleges and universities that participate in the National Space Grant program of the U.S. National Aeronautics and Space Administration (NASA) through their state consortium. Applicants must be interested in a program of study and/or research in a field of science, mathematics, engineering, or technology (SMET) related to space. A specific goal of the program is to increase preparation by members of underrepresented groups (minorities, women, and persons with disabilities) for SMET space-related careers. Financial need is not considered in the selection process.

Financial data Each consortium establishes the terms of the fellowship program in its state.

Additional information NASA established the Space Grant program in 1989. It operates through 52 consortia in each state, the District of Columbia, and Puerto Rico. Each consortium includes selected colleges and universities in that state as well as other affiliates from industry, museums, science centers, and state and local agencies. There are similar programs for postdoctorates and faculty at these institutions as well.

Number awarded Varies each year.

Deadline Each consortium sets its own deadlines.

[357]
NATIVE AMERICAN EDUCATION GRANTS

Presbyterian Church (USA)
Attn: Office of Financial Aid for Studies
100 Witherspoon Street, Room M-052
Louisville, KY 40202-1396
(502) 569-5776   Toll-free: (888) 728-7228, ext. 5776
Fax: (502) 569-8766   E-mail: fcook@ctr.pcusa.org
Web: www.pcusa.org

Purpose To provide financial assistance to needy Native American student members of the Presbyterian Church (USA) interested in continuing their college education, especially in selected fields.

Eligibility This program is open to Alaska Native and Native American students who have completed at least 2 years of full-time study at an accredited institution in the United States with a GPA of 2.5 or higher. Applicants must be making satisfactory progress toward a degree, able to provide proof of tribal membership, U.S. citizens or permanent residents, recommended by their church pastor, and able to demonstrate financial need. Preference is given to members of the PCUSA and to students who are majoring in the following fields of interest to missions of the church: education, health services and sciences, religious studies, sacred music, social services, and social sciences.
Financial data Stipends range from $200 to $3,000 per year, depending upon the recipient's financial need.
Duration 1 year; may be renewed.
Number awarded Varies each year.
Deadline June of each year.

[358]
NATIVE AMERICAN FINANCE OFFICERS ASSOCIATION STUDENT SCHOLARSHIP

Native American Finance Officers Association
Attn: Christina Morbelli, Program Coordinator
P.O. Box 50637
Phoenix, AZ 85076-0637
(602) 466-8697   Fax: (201) 447-0945
E-mail: christina@nafoa.org
Web: www.nafoa.org/education.html

Purpose To provide financial assistance to Native Americans who are studying a business-related field in college or graduate school.
Eligibility This program is open to enrolled members of a federally-recognized tribe who are currently a junior or senior in college or studying for an M.B.A. Applicants must be majoring in finance, accounting, business administration, or management and must maintain a GPA of 2.8 or higher. Along with their application, they must submit an essay of 200 to 400 words that includes information on their connection to their Native community, their history in the finance profession, and their future goals in finance.
Financial data A stipend is awarded (amount not specified).
Duration 1 year.
Number awarded Varies each year; recently, 3 of these scholarships were awarded.
Deadline October of each year.

[359]
NATIVE AMERICAN HEALTH EDUCATION FUND SCHOLARSHIP

Native American Health Education Fund
1701 Pleasant Green Road
Durham, NC 27705
(919) 383-1038   Fax: (919) 383-1038
E-mail: nahefscholarship@aol.com

Purpose To provide financial assistance to Native Americans who are attending college or graduate school to prepare for a career in a health-related field.
Eligibility This program is open to Native American students currently enrolled at a college or university. Applicants must be preparing for a career in medicine, nursing, dietetics and nutrition, medical technology, physical therapy, pharmacy, social work, medical research (biochemistry), or other health-related fields. They must be able to demonstrate a desire to return to their community or Reservation to improve health care.
Financial data A stipend is awarded (amount not specified).
Duration 1 year.
Additional information This program awarded its first scholarship in 1990. The fund operates as a member of the Triangle Community Foundation, 324 Blackwell Street, Suite 1220, Durham, NC 27701, (919) 474-8370, Fax: (919) 941-9208, E-mail: info@trianglecf.org.
Number awarded Varies each year. Since the program began, it has awarded 106 scholarships.
Deadline June of each year.

[360]
NATIVE AMERICAN SCHOLARSHIPS OF THE VERMONT SPACE GRANT CONSORTIUM

Vermont Space Grant Consortium
c/o University of Vermont
College of Engineering and Mathematics
Votey Building, Room 209
12 Colchester Avenue
Burlington, VT 05405-0156
(802) 656-1429   Fax: (802) 656-1102
E-mail: zeno@cems.uvm.edu
Web: www.vtspacegrant.org/vtmulticulture.htm

Purpose To provide financial assistance to Native American undergraduate students in space-related fields at selected colleges and universities in Vermont.
Eligibility This program is open to Native American residents of Vermont who are 1) enrolled in an undergraduate degree program at a Vermont institution of higher education with a GPA of 3.0 or higher or 2) seniors graduating from a high school in Vermont. Applicants must be planning to prepare for a professional career in a field that has direct relevance to the U.S. aerospace industry and the goal of the National Aeronautics and Space Administration (NASA), such as astronomy, biology, engineering, mathematics, physics, and other basic sciences (including earth sciences and medicine). They must submit an essay, up to 3 pages in length, on their career plans and the relationship of those plans to areas of interest to NASA. U.S. citizenship is required. Selection is based on academic standing, letters of recommendation, and the essay.
Financial data The stipend is $2,000 per year.
Duration 1 year; may be renewed upon reapplication.
Additional information This program is funded by NASA. Candidates are selected by the Northwest Supervisory District Indian Education Office. Participating institutions are the College of Engineering and Mathematics at the University of Vermont, St. Michael's College, Norwich University, Vermont Technical College, the Vermont State Mathematics Coalition, and Burlington Aviation Technology School/Burlington Technical Center.
Number awarded Up to 3 each year.
Deadline April of each year.

SCHOLARSHIPS

[361]
NATIVE AMERICAN WOMEN'S HEALTH EDUCATION RESOURCE CENTER SCHOLARSHIPS

Native American Women's Health Education Resource Center
P.O. Box 572
Lake Andes, SD 57356-0572
(605) 487-7072 Fax: (605) 487-7964
Web: www.nativeshop.org/nawherc.html

Purpose To provide financial assistance to American Indian women currently enrolled in college.
Eligibility This program is open to American Indian women who are currently enrolled in college and need financial assistance.
Financial data The stipend is either $300 or $500 per semester (up to $1,000 per year).
Duration The stipends are offered each semester.
Additional information The Native American Women's Health Education Resource Center is a project of the Native American Community Board.
Number awarded 2 per semester.
Deadline March of each year.

[362]
NATIVE HAWAIIAN CHAMBER OF COMMERCE SCHOLARSHIPS

Ke Ali'i Pauahi Foundation
Attn: Financial Aid & Scholarship Services
567 South King Street, Suite 160
Honolulu, HI 96813
(808) 534-3966   Toll-free: (800) 842-4682, ext. 43966
Fax: (808) 534-3890   E-mail: scholarships@pauahi.org
Web: www.pauahi.org

Purpose To provide financial assistance to students, especially Native Hawaiians, who are interested in working on an undergraduate or graduate degree in business.
Eligibility This program is open to undergraduate and graduate students who are working on a degree in business administration. Applicants must have a GPA of 3.0 or higher. Residency in Hawaii is not required. Preference is given to Native Hawaiians (descendants of the aboriginal inhabitants of the Hawaiian Islands prior to 1778).
Financial data A stipend is awarded (amount not specified).
Duration 1 year; may be renewed.
Additional information This program is sponsored by the Native Hawaiian Chamber of Commerce.
Number awarded Varies each year; recently, 6 of these scholarships were awarded.
Deadline April of each year.

[363]
NATIVE VISION SCHOLARSHIPS

Native Vision
c/o Johns Hopkins University
Center for American Indian Health
621 North Washington Street
Baltimore, MD 21205
(410) 955-6931 Fax: (410) 955-2010
E-mail: mhammen@jhsph.edu
Web: www.nativevision.org

Purpose To provide financial assistance for college to American Indian high school seniors who participate in a sports camp.
Eligibility This program is open to graduating high school seniors who are enrolled members of a federally-recognized tribe. Applicants must have been admitted to an accredited community college or 4-year undergraduate program. They must be able to demonstrate a sustained involvement in the community, an applied interest in American Indian concerns and initiatives, a GPA of 3.0 or higher, and involvement in extracurricular and/or athletic activities. Along with their application, they must submit a high school transcript, 2 letters of recommendation, and a 200-word essay on their goals for the future and how this scholarship will help them achieve their dreams; their essay should emphasize how their goals relate to their continued involvement in American Indian communities. The program is intended for students who also participate in the sponsor's summer Sports and Life Skills camp.
Financial data The stipend is $5,000.
Duration 1 year.
Additional information Native Vision was established in 2001 by the Center for American Indian Health at the Johns Hopkins Bloomberg School of Public Health and the National Football League Players Association. Each year, it sponsors a Sports and Life Skills camp, hosted by a tribal organization, for approximately 800 Native American students. In addition to training clinics in baseball, football, basketball, soccer, volleyball, and track, it conducts workshops on such topics as financial aid for college, leadership, crafts, and drunk driving prevention.
Number awarded 2 each year.
Deadline May of each year.

[364]
NAVAJO GENERATING STATION SCHOLARSHIP

Salt River Project
Navajo Generating Station
Attn: Linda Dawavendewa NGS 640
P.O. Box 850
Page, AZ 86040
(928) 645-6539 E-mail: ljdawave@srpnet.com
Web: www.srpnet.com/education/grants/navajo.aspx

Purpose To provide financial assistance to members of the Navajo Nation who have completed at least 2 years of college, particularly those who are majoring in selected sciences.
Eligibility This program is open to enrolled members of the Navajo Nation who are full-time students at an accredited college or university. Applicants must be entering their junior year of college and have a GPA of 3.0 or higher. Preference is given to students majoring in mathematics, engi-

neering, and environmental studies. Along with their application, they must submit a 1-page letter explaining their career goals, reasons for selecting that field of study, and why they believe the sponsor should provide funds; a current resume; official transcripts; 2 letters of recommendation; documentation of financial need; and a Certificate of Indian Blood. Selection is based on field of study, academic excellence, and achievement.

Financial data The stipend depends on the need of the recipient.

Duration 1 year; may be renewed until completion of a bachelor's degree.

Additional information This program was established in 1976.

Number awarded Varies each year; recently, 7 of these scholarships were awarded.

Deadline April of each year.

[365]
NAVAJO NATION COLLEGE DEVELOPMENTAL STUDIES PROGRAM

Navajo Nation
Attn: Office of Navajo Nation Scholarship and Financial Assistance
P.O. Box 1870
Window Rock, AZ 86515-1870
(928) 871-7640 Toll-free: (800) 243-2956
Fax: (928) 871-6561
E-mail: onnsfacentral@navajo.org
Web: www.onnsfa.org

Purpose To provide financial assistance to members of the Navajo Nation who require remedial education at the college level.

Eligibility This program is open to enrolled members of the Navajo Nation who are taking developmental studies courses to improve deficiencies in math, reading, or writing skills. Preference is given to students at Diné College. Selection is based on financial need.

Financial data The amount of the award depends on the need of the recipient.

Duration Recipients may enroll in up to 12 semester credit hours of college development courses during their first year in college.

Deadline June of each year for fall term; November of each year for winter or spring terms; April of each year for summer session.

[366]
NAVAJO NATION FINANCIAL NEED-BASED ASSISTANCE PROGRAM

Navajo Nation
Attn: Office of Navajo Nation Scholarship and Financial Assistance
P.O. Box 1870
Window Rock, AZ 86515-1870
(928) 871-7640 Toll-free: (800) 243-2956
Fax: (928) 871-6561
E-mail: onnsfacentral@navajo.org
Web: www.onnsfa.org

Purpose To provide financial assistance for college to members of the Navajo Nation.

Eligibility This program is open to enrolled members of the Navajo Nation who have proof of one-quarter or more Navajo Indian blood quantum on their Certificate of Indian Blood. Applicants must be attending or planning to attend an accredited institution of higher education to work on an associate or baccalaureate degree. Financial need must be demonstrated.

Financial data The stipend is $1,500 per year.

Duration 1 year; may be renewed (if the recipient maintains at least a 2.0 GPA) for up to a total of 10 semesters of full-time undergraduate study, 5 academic terms or 64 semester credit hours at 2-year institutions, or 50 semester credit hours of part-time undergraduate study.

Number awarded Varies each year; recently, 3,714 of these scholarships were awarded.

Deadline June of each year for fall term; November of each year for winter or spring terms; April of each year for summer session.

[367]
NAVAJO NATION TEACHER EDUCATION PROGRAM

Navajo Nation
Navajo Nation Scholarship and Financial Assistance
Attn: Navajo Nation Teacher Education Program
P.O. Box 4380
Window Rock, AZ 86515-4380
(928) 871-7453 Toll-free: (800) 243-2956
Fax: (928) 871-6443
E-mail: onnsfacentral@navajo.org
Web: www.onnsfa.org/nntep.asp

Purpose To provide financial assistance to members of the Navajo Nation who wish to prepare for a career as a bilingual or bicultural teacher.

Eligibility This program is open to enrolled members of the Navajo Nation who are enrolled in or planning to enroll in an undergraduate teacher education program, a post-baccalaureate program for teacher licensure, or a master's degree program in education. Applicants must complete an emphasis in either Navajo Language or Navajo Culture, taken concurrently each semester with teacher education courses. They may be specializing in elementary education, early childhood education, bilingual multicultural education, special education, educational leadership, school counseling, curriculum and instruction, library science, or science and mathematics secondary education. Students working on a second master's degree are not eligible. Financial need is not considered in the selection process.

Financial data Recipients are reimbursed for each course they complete at the rate of $250 per course for lower-division undergraduate courses or $500 for upper-division and graduate courses.

Duration 1 semester; may be renewed for undergraduate courses completed with a grade of "C" or better and for graduate courses completed with a grade of "B" or better.

Number awarded Varies each year; recently, 250 undergraduates and 225 graduate students were participating in the program.

Deadline June of each year for fall term; November of each year for winter or spring terms; April of each year for summer session.

SCHOLARSHIPS

[368]
NAVAJO NATION VOCATIONAL EDUCATION PROGRAM
Navajo Nation
Attn: Office of Navajo Nation Scholarship and Financial Assistance
P.O. Box 1870
Window Rock, AZ 86515-1870
(928) 871-7640 Toll-free: (800) 243-2956
Fax: (928) 871-6561
E-mail: onnsfacentral@navajo.org
Web: www.onnsfa.org

Purpose To provide financial assistance for vocational education to members of the Navajo Nation.
Eligibility This program is open to enrolled members of the Navajo Nation who are enrolled or planning to enroll full time at a regionally accredited vocational institution. Applicants must be interested in working on an associate of applied science degree or a vocational certificate. Selection is based on financial need.
Financial data The amount of the award depends on the need of the recipient.
Duration 1 year; may be renewed.
Number awarded Varies each year.
Deadline June of each year for fall term; November of each year for winter or spring terms; April of each year for summer session.

[369]
NCAI YOUTH AMBASSADOR LEADERSHIP PROGRAM SCHOLARSHIPS
National Congress of American Indians
Attn: Internship Program
1301 Connecticut Avenue, N.W., Suite 200
Washington, DC 20036
(202) 466-7767 Fax: (2020 466-7797
E-mail: ncai@ncai.org
Web: www.ncai.org/NCAI_Youth.10.0.html

Purpose To provide financial assistance to undergraduates and graduate students who participate in the Youth Commission Ambassador Leadership Program (ALP) of the National Congress of American Indians (NCAI).
Eligibility This program is open to youth between 17 and 25 years of age who are eligible for NCAI membership. Applicants must be graduating high school seniors or full-time undergraduate or graduate students. They must have support from their tribal council. Males and females are considered separately. Recipients are selected at the Congress on the basis of an oration, contemporary dress, extemporaneous question, cultural presentation, and debate; GPA and recommendations are also considered.
Financial data The stipend is $2,500. Funds are paid directly to the academic institution.
Duration The stipend is for 1 year; recipients serve as Youth Ambassadors for 2 years.
Additional information This program was established in 2006. Students selected as Youth Ambassadors lead the NCAI Youth Commission in its meetings and represent NCAI Youth when their presence is requested.
Number awarded 2 (1 male and 1 female) each even-numbered year.

[370]
NCEMNA AETNA SCHOLARS PROGRAM
National Coalition of Ethnic Minority Nurse Associations
c/o Dr. Betty Smith Williams, President
6101 West Centinela Avenue, Suite 378
Culver City, CA 90230
(310) 258-9515 Fax: (310) 258-9513
E-mail: bwilliams@ncemna.org
Web: www.ncemna.org/ncemna/scholarships.asp

Purpose To provide financial assistance to nursing students who are members of constituent organizations of the National Coalition of Ethnic Minority Nurse Associations (NCEMNA) and working on a 4-year or master's degree.
Eligibility This program is open to members of the 5 associations that comprise NCEMNA: the Asian American/Pacific Islander Nurses Association, Inc. (AAPINA), the National Alaska Native American Indian Nurses Association, Inc. (NANAINA), the National Association of Hispanic Nurses, Inc. (NAHN), the National Black Nurses Association, Inc. (NBNA), and the Philippine Nurses Association of America, Inc. (PNAA). Applicants must be currently attending or applying to a 4-year or master's degree program in nursing. Along with their application, they must submit a letter of reference, demonstration of leadership and involvement in the ethnic community, and a statement of career goals.
Financial data The stipend is $2,000.
Duration 1 year.
Additional information This program was established in 2004 with a grant from the Aetna Foundation.
Number awarded 5 each year: 1 nominee from each of the constituent associations.
Deadline April of each year.

[371]
NEW YORK AID TO NATIVE AMERICANS
New York State Education Department
Attn: Native American Education Unit
Education Building Annex, Room 374
Albany, NY 12234
(518) 474-0537 Fax: (518) 474-3666
Web: www.emsc.nysed.gov

Purpose To provide financial assistance for college to Native Americans in New York.
Eligibility Student aid is available to Native Americans who meet these qualifications: are on official tribal rolls of a New York State tribe or are the child of an enrolled member; are residents of New York State; and are or will be graduates of an accredited high school or have a New York State General Equivalency Diploma or are enrolled in college credit programs working for the State High School Equivalency Diploma. Recipients must be accepted by an approved accredited postsecondary institution within New York State.
Financial data The stipend is $2,000 per year for full-time study (at least 12 credit hours per semester or 24 credit hours per year); students registering for less than full-time study are funded on a prorated basis. Funding is available for summer course work on a special needs basis. Funds spent for summer school are deducted from the recipient's maximum entitlement.

Duration 1 year; renewable for up to 3 additional years (4 additional years for specific programs requiring 5 years to complete degree requirements).
Additional information The New York State tribes include members of the Iroquoian tribes (St. Regis Mohawk, Oneida, Onondaga, Cayuga, Seneca Nation, Tonawanda Band of Seneca, and Tuscarora), the Shinnecock tribe, and the Poospatuck tribe. Remedial, noncredit, and college preparation courses are not funded.
Number awarded Varies; approximately 500 each year.
Deadline July of each year for fall semester; December of each year for spring semester; May of each year for summer session.

[372]
NEZ PERCE HIGHER EDUCATION GRANTS
Nez Perce Tribe
Attn: Higher Education
116 Veterans Drive
P.O. Box 365
Lapwai, ID 83540
(206) 843-7316   Fax: (206) 843-7380
E-mail: kayk@nezperce.org
Web: www.nezperce.org

Purpose To provide financial assistance to members of the Nez Perce Tribe who are interested in attending college in any state.
Eligibility This program is open to enrolled members of the Nez Perce Tribe who are attending or planning to attend a college or university in any state to work on an associate or bachelor's degree. Applicants must submit documentation of financial need and a cover letter that explains how their education plan will help the Native American community, their role as a leader in their school or community, their personal and academic background, and how this assistance will help them achieve their goals.
Financial data A stipend is awarded (amount not specified).
Duration 1 semester; may be renewed.
Number awarded Varies each year.
Deadline June of each year for fall semester or quarter; October of each year for spring semester or winter quarter; January of each year for spring quarter.

[373]
NICKERSON WEST SHAKESPEARE/ARAPAHO TRUST UNDERGRADUATE SCHOLARSHIP
Northern Arapaho Tribe
Attn: Sky People Higher Education
P.O. Box 8480
Ethete, WY 82520
(307) 332-5286   Toll-free: (800) 815-6795
Fax: (307) 332-9104
E-mail: assistant@skypeopleed.org
Web: www.skypeopleed.org

Purpose To provide financial assistance to members of the Northern Arapaho Tribe who are working on an undergraduate degree in accounting or agribusiness.
Eligibility This program is open to full-time undergraduate students who have an undergraduate GPA of 2.0 or higher. Applicants must be one-fourth Northern Arapaho descent (enrolled or non-enrolled) and must submit a Certificate of Indian Blood or other verification of Northern Arapaho blood with at least one-fourth degree. They must be working on a degree in accounting or agribusiness. Along with their application, they must submit a 1-page personal statement that includes a brief history of their background, academic ability and achievement, work or leadership experience, participation in community-related activities, and career goals. Selection is based on that statement, potential to contribute to the community upon graduation, academic ability and achievement, and a letter of recommendation.
Financial data The stipend is $1,500 per year.
Duration 1 year; may be renewed.
Additional information Recipients are expected to apply for employment with the Northern Arapaho Tribe after graduation.
Number awarded 2 each year.
Deadline June of each year.

[374]
NIHEWAN SCHOLARSHIPS
Nihewan Foundation for Native American Education
9595 Wilshire Boulevard, Suite 1020
Beverly Hills, CA 90212
(808) 822-3111   Fax: (310) 278-0238
E-mail: info@nihewan.org
Web: www.nihewan.org/programs.html

Purpose To provide financial assistance to Native Americans interested in studying about their culture in college.
Eligibility This program is open to enrolled members of a Native American tribe or Canadian First nation. Applicants must be interested in working on a college degree in Native American/indigenous studies. Along with their application, they must include 3 essays: 1) their goals with regard to Native American/indigenous studies; 2) other foundations that are helping finance their studies (must have applied to at least 2 other foundations and still have unmet need); and 3) their current school expenses.
Financial data A stipend is awarded (amount not specified).
Duration 1 year.
Additional information The Nihewan Foundation was established by singer-songwriter Buffy Sainte-Marie in 1969.
Number awarded 1 or more each year.

[375]
NINILCHIK HIGHER EDUCATION GRANT PROGRAM
Ninilchik Traditional Council
Attn: Tribal Services Department
P.O. Box 39444
Ninilchik, AK 99639
(907) 567-3313   Fax: (907) 567-3308
E-mail: ntc@ninilchiktribe-nsn.gov
Web: www.ninilchiktribe-nsn.gov

Purpose To provide financial assistance for college or graduate school to Ninilchik Tribal members.
Eligibility Applicants must be an enrolled Ninilchik Tribal member or a one-quarter degree blood descendant of a member. They must be enrolled or accepted for enrollment

in a 4-year academic degree program at an accredited institution as a full-time undergraduate or graduate student. Financial need must be demonstrated.
Financial data Grants range from $400 to $1,500 per semester, depending on the availability of funds and the number of recipients. Total funds available for this program are approximately $12,000 per year.
Duration 1 year; may be renewed for up to 4 additional years if the recipient maintains full-time enrollment and a GPA of 2.0 or higher.
Number awarded 4 to 10 each year.
Deadline August of each year for fall semester; December of each year for spring semester; May of each year for summer semester.

[376]
NINILCHIK NATIVE ASSOCIATION SCHOLARSHIP AND VOCATIONAL GRANT
Cook Inlet Region, Inc.
Attn: The CIRI Foundation
3600 San Jeronimo Drive, Suite 256
Anchorage, AK 99508-2870
(907) 793-3575   Toll-free: (800) 764-3382
Fax: (907) 793-3585   E-mail: tcf@thecirifoundation.org
Web: www.thecirifoundation.org

Purpose To provide financial assistance for professional preparation after high school to Alaska Natives who are original enrollees or descendants of the Ninilchik Native Association.
Eligibility This program is open to 1) Alaska Native enrollees of the Ninilchik Native Association under the Alaska Native Claims Settlement Act (ANCSA) of 1971 and 2) their lineal descendants. Proof of eligibility must be submitted. There is no residency requirement. Applicants for the scholarships must be accepted or enrolled full time in an accredited or otherwise approved postsecondary college or university; applicants for the grants may be enrolled either part or full time in a technical skills certificate or degree program such as (but not limited to) craft/trade, automotive technology, office occupations, and computer technology. All applicants should have a GPA of 2.5 or higher. Along with their application, they must submit a 500-word statement on their educational and career goals and how they are contributing, or planning to contribute, to a positive Alaska Native community. Selection is based on that statement, academic achievement, rigor of course work or degree program, student financial contribution, financial need, grade level, previous work performance, community service, and relationship of degree program to career goals.
Financial data The stipend depends on the availability of funds.
Duration 1 semester for the general scholarship and 1 calendar year for the vocational technical grant; recipients may reapply.
Additional information This program was established in 1987.
Number awarded Varies each year.
Deadline May or November of each year for scholarships; June of each year for grants.

[377]
NISSAN NORTH AMERICA SCHOLARSHIP
American Indian College Fund
Attn: Scholarship Department
8333 Greenwood Boulevard
Denver, CO 80221
(303) 426-8900   Toll-free: (800) 776-FUND
Fax: (303) 426-1200   E-mail: info@collegefund.org
Web: www.collegefund.org

Purpose To provide financial assistance to Native American students enrolling in a bachelor's degree program at a mainstream college.
Eligibility This program is open to American Indians and Alaska Natives who can document proof of enrollment or descendancy. Applicants must be planning to enroll full time in a bachelor's degree program at a mainstream institution. They must have a GPA of 2.5 or higher and be able to demonstrate financial need. Along with their application, they must submit 1) short essays (up to 500 words each) on how they perceive themselves as leaders in their school or community and how their education will help the Native American community; and 2) a personal statement of 1,000 words that includes their personal background, their academic background, their educational and career goals, and how this scholarship will help them achieve those goals.
Financial data The stipend is $5,000 per year.
Duration 1 year; may be renewed.
Additional information This scholarship is sponsored by Nissan North America, Inc., in partnership with the American Indian College Fund.
Number awarded 20 each year.
Deadline May of each year.

[378]
NISSAN NORTH AMERICA TRIBAL COLLEGE SCHOLARSHIP PROGRAM
American Indian College Fund
Attn: Scholarship Department
8333 Greenwood Boulevard
Denver, CO 80221
(303) 426-8900   Toll-free: (800) 776-FUND
Fax: (303) 426-1200   E-mail: info@collegefund.org
Web: www.collegefund.org

Purpose To provide financial assistance to Native Americans who are attending or planning to attend a Tribal College or University (TCU).
Eligibility This program is open to American Indians or Alaska Natives who are enrolled or planning to enroll full time at an eligible TCU. Applicants must have a GPA of 2.5 or higher and be able to demonstrate financial need. Along with their application, they must submit 1) short essays (up to 500 words each) on how they perceive themselves as leaders in their school or community and how their education will help the Native American community; and 2) a personal statement of 1,000 words that includes their personal background, their academic background, their educational and career goals, and how this scholarship will help them achieve those goals.
Financial data The stipend is $3,000.
Duration 1 year.

Additional information This scholarship is sponsored by Nissan North America, Inc., in partnership with the American Indian College Fund.
Number awarded 1 or more each year.
Deadline May of each year.

[379]
NORMAN TECUBE SR. HIGHER EDUCATION FUND

Jicarilla Apache Tribe
Attn: Higher Education Program
P.O. Box 1099
Dulce, NM 87528
(505) 759-3242   Fax: (505) 759-9111
E-mail: jicarillahep@yahoo.com
Web: www.jicarillaonline.com

Purpose To provide financial assistance for undergraduate or graduate education to members of the Jicarilla Apache tribe.
Eligibility Enrolled members of the Jicarilla Apache tribe are eligible to apply if they are attending either undergraduate or graduate school. Recipients may enroll in any accredited postsecondary school and may major in any subject area. Financial need is considered in the selection process.
Financial data The amount awarded varies, depending on need, up to a maximum of $1,800 per year. Funds may not be used for extracurricular activities, trips out of the United States, non-credit courses, or unnecessary tools.
Duration 1 year; may be renewed.
Additional information This program was formerly called the Chester E. Faris Higher Education Fund.
Number awarded Varies each year.
Deadline February for fall semester or academic year applications; September of each year for spring semester applications.

[380]
NORTH CAROLINA AMERICAN INDIAN FUND SCHOLARSHIPS

North Carolina American Indian Fund
Attn: Mrs. Earlene Stacks, Chair
P.O. Box 25811
Raleigh, NC 27601-5811

Purpose To provide financial assistance to American Indian high school seniors from North Carolina who plan to attend college in any state.
Eligibility This program is open to graduating high school seniors who are enrolled members of a state or federally-recognized tribe. Applicants must be able to demonstrate a history of family residency in North Carolina. They must have a GPA of 2.0 or higher and have been admitted to a program of study at an accredited postsecondary institution in any state as a full-time student. Along with their application, they must submit a 1-page essay on their past and future involvement in American Indian communities or American Indian concerns and initiatives.
Financial data A stipend is awarded (amount not specified).
Duration 1 year.
Additional information This sponsoring organization was established in 2001.
Number awarded 1 or more each year.
Deadline May of each year.

[381]
NORTH DAKOTA INDIAN SCHOLARSHIP PROGRAM

North Dakota University System
Attn: Coordinator of Multicultural Education
919 South Seventh Street, Suite 603
Bismarck, ND 58504-5881
(701) 328-9661   Fax: (701) 328-9662
E-mail: rhonda_schauer@ndus.nodak.edu
Web: www.ndus.nodak.edu

Purpose To provide financial assistance to Native American students in North Dakota colleges and universities.
Eligibility Applicants must have at least one-quarter degree Indian blood, be residents of North Dakota or enrolled members of a tribe resident in North Dakota, and be accepted as full-time undergraduate students by an institution of higher learning or vocational education in North Dakota. Students must have at least a 2.0 GPA, although priority in funding is given to those with a GPA of 3.5 or higher. Participants in internships, student teaching, teaching assistance, or cooperative education programs are eligible only if participation in that program is required for the degree and only if tuition must be paid for the credits earned.
Financial data The amount of the stipend varies from $500 to $2,000 depending on scholastic ability, funds available, total number of applicants, and financial need. The award is divided into semester or quarter payments. The money is to be used to pay registration, health fees, board, room, books, and other necessary items handled by the institution. Any remaining balance may be used to cover the student's personal expenses.
Duration 1 academic year; renewable up to 3 additional years, if the recipient maintains a 2.0 GPA and continues to be in financial need.
Number awarded Varies; approximately 150 to 175 each year.
Deadline July of each year.

[382]
NORTHERN ARAPAHO ADULT VOCATIONAL TRAINING GRANTS

Northern Arapaho Tribe
Attn: Sky People Higher Education
P.O. Box 8480
Ethete, WY 82520
(307) 332-5286   Toll-free: (800) 815-6795
Fax: (307) 332-9104
E-mail: assistant@skypeopleed.org
Web: www.skypeopleed.org

Purpose To provide financial assistance for vocational training to members of the Northern Arapaho Tribe.
Eligibility This program is open to anyone who can certify at least one-fourth or more degree Northern Arapaho Indian Blood, but preference is given to enrolled members of the Northern Arapaho tribe. Applicants must be interested in enrolling in a vocational training program. They must have resided in Fremont or Hot Springs counties in Wyoming for at least 30 days prior to the beginning of training.

Financial data Grants provide partial payment of tuition and other costs of attendance.
Duration 1 year; may be renewed.
Number awarded Varies each year.
Deadline June of each year for the academic year; November of each year for the spring semester; April of each year for summer school.

[383]
NORTHERN ARAPAHO TRIBAL SCHOLARSHIPS
Northern Arapaho Tribe
Attn: Sky People Higher Education
P.O. Box 8480
Ethete, WY 82520
(307) 332-5286   Toll-free: (800) 815-6795
Fax: (307) 332-9104
E-mail: assistant@skypeopleed.org
Web: www.skypeopleed.org

Purpose To provide financial assistance for college to members of the Northern Arapaho Tribe.
Eligibility This program is open to anyone who can certify at least one-fourth or more degree Northern Arapaho Indian Blood, but preference is given to enrolled members of the Northern Arapaho tribe. Funding priorities are 1) college seniors ready to graduate; 2) continuing students with a GPA of 2.25 or higher; 3) high school or GED graduates; and 4) late applicants.
Financial data The amount of the awards depends on the financial need of the recipients.
Duration 1 year; may be renewed for a total of 5 academic years.
Additional information The scholarships may be used at any accredited college, university, or vocational/technical school. Recipients must attend college full time.
Number awarded Varies each year.
Deadline June of each year for the academic year; November of each year for the spring semester; April of each year for summer school.

[384]
NORTHERN CHEYENNE ADULT VOCATIONAL TRAINING PROGRAM
Northern Cheyenne Nation
Attn: Tribal Education Department
P.O. Box 307
Lame Deer, MT 59043
(406) 477-6567   Toll-free: (800) 353-8183
Fax: (406) 477-8150   E-mail: norma@rangeweb.net
Web: www.cheyennenation.com

Purpose To provide financial assistance to Northern Cheyenne tribal members who are interested in vocational training.
Eligibility Applicants must be enrolled members of the Northern Cheyenne tribe, be between the ages of 18 and 40, be high school graduates or have obtained a high school equivalency before applying, and be enrolled or accepted in a Bureau of Indian Affairs-approved school. Northern Cheyennes are not required to reside on the Northern Cheyenne Reservation; other eligible Indian members may qualify for this assistance if they reside on the Northern Cheyenne Reservation. The applicant must intend to enroll in a full-time trade or vocational program that can be completed in 3 to 24 months and that will prepare the student for employment. Selection is based on academic achievement, educational goals, need for financial support, choice of school, and plans after graduation. Awards are made according to the following priorities: 1) renewal of grants to continuing students in good standing; 2) new applicants who are enrolled Northern Cheyenne residing on or near the Northern Cheyenne Indian Reservation; 3) enrolled Northern Cheyenne new applicants who reside outside the service area of the reservation; 4) other Indian enrolled tribal members residing on the Northern Cheyenne Indian Reservation; and 5) individuals requesting retraining.
Financial data Funding under this program is supplemental to any other income. Grants are intended to cover living expenses, tuition, books, supplies related directly to the course, and child care. Transportation costs to training sites off the reservation are provided for the student and eligible family members. Medical coverage is provided by the Northern Cheyenne Indian Health Service for the duration of the training period.
Duration Up to 24 months for vocational training; up to 36 months for nursing training.
Additional information Individuals can request support for retraining, provided they can supply a physician's statement explaining why they cannot continue in their present occupation. Recipients must complete at least 12 units each semester or quarter with a GPA of 2.0 or higher. Recipients who voluntarily discontinue training without prior approval from the tribe or because of poor attendance or academic performance are not eligible for continued financial assistance.
Number awarded Varies each year.
Deadline February of each year for fall quarter/semester; September of each year for winter quarter/spring semester/spring quarter; March of each year for summer school.

[385]
NORTHERN CHEYENNE HIGHER EDUCATION SCHOLARSHIP PROGRAM
Northern Cheyenne Nation
Attn: Tribal Education Department
P.O. Box 307
Lame Deer, MT 59043
(406) 477-6567   Toll-free: (800) 353-8183
Fax: (406) 477-8150   E-mail: norma@rangeweb.net
Web: www.cheyennenation.com

Purpose To provide financial assistance for college or graduate school to Northern Cheyenne tribal members.
Eligibility This program is open to enrolled Northern Cheyenne tribal members who have been accepted to a degree program at an accredited college or university. The priority order for awards is 1) continuing and former college students in good standing; 2) graduating high school seniors in good standing or first-time adult college applicants not previously funded; 3) students or other individuals who have previously failed to meet the requirements of the scholarship program; and 4) graduate students (if funds are still available). All applicants must be able to demonstrate financial need.
Financial data The stipend depends on the need of the recipient, to a maximum of $6,000 per year. These awards

are intended to supplement other available sources of funding. The scholarship must be used for tuition, subsistence, required fees, and textbooks.
Duration 1 year; may be renewed if the recipient maintains a GPA of 2.0 or higher and completes at least 14 quarter or 16 semester units as a freshman and sophomore and at least 16 quarter or 18 semester units as a junior or senior.
Additional information Recipients who reside in Montana are expected to attend a postsecondary institution in the state. They must pay the difference in cost between Montana public postsecondary schools and private or out-of-state schools, if they elect to attend either of those. An exception is made if no comparable course of study exists in a Montana public institution. Eligible Northern Cheyenne Indians residing out of state are subject to the same regulation; however, they may enroll in a Montana institution of higher learning if there is no comparable course of study at a public institution in their home state.
Number awarded Approximately 80 each year.
Deadline February of each year for fall quarter/semester; September of each year for winter quarter/spring semester/spring quarter; March of each year for summer school.

[386]
NORTON SOUND HEALTH CORPORATION SCHOLARSHIPS
Norton Sound Health Corporation
Attn: Scholarships
P.O. Box 966
Nome, AK 99762
(907) 443-4530   Fax: (907) 443-2085
E-mail: info@nortonsoundhealth.org
Web: www.nortonsoundhealth.org/scholarship.html
Purpose To provide financial assistance to Native and other residents of Alaska who are interested in working on an undergraduate or graduate degree in a health-related field.
Eligibility This program is open to students enrolled in or planning to enrolled in an undergraduate or graduate program in a field of study relevant to employment at Norton Sound Health Corporation (NSHC). Priority is given to applicants in the following order: 1) Native residents of the Bering Straits region of Alaska; 2) Native residents of other regions of Alaska; and 3) non-Native residents of the Bering Straits region. They must submit brief statements on their educational goals and objectives, the activities in which they are currently participating, their community activities, and honors or awards they have received. Financial need is also considered in the selection process.
Financial data A stipend is awarded (amount not specified).
Duration 1 year; may be renewed if the recipient maintains full-time enrollment and a GPA of 2.5 or higher.
Additional information The Norton Sound Health Corporation was founded in 1970 to serve the health care need of the Inupiat, Yupik, and Siberian Yupik people of the Bering Straits region of northwest Alaska.
Number awarded Varies each year.
Deadline April of each year for fall terms; November of each year for spring terms.

[387]
NOTAY BEGAY III SCHOLARSHIP PROGRAM
Albuquerque Community Foundation
Attn: Scholarship Program
3301 Menaul N.E., Suite 2
P.O. Box 36960
Albuquerque, NM 87176-6960
(505) 883-6240   Fax: (505) 883-3629
E-mail: foundation@albuquerquefoundation.org
Web: www.albuquerquefoundation.org
Purpose To provide financial assistance to Native American high school seniors in New Mexico who have participated in athletics and plan to attend college in any state.
Eligibility This program is open to seniors graduating from high schools in New Mexico who are Native Americans. Applicants must be scholar-athletes with a varsity-level sports background and a GPA of 3.0 or higher. They must be planning to attend a college or university in any state as a full-time student. Along with their application, they must submit 1) a personal statement describing why they are going to college, what they plan to study, their career goals, any unusual challenges they face in continuing their education, and how they plan to give back to their community after college; 2) transcripts; 3) a reference from a current academic teacher or counselor; 4) a reference from an athletic coach; and 5) proof of tribal enrollment or Certificate of Indian Blood (at least 50%).
Financial data The stipend is $2,000.
Duration 1 year; nonrenewable.
Additional information This program began in 1999.
Number awarded 2 each year.
Deadline March of each year.

[388]
ODEN LUCE TRUST SCHOLARSHIPS
Charles and Nancy Oden Luce Trust
c/o Bank of America, N.A.
Attn: Private Bank Center, Seattle
CSC-10
P.O. Box 34345
Seattle, WA 98124-1345
(206) 358-7911   Toll-free: (800) 526-7307
Fax: (206) 358-1059
Purpose To provide financial assistance for college to high school seniors and graduates who are Umatilla Indians.
Eligibility This program is open to members of the Confederated Tribes of the Umatilla Indian Reservation who are graduating or have graduated from high school, need financial assistance to attend or continue attending college, and are interested in obtaining a liberal arts or professional degree.
Financial data The amount of each scholarship is determined by the funds available and the need of the recipients.
Duration 1 year; may be renewed.
Additional information Funds may also be used by qualified students who have completed the tenth grade and are interested in pursuing a vocational education.
Number awarded Varies each year.

[389]
OFFICE OF CIVILIAN RADIOACTIVE WASTE MANAGEMENT MINORITY SERVING INSTITUTIONS UNDERGRADUATE SCHOLARSHIP PROGRAM
Oak Ridge Institute for Science and Education
Attn: Science and Engineering Education
P.O. Box 117
Oak Ridge, TN 37831-0117
(865) 241-6704   Fax: (865) 241-9445
E-mail: MCarl.Wheeler@orau.gov
Web: see.orau.org

Purpose To provide scholarships and internship experience to students at Minority Serving Institutions (MEIs) working on undergraduate degrees in areas related to the Office of Civilian Radioactive Waste Management (OCRWM).

Eligibility This program is open to full time juniors and seniors at Historically Black Colleges and Universities (HBCUs), Hispanic Serving Institutions (HSIs), and Tribal Colleges and Universities (TCUs). Applicants must be working on a degree in science, mathematics, engineering, engineering technology, or social sciences (if their program focuses on public policy development of issues relevant to the OCRWM mission). As part of their program, they must be willing to participate in a summer internship at a U.S. Department of Energy (DOE) site conducting activities for the OCRWM. Along with their application, they must submit a 1- to 2-page statement of their career and academic goals and objectives. Selection is based on that statement, academic honors and awards, extracurricular activities, employment experience, and references.

Financial data The program provides for payment of tuition and fees (to a maximum of $8,000) plus a monthly stipend of $700 during the academic year and $1,400 during the summer internship.

Duration 2 years.

Additional information This program is funded by DOE/OCRWM and administered by Oak Ridge Institute for Science and Education (ORISE).

Number awarded 8 each year.

Deadline January of each year.

[390]
OFFICE OF HAWAIIAN AFFAIRS SCHOLARSHIPS
Hawai'i Community Foundation
Attn: Scholarship Department
1164 Bishop Street, Suite 800
Honolulu, HI 96813
(808) 566-5570   Toll-free: (888) 731-3863
Fax: (808) 521-6286
E-mail: scholarships@hcf-hawaii.org
Web: www.hawaiicommunityfoundation.org

Purpose To provide financial assistance for undergraduate studies to persons of Hawaiian descent.

Eligibility This program is open to students currently enrolled full-time at an accredited 2- or 4-year college or university in any state. Applicants must be able to document Hawaiian ancestry through the Office of Hawaiian Affairs Hawaiian Registry Program. Current Hawaiian residency is not required. Along with their application, they must submit a short statement indicating their reasons for attending college, their planned course of study, and their career goals. Selection is based on academic achievement (GPA of 2.7 or higher), good moral character, and financial need.

Financial data The amounts of the awards depend on the availability of funds and the need of the recipient; recently, stipends averaged $2,000.

Duration 1 year.

Number awarded Varies each year; recently, 110 of these scholarships were awarded.

Deadline February of each year.

[391]
OHKAY OWINGEH SCHOLARSHIPS
Pueblo of Ohkay Owingeh
Attn: Department of Education
P.O. Box 1269
San Juan Pueblo, NM 87566
(505) 852-3477   Fax: (505) 852-3030
E-mail: wevog68@valornet.com
Web: www.sanjuaned.org/higher_ed.html

Purpose To provide financial assistance to tribal members of the Pueblo of Ohkay Owingeh who are working on a certificate or undergraduate degree.

Eligibility This program is open to enrolled and verified members of the Ohkay Owingeh tribe who are enrolled or accepted for enrollment at an accredited college, university, or vocational/technical school in any state. Applicants must be working on or planning to work on a first-time certificate or undergraduate degree. They must agree to provide community service within the tribe of 20 hours per semester as a full-time student, 15 hours per semester as a half-time student, or 10 hours per semester if enrolled less than half time. Scholarships are awarded on a first-come, first-served basis; financial need is not considered.

Financial data The stipend is $600 per semester for full-time students, $300 per semester for half-time students, or $150 per semester for students enrolled less than half time.

Duration 1 semester; may be renewed, provided the recipient maintains a GPA of 2.0 or higher and fulfills the community service agreement.

Additional information Until 2005, the Pueblo of Ohkay Owingeh was known as the Pueblo of San Juan.

Number awarded 30 each semester.

Deadline June of each year for fall semester; December of each year for spring semester; April of each year for summer semester.

[392]
OLIVE WHITMAN MEMORIAL SCHOLARSHIP
Daughters of the American Revolution-New York State Organization
c/o Sharon DePuy, Recording Secretary
Wiltwyck Chapter DAR House and Museum
P.O. Box 3592
Kingston, NY 12402
(845) 339-0366   E-mail: S_DePuy@prodigy.net
Web: www.nydar.org/id26.htm

Purpose To provide financial assistance for college to Native American women in New York.

Eligibility This program is open to women who are at least 50% Native American and graduating seniors at high

schools in New York. Applicants must be planning to attend an accredited 4-year college or university in the state.
Financial data The stipend is $2,000.
Duration 1 year.
Number awarded 1 each year.
Deadline January of each year.

[393]
ONEIDA TRIBE HIGHER EDUCATION GRANT PROGRAM

Oneida Nation of Wisconsin
Attn: Higher Education Office
N7210 Seminary Road, North Wing
P.O. Box 365
Oneida, WI 54155-0365
(920) 869-4333   Toll-free: (800) 236-2214, ext. 4333
Fax: (920) 869-4039
E-mail: cvanden2@oneidanation.org
Web: www.oneidanation.org

Purpose To provide financial assistance for undergraduate or graduate study to members of the Oneida Tribe of Wisconsin.
Eligibility This program is open to enrolled members of the Oneida Tribe of Wisconsin who have a high school diploma, HSED diploma, or GED. Applicants must be working on or planning to work on a vocational/technical, undergraduate, graduate, or doctoral degree at a college, university, or vocational school in any state. They must be able to demonstrate financial need.
Financial data Stipends range up to $20,000 per year, depending on the need of the recipient.
Duration The total length of eligibility is 6 terms for vocation/technical students, 10 terms for undergraduate students, 6 terms for graduate students, and 10 terms for doctoral students. To be eligible for renewal, vocational/technical students and undergraduates must maintain a GPA of 2.0 or higher and graduate and doctoral students must maintain a GPA of 3.0 or higher.
Number awarded Varies each year, depending upon the availability of funds.
Deadline Applications must be submitted by April of each year for the fall term, by September of each year for the spring term, or by April of each year for the summer term.

[394]
OREGON NATIVE AMERICAN CHAMBER OF COMMERCE SCHOLARSHIPS

Oregon Native American Chamber of Commerce
c/o Kelly Anne Ilagan
P.O. Box 82068
Portland, OR 97282-0068
(503) 654-2138   Fax: (503) 654-3238
E-mail: kellyanne@geojem.com
Web: www.onacc.org/scholarship.htm

Purpose To provide financial assistance to Native American students from any state enrolled at colleges and universities in Oregon.
Eligibility This program is open to undergraduates at colleges and universities who can provide documentation of Native American blood. Applicants must submit brief statements on how receiving this scholarship would benefit them and their educational needs, how they are involved in their Native American community on or off campus, what they plan to do with their education to help "give back" to Native Americans after graduation, and how they view their Native American heritage and its importance to them. Financial need is not considered in the selection process.
Financial data The stipend is $1,000.
Duration 1 year.
Additional information This program began in 2000.
Number awarded Varies each year; recently, 2 of these scholarships were awarded.
Deadline December of each year.

[395]
OSAGE HIGHER EDUCATION GRANTS

Osage Nation Education Department
Attn: Scholarship Coordinator
HC 66
P.O. Box 990
Hominy, OK 74035
(918) 287-5301   Toll-free: (800) 390-6724
Fax: (918) 287-5567   E-mail: jholding@osagetribe.com
Web: www.osagetribe.com/education/index.aspx

Purpose To provide financial assistance for college or graduate school to members of the Osage Tribe.
Eligibility This program is open to Osage tribal students who are enrolled or planning to enroll in a 2-year or 4-year college or university. A point system is used to rank applicants, including such factors as student status (freshman through graduate student), number of previous full-time semesters in college, GPA from previous semester, full-time or part-time enrollment, qualification for federal Pell Grant, and Osage blood quantum.
Financial data The amount of the award depends on the number of points earned by the recipient.
Duration 1 semester; may be renewed.
Number awarded Varies each year.
Deadline June of each year for fall semester; December of each year for spring semester; April of each year for summer term.

[396]
OSAGE TRIBAL EDUCATION COMMITTEE PROGRAM

Osage Tribal Education Committee
c/o Oklahoma Area Education Office
4149 Highline Boulevard, Suite 380
Oklahoma City, OK 73108
(405) 605-6051, ext. 300   Fax: (405) 605-6057

Purpose To provide financial assistance to undergraduate and graduate Osage students.
Eligibility This program is open to students who can prove Osage Indian blood in any degree. Applicants must be enrolled in an accredited college, university, or technical vocational program. They may be residents of any state.
Financial data The amount of the award depends on the financial need of the recipient.
Duration 1 year; may be renewed for up to 4 additional years, provided the recipient reapplies each semester and maintains a GPA of 2.0 or higher.
Number awarded Varies each year.

[397]
OSMANN FAMILY NATIVE AMERICAN SCHOLARSHIP

Sioux Falls Area Community Foundation
Attn: Scholarship Coordinator
300 North Phillips Avenue, Suite 102
Sioux Falls, SD 57104-6035
(605) 336-7055, ext. 20   Fax: (605) 336-0038
E-mail: pgale@sfacf.org
Web: www.sfacf.org

Purpose To provide financial assistance to members of Indian tribes in South Dakota who are interested in attending college in the state.

Eligibility This program is open to enrolled members of South Dakota Indian tribes who are graduating from high school. Applicants must have a GPA of 2.5 or higher and a record of participation in school or community activities. They must be planning to attend an institution that is a member of the South Dakota university system or a vocational/technical school in Sioux Falls, Watertown, Mitchell, or Rapid City. Along with their application, they must submit a 250-word essay describing their educational goals.

Financial data The stipend is $500. Funds are paid in 2 equal installments and are to be used for tuition, fees, and/or books.

Duration 1 year.

Additional information This program was established in 1998.

Number awarded 1 or more each year.

Deadline March of each year.

[398]
OTTAWA TRIBE HIGHER EDUCATION GRANTS

Ottawa Tribe of Oklahoma
c/o Oklahoma Area Education Office
4149 Highline Boulevard, Suite 380
Oklahoma City, OK 73108
(405) 605-6051, ext. 304   Fax: (405) 605-6057
Web: ottawatribe.org/heducation.htm

Purpose To provide financial assistance to members of the Ottawa Tribe of Oklahoma who plan to attend college or graduate school in any state.

Eligibility This program is open to enrolled members of the Ottawa Tribe of Oklahoma who have been accepted at an accredited institution of higher education in any state as a full- or part-time undergraduate or graduate student. Applicants must be able to document financial need. Along with their application, they must submit a copy of their tribal enrollment card, a copy of their high school and/or college transcripts, documentation of financial need, and a letter of intent explaining why they wish to attend college.

Financial data The amount of the award depends on the financial need of the recipient.

Duration 1 year; may be renewed for up to 4 additional years, provided the recipient reapplies each semester and maintains a GPA of 2.0 or higher.

Number awarded Varies each year.

Deadline July of each year.

[399]
OTZ TELEPHONE COOPERATIVE SCHOLARSHIPS

OTZ Telephone Cooperative, Inc.
Attn: Scholarship Committee
P.O. Box 324
Kotzebue, AK 99752
(907) 442-1033   Toll-free: (800) 478-3111, ext. 1033
Fax: (907) 442-1026   E-mail: asieh@otz.net
Web: www.otz.net

Purpose To provide financial assistance to members of the OTZ Telephone Cooperative in northwestern Alaska and their descendants who plan to attend college in any state.

Eligibility This program is open to OTZ Telephone Cooperative members and their descendants who have a high school diploma or GED and a GPA of 2.0 or higher. Applicants must be enrolled or accepted for enrollment at an accredited college, university, or vocational school in any state. Along with their application, they must submit a statement of purpose that includes their personal history, a summary of their accomplishments, their field of study, their educational and career goals, their reasons for those goals, and how their specified area of study will enable them to reach those goals. Selection is based on that statement (30 points for content and 20 points for writing skills and grammar), the completed application (20 points), 3 letters of reference (10 points), official transcripts (10 points), and proof of acceptance (10 points).

Financial data The stipend is $1,500 per year for full-time students or $750 per year for part-time students.

Duration Up to 6 consecutive years.

Number awarded Varies each year.

Deadline June of each year.

[400]
PACIFIC ISLANDERS IN COMMUNICATIONS SCHOLARSHIPS

Pacific Islanders in Communications
Attn: Scholarship Committee
1221 Kapi'olani Boulevard, Suite 6A-4
Honolulu, HI 96814-3513
(808) 591-0059   Fax: (808) 591-1114
E-mail: gcobb-adams@piccom.org
Web: www.piccom.org/producers.php

Purpose To provide financial assistance to undergraduate and graduate students, especially Pacific Islanders, who are working on a degree in media and/or communications.

Eligibility This program is open to students who are working on a degree, certificate, and/or other certification in media and/or communications at the undergraduate, graduate, or unclassified level of study. Applicants must be 18 years of age or older and citizens, legal permanent residents, or nationals of the United States or its territories. All students are eligible, but the program especially encourages applications from Pacific Islanders, defined as descendants of the indigenous peoples of American Samoa, Guam, Hawai'i, the Northern Mariana Islands, and other Pacific Islands. Along with their application, they must submit a 500-word essay on why they feel Pacific Islander representation in media is important and their role in advancing equitable representation; their essay should include their reasons for attending school, their career goals and how this education will further those goals, prior and current ser-

Deadline June of each year for fall term; December of each year for spring term.

vice to school and community (in particular the Pacific Islander community), and a personal and professional history. Selection is based on the essay; academic proficiency; demonstrated experience in media, communications, and/or a related field; commitment to the Pacific Islander community; and financial need.
Financial data The stipend is $5,000.
Duration 1 year; nonrenewable.
Additional information This program began in 2002.
Number awarded Varies each year.
Deadline March of each year.

[401]
PASCUA YAQUI HIGHER EDUCATION SCHOLARSHIP

Pascua Yaqui Tribe
Attn: Higher Education Program
7474 South Camino de Oeste
Tucson, AZ 85746
(520) 883-5050   Toll-free: (800) 5-PASCUA
Fax: (520) 883-5021
Web: www.pascuayaqui-nsn.gov

Purpose To provide financial assistance to members of the Pascua Yaqui Tribe who are interested in attending a college or graduate school in any state.
Eligibility This program is open to enrolled members of the Pascua Yaqui Tribe who are attending or planning to attend a college, university, or vocational/technical institute in any state. Applicants must apply for all other available aid and still have unmet financial need. They may be planning to work on an undergraduate or graduate degree on a full- or part-time basis.
Financial data A stipend is awarded (amount not specified).
Duration 1 semester; may be renewed.
Number awarded Varies each year.
Deadline June of each year for fall; November of each year for spring; May of each year for summer.

[402]
PAUL AND EMILY SHAGEN SCHOLARSHIP

Chippewa County Community Foundation
P.O. Box 1979
Sault Ste. Marie, MI 49783
(906) 635-1046   Fax: (775) 417-7368
E-mail: cccf@lighthouse.net
Web: www.cccf4good4ever.org/main.asp?id=7

Purpose To provide financial assistance to members of the Sault Ste. Marie Tribe of Chippewa Indians who are interested in attending college or graduate school in any state.
Eligibility This program is open to enrolled members of the Sault Ste. Marie Tribe of Chippewa Indians who have been accepted for enrollment as a full-time undergraduate, graduate, or professional student at an accredited college, university, vocational school, or community college in any state. Applicants must submit an essay of 300 to 500 words on how they plan to use the education or training to contribute to the community, including the tribe. Selection is based on that essay, academic performance and progress, and financial need.
Financial data A stipend is awarded (amount not specified).
Duration 1 year.
Number awarded Varies each year.
Deadline June or November of each year.

[403]
PAULINE MIGUEL SCHOLARSHIP

Community Foundation for Southern Arizona
2250 East Broadway Boulevard
Tucson, AZ 85719
(520) 770-0800   Fax: (520) 770-1500
E-mail: philanthropy@cfsoaz.org
Web: www.cfsoaz.org/pagE17482.cfm

Purpose To provide financial assistance for college to members of the Tohono O'odham Nation in southern Arizona.
Eligibility This program is open to members of the Tohono O'odham Nation in southern Arizona. Applicants must be attending or planning to attend college. Selection is based on academic success, potential for post-high school academic achievement, interest and activities, and financial need.
Financial data The stipend is $1,000.
Duration 1 year.
Number awarded 1 each year.

[404]
PEARL CARTER SCOTT AVIATION SCHOLARSHIP

Chickasaw Foundation
110 West 12th Street
P.O. Box 1726
Ada, OK 74821-1726
(580) 421-9030   Fax: (580) 421-9031
E-mail: ChickasawFoundation@chickasaw.net
Web: www.chickasaw.net

Purpose To provide financial assistance to members of the Chickasaw Nation who are working on an undergraduate or graduate degree in a field related to aviation.
Eligibility This program is open to Chickasaw students who are currently enrolled at a college, university, or recognized private aviation school. Applicants must be working on an undergraduate or graduate degree in a field related to aviation (e.g., aviation maintenance technology, flight training, aviation law, air traffic control, aeronautical engineering, aerospace mechanical engineering, manufacturing engineering with an aviation emphasis, airline and airport operations, airport management, meteorology, aviation technology management, or a related field). Along with their application, they must submit high school or college transcripts, 2 letters of recommendation, a copy of their Chickasaw Nation citizenship card, and a 1-page essay on their long-term goals and plans for achieving them. Financial need is not considered in the selection process.
Financial data The stipend is $1,250 per year.
Duration 1 year; may be renewed if the recipient demonstrates appropriate progress toward a degree in an aviation program.
Number awarded 1 each year.
Deadline July of each year.

[405]
PEBBLE LIMITED PARTNERSHIP/BBNC SCHOLARSHIPS

Bristol Bay Native Corporation
Attn: BBNC Education Foundation
111 West 16th Avenue, Suite 400
Anchorage, AK 99501
(907) 278-3602 Toll-free: (800) 426-3602
Fax: (907) 276-3924 E-mail: pelagiol@bbnc.net
Web: www.bbnc.net/education/students

Purpose To provide financial assistance to shareholders of Bristol Bay Native Corporation (BBNC) who are entering freshmen at a postsecondary institution in any state and preparing for a career in the mining industry.

Eligibility This program is open to BBNC shareholders who are planning to enroll full time as a freshman at an accredited college, university, or vocational school in any state. Applicants must have a GPA of 2.0 or higher and be able to demonstrate financial need. They must be interested in preparing for a career in the mining industry. Along with their application, they must submit an essay on how they became interested in their proposed field of study, any special circumstances they want to be considered, and their desire to work in the region or for a BBNC subsidiary company. Selection is based on the essay (35%), cumulative GPA (40%), financial need (20%), and letters of recommendation (5%). Preference is given to graduates of the 4 Bristol Bay school districts.

Financial data The stipend is $5,000.

Duration 1 year.

Additional information This program is sponsored by the Pebble Limited Partnership.

Number awarded 1 or more each year.

Deadline April of each year.

[406]
PEGGY VATTER MEMORIAL SCHOLARSHIPS

Washington Science Teachers Association
c/o Patricia MacGowan, Washington MESA
University of Washington
P.O. Box 352181
Seattle, WA 98195-2181
(206) 543-0562 Fax: (206) 685-0666
E-mail: pmac@engr.washington.edu
Web: wsta.net/html

Purpose To provide financial assistance to minority and other upper-division students and teachers in Washington interested in training in science education.

Eligibility This program is open to 1) juniors and seniors at colleges and universities in Washington who are working on certification in science education or in elementary education with an emphasis on science; and 2) certified teachers in Washington interested in improving their skills in providing equitable science education through professional development. In the student category, preference is given to African Americans, Hispanics, Native Americans, and women. Applicants must submit a 1-page essay on why they are applying for this scholarship.

Financial data The stipend is $1,500.

Duration 1 year; nonrenewable.

Additional information This program was established in 2003.

Number awarded At least 2 each year: 1 to a student and 1 to a certified teacher.

Deadline April of each year.

[407]
PENOBSCOT NATION ADULT VOCATIONAL TRAINING

Penobscot Nation
Attn: Department of Education and Career Services
6 River Road
Indian Island, ME 04468
(207) 827-1649, ext. 148 Fax: (207) 827-2088
E-mail: pinedu@penobscotnation.org
Web: www.penobscotnation.org

Purpose To provide financial assistance to members of the Penobscot Nation who are working on 2-year degrees or training programs at schools in any state.

Eligibility This program is open to students who are members of the Penobscot Nation and are enrolled full time in an associate degree, diploma, or certificate training program at a school in any state. Awards are granted on the basis of financial need (as determined by the institution the student is attending).

Financial data The amount awarded varies, depending upon the needs of the recipient.

Duration 1 year or more.

Additional information Funding for this program is provided to the Penobscot Nation through the Bureau of Indian Affairs.

Number awarded Varies each year.

Deadline June of each year.

[408]
PENOBSCOT NATION HIGHER EDUCATION GRANT PROGRAM

Penobscot Nation
Attn: Department of Education and Career Services
6 River Road
Indian Island, ME 04468
(207) 827-1649, ext. 148 Fax: (207) 827-2088
E-mail: pinedu@penobscotnation.org
Web: www.penobscotnation.org

Purpose To provide financial assistance to members of the Penobscot Nation who are or will be working on a 4-year degree at a college in any state.

Eligibility This program is open to students who are members of the Penobscot Nation and are enrolled (or going to be enrolled) full time in a 4-year degree program in any state. Awards are granted on the basis of financial need as determined by the institution the student is attending.

Financial data The amount awarded varies, depending upon the needs of the recipient. Funds may be used to pay for tuition, fees, room, board, books, or living expenses.

Duration 1 year or more.

Additional information Funding for this program is provided to the Penobscot Nation through the Bureau of Indian Affairs.

Number awarded Varies each year.

Deadline June of each year.

[409]
PEORIA TRIBAL EDUCATION PROGRAM
Peoria Tribe of Indians of Oklahoma
Attn: Education Program
118 South Eight Tribes Trail
P.O. Box 1527
Miami, OK 74355
(918) 540-2535, ext. 10   Toll-free: (800) 259-9987
Fax: (918) 540-2538
Web: www.peoriatribe.com/services/education.php

Purpose To provide financial assistance for college to members of the Peoria Tribe of Indians of Oklahoma.

Eligibility This program is open to enrolled members of the Peoria Tribe of Indians of Oklahoma who have been accepted by an accredited college or vocational school as a full- or part-time student. Applicants must have a GPA of 2.5 or higher. They must submit high school transcripts, a copy of SAT or ACT scores, 2 letters of recommendation, and a short essay outlining their academic goals. Selection is based on academic achievement and the probability of completing the academic program; financial need is not considered.

Financial data The stipend is $3,500 per semester for full-time students or $1,750 per semester for part-time students.

Duration 1 semester; may be renewed up to 7 additional semesters if the recipient maintains a GPA of 2.5 or higher.

Number awarded Varies each year; recently, 225 of these scholarships (41 new awards, 169 renewals, and 15 part-time scholarships) were awarded.

Deadline July of each year for the fall semester; December of each year for the spring semester.

[410]
PERCY B. FEREBEE ENDOWMENT SCHOLARSHIP
Center for Scholarship Administration, Inc.
Attn: Wachovia Accounts
4320-G Wade Hampton Boulevard
Taylors, SC 29687
Toll-free: (866) 608-0001
E-mail: wachoviascholars@bellsouth.net
Web: https:

Purpose To provide financial assistance for college to residents of the Cherokee Nation or selected counties in North Carolina.

Eligibility This program is open to high school seniors who are residents of the counties of Cherokee, Clay, Graham, Jackson, Macon, or Swain (in North Carolina) or on the Cherokee Indian Reservation. Applicants must be able to demonstrate "worthy and talented characteristics," academic achievement, and financial need. They must be planning to attend a 4-year college or university in North Carolina.

Financial data A stipend is awarded (amount not specified).

Duration 1 year; may be renewed up to 3 additional years if the recipient maintains a GPA of 1.5 or higher for the freshman year and 2.0 or higher after the sophomore and junior years.

Number awarded 21 each year: 3 from each of the 6 counties, 2 from the Cherokee Indian Reservation, and 1 at large.

Deadline January of each year.

[411]
PETER DOCTOR MEMORIAL INDIAN EMLEN AWARDS
Peter Doctor Memorial Indian Scholarship Foundation, Inc.
c/o Clara Hill, Treasurer
P.O. Box 731
Basom, NY 14013
(716) 542-2025   E-mail: cehill@wnynet.net

Purpose To provide financial assistance to undergraduate or graduate students of New York Iroquois descent.

Eligibility This program is open to undergraduate or graduate students who are of Iroquois Indian descent (i.e., a parent or grandparent must be enrolled). Applicants must have completed at least 1 year in a technical school, college, or university. Interviews may be required. Selection is based on need.

Financial data Stipends range up to $2,000.

Duration 2 years for medical students; 1 year for all other recipients.

Deadline May of each year.

[412]
PETER DOCTOR MEMORIAL INDIAN SCHOLARSHIP GRANTS
Peter Doctor Memorial Indian Scholarship Foundation, Inc.
c/o Clara Hill, Treasurer
P.O. Box 731
Basom, NY 14013
(716) 542-2025   E-mail: cehill@wnynet.net

Purpose To provide financial assistance to New York Iroquois Indians currently enrolled in college on the undergraduate or graduate school level.

Eligibility This program is open to enrolled New York Iroquois Indian students who have completed at least 1 year in a technical school, college, or university. Both undergraduate and graduate students are eligible. There are no age limits or GPA requirements. Interviews may be required. Applicants must have tribal certification. Selection is based on need.

Financial data Stipends range up to $1,500.

Duration 2 years for medical students; 1 year for all other recipients.

Deadline May of each year.

[413]
PETER KALIFORNSKY MEMORIAL ENDOWMENT SCHOLARSHIP FUND
Cook Inlet Region, Inc.
Attn: The CIRI Foundation
3600 San Jeronimo Drive, Suite 256
Anchorage, AK 99508-2870
(907) 793-3575   Toll-free: (800) 764-3382
Fax: (907) 793-3585   E-mail: tcf@thecirifoundation.org
Web: www.thecirifoundation.org/designated.htm

Purpose To provide financial assistance for undergraduate or graduate studies to Alaska Natives who are original enrollees to Cook Inlet Region, Inc. (CIRI) and their lineal descendants.

Eligibility This program is open to Alaska Native enrollees to CIRI under the Alaska Native Claims Settlement Act (ANCSA) of 1971 and their lineal descendants. There are no Alaska residency requirements or age limitations. Applicants must be accepted or enrolled full time in a 4-year undergraduate or a graduate degree program. Preference is given to students in Alaska Native studies. They must have a GPA of 2.5 or higher. Along with their application, they must submit a 500-word statement on their educational and career goals and how they are contributing, or planning to contribute, to a positive Alaska Native community. Selection is based on that statement, academic achievement, rigor of course work or degree program, student financial contribution, financial need, grade level, previous work performance, community service, and relationship of degree program to career goals.

Financial data The stipend is $10,000 per year, $8,000 per year, or $2,500 per semester, depending on GPA.

Duration 1 semester or 1 year.

Additional information This program was established in 1993.

Number awarded Varies each year.

Deadline May of each year for annual scholarships; May or November of each year for semester scholarships.

[414]
PHYLLIS G. MEEKINS SCHOLARSHIP
Ladies Professional Golf Association
Attn: LPGA Foundation
100 International Golf Drive
Daytona Beach, FL 32124-1082
(386) 274-6200   Fax: (386) 274-1099
E-mail: foundation.scholarships@lpga.com
Web: www.lpgafoundation.org

Purpose To provide financial assistance to Native American and other minority female graduating high school seniors who played golf in high school and plan to continue to play in college.

Eligibility This program is open to female high school seniors who are members of a recognized minority group. Applicants must have a GPA of 3.0 or higher and a background in golf. They must be planning to enroll full time at a college or university in the United States and play competitive golf. Along with their application, they must submit a letter that describes how golf has been an integral part of their lives and includes their personal, academic, and professional goals; their chosen discipline of study; and how this scholarship will be of assistance. Financial need is considered in the selection process. U.S. citizenship or legal resident status is required.

Financial data The stipend is $1,250.

Duration 1 year.

Additional information This program was established in 2006.

Number awarded 1 each year.

Deadline May of each year.

[415]
PI STATE NATIVE AMERICAN GRANTS-IN-AID
Delta Kappa Gamma Society International-Pi State Organization
c/o Harlene Gilbert
5338 East Lake Road
Romulus, NY 14541
(315) 585-6691   E-mail: wilma@capital.net
Web: www.deltakappagamma.org/NY/awards.html

Purpose To provide funding to Native American women from New York who plan to work in education or another service field.

Eligibility This program is open to Native American women from New York who are attending a 2-year or 4-year college in the state. Applicants must be planning to work in education or another service field, but preference is given to those majoring in education. Both undergraduate and graduate students are eligible.

Financial data The grant is $500 per semester ($1,000 per year). Funds may be used for any career-related purpose, including purchase of textbooks.

Duration 1 semester; may be renewed for a total of 5 years and a total of $5,000 over a recipient's lifetime.

Number awarded Varies each year; recently, 3 of these grants were awarded.

[416]
P.O. PISTILLI SCHOLARSHIPS
Design Automation Conference
c/o Cherrice Traver
Union College
ECE Department
Schenectady, NY 12308
(518) 388-6326   Fax: (518) 388-6789
E-mail: traverc@union.edu
Web: doc.union.edu/acsee.html

Purpose To provide financial assistance to female, minority, or disabled high school seniors who are interested in preparing for a career in computer science or electrical engineering.

Eligibility This program is open to graduating high school seniors who are members of underrepresented groups: women, African Americans, Hispanics, Native Americans, and persons with disabilities. Applicants must be interested in preparing for a career in electrical engineering, computer engineering, or computer science. They must have at least a 3.0 GPA, have demonstrated high achievements in math and science courses, have demonstrated involvement in activities associated with the underrepresented group they represent, and be able to demonstrate significant financial need. U.S. citizenship is not required, but applicants must be U.S. residents when they apply and must plan to attend an accredited college or university. Along with their application, they must submit 3 letters of recommendation, official transcripts, ACT/SAT and/or PSAT scores, a personal statement outlining future goals and why they think they should receive this scholarship, a copy of their latest income tax return, and a copy of the FAFSA form they submitted.

Financial data Stipends are $4,000 per year. Awards are paid each year in 2 equal installments.

Duration 1 year; renewable for up to 4 additional years.

Additional information This program is funded by the Design Automation Conference and the IEEE Circuits and System Society. It is directed by the Association for Computing Machinery's Special Interest Group on Design Automation.
Number awarded 2 to 7 each year.
Deadline January of each year.

[417]
POARCH BAND OF CREEK INDIANS TUITION PAYMENT PROGRAM
Poarch Band of Creek Indians
Attn: Tuition Program Coordinator
5811 Jack Springs Road
Atmore, AL 36502
(251) 368-9136, ext. 2241 Fax: (251) 368-0809
E-mail: sfisher@poarchcreekindians-nsn.gov
Web: www.poarchcreekindians.org

Purpose To help pay the tuition costs of members of the Poarch Band of Creek Indians who are attending middle school, high school, or college in any state.
Eligibility This program is open to enrolled members of the Poarch Band of Creek Indians who are attending middle school, high school, or college in any state. Applicants must submit documentation of their tuition costs. College students may take courses by correspondence, from an online university, through a certification program, or on the usual college schedule.
Financial data Funds are paid toward the tuition expenses of qualified members.
Duration 1 semester; may be renewed.
Number awarded Varies each year.
Deadline Applications may be submitted at any time.

[418]
POKAGON BAND ADULT VOCATIONAL SCHOLARSHIP
Pokagon Band of Potawatomi Indians
Attn: Department of Education
58620 Sink Road
P.O. Box 180
Dowagiac, MI 49047
(269) 782-0887 Toll-free: (888) 330-1234
Fax: (269) 782-0985
E-mail: Joseph.morsaw@pokagon.com
Web: www.pokagon.com

Purpose To provide financial assistance to members of the Pokagon Band of Potawatomi Indians who are interested in working on a certificate in adult vocational education at a school in any state.
Eligibility This program is open to Pokagon Band members who are enrolled or planning to enroll in an adult vocational education program at an accredited institution in any state. Applicants must be able to document financial need.
Financial data Stipends are based on unmet financial need, to a lifetime total of $2,000 per member.
Duration 1 semester; may be renewed until completion of a vocational education certificate.
Number awarded Varies each year.

[419]
POKAGON BAND HIGHER EDUCATION SCHOLARSHIP
Pokagon Band of Potawatomi Indians
Attn: Department of Education
58620 Sink Road
P.O. Box 180
Dowagiac, MI 49047
(269) 782-0887 Toll-free: (888) 330-1234
Fax: (269) 782-0985
E-mail: Joseph.morsaw@pokagon.com
Web: www.pokagon.com

Purpose To provide financial assistance to members of the Pokagon Band of Potawatomi Indians who are interested in working on an undergraduate or graduate degree at a college in any state.
Eligibility This program is open to enrolled members of the Pokagon Band who are attending or planning to attend an accredited college or university in any state to work on an associate, bachelor's, master's, or doctoral degree. Applicants must apply for all campus-based financial aid for which they are eligible and be able to document that they still have an unmet financial need. If they plan to attend a public college or university in Michigan and have an Indian blood level of one-quarter or more, they must also apply for a Michigan Indian Tuition Waiver.
Financial data The maximum stipend is $1,000 per semester.
Duration 1 semester; may be renewed for 3 years of study for an associate degree, for 5 years of study for a bachelor's degree, or for 5 years of study for a graduate degree.
Number awarded Varies each year.

[420]
PONCA TRIBE OF NEBRASKA EDUCATIONAL GRANTS
Ponca Tribe of Nebraska
Attn: Departments of Education and Culture
1800 Syracuse Avenue
Norfolk, NE 68701
(402) 371-8834 Fax: (402) 371-7564
E-mail: pate@poncatribe-ne.org
Web: www.poncatribe-ne.org

Purpose To provide financial assistance to members of the Ponca Tribe of Nebraska who are interested in attending an undergraduate, graduate, or vocational school in any state.
Eligibility This program is open to enrolled members of the Ponca Tribe of Nebraska who are attending or planning to attend a college, university, or vocational/technical school in any state. Applicants must submit a letter of admission from the school they plan to attend, a Certificate of Indian Blood (CIB), and documentation of financial need.
Financial data A stipend is awarded (amount not specified).
Duration 1 semester or year. Full-time students may reapply each academic year (or summer session if they wish to attend summer school). Part-time students may reapply each semester or quarter. Renewals are approved if the student maintains a GPA of 2.0 or higher as an undergraduate or vocational student or 3.0 or higher as a graduate student.

Number awarded Varies each year.
Deadline August of each year for fall quarter or semester; November of each year for winter quarter; December of each year for spring quarter or semester; May of each year for summer session.

[421]
PO'PAY SCHOLARSHIPS

Pueblo of Ohkay Owingeh
Attn: Department of Education
P.O. Box 1269
San Juan Pueblo, NM 87566
(505) 852-3477   Fax: (505) 852-3030
E-mail: wevog68@valornet.com
Web: www.sanjuaned.org/higher_ed.html

Purpose To provide need-based financial assistance to tribal members of the Pueblo of Ohkay Owingeh who are working on an associate or bachelor's degree.
Eligibility This program is open to enrolled and verified members of the Ohkay Owingeh tribe who are enrolled or accepted for enrollment at an accredited 2- or 4-year college or university in any state. Applicants must be working on or planning to work on a first-time associate or bachelor's degree as a full-time student. They must agree to provide 20 hours of community service within the tribe each semester. Along with their application, they must submit a personal statement describing who they are, any activities in which they have been involved, and their personal and professional goals. Financial need is considered in the selection process.
Financial data The stipend depends on the unmet financial need of the recipient.
Duration 1 year; may be renewed up to 4 additional years, provided the recipient remains enrolled full time, maintains a GPA of 2.0 or higher, and fulfills the community service agreement.
Additional information Until 2005, the Pueblo of Ohkay Owingeh was known as the Pueblo of San Juan.
Number awarded Varies each year.
Deadline June of each year for fall semester; December of each year for spring semester.

[422]
PRAIRIE BAND POTAWATOMI NATION ADULT EDUCATION PROGRAM

Prairie Band Potawatomi Nation
Education Department
16281 Q Road
Mayetta, KS 66509
(785) 966-2255   Toll-free: (877) 715-6789
Fax: (785) 966-2956   E-mail: info@pbpnation.org
Web: www.pbpindiantribe.com/other-education.aspx

Purpose To provide funding to members of the Prairie Band Potawatomi Nation who are interested in continuing educational activities in any state.
Eligibility This program is open to members of the Prairie Band Potawatomi Nation who have a Certificate of Indian Blood. Applicants must be seeking assistance for GED preparation and examination fees, registration fees for conferences and/or workshops, tuition (if taking only 1 college course), employment enrichment training or courses, professional licensure fees, continuing education units, or other appropriate educational activity. Along with their application, they must submit a letter explaining why they need the grant and how it will be used.
Financial data The amount of the grant depends on the cost of the program for which support is requested.
Duration These are 1-time grants.
Number awarded Varies each year.
Deadline Applications must be submitted at least 4 weeks prior to beginning the program payment due date, whichever occurs first.

[423]
PRAIRIE BAND POTAWATOMI NATION ADULT VOCATIONAL TRAINING GRANT

Prairie Band Potawatomi Nation
Education Department
16281 Q Road
Mayetta, KS 66509
(785) 966-2255   Toll-free: (877) 715-6789
Fax: (785) 966-2956   E-mail: info@pbpnation.org
Web: www.pbpindiantribe.com/other-education.aspx

Purpose To provide financial assistance to members of the Prairie Band Potawatomi Nation who are interested in attending an adult vocational training program in any state.
Eligibility This program is open to members of the Prairie Band Potawatomi Nation who have a Certificate of Indian Blood. Applicants must be enrolled or planning to enroll in an adult vocational training program in any state. They may be attending a traditional (9 to 12 months) or nontraditional (less than 9 months) program. Along with their application, they must submit a letter explaining why they need the grant and how it will be used.
Financial data Grants provide partial payment of tuition and other costs. Funds may be used for tuition, fees, and books. Part-time students are eligible for exact costs only.
Duration 1 semester; may be renewed.
Number awarded Varies each year.
Deadline Applications must be submitted at least 2 months prior to beginning of attendance or payment due date, whichever occurs first.

[424]
PRAIRIE BAND POTAWATOMI NATION HIGHER EDUCATION UNDERGRADUATE PROGRAM

Prairie Band Potawatomi Nation
Education Department
16281 Q Road
Mayetta, KS 66509
(785) 966-2255   Toll-free: (877) 715-6789
Fax: (785) 966-2956   E-mail: info@pbpnation.org
Web: www.pbpindiantribe.com/other-education.aspx

Purpose To provide financial assistance to members of the Prairie Band Potawatomi Nation who are interested in attending college in any state.
Eligibility This program is open to members of the Prairie Band Potawatomi Nation who have a Certificate of Indian Blood. Applicants must be enrolled or planning to enroll at a college or university in any state to work on a bachelor's degree. Along with their application, they must submit a let-

ter explaining why they need the grant and how it will be used.

Financial data Full-time students receive a stipend of up to $3,000 per semester as a freshman, $3,500 per semester as a sophomore, $4,000 per semester as a junior, or $4,500 per semester as a senior. Funds may be used for tuition, fees, and books. Part-time students are eligible for exact costs only.

Duration 1 semester; may be renewed.

Number awarded Varies each year.

Deadline June of each year for fall semester; October of each year for spring semester.

[425]
PRINCE KUHIO HAWAIIAN CIVIC CLUB SCHOLARSHIP

Prince Kuhio Hawaiian Civic Club
Attn: Scholarship Chair
P.O. Box 4728
Honolulu, HI 96812
E-mail: Caztwin@aol.com
Web: www.pkhcc.com/scholarship

Purpose To provide financial assistance for undergraduate or graduate studies to persons of Hawaiian descent.

Eligibility Applicants must be of Hawaiian descent (descendants of the aboriginal inhabitants of the Hawaiian Islands prior to 1778) who are high school seniors, recent graduates, or full-time undergraduate or graduate students. Graduating high school seniors and current undergraduate students must have a GPA of 2.5 or higher; graduate students must have at least a 3.3 GPA. Priority is given to members of the Prince Kuhio Hawaiian Civic Club in good standing, including directly-related family members. Special consideration is given to applicants majoring in Hawaiian studies, Hawaiian language, or journalism.

Financial data Stipends range from $500 to $1,000.

Duration 1 year.

Additional information Information is also available from Cyr Pakele, Kamehameha Schools, Haleakala Counseling Center, 210 Konia Circle, Honolulu, HI 96817, (808) 842-8934, (800) 842-IMUA, E-mail: cypakele@ksbe.edu.

Number awarded Varies each year.

Deadline March of each year.

[426]
PRIVATE COLLEGES & UNIVERSITIES COMMUNITY SERVICE SCHOLARSHIP PROGRAM FOR MULTICULTURAL STUDENTS

Private Colleges & Universities, Inc.
Attn: *PC&U* Multicultural Edition Scholarship Program
2 LAN Drive, Suite 100
P.O. Box 349
Westford, MA 01886
(978) 692-5092
E-mail: mc.scholar@privatecolleges.com
Web: www.privatecolleges.com

Purpose To provide financial assistance to Native American and other high school seniors and graduates of color who are planning to enroll as a freshman in a private college or university.

Eligibility All students of color who are currently residents of the United States or its territories and who plan to enroll in a baccalaureate degree program at a participating private college or university (for a list, write to the sponsor) are eligible. Applicants must submit a 1,000-word statement about their community service activities, a high school transcript, and a recommendation by someone in their community (not a family member). Selection is based on academic merit (transcripts, class rank, and GPA) and on service to the community.

Financial data The stipend is $2,000.

Duration 1 year; nonrenewable.

Number awarded Up to 5 each year.

Deadline March of each year.

[427]
PROFESSIONAL GOLF MANAGEMENT DIVERSITY SCHOLARSHIP

Professional Golfers' Association of America
Attn: PGA Foundation
100 Avenue of the Champions
Palm Beach Gardens, FL 33418
Toll-free: (888) 532-6661
Web: www.pgafoundation.com/scholarships.cfm

Purpose To provide financial assistance to women and minorities interested in attending a designated college or university to prepare for a career as a golf professional.

Eligibility This program is open to women and minorities interested in becoming a licensed PGA Professional. Applicants must be interested in attending 1 of 20 colleges and universities that offer the Professional Golf Management (PGM) curriculum sanctioned by the PGA.

Financial data The stipend is $3,000 per year.

Duration 1 year; may be renewed.

Additional information This program began in 1993. Programs are offered at Arizona State University (Mesa, Arizona), Campbell University (Buies Creek, North Carolina), Clemson University (Clemson, South Carolina), Coastal Carolina University (Conway, South Carolina), Eastern Kentucky University (Richmond, Kentucky), Ferris State University (Big Rapids, Michigan), Florida Gulf Coast University (Fort Myers, Florida), Florida State University (Tallahassee, Florida), Methodist College (Fayetteville, North Carolina), Mississippi State University (Mississippi State, Mississippi), New Mexico State University (Las Cruces, New Mexico), North Carolina State University (Raleigh, North Carolina), Pennsylvania State University (University Park, Pennsylvania), Sam Houston University (Huntsville, Texas), University of Central Oklahoma (Edmond, Oklahoma), University of Colorado (Colorado Springs, Colorado), University of Idaho (Moscow, Idaho), University of Maryland Eastern Shore (Princess Anne, Maryland), University of Nebraska (Lincoln, Nebraska), and University of Nevada (Las Vegas, Nevada).

Number awarded 1 or more each year.

[428]
PUBLIC RELATIONS STUDENT SOCIETY OF AMERICA MULTICULTURAL AFFAIRS SCHOLARSHIPS

Public Relations Student Society of America
Attn: Vice President of Member Services
33 Maiden Lane, 11th Floor
New York, NY 10038-5150
(212) 460-1474   Fax: (212) 995-0757
E-mail: prssa@prsa.org
Web: www.prssa.org

Purpose To provide financial assistance to Native American and other minority college students who are interested in preparing for a career in public relations.

Eligibility This program is open to minority (African American/Black, Hispanic/Latino, Asian, Native American, Alaskan Native, or Pacific Islander) students who are at least juniors at an accredited 4-year college or university. Applicants must be attending full time, be able to demonstrate financial need, and have earned a GPA of 3.0 or higher. Membership in the Public Relations Student Society of America is preferred but not required. A major or minor in public relations is preferred; students who attend a school that does not offer a public relations degree or program must be enrolled in a communications degree program (e.g., journalism, mass communications).

Financial data The stipend is $1,500.

Duration 1 year.

Additional information This program was established in 1989.

Number awarded 2 each year.

Deadline April of each year.

[429]
PUEBLO OF ACOMA HIGHER EDUCATION GRANT PROGRAM

Pueblo of Acoma
Attn: Higher Education Coordinator
P.O. Box 307
Acoma, NM 87034
(505) 552-5121   Fax: (505) 552-6812
E-mail: acomahe@unm.edu

Purpose To provide financial assistance for college to Pueblo of Acoma high school graduates.

Eligibility This program is open to enrolled citizens of the Pueblo of Acoma who are residents of New Mexico, high school seniors or graduates, enrolled or planning to enroll in an accredited college or university in any state, and in financial need. Applicants must have a GPA of 3.0 or higher. Awards are made first to seniors, then juniors, then sophomores, and finally freshmen.

Financial data The amount awarded varies, depending upon the recipient's financial need. Generally, scholarships are considered supplemental to other assistance and range between $1,000 and $1,800 per year.

Duration 1 year; may be renewed for up to 3 additional years.

Number awarded Varies each year.

Deadline April of each year for the fall term; September of each year for the spring term.

[430]
PUEBLO OF ISLETA HIGHER EDUCATION PROGRAM

Pueblo of Isleta
Attn: Higher Education Program
P.O. Box 1270
Isleta, NM 87022
(505) 869-2680, ext. 433   Fax: (505) 869-7690
E-mail: poi08004@isletapueblo.com
Web: www.isletapueblo.com/higher%20ed.html

Purpose To provide financial assistance for undergraduate or graduate study to members of the Pueblo of Isleta.

Eligibility This program is open to undergraduate and graduate students who can document tribal membership in the Pueblo of Isleta or at least one-quarter Isleta blood. Applicants must have a GPA of 2.5 or higher and be able to demonstrate financial need They must have applied for federal aid by submitting a Free Application for Federal Student Aid (FAFSA).

Financial data The stipend depends on the need of the recipient.

Duration 1 year; may be renewed if the recipient maintains a GPA of 2.5 or higher.

Number awarded Varies each year.

Deadline June of each year for the academic year; October of each year for the spring semester or winter quarter; March of each year for summer term.

[431]
PUEBLO OF JEMEZ SCHOLARSHIP PROGRAM

Pueblo of Jemez
Attn: Higher Education Center
P.O. Box 60
Jemez Pueblo, NM 87024
(505) 834-9102   Toll-free: (888) 834-3936
Fax: (505) 834-7900
E-mail: Higher_Ed@jemezpueblo.org
Web: www.jemezpueblo.org

Purpose To provide financial assistance to Jemez Pueblo students who are interested in earning a college degree.

Eligibility This program is open to Jemez Pueblo students working on or planning to work on an associate or bachelor's degree at an accredited institution of higher education as a full-time student. Applicants must be at least one quarter Jemez and recognized by the Jemez Pueblo census office (a Certificate of Indian Blood must be provided). They must submit 2 letters of recommendation, a copy of their letter of acceptance from the institution they are or are planning to attend, and an official transcript from the high school or college they last attended. It is required that all students fill out the Free Application for Federal Student Aid (FAFSA) and apply for aid from the college they plan to attend.

Financial data The stipend depends on the need of the recipient.

Duration 1 semester; may be renewed if the recipient remains enrolled full time with a GPA of 2.0 or higher.

Number awarded Varies each year.

Deadline April of each year for fall semester; October of each year for spring semester.

[432]
PUEBLO OF LAGUNA HIGHER EDUCATION PROGRAM

Pueblo of Laguna
Attn: Higher Education Office
P.O. Box 207
Laguna, NM 87026
(505) 552-7182   Fax: (505) 552-7235
E-mail: m.conant@lagunaed.net
Web: www.ldoe.org/pfs%20programs.html

Purpose To provide financial assistance for college to regular members of the Pueblo of Laguna.

Eligibility This program is open to regular enrolled members of the Pueblo of Laguna. Applicants must have a high school diploma or GED certificate and be working on a bachelor's or transferable associate degree. They must have been accepted by an accredited college or university in the United States as a full-time student. Along with their application, they must submit documentation of financial need, a 1-page personal statement on their purpose for working on a degree in their chosen field of study and their career or professional goals, high school and/or college transcripts, ACT scores, and verification of tribal membership or Indian blood. Vocational students, part-time students, and "naturalized" Laguna tribal members are not eligible.

Financial data Stipends are intended to cover unmet financial need, to a maximum of $8,000 per year. Most awards range from $2,000 to $5,000 per academic year.

Duration 1 year; may be renewed for a maximum of 5 academic years if the recipient maintains full-time enrollment and a GPA of 2.0 or higher.

Number awarded Varies each year.

Deadline May of each year for the fall term or academic year; October of each year for the winter/spring term; April of each year for the summer term.

[433]
PUEBLO OF POJOAQUE HIGHER EDUCATION SCHOLARSHIP PROGRAM

Pueblo of Pojoaque
Attn: Education Department
101 C Lightning Loop
Santa Fe, NM 87506
(505) 455-3369   Fax: (505) 455-3360
E-mail: csuazo@puebloofpojoaque.org
Web: www.pojoaqueeducation.monkeymedia.org

Purpose To provide financial assistance to Pueblo of Pojoaque tribal members interested in working on an undergraduate or graduate degree at a school in any state.

Eligibility This program is open to Pueblo of Pojoaque tribal members who can provide a certificate of tribal verification. Applicants must be working on or planning to work on a certificate, associate, bachelor's, master's, or doctoral degree at a school of higher education in any state. They must be able to verify that they have applied for all other available financial aid and that they still have financial need. Both full- and part-time students are eligible.

Financial data Both full- and part-time students receive a grant to cover tuition, fees, and books, to a maximum of $2,000 per year. In addition, full-time students receive a monthly stipend (amount not specified).

Duration Students working on a certificate are eligible for up to 2 years of support to complete the requirements. Students working on an associate degree are eligible for up to 4 years of part-time support or 3 years of full-time support. Students working full time on a bachelor's degree are eligible for up to 5 years of support if they enter as a first-time student or up to 4 years of support if they transfer with an associate degree. Students working part time on a bachelor's degree are eligible for up to 7 years of support if they enter as a first-time student or up to 6 years of support if they transfer with an associate degree. Students working on a master's or Ph.D. degree are eligible for up to 4 years of support. Renewal for full-time students requires that they complete at least 20 hours of nonprofit community service per semester. Renewal for all students requires that they maintain a GPA of 2.0 or higher.

Number awarded Varies each year.

Deadline July of each year for fall semester; December of each year for spring semester; April of each year for summer semester.

[434]
PUEBLO OF SAN FELIPE HIGHER EDUCATION PROGRAM

Pueblo of San Felipe
Attn: Higher Education Program
P.O. Box 4339
San Felipe, NM 87001
(505) 867-5234   Fax: (505) 867-8867
E-mail: sanfelipeed@hotmail.com

Purpose To provide financial assistance to high school seniors who are enrolled members of the Pueblo of San Felipe and planning to attend college in any state.

Eligibility This program is open to recognized enrolled members of the Pueblo of San Felipe who are interested in working on an associate of arts degree or baccalaureate degree at an accredited institution of higher education in any state. Applicants must apply in either the second half of their junior year in high school or the first half of their senior year. Along with their application, they must submit a copy of their high school transcript, a copy of their letter of acceptance from a college or university, 2 letters of recommendation, a Certificate of Indian Blood (must be at least one quarter San Felipe and recognized under the Southern Pueblos Agency or the San Felipe Census Office), a certificate of tribal verification, and a needs analysis. Financial need is considered in the selection process.

Financial data A stipend is awarded (amount not specified).

Duration 1 semester; may be renewed for up to a total of 4 years.

Additional information Recipients must register for at least 12 units per semester in college. No remedial courses will be funded.

Number awarded Varies each year.

Deadline January of each year for the fall semester, October of each year for the spring semester, or February of each year for the summer term.

[435]
PURCELL POWLESS SCHOLARSHIP

Milwaukee Indian Education Committee
c/o American Indian Student Services
University of Wisconsin at Milwaukee
Holton G-48
P.O. Box 413
Milwaukee, WI 53201
(414) 229-5880   Fax: (414) 229-5930
E-mail: amour@uwm.edu
Web: www.indiansummer.org

Purpose To provide financial assistance to American Indians from Wisconsin who are studying or planning to study a medical field in college in any state.

Eligibility This program is open to Wisconsin residents who are American Indians by tribal enrollment or descendancy (having 1 or more ancestors who are tribally enrolled). Applicants must be accepted or in good standing at an institution of higher education in any state and majoring in a medical field. They must submit a 1-page statement describing their educational goals, the reasons they feel they should receive the scholarship, their community service, and any special needs. Preference is given to applicants who have provided service to the Indian community and have not previously received a scholarship.

Financial data The stipend is $1,000.

Duration 1 year.

Additional information Support for this program is provided by Indian Summer Festivals, Inc.

Number awarded 1 each year.

Deadline July of each year.

[436]
PYRAMID LAKE PAIUTE TRIBE ADULT VOCATIONAL TRAINING PROGRAM

Pyramid Lake Paiute Tribe
Attn: Consolidated Higher Education Office
P.O. Box 256
Nixon, NV 89424
(775) 574-0300   Fax: (775) 574-0302
E-mail: asampson@plpt.nsn.us
Web: www.plpt.nsn.us/highed/index.html

Purpose To provide financial assistance to members of the Pyramid Lake Paiute Tribe who are interested in adult vocational training at a school in any state.

Eligibility This program is open to members of the Pyramid Lake Paiute Tribe who can document financial need and tribal membership. Applicants must be interested in a program of adult vocational training at a school in any state. First-time applicants must submit a high school diploma, GED certificate, or adult education diploma. Continuing students must submit an official transcript of their most recent semester or quarter.

Financial data Stipends are intended to pay a portion of the costs of the vocational training program.

Duration 1 semester or quarter; may be renewed.

Additional information This program is funded in part by the U.S. Bureau of Indian Affairs.

Number awarded Varies each year.

Deadline June of each year for fall semester or academic year; October of each year for spring semester.

[437]
PYRAMID LAKE PAIUTE TRIBE ENRICHMENT SCHOLARSHIP

Pyramid Lake Paiute Tribe
Attn: Consolidated Higher Education Office
P.O. Box 256
Nixon, NV 89424
(775) 574-0300   Fax: (775) 574-0302
E-mail: asampson@plpt.nsn.us
Web: www.plpt.nsn.us/highed/index.html

Purpose To provide financial assistance to members of the Pyramid Lake Paiute Tribe who are interested in working part time on an undergraduate or graduate degree.

Eligibility This program is open to enrolled members of the Pyramid Lake Paiute Tribe who are working on an associate, bachelor's, master's, or doctoral (including law and medicine) degree. Applicants may take up to 9 credits per term (or 12 credits for law and medical students). They must have a GPA of 2.0 or higher for their most recent semester, certificate, or adult education diploma. Applicants must be interested in taking courses at a college, vocational school, or professional development program. They must have a GPA of 2.0 or higher for their most recent semester. Along with their application, they must submit a 75-word essay on how they will benefit from the courses they are taking.

Financial data The stipend is $1,000 per semester (or $2,000 per semester for law and medical students). A supplemental grant of $250 is provided for books and supplies.

Duration 1 semester; may be renewed, provided the recipient maintains a GPA of 2.0 or higher.

Number awarded Varies each year.

Deadline June of each year for fall; November of each year for spring.

[438]
RACE RELATIONS MULTIRACIAL STUDENT SCHOLARSHIP

Christian Reformed Church
Attn: Ministry of Race Relations
2850 Kalamazoo Avenue, S.E.
Grand Rapids, MI 49560-0200
(616) 224-5883   Toll-free: (800) 272-5125
E-mail: lugoe@crcna.org
Web: www.crcna.org

Purpose To provide financial assistance to Native American and other undergraduate and graduate minority students interested in attending colleges related to the Christian Reformed Church in North America (CRCNA).

Eligibility Students of color in the United States and Canada are eligible to apply. Normally, applicants are expected to be members of CRCNA congregations who plan to pursue their educational goals at Calvin Theological Seminary or any of the colleges affiliated with the CRCNA. Students who have no prior history with the CRCNA must attend a CRCNA-related college or seminary for a full academic year before they are eligible to apply for this program. Students entering their sophomore year must have earned a GPA of 2.0 or higher as freshmen; students entering their junior year must have earned a GPA of 2.3 or higher as sophomores; students entering their senior year must have earned a GPA of 2.6 or higher as juniors.

Financial data First-year students receive $500 per semester. Other levels of students may receive up to $2,000 per academic year.
Duration 1 year.
Additional information This program was first established in 1971 and revised in 1991. Recipients are expected to train to engage actively in the ministry of racial reconciliation in church and in society. They must be able to work in the United States or Canada upon graduating and must consider working for 1 of the agencies of the CRCNA.
Number awarded Varies each year; recently, 31 students received a total of $21,000 in support.
Deadline March of each year.

[439]
RALPH BUNCHE SUMMER INSTITUTE
American Political Science Association
Attn: Ralph Bunch Summer Institute
1527 New Hampshire Avenue, N.W.
Washington, DC 20036-1206
(202) 483-2512   Fax: (202) 483-2657
E-mail: minority@apsanet.org
Web: www.apsanet.org/section_397.cfm

Purpose To introduce Native American and other underrepresented minority undergraduate students to the world of graduate study and to encourage their eventual application to a Ph.D. program in political science.
Eligibility Applications are invited from African American, Latino(a), Native American, and Pacific Islander college students completing their junior year. They must be interested in attending graduate school and working on a degree in a field related to political science. U.S. citizenship is required.
Financial data Participants receive a stipend of $200 per week plus full support of tuition, transportation, room, board, books, and instructional materials.
Duration 5 weeks during the summer.
Additional information The institute includes 2 transferable credit courses (1 in quantitative analysis and the other on race and American politics). In addition, guest lecturers and recruiters from Ph.D. programs visit the students. Classes are held on the campus of Duke University. Most students who attend the institute excel in their senior year and go on to graduate school, many with full graduate fellowships and teaching assistantships. This program is funded by the National Science Foundation.
Number awarded 20 each year.
Deadline February of each year.

[440]
RED CLAY AWARD
Cherokee Nation
Attn: Cherokee Nation Education Corporation
17675 South Muskogee Avenue
P.O. Box 948
Tahlequah, OK 74465
(918) 453-5420   Toll-free: (800) 256-0671 (within OK)
Fax: (918) 458-6195   E-mail: cnec@cherokee.org
Web: www.cherokee.org

Purpose To provide financial assistance to high school seniors who are citizens of the Cherokee Nation, planning to attend college in any state, and residing within the tribal jurisdictional boundaries.
Eligibility This program is open to citizens of the Cherokee Nation who are graduating from high schools within the jurisdictional area of the tribe. Applicants must be planning to enroll at a college, university, or vocational/technical school in any state. They must have a record of active participation in their local JOM program. Selection is based on GPA, ACT score, cultural and community activities, personal academic goals, commitment to work with Cherokee people in the future, and financial need.
Financial data The stipend is $1,000 per semester ($2,000 per year).
Duration 1 year. Renewal for the second semester requires the recipient to earn a GPA of 2.5 or higher in the first semester.
Additional information The Cherokee Nation area covers all or part of the following Oklahoma counties: Adair, Cherokee, Craig, Delaware, Mayes, McIntosh, Muskogee, Nowata, Ottawa, Rogers, Sequoyah, Tulsa, Wagoner, and Washington.
Number awarded Varies each year; recently, 4 of these scholarships were awarded.
Deadline March of each year.

[441]
RICHARD B. FISHER SCHOLARSHIP
Morgan Stanley
Attn: Diversity Recruiting
750 Seventh Avenue, 31st Floor
New York, NY 10019
(212) 762-0211   Fax: (212) 507-4972
E-mail: diversityrecruiting@morganstanley.com
Web: www.morganstanley.com

Purpose To provide financial assistance and work experience to Native Americans and other minorities who are preparing for a career in technology within the financial services industry.
Eligibility This program is open to members of minority groups who are enrolled in their sophomore or junior year of college (or the third or fourth year of a 5-year program). Applicants must be enrolled full time and have a GPA of 3.0 or higher. They must be willing to commit to a paid summer internship in the Morgan Stanley Information Technology Division. All majors and disciplines are eligible, but preference is given to students preparing for a career in technology within the financial services industry. Along with their application, they must submit 1-page essays on 1) why they are applying for this scholarship and why they should be selected as a recipient; 2) a technical project on which they worked, either through a university course or previous work experience, their role in the project, and how they contributed to the end result; and 3) a software, hardware, or new innovative application of existing technology that they would create if they could and the impact it would have. Financial need is not considered in the selection process.
Financial data The stipend is $7,500 per year.
Duration 1 year (the junior year); may be renewed for the senior year.
Additional information The program, established in 1993, includes a paid summer internship in the Morgan

Stanley Information Technology Division in the summer following the time of application.
Number awarded 1 or more each year.
Deadline January of each year.

[442]
RICHARD HAGEN-MINERVA HARVEY MEMORIAL SCHOLARSHIP
South Dakota Department of Education
Attn: Office of the Secretary
700 Governors Drive
Pierre, SD 57501
(605) 773-3134   Fax: (605) 773-6139
Web: doe.sd.gov/scholarships/hagen

Purpose To provide financial assistance for college to American Indians whose reservation is located in South Dakota.
Eligibility This program is open to enrolled members of American Indian tribes whose reservation is located in whole or part in South Dakota. Applicants must be attending or planning to attend a public or non-public accredited college, university, or technical institute in South Dakota. They must apply within 5 years after high school graduation or within 1 year after release from active military duty (if that release is within 5 years of high school graduation). Along with their application, they must submit high school and/or college transcripts, verification of tribal enrollment, ACT scores, and an essay explaining why they deserve to receive this scholarship.
Financial data The stipend is at least $1,000 per year for the first 2 years of college, at least $1,500 for the third year, and at least $2,500 for the fourth year.
Duration 4 years, provided the recipient maintains a cumulative GPA of 2.5 or higher.
Number awarded Up to 7 each year.
Deadline April of each year.

[443]
RICHARD S. SMITH SCHOLARSHIP
United Methodist Church
Attn: General Board of Discipleship
Division on Ministries with Young People
P.O. Box 340003
Nashville, TN 37203-0003
(615) 340-7184   Toll-free: (877) 899-2780, ext. 7184
Fax: (615) 340-7063   E-mail: youngpeople@gbod.org
Web: www.gbod.org/youngpeople/grants/grants.htm

Purpose To provide financial assistance to Native American and other minority high school seniors who wish to prepare for a Methodist church-related career.
Eligibility This program is open to graduating high school seniors who are members of racial/ethnic minority groups and have been active members of a United Methodist Church for at least 1 year. Applicants must have been admitted to an accredited college or university to prepare for a church-related career. They must have maintained at least a "C" average throughout high school and be able to demonstrate financial need. Along with their application, they must submit brief essays on their participation in church projects and activities, a leadership experience, the role their faith plays in their life, the church-related vocation to which God is calling them, and their extracurricular interests and activities. U.S. citizenship or permanent resident status is required.
Financial data The stipend is $1,000.
Duration 1 year; nonrenewable.
Additional information This scholarship was first awarded in 1997. Recipients must enroll full time in their first year of undergraduate study.
Number awarded 2 each year.
Deadline May of each year.

[444]
RICHARD W. TANNER SCHOLARSHIP FUND
Saint Paul Foundation
Attn: Program Assistant
600 Fifth Street Center
55 Fifth Street East
St. Paul, MN 55101-1797
(651) 224-5463   Toll-free: (800) 875-6167
Fax: (651) 224-0436
E-mail: dlk@saintpaulfoundation.org
Web: www.saintpaulfoundation.org/pagE32236.cfm

Purpose To provide financial assistance for college to Indians who belong to a Minnesota tribe.
Eligibility This program is open to members of Indian tribes in Minnesota who are juniors or seniors in college. Applicants must have the following on file with the Minnesota Indian Scholarship Program: a Minnesota Indian Scholarship Application, their Free Application for Federal Student Aid, and proof of tribal enrollment and/or blood quantum from a federally-recognized American Indian tribe or community. They must submit a 250-word essay describing their involvement in the Indian community and how the accomplishment of their educational goals will benefit the American Indian community. Financial need is not considered in the selection process.
Financial data The stipend is $1,000.
Duration 1 year; nonrenewable.
Number awarded 1 each year.
Deadline June of each year.

[445]
RODNEY T. MATHEWS MEMORIAL SCHOLARSHIP FOR CALIFORNIA INDIANS
Morongo Band of Mission Indians
Attn: Scholarship Coordinator
11545 Potrero Road
Banning, CA 92220
(951) 572-6185   E-mail: trisha.smith@morongo.org
Web: www.morongonation.org/scholarship.asp

Purpose To provide financial assistance for college or graduate school to California Indians.
Eligibility This program is open to California Indians (must provide documentation of Native identity) who have been actively involved in the Native American community. Applicants must submit documentation of financial need, an academic letter of recommendation, and a letter of recommendation from the American Indian community. They must be enrolled full time at an accredited college or university. Undergraduates must have a GPA of 2.75 or higher; graduate students must have a GPA of 3.5 or higher. Along with

their application, they must submit 1) a 2-page personal statement on their academic, career, and personal goals; any extenuating circumstances they wish to have considered; how they view their Native American heritage and its importance to them; how they plan to "give back" to Native Americans after graduation; and their on-going active involvement in the Native American community both on and off campus; and 2) a 2-page essay, either on what they feel are the most critical issues facing tribal communities today and how they see themselves working in relationship to those issues, or on where they see Native people in the 21st century in terms of survival, governance, and cultural preservation, and what role they see themselves playing in that future.

Financial data The maximum stipend is $10,000 per year. Funds are paid directly to the recipient's school for tuition, housing, textbooks, and required fees.

Duration 1 year; may be renewed 1 additional year.

Additional information Recipients are required to complete 60 hours of service with a designated California Indian community agency: California Indian Museum and Cultural Center, Indian Health Care Services, National Indian Justice Center, California Indian Legal Services, California Indian Professors Association, California Indian Culture and Awareness Conference, or California Democratic Party Native American Caucus.

Number awarded 4 each year.

Deadline March of each year.

[446] RONALD H. BROWN MEMORIAL SCHOLARSHIP

Travel Industry Association of America
Attn: TIA Foundation
1100 New York Avenue, N.W., Suite 450
Washington, DC 20005-3934
(202) 408-8422   Fax: (202) 408-1255
Web: www.tia.org

Purpose To provide financial assistance to Native American and other minority undergraduate students interested in preparing for a career in travel and tourism.

Eligibility This program is open to minorities who are interested in working on an undergraduate degree in the travel and tourism field. Candidates must first be nominated by a department head at a 4-year college or university that has a travel and tourism program. Nominees are then contacted by the foundation and invited to complete an application, including an essay on what segment of the tourism industry interests them and why.

Financial data The stipend is $3,000 per year.

Duration 1 year.

Number awarded 1 each year.

[447] ROSEMARY GASKIN SCHOLARSHIP

Chippewa County Community Foundation
P.O. Box 1979
Sault Ste. Marie, MI 49783
(906) 635-1046   Fax: (775) 417-7368
E-mail: cccf@lighthouse.net
Web: www.cccf4good4ever.org/main.asp?id=7

Purpose To provide financial assistance to members of the Sault Ste. Marie Tribe of Chippewa Indians who are interested in attending a public college in any state.

Eligibility This program is open to enrolled members of the Sault Ste. Marie Tribe of Chippewa Indians who have been accepted for enrollment at a public institution of higher education in any state. Applicants are not required to demonstrate financial need, to enroll full time, or to have a minimum blood quantum level. Along with their application, they must submit a 500-word essay on their choice of the following topics: equality, American Indian rights, education, or reviving Indian culture and traditional beliefs.

Financial data The stipend is $1,000.

Duration 1 year.

Number awarded 1 each year.

Deadline July of each year.

[448] ROY M. HUHNDORF ENDOWMENT SCHOLARSHIP FUND

Cook Inlet Region, Inc.
Attn: The CIRI Foundation
3600 San Jeronimo Drive, Suite 256
Anchorage, AK 99508-2870
(907) 793-3575   Toll-free: (800) 764-3382
Fax: (907) 793-3585 E-mail: tcf@thecirifoundation.org
Web: www.thecirifoundation.org/designated.htm

Purpose To provide financial assistance for undergraduate or graduate studies in health science to Alaska Natives who are original enrollees to Cook Inlet Region, Inc. (CIRI) and their lineal descendants.

Eligibility This program is open to Alaska Native enrollees to CIRI under the Alaska Native Claims Settlement Act (ANCSA) of 1971 and their lineal descendants. There are no Alaska residency requirements or age limitations. Applicants must be accepted or enrolled full time in a 4-year undergraduate or a graduate degree program. They must be working on a degree in health science and have a GPA of 2.5 or higher. Along with their application, they must submit a 500-word statement on their educational and career goals and how they are contributing, or planning to contribute, to a positive Alaska Native community. Selection is based on that statement, academic achievement, rigor of course work or degree program, student financial contribution, financial need, grade level, previous work performance, community service, and relationship of degree program to career goals.

Financial data The stipend is $10,000 per year, $8,000 per year, or $2,500 per semester, depending on GPA.

Duration 1 semester or 1 year.

Additional information This program was established in 1995.

Number awarded Varies each year.

Deadline May of each year for annual scholarships; May or November of each year for semester scholarships.

[449]
ROYCE OSBORN MINORITY STUDENT SCHOLARSHIPS

American Society of Radiologic Technologists
Attn: ASRT Education and Research Foundation
15000 Central Avenue, S.E.
Albuquerque, NM 87123-3909
(505) 298-4500, ext. 2541
Toll-free: (800) 444-2778, ext. 2541
Fax: (505) 298-5063   E-mail: foundation@asrt.org
Web: www.asrt.org

Purpose To provide financial assistance to Native American and other minority students enrolled in entry-level radiologic sciences programs.

Eligibility This program is open to African Americans, Native Americans (including American Indians, Eskimos, Hawaiians, and Samoans), Hispanic Americans, Asian Americans, and Pacific Islanders who are enrolled in an entry-level radiologic sciences program. Applicants must have a GPA in radiologic sciences core courses of 3.0 or higher and be able to demonstrate financial need. They may not have a previous degree or certificate in the radiologic sciences. Along with their application, they must submit 150-word essays on 1) their reason for entering the radiologic sciences; 2) their career goals; 3) their financial need; and 4) why they should receive this scholarship. Only U.S. citizens nationals, and permanent residents are eligible.

Financial data The stipend is $4,000.
Duration 1 year; may be renewed for 1 additional year.
Number awarded 5 each year.
Deadline January of each year.

[450]
SAC AND FOX NATION HIGHER EDUCATION GRANTS

Sac and Fox Nation
Attn: Higher Education
Route 2 Box 246
Stroud, OK 74079
(918) 968-3526
Web: www.sacandfoxnation.com

Purpose To provide financial assistance for college or graduate school to members of the Sac and Fox Nation.

Eligibility This program is open to enrolled members of the Sac and Fox Nation who are enrolled or planning to enroll at an accredited college or university. Applicants must submit a personal letter describing the college major they plan to pursue and their career goals after graduation. They must be able to demonstrate financial need. Limited funding is available for graduate students.

Financial data Stipends are $800 per semester for full-time students, $400 per semester for part-time students, or $400 per semester for graduate students.
Duration 1 semester; may be renewed up to 9 additional semester for students at 4-year institutions, up to 5 additional semesters for students at 2-year institutions, or up to 5 additional semesters for graduate students. Freshmen and sophomores must earn a GPA of 2.0 to remain eligible; juniors and seniors must earn at GPA of 2.25 to remain eligible.
Number awarded Varies each year.
Deadline June of each year for fall semester; November of each year for spring semester.

[451]
SALAMATOF NATIVE ASSOCIATION, INC. SCHOLARSHIP PROGRAM

Cook Inlet Region, Inc.
Attn: The CIRI Foundation
3600 San Jeronimo Drive, Suite 256
Anchorage, AK 99508-2870
(907) 793-3575   Toll-free: (800) 764-3382
Fax: (907) 793-3585 E-mail: tcf@thecirifoundation.org
Web: www.thecirifoundation.org

Purpose To provide financial assistance for undergraduate or graduate studies to Alaska Natives who are original enrollees of the Salamatof Native Association, Inc. (SNAI) and their spouses and lineal descendants.

Eligibility This program is open to Alaska Native enrollees to SNAI under the Alaska Native Claims Settlement Act (ANCSA) of 1971 and their spouses and lineal descendants. There are no Alaska residency requirements or age limitations. Applicants must be accepted or enrolled full time in a 2-year, 4-year undergraduate, or graduate degree program. They must have a GPA of 2.5 or higher. Along with their application, they must submit a 500-word statement on their educational and career goals and how they are contributing, or planning to contribute, to a positive Alaska Native community. Selection is based on that statement, academic achievement, rigor of course work or degree program, student financial contribution, financial need, grade level, previous work performance, community service, and relationship of degree program to career goals.

Financial data The stipend depends on the availability of funds.
Duration 1 year; recipients must reapply each year.
Additional information This program was established in 1992 by the Salamatof Native Association, Inc. which provides funds matched by the CIRI Foundation.
Number awarded Varies each year; recently, 3 of these scholarships were awarded.
Deadline May of each year.

[452]
SANTA FE VETERANS FOR PEACE SCHOLARSHIPS

Veterans for Peace-Santa Fe Chapter
7 Avenida Vista Grande, Number 117
Santa Fe, NM 87508
(928) 871-7444   E-mail: info@vfp-santafe.org
Web: www.vfp-santafe.org

Purpose To provide financial assistance for college to members of the Navajo Nation who have a commitment to peace.

Eligibility This program is open to enrolled members of the Navajo Nation who are planning to attend an accredited college, junior college, community college, or vocational/technical school. Applicants must be able to demonstrate financial need and a commitment to the principles of Veterans for Peace. Along with their application, they must submit a 3-page essay on what peace means to them; how this concept of peace can relate to their life, their family, and

their community; and how this concept of peace relates to their educational goals.
Financial data The maximum stipend is $3,000.
Duration 1 year.
Additional information These scholarships were first awarded in 2006.
Number awarded Varies each year; recently, 4 of these scholarships were awarded.
Deadline November of each year.

[453]
SANTO DOMINGO SCHOLARSHIP PROGRAM
Santo Domingo Tribe
Attn: Education Office
P.O. Box 160
Santo Domingo Pueblo, NM 87052
(505) 465-2214, ext. 227   Fax: (505) 465-2688

Purpose To provide financial assistance for undergraduate education to members of the Santo Domingo Pueblo.
Eligibility This program is open to enrolled members of the Santo Domingo Pueblo who are at least one-quarter degree Indian blood. Applicants must be high school seniors or graduates who have been accepted or are enrolled at an accredited college or university in pursuit of a bachelor or associate of science/arts degree. They must have applied for all other sources of financial aid from their college or university.
Financial data The amount awarded depends on the financial need of the recipient, up to $1,200 per year.
Duration 1 year; may be renewed for up to 3 additional years if the recipient maintains full-time status and a GPA of 2.0 or higher.
Number awarded Varies each year.
Deadline February of each year for fall semester; October of each year for spring semester.

[454]
SARAH KELI'ILOLENA LUM KONIA NAKOA HAWAIIAN LANGUAGE PERPETUAL SCHOLARSHIP
Ke Ali'i Pauahi Foundation
Attn: Financial Aid & Scholarship Services
567 South King Street, Suite 160
Honolulu, HI 96813
(808) 534-3966   Toll-free: (800) 842-4682, ext. 43966
Fax: (808) 534-3890   E-mail: scholarships@pauahi.org
Web: www.pauahi.org

Purpose To provide financial assistance to undergraduate or graduate students, especially those of Hawaiian descent, who are working on a degree in Hawaiian language.
Eligibility This program is open to full-time undergraduate and graduate students who are residents of Hawaii. Applicants must be enrolled in a program for the study and perpetuation of the Hawaiian language, including Hawaiian culture and history. They must be able to demonstrate financial need and commitment to contribute to the greater community. Along with their application, they must submit an essay demonstrating their achievements in studying Hawaiian language, culture, and history; proposed action plan to complete college-level Hawaiian language studies; and plan to share this knowledge with others in the Hawaiian community. Preference is given to Native Hawaiians (descendants of the aboriginal inhabitants of the Hawaiian Islands prior to 1778).
Financial data A stipend is awarded (amount not specified).
Duration 1 year.
Number awarded 1 each year.
Deadline April each year.

[455]
SAULT HIGHER EDUCATION GRANT PROGRAM
Sault Tribe of Chippewa Indians
Attn: Education Department
Two Ice Circle
Sault Ste. Marie, MI 49783
(906) 635-7784   Toll-free: (800) 793-0660
Fax: (906) 635-7785   E-mail: jlewton@saulttribe.net
Web: www.saulttribe.com

Purpose To provide financial assistance for college to members of the Sault Tribe in Michigan.
Eligibility This program is open to members of the Sault Tribe who have been accepted at an accredited Michigan public college or university and have entered or will enter full time into a certificate- or degree-granting program. Students must apply for all institutional and governmental financial aid before tribal grant awards can be awarded.
Financial data The amounts of the awards depend on the availability of funds and the need of the recipient. Funds must be used for tuition, fees, books, supplies, room, and board.
Duration 1 year; may be renewed if the recipient maintains a GPA of 2.0 or higher.
Number awarded Varies each year.
Deadline February of each year.

[456]
SAULT TRIBE HIGHER EDUCATION SELF SUFFICIENCY FUND
Sault Tribe of Chippewa Indians
Attn: Education Department
Two Ice Circle
Sault Ste. Marie, MI 49783
(906) 635-7784   Toll-free: (800) 793-0660
Fax: (906) 635-7785   E-mail: jlewton@saulttribe.net
Web: www.saulttribe.com

Purpose To provide financial assistance to members of the Sault Tribe in Michigan who complete college-level courses.
Eligibility This program is open to members of the Sault Tribe who are enrolled in a certificate- or degree-granting program at a community college, 4-year college, or university in the United States, regardless of blood quantum or financial need.
Financial data For full-time students (12 credits or more), the award is $500 per semester or $333 per quarter. For part-time students (11 credits or less), the award is $40 per semester credit or $26.65 per quarter credit. The maximum award is $1,000 for a calendar year.
Duration The awards are granted each term the students complete their programs successfully.

Additional information Recipients need to complete their academic program successfully each term.
Number awarded Varies each year.
Deadline October of each year.

[457]
SAULT TRIBE HIGHER EDUCATION VOCATIONAL TRAINING PROGRAM

Sault Tribe of Chippewa Indians
Attn: Education Department
Two Ice Circle
Sault Ste. Marie, MI 49783
(906) 635-7784 Toll-free: (800) 793-0660
Fax: (906) 635-7785 E-mail: jlewton@saulttribe.net
Web: www.saulttribe.com

Purpose To provide financial assistance to members of the Sault Tribe in Michigan who wish to attend a vocational school.
Eligibility This program is open to members of the Sault Tribe who are 18 years of age or older. Applicants must have been accepted at a state-licensed vocational school in the United States. They may not be participating in the tribe's higher education grant program or higher education self-sufficiency program.
Financial data The maximum stipend is $3,000 for a calendar year.
Duration 1 year.
Number awarded Varies each year.
Deadline Applications may be submitted at any time, but they must be received at least 30 days before the program starts.

[458]
SCHOLARSHIP AWARDS FOR INCOMING MINORITY COLLEGE FRESHMEN IN CHEMICAL ENGINEERING

American Institute of Chemical Engineers
Attn: Awards Administrator
Three Park Avenue
New York, NY 10016-5991
(646) 495-1348 Fax: (646) 495-1504
E-mail: awards@aiche.org
Web: www.aiche.org

Purpose To provide financial assistance for study in science or engineering to Native American and other incoming minority freshmen.
Eligibility Eligible are members of a minority group that is underrepresented in chemical engineering (African Americans, Hispanics, Native Americans, and Alaskan Natives). Applicants must be graduating high school seniors planning to enroll at a 4-year university with a major in science or engineering. They must be nominated by an American Institute of Chemical Engineers (AIChE) local section. Selection is based on academic record (including a GPA of 3.0 or higher), participation in school and work activities, a 300-word letter outlining the reasons for choosing science or engineering, and financial need.
Financial data The stipend is $1,000.
Duration 1 year; nonrenewable.
Number awarded Approximately 10 each year.
Deadline Nominations must be submitted by May of each year.

[459]
SCHOLARSHIP AWARDS FOR MINORITY COLLEGE STUDENTS IN CHEMICAL ENGINEERING

American Institute of Chemical Engineers
Attn: Awards Administrator
Three Park Avenue
New York, NY 10016-5991
(646) 495-1348 Fax: (646) 495-1504
E-mail: awards@aiche.org
Web: www.aiche.org

Purpose To provide financial assistance for study in chemical engineering to Native American and other underrepresented minority college student members of the American Institute of Chemical Engineers (AIChE).
Eligibility This program is open to undergraduate student AIChE members who are also members of a minority group that is underrepresented in chemical engineering (African Americans, Hispanics, Native Americans, and Alaskan Natives). They must have a GPA of 3.0 or higher. Along with their application, they must submit a 300-word essay on their immediate plans after graduation, areas of chemical engineering of most interest, and long-range career plans. Selection is based on that essay, academic record, participation in AIChE student chapter and professional or civic activities, and financial need.
Financial data The stipend is $1,000.
Duration 1 year; nonrenewable.
Number awarded Approximately 10 each year.
Deadline Nominations must be submitted by May of each year.

[460]
SCHOLARSHIPS FOR MINORITY ACCOUNTING STUDENTS

American Institute of Certified Public Accountants
Attn: Academic and Career Development Division
220 Leigh Farm Road
Durham, NC 27707-8110
(919) 402-4931 Fax: (919) 419-4705
E-mail: MIC_Programs@aicpa.org
Web: www.aicpa.org

Purpose To provide financial assistance to Native Americans and other minorities interested in studying accounting at the undergraduate or graduate school level.
Eligibility This program is open to 1) minority undergraduate students who are enrolled full time, have completed at least 30 semester hours of college work (including at least 6 semester hours in accounting), are majoring in accounting with the intent to pursue a C.P.A. credential, and have a GPA (major and cumulative) of 3.3 or higher; and 2) minority graduate students who are enrolled full time in a master's-level accounting, finance, taxation, or related program and have a GPA (major and cumulative) of 3.3 or higher. Applicants must be U.S. citizens or permanent residents and student affiliate members of the American Institute of Certified Public Accountants (AICPA). The program defines minority students as those whose heritage is Black or African American, Hispanic or Latino, Asian, American Indian or Alaskan

Native, Native Hawaiian or other Pacific Islander, or of 2 or more races.
Financial data Stipends range from $1,500 to $5,000 per year.
Duration 1 year; may be renewed, if recipients are making satisfactory progress toward graduation.
Additional information These scholarships are granted by the institute's Minority Initiatives Committee.
Number awarded Varies each year; recently, 137 students received funding through this program.
Deadline May of each year.

[461]
SCOTTS COMPANY SCHOLARS PROGRAM
Golf Course Superintendents Association of America
Attn: Environmental Institute for Golf
1421 Research Park Drive
Lawrence, KS 66049-3859
(785) 832-4445   Toll-free: (800) 472-7878, ext. 4445
Fax: (785) 832-3643   E-mail: mwright@gcsaa.org
Web: www.gcsaa.org

Purpose To provide financial assistance and summer work experience to high school seniors and college students, particularly those from diverse backgrounds, who are preparing for a career in golf management.
Eligibility This program is open to high school seniors and college students (freshmen, sophomores, and juniors) who are interested in preparing for a career in golf management (the "green industry"). Applicants should come from diverse ethnic, cultural, and socioeconomic backgrounds, defined to include women, minorities, and people with disabilities. Selection is based on cultural diversity, academic achievement, extracurricular activities, leadership, employment potential, essay responses, and letters of recommendation. Financial need is not considered. Finalists are selected for summer internships and then compete for scholarships.
Financial data The finalists receive a $500 award to supplement their summer internship income. Scholarship stipends are $2,500.
Duration 1 year.
Additional information The program is funded from a permanent endowment established by Scotts Company. Finalists are responsible for securing their own internships.
Number awarded 5 finalists, of whom 2 receive scholarships, are selected each year.
Deadline February of each year.

[462]
SEALASKA HERITAGE INSTITUTE SCHOLARSHIPS
Sealaska Corporation
Attn: Sealaska Heritage Institute
One Sealaska Plaza, Suite 301
Juneau, AK 99801-1249
(907) 586-9166   Toll-free: (888) 311-4992
Fax: (907) 586-9293
E-mail: scholarship@sealaska.com
Web: www.sealaskaheritage.org

Purpose To provide financial assistance for undergraduate or graduate study to Native Alaskans who have a connection to Sealaska Corporation.
Eligibility This program is open to 1) Alaska Natives who are enrolled to Sealaska Corporation, and 2) Native lineal descendants of Alaska Natives enrolled to Sealaska Corporation, whether or not the applicant owns Sealaska Corporation stock. Applicants must be enrolled or accepted for enrollment as full-time undergraduate or graduate students. Along with their application, they must submit 2 essays: 1) their personal history and educational goals, and 2) their expected contributions to the Alaska Native or Native American community. Financial need is also considered in the selection process.
Financial data The amount of the award depends on the availability of funds, the number of qualified applicants, class standing, and cumulative GPA.
Duration 1 year; may be renewed up to 5 years for a bachelor's degree, up to 3 years for a master's degree, up to 2 years for a doctorate, or up to 3 years for vocational study. The maximum total support is limited to 9 years. Renewal depends on recipients' maintaining full-time enrollment and a GPA of 2.5 or higher as an undergraduate or 3.0 or higher as a graduate student.
Number awarded Varies each year.
Deadline February of each year.

[463]
SEALASKA HERITAGE INSTITUTE 7(I) SCHOLARSHIPS
Sealaska Corporation
Attn: Sealaska Heritage Institute
One Sealaska Plaza, Suite 301
Juneau, AK 99801-1249
(907) 586-9166   Toll-free: (888) 311-4992
Fax: (907) 586-9293
E-mail: scholarship@sealaska.com
Web: www.sealaskaheritage.org

Purpose To provide financial assistance for undergraduate or graduate study to Native Alaskans who have a connection to Sealaska Corporation and are majoring in designated fields.
Eligibility This program is open to 1) Alaska Natives who are enrolled to Sealaska Corporation, and 2) Native lineal descendants of Alaska Natives enrolled to Sealaska Corporation, whether or not the applicant owns Sealaska Corporation stock. Applicants must be enrolled or accepted for enrollment as full-time undergraduate or graduate students. Along with their application, they must submit 2 essays: 1) their personal history and educational goals, and 2) their expected contributions to the Alaska Native or Native American community. Financial need is also considered in the selection process. The following areas of study qualify for these awards: natural resources (environmental sciences, engineering, conservation biology, environmental law, fisheries, geology, marine science/biology, forestry, wildlife management, and mining technology); business administration (accounting, finance, marketing, international business, international commerce and trade, management of information systems, human resources management, economics, computer information systems, and industrial management); and other special fields (cadastral surveys, chemistry, equipment/machinery operators, industrial safety specialists, health specialists, plastics engineers, trade special-

ists, physics, mathematics, and marine trades and occupations).
Financial data The amount of the award depends on the availability of funds, the number of qualified applicants, class standing, and cumulative GPA.
Duration 1 year; may be renewed up to 5 years for a bachelor's degree, up to 3 years for a master's degree, up to 2 years for a doctorate, or up to 3 years for vocational study. The maximum total support is limited to 9 years. Renewal depends on recipients' maintaining full-time enrollment and a GPA of 2.5 or higher.
Additional information Funding for this program is provided from Alaska Native Claims Settlement Act (ANSCA) Section 7(i) revenue sharing provisions.
Number awarded Varies each year.
Deadline February of each year.

[464]
SENECA NATION HIGHER EDUCATION PROGRAM
Seneca Nation of Indians
Attn: Higher Education Program
12861 Route 438
Irving, NY 14081
(716) 532-3341　　　　　　　Fax: (716) 532-3269
E-mail: leann.bennett@sni.org
Web: www.sni.org/hep

Purpose To provide financial assistance for college or graduate school to members of the Seneca Nation of Indians in New York.
Eligibility This program is open to members of the Seneca Nation of Indians who are enrolled or planning to enroll in an associate, bachelor's, master's, or doctoral program. They must have applied for all other forms of financial aid for which they qualify, e.g., full-time undergraduates who are New York residents must apply for New York State Indian Aid (NYSIA) and the New York State Tuition Assistance Program (TAP); part-time undergraduates who are New York residents must apply for Aid for Part-Time Study (APTS); non-residents of New York must apply for funding from their state of residence; graduate students must apply for an American Indian Graduate Center (AIGC) fellowship. Applicants with permanent residence on the reservation qualify for level 1 awards; those with permanent residence within New York state qualify for level 2 awards; those with permanent residence outside New York state qualify for level 3 awards. Financial need is considered in the selection process.
Financial data Maximum awards per academic year for tuition and fees are $11,000 for level 1 students, $8,000 for level 2 students, or $6,000 for level 3 students. Other benefits for all recipients include $1,000 per year for books and supplies for full-time students or $100 per 3-credit hours for part-time students; payment of room and board in dormitories or college-approved housing for full-time students; a transportation allowance for commuters of $900 per year for full-time students or $85 per 3-credit hours for part-time students; and a personal expense allowance of $500 per year for full-time students or $50 per 3-credit hours for part-time students.
Duration 1 year; may be renewed.
Number awarded Varies each year.

Deadline June of each year for fall semester; July of each year for fall quarter; October of each year for winter quarter; November of each year for spring semester; January of each year for spring quarter; April of each year for summer semester or quarter.

[465]
SHEE ATIKA ACADEMIC SCHOLARSHIPS
Shee Atiká, Incorporated
Attn: Shee Atiká Benefits Trust
315 Lincoln Street, Suite 300
Sitka, AK 99835
(907) 747-3534　　　　　Toll-free: (800) 478-3534
Fax: (907) 747-5727　　　E-mail: info@sheeatika.com
Web: www.sheeatika.com/scholarships.shtml

Purpose To provide financial assistance for college or graduate school to shareholders of Shee Atiká, Incorporated, an urban corporation organized under the Alaska Native Claims Settlement Act (ANSCA).
Eligibility This program is open to Shee Atiká Class A and Class B shareholders enrolled or planning to enroll at a college, university, graduate school, or trade or vocational school. Relatives of shareholders are eligible only if they receive at least 1 share of stock from their family member allowed to make a gift under ANSCA. Students interested in a program of concentrated vocational training may petition for that status. Applicants must submit a statement covering their personal and professional goals, honors and activities, how this scholarship will assist them, and the reasons for their major or course of study. Selection is based on that statement, academic achievement, and financial need.
Financial data The maximum annual stipend is $2,200 for undergraduates, $4,400 for graduate students, or $6,600 for students enrolled in concentrated vocational training.
Duration 1 year; may be renewed up to 3 additional years of undergraduate study or 2 years of graduate study. The maximum that any shareholder may receive for both undergraduate and graduate study is $22,000.
Number awarded Varies each year.
Deadline January, April, July, or October of each year.

[466]
SHOSHONE TRIBAL SCHOLARSHIP PROGRAM
Shoshone Higher Education Program
P.O. Box 628
Fort Washakie, WY 82514
(307) 332-8052, ext. 13　　　　Fax: (307) 332-9932

Purpose To provide financial assistance to members of the Eastern Shoshone Tribe who are interested in undergraduate education.
Eligibility This program is open to enrolled members of the Eastern Shoshone Tribe who can demonstrate financial need. The tribal program provides funding for students who do not qualify for the Bureau of Indian Affairs (BIA) Higher Education Program or the BIA Adult Vocational Training Program. Aid is provided to students enrolled in 2-year or 4-year degree programs, in vocational training, or in extension-type college courses.
Financial data Up to $5,000 per year or the unmet financial need, whichever is less.

Duration 1 year; may be renewed, provided the recipient remains enrolled full time and maintains a GPA of 2.5 or higher.
Number awarded Varies; generally, at least 90 each year.
Deadline May of each year for the academic year; November of each year for the spring term; April of each year for the summer term.

[467]
SITKA TRIBE ADULT VOCATIONAL GRANT
Sitka Tribe of Alaska
Attn: Education and Training Department
456 Katlian Street
Sitka, AK 99835
(907) 747-6506   Toll-free: (866) 747-6506
Fax: (907) 747-3503   E-mail: cduncan@sitkatribe.org
Web: www.sitkatribe.org

Purpose To provide financial assistance to unemployed or underemployed enrolled citizens of the Sitka Tribe of Alaska who plan to enroll in a certified vocational education program or trade school.
Eligibility This program is open to enrolled members of the Sitka Tribe of Alaska who have been residents of Sitka for at least 6 months and are currently unemployed or underemployed. Members of other federally-recognized tribes are eligible if funding is available. Applicants must have been accepted into an accredited vocational training program, have a high school diploma or GED, and be able to demonstrate financial need. Their proposed course of study must be offered by a school/training program and lead to gainful employment.
Financial data A stipend is awarded (amount not specified). Funds are paid to the recipient's school. Emergency funding may be awarded to students in good standing, if funds are available.
Duration The maximum funding period is 24 months (36 months for students in a registered nursing program).
Additional information Funding may also be available for apprenticeship and on-the-job training programs that do not last more than 24 months.
Number awarded Varies each year.
Deadline Applications may be submitted at any time, but they must be received at least 90 days prior to the start of training.

[468]
SITKA TRIBE OF ALASKA HIGHER EDUCATION PROGRAM
Sitka Tribe of Alaska
Attn: Education and Training Department
456 Katlian Street
Sitka, AK 99835
(907) 747-6506   Toll-free: (866) 747-6506
Fax: (907) 747-3503   E-mail: cduncan@sitkatribe.org
Web: www.sitkatribe.org

Purpose To provide financial assistance for college or graduate school to enrolled members of the Sitka Tribe of Alaska.
Eligibility This program is open to enrolled members of the Sitka Tribe of Alaska as documented by the Bureau of Indian Affairs. Members of other federally-recognized tribes may also be eligible if funds are available. Applicants must be enrolled full time at an accredited 2-year college (credits must be transferable to a 4-year school) or a 4-year college or university. They must have a high school diploma or GED and be able to demonstrate financial need. Priority is given to eligible Sitka Tribe of Alaska students who have met the minimum requirements in the following order: 1) college seniors; 2) college juniors; 3) college sophomores; 4) entering freshmen; 5) graduate students (provided funds are available); and 6) other qualified applicants (provided funds are available).
Financial data The maximum stipend is $3,000 per year. Payments are made to students through the financial aid office at the college or university they attend.
Duration Up to 10 semesters for students working on a 4-year degree or up to 5 semesters for students working on a 2-year degree. Recipients must maintain a GPA of at least 2.0 as freshmen, 2.2 as sophomores, 2.25 as juniors, and 2.5 as seniors to remain eligible. Graduate students must remain enrolled full time and maintain minimum standards as set by their institution.
Number awarded Varies each year.
Deadline April of each year for students attending the fall semester/quarter or the full year; September of each year for students beginning the spring/winter semester/quarter.

[469]
SITNASUAK FOUNDATION SCHOLARSHIPS
Sitnasuak Native Corporation
Attn: Sitnasuak Foundation
P.O. Box 905
Nome, AK 99762
(907) 443-2632   Fax: (907) 443-3063
E-mail: foundation@snc.org
Web: www.snc.org/foundation.htm

Purpose To provide financial assistance to members of the Sitnasuak Native Corporation and other residents of the Bering Straits region of Alaska who plan to attend college or graduate school in any state.
Eligibility This program is open to students in the following order of priority: 1) residents of the Bering Straits region of Alaska with plans to return and contribute to the development of the region; 2) shareholders of the Sitnasuak Native Corporation and their descendants; and 3) continuing students. Applicants must be enrolled or accepted for enrollment at a college, graduate school, or vocational program in any state. They must have earned a GED or high school diploma with a GPA of 2.0 or higher and be able to demonstrate financial need. Along with their application, they must submit a 2-page essay describing their educational goals and future plans to contribute to the development of the Bering Straits region.
Financial data For full-time students, the stipend is $600 per semester for those with a GPA of 3.0 or higher, $500 per semester for those with a GPA of 2.5 to 2.9, or $400 per semester for those with a GPA of 2.0 to 2.4. For part-time students, the stipend is $200 per semester. For vocational training students, the stipend is $400 per semester or $800 per year.
Duration 1 year; may be renewed if undergraduate students maintain a GPA of 2.0 or higher, if graduate students

maintain a GPA of 2.5 or higher, and if vocational students provide a progress report at the end of each term.
Additional information The Sitnasuak Native Corporation is the largest of 16 native village corporations in the Bering Straits region of Alaska.
Number awarded Varies each year.
Deadline June of each year for fall semester; November of each year for spring semester; March of each year for summer session.

[470]
SNA FOUNDATION SCHOLARSHIPS
Seldovia Native Association, Inc.
Attn: SNA Foundation
P.O. Drawer L
Seldovia, AK 99663
(907) 234-7625   Toll-free: (800) 478-7898
Fax: (907) 234-7637
Web: www.snai.com/foundation.htm

Purpose To provide financial assistance to Alaska Natives who are shareholders in Seldovia Native Association (SNA) or their family members and who wish to attend college or graduate school in any state.
Eligibility This program is open to Alaska Natives who are enrolled as shareholders in SNA, their spouses, and their descendants. Applicants must be enrolled or accepted for enrollment as full-time undergraduate or graduate students at an accredited 2- or 4-year college or university in any state. They must have a GPA of 3.0 or higher for achievement scholarships or 2.0 or higher for general scholarships. Along with their application, they must submit a statement of purpose that includes their personal history, a summary of accomplishments, a description of their career goals, and how their degree program fits with their education and career plans. Selection is based on that statement, academic achievement, previous work experience, educational and community involvement, recommendations, seriousness of purpose, major field of study, practicality of educational and professional goals, completeness of the application, and financial need. Alaska residency is not required.
Financial data Achievement scholarships are $2,500 per year; general scholarships are $500 per year.
Duration 1 year; may be renewed.
Number awarded Varies each year.
Deadline June of each year.

[471]
SOCIETY OF AMERICAN INDIAN GOVERNMENT EMPLOYEES ACADEMIC SCHOLARSHIPS
Society of American Indian Government Employees
P.O. Box 7715
Washington, DC 20044
Web: www.saige.org

Purpose To provide financial assistance to American Indian and Alaska Native federal employees who are interested in working on an undergraduate or graduate degree.
Eligibility This program is open to American Indians and Alaska Natives who have term, seasonal, career conditional, or career appointments as federal employees. Applicants must be interested in working on a bachelor's, master's, or Ph.D. degree at an accredited postsecondary school. They must have a GPA of 2.5 or higher. Along with their application, they must submit a 1-page essay describing their educational and workforce advancement goals and how this scholarship will help them achieve their goals, a letter of recommendation, and a narrative of extracurricular and community service activities.
Financial data Stipends range from $300 to $500 per semester, or $500 to $1,000 per academic year. Funding is provided as reimbursement for tuition costs upon receipt of a passing grade.
Duration 1 semester; may be renewed upon reapplication.
Additional information This program was established in 2005. Information is also available from Veronica Vasquez, (805) 989-3254, E-mail: Veronica.Vasquez@navy.mil.
Number awarded 1 or more each semester.
Deadline May of each year for fall semester; October of each year for spring semester.

[472]
SOVEREIGN NATIONS SCHOLARSHIP FUND UNDERGRADUATE AWARDS
American Indian College Fund
Attn: Scholarship Department
8333 Greenwood Boulevard
Denver, CO 80221
(303) 426-8900   Toll-free: (800) 776-FUND
Fax: (303) 426-1200   E-mail: info@collegefund.org
Web: www.collegefund.org

Purpose To provide financial assistance for college to Native American students who are interested in working for a tribe or Indian organization after graduation.
Eligibility This program is open to American Indians and Alaska Natives who can document proof of enrollment or descendancy. Applicants must be planning to 1) enroll full time at a tribal college or in a bachelor's degree program at a mainstream institution, and 2) work for their tribe or an Indian organization after graduation. They must have a GPA of 3.0 GPA or higher and be able to demonstrate financial need. Along with their application, they must submit 1) short essays (up to 500 words each) on how they perceive themselves as leaders in their school or community and how their education will help the Native American community; and 2) a personal statement of 1,000 words that includes their personal background, their academic background, their educational and career goals, and how this scholarship will help them achieve those goals.
Financial data The stipend is $2,000 per year.
Duration 1 year; may be renewed.
Additional information Recipients are encouraged to work for their tribe or an Indian organization upon completion of their degree.
Number awarded Varies each year.
Deadline May of each year.

[473]
SPECPRO SCHOLARSHIPS
Bristol Bay Native Corporation
Attn: BBNC Education Foundation
111 West 16th Avenue, Suite 400
Anchorage, AK 99501
(907) 278-3602   Toll-free: (800) 426-3602
Fax: (907) 276-3924   E-mail: pelagiol@bbnc.net
Web: www.bbnc.net/education/students

Purpose To provide financial assistance to shareholders of Bristol Bay Native Corporation (BBNC) who are entering freshmen at a postsecondary institution in any state and preparing for a career in a field relevant to needs of the SpecPro company.

Eligibility This program is open to BBNC shareholders who are planning to enroll full time as a freshman at an accredited college, university, or vocational school in any state. Applicants must have a GPA of 3.0 or higher and be able to demonstrate financial need. They must be interested in preparing for a career in a field relevant to the technical and management needs of the SpecPro company (e.g., engineering, environmental studies, marketing, management, information technology, life science). Along with their application, they must submit an essay on how they became interested in their proposed field of study, any special circumstances they want to be considered, and their desire to work in the region or for a BBNC subsidiary company. Selection is based on the essay (35%), cumulative GPA (40%), financial need (20%), and letters of recommendation (5%).

Financial data The stipend ranges up to $10,000 per year.

Duration 1 year; may be renewed up to 3 and a half additional years.

Additional information This program was established in 2007 by SpecPro Inc.

Number awarded 1 each year.

Deadline April of each year.

[474]
SPIRIT OF SOVEREIGNTY SCHOLARSHIPS
National Indian Gaming Association
Attn: Spirit of Sovereignty Foundation
224 Second Street, S.E.
Washington, DC 20003
(480) 820-2464   E-mail: info@spiritfund.com
Web: www.spiritfund.com/student.htm

Purpose To provide financial assistance to Native American upper-division and graduate students who are working on a degree in a business-related field.

Eligibility This program is open to college juniors, seniors, and graduate students who are working on a degree in business or a related field (e.g., hotel management, information systems, computer science, economics, human resources). Applicants must submit a copy of their Certificate of Indian Blood (CIB), current transcript, 2 letters of recommendation, and a 250-word essay that describes their involvement in extracurricular American Indian programs at their institution, volunteer and community work related to American Indian communities, potential for future interaction and support to Indian communities, tribal and community involvement, and potential to represent the American Indian community to non-Native constituents.

Financial data A stipend is awarded (amount not specified).

Duration 1 year.

Additional information Information is also available from the American Indian Graduate Center, 4520 Montgomery Boulevard, N.E., Suite 1-B, Albuquerque, NM 87109, (505) 881-4584.

Number awarded 1 or more each year.

Deadline February of each year.

[475]
ST. LOUIS CHAPTER NATIONAL UNDERGRADUATE SCHOLARSHIP
National Black MBA Association-St. Louis Chapter
Attn: Scholarship Program
P.O. Box 5296
St. Louis, MO 63115
(636) 230-2404
E-mail: adrienne-thomas@sbcglobal.net
Web: www.stlbmbaa.org/drupal/?q=node/42

Purpose To provide financial assistance to underrepresented minority undergraduate students who are working on a degree in business.

Eligibility This program is open to minority (African American, Hispanic/Latino, or Native American) students who are currently enrolled full time in the second, third, or fourth year of a business or management bachelor's degree program at a college or university in any state. Applicants may be residents of any state, but they must be available to attend the corporate, scholarship, and membership reception of the St. Louis chapter of the National Black MBA Association. Along with their application, they must submit a 2-page essay on a topic that changes annually but relates to minorities and a current national issue. Selection is based on the essay, transcripts, and a list of extracurricular activities.

Financial data Stipends range from $1,000 to $4,500 each year.

Duration 1 year.

Number awarded 2 each year.

Deadline May of each year.

[476]
STABLES EDUCATION AWARD
Miami Nation
Attn: Education Committee
202 South Eight Tribes Trail
P.O. Box 1326
Miami, OK 74355
(918) 542-1445   Fax: (918) 542-7260
E-mail: edu@miaminaton.com
Web: www.miaminaton.com

Purpose To provide financial assistance for college to enrolled members of the Miami Tribe of Oklahoma.

Eligibility This program is open to enrolled members of the Miami Tribe of Oklahoma who are entering or attending a college or university as a full-time student. Applicants must have a GPA of 3.0 or higher. Along with their application, they must submit a high school and/or college tran-

script, 3 letters of recommendation, documentation of financial need, and a 1-page essay with the title, "Tell Us About Yourself."
Financial data The stipend is $1,000.
Duration 1 year; nonrenewable.
Number awarded 1 or more each year.
Deadline April of each year.

[477] STACIE LYNN HAYS MEMORIAL SCHOLARSHIP

Chickasaw Foundation
110 West 12th Street
P.O. Box 1726
Ada, OK 74821-1726
(580) 421-9030 Fax: (580) 421-9031
E-mail: ChickasawFoundation@chickasaw.net
Web: www.chickasaw.net

Purpose To provide financial assistance to members of the Chickasaw Nation who are working on an undergraduate degree in counseling.
Eligibility This program is open to Chickasaw students who are currently enrolled full time at a 2- or 4-year college or university and working on an undergraduate degree in counseling. Preference is given to students focusing on domestic violence prevention. Applicants must have a GPA of 2.5 or higher. Along with their application, they must submit high school or college transcripts, 2 letters of recommendation, a copy of their Chickasaw Nation citizenship card, and a 1-page essay on their long-term goals and plans for achieving them. Financial need is not considered in the selection process.
Financial data The stipend is $1,000.
Duration 1 year.
Number awarded 1 each year.
Deadline June of each year.

[478] STANDING ROCK SIOUX TRIBE HIGHER EDUCATION SCHOLARSHIPS

Standing Rock Sioux Tribe
Standing Rock Administrative Service Center
Attn: Office of Higher Education
North Standing Rock Avenue
Fort Yates, ND 58538
(701) 854-7408 Fax: (701) 854-2175
Web: www.standingrock.org

Purpose To provide financial assistance for college to members of the Standing Rock Sioux Tribe.
Eligibility This program is open to enrolled members of the Standing Rock Sioux Tribe in North Dakota and South Dakota. Applicants must be attending or planning to attend an accredited college or university. They must be able to demonstrate financial need.
Financial data The stipend depends on the need of the recipient.
Duration 1 semester; may be renewed until completion of an undergraduate degree.
Number awarded Varies each year.
Deadline May of each year for fall semester; November of each year for spring semester; April of each year for summer school.

[479] STOCKBRIDGE-MUNSEE COLLEGE AND VOCATIONAL ASSISTANCE

Stockbridge-Munsee Community
Attn: Education Department
W13447 Camp 14 Road
P.O. Box 70
Bowler, WI 54416
(715) 793-4111 Toll-free: (800) 720-2790
Fax: (715) 793-4830
E-mail: jolene.bowman@mohican-nsn.gov
Web: www.mohican-nsn.gov

Purpose To provide financial assistance to members of the Stockbridge-Munsee Community of Mohican Indians who are interested in attending college or graduate school in any state.
Eligibility This program is open to members of the Stockbridge-Munsee Community of Mohican Indians who are interested in working on a vocational, associate, baccalaureate, or graduate degree at a college or university in any state. Applicants must be able to demonstrate financial need. In the selection process, priority is given to students in the following order: new students, part-time students, students for whom the educational institution has made a determination of no financial need, and students who are repeating a degree level.
Financial data Stipends for full-time study are $2,625 per semester for 2-year college and vocational students, $5,000 per semester for 4-year baccalaureate students, or $6,670 per semester for graduate students. Stipends for part-time study are pro-rated appropriately.
Duration 1 semester; may be renewed up to 4 additional semesters for vocational and associate degree students, up to 9 additional semesters for baccalaureate students, up to 4 additional semesters for students in a 2-year graduate program, up to 6 additional semesters for students in a 3-year graduate program, or up to 8 additional semesters for students in a 4-year graduate program. Renewals require students to remain enrolled full time and to maintain a GPA of 2.0 or higher. Part-time students may renew proportionately.
Additional information This program is offered under contract with the U.S. Bureau of Indian Affairs.
Number awarded Varies each year.
Deadline May of each year for fall term; September of each year for spring term.

[480] STUDENT OPPORTUNITY SCHOLARSHIPS FOR ETHNIC MINORITY GROUPS

Presbyterian Church (USA)
Attn: Office of Financial Aid for Studies
100 Witherspoon Street, Room M-052
Louisville, KY 40202-1396
(502) 569-5745 Toll-free: (888) 728-7228, ext. 5745
Fax: (502) 569-8766 E-mail: KSmith@ctr.pcusa.org
Web: www.pcusa.org

Purpose To provide financial assistance to upper-division college students who are Presbyterians, especially those of racial/ethnic minority heritage majoring in designated fields.
Eligibility This program is open to members of the Presbyterian Church (USA), especially those from racial/ethnic

minority groups (Asian American, African American, Hispanic American, Native American, Alaska Native). Applicants must be able to demonstrate financial need, be entering their junior or senior year of college as full-time students, and be U.S. citizens or permanent residents. Preference is given to applicants who are majoring in the following fields of interest to missions of the church: education, health services and sciences, religious studies, sacred music, social services, and social sciences.

Financial data Stipends range from $200 to $2,000 per year, depending upon the financial need of the recipient.

Duration 1 year; may be renewed for up to 3 additional years if the recipient continues to need financial assistance and demonstrates satisfactory academic progress.

Number awarded Varies each year.

Deadline June of each year.

[481]
SUSIE QIMMIQSAK BEVINS ENDOWMENT SCHOLARSHIP FUND

Cook Inlet Region, Inc.
Attn: The CIRI Foundation
3600 San Jeronimo Drive, Suite 256
Anchorage, AK 99508-2870
(907) 793-3575   Toll-free: (800) 764-3382
Fax: (907) 793-3585 E-mail: tcf@thecirifoundation.org
Web: www.thecirifoundation.org/designated.htm

Purpose To provide financial assistance for undergraduate or graduate studies in the literary, performing, and visual arts to Alaska Natives who are original enrollees to Cook Inlet Region, Inc. (CIRI) and their lineal descendants.

Eligibility This program is open to Alaska Native enrollees to CIRI under the Alaska Native Claims Settlement Act (ANCSA) of 1971 and their lineal descendants. There are no Alaska residency requirements or age limitations. Applicants must be accepted or enrolled full time in a 2-year, 4-year, or graduate degree program in the literary, visual, or performing arts. They should have a GPA of 2.5 or higher. Along with their application, they must submit a 500-word statement on their educational and career goals and how they are contributing, or planning to contribute, to a positive Alaska Native community. Selection is based on that statement, academic achievement, rigor of course work or degree program, student financial contribution, financial need, grade level, previous work performance, community service, and relationship of degree program to career goals.

Financial data The stipend is $2,000 per semester.

Duration 1 semester; recipients may reapply.

Additional information This program was established in 1990.

Number awarded Varies each year.

Deadline May or November of each year.

[482]
SUULUTAAQ CONSTRUCTION SCHOLARSHIP

The Kuskokwim Corporation
Attn: Kuskokwim Educational Foundation, Inc.
P.O. Box 227
Aniak, AK 99557
(907) 675-4275   Toll-free: (800) 478-4275 (within AK)
Fax: (907) 675-4276   E-mail: dg@kuskokwim.com
Web: www.kuskokwim.com

Purpose To provide educational assistance for vocational study at a school in any state in a field related to construction to Native people with ties to the Middle Kuskokwim Region.

Eligibility This program is open to Native people and their descendants from the Middle Kuskokwim Region in Alaska. Applicants must 1) be attending an accredited college or vocational institution in any state or have been accepted at such an institution; 2) be enrolled in a construction-related vocational program (e.g., heavy equipment, electrical, carpentry); 3) have a GPA of 2.0 or higher; and 4) intend to return to southwestern Alaska after completing their program of study. Selection is based on academic and leadership potential, motivation, and financial need.

Financial data A stipend is awarded (amount not specified).

Duration 1 year; may be renewed if the recipient maintains full-time enrollment and a GPA of 2.0 or higher.

Additional information This program is sponsored by Nugget Construction and The Kuskokwim Corporation.

Number awarded 1 each year.

Deadline May of each year.

[483]
TANANA CHIEFS CONFERENCE HIGHER EDUCATION GRANTS

Tanana Chiefs Conference
Attn: Education Department
122 First Avenue, Suite 600
Fairbanks, AK 99701-4897
(907) 452-8251, ext. 3186   Toll-free: (800) 770-8251
Toll-free: (800) 478-6822 (within AK)
Fax: (907) 459-3885
Web: www.tanachiefs.org

Purpose To provide financial assistance to Native Alaskans who have a tie to the Tanana Chiefs Conference (TCC) and are interested in attending college or graduate school in any state.

Eligibility This program is open to Alaska Natives who are enrolled to Doyon, Limited or a member of a tribe or village served by TCC. Applicants must be attending or planning to attend an accredited college, university, graduate school, or vocational training program in any state. They must be able to demonstrate financial need and to apply for all other available financial aid.

Financial data A stipend is awarded (amount not specified).

Duration 1 semester; may be renewed if the recipient maintains a GPA of 2.0 or higher and full-time enrollment.

Additional information TCC serves 42 villages in interior Alaska; for a list, contact the conference.

Number awarded Varies each year.

Deadline April of each year for fall semester or quarter; November of each year for spring semester or winter or spring quarter; February of each year for summer school.

[484]
TIME WARNER TRIBAL SCHOLARS PROGRAM

American Indian College Fund
Attn: Scholarship Department
8333 Greenwood Boulevard
Denver, CO 80221
(303) 426-8900   Toll-free: (800) 776-FUND
Fax: (303) 426-1200   E-mail: info@collegefund.org
Web: www.collegefund.org

Purpose To provide financial assistance to Native Americans who are attending or planning to attend a Tribal College or University (TCU).

Eligibility This program is open to American Indians or Alaska Natives who are enrolled or planning to enroll full time at an eligible TCU. Applicants must have a GPA of 2.5 or higher and be able to demonstrate financial need. Along with their application, they must submit 1) short essays (up to 500 words each) on how they perceive themselves as leaders in their school or community and how their education will help the Native American community; and 2) a personal statement of 1,000 words that includes their personal background, their academic background, their educational and career goals, and how this scholarship will help them achieve those goals.

Financial data The stipend is $2,500.

Duration 1 year.

Additional information This scholarship is sponsored by Time Warner in partnership with the American Indian College Fund.

Number awarded 1 or more each year.

Deadline May of each year.

[485]
TLINGIT AND HAIDA INDIAN TRIBES OF ALASKA COLLEGE STUDENT ASSISTANCE PROGRAM

Central Council, Tlingit and Haida Indian Tribes of Alaska
Attn: Higher Education Services
3239 Hospital Drive
Juneau, AK 99801
(907) 463-7375   Toll-free: (800) 344-1432, ext. 7375
Fax: (907) 463-7321
Web: www.hied.org

Purpose To provide financial assistance for undergraduate and graduate study in any state to enrolled Tlingit or Haida tribal members.

Eligibility This program is open to both undergraduate and graduate students. Applicants must be Tlingit or Haida tribal members with a GPA of 2.0 or higher. Scholarship applications are given priority based on the following point system: 20 points for students residing in the following service areas of the Central Council: Craig, Juneau, Haines, Kasaan, Pelican, Saxman, Skagway, Tenakee, or Wrangell; 15 points for graduation from a high school within the service areas listed above; and 5 points if the applicant or the applicant's parents/guardians belong to a southeast Alaska IRA council, village, or regional corporation within the service areas listed above. Enrollment or corporation identification numbers must be supplied on the application form. In addition to this program, students are expected to apply for institution-sponsored financial aid, as well as funding from state and local community organizations or Native corporations. Financial need is considered in the selection process.

Financial data This assistance is intended to be supplemental. Funds are to be used solely for tuition, required fees, textbooks, supplies, and miscellaneous educational expenses. No part of the award may be used to repay tuition from previous terms, educational or personal loans, or previously incurred debts.

Duration 1 year; may be renewed. Undergraduate recipients must maintain a GPA of 2.0 or higher; graduate students must maintain a GPA of 3.0 or higher. All recipients must be full-time students.

Additional information Faxed applications are permitted. With the exception of distance education or independent learning courses, this program does not fund part-time attendance, vocational training, student conferences, seminars, developmental courses (i.e., professional skill involvement), or any professional licensing examinations.

Number awarded Varies each year.

Deadline May of each year.

[486]
TMA SYSTEMS SCHOLARSHIP

Choctaw Nation
Attn: Scholarship Advisement Program
16th and Locust
P.O. Drawer 1210
Durant, OK 74702-1210
(580) 924-8280
Toll-free: (800) 522-6170, ext. 2547 (within OK)
Fax: (580) 924-1267
E-mail: jomcdaniel@choctawnation.com
Web: www.choctawnation-sap.com/scholarships.html

Purpose To provide financial assistance to Choctaw Indian college students who can demonstrate academic excellence and interest in Native American activities.

Eligibility This program is open to college students who have a Choctaw Adult Membership card. Applicants must be able to demonstrate academic excellence and involvement or interest in Native American activities. They must register online with the Choctaw Honor Scholars Program.

Financial data The stipend is $5,000 per year.

Duration 1 year; may be renewed.

Additional information Funding for this program is provided by TMA Systems.

Number awarded 2 each year; TMA Systems provides funds for 1 scholarship and the Choctaw Nation matches that.

[487]
TONKAWA TRIBE HIGHER EDUCATION PROGRAM
Tonkawa Tribe of Oklahoma
Attn: Higher Education Program
1 Rush Buffalo Road
Tonkawa, OK 74653
(580) 628-7021   Fax: (580) 628-3375
E-mail: mmahtapene@tonkawatribe.com
Web: www.tonkawatribe.com/programs/edu.htm

Purpose To provide financial assistance for college to members of the Tonkawa Tribe of Oklahoma.
Eligibility This program is open to Tonkawa tribal members who are high school graduates or GED recipients. Applicants must be attending or planning to attend an accredited college or university. They must be able to demonstrate financial need and reasonable assurance they will be successful in completing a 4-year degree program.
Financial data The stipend depends on the need of the recipient.
Duration 1 year; may be renewed.
Number awarded Varies each year.

[488]
TRANSFER ENGINEERING STUDENT AWARD
National Association of Multicultural Engineering
  Program Advocates, Inc.
Attn: National Scholarship Selection Committee Chair
341 North Maitland Avenue, Suite 130
Maitland, FL 32751-4761
(407) 647-8839   Fax: (407) 629-2502
E-mail: namepa@namepa.org
Web: www.namepa.org/awards.html

Purpose To provide financial assistance to Native American and other underrepresented minority college transfer students who are planning to major in engineering.
Eligibility This program is open to African American, Hispanic, and American Indian college transfer students who are coming from a junior college, community college, or 3/2 dual-degree program. Applicants must be transferring to an engineering program at an institution affiliated with the National Association of Multicultural Engineering Program Advocates (NAMEPA). For a list of affiliated schools, write to the sponsor. They must have a GPA of 2.7 or higher. Along with their application, they must submit a copy of their college transcript, a letter of recommendation, and a 1-page essay on why they have chosen engineering as a profession, why they think they should be selected, and an overview of their future aspirations as an engineer. Financial need is not considered in the selection process.
Financial data The stipend is $1,000, paid in 2 equal installments.
Duration 1 year; nonrenewable.
Additional information Support for this program is provided by the ALCOA Foundation. NAMEPA formerly stood for the National Association of Minority Engineering Program Administrators, Inc.
Number awarded Varies each year; recently, NAMEPA awarded a total of 20 scholarships for its Beginning Freshman Awards and its Transfer Engineering Awards.
Deadline May of each year.

[489]
TRIANGLE NATIVE AMERICAN SOCIETY SCHOLARSHIPS
Triangle Native American Society
P.O. Box 26841
Raleigh, NC 27611-6841
(919) 779-5936   E-mail: tnasscholarship@tnasweb.org
Web: www.tnasweb.org/tnasfinancialaidhome.htm

Purpose To provide financial assistance to Native Americans in North Carolina who are enrolled at a public university in the state.
Eligibility This program is open to American Indians who have been North Carolina residents for at least 1 year and are entering their sophomore, junior, or senior year at a school in the University of North Carolina system. Applicants must be enrolled full time and have a GPA of 2.5 or higher. They must be able to demonstrate financial need, leadership abilities, and community involvement.
Financial data Stipends range from $500 to $1,000.
Duration 1 year; recipients may reapply.
Additional information This program was formerly known as the Mark Ulmer Native American Scholarship. Information is also available from Alisa Hunt-Lowery, 56 Livingston Place, Clayton, NC 27520.
Number awarded Varies each year; recently, 3 of these scholarships were awarded.
Deadline June of each year.

[490]
TRIBAL BUSINESS MANAGEMENT (TBM) PROGRAM
Catching the Dream
8200 Mountain Road, N.E., Suite 203
Albuquerque, NM 87110-7835
(505) 262-2351   Fax: (505) 262-0534
E-mail: NScholarsh@aol.com
Web: www.catchingthedream.org/Scholarship.htm

Purpose To provide financial assistance for college to American Indian students interested in studying a field related to economic development for tribes.
Eligibility This program is open to American Indians who can provide proof that they are at least one-quarter Indian blood and a member of a U.S. tribe that is federally-recognized, state-recognized, or terminated. Applicants must be enrolled or planning to enroll full time and major in the 1 of the following fields: business administration, finance, management, economics, banking, hotel management, or other fields related to economic development for tribes. They may be entering freshmen, undergraduate students, graduate students, or Ph.D. candidates. Along with their application, they must submit documentation of financial need, 3 letters of recommendation, copies of applications and responses for all other sources of funding for which they are eligible, official transcripts, standardized test scores (ACT, SAT, GRE, MCAT, LSAT, etc.), and an essay explaining their goals in life, college plans, and career plans (especially how those plans include working with and benefiting Indians). Selection is based on merit and potential for improving the lives of Indian people.
Financial data Stipends range from $500 to $5,000 per year.
Duration 1 year.

Additional information The sponsor was formerly known as the Native American Scholarship Fund. This program was established in 2003.
Number awarded Varies; generally, 30 to 35 each year.
Deadline April of each year for fall term; September of each year for spring and winter terms; March of each year for summer school.

[491]
TRUMAN D. PICARD SCHOLARSHIP PROGRAM

Intertribal Timber Council
Attn: Education Committee
1112 N.E. 21st Avenue, Suite 4
Portland, OR 97232-2114
(503) 282-4296   Fax: (503) 282-1274
E-mail: itc1@teleport.com
Web: www.itcnet.org/about_us/scholarships.html

Purpose To provide financial assistance to American Indians or Alaskan Natives who are interested in studying natural resources in college.
Eligibility This program is open to 1) graduating high school seniors, and 2) currently-enrolled college students. Applicants must be enrolled in a federally-recognized tribe or Native Alaska corporation. They must be majoring or planning to major in natural resources. Selection is based on interest in natural resources; commitment to education, community, and culture; academic merit; and financial need.
Financial data The stipend is $1,500 for high school seniors entering college or $2,000 for students already enrolled in college.
Duration 1 year.
Additional information Recipients who attend the University of Washington (Seattle) or Salish Kootenai College (Pablo, Montana) are also eligible for additional scholarships and tuition waivers.
Number awarded Varies each year. Recently, 21 of these scholarships were awarded.
Deadline January of each year.

[492]
TSAY CORPORATION "LET'S GET STARTED" SCHOLARSHIP

Pueblo of Ohkay Owingeh
Attn: Department of Education
P.O. Box 1269
San Juan Pueblo, NM 87566
(505) 852-3477   Fax: (505) 852-3030
E-mail: wevog68@valornet.com
Web: www.sanjuaned.org/higher_ed.html

Purpose To provide financial assistance to tribal members of the Pueblo of Ohkay Owingeh who are entering their freshman year of college.
Eligibility This program is open to enrolled and verified members of the Ohkay Owingeh tribe who have recently graduated from high school and are entering a 2- or 4-year college or university in any state as a full-time freshman. Applicants must have a high school GPA of 2.5 or higher. Along with their application, they must submit a 500-word essay on how a college degree will change their life. Financial need is not considered in the selection process.
Financial data The stipend is $3,000.
Duration 1 year.
Additional information Until 2005, the Pueblo of Ohkay Owingeh was known as the Pueblo of San Juan.
Number awarded 1 each year.
Deadline June of each year.

[493]
TSAY CORPORATION "MANY PATHS TO SUCCESS" SCHOLARSHIP

Pueblo of Ohkay Owingeh
Attn: Department of Education
P.O. Box 1269
San Juan Pueblo, NM 87566
(505) 852-3477   Fax: (505) 852-3030
E-mail: wevog68@valornet.com
Web: www.sanjuaned.org/higher_ed.html

Purpose To provide financial assistance to tribal members of the Pueblo of Ohkay Owingeh who are enrolled at a vocational or trade school.
Eligibility This program is open to enrolled and verified members of the Ohkay Owingeh tribe who are attending an accredited 2-year vocational or trade school as a full-time student. Applicants must have a GPA of 2.5 or higher. Along with their application, they must submit a 500-word essay on why they chose their field of study. Financial need is not considered in the selection process.
Financial data The stipend is $3,000.
Duration 1 year.
Additional information Until 2005, the Pueblo of Ohkay Owingeh was known as the Pueblo of San Juan.
Number awarded 1 each year.
Deadline June of each year.

[494]
TSAY CORPORATION "YOU'RE ALMOST THERE" SCHOLARSHIP

Pueblo of Ohkay Owingeh
Attn: Department of Education
P.O. Box 1269
San Juan Pueblo, NM 87566
(505) 852-3477   Fax: (505) 852-3030
E-mail: wevog68@valornet.com
Web: www.sanjuaned.org/higher_ed.html

Purpose To provide financial assistance to tribal members of the Pueblo of Ohkay Owingeh who are enrolled as juniors or seniors at a college or university in any state.
Eligibility This program is open to enrolled and verified members of the Ohkay Owingeh tribe who are attending an accredited 4-year college or university as a full-time junior or senior. Applicants must have a GPA of 2.5 or higher. Along with their application, they must submit a 500-word essay on what they consider to be the current needs of Ohkay Owingeh. Financial need is not considered in the selection process.
Financial data The stipend is $3,000.
Duration 1 year.
Additional information Until 2005, the Pueblo of Ohkay Owingeh was known as the Pueblo of San Juan.
Number awarded 1 each year.

Deadline June of each year.

[495]
TURTLE MOUNTAIN BAND OF CHIPPEWA INDIANS SCHOLARSHIP PROGRAM

Turtle Mountain Band of Chippewa Indians
P.O. Box 900
Belcourt, ND 58316
(701) 477-8102   Fax: (701) 477-8053
Web: www.tmbci.net

Purpose To provide financial assistance for full-time undergraduate or graduate study in any state to enrolled members of the Turtle Mountain Band of Chippewa.

Eligibility Applicants must be enrolled members of the Turtle Mountain Band of Chippewa, be full-time students enrolled in an academic program at an accredited postsecondary institution in any state on either the undergraduate or graduate school level, and have a GPA of 2.0 or higher. Undergraduate applicants must be enrolled for at least 12 quarter or 12 semester credit hours (or 6 semester/quarter hours for a summer session); graduate school applicants must be enrolled for at least 1 course. Along with their application, they must submit a Certificate of Indian Blood, a letter of acceptance/admission from their college, the Award Notice sent by the college's financial aid office, a high school transcript or GED certificate, and any college transcripts. Priority is given to applicants in the following order: seniors who need to attend summer school in order to graduate, seniors, juniors who need summer school in order to become seniors, students who need summer school to acquire their 2-year degree, sophomores, freshmen, and graduate students.

Financial data A stipend is awarded (amount not specified).

Duration The maximum number of terms the scholarship program will fund a student for an undergraduate degree is 10 semesters or 15 quarters; the maximum number of terms for a student at a 2-year college is 3 years, 6 semesters, or 9 quarters.

Additional information Once recipients earn 65 or more credit hours at a 2-year college, they must transfer to a 4-year institution.

Number awarded Varies each year.

Deadline August of each year.

[496]
TWO FEATHERS ENDOWMENT AMERICAN INDIAN SCHOLARSHIPS

Saint Paul Foundation
Attn: Program Assistant
600 Fifth Street Center
55 Fifth Street East
St. Paul, MN 55101-1797
(651) 224-5463   Toll-free: (800) 875-6167
Fax: (651) 224-0436
E-mail: dlk@saintpaulfoundation.org
Web: www.saintpaulfoundation.org/pagE32236.cfm

Purpose To provide financial assistance for college to Indians who belong to a Minnesota tribe.

Eligibility This program is open to members of Indian tribes in Minnesota. Applicants must have the following on file with the Minnesota Indian Scholarship Program: a Minnesota Indian Scholarship Application, their Free Application for Federal Student Aid, and proof of tribal enrollment and/or blood quantum from a federally-recognized American Indian tribe or community. They must submit a 250-word essay describing their involvement in the Indian community and how the accomplishment of their educational goals will benefit the American Indian community. Financial need is considered in the selection process.

Financial data The stipend is $1,000.

Duration 1 year; nonrenewable.

Number awarded Up to 5 each year.

Deadline June of each year.

[497]
TWO FEATHERS FUND HEALTH INITIATIVE SCHOLARSHIP

Saint Paul Foundation
Attn: Program Assistant
600 Fifth Street Center
55 Fifth Street East
St. Paul, MN 55101-1797
(651) 224-5463   Toll-free: (800) 875-6167
Fax: (651) 224-0436
E-mail: dlk@saintpaulfoundation.org
Web: www.saintpaulfoundation.org/pagE32236.cfm

Purpose To provide financial assistance to Indians who belong to a Minnesota tribe and are interested in studying a health-related field in college.

Eligibility This program is open to members of Indian tribes in Minnesota who are enrolled in college in a field of study related to health. Applicants must have the following on file with the Minnesota Indian Scholarship Program: a Minnesota Indian Scholarship Application, their Free Application for Federal Student Aid, and proof of tribal enrollment and/or blood quantum from a federally-recognized American Indian tribe or community. They must submit a 250-word essay describing their involvement in the Indian community and how the accomplishment of their educational goals will benefit the American Indian community. Financial need is considered in the selection process.

Financial data The stipend is $5,000.

Duration 1 year; nonrenewable.

Number awarded Several each year.

Deadline June of each year.

[498]
TYONEK NATIVE CORPORATION SCHOLARSHIP AND GRANT PROGRAM

Cook Inlet Region, Inc.
Attn: The CIRI Foundation
3600 San Jeronimo Drive, Suite 256
Anchorage, AK 99508-2870
(907) 793-3575   Toll-free: (800) 764-3382
Fax: (907) 793-3585   E-mail: tcf@thecirifoundation.org
Web: www.thecirifoundation.org

Purpose To provide financial assistance for professional preparation after high school to Alaska Natives who are original enrollees of the Tyonek Native Corporation (TNC) and their lineal descendants.

SCHOLARSHIPS

Eligibility This program is open to Alaska Native enrollees to TNC under the Alaska Native Claims Settlement Act (ANCSA) of 1971 and their lineal descendants as well as tribal members of the Native Village of Tyonek. Applicants must be accepted or enrolled full time in an accredited or otherwise approved postsecondary college, university, or technical skills education program. They must have a GPA of 2.0 or higher. Along with their application, they must submit a 500-word statement on their educational and career goals and how they are contributing, or planning to contribute, to a positive Alaska Native community. Selection is based on that statement, academic achievement, rigor of course work or degree program, student financial contribution, financial need, grade level, previous work performance, community service, and relationship of degree program to career goals.

Financial data The stipend depends on the availability of funds.

Duration 1 semester; recipients must reapply each semester.

Additional information This program was established in 1989. Funds are provided equally by the TNC and the CIRI Foundation.

Number awarded Varies each year; recently, 9 academic scholarships and 2 vocational training grants were awarded.

Deadline Applications for scholarships (for academic study) must be submitted by May or November of each year. Applications for grants (for vocational or technical programs) are due by March, June, September, or November of each year.

[499]
UNCF CORPORATE SCHOLARS PROGRAMS

United Negro College Fund
Attn: Corporate Scholars Program
P.O. Box 1435
Alexandria, VA 22313-9998
Toll-free: (866) 671-7237 E-mail: internship@uncf.org
Web: www.uncf.org

Purpose To provide financial assistance and work experience to Native American and other minority students pursuing a degree in designated fields of business, science, and engineering.

Eligibility A number of corporate sponsors provides funding for this program; each establishes its own specifications. All are open to undergraduates; some are also available to graduate students. Some allow students to be enrolled at the college or university of their choice, others are limited to students at Historically Black Colleges and Universities (HBCUs), and others are restricted to UNCF member institutions. Some are open to minority (African American, Alaskan Native, American Indian, Asian Pacific Islander American, Hispanic) students in general, but others are more restrictive. Fields of study vary, but most focus on areas of business, science, and engineering of interest to the corporate sponsor. All include summer internships at the sponsor. GPA requirements vary, but may be as high as 3.0.

Financial data The students selected for this program receive paid internships and need-based scholarships that range up to $15,000 per year.

Duration 8 to 10 weeks for the internships; 1 year for the scholarships, which may be renewed.

Additional information Current corporate sponsors include Booz Allen Hamilton, Dell Inc., Ford Motor Company, HSBC North America, JPMorganChase, Malcolm Pirnie Inc., Marathon Oil Corporation, Oracle Corporation, RR Donnelley, Sprint Nextel, United Parcel Service of America, Inc., and Weyerhaueser.

Number awarded Varies each year.

Deadline Each sponsor sets its own deadline.

[500]
UNDERGRADUATE AWARDS OF THE SEMINOLE NATION JUDGMENT FUND

Seminole Nation of Oklahoma
Attn: Judgment Fund Office
2007 West Wrangler Boulevard
Seminole, OK 74868
(405) 382-0549 Toll-free: (877) 382-0549
Fax: (405) 382-0571
Web: www.seminolenation.com

Purpose To provide financial assistance for undergraduate study to members of the Seminole Nation of Oklahoma.

Eligibility This program is open to enrolled members of the Seminole Nation who are descended from a member of the Seminole Nation as it existed in Florida on September 18, 1923. Applicants must be attending or planning to attend a college or university to work on an undergraduate degree.

Financial data The stipend for full-time students is $1,000 per year for freshmen, $1,200 per year for sophomores, $1,600 per year for juniors, or $1,800 for seniors. Part-time students receive the actual cost of tuition, books, and fees, to a maximum of $300 per semester. The total of all undergraduate degree awards to a student may not exceed $5,600.

Duration 1 year; may be renewed as long as the recipient maintains a GPA of 2.0 or higher.

Additional information The General Council of the Seminole Nation of Oklahoma approved a plan for use of the Judgment Fund Award in 1990. This aspect of the program went into effect in September of 1991.

Number awarded Varies each year.

Deadline November of each year for fall semester; April of each year for spring semester.

[501]
UNITED INDIANS OF VIRGINIA SCHOLARSHIP PROGRAM

United Indians of Virginia
Attn: Education Committee
12111 Indian Hill Lane
Providence Forge, VA 23140
(804) 966-2719 E-mail: mbradby@erols.com
Web: www.unitedindiansofva.org/education_fund.htm

Purpose To provide financial assistance for college to Virginia Native American Indians whose tribes are members of the United Indians of Virginia.

Eligibility Eligible to apply are Virginia Native Americans who belong to tribes that are members of the United Indians of Virginia. Applicants must be in good standing with their tribes. They must submit a completed application form, a letter of recommendation from the Chief of their tribe, 2 additional letters of reference, a resume, official school transcripts, and a 500-word essay that focuses on their career plans or future goals.

Financial data A stipend is awarded (amount not specified). Checks are sent to the recipient but made payable to the recipient's institution.

Duration 1 year.

Additional information The tribes that are included in the United Indians of Virginia are the Chickahominy, Eastern Chickahominy, Monacan, Nansemond, Pamunkey, Rappahannock, and Upper Mattaponi.

Number awarded Varies each year.

Deadline August of each year.

[502]
UNITED METHODIST CHURCH ONNSFA SCHOLARSHIPS

Navajo Nation
Attn: Office of Navajo Nation Scholarship and Financial Assistance
P.O. Box 1870
Window Rock, AZ 86515-1870
(928) 871-7640   Toll-free: (800) 243-2956
Fax: (928) 871-6561
E-mail: onnsfacentral@navajo.org
Web: www.onnsfa.org/corplist.asp

Purpose To provide financial assistance for college to Navajo college students who are affiliated with the United Methodist Church.

Eligibility This program is open to Navajo undergraduate students who belong to the United Methodist Church. Applicants may reside in any state. Both no-need and need-based scholarships are awarded.

Financial data The stipend is $1,000 per year.

Duration 1 year; may be renewed if the recipient maintains a GPA of 2.0 or higher and enrolls in at least 12 credit hours per semester.

Additional information Recipients must enroll as full-time students in college.

Number awarded 1 or more each year.

[503]
UNITED METHODIST ETHNIC MINORITY SCHOLARSHIPS

United Methodist Church
Attn: General Board of Higher Education and Ministry
Office of Loans and Scholarships
1001 19th Avenue South
P.O. Box 340007
Nashville, TN 37203-0007
(615) 340-7344   Fax: (615) 340-7367
E-mail: umscholar@gbhem.org
Web: www.gbhem.org/loansandscholarships

Purpose To provide financial assistance to undergraduate Methodist students who are of Native American or other ethnic minority ancestry.

Eligibility This program is open to full-time undergraduate students at accredited colleges and universities in the United States who have been active, full members of a United Methodist Church for at least 1 year prior to applying. Applicants must have at least 1 parent who is African American, Hispanic, Asian, Native American, Alaska Native, or Pacific Islander. They must have a GPA of 2.5 or higher and be able to demonstrate financial need. U.S. citizenship, permanent resident status, or membership in a central conference of the United Methodist Church is required. Selection is based on church membership, involvement in church and community activities, GPA, and financial need.

Financial data A stipend is awarded (amount not specified).

Duration 1 year; recipients may reapply.

Number awarded Varies each year.

Deadline April of each year.

[504]
UNITED METHODIST HIGHER EDUCATION FOUNDATION NATIVE ALASKAN FUND

United Methodist Higher Education Foundation
Attn: Scholarship Office
1001 19th Avenue South
P.O. Box 340005
Nashville, TN 37203-0005
(615) 340-7385   Toll-free: (800) 811-8110
Fax: (615) 340-7330
E-mail: umhefscholarships@gbhem.org
Web: www.umhef.org/othergroupa.html

Purpose To provide financial assistance to Native Alaskan Methodist undergraduate and graduate students at Methodist-related colleges and universities.

Eligibility This program is open to Native Alaskans enrolling as full-time undergraduate and graduate students at United Methodist-related colleges and universities. United Methodist students at Alaska Pacific University are also eligible. Applicants must have been active, full members of a United Methodist Church for at least 1 year prior to applying. They must be able to demonstrate financial need. U.S. citizenship or permanent resident status is required.

Financial data A stipend is awarded (amount not specified).

Duration 1 year; nonrenewable.

Number awarded Varies each year.

Deadline May of each year.

[505]
UNITED PARCEL SERVICE SCHOLARSHIP FOR MINORITY STUDENTS

Institute of Industrial Engineers
Attn: Scholarship Coordinator
3577 Parkway Lane, Suite 200
Norcross, GA 30092
(770) 449-0461, ext. 105   Toll-free: (800) 494-0460
Fax: (770) 441-3295   E-mail: bcameron@iienet.org
Web: www.iienet2.org/Details.aspx?id=857

Purpose To provide financial assistance to Native American and other minority undergraduates who are studying industrial engineering at a school in the United States, Canada, or Mexico.

Eligibility Eligible to be nominated are minority undergraduate students enrolled at any school in the United States and its territories, Canada, or Mexico, provided the

school's engineering program is accredited by an agency recognized by the Institute of Industrial Engineers (IIE) and the student is pursuing a full-time course of study in industrial engineering with a GPA of at least 3.4. Nominees must have at least 5 full quarters or 3 full semesters remaining until graduation. Students may not apply directly for these awards; they must be nominated by the head of their industrial engineering department. Nominees must be IIE members. Selection is based on scholastic ability, character, leadership, potential service to the industrial engineering profession, and need for financial assistance.
Financial data The stipend is $4,000.
Duration 1 year.
Additional information Funding for this program is provided by the UPS Foundation.
Number awarded 1 each year.
Deadline Schools must submit nominations by November of each year.

[506]
UNITED UTILITIES SCHOLARSHIPS
United Utilities, Inc.
Attn: Scholarship Committee
5450 A Street
P.O. Box 92730
Anchorage, AK 99518
(907) 561-1674   Toll-free: (800) 478-2020, ext. 5214
Fax: (907) 563-3185
E-mail: unicom@unicom-alaska.com
Web: www.unicom-alaska.com

Purpose To provide financial assistance to residents of selected Native communities in Alaska who are interested in attending college in any state.
Eligibility This program is open to high school seniors and graduates who live in a Native Alaska community where affiliates of United Utilities, Inc. provide communications services. Applicants must be enrolled or planning to enroll at a college, university, or vocational/trade school in any state. They must have a GPA of 2.0 or higher. Along with their application, they must submit a current transcript with GPA, the name of the college they plan to attend, estimated cost of education for 1 year, intended major or course of study, and an essay describing their future plans and goals.
Financial data The stipend is $2,000.
Duration 1 year.
Additional information United Utilities, Inc. is owned by Alaska Native corporations. Through its affiliates (United-KUC and Unicom, Inc.), it provides communications services to 58 native communities throughout Alaska.
Number awarded Approximately 150 each year.
Deadline April of each year.

[507]
UNIVERSITY OF NORTH CAROLINA CAMPUS SCHOLARSHIPS-PART II
North Carolina State Education Assistance Authority
Attn: Scholarship and Grant Services
10 Alexander Drive
P.O. Box 14103
Research Triangle Park, NC 27709-4103
(919) 549-8614   Toll-free: (800) 700-1775
Fax: (919) 549-8481   E-mail: information@ncseaa.edu
Web: www.ncseaa.edu

Purpose To provide financial assistance to Native American residents of North Carolina interested in working on an undergraduate degree at a public institution in the state.
Eligibility This program is open to residents of North Carolina who maintain cultural and political identification as a Native American through membership in an Indian tribe recognized by the United States or by the state of North Carolina, or through tribal affiliation or community recognition. Incoming freshmen must rank in the top half of their graduating class at a North Carolina high school; incoming transfers must have completed an associate degree and must have earned a GPA of 2.5 or higher at the 2-year college, or they must have a certificate in a program that articulates directly with an academic program at a constituent university and must have earned a GPA of 2.0 or higher at the college. Applicants must be admitted or enrolled in a regular undergraduate degree-granting program at 1 of the 16 constituent institutions of the University of North Carolina (UNC). They must be able to demonstrate financial need.
Financial data The maximum stipend is $3,000 per year.
Duration 1 year; may be renewed if the student maintains financial need and satisfactory academic progress.
Additional information This program was established in 2003 as a replacement for the former North Carolina Incentive Scholarship and Grant Program for Native Americans.
Number awarded Varies each year; recently, a total of 2,408 UNC Campus Scholarships, with a total value of $5,887,664, were awarded.
Deadline Deadline dates vary; check with the participating school.

[508]
UTAH NAVAJO TRUST FUND HIGHER EDUCATION SCHOLARSHIPS
Utah Navajo Trust Fund
Attn: Higher Education Office
151 East 500 North
Blanding, UT 84511
(435) 678-1460   Toll-free: (800) 378-2050
Fax: (435) 678-1464   E-mail: MHoliday@utah.gov
Web: ww.untf.utah.gov

Purpose To provide financial assistance for college or graduate school to members of the Navajo Nation in Utah.
Eligibility This program is open to students who can provide a letter of verification from their Chapter of the Navajo Nation or Blue Mountain Dine' Community to affirm residency in San Juan County, Utah. Applicants must be working on a 1-year or 2-year certificate or associate, bachelor's, master's, or doctoral degree. They must have maintained a GPA of 3.0 or higher during high school and be able to demonstrate financial need.

Financial data The stipend depends on the need of the recipient; funding is considered supplemental to that available from the Navajo Nation Scholarship and Financial Aid Office.
Duration 1 year; may be renewed, provided the recipient maintains a GPA of 2.0 or higher.
Number awarded Varies each year.
Deadline October of each year for fall quarter or semester; January of each year for winter quarter or spring semester; April of each year for spring quarter; June of each year for summer quarter or session.

[509]
UTAH SPORTS HALL OF FAME NATIVE AMERICAN SCHOLARSHIPS

Utah Sports Hall of Fame Foundation
c/o Berdean Jarman, Scholarship Chair
873 West 1200 North
Orem, UT 84057
(801) 225-3352
Web: www.utahsportshalloffame.org/AboutUs.html

Purpose To recognize and reward outstanding Native American high school seniors in Utah who have been involved in athletics and are interested in attending college in the state.
Eligibility Each high school in Utah may nominate 1 Native American high school senior. Nominees must be planning to attend college in the state. Selection is based on academic record, personal character, financial need, leadership qualities, and involvement in athletic activities, including football, basketball, cross country, volleyball, tennis, track and field, soccer, rodeo, baseball, swimming, wrestling, officiating, community recreation, or intramural sports.
Financial data The stipend is $2,000. Funds are paid to the recipient's institution.
Duration 1 year; nonrenewable.
Additional information Formerly, the sponsoring organization was known as the Old Time Athletes Association. Recipients must attend an academic institution in Utah.
Number awarded 2 each year.
Deadline March of each year.

[510]
VERL AND DOROTHY MILLER NATIVE AMERICAN VOCATIONAL SCHOLARSHIP

Oregon Community Foundation
Attn: Scholarship Department
1221 S.W. Yamhill Street, Suite 100
Portland, OR 97205-2108
(503) 227-6846, ext. 1418   Fax: (503) 274-7771
E-mail: diannec@ocf1.org
Web: www.ocf1.org

Purpose To provide financial assistance to American Indians from Oregon who are interested in studying at a trade or vocational school in the state.
Eligibility This program is open to American Indian residents of Oregon who can document tribal enrollment and/or blood quantum. Applicants must be attending or planning to attend a trade or vocational school in the state either full or part time. Selection is based on academic promise, participation in school or community activities, personal qualities (e.g., work ethic, dependability, stability, moral character, responsibility), aptitude for a particular trade or vocation, and financial need.
Financial data A stipend is awarded (amount not specified).
Duration 1 year; may be renewed up to 3 additional years.
Additional information This program was established in 2002.
Number awarded 1 or more each year.
Deadline February of each year.

[511]
VICTOR MATSON SR. TRIBUTARY SCHOLARSHIP

Sault Tribe of Chippewa Indians
Attn: Higher Education Department
Two Ice Circle
Sault Ste. Marie, MI 49783
(906) 635-7784   Toll-free: (800) 793-0660
Fax: (906) 635-7785   E-mail: jlewton@saulttribe.net
Web: www.saulttribe.com

Purpose To provide financial assistance to members of the Sault Tribe of Chippewa Indians interested in attending college to work on a fisheries-related degree.
Eligibility This program is open to enrolled members of the Sault Tribe who have been accepted at or are attending a 2-year or 4-year college or university. Applicants must be working on or planning to work on an undergraduate degree in a fisheries-related field. Along with their application, they must submit an essay of 300 to 500 words on how their education will benefit them and why they should receive the scholarship.
Financial data The stipend is $1,000 per year.
Duration 1 year.
Number awarded 1 each year.
Deadline May of each year.

[512]
VIRGINIA D. WILSON SCHOLARSHIP

Navajo Nation
Attn: Office of Navajo Nation Scholarship and Financial Assistance
P.O. Box 1870
Window Rock, AZ 86515-1870
(928) 871-7640   Toll-free: (800) 243-2956
Fax: (928) 871-6561
E-mail: onnsfacentral@navajo.org
Web: www.onnsfa.org/corplist.asp

Purpose To provide financial assistance for college to Navajo high school seniors in New Mexico.
Eligibility This program is open to high school seniors who are enrolled members of the Navajo Nation, reside in New Mexico, and are about to enter college. Financial need is not considered in the selection process.
Financial data The stipend is $2,000 per year.
Duration 1 year; may be renewed if the recipient maintains a GPA of 2.0 or higher and enrolls in at least 12 credit hours per semester.
Additional information Recipients may major in any field, but they must enroll as full-time students in college.

Number awarded 1 or more each year.

[513]
VOCATIONAL SCHOOL AWARDS OF THE SEMINOLE NATION JUDGMENT FUND
Seminole Nation of Oklahoma
Attn: Judgment Fund Office
2007 West Wrangler Boulevard
Seminole, OK 74868
(405) 382-0549
Web: www.cowboy.net

Purpose To provide financial assistance for vocational school to members of the Seminole Nation of Oklahoma.
Eligibility This program is open to enrolled members of the Seminole Nation who are descended from a member of the Seminole Nation as it existed in Florida on September 18, 1923. Applicants must be attending or planning to attend a vocational school.
Financial data The stipend for full-time students is $25 per week, to a maximum of $1,200 per year. The stipend for part-time students is $12 per week, to a maximum of $600 per year. Other benefits include a grant of $100 or the actual cost, whichever is less, of the fee to obtain a license upon completion of a vocational course. Students who take correspondence courses may receive up to $400 per year or the actual cost of tuition, books, or fees, whichever is less; no stipend is provided to those students. The total of all vocational school awards to an applicant may not exceed $2,400.
Duration 1 year; may be renewed for 1 additional year.
Additional information The General Council of the Seminole Nation of Oklahoma approved a plan for use of the Judgment Fund Award in 1990. This aspect of the program went into effect in September of 1991.
Number awarded Varies each year.
Deadline Applications must be submitted within 30 days of the completion of a vocational course.

[514]
WALTER CHARLEY MEMORIAL SCHOLARSHIPS
Ahtna, Incorporated
Attn: Walter Charley Memorial Scholarship
406 West Fireweed Lane, Suite 103
Anchorage, AK 99503
(907) 868-8227   Fax: (907) 868-8285
E-mail: cshade@ahtna.net
Web: www.ahtna-inc.com

Purpose To provide financial assistance to shareholders of Ahtna, Incorporated in Alaska and their descendants who plan to attend college in any state.
Eligibility This program is open to Ahtna shareholders and their descendants who are 1) attending or planning to attend a college, university, or vocational school in any state; or 2) accepted in a program specializing in a recognized area or field of study.
Financial data The stipend is $2,000 per semester ($4,000 per year) for full-time students or $1,000 per semester ($2,000 per year) for part-time students.
Duration 1 year; may be renewed, provided the recipient maintains a GPA of 2.0 or higher.

Additional information Ahtna, Incorporated is 1 of 13 regional corporations established according to the terms of the Alaska Native Claims Settlement Act (ANCSA) of 1971.
Number awarded Varies each year.
Deadline July of each year for fall semester; December of each year for spring semester.

[515]
WALTER "PORKY" WHITE SCHOLARSHIP FUND
MIGIZI Communications, Inc.
Attn: Scholarship Committee
3123 East Lake Street
Minneapolis, MN 55406
(612) 721-6631   Fax: (612) 721-3936
Web: migizi.org/mig/scholarships.html

Purpose To provide financial assistance to Native American students working on an undergraduate or graduate degree in natural resources or an environmental field.
Eligibility This program is open to Native American undergraduate and graduate students enrolled at an accredited 4-year college or university. Applicants must be working on a degree in environmental science, natural resource management, biology, marine biology, or a related discipline. Along with their application, they must submit documentation of financial need and a 500-word essay on 1) their current involvement in protecting and working with the environment and natural resources, 2) why it is important to protect and study our environment and natural resources, and 3) their plans for the future and how they plan to use their studies to help the community.
Financial data The stipend is $1,000.
Duration 1 year; nonrenewable.
Number awarded 1 each year.
Deadline May of each year.

[516]
WAMPANOAG HIGHER EDUCATION SCHOLARSHIP PROGRAM
Wampanoag Tribe of Gay Head
Attn: Education Director
20 Black Brook Road
Aquinnah, MA 02535-1546
(508) 645-9265, ext. 131   Fax: (508) 645-3790
Web: www.wampanoagtribe.net

Purpose To provide financial assistance to members of the Wampanoag Tribe of Gay Head who are interested in attending college or graduate school in any state.
Eligibility This program is open to enrolled members of the Wampanoag Tribe of Gay Head who are working on or planning to work on a baccalaureate or advanced degree. Applicants must submit a letter of acceptance from a college or university and documentation of financial need.
Financial data A stipend is awarded (amount not specified).
Duration 1 year; may be renewed.
Number awarded Varies each year.
Deadline June of each year.

[517]
WARNER NORCROSS & JUDD SECRETARIAL STUDIES SCHOLARSHIP

Grand Rapids Community Foundation
Attn: Scholarship Coordinator
209-C Waters Building
161 Ottawa Avenue N.W.
Grand Rapids, MI 49503-2757
(616) 454-1751, ext. 103   Fax: (616) 454-6455
E-mail: rbishop@grfoundation.org
Web: www.grfoundation.org

Purpose To provide financial assistance to minority residents of Michigan who are interested in enrolling in a legal assistant/secretarial program at an institution in the state.
Eligibility This program is open to minority students currently residing in Michigan. Applicants must be accepted at or enrolled in an accredited public or private 2- or 4-year college, university, vocational school, or business school with a declared major in legal assistant/legal secretarial studies. They must have a GPA of 2.5 or higher and be attending a school in Michigan.
Financial data The stipend is $1,000.
Duration 1 year.
Additional information Funding for this program is provided by the law firm Warner Norcross & Judd LLP.
Number awarded 1 each year.
Deadline March of each year.

[518]
WASHINGTON INDIAN GAMING ASSOCIATION SCHOLARSHIPS

Washington Indian Gaming Association
1110 Capitol Way South, Suite 404
Olympia, WA 98501
(360) 352-3248   Fax: (360) 352-4819
Web: www.washingtonindiangaming.org

Purpose To provide financial assistance for college or graduate school to members of Indian tribes in Washington.
Eligibility This program is open to Washington residents who are enrolled members of tribes affiliated with the Washington Indian Gaming Association (WIGA) and to urban Indian students in the state. Applicants must be attending or accepted at a community college, undergraduate institution, or community college in any state. Native American students from outside Washington who attend college in the state are also eligible. Along with their application, they must submit a personal essay on their academic and professional interests, how this scholarship will help support them in those interests, why they are considering their intended major, and their future career objectives. Financial need is also considered in the selection process.
Financial data Stipends are $1,200, $1,000, or $825.
Duration 1 year; may be renewed.
Number awarded Varies each year. Recently, 10 of these scholarships were awarded: 3 at $1,200, 3 at $1,000, and 4 at $825.
Deadline May of each year.

[519]
WASHINGTON STATE AMERICAN INDIAN ENDOWED SCHOLARSHIP PROGRAM

Washington Higher Education Coordinating Board
917 Lakeridge Way
P.O. Box 43430
Olympia, WA 98504-3430
(360) 753-7843   Fax: (360) 753-7808
TDD: (360) 753-7809   E-mail: aies@hecb.wa.gov
Web: www.hecb.wa.gov/paying/waaidprgm/aies.asp

Purpose To provide financial assistance to American Indian undergraduate and graduate students in Washington.
Eligibility This program is open to American Indian students who are Washington residents with close social and cultural ties to an American Indian tribe and/or community in the state. Applicants must demonstrate financial need and be enrolled, or planning to enroll, as a full-time undergraduate or graduate student at a Washington state public or independent college, university, or career school. They must agree to use their education to benefit other American Indians. Students who are working on a degree in religious, seminarian, or theological academic studies are not eligible.
Financial data Stipends range from about $500 to $2,000 per year.
Duration 1 year, may be renewed up to 4 additional years.
Additional information This program was created by the Washington legislature in 1990 with a state appropriation to an endowment fund and matching contributions from tribes, individuals, and organizations.
Number awarded Approximately 15 new and 10 renewal scholarships are awarded each year.
Deadline January of each year.

[520]
WASHOE TRIBE ADULT VOCATIONAL SCHOLARSHIPS

Washoe Tribe
Attn: Education Department
919 Highway 395 South
Gardnerville, NV 89410
(775) 265-4191, ext. 1132
Toll-free: (800) 76-WASHOE   Fax: (775) 265-6240
E-mail: education@washoetribe.us
Web: www.washoetribe.us/content/view/73/2

Purpose To provide financial assistance to members of the Washoe Tribe who are interested in obtaining a diploma or certificate at a vocational or technical junior college.
Eligibility Eligible to apply for these scholarships are adult members of the Washoe Tribe in Nevada and California who are pursuing (or planning to pursue) vocational education. Applicants are required to seek all other sources of funding, in addition to applying for this program. In the process, they must complete a Free Application for Federal Student Aid (FAFSA) and receive a Student Aid Report.
Financial data A stipend is awarded (amount not specified).
Duration The maximum training period is generally 24 months.
Number awarded Varies each year.
Deadline Applications may be submitted at any time.

[521]
WASHOE TRIBE HIGHER EDUCATION GRANT PROGRAM
Washoe Tribe
Attn: Education Department
919 Highway 395 South
Gardnerville, NV 89410
(775) 265-4191, ext. 1132
Toll-free: (800) 76-WASHOE   Fax: (775) 265-6240
E-mail: education@washoetribe.us
Web: www.washoetribe.us/content/view/74/2

Purpose To provide financial assistance for college or graduate school to members of the Washoe Tribe in Nevada and California.

Eligibility Eligible to apply for these scholarships are members of the Washoe Tribe who are working on (or planning to work on) an associate or bachelor's degree. Applicants are required to seek all other sources of funding, in addition to applying for this program. In the process, they must complete a Free Application for Federal Student Aid (FAFSA) and receive a Student Aid Report. Awards are granted in the following priority order: 1) continuing students with acceptable grades; 2) new students who reside near or within the boundaries of Washoe tribal colonies (Woodfords, Dresslerville, Carson, Stewart, Reno) and other Nevada and California residents; 3) students outside of Nevada and California; 4) graduate students; and 5) students who have a 4-year degree and are working to obtain a 4-year degree in a different field.

Financial data A stipend is awarded (amount not specified).

Duration 1 year; may be renewed if the recipient remains enrolled full time with a GPA of 1.8 or higher as a freshman and 2.0 or higher as a sophomore through senior.

Number awarded Varies each year.

Deadline August or December of each year.

[522]
WASHOE TRIBE INCENTIVE SCHOLARSHIPS
Washoe Tribe
Attn: Education Department
919 Highway 395 South
Gardnerville, NV 89410
(775) 265-4191, ext. 1132
Toll-free: (800) 76-WASHOE   Fax: (775) 265-6240
E-mail: education@washoetribe.us
Web: www.washoetribe.us/content/view/71/2

Purpose To provide financial assistance for college or graduate school to members of the Washoe Tribe.

Eligibility This program is open to members of the Washoe Tribe in Nevada and California who are currently working full time on an associate, baccalaureate, graduate, or postgraduate degree. Applicants must have a GPA of 3.0 or higher. Along with their application they must submit proof of Washoe enrollment, a copy of their college grade report, and a copy of their current class schedule. Selection is based on a first-come, first-served basis; financial need is not considered.

Financial data The stipend is $2,000 per year.

Duration 1 year; recipients may reapply.

Number awarded 20 each year.

Deadline January or September of each year.

[523]
WATSON MIDWIVES OF COLOR SCHOLARSHIP
American College of Nurse-Midwives
Attn: ACNM Foundation, Inc.
8403 Coleville Road, Suite 1550
Silver Spring, MD 20910-6374
(240) 485-1850   Fax: (240) 485-1818
Web: www.midwife.org/foundation_award.cfm

Purpose To provide financial assistance for midwifery education to students of color who belong to the American College of Nurse-Midwives (ACNM).

Eligibility This program is open to ACNM members of color who are currently enrolled in an accredited basic midwife education program and have successfully completed 1 academic or clinical semester/quarter or clinical module. Applicants must submit a 150-word essay on their midwifery career plans and a 100-word essay on their intended future participation in the local, regional, and/or national activities of the ACNM. Selection is based on leadership potential, financial need, academic history, and potential for future professional contribution to the organization.

Financial data The stipend is $3,000.

Duration 1 year.

Number awarded Varies each year; recently, 3 of these scholarships were awarded.

Deadline March of each year.

[524]
WELLS FARGO UNDERGRADUATE SCHOLARSHIPS
American Indian Graduate Center
Attn: Executive Director
4520 Montgomery Boulevard, N.E., Suite 1-B
Albuquerque, NM 87109-1291
(505) 881-4584   Toll-free: (800) 628-1920
Fax: (505) 884-0427   E-mail: aigc@aigc.com
Web: www.aigc.com

Purpose To provide financial assistance to Native American upper-division students working on a business-related degree.

Eligibility This program is open to enrolled members of U.S. federally-recognized American Indian tribes and Alaska Native groups and other students who can document one-fourth degree federally-recognized Indian blood. Applicants must be entering their junior or senior year as a full-time student and working on a degree to prepare for a career in banking, gaming operations, resort management, or administration, including accounting, finance, human resources, and information technology. They must have a GPA of 3.0 or higher. Along with their application, they must submit an essay on their personal, educational, and professional goals. Financial need is also considered in the selection process.

Financial data The stipend is $2,500.

Duration 1 year.

Additional information This program is supported by Wells Fargo Bank.

Number awarded 2 each year.

Deadline April of each year.

[525]
WELLS FARGO-BBNC SCHOLARSHIP FUND
Bristol Bay Native Corporation
Attn: BBNC Education Foundation
111 West 16th Avenue, Suite 400
Anchorage, AK 99501
(907) 278-3602   Toll-free: (800) 426-3602
Fax: (907) 276-3924   E-mail: pelagiol@bbnc.net
Web: www.bbnc.net/education/students

Purpose To provide financial assistance to shareholders of Bristol Bay Native Corporation (BBNC) who are majoring in banking at a college in any state.

Eligibility This program is open to BBNC shareholders who are enrolled full time as a junior or senior at a college or university in any state to prepare for a career in banking. Applicants must have a GPA of 2.0 or higher and be able to demonstrate financial need. Along with their application, they must submit an essay on how they became interested in their proposed field of study, any special circumstances they want to be considered, and their desire to work in the region or for a BBNC subsidiary company. Selection is based on the essay (35%), cumulative GPA (40%), financial need (20%), and letters of recommendation (5%).

Financial data The stipend is $5,000 per year.

Duration 1 year.

Additional information The funding for this program is provided equally by Wells Fargo Bank and the Bristol Bay Native Corporation Education Foundation.

Deadline April of each year.

[526]
WHITE EARTH SCHOLARSHIP PROGRAM
White Earth Indian Reservation Tribal Council
Attn: Scholarship Program
P.O. Box 418
White Earth, MN 56591
(218) 983-3285, ext. 1227   Toll-free: (800) 950-3248
Fax: (218) 983-3641
E-mail: highered@whiteearth.com
Web: www.whiteearth.com/education.htm

Purpose To provide financial assistance to Minnesota Chippewa Tribe enrolled members who are interested in attending college, vocational school, or graduate school in any state.

Eligibility This program is open to enrolled members of the White Earth Band of the Minnesota Chippewa Tribe who can demonstrate financial need. Applicants must be attending or planning to attend a college, university, or vocational school in any state. Graduate students in the fields of business, education, human services, law, and medicine are also eligible.

Financial data A stipend is awarded (amount not specified).

Duration 1 year; may be renewed, provided undergraduates maintain a GPA of 2.0 or higher and graduate students maintain a GPA of 3.0 or higher.

Additional information Applicants for this program must also apply for financial aid administered by their institution and any other aid for which they may be eligible (e.g., work-study, Social Security, veteran's benefits).

Number awarded Varies each year.

Deadline May of each year.

[527]
WINNEBAGO TRIBE HIGHER EDUCATION ASSISTANCE
Winnebago Tribe of Nebraska
Attn: Education Department
P.O. Box 687
Winnebago, NE 68071
(402) 878-3202   Fax: (402) 878-2632
E-mail: education@winnebagotribe.com
Web: www.winnebagotribe.com

Purpose To provide financial assistance to members of the Winnebago Tribe of Nebraska who are interested in attending college or graduate school in any state.

Eligibility This program is open to enrolled members of the Winnebago Tribe of Nebraska who are attending or planning to attend an institution of higher education in any state. Applicants must be working on an associate, bachelor's, master's, or doctoral degree or certificate. They must submit a copy of their Certificate of Indian Blood (CIB) and documentation of financial need.

Financial data A stipend is awarded (amount not specified). Funding is intended only to supplement other assistance available to the student.

Duration 1 semester; may be renewed.

Number awarded Varies each year.

Deadline April of each year for fall, academic year, or summer school; October of each year for spring or winter.

[528]
WINNERS FOR LIFE FOUNDATION SCHOLARSHIP
American Indian College Fund
Attn: Scholarship Department
8333 Greenwood Boulevard
Denver, CO 80221
(303) 426-8900   Toll-free: (800) 776-FUND
Fax: (303) 426-1200   E-mail: info@collegefund.org
Web: www.collegefund.org

Purpose To provide financial assistance to young Native Americans who are attending or planning to attend a Tribal College or University (TCU).

Eligibility This program is open to American Indians or Alaska Natives who are enrolled or planning to enroll full time at an eligible TCU. Applicants must have a GPA of 3.0 or higher and be able to demonstrate financial need. They must be between 17 and 24 years of age. Along with their application, they must submit 1) short essays (up to 500 words each) on how they perceive themselves as leaders in their school or community and how their education will help the Native American community; and 2) a personal statement of 1,000 words that includes their personal background, their academic background, their educational and career goals, and how this scholarship will help them achieve those goals.

Financial data The stipend is $2,000.

Duration 1 year.

Additional information This program is sponsored by Winners for Life Foundation in partnership with the American Indian College Fund.

Number awarded 1 or more each year.

Deadline May of each year.

[529]
WISCONSIN INDIAN EDUCATION ASSOCIATION SCHOLARSHIPS

Wisconsin Indian Education Association
Attn: Scholarship Coordinator
P.O. Box 910
Keshena, WI 54135
(715) 799-5110   Fax: (715) 799-5102
E-mail: vnuske@mitw.org
Web: www.wiea.org

Purpose To provide financial assistance for undergraduate or graduate study to members of Wisconsin Indian tribes.
Eligibility This program is open to residents of Wisconsin who can provide proof of tribal enrollment. Applicants must fall into 1 of the following categories: 1) graduating high school senior; 2) new or continuing student at a tribal or technical/vocational college; 3) undergraduate student at a 4-year college or university; or 4) graduate or Ph.D. student. All applicants must be full-time students. Along with their application, they must submit a 1-page personal essay on how they will apply their education. Selection is based on that essay (25 points), letters of recommendation (10 points), and GPA (15 points if 3.5 or higher, 10 points if 3.00 to 3.49, 5 points if 2.50 to 2.99). Financial need is not considered.
Financial data The stipend is $1,000 per year.
Duration 1 year; nonrenewable.
Additional information Eligible tribes include Menominee, Oneida, Stockbridge/Munsee, Mole Lake, Potowatomi, Ho-Chunk, Ba Chippewa, LCO Chippewa, St. Croix Chippewa, Red Cliff Chippewa, Sakoagon Chippewa, Brotherton, and Lac du Flam Chippewa.
Number awarded 4 each year: 1 in each of the 4 categories.
Deadline March of each year.

[530]
WISCONSIN INDIAN STUDENT ASSISTANCE GRANTS

Wisconsin Higher Educational Aids Board
131 West Wilson Street, Room 902
P.O. Box 7885
Madison, WI 53707-7885
(608) 266-0888   Fax: (608) 267-2808
E-mail: sandy.thomas@heab.state.wi.us
Web: heab.state.wi.us/programs.html

Purpose To provide financial aid for college or graduate school to Native Americans in Wisconsin.
Eligibility Wisconsin residents who have at least 25% Native American blood (of a certified tribe or band) are eligible to apply if they are able to demonstrate financial need and are interested in attending college on the undergraduate or graduate school level. Applicants must attend a Wisconsin institution (public, independent, or proprietary). They may be enrolled either full or part time.
Financial data Awards range from $250 to $1,100 per year. Additional funds are available on a matching basis from the U.S. Bureau of Indian Affairs.
Duration Up to 5 years.
Deadline Generally, applications can be submitted at any time.

[531]
WOKSAPE OYATE: "WISDOM OF THE PEOPLE" DISTINGUISHED SCHOLAR AWARD

American Indian College Fund
Attn: Scholarship Department
8333 Greenwood Boulevard
Denver, CO 80221
(303) 426-8900   Toll-free: (800) 776-FUND
Fax: (303) 426-1200   E-mail: info@collegefund.org
Web: www.collegefund.org

Purpose To provide financial assistance to Native American high school seniors who are the valedictorian or salutatorian of their class and planning to attend a Tribal College or University (TCU).
Eligibility This program is open to American Indians or Alaska Natives who are graduating from high school as the valedictorian or salutatorian of their class. Applicants must be planning to enroll full time at an eligible TCU. They must also be able to demonstrate financial need. Along with their application, they must submit 1) short essays (up to 500 words each) on how they perceive themselves as leaders in their school or community and how their education will help the Native American community; and 2) a personal statement of 1,000 words that includes their personal background, their academic background, their educational and career goals, and how this scholarship will help them achieve those goals.
Financial data The stipend is $8,000.
Duration 1 year.
Additional information This program was established in 2006 with an endowment grant from the Lilly Foundation.
Number awarded 1 each year.
Deadline May of each year.

[532]
WOKSAPE OYATE: "WISDOM OF THE PEOPLE" KEEPERS OF THE NEXT GENERATION AWARD

American Indian College Fund
Attn: Scholarship Department
8333 Greenwood Boulevard
Denver, CO 80221
(303) 426-8900   Toll-free: (800) 776-FUND
Fax: (303) 426-1200   E-mail: info@collegefund.org
Web: www.collegefund.org

Purpose To provide financial assistance to Native Americans who are single parents and attending or planning to attend a Tribal College or University (TCU).
Eligibility This program is open to American Indians or Alaska Natives who are enrolled or planning to enroll full time at an eligible TCU. Applicants must have a GPA of 3.5 or higher and be able to demonstrate financial need. They must be single parents. Along with their application, they must submit 1) short essays (up to 500 words each) on how they perceive themselves as leaders in their school or community and how their education will help the Native American community; and 2) a personal statement of 1,000 words that includes their personal background, their academic background, their educational and career goals, and how this scholarship will help them achieve those goals.
Financial data The stipend is $8,000.
Duration 1 year.

Additional information This program was established in 2006 with an endowment grant from the Lilly Foundation.
Number awarded 1 each year.
Deadline May of each year.

[533]
XEROX TECHNICAL MINORITY SCHOLARSHIP PROGRAM

Xerox Corporation
Attn: Technical Minority Scholarship Program
150 State Street, Fourth Floor
Rochester, NY 14614
(585) 422-7689   E-mail: xtmsp@rballiance.com
Web: www.xerox.com

Purpose To provide financial assistance to Native Americans and other minorities interested in undergraduate or graduate education in the sciences and/or engineering.
Eligibility This program is open to minorities (people of African American, Asian, Pacific Islander, Native American, Native Alaskan, or Hispanic descent) working full time on a bachelor's, master's, or doctoral degree in chemistry, computing and software systems, engineering (chemical, computer, electrical, imaging, manufacturing, mechanical, optical, or software), information management, laser optics, materials science, physics, or printing management science. Applicants must be U.S. citizens or permanent residents with a GPA of 3.0 or higher and attending a 4-year college or university.
Financial data Stipends range from $1,000 to $10,000.
Duration 1 year.
Number awarded Varies each year; recently, 118 of these scholarships were awarded.
Deadline September of each year.

[534]
YAKAMA ADULT VOCATIONAL TRAINING PROGRAM

Yakama Indian Nation
Department of Human Services
Attn: Adult Vocational Training Office
P.O. Box 151
Toppenish, WA 98948
(509) 865-5121, ext. 540   Toll-free: (800) 543-2802
Fax: (509) 865-6994

Purpose To provide financial assistance to Yakama Indians who are interested in attending an accredited vocational school, college, or trade institute.
Eligibility Yakama Indians who are at least 18 years of age, at least high school seniors, members of the Yakama Indian tribe, residents of the Yakama Indian Nation service area for the last 6 months, and unemployed or underemployed are eligible to apply for this program.
Financial data The amount awarded depends on the recipient's need.
Duration 1 year; may be renewed.
Additional information In addition to financial assistance, this program provides career guidance and vocational training.
Number awarded Varies each year.
Deadline Applications may be submitted at any time.

[535]
YAKAMA COLLEGE STUDENT ASSISTANCE PROGRAM

Yakama Indian Nation
Department of Human Services
Attn: Higher Education Programs
P.O. Box 151
Toppenish, WA 98948
(509) 865-5121, ext. 599   Fax: (509) 865-6994

Purpose To provide financial assistance to Yakama Indians who wish to attend an institution of higher education in any state.
Eligibility This program is open to enrolled members of U.S. Indian tribes; preference is given to enrolled Yakama members. Applicants must be high school seniors or graduates (or GED recipients), accepted at a 2-year or 4-year college or university in any state as full-time students, and in financial need.
Financial data The amounts of the awards depend on the need of the recipient, to a maximum of $2,000 per year.
Duration 1 year; may be renewed.
Additional information The Yakama Nation operates this program with funding from the Bureau of Indian Affairs.
Number awarded Varies each year.
Deadline June of each year for fall quarter or semester; October of each year for winter quarter or spring semester; January of each year for spring quarter; April of each year for summer term.

[536]
YAKAMA TRIBAL SCHOLARSHIP

Yakama Indian Nation
Department of Human Services
Attn: Higher Education Programs
P.O. Box 151
Toppenish, WA 98948
(509) 865-5121, ext. 519   Toll-free: (800) 543-2802
Fax: (509) 865-6994

Purpose To provide financial assistance to Yakama tribal members interested in working on an undergraduate or graduate degree in any state.
Eligibility Eligible to apply are Yakama students of one-quarter or more blood quantum. They must be at least high school graduates and enrolled or planning to enroll in a postsecondary institution in any state. Applicants must have at least a 2.0 GPA. Scholarships are awarded on the basis of academic achievement rather than financial need.
Financial data Eligible undergraduate students receive $1,500 per year; graduate students receive $3,000 per year. Part-time students receive funding for tuition, books, and transportation; this amount may never exceed the tribal scholarship amount.
Duration 1 year; may be renewed.
Additional information Before being awarded the scholarship, recipients must attend an orientation session. Students who drop out of school after receiving scholarship awards must refund the Yakama Tribal Scholarships before being granted additional funding. Tuition amounts kept by the student's college do not count against student refunds.
Number awarded Varies each year.

Deadline June of each year for fall quarter or semester; October of each year for winter quarter or spring semester; January of each year for spring quarter; April of each year for summer term.

[537] YDFDA VOCATIONAL TRAINING GRANTS

Yukon Delta Fisheries Development Association
Attn: Vocational Training Program
P.O. Box 210
Emmonak, AK 99581
(907) 949-1202   Toll-free: (877) 985-6625
Fax: (907) 949-1203   E-mail: info@ydfda.org
Web: www.ydfda.org

Purpose To provide financial assistance for vocational training to residents of Alaska Native villages served by the Yukon Delta Fisheries Development Association (YDFDA).

Eligibility This program is open to students who are interested in vocational training and have been residents for at least 5 continuous years of a Native village in the Lower Yukon Delta region of Alaska. Applicants must have a subsistence and/or commercial fishing relationship to the Lower Yukon Delta region. Selection criteria include motivation, academic achievement, and leadership potential.

Financial data The stipend depends on the cost of the program and the need of the recipient.

Duration At least 3 months.

Additional information YDFDA serves the Lower Delta Yukon region as 1 of 6 Community Development Quota (CDQ) organizations in the state.

Number awarded Varies each year; recently, 9 of these grants were awarded.

Deadline Applications may be submitted at any time, but they must be received at least 2 months prior to the start of the program.

[538] ZUNI HIGHER EDUCATION SCHOLARSHIPS

Pueblo of Zuni
Attn: Education and Career Development Center
P.O. Box 339
Zuni, NM 87327
(505) 782-7178   Fax: (505) 782-7223
E-mail: zunihe@hotmail.com
Web: www.ashiwi.org/highered/higheredhome.htm

Purpose To provide financial assistance for college or graduate school to members of the Pueblo of Zuni.

Eligibility This program is open to enrolled members of the Pueblo of Zuni who are high school seniors or graduates. Applicants must have earned a GPA of 2.0 or higher and be interested in working on an associate, bachelor's, or graduate degree as a full-time student. They must have also applied for a federal Pell Grant.

Financial data The amount awarded depends on the need of the recipient, up to $5,000 per year.

Duration 1 year; may be renewed if the recipient maintains a GPA of 2.0 or higher.

Number awarded Varies each year.

Deadline April of each year for the summer session; June of each year for the fall term; October of each year for the spring term.

[539] THE 13TH REGIONAL HERITAGE FOUNDATION SCHOLARSHIPS

The 13th Regional Corporation
Attn: The 13th Regional Heritage Foundation
1156 Industry Drive
Seattle, WA 98188
(206) 575-6229   Fax: (206) 575-6283
E-mail: info@thE13thregion.com
Web: www.thE13thregion.com/scholarships.html

Purpose To provide financial assistance for college or graduate school to Alaska Natives who are shareholders of The 13th Regional Corporation or their dependent children or grandchildren.

Eligibility This program is open to 1) original shareholders of The 13th Regional Corporation, and 2) their dependent children and grandchildren who are also Alaska Natives. Applicants must be accepted to or enrolled in an accredited community college, university, college, or vocational/trade school as an undergraduate, graduate, or vocational student. Along with their application, they must submit an essay of 500 to 1,000 words on their personal history, special talents and abilities, community involvement, plans for the future, philosophy of life, why they wish to attend college or graduate school, educational objective, major and minor field of interest, and school they plan to attend. Selection is based on leadership and initiative (20%), academic achievement (20%), educational goals (20%), completeness and neatness of application (20%), and financial need (20%).

Financial data The stipend is $500 per semester ($1,000 per year). Funds are disbursed directly to the school to be used for tuition, books, board, or laboratory fees.

Duration 1 semester; may be renewed.

Additional information The 13th Regional Corporation was established under provisions of the Alaska Native Claims Settlement Act of 1971. Its shareholders are Alaska Natives who no longer live in Alaska.

Number awarded Varies each year; recently, 12 of these scholarships were awarded.

Deadline February of each year for spring and summer terms; June of each year for fall and winter terms.

Fellowships

Described here are 369 funding programs open to Native Americans that are available to support studies on the graduate (for a master's degree, doctorate, professional degree, or specialist's certificate) or postgraduate level in the United States. Usually no return of service or repayment is required. Note: other funding opportunities for Native Americans on the graduate or postgraduate level are also described in the Grants, Awards, and Internships sections. So, if you are looking for a particular program and don't find it in this section, be sure to check the Program Title Index to see if it is covered elsewhere in the directory.

[540]
ACCENTURE GRADUATE FELLOWSHIPS
American Indian Graduate Center
Attn: Executive Director
4520 Montgomery Boulevard, N.E., Suite 1-B
Albuquerque, NM 87109-1291
(505) 881-4584   Toll-free: (800) 628-1920
Fax: (505) 884-0427   E-mail: aigc@aigc.com
Web: www.aigc.com/scholarships.index.asp

Purpose To provide financial assistance to Native American students interested in working on a graduate or professional degree in any field, especially high technology and business.

Eligibility This program is open to enrolled members of U.S. federally-recognized American Indian tribes and Alaska Native groups and other students who can document one-fourth degree federally-recognized Indian blood. Applicants must be entering their first year as a full-time student in a graduate or professional school in the United States and have a GPA of 3.25 or higher. They must be planning to work on a master's, doctoral, or professional degree in any field, including high technology and business. Along with their application, they must submit a 500-word essay on their vision and personal goals as an American Indian or Alaska native citizen, including their achievements in leadership, community service, extracurricular activities, and giving back to their community. Financial need is also considered in the selection process.

Financial data Awards are based on each applicant's unmet financial need.

Duration 1 year; may be renewed.

Additional information This program, established in 2005, is supported by Accenture. The application fee is $15. Since this a supplemental program, applicants must apply in a timely manner for federal financial aid and campus-based aid at the college they are attending to be considered for this program. Failure to apply will disqualify an applicant.

Number awarded Varies each year; recently, 5 of these fellowships were awarded.

Deadline May of each year.

[541]
ADRIENNE M. AND CHARLES SHELBY ROOKS FELLOWSHIP FOR RACIAL AND ETHNIC THEOLOGICAL STUDENTS
United Church of Christ
Attn: Local Church Ministries
700 Prospect Avenue East
Cleveland, OH 44115-1100
(216) 736-3865   Toll-free: (866) 822-8224, ext. 3865
Fax: (216) 736-3783   E-mail: lcm@ucc.org
Web: www.ucc.org/education/scholarships/index.html

Purpose To provide financial assistance to Native American and other minority students who are either enrolled at an accredited seminary preparing for a career of service in the United Church of Christ (UCC) or working on a doctoral degree in the field of religion.

Eligibility This program is open to members of underrepresented ethnic groups (African American, Hispanic American, Asian American, Native American Indian, or Pacific Islander) who have been a member of a UCC congregation for at least 1 year. Applicants must be either 1) enrolled in an accredited school of theology in the United States or Canada and working on an M.Div. degree with the intent of becoming a pastor or teacher within the United Church of Christ, or 2) doctoral (Ph.D., Th.D., or Ed.D.) students within a field related to religious studies. Seminary students must have a GPA in all postsecondary work of 3.0 or higher and must have begun the in-care process; preference is given to students who have demonstrated leadership (through a history of service to the church) and scholarship (through exceptional academic performance). For doctoral students, preference is given to applicants who have demonstrated academic excellence, teaching effectiveness, and commitment to the United Church of Christ and who intend to become professors in colleges, seminaries, or graduate schools.

Financial data Grants range from $500 to $5,000 per year.

Duration 1 year; may be renewed.

Number awarded Varies each year; recently, 14 of these scholarships, including 8 for M.Div. students and 6 for doctoral students, were awarded.

Deadline February of each year.

[542]
ADVANCED DEGREE SCHOLARSHIP FUND OF THE SEMINOLE NATION JUDGMENT FUND
Seminole Nation of Oklahoma
Attn: Judgment Fund Office
2007 West Wrangler Boulevard
Seminole, OK 74868
(405) 382-0549   Toll-free: (877) 382-0549
Fax: (405) 382-0571
Web: www.seminolenation.com

Purpose To provide financial assistance for graduate study to members of the Seminole Nation of Oklahoma.

Eligibility This program is open to enrolled members of the Seminole Nation who are descended from a member of the Seminole Nation as it existed in Florida on September 18, 1923. Applicants must be attending or planning to attend a college or university to work on a master's degree, Ph.D., J.D., medical degree, pharmacist degree, or other advanced degree.

Financial data The stipend for full-time students is $1,700 per year. Part-time students receive the actual cost of tuition, books, and fees, to a maximum of $250 per semester. Students attending summer school receive $500 per semester. The total of all advanced degree awards to an applicant may not exceed $5,100.

Duration 1 year; may be renewed as long as the recipient maintains a GPA of 2.0 or higher.

Additional information The General Council of the Seminole Nation of Oklahoma approved a plan for use of the Judgment Fund Award in 1990. This aspect of the program went into effect in September of 1991.

Number awarded Varies each year.

Deadline November of each year for fall semester; April of each year for spring semester.

[543]
AFOGNAK HIGHER EDUCATION PROGRAM
Afognak Native Corporation
215 Mission Road, Suite 212
Kodiak, AK 99615
(907) 486-6014 Toll-free: (800) 770-6014
Fax: (907) 486-2514
E-mail: scholarships@afognak.com
Web: afognak.com/scholarships.php

Purpose To provide financial assistance to members of the Afognak Native Corporation in Alaska who are interested in enrolling in a traditional college, university, graduate school, or vocational program.

Eligibility This program is open to Alaska Natives who are original Afognak Native Corporation enrollees and their lineal descendants. Applicants must be high school graduates or GED recipients who have been accepted to or are enrolled at an accredited college, university, or vocational school to work on an associate, bachelor's, master's, or doctoral degree. Along with their application, they must submit a letter that provides a personal history (information about their family and their special talents and abilities, community involvement, plans for the future, philosophy of life), future plans for education, and how their education may benefit the Alutiiq people and their commitment to the Alutiiq community. Financial need is considered in the selection process.

Financial data A stipend is awarded (amount not specified).

Duration 1 year; may be renewed if the recipient maintains a GPA of 2.0 or higher.

Number awarded Varies each year.

Deadline April of each year.

[544]
AICPA FELLOWSHIPS FOR MINORITY DOCTORAL STUDENTS
American Institute of Certified Public Accountants
Attn: Academic and Career Development Division
220 Leigh Farm Road
Durham, NC 27707-8110
(919) 402-4931 Fax: (919) 419-4705
E-mail: MIC_Programs@aicpa.org
Web: www.aicpa.org

Purpose To provide financial assistance to Native American and other minority doctoral students who wish to prepare for a career teaching accounting at the college level.

Eligibility This program is open to minority students who have applied to and/or been accepted into a doctoral program with a concentration in accounting. Applicants must have earned a master's degree or completed a minimum of 3 years of full-time work in accounting. They must be attending or planning to attend school full time and agree not to work full time in a paid position, teach more than 1 course as a teaching assistant, or work more than 25% as a research assistant. U.S. citizenship is required. Preference is given to applicants who have attained a C.P.A. designation. For purposes of this program, the American Institute of Certified Public Accountants (AICPA) defines minority students as those whose heritage is Black or African American, Hispanic or Latino, Asian, American Indian or Alaskan Native, Native Hawaiian or other Pacific Islander, or of 2 or more races.

Financial data Stipends range from $8,000 to $12,000 per year.

Duration 1 year; may be renewed up to 4 additional years.

Number awarded Varies each year; recently, 22 of these fellowships were awarded.

Deadline March of each year.

[545]
AISES GOOGLE SCHOLARSHIP
American Indian Science and Engineering Society
Attn: Scholarship Coordinator
2305 Renard, S.E., Suite 200
P.O. Box 9828
Albuquerque, NM 87119-9828
(505) 765-1052, ext. 106 Fax: (505) 765-5608
E-mail: shirley@aises.org
Web: www.aises.org

Purpose To provide financial assistance to members of the American Indian Science and Engineering Society (AISES) who are working on an undergraduate or graduate degree in a computer-related field.

Eligibility This program is open to AISES members who are full-time undergraduate or graduate students at a 4-year college or university or a full-time student at a 2-year college enrolled in a program leading to a 4-year degree. Applicants must be majoring in computer science, computer engineering, or management information systems. They must have a GPA of 3.5 or higher and be able to document ancestry as an American Indian, Alaskan Native, or Native Hawaiian. Along with their application, they must submit a 500-word essay on their educational and/or career goals, interest in and motivation to continue higher education, understanding of the importance of college and commitment to completion, commitment to learning, and giving back to the community. Financial need is not considered in the selection process. U.S. citizenship is required.

Financial data The total award is $10,000, disbursed equally over the recipient's course of study.

Duration Until completion of a degree.

Additional information This program, established in 2008, is funded by Google Inc.

Number awarded 20 each year.

Deadline June of each year.

[546]
ALASKA LIBRARY ASSOCIATION GRADUATE LIBRARY STUDIES SCHOLARSHIP
Alaska Library Association
Attn: Scholarship Committee
c/o Alaska State Library
P.O. Box 110571
Juneau, AK 99811-0571
(907) 465-2458 Fax: (907) 465-2665
E-mail: aja_razumny@alaska.gov
Web: www.akla.org/scholarships/index.html

Purpose To provide financial assistance to Native American and other Alaska residents who are interested in work-

ing on a library degree at a school in any state and, upon graduation, working in a library in Alaska.
Eligibility This program is open to Alaska residents who have earned a bachelor's degree or higher from an accredited college or university. Applicants must be eligible for acceptance or currently enrolled in an accredited graduate degree program in any state in library and information science; be or will be full-time students during the academic year, semester, or quarter for which the scholarship is awarded; and be willing to make a commitment to work in an Alaska library for at least 1 year after graduation as a paid employee or volunteer. Preference is given to applicants meeting the federal definition of Alaska Native ethnicity. Selection is based on financial need, demonstrated scholastic ability and writing skills, an essay on professional goals and objectives, and 3 letters of recommendation (at least 1 of which must be from a librarian).
Financial data The stipend is $3,000.
Duration 1 year.
Number awarded 1 each year.
Deadline January of each year.

[547]
ALASKA NATIVE TRIBAL HEALTH CONSORTIUM SCHOLARSHIPS
Alaska Native Tribal Health Consortium
Attn: Native Development Coordinator
4000 Ambassador Drive, Suite 114
Anchorage, AK 99508
(907) 729-1348   Toll-free: (800) 684-8361
Fax: (907) 729-1335   E-mail: kruesch@anthc.org
Web: www.anthc.org/jt/int

Purpose To provide financial assistance for college or graduate school to Natives and American Indians who are residents of Alaska and interested in a career in health care.
Eligibility This program is open to Alaska Natives and American Indians who are undergraduates or graduate students interested in preparing for a career in the field of health care. Applicants must be residents of Alaska enrolled full time. Along with their application, they must submit a resume, 3 letters of recommendation, documentation of financial need, and a 1-page personal statement that covers their personal and educational history, accomplishments, educational and career goals, involvement in the Native community, and how this scholarship and degree program contribute to their career goals.
Financial data The stipend is $5,000 per year.
Duration 1 year; may be renewed if they maintain a minimum GPA of 2.0 for undergraduates or 3.0 for graduate students.
Number awarded 10 each year: 5 for undergraduate students and 5 for graduate students.
Deadline February of each year.

[548]
ALBERT W. DENT STUDENT SCHOLARSHIP
American College of Healthcare Executives
One North Franklin Street, Suite 1700
Chicago, IL 60606-3529
(312) 424-2800   Fax: (312) 424-0023
E-mail: geninfo@ache.org
Web: www.ache.org

Purpose To provide financial assistance to Native American and other minority graduate student members of the American College of Healthcare Executives (ACHE).
Eligibility This program is open to ACHE student associates entering their final year of didactic work in a health care management graduate program. Applicants must be minority students, enrolled full time, able to demonstrate financial need, and U.S. or Canadian citizens. Along with their application, they must submit an 800-word essay describing their leadership abilities and experiences, their community and volunteer involvement, their goals as a health care executive, and how this scholarship can help them achieve their career goals.
Financial data The stipend is $4,000.
Duration 1 year.
Additional information The program was established and named in honor of Dr. Albert W. Dent, the foundation's first Black fellow and president emeritus of Dillard University.
Number awarded Varies each year.
Deadline March of each year.

[549]
ALEUT FOUNDATION GRADUATE SCHOLARSHIPS
The Aleut Corporation
Attn: Aleut Foundation
703 West Tudor Road, Suite 102
Anchorage, AK 99503-6650
(907) 646-1929   Toll-free: (800) 232-4882
Fax: (907) 646-1949
E-mail: taf@thealeutfoundation.org
Web: www.thealeutfoundation.org

Purpose To provide financial assistance to Native Alaskans with ties to the Aleutian Islands who plan to attend graduate school in any state.
Eligibility This program is open to residents of Alaska who are 1) an original enrollee or descendant of an original enrollee of The Aleut Corporation (TAC); 2) a beneficiary or a descendant of a beneficiary of the Aleutian Pribilof Islands Restitution Trust; or 3) an original enrollee or descendant of an original enrollee of the Isanotski Corporation (IC). Applicants must have a GPA of 3.0 or higher. They must be enrolled for at least 6 credit hours in a graduate degree program. Along with their application, they must include a letter of intent, up to 500 words in length, that covers their educational goals and how they intend to use their education in the Aleut community.
Financial data The stipend is $3,000 per year.
Duration 1 year; may be renewed.
Additional information The foundation established this program in 2008.
Number awarded Varies each year.

Deadline June of each year for annual scholarships; November of each year for spring scholarships.

[550]
ALEUT FOUNDATION PART-TIME SCHOLARSHIPS
The Aleut Corporation
Attn: Aleut Foundation
703 West Tudor Road, Suite 102
Anchorage, AK 99503-6650
(907) 646-1929   Toll-free: (800) 232-4882
Fax: (907) 646-1949
E-mail: taf@thealeutfoundation.org
Web: www.thealeutfoundation.org

Purpose To provide financial assistance for college or graduate school to Native Alaskans with ties to the Aleutian Islands who are enrolled part time.

Eligibility This program is open to residents of Alaska who are 1) an original enrollee or descendant of an original enrollee of The Aleut Corporation (TAC); 2) a beneficiary or a descendant of a beneficiary of the Aleutian Pribilof Islands Restitution Trust; or 3) an original enrollee or descendant of an original enrollee of the Isanotski Corporation (IC). Applicants must be enrolled in an associate, bachelor's, or higher degree program as a part-time student (at least 3 credit hours). They must have a GPA of 2.0 or higher. Along with their application, they must include a letter of intent, up to 500 words in length, that covers their educational goals and how they intend to use their education in the Aleut community.

Financial data The stipend depends on the number of credit hours in the undergraduate or graduate program, to a maximum of $1,200 per year.

Duration 1 year.

Additional information The foundation began awarding scholarships in 1987.

Number awarded Varies each year; recently, 2 of these scholarships were awarded.

Deadline June of each year for annual scholarships; November of each year for spring scholarships.

[551]
ALFRED J. DURAN SR. TRUST SCHOLARSHIP
Northern Arapaho Tribe
Attn: Sky People Higher Education
P.O. Box 8480
Ethete, WY 82520
(307) 332-5286   Toll-free: (800) 815-6795
Fax: (307) 332-9104
E-mail: assistant@skypeopleed.org
Web: www.skypeopleed.org

Purpose To provide financial assistance to members of the Northern Arapaho Tribe who are working on an undergraduate or graduate degree in any field.

Eligibility This program is open to full-time undergraduate and graduate students who have an undergraduate GPA of 2.0 or higher or the graduate GPA required by their school. Applicants must be of one-fourth Northern Arapaho descent (enrolled or non-enrolled) and must submit a Certificate of Indian Blood or other verification of Northern Arapaho blood with at least one-fourth degree. They may be working on a degree in any field. Along with their application, they must submit a 1-page personal statement that includes a brief history of their background, academic ability and achievement, work or leadership experience, participation in community-related activities, and career goals. Selection is based on that statement, potential to contribute to the community upon graduation, academic ability and achievement, and a letter of recommendation.

Financial data The stipend is $1,000 per year.

Duration 1 year; may be renewed.

Additional information Recipients are expected to apply for employment with the Northern Arapaho Tribe after graduation.

Number awarded 2 each year.

Deadline June of each year.

[552]
ALLOGAN SLAGLE SCHOLARSHIP
California Indian Law Association
c/o Mina Quintos
UCLA School of Law
P.O. Box 951476
Los Angeles, CA 90095-1476
(310) 206-6967   Fax: (310) 825-6023
E-mail: quintos@law.ucla.edu
Web: www.calindianlaw.org

Purpose To provide financial assistance to American Indian and Native Alaskan law students.

Eligibility This program is open to full-time American Indian and Native Alaskan law students. Preference is given to applicants in the following order: 1) entering law students who are enrolled or otherwise accepted members of federally-recognized or nonrecognized California Indian nations; 2) entering law students who are enrolled members of federally-recognized Indian nations outside California but attending law school in California; 3) continuing law students who are enrolled or otherwise accepted members of federally-recognized or nonrecognized California Indian nations; 4) continuing law students who are enrolled members of federally-recognized Indian nations outside California but attending law school in California; and 5) entering or continuing law students of demonstrated Native ancestry who will be or are attending law school in California. Along with their application, they must submit an essay on their educational goals. Selection is based on academic achievement, financial need, and community involvement.

Financial data The stipend is $2,000.

Duration 1 year. Recipients may reapply.

Additional information This program, established in 2004, is managed by the California Community Foundation, 445 South Figueroa Street, Suite 3400, Los Angeles, CA 90071-1638, (213) 413-4130, Fax: (213) 383-2046.

Number awarded 1 or more each year.

Deadline October of each year.

FELLOWSHIPS

[553]
AMA FOUNDATION MINORITY SCHOLARS AWARDS

American Medical Association
Attn: AMA Foundation
515 North State Street
Chicago, IL 60610
(312) 464-4193   Fax: (312) 464-4142
E-mail: dina.lindenberg@ama-assn.org
Web: www.ama-assn.org

Purpose To provide financial assistance to Native American and other medical school students who are members of underrepresented minority groups.

Eligibility This program is open to first- and second-year medical students who are members of the following minority groups: African American/Black, American Indian, Native Hawaiian, Alaska Native, and Hispanic/Latino. Only nominations are accepted. Each medical school is invited to submit 2 nominees.

Financial data The stipend is $10,000.

Duration 1 year.

Additional information This program is offered by the AMA Foundation of the American Medical Association in collaboration with the Minority Affairs Consortium (MAC) and with support from the Pfizer Medical Humanities Initiative.

Number awarded 10 each year.

Deadline April of each year.

[554]
AMELIA KEMP MEMORIAL SCHOLARSHIP

Women of the Evangelical Lutheran Church in America
Attn: Scholarships
8765 West Higgins Road
Chicago, IL 60631-4101
(773) 380-2736   Toll-free: (800) 638-3522, ext. 2736
Fax: (773) 380-2419   E-mail: emily.hansen@elca.org
Web: www.elca.org

Purpose To provide financial assistance to lay women of color who are members of Evangelical Lutheran Church of America (ELCA) congregations and who wish to study on the undergraduate, graduate, professional, or vocational school level.

Eligibility This program is open to ELCA lay women of color who are at least 21 years of age and have experienced an interruption of at least 2 years in their education since high school. Applicants must have been admitted to an educational institution to prepare for a career in other than a church-certified profession. U.S. citizenship is required.

Financial data The maximum stipend is $1,000.

Duration Up to 2 years.

Number awarded Varies each year, depending upon the funds available.

Deadline February of each year.

[555]
AMERICAN INDIAN ARTS COUNCIL SCHOLARSHIP PROGRAM

American Indian Arts Council, Inc.
Attn: Scholarship Committee
725 Preston Forest Shopping Center, Suite B
Dallas, TX 75230
(214) 891-9640   Fax: (214) 891-0221
E-mail: aiac@flash.net

Purpose To provide financial assistance to American Indian undergraduates or graduate students planning a career in the arts or arts administration.

Eligibility This program is open to American Indian undergraduate and graduate students who are preparing for a career in fine arts, visual and performing arts, communication arts, creative writing, or arts administration or management. Applicants must be currently enrolled in and attending a fully-accredited college or university. They must provide official tribal documentation verifying American Indian heritage and have a GPA of 2.5 or higher. Applicants majoring in the visual or performing arts (including writing) must submit slides, photographs, videotapes, audio tapes, or other examples of their work. Letters of recommendation are required. Awards are based on either merit or merit and financial need. If the applicants wish to be considered for a need-based award, a letter from their financial aid office is required to verify financial need.

Financial data Stipends range from $250 to $1,000 per semester.

Duration 1 semester; may be renewed if the recipient maintains a GPA of 2.5 or higher.

Additional information This program was established in 1993.

Number awarded Varies each year.

Deadline September of each year for the fall semester; February of each year for the spring semester.

[556]
AMERICAN INDIAN CHAMBER OF COMMERCE OF CALIFORNIA SCHOLARSHIP

American Indian Chamber of Commerce of California
Attn: AICC Scholarship
555 West Fifth Street, 31st Floor
Los Angeles, CA 90017
E-mail: stateadmin@aicccal.org
Web: www.aicccal.org/scholarship.html

Purpose To provide financial assistance for college or graduate school to American Indians who live or attend school in California.

Eligibility This program is open to American Indians who 1) are on a federal- or state-recognized tribal roll and identified by a tribal enrollment card; or 2) have an official letter from a federal- or state-recognized tribe or agency verifying tribal membership or Indian blood. Applicants must be full-time degree candidates at an accredited institution of higher learning (junior college, trade/vocational school, 4-year university, graduate school) in California or residents of California attending an institution of higher learning elsewhere in the United States. Along with their application, they must submit an educational commitment essay describing their chosen field of study, educational goals, career goals, involvement in the Indian community, and how this scholar-

ship will help in furthering their education. Selection is based on transcripts (30 points), a letter of recommendation (20 points), the educational commitment essay (50 points), and major chosen (bonus 10 points if majoring in business).
Financial data Stipends are $2,500 or $1,500.
Duration 1 year.
Additional information This program, which began in 1999, includes the Darlene Dyer Stanhoff Memorial Scholarship.
Number awarded 6 each year: 1 at $2,500 and 5 at $1,500.
Deadline October of each year.

[557]
AMERICAN INDIAN CHAMBER OF COMMERCE OF WISCONSIN SCHOLARSHIPS
American Indian Chamber of Commerce of Wisconsin, Inc.
Attn: Scholarship Program
10809 West Lincoln Avenue, Suite 102
West Allis, WI 53227
(414) 604-2044   Toll-free: (877) 603-2044
Fax: (414) 604-2070   E-mail: marie@aiccw.org
Web: www.aiccw.org/scholarship.php

Purpose To provide financial assistance for college or graduate school to American Indian students from Wisconsin.
Eligibility This program is open to residents of Wisconsin who can provide proof of enrollment in an American Indian tribe by at least 1 parent. Applicants must be enrolled full time in a vocational/technical school, 2-year or 4-year college or university, tribal college, or graduate school. Preference is given to students majoring in business administration or a related field at a 4-year college or university. Along with their application, they must submit a 1-page statement explaining their educational goals and any obstacles they may have to overcome to achieve those goals.
Financial data The stipend is $1,000.
Duration 1 year.
Additional information The program also provides a $2,000 scholarship to a student majoring in business at the University of Wisconsin at Oshkosh.
Number awarded 1 or more each year.
Deadline April of each year.

[558]
AMERICAN INDIAN FELLOWSHIP IN BUSINESS SCHOLARSHIP
National Center for American Indian Enterprise Development
Attn: Scholarship Committee
953 East Juanita Avenue
Mesa, AZ 85204
(480) 545-1298, ext. 243
Toll-free: (800) 4-NCAIED, ext. 243
Fax: (480) 545-4208   E-mail: events@ncaied.org
Web: www.ncaied.org/scholarships.php

Purpose To provide financial assistance to American Indian upper-division and graduate students working on a business degree.
Eligibility This program is open to American Indians who are currently enrolled full time in college at the upper-division or graduate school level and working on a business degree. Applicants must submit a letter on their reasons for pursuing higher education and their plans following completion of their degree. Selection is based on grades (30%), an essay on their community involvement (30%), an essay on personal challenges they have faced (25%), an essay on their paid or volunteer business experience (10%), and the quality of those essays (5%).
Financial data A stipend is awarded (amount not specified).
Duration 1 year.
Number awarded Up to 5 each year.
Deadline July of each year.

[559]
AMERICAN INDIAN GRADUATE CENTER FELLOWSHIPS
American Indian Graduate Center
Attn: Executive Director
4520 Montgomery Boulevard, N.E., Suite 1-B
Albuquerque, NM 87109-1291
(505) 881-4584   Toll-free: (800) 628-1920
Fax: (505) 884-0427   E-mail: aigc@aigc.com
Web: www.aigc.com/scholarships.index.asp

Purpose To provide financial assistance to Native American students interested in attending graduate school.
Eligibility This program is open to enrolled members of U.S. federally-recognized American Indian tribes and Alaska Native groups and other students who can document one-fourth degree federally-recognized Indian blood. Applicants must be enrolled as full-time students in a graduate or professional school in the United States working on a master's, doctoral, or professional degree in any field. Along with their application, they must submit a 500-word essay on their vision and personal goals as an American Indian or Alaska Native citizen, including their achievements in leadership, community service, extracurricular activities, and giving back to their community. Financial need is also considered in the selection process.
Financial data Awards are based on each applicant's unmet financial need.
Duration 1 year; may be renewed up to 1 additional year for master's degree students; up to 2 additional years for M.F.A. students; up to 3 additional years for doctoral degree students; up to 3 additional years for medicine, osteopathic medicine, dentistry, chiropractic, and veterinary degree students; or up to 2 additional years for law degree students.
Additional information The application fee is $15. Since this a supplemental program, students must apply in a timely manner for federal financial aid and campus-based aid at the college they are attending to be considered for this program. Failure to apply will disqualify an applicant.
Number awarded Varies each year; recently, 34 of these fellowships were awarded.
Deadline May of each year.

FELLOWSHIPS

[560]
AMERICAN LIBRARY ASSOCIATION SPECTRUM INITIATIVE SCHOLARSHIPS

American Library Association
Attn: Office for Diversity
50 East Huron Street
Chicago, IL 60611-2795
(312) 280-5048   Toll-free: (800) 545-2433, ext. 5048
Fax: (312) 280-3256   TDD: (312) 944-7298
TDD: (888) 814-7692   E-mail: spectrum@ala.org
Web: www.ala.org

Purpose To provide financial assistance to Native American and other minority students interested in working on a degree in librarianship.

Eligibility This program is open to ethnic minority students (African American or Black, Asian, Native Hawaiian or Pacific Islander, Latino or Hispanic, and American Indian or Alaska Native). Applicants must be U.S. or Canadian citizens or permanent residents who have completed a third of the requirements for a master's degree at an accredited school of library science. Selection is based on academic leadership, outstanding service, commitment to a career in librarianship, statements indicating the nature of the applicant's library and other work experience, letters of reference, and personal presentation.

Financial data The stipend is $5,000.

Duration 1 year; nonrenewable.

Additional information This program began in 1998. It is administered by a joint committee of the American Library Association (ALA).

Number awarded Varies each year; recently, 69 of these scholarships were awarded.

Deadline February of each year.

[561]
AMERICAN PLANNING ASSOCIATION PLANNING FELLOWSHIPS

American Planning Association
Attn: Leadership Affairs Associate
122 South Michigan Avenue, Suite 1600
Chicago, IL 60603-6107
(312) 431-9100   Fax: (312) 431-9985
E-mail: fellowship@planning.org
Web: www.planning.org/institutions/scholarship.htm

Purpose To provide financial assistance to Native American and other underrepresented minority students enrolled in master's degree programs at recognized planning schools.

Eligibility This program is open to first- and second-year graduate students in urban and regional planning who are members of the following minority groups: African American, Hispanic American, or Native American. Applicants must be citizens of the United States and able to document financial need. They must intend to work as practicing planners in the public sector. Along with their application, they must submit a 2- to 5-page personal statement describing how their graduate education will be applied to career goals and why they chose planning as a career path. Selection is based (in order of importance) on 1) commitment to planning as reflected in the personal statement and resume; 2) academic achievement and/or improvement during the past 2 years; 3) letters of recommendation; 4) financial need; and 5) professional presentation.

Financial data Stipends range from $1,000 to $5,000 per year. The money may be applied to tuition and living expenses only. Payment is made to the recipient's university and divided by terms in the school year.

Duration 1 year; recipients may reapply.

Additional information The fellowship program started in 1970 as a Ford Foundation Minority Fellowship Program.

Number awarded Varies each year; recently, 6 of these fellowships were awarded.

Deadline April of each year.

[562]
AMERICAN SOCIETY OF CRIMINOLOGY FELLOWSHIPS FOR ETHNIC MINORITIES

American Society of Criminology
Attn: Awards Committee
1314 Kinnear Road, Suite 212
Columbus, OH 43212-1156
(614) 292-9207   Fax: (614) 292-6767
E-mail: asc@osu.edu
Web: www.asc41.com/minorfel.htm

Purpose To provide financial assistance to Native American and other ethnic minority doctoral students in criminology and criminal justice.

Eligibility This program is open to African American, Asian American, Latino, and Native American doctoral students planning to enter the field of criminology and criminal justice. Applicants must submit an up-to-date curriculum vitae; an indication of race or ethnicity; copies of undergraduate and graduate transcripts; a statement of need and prospects for other financial assistance; a letter describing career plans, salient experiences, and nature of interest in criminology and criminal justice; and 3 letters of reference.

Financial data The stipend is $6,000.

Duration 1 year.

Additional information This fellowship was first awarded in 1989.

Number awarded 3 each year.

Deadline February of each year.

[563]
AMERICAN SOCIOLOGICAL ASSOCIATION MINORITY FELLOWSHIP PROGRAM

American Sociological Association
Attn: Minority Affairs Program
1430 K Street, N.W., Suite 600
Washington, DC 20005-2504
(202) 383-9005, ext. 322   Fax: (202) 638-0882
TDD: (202) 638-0981
E-mail: minority.affairs@asanet.org
Web: www.asanet.org

Purpose To provide financial assistance to Native American and other minority doctoral students in sociology who are interested in specializing in mental health and substance abuse issues.

Eligibility This program is open to U.S. citizens or permanent residents who are Blacks/African Americans, Latinos (e.g., Mexican Americans, Puerto Ricans, Cubans), American Indians or Alaskan Natives, Asian Americans (e.g.,

southeast Asians, Japanese, Chinese, Koreans), or Pacific Islanders (e.g., Filipinos, Samoans, Hawaiians, Guamanians). Applicants must be beginning or continuing students in sociology at the doctoral level, with an emphasis on mental disorders, mental illness, and/or drug and alcohol abuse. Selection is based on commitment to research, focus of research experience, academic achievement, writing ability, research potential, and financial need.
Financial data The stipend is $20,772 per year.
Duration 1 year; renewable for 2 additional years.
Additional information This program, which began in 1974, is funded by grants from the National Institute of Mental Health and the National Institute on Drug Abuse, components of the U.S. National Institutes of Health (NIH).
Number awarded 10 to 12 each year.
Deadline January of each year.

[564]
AMERICAN SPEECH-LANGUAGE-HEARING FOUNDATION SCHOLARSHIP FOR MINORITY STUDENTS

American Speech-Language-Hearing Foundation
Attn: Graduate Student Scholarship Competition
10801 Rockville Pike
Rockville, MD 20852-3279
(301) 897-5700   Toll-free: (800) 498-2071
Fax: (301) 571-0457   TTY: (800) 498-2071
E-mail: foundation@asha.org
Web: www.ashfoundation.org

Purpose To provide financial assistance to Native American and other minority graduate students in communication sciences and disorders programs.
Eligibility This program is open to full-time graduate students who are enrolled in communication sciences and disorders programs, with preference given to U.S. citizens who are members of a racial or ethnic minority group. Selection is based on academic promise and outstanding academic achievement. Master's (but not doctoral) candidates must be enrolled in an ASHA Educational Standards Board (ESB) accredited program.
Financial data The stipend is $4,000. Funds must be used for educational support (e.g., tuition, books, school living expenses), not for personal or conference travel.
Duration 1 year.
Number awarded 1 each year.
Deadline June of each year.

[565]
AMY LOUISE HUNTER-WILSON, M.D. MEMORIAL SCHOLARSHIP

Wisconsin Medical Society
Attn: Executive Director, Wisconsin Medical Society Foundation
330 East Lakeside Street
P.O. Box 1109
Madison, WI 53701-1109
(608) 442-3722   Toll-free: (866) 442-3800, ext. 3722
Fax: (608) 442-3851   E-mail: eileenw@wismed.org
Web: www.wisconsinmedicalsociety.org/foundation

Purpose To provide financial assistance to American Indians (especially those from Wisconsin) interested in working on a degree in medicine, nursing, or allied health care.
Eligibility This program is open to members of federally-recognized American Indian tribes who are 1) full-time students enrolled in a health career program at an accredited institution, 2) adults returning to school in an allied health field, and 3) adults working in a non-professional health-related field returning for a professional license or degree. Applicants must be working on a degree or advanced training as a doctor of medicine, nurse, physician assistant, technician, or other health-related professional. Preference is given to residents of Wisconsin who are students at educational institutions in the state. U.S. citizenship is required. Selection is based on financial need, academic achievement, personal qualities and strengths, and letters of recommendation.
Financial data Stipends range from $1,000 to $4,000.
Duration 1 year.
Number awarded Varies each year. Recently 7 of these scholarships were awarded: 3 at $1,000, 2 at $1,500, 1 at $2,000, and 1 at $4,000.
Deadline January of each year.

[566]
ANA CLINICAL RESEARCH PRE-DOCTORAL FELLOWSHIP PROGRAM

American Nurses Association
Attn: SAMHSA Minority Fellowship Programs
8515 Georgia Avenue, Suite 400
Silver Spring, MD 20910-3492
(301) 628-5247   Toll-free: (800) 274-4ANA
Fax: (301) 628-5339   E-mail: janet.jackson@ana.org
Web: www.emfp.org

Purpose To provide financial assistance to Native American and other minority nurses who are doctoral candidates interested in psychiatric, mental health, and substance abuse issues that impact the lives of ethnic minority people.
Eligibility This program is open to nurses who have a master's degree and are members of an ethnic or racial minority group, including but not limited to Blacks or African Americans, Hispanics or Latinos, American Indians and Alaska Natives, Asian Americans, and Native Hawaiians and other Pacific Islanders. Applicants must be able to demonstrate a commitment to a research career in nursing and psychiatric/mental health issues affecting ethnic minority populations. They must be interested in a program of full-time doctoral study, with a research focus on such issues of concern to minority populations as child abuse, violence in intimate relationships, mental health disorders, substance abuse, mental health service utilization, and stigma as a barrier to mental health care and personal resilience. U.S. citizenship or permanent resident status and membership in the American Nurses Association are required. Selection is based on research potential, scholarship, writing ability, knowledge of broad issues in mental health nursing, and professional commitment to ethnic minority concerns.
Financial data The program provides an annual stipend of $20,772 and tuition assistance.
Duration 3 to 5 years.
Additional information Funds for this program are provided by the Substance Abuse and Mental Health Services Administration (SAMHSA).

Number awarded 1 or more each year.
Deadline February of each year.

[567]
ANAC STUDENT DIVERSITY MENTORSHIP SCHOLARSHIP

Association of Nurses in AIDS Care
3538 Ridgewood Road
Akron, OH 44333-3122
(330) 670-0101 Toll-free: (800) 260-6780
Fax: (330) 670-0109 E-mail: anac@anacnet.org
Web: www.anacnet.org

Purpose To provide financial assistance to student nurses from Native American and other minority groups who are interested in HIV/AIDS nursing and in attending the national conference of the Association of Nurses in AIDS Care (ANAC).

Eligibility This program is open to student nurses from a diverse racial or ethnic background, defined to include African Americans, Hispanics/Latinos, Asians/Pacific Islanders, and American Indians/Alaskan Natives. Candidates must have a genuine interest in HIV/AIDS nursing, be interested in attending the ANAC national conference, and desire to develop a mentorship relationship with a member of the ANAC Diversity Specialty Committee. They must be currently enrolled in an accredited nursing program at any level (e.g., L.P.N., A.D.N., diploma, B.S.N., or graduate nursing). Nominees may be recommended by themselves, nursing faculty members, or ANAC members, but their nomination must be supported by an ANAC member. Along with their nomination form, they must submit a 500-word personal statement describing their interest or experience in HIV/AIDS care and why they want to attend the ANAC conference.

Financial data Recipients are awarded a $1,000 scholarship (paid directly to the school), up to $599 in reimbursement of travel expenses to attend the ANAC annual conference, free conference registration, an award plaque, a free ticket to the awards ceremony at the conference, and a 1-year ANAC membership.

Duration 1 year.

Additional information The mentor will be assigned at the conference and will maintain contact during the period of study.

Number awarded 1 each year.

Deadline May of each year.

[568]
ANNIE WAUNEKA VISITING FACULTY FELLOWSHIP

Johns Hopkins University
Attn: Center for American Indian Health
621 North Washington Street
Baltimore, MD 21205
(410) 955-6931 Fax: (410) 955-2010
E-mail: pjames@jhsph.edu
Web: www.jhsph.edu

Purpose To provide American Indian faculty members with an opportunity to further their research skills while in residence at Johns Hopkins Bloomberg School of Public Health.

Eligibility This program is open to American Indian faculty in the health sciences. Applicants must be interested in participating in a program that involves 1) research, under the mentorship of a senior Hopkins faculty member who has expertise in the fellow's area of interest; 2) teaching, in the Center for American Indian Health summer and winter institute courses; and 3) mentorship, to American Indian scholarship recipients at the school.

Financial data Fellows receive annual compensation (amount not specified) and travel funds.

Duration 1 year.

Additional information By the end of the fellowship, recipients are expected to have written a National Institutes of Health (NIH) grant.

Number awarded 1 each year.

[569]
APICDA HIGHER EDUCATION SCHOLARSHIPS

Aleutian Pribilof Island Community Development Association
Attn: Human Resources Director
509 West Third Avenue, Suite 101
Anchorage, AK 99501
(907) 929-5273 Toll-free: (800) 927-4232
Fax: (907) 929-5275 E-mail: ldelgado@apicda.com
Web: www.apicda.com

Purpose To provide financial assistance to Alaska residents who have ties to member communities of the Aleutian Pribilof Island Community Development Association (APICDA) and are planning to attend college or graduate school in any state.

Eligibility This program is open to residents of Alaska who have an affiliation with APICDA either through an historical relationship (Natives and non-Natives who have an historical relationship with 1 or more of the following communities: Akutan, Atka, False Pass, Nelson Lagoon, Nikolski, St. George, and Unalaska) or a residency relationship (full-time residents of those communities for at least the past 5 years). Applicants must intend to return to (or work for the benefit of) the APIDCA region upon completion of school. They must be working on or planning to work on an associate, bachelor's, master's, or doctoral degree. Along with their application, they must submit a personal statement that includes their educational and professional development goals, why they wish to attend school, what they plan to do after receiving their degree, and the contributions they believe they will be able to make to the communities of the APICDA region or to Alaska in general after achieving their goals.

Financial data The stipend is $2,500 per semester. Funds may be used for registration, tuition, books, room, board, and other reasonable educational expenses.

Duration 1 year; may be renewed as long as the recipient maintains full-time enrollment and a GPA of 2.0 or higher.

Number awarded Varies each year; recently 87 of these scholarships were awarded.

Deadline June of each year for full-year scholarships; November of each year for winter or spring terms.

[570]
APSA MINORITY FELLOWS PROGRAM
American Political Science Association
Attn: APSA Minority Fellows Program
1527 New Hampshire Avenue, N.W.
Washington, DC 20036-1206
(202) 483-2512 Fax: (202) 483-2657
E-mail: apsa@apsanet.org
Web: www.apsanet.org/section_427.cfm

Purpose To provide financial assistance to Native American and other underrepresented minorities interested in working on a doctoral degree in political science.

Eligibility This program is open to African Americans, Asian Pacific Americans, Latino(a)s, and Native Americans who are in their senior year at a college or university or currently enrolled in a master's degree program. Applicants must be planning to enroll in a doctoral program in the following academic year for the first time. They must be U.S. citizens and able to demonstrate financial need. Selection is based on interest in teaching and potential for research in political science.

Financial data The stipend is $2,000 per year.

Duration 2 years.

Additional information In addition to the fellows who receive stipends from this program, fellows without stipend are recommended for admission and financial support to every doctoral political science program in the country. This program was established in 1969.

Number awarded Up to 12 fellows receive stipends each year.

Deadline October of each year.

[571]
ARAPAHO EDUCATIONAL TRUST SCHOLARSHIP
Northern Arapaho Tribe
Attn: Sky People Higher Education
P.O. Box 8480
Ethete, WY 82520
(307) 332-5286 Toll-free: (800) 815-6795
Fax: (307) 332-9104
E-mail: assistant@skypeopleed.org
Web: www.skypeopleed.org

Purpose To provide financial assistance to members of the Northern Arapaho Tribe who are working on an undergraduate or graduate degree in engineering, law, or the sciences.

Eligibility This program is open to full-time undergraduate and graduate students who have an undergraduate GPA of 2.0 or higher or the graduate GPA required by their school. Applicants must be of one-fourth Northern Arapaho descent (enrolled or non-enrolled) and must submit a Certificate of Indian Blood or other verification of Northern Arapaho blood with at least one-fourth degree. They must be working on a degree in engineering, law, or the sciences. Along with their application, they must submit a 1-page personal statement that includes a brief history of their background, academic ability and achievement, work or leadership experience, participation in community-related activities, and career goals. Selection is based on that statement, potential to contribute to the community upon graduation, academic ability and achievement, and a letter of recommendation.

Financial data The stipend is $1,500 per year.

Duration 1 year; may be renewed.

Additional information The recipient is expected to apply for employment with the Northern Arapaho Tribe after graduation.

Number awarded 1 each year.

Deadline June of each year.

[572]
ARAPAHO RANCH EDUCATIONAL TRUST SCHOLARSHIP
Northern Arapaho Tribe
Attn: Sky People Higher Education
P.O. Box 8480
Ethete, WY 82520
(307) 332-5286 Toll-free: (800) 815-6795
Fax: (307) 332-9104
E-mail: assistant@skypeopleed.org
Web: www.skypeopleed.org

Purpose To provide financial assistance to members of the Northern Arapaho Tribe who are working on an undergraduate or graduate degree in conservation-related fields.

Eligibility This program is open to full-time undergraduate and graduate students who have an undergraduate GPA of 2.0 or higher or the graduate GPA required by their school. Applicants must be of one-fourth Northern Arapaho descent (enrolled or non-enrolled) and must submit a Certificate of Indian Blood or other verification of Northern Arapaho blood with at least one-fourth degree. They must be working on a degree in range conservation, forestry, animal sciences, or ranch and range management. Along with their application, they must submit a 1-page personal statement that includes a brief history of their background, academic ability and achievement, work or leadership experience, participation in community-related activities, and career goals. Selection is based on that statement, potential to contribute to the community upon graduation, academic ability and achievement, and a letter of recommendation.

Financial data The stipend is $2,000 per year.

Duration 1 year; may be renewed.

Number awarded 1 each year.

Deadline June of each year.

[573]
ARCTIC EDUCATION FOUNDATION SCHOLARSHIPS
Arctic Education Foundation
P.O. Box 129
Barrow, AK 99723
(907) 852-8633 Toll-free: (800) 770-2772
Fax: (907) 852-2774 E-mail: swilliams@asrc.com
Web: www.arcticed.com

Purpose To provide financial assistance Inupiat Natives who have ties to the Arctic Slope region of Alaska and plan to attend a college or graduate school in any state.

Eligibility This program is open to U.S. citizens who are 1) a northern Alaskan Inupiat Native currently residing in the Arctic Slope region of Alaska; 2) an original shareholder of the Arctic Slope Regional Corporation (ASRC); or 3) a direct lineal descendant of an original ASRC shareholder. Applicants must be attending or planning to attend a college, uni-

versity, or vocational/technical school in any state as a full- or part-time undergraduate or graduate student. Along with their application, they must submit documentation of financial need and a short paragraph on their personal plans upon completion of study.
Financial data The stipend depends on the need of the recipient.
Duration 1 year; may be renewed.
Number awarded Varies each year.
Deadline February of each year for spring quarter or early summer; May of each year for summer school; July of each year for fall semester or quarter; or November of each year for spring semester or winter quarter.

[574]
ARENT FOX DIVERSITY SCHOLARSHIPS
Arent Fox LLP
Attn: Senior Attorney Recruitment Coordinator
1050 Connecticut Avenue, N.W.
Washington, DC 20036-5339
(202) 857-6224   Fax: (202) 857-6395
E-mail: salvaterra.jessica@arentfox.com
Web: www.arentfox.com

Purpose To provide financial assistance and work experience to Native American and other minority law students.
Eligibility This program is open to first-year law students who are members of a diverse population that historically has been underrepresented in the legal profession. Applicants must be U.S. citizens or otherwise authorized to work in the United States. They must also be willing to work as a summer intern at the sponsoring law firm's offices in New York City or Washington, D.C. Along with their application, they must submit a resume, an undergraduate transcript and law school grades when available, a 5- to 10-page legal writing sample, 3 letters of recommendation, and an essay on how their background, skills, experience, and interest equip them to meet the sponsor's goal of commitment to diversity. Selection is based on academic performance during college and law school, oral and writing communication skills, leadership qualities, and community involvement.
Financial data The scholarship stipend is $15,000. The summer salary is $2,500 per week.
Duration 1 year.
Additional information These scholarships were first offered in 2006. Recipients are also offered summer internships with Arent Fox: 1 in New York City and 1 in Washington, D.C. Students interested in the summer program in New York should contact Attorney Recruitment Manager, 1675 Broadway, New York, NY 10019, (212) 484-3913, Fax: (212) 484-3990, E-mail: visconti.lisa@arentfox.com.
Number awarded 2 each year.
Deadline January of each year.

[575]
ARL INITIATIVE TO RECRUIT A DIVERSE WORKFORCE
Association of Research Libraries
Attn: Director of Diversity Initiatives
21 Dupont Circle, N.W., Suite 800
Washington, DC 20036
(202) 296-2296   Fax: (202) 872-0884
E-mail: jerome@arl.org
Web: www.arl.org/diversity/init

Purpose To provide financial assistance to Native Americans and members of other minority racial and ethnic groups who are interested in preparing for a career as an academic or research librarian.
Eligibility This program is open to members of racial and ethnic minority groups that are underrepresented as professionals in academic and research libraries (American Indian or Alaska Native, Asian, Black or African American, Native Hawaiian or other Pacific Islander, or Hispanic or Latino). Applicants must be interested in working on an M.L.S. degree in an ALA-accredited program. Along with their application, they must submit a 350-word essay on what attracts them to a career in a research library. The essays are judged on clarity and content of form, clear goals and benefits, enthusiasm, potential growth perceived, and professional goals.
Financial data The stipend is $5,000 per year.
Duration 2 years.
Additional information This program began in 2000. Recipients must agree to work for at least 2 years in a library that is a member of the Association of Research Libraries (ARL) after completing their degree.
Number awarded The program's goal is to award up to 15 of these scholarships each year.
Deadline August of each year.

[576]
ARTHUR C. PARKER SCHOLARSHIPS
Society for American Archaeology
900 Second Street, N.E., Suite 12
Washington, DC 20002-3560
(202) 789-8200   Fax: (202) 789-0284
E-mail: headquarters@saa.org
Web: ecommerce.saa.org

Purpose To provide financial assistance to Native American students and professionals interested in additional training in archaeological methods.
Eligibility This program is open to high school seniors, college undergraduates, graduate students, and personnel of tribal or other Native cultural preservation programs. Applicants must be Native Americans or Pacific Islanders from the United States, including U.S. Trust Territories, or indigenous people from Canada. Documentation of Native identity is required, but applicants do not have to be enrolled in a Native group, of certified Indian status, or a member of a group formally recognized by the U.S. or Canadian government to be eligible. Applicants must be interested in attending a training program in archaeological methods offered by an accredited college or university, including field work, analytical techniques, and curation. Other types of archaeological methods training programs are considered on a case-by-case basis. Individuals may

apply themselves, or they may be nominated by a high school teacher, current professor, or cultural preservation program supervisor. Along with the application, they must submit 1) a letter of nomination or recommendation; 2) a personal statement describing why they are interested in attending the archaeological methods training program and how the training will benefit them as well as their Native community; 3) a brief description of the training program; 4) an itemized budget; and 5) documentation of Native identity.

Financial data The stipend is $4,000.

Additional information Half of 1 of these scholarships is funded by the Society for American Archaeology. The other half of that scholarship and all of the other scholarships, designated as NSF Scholarships for Archaeological Training for Native Americans and Native Hawaiians, are funded by the National Science Foundation (NSF).

Number awarded 4 each year.

Deadline December of each year.

[577]
ASA GRADUATE FELLOWSHIP FOR MINORITIES

Acoustical Society of America
Attn: Office Manager
2 Huntington Quadrangle, Suite 1NO1
Melville, NY 11747-4502
(516) 576-2360   Fax: (516) 576-2377
E-mail: asa@aip.org
Web: asa.aip.org/fellowships.html

Purpose To provide financial assistance to Native American and other underrepresented minorities who are working on a graduate degree involving acoustics.

Eligibility This program is open to U.S. and Canadian citizens and permanent residents who are members of a minority group that is underrepresented in the sciences (Hispanic, African American, or Native American). Applicants must be enrolled in or accepted to a graduate degree program as a full-time student. Their program of study may be in any field of pure and applied science and engineering directly related to acoustics, including acoustical oceanography, architectural acoustics, animal bioacoustics, biomedical ultrasound and bioresponse to vibration, engineering acoustics, musical acoustics, noise, physical acoustics, psychological acoustics, physiological acoustics, signal processing in acoustics, speech communication, structural acoustics and vibration, and underwater acoustics. Along with their application, they must submit a statement on why they are enrolled in their present academic program, including how they intend to use their graduate education to develop a career and how the study of acoustics is relevant to their career objectives.

Financial data The stipend is $20,000 per year. The sponsor strongly encourages the host educational institution to waive all tuition costs and assessed fees. Fellows also receive $1,000 for travel to attend a national meeting of the sponsor.

Duration 1 year; may be renewed for 1 additional year if the recipient is making normal progress toward a degree and is enrolled full time.

Additional information This program was established in 1992.

Number awarded 1 or more each year.

Deadline April of each year.

[578]
ASA MINORITY FELLOWSHIP PROGRAM GENERAL FELLOWSHIP

American Sociological Association
Attn: Minority Affairs Program
1430 K Street, N.W., Suite 600
Washington, DC 20005-2504
(202) 383-9005, ext. 322   Fax: (202) 638-0882
TDD: (202) 638-0981
E-mail: minority.affairs@asanet.org
Web: www.asanet.org

Purpose To provide financial assistance to doctoral students in sociology who are Native Americans or members of minority groups.

Eligibility This program is open to U.S. citizens or permanent residents who are Blacks/African Americans, Latinos (e.g., Mexican Americans, Puerto Ricans, Cubans), American Indians or Alaskan Natives, Asian Americans (e.g., southeast Asians, Japanese, Chinese, Koreans), or Pacific Islanders (e.g., Filipinos, Samoans, Hawaiians, Guamanians). Applicants must be beginning or continuing students in sociology at the doctoral level. Selection is based on commitment to research, focus of research experience, academic achievement, writing ability, research potential, and financial need.

Financial data The stipend is $15,000 per year.

Duration 1 year; renewable for 2 additional years.

Additional information This program, which began in 1974, is supported by individual members of the American Sociological Association (ASA) and by several affiliated organizations (Alpha Kappa Delta, the Midwest Sociological Society, Sociologists for Women in Society, the Association of Black Sociologists, and the Southwestern Sociological Association.

Number awarded 1 each year.

Deadline January of each year.

[579]
ASSE DIVERSITY COMMITTEE SCHOLARSHIP

American Society of Safety Engineers
Attn: ASSE Foundation
1800 East Oakton Street
Des Plaines, IL 60018
(847) 768-3435   Fax: (847) 768-3434
E-mail: agabanski@asse.org
Web: www.asse.org

Purpose To provide financial assistance to upper-division and graduate student members of the American Society of Safety Engineers (ASSE) who come from diverse groups.

Eligibility This program is open to ASSE student members who are majoring in occupational safety, health, and environment or a closely-related field (e.g., industrial or environmental engineering, environmental science, industrial hygiene, occupational health nursing). Undergraduates must be full-time students who have completed at least 60 semester hours with a GPA of 3.0 or higher. Graduate students must also be enrolled full time, have completed at least 9 semester hours with a GPA of 3.5 or higher, and have had a GPA of 3.0 or higher as an undergraduate. Along with their application, they must submit 2 essays of 300 words or less: 1) why they are seeking a degree in occupational safety and health or a closely-related field, a brief description of their current activities, and how those relate to their career goals and objectives; and 2) why they should be awarded this scholarship (including career goals and financial need). A goal of this program is to support individuals regardless of race, ethnicity, gender, religion, personal beliefs, age, sexual orientation, physical challenges, geographic location, university, or specific area of study. U.S. citizenship is not required.

Financial data The stipend is $1,000 per year.
Duration 1 year; recipients may reapply.
Number awarded 1 each year.
Deadline November of each year.

[580]
A.T. ANDERSON MEMORIAL SCHOLARSHIP PROGRAM

American Indian Science and Engineering Society
Attn: Scholarship Coordinator
2305 Renard, S.E., Suite 200
P.O. Box 9828
Albuquerque, NM 87119-9828
(505) 765-1052, ext. 106   Fax: (505) 765-5608
E-mail: shirley@aises.org
Web: www.aises.org

Purpose To provide financial assistance to members of the American Indian Science and Engineering Society who are majoring in designated fields as undergraduate or graduate students.

Eligibility This program is open to members of the society who can furnish a Certificate of Indian Blood or proof of enrollment in an American Indian tribe or Alaskan Native group. Applicants must be full-time students at the undergraduate or graduate level attending an accredited 4-year college or university or a 2-year college leading to an academic degree in engineering, mathematics, medicine, natural resources, physical science, the sciences, or technology. They must submit a 500-word essay on their educational and career goals, including their interest in and motivation to continue higher education, an understanding of the importance of college and completing their educational and/or career goals, and a commitment to learning and giving back to the community. Selection is based on the essay, academic achievement (GPA of 3.0 or higher), leadership potential, and commitment to helping other American Indians. Financial need is not considered.

Financial data The annual stipend is $1,000 for undergraduates or $2,000 for graduate students.
Duration 1 year; nonrenewable.
Additional information This program was launched in 1983 in memory of A.T. Anderson, a Mohawk and a chemical engineer who worked with Albert Einstein. Anderson was 1 of the society's founders and was the society's first executive director. The program includes the following named awards: the Al Qöyawayma Award for an applicant who is majoring in science or engineering and also has a strong interest in the arts, the Norbert S. Hill, Jr. Leadership Award, the Polingaysi Qöyawayma Award for an applicant who is working on a teaching degree in order to teach mathematics or science in a Native community or an advanced degree for personal improvement or teaching at the college level, and the Robert W. Brocksbank Scholarship.

Number awarded Varies; generally, 200 or more each year, depending upon the availability of funds from corporate and other sponsors.
Deadline June of each year.

[581]
AT&T LABORATORIES FELLOWSHIP PROGRAM

AT&T Laboratories
Attn: Fellowship Administrator
180 Park Avenue, Room C103
P.O. Box 971
Florham Park, NJ 07932-0971
(973) 360-8109   Fax: (973) 360-8881
E-mail: recruiting@research.att.com
Web: www.research.att.com/index.cfm?portal=20

Purpose To provide financial assistance and work experience to Native American and other underrepresented minority and women students who are working on a doctoral degree in computer and communications-related fields.

Eligibility This program is open to minorities underrepresented in the sciences (Blacks, Hispanics, and Native Americans) and to women. Applicants must be U.S. citizens or permanent residents who are graduating college seniors or graduate students enrolled in their first or second year. They must be working on or planning to work on a Ph.D. in a field of study relevant to the business of AT&T; currently, those include computer science, electrical engineering, industrial engineering, mathematics, operations research, systems engineering, statistics, and related fields. Along with their application, they must submit a personal statement on why they are enrolled in their present academic program and how they intend to use their technical training, official transcripts, 3 academic references, and GRE scores. Selection is based on potential for success in scientific research.

Financial data This program covers all educational expenses during the school year, including tuition, books, fees, and approved travel expenses; educational expenses for summer study or university research; a stipend for living expenses of $2,380 per month (paid for 10 months of the year); a $500 book allowance; and support for attending approved scientific conferences.

Duration 1 year; may be renewed for up to 2 additional years, as long as the fellow continues making satisfactory progress toward the Ph.D.

Additional information The AT&T Laboratories Fellowship Program (ALFP) provides a mentor who is a staff member at AT&T Labs as well as a summer research internship within AT&T Laboratories during the first summer. The ALFP replaces the Graduate Research Program for Women (GRPW) and the Cooperative Research Fellowship Program (CRFP) run by the former AT&T Bell Laboratories. If recipients accept other support, the tuition payment and stipend received from that fellowship will replace that provided by this program. The other provisions of this fellowship will remain in force and the stipend will be replaced by an annual grant of $2,000.

Number awarded Approximately 8 each year.
Deadline January of each year.

[582]
BAKER DONELSON DIVERSITY SCHOLARSHIPS
Baker, Donelson, Bearman, Caldwell & Berkowitz, P.C.
Attn: Director of Attorney Recruiting
420 20th Street North, Suite 1600
Birmingham, AL 35203
(205) 328-0480   Fax: (205) 322-8007
E-mail: rsimon@bakerdonelson.com
Web: www.bakerdonelson.com

Purpose To provide financial assistance to law students who are Native Americans or members of other groups underrepresented at large law firms.

Eligibility This program is open to students who have completed the first year at an ABA-accredited law school. Applicants must be members of a group traditionally underrepresented at large law firms (American Indian or Alaskan Native, Native Hawaiian or Pacific Islander, Hispanic or Latino, Black, or Asian). Along with their application, they must submit a 10-page legal writing sample and a 1-page personal statement on challenges they have faced in pursuit of their legal career that have helped them to understand the value of diversity and its inclusion in the legal profession. Finalists are interviewed.

Financial data The stipend is $10,000.

Duration 1 year.

Additional information Recipients are also offered summer internships at Baker Donelson offices in Atlanta (Georgia), Birmingham (Alabama), Chattanooga (Tennessee), Jackson (Mississippi), Johnson City (Tennessee), Knoxville (Tennessee), Memphis (Tennessee), Nashville (Tennessee), and New Orleans (Louisiana).

Number awarded 3 each year.

Deadline June of each year.

[583]
BAKER HUGHES SCHOLARSHIPS
Society of Women Engineers
Attn: Scholarship Selection Committee
230 East Ohio Street, Suite 400
Chicago, IL 60611-3265
(312) 596-5223   Toll-free: (877) SWE-INFO
Fax: (312) 644-8557
E-mail: scholarshipapplication@swe.org
Web: societyofwomenengineers.swe.org

Purpose To provide financial assistance to minority and other women working on an undergraduate or graduate degree in designated engineering specialties.

Eligibility This program is open to women who are sophomores, juniors, seniors, or graduate students at 4-year ABET-accredited colleges and universities. Applicants must be working on a degree in computer science or chemical, electrical, mechanical, or petroleum engineering and have a GPA of 3.0 or higher. Preference is given to members of groups underrepresented in engineering or computer science. Selection is based on merit.

Financial data The stipend is $5,000.

Duration 1 year.

Additional information This program is sponsored by Baker Hughes Incorporated.

Number awarded 3 each year.

Deadline May of each year.

[584]
BALFOUR PHI DELTA PHI MINORITY SCHOLARSHIP PROGRAM
Phi Delta Phi International Legal Fraternity
1426 21st Street, N.W., First Floor
Washington, DC 20036
(202) 223-6801   Toll-free: (800) 368-5606
Fax: (202) 223-6808   E-mail: info@phideltaphi.org
Web: www.phideltaphi.org

Purpose To provide financial assistance to Native Americans and other minorities who are members of Phi Delta Phi International Legal Fraternity.

Eligibility All ethnic minority members of the legal fraternity are eligible to apply for this scholarship. Selection is based on participation, ethics, and scholastics.

Financial data The stipend is $3,000.

Duration 1 year.

Additional information This scholarship was established in 1997. Funding for this scholarship comes from the Lloyd G. Balfour Foundation.

Number awarded 1 each year.

Deadline October of each year.

[585]
BERING STRAITS FOUNDATION HIGHER EDUCATION AND VOCATIONAL TRAINING SCHOLARSHIPS
Bering Straits Native Corporation
Attn: Bering Straits Foundation
110 Front Street, Suite 300
P.O. Box 1008
Nome, AK 99762-1008
(907) 443-4305   Toll-free: (800) 478-5079 (within AK)
Fax: (907) 443-2985
E-mail: foundation@beringstraits.com
Web: www.beringstraits.com

Purpose To provide supplemental financial assistance to Alaska Natives with ties to the Bering Straits area who are entering or enrolled in an undergraduate or graduate program in any state.

Eligibility This program is open to Native Alaskans enrolled to the Bering Straits Native Corporation and lineal descendants (natural or adopted children) of persons enrolled to the Bering Straits Native Corporation. Applicants for higher education scholarships must be graduating or have graduated from high school with a GPA of 3.0 or higher (or have earned a GED); applicants for vocational training scholarships must be high school seniors with a GPA of 2.5 or higher. All applicants must be accepted or currently enrolled (as an undergraduate or graduate student) at an accredited college, university, or vocational school in any state as a full-time student and be able to demonstrate financial need. Along with their application, they must submit a personal statement outlining their educational goals and objectives.

Financial data Stipends range from $500 to $1,000 per semester for students who have a GPA of 3.0 or higher, up to $400 per semester for students who have a GPA less than 3.0, or up to $500 per semester for vocational students. Funds are paid directly to the recipient's school.

Duration 1 semester; may be renewed if the recipient maintains a GPA of 2.0 or higher during the first semester and 2.5 or higher in succeeding semesters.
Number awarded Varies each year.
Deadline June of each year for the fall semester; December of each year for the spring semester.

[586]
BILL THUNDER, JR./ARAPAHO RANCH TRUST SCHOLARSHIP

Northern Arapaho Tribe
Attn: Sky People Higher Education
P.O. Box 8480
Ethete, WY 82520
(307) 332-5286　　　　Toll-free: (800) 815-6795
Fax: (307) 332-9104
E-mail: assistant@skypeopleed.org
Web: www.skypeopleed.org

Purpose To provide financial assistance to members of the Northern Arapaho Tribe who are working on an undergraduate or graduate degree in agriculture or a related field.
Eligibility This program is open to full-time undergraduate and graduate students who have an undergraduate GPA of 2.0 or higher or the graduate GPA required by their school. Applicants must be of one-fourth Northern Arapaho descent (enrolled or non-enrolled) and must submit a Certificate of Indian Blood or other verification of Northern Arapaho blood with at least one-fourth degree. They must be working on a degree in agriculture or a related field (agribusiness, veterinary studies, animal science, horticulture, resource economics, rangeland ecosystem science, or agronomy). Along with their application, they must submit a 1-page personal statement that includes a brief history of their background, academic ability and achievement, work or leadership experience, participation in community-related activities, and career goals. Selection is based on that statement, potential to contribute to the community upon graduation, academic ability and achievement, and a letter of recommendation.
Financial data The stipend is $2,500 per year.
Duration 1 year; may be renewed.
Additional information The recipient is expected to apply for employment with the Northern Arapaho Tribe after graduation.
Number awarded 1 each year.
Deadline June of each year.

[587]
BLOSSOM KALAMA EVANS MEMORIAL SCHOLARSHIPS

Hawai'i Community Foundation
Attn: Scholarship Department
1164 Bishop Street, Suite 800
Honolulu, HI 96813
(808) 566-5570　　　　Toll-free: (888) 731-3863
Fax: (808) 521-6286
E-mail: scholarships@hcf-hawaii.org
Web: www.hawaiicommunityfoundation.org

Purpose To provide financial assistance to residents of Hawaii of native ancestry who are interested in working on an undergraduate or graduate degree at a school in any state.
Eligibility This program is open to residents of Hawaii who are of Hawaiian ancestry and enrolled as full-time juniors, seniors, or graduate students at a college or university in any state. Applicants must be able to demonstrate financial need and academic achievement (GPA of 2.7 or higher). Along with their application, they must submit an essay indicating their reasons for attending college, their planned course of study, their career goals, and how they plan to use their knowledge to serve the needs of the Native Hawaiian community.
Financial data The amounts of the awards depend on the availability of funds and the need of the recipient; recently, stipends averaged $1,166.
Duration 1 year.
Number awarded Varies each year; recently, 9 of these scholarships were awarded.
Deadline February of each year.

[588]
BOIS FORTE HIGHER EDUCATION PROGRAM

Bois Forte Band of Chippewa
Attn: Department of Education and Training
5344 Lake Shore Drive
P.O. Box 16
Nett Lake, MN 55772
(218) 757-3261　　　　Toll-free: (800) 221-8129
Fax: (218) 757-3312
E-mail: bmason@educ.boisforte.gov
Web: www.boisforte.com/divisions/education.htm

Purpose To provide financial assistance for undergraduate or graduate study to enrolled members of the Bois Forte Band of Chippewa Indians.
Eligibility Eligible to apply for this assistance are enrolled members of the Bois Forte Band of Chippewa Indians. Applicants must have been accepted at an institution of higher education and had their financial need determined by that institution based on the Free Application for Federal Student Aid (FAFSA). Minnesota residents must apply to the Indian Scholarship Assistance Program of the Minnesota Indian Scholarship Program. Applicants wishing to attend school outside of Minnesota must complete an out-of-state application form. Applicants must also apply for financial assistance from all other available sources, including but not limited to public and private grants and scholarships. They must not be in default of any tribal, federal, or state student education loan or in noncompliance with child support payments. Applicants are interviewed. Financial assistance is awarded on a first-come, first-served basis.
Financial data The maximum amount awarded is $5,000 per year for undergraduates or $6,250 per year for graduate students.
Duration 1 year; may be renewed for a total of 10 semesters of full-time enrollment or part-time equivalent provided recipients maintain a GPA of 2.0 or higher.
Additional information Students may receive financial assistance for summer school.
Number awarded Varies each year.
Deadline Applications may be submitted any time after January 1 but should be received no later than 8 weeks prior to the first day of school.

[589]
BRUCE T. AND JACKIE MAHI ERICKSON SCHOLARSHIP

Ke Ali'i Pauahi Foundation
Attn: Financial Aid & Scholarship Services
567 South King Street, Suite 160
Honolulu, HI 96813
(808) 534-3966 Toll-free: (800) 842-4682, ext. 43966
Fax: (808) 534-3890 E-mail: scholarships@pauahi.org
Web: www.pauahi.org

Purpose To provide financial assistance to undergraduate or graduate students, especially Native Hawaiians, who are working on research or a degree related to Hawaiian arts and crafts.

Eligibility This program is open to students working full time on an undergraduate or graduate degree related to the creation of crafts, art, and photography and/or independent research relating to historical Hawaiian crafts and arts. Financial need is considered in the selection process. Residency in Hawaii is not required. Preference is given to Native Hawaiians (descendants of the aboriginal inhabitants of the Hawaiian Islands prior to 1778).

Financial data A stipend is awarded (amount not specified).

Duration 1 year.

Additional information This program was established in 2006.

Number awarded 1 or more each year.

Deadline April of each year.

[590]
BULLIVANT HOUSER BAILEY LAW STUDENT DIVERSITY SCHOLARSHIP PROGRAM

Bullivant Houser Bailey PC
Attn: Recruitment and Diversity Manager
888 S.W. Fifth Avenue, Suite 300
Portland, OR 97204-2089
(503) 228-6351 Toll-free: (800) 654-8972
Fax: (503) 295-0915
E-mail: jill.valentine@bullivant.com
Web: www.bullivant.com/shownews.asp?Show=4795

Purpose To provide financial assistance and work experience to law students who come from a minority or disadvantaged background.

Eligibility This program is open to first-year law students who are members of a minority group (including any group underrepresented in the legal profession) and/or students coming from a disadvantaged educational or economic background. Applicants must have 1) a record of academic achievement and leadership in college and law school; 2) a willingness to complete a 12-week summer associateship at a California office of the firm; and 3) a record of contributions to the community that promote diversity within society, the legal community, and/or law school.

Financial data The program provides a salaried associate position at an office of the firm during the summer following the first year of law school and a stipend of $7,500 for the second year.

Duration 1 year.

Number awarded 2 each year: 1 assigned to an associateship in the Sacramento office and 1 assigned to an associateship in the San Francisco office.

Deadline January of each year.

[591]
BUTLER RUBIN DIVERSITY SCHOLARSHIP

Butler Rubin Saltarelli & Boyd LLP
Attn: Director of Marketing
70 West Madison Street, Suite 1800
Chicago, IL 60602
(312) 444-9660 Fax: (312) 444-9287
E-mail: agordon@butlerrubin.com
Web: www.butlerrubin.com

Purpose To provide financial assistance and summer work experience to Native Americans and other diverse law students who are interested in the area of business litigation.

Eligibility This program is open to law students of racial and ethnic backgrounds that will contribute to diversity in the legal profession. Applicants must be interested in the private practice of law in the area of business litigation and in a summer associateship in that field with Butler Rubin Saltarelli & Boyd in Chicago. Selection is based on academic performance and achievement, intention to remain in the Chicago area following graduation, and interpersonal and communication skills.

Financial data The stipend is $10,000 per year; funds are to be used for tuition and other expenses associated with law school. For the summer associateship, a stipend is paid.

Duration 1 year; may be renewed.

Additional information This program was established in 2006.

Number awarded 1 each year.

[592]
CAA PROFESSIONAL DEVELOPMENT FELLOWSHIPS

College Art Association of America
Attn: Fellowship Program
275 Seventh Avenue, 18th Floor
New York, NY 10001-6798
(212) 691-1051, ext. 249 Fax: (212) 627-2381
E-mail: mpotter@collegeart.org
Web: www.collegeart.org/fellowships

Purpose To provide financial assistance to graduate students from socially and economically diverse backgrounds who are completing an advanced degree in art history or the visual arts.

Eligibility This program is open to candidates for an M.F.A. degree in the visual arts or a Ph.D. in art history. Applicants must have been underrepresented in the field because of their race, religion, gender, age, national origin, sexual orientation, disability, or financial status. They must be U.S. citizens or permanent residents who can demonstrate financial need and an expected completion of their degree in the year following application.

Financial data Fellows receive a 1-time award of $15,000. Honorable mentions receive $1,000.

Duration 1 year: the final year of the degree program.

Additional information This program began in 1993. Funding for the M.F.A. program in the visual arts is provided by the National Endowment for the Arts. Funding for the Ph.D. program in art history is provided by the National

FELLOWSHIPS

Endowment for the Humanities. Other sponsors include the Wyeth Foundation for American Art and the Geraldine R. Dodge Foundation.

Number awarded Varies each year. Recently, 5 fellowships and 2 honorable mentions were awarded.

Deadline September of each year.

[593]
CALISTA SCHOLARSHIP FUND

Calista Corporation
Attn: Calista Scholarship Fund
301 Calista Court, Suite A
Anchorage, AK 99518-3028
(907) 279-5516   Toll-free: (800) 277-5516
Fax: (907) 644-6376
E-mail: scholarships@calistacorp.com
Web: www.calistacorp.com/scholarship/default.asp

Purpose To provide financial assistance to Alaska Natives with ties to the Calista region who are interested in working on an undergraduate or graduate degree.

Eligibility This program is open to Alaska Native shareholders and lineal descendants of Alaska Native shareholders with ties to the Calista region. Applicants must be at least a high school graduate or have earned a GED and be in good academic standing with a GPA of 2.0 or higher. Along with their application, they must submit an essay (up to 500 words) on their educational and career goals. Financial need is considered in the selection process.

Financial data The amount awarded depends upon the recipient's GPA. Recipients with a GPA of 2.0 to 2.49 are awarded $500 per semester, recipients with a GPA of 2.5 to 2.99 are awarded $750 per semester, and recipients with a GPA of 3.0 or higher are awarded $1,000 per semester. The funds are paid in 2 equal installments; the second semester check is not issued until grades from the previous semester's work are received.

Duration 1 year; recipients may reapply.

Additional information This program was established in 1994.

Number awarded Varies each year; recently, 79 of these scholarships were awarded.

Deadline June of each year.

[594]
CAP LATHROP ENDOWMENT SCHOLARSHIP FUND

Cook Inlet Region, Inc.
Attn: The CIRI Foundation
3600 San Jeronimo Drive, Suite 256
Anchorage, AK 99508-2870
(907) 793-3575   Toll-free: (800) 764-3382
Fax: (907) 793-3585   E-mail: tcf@thecirifoundation.org
Web: www.thecirifoundation.org/designated.htm

Purpose To provide financial assistance for undergraduate or graduate studies in media-related fields to Alaska Natives and their lineal descendants.

Eligibility This program is open to Alaska Native enrollees under the Alaska Native Claims Settlement Act (ANCSA) of 1971 and their lineal descendants. Proof of eligibility must be submitted. Applicants may be enrollees of any of the 13 ANCSA regional corporations, but preference is given to original enrollees/descendants of Cook Inlet Region, Inc. (CIRI) who have a GPA of 3.0 or higher. There are no Alaska residency requirements or age limitations. Applicants must be accepted or enrolled full time in a 2-year undergraduate, 4-year undergraduate, or graduate degree program. They must be majoring in a media-related field (e.g., telecommunications, broadcast, business, engineering, journalism) and planning to work in the telecommunications or broadcast industry in Alaska after graduation. Along with their application, they must submit a 500-word statement on their educational and career goals and how they are contributing, or planning to contribute, to a positive Alaska Native community. Selection is based on that statement, academic achievement, rigor of course work or degree program, student financial contribution, financial need, grade level, previous work performance, community service, and relationship of degree program to career goals.

Financial data The stipend is $3,500 per year. Funds must be used for tuition, university fees, books, required class supplies, and campus housing and meal plans for students who must live away from their permanent home to attend college. Checks are sent directly to the recipient's school.

Duration 1 year (2 semesters).

Additional information This program was established in 1997. Recipients must attend school on a full-time basis and must plan to work in the broadcast or telecommunications industry in Alaska upon completion of their academic degree.

Number awarded 1 each year.

Deadline May of each year.

[595]
CAPE FOX SCHOLARSHIPS

Sealaska Corporation
Attn: Sealaska Heritage Institute
One Sealaska Plaza, Suite 301
Juneau, AK 99801-1249
(907) 463-4844   Toll-free: (888) 311-4992
Fax: (907) 586-9293
E-mail: scholarship@sealaska.com
Web: www.sealaskaheritage.org

Purpose To provide financial assistance for undergraduate or graduate study to Native Alaskans who have a connection to the Cape Fox Corporation.

Eligibility This program is open to lineal descendants of Alaska Natives enrolled to Cape Fox Corporation, whether or not the applicant owns Cape Fox Corporation stock. Applicants must be enrolled or accepted for enrollment as full-time undergraduate or graduate students. Along with their application, they must submit 2 essays: 1) their personal history and educational goals, and 2) their expected contributions to the Alaska Native or Native American community. Financial need is also considered in the selection process.

Financial data The amount of the award depends on the availability of funds, the number of qualified applicants, class standing, and cumulative GPA.

Duration 1 year; may be renewed up to 5 years for a bachelor's degree, up to 3 years for a master's degree, up to 2 years for a doctorate, or up to 3 years for vocational study. The maximum total support is limited to 9 years. Renewal depends on recipients' maintaining full-time enroll-

ment and a GPA of 2.5 or higher as an undergraduate or 3.0 or higher as a graduate student.
Number awarded Varies each year.
Deadline February of each year.

[596]
CAREER AWARDS FOR MEDICAL SCIENTISTS
Burroughs Wellcome Fund
21 T.W. Alexander Drive, Suite 100
P.O. Box 13901
Research Triangle Park, NC 27709-3901
(919) 991-5100   Fax: (919) 991-5160
E-mail: info@bwfund.org
Web: www.bwfund.org/programs/CAMS/index.html

Purpose To provide funding to minority and other biomedical scientists in the United States and Canada who require assistance to make the transition from postdoctoral training to faculty appointment.
Eligibility Applicants must have an M.D., D.D.S., D.V.M., or equivalent degree. They must be interested in a program of research training in the area of basic biomedical, disease-oriented, translational, or molecular, genetic, or pharmacological epidemiology research. Training must take place at a degree-granting institution in the United States or Canada. Each U.S. and Canadian institution may nominate up to 5 candidates; nomination of underrepresented minorities and women is especially encouraged. Following their postdoctoral training, awardees may accept a faculty position at a U.S. or Canadian institution.
Financial data For each year of postdoctoral support, the stipend is $65,000, the research allowance is $20,500, and the administrative fee is $9,500. For each year of faculty support, the stipend is $150,000, the research allowance is $3,000, and the administrative fee is $17,000. The maximum portion of the award that can be used during the postdoctoral period is $190,000 or $95,000 per year. The faculty portion of the award is $700,000 minus the portion used during the postdoctoral years.
Duration The awards provide up to 2 years of postdoctoral support and up to 3 years of support during the faculty appointment.
Additional information This program began in 1995 as Career Awards in the Biomedical Sciences (CABS). It was revised to its current format in 2006 as a result of the NIH K99/R00 Pathway to Independence program. As the CABS, the program provided more than $100 million in support to 241 U.S. and Canadian scientists. Awardees are required to devote at least 75% of their time to research-related activities.
Number awarded Varies each year: recently, 22 of these awards were granted.
Deadline September of each year.

[597]
CARL H. MARRS SCHOLARSHIP FUND
Cook Inlet Region, Inc.
Attn: The CIRI Foundation
3600 San Jeronimo Drive, Suite 256
Anchorage, AK 99508-2870
(907) 793-3575   Toll-free: (800) 764-3382
Fax: (907) 793-3585   E-mail: tcf@thecirifoundation.org
Web: www.thecirifoundation.org/designated.htm

Purpose To provide financial assistance for undergraduate or graduate studies in business-related fields to Alaska Natives who are original enrollees to Cook Inlet Region, Inc. (CIRI) and their lineal descendants.
Eligibility This program is open to Alaska Native enrollees to CIRI under the Alaska Native Claims Settlement Act (ANCSA) of 1971 and their lineal descendants. There are no Alaska residency requirements or age limitations. Applicants must be accepted or enrolled full time in a 4-year undergraduate or a graduate degree program in business administration, economics, finance, organizational management, accounting, or a similar field. They must have a GPA of 3.7 or higher. Along with their application, they must submit a 500-word statement on their educational and career goals and how they are contributing, or planning to contribute, to a positive Alaska Native community. Selection is based on that statement, academic achievement, rigor of course work or degree program, student financial contribution, financial need, grade level, previous work performance, community service, and relationship of degree program to career goals.
Financial data The stipend is $20,000 per year.
Duration 1 year; may be renewed.
Additional information This program was established in 2001.
Number awarded Varies each year; recently, 2 of these scholarships were awarded.
Deadline May of each year.

[598]
CGSM FELLOWSHIPS
Consortium for Graduate Study in Management
5585 Pershing Avenue, Suite 240
St. Louis, MO 63112-4621
(314) 877-5500   Toll-free: (888) 658-6814
Fax: (314) 877-5505   E-mail: recruiting@cgsm.org
Web: www.cgsm.org

Purpose To provide financial assistance and work experience to Native American and other underrepresented racial minorities interested in preparing for a management career in business.
Eligibility This program is open to African Americans, Hispanic Americans (Chicanos, Cubans, Dominicans, and Puerto Ricans), and Native Americans who have graduated from college and are interested in a career in business. Other U.S. citizens and permanent residents who can demonstrate a commitment to the sponsor's mission of enhancing diversity in business education are also eligible. An undergraduate degree in business or economics is not required. Applicants must be planning to work on an M.B.A. degree at 1 of the consortium's 13 schools. Preference is given to applicants under 31 years of age.

Financial data The fellowship pays full tuition and required fees. Summer internships with the consortium's cooperative sponsors, providing paid practical experience, are also offered.
Duration Up to 4 semesters.
Additional information This program was established in 1966. The participating schools are Carnegie Mellon University, Dartmouth College, Emory University, Indiana University, University of Michigan, New York University, University of North Carolina at Chapel Hill, University of Rochester, University of Southern California, University of Texas at Austin, University of Virginia, Washington University, University of Wisconsin at Madison, and Yale. Fellowships are tenable at member schools only. Application fees are $150 for students applying to 1 to 3 schools, $210 for 4 schools, $270 for 5 schools, or $330 for 6 schools.
Number awarded Varies; up to 400 each year.
Deadline March of each year.

[599]
CHEROKEE NATION GRADUATE SCHOOL SCHOLARSHIP PROGRAM
Cherokee Nation
Attn: Office of Higher Education
17675 South Muskogee Avenue
P.O. Box 948
Tahlequah, OK 74465
(918) 453-5465   Toll-free: (800) 256-0671 (within OK)
Fax: (918) 458-6195
E-mail: highereducation@cherokee.org
Web: www.cherokee.org

Purpose To provide financial assistance for graduate study in any state to college graduates who belong to the Cherokee Nation.
Eligibility This program is open to graduate students at universities in any state who are citizens of the Cherokee Nation. First preference is given to students previously funded by this program. Second preference is given to residents of the Cherokee Nation area, defined as those counties within and contiguous to the Cherokee Nation boundaries (funding is not available to students living outside that area). Third preference is determined by cumulative undergraduate GPA.
Financial data The stipend is $1,000 per semester for full-time (6 or more credit hours) or $500 per semester for part-time (less than 6 credit hours).
Duration 1 year; may be renewed, but the maximum any student can receive for graduate study is $6,000.
Additional information The Cherokee Nation area covers all or part of the following Oklahoma counties: Adair, Cherokee, Craig, Delaware, Mayes, McIntosh, Muskogee, Nowata, Ottawa, Rogers, Sequoyah, Tulsa, Wagoner, and Washington. Contiguous counties include Haskell, Le Flore, Osage, and Pittsburg counties in Oklahoma, Benton, Crawford, and Washington counties in Arkansas; Cherokee, Labette, and Montgomery counties in Kansas; and McDonald County in Missouri.
Number awarded Approximately 60 each year.
Deadline June of each year.

[600]
CHEYENNE AND ARAPAHO HIGHER EDUCATION GRANTS
Cheyenne and Arapaho Tribes of Oklahoma
Attn: Higher Education Program
P.O. Box 38
Concho, OK 73022
(405) 262-7652   Toll-free: (800) 247-4612
Fax: (405) 262-5419   E-mail: mbell@c-a-tribes.org
Web: www.c-a-tribes.org/higher-education

Purpose To provide financial assistance to enrolled Cheyenne-Arapaho tribal members who are interested in working on an undergraduate or graduate degree at a college in any state.
Eligibility This program is open to Cheyenne-Arapaho Indians who are at least a high school graduate (or the equivalent), approved for admission by a college or university, and in financial need. Applicants may be enrolled or planning to enroll in a postsecondary school in any state. The vast majority of students assisted under this program are at the undergraduate level, although graduate and/or married students are eligible for consideration and assistance. Summer and part-time students may apply as well, as long as application is made well in advance of enrollment and is accompanied by an official need evaluation.
Financial data The amount of the award depends on the need of the applicant.
Duration 1 year; renewable.
Number awarded 40 to 80 each year.
Deadline May of each year for fall semester; October for spring semester; or March for summer session.

[601]
CHICKASAW NATION GENERAL SCHOLARSHIPS
Chickasaw Nation
Attn: Department of Education Services
122 East Main
Ada, OK 74820
(580) 421-7711   Fax: (580) 436-3733
E-mail: education.services@chickasaw.net
Web: www.chickasaweducationservices.com

Purpose To provide financial assistance to members of the Chickasaw Nation who are working on an undergraduate or graduate degree at a school in any state.
Eligibility This program is open to members of the Chickasaw Nation who are working full or part time on an undergraduate, graduate, or doctoral degree at an accredited college or university in any state. Applicants must have a GPA of 3.0 or higher.
Financial data Stipends depend on the level of academic study, the number of units the recipients are taking, and their GPA. The range is from $150 per semester (for part-time freshmen and sophomores with a GPA of 3.0 to 3.49) to $550 per semester (for full-time graduate students with a GPA of 4.0).
Duration 1 semester; recipients may reapply.
Number awarded Varies each year.
Deadline January of each year for spring semester; June of each year for summer semester; August of each year for fall semester for continuing students; March of each year for high school seniors.

[602]
CHICKASAW NATION HIGHER EDUCATION GRANTS
Chickasaw Nation
Attn: Department of Education Services
122 East Main
Ada, OK 74820
(580) 421-7711   Fax: (580) 436-3733
E-mail: education.services@chickasaw.net
Web: www.chickasaweducationservices.com

Purpose To provide financial assistance to needy members of the Chickasaw Nation who are working on an undergraduate or graduate degree at a school in any state.

Eligibility This program is open to members of the Chickasaw Nation who are working full or part time on an undergraduate, graduate, or doctoral degree at an accredited college or university in any state. Applicants must have a GPA of 2.0 or higher. They may be attending a community college, regional college or university, or research university.

Financial data For full-time undergraduates, stipends are $1,200 per semester at community colleges, $1,500 per semester at regional colleges and universities, or $2,400 per semester at research universities. For full-time graduate students, stipends are $2,400 per semester. For full-time doctoral students, stipends are $3,000 per semester. For part-time undergraduates, stipends are $100 per credit hour at community colleges, $125 per credit hour at regional colleges and universities, or $200 per credit hour at research universities. For part-time graduate students, stipends are $200 per credit hour at regional colleges and universities or $250 per credit hour at research universities. For part-time doctoral students, stipends are $250 per credit hour.

Duration 1 semester; recipients may reapply.

Number awarded Varies each year.

Deadline January of each year for spring semester; June of each year for summer semester; August of each year for fall semester for continuing students; March of each year for high school seniors.

[603]
CHICKASAW NATION LIFE-TIME SCHOLARSHIPS
Chickasaw Nation
Attn: Department of Education Services
122 East Main
Ada, OK 74820
(580) 421-7711   Fax: (580) 436-3733
E-mail: education.services@chickasaw.net
Web: www.chickasaweducationservices.com

Purpose To provide financial assistance to members of the Chickasaw Nation who are working on an undergraduate or graduate degree at a school in any state.

Eligibility This program is open to members of the Chickasaw Nation who are working full time on an undergraduate, graduate, or doctoral degree at an accredited college or university in any state. Applicants must have a GPA of 3.0 or higher, a GED score of 2800 or higher, or (for homeschooled students) an ACT score of 20 or higher. Along with their application, they must submit a 2- to 3-page essay on their past accomplishments, future goals, tribal involvement, and community involvement. Finalists are interviewed.

Financial data A stipend is awarded (amount not specified). Funds may be used for tuition, fees, supplies, books, room, and board.

Duration 1 year; may be renewed provided the recipient maintains a GPA of 3.0 or higher.

Number awarded 5 each year.

Deadline June of each year.

[604]
CHIEF FREEMAN JOHNSON SCHOLARSHIP
Rochester City School District
Attn: Native American Resource Center
494 Averill Avenue, Portable 15
Rochester, NY 14607
(585) 262-8966   Fax: (585) 262-8937

Purpose To provide financial assistance for college or graduate school to Native Americans from New York.

Eligibility This program is open to Native American students of at least one-quarter blood who are residents of New York. Applicants must be attending vocational, undergraduate, or graduate school and have applied for all other sources of financial aid.

Financial data A stipend is awarded (amount not specified).

Duration 1 year; may be renewed if the recipient maintains of GPA of 2.0 or higher.

Number awarded 1 or more each year.

Deadline July of each year.

[605]
CHUGACH HERITAGE FOUNDATION SCHOLARSHIPS
Chugach Alaska Corporation
Attn: Chugach Heritage Foundation
560 East 34th Avenue, Fourth Floor
Anchorage, AK 99503
(907) 563-8866   Toll-free: (800) 858-2768
Fax: (907) 550-4147
E-mail: scholarships@chugach-ak.com
Web: www.chugachheritagefoundation.org

Purpose To provide financial assistance to undergraduate and graduate students who are original enrollees of the Chugach Alaska Corporation or their descendants and attending college in any state.

Eligibility This program is open to original enrollees and the descendants of original enrollees of the Chugach Alaska Corporation. Applicants must be enrolled or planning to enroll at an accredited college, university, or vocational program in any state as an undergraduate or graduate student. They must have a GPA of 2.0 or higher.

Financial data For full-time students, stipends are $2,400 per year for students working on an associate degree or 1- or 2-year certificate, $3,000 per year for juniors and seniors, or $6,000 per year for graduate students. Stipends for part-time students are pro-rated appropriately.

Duration 1 year; may be renewed if the recipient maintains a GPA of 2.0 or higher.

Additional information Recipients who achieve a GPA of 3.5 or higher receive a bonus of $600 per academic year.

Number awarded Varies each year.

Deadline Applications may be submitted at any time, but they must be received at least 30 days prior to the first day of class.

[606]
CHUGACHMIUT HIGHER EDUCATION GRANTS
Chugachmiut
Attn: Education and Training Coordinator
1840 Bragaw Street, Suite 110
Anchorage, AK 99508-3463
(907) 562-4155   Toll-free: (800) 478-4155 (within AK)
Fax: (907) 563-2891   E-mail: Info@chugachmiut.org
Web: www.chugachmiut.org

Purpose To provide financial assistance to Alaska Natives from the Chugach Region who are interested in attending college or graduate school in any state.
Eligibility This program is open to enrolled tribal members of the Chugach Region who are working, full or part time, on an undergraduate or graduate degree at a college or university in any state. Applicants must be able to demonstrate financial need. Along with their application, they must submit a statement with their personal and educational history, accomplishments, educational and career goals, and how the degree program they are planning to attend fits in with their educational and career goals.
Financial data A stipend is awarded (amount not specified).
Duration 1 year; may be renewed if the recipient maintains of GPA of 2.0 or higher.
Additional information Chugachmiut is a tribal consortium of 7 native communities in the Chugach region of Alaska.
Number awarded Varies each year.
Deadline May of each year.

[607]
CIRI FOUNDATION ACHIEVEMENT SCHOLARSHIPS
Cook Inlet Region, Inc.
Attn: The CIRI Foundation
3600 San Jeronimo Drive, Suite 256
Anchorage, AK 99508-2870
(907) 793-3575   Toll-free: (800) 764-3382
Fax: (907) 793-3585   E-mail: tcf@thecirifoundation.org
Web: www.thecirifoundation.org/scholarships.htm

Purpose To provide financial assistance for undergraduate or graduate studies to Alaska Natives who are original enrollees to Cook Inlet Region, Inc. (CIRI) and their lineal descendants.
Eligibility This program is open to Alaska Native enrollees to CIRI under the Alaska Native Claims Settlement Act (ANCSA) of 1971 and their lineal descendants. There are no Alaska residency requirements or age limitations. Applicants must be accepted or enrolled full time in a 4-year or graduate degree program. They must have a GPA of 3.0 or higher. Along with their application, they must submit a 500-word statement on their educational and career goals and how they are contributing, or planning to contribute, to a positive Alaska Native community. Selection is based on that statement, academic achievement, rigor of course work or degree program, student financial contribution, financial need, grade level, previous work performance, community service, and relationship of degree program to career goals.
Financial data The stipend is $8,000 per year.
Duration 1 year (2 semesters).
Number awarded Varies each year.
Deadline May of each year.

[608]
CIRI FOUNDATION EXCELLENCE SCHOLARSHIPS
Cook Inlet Region, Inc.
Attn: The CIRI Foundation
3600 San Jeronimo Drive, Suite 256
Anchorage, AK 99508-2870
(907) 793-3575   Toll-free: (800) 764-3382
Fax: (907) 793-3585   E-mail: tcf@thecirifoundation.org
Web: www.thecirifoundation.org/scholarships.htm

Purpose To provide financial assistance for undergraduate or graduate studies to Alaska Natives who are original enrollees to Cook Inlet Region, Inc. (CIRI) and their lineal descendants.
Eligibility This program is open to Alaska Native enrollees to CIRI under the Alaska Native Claims Settlement Act (ANCSA) of 1971 and their lineal descendants. There are no Alaska residency requirements or age limitations. Applicants must be accepted or enrolled full time in a 4-year undergraduate or a graduate degree program. They must have a GPA of 3.5 or higher. Along with their application, they must submit a 500-word statement on their educational and career goals and how they are contributing, or planning to contribute, to a positive Alaska Native community. Selection is based on that statement, academic achievement, rigor of course work or degree program, student financial contribution, financial need, grade level, previous work performance, community service, and relationship of degree program to career goals.
Financial data The stipend is $10,000 per year.
Duration 1 year (2 semesters).
Number awarded Varies each year; recently, 7 of these scholarships were awarded.
Deadline May of each year.

[609]
CIRI FOUNDATION GENERAL SEMESTER SCHOLARSHIPS
Cook Inlet Region, Inc.
Attn: The CIRI Foundation
3600 San Jeronimo Drive, Suite 256
Anchorage, AK 99508-2870
(907) 793-3575   Toll-free: (800) 764-3382
Fax: (907) 793-3585   E-mail: tcf@thecirifoundation.org
Web: www.thecirifoundation.org/scholarships.htm

Purpose To provide financial assistance for undergraduate or graduate studies to Alaska Natives who are original enrollees to Cook Inlet Region, Inc. (CIRI) and their lineal descendants.
Eligibility This program is open to Alaska Native enrollees to CIRI under the Alaska Native Claims Settlement Act (ANCSA) of 1971 and their lineal descendants. There are no Alaska residency requirements or age limitations. Applicants must be accepted or enrolled full time in a 2-year, 4-year, or graduate degree program. They must have a GPA

of 2.5 or higher. Along with their application, they must submit a 500-word statement on their educational and career goals and how they are contributing, or planning to contribute, to a positive Alaska Native community. Selection is based on that statement, academic achievement, rigor of course work or degree program, student financial contribution, financial need, grade level, previous work performance, community service, and relationship of degree program to career goals.

Financial data The stipend is $2,500 per semester.
Duration 1 semester; recipients may reapply.
Number awarded Varies each year; recently, 213 of these scholarships were awarded.
Deadline May or November of each year.

[610]
CIRI FOUNDATION SPECIAL EXCELLENCE SCHOLARSHIPS

Cook Inlet Region, Inc.
Attn: The CIRI Foundation
3600 San Jeronimo Drive, Suite 256
Anchorage, AK 99508-2870
(907) 793-3575   Toll-free: (800) 764-3382
Fax: (907) 793-3585   E-mail: tcf@thecirifoundation.org
Web: www.thecirifoundation.org/scholarships.htm

Purpose To provide financial assistance for undergraduate or graduate studies in selected fields to Alaska Natives who are original enrollees to Cook Inlet Region, Inc. (CIRI) and their lineal descendants.
Eligibility This program is open to Alaska Native enrollees to CIRI under the Alaska Native Claims Settlement Act (ANCSA) of 1971 and their lineal descendants. There are no Alaska residency requirements or age limitations. Applicants must be accepted or enrolled full time in a 4-year undergraduate or a graduate degree program. They must have a GPA of 3.7 or higher. Preference is given to students working on a degree in business, education, mathematics, sciences, health services, or engineering. Along with their application, they must submit a 500-word statement on their educational and career goals and how they are contributing, or planning to contribute, to a positive Alaska Native community. Selection is based on that statement, academic achievement, rigor of course work or degree program, student financial contribution, financial need, grade level, previous work performance, community service, and relationship of degree program to career goals.
Financial data The stipend is $20,000 per year.
Duration 1 year; may be renewed.
Additional information This program was established in 1997.
Number awarded 1 or more each year.
Deadline May of each year.

[611]
CLA SCHOLARSHIP FOR MINORITY STUDENTS IN MEMORY OF EDNA YELLAND

California Library Association
717 20th Street, Suite 200
Sacramento, CA 95814
(916) 447-8541   Fax: (916) 447-8394
E-mail: info@cla-net.org
Web: www.cla-net.org/awards/ednayelland.php

Purpose To provide financial assistance to students of Native American or other ethnic minority origin from any state who are interested in working on a degree in library or information science in California.
Eligibility This program is open to California residents who are members of ethnic minority groups (American Indian, African American/Black, Mexican American/Chicano, Latino/Hispanic, Asian American, Pacific Islander, or Filipino). Applicants must be enrolled or accepted for enrollment in a master's program at an accredited graduate library school in California. Evidence of financial need and U.S. citizenship or permanent resident status must be submitted. Finalists are interviewed.
Financial data The stipend is $2,500.
Duration 1 academic year.
Additional information This fellowship is named for the executive secretary of the California Library Association from 1947 to 1963 who worked to promote the goals of the California Library Association and the profession. Until 1985, it was named the Edna Yelland Memorial Scholarship.
Number awarded 3 each year.
Deadline May of each year.

[612]
COCOPAH GRADUATE FELLOWSHIPS

Cocopah Indian Tribe
Attn: Education Department
County 15th and Avenue G
Somerton, AZ 85350
(928) 627-2101   Fax: (928) 627-3173
E-mail: cocopah@cocopah.com
Web: www.cocopah.com/docs/education.html

Purpose To provide financial assistance to members of the Cocopah Indian Nation who are attending or planning to attend a university to work on an graduate degree.
Eligibility This program is open to enrolled members of the Cocopah Indian Nation who are working full time on a master's or doctoral degree at an accredited college or university in the United States. Applicants must be able to document financial need. Along with their application, they must submit an essay of 500 to 1,000 words discussing their academic and career goals and how those goals will contribute to the long-term goals of the Cocopah Indian Nation. Priority is given to students in the fields of law, health professions, education, business, sciences, professional services, or social work.
Financial data Grants are intended to cover tuition, books, room and board, transportation, personal costs, and any other expenses deemed necessary by the institution's financial aid department.
Duration 1 year; may be renewed, provided the recipient maintains a GPA of 3.0 or higher and full-time enrollment.
Number awarded Varies each year.

Deadline April of each year for fall semester; September of each year for spring semester.

[613]
COCOPAH SUMMER TUITION ASSISTANCE

Cocopah Indian Tribe
Attn: Education Department
County 15th and Avenue G
Somerton, AZ 85350
(928) 627-2101 Fax: (928) 627-3173
E-mail: cocopah@cocopah.com
Web: www.cocopah.com/docs/education.html

Purpose To provide financial assistance to members of the Cocopah Indian Nation who are interested in working during the summer on an undergraduate or graduate degree.

Eligibility This program is open to enrolled members of the Cocopah Indian Nation who are enrolled at or accepted by an accredited college or university in the United States. Undergraduates should have a GPA of 2.0 or higher; graduate students should have a GPA of 3.0 or higher. Applicants must be interested in attending school during the summer. They must be able to document financial need.

Financial data Maximum grants are $2,500 for graduate students or $1,000 for undergraduates. Funds may be used for payment of direct costs only (tuition, fees, and textbooks).

Duration 1 summer term.

Number awarded Varies each year.

Deadline March of each year.

[614]
CONFEDERATED SALISH AND KOOTENAI TRIBES HIGHER EDUCATION SCHOLARSHIPS

Confederated Salish and Kootenai Tribes
Attn: Tribal Education Department
P.O. Box 278
Pablo, MT 59855
(406) 675-2700, ext. 1072 Toll-free: (877) 575-0086
Fax: (406) 275-2814 E-mail: tribaled@cskt.org
Web: www.cskt.org/services/education.htm

Purpose To provide financial assistance to members of the Confederated Salish and Kootenai Tribes who are interested in attending college or graduate school in any state.

Eligibility This program is open to enrolled members of the Confederated Salish and Kootenai Tribes who are enrolled or accepted for enrollment at an accredited college, university or vocational/technical school. Applicants must be able to demonstrate financial need. Assistance is available to students in the following priority order: 1) continuing students in good standing; 2) new students who have never received tribal higher education funding; 3) returning students who have taken a break from school for 1 or more quarters or semesters; and 4) part-time students. A small fund is set aside for graduate students.

Financial data For students at public colleges and universities in Montana, stipends supplement other funding available to the student to pay for tuition and fees, room and board, books, and miscellaneous expenses related to school. For students at private or out-of-state colleges and universities, support is limited to the level at public in-state colleges. Assistance for part-time students is capped at $3,000 per year and support for graduate students is limited to $2,000 per year.

Duration 1 year; may be renewed, provided recipients maintain a GPA of 2.0 or higher and full-time enrollment.

Number awarded Varies each year. Recently, 258 of these scholarships were awarded, including 141 to students at Salish Kootenai College, 39 to students at the University of Montana, 7 to students at the Bozeman or Billings campuses of Montana State University, 71 to students at colleges and universities outside Montana, and 10 to graduate students.

Deadline April of each year.

[615]
CONFEDERATED TRIBES OF THE UMATILLA INDIAN RESERVATION HIGHER EDUCATION SCHOLARSHIPS

Confederated Tribes of the Umatilla Indian Reservation
Attn: Education and Training Department
73239 Confederated Way
P.O. Box 638
Pendleton, OR 97801
(541) 966-2248 Fax: (541) 276-6543
E-mail: LouFarrow@ctuir.com
Web: www.umatilla.nsn.us/ed.html

Purpose To provide financial assistance for college or graduate school to Indians affiliated with the Confederated Tribes of the Umatilla Indian Reservation (CTUIR).

Eligibility This program is open to tribal members enrolled or planning to enroll in a bachelor's degree program at an accredited college or university; support for a master's or doctoral degree is also available if funds are available. Applicants must submit a complete information sheet, a personal letter outlining education goals, 3 letters of recommendation, high school or college transcripts or GED test scores, a college acceptance letter, documentation of financial need, and their Certificate of Indian Blood.

Financial data A stipend is awarded (amount not specified).

Duration 1 year; may be renewed.

Additional information The CTUIR was established in 1949 when the Cayuse, Walla Walla, and Umatilla tribes entered into an agreement regarding their reservation in northeastern Oregon and southeastern Washington.

Number awarded Varies each year.

Deadline June of each year for fall quarter or semester; October of each year of winter quarter or semester; January of each year for spring quarter; April of each year for summer quarter.

[616]
CONSUELO W. GOSNELL MEMORIAL SCHOLARSHIPS

National Association of Social Workers
Attn: NASW Foundation
750 First Street, N.E., Suite 700
Washington, DC 20002-4241
(202) 408-8600, ext. 298   Fax: (202) 336-8313
E-mail: naswfoundation@naswdc.org
Web: www.naswfoundation.org/gosnell.asp

Purpose To provide financial assistance to Native American, Hispanic American, and other students interested in working on a master's degree in social work.

Eligibility This program is open to students who have applied to or been accepted into an accredited M.S.W. program. Applicants must have demonstrated a commitment to working with, or have a special affinity with, American Indian, Alaska Native, or Hispanic/Latino populations in the United States. They must be members of the National Association of Social Workers (NASW), have the potential for completing an M.S.W. program, and have a GPA of 3.0 or higher. Applicants who have demonstrated a commitment to working with public or voluntary nonprofit agencies or with local grassroots groups in the United States are also eligible. Financial need is considered in the selection process.

Financial data The stipends range from $1,000 to $4,000 per year.

Duration Up to 1 year; may be renewed for 1 additional year.

Number awarded Up to 10 each year.

Deadline March of each year.

[617]
COOK INLET TRIBAL COUNCIL TRIBAL HIGHER EDUCATION PROGRAM

Cook Inlet Tribal Council, Inc.
Attn: Tribal Scholarships and Grants Program
3600 San Jeronimo Drive, Suite 286
Anchorage, AK 99508
(907) 793-3578   Toll-free: (877) 985-5900
Fax: (907) 793-3589   E-mail: scholarships@citci.com
Web: www.citci.com//page/42

Purpose To provide financial assistance to Alaska Native shareholders of the Cook Inlet Region, Inc. (CIRI) and their descendants who are working on an undergraduate or graduate degree.

Eligibility This program is open to Alaska Native shareholders of CIRI and their descendants, regardless of residence, who are enrolled or planning to enroll full time at an accredited college, university, or vocational training facility. Applicants must be working on a certificate, associate, bachelor's, or graduate degree. Along with their application they must submit a letter of reference, a 200-word statement of purpose, their Certificate of Indian Blood (CIB), a letter of acceptance from the school, transcripts, their Student Aid Report, a budget forecast, and (for males) documentation of Selective Service registration. Awards are presented on a first-come, first-served basis as long as funds are available.

Financial data This program provides supplementary matching financial aid. Awards are intended to be applied to tuition, fees, course-required books and supplies, and on-campus housing and meal plans only. Total funding over a lifetime educational career is limited to $15,000.

Duration 1 year; may be renewed up to 4 additional years if the recipient maintains a GPA of 2.0 or higher.

Additional information Students whose CIB gives their village as Tyonek, Kenai, Ninilchik, Knik, or Salamatof must apply directly to their village organization.

Number awarded Varies each year, depending on the availability of funds.

Deadline June of each year for fall; November of each year for spring.

[618]
COPPER RIVER NATIVE ASSOCIATION HIGHER EDUCATION SCHOLARSHIP

Copper River Native Association
Mile 104 Old Richardson Highway
P.O. Box H
Copper Center, AK 99573
(907) 822-8801   Fax: (907) 822-5241
E-mail: pbxoperator@crnative.org
Web: www.crnative.org

Purpose To provide financial assistance for undergraduate or graduate studies to Alaska Natives who are enrolled in the Copper River Native Association.

Eligibility Eligible for this program are Alaska Natives who are enrolled to Ahtna Inc., are at least one-quarter blood quantum, and are lineal descendants (children, grandchildren, natural or adopted). Applicants must be enrolled or accepted as full-time students at an accredited college or university on the undergraduate (4-year program) or graduate school level. They should have at least a 2.0 GPA. Alaska residency is not required. Applicants are expected to apply for other financial aid programs. Selection is based on scholastic achievement (primary factor), previous work performance, education and community involvement, financial need, recommendations, years in school, seriousness of purpose, major field of study, practicality of education and professional goals, and completeness of the application.

Financial data The stipend is $2,000 per semester. Funds are to be used for tuition, university fees, books, and campus related/approved room and board. The money is sent directly to the recipient's school.

Duration 1 year; may be renewed if the recipient maintains a GPA of 2.0 or higher.

Additional information The association is also known as Atna'T'Aene Nene.

Number awarded Varies each year.

[619]
COQUILLE INDIAN TRIBE COMPUTER EQUIPMENT PROGRAM

Coquille Indian Tribe
Attn: Education Department
3050 Tremont
P.O. Box 783
North Bend, OR 97459
(541) 756-0904, ext. 243   Toll-free: (800) 622-5869
Fax: (541) 756-0847
E-mail: ebryson@coquilletribe.org
Web: www.coquilletribe.org

Purpose To provide funding for purchase of computer equipment to members of the Coquille Indian Tribe who are working full time on an undergraduate or graduate degree.

Eligibility This program is open to enrolled members of the Coquille Indian Tribe who have been enrolled for at least 2 semester as full-time undergraduate or graduate students at an accredited college or university in any state. Applicants must be seeking funding for the purchase of computer equipment. Undergraduates must have a GPA of 2.0 or higher and graduate students must have a GPA of 3.0 or higher.

Financial data The grant is $1,000; funds must be used for purchase of computer equipment or programming, and not for training, shipping, and/or maintenance of equipment.

Duration This is a 1-time grant.

Number awarded Varies each year.

[620]
COQUILLE INDIAN TRIBE HIGHER EDUCATION GRANTS

Coquille Indian Tribe
Attn: Education Department
3050 Tremont
P.O. Box 783
North Bend, OR 97459
(541) 756-0904, ext. 243   Toll-free: (800) 622-5869
Fax: (541) 756-0847
E-mail: ebryson@coquilletribe.org
Web: www.coquilletribe.org

Purpose To provide financial assistance to members of the Coquille Indian Tribe who are attending or planning to attend college or graduate school in any state.

Eligibility This program is open to enrolled members of the Coquille Indian Tribe who are entering or continuing full-time undergraduate or graduate students at an accredited college or university in any state. Along with their application, they must submit 1) a personal essay on their career goals, why they chose their educational field, their past and present involvement with the Native American community, their past and present involvement with their school and/or community, and how they plan to use their education to benefit the Coquille Indian Tribe; 2) a description of their involvement with a Native American or diversity group on their campus (entering students must submit this statement after completion of their first semester); and 3) documentation of financial need.

Financial data A stipend is awarded (amount not specified).

Duration 1 year; may be renewed, provided the recipient remains enrolled full time and maintains a GPA of 2.0 or higher as an undergraduate or 3.0 or higher as a graduate student.

Number awarded Varies each year.

[621]
COUNCIL OF ENERGY RESOURCE TRIBES SCHOLARSHIPS

Council of Energy Resource Tribes
Attn: Education Program Director
695 South Colorado Boulevard, Suite 10
Denver, CO 80246-8008
(303) 282-7576, ext. 12   Fax: (303) 282-7584
E-mail: info@CERTRedEarth.com
Web: www.certredearth.com/education.php

Purpose To provide financial assistance to American Indians who are interested in studying fields related to mathematics, business, science, engineering, or other technical fields on the undergraduate or graduate school level.

Eligibility This program is open to Indian high school seniors, college students, and graduate students who have participated in a qualifying program conducted by the Council of Energy Resource Tribes (CERT). Applicants must be enrolled or planning to enroll full time at an accredited 2- or 4-year tribal, public, or private college or university and major in business, engineering, science, mathematics, computer technology, or a related field. Along with their application, they must submit official tribal affiliation documents, university or college enrollment verification, and their most recent academic transcripts. Financial need is also considered in the selection process.

Financial data The stipend is $1,000 per year.

Duration 1 year; may be renewed up to 4 additional years, provided the recipient maintains a GPA of 2.5 or higher.

Additional information From 1981 through 2005, CERT operated the Tribal Research Institute in Business, Engineering & Science (TRIBES) program for high school seniors. From 1986 through 2006 it also operated the CERT Intern Program for college students. Effective in 2006, it replaced those programs with the CERT Scholars Program. High school seniors who are accepted as CERT Scholars are eligible to apply for these scholarships. Undergraduate and graduate students who participated in the earlier programs are also eligible to apply for these scholarships.

Deadline September of each year for fall semester; February of each year for spring semester.

[622]
COW CREEK BAND CONTINUING AND DISTANCE EDUCATION PROGRAM

Cow Creek Band of Umpqua Tribe of Indians
Attn: Education Director
2371 N.E. Stephens Street, Suite 100
Roseburg, OR 97470
(541) 677-5575   Toll-free: (800) 929-8229
Fax: (541) 677-5574
Web: www.cowcreek.com

Purpose To provide financial assistance to members of the Cow Creek Bank of Umpqua Tribe of Indians who plan to work on a certificate or an undergraduate or graduate

degree through a continuing or distance education program.
Eligibility This program is open to Cow Creek members, regardless of where they live, who are interested in obtaining a certificate, 2-year degree, 4-year degree, master's degree, or doctoral degree through a continuing or distance education program. Applicants must submit a statement of their educational goals and plans and relevant transcripts. They are not required to apply for other financial aid.
Financial data The program provides partial payment of tuition, fees, and books, to a maximum that is adjusted annually.
Duration 1 year; may be renewed until completion of a certificate or degree.
Additional information Recipients may enroll for 1 to 7 credits each academic term.
Number awarded Varies each year.
Deadline Applications may be submitted at any time, but they must be received at least 1 month before the program begins.

[623]
COW CREEK BAND HIGHER EDUCATION PROGRAM
Cow Creek Band of Umpqua Tribe of Indians
Attn: Education Director
2371 N.E. Stephens Street, Suite 100
Roseburg, OR 97470
(541) 677-5575   Toll-free: (800) 929-8229
Fax: (541) 677-5574
Web: www.cowcreek.com

Purpose To provide financial assistance to members of the Cow Creek Bank of Umpqua Tribe of Indians who plan to attend college in any state to work on an undergraduate or graduate degree.
Eligibility This program is open to Cow Creek members, regardless of where they live, who are interested in obtaining a 4-year undergraduate degree, master's degree, or doctoral degree program at a college or university in any state. Applicants must submit a statement of their educational goals and plans and documentation of financial need. They must apply for all other financial aid for which they might be eligible. Full-time enrollment is required.
Financial data Stipends are $5,000 per academic year for students at 2-year colleges, $7,000 per academic year for students at 4-year colleges and universities, or $10,000 per academic year for graduate students.
Duration 1 year; may be renewed up to 4 additional years.
Number awarded Varies each year.
Deadline July of each year for fall quarter or semester; November of each year for winter quarter or spring semester; February of each year for spring quarter; or May of each year for summer session.

[624]
CRANE AWARD
Miami Nation
Attn: Education Committee
202 South Eight Tribes Trail
P.O. Box 1326
Miami, OK 74355
(918) 542-1445   Fax: (918) 542-7260
E-mail: edu@miamination.com
Web: www.miamination.com

Purpose To provide financial assistance for graduate study to enrolled members of the Miami Tribe of Oklahoma.
Eligibility This program is open to enrolled members of the Miami Tribe of Oklahoma who are working on or planning to work on a master's or doctoral degree. Applicants must have a GPA of 3.0 or higher. Along with their application, they must submit a high school and/or college transcript, 3 letters of recommendation, documentation of financial need, and a 1-page essay with the title, "Tell Us About Yourself."
Financial data The stipend is $1,500.
Duration 1 year; nonrenewable.
Number awarded 1 or more each year.
Deadline April of each year.

[625]
CREEK NATION POST GRADUATE PROGRAM
Muscogee (Creek) Nation of Oklahoma
Attn: Higher Education Program
P.O. Box 580
Okmulgee, OK 74447
(918) 732-7689   Toll-free: (800) 482-1979, ext. 7690
E-mail: (918) 732-7694
E-mail: cdavis@muscogeenation-nsn.gov
Web: www.muscogeenation-nsn.gov

Purpose To provide financial assistance to enrolled citizens of the Muscogee (Creek) Nation interested in working on a graduate degree at a college or university in any state.
Eligibility This program is open to enrolled citizens of the Muscogee (Creek) Nation (with no minimum blood quantum required) who are enrolled or planning to enroll in an accredited college or university in any state to work on a master's, doctoral, or professional degree. Applicants must have a GPA of 3.0 or higher. They must submit copies of their Certificate of Indian Blood (CIB) and tribal enrollment card.
Financial data The maximum award is $2,000 per semester for full-time study or $1,000 per semester for part-time study.
Duration 1 year; may be renewed for up to 1 additional year (for master's degree students) or up to 2 additional years (for doctoral students).
Number awarded Varies each year.
Deadline June of each year for summer; October of each year for fall.

[626]
CUMMINS SCHOLARSHIPS
Society of Women Engineers
Attn: Scholarship Selection Committee
230 East Ohio Street, Suite 400
Chicago, IL 60611-3265
(312) 596-5223 Toll-free: (877) SWE-INFO
Fax: (312) 644-8557
E-mail: scholarshipapplication@swe.org
Web: societyofwomenengineers.swe.org

Purpose To provide financial assistance to minority and other women working on an undergraduate or graduate degree in designated engineering specialties.

Eligibility This program is open to women who are sophomores, juniors, seniors, or graduate students at 4-year ABET-accredited colleges and universities. Applicants must be working on a degree in computer science or automotive, chemical, computer, electrical, industrial, manufacturing, materials, or mechanical engineering and have a GPA of 3.5 or higher. Preference is given to members of groups underrepresented in engineering or computer science. Selection is based on merit.

Financial data The stipend is $1,000.

Duration 1 year.

Additional information This program is sponsored by Cummins, Inc.

Number awarded 2 each year.

Deadline May of each year.

[627]
DAN AND RACHEL MAHI EDUCATIONAL SCHOLARSHIP
Ke Ali'i Pauahi Foundation
Attn: Financial Aid & Scholarship Services
567 South King Street, Suite 160
Honolulu, HI 96813
(808) 534-3966 Toll-free: (800) 842-4682, ext. 43966
Fax: (808) 534-3890 E-mail: scholarships@pauahi.org
Web: www.pauahi.org

Purpose To provide financial assistance to undergraduate or graduate students, especially those of Hawaiian descent.

Eligibility This program is open to students working full time on an undergraduate or graduate degree who have a GPA of 2.0 or higher. Financial need is considered in the selection process. Residency in Hawaii is not required. Preference is given to Native Hawaiians (descendants of the aboriginal inhabitants of the Hawaiian Islands prior to 1778).

Financial data A stipend is awarded (amount not specified).

Duration 1 year.

Number awarded 1 each year.

Deadline April of each year.

[628]
DANIEL KAHIKINA AND MILLIE AKAKA SCHOLARSHIP
Ke Ali'i Pauahi Foundation
Attn: Financial Aid & Scholarship Services
567 South King Street, Suite 160
Honolulu, HI 96813
(808) 534-3966 Toll-free: (800) 842-4682, ext. 43966
Fax: (808) 534-3890 E-mail: scholarships@pauahi.org
Web: www.pauahi.org

Purpose To provide financial assistance to undergraduate or graduate students, especially those of Hawaiian descent.

Eligibility This program is open to students working full time on an undergraduate or graduate degree who have a GPA of 3.2 or higher. Financial need is considered in the selection process. Residency in Hawaii is not required. Preference is given to Native Hawaiians (descendants of the aboriginal inhabitants of the Hawaiian Islands prior to 1778).

Financial data A stipend is awarded (amount not specified).

Duration 1 year.

Additional information Recipients are strongly encouraged to provide at least 10 hours of community service to the Council for Native Hawaiian Advancement.

Number awarded 1 each year.

Deadline April of each year.

[629]
DANIEL KOVACH FOUNDATION MINORITY STUDENT SCHOLARSHIP
Daniel Kovach Scholarship Foundation
5506 Red Robin Road
Raleigh, NC 27613
(919) 630-4895 E-mail: danielkovach@gmail.com
Web: www.collegescholarships.org

Purpose To provide financial assistance to undergraduate and graduate students who are members of minority groups.

Eligibility This program is open to full-time undergraduate and graduate students who are Black, Hispanic, Native American, or Pacific Islander. Applicants must have a GPA of 3.0 or higher. Along with their application, they must submit a 300-word essay on how being a minority affected their pre-college education, how being a minority has positively affected their character, and where they see themselves in 10 years. U.S. citizenship is required.

Financial data The stipend is $1,000.

Duration 1 year.

Additional information This scholarship was first awarded in 2006.

Number awarded 1 each year.

Deadline November of each year.

[630]
DAVID SANKEY MINORITY SCHOLARSHIP IN METEOROLOGY

National Weather Association
Attn: Executive Director
228 West Millbrook Road
Raleigh, NC 27609-4304
(919) 845-1546   Fax: (919) 845-1546
E-mail: exdir@nwas.org
Web: www.nwas.org/dsscholarship.html

Purpose To provide financial assistance to Native Americans and other minorities working on an undergraduate or graduate degree in meteorology.

Eligibility This program is open to members of minority ethnic groups who are either entering their sophomore or higher year of undergraduate study or enrolled as graduate students. Applicants must be working on a degree in meteorology. Along with their application, they must submit a 1-page letter describing their interest and involvement in meteorology. Selection is based on that letter, college transcripts, and 2 letters of recommendation.

Financial data The stipend is $1,000.

Duration 1 year.

Additional information This program was established in 2002.

Number awarded 1 each year.

Deadline April of each year.

[631]
DAVIS WRIGHT TREMAINE 1L DIVERSITY SCHOLARSHIP PROGRAM

Davis Wright Tremaine LLP
Attn: Diversity Scholarship Program
1201 Third Avenue, Suite 2200
Seattle, WA 98101-3045
(206) 622-3150   Toll-free: (877) 398-8416
Fax: (206) 757-7700   E-mail: carolyuly@dwt.com
Web: www.dwt.com/recruit/intro/scholarship.htm

Purpose To provide financial assistance and summer work experience to Native Americans and other law students of color.

Eligibility This program is open to first-year law students of color and others of diverse background. Applicants must have a record of academic achievement as an undergraduate and in the first year of law school that demonstrates promise for a successful career in law, a commitment to civic involvement that promotes diversity and will continue after entering the legal profession, and a willingness to become an associate in the sponsor's Seattle or Portland office during the summer between their first and second year of law school. They must submit a current resume, a complete undergraduate transcript, grades from the first semester of law school, a short personal essay indicating their interest in the scholarship, a legal writing sample, and 2 or 3 references. Although demonstrated need may be taken into account, applicants need not disclose their financial circumstances.

Financial data The award consists of a $7,500 stipend for second-year tuition and expenses and a paid summer clerkship.

Duration 1 academic year and summer.

Number awarded 3 each year: 2 in the Seattle office and 1 in the Portland office.

Deadline January of each year.

[632]
DENNIS WONG AND ASSOCIATES SCHOLARSHIP

Ke Ali'i Pauahi Foundation
Attn: Financial Aid & Scholarship Services
567 South King Street, Suite 160
Honolulu, HI 96813
(808) 534-3966   Toll-free: (800) 842-4682, ext. 43966
Fax: (808) 534-3890   E-mail: scholarships@pauahi.org
Web: www.pauahi.org

Purpose To provide financial assistance to undergraduate or graduate students in liberal arts or science, especially those of Hawaiian descent.

Eligibility This program is open to students working full time on an undergraduate degree in liberal arts or science or a graduate degree in a professional field. Applicants must have a well-rounded and balanced record of achievement in preparation for career objectives. Financial need is considered in the selection process. Residency in Hawaii is not required. Preference is given to Native Hawaiians (descendants of the aboriginal inhabitants of the Hawaiian Islands prior to 1778).

Financial data A stipend is awarded (amount not specified).

Duration 1 year.

Number awarded 2 each year.

Deadline April of each year.

[633]
DINSMORE & SHOHL LLP DIVERSITY SCHOLARSHIP PROGRAM

Dinsmore & Shohl LLP
Attn: Manager of Legal Recruiting
255 East Fifth Street, Suite 1900
Cincinnati, OH 45202
(513) 977-8488
E-mail: dinsmore.legalrecruiting@dinslaw.com
Web: www.dinslaw.com/careers/diversityscholarship

Purpose To provide financial assistance and summer work experience to Native American and other underrepresented minority law students.

Eligibility This program is open to first- and second-year law students who are members of groups traditionally underrepresented in the legal profession. Applicants must have a demonstrated record of academic or professional achievement and leadership qualities. They must also be interested in a summer associateship with Dinsmore & Shohl LLP.

Financial data The program provides an academic scholarship of $10,000 and a paid associateship at the firm.

Duration The academic scholarship is for 1 year. The summer associateship is for 12 weeks.

Additional information Associateships are available at firm offices in Charleston (West Virginia), Cincinnati (Ohio), Columbus (Ohio), Dayton (Ohio), Lexington (Kentucky), Louisville (Kentucky), Morgantown (West Virginia), Pittsburgh (Pennsylvania), and Wheeling (West Virginia). The program includes 1 associateship in which the student spends 6

weeks as a clerk in the legal department of the Procter & Gamble Company's worldwide headquarters in Cincinnati and 6 weeks at Dinsmore & Shohl's Cincinnati office. All associates are assigned to an attorney with the firm who serves as a mentor.
Number awarded Varies each year.
Deadline August of each year for second-year students; December of each year for first-year students.

[634]
DIVERSITY FELLOWSHIPS IN ENVIRONMENTAL REPORTING
University of Rhode Island
Graduate School of Oceanography
Attn: Metcalf Institute for Marine and Environmental Reporting
Narragansett, RI 02882
(401) 874-6211   Fax: (401) 874-6486
E-mail: sunshine@gso.uri.edu
Web: www.metcalfinstitute.org

Purpose To provide an opportunity for Native American and other minority journalists to gain experience in writing about the environment.
Eligibility This program is open to minority journalists who have less than 1 year of experience. Applicants must be interested in improving their environmental and science reporting skills through a program of independent study at the University of Rhode Island and mentored work at a media outlet.
Financial data The stipend is $28,000. Limited travel support is also provided.
Duration 10 months, including 4 weeks of independent study at the University of Rhode Island's Graduate School of Oceanography and 38 weeks of reporting on science and the environment with reporter and editor mentors at a radio, television, or print outlet of their choice.
Additional information This program, which began in 2006, is supported by the Geosciences Directorate of the National Science Foundation.
Number awarded 6 each year.
Deadline April of each year.

[635]
DIVERSITY PROGRAM IN NEUROSCIENCE PREDOCTORAL FELLOWSHIPS
American Psychological Association
Attn: Minority Fellowship Program
750 First Street, N.E.
Washington, DC 20002-4242
(202) 336-6127   Fax: (202) 336-6012
TDD: (202) 336-6123   E-mail: mfp@apa.org
Web: www.apa.org/mfp/prprogram.html

Purpose To provide financial assistance to graduate students who are interested in completing a doctorate in neuroscience, especially those whose participation will increase diversity in the field.
Eligibility This program is open to all U.S. citizens and permanent residents who are working full time on a Ph.D. degree. Applicants must have career goals that are consistent with those of this program: 1) to increase ethnic and racial diversity among neuroscience researchers; 2) to increase the number of neuroscience researchers with disabilities; 3) to increased the number of neuroscience researchers from disadvantaged backgrounds; and 4) to increase numbers of neuroscientists whose work is related to the federal initiative to eliminate health disparities. They may receive their training in a range of academic departments, provided their primary activity and career aspirations are research-oriented. Students identified as underrepresented in the neurosciences are especially encouraged to apply. Students working on a doctoral degree with a primarily clinical focus (e.g., M.D. or Psy.D) are not eligible. Selection is based on commitment to a research career in neuroscience, potential demonstrated through accomplishments and goals, fit between career goals and training environment selected, scholarship and grades, and letters of recommendation.
Financial data The stipend varies but is based on the amount established by the National Institutes of Health for predoctoral students; recently, that was $20,772 per year. The fellowship also provides travel funds to attend the annual meeting of the Society for Neuroscience and a program of summer training at the Marine Biological Laboratory in Woods Hole, Massachusetts.
Duration 1 year; may be renewed for up to 2 additional years.
Additional information The program was established in 1987. It is funded by 3 components of the U.S. National Institutes of Health: the National Institute of Mental Health (NIMH), the National Institute on Drug Abuse (NIDA), and the National Institute of Neurological Disorders and Stroke (NINDS).
Number awarded Varies each year.
Deadline January of each year.

[636]
DONALD W. BANNER DIVERSITY SCHOLARSHIP
Banner & Witcoff, Ltd.
Attn: Christopher Hummel
1100 13th Street, N.W., Suite 1200
Washington, DC 20005-4051
(202) 824-3000   Fax: (202) 824-3001
E-mail: chummel@bannerwitcoff.com
Web: www.bannerwitcoff.com/diversity.cfm

Purpose To provide financial assistance and work experience to law students who come from Native American and other groups historically underrepresented in intellectual property law.
Eligibility This program is open to students enrolled in the first or second year of a J.D. program at an ABA-accredited law school in the United States. Applicants must come from a group historically underrepresented in intellectual property law; that underrepresentation may be the result of race, sex, ethnicity, sexual orientation, or disability. Selection is based on academic merit, commitment to the pursuit of a career in intellectual property law, written communication skills, oral communication skills (determined through an interview), leadership qualities, and community involvement.
Financial data The stipend is $5,000 per year.
Duration 1 year (the second or third year of law school); students who accept and successfully complete the firm's

summer associate program may receive an additional $5,000 for a subsequent semester of law school.
Number awarded 1 or more each year.
Deadline September of each year.

[637]
DORA AMES LEE LEADERSHIP DEVELOPMENT FUND
United Methodist Church
General Board of Global Ministries
Attn: Health and Welfare Program
475 Riverside Drive, Room 330
New York, NY 10115
(212) 870-3871   Toll-free: (800) UMC-GBGM
E-mail: jyoung@gbgm-umc.org
Web: hbs.gbgm-umc.org

Purpose To provide financial assistance to Methodists and other Christians of Asian or Native American descent who are preparing for a career in a health-related field.
Eligibility This program is open to U.S. citizens who are of Asian American, Pacific Islander, or Native American descent. Applicants must be professed Christians, preferably United Methodists. They must be attending a college or university to enter or continue in a health-related field. Financial need is considered in the selection process.
Financial data The stipend is $2,000.
Duration 1 year.
Additional information This program was established in 1980.
Number awarded 6 each year.
Deadline June of each year.

[638]
DOYON FOUNDATION BASIC SCHOLARSHIPS
Doyon, Limited
Attn: Doyon Foundation
1 Doyon Place, Suite 300
Fairbanks, AK 99701-2941
(907) 459-2050   Toll-free: (888) 478-4755, ext. 2050
Fax: (907) 459-2065   E-mail: foundation@doyon.com
Web: www.doyonfoundation.com

Purpose To provide financial assistance to undergraduate and graduate students enrolled or descended from enrolled members of Doyon, Limited.
Eligibility This program is open to undergraduate or graduate students who are enrolled or the descendants of enrolled members of Doyon, Limited. Applicants must be accepted or enrolled at an accredited college, university, technical institute, or vocational school. Both part-time and full-time students are eligible, but full-time students must be accepted into a degree program.
Financial data Stipends are $800 per semester for full-time students or $400 per semester for part-time students.
Duration 1 year. Undergraduate students may reapply if they maintain a GPA of 2.0 or higher; graduate or master's degree students may reapply if they maintain a GPA of 3.0 or higher; and specialist or doctoral students may reapply if they maintain a GPA of 3.25 or higher.
Number awarded Varies each year; recently, scholarships were awarded to 228 full-time students and 40 part-time students.
Deadline March of each year for summer school, April of each year for fall semester, September of each year for winter term (vocational students only), November of each year for spring semester.

[639]
DOYON FOUNDATION COMPETITIVE SCHOLARSHIPS
Doyon, Limited
Attn: Doyon Foundation
1 Doyon Place, Suite 300
Fairbanks, AK 99701-2941
(907) 459-2050   Toll-free: (888) 478-4755, ext. 2050
Fax: (907) 459-2065   E-mail: foundation@doyon.com
Web: www.doyonfoundation.com

Purpose To provide financial assistance to undergraduate and graduate students enrolled or descended from enrolled members of Doyon, Limited.
Eligibility This program is open to undergraduate or graduate students who are enrolled or the descendants of enrolled members of Doyon, Limited. Applicants must be accepted or enrolled at an accredited college, university, or vocational/technical school in a program that lasts at least 6 weeks. Along with their application, they must submit a personal essay on their educational goals, professional goals, extracurricular and community service activities or volunteerism, and cultural awareness and contributions to a healthy Native community. Selection is based on the essay (40 points), GPA (40 points), letters of recommendation (30 points), and personal impression (10 points).
Financial data Stipends range from $2,000 to $7,000 per year.
Duration 1 year. Undergraduate students may reapply if they maintain a GPA of 2.0 or higher; graduate or master's degree students may reapply if they maintain a GPA of 3.0 or higher; and specialist or doctoral students may reapply if they maintain a GPA of 3.25 or higher. Students can receive a total of $10,000 throughout their entire undergraduate or vocational career. Students who continue in a 1- or 2-year master's degree program are eligible to receive an additional $10,000, for a total maximum of $20,000. Students who work on a 3- to 5-year graduate degree (e.g., Ph.D., M.D., J.D.) can receive an additional $10,000 for a total maximum of $30,000.
Additional information This program includes the Morris Thompson Scholarship Fund and the Rosemarie Maher Memorial Fund. Recipients must attend school on a full-time basis. Scholarship recipients of $5,000 or more are encouraged to complete at least 1 summer internship during their 4 years of study. Scholarship recipients of less than $5,000 are encouraged to do 1 of the following: serve on a local or regional board or commission, volunteer at least 20 hours, or give presentations on their field of study. A written report detailing the internship or service and lessons learned is required upon completion of the internship.
Number awarded Varies each year; recently, 52 new and renewal scholarships, with a total value of $178,352, were awarded.
Deadline April of each year.

[640]
DR. BESSIE ELIZABETH DELANEY FELLOWSHIP
National Dental Association
Attn: National Dental Association Foundation, Inc.
3517 16th Street, N.W.
Washington, DC 20010
(202) 588-1697   Fax: (202) 588-1242
E-mail: admin@ndaonline.org
Web: www.nadonline.org/ndafoundation.asp

Purpose To provide financial assistance to female dental postdoctoral students who are members of underrepresented minority groups.

Eligibility This program is open to members of underrepresented minority groups who are women dentists working on a degree in subspecialty areas of dentistry, public health, administration, research, or law. Students working on a master's degree beyond their residency may be considered. Applicants must be members of the National Dental Association (NDA) and U.S. citizens or permanent residents. Along with their application, they must submit a letter explaining why they should be considered for this scholarship, 2 letters of recommendation, a curriculum vitae, a description of the program, nomination by their program director, and documentation of financial need.

Financial data The stipend is $10,000.

Duration 1 year.

Additional information This program, established in 1990, is supported by the Colgate-Palmolive Company.

Number awarded 1 each year.

Deadline May of each year.

[641]
DR. CLIFTON O. DUMMETT AND LOIS DOYLE DUMMETT FELLOWSHIP
National Dental Association
Attn: National Dental Association Foundation, Inc.
3517 16th Street, N.W.
Washington, DC 20010
(202) 588-1697   Fax: (202) 588-1242
E-mail: admin@ndaonline.org
Web: www.nadonline.org/ndafoundation.asp

Purpose To provide financial assistance to Native American and other underrepresented minority dental postdoctoral students.

Eligibility This program is open to members of underrepresented minority groups who are dentists working on a degree in subspecialty areas of dentistry, public health, administration, research, or law. Students working on a master's degree beyond their residency may be considered. Applicants must be members of the National Dental Association (NDA) and U.S. citizens or permanent residents. Along with their application, they must submit a letter explaining why they should be considered for this scholarship, 2 letters of recommendation, a curriculum vitae, a description of the program, nomination by their program director, and documentation of financial need.

Financial data The stipend is $10,000.

Duration 1 year.

Additional information This program, established in 1990, is supported by the Colgate-Palmolive Company.

Number awarded 1 each year.

Deadline May of each year.

[642]
DR. JOSEPH L. HENRY SCHOLARSHIPS
National Dental Association
Attn: National Dental Association Foundation, Inc.
3517 16th Street, N.W.
Washington, DC 20010
(202) 588-1697   Fax: (202) 588-1242
E-mail: admin@ndaonline.org
Web: www.nadonline.org/ndafoundation.asp

Purpose To provide financial assistance to Native American and other underrepresented minorities entering their first year of dental school.

Eligibility This program is open to members of underrepresented minority groups who are entering their first year of dental school as full-time students. Applicants must have an undergraduate GPA of 3.5 or higher. Along with their application, they must submit information on their community service, a letter from their school verifying that they are attending, a letter of recommendation from an undergraduate professor, college transcripts, and documentation of financial need. They must be U.S. citizens or permanent residents. Selection is based on academic performance in undergraduate school and service to community and/or country.

Financial data The stipend is $2,000 per year.

Duration 1 year; may be renewed up to 3 additional years.

Additional information This program, established in 1990, is supported by the Colgate-Palmolive Company.

Number awarded 5 each year.

Deadline May of each year.

[643]
DR. ROE B. LEWIS MEMORIAL SCHOLARSHIPS
Southwest Indian Agricultural Association
P.O. Box 93524
Phoenix, AZ 85070-3524
(520) 562-6722   Fax: (520) 562-2840
E-mail: swiaa@att.net
Web: www.swindianag.com

Purpose To provide financial assistance to American Indians working on an undergraduate or graduate degree in a field related to agriculture or natural resources.

Eligibility This program is open to American Indians enrolled in a federally-recognized band, nation, or tribe. Applicants must be working on an undergraduate or graduate degree in agriculture or natural resources at an accredited vocational school, technical school, college, or university. Along with their application, they must submit an essay explaining how they plan to use their education to promote, educate, and/or improve agriculture on southwest reservations. First-year undergraduates must have a GPA of 2.5 or higher; all other students must have a GPA of 3.0 or higher. Financial need is not considered in the selection process.

Financial data The stipend is $1,000.

Duration 1 year.

Number awarded 3 each year: 2 to undergraduates and 1 to a graduate student.

Deadline November of each year.

[644]
DRI LAW STUDENT DIVERSITY SCHOLARSHIP
DRI-The Voice of the Defense Bar
Attn: Diversity Scholarship Committee
150 North Michigan Avenue, Suite 300
Chicago, IL 60601
(312) 795-1101　　　　　　　　Fax: (312) 795-0747
E-mail: dri@dri.org
Web: www.dri.org

Purpose To provide financial assistance to minority and women law students.

Eligibility This program is open to students entering their second year of law school who are African American, Hispanic, Asian, Pan Asian, Native American, or female. Applicants must submit an essay, up to 1,000 words, on the topic "With the Continuing Decline in the Number of Civil Trials, What Methods Can Defense Lawyers Adopt to Preserve the Civil Jury System?" Selection is based on that essay, demonstrated academic excellence, service to the profession, service to the community, and service to the cause of diversity. Students affiliated with the Association of Trial Lawyers of America as members, student members, or employees are not eligible. Finalists are invited to participate in personal interviews.

Financial data The stipend is $10,000 per year.

Duration 1 year.

Additional information This program was established in 2004.

Number awarded 2 each year.

Deadline July of each year.

[645]
DWIGHT DAVID EISENHOWER GRADUATE TRANSPORTATION FELLOWSHIPS
Department of Transportation
Federal Highway Administration
Attn: Office of Professional and Corporate
　Development, HPC-32
4600 North Fairfax Drive, Suite 800
Arlington, VA 22203-1553
(703) 235-0538　　　　　　　Toll-free: (877) 558-6873
Fax: (703) 235-0593
E-mail: transportationedu@dot.gov
Web: www.fhwa.dot.gov/opd/universitygrants.htm

Purpose To provide financial assistance to Native American and other graduate students working on a master's or doctoral degree in transportation-related fields.

Eligibility This program is open to students enrolled or planning to enroll full time to work on a master's or doctoral degree in a field of study directly related to transportation. Applicants must be planning to enter the transportation profession after completing their higher level education. They must be U.S. citizens or have an I-20 (foreign student) or I-551 (permanent resident) identification card. Selection is based on the proposed plan of study, academic records (class standing, GPA, and official transcripts), transportation work experience (including employer's endorsement), and recommendations. Students at Historically Black Colleges and Universities (HBCUs), Hispanic Serving Institutions (HSIs), and Tribal Colleges and Universities (TCUs) are especially encouraged to apply.

Financial data Fellows receive tuition and fees (to a maximum of $10,000 per year), monthly stipends of $1,700 for master's degree students or $2,000 for doctoral students, and a 1-time allowance of up to $1,500 for travel to an annual meeting of the Transportation Research Board to present the findings of their research.

Duration For master's degree students, 24 months, and the degree must be completed within 3 years; for doctoral students, 36 months, and the degree must be completed within 5 years.

Number awarded Approximately 100 to 150 each year.

Deadline February of each year.

[646]
ECIM SCHOLARSHIPS
Episcopal Church Center
Attn: Domestic and Foreign Missionary Society
Episcopal Council of Indigenous Ministries
815 Second Avenue, Seventh Floor
New York, NY 10017-4503
(212) 716-6175　　　　　　　Toll-free: (800) 334-7626
Fax: (212) 867-0395
E-mail: dcoy@episcopalchurch.org
Web: www.episcopalchurch.org

Purpose To provide financial assistance to Native Americans interested in theological education within the Episcopal Church in the United States of America (ECUSA).

Eligibility Applicants must be seminarians of American Indian/Alaska Native descent attending an accredited Episcopal institution. They must submit documentation of tribal membership, diocesan endorsement with a statement signed by the bishop that the applicant is in track for ordination, and a signed statement that the applicant intends to serve in Indian ministry upon completion of study.

Financial data The amount of the award depends on the needs of the recipient and the availability of funds, to a maximum of $2,000 per year.

Additional information The Episcopal Council of Indigenous Ministries (ECIM) also awards the David Oakerhater Merit Fellowship to a middler with outstanding achievement and the Oakerhater Award of $2,500 to a seminarian pursuing a Ph.D. This program relies on funds established as early as 1879 and includes the Episcopal Legacy Fund for Scholarships Honoring the Memory of the Rev. Dr. Martin Luther King, Jr., established in 1991.

Number awarded Varies each year.

Deadline May of each year for fall semester or October of each year for spring semester.

[647]
EDITH KANAKA'OLE FOUNDATION HIGHER EDUCATION SCHOLARSHIP
Edith Kanaka'ole Foundation
Attn: Higher Education Scholarship
1500 Kalaniana'ole Avenue
Hilo, HI 96720-4814
(808) 961-5242　　　　　　　　Fax: (808) 961-4789
Web: www.edithkanakaolefoundation.org

Purpose To provide financial assistance to Native Hawaiians who are attending or planning to attend a college or university on the island of Hawai'i.

Eligibility This program is open to students who are of Native Hawaiian ancestry in whole or in part. Applicants must be attending or planning to attend a college or university on Hawai'i island as a full-time student. They must have a GPA of 2.5 or higher and agree to complete a "give back" program. Preference is given to 1) students in a discipline that has little or no Native Hawaiian representation, very low Hawaiian enrollment, and/or low exit degree completion; 2) lessees in the Department of Hawaiian Homes or a child of a lessee; 3) students born and raised in the districts of Ka'u, Kohala, Puna, or Hilo; 4) upper-division or advanced standing students; and 5) Hawaiian cultural practitioners.
Financial data A stipend is awarded (amount not specified); funds are not intended to be the recipient's primary source of higher education funding.
Duration 1 year; may be renewed if the recipient maintains a GPA of 3.0 or higher.
Number awarded 1 each year.

[648]
EDUCATION AWARDS FOR HOPI TRIBAL MEMBERS
Hopi Tribe
Attn: Grants and Scholarship Program
P.O. Box 123
Kykotsmovi, AZ 86039
(928) 734-3533   Toll-free: (800) 762-9630
Fax: (928) 734-9575
E-mail: TLomakema@hopi.nsn.us
Web: www.hopi.nsn.us/education_htgsp.asp

Purpose To provide financial assistance to needy students of Hopi ancestry who are working on an undergraduate, graduate, or postgraduate degree.
Eligibility This program is open to students who are working on an associate, baccalaureate, graduate, or postgraduate degree. Applicants must be enrolled members of the Hopi Tribe. They must have a GPA of 2.5 or higher or a composite of 50% or higher on the GED and be able to demonstrate financial need.
Financial data The maximum grant is $2,500 per semester ($5,000 per year).
Duration 1 semester; may be renewed for up to 10 terms of undergraduate study or up to 5 terms of graduate study, provided the recipient maintains a GPA of 2.5 or higher as an undergraduate or 3.0 as a graduate student.
Additional information This grant is awarded as a secondary source of financial aid to eligible students who are also receiving aid from the Bureau of Indian Affairs (BIA) Higher Education program. Recipients must attend school on a full-time basis.
Number awarded Varies each year.
Deadline June of each year for fall or winter term; November of each year for spring term; March of each year for summer session.

[649]
EDWARD L. KRUGER MEMORIAL *ITTISH AAISHA* SCHOLARSHIP
Chickasaw Foundation
110 West 12th Street
P.O. Box 1726
Ada, OK 74821-1726
(580) 421-9030   Fax: (580) 421-9031
E-mail: ChickasawFoundation@chickasaw.net
Web: www.chickasaw.net

Purpose To provide financial assistance to members of the Chickasaw Nation who are working on a graduate degree in pharmacy.
Eligibility This program is open to Chickasaw students who are currently enrolled full time in a graduate school of pharmacy. Applicants must have a GPA of 3.0 or higher. Along with their application, they must submit high school or college transcripts, 2 letters of recommendation, a copy of their Chickasaw Nation citizenship card, and a 1-page essay on their long-term goals and plans for achieving them. Financial need is not considered in the selection process.
Financial data The stipend is $1,500 per year.
Duration 1 year.
Number awarded 1 each year.
Deadline June of each year.

[650]
ELIZABETH AND SHERMAN ASCHE MEMORIAL SCHOLARSHIP
Association on American Indian Affairs, Inc.
Attn: Director of Scholarship Programs
966 Hungerford Drive, Suite 12-B
Rockville, MD 20850
(240) 314-7155   Fax: (240) 314-7159
E-mail: lw.aaia@verizon.net
Web: www.indian-affairs.org

Purpose To provide financial assistance to Native Americans interested in working on an undergraduate or graduate degree in public health.
Eligibility This program is open to American Indian and Alaskan Native full-time undergraduate and graduate students working on a degree in public health. Applicants must submit documentation of financial need, a Certificate of Indian Blood showing at least one-quarter Indian blood, proof of tribal enrollment, an essay on their educational goals, 2 letters of recommendation, and their most recent transcript. Selection is based on merit and need.
Financial data The stipend is $1,500.
Duration 1 year.
Number awarded 1 or more each year.
Deadline June of each year.

[651]
ETHEL AND EMERY FAST SCHOLARSHIP
Ethel and Emery Fast Scholarship Foundation, Inc.
12620 Rolling Road
Potomac, MD 20854
(301) 762-1102   Fax: (301) 279-0201
E-mail: qccarol@erols.com

Purpose To provide financial assistance to qualified Native Americans enrolled as undergraduates or graduate students.

Eligibility Applicants must 1) be Native Americans enrolled in a federally-recognized tribe, 2) have successfully completed 1 year of their undergraduate or graduate school program, 3) be enrolled in school full time, and 4) be able to demonstrate financial need. Along with their application, they must submit documentation of Native American eligibility, an original transcript, a letter confirming enrollment, a federal income tax return, a statement of financial need, and a personal statement (up to 2 pages) describing they current situation, their future aspirations in terms of their academic pursuits, and how this scholarship will assist them in attaining their goals.

Financial data A stipend is awarded (amount not specified). Funds are paid directly to the recipient's college or university and can only be used to pay for tuition, room, board, and fees.

Duration 1 year.

Number awarded Varies each year.

Deadline August of each year for the fall semester; January of each year for the spring semester.

[652]
ETHEL CURRY SCHOLARSHIPS
Minnesota Department of Education
Attn: Manager, Minnesota Indian Education
1500 Highway 36 West
Roseville, MN 55113-4266
(651) 582-8832   Toll-free: (800) 657-3927
E-mail: mde.indian-education@state.mn.us
Web: education.state.mn.us

Purpose To provide financial assistance to Native Americans in Minnesota who are interested in working on an undergraduate or graduate degree.

Eligibility This program is open to Indians who are enrolled in a Minnesota-based tribe or community. Applicants must be attending an accredited postsecondary institution in Minnesota as a junior, senior, or graduate student. They must have a GPA of 3.0 or higher. Selection is based on merit.

Financial data The stipend is $3,000 per year for undergraduates or $6,000 per year for graduate students.

Duration Up to 4 years.

Number awarded Varies each year; recently, 12 of these scholarships were awarded.

Deadline May of each year.

[653]
ETHNIC IN-SERVICE TRAINING FUND
United Methodist Church
General Board of Higher Education and Ministry
Attn: Section of Chaplains and Related Ministries
1001 19th Avenue South
P.O. Box 340007
Nashville, TN 37203-0007
(615) 340-7366   Fax: (615) 340-7395
E-mail: sespino@gbhem.org
Web: www.gbhem.org/chaplains/mistscholarship.html

Purpose To provide funding to Methodists who are members of racial and ethnic minority groups involved in Clinical Pastoral Education (CPE) for pastoral counseling or hospital chaplaincy.

Eligibility This program is open to racial and ethnic minorities who have been active in a local United Methodist Church. Applicants must have been accepted into an accredited CPE program for pastoral counseling or hospital chaplaincy. They must submit a 2-page paper on their call to the ordained ministry and a 1-page paper on how CPE will enhance their ministry.

Financial data The stipend depends on the need of the recipient, the cost of the program, and the availability of funds.

Number awarded Varies each year.

Deadline August of each year.

[654]
ETHNIC MINORITY POSTGRADUATE SCHOLARSHIP FOR CAREERS IN ATHLETICS
Black Coaches Association
Attn: Director of Operations and Administration
Pan American Plaza
201 South Capital Avenue, Suite 495
Indianapolis, IN 46225
(217) 829-5619   Toll-free: (877) 789-1222
Fax: (217) 829-5601
Web: bcasports.cstv.com

Purpose To provide financial assistance to Native Americans and other minorities who participated in college athletics and are interested in working on a graduate degree in athletic administration.

Eligibility This program is open to former student-athletes on the college level who are of ethnic minority origin. Applicants must be entering or enrolled full time in a graduate program in sports administration or a related field to prepare for a career in athletics. They must have performed with distinction as student body members at their undergraduate institution and have a GPA of 2.5 or higher. U.S. citizenship is required. Selection is based on academic course work, extracurricular activities, commitment to preparing for a career in athletics, and promise of success in their career.

Financial data The stipend is $2,500. Funds are paid to the college or university of the recipient's choice.

Duration 1 year; nonrenewable.

Additional information This program was established in 1995.

Number awarded Varies each year; recently, 6 of these scholarships were awarded.

Deadline April of each year.

[655]
EYAK FOUNDATION SCHOLARSHIPS
Eyak Corporation
Attn: Eyak Foundation
901 LeFevre Street
P.O. Box 340
Cordova, AK 99574
(907) 424-7161　　　　　Fax: (907) 424-5161
Web: www.eyakcorporation.com

Purpose To provide financial assistance to Native Alaskans who are shareholders of the Eyak Corporation or their descendants and are interested in working on an undergraduate or graduate degree in any state.

Eligibility This program is open to Native Alaskans who are enrolled or planning to enroll in an accredited undergraduate or graduate program at a college or university, vocational education school, or continuing education program in any state. Applicants must be a shareholder of the Eyak Corporation or a lineal descendant of a Native shareholder. They must have a GPA of 2.5 or higher and be able to demonstrate financial need. Along with their application, they must submit a personal history and statement of educational goals.

Financial data The stipend is $1,000.

Duration 1 year.

Additional information The Eyak Foundation was formerly named the Cordova Native Foundation.

Number awarded 5 each year.

Deadline June of each year.

[656]
FAEGRE & BENSON DIVERSITY SCHOLARSHIP
Faegre & Benson LLP
Attn: Manager of Legal Personnel Services
2200 Wells Fargo Center
90 South Seventh Street
Minneapolis, MN 55402
(612) 766-7209　　　Toll-free: (800) 328-4393
Fax: (612) 766-1600　　　E-mail: dgray@faegre.com
Web: www.faegre.com/diversityscholarship

Purpose To provide financial assistance and work experience to Native American and other law students who will contribute to diversity in the legal profession.

Eligibility This program is open to students enrolled in the first year at an accredited law school in the United States. Applicants must submit a 500-word personal statement explaining their interest in the scholarship program, how diversity has influenced their life, and how it impacts the legal profession. Selection is based on that statement, a resume, undergraduate transcripts, a legal writing sample, and 2 professional recommendations.

Financial data The stipend is $6,000 per year.

Duration 2 years: the second and third year of law school.

Additional information Recipients are also offered an associateship during the summer between the first and second year at an office of the firm in Minneapolis, Denver, Boulder, or Des Moines. An attorney from the firm is assigned as a mentor to help them adjust to the firm and to the legal profession.

Number awarded 2 each year.

Deadline January of each year.

[657]
FERMILAB DOCTORAL FELLOWSHIP PROGRAM FOR MINORITY STUDENTS IN PHYSICS
Fermi National Accelerator Laboratory
Attn: Manager, Equal Opportunity Office
MS 117
P.O. Box 500
Batavia, IL 60510-0500
(630) 840-4633　　　　　Fax: (630) 840-5207
E-mail: engram@fnal.gov
Web: www.fnal.gov

Purpose To provide financial assistance for doctoral study in physics to Native American and other underrepresented minority students at universities that are members of the Universities Research Association, Inc. (URA).

Eligibility This program is open to doctoral students who are members of minority groups historically underrepresented in physics (Hispanics, African Americans, and Native Americans). Applicants must be enrolled at 1 of the 91 universities in the United States that are URA members. They must be U.S. citizens or permanent residents. Along with their application, they must submit a statement on why they want to participate in this program, why they are considering physics as their course of study in graduate school, how they intend to use their physics training after they complete their education, and whether they plan to work or do postdoctoral study after completing their education. Selection is based on that statement, financial need, university transcripts, and a progress letter from the thesis adviser.

Financial data The stipend depends on the availability of funds and the needs of the student.

Duration 1 year; may be renewed up to 6 additional years.

Additional information Fermilab scientists are assigned to all recipients as advisers to aid their progress in graduate school. In addition, students are encouraged to work summers at Fermilab under the supervision of a staff physicist. Funding support for this program is provided by the U.S. Department of Energy.

Number awarded Varies each year.

Deadline July of each year.

[658]
FINNEGAN HENDERSON DIVERSITY SCHOLARSHIP
Finnegan, Henderson, Farabow, Garrett & Dunner, LLP
Attn: Director of Professional Recruitment and Development
901 New York Avenue, N.W.
Washington, D.C. 20001-4413
(202) 408-4034　　　　　Fax: (202) 408-4400
E-mail: diversityscholarship@finnegan.com
Web: www.finnegan.com

Purpose To provide financial assistance and work experience to Native American and other underrepresented minority law students interested in a career in intellectual property law.

Eligibility This program is open to law students from underrepresented minority groups who have demonstrated a commitment to a career in intellectual property law and are currently enrolled either as a first-year full-time student or second-year part-time student. The sponsor defines

underrepresented minorities to include American Indians/Alaskan Natives, Blacks/African Americans, Asian Americans, Native Hawaiians or other Pacific Islanders, and Hispanics/Latinos. Applicants must have earned an undergraduate degree in life sciences, engineering, or computer science, or have substantial prior trademark experience. Selection is based on academic performance at the undergraduate, graduate (if applicable), and law school level; relevant work experience; community service; leadership skills; and special accomplishments.
Financial data The stipend is $15,000 per year.
Duration 1 year; may be renewed 1 additional year as long as the recipient completes a summer associateship with the sponsor and maintains of GPA of 3.0 or higher.
Additional information The sponsor, the world's largest intellectual property law firm, established this scholarship in 2003. Summer associateships are available at its offices in Washington, D.C.; Atlanta, Georgia; Cambridge, Massachusetts; Palo Alto, California; or Reston, Virginia.
Number awarded 1 each year.
Deadline February of each year.

[659]
FIRST PERSON JOURNALISM SCHOLARSHIP FUND

MIGIZI Communications, Inc.
Attn: Scholarship Committee
3123 East Lake Street
Minneapolis, MN 55406
(612) 721-6631   Fax: (612) 721-3936
Web: migizi.org/mig/scholarships.html

Purpose To provide financial assistance to Native American students working on an undergraduate or graduate degree in journalism.
Eligibility This program is open to Native American undergraduate and graduate students preparing for a career in journalism or mass communications. Applicants must be able to document financial need. Along with their application, they must submit a 500-word essay on 1) how and in what capacity they have been involved in journalism, 2) why journalism is important, and 3) their plans for the future and how they plan to use their studies to help the community.
Financial data The stipend is $1,000.
Duration 1 year; nonrenewable.
Number awarded 1 each year.
Deadline May of each year.

[660]
FIRST SERGEANT DOUGLAS AND CHARLOTTE DEHORSE SCHOLARSHIP

Catching the Dream
8200 Mountain Road, N.E., Suite 203
Albuquerque, NM 87110-7835
(505) 262-2351   Fax: (505) 262-0534
E-mail: NScholarsh@aol.com
Web: www.catchingthedream.org

Purpose To provide financial assistance to American Indians who have ties to the military and are working on an undergraduate or graduate degree.
Eligibility This program is open to American Indians who 1) have completed 1 year of an Army, Navy, or Air Force Junior Reserve Officer Training (JROTC) program; 2) are enrolled in an Army, Navy, or Air Force Reserve Officer Training (ROTC) program; or 3) are a veteran of the U.S. Army, Navy, Air Force, Marines, Merchant Marine, or Coast Guard. Applicants must be enrolled in an undergraduate or graduate program of study. Along with their application, they must submit a personal essay, high school transcripts, and letters of recommendation.
Financial data A stipend is awarded (amount not specified).
Duration 1 year.
Additional information This program was established in 2007.
Number awarded 1 or more each year.
Deadline April of each year for fall semester or quarter; September of each year for spring semester or winter quarter.

[661]
FISH & RICHARDSON DIVERSITY FELLOWSHIP PROGRAM

Fish & Richardson P.C.
Attn: Recruiting Department
1717 Main Street, Suite 5000
Dallas, TX 75201
(214) 760-6131   Fax: (214) 747-2091
E-mail: krassy@fr.com
Web: www.fr.com

Purpose To provide financial assistance and work experience to Native Americans and other students who will contribute to diversity in the legal profession.
Eligibility This program is open to students enrolled in the first year at a law school anywhere in the country. Applicants must be African American/Black, American Indian/Alaskan, Hispanic/Latino, Native Hawaiian/Pacific Islander, Asian, 2 or more races, disabled, or openly homosexual, bisexual, and/or transgender. Along with their application, they must submit a 500-word essay describing their background, what led them to the legal field, their interest in the sponsoring law firm, and what they could contribute to its practice and the profession. They must also indicate their first 3 choices of an office of the firm where they are interested in a summer associate clerkship.
Financial data The stipend is $5,000.
Duration 1 year: the second year of law school.
Additional information Recipients are also offered a paid associate clerkship during the summer following their first year of law school at an office of the firm in the location of their choice in Atlanta, Austin, Boston, Dallas, Delaware, New York, San Diego, Silicon Valley, Twin Cities, or Washington, D.C. This program began in 2005.
Number awarded 5 each year.
Deadline January of each year.

[662]
FLANDREAU SANTEE SIOUX STUDENT ASSISTANCE SCHOLARSHIPS

Flandreau Santee Sioux Tribe
Attn: Higher Education Committee
P.O. Box 283
Flandreau, SD 57028
(605) 997-2859 Fax: (605) 997-2951
E-mail: elaine.stephens@fsst.org
Web: www.fsst.org/Agnesrossedu_main.html

Purpose To provide financial assistance to members of the Flandreau Santee Sioux Tribe who live on the reservation and are interested in attending college or graduate school in any state.

Eligibility This program is open to enrolled members of the tribe who live on the reservation in Moody County, South Dakota. Applicants must be interested in attending a college, university, or vocational/technical institute in any state and working on an undergraduate or graduate degree. They must apply for all available federal funding, using the Free Application for Student Aid (FAFSA). Awards are granted on a first-come, first-served basis.

Financial data For the first semester of each year, full-time undergraduates receive $800 as freshmen, $900 as sophomores, $1,000 as juniors, or $1,100 as seniors. For the second semester of each year, full-time undergraduates who have a GPA of 2.0 to 3.0 during the first semester receive the same amounts; those who have less than 2.0 receive $640 as freshmen, $720 as sophomores, $800 as juniors, or $880 as seniors; those who have more than 3.0 receive $900 as freshmen, $1,000 as sophomores, $1,100 as juniors, or $1,200 as seniors. For full-time graduate students, stipends are $2,500 for the first semester, $2,500 for the second semester if they have a GPA between 3.0 and 3.5, $2,000 for the second semester if they a GPA less than 3.0, or $2,700 for the second semester if they have a GPA greater than 3.5. Part-time undergraduates and graduate students receive stipends equal to half the amount of full-time students in the same category. Vocational training students receive $500 at the beginning of the term and then $150 per month, to a total of $2,150 per year.

Duration 1 semester; may be renewed.

Additional information Funding for this program is provided by revenue from the Tribe's gaming operations.

Number awarded Varies each year.

Deadline July of each year for fall semester or quarter; December of each year for spring semester or winter quarter; January of each year for spring quarter; May of each year for summer session.

[663]
FLEMMIE D. KITTRELL FELLOWSHIP

American Association of Family and Consumer Sciences
Attn: Manager of Awards and Grants
400 North Columbus Street, Suite 202
Alexandria, VA 22314
(703) 706-4600 Toll-free: (800) 424-8080, ext. 119
Fax: (703) 706-4663 E-mail: staff@aafcs.org
Web: www.aafcs.org/programs/fellowships.html

Purpose To provide financial assistance to Native American and other minority graduate students in the field of family and consumer sciences.

Eligibility This program is open to minority students working full time on a graduate degree in an area of family and consumer sciences. Selection is based on ability to pursue graduate study (10 points); experience in relation to preparation for study in proposed field (15 points); special recognition and awards (5 points); voluntary participation in professional and community organizations and activities (10 points); evidence (or degree) of professional commitment and leadership (10 points); significance of proposed study or research interests to families and individuals (15 points); professional goals (10 points); written communication (5 points); and recommendations (10 points). Special consideration is given to applicants who have been members of the American Association of Family and Consumer Sciences (AAFCS) for up to 2 years (2 points) or for 2 or more years (10 points) or who have AAFCS credentials in family and consumer sciences (5 points). Preference is also given to applicants who have at least 1 year of work experience in family and consumer sciences, serving in such positions as a graduate/undergraduate assistant, trainee, or intern.

Financial data The stipend is $3,500.

Duration 1 year.

Additional information The fellowship, initiated in 1973, honors Flemmie D. Kittrell, who served for 27 years as the chair of the Home Economics Department (now the School of Human Ecology) at Howard University and pioneered in the development of international cooperation in home economics in Africa and India. The fellowship has been supported by annual gifts from the JCPenney Company, Inc. The application fee is $40. The association reserves the right to reconsider an award in the event the student receives a similar scholarship for the same academic year.

Number awarded 1 each year.

Deadline January of each year.

[664]
FLORENCE YOUNG MEMORIAL SCHOLARSHIP

Association on American Indian Affairs, Inc.
Attn: Director of Scholarship Programs
966 Hungerford Drive, Suite 12-B
Rockville, MD 20850
(240) 314-7155 Fax: (240) 314-7159
E-mail: lw.aaia@verizon.net
Web: www.indian-affairs.org

Purpose To provide financial assistance to Native Americans interested in working on a graduate degree in specified fields.

Eligibility This program is open to American Indian and Alaskan Native full-time graduate students working on a graduate degree in art, public health, or law. Applicants must submit documentation of financial need, a Certificate of Indian Blood showing at least one-quarter Indian blood, proof of tribal enrollment, an essay on their educational goals, 2 letters of recommendation, and their most recent transcript. Selection is based on merit and need.

Financial data The stipend is $1,500.

Duration 1 year; recipients may reapply.

Number awarded 1 or more each year.

Deadline June of each year.

[665]
FLORIDA LIBRARY ASSOCIATION MINORITY SCHOLARSHIPS

Florida Library Association
c/o Linda Alexander, Scholarship Committee Chair
University of South Florida
4202 East Fowler Avenue
CIS 1040
Tampa, FL 33620-7800
(813) 974-8966   E-mail: lindab.alexander@gmail.com
Web: www.flalib.org/scholarships.html

Purpose To provide financial assistance to Native American and other minority students from any state working on a graduate degree in library and information science in Florida.

Eligibility This program is open to residents of Florida who are working on a graduate degree in library and information science at schools in the state. Applicants must be members of a minority group: Black/African American, American Indian/Alaska Native, Asian/Pacific Islander, or Hispanic/Latino. They must have some experience in a Florida library and must commit to working in a Florida library for at least 1 year after graduation. Along with their application, they must submit 1) a list of activities, honors, awards, and/or offices held during college and outside college; and 2) a statement of their reasons for entering librarianship and their career goals with respect to Florida libraries.

Financial data The stipend is $2,000 per year.
Duration 1 year.
Number awarded 1 each year.
Deadline January of each year.

[666]
FOCUS PROFESSIONS GROUP FELLOWSHIPS

American Association of University Women
Attn: AAUW Educational Foundation
301 ACT Drive, Department 60
P.O. Box 4030
Iowa City, IA 52243-4030
(319) 337-1716, ext. 60   Fax: (319) 337-1204
E-mail: aauw@act.org
Web: www.aauw.org

Purpose To aid Native American and other women of color who are in their final year of graduate training in the fields of business administration, law, or medicine.

Eligibility This program is open to women of color who are working on a degree in these historically underrepresented fields: business administration (M.B.A., E.M.B.A.), law (J.D.), or medicine (M.D., D.O.). U.S. citizenship or permanent resident status is required. Applicants in business administration and medicine may be entering any year of study; applicants in law must be entering their second or third year of study. Special consideration is given to applicants who 1) demonstrate their intent to enter professional practice in disciplines in which women are underrepresented, to serve underserved populations and communities, or to pursue public interest areas; and 2) are nontraditional students. Selection is based on professional promise and personal attributes (50%), academic excellence and related academic success indicators (40%), and financial need (10%).

Financial data Stipends range from $5,000 to $12,000.
Duration 1 academic year, beginning in September.
Additional information The filing fee is $35.
Number awarded Varies each year.
Deadline January of each year.

[667]
FOUNDATION OF RESEARCH AND EDUCATION DIVERSITY SCHOLARSHIPS

American Health Information Management Association
Attn: Foundation of Research and Education
233 North Michigan Avenue, Suite 2150
Chicago, IL 60601-5806
(312) 233-1131   Fax: (312) 233-1431
E-mail: fore@ahima.org
Web: www.ahima.org/fore/student/programs.asp

Purpose To provide financial assistance to Native American and other minority members of the American Health Information Management Association (AHIMA) who are interested in working on an undergraduate or graduate degree in health information administration or technology.

Eligibility This program is open to AHIMA members who are enrolled in a health information administration or health information technology program accredited by the Commission on Accreditation of Allied Health Education Programs. Applicants must be minorities, be working on an undergraduate or graduate degree on at least a half-time basis, and have a GPA of 3.0 or higher. U.S. citizenship is required. Selection is based (in order of importance) on GPA and academic achievement, volunteer and work experience, commitment to the health information management profession, suitability to the health information management profession, quality and suitability of references provided, and clarity of application.

Financial data Stipends range from $1,000 to $5,000.
Duration 1 year; nonrenewable.
Number awarded Varies each year. Recently, 10 of these scholarships were awarded.
Deadline April of each year.

[668]
FRANCES JOHNSON MEMORIAL TRUST SCHOLARSHIP

Northern Arapaho Tribe
Attn: Sky People Higher Education
P.O. Box 8480
Ethete, WY 82520
(307) 332-5286   Toll-free: (800) 815-6795
Fax: (307) 332-9104
E-mail: assistant@skypeopleed.org
Web: www.skypeopleed.org

Purpose To provide financial assistance to members of the Northern Arapaho Tribe who are working on an undergraduate or graduate degree in nursing or a health-related field.

Eligibility This program is open to full-time undergraduate and graduate students who have an undergraduate GPA of 2.0 or higher or the graduate GPA required by their school. Applicants must be at least one-fourth Northern Arapaho descent (enrolled or non-enrolled) and must submit a Certificate of Indian Blood or other verification of Northern Arapaho blood with at least one-fourth degree. They must be working on a degree in nursing or a health-related field. Along with their application, they must submit a 1-page personal statement that includes a brief history of their background, academic ability and achievement, work or leadership experience, participation in community-related activities, and career goals. Selection is based on that statement, potential to contribute to the community upon graduation, academic ability and achievement, and a letter of recommendation.

Financial data The stipend is $1,500 per year.

Duration 1 year; may be renewed.

Additional information The recipient is expected to apply for employment, after graduation, at the Tribal Health Program, Indian Health Services, at health care facilities on the Wind River Indian Reservation, or in the local communities of Lander or Riverton.

Number awarded 1 each year.

Deadline June of each year.

[669]
FRANCHISE LAW DIVERSITY SCHOLARSHIP AWARD

International Franchise Association
Attn: President, Educational Foundation
1501 K Street, N.W., Suite 350
Washington, DC 20005
(202) 662-0764   Fax: (202) 628-0812
E-mail: jreynolds@franchise.org
Web: www.franchise.org/files/Scholarships.aspx

Purpose To provide financial assistance to Native American and other law students from diverse groups who are interested in taking courses related to franchise law.

Eligibility This program is open to second- and third-year students who are enrolled at ABA-accredited law schools and a member of a diverse group (defined as African Americans, American Indians, Hispanic Americans, Asian Americans or gays/lesbians). Applicants must be enrolled in at least 1 course oriented toward franchise law (e.g., torts, unfair trade practices, trade secrets, antitrust, trademarks, contracts, agency, or securities). Along with their application, they must submit current transcript, an essay explaining their interest in franchise law, and 2 letters of recommendation.

Financial data The stipend is $4,000. Funds are paid to the recipient's law school and are to be used for tuition.

Duration 1 year.

Additional information This award is cosponsored by the IFA Educational Foundation and DLA Piper US LLP. It may not be used by the recipient's law school to reduce the amount of any institutionally-awarded financial aid.

Number awarded 1 or more each year.

Deadline February of each year.

[670]
FREDRIKSON & BYRON FOUNDATION MINORITY SCHOLARSHIPS

Fredrikson & Byron Foundation
Attn: Attorney Recruiting Administrator
200 South Sixth Street, Suite 4000
Minneapolis, MN 55402-1425
(612) 492-7141   Fax: (612) 492-7077
E-mail: glarson@fredlaw.com
Web: www.fredlaw.com/firm/scholarship.htm

Purpose To provide financial assistance and summer work experience to Native American and other minority law students from any state who are interested in practicing in the Twin Cities area of Minnesota.

Eligibility This program is open to African American, Asian American, Pacific Islander, Hispanic, Native American, and Alaska Native students enrolled in their first year of law school. Applicants must be interested in practicing law in the Minneapolis-St. Paul area. Along with their application, they must submit 2 recommendations, a writing sample from their first-year legal writing course, transcripts from undergraduate and law school, and a resume. Financial need is not considered.

Financial data The fellowship stipend is $10,000. The internship portion of the program provides a $1,000 weekly stipend.

Duration 1 year.

Additional information Fellows are also eligible to participate in an internship at the firm's offices in Minneapolis.

Number awarded 1 each year.

Deadline March of each year.

[671]
GATES MILLENNIUM GRADUATE SCHOLARS PROGRAM

Bill and Melinda Gates Foundation
P.O. Box 10500
Fairfax, VA 22031-8044
Toll-free: (877) 690-GMSP   Fax: (703) 205-2079
Web: www.gmsp.org

Purpose To provide financial assistance for graduate studies in selected subject areas to Native Americans and other outstanding low-income minority students.

Eligibility This program is open to low-income African Americans, Native Alaskans, American Indians, Hispanic Americans, and Asian Pacific Islander Americans who are nominated by a professional educator. Nominees must be U.S. citizens who are enrolled or about to enroll in graduate school to work on a degree in computer science, education, engineering, library science, mathematics, public health, or science. They must have a GPA of 3.3 or higher, be able to demonstrate significant financial need, and have demonstrated leadership commitment through participation in community service (i.e., mentoring/tutoring, volunteer work in social service organizations, and involvement in church initiatives), extracurricular activities (student government and athletics), or other activities that reflect leadership abilities.

Financial data The program covers the full cost of graduate study: tuition, fees, books, and living expenses not paid for by grants and scholarships already committed as part of the recipient's financial aid package.

Duration Up to 4 years (up to and including the doctorate), if the recipient maintains at least a 3.0 GPA.
Additional information This program, established in 1999, is funded by the Bill and Melinda Gates Foundation and administered by the United Negro College Fund with support from the American Indian Graduate Center, the Hispanic Scholarship Fund, and the Asian & Pacific Islander American Scholarship Fund.
Number awarded Under the Gates Millennium Scholars Program, a total of 4,000 students receive support each year.
Deadline January of each year.

[672]
GEM M.S. ENGINEERING FELLOWSHIP PROGRAM
National Consortium for Graduate Degrees for
  Minorities in Engineering and Science (GEM)
Attn: Manager, Fellowships Administration
1800 K Street, N.W., Suite 900
Washington, DC 20006
(202) 457-8688   Fax: (202) 207-3518
E-mail: akee@genfellowship.org
Web: www.gemfellowship.org

Purpose To provide financial assistance and summer work experience to Native American and other underrepresented minority graduate students in engineering.
Eligibility This program is open to U.S. citizens who are members of ethnic groups underrepresented in engineering: Native Americans, African Americans, Latinos, Puerto Ricans, and other Hispanic Americans. Applicants must be enrolled as at least a junior in an ABET-accredited engineering discipline with an academic record that indicates the ability to pursue graduate studies in engineering (including a GPA of 2.8 or higher). Students in computer science and computer engineering may also apply, but engineering technology majors are not eligible. Applicants must be planning to attend 1 of the 100 GEM member universities that offer a master's degree.
Financial data The fellowship pays tuition, fees, and a stipend of $10,000 over its lifetime. In addition, each participant receives a salary during the summer work assignment as a GEM Summer Intern. Employer members reimburse GEM participants for travel expenses to and from the summer work site.
Duration Up to 3 semesters or 4 quarters, plus a summer work internship lasting 10 to 14 weeks for up to 3 summers, depending on whether the student applies as a junior, senior, or college graduate; recipients begin their internship upon acceptance into the program and work each summer until completion of their master's degree.
Additional information During the summer internship, each fellow is assigned an engineering project in a research setting. Each project is based on the fellow's interest and background and is carried out under the supervision of an experienced engineer. At the conclusion of the internship, each fellow writes a project report. Recipients must work on a master's degree in the same engineering discipline as their baccalaureate degree.
Number awarded Varies each year; recently, 327 of these fellowships were awarded.
Deadline October of each year.

[673]
GEM PH.D. ENGINEERING FELLOWSHIP PROGRAM
National Consortium for Graduate Degrees for
  Minorities in Engineering and Science (GEM)
Attn: Manager, Fellowships Administration
1800 K Street, N.W., Suite 900
Washington, DC 20006
(202) 457-8688   Fax: (202) 207-3518
E-mail: akee@genfellowship.org
Web: www.gemfellowship.org

Purpose To provide financial assistance and summer work experience to Native American and other underrepresented minority students interested in obtaining a Ph.D. degree in engineering.
Eligibility This program is open to U.S. citizens who are members of ethnic groups underrepresented in engineering: American Indians/Native Americans, Blacks/African Americans, and Latinos/Hispanic Americans. Applicants must have completed or be in the process of completing a master's degree in engineering with an academic record that indicates the ability to work on a doctoral degree in engineering (including a GPA of 3.0 or higher).
Financial data The stipend is $14,000 for the first year; in subsequent years, fellows receive full payment of tuition and fees plus a stipend and assistantship from their university that is equivalent to funding received by other doctoral students in their department.
Duration 3 to 5 years for the fellowship; 12 weeks during at least 1 summer for the internship.
Additional information This program is valid only at 1 of 100 participating GEM member universities; write to GEM for a list. The fellowship award is designed to support the student in the first year of the doctoral program without working. Subsequent years are subsidized by the respective universities and will usually include either a teaching or research assistantship. Recipients must participate in the GEM summer internship; failure to agree to accept the internship cancels the fellowship.
Number awarded Varies each year; recently, 49 of these fellowships were awarded.
Deadline October of each year.

[674]
GEM PH.D. SCIENCE FELLOWSHIP PROGRAM
National Consortium for Graduate Degrees for
  Minorities in Engineering and Science (GEM)
Attn: Manager, Fellowships Administration
1800 K Street, N.W., Suite 900
Washington, DC 20006
(202) 457-8688   Fax: (202) 207-3518
E-mail: akee@genfellowship.org
Web: www.gemfellowship.org

Purpose To provide financial assistance and summer work experience to Native American and other underrepresented minority students interested in working on a Ph.D. degree in the life sciences, mathematics, or physical sciences.
Eligibility This program is open to U.S. citizens who are members of ethnic groups underrepresented in the natural sciences: American Indians/Native Americans, Blacks/African Americans, and Latinos/Hispanic Americans.

Applicants must be college juniors, seniors, master's degree students, or recent graduates in the biological sciences, mathematics, or physical sciences (chemistry, computer science, earth sciences, and physics) with an academic record that indicates the ability to pursue doctoral studies (including a GPA of 3.0 or higher).

Financial data The stipend is $14,000 for the first year; in subsequent years, fellows receive full payment of tuition and fees plus a stipend and assistantship from their university that is equivalent to funding received by other doctoral students in their department.

Duration 3 to 5 years for the fellowship; 12 weeks during at least 1 summer for the internship. Fellows selected as juniors or seniors intern each summer until entrance to graduate school; fellows selected after college graduation intern at least 1 summer.

Additional information This program is valid only at 1 of 100 participating GEM member universities; write to GEM for a list. The fellowship award is designed to support the student in the first year of the doctoral program without working. Subsequent years are subsidized by the respective university and will usually include either a teaching or research assistantship. Recipients must participate in the GEM summer internship; failure to agree to accept the internship cancels the fellowship. Recipients must enroll in the same scientific discipline as their undergraduate major.

Number awarded Varies each year; recently, 40 of these fellowships were awarded.

Deadline October of each year.

[675]
GENERAL MOTORS ENGINEERING SCHOLARSHIP

American Indian Science and Engineering Society
Attn: Scholarship Coordinator
2305 Renard, S.E., Suite 200
P.O. Box 9828
Albuquerque, NM 87119-9828
(505) 765-1052, ext. 106   Fax: (505) 765-5608
E-mail: shirley@aises.org
Web: www.aises.org

Purpose To provide financial assistance to members of the American Indian Science and Engineering Society (AISES) who are working on an undergraduate or graduate degree in engineering.

Eligibility This program is open to AISES members who are full-time undergraduate or graduate students in engineering, with a preference given to electrical, industrial, or mechanical engineering majors. Applicants must have a GPA of 3.0 or higher and be members of an American Indian tribe or Alaskan Native group or otherwise considered to be an American Indian or Alaskan Native by the tribe or group with which affiliation is claimed. They must submit an essay that explains their knowledge of and experiences with American Indian tribal culture, discusses their specific interests in engineering, and states how they will contribute their knowledge or professional experience to a Native American community. Financial need is not considered in the selection process.

Financial data The stipend is $3,000.

Duration 1 year; nonrenewable.

Additional information This program, established in 2002, is funded by General Motors.

Number awarded 3 each year.

Deadline June of each year.

[676]
GEORGE A. STRAIT MINORITY SCHOLARSHIP ENDOWMENT

American Association of Law Libraries
Attn: Chair, Scholarships Committee
53 West Jackson Boulevard, Suite 940
Chicago, IL 60604
(312) 939-4764   Fax: (312) 431-1097
E-mail: scholarships@aall.org
Web: www.aallnet.org/services/sch_strait.asp

Purpose To provide financial assistance to Native American and other minority college seniors or college graduates who are interested in becoming law librarians.

Eligibility This program is open to college graduates with meaningful law library experience who are members of minority groups and intend to have a career in law librarianship. Applicants must be degree candidates at an ALA-accredited library school or an ABA-accredited law school. Along with their application, they must submit a personal statement that discusses their interest in law librarianship, reason for applying for this scholarship, career goals as a law librarian, and other pertinent information.

Financial data The stipend is $3,500.

Duration 1 year.

Additional information This program, established in 1990, is currently supported by Thomson West.

Number awarded 2 to 4 each year.

Deadline March of each year.

[677]
GEORGE HI'ILANI MILLS PERPETUAL FELLOWSHIP AWARD

Ke Ali'i Pauahi Foundation
Attn: Financial Aid & Scholarship Services
567 South King Street, Suite 160
Honolulu, HI 96813
(808) 534-3966   Toll-free: (800) 842-4682, ext. 43966
Fax: (808) 534-3890   E-mail: scholarships@pauahi.org
Web: www.pauahi.org

Purpose To provide financial assistance to students, especially Native Hawaiians, who are interested in working on a graduate degree in medicine or allied health.

Eligibility This program is open to students working full time on a graduate degree in medicine or the allied health-related fields. Applicants must be able to demonstrate financial need. Residency in Hawaii is not required. Preference is given to Native Hawaiians (descendants of the aboriginal inhabitants of the Hawaiian Islands prior to 1778).

Financial data A stipend is awarded (amount not specified).

Duration 1 year; may be renewed.

Number awarded Varies each year; recently, 2 of these fellowships were awarded.

Deadline April of each year.

[678]
GEORGE K. NOLAN TRIBAL JUDICIAL SCHOLARSHIP

Sault Tribe of Chippewa Indians
Attn: Higher Education Department
Two Ice Circle
Sault Ste. Marie, MI 49783
(906) 635-7784   Toll-free: (800) 793-0660
Fax: (906) 635-7785   E-mail: jlewton@saulttribe.net
Web: www.saulttribe.com

Purpose To provide financial assistance to members of the Sault Tribe of Chippewa Indians who are working on a degree in a field related to law.

Eligibility This program is open to enrolled members of the Sault Tribe who are attending a 2-year or 4-year college or university as a full-time sophomore or higher. Applicants must be majoring in law enforcement, legal studies, political science, public administration, or tribal law. They must submit documentation of financial need and an essay of 300 to 500 words on how the scholarship will help them realize their goals.

Financial data The stipend is $1,000 per year.

Duration 1 year.

Number awarded 1 each year.

Deadline May of each year.

[679]
GEORGE M. BROOKER COLLEGIATE SCHOLARSHIP FOR MINORITIES

Institute of Real Estate Management Foundation
Attn: Foundation Coordinator
430 North Michigan Avenue
Chicago, IL 60611-4090
(312) 329-6008   Toll-free: (800) 837-0706, ext. 6008
Fax: (312) 410-7908   E-mail: kholmes@irem.org
Web: www.irem.org

Purpose To provide financial assistance to Native Americans and other minorities interested in preparing (on the undergraduate or graduate school level) for a career in the real estate management industry.

Eligibility This program is open to junior, senior, and graduate minority (non-Caucasian) students majoring in real estate or, if their college has no real estate major, in a related field. Applicants must be preparing for a career in real estate, especially real estate management, after graduation. They must have completed at least 2 courses in real estate and have a GPA of 3.0 or higher in their major. Along with their application, they must submit an essay (up to 500 words) on why they want to follow a career in real estate management, what they hope to accomplish in the field, and why they believe that success in the field will come. Financial need is not considered in the selection process.

Financial data Stipends are $1,000 for undergraduates or $2,500 for graduate students. Funds are disbursed to the institution the student attends to be used only for tuition expenses.

Duration 1 year; nonrenewable.

Number awarded 3 each year: 2 for undergraduates and 1 for a graduate student.

Deadline March of each year.

[680]
GEORGE MILLER JR. MANAGEMENT LEADERSHIP ENDOWMENT FELLOWSHIP

Cook Inlet Region, Inc.
Attn: The CIRI Foundation
3600 San Jeronimo Drive, Suite 256
Anchorage, AK 99508-2870
(907) 793-3575   Toll-free: (800) 764-3382
Fax: (907) 793-3585   E-mail: tcf@thecirifoundation.org
Web: www.thecirifoundation.org/designated.htm

Purpose To provide financial assistance to Native Alaskan business leaders who are interested in enhancing their managerial skills.

Eligibility This program is open to Alaska Native enrollees to Cook Inlet Region, Inc. (CIRI) under the Alaska Native Claims Settlement Act (ANSCA) of 1971 and their lineal descendants. Applicants must be business leaders who are interested in improving their tribal, cultural, and business leadership and management skills for career advancement. Along with their application, they must submit a 1,000-word statement on the type of management education program for which they are applying, whether the program is full or part time, length of the program, why they want to take the program, significant management and personal attributes they have to offer, and the expected benefits to be gained by participating in the program.

Financial data Up to $6,000 a year is available to each recipient, to cover the costs of organizational management courses of study, internships, or specialized or general management or organizational training programs.

Duration 1 year.

Additional information The intent of this program, established in 1996, is to provide an opportunity for the recipient to learn, think, be reinvigorated with new ideas, and acquire new tribal, cultural, and managerial skills in order to be better prepared for the complex challenges of management and leadership. It is named for the first president of Cook Inlet Region, Inc., who was also president of Kenai Natives Association.

Deadline Applications may be submitted at any time.

[681]
GEORGE V. POWELL DIVERSITY SCHOLARSHIP

Lane Powell Spears Lubersky LLP
Attn: Manager of Attorney Recruiting
1420 Fifth Avenue, Suite 4100
Seattle, WA 98101-2338
(206) 223-6123   Fax: (206) 223-7107
E-mail: rodenl@lanepowell.com
Web: www.lanepowell.com/firm/scholarship.asp

Purpose To provide financial assistance and work experience to Native American and other law students who will contribute to the diversity of the legal community.

Eligibility This program is open to second-year students in good standing at an ABA-accredited law school. Applicants must be able to contribute meaningfully to the diversity of the legal community and have a demonstrated desire to work, live, and eventually practice law in Seattle or Portland. They must submit a cover letter including a statement indicating eligibility to participate in the program, resume, current copy of law school transcript, legal writing sample, and list of 2 or 3 professional or academic references.

Selection is based on academic achievement and record of leadership abilities, community service, and involvement in community issues.
Financial data The program provides a stipend of $6,000 for the third year of law school and a paid summer associate clerkship.
Duration 1 year, including the summer.
Additional information This program was established in 2005. Clerkships are provided at the offices of the sponsor in Seattle or Portland.
Number awarded 1 each year.
Deadline September of each year.

[682]
GEOSCIENCE MINORITY STUDENT SCHOLARSHIPS
American Geological Institute
Attn: Minority Participation Program
4220 King Street
Alexandria, VA 22302-1502
(703) 379-2480, ext. 227   Fax: (703) 379-7563
E-mail: cmm@agiweb.org
Web: www.agiweb.org/mpp/index.html

Purpose To provide financial assistance to Native American and other underrepresented minority undergraduate and graduate students interested in working on a degree in the geosciences.
Eligibility This program is open to members of ethnic minority groups underrepresented in the geosciences (Blacks, Hispanics, American Indians, Eskimos, Hawaiians, and Samoans). U.S. citizenship or permanent resident status is required. Applicants must be full-time students enrolled in an accredited institution working on an undergraduate or graduate degree in the geosciences, including geology, geochemistry, geophysics, hydrology, meteorology, physical oceanography, planetary geology, or earth science education; students in other natural sciences, mathematics, or engineering are not eligible. Selection is based on a 250-word essay on career goals and why the applicant has chosen a geoscience as a major, work experience, recommendations, honors and awards, extracurricular activities, and financial need.
Financial data Stipends range from $500 to $3,000 per year.
Duration 1 academic year; renewable if the recipient maintains satisfactory performance.
Additional information Funding for this program is provided by ExxonMobil Corporation, ConocoPhillips, ChevronTexaco Corporation, Marathon Corporation, and the Seismological Society of America.
Number awarded Varies each year; recently, 25 of these scholarships were awarded.
Deadline February of each year.

[683]
GLADYS KAMAKAKUOKALANI AINOA BRANDT SCHOLARSHIPS
Ke Ali'i Pauahi Foundation
Attn: Financial Aid & Scholarship Services
567 South King Street, Suite 160
Honolulu, HI 96813
(808) 534-3966   Toll-free: (800) 842-4682, ext. 43966
Fax: (808) 534-3890   E-mail: scholarships@pauahi.org
Web: www.pauahi.org

Purpose To provide financial assistance to undergraduate and graduate students, especially those of Hawaiian descent, who are preparing for a career in education.
Eligibility This program is open to full-time juniors, seniors, and graduate students who are planning to enter the education profession. Applicants must have a GPA of 2.5 or higher and be able to demonstrate financial need. Preference is given to Native Hawaiians (descendants of the aboriginal inhabitants of the Hawaiian Islands prior to 1778) and current or former residents of Kaua'i.
Financial data A stipend is awarded (amount not specified).
Duration 1 year.
Number awarded Varies each year; recently, 3 of these scholarships were awarded.
Deadline April of each year.

[684]
GOLDMAN SACHS MBA FELLOWSHIP
Goldman, Sachs & Company
Attn: Human Capital Management
Diversity Recruiting
180 Maiden Lane, 23rd Floor
New York, NY 10038
(212) 855-6184   E-mail: martin.rodriguez@gs.com
Web: www2.goldmansachs.com

Purpose To provide financial assistance and work experience to Native American and other underrepresented minority students interested in working on an M.B.A. degree at designated universities.
Eligibility This program is open to graduate students of Black, Hispanic, and Native American descent. Applicants must be interested in working on an M.B.A. degree at Columbia University Business School, the Fuqua School of Business at Duke University, Harvard Business School, Sloan School of Management at Massachusetts Institute of Technology, the Kellogg School of Management at Northwestern University, Stanford Graduate School of Business, Anderson School of Management at the University of California at Los Angeles, University of Chicago Graduate School of Business, the Ross School of Business at the University of Michigan, or the Wharton School at the University of Pennsylvania. Along with their application, they must submit 2 essays of 500 words or less on the following topics: 1) their interest in preparing for a career in the investment banking industry; and 2) their current involvement with a community-based organization. Selection is based on analytical skills and the ability to identify significant problems, gather facts, and analyze situations in depth; interpersonal skills, including, but not limited to, poise, confidence, and professionalism; academic record; evidence of hard

work and commitment; ability to work well with others; and commitment to community involvement.
Financial data Fellows receive tuition for the first year of business school; a summer internship at a domestic office of Goldman Sachs; and (after successful completion of the summer internship and acceptance of an offer to return to the firm after graduation as a full-time regular employee) payment of tuition costs for the second year of business school.
Duration Up to 2 years.
Additional information This program was initiated in 1997.
Number awarded 1 or more each year.
Deadline April of each year.

[685]
GOLDMAN SACHS/MATSUO TAKABUKE COMMEMORATIVE SCHOLARSHIPS
Ke Ali'i Pauahi Foundation
Attn: Financial Aid & Scholarship Services
567 South King Street, Suite 160
Honolulu, HI 96813
(808) 534-3966   Toll-free: (800) 842-4682, ext. 43966
Fax: (808) 534-3890   E-mail: scholarships@pauahi.org
Web: www.pauahi.org
Purpose To provide financial assistance to students, especially Native Hawaiians, who are interested in working on a graduate degree in business.
Eligibility This program is open to graduate students working full time on a degree in business or other field related to financial services. Preference is given to Native Hawaiians (descendants of the aboriginal inhabitants of the Hawaiian Islands prior to 1778), current residents of Hawaii, and applicants who can demonstrate financial need.
Financial data A stipend is awarded (amount not specified).
Duration 1 year; may be renewed.
Additional information This program is sponsored by Goldman Sachs, a global investment banking and securities firm.
Number awarded Varies each year; recently, 5 of these scholarships were awarded.
Deadline April of each year.

[686]
GOODWIN PROCTER DIVERSITY FELLOWSHIPS
Goodwin Procter LLP
Attn: Legal Recruitment Coordinator
53 State Street
Boston, MA 02109
(617) 570-1645
E-mail: fellowships@goodwinprocter.com
Web: www.goodwinprocter.com
Purpose To provide financial assistance and work experience to Native American and other minority students at law schools anywhere in the country.
Eligibility This program is open to students of color entering their second year at a law school in any state. Applicants must actively express an interest in working in the sponsoring firm's summer program. If they are applying for the Goodwin MassMutual Diversity, they must express an interest in working with MassMutual's legal department in Springfield, Massachusetts for 2 weeks as part of the summer program and specializing in the investment or insurance business or in a legal focus to advance business objectives. Selection is based on academic performance, leadership abilities, involvement in minority student organizations, commitment to community service, interpersonal skills, other special achievements and honors, and interest in working with the firm during the summer.
Financial data The stipend is $15,000.
Duration 1 year; nonrenewable.
Additional information This program was established in 2005. In 2007, it added the Goodwin MassMutual Diversity Fellowship, created in conjunction with its long-standing client, Massachusetts Mutual Life Insurance Company (MassMutual). Summer positions are available at the firm's offices in Boston, Los Angeles, New York, Palo Alto, San Diego, San Francisco, and Washington, D.C.
Number awarded 5 each year, including 1 Goodwin MassMutual Diversity Fellowship.
Deadline October of each year.

[687]
GRAND PORTAGE SCHOLARSHIP PROGRAM
Grand Portage Tribal Council
Attn: Education Director
P.O. Box 428
Grand Portage, MN 55605
(218) 475-0121   Fax: (218) 475-2284
E-mail: gpeduc@boreal.org
Web: www.grandportage.com/tribal.html
Purpose To provide financial assistance for undergraduate or graduate study to Minnesota Chippewa Tribe members.
Eligibility Applicants must be an enrolled member of the Grand Portage Band of Chippewa or have a parent who is enrolled. They must be enrolled at or accepted for enrollment at an accredited training program or degree-granting college or university and have applied for all other forms of financial aid. Residents of states other than Minnesota are eligible only for college or university study, not for vocational training.
Financial data The amount of the award is based on the need of the recipient.
Duration 1 year; may be renewed for a total of 10 semesters or 15 quarters to complete a 4-year degree program if recipients maintain full-time enrollment and a GPA of 2.0 or higher. Adjustments are considered for part-time and/or graduate study.
Number awarded Varies each year.
Deadline At least 8 weeks before school starts.

[688]
GRAND TRAVERSE BAND HIGHER EDUCATION GRANTS

Grand Traverse Band of Ottawa and Chippewa Indians
Attn: Higher Education
845 Business Park Drive
Traverse City, MI 49686
(231) 534-7760   Toll-free: (866) 534-7760
Fax: (231) 534-7773
E-mail: joyce.wilson@gtbindians.com
Web: www.gtbindians.org/departments/index.html

Purpose To provide financial assistance to members of the Grand Traverse Band (GTB) of Ottawa and Chippewa Indians who are interested in attending college or graduate school in any state.

Eligibility This program is open to enrolled GTB members who are working on or planning to work on an associate, bachelor's, master's, or doctoral degree at a college or university in any state. Applicants must be able to document financial need. Along with their application, they must submit a personal statement on how they plan to serve their Indian community after they have successfully completed their course of study.

Financial data Stipends for associate degree students are $200 per credit hour, to a maximum of $4,800 per year; stipends for bachelor's degree students are $250 per credit hour, to a maximum of $6,000 per year; stipends for graduate students are $600 per credit hour, to a maximum of $7,200 per year.

Duration 1 semester; may be renewed as long as the recipient maintains a GPA of 2.0 or higher.

Number awarded Varies each year.

[689]
HANA SCHOLARSHIPS

United Methodist Church
Attn: General Board of Higher Education and Ministry
Office of Loans and Scholarships
1001 19th Avenue South
P.O. Box 340007
Nashville, TN 37203-0007
(615) 340-7344   Fax: (615) 340-7367
E-mail: umscholar@gbhem.org
Web: www.gbhem.org/loansandscholarships

Purpose To provide financial assistance to upper-division and graduate Methodist students who are of Hispanic, Asian, Native American, Alaska Native, or Pacific Islander ancestry.

Eligibility This program is open to full-time juniors, seniors, and graduate students at accredited colleges and universities in the United States who have been active, full members of a United Methodist Church (UMC) for at least 1 year prior to applying. Applicants must have at least 1 parent who is Hispanic, Asian, Native American, Alaska Native, or Pacific Islander. They must be able to demonstrate involvement in their Hispanic, Asian, or Native American (HANA) community in the UMC. Selection is based on that involvement, academic ability (GPA of at least 2.85 for undergraduates or 3.0 for graduate students) and financial need. U.S. citizenship or permanent resident status is required.

Financial data The maximum stipend is $3,000 for undergraduates or $5,000 for graduate students.

Duration 1 year; recipients may reapply.

Number awarded 50 each year.

Deadline March of each year.

[690]
HAWAIIAN CIVIC CLUB OF HONOLULU SCHOLARSHIP

Hawaiian Civic Club of Honolulu
Attn: Scholarship Committee
P.O. Box 1513
Honolulu, HI 96806
E-mail: newmail@hotbot.com
Web: www.hcchonolulu.org/scholarship

Purpose To provide financial assistance for undergraduate or graduate studies to persons of Hawaiian descent.

Eligibility Applicants must be of Hawaiian descent (descendants of the aboriginal inhabitants of the Hawaiian Islands prior to 1778), residents of Hawaii, able to demonstrate academic achievement, and enrolled or planning to enroll full time in an accredited 2-year college, 4-year college, or graduate school. Graduating seniors and current undergraduate students must have a GPA of 2.5 or higher; graduate students must have at least a 3.0 GPA. Along with their application, they must submit a 2-page essay on a topic that changes annually but relates to issues of concern to the Hawaiian community; a recent topic related to the leadership, cultural and governmental, of the Hawaiian community. Selection is based on the quality of the essay, academic standing, financial need, and the completeness of the application package.

Financial data The amount of the stipend varies. Scholarship checks are made payable to the recipient and the institution and are mailed to the college or university financial aid office. Funds may be used for tuition, fees, books, and other educational expenses.

Duration 1 year.

Additional information Recipients may attend school in Hawaii or on the mainland. Information on this program is also available from Ke Ali'i Pauahi Foundation, Attn: Financial Aid and Scholarship Services, 567 King Street, Suite 160, Honolulu, HI 96813, (808) 534-3966.

Number awarded Varies each year; recently, 54 of these scholarships, worth $34,800, were awarded.

Deadline May of each year.

[691]
HAWAIIAN HOMES COMMISSION SCHOLARSHIPS

Hawai'i Community Foundation
Attn: Scholarship Department
1164 Bishop Street, Suite 800
Honolulu, HI 96813
(808) 566-5570   Toll-free: (888) 731-3863
Fax: (808) 521-6286
E-mail: scholarships@hcf-hawaii.org
Web: www.hawaiicommunityfoundation.org

Purpose To provide financial assistance for undergraduate or graduate studies to persons of Hawaiian descent.

Eligibility Applicants must be 50% or more of Hawaiian descent (descendants of the aboriginal inhabitants of the

Hawaiian Islands prior to 1778) or a homestead lessee (at least 25% Hawaiian ancestry). They must be U.S. citizens, enrolled in full-time study in an undergraduate or graduate degree program, and able to demonstrate financial need and academic excellence. Undergraduates must have a GPA of 2.0 or higher. Graduate students must have a GPA of 3.0 or higher. Current Hawaiian residency is not required. Special consideration is given to applicants with exceptional academic merit and proven commitment to serving the Native Hawaiian community. Along with their application, they must submit a short statement indicating their reasons for attending college, their planned course of study, and their career goals. Selection is based on academic achievement, good moral character, and financial need.

Financial data The amounts of the awards depend on the availability of funds and the need of the recipient; recently, stipends averaged $2,014.

Duration 1 year.

Additional information This program is sponsored by the state Department of Hawaiian Home Lands.

Number awarded Varies each year; recently, 111 of these scholarships were awarded.

Deadline February of each year.

[692]
HAYNES/HETTING AWARD

Philanthrofund Foundation
Attn: Scholarship Committee
1409 Willow Street, Suite 305
Minneapolis, MN 55403-3251
(612) 870-1806   Toll-free: (800) 435-1402
Fax: (612) 871-6587   E-mail: info@PfundOnline.org
Web: www.philanthrofund.org/scholarships.html

Purpose To provide funds to African American and Native American Minnesota students who are associated with gay, lesbian, bisexual, and transgender (GLBT) activities.

Eligibility This program is open to residents of Minnesota and students attending a Minnesota educational institution who are African American or Native American. Applicants must be self-identified as GLBT or from a GLBT family. They may be attending or planning to attend trade school, technical college, college, or university (as an undergraduate or graduate student). Preference is given to graduating high school seniors. Selection is based on the applicant's 1) affirmation of GLBT identity or commitment to GLBT communities; 2) evidence of experience and skills in service and leadership; and 3) evidence of service and leadership in GLBT communities, including serving as a role model, mentor, and/or adviser.

Financial data The stipend is $2,000. Funds must be used for tuition, books, fees, or dissertation expenses.

Duration 1 year.

Number awarded 1 each year.

Deadline January of each year.

[693]
HO-CHUNK NATION HIGHER EDUCATION SCHOLARSHIPS

Ho-Chunk Nation
Attn: Higher Education Division
P.O. Box 667
Black River Falls, WI 54615
(715) 284-4915   Toll-free: (800) 362-4476
Fax: (715) 284-1760
E-mail: higher.education@ho-chunk.com
Web: www.ho-chunknation.com/?PageId=47

Purpose To provide financial assistance to undergraduate or graduate students who are enrolled members of the Ho-Chunk Nation.

Eligibility Applicants must be enrolled members of the Ho-Chunk Nation who have been accepted at an accredited college, university, or vocational college in the United States as an undergraduate or graduate student. Applicants must intend to attend a nonprofit institution that is accredited by a regional agency and by the U.S. Department of Education as eligible to receive student financial aid funds. If they are determined by their school's financial aid office to have no financial need, they are eligible to receive non-need grants. If their school determines that they have financial need, they are eligible for need-based grants. Funds are awarded with the expectation that graduates will return to the Ho-Chunk Nation to use their knowledge and expertise to protect and strengthen the economic self-sufficiency and sovereignty of the nation.

Financial data Non-need grants cover direct costs of tuition, required fees, and books, up to the maximum award. Need-based grants are capped at $7,000 per academic year for full-time undergraduates or $12,000 per academic year for full-time graduate students. Awards for part-time students per academic year are for direct costs (tuition, required fees, and books) not covered by another source, to a maximum of $4,500 for undergraduates or $9,000 for graduate students. Funds are paid directly to the recipient's school.

Duration 1 year. Support is limited to 10 semesters for undergraduates, 6 semesters for master's degree students, or 10 semesters for doctoral students. Undergraduates must maintain a GPA of 2.0 or higher and graduate students 3.0 or higher in order to continue receiving funds.

Number awarded Varies each year.

Deadline April of each year or 4 months before the start of the term.

[694]
HO-CHUNK NATION SUMMER TUITION ASSISTANCE

Ho-Chunk Nation
Attn: Higher Education Division
P.O. Box 667
Black River Falls, WI 54615
(715) 284-4915   Toll-free: (800) 362-4476
Fax: (715) 284-1760
E-mail: higher.education@ho-chunk.com
Web: www.ho-chunknation.com/?PageId=47

Purpose To provide financial assistance to Ho-Chunk undergraduate or graduate students who wish to continue their postsecondary studies during the summer.

Eligibility Applicants must be enrolled members of the Ho-Chunk Nation; have been accepted at an accredited public vocational or technical school, college, or university in the United States in an undergraduate or graduate program; and be interested in attending summer school on a full-time basis.
Financial data This program pays up to $2,500 to undergraduate recipients and up to $5,000 to graduate school recipients. Funds must be used for tuition, fees, or books. Funds are paid directly to the recipient's school.
Duration Summer months. May be renewed for a total of 6 summers of support.
Additional information Undergraduate recipients must earn a GPA of 2.0 or higher in the summer classes; graduate school recipients must earn 3.0 or higher.
Number awarded Varies each year.
Deadline The priority deadline is the end of April of each year.

[695]
HOLLY A. CORNELL SCHOLARSHIP
American Water Works Association
Attn: Scholarship Coordinator
6666 West Quincy Avenue
Denver, CO 80235-3098
(303) 347-6201   Toll-free: (800) 926-7337
Fax: (303) 795-7603   E-mail: lmoody@awwa.org
Web: www.awwa.org

Purpose To provide financial assistance to outstanding minority and female students interested in working on an advanced degree in the field of water supply and treatment.
Eligibility Minority and female students who anticipate completing the requirements for a master's degree in engineering no sooner than December of the following year are eligible. Students who have been accepted into graduate school but have not yet begun graduate study are encouraged to apply. Recipients of the Larson Aquatic Research Support (LARS) M.S. Scholarship are not eligible for this program. Selection is based on the quality of the applicant's academic record and the potential to provide leadership in the field of water supply and treatment.
Financial data The stipend is $5,000.
Duration 1 year; nonrenewable.
Additional information Funding for this program comes from the consulting firm CH2M Hill.
Number awarded 1 each year.
Deadline January of each year.

[696]
HOOPA TRIBAL EDUCATION ASSOCIATION HIGHER EDUCATION AWARDS
Hoopa Valley Tribe
Attn: Hoopa Tribal Education Association
P.O. Box 428
Hoopa, CA 95546-0428
(530) 625-4413   Fax: (530) 625-5444
E-mail: hoopaeducation@gmail.com
Web: www.hoopa-nsn.gov

Purpose To provide financial assistance to members of the Hoopa Tribe who are attending or planning to attend college or graduate school in any state.
Eligibility This program is open to enrolled members of the Hoopa Tribe who are attending or planning to attend an accredited college or university in any state. Applicants must intend to work full time on an undergraduate or graduate degree. They must be able to demonstrate financial need. Along with their application, they must submit an educational plan that outlines the course work required for completing their degree and an estimate of the time remaining until completion.
Financial data A stipend is awarded (amount not specified).
Duration 1 semester; may be renewed up to a total of 3 years for a 2-year degree, 5 years for a 4-year, or until completion of a graduate degree.
Number awarded Varies each year.
Deadline June of each year for fall semester or academic year; November of each year for winter quarter; December of each year for spring semester; March of each year for spring quarter; May of each year for summer session.

[697]
HOPI TRIBAL MEMBERS BIA HIGHER EDUCATION GRANTS
Hopi Tribe
Attn: Grants and Scholarship Program
P.O. Box 123
Kykotsmovi, AZ 86039
(928) 734-3533   Toll-free: (800) 762-9630
Fax: (928) 734-9575
E-mail: TLomakema@hopi.nsn.us
Web: www.hopi.nsn.us/education_htgsp.asp

Purpose To provide financial assistance to needy students of Hopi ancestry who are working on an undergraduate, graduate, or postgraduate degree.
Eligibility This program is open to students who are working on an associate, baccalaureate, graduate, or postgraduate degree. Applicants must be enrolled members of the Hopi Tribe. They must have a GPA of 2.5 or higher or a composite of 50% or higher on the GED and be able to demonstrate financial need.
Financial data The maximum grant is $2,500 per semester ($5,000 per year).
Duration 1 semester; may be renewed for up to 10 terms of undergraduate study or up to 5 terms of graduate study, provided the recipient maintains a GPA of 2.5 or higher as an undergraduate or 3.0 as a graduate student.
Additional information This grant is awarded as a secondary source of financial aid to eligible students who are also receiving aid from the Bureau of Indian Affairs (BIA) Higher Education program. Recipients must attend school on a full-time basis.
Number awarded Varies each year.
Deadline June of each year for fall or winter term; November of each year for spring term; March of each year for summer session.

[698]
HOPI TUITION/BOOK SCHOLARSHIPS
Hopi Tribe
Attn: Grants and Scholarship Program
P.O. Box 123
Kykotsmovi, AZ 86039
(928) 734-3533 Toll-free: (800) 762-9630
Fax: (928) 734-9575
E-mail: TLomakema@hopi.nsn.us
Web: www.hopi.nsn.us/education_htgsp.asp

Purpose To provide financial assistance to students of Hopi ancestry who are working on an undergraduate, graduate, or postgraduate degree.

Eligibility This program is open to students who are working on an associate, baccalaureate, graduate, or postgraduate degree. Applicants must be an enrolled member of the Hopi Tribe. They must be pursuing a postsecondary degree for at least 1 of the following reasons: personal growth, career enhancement, career change, and/or continuing education. Both full- and part-time students may apply. Financial need is not required, but students must have applied for federal aid before applying for this award.

Financial data The scholarship covers the cost of tuition, fees, and books.

Duration 1 year; may be renewed if the recipient maintains a cumulative GPA of 2.5 or higher.

Number awarded Varies each year.

Deadline June of each year for fall or winter term; November of each year for spring term; March of each year for summer session.

[699]
HOWARD HUGHES MEDICAL INSTITUTE RESEARCH TRAINING FELLOWSHIPS FOR MEDICAL STUDENTS
Howard Hughes Medical Institute
Attn: Office of Grants and Special Programs
4000 Jones Bridge Road
Chevy Chase, MD 20815-6789
(301) 215-8889 Toll-free: (800) 448-4882, ext. 8889
Fax: (301) 215-8888 E-mail: fellows@hhmi.org
Web: www.hhmi.org

Purpose To provide financial assistance to Native American and other medical, dental, and veterinary students interested in pursuing research training.

Eligibility Applicants must be enrolled in a medical, dental, or veterinary school in the United States, although they may be citizens of any country. They must describe a proposed research project to be conducted at an academic or nonprofit research institution in the United States, other than a facility of the National Institutes of Health in Bethesda, Maryland. Research proposals should reflect the interests of the Howard Hughes Medical Institute (HHMI), especially in biochemistry, bioinformatics, biomedical engineering, biophysics, biostatistics, cell biology, developmental biology, epidemiology, genetics, immunology, mathematical and computational biology, microbiology, molecular biology, neuroscience, pharmacology, physiology, structural biology, or virology. Applications from women and minorities underrepresented in the sciences (Blacks, Hispanics, American Indians, Native Alaskans, and Native Pacific Islanders) are especially encouraged. Students enrolled in M.D./Ph.D., Ph.D., or Sc.D. programs and those who have completed a Ph.D. or Sc.D. in a laboratory-based science are not eligible. Selection is based on the applicant's ability and promise for a research career as a physician-scientist and the quality of training that will be provided.

Financial data Fellows receive a stipend of $27,000 per year; their institution receives an institutional allowance of $5,500 and a research allowance of $5,500.

Duration 1 year.

Additional information This program complements the HHMI-NIH Research Scholars Program; students may not apply to both programs in the same year.

Number awarded Up to 66 each year.

Deadline January of each year.

[700]
HOWARD KECK/WESTMIN ENDOWMENT SCHOLARSHIP FUND
Cook Inlet Region, Inc.
Attn: The CIRI Foundation
3600 San Jeronimo Drive, Suite 256
Anchorage, AK 99508-2870
(907) 793-3575 Toll-free: (800) 764-3382
Fax: (907) 793-3585 E-mail: tcf@thecirifoundation.org
Web: www.thecirifoundation.org/designated.htm

Purpose To provide financial assistance for undergraduate or graduate studies to Alaska Natives who are original enrollees to Cook Inlet Region, Inc. (CIRI) and their lineal descendants.

Eligibility This program is open to Alaska Native enrollees to CIRI under the Alaska Native Claims Settlement Act (ANCSA) of 1971 and their lineal descendants. There are no Alaska residency requirements or age limitations. Applicants must be accepted or enrolled full time in a 2-year undergraduate, 4-year undergraduate, or graduate degree program. They may be studying in any field but must have a GPA of 2.5 or higher. Along with their application, they must submit a 500-word statement on their educational and career goals and how they are contributing, or planning to contribute, to a positive Alaska Native community. Selection is based on that statement, academic achievement, rigor of course work or degree program, student financial contribution, financial need, grade level, previous work performance, community service, and relationship of degree program to career goals.

Financial data The stipend is $20,000 per year, $10,000 per year, $8,000 per year, or $2,500 per semester, depending on GPA.

Duration 1 semester or 1 year.

Additional information This fund was established in 1986.

Number awarded Varies each year; recently, 5 of these scholarships were awarded.

Deadline May of each year for annual scholarships; May or November of each year for semester scholarships.

[701]
HOWARD MAYER BROWN FELLOWSHIP
American Musicological Society
6010 College Station
Brunswick, ME 04011-8451
(207) 798-4243 Toll-free: (877) 679-7648
Fax: (207) 798-4254 E-mail: ams@ams-net.org
Web: www.ams-net.org/hmb.php

Purpose To provide financial assistance to Native American and other minority students who are working on a doctoral degree in the field of musicology.

Eligibility This program is open to members of minority groups historically underrepresented in the field of musicology. In the United States, that includes African Americans, Native Americans, Hispanic Americans, and Asian Americans. In Canada, it refers to visible minorities. Applicants must have completed at least 1 year of academic work at an institution with a graduate program in musicology and be planning to complete a Ph.D. degree in the field. There are no restrictions on research area, age, or sex. Candidates must submit a personal statement summarizing their musical and academic background and stating why they wish to work on an advanced degree in musicology, letters of support from 3 faculty members, a curriculum vitae, and samples of their work (such as term papers or published material). U.S. or Canadian citizenship or permanent resident status is required.

Financial data The stipend is $17,000.
Duration 1 year; nonrenewable.
Additional information This fellowship was first awarded in 1995. Information is also available from Martha Feldman, E-mail: rore@uchicago.edu.
Number awarded 1 each year.
Deadline January of each year.

[702]
HOWARD ROCK FOUNDATION GRADUATE SCHOLARSHIP PROGRAM
Cook Inlet Region, Inc.
Attn: The CIRI Foundation
3600 San Jeronimo Drive, Suite 256
Anchorage, AK 99508-2870
(907) 793-3575 Toll-free: (800) 764-3382
Fax: (907) 793-3585 E-mail: tcf@thecirifoundation.org
Web: www.thecirifoundation.org/designated.htm

Purpose To provide financial assistance for graduate study to Alaska Natives and their lineal descendants.

Eligibility This program is open to Alaska Natives who are original enrollees or lineal descendants of a regional or village corporation under the Alaska Native Claims Settlement Act (ANCSA) of 1971 or a member of a tribal organization or other Native organization. The corporation or other Native organization with which the applicant is affiliated must be a current member of Alaska Village Initiatives, Inc. Applicants must have a GPA of 3.0 or higher and must be able to demonstrate financial need. They must be accepted or enrolled full time in a graduate degree program. Along with their application, they must submit a 500-word statement on their educational and career goals and how they are contributing, or planning to contribute, to a positive Alaska Native community.

Financial data The stipend is $5,000 per year. Funds are to be used for tuition, university fees, books, course-required supplies, and (for students who must live away from their permanent home in order to attend college) room and board. Checks are made payable to the student and the university and are sent directly to the student's university.
Duration 1 year.
Additional information This program, established in 1986, is funded by Alaska Village Initiatives, Inc. The CIRI Foundation assumed its administration in 1999.
Number awarded Varies each year.
Deadline March of each year.

[703]
HUALAPAI GRADUATE STUDENT GRANTS
Hualapai Nation Education Office
Attn: Education and Training Department
460 Hualapai Way
P.O. Box 179
Peach Springs, AZ 86434-0179
(928) 769-2216 Fax: (928) 769-2243
Web: www.hualapai-nsn.gov

Purpose To provide financial assistance to members of the Hualapai Tribe who are interested in working on a graduate degree.

Eligibility This program is open to enrolled members of the Hualapai Tribe who are working full time on a graduate degree in any area. Financial need is considered in the selection process.

Financial data Up to $13,000 per year.
Duration 1 year; may be renewed.
Number awarded Varies each year.
Deadline June of each year for fall term and November of each year for spring term.

[704]
HUNA HERITAGE FOUNDATION EDUCATION ASSISTANCE PROGRAM
Huna Heritage Foundation
Attn: Education Programs
9301 Glacier Highway, Suite 210
Juneau, AK 99801
(907) 523-3682 Toll-free: (800) 428-8298
Fax: (907) 789-1896 E-mail: kmiller@hunaheritage.org
Web: www.hunaheritage.org/education.html

Purpose To provide financial assistance to Huna Totem shareholders and their descendants who are attending or planning to attend college or graduate school in any state.

Eligibility This program is open to Huna Totem shareholders and descendants who have a high school diploma or GED certificate. Applicants must be accepted by or attending a college or university in any state as a full-time undergraduate or graduate student. Internships, apprenticeships, and on-the-job training may also be funded. Students must have applied to other programs before they apply for this assistance. Proof of awards or denial by other programs must be supplied.

Financial data Stipends range up to $2,000 per year. Funding is intended to help pay for whatever costs other grant programs do not cover.
Duration 1 year; recipients may reapply.

Number awarded Varies each year; recently, 19 of these scholarships were awarded for the fall semester and 29 for the spring semester.
Deadline October of each year for first or second quarter or fall semester; January of each year for third or fourth quarter or spring or summer semester.

[705]
IBM PHD FELLOWSHIP PROGRAM
IBM Corporation
Attn: University Relations
1133 Westchester Avenue
White Plains, NY 10604
Toll-free: (800) IBM-4YOU   TTY: (800) IBM-3383
E-mail: phdfellow@us.ibm.com
Web: www-304.ibm.com

Purpose To provide funding and work experience to Native American and other students working on a Ph.D. in a research area of broad interest to IBM.
Eligibility Students nominated for this fellowship should be enrolled full time at an accredited college or university and should have completed at least 1 year of graduate study in the following fields: business sciences (including financial services, communication, and learning/knowledge); computer science and engineering; electrical and mechanical engineering; management; mathematical sciences (including optimization); physical sciences (including chemistry, materials sciences, and physics); or service sciences. They should be planning a career in research. Nominations must be made by a faculty member and endorsed by the department head. The program values diversity, and encourages nominations of women, minorities, and others who contribute to that diversity. Selection is based on the applicants' potential for research excellence, the degree to which their technical interests align with those of IBM, and academic progress to date.
Financial data Fellowships pay tuition, fees, and a stipend of $17,500 per year.
Duration 1 year; may be renewed up to 2 additional years, provided the recipient is renominated, interacts with IBM's technical community, and demonstrates continued progress and achievement.
Additional information Recipients are offered an internship at 1 of the IBM Research Division laboratories and are given an IBM computer.
Number awarded Varies each year; recently, 57 of these scholarships were awarded.
Deadline October of each year.

[706]
IDA M. POPE MEMORIAL TRUST SCHOLARSHIPS
Hawai'i Community Foundation
Attn: Scholarship Department
1164 Bishop Street, Suite 800
Honolulu, HI 96813
(808) 566-5570   Toll-free: (888) 731-3863
Fax: (808) 521-6286
E-mail: scholarships@hcf-hawaii.org
Web: www.hawaiicommunityfoundation.org

Purpose To provide financial assistance to Native Hawaiian women who are interested in working on an undergraduate or graduate degree.
Eligibility This program is open to female residents of Hawaii who are Native Hawaiian, defined as a descendant of the aboriginal inhabitants of the Hawaiian islands prior to 1778. Applicants must be enrolled in an accredited associate, bachelor's, or graduate degree program. They must be able to demonstrate academic achievement (GPA of 3.0 or higher), good moral character, and financial need. Along with their application, they must submit a short statement indicating their reasons for attending college, their planned course of study, and their career goals.
Financial data The amounts of the awards depend on the availability of funds and the need of the recipient; recently, stipends averaged $1,000.
Duration 1 year; may be renewed.
Number awarded Varies each year; recently, 61 of these scholarships were awarded.
Deadline February of each year.

[707]
INTEL SCHOLARSHIP
Society of Women Engineers
Attn: Scholarship Selection Committee
230 East Ohio Street, Suite 400
Chicago, IL 60611-3265
(312) 596-5223   Toll-free: (877) SWE-INFO
Fax: (312) 644-8557
E-mail: scholarshipapplication@swe.org
Web: societyofwomenengineers.swe.org

Purpose To provide financial assistance to Native American and other women working on a graduate degree in computer science or specified fields of engineering.
Eligibility This program is open to women working on a graduate degree in computer science or chemical, computer, electrical, industrial, manufacturing, materials, or mechanical engineering. Applicants must have a GPA of 3.5 or higher. Selection is based on merit. Preference is given to members of groups underrepresented in computer science and engineering.
Financial data The stipend is $1,000.
Duration 1 year.
Number awarded 3 each year.
Deadline May of each year.

[708]
IWALANI CARPENTER SOWA SCHOLARSHIP
Ke Ali'i Pauahi Foundation
Attn: Financial Aid & Scholarship Services
567 South King Street, Suite 160
Honolulu, HI 96813
(808) 534-3966   Toll-free: (800) 842-4682, ext. 43966
Fax: (808) 534-3890   E-mail: scholarships@pauahi.org
Web: www.pauahi.org

Purpose To provide financial assistance to graduate students, especially Native Hawaiians, who are preparing for a career in Protestant Christian ministry.
Eligibility This program is open to graduate students working full time on a degree that will prepare them for a career in Protestant Christian ministry. Applicants must express a desire to minister in Hawaii. Preference is given

to Native Hawaiians (descendants of the aboriginal inhabitants of the Hawaiian Islands prior to 1778), graduates of Kamehameha Schools, and applicants who can demonstrate financial need.
Financial data A stipend is awarded (amount not specified).
Duration 1 year; may be renewed.
Number awarded 1 or more each year.
Deadline April of each year.

[709]
J. ROBERT GLADDEN SOCIETY RESIDENT SCHOLARSHIPS
J. Robert Gladden Society
6300 North River Road, Suite 727
Rosemont, IL 60018-4226
(847) 698-1633   Fax: (847) 823-4921
E-mail: swift@aaos.org
Web: www.gladdensociety.org

Purpose To provide funding to Native American and other underrepresented minority orthopedic residents who are studying for their qualifying examinations.
Eligibility This program is open to members of underrepresented minority groups (African Americans, Pacific Islanders, Mexicans, Puerto Ricans, Native Americans) who are PGY 5 residents in accredited orthopedic programs. Applicants must be members of the J. Robert Gladden Society (JRGS) or recommended by a member. They must be interested in participating in a review course in preparation for their certifying examinations.
Financial data The grant is $1,000.
Duration Grants are awarded annually.
Number awarded 10 each year.
Deadline March of each year.

[710]
JALENE KANANI BELL 'OHANA SCHOLARSHIP
Ke Ali'i Pauahi Foundation
Attn: Financial Aid & Scholarship Services
567 South King Street, Suite 160
Honolulu, HI 96813
(808) 534-3966   Toll-free: (800) 842-4682, ext. 43966
Fax: (808) 534-3890   E-mail: scholarships@pauahi.org
Web: www.pauahi.org

Purpose To provide financial assistance to undergraduate and graduate students from Hawaii, especially those of Hawaiian descent, working on a degree in Hawaiian language.
Eligibility This program is open to full- and part-time undergraduate and graduate students who are residents of Hawaii. Applicants must be able to demonstrate financial need; interest in the Hawaiian, language, culture, and history; and a GPA of 2.5 or higher. Along with their application, they must submit an essay of 1 to 2 pages on their personal, community, and volunteer experiences; future goals; and source of their inspiration and strength. Preference is given to Native Hawaiians (descendants of the aboriginal inhabitants of the Hawaiian Islands prior to 1778).
Financial data A stipend is awarded (amount not specified).
Duration 1 year.
Number awarded 1 or more each year.
Deadline April each year.

[711]
JAMES D. VOELKER FOUNDATION NATIVE AMERICAN SCHOLARSHIP
James D. Voelker Foundation
P.O. Box 15222
Lansing, MI 48901-5222
Web: www.voelkerfdn.org/Scholarships.asp

Purpose To provide financial assistance to students enrolled in Wisconsin or Michigan tribes who live in any state and are interested in pursuing a legal education.
Eligibility This program is open to students who are enrolled members of a federally-recognized Michigan or Wisconsin tribe (applicants may live in any state) and are interested in studying law and working toward a career that will benefit Native American people. Applicants do not need to be currently enrolled in law school, but if they apply as undergraduates they must ultimately intend to attend law school. Selection is based on academic achievements and financial need (preference is given to applicants with the greatest need).
Financial data The amount awarded varies annually; recently, the scholarships were at least $4,000 each.
Duration 1 year.
Additional information Recipients must provide an annual report on their progress.
Number awarded 1 or more each year.

[712]
JO MORSE SCHOLARSHIP
Alaska Library Association
Attn: Scholarship Committee
c/o Alaska State Library
P.O. Box 110571
Juneau, AK 99811-0571
(907) 465-2458   Fax: (907) 465-2665
E-mail: aja_razumny@alaska.gov
Web: www.akla.org/scholarships/index.html

Purpose To provide financial assistance to Alaska Natives and other residents who are interested in working on a certificate in school librarianship and, upon graduation, working in a school library in Alaska.
Eligibility This program is open to Alaska residents who hold a State of Alaska teaching certificate. Applicants must be eligible for acceptance or currently enrolled in a graduate school library media specialist certificate program during the academic year, semester, or quarter for which the scholarship is awarded and be willing to make a commitment to work in an Alaska school library for at least 1 year after graduation as a paid employee or volunteer. Preference is given to applicants meeting the federal definition of Alaska Native ethnicity. Selection is based on financial need, demonstrated scholastic ability and writing skills, an essay on professional goals and objectives in pursuing a library media specialist certificate, and 3 letters of recommendation (at least 1 of which must be from a librarian).
Financial data The stipend is $3,000.
Duration 1 year.
Number awarded 1 each year.

Deadline January of each year.

[713]
JOHN AND MURIEL LANDIS SCHOLARSHIPS
American Nuclear Society
Attn: Scholarship Coordinator
555 North Kensington Avenue
La Grange Park, IL 60526-5592
(708) 352-6611   Toll-free: (800) 323-3044
Fax: (708) 352-0499   E-mail: outreach@ans.org
Web: www.ans.org/honors/scholarships

Purpose To provide financial assistance to Native American and other undergraduate or graduate students who are interested in preparing for a career in nuclear-related fields.

Eligibility This program is open to undergraduate and graduate students at colleges or universities located in the United States who are preparing for, or planning to prepare for, a career in nuclear science, nuclear engineering, or a nuclear-related field. Qualified high school seniors are also eligible. Applicants must have greater than average financial need and have experienced circumstances that render them disadvantaged. They must be sponsored by an organization (e.g., plant branch, local section, student section) within the American Nuclear Society (ANS). Along with their application, they must submit an essay on their academic and professional goals, experiences that have affected those goals, and other relevant information. Selection is based on that essay, academic achievement, letters of recommendation, and financial need. Women and members of minority groups are especially urged to apply. U.S. citizenship is not required.

Financial data The stipend is $4,000, to be used to cover tuition, books, fees, room, and board.

Duration 1 year; nonrenewable.

Number awarded Up to 8 each year.

Deadline January of each year.

[714]
JOHN C. ROUILLARD AND ALICE TONEMAH MEMORIAL SCHOLARSHIPS
National Indian Education Association
Attn: Awards Committee
110 Maryland Avenue, N.E., Suite 104
Washington, DC 20002
(202) 544-7290   Fax: (202) 544-7293
E-mail: niea@niea.org
Web: www.niea.org

Purpose To provide financial assistance for college or graduate school to members of the National Indian Education Association (NIEA).

Eligibility This program is open to American Indians, Native Hawaiians, and Alaska Natives working full time on an associate, bachelor's, master's, or doctoral degree. Applicants must be members of NIEA and be nominated by a member. They must have demonstrated leadership qualities, maintained high academic achievement, served as a role model for other students, and shown creativity or commitment in the following areas: 1) promoted an understanding and an appreciation of Native American culture in an educational setting; 2) demonstrated positive, active leadership in student affairs; 3) demonstrated and/or encouraged student involvement in educational or community activities; and/or 4) achieved their educational goals and objectives.

Financial data Stipends range from $1,000 to $2,500. Funds may be used for educational expenses not covered by other sources.

Duration 1 year.

Number awarded 1 or more each year.

Deadline September of each year.

[715]
JOHN MCLENDON MEMORIAL MINORITY POSTGRADUATE SCHOLARSHIP AWARD
National Association of Collegiate Directors of Athletics
Attn: NACDA Foundation
24651 Detroit Road
P.O. Box 16428
Cleveland, OH 44116-0426
(440) 892-4000   Fax: (440) 892-4007
E-mail: mclendon@nacda.com
Web: nacda.cstv.com

Purpose To provide financial assistance to Native American and other minority college seniors who are interested in working on a graduate degree in athletics administration.

Eligibility This program is open to minority college students who are seniors, are attending school on a full-time basis, have a GPA of 3.0 or higher, intend to attend graduate school to earn a degree in athletics administration, and are involved in college or community activities. Also eligible are college graduates who have at least 2 years' experience in an athletics administration or a sports business-related position. Students planning to work on an M.B.A. degree with a sports specialization may be eligible. All candidates must be nominated by an official of a member institution of the National Association of Collegiate Directors of Athletics (NACDA).

Financial data The stipend is $10,000.

Duration 1 year.

Additional information Recipients must maintain full-time status during the senior year to retain their eligibility. They must attend NACDA-member institutions.

Number awarded 6 each year.

Deadline Nominations must be submitted by June of each year.

[716]
JOHN N. COLBERG ENDOWMENT SCHOLARSHIP FUND
Cook Inlet Region, Inc.
Attn: The CIRI Foundation
3600 San Jeronimo Drive, Suite 256
Anchorage, AK 99508-2870
(907) 793-3575   Toll-free: (800) 764-3382
Fax: (907) 793-3585 E-mail: tcf@thecirifoundation.org
Web: www.thecirifoundation.org/designated.htm

Purpose To provide financial assistance for undergraduate or graduate studies leading to a career in the law to Alaska Natives who are original enrollees to Cook Inlet Region, Inc. (CIRI) and their lineal descendants.

Eligibility This program is open to Alaska Native enrollees to CIRI under the Alaska Native Claims Settlement Act (ANCSA) of 1971 and their lineal descendants. There are no

Alaska residency requirements or age limitations. Applicants must be accepted or enrolled full time in a 4-year undergraduate or a graduate degree program. Preference is given to students who are working on a degree leading to the study of law and have a GPA of 2.5 or higher. Along with their application, they must submit a 500-word statement on their educational and career goals and how they are contributing, or planning to contribute, to a positive Alaska Native community. Selection is based on that statement, academic achievement, rigor of course work or degree program, student financial contribution, financial need, grade level, previous work performance, community service, and relationship of degree program to career goals.
Financial data The stipend is $10,000 per year, $8,000 per year, or $2,500 per semester, depending on GPA.
Duration 1 semester or 1 year.
Additional information This program was established in 2003.
Number awarded 1 or more each year.
Deadline May of each year for annual scholarships; May or November of each year for semester scholarships.

[717]
JOHN SHURR JOURNALISM AWARD
Cherokee Nation
Attn: Cherokee Nation Education Corporation
17675 South Muskogee Avenue
P.O. Box 948
Tahlequah, OK 74465
(918) 453-5420   Toll-free: (800) 256-0671 (within OK)
Fax: (918) 458-6195   E-mail: cnec@cherokee.org
Web: www.cherokee.org

Purpose To provide financial assistance to citizens of the Cherokee Nation who are enrolled at a college or university in any state and working on an undergraduate or graduate degree in journalism.
Eligibility This program is open to citizens of the Cherokee Nation who are currently enrolled in an undergraduate or graduate program in journalism or mass communications at a college or university in any state. Applicants must have a GPA of 3.0 or higher. They are not required to reside in the Cherokee Nation area. Along with their application, they must submit a 1-page essay on how their background and interests make them want to be a modern journalist storyteller, what they hope to learn in college about journalism, what they want to accomplish with a career in the news business, and how their Cherokee heritage will come into play for those issues. Financial need is also considered in the selection process.
Financial data The stipend is $1,000 per semester ($2,000 per year).
Duration 1 year.
Additional information Recipients are expected to apply for an 8-week paid internship with *The Cherokee Phoenix* newspaper in Tahlequah, Oklahoma during the summer following their scholarship year.
Number awarded 1 each year.
Deadline Applications are accepted until the scholarship is awarded.

[718]
JOHN STANFORD MEMORIAL SCHOLARSHIP
Washington Library Media Association
P.O. Box 50194
Bellevue, WA 98015-0194
E-mail: wlma@earthlink.net
Web: www.wlma.org/scholarships

Purpose To provide financial assistance to Native Americans and other ethnic minorities from any state who are interested in preparing for a library media career in Washington.
Eligibility This program is open to students who are working toward a library media endorsement or graduate degree in Washington state. Applicants must be members of an ethnic minority group. They must be working or planning to work in a school library. Along with their application, they must submit documentation of financial need and a description of themselves that includes their plans for the future, interest in librarianship, and plans for further education.
Financial data The stipend is $1,000.
Duration 1 year.
Additional information Information is also available from Linda Riesterer, Scholarship Chair, 1800 Pitcher Canyon Road, Wenatchee, WA 98801.
Number awarded 1 each year.
Deadline April of each year.

[719]
JOSEPH K. LUMSDEN MEMORIAL SCHOLARSHIP
Sault Tribe of Chippewa Indians
Attn: Higher Education Department
Two Ice Circle
Sault Ste. Marie, MI 49783
(906) 635-7784   Toll-free: (800) 793-0660
Fax: (906) 635-7785   E-mail: jlewton@saulttribe.net
Web: www.saulttribe.com

Purpose To provide financial assistance to members of the Sault Tribe in Michigan who are upper-division or graduate students.
Eligibility This program is open to members of the Sault Tribe who are college juniors or higher and are one-quarter Indian blood quantum or more. Applicants must be attending an accredited Michigan 4-year public college or university on a full-time basis and have a cumulative GPA of 3.0 or higher. They must be able to demonstrate financial need.
Financial data The stipend is $1,000 per year.
Duration 1 year; may be renewed.
Number awarded 1 each year.
Deadline May of each year.

[720]
JOSEPH NAWAHI SCHOLARSHIP
Ke Ali'i Pauahi Foundation
Attn: Financial Aid & Scholarship Services
567 South King Street, Suite 160
Honolulu, HI 96813
(808) 534-3966   Toll-free: (800) 842-4682, ext. 43966
Fax: (808) 534-3890   E-mail: scholarships@pauahi.org
Web: www.pauahi.org

Purpose To provide financial assistance to graduate students at universities in Hawaii, especially those of Hawaiian descent, who are working on a degree in designated fields.

Eligibility This program is open to full-time graduate students at colleges and universities in Hawaii. Applicants must be working on a degree in Hawaiian studies, Hawaiian politics, law (specific to Hawaiian legal issues), or communications journalism (specific to Hawaiian history, culture, and politics). Applicants must have a GPA of 3.2 or higher and be able to demonstrate financial need. Along with their application, they must submit an essay describing their plan to maximize the potential of young people through communication as well as to demonstrate their leadership potential in the community. Preference is given to Native Hawaiians (descendants of the aboriginal inhabitants of the Hawaiian Islands prior to 1778).

Financial data A stipend is awarded (amount not specified).

Duration 1 year.

Additional information This program began in 2008.

Number awarded 1 or more each year.

Deadline April of each year.

[721]
JUANITA CORWIN SCHOLARSHIPS
Central Council, Tlingit and Haida Indian Tribes of Alaska
Attn: Higher Education Services
3239 Hospital Drive
Juneau, AK 99801
(907) 463-7375   Toll-free: (800) 344-1432, ext. 7375
Fax: (907) 463-7321
Web: www.hied.org

Purpose To provide financial assistance for undergraduate and graduate studies to enrolled Tlingit or Haida tribal members.

Eligibility This program is open to both undergraduate and graduate students. Applicants must be Tlingit or Haida tribal members, regardless of service area, community affiliation, origination, residence, tribal compact, or signatory status. They must have a GPA of 3.0 or higher and be attending (or planning to attend) school on a full-time basis. Selection is based on financial need, a statement of personal goals, and a list of academic, professional, and/or personal activities.

Financial data The stipend is $1,000.

Duration 1 year.

Number awarded 3 each year: 1 to a graduating high school senior, 1 to a current undergraduate student, and 1 to a current graduate student.

Deadline September of each year.

[722]
JUDITH MCMANUS PRICE SCHOLARSHIPS
American Planning Association
Attn: Leadership Affairs Associate
122 South Michigan Avenue, Suite 1600
Chicago, IL 60603-6107
(312) 431-9100   Fax: (312) 431-9985
E-mail: fellowship@planning.org
Web: www.planning.org/institutions/scholarship.htm

Purpose To provide financial assistance to women and underrepresented minority students enrolled in undergraduate or graduate degree programs at recognized planning schools.

Eligibility This program is open to undergraduate and graduate students in urban and regional planning who are women or members of the following minority groups: African American, Hispanic American, or Native American. Applicants must be citizens of the United States and able to document financial need. They must intend to work as practicing planners in the public sector. Along with their application, they must submit a 2- to 5-page personal statement describing how their education will be applied to career goals and why they chose planning as a career path. Selection is based (in order of importance) on 1) commitment to planning as reflected in the personal statement and resume; 2) academic achievement and/or improvement during the past 2 years; 3) letters of recommendation; 4) financial need; and 5) professional presentation.

Financial data Stipends range from $2,000 to $4,000 per year. The money may be applied to tuition and living expenses only. Payment is made to the recipient's university and divided by terms in the school year.

Duration 1 year; recipients may reapply.

Additional information This program was established in 2002.

Number awarded Varies each year; recently, 2 of these scholarships were awarded.

Deadline April of each year.

[723]
KAW NATION GRADUATE PROGRAM
Kaw Nation
Attn: Education and Social Services Department
P.O. Box 50
Kaw City, OK 74641
(580) 269-1186   Fax: (580) 269-2116
E-mail: khowe@kawnation.com
Web: www.kawnation.com/Programs/edsvcs.html

Purpose To provide financial assistance for graduate school to members of the Kaw Nation who can demonstrate need.

Eligibility This program is open to Kaw tribal members who are working on or planning to work on a graduate degree. Applicants must be able to demonstrate financial need and be eligible for other types of assistance, such as loans.

Financial data A stipend is awarded (amount not specified).

Duration 1 year; may be renewed.

Number awarded Varies each year.

Deadline May of each year for fall semester; October of each year for spring semester.

[724]
KENAI NATIVES ASSOCIATION SCHOLARSHIP AND GRANT FUND

Cook Inlet Region, Inc.
Attn: The CIRI Foundation
3600 San Jeronimo Drive, Suite 256
Anchorage, AK 99508-2870
(907) 793-3575   Toll-free: (800) 764-3382
Fax: (907) 793-3585   E-mail: tcf@thecirifoundation.org
Web: www.thecirifoundation.org

Purpose To provide financial assistance for undergraduate or graduate studies to Alaska Natives who are original enrollees of the Kenai Natives Association (KNA) and their lineal descendants.

Eligibility This program is open to Alaska Native enrollees of KNA under the Alaska Native Claims Settlement Act (ANCSA) of 1971 and their lineal descendants. There are no Alaska residency requirements or age limitations. Applicants must be accepted or enrolled full time in a 2-year, 4-year, or graduate degree program or technical skills training program. They must have a GPA of 2.5 or higher. Along with their application, they must submit a 500-word statement on their educational and career goals and how they are contributing, or planning to contribute, to a positive Alaska Native community. Selection is based on that statement, academic achievement, rigor of course work or degree program, student financial contribution, financial need, grade level, previous work performance, community service, and relationship of degree program to career goals.

Financial data The stipend depends on the availability of funds.

Duration 1 semester; recipients must reapply each semester.

Additional information This program was established in 1989. Funds are provided by the KNA and the Tanaina Corporation with matching funds from the CIRI Foundation.

Number awarded 1 or more each year.

Deadline May or November of each year.

[725]
KENAITZE INDIAN TRIBE HIGHER EDUCATION SCHOLARSHIP PROGRAM

Kenaitze Indian Tribe
P.O. Box 988
Kenai, AK 99611
(907) 283-3633   Fax: (907) 283-3052
E-mail: education@kenaitze.org
Web: www.kenaitze.org/education/index.html

Purpose To provide financial assistance to members of recognized Native Alaskan Tribes who plan to attend college or graduate school in any state.

Eligibility This program is open to members of federally-recognized tribes and Native Alaskans of at least one-quarter degree blood. Applicants must be enrolled or planning to enroll full time at a college or university in any state and work on a baccalaureate degree. They are also expected to apply for federal financial aid through the FAFSA. Along with their application, they must submit a letter on their goals and educational plans, verification of Indian ancestry (CIB or tribal card), a letter of acceptance to the school they plan to attend, transcripts, a completed FAFSA application, and an Alaska driver's license. Limited support may be provided to graduate students if funds are available.

Financial data The amount awarded varies, depending upon the available funds and the recipient's unmet needs. Funds are paid directly to the educational institution.

Duration 1 year; may be renewed if the recipient maintains a GPA of 2.5 of higher.

Additional information This program is funded by the U.S. Bureau of Indian Affairs.

Number awarded Varies each year.

Deadline May of each year for fall; November of each year for spring or winter.

[726]
KIRBY MCDONALD EDUCATION ENDOWMENT SCHOLARSHIP FUND

Cook Inlet Region, Inc.
Attn: The CIRI Foundation
3600 San Jeronimo Drive, Suite 256
Anchorage, AK 99508-2870
(907) 793-3575   Toll-free: (800) 764-3382
Fax: (907) 793-3585   E-mail: tcf@thecirifoundation.org
Web: www.thecirifoundation.org/designated.htm

Purpose To provide financial assistance for undergraduate or graduate studies to Alaska Natives who are original enrollees to Cook Inlet Region, Inc. (CIRI) and their lineal descendants.

Eligibility This program is open to Alaska Native enrollees to CIRI under the Alaska Native Claims Settlement Act (ANCSA) of 1971 and their lineal descendants. There are no Alaska residency requirements or age limitations. Applicants must be accepted or enrolled full time in a 4-year undergraduate or a graduate degree program. Preference is given to students in the culinary arts, but students in business administration and engineering are also eligible. They must have a GPA of 2.5 or higher. Along with their application, they must submit a 500-word statement on their educational and career goals and how they are contributing, or planning to contribute, to a positive Alaska Native community. Selection is based on that statement, academic achievement, rigor of course work or degree program, student financial contribution, financial need, grade level, previous work performance, community service, and relationship of degree program to career goals.

Financial data The stipend is $10,000 per year, $8,000 per year, or $2,500 per semester, depending on GPA.

Duration 1 semester or 1 year.

Additional information This program was established in 1991.

Number awarded 1 or more each year.

Deadline May of each year for annual scholarships; May or November of each year for semester scholarships.

[727]
K&L GATES DIVERSITY FELLOWSHIP

Kirkpatrick & Lockhart Preston Gates Ellis LLP
Attn: Recruiting Coordinator
925 Fourth Avenue, Suite 2900
Seattle, WA 98104
(206) 623-7580
Web: www.klgates.com/lawstudents/studentsdiversity

Purpose To provide financial assistance and summer work experience (in Seattle) to Native American or other minority law students from any state.

Eligibility This program is open to first-year students at ABA-accredited law schools in the United States. Applicants must be Native American or members of other minority racial and ethnic groups.

Financial data Fellows receive a paid associateship with the Seattle office of the sponsoring firm during the summer following their first year of law school and an academic scholarship of $7,500 for their second year of law school.

Duration 1 year.

Number awarded 2 each year: 1 for a law student nationally and 1 for a student at the University of Washington School of Law.

Deadline January of each year.

[728]
KONIAG EDUCATION FOUNDATION ACADEMIC ACHIEVEMENT/GRADUATE SCHOLARSHIPS

Koniag Incorporated
Attn: Koniag Education Foundation
6927 Old Seward Highway, Suite 103
Anchorage, AK 99518-2283
(907) 562-9093   Toll-free: (888) 562-9093
Fax: (907) 562-9023   E-mail: kef@alaska.com
Web: www.koniageducation.org/KEFScholarship.html

Purpose To provide financial assistance to Alaska Natives with ties to the Koniag region who plan to attend college or graduate school in any state.

Eligibility This program is open to high school seniors, high school and GED graduates, college students, and graduate students who are Alaska Native shareholders of the Koniag region or descendants of those original enrollees. Applicants must supply proof of eligibility and documentation of financial need. They must have a GPA of 3.0 or higher and be enrolled or planning to enroll at a college or university in any state. Along with their application, they must submit a 300- to 600-word letter that includes their personal and family history, their schooling, and their educational and life goals.

Financial data Stipends range up to $2,500 per year. Funds are sent directly to the recipient's school and may be used for tuition, books, supplies, room, board, and transportation.

Duration 1 year; may be renewed, provided recipients maintain a GPA of 3.0 or higher.

Additional information The Koniag Education Foundation was established in 1993 by the directors of Koniag, Inc. The Koniag region covers Kodiak Island, many smaller islands, and a portion of the Alaska Peninsula.

Number awarded Varies each year.

Deadline March of each year for summer term; May of each year for fall or spring term.

[729]
KUSKOKWIM EDUCATIONAL FOUNDATION GENERAL SCHOLARSHIPS

The Kuskokwim Corporation
Attn: Kuskokwim Educational Foundation, Inc.
P.O. Box 227
Aniak, AK 99557
(907) 675-4275   Toll-free: (800) 478-4275 (within AK)
Fax: (907) 675-4276   E-mail: dg@kuskokwim.com
Web: www.kuskokwim.com

Purpose To provide financial assistance for college or graduate school to Native people and their descendants with ties to The Kuskokwim Corporation (TKC) region.

Eligibility This program is open to Native people and their descendants from The Kuskokwim Corporation region in Alaska. Applicants may be high school seniors, high school graduates, currently-enrolled college students, college graduates, or graduate students. They must be interested in attending school on a full-time basis. Along with their application, they must submit a letter or essay describing their talents, special interests, accomplishments, educational objectives, reasons for selecting those objectives, and progress toward achieving those objectives; documentation of financial need; transcripts; and 2 letters of recommendation.

Financial data Stipends range from $100 to $1,500 per year. Funds are sent to the recipient's school in 2 equal installments.

Duration 1 year; may be renewed if the recipient maintains full-time enrollment and a GPA of 2.0 or higher as an undergraduate, a GPA of 3.0 or higher as a graduate student, or satisfactory progress as a vocational student.

Additional information Recipients may use the funds for college and university courses, vocational and continuing education, student exchange programs, and other educational opportunities approved by the board.

Number awarded Varies each year; recently, 20 of these scholarships were awarded.

Deadline June of each year for fall semester; November of each year for spring semester.

[730]
LAGRANT FOUNDATION GRADUATE SCHOLARSHIPS

Lagrant Foundation
Attn: Programs Manager
626 Wilshire Boulevard, Suite 700
Los Angeles, CA 90071-2920
(323) 469-8680   Fax: (323) 469-8683
E-mail: erickaavila@lagrant.com
Web: www.lagrantfoundation.org/site/?page_id=3

Purpose To provide financial assistance to Native American and other minority graduate students who are working on a degree in advertising, public relations, or marketing.

Eligibility This program is open to African Americans, Asian Pacific Americans, Hispanics, and Native Americans who are full-time graduate students at an accredited institution. Applicants must have a GPA of 3.2 or higher and be working on a master's degree in advertising, marketing, or public relations. They must have at least 2 academic semesters remaining to complete their degree. Along with their application, they must submit 1) a 1- to 2-page essay outlin-

ing their career goals; why it is important to increase ethnic representation in the fields of advertising, marketing, and public relations; and the role of an advertising, marketing, or public relations practitioner; 2) a paragraph describing the graduate school and/or community activities in which they are involved; 3) a brief paragraph describing any honors and awards they have received; 4) a letter of reference; 5) a resume; and 6) an official transcript. Applicants majoring in public relations must also submit an essay on the importance and relevance of the Arthur W. Page Society Principles.
Financial data The stipend is $10,000 per year.
Duration 1 year.
Additional information Support for the public relations scholarships is provided by the Arthur W. Page Society.
Number awarded 5 each year, including 2 supported by the Arthur W. Page Society.
Deadline February of each year.

[731]
LAGUNA EDUCATION FOUNDATION GRADUATE SCHOLARSHIPS
Laguna Education Foundation
P.O. Box 645
Laguna, NM 87026
(505) 552-6377   Fax: (505) 552-6398
E-mail: r.johnson@lagunaed.net
Web: www.lagunaedfoundation.org

Purpose To provide financial assistance for graduate school to regular members of the Pueblo of Laguna.
Eligibility This program is open to regular enrolled members of the Pueblo of Laguna who are attending an accredited college or university. Applicants must be working on a graduate or professional degree. Along with their application, they must submit an essay of 2 to 3 pages that covers their philosophy of leadership, enriching the lives of others, belief systems, cultural experiences, traditions, extracurricular activities at their institution relative to Native issues, tribal and community involvement, previous experience with Laguna, and how they will give back to Laguna Pueblo. Preference is given to students enrolled in fields of study that will build and enhance local tribal community efforts, followed by fields that address Native American interests and national perspectives.
Financial data Stipends are $2,000 per year.
Duration 1 year; may be renewed.
Number awarded Varies each year.
Deadline May of each year.

[732]
LARRY MATFAY SCHOLARSHIP
Koniag Incorporated
Attn: Koniag Education Foundation
6927 Old Seward Highway, Suite 103
Anchorage, AK 99518-2283
(907) 562-9093   Toll-free: (888) 562-9093
Fax: (907) 562-9023   E-mail: kef@alaska.com
Web: www.koniageducation.org

Purpose To provide financial assistance to Alaska Natives with ties to the Koniag region who are enrolled in undergraduate or graduate study in a field related to Alutiiq culture.
Eligibility This program is open to college juniors, seniors, and graduate students who are Alaska Native shareholders of the Koniag region or descendants of those original enrollees. Applicants must supply proof of eligibility and documentation of financial need. They must have a GPA of 2.5 or higher cumulatively (3.0 or higher within their major) and be majoring in anthropology, history, Alaska Native or American Indian studies, or another discipline that involves research and learning about Alutiiq culture. Along with their application, they must submit a 300- to 600-word letter that includes their personal and family history, their schooling or work history, and their educational and life goals.
Financial data The stipend is $1,000 per year. Funds are sent directly to the recipient's school and may be used for tuition, books, supplies, room, board, and transportation.
Duration 1 year; may be renewed.
Additional information Recipients are also eligible to apply for a Koniag Education Foundation Academic Achievement/Graduate Scholarship. The Koniag Education Foundation was established in 1993 by the directors of Koniag, Inc. The Koniag region covers Kodiak Island, many smaller islands, and a portion of the Alaska Peninsula.
Number awarded 1 each year.
Deadline March of each year for summer term; May of each year for fall or spring term.

[733]
LATHAM & WATKINS DIVERSITY SCHOLARS PROGRAM
Latham & Watkins LLP
Attn: Global Recruiting Manager-Diversity and Law School Outreach
12636 High Bluff Drive, Suite 400
San Diego, CA 92130
(858) 523-5459   Fax: (858) 523-5450
Web: www.lw.com/AboutLatham.aspx?page=Diversity

Purpose To provide financial assistance to Native American and other minority law students interested in working for a global law firm.
Eligibility Applicants must be second-year law students at an accredited law school and plan to practice law in a major city in the United States. Students who have received a similar scholarship from another sponsor are not eligible to apply. Applicants must have the ability to contribute to the diversity objects of global law firms, be able to identify obstacles or challenges they have overcome, have a record of academic and/or leadership achievements, and intend to practice in a global law firm environment. Along with their application, they must submit a personal statement, resume, and transcript.
Financial data The stipend is $10,000.
Duration 1 year; nonrenewable.
Additional information This program was established in 2005. Recipients are not required to work for Latham & Watkins after graduation.
Number awarded 4 each year.
Deadline November of each year.

[734]
LAUNCHING LEADERS MBA SCHOLARSHIP
JPMorgan Chase
Campus Recruiting
Attn: Launching Leaders
277 Park Avenue, Second Floor
New York, NY 10172
(212) 270-6000
E-mail: bronwen.x.baumgardner@jpmorgan.com
Web: launchingleaders.jpmorgan.com/02.0.ashx

Purpose To provide financial assistance and work experience to Native American and other underrepresented minority students enrolled in the first year of an M.B.A. program.

Eligibility This program is open to Black, Hispanic, and Native American students enrolled in the first year of an M.B.A. program. Applicants must have a demonstrated commitment to working in financial services. Along with their application, they must submit essays on 1) a hypothetical proposal on how to use $50 million from a donor to their school to benefit all of its students; and 2) the special background and attributes they would contribute to the sponsor's diversity agenda and their motivation for applying to this scholarship program. They must be interested in a summer associate position in the sponsor's investment banking, sales and trading, or research divisions.

Financial data The stipend is $40,000 for the first year of study; a paid summer associate position is also provided.

Duration 1 year; may be renewed 1 additional year if the recipient successfully completes the 10-week summer associate program.

Number awarded Varies each year.

Deadline October of each year.

[735]
LAWRENCE MATSON MEMORIAL ENDOWMENT FUND SCHOLARSHIPS
Cook Inlet Region, Inc.
Attn: The CIRI Foundation
3600 San Jeronimo Drive, Suite 256
Anchorage, AK 99508-2870
(907) 793-3575   Toll-free: (800) 764-3382
Fax: (907) 793-3585   E-mail: tcf@thecirifoundation.org
Web: www.thecirifoundation.org/designated.htm

Purpose To provide financial assistance for undergraduate or graduate studies in selected liberal arts to Alaska Natives who are original enrollees to Cook Inlet Region, Inc. (CIRI) and their lineal descendants.

Eligibility This program is open to Alaska Native enrollees to CIRI under the Alaska Native Claims Settlement Act (ANCSA) of 1971 and their lineal descendants. There are no Alaska residency requirements or age limitations. Applicants must be accepted or enrolled full time in a 4-year undergraduate or a graduate degree program in the following liberal arts fields: language, education, social sciences, arts, communications, or law. They must have a GPA of 2.5 or higher. Along with their application, they must submit a 500-word statement on their educational and career goals and how they are contributing, or planning to contribute, to a positive Alaska Native community. Selection is based on that statement, academic achievement, rigor of course work or degree program, student financial contribution, financial need, grade level, previous work performance, community service, and relationship of degree program to career goals.

Financial data The stipend is $10,000 per year, $8,000 per year, or $2,500 per semester, depending on GPA.

Duration 1 semester or 1 year.

Additional information This fund was established in 1989.

Number awarded Varies each year. Recently, 3 of these scholarships were awarded: 1 at $10,000 per year, 1 at $8,000 per year, and 1 at $2,500 per semester.

Deadline May of each year for annual scholarships; May or November of each year for semester scholarships.

[736]
LEADERSHIP AND CAREER DEVELOPMENT PROGRAM
Medical Library Association
Attn: Professional Development Department
65 East Wacker Place, Suite 1900
Chicago, IL 60601-7246
(312) 419-9094, ext. 28   Fax: (312) 419-8950
E-mail: mlapd2@mlahq.org
Web: www.mlanet.org

Purpose To provide an opportunity for Native American and other minority mid-career librarians to engage in leadership and career development activities.

Eligibility This program is open to professionals with 3 to 10 years of experience at academic and research libraries. Applicants must be members of minority ethnic groups (African Americans, Hispanics, Asians, Native Americans, or Pacific Islanders). They must be interested in taking advantage of advancement and leadership opportunities. Along with their application, they must submit a resume, a 500-word essay describing their interest in the program, a 1-page description of their proposed research project, and a letter from their immediate supervisor describing their demonstrated and potential skills for leadership roles in research libraries.

Financial data The grant is $4,500.

Duration 1 year.

Additional information This program is jointly managed by the Medical Library Association (MLA) and the Association of Research Libraries (ARL) with funding from the National Library of Medicine.

Number awarded 2 each year.

Deadline September of each year.

[737]
LEADERSHIP FOR DIVERSITY SCHOLARSHIP
California School Library Association
1001 26th Street
Sacramento, CA 95816
(916) 447-2684   Fax: (916) 447-2695
E-mail: csla@pacbell.net
Web: www.csla.net/awa/scholarships.htm

Purpose To provide financial assistance to Native American and other minority students who any state interested in earning a credential as a library media teacher in California.

Eligibility This program is open to students who are members of a traditionally underrepresented group enrolled

in a college or university library media teacher credential program in California. Applicants must intend to work as a library media teacher in a California school library media center for a minimum of 3 years. Along with their application, they must submit a 250-word statement on their school library media career interests and goals, why they should be considered, what they can contribute, their commitment to serving the needs of our multicultural and multilingual students, and their financial situation.
Financial data The stipend is $1,500.
Duration 1 year.
Number awarded 1 each year.
Deadline April of each year.

[738]
LEGAL OPPORTUNITY SCHOLARSHIP
American Bar Association
Attn: Fund for Justice and Education
321 North Clark Street
Chicago, IL 60610
(312) 988-5415 Fax: (312) 988-6392
E-mail: fje@staff.abanet.org
Web: www.abanet.org/fje/losfpage.html

Purpose To provide financial assistance to Native American and other minority students who are interested in attending law school.
Eligibility This program is open to racial and ethnic minority college graduates who are interested in attending an ABA-accredited law school. Only students beginning law school may apply; students who have completed 1 or more semesters of law school are not eligible. Applicants must have a cumulative GPA of 2.5 or higher and be citizens or permanent residents of the United States. Along with their application, they must submit a 1,000-word statement describing their personal and family background, community service activities, and other connections to their racial and ethnic minority community. Financial need is also considered in the selection process.
Financial data The stipend is $5,000 per year.
Duration 1 year; may be renewed for 2 additional years if satisfactory performance in law school has been achieved.
Additional information This program began in the 2000-01 academic year.
Number awarded Approximately 20 each year.
Deadline February of each year.

[739]
LIKO A'E SCHOLARSHIPS
Liko A'e Native Hawaiian Scholarship Program
c/o Maui Community College
310 West Ka'ahumanu Avenue
Kahului, HI 96732-1617
(808) 984-3366 Fax: (808) 984-3562
E-mail: lhokoana@hawaii.edu
Web: www.likoae.org/scholarship_info.asp

Purpose To provide financial assistance for college or graduate school to Native Hawaiian students.
Eligibility This program is open to U.S. citizens who are descendants of the aboriginal inhabitants of the Hawaiian Islands prior to 1778. Applicants must be enrolled or accepted as full- or part-time students in an accredited 2- or 4-year degree-granting institution of higher education. Undergraduates must have a GPA of 2.0 or higher and graduate students must have a GPA of 3.0 or higher. Selection is based on merit (as judged by GPA and responses to essay questions) and financial need. Preference is given to students working on degrees in professions in which Native Hawaiians are underrepresented. Some of the scholarships are designated for students from smaller rural communities who are working on a degree in education.
Financial data A stipend is awarded (amount not specified). Child care assistance is also provided.
Duration 1 year.
Additional information This program was established in 2003 by a grant from the U.S. Department of Education and is administered by Maui Community College.
Number awarded Varies each year.
Deadline Deadlines are in May, August, November, and February.

[740]
LIONEL C. BARROW MINORITY DOCTORAL STUDENT SCHOLARSHIP
Association for Education in Journalism and Mass Communication
Attn: Communication Theory and Methodology Division
234 Outlet Pointe Boulevard, Suite A
Columbia, SC 29210-5667
(803) 798-0271 Fax: (803) 772-3509
E-mail: aejmc@aejmc.org
Web: aejmcctm.blogspot.com

Purpose To provide financial assistance to minorities who are interested in working on a doctorate in mass communication.
Eligibility This program is open to minority students enrolled in a Ph.D. program in journalism and/or mass communication. Applicants must submit 2 letters of recommendation, a resume, and a brief letter outlining their research interests and career plans. Membership in the association is not required, but applicants must be U.S. citizens or permanent residents. Selection is based on the likelihood that the applicant's work will contribute to communication theory and/or methodology.
Financial data The stipend is $1,400.
Duration 1 year.
Additional information This program began in 1972. Information is also available from Edward Horowitz, Cleveland State University, School of Communication, 2121 Euclid Avenue, MU 239, Cleveland, OH 44115-2214, E-mail: e.horowitz@csuohio.edu.
Number awarded 1 each year.
Deadline May of each year.

[741]
LITA/OCLC MINORITY SCHOLARSHIP
American Library Association
Attn: Library and Information Technology Association
50 East Huron Street
Chicago, IL 60611-2795
(312) 280-4270   Toll-free: (800) 545-2433, ext. 4270
Fax: (312) 280-3257   TDD: (312) 944-7298
TDD: (888) 814-7692   E-mail: lita@ala.org
Web: www.ala.org

Purpose To provide financial assistance to Native American and other minority graduate students interested in preparing for a career in library automation.
Eligibility This program is open to U.S. or Canadian citizens who are interested in working on a master's degree in library/information science and preparing for a career in the field of library and automated systems. Applicants must be a member of 1 of the following ethnic groups: American Indian, Alaskan Native, Asian, Pacific Islander, African American, or Hispanic. They may not have completed more than 12 credit hours of course work for their degree. Selection is based on academic excellence, leadership potential, evidence of a commitment to a career in library automation and information technology, and prior activity and experience in those fields. Financial need is considered when all other factors are equal.
Financial data The stipend is $3,000.
Duration 1 year.
Additional information This scholarship, first awarded in 1991, is funded by Online Computer Library Center (OCLC) and administered by the Library and Information Technology Association (LITA) of the American Library Association.
Number awarded 1 each year.
Deadline February of each year.

[742]
LSSI MINORITY SCHOLARSHIP
American Library Association
Attn: Library and Information Technology Association
50 East Huron Street
Chicago, IL 60611-2795
(312) 280-4270   Toll-free: (800) 545-2433, ext. 4270
Fax: (312) 280-3257   TDD: (312) 944-7298
TDD: (888) 814-7692   E-mail: lita@ala.org
Web: www.ala.org

Purpose To provide financial assistance to Native American and other minority graduate students interested in preparing for a career in library automation.
Eligibility This program is open to U.S. or Canadian citizens who are interested in working on a master's degree in library/information science and preparing for a career in the field of library and automated systems. Applicants must be a member of 1 of the following ethnic groups: American Indian, Alaskan Native, Asian, Pacific Islander, African American, or Hispanic. They may not have completed more than 12 credit hours of course work for their degree. Selection is based on academic excellence, leadership potential, evidence of a commitment to a career in library automation and information technology, and prior activity and experience in those fields. Financial need is considered when all other factors are equal.
Financial data The stipend is $2,500.
Duration 1 year.
Additional information This scholarship, first awarded in 1995, is funded by Library Systems & Services, Inc. (LSSI) and administered by the Library and Information Technology Association (LITA) of the American Library Association.
Number awarded 1 each year.
Deadline February of each year.

[743]
MAE LASLEY/OSAGE SCHOLARSHIPS
Osage Scholarship Fund
c/o Roman Catholic Diocese of Tulsa
P.O. Box 690240
Tulsa, OK 74169-0240
(918) 294-1904   Fax: (918) 294-0920
E-mail: sarah.jameson@dioceseoftulsa.org
Web: www.osagetribe.com

Purpose To provide financial assistance to Osage Indians who are Roman Catholics attending college or graduate school.
Eligibility This program is open to Roman Catholics who are attending or planning to attend a college or university as an undergraduate or graduate student. Applicants must be Osage Indians on the rolls in Pawhuska, Oklahoma and have of copy of their Certificate of Indian Blood (CIB) or Osage tribal membership card. Selection is based on academic ability and financial need.
Financial data The stipend is $1,000 per year.
Duration 1 year; may be renewed if the recipient maintains full-time enrollment and a GPA of 2.5 or higher as an undergraduate or 3.0 or higher as a graduate student.
Number awarded Normally, 10 each year: 2 for students attending St. Gregory's University in Shawnee, Oklahoma as freshmen and 8 for any college or university.
Deadline April of each year.

[744]
MAKIA AND ANN MALO SCHOLARSHIP
Hawai'i Community Foundation
Attn: Scholarship Department
1164 Bishop Street, Suite 800
Honolulu, HI 96813
(808) 566-5570   Toll-free: (888) 731-3863
Fax: (808) 521-6286
E-mail: scholarships@hcf-hawaii.org
Web: www.hawaiicommunityfoundation.org

Purpose To provide financial assistance to Native Hawaiians who are working on a degree in law.
Eligibility This program is open to Hawaii residents who are entering the second or third year of law school. Applicants must be able to document Native Hawaiian ancestry, academic achievement (GPA of 2.7 or higher), good moral character, and financial need. Along with their application, they must submit an essay on the major issues facing Native Hawaiians today and how they plan to use their education to resolve those issues.
Financial data The amounts of the awards depend on the availability of funds and the need of the recipient; recently, the stipend was $1,500.
Duration 1 year.

Additional information This program began in 2001.
Number awarded Varies each year; recently, 1 of these scholarships was awarded.
Deadline February of each year.

[745]
MARILYN A. JACKSON SCHOLARSHIP AWARD

Omaha Presbyterian Seminary Foundation
2120 South 72nd Street, Suite 630
Omaha, NE 68124
(402) 397-5138   Fax: (402) 397-4944
E-mail: OPSF@omaha-sem-found.org
Web: www.omaha-sem-found.org

Purpose To provide financial assistance to Native American and other minority students at Presbyterian theological seminaries.
Eligibility This program is open to students of ethnic minority (African American, Alaska Native, Asian American, Hispanic American, or Native American) descent. Applicants must be members of a Presbyterian Church, under the care of a presbytery as a candidate/inquirer, and accepted or enrolled in 1 of the following 10 theological institutions: Austin Presbyterian Theological Seminary (Austin, Texas); Columbia Theological Seminary (Decatur, Georgia); University of Dubuque Theological Seminary (Dubuque, Iowa); Johnson C. Smith Theological Seminary (Atlanta, Georgia); Louisville Presbyterian Theological Seminary (Louisville, Kentucky); McCormick Theological Seminary (Chicago, Illinois); Pittsburgh Theological Seminary (Pittsburgh, Pennsylvania); Princeton Theological Seminary (Princeton, New Jersey); San Francisco Theological Seminary (San Anselmo, California); or Union Theological Seminary and Presbyterian School of Christian Education (Richmond, Virginia). They must be serving, or planning to serve, in a small Presbyterian church for at least 5 years in the 13-state area served by the foundation. Along with their application, they must submit essays on 1) why they consider themselves to be a racial ethnic or minority student, and 2) how they will use their leadership and administrative skills and abilities in the life and work of the small church they will be called to serve. Financial need is also considered in the selection process.
Financial data A stipend is awarded (amount not specified).
Duration 1 year; nonrenewable.
Number awarded 1 or more each year.
Deadline April of each year.

[746]
MARRIAGE AND FAMILY THERAPY MINORITY FELLOWSHIP PROGRAM

American Association for Marriage and Family Therapy
Attn: Awards Committee
112 South Alfred Street
Alexandria, VA 22314
(703) 838-9808   Fax: (703) 838-9805
Web: www.aamft.org

Purpose To provide financial assistance to Native American and other minority students enrolled in graduate and post-degree training programs in marriage and family therapy.
Eligibility This program is open to minority students (including African Americans, Hispanics, Native Americans, Asian Americans, and Pacific Islanders) enrolled in graduate programs or post-degree institutes that provide training in marriage and family therapy. Applicants must be members of the American Association for Marriage and Family Therapy (AAMFT). They must be citizens of the United States or Canada and show promise in and commitment to a career in marital and family therapy education, research, or practice. Along with their application, they must submit a personal statement explaining how their racial or ethnic background has had an impact on them and their career decision; the statement should include their professional interests, goals, and commitment to the field of marriage and family therapy.
Financial data The stipend is $1,000. Awardees also receive a plaque and funding up to $500 to attend the association's annual conference.
Duration 1 year.
Additional information This program began in 1986.
Number awarded Up to 3 each year.
Deadline January of each year.

[747]
MARTIN LUTHER KING JR. SCHOLARSHIP AWARDS

American Correctional Association
Attn: Scholarship Award Committee
206 North Washington Street, Suite 200
Alexandria, VA 22314
(703) 224-0000   Toll-free: (800) ACA-JOIN
E-mail: jenniferb@aca.org
Web: www.aca.org/pastpresentfuture/awards.asp

Purpose To provide financial assistance for undergraduate or graduate study to Native American and other minorities interested in a career in the criminal justice field.
Eligibility Members of the American Correctional Association (ACA) may nominate a minority person for these awards. Nominees do not need to be ACA members, but they must have been accepted to or be enrolled in an undergraduate or graduate program in criminal justice at a 4-year college or university. Along with the nomination package, they must submit a 250-word essay describing their reflections on the ideals and philosophies of Dr. Martin Luther King and how they have attempted to emulate those qualities in their lives. They must provide documentation of financial need, academic achievement, and commitment to the principles of Dr. King.
Financial data A stipend is awarded (amount not specified). Funds are paid directly to the recipient's college or university.
Number awarded 1 each year.
Deadline May of each year.

[748]
MARTIN OLSON MEMORIAL SCHOLARSHIP
Bering Straits Native Corporation
Attn: Bering Straits Foundation
110 Front Street, Suite 300
P.O. Box 1008
Nome, AK 99762-1008
(907) 443-4305   Toll-free: (800) 478-5079 (within AK)
Fax: (907) 443-2985
E-mail: foundation@beringstraits.com
Web: www.beringstraits.com

Purpose To provide supplemental financial assistance to Alaska Natives with ties to the Bering Straits area who are enrolled in an undergraduate or graduate program in any state.

Eligibility This program is open to Native Alaskans enrolled to the Bering Straits Native Corporation or as an "At Large" member. Applicants must be enrolled full time in an accredited institution or vocational school in any state as an undergraduate or graduate student. Along with their application, they must submit transcripts, 2 letters of recommendation, documentation of financial need, and a short personal statement outlining their career goals.

Financial data A stipend is awarded (amount not specified). Funds are paid directly to the recipient's school.

Duration 1 year; may be renewed if the recipient maintains a GPA of 2.0 or higher and full-time enrollment.

Number awarded 1 each year.

Deadline June of each year.

[749]
MARY TINKER SCHOLARSHIP FUND
Osage Nation Education Department
Attn: Scholarship Coordinator
HC 66
P.O. Box 990
Hominy, OK 74035
(918) 287-5301   Toll-free: (800) 390-6724
Fax: (918) 287-5567   E-mail: jholding@osagetribe.com
Web: www.osagetribe.com/education/index.aspx

Purpose To provide financial assistance for college or graduate school to members of the Osage Tribe.

Eligibility This program is open to Osage tribal students who are enrolled or planning to enroll in a 2-year or 4-year college or university. A point system is used to rank applicants, including such factors as student status (freshman through graduate student), number of previous full-time semesters in college, GPA from previous semester, full-time or part-time enrollment, qualification for federal Pell Grant, and Osage blood quantum.

Financial data The amount of the award depends on the number of points earned by the recipient.

Duration 1 semester; may be renewed.

Number awarded Varies each year.

Deadline June of each year for fall semester; December of each year for spring semester; April of each year for summer school.

[750]
MASSACHUSETTS INDIAN ASSOCIATION SCHOLARSHIP FUND
Massachusetts Indian Association
c/o Marjorie Findlay
245 Rockland Road
Carlisle, MA 01741
Fax: (978) 369-5828

Purpose To provide financial assistance for college or graduate school to Native Americans.

Eligibility Native American students anywhere in the United States may apply for these scholarships if they have a tribal number, are in good academic standing, and can demonstrate financial need.

Financial data The stipends range up to $750 for undergraduate students and $1,500 for graduate students. The funds are intended to supplement other aid by paying for books, lab fees, and other course-related expenses. Grants may be used for tuition, if necessary.

Duration 1 year; may be renewed.

Number awarded Varies each year.

Deadline September of each year.

[751]
MCANDREWS DIVERSITY IN PATENT LAW FELLOWSHIP
McAndrews, Held & Malloy, Ltd.
500 West Madison Street, 34th Floor
Chicago, IL 60661
(312) 775-8000   Fax: (312) 775-8100
E-mail: info@mcandrews-ip.com
Web: www.mcandrews-ip.com/diversity_fellowship

Purpose To provide financial assistance to Native American and other law students who come from a diverse background and are interested in patent law.

Eligibility This program is open to first-year students at ABA-accredited law schools who come from a diverse background. Applicants must have a degree in science or engineering and be planning to practice patent law in the Chicago area. Along with their application, they must submit a 500-word personal statement on why they wish to prepare for a career in patent law, why they are interested in the sponsoring firm as a place to work, and how their background and/or life experiences would improved diversity in the field of intellectual property law. Selection is based on that statement, a resume (including their science or engineering educational credentials), a legal writing sample, undergraduate transcript, and at least 1 letter of recommendation.

Financial data The stipend is $5,000.

Duration 1 year (the second year of law school).

Additional information This fellowship was first awarded in 2008. It includes a paid clerkship position at McAndrews, Held & Malloy during the summer after the first year of law school and possibly another clerkship during the summer after the second year.

Number awarded 1 each year.

Deadline January of each year.

[752]
MCDERMOTT MINORITY SCHOLARSHIP
McDermott Will & Emery
Attn: Recruiting Committee Chair
227 West Monroe Street
Chicago, IL 60606
(312) 984-6470   Fax: (312) 984-7700
E-mail: mcdermottscholarship@mwe.com
Web: www.mwe.com

Purpose To provide financial assistance and work experience to Native American and other minority law students.

Eligibility This program is open to second-year minority (African American, Asian, Hispanic, Middle Eastern, Native American) law students at ABA-accredited U.S. law schools. Applicants must be able to demonstrate leadership, community involvement, and a commitment to improving diversity in the legal community. They must be interested in participating in the sponsor's summer program and be able to meet its hiring criteria. Along with their application, they must submit an essay of 1 to 2 pages that provides ideas they have on how the number of minority students in law schools can be increased and how they have improved and intend to help improve diversity in the legal profession throughout their law school and legal career.

Financial data The stipend is $15,000.

Duration 1 year.

Additional information Recipients also participate in a summer program at the sponsor's offices in Boston, Chicago, Los Angeles, Miami, New York, Orange County, Silicon Valley, or Washington, D.C.

Number awarded 2 each year.

Deadline October of each year.

[753]
MEDICAL LIBRARY ASSOCIATION SCHOLARSHIP FOR MINORITY STUDENTS
Medical Library Association
Attn: Professional Development Department
65 East Wacker Place, Suite 1900
Chicago, IL 60601-7246
(312) 419-9094, ext. 28   Fax: (312) 419-8950
E-mail: mlapd2@mlahq.org
Web: www.mlanet.org/awards/grants/minstud.html

Purpose To assist Native American and other minority students interested in preparing for a career in medical librarianship.

Eligibility This program is open to racial minority students (Asians, African Americans, Hispanics, Native Americans, or Pacific Islander Americans) who are entering a graduate program in librarianship or who have completed less than half of their academic requirements for the master's degree in library science. They must be interested in preparing for a career in medical librarianship. Selection is based on academic record, letters of reference, professional potential, and the applicant's statement of career objectives. U.S. or Canadian citizenship or permanent resident status is required.

Financial data The stipend is $5,000.

Duration 1 year.

Additional information This scholarship was first awarded in 1973.

Number awarded 1 each year.

Deadline November of each year.

[754]
MESBEC PROGRAM
Catching the Dream
8200 Mountain Road, N.E., Suite 203
Albuquerque, NM 87110-7835
(505) 262-2351   Fax: (505) 262-0534
E-mail: NScholarsh@aol.com
Web: www.catchingthedream.org/Scholarship.htm

Purpose To provide financial assistance to American Indian students who are interested in working on an undergraduate or graduate degree in selected fields.

Eligibility This program is open to American Indians who can provide proof that they have at least one-quarter Indian blood and are a member of a U.S. tribe that is federally-recognized, state-recognized, or terminated. Applicants must be enrolled or planning to enroll full time and major in the 1 of the following fields: mathematics, engineering, science (including medicine), business administration, education, or computer science. They may be entering freshmen, undergraduate students, graduate students, or Ph.D. candidates. Along with their application, they must submit documentation of financial need, 3 letters of recommendation, copies of applications and responses from all other sources of funding for which they are eligible, official transcripts, standardized test scores (ACT, SAT, GRE, MCAT, LSAT, etc.), and an essay explaining their goals in life, college plans, and career plans (especially how those plans include working with and benefiting Indians). Selection is based on merit and potential for improving the lives of Indian people.

Financial data Stipends range from $500 to $5,000 per year.

Duration 1 year; may be renewed.

Additional information MESBEC is an acronym that stands for the priority areas of this program: mathematics, engineering, science, business, education, and computers. The sponsor was formerly known as the Native American Scholarship Fund.

Number awarded Varies; generally, 30 to 35 each year.

Deadline April of each year for fall term; September of each year for spring and winter terms; March of each year for summer school.

[755]
MESCALERO APACHE TRIBAL SCHOLARSHIP
Mescalero Apache Tribe
Attn: Tribal Education Department
P.O. Box 176
Mescalero, NM 88340
(505) 671-4494   Fax: (505) 671-4454

Purpose To provide financial assistance for undergraduate or graduate education to members of the Mescalero Apache Tribe.

Eligibility This program is open to enrolled members of the Mescalero Apache Tribe who are high school seniors, high school graduates, or currently-enrolled undergraduate or graduate students. Applicants must have a GPA of 2.0 or higher, Financial need is considered in the selection process.

Financial data The amount awarded varies, up to $8,000 per year.
Duration 1 year; may be renewed for up to 3 additional years.
Number awarded Varies each year.
Deadline May of each year for the fall term; October for the spring term.

[756]
METROPOLITAN LIFE FOUNDATION AWARDS PROGRAM FOR ACADEMIC EXCELLENCE IN MEDICINE

National Medical Fellowships, Inc.
Attn: Scholarship Program
5 Hanover Square, 15th Floor
New York, NY 10004
(212) 483-8880   Fax: (212) 483-8897
E-mail: info@nmfonline.org
Web: www.nmfonline.org

Purpose To provide financial assistance to Native American and other underrepresented minority medical students who reside or attend school in designated cities throughout the country.
Eligibility This program is open to African American, mainland Puerto Rican, Mexican American, Native Hawaiian, Alaska Native, or American Indian medical students in their second through fourth year who are nominated by their dean. Nominees must be enrolled in medical schools located in (or residents of) the following cities: Phoenix, Arizona; San Francisco/Oakland/Bay area, California; Los Angeles, California; Denver, Colorado; Miami, Florida; Tampa/St. Petersburg, Florida; Atlanta, Georgia; Aurora/Chicago, Illinois; Boston, Massachusetts; St. Louis, Missouri; Albany, New York; metropolitan New York area (including New York City, southern New York, Long Island, central and northern New Jersey, and southern Connecticut); Rensselaer, New York; Utica, New York; Dayton, Ohio; Tulsa, Oklahoma; Philadelphia, Pennsylvania; Pittsburgh, Pennsylvania; Scranton, Pennsylvania; Warwick/Providence, Rhode Island; Greenville, South Carolina; Austin, Texas; Dallas/Fort Worth, Texas; or Houston, Texas. Selection is based on demonstrated financial need, outstanding academic achievement, leadership, and potential for distinguished contributions to medicine.
Financial data The stipend is $4,000.
Duration 1 year; nonrenewable.
Additional information Funding for this program, established in 1987, is provided by the Metropolitan Life Foundation of New York, New York.
Number awarded 17 each year.
Deadline February of each year.

[757]
MICHELE CLARK FELLOWSHIP

Radio and Television News Directors Foundation
Attn: RTNDF Fellowship Program
4121 Plank Road, Suite 512
Fredericksburg, VA 22407
(202) 467-5214   Fax: (202) 223-4007
E-mail: staceys@rtnda.org
Web: www.rtnda.org/pages/education.php

Purpose To provide financial assistance for professional development to minority journalists employed in electronic news.
Eligibility This program is open to minority journalists employed in television or radio news who have 10 years or less of full-time experience. Applications must include samples of the journalist's work done as the member of a news staff, with a script and tape (audio or video) up to 15 minutes.
Financial data The grant is $1,000 plus an all-expense paid trip to the international convention of the Radio-Television News Directors Association held that year.
Duration The grant is presented annually.
Additional information The grant, named for CBS journalist Michele Clark, may be used in any way to improve the craft and enhance the excellence of the recipient's news operation.
Number awarded 1 each year.
Deadline May of each year.

[758]
MICHIGAN INDIAN TUITION WAIVER PROGRAM

Inter-Tribal Council of Michigan, Inc.
Attn: Michigan Indian Tuition Waiver
2956 Ashmun Street
Sault Ste. Marie, MI 49783-3720'
(906) 632-6896   Toll-free: (800) 562-4957
Fax: (906) 632-1810   E-mail: christin@itcmi.org
Web: www.itcmi.org/ituition.html

Purpose To exempt members of Indian tribes from tuition at Michigan postsecondary institutions.
Eligibility This program is open to Michigan residents who have lived in the state for at least 12 months and can certify at least one-quarter North American Indian blood from a federally-recognized or state historic tribe. Applicants must be attending a public college, university, or community college in Michigan. The program includes full- and part-time study, academic-year and summer school, and undergraduate and graduate work.
Financial data All qualified applicants are entitled to waiver of tuition at Michigan public institutions.
Duration Indian students are entitled to the waiver as long as they attend college in Michigan.
Additional information This program was established in 1976 as the result of an agreement between the state of Michigan and the federal government under which the state agreed to provide free tuition to North American Indians in exchange for the Mt. Pleasant Indian School, which the state acquired as a training facility for the developmentally disabled.
Number awarded Varies each year.

[759]
MILBANK DIVERSITY SCHOLARS PROGRAM

Milbank, Tweed, Hadley & McCloy LLP
Attn: Director, Law School Recruiting
One Chase Manhattan Plaza
New York, NY 10005
(212) 530-5687 Fax: (212) 822-5872
E-mail: recruiting@milbank.com
Web: www.milbank.com/careers

Purpose To provide financial assistance to law students, especially those who are Native Americans or other members of groups underrepresented at large law firms.

Eligibility This program is open to students who have completed their first year of a full-time J.D. program at an ABA-accredited law school. Joint degree candidates must have successfully completed 2 years of a J.D. program. Applications are particularly encouraged from members of groups traditionally underrepresented at large law firms. Applicants must submit a 500-word essay on 1) the challenges they have faced in pursuit of a legal career that have helped them understand the value of diversity and inclusion in the legal profession; and 2) the personal contributions they would make to furthering the diversity objectives of the sponsoring law firm. Selection is based on academic achievement, demonstrated leadership ability, writing and interpersonal skills, and interest in the firm's practice.

Financial data The stipend is $15,000. A paid associate position during the summer after the second year of law school is also provided. If the student is offered and accepts a permanent position with the firm after graduation, an additional $35,000 scholarship stipend is also awarded.

Duration 1 year (the third year of law school).

Additional information Scholars may be offered a permanent position with the firm, but there is no guarantee of such an offer.

Number awarded At least 2 each year.

Deadline August of each year.

[760]
MILLE LACS BAND POST GRADUATE DEGREE PROGRAM

Mille Lacs Band of Ojibwe
Attn: Higher Education Office
43408 Oodena Avenue
Onamia, MN 56359-2236
(320) 532-7508 Toll-free: (800) 532-9059
Fax: (320) 532-3785
E-mail: mlbsp@MilleLacsOjibwe.nsn.us
Web: www.millelacsojibwe.org/scholarship.asp

Purpose To provide financial assistance to members of the Mille Lacs Band of Ojibwe interested in working on a graduate degree in any field.

Eligibility This program is open to enrolled members of the band, their non-enrolled biological children, and legally adopted children of enrolled band members. Applicants must have received a baccalaureate degree from an accredited college or university and have been accepted at an accredited graduate degree program. They must be able to demonstrate financial need.

Financial data This program provides a stipend of up to $12,000 per year and an allowance of up to $375 per semester for books and supplies.

Duration 1 year; may be renewed.

Number awarded Varies each year.

Deadline March of each year.

[761]
MINNESOTA INDIAN SCHOLARSHIP PROGRAM

Minnesota Office of Higher Education
Attn: Manager of State Financial Aid Programs
1450 Energy Park Drive, Suite 350
St. Paul, MN 55108-5227
(651) 642-0567 Toll-free: (800) 657-3866
Fax: (651) 642-0675 TTY: (800) 627-3529
E-mail: Ginny.Dodds@state.mn.us
Web: www.ohe.state.mn.us

Purpose To provide financial assistance to Native Americans in Minnesota who are interested in working on an undergraduate or graduate degree in any field.

Eligibility Applicants must be at least one-fourth degree Indian ancestry; members of a recognized Indian tribe; at least high school graduates (or approved equivalent); accepted by an accredited college, university, or vocational school in Minnesota; and residents of Minnesota for at least 1 year. They must be attending college or graduate school at least three-fourths time.

Financial data The stipend depends on need, to a maximum of $4,000 per year for undergraduates or $6,600 per year for graduate students. Awards are paid directly to the student's school or college.

Duration 1 year; may be renewed up to 4 additional years, provided the recipient maintains a GPA of 2.0 or higher and sends official grade transcripts to the office for review after each quarter or semester.

Number awarded Approximately 700 each year.

Deadline June of each year.

[762]
MINORITIES IN GOVERNMENT FINANCE SCHOLARSHIP

Government Finance Officers Association
Attn: Scholarship Committee
203 North LaSalle Street, Suite 2700
Chicago, IL 60601-1210
(312) 977-9700 Fax: (312) 977-4806
Web: www.gfoa.org

Purpose To provide financial assistance to Native American and other minority upper-division and graduate students who are preparing for a career in state and local government finance.

Eligibility This program is open to upper-division and graduate students who are preparing for a career in public finance with a major in public administration, accounting, finance, political science, economics, or business administration (with a specific focus on government or nonprofit management). Applicants must be members of a minority group, citizens or permanent residents of the United States or Canada, and able to provide a letter of recommendation from a representative of their school. Selection is based on career plans, academic record, plan of study, letters of recommendation, and GPA. Financial need is not considered.

Financial data The stipend is $5,000.

Duration 1 year.

Additional information This program defines minorities as Black or African Americans, American Indians or Alaskan Natives, Hispanics or Latinos, Native Hawaiians or other Pacific Islanders, or Asians.
Number awarded 1 or more each year.
Deadline February of each year.

[763]
MINORITY DENTAL STUDENT SCHOLARSHIP
American Dental Association
Attn: ADA Foundation
211 East Chicago Avenue
Chicago, IL 60611
(312) 440-2547   Fax: (312) 440-3526
E-mail: adaf@ada.org
Web: www.ada.org

Purpose To provide financial assistance to Native American and other underrepresented minorities who wish to enter the field of dentistry.
Eligibility This program is open to U.S. citizens from a minority group that is currently underrepresented in the dental profession: Native American, African American, or Hispanic. Applicants must have a GPA of 3.0 or higher and be entering their second year of study at a dental school in the United States accredited by the Commission on Dental Accreditation. Selection is based upon academic achievement, a written summary of personal and professional goals, letters of reference, and demonstrated financial need.
Financial data The maximum stipend is $2,500. Funds are sent directly to the student's financial aid office to be used to cover tuition, fees, books, supplies, and living expenses.
Duration 1 year.
Additional information This program, established in 1991, is supported by the Harry J. Bosworth Company, Colgate-Palmolive, Sunstar Americas, and Procter & Gamble Company. Students receiving a full scholarship from any other source are ineligible to receive this scholarship.
Number awarded 25 each year.
Deadline October of each year.

[764]
MINORITY FACULTY DEVELOPMENT SCHOLARSHIP AWARD IN PHYSICAL THERAPY
American Physical Therapy Association
Attn: Department of Minority/International Affairs
1111 North Fairfax Street
Alexandria, VA 22314-1488
(703) 706-3143   Toll-free: (800) 999-APTA, ext. 3143
Fax: (703) 706-8519   TDD: (703) 683-6748
E-mail: min-intl@apta.org
Web: www.apta.org

Purpose To provide financial assistance to Native American and other minority faculty members in physical therapy who are interested in working on a doctoral degree.
Eligibility This program is open to U.S. citizens and permanent residents who are members of the following minority groups: African American or Black, Asian, Native Hawaiian or other Pacific Islander, American Indian or Alaska Native, or Hispanic/Latino. Applicants must be full-time faculty members, teaching in an accredited or developing professional physical therapist education program, who will have completed the equivalent of 2 full semesters of post-professional doctoral course work. They must possess a license to practice physical therapy in a U.S. jurisdiction and be enrolled as a student in an accredited post-professional doctoral program whose content has a demonstrated relationship to physical therapy. Along with their application, they must submit transcripts of all post-professional doctoral course work, a curriculum vitae, and their plan of study for attaining the doctoral degree. Selection is based on 1) demonstrated evidence of contributions in the area of minority affairs and services; 2) contributions to the profession of physical therapy; and 3) scholastic achievement.
Financial data The stipend is $7,000.
Duration 1 year.
Additional information This program was established in 1999.
Number awarded Varies each year; recently, 1 of these scholarships was awarded.
Deadline November of each year.

[765]
MINORITY MEDICAL STUDENTS ELECTIVE IN HIV PSYCHIATRY
American Psychiatric Association
Attn: Institute for Research and Education
1000 Wilson Boulevard, Suite 1825
Arlington, VA 22209-3901
(703) 907-8668   Toll-free: (888) 357-7849
Fax: (703) 907-1089   E-mail: dpennessi@psych.org
Web: www.psych.org/aids

Purpose To provide an opportunity for Native American and other minority medical students to spend an elective residency learning about HIV psychiatry.
Eligibility This program is open to minority medical students entering their fourth year at an accredited M.D. or D.O. degree-granting institution. Applicants must be interested in a psychiatry, internal medicine, pediatrics, or research career. They must be interested in participating in a program that includes intense training in HIV mental health (including neuropsychiatry), a clinical and/or research experience working with a mentor, and participation in the Committee on AIDS of the American Psychiatric Association (APA). U.S. citizenship is required.
Financial data A stipend is provided (amount not specified).
Duration 1 year.
Additional information The heart of the program is in establishing a mentor relationship at 1 of 5 sites, becoming involved with a cohort of medical students interested in HIV medicine/psychiatry, participating in an interactive didactic/experimental learning program, and developing expertise in areas related to ethnic minority mental health research or psychiatric services. Students selected for this program who are not APA members automatically receive membership.
Number awarded Varies each year.
Deadline March of each year.

FELLOWSHIPS

[766]
MINORITY NURSE MAGAZINE SCHOLARSHIP PROGRAM
Minority Nurse Magazine
Attn: Career Recruitment Media
211 West Wacker Drive, Suite 900
Chicago, IL 60606
(312) 525-3095   Fax: (312) 429-3336
E-mail: pchwedyk@alloyeducation.com
Web: www.minoritynurse.com

Purpose To provide financial assistance to Native Americans and other minorities who are working on a bachelor's or master's degree in nursing.

Eligibility This program is open to minority nursing students currently enrolled in 1) the third or fourth year of an accredited B.S.N. program; 2) an accelerated program leading to a B.S.N. degree (e.g., R.N. to B.S.N., B.A. to B.S.N.); or 3) an accelerated master's entry nursing program (e.g., R.N. to M.S.N., B.S. to M.S.N.). Along with their application, they must submit a 250-word essay on their academic and personal accomplishments, community service, and goals for their future nursing career. Selection is based on academic excellence (GPA of 3.0 or higher), demonstrated commitment of service to the student's minority community, and financial need. U.S. citizenship of permanent resident status is required.

Financial data The stipends are $1,000 or $500.

Duration 1 year.

Additional information These scholarships were first offered in 2000. Winners are announced in the fall issue of *Minority Nurse* magazine.

Number awarded 4 each year: 2 at $1,000 and 2 at $500.

Deadline June of each year.

[767]
MINORITY RESEARCH TRAINING IN PSYCHIATRY
American Psychiatric Association
Attn: Institute for Research and Education
1000 Wilson Boulevard, Suite 1825
Arlington, VA 22209-3901
(703) 907-8622   Toll-free: (800) 852-1390
Fax: (703) 907-1085   E-mail: eguerra@psych.org
Web: www.psych.org

Purpose To provide financial assistance to Native American and other underrepresented minority medical students, residents, and postresidency fellows interested in psychiatric research training.

Eligibility This program is open to 3 levels of applicants: medical students, residents at the PGY-4 level of psychiatry training, and postdoctoral fellows who have completed residency training in psychiatry. Preference is given to members of underrepresented minority groups (American Indians, Blacks/African Americans, Hispanics, and Pacific Islanders). Candidates must be interested in training at research-intensive departments of psychiatry in major U.S. medical schools. Training sites with excellent research facilities and resources, funded research record, research faculty (including minority researchers), and training history are preferred. U.S. citizenship or permanent resident status is required.

Financial data Stipends for medical students are paid at the rate of $20,772 per year, or $1,731 per month for the months actually involved in research training. Stipends for residents are paid at the rate of $45,048 per year. For postresidency fellows, stipends depend on the number of years of experience, ranging from $45,048 to $51,036 per year.

Duration Medical students can receive support for 3 to 4 months or as a summer experience. Residents can receive support for 2 months to 1 year. For postresidency fellows, the duration is generally 2 years.

Additional information This program is funded by the National Institute of Mental Health and administered by the APA's American Psychiatric Institute for Research and Education.

Number awarded Varies each year.

Deadline For a summer research training program for medical students, applications are due by March of each year. For medical student programs at other times of the year, applications should be received at least 2 months prior to the start of the program. For residents and postresidency fellows, applications are due by November of each year.

[768]
MISHKOSWIN (STRENGTH) SCHOLARSHIP PROGRAM
Indigenous Early Intervention Alliance
Attn: Office of American Indian Projects
411 North Central Avenue, Suite 880M
Phoenix, AZ 85004
(602) 496-0102
E-mail: mdniles@indigenous-early-intervention.com
Web: indigenous-early-intervention.com

Purpose To provide financial assistance for college or graduate school to members of American Indian tribes.

Eligibility This program is open to enrolled members of any tribe who are working on or planning to work on an undergraduate or graduate degree at a college or university. Applicants must have demonstrated "courage, bravery, and dedication to their college education." Along with their application, they must submit a short essay on their plans following graduation from college. Preference is given to students who 1) are residing on their reservation at the time of application, and 2) plan to return to their tribe following college graduation.

Financial data A stipend is awarded (amount not specified).

Duration 1 year; nonrenewable.

Number awarded 1 each year.

Deadline August of each year.

[769]
MONTANA AMERICAN INDIAN STUDENT WAIVER
Montana Guaranteed Student Loan Program
2500 Broadway
P.O. Box 203101
Helena, MT 59620-3101
(406) 444-6570   Toll-free: (800) 537-7508
Fax: (406) 444-1869
E-mail: scholarships@mgslp.state.mt.us
Web: www.mgslp.state.mt.us

Purpose To provide financial assistance to Montana Indians interested in attending college or graduate school in the state.

Eligibility Eligible to apply are Native American students (one-quarter Indian blood or more) who have been residents of Montana for at least 1 year prior to application, have graduated from an accredited high school or federal Indian school, and can demonstrate financial need.

Financial data Students eligible for this benefit are entitled to attend any unit of the Montana University System without payment of undergraduate or graduate registration or incidental fees.

Duration Students are eligible for continued fee waiver as long as they maintain reasonable academic progress and full-time status (12 or more credits for undergraduates, 9 or more credits for graduate students).

Number awarded Varies; more than $1 million in waivers are approved each year.

[770]
MORGAN STANLEY MBA FELLOWSHIP

Morgan Stanley
Attn: Diversity Recruiting
750 Seventh Avenue, 31st Floor
New York, NY 10019
(212) 762-0211   Fax: (212) 507-4972
E-mail: diversityrecruiting@morganstanley.com
Web: www.morganstanley.com

Purpose To provide financial assistance and work experience to Native Americans and members of other underrepresented minority groups who are working on an M.B.A. degree.

Eligibility This program is open to M.B.A. students of African American, Hispanic, and Native American descent. Selection is based on assigned essays, academic achievement, recommendations, extracurricular activities, leadership qualities, and on-site interviews.

Financial data The program provides full payment of tuition and fees and a paid summer internship.

Duration 1 year; may be renewed for a second year, providing the student remains enrolled full time in good academic standing and completes the summer internship following the first year.

Additional information The paid summer internship is offered within Morgan Stanley institutional securities (equity research, fixed income, institutional equity, investment banking), investment management, or private wealth management. This program was established in 1999.

Number awarded 1 or more each year.

Deadline April of each year.

[771]
MYRON AND LAURA THOMPSON SCHOLARSHIP

Ke Ali'i Pauahi Foundation
Attn: Financial Aid & Scholarship Services
567 South King Street, Suite 160
Honolulu, HI 96813
(808) 534-3966   Toll-free: (800) 842-4682, ext. 43966
Fax: (808) 534-3890   E-mail: scholarships@pauahi.org
Web: www.pauahi.org

Purpose To provide financial assistance to undergraduate or graduate students, especially those of Hawaiian descent, working on a degree in early childhood education.

Eligibility This program is open to full-time undergraduate and graduate students working on a degree in early childhood education. Applicants must be able to demonstrate financial need; an interest in the Hawaiian language, culture, history, and values; and commitment to contribute to the greater community. Preference is given to Native Hawaiians (descendants of the aboriginal inhabitants of the Hawaiian Islands prior to 1778) and students who demonstrate an interest in working with Hawaiian children in Hawaii after completion of their education.

Financial data A stipend is awarded (amount not specified).

Duration 1 year.

Number awarded 1 each year.

Deadline April each year.

[772]
NAAJ SCHOLARSHIPS

Native American Journalists Association
c/o University of Oklahoma
Gaylord College
395 West Lindsey
Norman, OK 73019-0001
(405) 325-9008   Fax: (405) 325-7565
E-mail: info@naja.com
Web: www.naja.com

Purpose To provide financial assistance to student members of the Native American Journalists Association (NAJA) who are interested in a career in journalism or journalism education.

Eligibility This program is open to NAJA members who are high school seniors, undergraduates, or graduate students working on or planning to work on a degree in journalism. Applicants must include proof of enrollment in a federal- or state-recognized tribe; work samples; transcripts; a personal statement that demonstrates financial need, area of interest (print, broadcast, photojournalism, new media, journalism education), and the student's reasons for preparing for a career in journalism; and 3 letters of recommendation.

Financial data The stipends range from $500 to $5,000.

Duration 1 year.

Additional information Support for this program is provided by GMAC, the James M. Cox Foundation, the Samuel I. Newhouse Foundation, *The Arizona Republic,* and CNN.

Number awarded Varies each year; recently, 10 of these scholarships were awarded.

Deadline March of each year.

[773]
NAJA PROFESSIONAL DEVELOPMENT FELLOWSHIPS

Native American Journalists Association
c/o University of Oklahoma
Gaylord College
395 West Lindsey
Norman, OK 73019-0001
(405) 325-9008   Fax: (405) 325-7565
E-mail: info@naja.com
Web: www.naja.com

Purpose To provide financial assistance to Native American journalists interested in enhancing and developing their skills.

Eligibility This program is open to members of the Native American Journalists Association (NAJA) who have been working journalists for at least 2 years, earning more than 50% of their income as journalists in tribal or mainstream organizations or freelance. Students are not eligible. Applicants must be interested in attending skills-building seminars or classes or purchasing job-related equipment. They must submit a resume, a letter of recommendation from a supervisor or other media professional, a detailed budget, and either 1) a description of the seminar or class, or 2) a detailed explanation why the equipment is essential to career development.

Financial data The grants range up to $500 or $1,000.

Number awarded 2 each year: 1 from $100 to $500 and 1 from $500 to $1,000.

Deadline May of each year for the $500 grant; December of each year for the $1,000 grant.

[774]
NALE PROGRAM

Catching the Dream
8200 Mountain Road, N.E., Suite 203
Albuquerque, NM 87110-7835
(505) 262-2351   Fax: (505) 262-0534
E-mail: NScholarsh@aol.com
Web: www.catchingthedream.org/Scholarship.htm

Purpose To provide financial assistance to American Indian paraprofessionals in the education field who wish to return to college or graduate school.

Eligibility This program is open to paraprofessionals who are working in Indian schools and who plan to return to college or graduate school to complete their degree in education, counseling, or school administration. Applicants must be able to provide proof that they are at least one-quarter Indian blood and a member of a U.S. tribe that is federally-recognized, state-recognized, or terminated. Along with their application, they must submit documentation of financial need, 3 letters of recommendation, copies of applications and responses from all other sources of funding for which they are eligible, official transcripts, standardized test scores (ACT, SAT, GRE, MCAT, LSAT, etc.), and an essay explaining their goals in life, college plans, and career plans (especially how those plans include working with and benefiting Indians). Selection is based on merit and potential for improving the lives of Indian people.

Financial data Stipends range from $500 to $5,000 per year.

Duration 1 year; may be renewed.

Additional information The sponsor was formerly known as the Native American Scholarship Fund.

Number awarded Varies; generally, 15 or more each year.

Deadline April of each year for fall term; September of each year for spring and winter terms; March of each year for summer school.

[775]
NATIONAL ASSOCIATION OF SCHOOL PSYCHOLOGISTS MINORITY SCHOLARSHIP

National Association of School Psychologists
Attn: Education and Research Trust
4340 East-West Highway, Suite 402
Bethesda, MD 20814
(301) 657-0270, ext. 234   Toll-free: (866) 331-NASP
Fax: (301) 657-0275   TTY: (301) 657-4155
E-mail: kbritton@naspweb.org
Web: www.nasponline.org/about_nasp/minority.aspx

Purpose To provide financial assistance to Native American and other minority graduate students enrolled in a school psychology program.

Eligibility This program is open to minority students who are U.S. citizens enrolled in a regionally-accredited school psychology program in the United States. Applicants must have a GPA of 3.0 or higher. Doctoral candidates are not eligible. Applications must be accompanied by 1) a resume that includes undergraduate and/or graduate schools attended, awards and honors, student and professional activities, work and volunteer experiences, research and publications, workshops or other presentations, and any special skills, training, or experience, such as bilingualism, teaching experience, or mental health experience; 2) a statement, up to 1,000 words, of professional goals; 3) at least 2 letters of recommendation, including at least 1 from a faculty member from their undergraduate or graduate studies (if a first-year student) or at least 1 from a faculty member of their school psychology program (if a second- or third-year student); 4) a completed financial statement; 5) an official transcript of all graduate course work (first-year students may submit an official undergraduate transcript); 6) other personal accomplishments that the applicant wishes to be considered; and 7) a letter of acceptance from a school psychology program for first-year applicants.

Financial data The stipend is $5,000.

Duration 1 year; may be renewed up to 2 additional years.

Additional information Recipients must become a member of the National Association of School Psychologists (NASP).

Number awarded 5 each year.

Deadline October of each year.

[776]
NATIONAL CENTER FOR COOPERATIVE EDUCATION SCHOLARSHIPS

National Center for Cooperative Education
c/o Haskell Indian Nations University
Natural Resources Liaison Office
155 Indian Avenue, Box 5018
Lawrence, KS 66046
(785) 749-8414   E-mail: daeifler@fs.fed.us
Web: www.haskell.edu

Purpose To provide financial assistance and work experience to American Indian and Alaska Native students interested in preparing for a career in a natural resource field.

Eligibility This program is open to American Indian and Alaska Native students who have finished at least their freshman year at an accredited college or university. Applicants must be working on a bachelor's or higher degree in a natural resources field, including forestry, soil conservation, range management, geographic information systems (GIS), wildlife management, watershed/hydrology, fisheries management, or civil engineering. They must be interested in preparing for a career with tribes, the Bureau of Indian Affairs (BIA), or other natural resources agencies. Along with their application, they must submit a letter that includes their perception of their academic and professional strengths and a description of their academic and career potential. They must also be interested in summer employment related to their academic field of study.

Financial data The scholarship stipend is $5,000 per year. The salary for summer employment ranges from $9 to $11 per hour.

Duration 1 academic year and 1 summer; may be renewed.

Additional information The National Center for Cooperative Education (NCCE) was established in 1997 by the BIA.

Number awarded Varies each year.

Deadline March of each year.

[777]
NATIONAL COLLEGIATE ATHLETIC ASSOCIATION ETHNIC MINORITY POSTGRADUATE SCHOLARSHIP PROGRAM

National Collegiate Athletic Association
Attn: Office for Diversity and Inclusion
700 West Washington Avenue
P.O. Box 6222
Indianapolis, IN 46206-6222
(317) 917-6222   Fax: (317) 917-6888
E-mail: ncastro@ncaa.org
Web: www.ncaa.org/about/scholarships.html

Purpose To provide funding to Native American and other minority graduate students who are interested in preparing for a career in intercollegiate athletics.

Eligibility This program is open to members of minority groups who have been accepted into a program at a National Collegiate Athletic Association (NCAA) member institution that will prepare them for a career in intercollegiate athletics (athletics administrator, coach, athletic trainer, or other career that provides a direct service to intercollegiate athletics). Applicants must be U.S. citizens, have performed with distinction as a student body member at their respective undergraduate institution, and be entering the first semester or term of full time postgraduate study. Selection is based on the applicant's involvement in extracurricular activities, course work, commitment to preparing for a career in intercollegiate athletics, and promise for success in that career. Financial need is not considered.

Financial data The stipend is $6,000; funds are paid to the college or university of the recipient's choice.

Duration 1 year; nonrenewable.

Number awarded 13 each year.

Deadline December of each year.

[778]
NATIONAL CRUSADE SCHOLARSHIP PROGRAM

United Methodist Church
General Board of Global Ministries
Attn: Scholarship Office
475 Riverside Drive, Room 1351
New York, NY 10115
(212) 870-3787   Toll-free: (800) UMC-GBGM
E-mail: scholars@gbgm-umc.org
Web: new.gbgm-umc.org

Purpose To provide financial assistance to Native American and other minority students who are interested in attending graduate school to prepare for leadership within the United Methodist Church.

Eligibility This program is open to U.S. citizens and permanent residents who are ethnic and racial minority graduate students (African Americans, Hispanic Americans, Pacific/Asian Americans, and Native Americans). They must have applied to or been admitted to a graduate program at an institution of higher education. Preference is given to members of the United Methodist Church. Applicants should be committed to preparing themselves for leadership in mission to church and society and serving for at least 10 years. Financial need must be demonstrated.

Financial data The stipend ranges from $250 to $12,500, depending on the recipient's related needs and school expenses.

Duration 1 year.

Additional information These awards are funded by the World Communion Offering received in United Methodist Churches on the first Sunday in October.

Number awarded 5 to 10 each year.

Deadline November of each year.

[779]
NATIONAL DENTAL ASSOCIATION FOUNDATION MEMORIAL AWARD

National Dental Association
Attn: National Dental Association Foundation, Inc.
3517 16th Street, N.W.
Washington, DC 20010
(202) 588-1697   Fax: (202) 588-1242
E-mail: admin@ndaonline.org
Web: www.nadonline.org/ndafoundation.asp

Purpose To provide financial assistance to Native American and other underrepresented minority dental postdoctoral students.

Eligibility This program is open to members of underrepresented minority groups who are dentists working on a degree in subspecialty areas of dentistry, public health, administration, research, or law. Students working on a master's degree beyond their residency may be considered. Applicants must be members of the National Dental Association (NDA) and U.S. citizens or permanent residents. Along with their application, they must submit a letter explaining why they should be considered for this scholarship, 2 letters of recommendation, a curriculum vitae, a description of the program, nomination by their program director, and documentation of financial need.

Financial data The stipend is $10,000.
Duration 1 year.
Additional information This program, established in 1990, is supported by the Colgate-Palmolive Company.
Number awarded 1 each year.
Deadline May of each year.

[780]
NATIONAL DENTAL ASSOCIATION FOUNDATION PRE-DOCTORAL SCHOLARSHIP PROGRAM

National Dental Association
Attn: National Dental Association Foundation, Inc.
3517 16th Street, N.W.
Washington, DC 20010
(202) 588-1697   Fax: (202) 588-1242
E-mail: admin@ndaonline.org
Web: www.nadonline.org/ndafoundation.asp

Purpose To provide financial assistance to Native American and other underrepresented minority dental students.
Eligibility This program is open to members of underrepresented minority groups who are entering their second, third, or fourth year of dental school. Applicants must be members of the Student National Dental Association (SNDA) and U.S. citizens or permanent residents. Along with their application, they must submit a letter explaining why they should be considered for this scholarship, 2 letters of recommendation, and documentation of financial need. Selection is based on academic performance and service to community and/or country.
Financial data The stipend is $1,000 per year.
Duration 1 year. Recipients may reapply.
Additional information This program, established in 1990, is supported by the Colgate-Palmolive Company.
Number awarded Varies each year.
Deadline May of each year.

[781]
NATIONAL MEDICAL FELLOWSHIP PROGRAM IN AIDS CARE

National Medical Fellowships, Inc.
Attn: Scholarship Program
5 Hanover Square, 15th Floor
New York, NY 10004
(212) 483-8880   Fax: (212) 483-8897
E-mail: info@nmfonline.org
Web: www.nmfonline.org

Purpose To provide funding to Native American and other underrepresented minority medical students who wish to receive specialized training in treating AIDS.
Eligibility This program is open to African American, Native Hawaiian, Alaskan Native, American Indian, Mexican American, and mainland Puerto Rican students enrolled in the second or third year of medical school. Candidates must be interested in participating in a multidisciplinary training program in HIV/AIDS clinical care and research at the University of California at San Francisco's AIDS Research Institute. Along with their application, they must submit a personal statement on their reasons for applying for this fellowship and what they expect to gain from the experience, including career plans over the next 10 years. Selection is based on academic achievement, leadership potential, and potential for distinguished contributions to medicine.
Financial data The stipend of $7,000 is intended to cover room, board, travel, and other related expenses.
Duration 4 weeks, during October of the participants' third or fourth year.
Additional information This program is a joint initiative of the University of California at San Francisco's AIDS Research Institute and National Medical Fellowships, Inc. Funding is provided by Kaiser Permanente, the California HealthCare Foundation, and Aetna Foundation, Inc.
Number awarded Up to 8 each year.
Deadline November of each year.

[782]
NATIONAL MUSEUM OF THE AMERICAN INDIAN WORKSHOPS IN MUSEUM TRAINING

National Museum of the American Indian
Attn: Museum Training Program
Cultural Resources Center
4220 Silver Hill Road
Suitland, MD 20746-2863
(301) 238-1540   Fax: (301) 238-3200
E-mail: NMAI-CSinfo@si.edu
Web: www.nmai.si.edu

Purpose To provide an opportunity for professionals at tribal museums to participate in training workshops sponsored by the Smithsonian Institution.
Eligibility Native Americans working in tribal museums and American Indian cultural centers are eligible to participate in this program. Workshops are held at various tribal locations in North America to assist museum professionals in the continuation and interpretation of tribal cultures as they define them. Topics include museum basics, collections, audience development, exhibitions, archives and research, fund raising, and language preservation in museums.
Financial data Stipends are provided to assist with travel and lodging expenses.
Duration Workshops normally last 3 to 4 weeks.
Number awarded 3 to 4 workshops are held each year; up to 15 participants are selected per workshop.

[783]
NATIONAL OCEANIC AND ATMOSPHERIC ADMINISTRATION EDUCATIONAL PARTNERSHIP PROGRAM WITH MINORITY SERVING INSTITUTIONS GRADUATE SCIENCES PROGRAM

Oak Ridge Institute for Science and Education
Attn: Science and Engineering Education
P.O. Box 117
Oak Ridge, TN 37831-0117
(865) 241-6704   Fax: (865) 576-8293
E-mail: MCarl.Wheeler@orau.gov
Web: see.orau.org

Purpose To provide financial assistance and summer research experience to graduate students at Minority Serving Institutions who are majoring in scientific fields of interest to the National Oceanic and Atmospheric Administration (NOAA).

Eligibility This program is open to graduate students working on master's or doctoral degrees at Minority Serving Institutions, including Alaska Native Serving Institutions (ANSIs), Hispanic Serving Institutions (HSIs), Historically Black Colleges and Universities (HBCUs), Native Hawaiian Serving Institutions (NHSIs), and Tribal Colleges and Universities (TCUs). Applicants must be working on a degree in biology, cartography, chemistry, computer science, economics, engineering, environmental planning, fishery biology, geography, geology, hydrology, mathematics, meteorology, oceanography, physical science, physics, or social science. The program includes a training program during the summer at a NOAA research facility.

Financial data During the school year, the program provides payment of tuition, fees, books, housing, meals, travel expenses, and a 1-time academic allowance. During the summer, students receive a salary and benefits from NOAA.

Duration 2 years of study plus 16 weeks of research training during the summer.

Additional information This program is funded by NOAA and administered by Oak Ridge Institute for Science and Education (ORISE). Summer assignments are available in the following sections of NOAA: National Environmental, Satellite, Data and Information Service; National Weather Service; National Ocean Service; National Marine Fisheries Service; and Office of Oceanic and Atmospheric Research.

Number awarded 5 each year.

Deadline January of each year.

[784]
NATIONAL SPACE GRANT COLLEGE AND FELLOWSHIP PROGRAM

National Aeronautics and Space Administration
Attn: Program Manager
NASA Headquarters
Washington, DC 20546-0001
(202) 358-1523   Fax: (202) 358-3048
E-mail: jdasch@hq.nasa.gov
Web: www.nasa.gov

Purpose To provide financial assistance to minority and other undergraduate and graduate students interested in preparing for a career in a space-related field at a college or university participating in the National Space Grant program.

Eligibility This program is open to undergraduate and graduate students at colleges and universities that participate in the National Space Grant program of the U.S. National Aeronautics and Space Administration (NASA) through their state consortium. Applicants must be interested in a program of study and/or research in a field of science, mathematics, engineering, or technology (SMET) related to space. A specific goal of the program is to increase preparation by members of underrepresented groups (minorities, women, and persons with disabilities) for SMET space-related careers. Financial need is not considered in the selection process.

Financial data Each consortium establishes the terms of the fellowship program in its state.

Additional information NASA established the Space Grant program in 1989. It operates through 52 consortia in each state, the District of Columbia, and Puerto Rico. Each consortium includes selected colleges and universities in that state as well as other affiliates from industry, museums, science centers, and state and local agencies. There are similar programs for postdoctorates and faculty at these institutions as well.

Number awarded Varies each year.

Deadline Each consortium sets its own deadlines.

[785]
NATIONAL STRENGTH AND CONDITIONING ASSOCIATION MINORITY SCHOLARSHIPS

National Strength and Conditioning Association
Attn: Grants and Scholarships Program
1885 Bob Johnson Drive
Colorado Springs, CO 80906
(719) 632-6722, ext. 105   Toll-free: (800) 815-6826
Fax: (719) 632-6367   E-mail: nsca@nsca-lift.org
Web: www.nsca-lift.org

Purpose To provide financial assistance to Native American and other minorities who are members of the National Strength and Conditioning Association (NSCA) and interested in preparing for a career in strength training and conditioning.

Eligibility This program is open to minorities 17 years of age and older who have been members of the association for at least 1 year. Applicants must have been accepted into an accredited postsecondary institution to work on a graduate degree in the strength and conditioning field. They must submit a 500-word essay describing their course of study, career goals, and financial need.

Financial data The stipend is $1,000.

Duration 1 year.

Additional information The NSCA is a nonprofit organization of strength and conditioning professionals, including coaches, athletic trainers, physical therapists, educators, researchers, and physicians. This program was first offered in 2003.

Number awarded 2 each year.

Deadline March of each year.

[786]
NATIONAL URBAN FELLOWS PROGRAM

National Urban Fellows, Inc.
Attn: Program Director
102 West 38th Street, Suite 700
New York, NY 10018-3675
(212) 730-1700   Fax: (212) 730-1823
E-mail: mgarciajr@nuf.org
Web: www.nuf.org

Purpose To provide mid-career public sector professionals, especially minorities and women, with an opportunity to strengthen leadership skills through a master's degree program coupled with a mentorship.

Eligibility This program is open to U.S. citizens who have a bachelor's degree, have at least 3 years of administrative or managerial experience, have demonstrated exceptional ability and leadership potential, meet academic admission requirements, have a high standard of integrity and work ethic, and are committed to the solution of urban problems. Applicants must a 1,000-word autobiographical statement and a 1,000-word statement on their career goals. They may be of any racial or ethnic background, but the program's goal is to increase the number of competent administrators from underrepresented ethnic and cultural groups at all levels of public and private urban management organizations. Semifinalists are interviewed.

Financial data The stipend is $25,000. The program also provides full payment of tuition, a relocation allowance of $500, a book allowance of $500, and reimbursement for program-related travel.

Duration 14 months.

Additional information The program begins with a summer semester of study at Bernard M. Baruch College of the City University of New York. Following this, fellows spend 9 months in mentorship assignments with a senior administrator in a government agency, a major nonprofit, or a foundation. The final summer is spent in another semester of study at Baruch College. Fellows who successfully complete all requirements are granted a master's of public administration from that college. A $75 processing fee must accompany each application.

Number awarded Varies; approximately 20 each year.

Deadline February of each year.

[787]
NATIVE AMERICAN FINANCE OFFICERS ASSOCIATION STUDENT SCHOLARSHIP

Native American Finance Officers Association
Attn: Christina Morbelli, Program Coordinator
P.O. Box 50637
Phoenix, AZ 85076-0637
(602) 466-8697   Fax: (201) 447-0945
E-mail: christina@nafoa.org
Web: www.nafoa.org/education.html

Purpose To provide financial assistance to Native Americans who are studying a business-related field in college or graduate school.

Eligibility This program is open to enrolled members of a federally-recognized tribe who are currently a junior or senior in college or studying for an M.B.A. Applicants must be majoring in finance, accounting, business administration, or management and must maintain a GPA of 2.8 or higher. Along with their application, they must submit an essay of 200 to 400 words that includes information on their connection to their Native community, their history in the finance profession, and their future goals in finance.

Financial data A stipend is awarded (amount not specified).

Duration 1 year.

Number awarded Varies each year; recently, 3 of these scholarships were awarded.

Deadline October of each year.

[788]
NATIVE AMERICAN HEALTH EDUCATION FUND SCHOLARSHIP

Native American Health Education Fund
1701 Pleasant Green Road
Durham, NC 27705
(919) 383-1038   Fax: (919) 383-1038
E-mail: nahefscholarship@aol.com

Purpose To provide financial assistance to Native Americans who are attending college or graduate school to prepare for a career in a health-related field.

Eligibility This program is open to Native American students currently enrolled at a college or university. Applicants must be preparing for a career in medicine, nursing, dietetics and nutrition, medical technology, physical therapy, pharmacy, social work, medical research (biochemistry), or other health-related fields. They must be able to demonstrate a desire to return to their community or Reservation to improve health care.

Financial data A stipend is awarded (amount not specified).

Duration 1 year.

Additional information This program awarded its first scholarship in 1990. The fund operates as a member of the Triangle Community Foundation, 324 Blackwell Street, Suite 1220, Durham, NC 27701, (919) 474-8370, Fax: (919) 941-9208, E-mail: info@trianglecf.org.

Number awarded Varies each year. Since the program began, it has awarded 106 scholarships.

Deadline June of each year.

[789]
NATIVE AMERICAN SUPPLEMENTAL GRANTS

Presbyterian Church (USA)
Attn: Office of Financial Aid for Studies
100 Witherspoon Street, Room M-052
Louisville, KY 40202-1396
(502) 569-5735   Toll-free: (888) 728-7228, ext. 5735
Fax: (502) 569-8766   E-mail: Lbryan@ctr.pcusa.org
Web: www.pcusa.org

Purpose To provide financial assistance to Native American students interested in preparing for church occupations within the Presbyterian Church (USA).

Eligibility This program is open to Native American and Alaska Native students who are enrolled full time at a PCUSA seminary or accredited theological institution approved by their presbytery's Committee on Preparation for Ministry (CPM). Applicants must be working on 1) an M.Div. degree and enrolled as an inquirer or candidate by a PCUSA presbytery, or 2) an M.A.C.E. degree and preparing for a church occupation. They must be PCUSA members, U.S. citizens or permanent residents, able to demonstrate financial need, and recommended by the financial aid officer at their theological institution.

Financial data Stipends range from $500 to $1,500 per year. Funds are intended as supplements to students who have been awarded a Presbyterian Study Grant but still demonstrate remaining financial need.

Duration 1 year; may be renewed up to 2 additional years.

Number awarded Varies each year.

Deadline June of each year.

[790]
NATIVE HAWAIIAN CHAMBER OF COMMERCE SCHOLARSHIPS

Ke Ali'i Pauahi Foundation
Attn: Financial Aid & Scholarship Services
567 South King Street, Suite 160
Honolulu, HI 96813
(808) 534-3966   Toll-free: (800) 842-4682, ext. 43966
Fax: (808) 534-3890   E-mail: scholarships@pauahi.org
Web: www.pauahi.org

Purpose To provide financial assistance to students, especially Native Hawaiians, who are interested in working on an undergraduate or graduate degree in business.

Eligibility This program is open to undergraduate and graduate students who are working on a degree in business administration. Applicants must have a GPA of 3.0 or higher. Residency in Hawaii is not required. Preference is given to Native Hawaiians (descendants of the aboriginal inhabitants of the Hawaiian Islands prior to 1778).

Financial data A stipend is awarded (amount not specified).

Duration 1 year; may be renewed.

Additional information This program is sponsored by the Native Hawaiian Chamber of Commerce.

Number awarded Varies each year; recently, 6 of these scholarships were awarded.

Deadline April of each year.

[791]
NAVAJO NATION GRADUATE TRUST FUND AND FELLOWSHIP

Navajo Nation
Attn: Office of Navajo Nation Scholarship and Financial Assistance
P.O. Box 1870
Window Rock, AZ 86515-1870
(928) 871-7640   Toll-free: (800) 243-2956
Fax: (928) 871-6561
E-mail: onnsfacentral@navajo.org
Web: www.onnsfa.org/gradfund.asp

Purpose To provide financial assistance to members of the Navajo Nation who wish to work on a graduate degree.

Eligibility This program is open to enrolled members of the Navajo Nation who are enrolled or planning to enroll as graduate students. Preference is given to students at institutions that provide matching funds to the Navajo Nation or its student participants. Candidates for a second graduate degree at the same level (master's, education terminal degree, or doctorate) are not eligible. Applicants must submit transcripts and documentation of financial need.

Financial data Stipends for full-time graduate students range from $5,000 to $10,000 per year, depending on the need of the recipient; for part-time graduate students, the stipend is $500 per 3 semester credit hours or equivalent amount of quarter credit hours.

Duration 1 year; may be renewed for a total of 5 semesters (6 semesters for law students) provided the recipient maintains a GPA of at least 3.0 (or 2.0 for medical, veterinary, and law students).

Deadline April of each year.

[792]
NAVAJO NATION TEACHER EDUCATION PROGRAM

Navajo Nation
Navajo Nation Scholarship and Financial Assistance
Attn: Navajo Nation Teacher Education Program
P.O. Box 4380
Window Rock, AZ 86515-4380
(928) 871-7453   Toll-free: (800) 243-2956
Fax: (928) 871-6443
E-mail: onnsfacentral@navajo.org
Web: www.onnsfa.org/nntep.asp

Purpose To provide financial assistance to members of the Navajo Nation who wish to prepare for a career as a bilingual or bicultural teacher.

Eligibility This program is open to enrolled members of the Navajo Nation who are enrolled in or planning to enroll in an undergraduate teacher education program, a post-baccalaureate program for teacher licensure, or a master's degree program in education. Applicants must complete an emphasis in either Navajo Language or Navajo Culture, taken concurrently each semester with teacher education courses. They may be specializing in elementary education, early childhood education, bilingual multicultural education, special education, educational leadership, school counseling, curriculum and instruction, library science, or science and mathematics secondary education. Students working on a second master's degree are not eligible. Financial need is not considered in the selection process.

Financial data Recipients are reimbursed for each course they complete at the rate of $250 per course for lower-division undergraduate courses or $500 for upper-division and graduate courses.

Duration 1 semester; may be renewed for undergraduate courses completed with a grade of "C" or better and for graduate courses completed with a grade of "B" or better.

Number awarded Varies each year; recently, 250 undergraduates and 225 graduate students were participating in the program.

Deadline June of each year for fall term; November of each year for winter or spring terms; April of each year for summer session.

[793]
NCEMNA AETNA SCHOLARS PROGRAM
National Coalition of Ethnic Minority Nurse
  Associations
c/o Dr. Betty Smith Williams, President
6101 West Centinela Avenue, Suite 378
Culver City, CA 90230
(310) 258-9515   Fax: (310) 258-9513
E-mail: bwilliams@ncemna.org
Web: www.ncemna.org/ncemna/scholarships.asp

Purpose To provide financial assistance to nursing students who are members of constituent organizations of the National Coalition of Ethnic Minority Nurse Associations (NCEMNA) and working on a 4-year or master's degree.

Eligibility This program is open to members of the 5 associations that comprise NCEMNA: the Asian American/Pacific Islander Nurses Association, Inc. (AAPINA), the National Alaska Native American Indian Nurses Association, Inc. (NANAINA), the National Association of Hispanic Nurses, Inc. (NAHN), the National Black Nurses Association, Inc. (NBNA), and the Philippine Nurses Association of America, Inc. (PNAA). Applicants must be currently attending or applying to a 4-year or master's degree program in nursing. Along with their application, they must submit a letter of reference, demonstration of leadership and involvement in the ethnic community, and a statement of career goals.

Financial data The stipend is $2,000.

Duration 1 year.

Additional information This program was established in 2004 with a grant from the Aetna Foundation.

Number awarded 5 each year: 1 nominee from each of the constituent associations.

Deadline April of each year.

[794]
NELL B. BROWN MEMORIAL AWARD
Cherokee Nation
Attn: Cherokee Nation Education Corporation
17675 South Muskogee Avenue
P.O. Box 948
Tahlequah, OK 74465
(918) 453-5420   Toll-free: (800) 256-0671 (within OK)
Fax: (918) 458-6195   E-mail: cnec@cherokee.org
Web: www.cherokee.org

Purpose To provide financial assistance to graduate student citizens of the Cherokee Nation who are working on a degree in a field related to American Indian or Cherokee studies at a university in any state.

Eligibility This program is open to citizens of the Cherokee Nation who live within or outside the jurisdictional area of the tribe. Applicants must be working on a graduate degree in history, anthropology, or archaeology with an emphasis on American Indian or Cherokee studies. Selection is based on GPA, ACT score, cultural and community activities, personal academic goals, commitment to work with Cherokee people in the future, and financial need.

Financial data The stipend is $1,000 per semester ($2,000 per year).

Duration 1 year. Renewal for the second semester requires the recipient to earn a GPA of 2.5 or higher in the first semester.

Number awarded 1 each year.

Deadline March of each year.

[795]
NICKERSON WEST SHAKESPEARE/ARAPAHO TRUST GRADUATE SCHOLARSHIP
Northern Arapaho Tribe
Attn: Sky People Higher Education
P.O. Box 8480
Ethete, WY 82520
(307) 332-5286   Toll-free: (800) 815-6795
Fax: (307) 332-9104
E-mail: assistant@skypeopleed.org
Web: www.skypeopleed.org

Purpose To provide financial assistance to members of the Northern Arapaho Tribe who are working on a graduate degree in any field.

Eligibility This program is open to full-time graduate students who have a GPA required by their school. Applicants must be of one-fourth Northern Arapaho descent (enrolled or non-enrolled) and must submit a Certificate of Indian Blood or other verification of Northern Arapaho blood with at least one-fourth degree. They may be working on a degree in any field. Along with their application, they must submit a 1-page personal statement that includes a brief history of their background, academic ability and achievement, work or leadership experience, participation in community-related activities, and career goals. Selection is based on that statement, potential to contribute to the community upon graduation, academic ability and achievement, and a letter of recommendation.

Financial data The stipend is $1,500 per year.

Duration 1 year; may be renewed.

Additional information Recipients are expected to apply for employment with the Northern Arapaho Tribe after graduation.

Number awarded 2 each year.

Deadline June of each year.

[796]
NINILCHIK HIGHER EDUCATION GRANT PROGRAM
Ninilchik Traditional Council
Attn: Tribal Services Department
P.O. Box 39444
Ninilchik, AK 99639
(907) 567-3313   Fax: (907) 567-3308
E-mail: ntc@ninilchiktribe-nsn.gov
Web: www.ninilchiktribe-nsn.gov

Purpose To provide financial assistance for college or graduate school to Ninilchik Tribal members.

Eligibility Applicants must be an enrolled Ninilchik Tribal member or a one-quarter degree blood descendant of a member. They must be enrolled or accepted for enrollment in a 4-year academic degree program at an accredited institution as a full-time undergraduate or graduate student. Financial need must be demonstrated.

Financial data Grants range from $400 to $1,500 per semester, depending on the availability of funds and the number of recipients. Total funds available for this program are approximately $12,000 per year.

Duration 1 year; may be renewed for up to 4 additional years if the recipient maintains full-time enrollment and a GPA of 2.0 or higher.
Number awarded 4 to 10 each year.
Deadline August of each year for fall semester; December of each year for spring semester; May of each year for summer semester.

[797]
NJLA DIVERSITY SCHOLARSHIP
New Jersey Library Association
4 Lafayette Street
P.O. Box 1534
Trenton, NJ 08607
(609) 394-8032   Fax: (609) 394-8164
E-mail: ptumulty@njla.org
Web: www.njla.org/honorsawards/scholarship

Purpose To provide financial assistance to New Jersey residents who are Native Americans or members of other minority groups and interested in working on a graduate or postgraduate degree in public librarianship at a school in any state.
Eligibility This program is open to residents of New Jersey and individuals who have worked in a New Jersey library for at least 12 months. Applicants must be members of a minority group (African American, Asian/Pacific Islander, Latino/Hispanic, or Native American/Native Alaskan). They must be enrolled or planning to enroll at an ALA-accredited school of library science in any state to work on a graduate or postgraduate degree in librarianship. Along with their application, they must submit an essay of 150 to 250 words explaining their choice of librarianship as a profession. An interview is required. Selection is based on academic ability and financial need.
Financial data The stipend is $1,000.
Duration 1 year.
Additional information Information is also available from Arlene Sahraie, Scholarship Committee Chair, Bergen County Cooperative Library System, 810 Main Street, Hackensack, NJ 07601, (201) 489-1904, E-mail: arlene@bccls.org.
Number awarded 1 each year.
Deadline February of each year.

[798]
NLM INDIVIDUAL FELLOWSHIP FOR INFORMATIONIST TRAINING
National Library of Medicine
Attn: Extramural Programs
6705 Rockledge Drive, Suite 301
Bethesda, MD 20892-7968
(301) 594-4882   Fax: (301) 402-2952
TTY: (301) 451-0088   E-mail: florancev@mail.nih.gov
Web: www.nlm.nih.gov/grants.html

Purpose To provide financial assistance to Native American and other health science librarians and health professionals who are interested in additional training to prepare for a career as an informationist.
Eligibility This program is open to health sciences librarians, scientists, health professionals, and others interested in broadening their existing scientific background by acquiring additional disciplinary knowledge and experience to function as an informationist. Applicants must have a master's or doctoral degree, preferably in library and information sciences, health fields, biomedical and behavioral sciences, public health, engineering, or computer science. They must be interested in a mentored training program under the supervision of an experienced informationist at a domestic nonprofit institution, such as a university, college, hospital, laboratories, unit of state or local government, or eligible agency of the federal government (including intramural laboratories of the National Institutes of Health). The program must include formal course work, a practicum, and a research project. Members of underrepresented racial and ethnic groups and individuals with disabilities are especially encouraged to apply. Only U.S. citizens, nationals, and permanent residents are eligible.
Financial data The award provides an annual stipend based on the number of years of experience beyond the graduate degree, ranging from $36,996 for less than 1 year to $51,036 for 7 or more years. Institutions also receive an allowance to help defray such awardee expenses as self-only health insurance, research supplies, equipment, travel to scientific meetings, and related items; the allowance is $7,850 per 12-month period for fellows at nonfederal, nonprofit institutions and $6,750 per 12-month period at federal laboratories and for-profit institutions. In addition, tuition and fees are reimbursed at a rate of 60%, up to $4,500; if the fellow's program supports postdoctoral individuals in formal degree-granting training, tuition is supported at the rate of 60%, up to $16,000 for an additional degree.
Duration 1 or 2 years; nonrenewable.
Number awarded Varies each year.
Deadline April, August, or December of each year.

[799]
NMF NEED-BASED SCHOLARSHIP PROGRAM
National Medical Fellowships, Inc.
Attn: Scholarship Program
5 Hanover Square, 15th Floor
New York, NY 10004
(212) 483-8880   Fax: (212) 483-8897
E-mail: info@nmfonline.org
Web: www.nmfonline.org

Purpose To provide financial assistance to Native American and other underrepresented minority medical students.
Eligibility This program is open to U.S. citizens enrolled in the first or second year of an accredited M.D. or D.O. degree-granting program in the United States. Applicants must be African American, Mexican American, Native Hawaiian, Alaska Native, American Indian, or mainland Puerto Rican. They must submit an essay of 500 to 1,000 words on their motivation for a career in medicine and their personal and professional goals over the next 10 years. Selection is based primarily on financial need.
Financial data The amount of the award depends on the student's total resources (including parental and spousal support), cost of education, and receipt of additional scholarships; recently, individual awards ranged from $500 to $10,000 per year.
Duration 1 year for first-year students; may be renewed for the second year only.
Number awarded Varies each year; recently, more than 300 students received support from this program.

Deadline June of each year.

[800]
NORMAN TECUBE SR. HIGHER EDUCATION FUND
Jicarilla Apache Tribe
Attn: Higher Education Program
P.O. Box 1099
Dulce, NM 87528
(505) 759-3242 Fax: (505) 759-9111
E-mail: jicarillahep@yahoo.com
Web: www.jicarillaonline.com

Purpose To provide financial assistance for undergraduate or graduate education to members of the Jicarilla Apache tribe.

Eligibility Enrolled members of the Jicarilla Apache tribe are eligible to apply if they are attending either undergraduate or graduate school. Recipients may enroll in any accredited postsecondary school and may major in any subject area. Financial need is considered in the selection process.

Financial data The amount awarded varies, depending on need, up to a maximum of $1,800 per year. Funds may not be used for extracurricular activities, trips out of the United States, non-credit courses, or unnecessary tools.

Duration 1 year; may be renewed.

Additional information This program was formerly called the Chester E. Faris Higher Education Fund.

Number awarded Varies each year.

Deadline February for fall semester or academic year applications; September of each year for spring semester applications.

[801]
NORTH AMERICAN DOCTORAL FELLOWSHIPS
The Fund for Theological Education, Inc.
825 Houston Mill Road, Suite 250
Atlanta, GA 30329
(404) 727-1450 Fax: (404) 727-1490
E-mail: fellowships@thefund.org
Web: www.thefund.org/programs/racialethnic.phtml

Purpose To provide financial assistance to North American and other underrepresented racial and ethnic minority students enrolled in a doctoral program in religious or theological studies.

Eligibility This program is open to continuing students enrolled full time in a Ph.D. or Th.D. program in religious or theological studies. Applicants must be citizens or permanent residents of the United States or Canada who are racial or ethnic minority students traditionally underrepresented in graduate education. D.Min. students are ineligible. Preference is given to students nearing completion of their degree. Selection is based on commitment to teaching and scholarship, academic achievement, capacity for leadership in theological scholarship, and financial need.

Financial data Stipends range from $5,000 to $10,000 per year, depending on financial need.

Duration 1 year; may be renewed up to 2 additional years.

Additional information Funding for this program is provided by the National Council of Churches, proceeds from the book *Stony the Road We Trod: African American Biblical Interpretation,* an endowment from the Hearst Foundation, and the previously established FTE Black Doctoral Program supported by Lilly Endowment, Inc.

Number awarded Varies each year; recently, 12 of these fellowships were awarded.

Deadline February of each year.

[802]
NORTHERN CHEYENNE HIGHER EDUCATION SCHOLARSHIP PROGRAM
Northern Cheyenne Nation
Attn: Tribal Education Department
P.O. Box 307
Lame Deer, MT 59043
(406) 477-6567 Toll-free: (800) 353-8183
Fax: (406) 477-8150 E-mail: norma@rangeweb.net
Web: www.cheyennenation.com

Purpose To provide financial assistance for college or graduate school to Northern Cheyenne tribal members.

Eligibility This program is open to enrolled Northern Cheyenne tribal members who have been accepted to a degree program at an accredited college or university. The priority order for awards is 1) continuing and former college students in good standing; 2) graduating high school seniors in good standing or first-time adult college applicants not previously funded; 3) students or other individuals who have previously failed to meet the requirements of the scholarship program; and 4) graduate students (if funds are still available). All applicants must be able to demonstrate financial need.

Financial data The stipend depends on the need of the recipient, to a maximum of $6,000 per year. These awards are intended to supplement other available sources of funding. The scholarship must be used for tuition, subsistence, required fees, and textbooks.

Duration 1 year; may be renewed if the recipient maintains a GPA of 2.0 or higher and completes at least 14 quarter or 16 semester units as a freshman and sophomore and at least 16 quarter or 18 semester units as a junior or senior.

Additional information Recipients who reside in Montana are expected to attend a postsecondary institution in the state. They must pay the difference in cost between Montana public postsecondary schools and private or out-of-state schools, if they elect to attend either of those. An exception is made if no comparable course of study exists in a Montana public institution. Eligible Northern Cheyenne Indians residing out of state are subject to the same regulation; however, they may enroll in a Montana institution of higher learning if there is no comparable course of study at a public institution in their home state.

Number awarded Approximately 80 each year.

Deadline February of each year for fall quarter/semester; September of each year for winter quarter/spring semester/spring quarter; March of each year for summer school.

[803]
NORTON SOUND HEALTH CORPORATION SCHOLARSHIPS

Norton Sound Health Corporation
Attn: Scholarships
P.O. Box 966
Nome, AK 99762
(907) 443-4530   Fax: (907) 443-2085
E-mail: info@nortonsoundhealth.org
Web: www.nortonsoundhealth.org/scholarship.html

Purpose To provide financial assistance to Native and other residents of Alaska who are interested in working on an undergraduate or graduate degree in a health-related field.

Eligibility This program is open to students enrolled in or planning to enrolled in an undergraduate or graduate program in a field of study relevant to employment at Norton Sound Health Corporation (NSHC). Priority is given to applicants in the following order: 1) Native residents of the Bering Straits region of Alaska; 2) Native residents of other regions of Alaska; and 3) non-Native residents of the Bering Straits region. They must submit brief statements on their educational goals and objectives, the activities in which they are currently participating, their community activities, and honors or awards they have received. Financial need is also considered in the selection process.

Financial data A stipend is awarded (amount not specified).

Duration 1 year; may be renewed if the recipient maintains full-time enrollment and a GPA of 2.5 or higher.

Additional information The Norton Sound Health Corporation was founded in 1970 to serve the health care need of the Inupiat, Yupik, and Siberian Yupik people of the Bering Straits region of northwest Alaska.

Number awarded Varies each year.

Deadline April of each year for fall terms; November of each year for spring terms.

[804]
NPSC GRADUATE FELLOWSHIPS

National Physical Science Consortium
c/o University of Southern California
3716 South Hope Street, Suite 348
Los Angeles, CA 90007-4344
(213) 743-2409   Toll-free: (800) 854-NPSC
Fax: (213) 743-2407   E-mail: npschq@npsc.org
Web: www.npsc.org/students/info.html

Purpose To provide financial assistance and summer work experience to underrepresented minorities and women interested in working on a Ph.D. in designated science and engineering fields.

Eligibility This program is open to U.S. citizens who are seniors graduating from college with a GPA of 3.0 or higher, enrolled in the first year of a doctoral program, completing a terminal master's degree, or returning from the work force and holding no more than a master's degree. Students currently in the third or subsequent year of a Ph.D. program or who already have a doctoral degree in any field (Ph.D., M.D., J.D., Ed.D.) are ineligible. Applicants must be interested in working on a Ph.D. in the physical sciences or related fields of science or engineering. The program welcomes applications from all qualified students and continues to emphasize the recruitment of underrepresented minority (African American, Hispanic, Native American Indian, Eskimo, Aleut, and Pacific Islander) and women physical science and engineering students. Fellowships are provided to students at the 116 universities that are members of the consortium. Selection is based on academic standing (GPA), course work taken in preparation for graduate school, university and/or industry research experience, letters of recommendation, and GRE scores.

Financial data The fellowship pays tuition and fees plus an annual stipend of $16,000. It also provides on-site paid summer employment to enhance technical experience. The exact value of the fellowship depends on academic standing, summer employment, and graduate school attended; the total amount generally exceeds $200,000.

Duration Support is initially provided for 2 or 3 years, depending on the employer-sponsor. If the fellow makes satisfactory progress and continues to meet the conditions of the award, support may continue for a total of up to 6 years or completion of the Ph.D., whichever comes first.

Additional information This program began in 1989. Tuition and fees are provided by the participating universities. Stipends and summer internships are provided by sponsoring organizations. Students must submit separate applications for internships, which may have additional eligibility requirements. Internships are currently available at Lawrence Livermore National Laboratory in Livermore, California (astronomy, chemistry, computer science, geology, materials science, mathematics, and physics); Los Alamos National Laboratory in Los Alamos, New Mexico (computer science, engineering, mathematics, and physics); National Security Agency in Fort Meade, Maryland (astronomy, chemistry, computer science, geology, materials science, mathematics, and physics); Sandia National Laboratory in Livermore, California (biology, chemistry, computer science, environmental science, geology, materials science, mathematics, and physics); and Sandia National Laboratory in Albuquerque, New Mexico (chemical engineering, chemistry, computer science, materials science, mathematics, mechanical engineering, and physics). Fellows must submit a separate application for dissertation support in the year prior to the beginning of their dissertation research program, but not until they can describe their intended research in general terms.

Number awarded Varies each year; recently, 11 of these fellowships were awarded.

Deadline November of each year.

[805]
N.S. BIENSTOCK FELLOWSHIP

Radio and Television News Directors Foundation
Attn: RTNDF Fellowship Program
4121 Plank Road, Suite 512
Fredericksburg, VA 22407
(202) 467-5214   Fax: (202) 223-4007
E-mail: staceys@rtnda.org
Web: www.rtnda.org/pages/education.php

Purpose To provide financial assistance for professional development to Native American and other minority journalists employed in electronic news.

Eligibility This program is open to minority journalists employed in electronic news who have 10 years of less of

full-time experience. Applications must include samples of the journalist's work done as the member of a news staff, with a script and tape (audio or video) up to 15 minutes.
Financial data The grant is $2,500 plus an all-expense paid trip to the international convention of the Radio-Television News Directors Association held that year.
Duration The grant is presented annually.
Additional information The grant, established in 1999, may be used in any way to improve the craft and enhance the excellence of the recipient's news operation.
Number awarded 1 each year.
Deadline May of each year.

[806]
NSF GRADUATE RESEARCH FELLOWSHIPS
National Science Foundation
Directorate for Education and Human Resources
Attn: Division of Graduate Education
4201 Wilson Boulevard, Room 907N
Arlington, VA 22230
(703) 331-3424   Toll-free: (866) NSF-GRFP
Fax: (703) 292-9048   E-mail: help@nsfgradfellows.org
Web: www.nsf.gov

Purpose To provide financial assistance to graduate students, especially those who will increase diversity, who are interested in working on a master's or doctoral degree in fields supported by the National Science Foundation (NSF).
Eligibility This program is open to U.S. citizens, nationals, and permanent residents who wish to work on research-based master's or doctoral degrees in a field of science (including social science), technology, engineering, or mathematics (STEM) supported by NSF. Research in bioengineering is eligible if it involves 1) diagnosis or treatment-related goals that apply engineering principles to problems in biology and medicine while advancing engineering knowledge, or 2) aiding persons with disabilities. Other work in medical, dental, law, public health, or practice-oriented professional degree programs, or in joint science-professional degree programs, such as M.D./Ph.D. and J.D./Ph.D. programs, is not eligible. Other categories of ineligible support include 1) clinical, counseling, business, or management fields; 2) education (except science education); 3) history (except the history of science); 4) social work; 5) medical sciences or research with disease-related goals, including work on the etiology, diagnosis, or treatment of physical or mental disease, abnormality, or malfunction in human beings or animals; 6) research involving animal models with disease-related goals; and 7) testing of drugs or other procedures for disease-related goals. Applications normally should be submitted during the senior year in college or in the first year of graduate study; eligibility is limited to those who have completed no more than 12 months of graduate study since completion of a baccalaureate degree. Applicants who have already earned an advanced degree in science, engineering, or medicine (including an M.D., D.D.S., or D.V.M.) are ineligible. Selection is based on intellectual merit and broader impacts. Intellectual merit includes intellectual ability and other accepted requisites for scholarly scientific study, such as the ability to work as a member of a team as well as independently, to interpret and communicate research findings, and to plan and conduct research. The broader impacts criterion includes contributions that 1) effectively integrate research and education at all levels, infuse learning with the excitement of discovery, and assure that the findings and methods of research are communicated in a broad context and to a large audience; 2) encourage diversity, broaden opportunities, and enable the participation of women, underrepresented minorities, and persons with disabilities in science and engineering; 3) enhance scientific and technical understanding; and 4) benefit society.
Financial data The stipend is $30,000 per year; an additional $10,500 cost-of-education allowance is provided to the recipient's institution. If a fellow affiliates with a foreign institution, tuition and fees are reimbursed to the fellow up to a maximum of $10,500 per tenure year and an additional international research travel allowance of $1,000 is provided.
Duration Up to 3 years, usable over a 5-year period.
Additional information Fellows may choose as their fellowship institution any appropriate nonprofit U.S. or foreign institution of higher education.
Number awarded Approximately 1,100 each year.
Deadline October of each year.

[807]
OLIVER GOLDSMITH, M.D. SCHOLARSHIP
Kaiser Permanente, Southern California
Attn: Resident Recruitment and Outreach
94 South Los Robles
Pasadena, CA 91101
Toll-free: (877) 574-0002   Fax: (626) 564-5822
E-mail: socal.residency@kp.org
Web: residency.kp.org/scal/scholarship.html

Purpose To provide financial assistance to Native American and other medical students who will help bring diversity to the profession.
Eligibility This program is open to students entering their third or fourth year of allopathic or osteopathic medical school. Applicants must have demonstrated their commitment to diversity through community service, clinical volunteering, or research. They may be attending medical school in any state, but they must intend to practice in southern California and they must be available to participate in a mentoring program and a clinical rotation at a Kaiser Permanente facility in that region.
Financial data The stipend is $5,000.
Duration 1 year.
Additional information These scholarships were first awarded in 2004.
Number awarded 10 each year.
Deadline February of each year.

[808]
ONEIDA TRIBE HIGHER EDUCATION GRANT PROGRAM

Oneida Nation of Wisconsin
Attn: Higher Education Office
N7210 Seminary Road, North Wing
P.O. Box 365
Oneida, WI 54155-0365
(920) 869-4333   Toll-free: (800) 236-2214, ext. 4333
Fax: (920) 869-4039
E-mail: cvanden2@oneidanation.org
Web: www.oneidanation.org

Purpose To provide financial assistance for undergraduate or graduate study to members of the Oneida Tribe of Wisconsin.

Eligibility This program is open to enrolled members of the Oneida Tribe of Wisconsin who have a high school diploma, HSED diploma, or GED. Applicants must be working on or planning to work on a vocational/technical, undergraduate, graduate, or doctoral degree at a college, university, or vocational school in any state. They must be able to demonstrate financial need.

Financial data Stipends range up to $20,000 per year, depending on the need of the recipient.

Duration The total length of eligibility is 6 terms for vocation/technical students, 10 terms for undergraduate students, 6 terms for graduate students, and 10 terms for doctoral students. To be eligible for renewal, vocational/technical students and undergraduates must maintain a GPA of 2.0 or higher and graduate and doctoral students must maintain a GPA of 3.0 or higher.

Number awarded Varies each year, depending upon the availability of funds.

Deadline Applications must be submitted by April of each year for the fall term, by September of each year for the spring term, or by April of each year for the summer term.

[809]
OPERATION JUMP START III SCHOLARSHIPS

American Association of Advertising Agencies
Attn: AAAA Foundation
405 Lexington Avenue, 18th Floor
New York, NY 10174-1801
(212) 682-2500   Toll-free: (800) 676-9333
Fax: (212) 682-2028   E-mail: ameadows@aaaa.org
Web: www.aaaa.org

Purpose To provide financial assistance to multicultural art directors and copywriters interested in working on a graduate degree in advertising.

Eligibility This program is open to African Americans, Asian Americans, Hispanic Americans, and Native Americans who are interested in studying the advertising creative arts at designated institutions. Applicants must have already received an undergraduate degree and be able to demonstrate financial need. As part of the selection process, they must submit 10 samples of creative work in their respective field of expertise.

Financial data The stipend is $5,000 per year.

Duration Most awards are for 2 years.

Additional information Operation Jump Start began in 1997 and was followed by Operation Jump Start II in 2002. The current program began in 2006. Participating schools are the AdCenter at Virginia Commonwealth University, the Creative Circus and the Portfolio Center in Atlanta, the Miami Ad School, the University of Texas at Austin, Pratt Institute, the Minneapolis College of Art and Design, and the Art Center College of Design at Pasadena, California.

Number awarded 20 each year.

[810]
OSAGE HIGHER EDUCATION GRANTS

Osage Nation Education Department
Attn: Scholarship Coordinator
HC 66
P.O. Box 990
Hominy, OK 74035
(918) 287-5301   Toll-free: (800) 390-6724
Fax: (918) 287-5567   E-mail: jholding@osagetribe.com
Web: www.osagetribe.com/education/index.aspx

Purpose To provide financial assistance for college or graduate school to members of the Osage Tribe.

Eligibility This program is open to Osage tribal students who are enrolled or planning to enroll in a 2-year or 4-year college or university. A point system is used to rank applicants, including such factors as student status (freshman through graduate student), number of previous full-time semesters in college, GPA from previous semester, full-time or part-time enrollment, qualification for federal Pell Grant, and Osage blood quantum.

Financial data The amount of the award depends on the number of points earned by the recipient.

Duration 1 semester; may be renewed.

Number awarded Varies each year.

Deadline June of each year for fall semester; December of each year for spring semester; April of each year for summer term.

[811]
OSAGE TRIBAL EDUCATION COMMITTEE PROGRAM

Osage Tribal Education Committee
c/o Oklahoma Area Education Office
4149 Highline Boulevard, Suite 380
Oklahoma City, OK 73108
(405) 605-6051, ext. 300   Fax: (405) 605-6057

Purpose To provide financial assistance to undergraduate and graduate Osage students.

Eligibility This program is open to students who can prove Osage Indian blood in any degree. Applicants must be enrolled in an accredited college, university, or technical vocational program. They may be residents of any state.

Financial data The amount of the award depends on the financial need of the recipient.

Duration 1 year; may be renewed for up to 4 additional years, provided the recipient reapplies each semester and maintains a GPA of 2.0 or higher.

Number awarded Varies each year.

Deadline June of each year for fall term; December of each year for spring term.

[812]
OTTAWA TRIBE HIGHER EDUCATION GRANTS
Ottawa Tribe of Oklahoma
c/o Oklahoma Area Education Office
4149 Highline Boulevard, Suite 380
Oklahoma City, OK 73108
(405) 605-6051, ext. 304   Fax: (405) 605-6057
Web: ottawatribe.org/heducation.htm

Purpose To provide financial assistance to members of the Ottawa Tribe of Oklahoma who plan to attend college or graduate school in any state.

Eligibility This program is open to enrolled members of the Ottawa Tribe of Oklahoma who have been accepted at an accredited institution of higher education in any state as a full- or part-time undergraduate or graduate student. Applicants must be able to document financial need. Along with their application, they must submit a copy of their tribal enrollment card, a copy of their high school and/or college transcripts, documentation of financial need, and a letter of intent explaining why they wish to attend college.

Financial data The amount of the award depends on the financial need of the recipient.

Duration 1 year; may be renewed for up to 4 additional years, provided the recipient reapplies each semester and maintains a GPA of 2.0 or higher.

Number awarded Varies each year.

Deadline July of each year.

[813]
PACIFIC ISLANDERS IN COMMUNICATIONS SCHOLARSHIPS
Pacific Islanders in Communications
Attn: Scholarship Committee
1221 Kapi'olani Boulevard, Suite 6A-4
Honolulu, HI 96814-3513
(808) 591-0059   Fax: (808) 591-1114
E-mail: gcobb-adams@piccom.org
Web: www.piccom.org/producers.php

Purpose To provide financial assistance to undergraduate and graduate students, especially Pacific Islanders, who are working on a degree in media and/or communications.

Eligibility This program is open to students who are working on a degree, certificate, and/or other certification in media and/or communications at the undergraduate, graduate, or unclassified level of study. Applicants must be 18 years of age or older and citizens, legal permanent residents, or nationals of the United States or its territories. All students are eligible, but the program especially encourages applications from Pacific Islanders, defined as descendants of the indigenous peoples of American Samoa, Guam, Hawai'i, the Northern Mariana Islands, and other Pacific Islands. Along with their application, they must submit a 500-word essay on why they feel Pacific Islander representation in media is important and their role in advancing equitable representation; their essay should include their reasons for attending school, their career goals and how this education will further those goals, prior and current service to school and community (in particular the Pacific Islander community), and a personal and professional history. Selection is based on the essay; academic proficiency; demonstrated experience in media, communications, and/or a related field; commitment to the Pacific Islander community; and financial need.

Financial data The stipend is $5,000.

Duration 1 year; nonrenewable.

Additional information This program began in 2002.

Number awarded Varies each year.

Deadline March of each year.

[814]
PASCUA YAQUI HIGHER EDUCATION SCHOLARSHIP
Pascua Yaqui Tribe
Attn: Higher Education Program
7474 South Camino de Oeste
Tucson, AZ 85746
(520) 883-5050   Toll-free: (800) 5-PASCUA
Fax: (520) 883-5021
Web: www.pascuayaqui-nsn.gov

Purpose To provide financial assistance to members of the Pascua Yaqui Tribe who are interested in attending a college or graduate school in any state.

Eligibility This program is open to enrolled members of the Pascua Yaqui Tribe who are attending or planning to attend a college, university, or vocational/technical institute in any state. Applicants must apply for all other available aid and still have unmet financial need. They may be planning to work on an undergraduate or graduate degree on a full- or part-time basis.

Financial data A stipend is awarded (amount not specified).

Duration 1 semester; may be renewed.

Number awarded Varies each year.

Deadline June of each year for fall; November of each year for spring; May of each year for summer.

[815]
PATRICK D. MCJULIEN MINORITY GRADUATE SCHOLARSHIP
Association for Educational Communications and Technology
Attn: ECT Foundation
1800 North Stonelake Drive, Suite 2
Bloomington, IN 47408
(812) 335-7675   Toll-free: (877) 677-AECT
Fax: (812) 335-7678
Web: www.aect.org/Foundation/Awards/McJulien.asp

Purpose To provide financial assistance to Native American and other minority members of the Association for Educational Communications and Technology (AECT) working on a graduate degree in the field of educational communications and technology.

Eligibility This program is open to AECT members who are members of minority groups. Applicants must be full-time graduate students enrolled in a degree-granting program in educational technology at the masters (M.S.), specialist (Ed.S.), or doctoral (Ph.D., Ed.D.) levels with a GPA of 3.0 or higher.

Financial data A stipend is awarded (amount not specified).

Duration 1 year.

Number awarded 1 each year.
Deadline July of each year.

[816]
PAUL AND EMILY SHAGEN SCHOLARSHIP
Chippewa County Community Foundation
P.O. Box 1979
Sault Ste. Marie, MI 49783
(906) 635-1046   Fax: (775) 417-7368
E-mail: cccf@lighthouse.net
Web: www.cccf4good4ever.org/main.asp?id=7

Purpose To provide financial assistance to members of the Sault Ste. Marie Tribe of Chippewa Indians who are interested in attending college or graduate school in any state.
Eligibility This program is open to enrolled members of the Sault Ste. Marie Tribe of Chippewa Indians who have been accepted for enrollment as a full-time undergraduate, graduate, or professional student at an accredited college, university, vocational school, or community college in any state. Applicants must submit an essay of 300 to 500 words on how they plan to use the education or training to contribute to the community, including the tribe. Selection is based on that essay, academic performance and progress, and financial need.
Financial data A stipend is awarded (amount not specified).
Duration 1 year.
Number awarded Varies each year.
Deadline June or November of each year.

[817]
PAUL D. WHITE SCHOLARSHIP
Baker Hostetler LLP
Attn: Attorney Recruitment and Development Manager
3200 National City Center
1900 East Ninth Street
Cleveland, OH 44114-3485
(216) 861-7092   Fax: (216) 696-0740
E-mail: ddriscole@bakerlaw.com
Web: www.bakerlaw.com

Purpose To provide financial assistance and summer work experience to minority law school students.
Eligibility This program is open to first- and second-year law students of African American, Hispanic, Asian American, or American Indian descent. Selection is based on law school performance, demonstrated leadership abilities (as evidenced by community and collegiate involvement), collegiate academic record, extracurricular activities, work experience, and a written personal statement.
Financial data The program provides a stipend of $6,000 for the scholarship and $8,400 per month for a summer clerkship with the sponsoring firm. To date, the firm has paid out more than $1.5 million in scholarships and clerkships.
Duration 1 year, including the following summer.
Additional information This program was established in 1997.
Number awarded 2 each year: 1 in the Cincinnati office and 1 in the Columbus office.
Deadline January of each year.

[818]
PAULA DE MERIEUX RHEUMATOLOGY FELLOWSHIP AWARD
American College of Rheumatology
Attn: Research and Education Foundation
1800 Century Place, Suite 250
Atlanta, GA 30345
(404) 633-3777   Fax: (404) 633-1870
E-mail: ref@rheumatology.org
Web: www.rheumatology.org

Purpose To provide funding to women and underrepresented minorities interested in a program of training for a career providing clinical care to people affected by rheumatic diseases.
Eligibility This program is open to trainees at ACGME-accredited institutions. Applications must be submitted by the training program director at the institution who is responsible for selection and appointment of trainees. The program must train and prepare fellows to provide clinical care to those affected by rheumatic diseases. Trainees must be women or members of underrepresented minority groups, defined as Black Americans, Native Americans (Native Hawaiians, Alaska Natives, and American Indians), Mexican Americans, Puerto Ricans, or other minorities. They must be U.S. citizens, nationals, or permanent residents. Selection is based on the institution's pass rate of rheumatology fellows, publication history of staff and previous fellows, current positions of previous fellows, and status of clinical faculty.
Financial data The grant is $25,000 per year, to be used as salary for the trainee. Other trainee costs (e.g., fees, health insurance, travel, attendance at scientific meetings) are to be incurred by the recipient's institutional program. Supplemental or additional support to offset the cost of living may be provided by the grantee institution.
Duration Up to 1 year.
Additional information This fellowship was first awarded in 2005.
Number awarded 1 each year.
Deadline July of each year.

[819]
PEARL CARTER SCOTT AVIATION SCHOLARSHIP
Chickasaw Foundation
110 West 12th Street
P.O. Box 1726
Ada, OK 74821-1726
(580) 421-9030   Fax: (580) 421-9031
E-mail: ChickasawFoundation@chickasaw.net
Web: www.chickasaw.net

Purpose To provide financial assistance to members of the Chickasaw Nation who are working on an undergraduate or graduate degree in a field related to aviation.
Eligibility This program is open to Chickasaw students who are currently enrolled at a college, university, or recognized private aviation school. Applicants must be working on an undergraduate or graduate degree in a field related to aviation (e.g., aviation maintenance technology, flight training, aviation law, air traffic control, aeronautical engineering, aerospace mechanical engineering, manufacturing engineering with an aviation emphasis, airline and airport operations, airport management, meteorology, aviation

technology management, or a related field). Along with their application, they must submit high school or college transcripts, 2 letters of recommendation, a copy of their Chickasaw Nation citizenship card, and a 1-page essay on their long-term goals and plans for achieving them. Financial need is not considered in the selection process.
Financial data The stipend is $1,250 per year.
Duration 1 year; may be renewed if the recipient demonstrates appropriate progress toward a degree in an aviation program.
Number awarded 1 each year.
Deadline July of each year.

[820]
PENOBSCOT NATION FELLOWSHIP
Penobscot Nation
Attn: Department of Education and Career Services
6 River Road
Indian Island, ME 04468
(207) 827-1649, ext. 148   Fax: (207) 827-2088
E-mail: pinedu@penobscotnation.org
Web: www.penobscotnation.org

Purpose To provide financial assistance to members of the Penobscot Nation who are working on a graduate degree at a college or university in any state.
Eligibility This program is open to students who are members of the Penobscot Nation and are enrolled either full or part time in a graduate degree program at a college or university in any state. Selection is not based on financial need.
Financial data A stipend is awarded (amount not specified). Funds may be used for any educational expense.
Duration 1 year or more.
Number awarded Varies each year.
Deadline June of each year.

[821]
PETER DOCTOR MEMORIAL INDIAN EMLEN AWARDS
Peter Doctor Memorial Indian Scholarship Foundation, Inc.
c/o Clara Hill, Treasurer
P.O. Box 731
Basom, NY 14013
(716) 542-2025   E-mail: cehill@wnynet.net

Purpose To provide financial assistance to undergraduate or graduate students of New York Iroquois descent.
Eligibility This program is open to undergraduate or graduate students who are of Iroquois Indian descent (i.e., a parent or grandparent must be enrolled). Applicants must have completed at least 1 year in a technical school, college, or university. Interviews may be required. Selection is based on need.
Financial data Stipends range up to $2,000.
Duration 2 years for medical students; 1 year for all other recipients.
Deadline May of each year.

[822]
PETER DOCTOR MEMORIAL INDIAN SCHOLARSHIP GRANTS
Peter Doctor Memorial Indian Scholarship Foundation, Inc.
c/o Clara Hill, Treasurer
P.O. Box 731
Basom, NY 14013
(716) 542-2025   E-mail: cehill@wnynet.net

Purpose To provide financial assistance to New York Iroquois Indians currently enrolled in college on the undergraduate or graduate school level.
Eligibility This program is open to enrolled New York Iroquois Indian students who have completed at least 1 year in a technical school, college, or university. Both undergraduate and graduate students are eligible. There are no age limits or GPA requirements. Interviews may be required. Applicants must have tribal certification. Selection is based on need.
Financial data Stipends range up to $1,500.
Duration 2 years for medical students; 1 year for all other recipients.
Deadline May of each year.

[823]
PETER KALIFORNSKY MEMORIAL ENDOWMENT SCHOLARSHIP FUND
Cook Inlet Region, Inc.
Attn: The CIRI Foundation
3600 San Jeronimo Drive, Suite 256
Anchorage, AK 99508-2870
(907) 793-3575   Toll-free: (800) 764-3382
Fax: (907) 793-3585   E-mail: tcf@thecirifoundation.org
Web: www.thecirifoundation.org/designated.htm

Purpose To provide financial assistance for undergraduate or graduate studies to Alaska Natives who are original enrollees to Cook Inlet Region, Inc. (CIRI) and their lineal descendants.
Eligibility This program is open to Alaska Native enrollees to CIRI under the Alaska Native Claims Settlement Act (ANCSA) of 1971 and their lineal descendants. There are no Alaska residency requirements or age limitations. Applicants must be accepted or enrolled full time in a 4-year undergraduate or a graduate degree program. Preference is given to students in Alaska Native studies. They must have a GPA of 2.5 or higher. Along with their application, they must submit a 500-word statement on their educational and career goals and how they are contributing, or planning to contribute, to a positive Alaska Native community. Selection is based on that statement, academic achievement, rigor of course work or degree program, student financial contribution, financial need, grade level, previous work performance, community service, and relationship of degree program to career goals.
Financial data The stipend is $10,000 per year, $8,000 per year, or $2,500 per semester, depending on GPA.
Duration 1 semester or 1 year.
Additional information This program was established in 1993.
Number awarded Varies each year.
Deadline May of each year for annual scholarships; May or November of each year for semester scholarships.

[824]
PI STATE NATIVE AMERICAN GRANTS-IN-AID

Delta Kappa Gamma Society International-Pi State
   Organization
c/o Harlene Gilbert
5338 East Lake Road
Romulus, NY 14541
(315) 585-6691 E-mail: wilma@capital.net
Web: www.deltakappagamma.org/NY/awards.html

Purpose To provide funding to Native American women from New York who plan to work in education or another service field.

Eligibility This program is open to Native American women from New York who are attending a 2-year or 4-year college in the state. Applicants must be planning to work in education or another service field, but preference is given to those majoring in education. Both undergraduate and graduate students are eligible.

Financial data The grant is $500 per semester ($1,000 per year). Funds may be used for any career-related purpose, including purchase of textbooks.

Duration 1 semester; may be renewed for a total of 5 years and a total of $5,000 over a recipient's lifetime.

Number awarded Varies each year; recently, 3 of these grants were awarded.

[825]
POKAGON BAND HIGHER EDUCATION SCHOLARSHIP

Pokagon Band of Potawatomi Indians
Attn: Department of Education
58620 Sink Road
P.O. Box 180
Dowagiac, MI 49047
(269) 782-0887 Toll-free: (888) 330-1234
Fax: (269) 782-0985
E-mail: Joseph.morsaw@pokagon.com
Web: www.pokagon.com

Purpose To provide financial assistance to members of the Pokagon Band of Potawatomi Indians who are interested in working on an undergraduate or graduate degree at a college in any state.

Eligibility This program is open to enrolled members of the Pokagon Band who are attending or planning to attend an accredited college or university in any state to work on an associate, bachelor's, master's, or doctoral degree. Applicants must apply for all campus-based financial aid for which they are eligible and be able to document that they still have an unmet financial need. If they plan to attend a public college or university in Michigan and have an Indian blood level of one-quarter or more, they must also apply for a Michigan Indian Tuition Waiver.

Financial data The maximum stipend is $1,000 per semester.

Duration 1 semester; may be renewed for 3 years of study for an associate degree, for 5 years of study for a bachelor's degree, or for 5 years of study for a graduate degree.

Number awarded Varies each year.

[826]
PONCA TRIBE OF NEBRASKA EDUCATIONAL GRANTS

Ponca Tribe of Nebraska
Attn: Departments of Education and Culture
1800 Syracuse Avenue
Norfolk, NE 68701
(402) 371-8834 Fax: (402) 371-7564
E-mail: pate@poncatribe-ne.org
Web: www.poncatribe-ne.org

Purpose To provide financial assistance to members of the Ponca Tribe of Nebraska who are interested in attending an undergraduate, graduate, or vocational school in any state.

Eligibility This program is open to enrolled members of the Ponca Tribe of Nebraska who are attending or planning to attend a college, university, or vocational/technical school in any state. Applicants must submit a letter of admission from the school they plan to attend, a Certificate of Indian Blood (CIB), and documentation of financial need.

Financial data A stipend is awarded (amount not specified).

Duration 1 semester or year. Full-time students may reapply each academic year (or summer session if they wish to attend summer school). Part-time students may reapply each semester or quarter. Renewals are approved if the student maintains a GPA of 2.0 or higher as an undergraduate or vocational student or 3.0 or higher as a graduate student.

Number awarded Varies each year.

Deadline August of each year for fall quarter or semester; November of each year for winter quarter; December of each year for spring quarter or semester; May of each year for summer session.

[827]
PORTER PHYSIOLOGY DEVELOPMENT AWARDS

American Physiological Society
Attn: Education Office
9650 Rockville Pike, Room 3111
Bethesda, MD 20814-3991
(301) 634-7132 Fax: (301) 634-7098
E-mail: education@the-aps.org
Web: www.the-aps.org

Purpose To provide financial assistance to Native American and other minorities interested in working on a doctoral degree in physiology.

Eligibility This program is open to U.S. citizens and permanent residents who are members of racial or ethnic minority groups (Hispanic or Latino, American Indian or Alaska Native, Asian, Black or African American, and Native Hawaiian or other Pacific Islander). Applicants must be currently enrolled in or accepted to a doctoral program in physiology at a university as full-time students. They must be planning a program of research training under the supervision of a qualified preceptor. Selection is based on the applicant's potential for success (academic record, statement of interest, previous awards and experiences, letters of recommendation); applicant's proposed training environment (including quality of preceptor); and applicant's research and training plan (clarity and quality).

Financial data The stipend is $20,772. No provision is made for a dependency allowance or tuition and fees.

Duration 1 year; may be renewed for 1 additional year and, in exceptional cases, for a third year.
Additional information This program is supported by the William Townsend Porter Foundation (formerly the Harvard Apparatus Foundation). The first Porter Fellowship was awarded in 1920. In 1966 and 1967, the American Physiological Society established the Porter Physiology Development Committee to award fellowships to minority students engaged in graduate study in physiology.
Number awarded Varies each year; recently, 5 of these fellowships were awarded.
Deadline January of each year.

[828]
PORTER WRIGHT MORRIS & ARTHUR LLP/RALPH K. FRASIER SCHOLARSHIP
Porter Wright Morris & Arthur LLP
Huntington Center
41 South High Street
Columbus, OH 43215
(614) 227-2000   Toll-free: (800) 533-2794
Fax: (614) 227-2100
Web: www.porterwright.com

Purpose To provide financial assistance and summer work experience to minority students from any state who are enrolled at designated law schools in Ohio.
Eligibility This program is open to minority students enrolled in the first year at the following law schools: Ohio State University Moritz College of Law, Capital University Law School, Case Western Reserve University School of Law, Cleveland-Marshall College of Law, University of Cincinnati College of Law, University of Dayton School of Law, and University of Toledo College of Law. Applicants must submit undergraduate and law school transcripts, a resume, and an essay in the form of a legal memorandum on a hypothetical law case. They must also indicate their choice of the sponsoring firm's offices in Cleveland and Columbus for a summer clerkship.
Financial data The program provides a competitive salary for the summer clerkship and a stipend of $5,000 for the second year of law school.
Duration 1 year.
Additional information This program was established in 2005.
Number awarded 2 each year: 1 for a clerkship in Cleveland and 1 for a clerkship in Columbus.
Deadline January of each year.

[829]
PRAIRIE BAND POTAWATOMI NATION HIGHER EDUCATION GRADUATE PROGRAM
Prairie Band Potawatomi Nation
Education Department
16281 Q Road
Mayetta, KS 66509
(785) 966-2255   Toll-free: (877) 715-6789
Fax: (785) 966-2956   E-mail: info@pbpnation.org
Web: www.pbpindiantribe.com/other-education.aspx

Purpose To provide financial assistance to members of the Prairie Band Potawatomi Nation who are interested in attending graduate school in any state.
Eligibility This program is open to members of the Prairie Band Potawatomi Nation who have a Certificate of Indian Blood. Applicants must be enrolled or planning to enroll at a college or university in any state to work on a master's or doctoral degree. Along with their application, they must submit a letter explaining why they need the grant and how it will be used.
Financial data Full-time students receive a stipend of up to $5,000 per semester. Funds may be used for tuition, fees, and books. Part-time students are eligible for exact costs only.
Duration 1 semester; may be renewed.
Number awarded Varies each year.
Deadline Applications must be submitted at least 2 months prior to beginning of attendance or payment due date, whichever occurs first.

[830]
PREDOCTORAL FELLOWSHIPS OF THE FORD FOUNDATION DIVERSITY FELLOWSHIP PROGRAM
National Research Council
Attn: Fellowships Office, GR 346A
500 Fifth Street, N.W.
Washington, DC 20001
(202) 334-2872   Fax: (202) 334-3419
E-mail: infofell@nas.edu
Web: www7.nationalacademies.org

Purpose To provide financial assistance for graduate school to students whose success will increase the racial and ethnic diversity of U.S. colleges and universities.
Eligibility This program is open to citizens and nationals of the United States who are enrolled or planning to enroll full time in a Ph.D. or Sc.D. degree program and are committed to a career in teaching and research at the college or university level. Applicants may be undergraduates in their senior year, individuals who have completed undergraduate study or some graduate study, or current Ph.D. or Sc.D. students who can demonstrate that they can fully utilize a 3-year fellowship award. The following are considered as positive factors in the selection process: evidence of superior academic achievement; promise of continuing achievement as scholars and teachers; membership in a group whose underrepresentation in the American professoriate has been severe and longstanding, including Black/African Americans, Puerto Ricans, Mexican Americans/Chicanos/Chicanas, Native American Indians, Alaska Natives (Eskimos or Aleuts), and Native Pacific Islanders (Micronesians or Polynesians); capacity to respond in pedagogically productive ways to the learning needs of students from diverse backgrounds; sustained personal engagement with communities that are underrepresented in the academy and an ability to bring this asset to learning, teaching, and scholarship at the college and university level; and likelihood of using the diversity of human experience as an educational resource in teaching and scholarship. Applicants must be working on or planning to work on a degree in the following fields: American studies, anthropology, archaeology, art and theater history, astronomy, chemistry, communications, computer science, earth sciences, economics, engineering, ethnomusicology, geography, history, international relations, language, life sciences, linguistics, literature, mathematics, performance study, philosophy, physics,

political science, psychology, religion, sociology, urban planning, and women's studies. Also eligible are interdisciplinary ethnic studies programs, such as African American studies and Native American studies, and other interdisciplinary programs, such as area studies, peace studies, and social justice. Awards are not made for such practice-oriented areas as administration and management, audiology, business, educational administration and leadership, filmmaking, fine arts, guidance, home economics, library and information science, nursing, occupational health, performing arts, personnel, physical education, social welfare, social work, or speech pathology. Ineligibility also includes students working on a terminal master's degree; the Ed.D. degree; the degrees of Doctor of Fine Arts (D.F.A.) or Doctor of Psychology (Psy.D.); professional degrees in such areas as medicine, law, and public health; or such joint degrees as M.D./Ph.D., J.D./Ph.D., and M.F.A./Ph.D.

Financial data The program provides a stipend to the student of $20,000 per year and an award to the host institution of $3,000 per year in lieu of tuition and fees.

Duration 3 years of support is provided, to be used within a 5-year period.

Additional information The competition for this program is conducted by the National Research Council on behalf of the Ford Foundation. Applicants who merit receiving the fellowship but to whom awards cannot be made because of insufficient funds are given Honorable Mentions; this recognition does not carry with it a monetary award but honors applicants who have demonstrated substantial academic achievement. The National Research Council publishes a list of those Honorable Mentions who wish their names publicized. Fellows may not accept remuneration from another fellowship or similar external award while on this program; however, supplementation from institutional funds, educational benefits from the Department of Veterans Affairs, or educational incentive funds may be received concurrently with Ford Foundation support. Predoctoral fellows are required to submit an interim progress report 6 months after the start of the fellowship and a final report at the end of the 12 month tenure.

Number awarded Approximately 60 each year.

Deadline November of each year.

[831]
PRINCE KUHIO HAWAIIAN CIVIC CLUB SCHOLARSHIP

Prince Kuhio Hawaiian Civic Club
Attn: Scholarship Chair
P.O. Box 4728
Honolulu, HI 96812
E-mail: Caztwin@aol.com
Web: www.pkhcc.com/scholarship

Purpose To provide financial assistance for undergraduate or graduate studies to persons of Hawaiian descent.

Eligibility Applicants must be of Hawaiian descent (descendants of the aboriginal inhabitants of the Hawaiian Islands prior to 1778) who are high school seniors, recent graduates, or full-time undergraduate or graduate students. Graduating high school seniors and current undergraduate students must have a GPA of 2.5 or higher; graduate students must have at least a 3.3 GPA. Priority is given to members of the Prince Kuhio Hawaiian Civic Club in good standing, including directly-related family members. Special consideration is given to applicants majoring in Hawaiian studies, Hawaiian language, or journalism.

Financial data Stipends range from $500 to $1,000.

Duration 1 year.

Additional information Information is also available from Cyr Pakele, Kamehameha Schools, Haleakala Counseling Center, 210 Konia Circle, Honolulu, HI 96817, (808) 842-8934, (800) 842-IMUA, E-mail: cypakele@ksbe.edu.

Number awarded Varies each year.

Deadline March of each year.

[832]
PUBLIC POLICY AND INTERNATIONAL AFFAIRS FELLOWSHIPS

Public Policy and International Affairs Fellowship Program
1029 Vermont Avenue, N.W., Suite 800
Washington, DC 20005
(202) 496-0130   Fax: (202) 496-0134
E-mail: ppia@ppiaprogram.org
Web: www.ppiaprogram.org

Purpose To provide financial assistance to Native American and other minority undergraduate students who are interested in preparing for graduate study in the fields of public policy and/or international affairs.

Eligibility This program is open to people of color historically underrepresented in public policy and international affairs, including African Americans, Asian Americans, Pacific Islanders, Hispanic Americans, Alaska Natives, and Native Americans. Students must enter the program when they apply to participate in a summer institute following the junior year of college. Applicants must be U.S. citizens or permanent residents interested in a summer institute in public policy and international affairs. They must first apply directly to the summer institute. Following participation in that institute, they apply for graduate study in fields of their choice at 38 designated universities. For a list of participating institutions, contact the sponsor.

Financial data During the summer institute portion of the program, participants receive transportation to and from the institute site, room and board, and a $1,000 stipend. The participating programs in public policy and/or international affairs have agreed to waive application fees and grant fellowships of at least $5,000 to students who have participated in the summer institutes.

Duration 1 summer and 1 academic year.

Additional information This program was established in 1981 when the Alfred P. Sloan Foundation provided a grant to the Association for Public Policy Analysis and Management (APPAM). From 1981 through 1988, participants were known as Sloan Fellows. From 1889 through 1995, the program was supported by the Ford Foundation and administered by the Woodrow Wilson National Fellowship Administration, so participants were known as Woodrow Wilson Fellows in Public Policy and International Affairs. Beginning in 1995, the program's name was shortened to the Public Policy and International Affairs Fellowship Program (PPIA) and its administration was moved to the Academy for Educational Development. To complement APPAM's role, the Association of Professional Schools of International Affairs

(APSIA) also became an institutional sponsor. In 1999, the Ford Foundation ended its support for PPIA effective with the student cohort that participated in summer institutes in 1999. The APPAM and APSIA incorporated PPIA as an independent organization and operated the summer institutes in 2000. In 2001, the National Association of Schools of Public Affairs and Administration (NASPAA) also became a sponsor of PPIA. Since in summer of that year, summer institutes have been held at 5 universities: the Summer Program in Public Policy and International Affairs at the Gerald R. Ford School of Public Policy at the University of Michigan, the Maryland Leadership Institute at the School of Public Policy at the University of Maryland, the UCPPIA Summer Institute at the Richard & Rhoda Goldman School of Public Policy at the University of California at Berkeley, the PPIA Junior Summer Institute at the Woodrow Wilson School of Public and International Affairs at Princeton University, and the PPIA Junior Summer Institute at the Heinz School of Public Policy and Management at Carnegie Mellon University. For information on those institutes, contact the respective school. Additional support is currently provided by the Foundation for Child Development and the William T. Grant Foundation.

Number awarded Varies each year.

[833]
PUEBLO OF ISLETA HIGHER EDUCATION PROGRAM

Pueblo of Isleta
Attn: Higher Education Program
P.O. Box 1270
Isleta, NM 87022
(505) 869-2680, ext. 433   Fax: (505) 869-7690
E-mail: poi08004@isletapueblo.com
Web: www.isletapueblo.com/higher%20ed.html

Purpose To provide financial assistance for undergraduate or graduate study to members of the Pueblo of Isleta.

Eligibility This program is open to undergraduate and graduate students who can document tribal membership in the Pueblo of Isleta or at least one-quarter Isleta blood. Applicants must have a GPA of 2.5 or higher and be able to demonstrate financial need They must have applied for federal aid by submitting a Free Application for Federal Student Aid (FAFSA).

Financial data The stipend depends on the need of the recipient.

Duration 1 year; may be renewed if the recipient maintains a GPA of 2.5 or higher.

Number awarded Varies each year.

Deadline June of each year for the academic year; October of each year for the spring semester or winter quarter; March of each year for summer term.

[834]
PUEBLO OF POJOAQUE HIGHER EDUCATION SCHOLARSHIP PROGRAM

Pueblo of Pojoaque
Attn: Education Department
101 C Lightning Loop
Santa Fe, NM 87506
(505) 455-3369   Fax: (505) 455-3360
E-mail: csuazo@puebloofpojoaque.org
Web: www.pojoaqueeducation.monkeymedia.org

Purpose To provide financial assistance to Pueblo of Pojoaque tribal members interested in working on an undergraduate or graduate degree at a school in any state.

Eligibility This program is open to Pueblo of Pojoaque tribal members who can provide a certificate of tribal verification. Applicants must be working on or planning to work on a certificate, associate, bachelor's, master's, or doctoral degree at a school of higher education in any state. They must be able to verify that they have applied for all other available financial aid and that they still have financial need. Both full- and part-time students are eligible.

Financial data Both full- and part-time students receive a grant to cover tuition, fees, and books, to a maximum of $2,000 per year. In addition, full-time students receive a monthly stipend (amount not specified).

Duration Students working on a certificate are eligible for up to 2 years of support to complete the requirements. Students working on an associate degree are eligible for up to 4 years of part-time support or 3 years of full-time support. Students working full time on a bachelor's degree are eligible for up to 5 years of support if they enter as a first-time student or up to 4 years of support if they transfer with an associate degree. Students working part time on a bachelor's degree are eligible for up to 7 years of support if they enter as a first-time student or up to 6 years of support if they transfer with an associate degree. Students working on a master's or Ph.D. degree are eligible for up to 4 years of support. Renewal for full-time students requires that they complete at least 20 hours of nonprofit community service per semester. Renewal for all students requires that they maintain a GPA of 2.0 or higher.

Number awarded Varies each year.

Deadline July of each year for fall semester; December of each year for spring semester; April of each year for summer semester.

[835]
RACE RELATIONS MULTIRACIAL STUDENT SCHOLARSHIP

Christian Reformed Church
Attn: Ministry of Race Relations
2850 Kalamazoo Avenue, S.E.
Grand Rapids, MI 49560-0200
(616) 224-5883   Toll-free: (800) 272-5125
E-mail: lugoe@crcna.org
Web: www.crcna.org

Purpose To provide financial assistance to Native American and other undergraduate and graduate minority students interested in attending colleges related to the Christian Reformed Church in North America (CRCNA).

Eligibility Students of color in the United States and Canada are eligible to apply. Normally, applicants are expected to be members of CRCNA congregations who plan to pursue their educational goals at Calvin Theological Seminary or any of the colleges affiliated with the CRCNA. Students who have no prior history with the CRCNA must attend a CRCNA-related college or seminary for a full academic year before they are eligible to apply for this program. Students entering their sophomore year must have earned a GPA of 2.0 or higher as freshmen; students entering their junior year must have earned a GPA of 2.3 or higher as sophomores; students entering their senior year must have earned a GPA of 2.6 or higher as juniors.

Financial data First-year students receive $500 per semester. Other levels of students may receive up to $2,000 per academic year.

Duration 1 year.

Additional information This program was first established in 1971 and revised in 1991. Recipients are expected to train to engage actively in the ministry of racial reconciliation in church and in society. They must be able to work in the United States or Canada upon graduating and must consider working for 1 of the agencies of the CRCNA.

Number awarded Varies each year; recently, 31 students received a total of $21,000 in support.

Deadline March of each year.

[836]
RACIAL ETHNIC SUPPLEMENTAL GRANTS
Presbyterian Church (USA)
Attn: Office of Financial Aid for Studies
100 Witherspoon Street, Room M-052
Louisville, KY 40202-1396
(502) 569-5735   Toll-free: (888) 728-7228, ext. 5735
Fax: (502) 569-8766   E-mail: LBryan@ctr.pcusa.org
Web: www.pcusa.org/financialaid/programs/grant.htm

Purpose To provide financial assistance to Native American and other minority graduate students who are Presbyterian Church (USA) members interested in preparing for church occupations.

Eligibility This program is open to racial/ethnic graduate students (Asian American, African American, Hispanic American, Native American, or Alaska Native) who are enrolled full time at a PCUSA seminary or accredited theological institution approved by their Committee on Preparation for Ministry. Applicants must be working on 1) an M.Div. degree and enrolled as an inquirer or candidate by a PCUSA presbytery, or 2) an M.A.C.E. degree and preparing for a church occupation. They must be PCUSA members, U.S. citizens or permanent residents, able to demonstrate financial need, and recommended by the financial aid officer at their theological institution.

Financial data Stipends range from $500 to $1,000 per year. Funds are intended as supplements to students who have been awarded a Presbyterian Study Grant but still demonstrate remaining financial need.

Duration 1 year; may be renewed up to 2 additional years.

Number awarded Varies each year.

Deadline June of each year.

[837]
THE REV. FRANCENE EAGLE BIG GOOSE MEMORIAL SCHOLARSHIP
United Methodist Church-Arkansas Conference
Attn: Committee on Native American Ministries
Two Trudie Kibbe Reed Drive
Little Rock, AR 72202-3770
(501) 324-8045   Toll-free: (877) 646-1816
Fax: (501) 324-8018   E-mail: conference@arumc.org
Web: www.arumc.org

Purpose To provide book scholarships to Native American Methodist seminary students from Arkansas.

Eligibility This program is open to seminary students of Native American/Indigenous Heritage, including Native Indians, Native Alaskans, Native Hawaiians, and Pacific Island populations. Applicants must be active members of local congregations affiliated with the Arkansas Conference of the United Methodist Church. If no applications are received from students within Arkansas, the program is open to students from the Oklahoma Indian Missionary Conference. The seminary they are attending must be approved by the University Senate of the United Methodist Church. Along with their application, they must submit brief essays on their educational goals, how they contribute to the Native American community, and a personal accomplishment of which they are particularly proud that related to their Native American/Indigenous Heritage. They must be able to demonstrate financial need.

Financial data The stipend is $500 per semester ($1,000 per year). Funds are intended to assist in the purchase of books.

Duration 1 semester; may be renewed.

Additional information Information is also available from Rev. Angie Gage, P.O. Box 69, Bay, AR 72411, (870) 781-3262, E-mail: bayumcpastor@suddenlinkmail.com.

Number awarded 1 or more each year.

Deadline July of each year for fall semester; December of each year for spring semester.

[838]
RICHARD AND HELEN BROWN COREM SCHOLARSHIPS
United Church of Christ
Parish Life and Leadership Ministry Team
Attn: COREM Administrator
700 Prospect Avenue East
Cleveland, OH 44115-1100
(216) 736-2113   Toll-free: (866) 822-8224, ext. 2113
Fax: (216) 736-3783
Web: www.ucc.org/education/scholarships/index.html

Purpose To provide financial assistance to Native American and other minority seminary students who are interested in becoming a pastor in the United Church of Christ (UCC).

Eligibility This program is open to students at accredited seminaries who have been members of a UCC congregation for at least 1 year. Applicants must work through 1 of the member bodies of the Council for Racial and Ethnic Ministries (COREM): United Black Christians (UBC), Council for Hispanic Ministries (CHM), Pacific Islander and Asian American Ministries (PAAM), or Council for American Indian Ministries (CAIM). They must 1) have a GPA of 3.0 or higher, 2)

be enrolled in a course of study leading to ordained ministry, 3) be in care of an association or conference at the time of application, and 4) demonstrate leadership ability through participation in their local church, association, conference, or academic environment.
Financial data Stipends are approximately $10,000 per year.
Duration 1 year.
Additional information Information on UBC is available from the Minister for African American Relations, (216) 736-2189. Information on CHM is available from the Minister for Hispanic Relations, (216) 736-2193. Information on PAAM is available from the Minister for Pacific Islander and Asian American Relations, (216) 736-2195. Information on CAIM is available from the Minister for Native American Relations, (216) 736-2194.
Number awarded Varies each year; recently, 4 scholarships were awarded by UBC, 1 by CHM, 1 by PAAM, and 1 by CAIM.

[839]
RICHARD D. HAILEY AAJ LAW STUDENT SCHOLARSHIPS
American Association for Justice
Attn: Minority Caucus
1050 31st Street, N.W.
Washington, DC 20007
(202) 965-3500, ext. 272
Toll-free: (800) 424-2725, ext 272
Fax: (202) 298-6849   E-mail: info@justice.org
Web: www.justice.org/networking/tier3/Hailey.aspx

Purpose To provide financial assistance for law school to Native American and other minority student members of the American Association for Justice (AAJ).
Eligibility This program is open to African American, Hispanic, Asian American, Native American, and biracial members of the association who are enrolled in the first or second year of law school. Selection is based on commitment to the association, involvement in student chapter and minority caucus activities, desire to represent victims, interest and proficiency of skills in trial advocacy, and financial need. Applicants must submit a 500-word essay on how they meet those criteria and 3 letters of recommendation.
Financial data The stipend is $1,000.
Duration 1 year.
Additional information The American Association for Justice was formerly the Association of Trial Lawyers of America.
Number awarded Up to 6 each year.
Deadline April of each year.

[840]
RICHARD (YOGI) CROWE MEMORIAL SCHOLARSHIP
Richard (Yogi) Crowe Memorial Scholarship Fund
P.O. Box 892
Cherokee, NC 28719
Web: www.yogicrowecherokeescholarship.org

Purpose To provide financial assistance to members of the Eastern Band of Cherokee Indians who are working on a graduate degree.
Eligibility This program is open to enrolled members of the Eastern Band of Cherokee Indians who have been accepted by a graduate or doctoral school that requires the GMAT, GRE, LSAT, or MCAT for admission. Applicants must be willing to return to Cherokee, North Carolina and contribute to the betterment of the tribe for at least 2 years. Both part- and full-time students are eligible. Financial need is considered in the selection process.
Financial data The stipend depends on the availability of funds.
Duration 1 year.
Number awarded 1 or more each year.
Deadline March of each year for summer term; June of each year for fall semester; October of each year for spring semester.

[841]
ROBERT TOIGO FOUNDATION FELLOWSHIPS
Robert Toigo Foundation
Attn: Fellowship Program Administrator
1230 Preservation Park Way
Oakland, CA 94612
(510) 763-5771   Fax: (510) 763-5778
E-mail: info@toigofoundation.org
Web: www.toigofoundation.org

Purpose To provide financial assistance to Native American and other minority students working on a master's degree in business administration or related field.
Eligibility This program is open to members of minority groups (of African American, Hispanic, Native American/Alaskan Native, or Asian/Pacific Islander descent) who are entering or enrolled in an M.B.A. program as a full-time student. Applicants must be preparing for a career in finance, including (but not limited to) investment management, investment banking, corporate finance, real estate, private equity, venture capital, sales and trading, research, or financial services consulting. Also eligible are students enrolled in programs in real estate with a concentration in finance, master's degree programs in public policy with a concentration in finance, master's in financial engineering, and J.D./M.B.A. programs.
Financial data The stipend is $5,000 per year.
Duration Up to 2 years.
Number awarded Approximately 60 each year.
Deadline January of each year for entering students; April of each year for continuing students.

[842]
RODNEY T. MATHEWS MEMORIAL SCHOLARSHIP FOR CALIFORNIA INDIANS
Morongo Band of Mission Indians
Attn: Scholarship Coordinator
11545 Potrero Road
Banning, CA 92220
(951) 572-6185   E-mail: trisha.smith@morongo.org
Web: www.morongonation.org/scholarship.asp

Purpose To provide financial assistance for college or graduate school to California Indians.
Eligibility This program is open to California Indians (must provide documentation of Native identity) who have been actively involved in the Native American community.

Applicants must submit documentation of financial need, an academic letter of recommendation, and a letter of recommendation from the American Indian community. They must be enrolled full time at an accredited college or university. Undergraduates must have a GPA of 2.75 or higher; graduate students must have a GPA of 3.5 or higher. Along with their application, they must submit 1) a 2-page personal statement on their academic, career, and personal goals; any extenuating circumstances they wish to have considered; how they view their Native American heritage and its importance to them; how they plan to "give back" to Native Americans after graduation; and their on-going active involvement in the Native American community both on and off campus; and 2) a 2-page essay, either on what they feel are the most critical issues facing tribal communities today and how they see themselves working in relationship to those issues, or on where they see Native people in the 21st century in terms of survival, governance, and cultural preservation, and what role they see themselves playing in that future.

Financial data The maximum stipend is $10,000 per year. Funds are paid directly to the recipient's school for tuition, housing, textbooks, and required fees.

Duration 1 year; may be renewed 1 additional year.

Additional information Recipients are required to complete 60 hours of service with a designated California Indian community agency: California Indian Museum and Cultural Center, Indian Health Care Services, National Indian Justice Center, California Indian Legal Services, California Indian Professors Association, California Indian Culture and Awareness Conference, or California Democratic Party Native American Caucus.

Number awarded 4 each year.

Deadline March of each year.

[843]
ROY M. HUHNDORF ENDOWMENT SCHOLARSHIP FUND

Cook Inlet Region, Inc.
Attn: The CIRI Foundation
3600 San Jeronimo Drive, Suite 256
Anchorage, AK 99508-2870
(907) 793-3575   Toll-free: (800) 764-3382
Fax: (907) 793-3585   E-mail: tcf@thecirifoundation.org
Web: www.thecirifoundation.org/designated.htm

Purpose To provide financial assistance for undergraduate or graduate studies in health science to Alaska Natives who are original enrollees to Cook Inlet Region, Inc. (CIRI) and their lineal descendants.

Eligibility This program is open to Alaska Native enrollees to CIRI under the Alaska Native Claims Settlement Act (ANCSA) of 1971 and their lineal descendants. There are no Alaska residency requirements or age limitations. Applicants must be accepted or enrolled full time in a 4-year undergraduate or a graduate degree program. They must be working on a degree in health science and have a GPA of 2.5 or higher. Along with their application, they must submit a 500-word statement on their educational and career goals and how they are contributing, or planning to contribute, to a positive Alaska Native community. Selection is based on that statement, academic achievement, rigor of course work or degree program, student financial contribution, financial need, grade level, previous work performance, community service, and relationship of degree program to career goals.

Financial data The stipend is $10,000 per year, $8,000 per year, or $2,500 per semester, depending on GPA.

Duration 1 semester or 1 year.

Additional information This program was established in 1995.

Number awarded Varies each year.

Deadline May of each year for annual scholarships; May or November of each year for semester scholarships.

[844]
SAC AND FOX NATION HIGHER EDUCATION GRANTS

Sac and Fox Nation
Attn: Higher Education
Route 2 Box 246
Stroud, OK 74079
(918) 968-3526
Web: www.sacandfoxnation.com

Purpose To provide financial assistance for college or graduate school to members of the Sac and Fox Nation.

Eligibility This program is open to enrolled members of the Sac and Fox Nation who are enrolled or planning to enroll at an accredited college or university. Applicants must submit a personal letter describing the college major they plan to pursue and their career goals after graduation. They must be able to demonstrate financial need. Limited funding is available for graduate students.

Financial data Stipends are $800 per semester for full-time students, $400 per semester for part-time students, or $400 per semester for graduate students.

Duration 1 semester; may be renewed up to 9 additional semester for students at 4-year institutions, up to 5 additional semesters for students at 2-year institutions, or up to 5 additional semesters for graduate students. Freshmen and sophomores must earn a GPA of 2.0 to remain eligible; juniors and seniors must earn at GPA of 2.25 to remain eligible.

Number awarded Varies each year.

Deadline June of each year for fall semester; November of each year for spring semester.

[845]
SACNAS GENOME SCHOLARS PROGRAM

Society for Advancement of Chicanos and Native
  Americans in Science
333 Front Street, Suite 104
P.O. Box 8526
Santa Cruz, CA 95061-8526
(831) 459-0170   Toll-free: (877) SACNAS-1
Fax: (831) 459-0194   E-mail: info@sacnas.org
Web: www.sacnas.org/genomicsOpportunities.cfm

Purpose To provide financial assistance to members of the Society for Advancement of Chicanos and Native Americans in Science (SACNAS) who are interested in working on a graduate degree in genomics.

Eligibility This program is open to SACNAS members who are enrolled or planning to enroll in a graduate program in a field related to genomics (including ethical, legal, and social implications of genomic research, computational biology as it relates to genomics, and bioengineering as it relates to genomics). Applicants must be U.S. citizens or permanent residents. Along with their application, they must submit 3 essays describing 1) personal, professional, or educational experiences that have contributed to their desire to pursue advanced study in science, mathematics, or engineering; 2) their experiences in integrating research and education, advancing diversity in science, enhancing scientific and technical understanding, and otherwise benefiting society; and 3) their proposed plan of research.

Financial data The stipend is $25,000. Scholars also receive full support to attend the SACNAS national conference and present research in a poster or oral presentation and to attend an additional national genomics or bioinformatics conference.

Duration 1 year.

Number awarded 1 each year.

Deadline February of each year.

[846]
SALAMATOF NATIVE ASSOCIATION, INC. SCHOLARSHIP PROGRAM

Cook Inlet Region, Inc.
Attn: The CIRI Foundation
3600 San Jeronimo Drive, Suite 256
Anchorage, AK 99508-2870
(907) 793-3575 Toll-free: (800) 764-3382
Fax: (907) 793-3585 E-mail: tcf@thecirifoundation.org
Web: www.thecirifoundation.org

Purpose To provide financial assistance for undergraduate or graduate studies to Alaska Natives who are original enrollees of the Salamatof Native Association, Inc. (SNAI) and their spouses and lineal descendants.

Eligibility This program is open to Alaska Native enrollees to SNAI under the Alaska Native Claims Settlement Act (ANCSA) of 1971 and their spouses and lineal descendants. There are no Alaska residency requirements or age limitations. Applicants must be accepted or enrolled full time in a 2-year, 4-year undergraduate, or graduate degree program. They must have a GPA of 2.5 or higher. Along with their application, they must submit a 500-word statement on their educational and career goals and how they are contributing, or planning to contribute, to a positive Alaska Native community. Selection is based on that statement, academic achievement, rigor of course work or degree program, student financial contribution, financial need, grade level, previous work performance, community service, and relationship of degree program to career goals.

Financial data The stipend depends on the availability of funds.

Duration 1 year; recipients must reapply each year.

Additional information This program was established in 1992 by the Salamatof Native Association, Inc. which provides funds matched by the CIRI Foundation.

Number awarded Varies each year; recently, 3 of these scholarships were awarded.

Deadline May of each year.

[847]
SANDIA MASTER'S FELLOWSHIP PROGRAM

Sandia National Laboratories
Attn: Staffing Department 3535
MS-1023
P.O. Box 5800
Albuquerque, NM 87185-1023
(505) 844-3441 Fax: (505) 844-6636
E-mail: pacover@sandia.gov
Web: www.sandia.gov

Purpose To enable Native American and other minority students to obtain a master's degree in engineering or computer science and also work at Sandia National Laboratories.

Eligibility This program is open to minority (American Indian, Asian, Black, or Hispanic) students with a bachelor's degree in engineering or computer science and a GPA of 3.2 or higher. Participants must apply to 3 schools jointly selected by the program and themselves. They must be prepared to obtain a master's degree within 1 year. The fields of study (not all fields are available at all participating universities) include computer science, electrical engineering, mechanical engineering, civil engineering, chemical engineering, nuclear engineering, materials sciences, and petroleum engineering. Applicants must be interested in working at the sponsor's laboratories during the summer between graduation from college and the beginning of their graduate program, and then following completion of their master's degree.

Financial data Participants receive a competitive salary while working at the laboratories on a full-time basis and a stipend while attending school.

Duration 1 year.

Additional information During their summer assignment, participants work at the laboratories, either in Albuquerque, New Mexico or in Livermore, California. Upon successful completion of the program, they return to Sandia's hiring organization as a full-time member of the technical staff. This program began in 1968. Application to schools where students received their undergraduate degree is not recommended. After the schools accept an applicant, the choice of a school is made jointly by the laboratories and the participant.

Number awarded Varies each year; since the program began, more than 350 engineers and computer scientists have gone to work at Sandia with master's degrees.

[848]
SARAH KELI'ILOLENA LUM KONIA NAKOA HAWAIIAN LANGUAGE PERPETUAL SCHOLARSHIP

Ke Ali'i Pauahi Foundation
Attn: Financial Aid & Scholarship Services
567 South King Street, Suite 160
Honolulu, HI 96813
(808) 534-3966 Toll-free: (800) 842-4682, ext. 43966
Fax: (808) 534-3890 E-mail: scholarships@pauahi.org
Web: www.pauahi.org

Purpose To provide financial assistance to undergraduate or graduate students, especially those of Hawaiian descent, who are working on a degree in Hawaiian language.

Eligibility This program is open to full-time undergraduate and graduate students who are residents of Hawaii. Applicants must be enrolled in a program for the study and perpetuation of the Hawaiian language, including Hawaiian culture and history. They must be able to demonstrate financial need and commitment to contribute to the greater community. Along with their application, they must submit an essay demonstrating their achievements in studying Hawaiian language, culture, and history; proposed action plan to complete college-level Hawaiian language studies; and plan to share this knowledge with others in the Hawaiian community. Preference is given to Native Hawaiians (descendants of the aboriginal inhabitants of the Hawaiian Islands prior to 1778).
Financial data A stipend is awarded (amount not specified).
Duration 1 year.
Number awarded 1 each year.
Deadline April each year.

[849]
SCHOLARSHIPS FOR MINORITY ACCOUNTING STUDENTS
American Institute of Certified Public Accountants
Attn: Academic and Career Development Division
220 Leigh Farm Road
Durham, NC 27707-8110
(919) 402-4931   Fax: (919) 419-4705
E-mail: MIC_Programs@aicpa.org
Web: www.aicpa.org

Purpose To provide financial assistance to Native Americans and other minorities interested in studying accounting at the undergraduate or graduate school level.
Eligibility This program is open to 1) minority undergraduate students who are enrolled full time, have completed at least 30 semester hours of college work (including at least 6 semester hours in accounting), are majoring in accounting with the intent to pursue a C.P.A. credential, and have a GPA (major and cumulative) of 3.3 or higher; and 2) minority graduate students who are enrolled full time in a master's-level accounting, finance, taxation, or related program and have a GPA (major and cumulative) of 3.3 or higher. Applicants must be U.S. citizens or permanent residents and student affiliate members of the American Institute of Certified Public Accountants (AICPA). The program defines minority students as those whose heritage is Black or African American, Hispanic or Latino, Asian, American Indian or Alaskan Native, Native Hawaiian or other Pacific Islander, or of 2 or more races.
Financial data Stipends range from $1,500 to $5,000 per year.
Duration 1 year; may be renewed, if recipients are making satisfactory progress toward graduation.
Additional information These scholarships are granted by the institute's Minority Initiatives Committee.
Number awarded Varies each year; recently, 137 students received funding through this program.
Deadline May of each year.

[850]
SEALASKA HERITAGE INSTITUTE SCHOLARSHIPS
Sealaska Corporation
Attn: Sealaska Heritage Institute
One Sealaska Plaza, Suite 301
Juneau, AK 99801-1249
(907) 586-9166   Toll-free: (888) 311-4992
Fax: (907) 586-9293
E-mail: scholarship@sealaska.com
Web: www.sealaskaheritage.org

Purpose To provide financial assistance for undergraduate or graduate study to Native Alaskans who have a connection to Sealaska Corporation.
Eligibility This program is open to 1) Alaska Natives who are enrolled to Sealaska Corporation, and 2) Native lineal descendants of Alaska Natives enrolled to Sealaska Corporation, whether or not the applicant owns Sealaska Corporation stock. Applicants must be enrolled or accepted for enrollment as full-time undergraduate or graduate students. Along with their application, they must submit 2 essays: 1) their personal history and educational goals, and 2) their expected contributions to the Alaska Native or Native American community. Financial need is also considered in the selection process.
Financial data The amount of the award depends on the availability of funds, the number of qualified applicants, class standing, and cumulative GPA.
Duration 1 year; may be renewed up to 5 years for a bachelor's degree, up to 3 years for a master's degree, up to 2 years for a doctorate, or up to 3 years for vocational study. The maximum total support is limited to 9 years. Renewal depends on recipients' maintaining full-time enrollment and a GPA of 2.5 or higher as an undergraduate or 3.0 or higher as a graduate student.
Number awarded Varies each year.
Deadline February of each year.

[851]
SEALASKA HERITAGE INSTITUTE 7(I) SCHOLARSHIPS
Sealaska Corporation
Attn: Sealaska Heritage Institute
One Sealaska Plaza, Suite 301
Juneau, AK 99801-1249
(907) 586-9166   Toll-free: (888) 311-4992
Fax: (907) 586-9293
E-mail: scholarship@sealaska.com
Web: www.sealaskaheritage.org

Purpose To provide financial assistance for undergraduate or graduate study to Native Alaskans who have a connection to Sealaska Corporation and are majoring in designated fields.
Eligibility This program is open to 1) Alaska Natives who are enrolled to Sealaska Corporation, and 2) Native lineal descendants of Alaska Natives enrolled to Sealaska Corporation, whether or not the applicant owns Sealaska Corporation stock. Applicants must be enrolled or accepted for enrollment as full-time undergraduate or graduate students. Along with their application, they must submit 2 essays: 1) their personal history and educational goals, and 2) their expected contributions to the Alaska Native or Native American community. Financial need is also considered in the

selection process. The following areas of study qualify for these awards: natural resources (environmental sciences, engineering, conservation biology, environmental law, fisheries, geology, marine science/biology, forestry, wildlife management, and mining technology); business administration (accounting, finance, marketing, international business, international commerce and trade, management of information systems, human resources management, economics, computer information systems, and industrial management); and other special fields (cadastral surveys, chemistry, equipment/machinery operators, industrial safety specialists, health specialists, plastics engineers, trade specialists, physics, mathematics, and marine trades and occupations).

Financial data The amount of the award depends on the availability of funds, the number of qualified applicants, class standing, and cumulative GPA.

Duration 1 year; may be renewed up to 5 years for a bachelor's degree, up to 3 years for a master's degree, up to 2 years for a doctorate, or up to 3 years for vocational study. The maximum total support is limited to 9 years. Renewal depends on recipients' maintaining full-time enrollment and a GPA of 2.5 or higher.

Additional information Funding for this program is provided from Alaska Native Claims Settlement Act (ANSCA) Section 7(i) revenue sharing provisions.

Number awarded Varies each year.

Deadline February of each year.

[852]
SEMICONDUCTOR RESEARCH CORPORATION MASTER'S SCHOLARSHIP PROGRAM

Semiconductor Research Corporation
Attn: Global Research Collaboration
1101 Slater Road, Suite 120
P.O. Box 12053
Research Triangle Park, NC 27709-2053
(919) 941-9400   Fax: (919) 941-9450
E-mail: students@src.org
Web: grc.src.org/member/about/aboutmas.asp

Purpose To provide financial assistance to minorities and women interested in working on a master's degree in a field of microelectronics relevant to the interests of the Semiconductor Research Corporation (SRC).

Eligibility This program is open to women and members of underrepresented minority groups (African Americans, Hispanics, and Native Americans). Applicants must be U.S. citizens or permanent residents admitted to an SRC participating university to work on a master's degree in a field relevant to microelectronics under the guidance of an SRC-sponsored faculty member and under an SRC-funded contract. Selection is based on academic achievement.

Financial data The fellowship provides full tuition and fee support, a monthly stipend of $2,060, an annual grant of $2,000 to the university department with which the student recipient is associated, and travel expenses to the Graduate Fellowship Program Annual Conference.

Duration Up to 2 years.

Additional information This program was established in 1997 for underrepresented minorities and expanded to include women in 1999.

Number awarded Varies each year; recently 9 new scholars were appointed to this program.

Deadline February of each year.

[853]
SENECA NATION HIGHER EDUCATION PROGRAM

Seneca Nation of Indians
Attn: Higher Education Program
12861 Route 438
Irving, NY 14081
(716) 532-3341   Fax: (716) 532-3269
E-mail: leann.bennett@sni.org
Web: www.sni.org/hep

Purpose To provide financial assistance for college or graduate school to members of the Seneca Nation of Indians in New York.

Eligibility This program is open to members of the Seneca Nation of Indians who are enrolled or planning to enroll in an associate, bachelor's, master's, or doctoral program. They must have applied for all other forms of financial aid for which they qualify, e.g., full-time undergraduates who are New York residents must apply for New York State Indian Aid (NYSIA) and the New York State Tuition Assistance Program (TAP); part-time undergraduates who are New York residents must apply for Aid for Part-Time Study (APTS); non-residents of New York must apply for funding from their state of residence; graduate students must apply for an American Indian Graduate Center (AIGC) fellowship. Applicants with permanent residence on the reservation qualify for level 1 awards; those with permanent residence within New York state qualify for level 2 awards; those with permanent residence outside New York state qualify for level 3 awards. Financial need is considered in the selection process.

Financial data Maximum awards per academic year for tuition and fees are $11,000 for level 1 students, $8,000 for level 2 students, or $6,000 for level 3 students. Other benefits for all recipients include $1,000 per year for books and supplies for full-time students or $100 per 3-credit hours for part-time students; payment of room and board in dormitories or college-approved housing for full-time students; a transportation allowance for commuters of $900 per year for full-time students or $85 per 3-credit hours for part-time students; and a personal expense allowance of $500 per year for full-time students or $50 per 3-credit hours for part-time students.

Duration 1 year; may be renewed.

Number awarded Varies each year.

Deadline June of each year for fall semester; July of each year for fall quarter; October of each year for winter quarter; November of each year for spring semester; January of each year for spring quarter; April of each year for summer semester or quarter.

[854]
SEQUOYAH GRADUATE FELLOWSHIPS
Association on American Indian Affairs, Inc.
Attn: Director of Scholarship Programs
966 Hungerford Drive, Suite 12-B
Rockville, MD 20850
(240) 314-7155   Fax: (240) 314-7159
E-mail: lw.aaia@verizon.net
Web: www.indian-affairs.org

Purpose To provide financial assistance to Native Americans interested in working on a graduate degree in any field.

Eligibility This program is open to American Indians and Alaskan Natives working full time on a graduate degree. Applicants must submit documentation of financial need, a Certificate of Indian Blood showing at least one-quarter Indian blood, proof of tribal enrollment, an essay on their educational goals, 2 letters of recommendation, and their most recent transcript.

Financial data The stipend is $1,500.

Duration 1 year; recipients may reapply.

Number awarded Varies each year.

Deadline June of each year.

[855]
SHEE ATIKA ACADEMIC SCHOLARSHIPS
Shee Atiká, Incorporated
Attn: Shee Atiká Benefits Trust
315 Lincoln Street, Suite 300
Sitka, AK 99835
(907) 747-3534   Toll-free: (800) 478-3534
Fax: (907) 747-5727   E-mail: info@sheeatika.com
Web: www.sheeatika.com/scholarships.shtml

Purpose To provide financial assistance for college or graduate school to shareholders of Shee Atiká, Incorporated, an urban corporation organized under the Alaska Native Claims Settlement Act (ANSCA).

Eligibility This program is open to Shee Atiká Class A and Class B shareholders enrolled or planning to enroll at a college, university, graduate school, or trade or vocational school. Relatives of shareholders are eligible only if they receive at least 1 share of stock from their family member allowed to make a gift under ANSCA. Students interested in a program of concentrated vocational training may petition for that status. Applicants must submit a statement covering their personal and professional goals, honors and activities, how this scholarship will assist them, and the reasons for their major or course of study. Selection is based on that statement, academic achievement, and financial need.

Financial data The maximum annual stipend is $2,200 for undergraduates, $4,400 for graduate students, or $6,600 for students enrolled in concentrated vocational training.

Duration 1 year; may be renewed up to 3 additional years of undergraduate study or 2 years of graduate study. The maximum that any shareholder may receive for both undergraduate and graduate study is $22,000.

Number awarded Varies each year.

Deadline January, April, July, or October of each year.

[856]
SHERRY R. ARNSTEIN MINORITY STUDENT SCHOLARSHIP
American Association of Colleges of Osteopathic Medicine
Attn: Office of Government Relations
5550 Friendship Boulevard, Suite 310
Chevy Chase, MD 20815-7231
(301) 968-4151   Fax: (301) 968-4101
Web: www.aacom.org

Purpose To provide financial assistance to Native American and other underrepresented minority students already enrolled in osteopathic medical school.

Eligibility This program is open to Black, Hispanic, and Native American students currently enrolled in good standing in their first, second, or third year of osteopathic medical school. Applicants must submit a 750-word essay on what osteopathic medical schools can do to recruit and retain more underrepresented minority students, what they personally plan to do as a student and as a future D.O. to help increase minority student enrollment at a college of osteopathic medicine, and how and why they were drawn to osteopathic medicine.

Financial data Stipends are generally $1,000.

Duration 1 year; nonrenewable.

Deadline March of each year.

[857]
SHERRY R. ARNSTEIN NEW STUDENT MINORITY STUDENT SCHOLARSHIP
American Association of Colleges of Osteopathic Medicine
Attn: Office of Government Relations
5550 Friendship Boulevard, Suite 310
Chevy Chase, MD 20815-7231
(301) 968-4151   Fax: (301) 968-4101
Web: www.aacom.org

Purpose To provide financial assistance to underrepresented minority students planning to enroll at an osteopathic medical school.

Eligibility This program is open to Black, Hispanic, and Native American students who have been accepted and are planning to enroll as a first-time student at any of the 20 colleges of osteopathic medicine that are members of the American Association of Colleges of Osteopathic Medicine (AACOM). Applicants must submit a 750-word essay on what osteopathic medical schools can do to recruit and retain more underrepresented minority students, what they personally plan to do as a student and as a future D.O. to help increase minority student enrollment at a college of osteopathic medicine, and how and why they were drawn to osteopathic medicine.

Financial data Stipends are generally $1,000.

Duration 1 year; nonrenewable.

Deadline March of each year.

[858]
SIDNEY B. WILLIAMS, JR. INTELLECTUAL PROPERTY LAW SCHOOL SCHOLARSHIPS

American Intellectual Property Law Education
 Foundation
485 Kinderkamack Road
Oradell, NJ 07649
(201) 634-1870 Fax: (201) 634-1871
E-mail: admin@aiplef.org
Web: www.aiplef.org/scholarships/sidney_b_williams

Purpose To provide financial assistance to Native American and other minority law school students who are interested in preparing for a career in intellectual property law.

Eligibility This program is open to members of minority groups currently enrolled in or accepted to an ABA-accredited law school. Applicants must be U.S. citizens with a demonstrated intent to engage in the full-time practice of intellectual property law. Along with their application, they must submit a 250-word essay on how this scholarship will make a difference to them in meeting their goal of engaging in the full-time practice of intellectual property law and why they intend to do so. Selection is based on 1) demonstrated commitment to developing a career in intellectual property law; 2) academic performance at the undergraduate, graduate, and law school levels (as applicable); 3) general factors, such as leadership skills, community activities, or special accomplishments; and 4) financial need.

Financial data The stipend is $10,000 per year. Funds may be used for tuition, fees, books, supplies, room, board, and a patent bar review course.

Duration 1 year; may be renewed if the recipient maintains a GPA of 2.0 or higher.

Additional information This program, which began in 2002, is administered by the Thurgood Marshall Scholarship Fund, 80 Maiden Lane, Suite 2204, New York, NY 10038, (212) 573-8487, Fax: (212) 573-8497, E-mail: srogers@tmcfund.org. Additional funding is provided by the American Intellectual Property Law Association, the American Bar Association's Section of Intellectual Property Law, and the Minority Corporate Counsel Association. The first class of recipients included a Chinese American, an Asian Pacific American, Mexican Americans, and African Americans. Recipients are required to join and maintain membership in the American Intellectual Property Law Association.

Number awarded Varies each year; recently, 14 of these scholarships were awarded.

Deadline February of each year.

[859]
SITKA TRIBE OF ALASKA HIGHER EDUCATION PROGRAM

Sitka Tribe of Alaska
Attn: Education and Training Department
456 Katlian Street
Sitka, AK 99835
(907) 747-6506 Toll-free: (866) 747-6506
Fax: (907) 747-3503 E-mail: cduncan@sitkatribe.org
Web: www.sitkatribe.org

Purpose To provide financial assistance for college or graduate school to enrolled members of the Sitka Tribe of Alaska.

Eligibility This program is open to enrolled members of the Sitka Tribe of Alaska as documented by the Bureau of Indian Affairs. Members of other federally-recognized tribes may also be eligible if funds are available. Applicants must be enrolled full time at an accredited 2-year college (credits must be transferable to a 4-year school) or a 4-year college or university. They must have a high school diploma or GED and be able to demonstrate financial need. Priority is given to eligible Sitka Tribe of Alaska students who have met the minimum requirements in the following order: 1) college seniors; 2) college juniors; 3) college sophomores; 4) entering freshmen; 5) graduate students (provided funds are available); and 6) other qualified applicants (provided funds are available).

Financial data The maximum stipend is $3,000 per year. Payments are made to students through the financial aid office at the college or university they attend.

Duration Up to 10 semesters for students working on a 4-year degree or up to 5 semesters for students working on a 2-year degree. Recipients must maintain a GPA of at least 2.0 as freshmen, 2.2 as sophomores, 2.25 as juniors, and 2.5 as seniors to remain eligible. Graduate students must remain enrolled full time and maintain minimum standards as set by their institution.

Number awarded Varies each year.

Deadline April of each year for students attending the fall semester/quarter or the full year; September of each year for students beginning the spring/winter semester/quarter.

[860]
SITNASUAK FOUNDATION SCHOLARSHIPS

Sitnasuak Native Corporation
Attn: Sitnasuak Foundation
P.O. Box 905
Nome, AK 99762
(907) 443-2632 Fax: (907) 443-3063
E-mail: foundation@snc.org
Web: www.snc.org/foundation.htm

Purpose To provide financial assistance to members of the Sitnasuak Native Corporation and other residents of the Bering Straits region of Alaska who plan to attend college or graduate school in any state.

Eligibility This program is open to students in the following order of priority: 1) residents of the Bering Straits region of Alaska with plans to return and contribute to the development of the region; 2) shareholders of the Sitnasuak Native Corporation and their descendants; and 3) continuing students. Applicants must be enrolled or accepted for enrollment at a college, graduate school, or vocational program in any state. They must have earned a GED or high school diploma with a GPA of 2.0 or higher and be able to demonstrate financial need. Along with their application, they must submit a 2-page essay describing their educational goals and future plans to contribute to the development of the Bering Straits region.

Financial data For full-time students, the stipend is $600 per semester for those with a GPA of 3.0 or higher, $500 per semester for those with a GPA of 2.5 to 2.9, or $400 per semester for those with a GPA of 2.0 to 2.4. For part-time students, the stipend is $200 per semester. For vocational training students, the stipend is $400 per semester or $800 per year.

Duration 1 year; may be renewed if undergraduate students maintain a GPA of 2.0 or higher, if graduate students maintain a GPA of 2.5 or higher, and if vocational students provide a progress report at the end of each term.
Additional information The Sitnasuak Native Corporation is the largest of 16 native village corporations in the Bering Straits region of Alaska.
Number awarded Varies each year.
Deadline June of each year for fall semester; November of each year for spring semester; March of each year for summer session.

[861]
SKY PEOPLE GRADUATE SCHOLARSHIP PROGRAM

Northern Arapaho Tribe
Attn: Sky People Higher Education
P.O. Box 8480
Ethete, WY 82520
(307) 332-5286   Toll-free: (800) 815-6795
Fax: (307) 332-9104
E-mail: assistant@skypeopleed.org
Web: www.skypeopleed.org

Purpose To provide financial assistance for graduate school to members of the Northern Arapaho Tribe.
Eligibility This program is open to full-time and part-time graduate students who have a GPA of 3.0 or higher. Applicants must be of one-fourth Northern Arapaho descent (enrolled or non-enrolled) and must submit a Certificate of Indian Blood or other verification of Northern Arapaho blood with at least one-fourth degree. Along with their application, they must submit a 1-page personal statement that includes a brief history of their background, academic ability and achievement, work or leadership experience, participation in community-related activities, and career goals. Selection is based on that statement, potential to contribute to the community upon graduation, academic ability and achievement, and a letter of recommendation.
Financial data The stipend depends on the availability of funds.
Duration 1 year; may be renewed.
Number awarded Varies each year.

[862]
SNA FOUNDATION SCHOLARSHIPS

Seldovia Native Association, Inc.
Attn: SNA Foundation
P.O. Drawer L
Seldovia, AK 99663
(907) 234-7625   Toll-free: (800) 478-7898
Fax: (907) 234-7637
Web: www.snai.com/foundation.htm

Purpose To provide financial assistance to Alaska Natives who are shareholders in Seldovia Native Association (SNA) or their family members and who wish to attend college or graduate school in any state.
Eligibility This program is open to Alaska Natives who are enrolled as shareholders in SNA, their spouses, and their descendants. Applicants must be enrolled or accepted for enrollment as full-time undergraduate or graduate students at an accredited 2- or 4-year college or university in any state. They must have a GPA of 3.0 or higher for achievement scholarships or 2.0 or higher for general scholarships. Along with their application, they must submit a statement of purpose that includes their personal history, a summary of accomplishments, a description of their career goals, and how their degree program fits with their education and career plans. Selection is based on that statement, academic achievement, previous work experience, educational and community involvement, recommendations, seriousness of purpose, major field of study, practicality of educational and professional goals, completeness of the application, and financial need. Alaska residency is not required.
Financial data Achievement scholarships are $2,500 per year; general scholarships are $500 per year.
Duration 1 year; may be renewed.
Number awarded Varies each year.
Deadline June of each year.

[863]
SOCIETY OF AMERICAN INDIAN GOVERNMENT EMPLOYEES ACADEMIC SCHOLARSHIPS

Society of American Indian Government Employees
P.O. Box 7715
Washington, DC 20044
Web: www.saige.org

Purpose To provide financial assistance to American Indian and Alaska Native federal employees who are interested in working on an undergraduate or graduate degree.
Eligibility This program is open to American Indians and Alaska Natives who have term, seasonal, career conditional, or career appointments as federal employees. Applicants must be interested in working on a bachelor's, master's, or Ph.D. degree at an accredited postsecondary school. They must have a GPA of 2.5 or higher. Along with their application, they must submit a 1-page essay describing their educational and workforce advancement goals and how this scholarship will help them achieve their goals, a letter of recommendation, and a narrative of extracurricular and community service activities.
Financial data Stipends range from $300 to $500 per semester, or $500 to $1,000 per academic year. Funding is provided as reimbursement for tuition costs upon receipt of a passing grade.
Duration 1 semester; may be renewed upon reapplication.
Additional information This program was established in 2005. Information is also available from Veronica Vasquez, (805) 989-3254, E-mail: Veronica.Vasquez@navy.mil.
Number awarded 1 or more each semester.
Deadline May of each year for fall semester; October of each year for spring semester.

[864]
SOCIETY OF AMERICAN INDIAN GOVERNMENT EMPLOYEES PROFESSIONAL DEVELOPMENT SCHOLARSHIPS

Society of American Indian Government Employees
P.O. Box 7715
Washington, DC 20044
Web: www.saige.org

Purpose To provide financial assistance to American Indian and Alaska Native federal employees who are interested in taking professional development courses or training.

Eligibility This program is open to American Indians and Alaska Natives who have term, seasonal, career conditional, or career appointments as federal employees. Applicants must be interested in participating in a professional development course or training activity. Along with their application, they must submit a 1-page essay describing their educational and workforce advancement goals and how this scholarship will help them achieve their goals, an Individual Development Plan (IDP) signed by their supervisor, a letter of recommendation, and a narrative of extracurricular and community service activities.

Financial data Grants provide for reimbursement of registration costs.

Duration These are 1-time grants.

Additional information This program was established in 2005. Information is also available from Veronica Vasquez, (805) 989-3254, E-mail: Veronica.Vasquez@navy.mil.

Number awarded 1 or more each year.

Deadline May or October of each year.

[865]
SOVEREIGN NATIONS SCHOLARSHIP FUND GRADUATE AWARDS

American Indian College Fund
Attn: Scholarship Department
8333 Greenwood Boulevard
Denver, CO 80221
(303) 426-8900   Toll-free: (800) 776-FUND
Fax: (303) 426-1200   E-mail: info@collegefund.org
Web: www.collegefund.org

Purpose To provide financial assistance for graduate school to Native American students who are interested in working for a tribe or Indian organization after completing their degree.

Eligibility This program is open to American Indians and Alaska Natives who can document proof of enrollment or descendancy. Applicants must be planning to 1) enroll full time in an advanced degree (e.g., M.A., M.S., J.D., Ph.D., M.D.) program at a mainstream institution, and 2) work for their tribe or an Indian organization after graduation. They must have a GPA of 3.0 GPA or higher and be able to demonstrate financial need. Along with their application, they must submit 1) short essays (up to 500 words each) on how they perceive themselves as leaders in their school or community and how their education will help the Native American community; and 2) a personal statement of 1,000 words that includes their personal background, their academic background, their educational and career goals, and how this scholarship will help them achieve those goals.

Financial data The stipend is $2,000 per year.

Duration 1 year; may be renewed.

Additional information Recipients are encouraged to work for their tribe or an Indian organization upon completion of their degree.

Number awarded Varies each year.

Deadline May of each year.

[866]
SPECIAL LIBRARIES ASSOCIATION AFFIRMATIVE ACTION SCHOLARSHIP

Special Libraries Association
Attn: Scholarship Committee
331 South Patrick Street
Alexandria, VA 22314-3501
(703) 647-4900   Fax: (703) 647-4901
E-mail: sla@sla.org
Web: www.sla.org

Purpose To provide financial assistance to Native Americans and other minorities who are interested in preparing for a career in the fields of library or information science in the United States or Canada.

Eligibility This program is open to members of a racial minority group, defined as Black (African American), Hispanic, Asian, Pacific Islander, American Indian, Native Hawaiian, or Alaskan Native. Applicants must be enrolled or accepted for enrollment in a recognized school of library or information science and in financial need. Preference is given to members of the Special Libraries Association and to persons who have worked in and for special libraries.

Financial data The stipend is $6,000.

Duration 1 year.

Number awarded 1 each year.

Deadline September of each year.

[867]
SPIRIT OF SOVEREIGNTY SCHOLARSHIPS

National Indian Gaming Association
Attn: Spirit of Sovereignty Foundation
224 Second Street, S.E.
Washington, DC 20003
(480) 820-2464   E-mail: info@spiritfund.com
Web: www.spiritfund.com/student.htm

Purpose To provide financial assistance to Native American upper-division and graduate students who are working on a degree in a business-related field.

Eligibility This program is open to college juniors, seniors, and graduate students who are working on a degree in business or a related field (e.g., hotel management, information systems, computer science, economics, human resources). Applicants must submit a copy of their Certificate of Indian Blood (CIB), current transcript, 2 letters of recommendation, and a 250-word essay that describes their involvement in extracurricular American Indian programs at their institution, volunteer and community work related to American Indian communities, potential for future interaction and support to Indian communities, tribal and community involvement, and potential to represent the American Indian community to non-Native constituents.

Financial data A stipend is awarded (amount not specified).

Duration 1 year.

Additional information Information is also available from the American Indian Graduate Center, 4520 Montgomery Boulevard, N.E., Suite 1-B, Albuquerque, NM 87109, (505) 881-4584.
Number awarded 1 or more each year.
Deadline February of each year.

[868]
SREB DOCTORAL SCHOLARS PROGRAM
Southern Regional Education Board
592 10th Street N.W.
Atlanta, GA 30318-5776
(404) 875-9211, ext. 273   Fax: (404) 872-1477
E-mail: doctoral.scholars@sreb.org
Web: www.sreb.org/programs/dsp/dspindex.asp

Purpose To provide financial assistance to Native American and other minority students who wish to work on a doctoral degree in the sciences at designated universities in the southern states.
Eligibility This program is open to U.S. citizens who are members of racial/ethnic minority groups (Native Americans, Hispanic Americans, Asian Americans, and African Americans) and have or will receive a bachelor's degree from an accredited college or university. Applicants must intend to work on a Ph.D. in science, mathematics, engineering, or science or mathematics education at a participating institution. They must indicate an interest in becoming a college professor at an institution in the South. Students who are already enrolled in a doctoral program are not eligible. Study for professional degrees, such as the M.D., D.D.S., J.D., or D.V.M., as well as graduate study in education leading to an Ed.D., does not qualify.
Financial data Scholars receive a waiver of tuition and fees (in or out of state) for up to 5 years, an annual stipend of $15,000 for 3 years, an annual allowance for professional development activities, and reimbursement of travel expenses to attend the Company for Faculty Diversity's annual Institute on Teaching and Mentoring.
Duration Up to 5 years.
Additional information This program was established in 1993 as part of the Compact for Faculty Diversity, supported by the Pew Charitable Trusts and the Ford Foundation.
Number awarded Varies each year; recently, the program was supporting more than 300 scholars. Since its founding, it has supported more than 800 scholars at 83 institutions in 29 states.
Deadline March of each year.

[869]
ST. LOUIS CHAPTER NATIONAL GRADUATE SCHOLARSHIP
National Black MBA Association-St. Louis Chapter
Attn: Scholarship Program
P.O. Box 5296
St. Louis, MO 63115
(636) 230-2404
E-mail: adrienne-thomas@sbcglobal.net
Web: www.stlbmbaa.org/drupal/?q=node/42

Purpose To provide financial assistance to Native American and other underrepresented minority graduate students who are working on a degree in business.
Eligibility This program is open to minority (African American, Hispanic/Latino, or Native American) students who are currently enrolled full time in a graduate business or management program at a college or university anywhere in the country. Applicants may be residents of any state, but they must be available to attend the corporate, scholarship, and membership reception of the St. Louis chapter of the National Black MBA Association and they must agree to become an active member of that chapter. Along with their application, they must submit a 2-page essay on 1 of 2 assigned topics that change annually but relate to minorities and business. Selection is based on the essay, resume, transcripts, and a list of extracurricular activities.
Financial data Stipends range from $1,000 to $4,500 each year.
Duration 1 year.
Number awarded 2 each year.
Deadline May of each year.

[870]
STOCKBRIDGE-MUNSEE COLLEGE AND VOCATIONAL ASSISTANCE
Stockbridge-Munsee Community
Attn: Education Department
W13447 Camp 14 Road
P.O. Box 70
Bowler, WI 54416
(715) 793-4111   Toll-free: (800) 720-2790
Fax: (715) 793-4830
E-mail: jolene.bowman@mohican-nsn.gov
Web: www.mohican-nsn.gov

Purpose To provide financial assistance to members of the Stockbridge-Munsee Community of Mohican Indians who are interested in attending college or graduate school in any state.
Eligibility This program is open to members of the Stockbridge-Munsee Community of Mohican Indians who are interested in working on a vocational, associate, baccalaureate, or graduate degree at a college or university in any state. Applicants must be able to demonstrate financial need. In the selection process, priority is given to students in the following order: new students, part-time students, students for whom the educational institution has made a determination of no financial need, and students who are repeating a degree level.
Financial data Stipends for full-time study are $2,625 per semester for 2-year college and vocational students, $5,000 per semester for 4-year baccalaureate students, or $6,670 per semester for graduate students. Stipends for part-time study are pro-rated appropriately.
Duration 1 semester; may be renewed up to 4 additional semesters for vocational and associate degree students, up to 9 additional semesters for baccalaureate students, up to 4 additional semesters for students in a 2-year graduate program, up to 6 additional semesters for students in a 3-year graduate program, or up to 8 additional semesters for students in a 4-year graduate program. Renewals require students to remain enrolled full time and to maintain a GPA of 2.0 or higher. Part-time students may renew proportionately.

Additional information This program is offered under contract with the U.S. Bureau of Indian Affairs.
Number awarded Varies each year.
Deadline May of each year for fall term; September of each year for spring term.

[871]
STOKES EDUCATIONAL SCHOLARSHIP PROGRAM
National Security Agency
Attn: Office of Recruitment and Hiring
9800 Savage Road, Suite 6779
P.O. Box 1661
Fort Meade, MD 20755-6779
(410) 854-4725   Toll-free: (866) NSA-HIRE
Web: www.nsa.gov

Purpose To provide minority and other high school seniors and college sophomores with financial assistance and work experience at the National Security Agency (NSA).
Eligibility This program is open to 1) graduating high school seniors, particularly minorities, who are planning a college major in electrical or computer engineering or computer science; and 2) college sophomores who are majoring in mathematics, foreign language (currently, Russian or Farsi only), or fields related to intelligence analysis, such as regional studies (Middle East; south, east, or central Asia), topical studies (terrorism, proliferation, or related sciences), international banking and finance, telecommunications and information system networks, intelligence or information analysis, international relations, or security studies. High school seniors must have minimum scores of 1600 on the SAT (1100 on critical reading and mathematics, 500 in writing) or 25 on the ACT. All applicants must have a GPA of 3.0 or higher. Along with their application, they must submit a 1-page essay on why they want to have a career with the NSA. U.S. citizenship and eligibility to obtain a high-level security clearance are required.
Financial data Participants receive college tuition for up to 4 years, reimbursement for books and certain fees, a year-round salary, and a housing allowance and travel reimbursement during summer employment if the distance between the agency and school exceeds 75 miles. Following graduation, participants must work for the agency for 1 and a half times their length of study, usually 5 years. Students who leave agency employment earlier must repay the tuition cost.
Duration Up to 4 years, followed by employment at the agency for 5 years.
Additional information Participants must attend classes full time and work at the agency during the summer in jobs tailored to their course of study. They must maintain at least a 3.0 GPA. This program, established in 1986, was formerly known as the National Security Agency Undergraduate Training Program.
Number awarded Varies each year.
Deadline November of each year.

[872]
SUSIE QIMMIQSAK BEVINS ENDOWMENT SCHOLARSHIP FUND
Cook Inlet Region, Inc.
Attn: The CIRI Foundation
3600 San Jeronimo Drive, Suite 256
Anchorage, AK 99508-2870
(907) 793-3575   Toll-free: (800) 764-3382
Fax: (907) 793-3585   E-mail: tcf@thecirifoundation.org
Web: www.thecirifoundation.org/designated.htm

Purpose To provide financial assistance for undergraduate or graduate studies in the literary, performing, and visual arts to Alaska Natives who are original enrollees to Cook Inlet Region, Inc. (CIRI) and their lineal descendants.
Eligibility This program is open to Alaska Native enrollees to CIRI under the Alaska Native Claims Settlement Act (ANCSA) of 1971 and their lineal descendants. There are no Alaska residency requirements or age limitations. Applicants must be accepted or enrolled full time in a 2-year, 4-year, or graduate degree program in the literary, visual, or performing arts. They should have a GPA of 2.5 or higher. Along with their application, they must submit a 500-word statement on their educational and career goals and how they are contributing, or planning to contribute, to a positive Alaska Native community. Selection is based on that statement, academic achievement, rigor of course work or degree program, student financial contribution, financial need, grade level, previous work performance, community service, and relationship of degree program to career goals.
Financial data The stipend is $2,000 per semester.
Duration 1 semester; recipients may reapply.
Additional information This program was established in 1990.
Number awarded Varies each year.
Deadline May or November of each year.

[873]
TANANA CHIEFS CONFERENCE HIGHER EDUCATION GRANTS
Tanana Chiefs Conference
Attn: Education Department
122 First Avenue, Suite 600
Fairbanks, AK 99701-4897
(907) 452-8251, ext. 3186   Toll-free: (800) 770-8251
Toll-free: (800) 478-6822 (within AK)
Fax: (907) 459-3885
Web: www.tanachiefs.org

Purpose To provide financial assistance to Native Alaskans who have a tie to the Tanana Chiefs Conference (TCC) and are interested in attending college or graduate school in any state.
Eligibility This program is open to Alaska Natives who are enrolled to Doyon, Limited or a member of a tribe or village served by TCC. Applicants must be attending or planning to attend an accredited college, university, graduate school, or vocational training program in any state. They must be able to demonstrate financial need and to apply for all other available financial aid.
Financial data A stipend is awarded (amount not specified).
Duration 1 semester; may be renewed if the recipient maintains a GPA of 2.0 or higher and full-time enrollment.

Additional information TCC serves 42 villages in interior Alaska; for a list, contact the conference.
Number awarded Varies each year.
Deadline April of each year for fall semester or quarter; November of each year for spring semester or winter or spring quarter; February of each year for summer school.

[874]
TED SCRIPPS FELLOWSHIPS IN ENVIRONMENTAL JOURNALISM
University of Colorado at Boulder
Attn: Center for Environmental Journalism
1511 University Avenue
Campus Box 478
Boulder, CO 80309-0478
(303) 492-4114   E-mail: cej@colorado.edu
Web: www.colorado.edu

Purpose To provide minority and other journalists with an opportunity to gain more knowledge about environmental issues at the University of Colorado at Boulder.
Eligibility This program is open to full-time U.S. print and broadcast journalists who have at least 5 years' professional experience and have completed an undergraduate degree. Applicants may be general assignment reporters, editors, producers, environmental reporters, full-time freelancers. or photojournalists. Prior experience in covering the environment is not required. Professionals in such related fields as teaching, public relations, or advertising are not eligible. Applicants must be interested in a program at the university that includes classes, weekly seminars, and field trips. They also must engage in independent study expected to lead to a significant piece of journalistic work. Applications are especially encouraged from women, ethnic minorities, and disabled persons.
Financial data The program covers tuition and fees and pays a $46,000 stipend. Employers are strongly encouraged to continue benefits, including health insurance.
Duration 9 months.
Additional information This program, established in 1992 at the University of Michigan and transferred to the University of Colorado in 1997, is supported by the Scripps Howard Foundation. This is a non-degree program. Fellows must obtain a leave of absence from their regular employment and must return to their job following the fellowship.
Number awarded 5 each year.
Deadline February of each year.

[875]
TEXAS MEDICAL ASSOCIATION MINORITY SCHOLARSHIP PROGRAM
Texas Medical Association
Attn: Educational Loans Department
401 West 15th Street
P.O. Box 143026
Austin, TX 78714-3026
(512) 370-2828   Toll-free: (800) 880-2828
Fax: (512) 370-1635   E-mail: info@tmaloanfunds.com
Web: www.tmaloanfunds.com

Purpose To provide financial assistance to members of underrepresented minority groups from any state who are entering medical school in Texas.
Eligibility This program is open to members of minority groups that are underrepresented in the medical profession (Black, Hispanic, Native American). Applicants must have been accepted at a medical school in Texas. Along with their application, they must submit a 750-word essay on how they, as a physician, would improve the health of all Texans.
Financial data The stipend is $5,000.
Duration 1 year; renewable.
Additional information This program began in 1999.
Number awarded Varies each year; recently, 8 of these scholarships were awarded.
Deadline April of each year.

[876]
TLINGIT AND HAIDA INDIAN TRIBES OF ALASKA COLLEGE STUDENT ASSISTANCE PROGRAM
Central Council, Tlingit and Haida Indian Tribes of Alaska
Attn: Higher Education Services
3239 Hospital Drive
Juneau, AK 99801
(907) 463-7375   Toll-free: (800) 344-1432, ext. 7375
Fax: (907) 463-7321
Web: www.hied.org

Purpose To provide financial assistance for undergraduate and graduate study in any state to enrolled Tlingit or Haida tribal members.
Eligibility This program is open to both undergraduate and graduate students. Applicants must be Tlingit or Haida tribal members with a GPA of 2.0 or higher. Scholarship applications are given priority based on the following point system: 20 points for students residing in the following service areas of the Central Council: Craig, Juneau, Haines, Kasaan, Pelican, Saxman, Skagway, Tenakee, or Wrangell; 15 points for graduation from a high school within the service areas listed above; and 5 points if the applicant or the applicant's parents/guardians belong to a southeast Alaska IRA council, village, or regional corporation within the service areas listed above. Enrollment or corporation identification numbers must be supplied on the application form. In addition to this program, students are expected to apply for institution-sponsored financial aid, as well as funding from state and local community organizations or Native corporations. Financial need is considered in the selection process.
Financial data This assistance is intended to be supplemental. Funds are to be used solely for tuition, required fees, textbooks, supplies, and miscellaneous educational expenses. No part of the award may be used to repay tuition from previous terms, educational or personal loans, or previously incurred debts.
Duration 1 year; may be renewed. Undergraduate recipients must maintain a GPA of 2.0 or higher; graduate students must maintain a GPA of 3.0 or higher. All recipients must be full-time students.
Additional information Faxed applications are permitted. With the exception of distance education or independent learning courses, this program does not fund part-time attendance, vocational training, student conferences, seminars, developmental courses (i.e., professional skill involvement), or any professional licensing examinations.

Number awarded Varies each year.
Deadline May of each year.

[877]
TONKON TORP FIRST-YEAR DIVERSITY FELLOWSHIP PROGRAM

Tonkon Torp LLP
Attn: Manager of Attorney Recruiting
1600 Pioneer Tower
888 S.W. Fifth Avenue
Portland, OR 97204
(503) 221-1440   Fax: (503) 274-8779
E-mail: LoreeD@tonkon.com
Web: www.tonkon.com

Purpose To provide financial assistance and summer work experience (in Portland, Oregon) to Native American and other first-year minority law students from any state.

Eligibility This program is open to members of racial and ethnic minority groups who are currently enrolled in their first year at an ABA-accredited law school. Applicants must be able to demonstrate 1) a record of academic achievement that indicates a strong likelihood of a successful career during the remainder of law school and in the legal profession; 2) a commitment to practice law in Portland, Oregon following graduation from law school; and 3) an ability to contribute meaningfully to the diversity of the law school student body and, after entering the legal profession, the legal community. They are not required to disclose their financial circumstances, but a demonstrated need for financial assistance may be taken into consideration.

Financial data The recipient is offered a paid summer associateship at Tonkon Torp in Portland, Oregon for the summer following the first year of law school and, depending on the outcome of that experience, may be invited for a second summer following the second year of law school. Following the successful completion of that second associateship, the recipient is awarded an academic scholarship of $7,500 for the third year of law school.

Duration The program covers 2 summers and 1 academic year.

Number awarded 1 each year.
Deadline January of each year.

[878]
TOWNSEND AND TOWNSEND AND CREW DIVERSITY SCHOLARSHIP

Townsend and Townsend and Crew LLP
Attn: Lindy Yurich
Two Embarcadero Center, Eighth Floor
San Francisco, CA 94111-3834
(415) 576-0200   Fax: (415) 576-0300
E-mail: mvyurich@townsend.com
Web: www.townsend.com/who/div_scholarship.asp

Purpose To provide financial assistance to women and minority students attending law school to prepare for a career in patent law.

Eligibility This program is open to students enrolled at ABA-accredited law schools who are women or members of minority groups that have historically been underrepresented in the field of patent law (American Indians/Alaskan Natives, Blacks/African Americans, Hispanics/Latinos, and Asian Americans/Pacific Islanders). Applicants must have an undergraduate or graduate degree in a field that will help prepare them for a career in patent law (e.g., life sciences, engineering). They must have a demonstrated commitment to preparing for a career in patent law in a city in which the sponsoring law firm has an office. Selection is based on academic performance; work experience related to science, engineering, or patent law; community service; and demonstrated leadership ability.

Financial data The stipend is $2,000 per year.
Duration 1 year; recipients may reapply.
Additional information This program was established in 2005. Townsend and Townsend and Crew has offices in San Francisco, Palo Alto (California), Denver, Walnut Creek (California), San Diego, Denver, Tokyo, and Washington, D.C.

Number awarded Varies each year; recently, 11 of these scholarships were awarded.
Deadline August of each year.

[879]
TRIAD HOSPITALS CORRIS BOYD SCHOLARSHIP

Association of University Programs in Health Administration
Attn: Prizes, Fellowships and Scholarships
2000 14th Street North, Suite 780
Arlington, VA 22201
(703) 894-0940, ext. 131   Fax: (703) 894-0941
E-mail: aupha@aupha.org
Web: www.aupha.org

Purpose To provide financial assistance to Native American and other minority students entering graduate schools affiliated with the Association of University Programs in Health Administration (AUPHA).

Eligibility This program is open to members of racial and ethnic minority groups (African Americans, American Indians, Alaska Natives, Asian Americans, Hispanic Americans, Native Hawaiians, and other Pacific Islanders) who have applied to but not yet enrolled in a master's degree program in health care management at an AUPHA member institution. Applicants must be U.S. citizens and have a GPA of 3.0 or higher. Selection is based on leadership qualities, academic achievement, community involvement, and commitment to health care; financial need may be considered if all other factors are equal.

Financial data Fellows receive full payment of tuition at the AUPHA member institution of their choice. The school receives a grant of $13,000 to provide the student with an assistantship and a stipend loan sufficient to cover additional out-of-pocket expenses for the student.

Duration 1 year.
Additional information These fellowships are funded by Triad Hospitals, Inc. The program is jointly administered by AUPHA and the Institute for Diversity in Healthcare Management. Recipients are offered, and required to accept, a residency placement with Triad Hospitals upon graduation.

Number awarded 2 each year.
Deadline March of each year.

[880]
TURTLE MOUNTAIN BAND OF CHIPPEWA INDIANS SCHOLARSHIP PROGRAM

Turtle Mountain Band of Chippewa Indians
P.O. Box 900
Belcourt, ND 58316
(701) 477-8102   Fax: (701) 477-8053
Web: www.tmbci.net

Purpose To provide financial assistance for full-time undergraduate or graduate study in any state to enrolled members of the Turtle Mountain Band of Chippewa.

Eligibility Applicants must be enrolled members of the Turtle Mountain Band of Chippewa, be full-time students enrolled in an academic program at an accredited postsecondary institution in any state on either the undergraduate or graduate school level, and have a GPA of 2.0 or higher. Undergraduate applicants must be enrolled for at least 12 quarter or 12 semester credit hours (or 6 semester/quarter hours for a summer session); graduate school applicants must be enrolled for at least 1 course. Along with their application, they must submit a Certificate of Indian Blood, a letter of acceptance/admission from their college, the Award Notice sent by the college's financial aid office, a high school transcript or GED certificate, and any college transcripts. Priority is given to applicants in the following order: seniors who need to attend summer school in order to graduate, seniors, juniors who need summer school in order to become seniors, students who need summer school to acquire their 2-year degree, sophomores, freshmen, and graduate students.

Financial data A stipend is awarded (amount not specified).

Duration The maximum number of terms the scholarship program will fund a student for an undergraduate degree is 10 semesters or 15 quarters; the maximum number of terms for a student at a 2-year college is 3 years, 6 semesters, or 9 quarters.

Additional information Once recipients earn 65 or more credit hours at a 2-year college, they must transfer to a 4-year institution.

Number awarded Varies each year.

Deadline August of each year.

[881]
UNCF CORPORATE SCHOLARS PROGRAMS

United Negro College Fund
Attn: Corporate Scholars Program
P.O. Box 1435
Alexandria, VA 22313-9998
Toll-free: (866) 671-7237 E-mail: internship@uncf.org
Web: www.uncf.org

Purpose To provide financial assistance and work experience to Native American and other minority students pursuing a degree in designated fields of business, science, and engineering.

Eligibility A number of corporate sponsors provides funding for this program; each establishes its own specifications. All are open to undergraduates; some are also available to graduate students. Some allow students to be enrolled at the college or university of their choice, others are limited to students at Historically Black Colleges and Universities (HBCUs), and others are restricted to UNCF member institutions. Some are open to minority (African American, Alaskan Native, American Indian, Asian Pacific Islander American, Hispanic) students in general, but others are more restrictive. Fields of study vary, but most focus on areas of business, science, and engineering of interest to the corporate sponsor. All include summer internships at the sponsor. GPA requirements vary, but may be as high as 3.0.

Financial data The students selected for this program receive paid internships and need-based scholarships that range up to $15,000 per year.

Duration 8 to 10 weeks for the internships; 1 year for the scholarships, which may be renewed.

Additional information Current corporate sponsors include Booz Allen Hamilton, Dell Inc., Ford Motor Company, HSBC North America, JPMorganChase, Malcolm Pirnie Inc., Marathon Oil Corporation, Oracle Corporation, RR Donnelley, Sprint Nextel, United Parcel Service of America, Inc., and Weyerhaueser.

Number awarded Varies each year.

Deadline Each sponsor sets its own deadline.

[882]
UNDERREPRESENTED MENTAL HEALTH RESEARCH FELLOWSHIP PROGRAM

Council on Social Work Education
Attn: Minority Fellowship Program
1725 Duke Street, Suite 500
Alexandria, VA 22314-3457
(703) 683-8080, ext. 217   Fax: (703) 683-8099
E-mail: mfp@cswe.org
Web: www.cswe.org/CSWE/scholarships/fellowships

Purpose To provide funding to Native American and other racial minority members interested in preparing for a career in mental health research.

Eligibility This program is open to U.S. citizens and permanent residents who have been underrepresented in the field of social work. These include but are not limited to the following groups: American Indians/Alaskan Natives, Asian/Pacific Islanders (e.g., Chinese, East Indians, South Asians, Filipinos, Hawaiians, Japanese, Koreans, and Samoans), Blacks, and Hispanics (e.g., Mexicans/Chicanos, Puerto Ricans, Cubans, Central or South Americans). Applicants must be interested in enrolling in a doctoral-level social work program that provides strong research courses and research training in mental health. They must be interested in working on a doctoral degree as a full-time student. Selection is based on potential and interest in mental health research, potential for success in doctoral studies, and commitment to a career in mental health research.

Financial data Awards provide a stipend of $20,772 per year and tuition support at the rate of 100% of the first $3,000 and 60% of the remaining tuition.

Duration 1 academic year; renewable for 2 additional years if funds are available and the recipient makes satisfactory progress toward the degree objectives.

Additional information This program has been funded since 1974 by the National Institute of Mental Health of the National Institutes of Health.

Deadline February of each year.

[883]
UNITARIAN UNIVERSALIST ASSOCIATION INCENTIVE GRANTS

Unitarian Universalist Association
Attn: Office of Ministerial Credentialing
25 Beacon Street
Boston, MA 02108-2800
(617) 948-6403   Fax: (617) 742-2875
E-mail: cmay@uua.org
Web: www.uua.org

Purpose To provide financial aid to Native American and other persons of color who the Unitarian Universalist Association is interested in attracting to the ministry.
Eligibility These grants are offered to persons of color who the association is particularly interested in attracting to Unitarian Universalist ministry to promote racial, cultural, or class diversity. Applicants must be in their first year of study. Decisions regarding potential recipients are made in consultation with the schools. Selection is based on merit.
Financial data A stipend is awarded (amount not specified).
Duration 1 year; nonrenewable.
Additional information In subsequent years, recipients may apply for the association's General Financial Aid Grants.
Number awarded Varies each year.
Deadline April of each year.

[884]
UNITED METHODIST HIGHER EDUCATION FOUNDATION NATIVE ALASKAN FUND

United Methodist Higher Education Foundation
Attn: Scholarship Office
1001 19th Avenue South
P.O. Box 340005
Nashville, TN 37203-0005
(615) 340-7385   Toll-free: (800) 811-8110
Fax: (615) 340-7330
E-mail: umhefscholarships@gbhem.org
Web: www.umhef.org/othergroupa.html

Purpose To provide financial assistance to Native Alaskan Methodist undergraduate and graduate students at Methodist-related colleges and universities.
Eligibility This program is open to Native Alaskans enrolling as full-time undergraduate and graduate students at United Methodist-related colleges and universities. United Methodist students at Alaska Pacific University are also eligible. Applicants must have been active, full members of a United Methodist Church for at least 1 year prior to applying. They must be able to demonstrate financial need. U.S. citizenship or permanent resident status is required.
Financial data A stipend is awarded (amount not specified).
Duration 1 year; nonrenewable.
Number awarded Varies each year.
Deadline May of each year.

[885]
UNITED METHODIST NATIVE AMERICAN SEMINARY AWARDS

United Methodist Church
Attn: General Board of Higher Education and Ministry
Office of Loans and Scholarships
1001 19th Avenue South
P.O. Box 340007
Nashville, TN 37203-0007
(615) 340-7344   Fax: (615) 340-7367
E-mail: umscholar@gbhem.org
Web: www.gbhem.org/loansandscholarships

Purpose To provide financial assistance to Native American seminary students preparing for ministry within the United Methodist Church.
Eligibility This program is open to Native Americans accepted and/or enrolled as a full-time student at a school of theology approved by the University Senate of the United Methodist Church. At least 1 parent must be Native American, American Indian, or Alaska Native Applicants must have been active, full members of a United Methodist Church for at least 3 years prior to applying They must be able to demonstrate financial need, a GPA of 2.5 or higher, and involvement in their Native American community.
Financial data The average stipend is $12,000. Half of the funds are provided in the form of a grant and half in the form of a loan that is forgiven if the recipient serves at least 2 years in a Native American congregation or ministry/fellowship that is recognized by the United Methodist Church.
Duration 1 year.
Number awarded Varies each year; recently, 12 of these scholarships were awarded.
Deadline April of each year.

[886]
UNITED METHODIST WOMEN OF COLOR SCHOLARS PROGRAM

United Methodist Church
Attn: General Board of Higher Education and Ministry
Office of Loans and Scholarships
1001 19th Avenue South
P.O. Box 340007
Nashville, TN 37203-0007
(615) 340-7344   Fax: (615) 340-7367
E-mail: umscholar@gbhem.org
Web: www.gbhem.org/loansandscholarships

Purpose To provide financial assistance to Native American and other Methodist women of color who are working on a doctoral degree to prepare for a career as an educator at a United Methodist seminary.
Eligibility This program is open to women of color (have at least 1 parent who is African American, African, Hispanic, Asian, Native American, Alaska Native, or Pacific Islander) who have an M.Div. degree. Applicants must have been active, full members of a United Methodist Church for at least 3 years prior to applying. They must be enrolled full time in a degree program at the Ph.D. or Th.D. level to prepare for a career teaching at a United Methodist seminary.
Financial data The maximum stipend is $10,000 per year.
Duration 1 year; may be renewed up to 3 additional years.

Number awarded Varies each year; recently, 10 of these scholarships were awarded.
Deadline January of each year.

[887]
UTAH NAVAJO TRUST FUND HIGHER EDUCATION SCHOLARSHIPS
Utah Navajo Trust Fund
Attn: Higher Education Office
151 East 500 North
Blanding, UT 84511
(435) 678-1460   Toll-free: (800) 378-2050
Fax: (435) 678-1464   E-mail: MHoliday@utah.gov
Web: ww.untf.utah.gov

Purpose To provide financial assistance for college or graduate school to members of the Navajo Nation in Utah.
Eligibility This program is open to students who can provide a letter of verification from their Chapter of the Navajo Nation or Blue Mountain Dine' Community to affirm residency in San Juan County, Utah. Applicants must be working on a 1-year or 2-year certificate or associate, bachelor's, master's, or doctoral degree. They must have maintained a GPA of 3.0 or higher during high school and be able to demonstrate financial need.
Financial data The stipend depends on the need of the recipient; funding is considered supplemental to that available from the Navajo Nation Scholarship and Financial Aid Office.
Duration 1 year; may be renewed, provided the recipient maintains a GPA of 2.0 or higher.
Number awarded Varies each year.
Deadline October of each year for fall quarter or semester; January of each year for winter quarter or spring semester; April of each year for spring quarter; June of each year for summer quarter or session.

[888]
VINE DELORIA JR. MEMORIAL SCHOLARSHIP
American Indian College Fund
Attn: Scholarship Department
8333 Greenwood Boulevard
Denver, CO 80221
(303) 426-8900   Toll-free: (800) 776-FUND
Fax: (303) 426-1200   E-mail: info@collegefund.org
Web: www.collegefund.org

Purpose To provide financial assistance for graduate school to Native American students.
Eligibility This program is open to American Indians and Alaska Natives who can document proof of enrollment or descendancy. Applicants must be enrolled in an advanced degree (e.g., M.A., M.S., J.D., Ph.D., M.D.) program. They must be able to demonstrate financial need. Along with their application, they must submit 1) short essays (up to 500 words each) on how they perceive themselves as leaders in their school or community and how their education will help the Native American community; and 2) a personal statement of 1,000 words that includes their personal background, their academic background, their educational and career goals, and how this scholarship will help them achieve those goals.

Financial data A stipend is awarded (amount not specified).
Duration 1 year.
Number awarded Varies each year.
Deadline May of each year.

[889]
VISITING INDIGENOUS PROFESSIONAL (VIP) MUSEUM STUDIES PROGRAM OF THE NATIONAL MUSEUM OF THE AMERICAN INDIAN
National Museum of the American Indian
Attn: Museum Training Program
Cultural Resources Center
4220 Silver Hill Road
Suitland, MD 20746-2863
(301) 238-1540   Fax: (301) 238-3200
E-mail: NMAI-CSinfo@si.edu
Web: www.nmai.si.edu

Purpose To provide professionals currently working in Native museums and cultural centers with an opportunity to obtain hands-on training at facilities of the Smithsonian Institution's National Museum of the American Indian (NMAI).
Eligibility This program is open to professionals currently working in various disciplines at Native museums and cultural centers. Applicants must be interested in visiting the Cultural Resources Center of the NMAI to obtain technical advice in the planning and development of a museum or cultural center. Areas of interest include collections management, conservation, registration, library services, membership and visitor services, and exhibition development. Along with their application, they must submit 1) a study plan that includes their goals, why they are best suited for conducting this study, their ability to conduct thorough and relevant research, and expected outcomes for Native community enrichment; 2) a personal statement of their goals and how their community ties, personal attributes, and experiences will further their work; 3) a resume or curriculum vitae; 4) 2 letters of recommendation; and 5) a description of the institution with which they are affiliated.
Financial data The program provides limited reimbursement of expenses associated with participating in the training.
Duration 3 days to 6 weeks.
Number awarded Varies each year.
Deadline March or September of each year.

[890]
WALTER "PORKY" WHITE SCHOLARSHIP FUND
MIGIZI Communications, Inc.
Attn: Scholarship Committee
3123 East Lake Street
Minneapolis, MN 55406
(612) 721-6631   Fax: (612) 721-3936
Web: migizi.org/mig/scholarships.html

Purpose To provide financial assistance to Native American students working on an undergraduate or graduate degree in natural resources or an environmental field.
Eligibility This program is open to Native American undergraduate and graduate students enrolled at an accredited 4-year college or university. Applicants must be

working on a degree in environmental science, natural resource management, biology, marine biology, or a related discipline. Along with their application, they must submit documentation of financial need and a 500-word essay on 1) their current involvement in protecting and working with the environment and natural resources, 2) why it is important to protect and study our environment and natural resources, and 3) their plans for the future and how they plan to use their studies to help the community.
Financial data The stipend is $1,000.
Duration 1 year; nonrenewable.
Number awarded 1 each year.
Deadline May of each year.

[891]
WAMPANOAG HIGHER EDUCATION SCHOLARSHIP PROGRAM
Wampanoag Tribe of Gay Head
Attn: Education Director
20 Black Brook Road
Aquinnah, MA 02535-1546
(508) 645-9265, ext. 131   Fax: (508) 645-3790
Web: www.wampanoagtribe.net

Purpose To provide financial assistance to members of the Wampanoag Tribe of Gay Head who are interested in attending college or graduate school in any state.
Eligibility This program is open to enrolled members of the Wampanoag Tribe of Gay Head who are working on or planning to work on a baccalaureate or advanced degree. Applicants must submit a letter of acceptance from a college or university and documentation of financial need.
Financial data A stipend is awarded (amount not specified).
Duration 1 year; may be renewed.
Number awarded Varies each year.
Deadline June of each year.

[892]
WASHINGTON STATE AMERICAN INDIAN ENDOWED SCHOLARSHIP PROGRAM
Washington Higher Education Coordinating Board
917 Lakeridge Way
P.O. Box 43430
Olympia, WA 98504-3430
(360) 753-7843   Fax: (360) 753-7808
TDD: (360) 753-7809   E-mail: aies@hecb.wa.gov
Web: www.hecb.wa.gov/paying/waaidprgm/aies.asp

Purpose To provide financial assistance to American Indian undergraduate and graduate students in Washington.
Eligibility This program is open to American Indian students who are Washington residents with close social and cultural ties to an American Indian tribe and/or community in the state. Applicants must demonstrate financial need and be enrolled, or planning to enroll, as a full-time undergraduate or graduate student at a Washington state public or independent college, university, or career school. They must agree to use their education to benefit other American Indians. Students who are working on a degree in religious, seminarian, or theological academic studies are not eligible.
Financial data Stipends range from about $500 to $2,000 per year.
Duration 1 year, may be renewed up to 4 additional years.
Additional information This program was created by the Washington legislature in 1990 with a state appropriation to an endowment fund and matching contributions from tribes, individuals, and organizations.
Number awarded Approximately 15 new and 10 renewal scholarships are awarded each year.
Deadline January of each year.

[893]
WASHOE TRIBE HIGHER EDUCATION GRANT PROGRAM
Washoe Tribe
Attn: Education Department
919 Highway 395 South
Gardnerville, NV 89410
(775) 265-4191, ext. 1132
Toll-free: (800) 76-WASHOE   Fax: (775) 265-6240
E-mail: education@washoetribe.us
Web: www.washoetribe.us/content/view/74/2

Purpose To provide financial assistance for college or graduate school to members of the Washoe Tribe in Nevada and California.
Eligibility Eligible to apply for these scholarships are members of the Washoe Tribe who are working on (or planning to work on) an associate or bachelor's degree. Applicants are required to seek all other sources of funding, in addition to applying for this program. In the process, they must complete a Free Application for Federal Student Aid (FAFSA) and receive a Student Aid Report. Awards are granted in the following priority order: 1) continuing students with acceptable grades; 2) new students who reside near or within the boundaries of Washoe tribal colonies (Woodfords, Dresslerville, Carson, Stewart, Reno) and other Nevada and California residents; 3) students outside of Nevada and California; 4) graduate students; and 5) students who have a 4-year degree and are working to obtain a 4-year degree in a different field.
Financial data A stipend is awarded (amount not specified).
Duration 1 year; may be renewed if the recipient remains enrolled full time with a GPA of 1.8 or higher as a freshman and 2.0 or higher as a sophomore through senior.
Number awarded Varies each year.
Deadline August or December of each year.

[894]
WASHOE TRIBE INCENTIVE SCHOLARSHIPS
Washoe Tribe
Attn: Education Department
919 Highway 395 South
Gardnerville, NV 89410
(775) 265-4191, ext. 1132
Toll-free: (800) 76-WASHOE   Fax: (775) 265-6240
E-mail: education@washoetribe.us
Web: www.washoetribe.us/content/view/71/2

Purpose To provide financial assistance for college or graduate school to members of the Washoe Tribe.
Eligibility This program is open to members of the Washoe Tribe in Nevada and California who are currently

working full time on an associate, baccalaureate, graduate, or postgraduate degree. Applicants must have a GPA of 3.0 or higher. Along with their application they must submit proof of Washoe enrollment, a copy of their college grade report, and a copy of their current class schedule. Selection is based on a first-come, first-served basis; financial need is not considered.
Financial data The stipend is $2,000 per year.
Duration 1 year; recipients may reapply.
Number awarded 20 each year.
Deadline January or September of each year.

[895]
WATSON MIDWIVES OF COLOR SCHOLARSHIP
American College of Nurse-Midwives
Attn: ACNM Foundation, Inc.
8403 Coleville Road, Suite 1550
Silver Spring, MD 20910-6374
(240) 485-1850   Fax: (240) 485-1818
Web: www.midwife.org/foundation_award.cfm

Purpose To provide financial assistance for midwifery education to students of color who belong to the American College of Nurse-Midwives (ACNM).
Eligibility This program is open to ACNM members of color who are currently enrolled in an accredited basic midwife education program and have successfully completed 1 academic or clinical semester/quarter or clinical module. Applicants must submit a 150-word essay on their midwifery career plans and a 100-word essay on their intended future participation in the local, regional, and/or national activities of the ACNM. Selection is based on leadership potential, financial need, academic history, and potential for future professional contribution to the organization.
Financial data The stipend is $3,000.
Duration 1 year.
Number awarded Varies each year; recently, 3 of these scholarships were awarded.
Deadline March of each year.

[896]
WELLS FARGO GRADUATE SCHOLARSHIPS
American Indian Graduate Center
Attn: Executive Director
4520 Montgomery Boulevard, N.E., Suite 1-B
Albuquerque, NM 87109-1291
(505) 881-4584   Toll-free: (800) 628-1920
Fax: (505) 884-0427   E-mail: aigc@aigc.com
Web: www.aigc.com/scholarships.index.asp

Purpose To provide financial assistance to Native American graduate students interested in preparing for a career in banking, gaming operations, resort management, or administration.
Eligibility This program is open to enrolled members of U.S. federally-recognized American Indian tribes and Alaska Native groups and other students who can document one-fourth degree federally-recognized Indian blood. Applicants must be working full time on a graduate or professional degree to prepare for a career in banking, gaming operations, resort management, or administration, including accounting, finance, human resources, and information technology. They must have a GPA of 3.0 or higher. Along with their application, they must submit an essay on their personal, educational, and professional goals. Financial need is also considered in the selection process.
Financial data Awards are based on each applicant's unmet financial need. The stipend is $10,000.
Duration 1 year.
Additional information This program is supported by Wells Fargo Bank. The application fee is $15. Since this a supplemental program, applicants must apply in a timely manner for federal financial aid and campus-based aid at the college they are attending to be considered for this program. Failure to apply will disqualify an applicant.
Number awarded 2 each year.
Deadline May of each year.

[897]
WHITE EARTH SCHOLARSHIP PROGRAM
White Earth Indian Reservation Tribal Council
Attn: Scholarship Program
P.O. Box 418
White Earth, MN 56591
(218) 983-3285, ext. 1227   Toll-free: (800) 950-3248
Fax: (218) 983-3641
E-mail: highered@whiteearth.com
Web: www.whiteearth.com/education.htm

Purpose To provide financial assistance to Minnesota Chippewa Tribe enrolled members who are interested in attending college, vocational school, or graduate school in any state.
Eligibility This program is open to enrolled members of the White Earth Band of the Minnesota Chippewa Tribe who can demonstrate financial need. Applicants must be attending or planning to attend a college, university, or vocational school in any state. Graduate students in the fields of business, education, human services, law, and medicine are also eligible.
Financial data A stipend is awarded (amount not specified).
Duration 1 year; may be renewed, provided undergraduates maintain a GPA of 2.0 or higher and graduate students maintain a GPA of 3.0 or higher.
Additional information Applicants for this program must also apply for financial aid administered by their institution and any other aid for which they may be eligible (e.g., work-study, Social Security, veteran's benefits).
Number awarded Varies each year.
Deadline May of each year.

[898]
WILLIAM G. ANDERSON, D.O. MINORITY SCHOLARSHIP
American Osteopathic Foundation
Attn: Program Manager
142 East Ontario Street
Chicago, IL 60611-2864
(312) 202-8232   Toll-free: (800) 621-1773
Fax: (312) 202-8216
E-mail: vheck@aof-foundation.org
Web: www.aof-foundation.org/stu.asp

Purpose To provide financial assistance to Native American and other minority students enrolled in colleges of osteopathic medicine.

Eligibility This program is open to minority (African American, Native American, Asian American, Pacific Islander, or Hispanic) students entering their second, third, or fourth year at an accredited college of osteopathic medicine. Applicants must demonstrate 1) interest in osteopathic medicine, its philosophy, and its principles; 2) academic achievement; 3) leadership efforts in addressing the educational, societal, and health needs of minorities; 4) leadership efforts to eliminate inequities in medical education and health care; 5) accomplishments, awards and honors, clerkships or special projects; and extracurricular activities in which the student has shown leadership abilities; and 6) financial need.

Financial data The stipend is $5,000.
Duration 1 year.
Additional information This program was established in 1998.
Number awarded 1 each year.
Deadline March of each year.

[899]
WINNEBAGO TRIBE HIGHER EDUCATION ASSISTANCE

Winnebago Tribe of Nebraska
Attn: Education Department
P.O. Box 687
Winnebago, NE 68071
(402) 878-3202 Fax: (402) 878-2632
E-mail: education@winnebagotribe.com
Web: www.winnebagotribe.com

Purpose To provide financial assistance to members of the Winnebago Tribe of Nebraska who are interested in attending college or graduate school in any state.

Eligibility This program is open to enrolled members of the Winnebago Tribe of Nebraska who are attending or planning to attend an institution of higher education in any state. Applicants must be working on an associate, bachelor's, master's, or doctoral degree or certificate. They must submit a copy of their Certificate of Indian Blood (CIB) and documentation of financial need.

Financial data A stipend is awarded (amount not specified). Funding is intended only to supplement other assistance available to the student.
Duration 1 semester; may be renewed.
Number awarded Varies each year.
Deadline April of each year for fall, academic year, or summer school; October of each year for spring or winter.

[900]
WINSTON & STRAWN DIVERSITY SCHOLARSHIP PROGRAM

Winston & Strawn LLP
Attn: Director of Attorney Recruitment
35 West Wacker Drive
Chicago, IL 60601-9703
(312) 558-7334
E-mail: diversityscholarship@winston.com
Web: www.winston.com

Purpose To provide financial assistance to Native American and other diverse law students who are interested in practicing in a city in which Winston & Strawn LLP has an office.

Eligibility This program is open to second-year law students who self-identify as a member of 1 of the following groups: American Indian or Alaska Native, Asian or Pacific Islander, Black or African American, or Hispanic or Latino. Applicants must submit a resume, law school transcript, and 500-word personal statement. Selection is based on 1) interest in practicing law after graduation in a large law firm in a city in which Winston & Strawn has an office (currently, Charlotte, Chicago, Los Angeles, New York, San Francisco, and Washington, D.C.); 2) law school and undergraduate record, including academic achievements and involvement in extracurricular activities; 3) demonstrated leadership skills; 4) and interpersonal skills.

Financial data The stipend is $10,000.
Duration 1 year (the third year of law school).
Number awarded 5 each year.
Deadline October of each year.

[901]
WISCONSIN INDIAN EDUCATION ASSOCIATION SCHOLARSHIPS

Wisconsin Indian Education Association
Attn: Scholarship Coordinator
P.O. Box 910
Keshena, WI 54135
(715) 799-5110 Fax: (715) 799-5102
E-mail: vnuske@mitw.org
Web: www.wiea.org

Purpose To provide financial assistance for undergraduate or graduate study to members of Wisconsin Indian tribes.

Eligibility This program is open to residents of Wisconsin who can provide proof of tribal enrollment. Applicants must fall into 1 of the following categories: 1) graduating high school senior; 2) new or continuing student at a tribal or technical/vocational college; 3) undergraduate student at a 4-year college or university; or 4) graduate or Ph.D. student. All applicants must be full-time students. Along with their application, they must submit a 1-page personal essay on how they will apply their education. Selection is based on that essay (25 points), letters of recommendation (10 points), and GPA (15 points if 3.5 or higher, 10 points if 3.00 to 3.49, 5 points if 2.50 to 2.99). Financial need is not considered.

Financial data The stipend is $1,000 per year.
Duration 1 year; nonrenewable.
Additional information Eligible tribes include Menominee, Oneida, Stockbridge/Munsee, Mole Lake, Potowatomi,

Ho-Chunk, Ba Chippewa, LCO Chippewa, St. Croix Chippewa, Red Cliff Chippewa, Sakoagon Chippewa, Brotherton, and Lac du Flam Chippewa.
Number awarded 4 each year: 1 in each of the 4 categories.
Deadline March of each year.

[902]
WISCONSIN INDIAN STUDENT ASSISTANCE GRANTS

Wisconsin Higher Educational Aids Board
131 West Wilson Street, Room 902
P.O. Box 7885
Madison, WI 53707-7885
(608) 266-0888   Fax: (608) 267-2808
E-mail: sandy.thomas@heab.state.wi.us
Web: heab.state.wi.us/programs.html

Purpose To provide financial aid for college or graduate school to Native Americans in Wisconsin.
Eligibility Wisconsin residents who have at least 25% Native American blood (of a certified tribe or band) are eligible to apply if they are able to demonstrate financial need and are interested in attending college on the undergraduate or graduate school level. Applicants must attend a Wisconsin institution (public, independent, or proprietary). They may be enrolled either full or part time.
Financial data Awards range from $250 to $1,100 per year. Additional funds are available on a matching basis from the U.S. Bureau of Indian Affairs.
Duration Up to 5 years.
Deadline Generally, applications can be submitted at any time.

[903]
W.K. KELLOGG FOUNDATION DOCTORAL FELLOWSHIP IN HEALTH POLICY

National Medical Fellowships, Inc.
Attn: Scholarship Program
5 Hanover Square, 15th Floor
New York, NY 10004
(212) 483-8880   Fax: (212) 483-8897
E-mail: info@nmfonline.org
Web: www.nmfonline.org

Purpose To provide financial assistance to Native Americans and other minorities enrolled in a doctoral program in health policy research who are committed to working with underserved populations.
Eligibility This program is open to members of minority groups (African Americans, Native Americans, Asians, and Hispanics) enrolled in doctoral programs in public health, social policy, or health policy (Ph.D., Dr.P.H., or Sc.D.). Applicants must demonstrate a willingness to complete relevant dissertation research and a commitment to work with underserved populations upon completion of the doctorate. They must include an essay of 500 to 1,000 words discussing their reasons for applying for a fellowship, their qualifications, how it will support their career plans, and which of 4 areas of focus (health policy, men's health, mental health, substance abuse) most interests them and why.
Financial data Fellowships cover tuition, fees, and a partial living stipend.
Duration Up to 5 years: 2 years to do the necessary course work and 3 years to complete the dissertation.
Additional information The program was created in 1998 with grant support from the W.K. Kellogg Foundation. Recently, it operated at 8 institutions: the RAND Graduate School, the Heller Graduate School at Brandeis University, the Joseph L. Mailman School of Public Health at Columbia University, the Harvard School of Public Health, the Johns Hopkins School of Hygiene and Public Health, the UCLA School of Public Health, the University of Michigan School of Public Health, and the University of Pennsylvania. Information is also available from the sponsor's Washington office at 1627 K Street, N.W., Suite 1200, Washington, DC 20006-1702, (202) 296-4431, Fax: (202) 293-1990.
Number awarded 5 each year.
Deadline June of each year.

[904]
WOMBLE CARLYLE SCHOLARS PROGRAM

Womble Carlyle Sandridge & Rice, PLLC
Attn: Director of Diversity and Workplace Initiatives
One West Fourth Street
Winston-Salem, NC 27101
(336) 728-7055   Fax: (336) 733-8306
E-mail: gagard@wcsr.com
Web: www.wcsr.com/?id=149

Purpose To provide financial assistance and summer work experience to Native American and other underrepresented students at designated law schools.
Eligibility This program is open to students at designated law schools who are members of underrepresented groups. Applicants must be able to demonstrate solid academic credentials, personal or professional achievement outside the classroom, and significant participation in community service. Along with their application, they must submit a 300-word essay on either 1) a situation in which they and a person they respect disagreed over values or ideals and what they did, or 2) what idea has most influenced their life and why.
Financial data The stipend is $4,000. Recipients are also offered summer employment at an office of the sponsoring law firm. Salaries are the same as the firm's other summer associates in each office.
Duration 1 year (the second year of law school); may be renewed 1 additional year.
Additional information This program was established in 2004. The eligible law schools are North Carolina Central University School of Law (Durham, North Carolina), University of North Carolina at Chapel Hill School of Law (Chapel Hill, North Carolina), Duke University School of Law (Durham, North Carolina), Wake Forest University School of Law (Winston-Salem, North Carolina), University of South Carolina School of Law (Columbia, South Carolina), Howard University School of Law (Washington, D.C.), University of Virginia School of Law (Charlottesville, Virginia), University of Georgia School of Law (Athens, Georgia), Georgia Washington University Law School (Washington, D.C.), and Emory University School of Law (Atlanta, Georgia). The sponsoring law firm has offices in Atlanta (Georgia), Baltimore (Maryland), Charlotte (North Carolina), Greensboro (North Carolina), Greenville (South Carolina), Raleigh (North Carolina), Research Triangle Park (North Carolina), Tysons Corner (Vir-

ginia), Washington (D.C.), Wilmington (Delaware), and Winston-Salem (North Carolina).
Number awarded Varies each year; recently, 9 of these scholarships were awarded.
Deadline May of each year.

[905]
XEROX TECHNICAL MINORITY SCHOLARSHIP PROGRAM
Xerox Corporation
Attn: Technical Minority Scholarship Program
150 State Street, Fourth Floor
Rochester, NY 14614
(585) 422-7689 E-mail: xtmsp@rballiance.com
Web: www.xerox.com

Purpose To provide financial assistance to Native Americans and other minorities interested in undergraduate or graduate education in the sciences and/or engineering.
Eligibility This program is open to minorities (people of African American, Asian, Pacific Islander, Native American, Native Alaskan, or Hispanic descent) working full time on a bachelor's, master's, or doctoral degree in chemistry, computing and software systems, engineering (chemical, computer, electrical, imaging, manufacturing, mechanical, optical, or software), information management, laser optics, materials science, physics, or printing management science. Applicants must be U.S. citizens or permanent residents with a GPA of 3.0 or higher and attending a 4-year college or university.
Financial data Stipends range from $1,000 to $10,000.
Duration 1 year.
Number awarded Varies each year, recently, 118 of these scholarships were awarded.
Deadline September of each year.

[906]
YAKAMA TRIBAL SCHOLARSHIP
Yakama Indian Nation
Department of Human Services
Attn: Higher Education Programs
P.O. Box 151
Toppenish, WA 98948
(509) 865-5121, ext. 519 Toll-free: (800) 543-2802
Fax: (509) 865-6994

Purpose To provide financial assistance to Yakama tribal members interested in working on an undergraduate or graduate degree in any state.
Eligibility Eligible to apply are Yakama students of one-quarter or more blood quantum. They must be at least high school graduates and enrolled or planning to enroll in a postsecondary institution in any state. Applicants must have at least a 2.0 GPA. Scholarships are awarded on the basis of academic achievement rather than financial need.
Financial data Eligible undergraduate students receive $1,500 per year; graduate students receive $3,000 per year. Part-time students receive funding for tuition, books, and transportation; this amount may never exceed the tribal scholarship amount.
Duration 1 year; may be renewed.
Additional information Before being awarded the scholarship, recipients must attend an orientation session. Students who drop out of school after receiving scholarship awards must refund the Yakama Tribal Scholarships before being granted additional funding. Tuition amounts kept by the student's college do not count against student refunds.
Number awarded Varies each year.
Deadline June of each year for fall quarter or semester; October of each year for winter quarter or spring semester; January of each year for spring quarter; April of each year for summer term.

[907]
ZUNI HIGHER EDUCATION SCHOLARSHIPS
Pueblo of Zuni
Attn: Education and Career Development Center
P.O. Box 339
Zuni, NM 87327
(505) 782-7178 Fax: (505) 782-7223
E-mail: zunihe@hotmail.com
Web: www.ashiwi.org/highered/higheredhome.htm

Purpose To provide financial assistance for college or graduate school to members of the Pueblo of Zuni.
Eligibility This program is open to enrolled members of the Pueblo of Zuni who are high school seniors or graduates. Applicants must have earned a GPA of 2.0 or higher and be interested in working on an associate, bachelor's, or graduate degree as a full-time student. They must have also applied for a federal Pell Grant.
Financial data The amount awarded depends on the need of the recipient, up to $5,000 per year.
Duration 1 year; may be renewed if the recipient maintains a GPA of 2.0 or higher.
Number awarded Varies each year.
Deadline April of each year for the summer session; June of each year for the fall term; October of each year for the spring term.

[908]
THE 13TH REGIONAL HERITAGE FOUNDATION SCHOLARSHIPS
The 13th Regional Corporation
Attn: The 13th Regional Heritage Foundation
1156 Industry Drive
Seattle, WA 98188
(206) 575-6229 Fax: (206) 575-6283
E-mail: info@thE13thregion.com
Web: www.thE13thregion.com/scholarships.html

Purpose To provide financial assistance for college or graduate school to Alaska Natives who are shareholders of The 13th Regional Corporation or their dependent children or grandchildren.
Eligibility This program is open to 1) original shareholders of The 13th Regional Corporation, and 2) their dependent children and grandchildren who are also Alaska Natives. Applicants must be accepted to or enrolled in an accredited community college, university, college, or vocational/trade school as an undergraduate, graduate, or vocational student. Along with their application, they must submit an essay of 500 to 1,000 words on their personal history, special talents and abilities, community involvement, plans for the future, philosophy of life, why they wish to attend college or graduate school, educational objective, major

and minor field of interest, and school they plan to attend. Selection is based on leadership and initiative (20%), academic achievement (20%), educational goals (20%), completeness and neatness of application (20%), and financial need (20%).

Financial data The stipend is $500 per semester ($1,000 per year). Funds are disbursed directly to the school to be used for tuition, books, board, or laboratory fees.

Duration 1 semester; may be renewed.

Additional information The 13th Regional Corporation was established under provisions of the Alaska Native Claims Settlement Act of 1971. Its shareholders are Alaska Natives who no longer live in Alaska.

Number awarded Varies each year; recently, 12 of these scholarships were awarded.

Deadline February of each year for spring and summer terms; June of each year for fall and winter terms.

Grants

Described here are 234 programs that provide funds to Native Americans for innovative efforts, travel, projects, creative activities, or research on any level (from undergraduate to postdoctorates and professional). If you are looking for a particular program and don't find it in this section, be sure to check the Program Title Index to see if it is covered elsewhere in the directory.

[909]
AAUW POSTDOCTORAL RESEARCH LEAVE FELLOWSHIPS

American Association of University Women
Attn: AAUW Educational Foundation
301 ACT Drive, Department 60
P.O. Box 4030
Iowa City, IA 52243-4030
(319) 337-1716, ext. 60   Fax: (319) 337-1204
E-mail: aauw@act.org
Web: www.aauw.org

Purpose To enable Native American and other women who have achieved distinction or promise of distinction in their fields of scholarly work to engage in additional research.

Eligibility This program is open to women who have a research doctorate (e.g., Ph.D., Ed.D., D.B.A., D.M.) or an M.F.A. degree as of the application deadline. Applicants must be interested in conducting independent research; preference is given to projects that are not simply a revision of a doctoral dissertation. Fields of study include the arts and humanities, social sciences, and natural sciences. Selection is based on scholarly excellence, quality of project design, originality of project, scholarly significance of project to discipline, feasibility of project and proposed schedule, qualifications of applicant, potential of applicant to make a significant contribution to field, applicant's commitment to women's issues in profession and community, applicant's teaching experience, and applicant's mentoring of other women. U.S. citizenship or permanent resident status is required. At least 1 fellowship is designated for a woman from a Native American tribe or another underrepresented group.

Financial data The stipend is $30,000. Funding is not provided for laboratory supplies and equipment, research assistants, publication costs, travel to professional meetings or seminars, tuition for additional course work, repayment of loans or other personal obligations, or tuition for a dependent's education.

Duration 1 year, beginning in July.

Additional information The filing fee is $45.

Number awarded Varies each year; recently, 20 of these fellowships were awarded.

Deadline November of each year.

[910]
ACADEMIC RESEARCH ENHANCEMENT AWARD

National Institutes of Health
Office of Extramural Research
Attn: Grants Information
6705 Rockledge Drive
Bethesda, MD 20892-7974
(301) 451-7972   Fax: (301) 480-0146
TTY: (301) 451-0088   E-mail: drusso1@mail.nih.gov
Web: grants.nih.gov/grants/guide/index.html

Purpose To stimulate research in educational institutions (particularly minority and women's institutions) that provide baccalaureate training for a significant number of American research scientists but that have not been major participants in National Institutes of Health (NIH) programs.

Eligibility This grant program is offered to researchers at domestic institutions that award baccalaureate or advanced degrees in the sciences related to health, except those that have received research grants and cooperative agreements from the National Institutes of Health (NIH) totaling more than $3 million per year in each of 4 or more of the preceding 7 years. Health professional schools (e.g., schools of medicine, dentistry, nursing, osteopathy, pharmacy, veterinary medicine, public health, allied health, optometry, chiropractic, podiatry, naturopath) are eligible, as are officially discrete campuses of a university. Investigators eligible for the program are those who will not have active research grant support from the NIH at the time of application. Members of underrepresented racial or ethnic groups and individuals with disabilities are always encouraged to apply for NIH programs. Scientists working in eligible minority and women's educational institutions are particularly encouraged to submit an application for this program.

Financial data Grants provide up to $150,000 in direct costs, plus applicable facilities and administrative costs, for a 36-month period. Allowable direct costs include salaries for the principal investigator and other research personnel (including students), supplies, equipment, travel, and other items specifically associated with the proposed research project.

Duration Up to 36 months.

Additional information Investigators applying for this program may not submit a separate grant application for essentially the same project to the NIH. Principal investigators are expected to conduct the majority of their research at their own institution, although limited access to special facilities or equipment at another institution is permitted.

Number awarded Varies each year; recently, 214 of these grants, with funding of $31,055,000, were awarded.

Deadline February, June, or October of each year.

[911]
ADVANCED POSTDOCTORAL FELLOWSHIPS IN DIABETES RESEARCH

Juvenile Diabetes Research Foundation
Attn: Grant Administrator
120 Wall Street, 19th Floor
New York, NY 10005-4001
(212) 479-7572   Toll-free: (800) 533-CURE
Fax: (212) 785-9595   E-mail: info@jdrf.org
Web: www.jdrf.org/index.cfm?page_id=103207

Purpose To provide advanced research training to minority and other scientists who are beginning their professional careers and are interested in conducting research on the causes, treatment, prevention, or cure of diabetes or its complications.

Eligibility This program is open to postdoctorates who show extraordinary promise for a career in diabetes research. Applicants must have received their first doctoral degree (M.D., Ph.D., D.M.D., or D.V.M.) within the past 5 years and should have completed 1 to 3 years of postdoctoral training. They may not have a faculty appointment. There are no citizenship requirements. Applications are encouraged from women, members of minority groups underrepresented in the sciences, and people with disabilities. The proposed research training may be conducted at foreign and domestic, for-profit and nonprofit, and public and private institutions, including universities, colleges, hospitals, laboratories, units of state and local government, and eligible agencies of the federal government. Selection is based on the applicant's previous experience and academic record; the caliber of the proposed research; the quality of the mentor, training program, and environment; and the applicant's potential to obtain an independent research position in the future. Fellows who obtain a faculty position at any time during the term of the fellowship may apply for a transition award for support during their first year as a faculty member.

Financial data The total award is $90,000 per year, including salary that depends on number of years of experience, ranging from $35,568 for zero up to $51,036 for 7 or more years of experience. In the first year only, funds in excess of the grant may be used for travel to scientific meetings (up to $2,000), journal subscriptions, books, training courses, laboratory supplies, equipment, or purchase of a personal computer (up to $2,000). Indirect costs are not allowed. Fellows who receive a faculty position are granted a transition award of up to $110,000 for 1 year, including up to 10% in indirect costs.

Duration Up to 3 years.

Deadline January or July of each year.

[912]
AERA MINORITY FELLOWSHIPS IN EDUCATION RESEARCH

American Educational Research Association
1430 K Street, N.W.
Washington, DC 20005
(202) 238-3200   Fax: (202) 238-3250
E-mail: fellowships@aera.net
Web: www.aera.net

Purpose To provide funding to Native American and other minority doctoral students writing their dissertation on educational research.

Eligibility This program is open to U.S. citizens and permanent residents who have advanced to candidacy and successfully defended their Ph.D./Ed.D. dissertation research proposal. Applicants must plan to work full time on their dissertation in educational research. This program is targeted for members of groups historically underrepresented in higher education (African Americans, American Indians, Alaskan Natives, Asian Americans, Native Hawaiian or Pacific Islanders, and Hispanics or Latinos). Selection is based on scholarly achievements and publications, letters of recommendation, quality and significance of the proposed research, and commitment of the applicant's faculty mentor to the goals of the program.

Financial data The grant is $12,000. Up to $1,000 is provided to pay for travel to the sponsor's annual conference.

Duration 1 year; nonrenewable.

Additional information This program was established in 1991.

Number awarded Up to 3 each year.

Deadline December of each year.

[913]
AGA STUDENT RESEARCH FELLOWSHIP AWARDS

Foundation for Digestive Health and Nutrition
Attn: Research Awards Program
4930 Del Ray Avenue
Bethesda, MD 20814-2512
(301) 222-4012   Fax: (301) 652-3890
E-mail: awards@fdhn.org
Web: www.fdhn.org/wmspage.cfm?parm1=115

Purpose To provide funding for research on digestive diseases or nutrition to minority and other students.

Eligibility This program is open to high school, college, graduate, and medical students at accredited institutions in North America who are not yet engaged in thesis research. They must be interested in conducting research on digestive diseases or nutrition. Candidates must not hold similar salary support awards from other agencies (e.g., American Liver Foundation, Crohn's and Colitis Foundation). Women and underrepresented minority students are strongly encouraged to apply. Research must be conducted under the supervision of a preceptor who is a full-time faculty member at a North American institution, directing a research project in a gastroenterology-related area, and a member of the American Gastroenterological Association (AGA). Selection is based on novelty, feasibility, and significance of the proposal; attributes of the candidate; record of the preceptor; evidence of institutional commitment; and laboratory environment. Applicants are grouped and evaluated according to educational level.

Financial data Grants range from $2,000 to $3,000. No indirect costs are allowed. The award is paid directly to the student and is to be used as a stipend or for thesis research.

Duration At least 10 weeks. The work may take place at any time during the year.

Additional information In an effort to attract and encourage minorities, several of the awards are set aside specifically for underrepresented minority students, defined as African Americans, Mexican Americans, Mainland Puerto Ricans, and Native Americans (Alaskan Natives, American Indians, and Native Hawaiians). This award is administered by the Foundation for Digestive Health and Nutrition (FDHN) and sponsored by the AGA. Funds may not be used to support thesis research.

Number awarded Varies each year. Recently, 21 of these awards were granted, including several set aside specifically for underrepresented minorities (African Americans, American Indians, Alaska and Hawaiian Natives, Mexican Americans, and Mainland Puerto Ricans).

Deadline March of each year.

[914]
AGING RESEARCH DISSERTATION AWARDS TO INCREASE DIVERSITY

National Institute on Aging
Attn: Office of Extramural Affairs
7201 Wisconsin Avenue, Room 2C-218
Bethesda, MD 20892-9205
(301) 496-9322   Fax: (301) 402-2945
TTY: (301) 451-0088   E-mail: BarrR@mail.nih.gov
Web: www.nia.nih.gov

Purpose To provide financial assistance to doctoral candidates from Native American and other underrepresented groups who wish to conduct research on aging.

Eligibility This program is open to doctoral candidates conducting research on a dissertation with an aging-related focus, including the 4 extramural programs within the National Institute on Aging (NIA): the biology of aging program, the behavioral and social research program, the neuroscience and neuropsychology of aging program, and the geriatrics and clinical gerontology program. Applicants must be 1) members of an ethnic or racial group underrepresented in biomedical or behavioral research; 2) individuals with disabilities; or 3) individuals from socially, culturally, economically, or educationally disadvantaged backgrounds that have inhibited their ability to prepare for a career in health-related research. They must be U.S. citizens, nationals, or permanent residents.

Financial data Grants provide $20,772 per year for stipend and up to $15,000 for additional expenses. No funds may be used to pay tuition or fees associated with completion of doctoral studies. The institution may receive up to 8% of direct costs as facilities and administrative costs per year.

Duration Up to 2 years.

Number awarded 6 to 8 each year.

Deadline Letters of intent must be submitted by February or October of each year.

[915]
ALFRED P. SLOAN FOUNDATION RESEARCH FELLOWSHIPS

Alfred P. Sloan Foundation
630 Fifth Avenue, Suite 2550
New York, NY 10111-0242
(212) 649-1649   Fax: (212) 757-5117
E-mail: teitelbaum@sloan.org
Web: www.sloan.org

Purpose To provide funding for research in selected fields of science to minority and other recent doctorates.

Eligibility This program is open to scholars who are no more than 6 years from completion of the most recent Ph.D. or equivalent in computational and evolutionary molecular biology, chemistry, physics, mathematics, computer science, economics, neuroscience, or a related interdisciplinary field. Direct applications are not accepted; candidates must be nominated by department heads or other senior scholars. Although fellows must be at an early stage of their research careers, they should give strong evidence of independent research accomplishments and creativity. The sponsor strongly encourages the participation of women and members of underrepresented minority groups.

Financial data The stipend is $22,500 per year. Funds are paid directly to the fellow's institution to be used by the fellow for such purposes as equipment, technical assistance, professional travel, trainee support, or any other research-related expense; they may not be used to augment an existing full-time salary.

Duration 2 years; may be extended if unexpended funds still remain.

Additional information This program began in 1955 when it awarded $235,000 to 22 chemists, physicists, and pure mathematicians. Neuroscience was added in 1972, economics and applied mathematics in 1980, computer science in 1993, and computational and evolutionary molecular biology in 2002. Currently, the program awards $5.22 million in grants annually.

Number awarded 116 each year: 23 in chemistry, 12 in computational and evolutionary molecular biology, 14 in computer science, 8 in economics, 20 in mathematics, 16 in neuroscience, and 23 in physics.

Deadline September of each year.

[916]
ALLERGY/IMMUNOLOGY FELLOWSHIP OF EXCELLENCE TRAINING AWARD

American Academy of Allergy, Asthma & Immunology
555 East Wells Street, Suite 1100
Milwaukee, WI 53202-3823
(414) 272-6071   Fax: (414) 272-6070
E-mail: info@aaaai.org
Web: www.aaaai.org

Purpose To provide financial assistance for a program of research training in allergy and immunology to postdoctoral fellows who are Native Americans or members of other underrepresented minority groups.

Eligibility This program is open to members of underrepresented minority communities who have graduated from a U.S. medical school certified in internal medicine or pediatrics. Applicants must be interested in enrolling in an ACGME-accredited allergy/immunology training program in the United States. Along with their application, they must submit a career statement of 1 to 2 pages that covers their interest in the field of allergy/immunology, their interest in teaching and/or research, how they will use their allergy/immunology expertise to advance opportunities for individuals from underrepresented minority communities, and their planned career path following completion of allergy/immunology training. U.S. citizenship is required.

Financial data The stipend is $50,000 per year. Funds may not be used for institutional indirect costs.

Duration 2 years.

Number awarded 1 each year.

Deadline March of each year.

[917]
ALZHEIMER'S ASSOCIATION INVESTIGATOR-INITIATED RESEARCH GRANTS

Alzheimer's Association
Attn: Medical and Scientific Affairs
225 North Michigan Avenue, 17th Floor
Chicago, IL 60601-7633
(312) 335-5747   Toll-free: (800) 272-3900
Fax: (312) 335-4034   E-mail: grantsapp@alz.org
Web: www.alz.org

Purpose To provide funding to minority and other scientists interested in conducting research on Alzheimer's Disease.

Eligibility This program is open to postdoctoral investigators at public, private, domestic, and foreign research laboratories, medical centers, hospitals, and universities. Applicants must be proposing to conduct research with focus areas that change annually but are related to Alzheimer's Disease. Investigators from all stages of research career development are eligible. Scientists from underrepresented groups are especially encouraged to apply.

Financial data Grants up to $100,000 per year, including direct expenses and up to 10% for overhead costs, are available. The total award for the life of the grant may not exceed $240,000.

Duration Up to 3 years.

Number awarded Up to 55 each year.

Deadline Letters of intent must be submitted by November of each year.

[918]
AMERICAN ANTHROPOLOGICAL ASSOCIATION MINORITY DISSERTATION FELLOWSHIP PROGRAM

American Anthropological Association
Attn: Department of Academic Relations
2200 Wilson Boulevard, Suite 600
Arlington, VA 22201-3357
(703) 528-1902   Fax: (703) 528-3546
E-mail: academic@aaanet.org
Web: www.aaanet.org/about/prizes-awards

Purpose To provide funding to Native Americans and other minorities who are working on a Ph.D. dissertation in anthropology.

Eligibility This program is open to Native American, African American, Latino(a), Pacific Islander, and Asian American doctoral students who have been admitted to degree candidacy in anthropology. Applicants must be U.S. citizens, enrolled in a full-time academic program leading to a doctoral degree in anthropology, and members of the American Anthropological Association. They must have a record of outstanding academic success, have had their dissertation proposal approved by their dissertation committee prior to application, be writing a dissertation in an area of anthropological research, and need funding to complete the dissertation. Along with their application, they must submit a cover letter, a research plan summary, a curriculum vitae, a statement regarding employment, a disclosure statement providing information about other sources of available and pending financial support, 3 letters of recommendation, and an official transcript from their doctoral program. Selection is based on the quality of the submitted information and the judged likelihood that the applicant will have a good chance of completing the dissertation. Consideration is also given to the implications of the applicant's research to issues and concerns of the U.S. historically disadvantaged populations, relevant service to the community, and future plans.

Financial data The stipend is $10,000. Funds are sent in 2 installments (in September and in January) to the recipient's institution.

Duration 1 year; nonrenewable.

Number awarded 1 each year.

Deadline February of each year.

[919]
AMERICAN COUNCIL OF LEARNED SOCIETIES FELLOWSHIPS

American Council of Learned Societies
Attn: Office of Fellowships and Grants
633 Third Avenue
New York, NY 10017-6795
(212) 697-1505   Fax: (212) 949-8058
E-mail: fellowships@acls.org
Web: www.acls.org/felguide.htm

Purpose To provide research funding to minority and other scholars in all disciplines of the humanities and the humanities-related social sciences.

Eligibility This program is open to scholars at all stages of their careers who received a Ph.D. degree at least 2 years previously. Established scholars who can demonstrate the equivalent of the Ph.D. in publications and professional experience may also qualify. Applicants must be U.S. citizens or permanent residents who have not had supported leave time for at least 2 years prior to the start of the proposed research. Appropriate fields of specialization include, but are not limited to, American studies; anthropology; archaeology; art and architectural history; classics; economics; film; geography; history; languages and literatures; legal studies; linguistics; musicology; philosophy; political science; psychology; religious studies; rhetoric, communication, and media studies; science, technology, and medicine studies; sociology; and theater, dance, and performance studies. Proposals in those fields of the social sciences are eligible only if they employ predominantly humanistic approaches (e.g., economic history, law and literature, political philosophy). Proposals in interdisciplinary and cross-disciplinary studies are welcome, as are proposals focused on a geographic region or on a cultural or linguistic group. Awards are available at 3 academic levels: full professor, associate professor, and assistant professor. Applications are particularly invited from women and members of minority groups.

Financial data The maximum grant is $60,000 for full professors and equivalent, $40,000 for associate professors and equivalent, or $30,000 for assistant professors and equivalent. Normally, fellowships are intended as salary replacement and may be held concurrently with other fellowships, grants, and sabbatical pay, up to an amount equal to the candidate's current academic year salary.

Duration 6 to 12 months.

Additional information This program is supported in part by funding from the Ford Foundation, the Andrew W. Mellon Foundation, the National Endowment for the Human-

ities, the William and Flora Hewlett Foundation, and the Rockefeller Foundation.
Number awarded Approximately 45 each year: 25 at the full professor level and 20 at the assistant and associate professor level.
Deadline September of each year.

[920]
AMERICAN INDIAN PROGRAM
National Museum of Natural History
Attn: Department of Anthropology
P.O. Box 37012, MRC 112
Washington, DC 20013-7012
(202) 357-4760   Fax: (202) 357-2208
E-mail: archambj@si.edu
Web: anthropology.si.edu/research.htm

Purpose To provide assistance for research, exhibitions, and public programming by and about Indian people.
Eligibility This program works with Native individuals, communities, schools, and other cultural and educational institutions on a variety of collaborative projects. It encourages collection and archival research activities as well as exhibition and public program development. It also provides opportunities for museum training and supervised research projects in any aspect of Indian culture and history that is appropriate for the museum's holdings and staff expertise, including ethnology, archaeology, language, biological anthropology, and history. No educational requirements are imposed; prior fellows have come from age groups ranging from 16 to 82 and from all walks of life.
Financial data The amount of the award depends on the nature of the project.
Duration Project length varies.
Additional information This program was established in 1986 to encourage participation of Native Americans in Smithsonian activities and to support collection research, exhibitions, and public programming as they relate to Native peoples. The program is particularly interested in collaborative projects with Indian-controlled museums, colleges, and other cultural and educational institutions, but inquiries about research, exhibitions, and other outreach activities are welcomed from all interested parties.
Number awarded 3 to 5 each year.
Deadline Applications may be submitted at any time.

[921]
AMERICAN INDIAN STUDIES POSTDOCTORAL AND VISITING SCHOLARS FELLOWSHIP PROGRAM
University of California at Los Angeles
American Indian Studies Center
Attn: IAC Coordinator
3220 Campbell Hall
P.O. Box 951548
Los Angeles, CA 90095-1548
(310) 825-7315
Web: www.gdnet.ucla.edu/iacweb/pstweber.htm

Purpose To provide funding support to scholars interested in conducting research in Native American studies at UCLA's American Indian Studies Center.
Eligibility Applicants must have completed a doctoral degree in Native American or related studies. They must be interested in teaching or conducting research at UCLA's American Indian Studies Center. UCLA faculty, students, and staff are not eligible. U.S. citizenship or permanent resident status is required.
Financial data Fellows receive a stipend of $33,000 to $35,000 (depending on rank, experience, and date of completion of the Ph.D.), health benefits, and up to $4,000 in research support.
Duration 9 months, beginning in October.
Additional information Fellows must teach or do research in the programs of the center. The award is offered in conjunction with UCLA's Institute of American Cultures (IAC).
Number awarded 1 each year.
Deadline January of each year.

[922]
AMERICAN SOCIETY OF CRIMINOLOGY UNDERGRADUATE STUDENT MINORITY/MENTOR RESEARCH GRANT
American Society of Criminology
Attn: Awards Committee
1314 Kinnear Road, Suite 212
Columbus, OH 43212-1156
(614) 292-9207   Fax: (614) 292-6767
E-mail: asc@osu.edu
Web: www.asc41.com/uminorfel.htm

Purpose To provide funding to Native American and other ethnic minority undergraduate students interested in conducting a research project in criminology and criminal justice.
Eligibility This program is open to undergraduate students who are members of historically disadvantaged and underrepresented ethnic and racial groups (including African Americans, Asian Americans, Hispanics, and Native Americans). Applicants must be entering their junior year in a program in criminology and criminal justice. They must be interested in conducting a research project under the mentorship of a faculty member, who must act as a co-applicant for the funding. Along with the application, students must provide a personal statement on their career goals in criminology and another statement on how the grant would enable them to focus more time on their academic work and better achieve their career goals. Faculty members must provide 1) a written recommendation for why the student has the academic potential and career aspirations to complete graduate study in criminology successfully and prepare for an academic career; 2) student transcripts and other supporting materials; 3) a description of the proposed collaborative research project that will result in a presentation at the annual meeting of the American Society of Criminology (ASC) in the student's senior years; and 4) a description of other mentoring activities and proposed contact with the student during the junior and senior years. Selection is based on the student's potential for completing doctoral work in criminology and the quality of the proposed mentoring relationship.
Financial data The grant provides $5,000 per year for research support and a $1,500 travel grant to attend the ASC annual meetings.
Duration 2 years (the junior and senior year of college).
Additional information This program began in 2004.

Number awarded Up to 4 each year.
Deadline April of each year.

[923]
AMTA FELLOWSHIP FOR MEMBRANE TECHNOLOGY

National Water Research Institute
Attn: Fellowship Program
18700 Ward Street
P.O. Box 8096
Fountain Valley, CA 92728-8096
(714) 378-3278   Fax: (714) 378-3375
E-mail: fellow@nwri-usa.org
Web: www.nwri-usa.org/fellowship.htm

Purpose To provide funding to minority and other graduate students interested in conducting research on the use of membranes in water science and technology.

Eligibility This program is open to full-time graduate students interested in conducting research in areas of interest to the American Membrane Technology Association (AMTA): to promote, advocate, and advance the understanding and application of membrane technology to create safe, affordable, and reliable water supplies, and to treat municipal, industrial, agricultural, and waste waters for beneficial use. Possible topics include innovative membrane treatment technologies, use of advanced materials, membrane bioreactors, membrane fouling/scaling control, membrane removal efficiency, membrane pretreatment, or improved feedwater recovery. Research areas include, but are not limited to, engineering, physical and chemical sciences, biological sciences, health sciences, political sciences, economics, and planning and public policy that are related to water and/or water resources. Preference is given to doctoral candidates, but outstanding students in master's programs may be considered. Applicants must submit a letter of inquiry describing the importance of the research to them and the water community, how their research will contribute to water science in general, what they expect to accomplish, and how their research relates to the mission of the National Water Research Institute (NWRI) to create new sources of water through research and technology and to protect the freshwater and marine environments. Women and members of minority groups underrepresented in academia are strongly encouraged to apply.

Financial data Grants range from $2,000 to $20,000 per year, but they are typically $10,000 per year.

Duration 2 years.

Additional information This fellowship is jointly sponsored by AMTA and the NWRI.

Number awarded 2 each even-numbered year.

Deadline February of each even-numbered year.

[924]
ANA CLINICAL RESEARCH PRE-DOCTORAL FELLOWSHIP PROGRAM

American Nurses Association
Attn: SAMHSA Minority Fellowship Programs
8515 Georgia Avenue, Suite 400
Silver Spring, MD 20910-3492
(301) 628-5247   Toll-free: (800) 274-4ANA
Fax: (301) 628-5339   E-mail: janet.jackson@ana.org
Web: www.emfp.org

Purpose To provide financial assistance to Native American and other minority nurses who are doctoral candidates interested in psychiatric, mental health, and substance abuse issues that impact the lives of ethnic minority people.

Eligibility This program is open to nurses who have a master's degree and are members of an ethnic or racial minority group, including but not limited to Blacks or African Americans, Hispanics or Latinos, American Indians and Alaska Natives, Asian Americans, and Native Hawaiians and other Pacific Islanders. Applicants must be able to demonstrate a commitment to a research career in nursing and psychiatric/mental health issues affecting ethnic minority populations. They must be interested in a program of full-time doctoral study, with a research focus on such issues of concern to minority populations as child abuse, violence in intimate relationships, mental health disorders, substance abuse, mental health service utilization, and stigma as a barrier to mental health care and personal resilience. U.S. citizenship or permanent resident status and membership in the American Nurses Association are required. Selection is based on research potential, scholarship, writing ability, knowledge of broad issues in mental health nursing, and professional commitment to ethnic minority concerns.

Financial data The program provides an annual stipend of $20,772 and tuition assistance.

Duration 3 to 5 years.

Additional information Funds for this program are provided by the Substance Abuse and Mental Health Services Administration (SAMHSA).

Number awarded 1 or more each year.

Deadline February of each year.

[925]
ANL LABORATORY–GRADUATE RESEARCH APPOINTMENTS

Argonne National Laboratory
Division of Educational Programs
Attn: Graduate Student Program Office
9700 South Cass Avenue/DEP 223
Argonne, IL 60439-4845
(630) 252-3366   Fax: (630) 252-3193
E-mail: Lreed@dep.anl.gov
Web: www.dep.anl.gov/p_graduate/labgrad.htm

Purpose To offer opportunities for minority and other graduate students to carry out their master's or doctoral thesis research at the Argonne National Laboratory (ANL).

Eligibility Appointments are available for graduate students at U.S. universities who wish to carry out their thesis research under the co-sponsorship of an Argonne National Laboratory staff member and a faculty member. Research may be conducted in the basic physical and life sciences, mathematics, computer science, and engineering, as well as in a variety of applied areas relating to conservation, environment, fission and fusion energy, and other energy technologies. Applicants must be U.S. citizens or permanent residents. The laboratory encourages applications from all qualified persons, especially women and members of underrepresented minority groups.

Financial data Support consists of a stipend, tuition payments up to $5,000 per year, and payment of certain travel expenses. In addition, the student's faculty sponsor may receive payment for limited travel expenses.

Duration 1 year; may be renewed.

Additional information This program, which is also referred to as the Lab–Grad Program, is sponsored by the U.S. Department of Energy. In certain cases, students may be awarded support for pre-thesis studies on campus, provided they intend to carry out their thesis research at Argonne. Mutual interest in an area of research by the student and the Argonne staff sponsor is essential for the successful arrangement of a Lab-Grad appointment. To help the parties gauge their mutual interest, a limited number of temporary appointments are available for qualified graduate students, so they may work with an Argonne staff member and become familiar with his/her research program. These temporary appointments have a tenure of 3 months and support consists of a per diem payment to help cover the cost of living away from home, plus travel expenses.

Number awarded Varies each year.

Deadline Applications may be submitted at any time, but a complete application should be submitted at least 2 months prior to the proposed starting date.

[926]
ANTARCTIC RESEARCH PROGRAM

National Science Foundation
Attn: Office of Polar Programs
4201 Wilson Boulevard, Room 755 S
Arlington, VA 22230
(703) 292-4746   Fax: (703) 292-9079
TDD: (800) 281-8749   E-mail: twagner@nsf.gov
Web: www.nsf.gov

Purpose To provide funding to minority and other scientists interested in conducting research related to Antarctica.

Eligibility This program is open to investigators at U.S. institutions, primarily universities and, to a lesser extent, federal agencies and other organizations. Applicants must be proposing to conduct Antarctic-related research in the following major areas: aeronomy and astrophysics, organisms and ecosystems, earth sciences, ocean and atmospheric sciences, glaciology, and integrated and system science. The program encourages applications from women, underrepresented minorities, and persons with disabilities.

Financial data The amounts of the awards depend on the nature of the proposal and the availability of funds.

Additional information The NSF operates 3 year-round research stations in Antarctica, additional research facilities and camps, airplanes, helicopters, various types of surface vehicles, and ships.

Number awarded Varies each year; recently, the program planned to make 35 awards with a total budget of $10 million for new and continuing awards.

Deadline June of each year.

[927]
ARCTIC RESEARCH OPPORTUNITIES

National Science Foundation
Attn: Office of Polar Programs
4201 Wilson Boulevard, Suite 755
Arlington, VA 22230
(703) 292-8030   Fax: (703) 292-9081
TDD: (800) 281-8749
Web: www.nsf.gov

Purpose To provide funding to minorities and other disadvantaged groups for research related to the Arctic.

Eligibility This program is open to investigators affiliated with U.S. universities, research institutions, or other organizations, including local or state governments. Applicants must be proposing to conduct research in the 6 program areas of Arctic science: 1) Arctic Natural Sciences, with areas of special interest in marine and terrestrial ecosystems, Arctic atmospheric and oceanic dynamics and climatology, Arctic geological and glaciological processes, and their connectivity to lower latitudes; 2) Arctic Social Sciences, including (but not limited to) anthropology, archaeology, economics, geography, linguistics, political science, psychology, science and technology studies, sociology, traditional knowledge, and related subjects; 3) Arctic System Science, for research focused on a system understanding of the Arctic, understanding the behavior of the Arctic system (past, present, and future), understanding the role of the Arctic as a component of the global system, and society as an integral part of the Arctic system; 4) Arctic Research Support and Logistics Program, for proposals that support long-term observations of the Arctic, support the acquisition of data sets useful to a broad segment of the Arctic research community, will lead to cooperative agreements to operate multi-use Arctic research facilities, or provide services that broadly support the Arctic research community; 5) Arctic Research and Education Program, for proposals that promote science literacy and widespread understanding of polar research, increase diversity in the polar sciences, contribute to improved K-12 science instruction, attract and retain students in STEM (science, technology, engineering, and mathematics) fields, and develop long-term collaborations between Arctic research and science education; and 6) International Polar Year activities. The program encourages proposals from all women, underrepresented minorities, and persons with disabilities.

Financial data The amounts of the awards depend on the nature of the proposal and the availability of funds.

Number awarded Approximately 40 each year. Recently, this program awarded approximately $16 million in grants.

Deadline November of each year.

[928]
ASCO MEDICAL STUDENT ROTATION

American Society of Clinical Oncology
Attn: ASCO Cancer Foundation
2318 Mill Road, Suite 800
Alexandria, VA 22314
(571) 483-1300   E-mail: grants@asco.org
Web: www.asco.org

Purpose To provide funding to medical students from underrepresented groups (including Native Americans) interested in a clinical research oncology rotation.

Eligibility This program is open to U.S. citizens, nationals, and permanent residents who are currently enrolled at a U.S. medical school. Applicants must be a member of a group currently underrepresented in medicine, defined as American Indian/Alaska Native, Black/African American, Hispanic/Latino, or Native Hawaiian/Pacific Islander. They must be interested in a clinical or clinical research oncology rotation at their home institution or at another institution that has agreed to host program participants.
Financial data Students receive a stipend of $5,000 plus $1,500 for future travel to the annual meeting of the American Society of Clinical Oncology (ASCO). Their mentor receives a grant of $2,000.
Duration 8 to 10 weeks.
Additional information This program is sponsored by Susan G. Komen for the Cure.
Number awarded Varies each year.
Deadline January of each year.

[929]
ASH-AMFDP RESEARCH GRANTS
American Society of Hematology
Attn: Award Program Coordinator
1900 M Street, N.W., Suite 200
Washington, DC 20036
(202) 776-0544, ext. 1168   Fax: (202) 776-0545
E-mail: ASH@hematology.org
Web: www.hematology.org

Purpose To provide an opportunity for historically disadvantaged postdoctoral physicians to conduct a research project in hematology.
Eligibility This program is open to postdoctoral physicians who are members of historically disadvantaged groups, defined as individuals who face challenges because of their race, ethnicity, socioeconomic status, or other similar factors. Applicants must be committed to a career in academic medicine in hematology and to serving as a role model for students and faculty of similar backgrounds. They must identify a mentor at their institution to work with them and give them research and career guidance. Selection is based on excellence in educational career; willingness to devote 4 consecutive years to research; and commitment to an academic career, improving the health status of the underserved, and decreasing health disparities.
Financial data The grant includes a stipend of up to $75,000 per year, a grant of $29,139 per year for support of research activities, complimentary membership in the American Society of Hematology (ASH), and travel support to attend the ASH annual meeting.
Duration 4 years.
Additional information This program, first offered in 2006, is a partnership between the ASH and the Robert Wood Johnson Foundation, whose Minority Medical Faculty Development Program (MMFDP) was subsequently renamed the Harold Amos Medical Faculty Development Program (AMFDP) in honor of the first African American to chair a department at the Harvard Medical School.
Number awarded At least 1 each year.

[930]
ASTRONOMY AND ASTROPHYSICS POSTDOCTORAL FELLOWSHIPS
National Science Foundation
Directorate for Mathematical and Physical Sciences
Attn: Division of Astronomical Sciences
4201 Wilson Boulevard, Room 1045
Arlington, VA 22230
(703) 292-7456   TDD: (800) 281-8749
E-mail: dlehr@nsf.gov
Web: www.nsf.gov

Purpose To provide funding to minority and other recent doctoral recipients in astronomy or astrophysics who are interested in pursuing a program of research and education.
Eligibility This program is open to U.S. citizens, nationals, and permanent residents who completed a Ph.D. in astronomy or astrophysics during the previous 3 years. Applicants must be interested in a program of research of an observational, instrumental, or theoretical nature, especially research that is particularly facilitated or enabled by new ground-based capability in radio, optical/IR, or solar astrophysics. The proposal must include a coherent program of educational activities, such as teaching a course each year at the host institution or an academic institution with ties to the host institution, developing educational materials, or engaging in a significant program of outreach or general education. The program encourages applications from women, underrepresented minorities, and persons with disabilities.
Financial data Grants up to $67,000 per year are available, including stipends of $50,000 per year, a research allowance of $10,000 per year, and an institutional allowance of $7,000 per year.
Duration Up to 3 years.
Number awarded Up to 10 each year.
Deadline October of each year.

[931]
BAY AREA COMMUNITY SERVICE SCHOLARSHIPS
National Medical Fellowships, Inc.
Attn: Scholarship Program
5 Hanover Square, 15th Floor
New York, NY 10004
(212) 483-8880   Fax: (212) 483-8897
E-mail: info@nmfonline.org
Web: www.nmfonline.org

Purpose To provide clinical experience and financial assistance to Native American and other underrepresented minority medical students at designated schools in California.
Eligibility This program is open to third- or fourth-year medical students from any state who are African Americans, mainland Puerto Ricans, Mexican Americans, Native Hawaiians, Alaska Natives, or American Indians. Applicants must be enrolled at a California M.D.-granting school and planning to practice in the San Francisco Bay area. They must be interested in either 1) clinical rotation at an approved community health center in the San Francisco Bay area dedicated to medically underserved populations, or 2) a basic science or clinical science research project in an area of critical need (e.g., HIV/AIDS care and research, hypertension, tuberculosis, cardiovascular disease, diabetes,

asthma, substance abuse, women's health research). Selection is based on demonstrated commitment to practice in California, interest in community-based primary care or research, academic performance, financial need, and leadership.
Financial data The stipend is $7,500 for 6-week clinical rotations or 8-week research projects, or $15,000 for 12-week clinical rotations or research projects.
Duration Clinical rotations may be either 6 weeks or 12 weeks. Research projects may extend either 8 weeks or 12 weeks.
Additional information This program was established in 2002 with support from the San Francisco Foundation, the McKesson Foundation, and the California Endowment. Information is also available from the administrator's California Regional Office, The Chancery Building, 564 Market Street, Suite 209, San Francisco, CA 94101, (415) 397-2526, Fax: (415) 397-2556. Students who choose a 12-week clinical rotation must plan and implement a clinical project at their site. Projects may involve qualitative or quantitative research, health education, or another area of relevance to the site.
Number awarded 6 each year.
Deadline January of each year.

[932]
BETTY LEA STONE RESEARCH FELLOWSHIP
American Cancer Society-New England Division
30 Speen Street
P.O. Box 9376
Framingham, MA 01701-9376
(508) 270-4690   Toll-free: (800) 952-7664, ext. 4690
Fax: (508) 270-4699   E-mail: koconnor@cancer.org
Web: www.cancer.org

Purpose To provide funding for summer cancer research to minority and other medical students in New England.
Eligibility This program is open to first-year students at medical schools in New England. Applicants must be interested in working on a summer research project under the supervision of a faculty sponsor. Minority students are encouraged to apply.
Financial data The grant is $4,500.
Duration 10 weeks during the summer.
Deadline February of each year.

[933]
BREAST CANCER DISPARITIES RESEARCH GRANTS
Susan G. Komen Breast Cancer Foundation
Attn: Grants Department
5005 LBJ Freeway, Suite 250
Dallas, TX 75244
(972) 855-1616   Toll-free: (888) 300-5582
Fax: (972) 855-1640   E-mail: grants@komen.org
Web: www.komen.org

Purpose To provide funding to minority and other scholars interested in conducting innovative projects focusing on the epidemiology of breast cancer within specific populations at risk for the disease.
Eligibility This program is open to scientists interested in conducting research on aspects of disparity in breast cancer education, screening, treatment, incidence, mortality, and/or morbidity among populations at risk for breast cancer, including African Americans, Asian Americans, Native Hawaiians, Pacific Islanders, Alaskan Natives, Hispanics/Latinas, Native Americans, lesbians, low literacy individuals, breast cancer survivors, women with disabilities, persons of high risk, and men. Studies focusing on the following are encouraged: epidemiological studies; identification and examination of the gaps in breast health care for minority, underserved communities, and breast cancer survivors; development and evaluation of models to improve access and utilization of breast health services; strategies to educate health care professionals to communicate more effectively with minorities and to reduce treatment bias; breast cancer prevention and control in underserved communities; behavioral science related to barriers to breast health education and breast cancer care; and quality of life, medical/physical, and psychosocial issues related to breast cancer survivorship. Preference is given to applicants who demonstrate collaboration with a community-based organization. U.S. citizenship or residency is not required. Women and members of groups historically underrepresented in the sciences are especially encouraged to apply.
Financial data The maximum total grant is $300,000 (combined direct and indirect costs). A salary for the principal investigator is allowed but limited to $125,900 per year. Equipment is limited to 30% of direct costs.
Duration 2 or 3 years.
Number awarded Varies each year; recently, 18 of these grants were awarded.
Deadline August of each year.

[934]
BRUCE T. AND JACKIE MAHI ERICKSON SCHOLARSHIP
Ke Ali'i Pauahi Foundation
Attn: Financial Aid & Scholarship Services
567 South King Street, Suite 160
Honolulu, HI 96813
(808) 534-3966   Toll-free: (800) 842-4682, ext. 43966
Fax: (808) 534-3890   E-mail: scholarships@pauahi.org
Web: www.pauahi.org

Purpose To provide financial assistance to undergraduate or graduate students, especially Native Hawaiians, who are working on research or a degree related to Hawaiian arts and crafts.
Eligibility This program is open to students working full time on an undergraduate or graduate degree related to the creation of crafts, art, and photography and/or independent research relating to historical Hawaiian crafts and arts. Financial need is considered in the selection process. Residency in Hawaii is not required. Preference is given to Native Hawaiians (descendants of the aboriginal inhabitants of the Hawaiian Islands prior to 1778).
Financial data A stipend is awarded (amount not specified).
Duration 1 year.
Additional information This program was established in 2006.
Number awarded 1 or more each year.
Deadline April of each year.

[935]
CALDER SUMMER UNDERGRADUATE RESEARCH PROGRAM

Fordham University
Attn: Louis Calder Center Biological Field Station
53 Whippoorwill Road
P.O. Box 887
Armonk, NY 10504
(914) 273-3078, ext. 10   Fax: (914) 273-2167
E-mail: REUatCalder@fordham.edu
Web: www.fordham.edu/calder_center

Purpose To provide an opportunity for minority and other undergraduates to pursue summer research activities in biology at Fordham University's Louis Calder Center Biological Field Station.

Eligibility This program is open to undergraduates interested in conducting a summer research project of their own design at the center. Fields of interest must relate to the activities of staff who will serve as mentors on the projects; those include forest ecology, limnology, wildlife ecology, microbial ecology, Lyme disease, insect-plant interactions, evolutionary ecology, and the effects of urbanization on ecosystem processes. Applications from underrepresented minorities and women are especially encouraged.

Financial data The program provides a stipend of $4,800, housing on the site, and support for research supplies and local travel.

Duration 12 weeks during the summer.

Additional information This program has operated since 1967.

Number awarded Up to 12 each year.

Deadline February of each year.

[936]
CANCER PREVENTION, CONTROL, BEHAVIORAL, AND POPULATION SCIENCES CAREER DEVELOPMENT AWARD

National Cancer Institute
Attn: Cancer Training Branch
6116 Executive Boulevard, Suite 7025
Bethesda, MD 20892-8346
(301) 496-8580   Fax: (301) 402-0181
TTY: (301) 451-0088   E-mail: gorelicl@mail.nih.gov
Web: www.cancer.gov/researchandfunding/training

Purpose To provide support to minority and other scientists who already have a doctorate and wish to obtain additional research training related to cancer.

Eligibility This program is open to U.S. citizens, nationals, and permanent residents who have a Ph.D. degree, have a health professional doctoral degree (e.g., M.D., Dr.P.H., D.D.S., D.O., D.V.M., Pharm.D.), or are a doctoral-level oncology nurse. Applicants must be interested in a program of didactic study and mentored research in scientific areas relevant to cancer prevention, cancer control, and behavioral and population sciences research. They must have a research or academic appointment at the sponsoring institution, which must be a for-profit or nonprofit organization, public or private institution (e.g., university, college, hospital, laboratory), unit of state and local government, and a domestic institution. Members of underrepresented racial and ethnic groups and individuals with disabilities are especially encouraged to apply.

Financial data The award provides salary up to $75,000 per year plus related fringe benefits. In addition, up to $30,000 per year is provided for the following types of expenses: tuition, fees, and books related to career development; research expenses, such as supplies, equipment, and technical personnel; statistical services, including personnel and computer time; tuition, fees, and books related to career development; and travel to research meetings or for training. Facilities and administrative costs are reimbursed at 8% of modified total direct costs.

Duration Up to 5 years.

Additional information Recipients must devote at least 75% of their full-time professional effort to cancer-related research and training activities.

Number awarded Varies each year.

Deadline February, June, or October of each year.

[937]
CAREER AWARDS FOR MEDICAL SCIENTISTS

Burroughs Wellcome Fund
21 T.W. Alexander Drive, Suite 100
P.O. Box 13901
Research Triangle Park, NC 27709-3901
(919) 991-5100   Fax: (919) 991-5160
E-mail: info@bwfund.org
Web: www.bwfund.org/programs/CAMS/index.html

Purpose To provide funding to minority and other biomedical scientists in the United States and Canada who require assistance to make the transition from postdoctoral training to faculty appointment.

Eligibility Applicants must have an M.D., D.D.S., D.V.M., or equivalent degree. They must be interested in a program of research training in the area of basic biomedical, disease-oriented, translational, or molecular, genetic, or pharmacological epidemiology research. Training must take place at a degree-granting institution in the United States or Canada. Each U.S. and Canadian institution may nominate up to 5 candidates; nomination of underrepresented minorities and women is especially encouraged. Following their postdoctoral training, awardees may accept a faculty position at a U.S. or Canadian institution.

Financial data For each year of postdoctoral support, the stipend is $65,000, the research allowance is $20,500, and the administrative fee is $9,500. For each year of faculty support, the stipend is $150,000, the research allowance is $3,000, and the administrative fee is $17,000. The maximum portion of the award that can be used during the postdoctoral period is $190,000 or $95,000 per year. The faculty portion of the award is $700,000 minus the portion used during the postdoctoral years.

Duration The awards provide up to 2 years of postdoctoral support and up to 3 years of support during the faculty appointment.

Additional information This program began in 1995 as Career Awards in the Biomedical Sciences (CABS). It was revised to its current format in 2006 as a result of the NIH K99/R00 Pathway to Independence program. As the CABS, the program provided more than $100 million in support to 241 U.S. and Canadian scientists. Awardees are required to devote at least 75% of their time to research-related activities.

Number awarded Varies each year: recently, 22 of these awards were granted.
Deadline September of each year.

[938]
CAREER DEVELOPMENT AWARD TO PROMOTE DIVERSITY IN NEUROSCIENCE

National Institute of Neurological Disorders and Stroke
Attn: Office of Minority Health and Research
6001 Executive Boulevard, Suite 2150
Bethesda, MD 20892-9527
(301) 496-6035 Fax: (301) 594-5929
TTY: (301) 451-0088 E-mail: jettd@ninds.nih.gov
Web: www.ninds.nih.gov

Purpose To provide funding to neurological research scientists who are Native Americans or members of other underrepresented groups interested in making a transition to a career as an independent investigator.

Eligibility This program is open to full-time faculty members at domestic, for-profit and nonprofit, public and private institutions, such as universities, colleges, hospitals, and laboratories. Applicants must be junior neuroscience investigators making the transition to an independent scientific career at the senior postdoctoral and junior faculty stages under the supervision of a qualified mentor. They must qualify as 1) a member of an ethnic or racial group shown to be underrepresented in health-related sciences on a national basis; 2) an individual with a disability; or 3) an individual from a disadvantaged background, including those from a low-income family and those from a social, cultural, and/or educational environment that has inhibited them from preparation for a research career. Selection is based on qualifications of the applicant, soundness of the proposed career development plan, training in the responsible conduct of research, nature and scientific/technical merit of the proposed research plan, qualifications and appropriateness of the mentor, environment and institutional commitment to the applicant's career, and strength of the description of how this particular award will promote diversity within the institution or in science nationally. Only U.S. citizens, nationals, and permanent residents are eligible.

Financial data Grants provide an annual award of up to $85,000 for salary and fringe benefits and an annual research allowance of up to $50,000 for direct research costs. The institution may apply for up to 8% of direct costs for facilities and administrative costs.

Duration 3 to 5 years.

Number awarded Varies each year.

Deadline February, June, or October of each year.

[939]
CAREER TRANSITION AWARDS OF THE TUBEROUS SCLEROSIS COMPLEX RESEARCH PROGRAM

U.S. Army
Attn: MCMR-ZB-C
1077 Patchel Street (Building 1077)
Fort Detrick, MD 21702-5024
(301) 619-7079 Fax: (301) 619-7792
E-mail: cdmrp.pa@amedd.army.mil
Web: cdmrp.army.mil/funding/tscrp.htm

Purpose To provide funding to minority and other scientists who are completing postdoctoral training and entering a career as an independent investigator conducting research related to Tuberous Sclerosis Complex (TSC).

Eligibility This program is open to postdoctoral investigators within 2 or 3 years of completing the postdoctoral work at universities, colleges, hospitals, laboratories, companies, and agencies of local, state, and federal governments. The sponsor is especially interested in receiving applications from Historically Black Colleges and Universities and Minority Institutions (HBCU/MI). Applicants must be able to complete their postdoctoral training and obtain a faculty position as an independent investigator in TSC research. They must clearly and explicitly articulate their proposed project's innovation and the impact it may have on the field of TSC research. Clinical trials are not acceptable. Proposals that address the needs of minority, low-income, rural, and other underrepresented and/or medically underserved populations are especially encouraged.

Financial data The maximum grant is $338,000 for direct costs over the full term of the award, plus indirect costs as appropriate. That includes up to $69,000 per year for the postdoctoral phase and up to $100,000 per year for the faculty phase.

Duration 4 years: 2 years as a postdoctoral fellow and 2 years as a junior faculty member. Continuation of the grant depends on the recipient's completing postdoctoral study and obtaining a faculty position.

Additional information The Tuberous Sclerosis Complex Research Program was established in 2002 as part of the Congressionally Directed Medical Research Programs (CDMRP) of the U.S. Department of Defense. The Career Transition Awards mechanism was introduced in 2008.

Number awarded 1 each year.

Deadline Pre-applications must be submitted by May of each year; full proposals are due in June.

[940]
CAROLINA POSTDOCTORAL PROGRAM FOR FACULTY DIVERSITY

University of North Carolina at Chapel Hill
Attn: Office of the Vice Chancellor for Research and Economic Development
312 South Building, CB #4000
Chapel Hill, NC 27599-4000
(919) 962-1319 Fax: (919) 962-1476
E-mail: twaldrop@mail.unc.edu
Web: research.unc.edu/red/postdoc.php

Purpose To support Native American and other minority scholars who are interested in teaching and conducting research at the University of North Carolina (UNC).

Eligibility This program is open to scholars from underrepresented groups who have completed their doctoral degree within the past 4 years. Applicants must be interested in teaching and conducting research at UNC. Preference is given to U.S. citizens and permanent residents. Selection is based on the evidence of scholarship potential and ability to compete for tenure-track appointments at UNC and other research universities.
Financial data Fellows receive $35,625 per year, plus an allowance for research and travel. Health benefits are also available.
Duration Up to 2 years.
Additional information Fellows must be in residence at the Chapel Hill campus for the duration of the program. They teach 1 course per year and spend the rest of the time in research. This program began in 1983.
Number awarded 5 or 6 each year.
Deadline January of each year.

[941]
CARY INSTITUTE OF ECOSYSTEM STUDIES RESEARCH EXPERIENCES FOR UNDERGRADUATES PROGRAM

Cary Institute of Ecosystem Studies
Attn: Undergraduate Research Program
181 Sharon Turnpike
P.O. Box R
Millbrook, NY 12545
(845) 677-7600, ext. 326   Fax: (845) 677-6455
E-mail: zolnikp@ecostudies.org
Web: www.ecostudies.org/reu.html

Purpose To provide minority and other undergraduate students with an opportunity to conduct research during the summer at the Cary Institute of Ecosystem Studies (IES) at Millbrook, New York.
Eligibility This program is open to undergraduate freshmen, sophomores, juniors, and first semester seniors. Applicants must be interested in conducting an independent research project of their own design under the guidance of a mentor scientist. They must identify their interest in ecological research, their current career plans, and how participating in this program could help them in their degree program and their future pursuits. Each year, a variety of research topics underway at IES are open to undergraduate participation; some recent topics included microbial processes in urban ecosystems, segregation of tree species along soil nutrient gradients, effects of air pollutants on the forests of the Catskill Mountains, and groundwater ecology. The program welcomes applications from students of diverse backgrounds at schools in all part of the country. U.S. citizenship or permanent resident status is required.
Financial data The stipend is $4,000. Housing and a $600 allowance for food are also provided.
Duration 12 weeks during the summer.
Additional information This program is supported by the National Science Foundation as part of its Research Experiences for Undergraduates (REU) program.
Deadline February of each year.

[942]
CDC/PRC MINORITY FELLOWSHIPS

Association of Schools of Public Health
Attn: Senior Manager, Graduate Training Programs
1101 15th Street, N.W., Suite 910
Washington, DC 20005
(202) 296-1099, ext. 143   Fax: (202) 296-1252
E-mail: mstadtler@asph.org
Web: www.asph.org

Purpose To provide an opportunity for Native American and other minority doctoral students to conduct research at Prevention Research Centers (PRCs) funded by the U.S. Centers for Disease Control and Prevention (CDC).
Eligibility This program is open to minority (African American/Black American, Hispanic/Latino, American Indian/Alaska Native, and Asian/Pacific Islander) students working on a doctoral degree at a school of public health with a CDC-funded PRC. Applicants must be proposing to conduct a research project that is related to the PRC activities and is endorsed by the PRC director. Along with their application, they must submit a personal statement (2 pages or less) on why they are interested in this fellowship, including specifics regarding their interest in the opportunity, benefits they expect to receive from the fellowship experience, how the experience will shape their future career plans, and how the proposed project will advance the field of public health prevention research. Selection is based on the personal statement (30 points), curriculum vitae and transcripts (20 points), and the project proposal (50 points). U.S. citizenship or permanent resident status is required.
Financial data The stipend is $22,500 per year. Fellows are also reimbursed up to $3,000 per year for health-related expenses, project-related travel, tuition, journal subscriptions, and association dues.
Duration 2 years.
Number awarded Varies each year; recently, 11 of these fellowships were awarded.
Deadline February of each year.

[943]
CEDAR, GEM, AND SHINE POSTDOCTORAL RESEARCH GRANTS

National Science Foundation
Directorate for Geosciences
Attn: Division of Atmospheric Sciences
4201 Wilson Boulevard, Room 775 S
Arlington, VA 22230
(703) 292-8529   Fax: (703) 292-9022
TDD: (800) 281-8749   E-mail: rmrobins@nsf.gov
Web: www.nsf.gov

Purpose To provide funding to minority and other postdoctoral scientists interested in conducting research related to 3 programs of the National Science Foundation (NSF) Division of Atmospheric Sciences: Coupling, Energetics, and Dynamics of Atmospheric Regions (CEDAR), Geospace Environmental Modeling (GEM), or Solar, Heliosphere, and INterplanetary Environment (SHINE).
Eligibility This program is open to U.S. citizens, nationals, and permanent residents who either received a Ph.D. within the past 3 years or expect to be in a postdoctoral research position by the time the award is made. Applicants

must be interested in conducting a research project that is relevant to the activities of the CEDAR, GEM, or SHINE ongoing programs supported by NSF. Proposals for cross-cutting research that would be appropriate for 2 or all 3 of those programs is encouraged. Applications are encouraged from women, underrepresented minorities, and persons with disabilities.
Financial data Grants are approximately $80,000 per year. Funds must be used as salary or stipend support for the postdoctoral researcher.
Duration 2 years.
Number awarded 3 to 6 each year. A total of $360,000 is available for this program annually.
Deadline January of each year.

[944]
CHANCELLOR'S POSTDOCTORAL FELLOWSHIPS FOR ACADEMIC DIVERSITY
University of California at Berkeley
Attn: Office of the Chancellor
Office for Faculty Equity
200 California Hall
Berkeley, CA 94720-1500
(510) 643-5878　　　E-mail: cbernal@berkeley.edu
Web: facultyequity.chance.berkeley.edu

Purpose To provide an opportunity for Native American and other recent postdoctorates who will increase diversity at the University of California at Berkeley to conduct research on campus.
Eligibility This program is open to U.S. citizens and permanent residents who received a doctorate within 3 years of the start of the fellowship. The program particularly solicits applications from individuals who are members of ethnic minority groups that are underrepresented in American universities. Special consideration is given to applicants committed to careers in university research and teaching and whose life experience, research, or employment background will contribute significantly to academic diversity and excellence at the Berkeley campus. An application form is not required. Interested applicants should submit a curriculum vitae, a statement of proposed research (up to 5 pages), sample publications, and 1 dissertation chapter. In addition, 3 letters of recommendation are required (1 must be from the dissertation adviser).
Financial data The stipend is $40,000 per year (11 months, plus 1 month vacation). Costs associated with 1-way transportation to Berkeley for the fellow and immediate family members and removal expenses are reimbursable, up to $2,000. In addition, up to $500 is available each year for supplies and related expenses, $3,000 for research-related expenses, and $1,000 for health insurance.
Duration 2 years.
Additional information Research opportunities, mentoring, and guidance are provided as part of the program.
Number awarded Varies each year; recently, 5 of these fellowships were awarded.
Deadline October of each year.

[945]
CHARLES A. EASTMAN DISSERTATION FELLOWSHIP FOR NATIVE AMERICAN SCHOLARS
Dartmouth College
Attn: Office of Graduate Studies
6062 Wentworth Hall, Room 304
Hanover, NH 03755-3526
(603) 646-6578　　　Fax: (603) 646-8762
Web: www.dartmouth.edu

Purpose To provide funding to Native American and other doctoral students who are interested in working on their dissertation at Dartmouth College.
Eligibility This program is open to doctoral candidates who have completed all requirements for the Ph.D. except the dissertation and are planning a career in higher education. Applicants must be Native Americans or other graduate students with a demonstrated commitment and ability to advance educational diversity. They must be interested in working on their dissertation at Dartmouth College. All academic fields that are taught in the Dartmouth undergraduate Arts and Sciences curriculum are eligible. Selection is based on academic achievement and promise; demonstrated commitment to increasing opportunities for underrepresented minorities and increasing cross-racial understanding; and potential for serving as an advocate and mentor for minority undergraduate and graduate students.
Financial data The stipend is $30,000. In addition, fellows receive office space, library privileges, and a $2,500 research allowance.
Duration 1 year, beginning in September.
Additional information The fellows are affiliated with a department or program at Dartmouth College. Fellows are expected to be in residence at Dartmouth College for the duration of the program and to complete their dissertation during that time. They are also expected to teach a course, either as the primary instructor or as part of a team.
Number awarded 1 each year.
Deadline January of each year.

[946]
CIRI EDUCATION PROJECT GRANTS
Cook Inlet Region, Inc.
Attn: The CIRI Foundation
3600 San Jeronimo Drive, Suite 256
Anchorage, AK 99508-2870
(907) 793-3575　　　Toll-free: (800) 764-3382
Fax: (907) 793-3585　E-mail: tcf@thecirifoundation.org
Web: www.thecirifoundation.org/project_grants.htm

Purpose To provide funding to individuals and nonprofit organizations interested in developing projects that further the quality of education and life for Alaska Natives, especially of the Cook Inlet region.
Eligibility This program is open to public nonprofit organizations and tribal councils, with preference given to organizations located within Cook Inlet region. Alaska Natives enrolled to Cook Inlet Region, Inc. (CIRI) and their lineal descendants may also submit applications if they are sponsored by a nonprofit organization. Applicants must be proposing projects that 1) promote quality of learning and educational experiences for Alaska Natives from middle school through adulthood; 2) examine educational issues and opportunities and identify possible solutions to eliminate

those factors that hinder successful achievement by Alaska Natives in their educational pursuits; or 3) foster educational enrichment programs that improve the quality of life for Alaska Natives. Selection is based on the appropriateness of the applicant's project to the foundation's education goals and grant guidelines, need for the project, involvement and direct impact upon Alaska Native enrollees and lineal descendants of CIRI, extent to which the project impacts the targeted audience, extent to which the project impacts the general public, clarity of purpose, realistically-defined program and budget plans that can be reasonably accomplished, demonstration of available funds that at least match the amount of funds requested from the foundation, feasibility of project budget and timeline, innovation of project plan, appropriate and clearly-stated project evaluation plan, and ability to complete project within the projected timeline.

Financial data The maximum grant is $6,000. Preference is given to applications that demonstrate a funding match of at least a 1:1 basis.

Additional information This program was established in 1989.

Number awarded Varies each year.

Deadline Grant applications must be submitted by February, May, August, or October of each year.

[947]
CLINICAL RESEARCH POST-DOCTORAL FELLOWSHIP PROGRAM

American Nurses Association
Attn: SAMHSA Minority Fellowship Programs
8515 Georgia Avenue, Suite 400
Silver Spring, MD 20910-3492
(301) 628-5247   Toll-free: (800) 274-4ANA
Fax: (301) 628-5339   E-mail: janet.jackson@ana.org
Web: www.emfp.org

Purpose To provide funding to postdoctoral minority nurses interested in a program of research and study on psychiatric, mental health, and substance abuse issues that impact the lives of ethnic minority people.

Eligibility This program is open to doctoral-prepared nurses who are members of an ethnic or racial minority group, including but not limited to Blacks or African Americans, Hispanics or Latinos, American Indians and Alaska Natives, Asian Americans, and Native Hawaiians and other Pacific Islanders. Applicants must be able to demonstrate a commitment to a research career in nursing and psychiatric/mental health issues affecting ethnic minority populations. They must be interested in a program of full-time postdoctoral study, with a research focus on such issues of concern to minority populations as substance abuse treatment capacity, mental health system transformation, prevention, co-occurring disorders, seclusion and restraint, children and families, disaster readiness and response, homelessness, older adults, HIV/AIDS and hepatitis, and criminal and juvenile justice. U.S. citizenship or permanent resident status and membership in the American Nurses Association are required.

Financial data The stipend depends on the number of years of postdoctoral experience, ranging from $36,996 for less than 1 year to $51,036 for 7 or more years.

Duration 1 to 2 years.

Additional information Funds for this program are provided by the Substance Abuse and Mental Health Services Administration (SAMHSA).

Number awarded 1 or more each year.

Deadline February of each year.

[948]
CLINICAL SCIENCE FACULTY DEVELOPMENT GRANT

American Society of Transplantation
Attn: Chair, Awards and Grants Committee
15000 Commerce Parkway, Suite C
Mt. Laurel, NJ 08054
(856) 439-9986   Fax: (856) 439-9982
E-mail: ast@ahint.com
Web: cmeplanning.com/ast/event/category/10

Purpose To provide funding for research to underrepresented minority and other junior members of the American Society of Transplantation (AST) who are interested in conducting clinical research.

Eligibility This program is open to AST members who have an M.D., D.O., Ph.D., D.V.M. or equivalent graduate degree and have completed postgraduate training. Applicants must have an academic appointment at an accredited institution of higher education and be within 5 years of their initial faculty appointment. They must be citizens, permanent residents, or lawfully-admitted foreign nationals of Canada, Mexico, or the United States. Their proposed research project must involve clinical outcomes or observational studies to better define the causes and/or consequences of pathological or biological processes in transplantation. Research topics that involve underrepresented areas (minorities, women, and pediatrics) are strongly encouraged. The AST also encourages applications from women and underrepresented minority investigators.

Financial data The grant is $40,000 per year. No more than 15% of funding can be used for indirect costs.

Duration 2 years.

Number awarded 1 or more each year.

Deadline December of each year.

[949]
COLLABORATIVE NEUROLOGICAL SCIENCES AWARD

National Institute of Neurological Disorders and Stroke
Attn: Office of Minority Health and Research
6001 Executive Boulevard, Suite 2149
Bethesda, MD 20892-5929
(301) 496-3102   Fax: (301) 594-5929
TTY: (301) 451-0088   E-mail: lynchj@ninds.nih.gov
Web: www.ninds.nih.gov

Purpose To provide funding for neurological science research to scientists at predominantly minority institutions.

Eligibility This program is open to new investigators who hold a doctoral degree in a basic or clinical neuroscience area, have completed 2 or more years of formal postdoctoral training in neuroscience research, and have an appointment equivalent to assistant professor at a minority institution (including an Hispanic-Service Institution (HSI), Historically Black College or University (HBCU), Tribal College or University (TCU), Alaska Native-Service Institution, or Native Hawaiian-Serving Institution). Applications must be submitted in collaboration with an investigator who is a grantee from a research-intensive institution and who has current support from the National Institutes of Health (NIH) to conduct neurological science research. The applicant investigator must document the potential for excellence in research and teaching and provide evidence of the intent to develop a career in neurological science research. The collaborating investigator must be an individual holding a senior academic position, such as an associate or full professor, and must have demonstrated research competency by competing successfully for current NIH research grant support. The applicant investigator must also be a U.S. citizen, national, or permanent resident. The proposal must involve joint research efforts, specialized training in research techniques, and participation in research seminars.

Financial data Awards range up to $200,000 per year in direct costs, including up to $75,000 for the collaborator.

Duration Up to 5 years.

Additional information This program is also offered by the National Institute on Alcohol Abuse and Alcoholism, Division of Neuroscience and Behavior, 5635 Fishers Lane, Room 2053, Bethesda, MD 20892-9304, (301) 443-2678, Fax: (301) 443-1650, E-mail: rsorense@mail.nih.gov.

Number awarded Varies each year.

Deadline January, May, or September of each year.

[950]
COLLABORATIVE RESEARCH EXPERIENCE FOR UNDERGRADUATES IN COMPUTER SCIENCE AND ENGINEERING

Computing Research Association
1100 17th Street, N.W., Suite 507
Washington, DC 20036-4632
(202) 234-2111   Fax: (202) 667-1066
E-mail: creu@cra.org
Web: www.cra.org/Activities/craw/creu/index.php

Purpose To provide funding to undergraduate students, especially minorities and women, who are interested in conducting a research project in computer science or engineering.

Eligibility This program is open to teams of 2 or 3 undergraduates who have completed 2 years of study, including at least 4 courses in computer science or computer engineering, at a college or university in the United States or Canada. Applicants must be interested in conducting a research project directly related to computer science or computer engineering. They must apply jointly with 1 or 2 sponsoring faculty members. Teams consisting of all women or all underrepresented minorities are especially encouraged to apply. Selection is based on the following criteria: the scope and goals of the project should be reasonable and realistic, based upon the students' prior education and experience; the plan for the project should be well-defined and should describe a collaborative approach to be taken; the project should warrant background research on the part of the students and should have an active, investigative, and experiential nature by which the students can discover their results; the proposal should be complete and well-written; students should be actively involved in writing the proposal, with guidance and support of the sponsoring faculty member; the project should further the goal of the program to increase the numbers of women and minorities who continue on to graduate school in computer science and engineering; the project should enable student empowerment, leadership development, confidence-building, and skill-building in project management; the students should have good potential for doing independent work; the sponsor(s) should have the background necessary to oversee the research and an appropriate strategy for keeping the students on track; and the sponsor(s) and students must have enough time to devote to the research project so that weekly meetings can occur and additional independent work can take place outside of those meetings.

Financial data Each student participant receives a stipend of $3,000. Each project receives an additional grant of $500 to be used for special equipment, travel, supporting materials, or as an honorarium for the faculty member(s).

Duration 1 academic year.

Additional information This program is sponsored by the Computing Research Association's Committee on the Status of Women in Computing Research (CRA-W) and the Coalition to Diversify Computing (CDC). Information is also available from Sheila Casteñeda, Clarke College, Computer Science Department, Dubuque, IA 52001, (563) 588-6401, Fax: (563) 588-6789, E-mail: cast@clarke.edu.

Number awarded Varies each year; recently, 11 teams of students received support from this program.

Deadline May of each year.

[951]
COMMUNITY ARTS SYMPOSIUM PROGRAM OF THE NATIONAL MUSEUM OF THE AMERICAN INDIAN

National Museum of the American Indian
Attn: Native Arts Program
Cultural Resources Center
4220 Silver Hill Road
Suitland, MD 20746-2863
(301) 238-1540   Fax: (301) 238-3200
E-mail: NAP@si.edu
Web: www.nmai.si.edu

Purpose To provide Native American professional artists with an opportunity to organize and conduct a symposium on an art-related topic in their local community.

Eligibility This program is open to Native artists from the western Hemisphere and Hawaii who are recognized by their community, have at least 10 years of experience, and can demonstrate significant artistic accomplishments in any media (e.g., visual arts, media arts, performance arts, literature). Students enrolled in a degree program are ineligible. Applicants must be interested in developing a symposium discussing an art-related topic of relevance to their local community. They must be able to propose a topic of discussion; create a timeline for planning and execution; coordinate logistics of the symposium; and assist in dissemination of the discussion via radio, publications, and/or the Internet. In addition to the coordinating artist, the symposium should feature a panel of up to 4 participants, including at least 2 local community members. Its discussion may focus on such wide-ranging themes as art theory, traditional knowledge, Native American art history, politics and Native art,

Native representations in art, or other issues related to Native art.

Financial data The grant is $6,000. Funds are to be distributed among required tasks, including symposium preparation and planning, oversight, and documentation and dissemination. Additional support is available to provide such services as audio/visual documentation, transcription, travel and lodging (for up to 2 panelists), honoraria (for all 4 panel members), and symposium moderator.

Duration The symposium is to last 1 day. The artist may utilize as much time as necessary to plan and organize the activity.

Additional information Following the symposium, the artist must submit a 1-page report (that may include slides, photos, or videos) describing the symposium's highlights.

Number awarded 1 each year.

Deadline April of each year.

[952]
COOK INLET REGION, INC. HERITAGE PROJECT GRANTS

Cook Inlet Region, Inc.
Attn: The CIRI Foundation
3600 San Jeronimo Drive, Suite 256
Anchorage, AK 99508-2870
(907) 793-3575   Toll-free: (800) 764-3382
Fax: (907) 793-3585 E-mail: tcf@thecirifoundation.org
Web: www.thecirifoundation.org/project_grants.htm

Purpose To provide funding to individuals and nonprofit organizations interested in developing projects that further the heritage of Alaska Native beneficiaries of the Cook Inlet region.

Eligibility This program is open to nonprofit organizations (including, but not limited to, schools, colleges, cultural centers, and museums) and tribal councils, with preference given to organizations located within Cook Inlet region. Alaska Natives enrolled to Cook Inlet Region, Inc. (CIRI) and their lineal descendants may also submit applications if they are sponsored by a nonprofit organization. Applicants must be proposing projects that help promote the sponsor's heritage goals: 1) support educational projects, research, and development of materials on subjects that enhance the understanding and appreciation by Natives and the general public about traditional and contemporary Native history, ethnology, anthropology, philosophy, literature, the arts, and other related fields; 2) promote enrichment programs about the cultural traditions of Alaska Natives of Cook Inlet region and encourage contemporary Native tradition bearers in pursuit of their work; 3) foster the identification, preservation, curation, and interpretation of traditional and contemporary Alaska Native cultural resource materials of Cook Inlet region; 4) encourage excellence in the development and exhibition of traditional and contemporary Native art, music, literature, and other works for appreciation by the general public; 5) conduct consultation and cooperation to protect traditional and cultural values ascribed to Native lands in the Cook Inlet region; and 6) promote cooperation and involvement of Natives within Cook Inlet region as well as with civic and private organizations to accomplish the foundation's heritage programs. Selection is based on the appropriateness of the applicant's project to the foundation's heritage goals and grant guidelines, need for the project, involvement and direct impact upon Alaska Native enrollees and their lineal descendants of CIRI, extent to which the project impacts the targeted audience, extent to which the project impacts the general public, clarity of purpose, realistically-defined tasks to achieve the project's goals and objectives, demonstration of available funds that at least match the amount of funds requested from the foundation, feasibility of project budget and timeline, innovation of project plan, and appropriateness of a project evaluation plan.

Financial data The maximum grant is $6,000. Preference is given to applications that demonstrate a funding match of at least a 1:1 basis.

Additional information This program was established in 1996.

Number awarded Varies each year.

Deadline Grant applications must be submitted by February, May, August, or October of each year.

[953]
CORNELL UNIVERSITY LIBRARY FELLOWSHIP PROGRAM

Cornell University
Attn: Director of Library Human Resources
201 Olin Library
Ithaca, NY 14853-5301
(607) 255-5181   E-mail: sem2@cornell.edu
Web: www.library.cornell.edu

Purpose To increase the number of Native American and other underrepresented minority staff members at Cornell University's academic libraries.

Eligibility This program is open to recent recipients of M.L.S. degrees who are interested in a career in academic librarianship. Applicants must be able to demonstrate critical thinking skills and have excellent oral and written communication skills. Experience and interest in emerging library technologies are strongly desired. African Americans, Latinos/Hispanics, and Native Americans are especially encouraged to apply.

Financial data The appointment is at the Assistant Librarian level, with full benefits, including 22 vacation days, 11 paid holidays, health insurance, life insurance, and university retirement contributions.

Duration 2 years.

Additional information The program allows fellows to work in at least 2 department or functional areas, to explore new information technologies, to work on a variety of grant-funded projects, and to participate in a challenging work environment. In addition, the program provides conference travel funding, a mentoring program, specialized training, continuing education, library committee assignments, and administrative assignments. Fellows will be considered for regular continuing appointments that might arise during their tenure.

Number awarded 2 each year.

Deadline November of each year.

[954]
CULTURAL ANTHROPOLOGY SCHOLARS AWARDS
National Science Foundation
Social, Behavioral, and Economic Sciences
Attn: Division of Behavioral and Cognitive Sciences
4201 Wilson Boulevard, Room 995
Arlington, VA 22230
(703) 292-7315   Fax: (703) 292-9068
TDD: (800) 281-8749   E-mail: dwinslow@nsf.gov
Web: www.nsf.gov

Purpose To provide funding to minority and other cultural anthropologists interested in upgrading their methodological skills.

Eligibility This program is open to cultural anthropologists who are active researchers. Applicants must be interested in a program to upgrade their methodological skills by learning a specific analytical technique that will improve their research abilities. The program encourages applications from women, underrepresented minorities, and persons with disabilities.

Financial data Grants up to $50,000 are available.

Duration Up to 12 months.

Number awarded 2 each year.

Deadline January or August of each year.

[955]
DEPARTMENT OF DEFENSE EXPERIMENTAL PROGRAM TO STIMULATE COMPETITIVE RESEARCH
Army Research Office
Attn: AMSRL-RO-RI
4300 South Miami Boulevard
P.O. Box 12211
Research Triangle Park, NC 27709-2211
(919) 549-4207   Fax: (919) 549-4248
Web: www.arl.army.mil

Purpose To provide funding to researchers at colleges and universities in designated states, especially those at Minority Institutions (MIs).

Eligibility This program is open to researchers at colleges and universities in states and territories that have traditionally not received a large number of research awards (Alaska, Arkansas, Delaware, Hawaii, Idaho, Kansas, Kentucky, Maine, Montana, Nebraska, Nevada, New Hampshire, North Dakota, Oklahoma, Puerto Rico, Rhode Island, South Carolina, South Dakota, Tennessee, Vermont, U.S. Virgin Islands, West Virginia, and Wyoming). Special consideration is given to applications from scholars at HBCUs and MIs. All applying institutions must have an accredited, degree-granting program in science, engineering, or mathematics and a history of graduating students in those fields. Applicants must be proposing a program of research in a science, engineering, or mathematics field of interest to the Department of Defense.

Financial data Grants range up to $100,000.

Additional information Information about this program is also available from the Air Force Office of Scientific Research, 4015 Wilson Boulevard, Room 713, Arlington, VA 22203-1954, (703) 696-7312, Fax: (703) 696-7320, E-mail: info@afosr.af.mil; and the Office of Naval Research, 875 North Randolph Street, Suite 1425, Arlington, VA 22203-1995, (703) 696-4111, E-mail: 363_DEPSCOR@onr.navy.mil.

Number awarded Varies; a total of approximately $10 million in new awards is available through the participating Department of Defense agencies each year.

Deadline October of each year.

[956]
DEPARTMENT OF DEFENSE SMALL BUSINESS INNOVATION RESEARCH GRANTS
Department of Defense
Attn: Office of Small Business Programs
Crystal Gateway North, West Tower
201 12th Street South, Suite 406
Arlington, VA 22202
(703) 604-0157   Toll-free: (866) SBIR-HLP
Fax: (703) 604-0025   E-mail: SBIRHelp@brtrc.com
Web: www.acq.osd.mil/osbp/sbir

Purpose To support small businesses (especially those owned by minorities and women) that have the technological expertise to contribute to the research and development mission of various agencies within the Department of Defense.

Eligibility For the purposes of this program, a "small business" is defined as a firm that is organized for profit with a location in the United States; is in the legal form of an individual proprietorship, partnership, limited liability company, corporation, joint venture, association, trust, or cooperative; is at least 51% owned and controlled by 1 or more individuals who are citizens or permanent residents of the United States; and has (including its affiliates) fewer than 500 employees. The primary employment of the principal investigator must be with the firm at the time of award and during the conduct of the proposed project. Preference is given to women-owned small business concerns and to socially and economically disadvantaged small business concerns. Women-owned small business concerns are those that are at least 51% owned by a woman or women who also control and operate them. Socially and economically disadvantaged small business concerns are at least 51% owned by an Indian tribe, a Native Hawaiian organization, a Community Development Corporation, or 1 or more socially and economically disadvantaged individuals (African Americans, Hispanic Americans, Native Americans, Asian Pacific Americans, or subcontinent Asian Americans). The project must be performed in the United States. Agencies that have Department of Defense Small Business Innovation Research (SBIR) programs are the Department of the Army, Department of the Navy, Department of the Air Force, Defense Advanced Research Projects Agency (DARPA), Defense Threat Reduction Agency (DTRA), Chemical Biological Defense (CBD), Defense Logistics Agency (DLA), Special Operations Command (SOCOM), Missile Defense Agency (MDA), National Geospatial-Intelligence Agency (NGA), Defense Microelectronics Activity (DMEA), and Office of Secretary of Defense (OSD). Selection is based on the soundness, technical merit, and innovation of the proposed approach and its incremental progress toward topic or subtopic solution; the qualifications of the proposed principal investigators, supporting staff, and consultants; and the potential for commercial application and the benefits expected to accrue from this commercialization.

Financial data Grants are offered in 2 phases. In phase 1, awards normally range from $70,000 to $100,000 (for both direct and indirect costs); in phase 2, awards normally range from $500,000 to $750,000 (including both direct and indirect costs).

Duration Phase 1 awards may extend up to 6 months; phase 2 awards may extend up to 2 years.

Number awarded Varies each year. Recently, 1,862 Phase 1 awards were granted: 446 for Department of the Navy, 352 for Department of the Army, 577 for Department of the Air Force, 25 for DARPA, 23 for DTRA, 17 for CBD, 49 for SOCOM, 174 for MDA, 2 for NGA, and 197 for OSD. The number of Phase 2 awards was 1,172, including 232 for Department of the Navy, 390 for Department of the Army, 312 for Department of the Air Force, 48 for DARPA, 17 for DTRA, 9 for CBD, 5 for SOCOM, 119 for MDA 1 for NGA, and 39 for OSD. Total funding was approximately $1.13 billion.

Deadline January, March, June, or September of each year.

[957]
DEPARTMENT OF DEFENSE SMALL BUSINESS TECHNOLOGY TRANSFER GRANTS
Department of Defense
Attn: Office of Small Business Programs
Crystal Gateway North, West Tower
201 12th Street South, Suite 406
Arlington, VA 22202
(703) 604-0157   Toll-free: (866) SBIR-HLP
Fax: (703) 604-0025   E-mail: SBIRHelp@brtrc.com
Web: www.acq.osd.mil/osbp/sbir

Purpose To provide financial support to cooperative research and development projects carried out between small business concerns (especially those owned by minorities) and research institutions in areas of interest to various agencies within the Department of Defense.

Eligibility For the purposes of this program, a "small business" is defined as a firm that is organized for profit with a location in the United States; is in the legal form of an individual proprietorship, partnership, limited liability company, corporation, joint venture, association, trust, or cooperative; is at least 51% owned and controlled by 1 or more individuals who are citizens or permanent residents of the United States; and has (including its affiliates) fewer than 500 employees. Unlike the Department of Defense Small Business Innovation Research Grants, the primary employment of the principal investigator does not need to be with the business concern. This program, however, requires that the small business apply in collaboration with a nonprofit research institution for conduct of a project that has potential for commercialization. At least 40% of the work must be performed by the small business and at least 30% of the work must be performed by the research institution. The principal investigator may have his/her primary employment with an organization other than the small business concern, including the research institution. Preference is given to women-owned small business concerns and to socially and economically disadvantaged small business concerns. Women-owned small business concerns are those that are at least 51% owned by a woman or women who also control and operate them. Socially and economically disadvantaged small business concerns are at least 51% owned by an Indian tribe, a Native Hawaiian organization, or 1 or more socially and economically disadvantaged individuals (African Americans, Hispanic Americans, Native Americans, Asian Pacific Americans, or subcontinent Asian Americans). Partnerships between small businesses and Historically Black Colleges and Universities (HBCUs) and Minority Institutions (MIs) are especially encouraged. The project must be performed in the United States. Agencies of the Department of Defense currently participating in this program are the Department of the Army, Department of the Navy, Department of the Air Force, Defense Advanced Research Projects Agency (DARPA), Missile Defense Agency (MDA), and Office of Secretary of Defense (OSD). Selection is based on the soundness, technical merit, and innovation of the proposed approach and its incremental progress toward topic or subtopic solution; the qualifications of the proposed principal investigators, supporting staff, and consultants; and the potential for commercial application and the benefits expected to accrue from this commercialization.

Financial data In the first phase, annual awards range from $70,000 to $100,000 for direct costs, indirect costs, and negotiated fixed fees. In the second phase, awards from $500,000 to $750,000 for the full period are available.

Duration Generally 1 year for the first phase and 2 years for the second phase.

Additional information Grants in the first phase are to determine the scientific, technical, and commercial merit and feasibility of the proposed cooperative effort and the quality of performance of the small business concern. In the second phase, the research and development efforts continue, depending on the results of the first phase.

Number awarded Varies each year. Recently, 340 Phase 1 awards were granted: 79 for Department of the Army, 116 for Department of the Navy, 87 for Department of the Air Force, 17 for DARPA, 13 for OSD, and 28 for MDA. The number of Phase 2 awards was 153, including 36 for Department of the Army, 42 for Department of the Navy, 43 for Department of the Air Force, 8 for DARPA, 8 for OSD, and 16 for MDA. Total funding was approximately $131 million.

Deadline April of each year.

[958]
DEPARTMENT OF EDUCATION SMALL BUSINESS INNOVATION RESEARCH GRANTS
Department of Education
Attn: Institute of Education Sciences
555 New Jersey Avenue, N.W., Room 608D
Washington, DC 20208-5544
(202) 208-1983   Fax: (202) 219-2030
E-mail: Edward.metz@ed.gov
Web: www.ed.gov/programs/sbir/index.html

Purpose To support small businesses (especially those owned by minorities and women) that have the technological expertise to contribute to the research and development mission of the Department of Education.

Eligibility For the purposes of this program, a "small business" is defined as a firm that is organized for profit with a location in the United States; is in the legal form of an individual proprietorship, partnership, limited liability company, corporation, joint venture, association, trust, or cooperative; is at least 51% owned and controlled by 1 or more individuals who are citizens or permanent residents of the United States; and has (including its affiliates) fewer than 500 employees. The primary employment of the principal investigator must be with the firm at the time of award and during the conduct of the proposed project. Applications are encouraged from women-owned small business concerns and from socially and economically disadvantaged small business concerns. Women-owned small business concerns are those that are at least 51% owned by a woman or women who also control and operate them. Socially and economically disadvantaged small business concerns are at least 51% owned by an Indian tribe, a Native Hawaiian organization, or 1 or more socially and economically disadvantaged individuals (African Americans, Hispanic Americans, Native Americans, Asian Pacific Americans, or subcontinent Asian Americans). The project must be performed in the United States. Firms with strong research capabilities in science, engineering, or educational technology in any of the topic areas are encouraged to participate. Recently, the program operated in 2 branches of the Department of Education: 1) the National Institute on Disability and Rehabilitations Research (NIDRR) within the Office of Special Education and Rehabilitative Services (OSERS); and 2) the Institute of Education Sciences (IES), formerly the Office of Educational Research and Improvement (OERI). Selection is based on quality of project design (45 points), significance (25 points), quality of project personnel (20 points), and adequacy of resources (10 points).

Financial data Grants are offered in 2 phases. Phase 1 awards normally do not exceed $100,000 for IES programs or $75,000 for OSERS/NIDRR programs; phase 2 awards normally do not exceed $750,000 for IES programs or $500,000 for OSERS/NIDRR programs.

Duration Phase 1 awards may extend up to 6 months; phase 2 awards may extend up to 2 years.

Number awarded Varies each year; recently, approximately 40 phase 1 awards were available. Approximately one third of those were expected to receive phase 2 awards.

Deadline January of each year.

[959]
DEPARTMENT OF HOMELAND SECURITY SMALL BUSINESS INNOVATION RESEARCH GRANTS

Department of Homeland Security
Homeland Security Advanced Research Projects Agency
Attn: SBIR Program Manager
Washington, DC 20528
(202) 254-6768   Toll-free: (800) 754-3043
Fax: (202) 254-7170
E-mail: elissa.sobolewski@dhs.gov
Web: www.hsarpasbir.com

Purpose To support small businesses (especially those owned by minorities and women) that have the technological expertise to contribute to the research and development mission of the Department of Homeland Security (DHS).

Eligibility For the purposes of this program, a "small business" is defined as a firm that is organized for profit with a location in the United States; is in the legal form of an individual proprietorship, partnership, limited liability company, corporation, joint venture, association, trust, or cooperative; is at least 51% owned and controlled by 1 or more individuals who are citizens or permanent residents of the United States; and has (including its affiliates) fewer than 500 employees. The primary employment of the principal investigator must be with the firm at the time of award and during the conduct of the proposed project. Preference is given to women-owned small business concerns, service-disabled veteran small business concerns, veteran small business concerns, and socially and economically disadvantaged small business concerns. Women-owned small business concerns are those that are at least 51% owned by a woman or women who also control and operate them. Service-disabled veteran small business concerns are those that are at least 51% owned by a service-disabled veteran and controlled by such a veteran or (for veterans with permanent and severe disability) the spouse of permanent caregiver of such a veteran. Veteran small business concerns are those that are at least 51% owned by a veteran or veterans who also control and manage them. Socially and economically disadvantaged small business concerns are at least 51% owned by an Indian tribe, a Native Hawaiian organization, a Community Development Corporation, or 1 or more socially and economically disadvantaged individuals (African Americans, Hispanic Americans, Native Americans, Asian Pacific Americans, or subcontinent Asian Americans). The project must be performed in the United States. Currently, DHS has 7 research priorities: explosives; border and maritime security; command, control, and interoperability; human factors; infrastructure and geophysical; chemical and biological; and domestic nuclear detection. Selection is based on the soundness, technical merit, and innovation of the proposed approach and its incremental progress toward topic or subtopic solution; the qualifications of the proposed principal investigators, supporting staff, and consultants; and the potential for commercial application and the benefits expected to accrue from this commercialization.

Financial data Grants are offered in 2 phases. In phase 1, awards normally range up to $100,000 (or $150,000 for domestic nuclear detection); in phase 2, awards normally range up to $750,000 (or $1,000,000 for domestic nuclear detection).

Duration Phase 1 awards may extend up to 6 months; phase 2 awards may extend up to 2 years.

Number awarded Varies each year. Recently, 61 Phase 1 awards were granted.

Deadline February of each year.

[960]
DEPARTMENT OF HOMELAND SECURITY SUMMER FACULTY AND STUDENT RESEARCH TEAM PROGRAM

Oak Ridge Institute for Science and Education
Attn: Science and Engineering Education
P.O. Box 117
Oak Ridge, TN 37831-0117
(865) 241-2722   Fax: (865) 241-5219
E-mail: leigh.ann.pennington@orau.gov
Web: see.orau.org

Purpose To provide an opportunity for teams of students and faculty from minority-serving educational institutions to conduct summer research in areas of interest to the Department of Homeland Security (DHS).

Eligibility This program is open to teams of up to 2 students (undergraduate and/or graduate) and 1 faculty from

Historically Black Colleges and Universities (HBCUs), Hispanic Serving Institutions (HSIs), Tribal Colleges and Universities (TCUs), Alaska Native Serving Institutions (ANSIs), and Native Hawaiian Serving Institutions (NHSIs). Applicants must be interested in conducting research at designated DHS Centers of Excellence in science, technology, engineering, or mathematics related to homeland security (HS-STEM), including explosives detection, mitigation, and response; social, behavioral, and economic sciences; risk and decision sciences; human factors aspects of technology; chemical threats and countermeasures; biological threats and countermeasures; food and agricultural security; transportation security; border security; immigration studies; maritime and port security; infrastructure protection; natural disasters and related geophysical studies; emergency preparedness and response; communications and interoperability; or advanced data analysis and visualization. Faculty must have a full-time appointment at an eligible institution and have received a Ph.D. in an HS-STEM discipline no more than 7 years previously; at least 2 years of full-time research and/or teaching experience is preferred. Students must have a GPA of 3.0 or higher and be enrolled full time. Undergraduates must be entering their junior or senior year. U.S. citizenship is required. Selection is based on relevance and intrinsic merit of the research (40%), faculty applicant qualifications (30%), academic benefit to the faculty applicant and his/her institution (10%), and student applicant qualifications (20%).

Financial data Stipends are $1,200 per week for faculty, $600 per week for graduate students, and $500 per week for undergraduates. Faculty members who live more than 50 miles from their assigned site may receive a relocation allowance of $1,500 and travel expenses up to an additional $500. Limited travel expenses for 1 round trip are reimbursed for undergraduate and graduate students living more than 50 miles from their assigned site.

Duration 12 weeks during the summer.

Additional information This program is funded by DHS and administered by Oak Ridge Institute for Science and Education (ORISE). Recently, the available DHS Centers of Excellence were the Center for Advancing Microbial Risk Assessment (Michigan State University and Drexel University); the Center for Risk and Economic Analysis of Terrorism Events (University of Southern California, University of Wisconsin at Madison, or New York University); the National Center for Food Protection and Defense (University of Minnesota, Michigan State University, University of Wisconsin at Madison, North Dakota State University, Georgia Institute of Technology, or University of Tennessee at Knoxville); the National Center for Foreign Animal and Zoonotic Disease Defense (Texas A&M University, University of Texas Medical Branch, University of California at Davis, or University of Southern California); the National Center for the Study of Preparedness and Catastrophic Event Response (Johns Hopkins University and 12 partner institutions); the National Consortium for the Study of Terrorism and Responses to Terrorism (University of Maryland, University of California at Los Angeles, University of Colorado, Monterey Institute of International Studies, University of Pennsylvania, or University of South Carolina); the National Visualization and Analytics Center (Pacific Northwest National Laboratory) and Regional Visualization and Analytics Centers (Pennsylvania State University, Purdue University, Stanford University, University of North Carolina at Charlotte, Georgia Institute of Technology, and University of Washington); and University Affiliate Centers to the Institute for Discrete Sciences (Rutgers University, University of Illinois, University of Pittsburgh, and University of Southern California).

Number awarded Approximately 12 teams are selected each year.

Deadline January of each year.

[961]
DEPARTMENT OF TRANSPORTATION SMALL BUSINESS INNOVATION RESEARCH GRANTS

Department of Transportation
Attn: Research and Innovative Technology
 Administration
John A. Volpe National Transportation Systems Center
55 Broadway, Kendall Square
Cambridge, MA 02142-1093
(617) 494-2051 Fax: (617) 494-2370
E-mail: henebury@volpe.dot.gov
Web: www.volpe.dot.gov/sbir

Purpose To support small businesses (especially those owned by minorities, veterans, and women) that have the technological expertise to contribute to the research and development mission of the Department of Transportation.

Eligibility For the purposes of this program, a "small business" is defined as a firm that is organized for profit with a location in the United States; is in the legal form of an individual proprietorship, partnership, limited liability company, corporation, joint venture, association, trust, or cooperative; is at least 51% owned and controlled by 1 or more individuals who are citizens or permanent residents of the United States; and has (including its affiliates) fewer than 500 employees. The primary employment of the principal investigator must be with the firm at the time of award and during the conduct of the proposed project. Preference is given to 1) women-owned small business concerns; 2) veteran-owned small businesses; and 3) socially and economically disadvantaged small business concerns. Women-owned small business concerns are those that are at least 51% owned by a woman or women who also control and operate them. Veteran-owned small businesses are those that are at least 51% owned and controlled by 1 or more veterans. Socially and economically disadvantaged small business concerns are at least 51% owned by an Indian tribe, a Native Hawaiian organization, or 1 or more socially and economically disadvantaged individuals (African Americans, Hispanic Americans, Native Americans, Asian Pacific Americans, or subcontinent Asian Americans). The project must be performed in the United States. Selection is based on scientific and technical merit, the feasibility of the proposal's commercial potential, the adequacy of the work plan, qualifications of the principal investigator, and adequacy of supporting staff and facilities, equipment, and data.

Financial data Support is offered in 2 phases. In phase 1, awards normally do not exceed $100,000 (for both direct and indirect costs); in phase 2, awards normally do not exceed $750,000 (including both direct and indirect costs).

Duration Phase 1 awards may extend up to 6 months; phase 2 awards may extend up to 2 years.

Number awarded Varies each year. Recently, DOT planned to award 19 of these grants: 4 to the Federal High-

way Administration, 1 to the Federal Motor Carrier Safety Administration, 4 to the Pipeline and Hazardous Materials Safety Administration, 2 to the National Highway and Traffic Safety Administration, 5 to the Federal Transit Administration, and 3 to the Federal Railroad Administration.
Deadline April of each year.

[962]
DIBNER MATH AND SCIENCE TEACHING PROGRAM
Catching the Dream
8200 Mountain Road, N.E., Suite 203
Albuquerque, NM 87110-7835
(505) 262-2351   Fax: (505) 262-0534
E-mail: NScholarsh@aol.com
Web: www.catchingthedream.org/grants.htm

Purpose To provide funding to teachers and schools for projects that are designed to improve mathematics and science teaching for Indian high school students.
Eligibility This program is open to Indian high schools that wish to offer more advanced mathematics and science courses and to enroll more Indian students in advanced classes. Applicants must describe their school, the students to be served, the current number of Indian students enrolling in their advanced mathematics and science classes, how the program will work, how the funds from the grant will be used, the background of the person in charge, and the goals and objectives of the proposed program.
Financial data Grants are $5,000. Some of the previous acceptable uses of funds have included purchase of advanced mathematics or science books, purchase of science supplies, purchase of mathematics supplies, or taking students on field trips.
Duration Grants are awarded annually.
Additional information The sponsor was formerly known as the Native American Scholarship Fund.
Number awarded 1 or more each year.
Deadline October of each year.

[963]
DISSERTATION YEAR VISITING DIVERSITY FELLOWSHIPS FOR ADVANCED GRADUATE STUDENTS
Northeast Consortium for Faculty Diversity
Attn: JoAnn Moody
13345 Benchley Road
San Diego, CA 92130-1247
E-mail: joann.moody@earthlink.net
Web: www.diversityoncampus.com/id2.html

Purpose To provide an opportunity for Native American and other doctoral candidates from underrepresented minority groups to complete their dissertation while in residence at participating colleges and universities in the Northeast.
Eligibility This program is open to members of underrepresented minority groups who are at the dissertation writing stage of their doctoral program in any field. Applicants may be working at a university anywhere in the country but must be interested in completing their dissertation at a college or university in the Northeast. They must be able to demonstrate that they can complete the dissertation while at the host campus. Along with their application, they must submit a curriculum vitae, a statement of scholarship and teaching goals, 3 letters of recommendation (including 1 from the dissertation advisor at their home campus), a copy of the dissertation prospectus, and a graduate school transcript.
Financial data The stipend ranges from $25,000 to $32,000. The host campus will provide computer and library privileges, office space, and health insurance.
Duration 12 months.
Additional information This program began in 2001. Recently, the host campuses were Northeastern University, Colgate University, Middlebury College, Allegheny College, Monmouth University, and the University of Vermont. Although the scholars have no formal teaching assignment, they are expected to present their work-in-progress at 2 or 3 campus-wide or department-wide forums during the year and to teach or co-teach a course.
Number awarded Varies each year. Each participating college or university hosts 1 or more dissertation scholars.
Deadline January of each year.

[964]
DIVERSITY PROGRAM IN NEUROSCIENCE POSTDOCTORAL FELLOWSHIPS
American Psychological Association
Attn: Minority Fellowship Program
750 First Street, N.E.
Washington, DC 20002-4242
(202) 336-6127   Fax: (202) 336-6012
TDD: (202) 336-6123   E-mail: mfp@apa.org
Web: www.apa.org/mfp/pdprogram.html

Purpose To provide funding to postdoctorates who are interested in pursuing research training in neuroscience, especially those whose participation will increase diversity in the field.
Eligibility This program is open to all U.S. citizens and permanent residents who have a Ph.D. or M.D. degree with appropriate research experience in neuroscience or an applied discipline, such as cell or molecular biology or immunology. Applicants must have career goals that are consistent with those of the program: 1) to increase ethnic and racial diversity among neuroscience researchers; 2) to increase the number of neuroscience researchers with disabilities; 3) to increased the number of neuroscience researchers from disadvantaged backgrounds; and 4) to increase numbers of neuroscientists whose work is related to the federal initiative to eliminate health disparities. They must be interested in engaging in postdoctoral research training in neuroscience under the guidance of an established, grant-funded research mentor or sponsor. Students identified as underrepresented in the neurosciences are especially encouraged to apply. Selection is based on scholarship, research experience and potential, a research proposal, the suitability of the proposed laboratory and mentor, commitment to a research career in neuroscience, writing ability, and appropriateness to program goal.
Financial data The stipend depends on the number of years of research experience and is equivalent to the standard postdoctoral stipend level of the National Institutes of Health (currently ranging from $36,996 for no years of experience to $51,036 for 7 or more years of experience). The

fellowship also provides travel funds to attend the annual meeting of the Society for Neuroscience.
Duration 1 year; may be renewed for up to 1 additional year.
Additional information The program was established in 1987. It is funded by the U.S. National Institute of Mental Health of the National Institutes of Health and administered by the American Psychological Association.
Number awarded Varies each year.
Deadline January of each year.

[965]
DOCTORAL DISSERTATION IMPROVEMENT GRANTS IN THE DIRECTORATE FOR BIOLOGICAL SCIENCES

National Science Foundation
Directorate for Biological Sciences
Attn: Division of Environmental Biology
4201 Wilson Boulevard
Arlington, VA 22230
(703) 292-8480   TDD: (800) 281-8749
E-mail: ddig-deb@nsf.gov
Web: www.nsf.gov

Purpose To provide partial support to underrepresented minorities and others for dissertation research in selected areas supported by the National Science Foundation (NSF) Directorate for Biological Sciences (DBS).
Eligibility Applications may be submitted through regular university channels by dissertation advisers on behalf of graduate students who have advanced to candidacy and have begun or are about to begin dissertation research. Students must be enrolled at U.S. institutions but need not be U.S. citizens. Proposals should focus on the ecology, ecosystems, systematics, or population biology programs in the DBS Division of Environmental Biology, or the animal behavior or ecological and evolutionary physiology programs in the DBS Division of Integrative Organismal Biology. The program encourages applications from women, underrepresented minorities, and persons with disabilities.
Financial data Grants range up to $12,000; funds may be used for travel to specialized facilities or field research locations, specialized research equipment, purchase of supplies and services not otherwise available, fees for computerized or other forms of data, and rental of environmental chambers or other research facilities. Funding is not provided for stipends, tuition, textbooks, journals, allowances for dependents, travel to scientific meetings, publication costs, dissertation preparation or reproduction, or indirect costs.
Duration Normally 2 years.
Additional information Information on programs in the Division of Environmental Biology is available at the address and telephone number above; information from the Division of Integrative Organismal Biology is available at (703) 292-8423, E-mail: ddig-iob@nsf.gov.
Number awarded 120 each year; approximately $1,300,000 is available for this program each year.
Deadline November of each year.

[966]
DOE FACULTY SABBATICAL PROGRAM

Department of Energy
Attn: Office of Science
1000 Independence Avenue, S.W.
Washington, DC 20585
(202) 586-9742   Toll-free: (800) DIAL-DOE
Fax: (202) 586-4039
E-mail: sc.helpwithapplication@science.doe.gov
Web: www.scied.science.doe.gov

Purpose To provide an opportunity for faculty at community colleges and Minority Serving Institutions to work on research projects under the guidance of staff members of the U.S. Department of Energy (DOE).
Eligibility This program is open to full-time tenured or tenure-track faculty at accredited community colleges, Hispanic Serving Institutions (HSIs), Historically Black Colleges and Universities (HBCUs), and Tribal Colleges and Universities (TCUs). Applicants must be interested in working on a research project at a DOE national laboratory resident scientist while on sabbatical from their home institution. U.S. citizenship or permanent resident status is required.
Financial data Participants receive regular sabbatical pay from their home institution plus supplemental funds from DOE so their salary matches that of a national laboratory scientist with similar background and experience.
Duration 1 semester or 1 academic year.
Additional information At the conclusion of their time at a national laboratory, participants are expected to complete and submit a grant proposal to DOE or another federal agency.
Number awarded Varies each year.

[967]
DOE SMALL BUSINESS INNOVATION RESEARCH GRANTS

Department of Energy
Attn: SBIR/STTR Program, SC-32
Germantown Building
1000 Independence Avenue, S.W.
Washington, DC 20585-1290
(301) 903-1414   Fax: (301) 903-5488
E-mail: sbir-sttr@science.doe.gov
Web: www.science.doe.gov/sbir

Purpose To support small businesses (especially those owned by minorities and women) that have the technological expertise to contribute to the research and development mission of the Department of Energy (DOE).
Eligibility For the purposes of this program, a "small business" is defined as a firm that is organized for profit with a location in the United States; is in the legal form of an individual proprietorship, partnership, limited liability company, corporation, joint venture, association, trust, or cooperative; is at least 51% owned and controlled by 1 or more individuals who are citizens or permanent residents of the United States; and has (including its affiliates) fewer than 500 employees. The primary employment of the principal investigator must be with the firm at the time of award and during the conduct of the proposed project. Preference is given to women-owned small business concerns and socially and economically disadvantaged small business concerns. Women-owned small business concerns are

those that are at least 51% owned by a woman or women who also control and operate them. Socially and economically disadvantaged small business concerns are at least 51% owned by an Indian tribe, a Native Hawaiian organization, or 1 or more socially and economically disadvantaged individuals (African Americans, Hispanic Americans, Native Americans, Asian Pacific Americans, or subcontinent Asian Americans). The project must be performed in the United States. Each office within DOE defines technical topics eligible for research.

Financial data Support is offered in 2 phases: in phase 1, awards normally do not exceed $100,000 (for both direct and indirect costs); in phase 2, awards normally do not exceed $750,000 (including both direct and indirect costs).

Duration Phase 1: up to 9 months; phase 2: up to 2 years.

Additional information The objectives of this program include increasing private sector commercialization of technology developed through research and development supported by the Department of Energy, stimulating technological innovation in the private sector, strengthening the role of small business in meeting federal research and development needs, and improving the return on investment from federally-funded research for economic and social benefits to the nation.

Number awarded Varies each year; recently 279 Phase 1 and 113 Phase 2 grants were awarded.

Deadline November of each year.

[968]
DOE SMALL BUSINESS TECHNOLOGY TRANSFER GRANTS

Department of Energy
Attn: SBIR/STTR Program, SC-32
Germantown Building
1000 Independence Avenue, S.W.
Washington, DC 20585-1290
(301) 903-1414   Fax: (301) 903-5488
E-mail: sbir-sttr@science.doe.gov
Web: www.science.doe.gov/sbir

Purpose To provide financial support to cooperative research and development projects carried out between small business concerns (especially those owned by minorities) and research institutions in areas of interest to the Department of Energy.

Eligibility For the purposes of this program, a "small business" is defined as a firm that is organized for profit with a location in the United States; is in the legal form of an individual proprietorship, partnership, limited liability company, corporation, joint venture, association, trust, or cooperative; is at least 51% owned and controlled by 1 or more individuals who are citizens or permanent residents of the United States; and has (including its affiliates) fewer than 500 employees. Unlike the Department of Energy Small Business Innovation Research Grants, the primary employment of the principal investigator does not need to be with the business concern. This program, however, requires that the small business apply in collaboration with a nonprofit research institution for conduct of a project that has potential for commercialization. At least 40% of the work must be performed by the small business and at least 30% of the work must be performed by the research institution. The principal investigator may have his/her primary employment with an organization other than the small business concern, including the research institution. Preference is given to women-owned small business concerns and to socially and economically disadvantaged small business concerns. Women-owned small business concerns are those that are at least 51% owned by a woman or women who also control and operate them. Socially and economically disadvantaged small business concerns are at least 51% owned by an Indian tribe, a Native Hawaiian organization, or 1 or more socially and economically disadvantaged individuals (African Americans, Hispanic Americans, Native Americans, Asian Pacific Americans, or subcontinent Asian Americans). The project must be performed in the United States. Each office within DOE defines technical topics eligible for research.

Financial data In the first phase, annual awards do not exceed $100,000 for direct costs, indirect costs, and negotiated fixed fees. In the second phase, awards up to $500,000 are available.

Duration Generally 9 months for the first phase and 2 years for the second phase.

Additional information Grants in the first phase are to determine the scientific, technical, and commercial merit and feasibility of the proposed cooperative effort and the quality of performance of the small business concern. In the second phase, the research and development efforts continue, depending on the results of the first phase.

Number awarded Varies each year; recently 39 Phase 1 and 15 Phase 2 grants were awarded.

Deadline January of each year.

[969]
DORIS DUKE CLINICAL SCIENTIST DEVELOPMENT AWARDS

Doris Duke Charitable Foundation
Attn: Grantmaking Programs
650 Fifth Avenue, 19th Floor
New York, NY 10019
(212) 974-7000   Fax: (212) 974-7590
E-mail: ddcf@aibs.org
Web: www.ddcf.org/page.asp?pageId=291

Purpose To provide funding to minority and other junior physician-scientists interested in conducting clinical research.

Eligibility This program is open to physician-scientists who have received an M.D., M.D./Ph.D., or foreign equivalent and are working in a U.S. degree-granting institution (although U.S. citizenship is not required). Applicants must have a full-time faculty level position not higher than the assistant professor level and have been appointed to their first full-time faculty position within the past 5 years. They must be conducting clinical research in a disease area; clinical research includes studies on the etiology and pathogenesis of human disease, therapeutic interventions, clinical trials, disease control research, epidemiological studies, and health outcomes research. Experiments that utilize animals or primary tissues derived from animals are not supported by this program. Each institution may nominate up to 3 candidates for this program. Institutions are strongly encouraged to nominate women and underrepresented minorities (Blacks or African Americans, Hispanics or Latinos, American Indians, Native Hawaiians, and Alaskan Natives).

Financial data Grants provide $125,000 per year for direct costs and $10,000 per year for indirect costs.
Duration 3 years.
Additional information This program began in 1998.
Number awarded At least 17 each year. Since this program was established, it has awarded 105 grants worth more than $47 million.
Deadline Nominations must be submitted by January of each year.

[970]
DR. JULES M. ROTHSTEIN MINORITY RESEARCH FELLOWSHIP AWARD

American Physical Therapy Association
Attn: Department of Minority/International Affairs
1111 North Fairfax Street
Alexandria, VA 22314-1488
(703) 706-3143   Toll-free: (800) 999-APTA, ext. 3143
Fax: (703) 706-8519   TDD: (703) 683-6748
E-mail: min-intl@apta.org
Web: www.apta.org

Purpose To provide funding for a program of research training in physical therapy to Native American and other minority postdoctorates.
Eligibility This program is open to physical therapists who have an academic or clinical doctoral degree and are members of the following minority groups: African American or Black, Asian, Native Hawaiian or other Pacific Islander, American Indian or Alaska Native, or Hispanic/Latino. Applicants must have a full-time faculty appointment at an accredited or developing professional physical therapy education program and be in the first 5 years of postdoctoral work or the first 3 years in a tenure-track position. They must be seeking funding for additional training in an area that is relevant to physical therapy, health disparities, and/or minority health research. Appropriate activities include planning research proposals and securing research assistants, conducting pilot studies, developing and planning on site short-term visits with potential research collaborators and/or mentors, paying fees for courses related to areas of scientific inquiry, or paying travel costs for attendance at scientific meetings or other networking experiences. U.S. citizenship or permanent resident status is required.
Financial data The stipend is $5,000.
Duration 1 year, beginning in January.
Number awarded 1 each year.
Deadline August of each year.

[971]
DRUG ABUSE DISSERTATION RESEARCH: EPIDEMIOLOGY, PREVENTION, TREATMENT, SERVICES, AND WOMEN AND SEX/GENDER DIFFERENCES

National Institute on Drug Abuse
Attn: Division of Clinical Neuroscience, Development, and Behavioral Treatment
6101 Executive Boulevard, Room 4230
Bethesda, MD 20892-9593
(301) 443-2261   Fax: (301) 443-6814
E-mail: mraciopp@nida.nih.gov
Web: www.nida.nih.gov

Purpose To provide financial assistance to minority and other doctoral candidates interested in conducting dissertation research on drug abuse treatment and health services.
Eligibility This program is open to doctoral candidates who are conducting dissertation research in a field of the behavioral, biomedical, or social sciences related to drug abuse treatment, including research in epidemiology, prevention, treatment, services, and women and sex/gender differences. Students working on an M.D., D.O., D.D.S., or similar professional degree are not eligible. Applicants must be U.S. citizens nationals, or permanent residents and must have completed all requirements for the doctoral degree except the dissertation. Special attention is paid to recruiting members of racial and ethnic groups underrepresented in the biomedical and behavioral sciences (African Americans, Hispanic Americans, Native Americans, Alaskan Natives, and Pacific Islanders).
Financial data The maximum grant is $50,000 per year, including support for the recipient's salary (up to $20,772 per year), research assistant's salary and direct research project expenses. Funding may not be used for tuition, alterations or renovations, faculty salary, contracting costs, or space rental. The recipient's institution may receive facilities and administrative costs of up to 8% of total direct costs.
Duration Up to 2 years; may be extended for 1 additional year.
Number awarded Varies each year, depending on the availability of funds.
Deadline April, August, or December of each year.

[972]
ECOLOGY OF INFECTIOUS DISEASES INITIATIVE

Fogarty International Center
Attn: Division of International Training and Research
31 Center Drive, Room B2C39
Bethesda, MD 20892-2220
(301) 496-1653   Fax: (301) 402-2056
TTY: (301) 451-0088
E-mail: Joshua_Rosenthal@nih.gov
Web: www.fic.nih.gov

Purpose To provide funding to minority and other U.S. scientists interested in conducting research on the underlying ecological and biological mechanisms that govern relationships between human-induced environmental changes and the emergence and transmission of infectious diseases.
Eligibility This program is open to investigators at domestic and foreign for-profit and nonprofit organizations, both public and private, such as universities, colleges, hos-

pitals, laboratories, units of state and local governments, and eligible agencies of the federal government. Applicants should be proposing to conduct research on the ecological and socio-ecological determinants of transmission by vectors or abiotic agents, the population dynamics of reservoir species, the transmission to humans or other hosts, or the cultural, social, behavioral, and economic dimensions of disease communication. Proposals for research on disease systems of public health concern to developing countries are strongly encouraged. Applicants are also encouraged to include links to the public health research community in the United States and developing countries, including participation by epidemiologists, physicians, veterinarians, medical social scientists, medical entomologists, virologists, or parasitologists. The program encourages applications from women, underrepresented minorities, and persons with disabilities.

Financial data Grants provide up to $500,000 per year.
Duration Up to 5 years.
Additional information This program, established in 2000, is jointly funded by 3 components National Science Foundation (NSF): the Directorate for Biological Sciences, the Directorate for Geosciences, and the Directorate for Social, Behavioral, and Economic Sciences, and 4 components of the National Institutes of Health (NIH): the Fogarty International Center, the National Institute of Environmental Health Sciences, the National Institute of Allergy and Infectious Diseases, and the National Institute of General Medical Sciences.
Number awarded Up to 7 each year.
Deadline December of each year.

[973]
EISENHOWER GRANTS FOR RESEARCH AND INTERN FELLOWSHIPS

Department of Transportation
Federal Highway Administration
Attn: Office of Professional and Corporate
   Development, HPC-32
4600 North Fairfax Drive, Suite 800
Arlington, VA 22203-1553
(703) 235-0538   Toll-free: (877) 558-6873
Fax: (703) 235-0593
E-mail: transportationedu@dot.gov
Web: www.fhwa.dot.gov/opd/universitygrants.htm

Purpose To enable minority and other students to participate in transportation-related research activities either at facilities of the U.S. Department of Transportation (DOT) Federal Highway Administration in the Washington, D.C. area or as interns for private or public organizations.
Eligibility This program is open to 1) students in their junior year of a baccalaureate program who will complete their junior year before being awarded a fellowship; 2) students in their senior year of a baccalaureate program; and 3) students who have completed their baccalaureate degree and are enrolled in a program leading to a master's, Ph.D., or equivalent degree. Applicants must be enrolled full time at an accredited U.S institution of higher education and planning to enter the transportation profession after completing their higher education. They must be U.S. citizens or have an I-20 (foreign student) or I-551 (permanent resident) identification card. For research fellowships, they select 1 or more projects from a current list of research activities underway at various DOT facilities; the research is conducted with academic supervision provided by a faculty adviser from their home university (which grants academic credit for the research project) and with technical direction provided by the DOT staff. Intern fellowships provide students with opportunities to perform transportation-related research, development, technology transfer, and other activities at public and private sector organizations. Specific requirements for the target projects vary; most require engineering backgrounds, but others involve transportation planning, information management, public administration, physics, materials science, statistical analysis, operations research, chemistry, economics, technology transfer, urban studies, geography, and urban and regional planning. The DOT encourages students at Historically Black Colleges and Universities (HBCUs), Hispanic Serving Institutions (HSIs), and Tribal Colleges and Universities (TCUs) to apply for these grants. Selection is based on the match of the student's qualifications with the proposed research project (including the student's ability to accomplish the project in the available time), recommendation letters regarding the nominee's qualifications to conduct the research, academic records (including class standing, GPA, and transcripts), and transportation work experience (if any), including the employer's endorsement.

Financial data Fellows receive full tuition and fees that relate to the academic credits for the approved research project (to a maximum of $10,000) and a monthly stipend of $1,450 for undergraduates, $1,700 for master's students, or $2,000 for doctoral students. An allowance for travel to and from the DOT facility where the research is conducted is also provided, but selectees are responsible for their own housing accommodations. Recipients are also provided with a 1-time allowance of up to $1,500 to attend the annual Transportation Research Board (TRB) meeting.
Duration Projects normally range from 3 to 12 months.
Number awarded Varies each year; recently, 9 students participated in this program.
Deadline Applications remain open until each project is filled.

[974]
ENDOCRINE SOCIETY SUMMER RESEARCH FELLOWSHIPS

Endocrine Society
Attn: Summer Research Fellowships
8401 Connecticut Avenue, Suite 900
Chevy Chase, MD 20815
(301) 951-2616   Toll-free: (888) 363-6274
Fax: (301) 576-7787
E-mail: awards@endo-society.org
Web: www.endo-society.org

Purpose To provide funding to minority and other undergraduate, medical, and graduate students interested in conducting a summer research project in endocrinology.
Eligibility This program is open to full-time students who are undergraduates in the third year of study or higher, medical students beyond their first year of study, and first-year graduate students. Applicants must be interested in participating in a research project under the supervision of a mentor. The mentor must be an active member of the

Endocrine Society. Each member may sponsor only 1 student. Projects must be relevant to an aspect of endocrinology and are expected to have clearly defined research goals; students should not function as aides or general research assistants. Applications on behalf of underrepresented minority students are especially encouraged.

Financial data The grant of $4,000 provides funding for a stipend, fringe benefits, and indirect costs.

Duration 10 to 12 weeks during the summer.

Additional information At the conclusion of the fellowship period, students must submit a 1-page summary of their research project explaining how the fellowship affected their consideration of a career in endocrinology.

Number awarded 20 each year.

Deadline January of each year.

[975]
EPA SMALL BUSINESS INNOVATION RESEARCH GRANTS

Environmental Protection Agency
Attn: Office of Research and Development
ORD/NCER (8722F)
1200 Pennsylvania Avenue, N.W.
Washington, DC 20460
(202) 343-9703   Toll-free: (800) 490-9194
Fax: (202) 233-0678   E-mail: Gallup.James@epa.gov
Web: es.epa.gov/ncer/sbir

Purpose To support small businesses (especially those owned by minorities and women) that have the technological experience to contribute to the research and development mission of the Environmental Protection Agency (EPA).

Eligibility For the purposes of this program, a "small business" is defined as a firm that is organized for profit with a location in the United States; is in the legal form of an individual proprietorship, partnership, limited liability company, corporation, joint venture, association, trust, or cooperative; is at least 51% owned and controlled by 1 or more individuals who are citizens or permanent residents of the United States; and has (including its affiliates) fewer than 500 employees. The primary employment of the principal investigator must be with the firm at the time of award and during the conduct of the proposed project. Preference is given to women-owned small business concerns and to socially and economically disadvantaged small business concerns. Women-owned small business concerns are those that are at least 51% owned by a woman or women who also control and operate them. Socially and economically disadvantaged small business concerns are at least 51% owned by an Indian tribe, a Native Hawaiian organization, or 1 or more socially and economically disadvantaged individuals (African Americans, Hispanic Americans, Native Americans, Asian Pacific Americans, or subcontinent Asian Americans). The project must be performed in the United States. The proposed research must relate to the following EPA topics: innovation in manufacturing, nanotechnology, green buildings, drinking water and water monitoring, water and wasterwater management, control of air pollution, air monitoring and remote sensing, engine and vehicle emissions reduction, animal waste and waste to energy, waste management and monitoring, coal bed methane and oil and gas drilling, large-scale disaster debris management, technology for villages and small communities, and homeland security. Selection is based on the scientific and technical significance of the proposed technology and its appropriateness to the research topic; quality and soundness of the research plan to establish the technical and commercial feasibility of the concept; the uniqueness/ingenuity of the proposed concept or application as technology innovation; originality and innovativeness of the proposed research toward meeting customer needs and achieving commercialization of the technology; potential demonstration of performance/cost effectiveness and environmental benefits associated with the proposed research; qualifications of the principal investigator, supporting staff, and consultants; and potential of the proposed concept for significant commercial applications.

Financial data Grants are offered in 2 phases. In phase 1, awards normally do not exceed $70,000 (for both direct and indirect costs); in phase 2, awards normally do not exceed $225,000 plus up to $120,000 for firms with third-party financing for accelerating commercialization and for technologies accepted into an EPA technology verification testing program.

Duration Phase 1 awards may extend up to 6 months; phase 2 awards may extend up to 2 years.

Number awarded Varies each year, recently, 41 phase 1 and 14 phase 2 awards were granted.

Deadline May of each year.

[976]
EPILEPSY FOUNDATION RESEARCH GRANTS PROGRAM

Epilepsy Foundation
Attn: Research Department
8301 Professional Place
Landover, MD 20785-2237
(301) 459-3700   Toll-free: (800) EFA-1000
Fax: (301) 577-2684   TDD: (800) 332-2070
E-mail: grants@efa.org
Web: www.epilepsyfoundation.org

Purpose To provide funding to minority and other junior investigators interested in conducting research that will advance the understanding, treatment, and prevention of epilepsy.

Eligibility Applicants must have a doctoral degree and an academic appointment at the level of assistant professor in a university or medical school (or equivalent standing at a research institution or medical center). They must be interested in conducting basic or clinical research in the biological, behavioral, or social sciences related to the causes of epilepsy. Faculty with appointments at the level of associate professor or higher are not eligible. Applications from women, members of minority groups, and people with disabilities are especially encouraged. U.S. citizenship is not required, but the research must be conducted in the United States. Selection is based on the scientific quality of the research plan, the relevance of the proposed research to epilepsy, the applicant's qualifications, and the adequacy of the institution and facility where research will be conducted.

Financial data The maximum grant is $50,000 per year.

Duration Up to 2 years.

Additional information Support for this program is provided by many individuals, families, and corporations, especially the American Epilepsy Society, Abbott Laboratories, Ortho-McNeil Pharmaceutical, and Pfizer Inc.

Number awarded Varies each year.

Deadline August of each year.

[977]
ERIC AND BARBARA DOBKIN NATIVE AMERICAN ARTIST FELLOWSHIP

School for Advanced Research
Attn: Indian Arts Research Center
660 Garcia Street
P.O. Box 2188
Santa Fe, NM 87504-2188
(505) 954-7205 Fax: (505) 954-7207
E-mail: iarc@sarsf.org
Web: www.sarweb.org/iarc/dobkin/dobkin.htm

Purpose To provide an opportunity for Native American women artists to improve their skills through a spring residency at the Indian Arts Research Center in Santa Fe, New Mexico.

Eligibility This program is open to Native American women who excel in the visual, written, or performing arts. Applicants should be attempting to realize personal goals in growth, enhancement, excellence, and continued artistic achievement. Along with their application, they must submit a statement describing the project they plan to complete during the residency.

Financial data The fellowship provides financial support, an opportunity to study the collections, and interaction with the staff.

Duration 3 months, beginning in March.

Additional information Fellows work with the staff and research curators at the Indian Arts Research Center, an academic division of the School of Advanced Research that is devoted solely to Native American art scholarship. The center has a significant collection of Pueblo pottery, Navajo and Pueblo Indian textiles, and early 20th-century Indian paintings, as well as holdings of jewelry and silverwork, basketry, clothing, and other ethnological materials. This fellowship was established in 2001.

Number awarded 1 each year.

Deadline November of each year.

[978]
ETS VISITING SCHOLAR PROGRAM

Educational Testing Service
Attn: Visiting Scholar Program
Rosedale Road
MS O2-D
Princeton, NJ 08541-0001
(609) 734-1972 Fax: (609) 734-1900
E-mail: visitingscholars@ets.org
Web: www.ets.org

Purpose To provide funding to Native American and other postdoctoral scholars of color who wish to learn more about issues related to minorities at the Educational Testing Service (ETS).

Eligibility This program is open to members of underrepresented groups who are experienced liberal arts community college or university teachers. Applicants must have completed at least 3 years of recent teaching experience in the United States in English, ESL, foreign languages, education, mathematics, psychometrics, statistics, science, or social science. They must be interested in spending time at the ETS campus studying issues related to test design and learning to develop test questions and related materials for a variety of assessment programs. They may also work on educational measurement and policy issues related to assessment equity and attend seminars on fairness in testing, from question conception through test administration and research.

Financial data The award includes an honorarium of $3,500, limited round-trip travel reimbursement, hotel accommodations, and compensation for additional services provided subsequent to the summer program.

Duration 4 weeks during the summer.

Additional information Fellows work with senior staff at ETS in Princeton, New Jersey and have access to senior research staff. This program was established in 2000.

Number awarded Several each year.

Deadline December of each year.

[979]
EXPLORATION-HYPOTHESIS DEVELOPMENT AWARDS OF THE NEUROFIBROMATOSIS RESEARCH PROGRAM

U.S. Army
Medical Research and Materiel Command
Attn: MCMR-ZB-C
1077 Patchel Street (Building 1077)
Fort Detrick, MD 21702-5024
(301) 619-7079 Fax: (301) 619-7792
E-mail: cdmrp.pa@amedd.army.mil
Web: cdmrp.army.mil/funding/nfrp.htm

Purpose To provide funding to minority and other scientists interested in conducting innovative and untested research on neurofibromatosis.

Eligibility This program is open to researchers at all academic levels at universities, colleges, hospitals, laboratories, companies, and agencies of local, state, and federal governments. The sponsor is especially interested in receiving applications from Historically Black Colleges and Universities and Minority Institutions (HBCU/MI). Applicants must be interested in conducting research that explores innovative, untested, high-risk/high-gain, and potentially groundbreaking concepts relevant to neurofibromatosis and/or Schwannomatosis. Results of studies conducted through this award may provide the scientific rationale upon which a new hypothesis can be based or the initial principles of an innovative hypothesis. The presentation of preliminary data is encouraged but not required. All areas of laboratory, clinical, behavioral, and epidemiological research are eligible, as are the environmental basic, clinical, psychosocial, behavioral, sociocultural, and environmental sciences, nursing, occupational health, alternative therapies, public health and policy, ethics, and economics. Proposals that address the needs of minority, low-income, rural, and other underrepresented and/or medically underserved populations are especially welcome.

Financial data Grants range up to $100,000 for direct costs over the term of the award, plus indirect costs as appropriate.
Duration 2 years.
Additional information The Neurofibromatosis Research Program was established in 1996 as part of the Congressionally Directed Medical Research Programs (CDMRP) of the U.S. Department of Defense. The Exploration-Hypothesis Development Award mechanism was first offered in 2008.
Number awarded 2 to 3 each year. Approximately $350,000 is available for this program annually.
Deadline Pre-applications must be submitted by March of each year; full proposals are due in April.

[980]
EXPLORATIONS IN BIOMEDICINE SUMMER RESEARCH FELLOWSHIPS

American Physiological Society
Attn: Education Office
9650 Rockville Pike, Room 3111
Bethesda, MD 20814-3991
(301) 634-7132   Fax: (301) 634-7098
E-mail: education@the-aps.org
Web: www.the-aps.org/education/expl/research.htm

Purpose To provide an opportunity for Tribal College and University (TCU) science faculty and middle/high school life science teachers of Native American students in Montana to participate in a summer research project in physiology.
Eligibility This program is open to 1) science faculty members at Montana TCUs that are members of the American Indian Research Opportunities Consortium (Blackfeet Community College, Dull Knife Memorial College, Fort Belknap College, Fort Peck Community College, Little Big Horn College, Salish Kootenai College, and Stone Child College); and 2) science teachers at middle schools (grades 6-9) and high schools (grades 9-12) in Montana serving primarily Native American students. Applicants do not need to have extensive mathematics skills, but they must be able to demonstrate a commitment to excellence in teaching, strong observation skills, interest in learning about research firsthand and in making contact with researchers in other parts of the country, and a willingness to travel away from home during the summer.
Financial data Selectees receive a stipend of $500 per week (to a maximum of $4,000) and reimbursement of living expenses to travel away from home (up to $3,500).
Duration 7 to 8 weeks during the summer.
Additional information This program, which began in 1997, includes 3 components: 1) experiencing scientific research, in which teachers explore a research project in a physiology laboratory at a location of their preference in the continental United States; 2) exploring effective pedagogy, in which participants use the Internet to expand their repertory of teaching methods and their network of colleagues; and 3) developing and presenting new materials, in which teachers develop an inquiry-based classroom activity or laboratory, along with a corresponding web page. Support is provided by the Minority Access to Research Careers (MARC) program of the National Institute of General Medical Sciences (NIGMS), a component of the National Institute of Health (NIH).

Number awarded Varies each year; since this program began, 27 Montana science educators have participated in it.
Deadline January of each year.

[981]
EXTRAMURAL ASSOCIATES RESEARCH DEVELOPMENT AWARD

National Institute of Child Health and Human Development
Attn: Director, Extramural Associates Program
6100 Executive Boulevard, Room 5E03
Bethesda, MD 20892-7510
(301) 435-2736   Fax: (301) 480-0393
TTY: (301) 451-0088   E-mail: kinnardm@mail.nih.gov
Web: www.nichd.nih.gov

Purpose To provide opportunities for faculty at minority and women's colleges and universities to participate in a program at the National Institutes of Health (NIH) in Bethesda, Maryland during the summer.
Eligibility This program is open to faculty at 1) domestic private and public women's colleges and educational institutions with significant underrepresented minority student populations that offer programs in the biomedical or behavioral sciences; and 2) community colleges that meet those enrollment criteria and have established significant collaborative research activities or bridge programs with institutions that award at least a baccalaureate science degree. Applicants should be full-time faculty who have earned degrees in the life sciences (biomedical or behavioral sciences) or in the physical sciences (chemistry, mathematics, engineering, or physics). Academic science administrators and mid-level and senior faculty are preferable. Members of underrepresented racial and ethnic groups and individuals with disabilities are especially encouraged to apply.
Financial data During their tenure at the NIH, associates receive a salary that is comparable to that at their home institution. Travel, housing, and subsistence expenses while at NIH, and any costs incurred that are directly related to the training, are reimbursed by the NIH. The maximum grant to sponsoring institutions is $60,000 in direct costs per year, plus reimbursement of facilities and administrative costs at 8% of total direct costs. An additional $40,000 in direct costs (plus facilities and administrative costs at 8%) may be requested for faculty pilot research grants.
Duration 10 weeks during the summer. Awards to institutions are up to 5 years, with a possible extension for an additional 3 years.
Additional information During their tenure at the NIH, associates acquire a thorough knowledge of the NIH, the support mechanisms through which research is being accomplished, and the policies and procedures which govern the awarding of grants and contracts. Associates also obtain information about other federal health-related programs; grant and contract activities; legislative, budgetary and similar processes; and administrative procedures, including participation in staff meetings, review meetings, site visits, workshops, and conferences. Following completion of the summer program, associates return to their institutions with a grant that provides developmental funding. This program is also offered by the National Institute of Biomedical Imaging and Bioengineering, Attn: Extramural

Science Programs, 6707 Democracy Boulevard, Suite 200, Bethesda, MD 20892-5477, (301) 451-4792, (301) 480-1614, E-mail: templeocm@mail.nih.gov.

Number awarded Varies each year; recently, 3 to 5 awards have been available through this program.

Deadline Letters of intent must be submitted by February of each year; completed applications are due in March.

[982]
FACULTY AT FDA GRANTS

National Science Foundation
Directorate for Engineering
Attn: Division of Bioengineering and Environmental Systems
4201 Wilson Boulevard, Room 565 S
Arlington, VA 22230
(703) 292-7943   Fax: (703) 292-9098
TDD: (800) 281-8749   E-mail: gdevey@nsf.gov
Web: www.nsf.gov

Purpose To provide an opportunity for minority and other faculty members to conduct research at an intramural laboratory of the U.S. Food and Drug Administration (FDA).

Eligibility This program is open to full-time faculty members at U.S. colleges and universities in science, engineering, and mathematics fields of interest to the National Science Foundation (NSF). Applicants must be U.S. citizens, nationals, or permanent residents. They must present a plan for collaboration between their institution and the FDA, with a description of the facilities and resources that will be available at an FDA laboratory to support the proposed research. The program encourages applications from women, underrepresented minorities, and persons with disabilities.

Financial data Grants range from $25,000 to $150,000, including 85% of the faculty member's salary and fringe benefits during the industrial residency period. Up to 20% of the total requested amount may be used for travel and research expenses for the faculty and his/her students, including materials but excluding equipment. In lieu of indirect costs, up to 15% of the total cost may be allocated for administrative expenses. The fellow's home institution must commit to support the other 15% of the faculty salary and fringe benefits. FDA provides office space, research facilities, research costs in the form of expendable and minor equipment purchases in the host laboratory, and the time of its research staff.

Duration 3 to 12 months.

Additional information This program is also offered by the NSF Directorate for Computer and Information Science and Engineering; for information, contact its Division of Computer-Communications Research, (703) 292-8910, Fax: (703) 292-9059, E-mail: hgill@nsf.gov. The FDA contact is William A. Herman, Director, Division of Physical Sciences, Center for Devices and Radiological Health, 12725 Twinbrook Parkway, Rockville, MD 20852, (301)827-5599, E-mail: wah@cdrh.fda.gov.

Number awarded A total of 3 to 10 grants for all FDA programs is awarded each year; total funding is approximately $500,000.

Deadline March of each year.

[983]
FACULTY EARLY CAREER DEVELOPMENT PROGRAM

National Science Foundation
Directorate for Education and Human Resources
Senior Staff Associate for Cross Directorate Programs
4201 Wilson Boulevard, Room 805
Arlington, VA 22230
(703) 292-8600   TDD: (800) 281-8749
Web: www.nsf.gov

Purpose To provide support for science and engineering research to minority and other outstanding new faculty who intend to develop academic careers involving both research and education.

Eligibility This program, identified as the CAREER program, is open to faculty members who meet all of the following requirements: 1) be employed in a tenure-track (or equivalent) position at an institution in the United States, its territories or possessions, or the Commonwealth of Puerto Rico that awards degrees in a field supported by the National Science Foundation (NSF) or that is a nonprofit, non-degree granting organization such as a museum, observatory, or research laboratory; 2) have a doctoral degree in a field of science or engineering supported by NSF: 3) not have competed more than 3 times in this program; 4) be untenured; and 5) not be a current or former recipient of a Presidential Early Career Award for Scientists and Engineers (PECASE) or CAREER award. Applicants must be U.S. citizens, nationals, or permanent residents. They must submit a career development plan that indicates a description of the proposed research project, including preliminary supporting data if appropriate, specific objectives, methods, and procedures to be used, and expected significance of the results; a description of the proposed educational activities, including plans to evaluate their impact; a description of how the research and educational activities are integrated with each other; and results of prior NSF support, if applicable. Proposals from women, underrepresented minorities, and persons with disabilities are especially encouraged.

Financial data The total grant is $400,000 (or $500,000 for the Directorate of Biological Sciences) over the full period of the award.

Duration 5 years.

Additional information This program is operated by various disciplinary divisions within the NSF; for a list of the participating divisions and their telephone numbers, contact the sponsor. Outstanding recipients of these grants are nominated for the NSF component of the PECASE awards, which are awarded to 20 recipients of these grants as an honorary award.

Number awarded 300 to 400 each year. Approximately $85 million is budgeted to support this program annually.

Deadline July of each year.

[984]
FACULTY FELLOWSHIPS AT THE NEWBERRY LIBRARY

Newberry Library
Attn: McNickle Center for American Indian History
60 West Walton Street
Chicago, IL 60610-3305
(312) 255-3564   Fax: (312) 255-3513
E-mail: mcnickle@newberry.org
Web: www.newberry.org/mcnickle/darcyhome.html

Purpose To provide funding to faculty members at member institutions of the Committee on Institutional Cooperation (CIC) who wish to conduct research in American Indian studies at the D'Arcy McNickle Center for the History of the American Indian at the Newberry Library.

Eligibility This program is open to faculty members at CIC institutions who are interested in conducting research in American Indian studies at the Newberry Library. Applicants must submit their curriculum vitae; a 3- to 5-page research proposal that discusses the topic, significance, methodological approach, and Newberry collections to be used; and a 1- to 2-page syllabus for a spring semester seminar.

Financial data Grants provide a stipend of $40,000.

Duration 1 academic year.

Additional information The fellow also leads a seminar during the spring semester for graduate students at CIC institutions on a topic appropriate to the Newberry's collections and the expertise of the fellow. The CIC institutions are Indiana University, Michigan State University, Northwestern University, Ohio State University, Pennsylvania State University, Purdue University, University of Chicago, University of Illinois at Chicago, University of Illinois at Urbana-Champaign, University of Iowa, University of Michigan, University of Minnesota, and University of Wisconsin at Madison. Fellows must spend a significant portion of their time at the library's D'Arcy McNickle Center.

Number awarded 1 each year.

Deadline January of each year.

[985]
FACULTY RESEARCH AWARDS FOR HISTORICALLY BLACK AND TRIBAL COLLEGES AND UNIVERSITIES AND INSTITUTIONS WITH HIGH HISPANIC ENROLLMENT

National Endowment for the Humanities
Attn: Division of Research Programs
1100 Pennsylvania Avenue, N.W., Room 318
Washington, DC 20506
(202) 606-8200   Toll-free: (800) NEH-1121
Fax: (202) 606-8204   TDD: (866) 372-2930
E-mail: FacultyResearch@neh.gov
Web: www.neh.gov

Purpose To provide funding to faculty members at Historically Black Colleges and Universities (HBCUs), Hispanic Serving Institutions (HSIs), and Tribal Colleges and Universities (TCUs) who are interested in working on a research project in the humanities.

Eligibility This program is open to faculty members at HBCUs, HSIs, and TCUs who hold a full-time tenured, tenure-track, or annual contract position. Applicants must be U.S. citizens or foreign nationals who have resided in the United States or its jurisdictions for at least 3 years. The proposed project should contribute to scholarly knowledge or to the public's understanding of the humanities in the form of publications, presentations, and classroom teaching. Grants may be awarded to individual faculty or 2 faculty collaborating on a single project. Support is not provided for graduate course work, but the proposed project may contribute to the completion of a doctoral dissertation. Grants are not provided for curricular or pedagogical methods, theories, or surveys; preparation or revision of textbooks; works in the creative or performing arts; projects that seek to promote a particular political, philosophical, religious, or ideological point of view; or projects that advocate a particular program of social action. Selection is based on: 1) the intellectual significance of the proposed project, including its value to scholars and general audiences in the humanities; 2) the quality or promise of quality of the applicant's work as an interpreter of the humanities; 3) the quality of the conception, definition, organization, and description of the project; and 4) the feasibility of the proposed plan of work; and 5) the likelihood that the applicant will complete the project.

Financial data The grant is $4,200 per month, to a maximum of $50,400 for 12 months.

Duration 6 to 12 months.

Number awarded Varies each year.

Deadline April of each year.

[986]
FELLOWSHIPS FOR HUMAN EMBRYONIC STEM CELL RESEARCH

National Institutes of Health
Office of Extramural Research
Attn: Grants Information
6705 Rockledge Drive
Bethesda, MD 20892-7974
(301) 435-0714   Fax: (301) 480-0525
TTY: (301) 451-0088   E-mail: GrantsInfo@nih.gov
Web: grants.nih.gov/grants/guide/index.html

Purpose To provide funding to minority and other postdoctorates and senior scientists interested in a program of research training that involves the use of human embryonic stem cells.

Eligibility This program is open to scientists who have received a Ph.D., M.D., D.O., D.C., D.D.S., D.V.M., O.D., D.P.M., Sc.D., Eng.D., D.N.S., N.D., Pharm.D., D.S.W., Psy.D., or equivalent doctoral degree. They may be either recent postdoctorates or senior scholars who are at least 7 years beyond their doctorate, have had at least 7 years of post-degree relevant research or professional experience, and have established an independent research career. Applicants must be interested in a program of mentored research training in the use of human embryonic stem cells at a domestic or foreign, for-profit or nonprofit, public or private institution, such as a university, college, hospital, laboratory, unit of state or local government, or eligible agency of the federal government. Members of underrepresented racial and ethnic groups and individuals with disabilities are especially encouraged to apply. Only U.S. citizens, nationals, and permanent residents are eligible.

Financial data The grant provides an annual stipend based on the number of years of postdoctoral experience, ranging from $36,996 for less than 1 year to $51,036 for 7 or more years. For fellows sponsored by domestic nonfederal institutions, the stipend is paid through the sponsoring institution; for fellows sponsored by federal or foreign institutions, the monthly stipend is paid directly to the fellow. Institutions also receive an allowance to help defray such awardee expenses as self-only health insurance, research supplies, equipment, travel to scientific meetings, and related items; the allowance is $7,850 per 12-month period for fellows at nonfederal, nonprofit, and foreign institutions and $6,750 per 12-month period at federal laboratories and for-profit institutions. In addition, tuition and fees are reimbursed at a rate of 60%, up to $4,500; if the fellow's program supports postdoctoral individuals in formal degree-granting training, tuition is supported at the rate of 60%, up to $16,000 for an additional degree. Grants for training at a foreign site may include a single economy or coach round-trip travel fare; no allowance is provided for dependents. The initial 12 months of National Research Service Award postdoctoral support carries a service payback requirement, which can be fulfilled by continued training under the award or by engaging in other health-related research training, health-related research, or health-related teaching. Fellows who fail to fulfill the payback requirement of 1 month of acceptable service for each month of the initial 12 months of support received must repay all funds received with interest.

Duration Up to 3 years for postdoctorates; up to 2 years for senior scientists.

Additional information This program is supported by 6 of the NIH component organizations: the National Heart, Lung, and Blood Institute, the National Institute of General Medical Sciences, the National Institute of Diabetes and Digestive and Kidney Diseases, the National Institute of Child Health and Development, the National Institute on Deafness and Other Communication Disorders, and the National Institute of Environmental Health Sciences. Awardees are expected to devote at least 50% of their effort to the project supported by the award, although a full-time commitment is allowed.

Number awarded Varies each year.

Deadline April, August, or December of each year.

[987]
FIRST BOOK GRANT PROGRAM FOR MINORITY SCHOLARS

Louisville Institute
Attn: Executive Director
1044 Alta Vista Road
Louisville, KY 40205-1798
(502) 992-5432   Fax: (502) 894-2286
E-mail: info@louisville-institute.org
Web: www.louisville-institute.org

Purpose To provide funding to Native Americans and other scholars of color interested in completing a major research and book project that focuses on an aspect of Christianity in North America.

Eligibility This program is open to members of a racial/ethnic minority group (African Americans, Hispanics, Native Americans, Asian Americans, Arab Americans, and Pacific Islanders) who have an earned doctoral degree (normally the Ph.D. or Th.D.). Applicants must be a pre-tenured faculty member in a full-time, tenure-track position at an accredited institution of higher education (college, university, or seminary) in North America. They must be able to negotiate a full academic year free from teaching and committee responsibilities in order to engage in a scholarly research project leading to the publication of their first (or second) book focusing on an aspect of Christianity in North America. Selection is based on the intellectual quality of the research and writing project, its potential to contribute to scholarship in religion, and the potential contribution of the research to the vitality of North American Christianity.

Financial data The grant is $40,000. Awards are intended to make possible a full academic year of sabbatical research and writing by providing up to half of the grantee's salary and benefits for that year. Funds are paid directly to the grantee's institution, but no indirect costs are allowed.

Duration 1 academic year; nonrenewable.

Additional information The Louisville Institute is located at Louisville Presbyterian Theological Seminary and is supported by the Lilly Endowment. Grantees may not accept other awards that provide a stipend during the tenure of this award, and they must be released from all teaching and committee responsibilities during the award year.

Number awarded Up to 3 each year.

Deadline February of each year.

[988]
FIVE COLLEGE FELLOWSHIP PROGRAM

Five Colleges, Incorporated
Attn: Five Colleges Fellowship Program Committee
97 Spring Street
Amherst, MA 01002-2324
(413) 256-8316   Fax: (413) 256-0249
E-mail: neckert@fivecolleges.edu
Web: www.fivecolleges.edu

Purpose To provide funding to graduate students from Native American and other underrepresented groups who have completed all the requirements for the Ph.D. except the dissertation and are interested in teaching at selected colleges in Massachusetts.

Eligibility Fellows are chosen by the host department in each of the 5 participating campuses (Amherst, Hampshire, Mount Holyoke, Smith, and the University of Massachusetts). Applicants must be graduate students at an accredited school who have completed all doctoral requirements except the dissertation and are interested in devoting full time to the completion of the dissertation. The chief goal of the program is to promote diversity in American higher education by enabling more scholars of underrepresented groups and/or unique interests, experiences, or histories to prepare for an academic career.

Financial data The stipend is $30,000 plus a research grant, fringe benefits, office space, library privileges, and housing assistance.

Duration 9 months, beginning in September.

Additional information Although the primary goal is completion of the dissertation, each fellow also has many opportunities to experience working with students and faculty colleagues on the host campus as well as with those at the other colleges. The fellows are also given an opportunity to teach (generally as a team teacher, in a section of a core course, or in a component within a course). Fellows

meet monthly with each other to share their experiences. At Smith College, this program is named Mendenhall Fellowships.
Number awarded 5 each year: 1 at each of the participating colleges.
Deadline January of each year.

[989]
FORD FOUNDATION DIVERSITY DISSERTATION FELLOWSHIP PROGRAM

National Research Council
Attn: Fellowships Office, GR 346A
500 Fifth Street, N.W.
Washington, DC 20001
(202) 334-2872 Fax: (202) 334-3419
E-mail: infofell@nas.edu
Web: www7.nationalacademies.org

Purpose To provide funding for dissertation research to graduate students whose success will increase the racial and ethnic diversity of U.S. colleges and universities.
Eligibility This program is open to citizens and nationals of the United States who are Ph.D. or Sc.D. degree candidates committed to a career in teaching and research at the college or university level. The following are considered as positive factors in the selection process: evidence of superior academic achievement; promise of continuing achievement as scholars and teachers; membership in a group whose underrepresentation in the American professoriate has been severe and longstanding, including Black/African Americans, Puerto Ricans, Mexican Americans, Native American Indians, Alaska Natives (Eskimos or Aleuts), and Native Pacific Islanders (Micronesians or Polynesians); capacity to respond in pedagogically productive ways to the learning needs of students from diverse backgrounds; sustained personal engagement with communities that are underrepresented in the academy and an ability to bring this asset to learning, teaching, and scholarship at the college and university level; and likelihood of using the diversity of human experience as an educational resource in teaching and scholarship. Applicants must be working to complete their dissertation in the following fields: American studies, anthropology, archaeology, art and theater history, astronomy, chemistry, communications, computer science, earth sciences, economics, education, engineering, ethnomusicology, geography, history, international relations, language, life sciences, linguistics, literature, mathematics, performance study, philosophy, physics, political science, psychology, religion, sociology, urban planning, and women's studies. Awards are not made for such practice-oriented areas as administration and management, audiology, business, educational administration and leadership, filmmaking, fine arts, guidance, home economics, library and information science, nursing, occupational health, performing arts, personnel, physical education, social welfare, social work, or speech pathology. Ineligibility also includes students working on a terminal master's degree; the Ed.D. degree; the degrees of Doctor of Fine Arts (D.F.A.) or Doctor of Psychology (Psy.D.); professional degrees in such areas as medicine, law, and public health; or such joint degrees as M.D./Ph.D., J.D./Ph.D., and M.F.A./Ph.D.
Financial data The stipend is $21,000 per year; stipend payments are made through fellowship institutions.
Duration 9 to 12 months.
Additional information The competition for this program is conducted by the National Research Council on behalf of the Ford Foundation. Fellows may not accept remuneration from another fellowship or similar external award while on this program; however, supplementation from institutional funds, educational benefits from the Department of Veterans Affairs, or educational incentive funds may be received concurrently with Ford Foundation support. Dissertation fellows are required to submit an interim progress report 6 months after the start of the fellowship and a final report at the end of the 12 month tenure.
Number awarded Approximately 35 each year.
Deadline November of each year.

[990]
FOUNDATION FOR DIGESTIVE HEALTH AND NUTRITION/AGA RESEARCH SCHOLAR AWARDS

Foundation for Digestive Health and Nutrition
Attn: Research Awards Program
4930 Del Ray Avenue
Bethesda, MD 20814-2512
(301) 222-4012 Fax: (301) 652-3890
E-mail: awards@fdhn.org
Web: www.fdhn.org/wmspage.cfm?parm1=103

Purpose To provide salary support for minority and other young investigators developing an independent career in an area of gastroenterology, hepatology, or related fields.
Eligibility Applicants must hold full-time faculty positions at North American universities or professional institutes at the time of application. They should be early in their careers (fellows and established investigators are not appropriate candidates). Candidates with an M.D. degree must have completed clinical training within the past 5 years and those with a Ph.D. must have completed postdoctoral training within the past 5 years. Membership in the American Gastroenterological Association (AGA) is required. Selection is based on novelty, feasibility, and significance of the proposal; attributes of the candidate, including potential for independence; evidence of institutional commitment; and the research environment. Special consideration is given to applications with a focus on nutrition or geriatrics. Women, minorities, and physician/scientist investigators are strongly encouraged to apply.
Financial data The grant is $75,000 per year. Funds are to be used for project costs, including salary, supplies, and equipment but excluding travel. Indirect costs are not allowed.
Duration 3 years.
Additional information This program is administered by the Foundation for Digestive Health and Nutrition (FDHN) and sponsored by the AGA. Funding is provided by TAP Pharmaceuticals, Inc., AstraZeneca Pharmaceuticals, L.P., Janssen Pharmaceutica Products, L.P., Johnson & Johnson/Merck Consumer Pharmaceuticals, Roche Pharmaceuticals, and Wyeth-Ayerst Laboratories. At least 70% of the recipient's research effort should relate to the gastrointestinal tract or liver. Recipients cannot hold or have held an R01, R29, K121, K08, VA Research Award, or any award with similar objectives from nonfederal sources.
Number awarded 6 each year.
Deadline September of each year.

[991]
FRANCES C. ALLEN FELLOWSHIPS
Newberry Library
Attn: McNickle Center for American Indian History
60 West Walton Street
Chicago, IL 60610-3305
(312) 255-3564 Fax: (312) 255-3513
E-mail: mcnickle@newberry.org
Web: www.newberry.org/mcnickle/frances.html

Purpose To provide funding to Native American women graduate students who wish to use the resources of the D'Arcy McNickle Center for the History of the American Indian at the Newberry Library.
Eligibility This program is open to women of American Indian heritage who are interested in using the library for a project appropriate to its collections. Applicants must be enrolled in a graduate or pre-professional program, especially in the humanities or social sciences. Recommendations are required; at least 2 must come from academic advisers or instructors who can comment on the significance of the applicant's proposed project and explain how it will help in the achievement of professional goals.
Financial data Grants range from $1,200 to $8,000 in approved expenses, which may include travel expenses.
Duration From 1 month to 1 year.
Additional information These grants were first awarded in 1983. Fellows must spend a significant portion of their time at the library's D'Arcy McNickle Center.
Number awarded Varies each year; recently, 4 of these fellowships were awarded.
Deadline February of each year.

[992]
FRONTIERS IN PHYSIOLOGY PROFESSIONAL DEVELOPMENT FELLOWSHIPS
American Physiological Society
Attn: Education Office
9650 Rockville Pike, Room 3111
Bethesda, MD 20814-3991
(301) 634-7132 Fax: (301) 634-7098
E-mail: education@the-aps.org
Web: www.the-aps.org/education/frontiers/index.htm

Purpose To provide an opportunity for minority and other middle/high school life science teachers to participate in a summer research project in physiology.
Eligibility This program is open to science teachers at middle schools (grades 6-9) and high schools (grades 9-12) who do not have recent (within 10 years) laboratory experience in physiology or the life sciences, do not have an advanced degree in laboratory science, and are not a candidate for an advanced degree in a laboratory science. Applicants do not need to have extensive mathematics skills, but they must be able to demonstrate a commitment to excellence in teaching, strong observation skills, and a desire to learn about research first-hand. Teachers who are members of minority groups underrepresented in science (African Americans, Hispanics, Native Americans, and Pacific Islanders) or who teach in schools with a predominance of underrepresented minority students are especially encouraged to apply. Teachers must apply jointly with a member of the American Physiological Society (APS) at a research institution in the same geographic area as their home and school. Selection is based on the quality of the summer research experience and potential long-term impact on teaching and on students.
Financial data For the summer research experience, teachers receive a stipend of $500 per week (to a maximum of $4,000), a grant of $250 for participation in the summer forum, a grant of $250 for development and field testing of new inquiry-based laboratory or lesson, $400 for completion of online reflections and reading assignments, and $100 for completion of project evaluation activities. For the remainder of the year, they receive $2,500 for reimbursement of travel costs to attend the Science Teaching Forum, $1,000 for reimbursement of travel costs to attend the Experimental Biology meeting, and $300 for materials to field-test a new inquiry-based laboratory or lesson. The maximum total value of the fellowship is $8,800.
Duration 1 year, including 7 to 8 weeks during the summer for participation in the research experience.
Additional information This program enables teachers to work on a summer research project in the laboratory of their APS sponsor, use the Internet to expand their repertory of teaching methods and their network of colleagues, and develop an inquiry-based classroom activity or laboratory, along with a corresponding web page. They also take a break from their summer research to attend a 1-week Science Teaching Forum in Washington D.C. where they work with APS staff, physiologists, and mentors to explore and practice effective teaching methods focused on how to integrate inquiry, equity, and the Internet into their classrooms. This program is supported by the National Center for Research Resources (NCRR) and the National Institute of Diabetes and Digestive and Kidney Diseases (NIDDK). both components of the National Institutes of Health (NIH).
Number awarded Varies each year; recently 17 of these fellowships were awarded.
Deadline January of each year.

[993]
GAIUS CHARLES BOLIN DISSERTATION FELLOWSHIPS
Williams College
Attn: Dean of the Faculty
Hopkins Hall
P.O. Box 141
Williamstown, MA 01267
(413) 597-4351 E-mail: Gail.Burda@williams.edu
Web: www.williams.edu

Purpose To provide financial assistance to Native Americans and other doctoral students from underrepresented groups at any school who are interested in teaching courses at Williams College while working on their dissertation.
Eligibility This program is open to graduate students from underrepresented groups who have completed all doctoral work except for the dissertation. Applicants must be working on a Ph.D. in the humanities or the natural, social, or behavioral sciences, and be willing to teach a course at Williams College. They must submit a full curriculum vitae, a graduate school transcript, 3 letters of recommendation, a copy of their dissertation prospectus, and a description of their teaching interests within a department or program at Williams College.

Financial data Fellows receive $33,000 for the academic year, plus housing assistance, office space, computer and library privileges, and a research allowance of up to $4,000.
Duration 1 academic year, beginning in September.
Additional information Bolin fellows are assigned a faculty advisor in the appropriate department. This program was established in 1985. Fellows are expected to teach a 1-semester course. They must be in residence at Williams College for the duration of the fellowship.
Number awarded 2 each year.
Deadline November of each year.

[994]
GEOPHYSICAL FLUID DYNAMICS FELLOWSHIPS
Woods Hole Oceanographic Institution
Attn: Education Office
Clark Laboratory 223, MS 31
360 Woods Hole Road
Woods Hole, MA 02543-1541
(508) 289-2219   Fax: (508) 457-2188
E-mail: gfd@whoi.edu
Web: gfd.whoi.edu/index.html

Purpose To provide research and study opportunities at Woods Hole Oceanographic Institution (WHOI) to minority and other pre- and postdoctoral scholars interested in geophysical fluid dynamics.
Eligibility This program is open to pre- and postdoctorates who are interested in pursuing research or study opportunities in a field that involves nonlinear dynamics of rotating, stratified fluids. Fields of specialization include oceanography, meteorology, geophysics, astrophysics, engineering, physics, and applied mathematics. Applications from women and members of underrepresented groups are particularly encouraged.
Financial data Participants receive a stipend of $4,900 and an allowance for travel expenses within the United States.
Duration 10 weeks during the summer.
Additional information Each summer, the program at WHOI revolves around a central theme. A recent theme related to boundary layers. The main components of the summer program are a series of principal lectures, a set of supplementary research seminars, and research projects conducted by the student fellows with the active support of the staff. Funding for this program, which began in 1959, is provided by the National Science Foundation and Office of Naval Research.
Number awarded Up to 10 graduate students are supported each year.
Deadline February of each year.

[995]
GEORGETOWN UNIVERSITY LAW CENTER LIBRARY RESIDENT PROGRAM
Georgetown University Law Center
Attn: Edward Bennett Williams Law Library
Attn: Association Law Librarian for Administration
111 G Street, N.W.
Washington, DC 20001
(202) 662-9162   Fax: (202) 662-9168
E-mail: libraryjobs@law.georgetown.edu
Web: www.ll.georgetown.edu/staff/resident/index.cfm

Purpose To provide an opportunity for members of Native Americans and other minority groups to learn more about law librarianship during a residency at Georgetown University Law Center.
Eligibility This program is open to members of minority groups (Asian American/Pacific Islander, Native American, Hispanic American, African American) who received an M.L.S. or equivalent from an ALA-accredited school and have no more than 2 years of experience as a professional librarian. Applicants must be interested in a residency at the Georgetown University Law Center in Washington, D.C. Along with their application, they must submit a resume, names of 3 references, library school or law school transcript, and a personal statement on their reasons for applying for the residency, career goals, and any other relevant information.
Financial data A competitive stipend is paid (amount not specified).
Duration 2 years.
Additional information Residents work with an experienced law librarian mentor in patron services, collection services, scholarly resources, and/or administrative services. They also assist patrons with legal research, create research guides, and teach legal research classes under the supervision of experienced librarians. During the second year, they design and carry out a significant research, instructional, or service-based project.
Number awarded 1 each year.
Deadline February of each year.

[996]
GERALD OSHITA MEMORIAL FELLOWSHIP
Djerassi Resident Artists Program
Attn: Admissions
2325 Bear Gulch Road
Woodside, CA 94062-4405
(650) 747-1250   Fax: (650) 747-0105
E-mail: drap@djerassi.org
Web: www.djerassi.org/oshita.html

Purpose To provide an opportunity for Native Americans and other composers of color to participate in the Djerassi Resident Artists Program.
Eligibility This program is open to composers of Asian, African, Latino, or Native American ethnic background. Applicants must be interested in utilizing a residency to compose, study, rehearse, and otherwise advance their own creative projects.
Financial data The fellow is offered housing, meals, studio space, and a stipend of $2,500.
Duration 4 to 5 weeks, from late March through mid-November.

[997]
GERBER FELLOWSHIP IN PEDIATRIC NUTRITION
National Medical Fellowships, Inc.
Attn: Scholarship Program
5 Hanover Square, 15th Floor
New York, NY 10004
(212) 483-8880   Fax: (212) 483-8897
E-mail: info@nmfonline.org
Web: www.nmfonline.org

Purpose To provide funding to Native American and other underrepresented minority medical students and residents who are interested in conducting research on pediatric nutrition.

Eligibility This program is open to African Americans, Native Hawaiians, Alaska Natives, American Indians, Mexican Americans, and mainland Puerto Ricans who are 1) students enrolled in accredited medical schools, 2) students enrolled in U.S. colleges of osteopathic medicine, or 3) medical residents in U.S. programs. Candidates must be nominated by their deans or graduate education directors. They must be participating in ongoing research in the area of pediatric nutrition. U.S. citizenship is required. Selection is based on academic achievement and motivation to prepare for a career in pediatric nutrition research.

Financial data The grant is $3,000.

Duration 1 year; nonrenewable.

Additional information This award was established in 1997 with grant support from the Gerber Companies Foundation.

Number awarded 1 each year.

Deadline October of each year.

[998]
GISA BERDACH RESEARCH GRANTS
Gay Indian Studies Association
Attn: Foundation
13730 Loumont Street
Whittier, CA 90601

Purpose To provide financial assistance to American Indian graduate students interested in conducting research on the phenomenon of berdaches in the southwestern United States.

Eligibility This program is open to graduate students who wish to conduct research (for a master's degree thesis or a doctoral dissertation) on the topic of berdaches (male Indians who lived as women) among the tribes of the southwestern United States. Applicants must be gay males who are enrolled members of a federally-recognized Indian tribal organization in the United States. They must be able to demonstrate a "congruence between their own personal experiences and the topic of their proposed research."

Financial data The grant is $10,000. Funds must be used for research purposes only; the research may be historical (in libraries and archives) or contemporary (involving field studies as well as library research).

Duration This is a 1-time grant.

Additional information Funding for this program is provided by the National Science Foundation. Requests for applications should be accompanied by a self-addressed stamped envelope, the student's e-mail address, and the source where they found the scholarship information.

Number awarded 2 or more each year.

Deadline December of each year.

[999]
GLENN-STOKES ACADEMIC YEAR RESEARCH INTERNSHIP PROGRAM
Ohio Science and Engineering Alliance
c/o Ohio State University
247 University Hall
230 North Oval Mall
Columbus, OH 43210-1366
(614) 247-7267
Web: www.ohiosea.org/research/ay_prog.html

Purpose To provide an opportunity for Native American and other underrepresented minority students at designated institutions in Ohio to work on a research project in a field of science, technology, engineering, or mathematics (STEM).

Eligibility This program is open to students at the 15 member institutions of the Ohio Science and Engineering Alliance (OSEA) who are members of underrepresented minority racial or ethnic groups (African Americans, Hispanics, American Indians, Pacific Islanders, and Puerto Ricans). Applicants must be interested in conducting a research project at their home university under the mentorship of a faculty member. The proposed research may relate to any approved STEM field.

Financial data The stipend is $1,800 per academic year ($600 per quarter or $900 per semester).

Duration 1 quarter, semester, or academic year.

Additional information The OSEA, funded by the National Science Foundation, consists of the following Ohio institutions: Bowling Green State University, Case Western Reserve University, Central State University, Cleveland State University, Kent State University, Miami University, Ohio State University, Ohio University, University of Akron, University of Cincinnati, University of Dayton, University of Toledo, Wilberforce University, Wright State University, and Youngstown State University. This program is named in honor of John Glenn (Ohio Senator and astronaut) and Louis Stokes (Ohio Congressman).

Number awarded Varies each year.

Deadline Applications may be submitted at any time, but they should be received at least 30 days prior to the beginning of the semester or quarter of the proposed research.

[1000]
GOALI FACULTY IN INDUSTRY AWARDS
National Science Foundation
Directorate for Engineering
Attn: Division of Industrial Innovation and Partnerships
4201 Wilson Boulevard, Room 550 S
Arlington, VA 22230
(703) 292-7082 Fax: (703) 292-9056
TDD: (800) 281-8749 E-mail: dsenich@nsf.gov
Web: www.nsf.gov

Purpose To provide funding to minority and other science, engineering, and mathematics faculty who wish to conduct research in an industrial setting as part of the Grant Opportunities for Academic Liaison with Industry (GOALI) program of the National Science Foundation (NSF).

Eligibility This program is open to full-time faculty members at U.S. colleges and universities in science, engineering, and mathematics fields of interest to NSF. Applicants must be U.S. citizens, nationals, or permanent residents. They must present a plan for collaboration between their institution and industry, with a description of the facilities and resources that will be available at the industrial site to support the proposed research. The program encourages applications from women, underrepresented minorities, and persons with disabilities.

Financial data Grants range from $30,000 to $75,000, including 50% of the faculty member's salary and fringe benefits during the industrial residency period. Up to 20% of the total requested amount may be used for travel and research expenses for the faculty and his/her students, including materials but excluding equipment. The industrial partner must commit to support the other 50% of the faculty salary and fringe benefits.

Duration 1 year.

Additional information This program is also offered by most other NSF directorates. Check the website for a name and e-mail address of the contact person in each directorate.

Number awarded A total of 60 to 80 grants for all GOALI programs is awarded each year; total funding is approximately $5 million.

Deadline Applications may be submitted at any time.

[1001]
GRADUATE FELLOWSHIP IN THE HISTORY OF SCIENCE
American Meteorological Society
Attn: Fellowship/Scholarship Program
45 Beacon Street
Boston, MA 02108-3693
(617) 227-2426, ext. 246 Fax: (617) 742-8718
E-mail: scholar@ametsoc.org
Web: www.ametsoc.org

Purpose To provide funding to minority and other graduate students interested in conducting dissertation research on the history of meteorology.

Eligibility This program is open to graduate students who are planning to complete a dissertation on the history of the atmospheric or related oceanic or hydrologic sciences. Applicants must be U.S. citizens or permanent residents and working on a degree at a U.S. institution. Fellowships may be used to support research at a location away from the student's institution, provided the plan is approved by the student's thesis adviser. In such an instance, an effort is made to place the student into a mentoring relationship with a member of the society at an appropriate institution. The sponsor specifically encourages applications from women, minorities, and students with disabilities who are traditionally underrepresented in the atmospheric and related oceanic sciences.

Financial data The stipend is $15,000.

Duration 1 year.

Number awarded 1 each year.

Deadline February of each year.

[1002]
GRADUATE STUDENT FELLOWSHIPS AT FDA
National Science Foundation
Directorate for Engineering
Attn: Division of Bioengineering and Environmental Systems
4201 Wilson Boulevard, Room 565 S
Arlington, VA 22230
(703) 292-7943 Fax: (703) 292-9098
TDD: (800) 281-8749 E-mail: gdevey@nsf.gov
Web: www.nsf.gov

Purpose To provide an opportunity for minority and other graduate students to conduct research at an intramural laboratory of the U.S. Food and Drug Administration (FDA).

Eligibility This program is open to graduate students (preferably Ph.D. students) in science, engineering, and mathematics fields of interest to the National Science Foundation (NSF). Applicants must be U.S. citizens, nationals, or permanent residents. They must be proposing a program of full- or part-time work at an FDA intramural laboratory in an area related to their research, conducted under the guidance of an academic adviser and an FDA mentor. The program encourages applications from women, underrepresented minorities, and persons with disabilities.

Financial data Graduate students may receive stipends from $1,500 to $1,800 per month, plus transportation expenses. The faculty adviser may receive 10% of the total award for research-related expenses, excluding equipment. The academic institution receives an allowance of 15% of total direct costs for administrative expenses. The total award may be up to $30,000 for a fellowship for a single student. FDA provides office space, research facilities, research costs in the form of expendable and minor equipment purchases in the host laboratory, and the time of its research staff.

Duration 1 to 4 semesters.

Additional information This program is also offered by the NSF Directorate for Computer and Information Science and Engineering; for information, contact its Division of Computer-Communications Research, (703) 292-8910, Fax: (703) 292-9059, E-mail: hgill@nsf.gov. The FDA contact is William A. Herman, Director, Division of Physical Sciences, Center for Devices and Radiological Health, 12725 Twinbrook Parkway, Rockville, MD 20852, (301)827-5599, E-mail: wah@cdrh.fda.gov.

Number awarded A total of 3 to 10 grants for all FDA programs is awarded each year; total funding is approximately $500,000.

Deadline March of each year.

[1003]
GRADUATE STUDENT FELLOWSHIPS IN AMERICAN INDIAN STUDIES

Newberry Library
Attn: McNickle Center for American Indian History
60 West Walton Street
Chicago, IL 60610-3305
(312) 255-3564 Fax: (312) 255-3513
E-mail: mcnickle@newberry.org
Web: www.newberry.org/mcnickle/darcyhome.html

Purpose To provide funding to doctoral students at member institutions of the Committee on Institutional Cooperation (CIC) who wish to conduct dissertation research in American Indian studies at the D'Arcy McNickle Center for the History of the American Indian at the Newberry Library.

Eligibility This program is open to advanced graduate students at CIC institutions who are interested in conducting dissertation research in American Indian studies at the Newberry Library. Applicants must submit their curriculum vitae, 2 letters of recommendation, and a 2- to 3-page summary of an approved dissertation proposal.

Financial data Grants provide a stipend of $1,500 per month.

Duration From 1 to 3 months.

Additional information The CIC institutions are Indiana University, Michigan State University, Northwestern University, Ohio State University, Pennsylvania State University, Purdue University, University of Chicago, University of Illinois at Chicago, University of Illinois at Urbana-Champaign, University of Iowa, University of Michigan, University of Minnesota, and University of Wisconsin at Madison. Fellows must spend a significant portion of their time at the library's D'Arcy McNickle Center.

Number awarded Varies each year; recently, 7 of these fellowships were awarded.

Deadline January of each year.

[1004]
GRANTS FOR HEALTH SERVICES RESEARCH DISSERTATIONS

Agency for Healthcare Research and Quality
Attn: Office of Extramural Research, Education, and Priority Populations
540 Gaither Road
Rockville, MD 20850
(301) 427-1527 Fax: (301) 427-1562
TTY: (301) 451-0088 E-mail: bharding@ahrq.gov
Web: www.ahrq.gov/fund

Purpose To provide funding to minority and other doctoral candidates engaged in research for a dissertation that examines an aspect of the health care system.

Eligibility This program is open to students enrolled in an accredited research doctoral degree (e.g., Ph.D., Sc.D., Dr.P.H., Ed.D.) program. Applicants must have completed all requirements for the doctoral degree other than the dissertation. The dissertation topic must relate to the strategic goals of the Agency for Healthcare Research and Quality (AHRQ) to enhance patient safety and quality of care. Priority is given to research on health issues related to designated populations, including individuals living in inner city and rural areas, low-income and minority groups, women, children, the elderly, and individuals with special health care needs (such as individuals with disabilities and individuals who need chronic care or end-of-life health care). U.S. citizenship or permanent resident status is required. Members of underrepresented racial and ethnic groups and individuals with disabilities are especially encouraged to apply.

Financial data Total direct costs may not exceed $35,000. Funds may be used for the investigator's salary, direct project expenses (travel, data purchasing, data processing, and supplies), and matriculation fees. The institution will receive facilities and administrative costs of 8% of total allowable direct costs exclusive of tuition and related fees, health insurance, and expenditures for equipment.

Duration 9 to 17 months.

Number awarded Up to 30 each year.

Deadline February, June, or October of each year.

[1005]
HAROLD AMOS MEDICAL FACULTY DEVELOPMENT PROGRAM

Robert Wood Johnson Foundation
College Road East and U.S. Route 1
P.O. Box 2316
Princeton, NJ 08543-2316
(609) 452-8701 Toll-free: (877) 843-RWJF
E-mail: mail@rwjf.org
Web: www.rwjf.org

Purpose To provide funding to physicians from historically disadvantaged backgrounds who are interested in preparing for a career in academic medicine.

Eligibility This program is open to physicians who are now completing or have completed their formal clinical training; preference is given to physicians who have recently completed their formal clinical training. Applicants must be from a background that is historically disadvantaged, defined to refer to challenges they have faced because of their race, ethnicity, socioeconomic status, gender, or similar factors. They must be interested in a program of postdoctoral training and research to prepare for a career in academic medicine in which they will be able to serve as role models for other students and faculty from historically disadvantaged backgrounds, improve the health status of the underserved, and/or decrease health disparities. U.S. citizenship or permanent resident status is required.

Financial data Scholars receive an annual stipend of up to $75,000 and an annual grant of $30,000 toward support of research activities.

Duration 4 years.

Additional information Information is also available from the national program office, 714 North Senate Avenue, EF212, Indianapolis, IN 46202, (317) 278-0500, Fax: (317) 278-0508, E-mail: amfdp@indiana.edu.

Number awarded Up to 12 each year.

Deadline March of each year.

[1006]
HEALTH DISPARITY RESEARCH AWARDS IN PROSTATE CANCER

U.S. Army
Medical Research and Materiel Command
Attn: MCMR-ZB-C
1077 Patchel Street (Building 1077)
Fort Detrick, MD 21702-5024
(301) 619-7079　　　　　　　Fax: (301) 619-7792
E-mail: cdmrp.pa@amedd.army.mil
Web: cdmrp.army.mil/funding/pcrp.htm

Purpose To provide funding to minority and other scientists interested in conducting research related to health disparities in prostate cancer.

Eligibility This program is open to independent investigators at universities, colleges, hospitals, laboratories, companies, and agencies of local, state, and federal governments. The sponsor is especially interested in receiving applications from Historically Black Colleges and Universities and Minority Institutions (HBCU/MI). Applicants must be interested in conducting research to resolve disparities in prostate cancer incidence, morbidity, and mortality. They may be at 1 of 3 career levels; 1) transitioning investigators who have a Ph.D. and/or M.D. degree, have received no more than $300,000 in direct costs on prior grants, have less than 3 years since they started their first independent faculty position, and have a designated mentor with experience in prostate cancer health disparity research; 2) early-career investigators who have received no more than $300,000 in direct costs on prior grants, are within 6 years of completion of postdoctoral or fellowship training, have a position at the level of instructor or assistant professor, and are encouraged to have a collaborator with appropriate prostate cancer or health disparity research experience; 3) established investigators who have 6 or more years of experience since completion of postdoctoral or fellowship training, have access to facilities appropriate for health disparity research, and may have a collaborator with prostate cancer or health disparity research experience. The experience of collaborators may include being a member of the affected population or community with a demonstrated commitment to the affected population or community; having experience working with the affected population or community; or having interactions with or active membership in such organizations as the Urban League, National Medical Association, National Alliance for Hispanic Health, American Indian Health Care Association, National Rural Health Association, Patient Advocate Foundation, National African American Outreach Program, or Prostate Health Education Network. Appropriate disparity focus areas include, but are not limited to, race and ethnicity, socioeconomic status, access to health care, insurance status, age, geography, and cultural beliefs.

Financial data For transitioning investigators and early-career investigators, grants range up to $225,000 for direct costs over the term of the award, plus indirect costs as appropriate. For established investigators, grants range up to $375,000 for direct costs over the term of the award, plus indirect costs as appropriate.

Duration 3 years.

Additional information The Prostate Cancer Research Program was established in 1997 as part of the Congressionally Directed Medical Research Programs (CDMRP) of the U.S. Department of Defense. The Health Disparity Research Award mechanism was introduced in 2001.

Number awarded Approximately 8 each year. Approximately $3.2 million is available for this program annually.

Deadline Pre-applications must be submitted by June of each year; full proposals are due in early July.

[1007]
HIGH RISK RESEARCH IN ANTHROPOLOGY GRANTS

National Science Foundation
Social, Behavioral, and Economic Sciences
Attn: Division of Behavioral and Cognitive Sciences
4201 Wilson Boulevard, Room 995
Arlington, VA 22230
(703) 292-7315　　　　　　　Fax: (703) 292-9068
TDD: (800) 281-8749　　　　E-mail: dwinslow@nsf.gov
Web: www.nsf.gov

Purpose To provide funding to minority and other scholars interested in conducting high-risk research in anthropology.

Eligibility This program is open to scholars interested in conducting research projects in cultural anthropology, archaeology, or physical anthropology that might be considered too risky for normal review procedures. A project is considered risky if the data may not be obtainable in spite of all reasonable preparation on the researcher's part. Proposals for extremely urgent research where access to the data may not be available in the normal review schedule, even with all reasonable preparation by the researcher, are also appropriate for this program. Graduate students are not eligible. Applications are encouraged from women, underrepresented minorities, and persons with disabilities.

Financial data Grants up to $25,000, including indirect costs, are available.

Number awarded Generally, 5 of these grants are awarded each year.

Deadline Applications may be submitted at any time.

[1008]
HISTORICALLY BLACK COLLEGES AND UNIVERSITIES AND OTHER MINORITY INSTITUTIONS EDUCATION AND TRAINING PROGRAM IN FOSSIL ENERGY

Department of Energy
Attn: National Energy Technology Laboratory
3610 Collins Ferry Road
P.O. Box 880
Morgantown, WV 26507
(304) 285-4721
E-mail: robert.romanosky@netl.doe.gov
Web: fossil.energy.gov/education/index.html

Purpose To provide support to researchers at minority institutions for research projects on advanced coal, oil, and natural gas concepts.

Eligibility Applications are solicited from federally-recognized HBCUs and other minority institutions to conduct research projects on fossil energy. Proposals must involve collaboration with an industrial partner, and each research team must include a teaching professor and at least 30% of personnel time must be to pay for student

assistance. Recently, priority has been given to research on sensors and controls, computational energy sources, and advanced materials for power generation and for hydrogen separation and storage.
Financial data Grant amounts vary; recently, total project awards were $200,000.
Duration Funding is normally provided for 3 years.
Additional information This program, which began in 1984, is supported by the Office of Fossil Energy within the U.S. Department of Energy.
Number awarded Approximately 4 to 5 grants are awarded each year.
Deadline January of each year.

[1009]
HOWARD HUGHES MEDICAL INSTITUTE RESEARCH TRAINING FELLOWSHIPS FOR MEDICAL STUDENTS

Howard Hughes Medical Institute
Attn: Office of Grants and Special Programs
4000 Jones Bridge Road
Chevy Chase, MD 20815-6789
(301) 215-8889   Toll-free: (800) 448-4882, ext. 8889
Fax: (301) 215-8888   E-mail: fellows@hhmi.org
Web: www.hhmi.org

Purpose To provide financial assistance to Native American and other medical, dental, and veterinary students interested in pursuing research training.
Eligibility Applicants must be enrolled in a medical, dental, or veterinary school in the United States, although they may be citizens of any country. They must describe a proposed research project to be conducted at an academic or nonprofit research institution in the United States, other than a facility of the National Institutes of Health in Bethesda, Maryland. Research proposals should reflect the interests of the Howard Hughes Medical Institute (HHMI), especially in biochemistry, bioinformatics, biomedical engineering, biophysics, biostatistics, cell biology, developmental biology, epidemiology, genetics, immunology, mathematical and computational biology, microbiology, molecular biology, neuroscience, pharmacology, physiology, structural biology, or virology. Applications from women and minorities underrepresented in the sciences (Blacks, Hispanics, American Indians, Native Alaskans, and Native Pacific Islanders) are especially encouraged. Students enrolled in M.D./Ph.D., Ph.D., or Sc.D. programs and those who have completed a Ph.D. or Sc.D. in a laboratory-based science are not eligible. Selection is based on the applicant's ability and promise for a research career as a physician-scientist and the quality of training that will be provided.
Financial data Fellows receive a stipend of $27,000 per year; their institution receives an institutional allowance of $5,500 and a research allowance of $5,500.
Duration 1 year.
Additional information This program complements the HHMI-NIH Research Scholars Program; students may not apply to both programs in the same year.
Number awarded Up to 66 each year.
Deadline January of each year.

[1010]
HUD URBAN SCHOLARS POSTDOCTORAL FELLOWSHIP PROGRAM

National Research Council
Attn: Fellowships Office, GR 346A
500 Fifth Street, N.W.
Washington, DC 20001
(202) 334-2872   Fax: (202) 334-3419
E-mail: infofell@nas.edu
Web: www7.nationalacademies.org

Purpose To provide funding to minority and other recent postdoctorates interested in conducting research on topics of interest to the U.S. Department of Housing and Urban Development (HUD).
Eligibility Applicants must have received a Ph.D. degree within the past 7 years and currently have an academic appointment at an institution of higher learning. They must be interested in conducting research on 1 of HUD's strategic goals for the year; recently, those goals included topics related to providing increased homeownership and rental opportunities for low- and moderate-income persons with disabilities, the elderly, minorities, and families with limited English proficiency; improving our nation's communities; encouraging accessible design features; providing full and equal access to grass-roots faith-based and other community-based organizations; improved housing conditions for families living in colonies (rural communities located within 150 miles of the border between the United States and Mexico), Appalachia, the Mississippi Delta, and tribal areas; participation in minority-serving institutions in HUD programs; participation in the HUD Energy Star program; ending chronic homelessness; ensuring equal opportunity in housing; or embracing high standards of ethics, management, and accountability. Applicants must work with a mentor, who can be someone in their institution or elsewhere but must be a well-respected scholar in the area of the proposed research. Selection is based on appropriateness of the methodology and approach to the topic (25 points), need for the research (20 points), relevance of the research to HUD's strategic goals (15 points), applicant's capacity to do the research (15 points), commitment of the university (10 points), likelihood of timely completion of the research project (10 points), and quality of the mentoring plan (5 points).
Financial data The maximum grant is $55,000. The following items may be included: salary for 1 summer and the last 3 months of the fellowship; graduate assistants to work on the project; up to $2,500 per course for the cost of employing a replacement for the courses if the university relieves the applicant from teaching responsibilities; computer software, survey development and administration, and the purchase of data; travel expenses to collect data or to make presentations at meetings on findings; transcription services and compensation for interviews; and up to 8% for the university's indirect costs.
Duration Up to 15 months.
Number awarded Approximately 10 each year.
Deadline December of each year.

[1011]
INDEPENDENT SCIENTIST AWARDS

National Institutes of Health
Office of Extramural Research
Attn: Grants Information
6705 Rockledge Drive
Bethesda, MD 20892-7974
(301) 435-0714   Fax: (301) 480-0525
TTY: (301) 451-0088   E-mail: NIHTrain@mail.nih.gov
Web: grants.nih.gov/grants/guide/index.html

Purpose To provide financial support to minority and other scientists in health-related fields who have recently become independent investigators and are seeking funding for research.

Eligibility This program is open to candidates who have a doctoral degree and peer-reviewed, independent research support at the time the award is made. They must be willing to spend a minimum of 75% of full-time professional effort conducting research and research career development activities for the period of the award. Candidates must demonstrate that the requested period of research focus will foster their career as highly productive scientists in the indicated field of research. Applications may be submitted on behalf of candidates by domestic, nonfederal public or private organizations, such as universities, colleges, hospitals, or laboratories. Members of underrepresented ethnic and racial groups, individuals with disabilities, and individuals from disadvantaged backgrounds are especially encouraged to apply. Only U.S. citizens, nationals, and permanent residents are eligible.

Financial data This program provides salary and fringe benefits for the candidate only; each component establishes its own salary limits on career awards. Facilities and administrative costs are reimbursed at 8% of modified total direct costs, or at the actual indirect cost rate, whichever is less.

Duration 3, 4, or 5 years.

Additional information Awards under this program are available from 13 agencies of the National Institutes of Health (NIH): the National Institute on Aging, the National Institute on Alcohol Abuse and Alcoholism, the National Institute of Allergy and Infectious Diseases, the National Institute of Arthritis and Musculoskeletal and Skin Diseases, the National Institute of Child Health and Human Development, the National Institute on Deafness and Other Communication Disorders, the National Institute of Dental and Craniofacial Research, the National Institute of Neurological Disorders and Stroke, the National Institute on Drug Abuse, the National Institute of Environmental Health Sciences, the National Heart, Lung, and Blood Institute, the National Institute of Mental Health, and the Office of Dietary Supplements. The names and addresses of staff people at each agency are available from NIH Grants Information.

Number awarded Varies each year.

Deadline February, June, or October of each year.

[1012]
INDUSTRY STUDIES FELLOWSHIPS

Alfred P. Sloan Foundation
630 Fifth Avenue, Suite 2550
New York, NY 10111-0242
(212) 649-1649   Fax: (212) 757-5117
E-mail: pesyna@sloan.org
Web: www.sloan.org/programs/fellow_announ.shtml

Purpose To provide funding to minority and other scholars interested in conducting research related to the field of industry studies.

Eligibility This program is open to faculty members at colleges and universities in Canada and the United States who have a Ph.D. in economics, management, engineering, political science, sociology, or a related or interdisciplinary field. Applicants may be no more than 6 years from completion of their most recent Ph.D. and normally should not have tenure. They must be interested in conducting research that relates to "the complex systems of companies, product and labor markets, institutions and their interactions that shape the multifaceted environment of modern industrial enterprises." Their research record should demonstrate past efforts to develop an understanding of the markets, firms, and institutions that characterize a particular industry. The proposed research may be multidisciplinary or it may contribute to a single discipline; narrowly technical research within a single discipline does not usually qualify. The sponsor strongly encourages the participation of women and members of underrepresented minority groups.

Financial data The grant is $45,000 for the full period.

Duration 2 years.

Number awarded Up to 5 each year.

Deadline October of each year.

[1013]
INSTITUTE FOR RESEARCH ON POVERTY VISITING SCHOLARS PROGRAM

University of Wisconsin at Madison
Attn: Institute for Research on Poverty
3412 Social Science Building
1180 Observatory Drive
Madison, WI 53706-1393
(608) 262-6358   Fax: (608) 265-3119
E-mail: rsnell@ssc.wisc.edu
Web: www.irp.wisc.edu

Purpose To provide Native American and other minority scholars with an opportunity to visit the Institute for Research on Poverty (IRP) at the University of Wisconsin at Madison.

Eligibility This program is open to minority scholars in the social sciences, especially those in the beginning years of their academic careers. Applicants should submit a letter describing their poverty research interests and experience, the proposed dates for a visit, a current curriculum vitae, and 2 examples of written material.

Financial data The program provides transportation, lodging, and meal expenses.

Duration 1 to 2 weeks.

Additional information During their visit, scholars are invited to give a seminar, to work on their own projects, and to confer with an IRP adviser who will arrange for an interchange with other IRP affiliates.

Number awarded Up to 3 each year.
Deadline June of each year.

[1014]
INSTITUTIONAL RESEARCH AND ACADEMIC CAREER DEVELOPMENT AWARDS

National Institute of General Medical Sciences
Attn: Division of Minority Opportunities in Research
45 Center Drive, Suite 2AS37
Bethesda, MD 20892-6200
(301) 594-3900   Fax: (301) 480-2753
TTY: (301) 451-0088   E-mail: poodryc@nigms.nih.gov
Web: www.nigms.nih.gov/Research/Funding

Purpose To provide an opportunity for minority and other postdoctoral biomedical scientists to gain experience at a research-intensive institution while they complete a teaching assignment at a Minority Serving Institution (MSI).
Eligibility This program is open to members of minority groups underrepresented in the biomedical and behavioral sciences, defined as African Americans, Hispanic Americans, Native Americans (including Alaska Natives), and natives of the U.S. Pacific Islands. Candidates must have a Ph.D., M.D., or comparable doctoral degree, be committed to research, and have the potential to develop as independent investigators. They must be interested in a mentored research experience typical of other competitive postdoctoral opportunities, combined with a mentored teaching experience at an MSI.
Financial data Grants up to $500,000 per year are available. Funding includes salary support for the scholar at a rate consistent with the established salary structure at the sponsoring institution, research development support (e.g., tuition and fees related to career development, supplies and other modest research expenses, travel to a scientific meeting, statistical services such as personnel and computer time), academic development support, and program administration. Facilities and administrative costs are reimbursed at 8% of modified total direct costs.
Duration 1 or more years.
Additional information The National Institute of General Medical Sciences, a component of the National Institutes of Health (NIH), operates this program as part of its Minority Opportunities for Research (MORE) Division. Scholars are expected to devote approximately 25% of their time to their teaching experience.
Number awarded 1 or 2 each year.
Deadline September of each year.

[1015]
ISAAC "IKE" CRUMBLY MINORITIES IN ENERGY GRANT

American Association of Petroleum Geologists Foundation
Attn: GIA Coordinator
1444 South Boulder Avenue
P.O. Box 979
Tulsa, OK 74101-0979
(918) 560-2644   Toll-free: (888) 945-2274, ext. 644
Fax: (918) 560-2642   E-mail: rgriffin@aapg.org
Web: foundation.aapg.org/gia/crumbly.cfm

Purpose To provide funding to minority and female graduate students who are interested in conducting research related to earth science aspects of the petroleum industry.
Eligibility This program is open to women and ethnic minorities (Black, Hispanic, Asian, or Native American, including American Indian, Eskimo, Hawaiian, or Samoan) who are working on a master's or doctoral degree and interested in conducting research related to the search for and development of petroleum and energy-minerals resources and to related environmental geology issues. Selection is based on merit and, in part, on financial need. Factors weighed in selecting the successful applicants include: the applicant's past academic performance, originality and imagination of the proposed project, departmental support, and significance of the project to petroleum, energy minerals, and related environmental geology.
Financial data Grants range from $500 to $3,000. Funds are to be applied to research-related expenses (e.g., a summer of field work). They may not be used to purchase capital equipment or to pay salaries, tuition, room, or board.
Duration 1 year. Doctoral candidates may receive a 1-year renewal.
Number awarded 1 each year.
Deadline January of each year.

[1016]
JDRF FACULTY GRANT

American Society of Transplantation
Attn: Chair, Awards and Grants Committee
15000 Commerce Parkway, Suite C
Mt. Laurel, NJ 08054
(856) 439-9986   Fax: (856) 439-9982
E-mail: ast@ahint.com
Web: cmeplanning.com/ast/event/category/10

Purpose To provide funding for research to minority and other junior members of the American Society of Transplantation (AST) who are interested in conducting research related to juvenile diabetes.
Eligibility This program is open to AST members who have an M.D., D.O., Ph.D., D.V.M. or equivalent graduate degree and have completed postgraduate training. Applicants must have an academic appointment at an accredited institution of higher education and be within 5 years of their initial faculty appointment. They must be citizens, permanent residents, or lawfully-admitted foreign nationals of Canada, Mexico, or the United States. Their proposed research project must involve the application of transplantation, understanding, and treatment of juvenile onset (i.e., type I) diabetes mellitus (e.g., studies of islet transplantation, autoimmunity). Research topics that involve underre-

presented areas (e.g., minorities, women) are strongly encouraged. The AST also encourages applications from women and underrepresented minority investigators.
Financial data The grant is $40,000 per year. No more than 15% of funding can be used for indirect costs.
Duration 2 years.
Additional information This program is jointly sponsored by the American Society of Transplantation (AST) and the Juvenile Diabetes Research Foundation (JDRF).
Number awarded 1 or more each year.
Deadline December of each year.

[1017]
JEFFREY CAMPBELL GRADUATE FELLOWS PROGRAM

St. Lawrence University
Attn: Human Resources/Office of Equity Programs
Jeffrey Campbell Graduate Fellowship Program
Canton, NY 13617
(315) 229-5509   E-mail: humanresources@stlawu.edu
Web: www.stlawu.edu

Purpose To provide funding to Native American and other minority graduate students who have completed their course work and are interested in conducting research at St. Lawrence University in New York.
Eligibility This program is open to graduate students who are members of racial or ethnic groups historically underrepresented at the university and in American higher education. Applicants must have completed their course work and preliminary examinations for the Ph.D. They must be interested in working on their dissertations or terminal degree projects while in residence at the University.
Financial data The stipend is $28,500 per academic year. Additional funds may be available to support travel to conferences and professional meetings. Office space and a personal computer are provided.
Duration 1 academic year.
Additional information This program is named for 1 of the university's early African American graduates. Recipients must teach 1 course a semester in a department or program at St. Lawrence University related to their research interests. In addition, they must present a research-based paper in the fellows' lecture series each semester.
Deadline January of each year.

[1018]
JOHN HOPE FRANKLIN DISSERTATION FELLOWSHIP

American Philosophical Society
Attn: Committee on Research
104 South Fifth Street
Philadelphia, PA 19106-3387
(215) 440-3429   Fax: (215) 440-3436
E-mail: LMusumeci@amphilsoc.org
Web: www.amphilsoc.org

Purpose To provide funding to Native American and other underrepresented minority graduate students conducting research for a doctoral dissertation.
Eligibility This program is open to African American, Hispanic American, and Native American graduate students working on a degree at a Ph.D. granting institution in the United States. Other talented students who have a demonstrated commitment to eradicating racial disparities and enlarging minority representation in academia are also eligible. Applicants must have completed all course work and examinations preliminary to the doctoral dissertation and be able to devote full-time effort, with no teaching obligations, to researching or writing their dissertation. The proposed research should relate to a topic in which the holdings of the Library of the American Philosophical Society (APS) are particularly strong: quantum mechanics, nuclear physics, computer development, the history of genetics and eugenics, the history of medicine, Early American political and cultural history, natural history in the 18th and 19th centuries, the development of cultural anthropology, or American Indian culture and linguistics.
Financial data The grant is $25,000; an additional grant of $5,000 is provided to support the cost of residency in Philadelphia.
Duration 12 months, to begin at the discretion of the grantee.
Additional information This program was established in 2005. Recipients are expected to spend a significant amount of time in residence at the APS Library.
Number awarded 1 each year.
Deadline March of each year.

[1019]
JOHN MERRILL TRANSPLANT SCHOLAR GRANT

American Society of Transplantation
Attn: Chair, Awards and Grants Committee
15000 Commerce Parkway, Suite C
Mt. Laurel, NJ 08054
(856) 439-9986   Fax: (856) 439-9982
E-mail: ast@ahint.com
Web: cmeplanning.com/ast/event/category/10

Purpose To provide funding for research to minority and other junior members of the American Society of Transplantation (AST) and the American Society of Nephrology (ASN) who are interested in conducting biomedical research.
Eligibility This program is open to investigators who are members of both AST and ASN. Applicants must have an M.D., Ph.D., or equivalent graduate degree and be within 7 years of their initial faculty appointment at an accredited institution of higher education. They must be citizens, permanent residents, or lawfully-admitted foreign nationals of Canada, Mexico, or the United States. Their proposed research must involve a biomedical study related to transplantation. Research topics that involve underrepresented areas (minorities, women, and pediatrics) are strongly encouraged. The AST also encourages applications from women and underrepresented minority investigators. Selection is based on scientific merit of the project and the applicant's prior training, productivity, and independence.
Financial data The grant is $100,000 per year. No more than 10% of funding can be used for indirect costs.
Duration 2 years.
Number awarded 1 each year.
Deadline January of each year.

[1020]
JUVENILE DIABETES RESEARCH FOUNDATION SCHOLAR AWARDS

Juvenile Diabetes Research Foundation
Attn: Grant Administrator
120 Wall Street, 19th Floor
New York, NY 10005-4001
(212) 479-7572　　　　Toll-free: (800) 533-CURE
Fax: (212) 785-9595　　　E-mail: info@jdrf.org
Web: www.jdrf.org/index.cfm?page_id=103207

Purpose To provide funding to minority and other established independent physician scientists interested in conducting basic or clinical diabetes-related research.

Eligibility This program is open to established investigators in diabetes-related research who have an M.D., D.M.D., D.O., Ph.D., D.V.M., or equivalent degree and an independent investigator position at a university, health science center, or comparable institution. Normally, applicants should have at least 7 years of relevant experience since receiving their doctoral degree. They must be willing to take risks and attempt new approaches to accelerate Type 1 diabetes research. This program is not intended to expand the funding of scientists already well supported for exploring this concept. There are no citizenship requirements. Applications are encouraged from women, members of minority groups underrepresented in the sciences, and people with disabilities. The proposed research may be conducted at foreign or domestic, for-profit or nonprofit, or public or private institutions, including universities, colleges, hospitals, laboratories, units of state or local government, or eligible agencies of the federal government. Selection is based on relevance on the research to and impact on the mission of the Juvenile Diabetes Research Foundation (JDRF); innovation, creativity, and the potential for future innovation relative to the applicant's career stage; and the applicant's motivation, enthusiasm, and intellectual energy to pursue a challenging problem.

Financial data The total award may be up to $250,000 each year, including indirect costs.

Duration Up to 5 years.

Number awarded Up to 4 each year.

Deadline An intent to submit must be received by August of each year. Completed applications are due in September.

[1021]
KATRIN H. LAMON FELLOWSHIP

School for Advanced Research
Attn: Director of Academic Programs
660 Garcia Street
P.O. Box 2188
Santa Fe, NM 87504-2188
(505) 954-7201　　　　E-mail: scholar@sarsf.org
Web: www.sarweb.org/scholars/description.htm

Purpose To provide funding for Native American scholars and graduate students who would benefit from a residency at the School of American Research in Santa Fe, New Mexico.

Eligibility Eligible to apply are Native Americans who are interested in conducting research from the perspective of anthropology or from anthropologically-informed perspectives in allied fields, such as history, sociology, art, law, and philosophy. They may be postdoctoral scholars, retired scholars, or Ph.D. candidates who are working on their dissertation. Selection is based on overall excellence and significance of the proposed project, clarity of presentation, and applicant's record of academic accomplishment. Preference is given to applicants whose field work or basic research and analysis are complete and who need time to write up their research.

Financial data Fellowships provide apartments and offices on the campus of the School of American Research, a stipend up to $40,000, library assistance, and other benefits.

Duration 9 months, beginning in September.

Additional information Participants are given an opportunity to interact with scholars, visiting anthropologists, and staff at the School for Advanced Research. Funding for this program is provided by the Katrin H. Lamon Endowment for Native American Art and Education. Participants must spend their 9-month residency at the school in New Mexico.

Number awarded 1 each year.

Deadline October of each year.

[1022]
KING-CHAVEZ-PARKS VISITING PROFESSORS PROGRAM

University of Michigan
Attn: Office of the Senior Vice Provost—Academic
　Affairs
503 Thompson Street
3084 Fleming Administration Building
Ann Arbor, MI 48109-1340
(734) 764-3982　　　　Fax: (734) 764-4546
E-mail: provost@umich.edu
Web: www.provost.umich.edu

Purpose To provide an opportunity for Native American and other minority scholars to visit and teach at the University of Michigan.

Eligibility Outstanding minority (African American, Asian/Pacific American, Latino/a (Hispanic) American, and Native American) postdoctorates or scholars/practitioners are eligible to be nominated by University of Michigan department chairs or deans to visit and lecture there. Nominations that include collaborations with other educational institutions in Michigan are of high priority.

Financial data Visiting Professors receive round-trip transportation and an appropriate honorarium.

Duration Visits range from 1 to 5 days.

Additional information This program was established in 1986. Visiting Professors are expected to lecture or teach at the university, offer at least 1 event open to the general public, and meet with minority campus/community groups, including local K-12 schools.

Number awarded Varies each year.

Deadline January for the summer term; March for the fall term; August for the winter term; and November for the spring term.

[1023]
LASPACE RESEARCH INITIATION GRANTS PROGRAM

Louisiana Space Consortium
c/o Louisiana State University
Department of Physics and Astronomy
371 Nicholson Hall
Baton Rouge, LA 70803-4001
(225) 578-8697　　　　　　　Fax: (225) 578-1222
E-mail: laspace@lsu.edu
Web: laspace.lsu.edu/grantopps.html

Purpose To provide seed grant funding for research to minority and other faculty at Louisiana Space Consortium (LaSPACE) institutions that are 4-year colleges without major graduate programs or Minority Serving Institutions.

Eligibility This program is open to faculty at LaSPACE member schools that are 4-year colleges without major graduate programs or HBCUs. Applicants may be proposing projects to provide research support for such aerospace-related activities as pre-proposal travel to a National Aeronautics and Space Administration (NASA) field center, support for a graduate student to join a faculty member at a NASA field center for part of a summer term, support to develop a new research project among scientists at several LaSPACE campuses, or development of new interdisciplinary areas of research or technology that can contribute to the NASA mission. A goal of NASA is to increase diversity in science, technology, engineering, and mathematics (STEM) disciplines. Traditionally, minority groups, women, and people with disabilities have been underrepresented in STEM disciplines; applicants are encouraged to help address the diversity objective. Selection is based on scientific and technical merit of the proposed project; relevance of the proposal to aerospace goals and alignment with the NASA mission; contribution of the proposed project to increasing diversity, particularly underrepresented groups, women, and persons with disabilities; competency of the project personnel, with emphasis on the potential degree of enhancement and of the probability for the project to lead to increased competitiveness and subsequently funded work; degree to which new research directions and capabilities are to be developed; and degree to which the project will contribute to workforce development and human capital needs, both locally and nationally.

Financial data The maximum grant is $20,000. Funds may be used for summer salary, student support, laboratory supplies, and research travel. A match of 2:1 (i.e., $1 in match for every $2 in LaSPACE funds requested) is required.

Duration 1 year or less.

Additional information The LaSPACE member institutions eligible for this program are Dillard University, Grambling State University, Loyola University, McNeese State University, Nicholls State University, Northwestern State University of Louisiana, Southeastern Louisiana University, Southern University and A&M College, Southern University in New Orleans, University of Louisiana at Monroe, and Xavier University of Louisiana. Funding for this program is provided by NASA.

Number awarded Varies each year.

Deadline Applications are accepted on a first-come, first-served basis.

[1024]
LAW AND SOCIAL SCIENCE DOCTORAL DISSERTATION FELLOWSHIPS

American Bar Foundation
Attn: Assistant Director
750 North Lake Shore Drive
Chicago, IL 60611
(312) 988-6560　　　　　　　Fax: (312) 988-6579
E-mail: fellowships@abfn.org
Web: www.abf-sociolegal.org/abffellow.html

Purpose To provide funding to minority and other doctoral candidates who wish to conduct research on law, the legal profession, and legal institutions.

Eligibility Applications are invited from outstanding students who are candidates for a Ph.D. degree in the social sciences. They must have completed all doctoral requirements except the dissertation. Proposed research must be in the general area of sociolegal studies or in social scientific approaches to law, the legal profession, or legal institutions. The dissertation must address critical issues in the field and show promise of making a major contribution to social scientific understanding of law and legal processes. Applications must include 1) transcripts of graduate work; 2) 2 letters of recommendation; 3) a curriculum vitae; and 4) a dissertation prospectus or proposal with an outline of the substance and methodology of the intended research. Minority students are especially encouraged to apply.

Financial data The stipend is $25,000 per year. Fellows also may request up to $1,500 each fellowship year to reimburse expenses associated with dissertation research, travel to meet with dissertation advisers, and travel to conferences at which papers are presented. Relocation expenses of up to $1,000 may be reimbursed on application.

Duration 1 year; may be renewed for 1 additional year.

Additional information Fellows are offered access to the computing and word processing facilities of the American Bar Foundation and the libraries of Northwestern University and the University of Chicago. This program was established in 1987. Fellowships must be held in residence at the American Bar Foundation. Appointments to the fellowship are full time; fellows are not permitted to undertake other work.

Number awarded 2 each year.

Deadline January of each year.

[1025]
LEO GOLDBERG FELLOWSHIPS

National Optical Astronomy Observatories
Attn: Human Resources Office
950 North Cherry Avenue
P.O. Box 26732
Tucson, AZ 85726-6732
(520) 318-8o00　　　　　　　Fax: (520) 318-8494
E-mail: hrnoao@noao.edu
Web: www.noao.edu/goldberg/fellows.html

Purpose To provide an opportunity for minority and other postdoctorates in astronomy to conduct research at the facilities of the National Optical Astronomy Observatories (NOAO) in Arizona or Chile.

Eligibility This program is open to recent Ph.D. recipients in observational astronomy, astronomical instrumentation, or theoretical astrophysics. Applicants must be interested in conducting a research program of their own choosing or participating in a current NOAO initiative at Kitt Peak National Observatory (KPNO) near Tucson, Arizona or Cerro Tololo Inter-American Observatory (CTIO) in La Serena, Chile. Women and candidates from underrepresented minorities are particularly encouraged to apply. Selection is based on the applicants' promise for an outstanding career in astronomy, their proposed use of KPNO or CTIO facilities, the relationship of their research to a proposed interaction with NOAO programs to plan the next generation of community facilities, and the relationship of their research to programs conducted by NOAO staff.

Financial data A competitive salary is paid. Additional support is provided to fellows and their families in Chile.

Duration 5 years. The first 4 years are spent either at Kitt Peak or in La Serena; the final year is spent at an U.S. university or astronomical institute willing to host the fellow.

Additional information NOAO is supported under a contract between the National Science Foundation and the Association of Universities for Research in Astronomy, Inc. This program was formerly known as the NOAO 5-Year Science Fellowship.

Number awarded 1 each year.

Deadline November of each year.

[1026]
LEROY C. MERRITT HUMANITARIAN FUND AWARD

LeRoy C. Merritt Humanitarian Fund
Attn: Secretary
50 East Huron Street
Chicago, IL 60611
(312) 280-4226   Toll-free: (800) 545-2433, ext. 4226
Fax: (312) 280-4227   E-mail: merrittfund@ala.org
Web: www.merrittfund.org

Purpose To provide financial support to librarians facing discrimination on the basis of race, sex, or other factors.

Eligibility The fund was established in 1970 to provide direct financial aid for the support, maintenance, medical care, legal fees, and welfare of librarians who are or have been "threatened with loss of employment or discharged because of their stand for the cause of intellectual freedom." In 1975, the scope of the fund was broadened to include librarians who had been discriminated against on the basis of gender, age, race, color, creed, sexual orientation, place of national origin, or defense of intellectual freedom. Applicants should describe their situation, including a brief explanation of its financial ramifications and of the amount of aid requested.

Financial data The amount awarded varies, depending upon the needs of the recipient.

Duration The award is granted annually.

Number awarded Varies each year.

Deadline Applications may be submitted at any time.

[1027]
LYMAN T. JOHNSON POSTDOCTORAL FELLOWSHIP

University of Kentucky
Attn: Vice President for Research
311 Main Building
Lexington, KY 40506-0032
(859) 257-5294   Fax: (859) 323-2800
E-mail: vpr@email.uky.edu
Web: www.research.uky.edu

Purpose To provide an opportunity for recent postdoctorates, especially minorities, to conduct research at the University of Kentucky (U.K.).

Eligibility This program is open to U.S. citizens and permanent residents who have completed a doctoral degree within the past 2 years. Applicants must be interested in conducting an individualized research program under the mentorship of a U.K. professor. They should indicate, in their letter of application, how their participation in this program would contribute to the compelling interest of diversity at U.K. Race, ethnicity, and national origin are among the factors that contribute to diversity. Selection is based on evidence of scholarship with competitive potential for a tenure-track faculty appointment at a research university, compatibility of specific research interests with those in doctorate-granting units at U.K., quality of the research proposal, support from mentor and references, and effect of the appointment on the educational benefit of diversity within the research or professional area.

Financial data The fellowship provides a stipend of $35,000 plus $5,000 for support of research activities.

Duration Up to 2 years.

Additional information In addition to conducting an individualized research program under the mentorship of a U.K. professor, fellows actively participate in research, teaching, and service to the university, their profession, and the community. This program began in 1992.

Number awarded 1 each year.

Deadline October of each year.

[1028]
MANY VOICES RESIDENCIES

Playwrights' Center
2301 East Franklin Avenue
Minneapolis, MN 55406-1024
(612) 332-7481   Fax: (612) 332-6037
E-mail: info@pwcenter.org
Web: www.pwcenter.org/fellows_voices.php

Purpose To provide funding to Native American and other Minnesota playwrights of color so they can spend a year in residence at the Playwrights' Center in Minneapolis.

Eligibility This program is open to playwrights of color who have been citizens or permanent residents of the United States and residents of Minnesota for at least 1 year. Applicants must be interested in playwriting and creating theater in a supportive artists' community at the Playwrights' Center. Selection is based on the applicant's commitment, proven talent, and artistic potential.

Financial data The program provides a stipend of $1,250; a mentorship with an established playwright or theater artist of their choosing; a full scholarship to a center class; a private script workshop with professional actors, directors,

and dramaturgs; a public reading with professional actors and an audience discussion; and a 1-year membership in the Playwrights' Center.
Duration 9 months, beginning in October.
Additional information This program, which began in 1994, is funded by the Jerome Foundation. Fellows must be in residence at the Playwrights' Center for the duration of the program.
Number awarded 8 each year.
Deadline August of each year.

[1029]
MARY P. KEY DIVERSITY RESIDENCY PROGRAM
Ohio State University Libraries
Attn: Assistance Director for Administrative Services
5810 Ackerman Library
610 Ackerman Road
Columbus, OH 43202
(614) 292-5863   Fax: (614) 292-7859
E-mail: gonzalez.107@osu.edu
Web: library.osu.edu

Purpose To provide an opportunity for librarians who will increase the diversity of the library to gain work experience at Ohio State University.
Eligibility Eligible to apply are recent library school graduates who are interested in working in a university/research library. The program is designed to increase diversity at Ohio State University so encourages all interested library graduates to apply.
Financial data A competitive stipend is paid (amount not specified).
Duration 2 years.
Additional information This program began in 1989. The first year of the residency includes introduction/orientation to the various departments and operations within the library; the second year emphasizes 1 or more areas of special interest to the resident.
Number awarded 1 each year.
Deadline December of each year (or until the internship is filled).

[1030]
MARYLAND SEA GRANT RESEARCH EXPERIENCES FOR UNDERGRADUATES
Maryland Sea Grant College
c/o University of Maryland
4321 Hartwick Road, Suite 300
College Park, MD 20740
(301) 405-7500   Fax: (301) 314-5780
E-mail: moser@mdsg.umd.edu
Web: www.mdsg.umd.edu/Education/REU/index.html

Purpose To provide minority and other undergraduate students with an opportunity to conduct marine research during the summer in biology, chemistry, and physical oceanography on Chesapeake Bay.
Eligibility This program is open to undergraduate students who have completed at least 2 years of study towards a bachelor's degree. Applicants must be interested in conducting individual research projects (under the mentorship of scientists from the University of Maryland or the Academy of Natural Science Estuarine Research Center) in such areas as estuarine processes, biochemistry, coastal technologies, modeling and analysis, contaminants, fisheries, physical oceanography, the benthic environment, and submerged aquatic vegetation. U.S. citizenship or permanent resident status is required. Selection is based on a 1-page description of interests, course work and grades, letters of recommendation, and the potential benefits students will gain from the research experience. Preference is given to rising seniors. Students from underrepresented groups and institutions with limited research opportunities are especially encouraged to apply.
Financial data Fellows receive a stipend of $3,700, payment of dormitory costs, round-trip travel expenses, and funding to assist in publishing or presenting the results of summer research.
Duration 12 weeks during the summer.
Additional information This program is supported by the National Science Foundation as part of the Research Experiences for Undergraduates Program.
Number awarded 13 each year.
Deadline February of each year.

[1031]
MENTAL HEALTH DISSERTATION RESEARCH GRANTS TO INCREASE DIVERSITY IN THE MENTAL HEALTH RESEARCH ARENA
National Institute of Mental Health
Attn: Division of Extramural Activities
6001 Executive Boulevard, Room 6138
Bethesda, MD 20892-9609
(301) 443-3534   Fax: (301) 443-4720
TTY: (301) 451-0088 E-mail: armstrda@mail.nih.gov
Web: www.nimh.nih.gov/researchfunding/index.cfm

Purpose To provide financial support to Native American and other doctoral candidates from underrepresented groups planning to prepare for a research career in any area relevant to mental health and/or mental disorders.
Eligibility This program is open to doctoral candidates conducting dissertation research in a field related to mental health and/or mental disorders at a university, college, or professional school with an accredited doctoral degree granting program. Applicants must be 1) members of an ethnic or racial group that has been determined by their institution to be underrepresented in biomedical or behavioral research; 2) individuals with disabilities; or 3) individuals from socially, culturally, economically, or educationally disadvantaged backgrounds that have inhibited their ability to prepare for a career in health-related research. They must be U.S. citizens, nationals, or permanent residents.
Financial data Grants provide up to $35,000 per year in direct costs. Facilities and administrative costs are limited to 8% of direct costs.
Duration Up to 2 years.
Number awarded Varies each year.
Deadline April, August, or December of each year.

[1032]
MENTOR-BASED MINORITY POSTDOCTORAL FELLOWSHIPS IN DIABETES

American Diabetes Association
Attn: Research Program Specialist
1701 North Beauregard Street
Alexandria, VA 22311
(703) 549-1500, ext. 2250   Toll-free: (800) DIABETES
Fax: (703) 549-1715   E-mail: mrowan@diabetes.org
Web: www.diabetes.org

Purpose To provide funding to Native American and other minority postdoctoral fellows working with established diabetes investigators.

Eligibility Applications for these fellowships may be submitted by established and active investigators in diabetes research who wish to supervise the work of a postdoctoral fellow, whom they will select. They must currently hold a grant from the American Diabetes Association. The fellow selected by the investigator must be a member of an underrepresented minority group (African American; Spanish, Hispanic, or Latino; American Indian and Alaskan Native; Native Hawaiian and Pacific Islander), must have an M.D. or Ph.D. degree, must not be serving an internship or residency during the fellowship period, and must not have more than 3 years of postdoctoral research experience in the field of diabetes/endocrinology. Applicant investigators and fellows must be U.S. citizens or permanent residents. The applicant investigator must also hold an appointment at a U.S. research institution and have sufficient research support to provide an appropriate training environment for the fellow. The applicant investigator must be a member of the Professional Section of the American Diabetes Association; the fellow must also be, or agree to become, a member. Selection is based on the quality and activity of the applicant investigator's diabetes research program, the likelihood that the fellow trained by the mentor will actively pursue a career in diabetes research, the applicant investigator's past training record, and evidence of sufficient research support and adequate facilities to provide an appropriate training environment for a postdoctoral fellow.

Financial data The grant is $45,000 per year. Within that total, the applicant investigator may determine the salary of the fellow; up to $3,000 per year of the total may be used for laboratory supply costs, and up to $1,000 may be used for travel by the fellow to attend diabetes-related scientific meetings.

Duration 2 to 3 years.

Number awarded Varies each year.

Deadline January of each year.

[1033]
MENTORED CLINICAL SCIENTIST RESEARCH CAREER DEVELOPMENT AWARDS

National Institutes of Health
Office of Extramural Research
Attn: Grants Information
6705 Rockledge Drive
Bethesda, MD 20892-7974
(301) 435-0714   Fax: (301) 480-0525
TTY: (301) 451-0088   E-mail: NIHTrain@mail.nih.gov
Web: grants.nih.gov/grants/guide/index.html

Purpose To provide financial support for specialized study to clinically-trained minorities and other professionals who are committed to a career in research and have the potential to develop into independent investigators.

Eligibility This program is open to candidates who 1) have a clinical doctoral degree (e.g., M.D., D.D.S., D.M.D., D.O., D.C., O.D., D.V.M., Pharm.D., or Ph.D.) in such clinical disciplines as nursing, speech-language pathology, clinical psychology, audiology, rehabilitation, or clinical genetics; 2) can identify a mentor with extensive research experience; and 3) are willing to spend a minimum of 75% of full-time professional effort conducting research and research career development activities for the period of the award. Applications may be submitted on behalf of candidates by domestic, nonfederal organizations, public or private, such as universities, colleges, hospitals, or laboratories. Members of underrepresented ethnic and racial groups, individuals with disabilities, and individuals from disadvantaged backgrounds are especially encouraged to apply. Only U.S. citizens, nationals, and permanent residents are eligible.

Financial data This program provides salary and fringe benefits for the candidate only; each component establishes its own salary limits on career awards. Additional funding is provided for tuition and fees related to career development; research expenses, such as supplies, equipment, and technical personnel; travel to research meetings or training; and statistical services, including personnel and computer time. Facilities and administrative costs are reimbursed at 8% of modified total direct costs.

Duration 3 to 5 years.

Additional information Awards under this program are available from 19 agencies of the National Institutes of Health (NIH): the National Institute on Aging, the National Institute on Alcohol Abuse and Alcoholism, the National Institute of Allergy and Infectious Diseases, the National Institute of Arthritis and Musculoskeletal and Skin Diseases, the National Cancer Institute, the National Institute of Child Health and Human Development, the National Institute on Deafness and Other Communication Disorders, the National Institute of Dental and Craniofacial Research, the National Institute of Diabetes and Digestive and Kidney Diseases, the National Institute on Drug Abuse, the National Institute of Environmental Health Sciences, the National Eye Institute, the National Heart, Lung, and Blood Institute, the National Institute of Mental Health, the National Institute of Neurological Disorders and Stroke, the National Institute for Biomedical Imaging and Bioengineering, the National Institute of General Medical Sciences, the National Center for Complementary and Alternative Medicine, and the Office of Dietary Supplements. The names and addresses of staff people at each agency are available from NIH Grants Information.

Number awarded Varies each year.

Deadline February, June, or October of each year.

[1034]
MENTORED RESEARCH SCIENTIST DEVELOPMENT AWARDS

National Institutes of Health
Office of Extramural Research
Attn: Grants Information
6705 Rockledge Drive
Bethesda, MD 20892-7974
(301) 435-0714   Fax: (301) 480-0525
TTY: (301) 451-0088   E-mail: NIHTrain@mail.nih.gov
Web: grants.nih.gov/grants/guide/index.html

Purpose To provide financial support to minority and other research scientists who need an additional period of sponsored research training as a way to gain expertise in an area new to them or in an area that would demonstrably enhance their scientific career.

Eligibility This program is open to candidates who have a health-professional doctorate or its equivalent and have demonstrated the capacity or potential for highly productive independent research in the period after the doctorate. Candidates must identify a mentor with extensive research experience and must be willing to spend a minimum of 75% of full-time professional effort conducting research and research career development activities for the period of the award. Applications may be submitted on behalf of candidates by domestic, for-profit or nonprofit, public or private institutions (such as universities, colleges, hospitals, or laboratories). Members of underrepresented ethnic and racial groups and individual with disabilities are especially encouraged to apply. Only U.S. citizens, nationals, and permanent residents are eligible.

Financial data This program provides salary and fringe benefits for the scholar based on the established scale at the sponsoring institution; limits are not uniform but range from $50,000 to $180,000 per year. Support ranging from $20,000 to $50,000 per year is also provided for tuition, fees, and books related to career development; research expenses, such as supplies, equipment, and technical personnel; travel to research meetings or training; and statistical services, including personnel and computer time. Facilities and administrative costs are reimbursed at 8% of modified total direct costs.

Duration 3 to 5 years.

Additional information Awards under this program are available from 18 agencies of the National Institutes of Health (NIH): the National Institute on Aging, the National Institute on Alcohol Abuse and Alcoholism, the National Institute of Allergy and Infectious Diseases, the National Institute of Arthritis and Musculoskeletal and Skin Diseases, the National Institute of Biomedical Imaging and Bioengineering, the National Cancer Institute, the National Institute of Child Health and Human Development, the National Institute on Deafness and Other Communication Disorders, the National Institute of Diabetes and Digestive and Kidney Diseases, the National Institute on Drug Abuse, the National Institute of Environmental Health Sciences, the National Institute of Mental Health, the National Institute of Neurological Disorders and Stroke, the National Institute of Nursing Research, the National Human Genome Research Institute, the National Center for Complementary and Alternative Medicine, the National Center for Research Resources, and the Office of Dietary Supplements. The names and addresses of staff people at each agency are available from NIH Grants Information.

Number awarded Varies each year.

Deadline February, June, or October of each year.

[1035]
MIAMI UNIVERSITY RESIDENT LIBRARIAN

Miami University
University Libraries
Attn: Dean and University Librarian
King Library, Room 271
Oxford, OH 45056-1878
(513) 529-2800   E-mail: hendribn@lib.muohio.edu
Web: www.lib.muohio.edu

Purpose To provide a residency at Miami University for librarians who can provide outreach to multicultural constituents.

Eligibility This program is open to recent (within the past 2 years) recipients of a master's degree from a library school accredited by the American Library Association who are interested in a career in academic librarianship. Applicants must have a familiarity with and the skills necessary to provide outreach to multicultural constituents throughout the university (e.g., Black World Studies, Latin American Studies). They should be able to demonstrate familiarity with and knowledge of advancing technologies, an ability to work collegially in a team environment, a knowledge of and interest in academic libraries, excellent oral and written communication skills, the initiative and ability to conceive and carry out projects, and the ability to establish and maintain good working relationships with faculty, students, and other library users as well as library staff.

Financial data The stipend is negotiable, depending on experience and qualifications. Benefits include the standard insurance package.

Duration 12 months; may be renewed for 1 additional year.

Additional information Interns are exposed to all areas of the university library's operations, including public, technical, and administrative services.

Number awarded 1 each year.

Deadline December of each year.

[1036]
MICHIGAN SPACE GRANT CONSORTIUM UNDERGRADUATE UNDERREPRESENTED MINORITY FELLOWSHIPS

Michigan Space Grant Consortium
c/o University of Michigan
1320 Beal Avenue
1216-C FXB
Ann Arbor, MI 48109-2140
(734) 764-9508   Fax: (734) 763-6904
E-mail: blbryant@umich.edu
Web: sgc.engin.umich.edu

Purpose To provide funding to Native American and other underrepresented minority undergraduate students at member institutions of the Michigan Space Grant Consortium who wish to conduct space-related research.

Eligibility This program is open to undergraduate students at affiliates of the Michigan consortium who members of underrepresented minority groups (African American, Hispanic, Latino, Native American, and Pacific Islander). Applicants must be proposing to conduct research in aerospace, space science, earth system science, and other related fields in science, engineering, or mathematics; students working on educational research topics in mathematics, science, or technology are also eligible. They must identify a mentor in the faculty research, education, or public service communities with whom they intend to work and who is available to write a letter of recommendation. Normally, they should have a GPA of 3.0 or higher, but students with a lower GPA may be eligible if they have strong mentorship. U.S. citizenship is required.
Financial data The maximum grant is $2,500. Mentors qualify for $2,000 in additional salary, with a minimum salary match of 1:1 required from their institution.
Additional information The consortium consists of Eastern Michigan University, Grand Valley State University, Hope College, Michigan State University, Michigan Technological University, Oakland University, Saginaw Valley State University, University of Michigan, Wayne State University, and Western Michigan University. This program is supported by the U.S. National Aeronautics and Space Administration (NASA).
Number awarded Varies each year; a total of $14,000 is available for this program annually.
Deadline November of each year.

[1037]
MICROBIOLOGY UNDERGRADUATE RESEARCH FELLOWSHIP

American Society for Microbiology
Attn: Education Board
1752 N Street, N.W.
Washington, DC 20036-2904
(202) 942-9283 Fax: (202) 942-9329
E-mail: fellowships-careerinformation@asmusa.org
Web: www.asm.org/Education/index.asp?bid=4322

Purpose To provide Native American and other underrepresented minority college students with the opportunity to work on a summer research project in microbiology under the mentorship of a member of the American Society for Microbiology (ASM).
Eligibility This program is open to African Americans, Hispanic Americans, Native Americans, Alaskan Native Americans, and Native Pacific Islanders who 1) are enrolled as full-time undergraduate students; 2) have taken introductory courses in biology, chemistry, and (preferably) microbiology prior to applying; 3) have a strong interest in obtaining a Ph.D. or M.D./Ph.D. in the microbiological sciences; 4) have laboratory research experience; and 5) are U.S. citizens or permanent residents. Applicants must be interested in conducting basic science research at a host institution during the summer under an ASM mentor. Selection is based on academic achievement, achievement in previous research experiences or independent projects, career goals as a research scientist, commitment to research, personal motivation to participate in the project, willingness to conduct summer research with an ASM member located at an institution other than their own, and leadership skills.

Financial data Students receive $3,500 as a stipend, up to $850 for student lodging, up to $500 for round-trip travel to the host institution, 2-year student membership in the ASM, and travel support up to $1,000 if they present the results of the research project at the ASM general meeting the following year.
Duration 10 to 12 weeks during the summer.
Additional information Recently, placements were available at Albert Einstein College of Medicine (Bronx, New York) and Tufts University School of Medicine (Boston, Massachusetts). In addition to their research activities, fellows participate in a weekly seminar series, journal club, GRE preparatory course, graduate admission counseling, and career counseling.
Number awarded 5 to 8 students are placed at each institution.
Deadline January of each year.

[1038]
MINORITY MEDICAL STUDENT AWARD PROGRAM OF THE AMERICAN SOCIETY OF HEMATOLOGY

American Society of Hematology
Attn: Award Program Coordinator
1900 M Street, N.W., Suite 200
Washington, DC 20036
(202) 776-0544, ext. 1168 Fax: (202) 776-0545
E-mail: ASH@hematology.org
Web: www.hematology.org

Purpose To provide an opportunity for Native American and other underrepresented minority medical students to conduct a research project in hematology.
Eligibility This program is open to medical students enrolled in D.O., M.D., or M.D./Ph.D. programs in the United States or Canada who are members of minority groups. For purposes of this program, minority is defined as those groups that the sponsor has identified as underrepresented in the field of hematology related to biomedical, behavioral, clinical, or social science research, including racial/ethnic minorities and persons from disadvantaged socioeconomic groups. Applicants must be interested in conducting a research project in hematology with a mentor who focuses on the research experience and another mentor who serves as an adviser. Mentors must be members of the American Society of Hematology (ASH) and the advisory mentor must be from a minority group. Students must self-identify as minorities. Along with their application, they must submit a brief essay on their interest in learning more about hematology and hematology research. U.S. or Canadian citizenship or permanent resident status is required.
Financial data The grant includes $5,000 for research support and an additional $2,000 to support travel to the annual meeting of the ASH. During subsequent years of medical school and residency, travel support of $1,000 for the annual meeting is also provided. Research mentors receive an allowance for supplies of $2,000 and a travel allowance of $1,000 if they accompany the student to the ASH annual meeting. Advisory mentors receive a $1,000 travel allowance every time they accompany the student to an ASH annual meeting.
Duration 8 to 12 weeks.
Additional information This program is supported by Genentech BioOncology.

Number awarded Up to 10 each year.
Deadline March of each year.

[1039]
MINORITY POSTDOCTORAL RESEARCH FELLOWSHIPS
National Science Foundation
Directorate for Biological Sciences
Attn: Division of Biological Infrastructure
4201 Wilson Boulevard, Room 615 N
Arlington, VA 22230
(703) 292-8470   Fax: (703) 292-9063
TDD: (800) 281-8749   E-mail: ckimsey@nsf.gov
Web: www.nsf.gov

Purpose To provide financial assistance for postdoctoral research training in the United States or abroad to Native American and other underrepresented minority scientists in the biological, social, economic, and behavioral sciences.

Eligibility This program is open to U.S. citizens, nationals, and permanent residents who will complete their doctorate within a year or have completed it within the previous 4 years but have not completed more than 12 months in a postdoctoral research position. Applicants must be a member of an ethnic group that is significantly underrepresented at advanced levels of science and engineering in the United States, including Native Americans (Alaska Natives and American Indians), African Americans, Hispanics, and Native Pacific Islanders. They must be proposing research training that falls within the program areas of the National Science Foundation (NSF) Directorate for Biological Sciences or the Directorate for Social, Behavioral, and Economic Sciences to be conducted at any appropriate nonprofit U.S. or foreign institution (government laboratory, institution of higher education, national laboratory, or public or private research institute), but not at the same institution where the doctorate was obtained.

Financial data The grant is $60,000 per year, including an annual stipend of $45,000, a research allowance of $10,000 per year, and an institutional allowance of $5,000 per year for partial reimbursement of indirect research costs (space, equipment, general purpose supplies, and fringe benefits).

Duration 2 years; applicants who propose to spend their 2-year tenure at a foreign institution may apply for a third year of support at an appropriate U.S. institution.

Additional information Information on the programs from the Directorate for Social, Behavioral, and Economic Sciences is available at (703) 292-7279, Fax: (703) 292-9068, E-mail: jperhoni@nsf.gov.

Number awarded Approximately 25 each year.
Deadline November of each year.

[1040]
MINORITY RESEARCH TRAINING IN PSYCHIATRY
American Psychiatric Association
Attn: Institute for Research and Education
1000 Wilson Boulevard, Suite 1825
Arlington, VA 22209-3901
(703) 907-8622   Toll-free: (800) 852-1390
Fax: (703) 907-1085   E-mail: eguerra@psych.org
Web: www.psych.org

Purpose To provide financial assistance to Native American and other underrepresented minority medical students, residents, and postresidency fellows interested in psychiatric research training.

Eligibility This program is open to 3 levels of applicants: medical students, residents at the PGY-4 level of psychiatry training, and postdoctoral fellows who have completed residency training in psychiatry. Preference is given to members of underrepresented minority groups (American Indians, Blacks/African Americans, Hispanics, and Pacific Islanders). Candidates must be interested in training at research-intensive departments of psychiatry in major U.S. medical schools. Training sites with excellent research facilities and resources, funded research record, research faculty (including minority researchers), and training history are preferred. U.S. citizenship or permanent resident status is required.

Financial data Stipends for medical students are paid at the rate of $20,772 per year, or $1,731 per month for the months actually involved in research training. Stipends for residents are paid at the rate of $45,048 per year. For postresidency fellows, stipends depend on the number of years of experience, ranging from $45,048 to $51,036 per year.

Duration Medical students can receive support for 3 to 4 months or as a summer experience. Residents can receive support for 2 months to 1 year. For postresidency fellows, the duration is generally 2 years.

Additional information This program is funded by the National Institute of Mental Health and administered by the APA's American Psychiatric Institute for Research and Education.

Number awarded Varies each year.

Deadline For a summer research training program for medical students, applications are due by March of each year. For medical student programs at other times of the year, applications should be received at least 2 months prior to the start of the program. For residents and postresidency fellows, applications are due by November of each year.

[1041]
MINORITY SCHOLAR-IN-RESIDENCE DISSERTATION FELLOWSHIPS

Consortium for Faculty Diversity at Liberal Arts Colleges
c/o DePauw University
Academic Affairs Office
305 Harrison Hall
7 East Larabee Street
Greencastle, IN 461350
(765) 658-4553   Fax: (765) 658-6595
E-mail: cfd@depauw.edu
Web: www.depauw.edu

Purpose To provide an opportunity for Native American and other minority students to work on their dissertation while in residence at selected liberal arts colleges.

Eligibility This program is open to African American, Asian American, Hispanic American, and Native American doctoral candidates who have completed all the requirements for the Ph.D. or M.F.A. except the dissertation. Applicants must be interested in a residency at a member institution of the Consortium for Faculty Diversity at Liberal Arts Colleges during which they will complete their dissertation.

Financial data Dissertation fellows receive a stipend based on the average salary paid to instructors at the participating college. Modest funds are made available to finance the fellow's proposed research, subject to the usual institutional procedures.

Duration 1 year.

Additional information The following schools are participating in the program: Bowdoin College, Bryn Mawr College, Carleton College, Centre College, Claremont McKenna College, Coe College, College of Wooster, Colorado College, Denison University, DePauw University, Dickinson College, Gettysburg College, Grinnell College, Hamilton College, Haverford College, Hobart and William Smith Colleges, Hope College, Juniata College, Lewis and Clark College, Luther College, Macalester College, Mount Holyoke College, Oberlin College, Occidental College, Pomona College, Reed College, Rhodes College, University of Richmond, St. Olaf College, Sewanee: The University of the South, Skidmore College, Southwestern University, Swarthmore College, Vassar College, Wellesley College, Wheaton College, Whitman College, and Willamette University. Fellows are expected to teach at least 1 course, participate in departmental seminars, and interact with students.

Number awarded Varies each year.

Deadline November of each year.

[1042]
MINORITY SCHOLAR-IN-RESIDENCE PROGRAM POSTDOCTORAL FELLOWSHIPS

Consortium for Faculty Diversity at Liberal Arts Colleges
c/o DePauw University
Academic Affairs Office
305 Harrison Hall
7 East Larabee Street
Greencastle, IN 461350
(765) 658-4553   Fax: (765) 658-6595
E-mail: cfd@depauw.edu
Web: www.depauw.edu

Purpose To make available the facilities of liberal arts colleges to Native American and other minority scholars who recently received their doctoral/advanced degree.

Eligibility This program is open to African American, Asian American, Hispanic American, and Native American scholars in the liberal arts and engineering who received the Ph.D. or M.F.A. degree within the past 5 years. Applicants must be interested in a residency at a participating institution that is part of the Consortium for a Strong Minority Presence at Liberal Arts Colleges.

Financial data Fellows receive a stipend equivalent to the average salary paid by the host college to beginning assistant professors. Modest funds are made available to finance the fellow's proposed research, subject to the usual institutional procedures.

Duration 1 year.

Additional information The following schools are participating in the program: Bowdoin College, Bryn Mawr College, Carleton College, Centre College, Claremont McKenna College, Coe College, College of Wooster, Colorado College, Denison University, DePauw University, Dickinson College, Gettysburg College, Grinnell College, Hamilton College, Haverford College, Hobart and William Smith Colleges, Hope College, Juniata College, Lewis and Clark College, Luther College, Macalester College, Mount Holyoke College, Oberlin College, Occidental College, Pomona College, Reed College, Rhodes College, University of Richmond, St. Olaf College, Sewanee: The University of the South, Skidmore College, Southwestern University, Swarthmore College, Vassar College, Wellesley College, Wheaton College, Whitman College, and Willamette University. Fellows are expected to teach at least 1 course in each academic term of residency, participate in departmental seminars, and interact with students.

Number awarded Varies each year.

Deadline November of each year.

[1043]
MINORITY VISITING STUDENT AWARDS PROGRAM

Smithsonian Institution
Attn: Office of Research Training and Services
470 L'Enfant Plaza, Suite 7102
P.O. Box 37012, MRC 902
Washington, DC 20013-7012
(202) 633-7070 Fax: (202) 633-7069
E-mail: siofg@si.edu
Web: www.si.edu/ofg/ofgapp.htm

Purpose To provide funding to Native American and other minority graduate students interested in conducting research at the Smithsonian Institution.

Eligibility This program is open to members of U.S. minority groups underrepresented in Smithsonian scholarly programs. Applicants must be advanced graduate students interested in conducting research in the Institution's disciplines and in the museum field.

Financial data Students receive a grant of $500 per week.

Duration Up to 10 weeks.

Additional information Recipients carry out independent research projects in association with the Smithsonian's research staff. Eligible fields of study currently available include animal behavior, ecology, and environmental science (including an emphasis on the tropics); anthropology (including archaeology); astrophysics and astronomy; earth sciences and paleobiology; evolutionary and systematic biology; history of science and technology; history of art (especially American, contemporary, African, Asian, and 20th-century art); American crafts and decorative arts; social and cultural history of the United States; folklife; and materials research. Fellows are required to be in residence at the Smithsonian for the duration of the fellowship.

Number awarded Varies each year.

Deadline January of each year for summer and fall residency; September of each year for spring residency.

[1044]
MISSILE DEFENSE AGENCY HISTORICALLY BLACK COLLEGES AND UNIVERSITIES AND MINORITY INSTITUTIONS BROAD AGENCY ANNOUNCEMENT

Missile Defense Agency
Attn: Advanced Technology Deputate (MDA/DV)
7100 Defense Pentagon
Washington, DC 20301-7100
(703) 882-6894 Fax: (703) 882-6356
E-mail: millie.abdi@mda.mil
Web: www.mda.mil/mdalink/html/asacquisition.htm.

Purpose To provide funding to investigators at Historically Black Colleges and Universities (HBCUs) and Minority Institutions (MIs) interested in conducting research related to the mission of the Missile Defense Agency (MDA).

Eligibility This program is open to investigators at HBCUs and MIs interested in conducting research in the following general areas: 1) radar systems; 2) lasers and electro-optical systems; 3) integrated active/passive IR sensor systems; 4) computer science, signal, and data processing; 5) mathematics, probability, and decision theory; 6) physics, chemistry, and materials; 7) mechanical and aerospace engineering; and 8) battle management, command, and control. Selection is based on anticipated benefits of the research effort to the MDA mission; scientific/technical quality of the research proposal and its relevance to the topic description; qualifications of the principal investigator, other key staff, and consultants; and adequacy of management planning and controls.

Financial data The maximum grant is $150,000 per year.

Duration 12 to 24 months.

Number awarded Varies each year.

Deadline June of each year.

[1045]
MORE FACULTY DEVELOPMENT AWARDS

National Institute of General Medical Sciences
Attn: Division of Minority Opportunities in Research
45 Center Drive, Suite 2AS37
Bethesda, MD 20892-6200
(301) 594-3900 Fax: (301) 480-2753
TTY: (301) 451-0088 E-mail: at21z@nih.gov
Web: www.nigms.nih.gov/Research/Funding

Purpose To enable faculty at minority institutions to sharpen their research skills by spending intervals conducting full-time research in a research-intensive laboratory.

Eligibility Candidates for this program must have been full-time permanent faculty in a biomedically-related science, including behavioral science, or mathematics at the home institution for at least 3 years; have received the Ph.D. or equivalent at least 5 years before the date of the application; intend to remain at the home institution at the end of the training period; demonstrate a commitment to research and teaching in a minority institution; plan to conduct research in a science (including mathematics) related to biomedical or behavioral research; and be a citizen or permanent resident of the United States. The home institution must be a domestic private or public educational institution with a significant enrollment of underrepresented minorities, defined as African Americans, Hispanic Americans, Native Americans, and Pacific Islanders, that offers at least the baccalaureate degree in the biomedical or behavioral sciences or mathematics. The research institution is the university or other institution at which the candidate conducts full-time research and takes courses; the research institution may not be the same as the home institution.

Financial data Candidates may request a salary equal to their actual annual salary and appropriate fringe benefits prorated for the time during which they are engaged in full-time research (salary support is not provided for the time candidates are enrolled in academic courses); up to $3,000 per year for supplies, equipment, travel, and other costs directly related to their full-time research experience; and funds to pay tuition and fees for 1 course per academic term to be taken at the research institution. Any expected concurrent sabbatical or any other salary support for the proposed period in residence is taken into account. A travel allowance equivalent to round-trip coach airfare between the visiting scientist's home institution and the sponsoring institution is provided. The sponsoring institution may receive up to $3,000 as an allowance for costs of supplies, supporting services, and demonstration costs related to activities proposed for the visiting scientist.

Duration Research may be conducted at intervals over a period of 2 to 5 years.
Additional information The National Institute of General Medical Sciences, a component of the National Institutes of Health (NIH), operates this program as part of its Minority Opportunities for Research (MORE) Division.
Number awarded Varies each year.
Deadline January, May, or September of each year.

[1046]
MWH FELLOWSHIP FOR ADVANCED WATER/WASTEWATER TREATMENT TECHNOLOGIES

National Water Research Institute
Attn: Fellowship Program
18700 Ward Street
P.O. Box 8096
Fountain Valley, CA 92728-8096
(714) 378-3278   Fax: (714) 378-3375
E-mail: fellow@nwri-usa.org
Web: www.nwri-usa.org/fellowship.htm

Purpose To provide funding to minority and other graduate students interested in conducting science and technology research, especially research that relates to advanced water and wastewater technologies.
Eligibility This program is open to full-time graduate students interested in conducting research on the development of novel and innovative advanced water and wastewater treatment, disinfection, or oxidation technologies. These technologies should address the need to create new sources of water supply from impaired and nontraditional water sources. Research areas include, but are not limited to, engineering, physical and chemical sciences, biological sciences, health sciences, political sciences, economics, and planning and public policy that are related to water and/or water resources. Preference is given to doctoral candidates, but outstanding students in master's programs may be considered. Applicants must submit a letter of inquiry describing the importance of the research to them and the water community, how their research will contribute to water science in general, what they expect to accomplish, and how their research relates to the mission of the (National Water Research Institute) NWRI to create new sources of water through research and technology and to protect the freshwater and marine environments. Women and members of minority groups underrepresented in academia are strongly encouraged to apply.
Financial data Grants range from $2,000 to $20,000 per year, but are typically $10,000 per year.
Duration 2 years.
Additional information This fellowship is jointly sponsored by the NWRI and MWH, an environmental consulting firm based in Broomfield, Colorado.
Number awarded 1 each year.
Deadline February of each year.

[1047]
NASA ADMINISTRATOR'S FELLOWSHIP PROGRAM

United Negro College Fund Special Programs Corporation
2750 Prosperity Avenue, Suite 600
Fairfax, VA 22031
(703) 205-8137   Toll-free: (800) 530-6232
Fax: (703) 205-7645   E-mail: nafp@uncfsp.org
Web: www.uncfsp.org

Purpose To provide funding to faculty members at Minority Institutions (MIs) who wish to conduct research in a field of interest to the National Aeronautics and Space Administration (NASA).
Eligibility This program is open to full-time, tenure-track faculty members at MIs (Historically Black Colleges and Universities, Hispanic Serving Institutions, and Tribal Colleges and Universities) who either 1) have a Ph.D., Sc.D., or equivalent degree in science, technology, engineering, or mathematics (STEM), or 2) have expertise in NASA-related fields (aerospace, biology, chemistry, computer science, electrical engineering, mathematics, mechanical engineering, physics, physiology, and structural engineering). Applicants must be proposing to conduct research at a NASA center, another government agency, a research university, or a private sector organization. U.S. citizenship is required.
Financial data Fellows remain on the payroll of the institution where they are employed and the fellowship provides the institution with their current salary and benefits. Fellows also receive an additional 55% of the host site per diem rate if it is necessary to relocate for participation in the program.
Duration 12 months.
Additional information This program is funded by NASA and administered by the United Negro College Fund Special Programs Corporation. In addition to STEM faculty at MIs, the program is open to NASA employees who spend 18 to 22 months teaching and/or conducting research at an MI. Fellows must agree to return to their home institution for at least 2 years after conclusion of the program.
Number awarded 12 each year: 6 STEM faculty members and 6 NASA employees.
Deadline January of each year.

[1048]
NASA FACULTY FELLOWSHIP PROGRAM

American Society for Engineering Education
Attn: Projects Department
1818 N Street, N.W., Suite 600
Washington, DC 20036-2479
(202) 331-3509   Fax: (202) 265-8504
E-mail: nasa@asee.org
Web: www.asee.org/nffp

Purpose To provide support to minority and other faculty members in engineering and science who wish to conduct summer research at facilities of the National Aeronautics and Space Administration (NASA).
Eligibility This program is open to tenured or tenure-track faculty at 4-year institutions and full-time faculty at 2-year institutions. Applicants must be U.S. citizens who have a Ph.D. in an engineering, mathematics, or science discipline applicable to the research and/or technology development needs of the National Aeronautics and Space Administration (NASA). They must be interested in conducting a sum-

mer research project at a participating NASA center. Faculty who participated in this program within the past 5 years, who have received more than $300,000 in NASA funding within the past 5 years, or who have received a NASA Faculty Awards for Research grant are not eligible. Women, underrepresented minorities, and persons with disabilities are strongly encouraged to apply. Selection is based on relevance and merit of the research (40%), qualifications of the faculty applicant (40%), and overall academic benefit to the faculty applicant and his or her institution (20%).

Financial data The stipend is $1,200 per week, for a maximum of $12,000. A relocation allowance is available for fellows who live more than 50 miles from their assigned center and reasonable travel expenses for a round-trip are also reimbursed for fellows who receive the relocation allowance. The maximum allowance for relocation and travel is $2,000. To facilitate the participation of individuals with disabilities, NASA provides up to $1,500 in supplemental funding for special assistance and/or equipment necessary to enable the principal investigator to perform the work under the award.

Duration 10 weeks during the summer.

Additional information Participating NASA centers are Hugh L. Dryden Flight Research Facility (Edwards, California); Goddard Space Flight Center (Greenbelt, Maryland) and its Wallops Flight Facility (Wallops Island, Virginia) and Goddard Institute for Space Studies (New York, New York); Jet Propulsion Laboratory (Pasadena, California); Lyndon B. Johnson Space Center (Houston, Texas) and its White Sands Test Facility (Las Cruces, New Mexico); John F. Kennedy Space Center (Cape Canaveral, Florida); Langley Research Center (Hampton, Virginia); Glenn Research Center (Cleveland, Ohio); George C. Marshall Space Flight Center (Huntsville, Alabama); and John C. Stennis Space Center (Stennis Space Center, Mississippi). This program is funded by NASA and administered by the American Society for Engineering Education (ASEE) and the Universities Space Research Association (USRA).

Number awarded Varies each year.

Deadline January of each year.

[1049]
NASA GRADUATE STUDENT RESEARCHERS PROGRAM

National Aeronautics and Space Administration
Attn: Office of Education
500 E Street, S.W., Suite 200
Washington, DC 20024-2760
(202) 358-0402   Fax: (202) 358-3523
E-mail: katie.blanding@nasa.gov
Web: fellowships.hq.nasa.gov/gsrp/program

Purpose To provide funding to minority and other graduate students interested in conducting research in fields of interest to the U.S. National Aeronautics and Space Administration (NASA).

Eligibility This program is open to full-time students enrolled or planning to enroll in an accredited graduate program at a U.S. college or university. Applicants must be citizens of the United States, sponsored by a faculty adviser or department chair, and interested in conducting research in space sciences. They must also be interested in a summer internship at a NASA field center. Selection is based on academic qualifications, quality of the proposed research and its relevance to NASA's program, proposed utilization of center research facilities (except for NASA headquarters), and ability of the student to accomplish the defined research. Individuals from underrepresented groups in science, technology, engineering, and mathematics (STEM) fields (African Americans, Native Americans, Alaskan Natives, Mexican Americans, Puerto Ricans, Native Pacific Islanders, women, and persons with disabilities) are strongly urged to apply. First-time applicants are eligible only for research opportunities offered by NASA field centers or the Aeronautics Research Mission Directorate; renewal awards are available from NASA field centers and all Mission Directorates.

Financial data The program provides a $21,000 student stipend, a $4,000 student travel allowance, up to $1,000 for health insurance, and a $4,000 university allowance. The student stipend may cover tuition, room and board, books, software, meal plans, school and laboratory supplies, and other related expenses. The student travel allowance may be used for national and international conferences and data collection. The university allowance is a discretionary award that typically goes to the research adviser. If the student already has health insurance, that $1,000 grant may be added to the student stipend or student travel allowance. An additional stipend of $10,000 for the first year is available to students approved for the Aeronautics Fellowship.

Duration 1 year; may be renewed for up to 2 additional years.

Additional information This program was established in 1980. Under the current NASA organizational structure, the Aeronautics Research Mission Directorate (ARMD) supports research in aeronautical engineering; the Exploration Systems Mission Directorate (ESMD) supports research in chemical, electrical, materials, mechanical, and metallurgical engineering, chemistry, physics, biological and life science, environmental science, and other sciences; the Science Mission Directorate, Office of Earth Science Division (SMD-ES) supports research in mechanical engineering, chemistry, physics, physical science, mathematics, computer science, biological science, social science, atmospheric science, geological science, oceanography, and environmental science; the Science Mission Directorate-Office of Space Science (SMD-SS) supports research in astronomy, chemistry, physics, physical science, computer science, biological science, and atmospheric science; the Space Operations Mission Directorate (SOMD) supports research in materials, mechanical, and metallurgical engineering, mathematics, and computer science. Other awards are distributed through NASA field centers, each of which has its own research agenda and facilities. These centers include Ames Research Center (Moffett Field, California), Dryden Flight Research Facility (Edwards, California), Goddard Space Flight Center (Greenbelt, Maryland), Jet Propulsion Laboratory (Pasadena, California), Johnson Space Center (Houston, Texas), Kennedy Space Center (Kennedy Space Center, Florida), Langley Research Center (Hampton, Virginia), Glenn Research Center (Cleveland, Ohio), Marshall Space Flight Center (Huntsville, Alabama), and Stennis Space Center (Stennis Space Center, Mississippi). Fellows spend some period of time in residence at the center, taking advantage of the unique research facilities of the installation and working with center personnel. They also conduct an internship there during the summers. Travel outside the

United States is allowed if it is essential to the research effort and charged to a grant.
Number awarded This program supports approximately 300 graduate students each year.
Deadline January of each year.

[1050]
NASA SMALL BUSINESS INNOVATION RESEARCH GRANTS

National Aeronautics and Space Administration
c/o REI Systems, Inc.
NASA SBIR/STTR Support Office
4041 Powder Mill Road, Suite 311
Calverton, MD 20705
(301) 937-0888   Fax: (301) 937-0204
E-mail: sbir@reisys.com
Web: sbir.nasa.gov

Purpose To support small businesses (especially those owned by minorities and women) that have the technological experience to contribute to the research and development mission of the National Aeronautics and Space Administration (NASA).
Eligibility For the purposes of this program, a "small business" is defined as a firm that is organized for profit with a location in the United States; is in the legal form of an individual proprietorship, partnership, limited liability company, corporation, joint venture, association, trust, or cooperative; is at least 51% owned and controlled by 1 or more individuals who are citizens or permanent residents of the United States; and has (including its affiliates) fewer than 500 employees. The primary employment of the principal investigator must be with the firm at the time of award and during the conduct of the proposed project. Preference is given to women-owned small business concerns and to socially and economically disadvantaged small business concerns. Women-owned small business concerns are those that are at least 51% owned by a woman or women who also control and operate them. Socially and economically disadvantaged small business concerns are at least 51% owned by an Indian tribe, a Native Hawaiian organization, or 1 or more socially and economically disadvantaged individuals (African Americans, Hispanic Americans, Native Americans, Asian Pacific Americans, or subcontinent Asian Americans). Currently, the program is aligned with NASA's 4 mission directorates: aeronautics research, exploration systems, science, and space operations. Selection is based on the project's scientific/technical merit and feasibility; technical capabilities and experience of the principal investigator or project manager, key personnel, staff, consultants, and subcontractors; effectiveness of the proposed work plan; and commercial merit and feasibility.
Financial data Grants are offered in 2 phases. In phase 1, awards normally do not exceed $100,000 (for both direct and indirect costs); in phase 2, awards normally do not exceed $600,000 (including both direct and indirect costs).
Duration Phase 1 awards may extend up to 6 months; phase 2 awards may extend up to 2 years.
Additional information Information is also available from each NASA center. The lead center for the SBIR/STTR program is Ames Research Center, MS 239-11, Moffett Field, CA 94035-1000, (650) 604-6595, E-mail: Gary.C.Jahns@nasa.gov.
Number awarded Varies each year; recently, NASA issued 276 phase 1 awards worth approximately $27.6 million; it planned to offer approximately 40% of those phase 2 awards.
Deadline September of each year.

[1051]
NATIONAL CANCER INSTITUTE MENTORED CLINICAL SCIENTIST AWARD TO PROMOTE DIVERSITY

National Cancer Institute
Attn: Comprehensive Minority Biomedical Branch
6116 Executive Boulevard, Suite 7031
Bethesda, MD 20892-8350
(301) 496-7344   Fax: (301) 402-4551
TTY: (301) 451-0088   E-mail: lockeb@mail.nih.gov
Web: www.cancer.gov/researchandfunding/training

Purpose To provide funding to Native Americans and members of other underrepresented groups who are interested in a program of training in cancer research under the supervision of an experienced mentor.
Eligibility This program is open to U.S. citizens, nationals, and permanent residents who have a health professional doctorate or are doctorally-trained oncology nurses. Applicants must be interested in a program of training to prepare for a career in laboratory or field-based cancer research. Candidates must be sponsored by a domestic, nonprofit or for-profit public or private institution (such as a university, college, hospital, or laboratory); a unit of state or local government; or an eligible agency of the federal government. They must qualify as 1) members of an ethnic or racial group shown to be underrepresented in health-related sciences on a national basis; 2) individuals with a disability; or 3) individuals from a disadvantaged background, including those from a low-income family and those from a social, cultural, and/or educational environment that has inhibited them from preparation for a research career. The mentor must 1) have extensive research experience; 2) be able to demonstrate an appreciation of the cultural, socioeconomic, and research background of the individual candidate; and 3) recognize the personal attention that minority candidates often need to pursue successful research careers. Selection is based on the applicant's qualifications, interests, accomplishments, motivation, and potential for a career in laboratory or field-based cancer research.
Financial data The award provides salary up to $75,000 per year plus related fringe benefits. In addition, up to $30,000 per year is provided for the following types of expenses: tuition, fees, and books related to career development; research expenses, such as supplies, equipment, and technical personnel; statistical services, including personnel and computer time; tuition, fees, and books related to career development; and travel to research meetings or for training. Facilities and administrative costs are reimbursed at 8% of modified total direct costs.
Duration Up to 5 years.
Additional information This program was originally established in 2002 as the successor of a program designated the Minorities in Clinical Oncology Program Grants. Recipients must devote at least 75% of their full-time pro-

fessional effort to cancer-related research and training activities.
Number awarded Varies each year, depending on the availability of funds.
Deadline February, June, or October of each year.

[1052]
NATIONAL EDUCATIONAL ENRICHMENT PROGRAM FOR MINORITY GRADUATE STUDENTS FELLOWSHIP IN GERONTOLOGY

National Hispanic Council on Aging
734 15th Street, N.W., Suite 1050
Washington, DC 20005
(202) 347-9733   Fax: (202) 347-9735
E-mail: nhcoa@nhcoa.org
Web: www.nhcoa.org/andrus_foundation.htm

Purpose To provide funding to graduate students from Native American or other underrepresented minority groups interested in conducting research and attending a seminar about current developments related to elderly minorities.
Eligibility This program is open to Latino, African American, and Native American graduate students. Applicants must be interested in participating in a program that includes 1) research activities at their home academic institutions or another campus, and 2) a seminar at the sponsoring organization.
Financial data Fellows receive a $2,000 stipend, travel and per diem for the seminar, and reimbursement for books and other approved expenses.
Duration 2 months, including 1 week for the seminar in Washington, D.C.
Additional information The seminar includes study of the policy-making process, the resource allocation process in relation to minority aging, a review of research being conducted presently that addresses issues of minority elderly, the research topic of each fellow, and an examination of leadership roles that future minority gerontologists must assume to improve the quality of life for minority elderly. This program is jointly sponsored by the National Caucus and Center on Black Aged, the National Hispanic Council on Aging, and the National Indian Council on Aging. Funding is provided by the Andrus Foundation of the American Association of Retired Persons.
Number awarded 9 each year: 3 selected by each sponsoring organization.

[1053]
NATIONAL HEART, LUNG, AND BLOOD INSTITUTE CAREER TRANSITION AWARD

National Heart, Lung, and Blood Institute
Attn: Office of Minority Health Affairs
6701 Rockledge Drive, Suite 8186
Bethesda, MD 20892-7913
(301) 451-5081   Fax: (301) 480-0862
TTY: (301) 451-0088   E-mail: krishnac@nhlbi.nih.gov
Web: www.nhlbi.nih.gov/funding/inits/index.htm

Purpose To provide funding to minority and other recent postdoctorates interested in a program of research training in diseases of the heart, lungs, and blood at intramural laboratories of the National Heart, Lung, and Blood Institute (NHLBI), followed by a transition as a new investigator at an extramural institution.
Eligibility This program is open to U.S. citizens, nationals, and permanent residents who have a research or health-professional doctorate and postdoctoral research experience. Applicants must be interested in a program of training at an NHLBI intramural laboratory in diseases of the heart, blood vessels, blood, and lungs. After that experience, they must obtain a tenure-track position at an eligible domestic, for-profit or nonprofit, public or private institution, such as a university, college, hospital, laboratory, unit of state or local government, or eligible agency of the federal government. Members of underrepresented racial and ethnic groups and individuals with disabilities are especially encouraged to apply.
Financial data During the intramural phase, the salary is at the regular NHLBI rate for the awardee's level of experience. For the extramural phase, total direct costs up to $150,000 per year are supported.
Duration 4 or 5 years, including 2 or 3 years of intramural support at NHLBI and 2 years at an extramural institution.
Additional information During the intramural phase, awardees must work full time on research; during the extramural phase, they must devote 75% of full-time professional effort to research and career development activities.
Number awarded 5 each year.
Deadline February, June, or October of each year.

[1054]
NATIONAL INSTITUTES OF HEALTH SMALL BUSINESS TECHNOLOGY TRANSFER GRANTS

National Institutes of Health
Attn: SBIR/STTR Program Coordinator
6705 Rockledge Drive, Room 3534
Bethesda, MD 20892-7911
(301) 435-2688   Fax: (301) 480-0146
TTY: (301) 451-0088   E-mail: jg128w@nih.gov
Web: grants.nih.gov/grants/guide/index.html

Purpose To provide financial support to cooperative research and development projects carried out between small business concerns (especially those owned by minorities) and research institutions in areas of interest to the National Institutes of Health (NIH).
Eligibility For the purposes of this program, a "small business" is defined as those organized for profit with a location in the United States; is in the legal form of an individual proprietorship, partnership, limited liability company, corporation, joint venture, association, trust, or cooperative; is at least 51% owned and controlled by 1 or more individuals who are citizens or permanent residents of the United States; and has (including its affiliates) fewer than 500 employees. Unlike the Public Health Service Small Business Innovation Research Grants, the primary employment of the principal investigator does not need to be with the business concern. This program, however, requires that the small business apply in collaboration with a nonprofit research institution for conduct of a project that has potential for commercialization. At least 40% of the work must be performed by the small business and at least 30% of the work must be performed by the research institution. The principal investigator may have his/her primary employment with an organization other than the small business concern, includ-

ing the research institution. Preference is given to women-owned small business concerns and to socially and economically disadvantaged small business concerns. Women-owned small business concerns are those that are at least 51% owned by a woman or women who also control and operate them. Socially and economically disadvantaged small business concerns are at least 51% owned by an Indian tribe, a Native Hawaiian organization, or 1 or more socially and economically disadvantaged individuals (African Americans, Hispanic Americans, Native Americans, Asian Pacific Americans, or subcontinent Asian Americans). Partnerships between small business and Historically Black Colleges and Universities (HBCUs) and Minority Institutions (MIs) are especially encouraged. The project must be performed in the United States. Research is supported in all areas of biomedical and behavioral science that fall within the mission of the NIH.
Financial data Support is offered in 2 phases. In phase 1, awards normally do not exceed $100,000 (for both direct and indirect costs); in phase 2, awards normally do not exceed $500,000 (including both direct and indirect costs).
Duration Phase 1 awards may extend up to 1 year; phase 2 awards may extend up to 2 years.
Additional information The NIH is the only component of the U.S. Public Health Service (PHS) that participates in this program.
Number awarded Each year, approximately 100 awards are made by NIH. The total budget for this program recently was approximately $69 million.
Deadline April, August, or December of each year.

[1055]
NATIONAL INSTITUTES OF HEALTH SMALL RESEARCH GRANT PROGRAM

National Institutes of Health
Office of Extramural Research
Attn: Grants Information
6705 Rockledge Drive
Bethesda, MD 20892-7974
(301) 435-0714 Fax: (301) 480-0525
TTY: (301) 451-0088 E-mail: GrantsInfo@nih.gov
Web: grants.nih.gov/grants/guide/index.html

Purpose To provide funding to minority and other investigators in the biomedical and behavioral sciences who are interested in conducting pilot or other small research projects.
Eligibility This program is open to 1) investigators in the biomedical and behavioral sciences at domestic and foreign, for-profit and nonprofit, public and private institutions (such as universities, colleges, hospitals, and laboratories); 2) units of state and local governments; and 3) eligible agencies of the federal government. Applicants must be interested in conducting limited research projects, such as pilot or feasibility studies; secondary analysis of existing data; small, self-contained research projects; development of research methodology; or development of new research technology. Members of underrepresented ethnic or racial groups and individuals with disabilities are especially encouraged to apply.
Financial data Applicants may request up to $50,000 per year (direct costs) or $25,000 per module for 2 modules per year for supplies, travel, small items of equipment, and salary for technical personnel.
Duration Up to 24 months.
Additional information These grants are offered by 12 component institutes and centers within the National Institutes of Health (NIH): the National Human Genome Research Institute, the National Institute on Drug Abuse, the National Institute on Aging, the National Institute on Alcohol Abuse and Alcoholism, the National Institute of Allergy and Infectious Diseases, the National Institute of Biomedical Imaging and Bioengineering, the National Institute of Child Health and Human Development, the National Institute of Environmental Health Sciences, the National Institute of Mental Health, the National Institute of Neurological Disorders and Stroke, the National Institute of Nursing Research, and the National Library of Medicine. Other components operate their own specialized programs.
Number awarded Varies each year.
Deadline February, June, or October of each year.

[1056]
NATIONAL MUSEUM OF THE AMERICAN INDIAN VISITING ARTIST PROGRAM

National Museum of the American Indian
Attn: Native Arts Program
Cultural Resources Center
4220 Silver Hill Road
Suitland, MD 20746-2863
(301) 238-1540 Fax: (301) 238-3200
E-mail: NAP@si.edu
Web: www.nmai.si.edu

Purpose To provide Native American professional artists with an opportunity to collaborate and consult with the National Museum of the American Indian (NMAI) in conducting museum research and collection study.
Eligibility This program is open to Native artists from the western Hemisphere and Hawaii who are recognized by their community, have at least 10 years of experience, and can demonstrate significant artistic accomplishments in any media (e.g., visual arts, media arts, performance arts, literature). Students enrolled in a degree program are ineligible. Applicants must be interested in visiting and conducting research in NMAI collections and other museums and cultural institutions on the East Coast. Along with their application, they must submit a research proposal that includes descriptions of the cultural area or community, type of objects, and time period to be researched; the relationship between the proposed collections research and their art; any culturally sensitive objects they wish to research; how the research will benefit their career and advance their artistic endeavors; and how they plan to document their research.
Financial data The grant is $6,000. Round-trip air transportation and lodging are also provided, but participants are responsible for such personal and incidental expenses as meals and local travel.
Duration 2 to 3 weeks.
Additional information Fellowships provide support for travel to the NMAI Cultural Resources Center in Suitland, Maryland and to museums in New York, Philadelphia, Boston, and Washington, D.C. Artists must conduct a community-based project within 6 months of the research period and

submit a 1-page written report (that may include slides, photos, or videos) describing the outcome of the project.
Number awarded 4 each year.
Deadline April of each year.

[1057]
NATIONAL NATIVE CREATIVE DEVELOPMENT GRANT PROGRAM

Evergreen State College
Attn: Longhouse Education and Cultural Center
2700 Evergreen Parkway N.W.
Olympia, WA 98505
(360) 867-6413   Fax: (360) 867-6699
E-mail: longhouse@evergreen.edu
Web: www.evergreen.edu

Purpose To provide funding for professional development to Native artists.
Eligibility This program is open to Native artists (defined to include American Indians, Alaska Natives, and Native Hawaiians) working in any form of visual, performance, literary, and performing arts. Applicants must be seeking funding for professional development needs (e.g., training in marketing, supplies and materials, harvesting resources, portfolio development, apprenticeships). They must submit a letter of inquiry that includes a description of their proposed project, the intended outcome of their project, how the project would advance their professional and personal development, and how their project would contribute to the field of Native art. U.S. citizenship is required.
Financial data The maximum grant is $2,000.
Duration Up to 1 year.
Additional information This program began in 2005 as a project of the Artist Trust of Seattle and limited to artists living in the Northwest. In 2007, the Longhouse Education and Cultural Center at Evergreen State College, with support from the Ford Foundation, assumed management and made the project national.
Number awarded Up to 16 each year.
Deadline Letters of inquiry must be submitted by May of each year.

[1058]
NATIONAL NATIVE MASTER ARTIST INITIATIVE: ARTIST TEACHING ARTISTS

Evergreen State College
Attn: Longhouse Education and Cultural Center
2700 Evergreen Parkway N.W.
Olympia, WA 98505
(360) 867-6413   Fax: (360) 867-6699
E-mail: longhouse@evergreen.edu
Web: www.evergreen.edu

Purpose To provide funding to organizations and individuals interested in developing a project in which master Native artists provide training to other artists in their community.
Eligibility This program provides an opportunity for a master Native artist to teach other Native artists, within a community setting. Native is defined to include American Indians, Alaska Natives, and Native Hawaiians; acceptable disciplines include all forms of visual, performance, literary, and performing arts. Applications may be submitted by either a master Native artist (defined as a person who is considered a master by his or her peers or by the Native community) or a sponsoring organization (tribal government, urban Native center, educational institution, or other organization that works in support of Native arts and cultures). Initial letters of inquiry must include a description of the proposed project and the art form to be taught, a brief description of the host community, the host organization's mission statement, an explanation of how the host organization's mission statement addresses Native art, evidence of previous successful programs with Native communities for the host organization and master artist, and a statement of why this project is needed in the host community.
Financial data The maximum grant is $5,000.
Duration The training program may be as short as 2 weeks, or it may be for up to 1 year, depending on the art form.
Additional information This program is supported by the Ford Foundation.
Number awarded 5 each year.
Deadline Letters of inquiry must be submitted by May of each year.

[1059]
NATIONAL PHYSICAL SCIENCE CONSORTIUM DISSERTATION SUPPORT PROGRAM

National Physical Science Consortium
c/o University of Southern California
3716 South Hope Street, Suite 348
Los Angeles, CA 90007-4344
(213) 743-2409   Toll-free: (800) 854-NPSC
Fax: (213) 743-2407   E-mail: npschq@npsc.org
Web: www.npsc.org/students/info.html

Purpose To provide funding to Native American and other underrepresented minorities and women conducting dissertation research in designated science and engineering fields.
Eligibility This program is open to U.S. citizens who are enrolled in a doctoral program and about to begin dissertation research. Eligible fields of study are generally limited to astronomy, chemistry, computer science, geology, materials science, mathematical sciences, physics, their subdisciplines, and related engineering fields (chemical, computer, electrical, environmental, and mechanical). The program welcomes applications from all qualified students and continues to emphasize the recruitment of underrepresented minority (African American, Hispanic, Native American Indian, Eskimo, Aleut, and Pacific Islander) and women physical science and engineering students. Fellowships are provided to students at the 116 universities that are members of the consortium. Selection is based on academic standing (GPA), undergraduate and graduate course work and grades, university and/or industry research experience, letters of recommendation, and GRE scores.
Financial data The fellowship pays tuition and fees plus an annual stipend of $16,000.
Duration Up to 4 years.
Number awarded Varies each year.
Deadline November of each year.

[1060]
NATIONAL SPACE GRANT COLLEGE AND FELLOWSHIP PROGRAM
National Aeronautics and Space Administration
Attn: Program Manager
NASA Headquarters
Washington, DC 20546-0001
(202) 358-1523 Fax: (202) 358-3048
E-mail: jdasch@hq.nasa.gov
Web: www.nasa.gov

Purpose To provide financial assistance to minority and other undergraduate and graduate students interested in preparing for a career in a space-related field at a college or university participating in the National Space Grant program.

Eligibility This program is open to undergraduate and graduate students at colleges and universities that participate in the National Space Grant program of the U.S. National Aeronautics and Space Administration (NASA) through their state consortium. Applicants must be interested in a program of study and/or research in a field of science, mathematics, engineering, or technology (SMET) related to space. A specific goal of the program is to increase preparation by members of underrepresented groups (minorities, women, and persons with disabilities) for SMET space-related careers. Financial need is not considered in the selection process.

Financial data Each consortium establishes the terms of the fellowship program in its state.

Additional information NASA established the Space Grant program in 1989. It operates through 52 consortia in each state, the District of Columbia, and Puerto Rico. Each consortium includes selected colleges and universities in that state as well as other affiliates from industry, museums, science centers, and state and local agencies. There are similar programs for postdoctorates and faculty at these institutions as well.

Number awarded Varies each year.

Deadline Each consortium sets its own deadlines.

[1061]
NATIVE AMERICAN PUBLIC TELECOMMUNICATIONS PUBLIC TELEVISION PROGRAM FUND
Native American Public Telecommunications, Inc.
1800 North 33rd Street
P.O. Box 83111
Lincoln, NE 68501
(402) 472-3522 Fax: (402) 472-8675
E-mail: native@unl.edu
Web: www.nativetelecom.org

Purpose To provide funding for the creation of Native American theme programs intended for broadcast to public television audiences.

Eligibility This program invites producers to submit competitive proposals for the research and development, scripting, or completion of culture-specific programs that originate from the Native North American experience and are intended for national public television audiences. All program categories are eligible, except industrial or promotional films and videos, student productions, projects that are commercial in nature, projects for which 4-year exclusive public television broadcast rights are not available, projects or production entities that are foreign-owned or controlled, projects intended solely for theatrical release, and projects funded in part by a government entity or group featured in the content of the program. Applicants must be U.S. citizens or legal residents at least 21 years of age. They must have previous television or filmmaking experience. Applications must be accompanied by a project description, itemized budget, list of key personnel, and sample of a completed work or a work-in-progress by the director. Selection is based on quantity and quality of Native American participation in creative, technical, and advisory personnel; power of the finished program to illuminate the Native American experience through public television; originality of concept and style; strength of the production team to complete the project within budget, schedule, and the highest quality standards; sound production and fundraising plans; reasonable budget estimates and considerations; potential interest to a national audience; and strength of sample work.

Financial data Grants range up to $25,000 for research and development, or up to $100,000 for production or completion.

Duration Up to 1 year.

Additional information This program is underwritten by the Corporation for Public Broadcasting.

Number awarded Varies each year.

Deadline July of each year.

[1062]
NATIVE AMERICAN VISITING STUDENT AWARDS
Smithsonian Institution
Attn: Office of Research Training and Services
470 L'Enfant Plaza, Suite 7102
P.O. Box 37012, MRC 902
Washington, DC 20013-7012
(202) 633-7070 Fax: (202) 633-7069
E-mail: siofg@si.edu
Web: www.si.edu/ofg/ofgapp.htm

Purpose To provide funding to Native American graduate students interested in working on a project related to Native American topics at the Smithsonian Institution.

Eligibility Native Americans who are formally or informally related to a Native American community are eligible to apply. Applicants must be advanced graduate students who are proposing to undertake a project that is related to a Native American topic and requires the use of Native American resources at the Smithsonian Institution.

Financial data Students receive a grant of $100 per day for short-term awards or $500 per week for long-term awards. Also provided are allowances for travel and research.

Duration Up to 21 days for short-term awards; 3 to 10 weeks for long-term awards.

Additional information Recipients carry out independent research projects in association with the Smithsonian's research staff. Fellows are required to be in residence at the Smithsonian for the duration of the fellowship.

Number awarded Varies each year.

Deadline January of each year for summer or fall residency; September of each year for spring residency.

[1063]
NAVAJO NATION DISSERTATION FUNDING
Navajo Nation
Attn: Office of Navajo Nation Scholarship and Financial Assistance
P.O. Box 1870
Window Rock, AZ 86515-1870
(928) 871-7640   Toll-free: (800) 243-2956
Fax: (928) 871-6561
E-mail: onnsfacentral@navajo.org
Web: www.onnsfa.org/gradfund.asp

Purpose To provide financial assistance to members of the Navajo Nation who are working on a doctoral dissertation.

Eligibility This program is open to enrolled members of the Navajo Nation who are conducting dissertation research for a doctoral degree. Applicants must have completed all course work and have been advanced to candidacy. They must submit an itemized dissertation budget.

Financial data Funding is limited to direct costs for field work and research necessary to complete the dissertation.

Duration 1 year; may be renewed if the recipient is making satisfactory progress on the dissertation.

Deadline April of each year.

[1064]
NAVAL RESEARCH LABORATORY BROAD AGENCY ANNOUNCEMENT
Naval Research Laboratory
Attn: Deputy for Small Business
4555 Overlook Avenue, S.W.
Washington, DC 20375-5320
(202) 767-0666   Fax: (202) 767-0494
E-mail: marita.thompson@nrl.navy.mil
Web: heron.nrl.navy.mil/contracts/home.htm

Purpose To provide funding to minority and other investigators interested in conducting scientific research of interest to the U.S. Navy.

Eligibility This program is open to investigators qualified to conduct research in designated scientific and technical areas. Topics cover a wide range of technical and scientific areas; recent programs included radar technology, information technology, optical sciences, tactical electronic warfare, materials science and component technology, chemistry, computational physics and fluid dynamics, plasma physics, electronics science and technology, biomolecular science and engineering, ocean and atmospheric science and technology, acoustics, remote sensing, oceanography, marine geosciences, marine meteorology, and space science. Proposals may be submitted by any non-governmental entity, including commercial firms, institutions of higher education with degree-granting programs in science or engineering, or by consortia led by such concerns. The Naval Research Laboratory (NRL) encourages participation by small businesses, small disadvantaged business concerns, women-owned small businesses, veteran-owned small businesses, service-disabled veteran-owned small businesses, HUBZone small businesses, Historically Black Colleges and Universities, and Minority Institutions. Selection is based on the degree to which new and creative solutions to technical issues important to NRL programs are proposed and the offeror's understanding of the proposed approach and technical objectives; the offeror's ability to implement the proposed approach; the degree to which technical data and/or computer software developed under the proposed contract are to be delivered to the NRL with rights compatible with NRL research and development objectives; proposed cost and cost realism; and the extent to which offerors identify and commit to small business, small disadvantaged business, veteran-owned small business, women-owned small business, HUBZone small business, Historically Black College and University, or Minority Institution participation in the proposed effort (as a joint venture, teaming arrangement, or subcontractor).

Financial data The typical range of funding is from $100,000 to $2,000,000.

Duration 1 year.

Additional information The Naval Research Laboratory conducts most of its research in its own facilities in Washington, D.C., Stennis Space Center, Mississippi, and Monterey, California, but it also funds some related research.

Number awarded Varies each year.

Deadline Each program establishes its own application deadline; for a complete list of all the programs, including their deadlines, contact the NRL.

[1065]
NCI MENTORED CAREER DEVELOPMENT AWARD TO PROMOTE DIVERSITY
National Cancer Institute
Attn: Comprehensive Minority Biomedical Branch
6116 Executive Boulevard, Suite 7031
Bethesda, MD 20892-8350
(301) 496-7344   Fax: (301) 402-4551
TTY: (301) 451-0088   E-mail: lockeb@mail.nih.gov
Web: www.cancer.gov/researchandfunding/training

Purpose To provide funding to Native Americans and members of other underrepresented groups who need a period of "protected time" for intensive cancer research career development under the guidance of an experienced mentor.

Eligibility This program is open to U.S. citizens, nationals, and permanent residents who have a health professional doctorate and have completed a mentored research training experience. They must be in an intensive, supervised research experience in the basic, clinical, prevention, and/or population sciences to prepare for an independent research career related to cancer biology, etiology, pathogenesis, prevention, diagnosis, and/or treatment. Candidates must be sponsored by a domestic, nonprofit or for-profit organization, public or private (such as a university, college, hospital, or laboratory) that can demonstrate a commitment to the development of the research careers of junior underrepresented minority health professionals in clinical oncology. They must qualify as 1) a member of an ethnic or racial group shown to be underrepresented in health-related sciences on a national basis; 2) an individual with a disability; or 3) an individual from a disadvantaged background, including those from a low-income family and those from a social, cultural, and/or educational environment that have inhibited them from preparation for a research career. The mentor must have extensive research experience and an appreciation of the cultural, socioeconomic, and research background of the candidate.

Financial data The award provides salary up to $75,000 per year plus related fringe benefits. In addition, up to $30,000 per year is provided for the following types of expenses: tuition, fees, and books related to career development; research expenses, such as supplies, equipment, and technical personnel; statistical services, including personnel and computer time; tuition, fees, and books related to career development; and travel to research meetings or for training. Facilities and administrative costs are reimbursed at 8% of modified total direct costs.
Duration 3, 4, or 5 years.
Additional information Recipients must devote at least 75% of their full-time professional effort to cancer-related research and training activities.
Number awarded Varies each year.
Deadline February, June, or October of each year.

[1066]
NCI MENTORED PATIENT-ORIENTED RESEARCH AWARD TO PROMOTE DIVERSITY

National Cancer Institute
Attn: Comprehensive Minority Biomedical Branch
6116 Executive Boulevard, Suite 7031
Bethesda, MD 20892-8350
(301) 496-7344   Fax: (301) 402-4551
TTY: (301) 451-0088   E-mail: lockeb@mail.nih.gov
Web: www.cancer.gov/researchandfunding/training

Purpose To provide funding to Native Americans and members of other underrepresented groups who are interested in a program of research training in patient-oriented oncology under the supervision of an experienced mentor.
Eligibility This program is open to U.S. citizens, nationals, and permanent residents who have a health professional doctorate and are committed to a career in patient-oriented cancer research. Their doctorate may be a health professional degree (e.g., M.D., D.D.S., D.O., D.V.M., D.N.Sc., Pharm.D.), but they may also have a Ph.D. in such disciplines as clinical psychology, nursing, clinical genetics, speech-language pathology, audiology, and rehabilitation. Candidates must be sponsored by a domestic, nonprofit or for-profit organization, public or private (such as a university, college, hospital, laboratory, unit of state or local government, or eligible agency of the federal government) that can demonstrate a commitment to the development of the research careers of junior underrepresented minority health professionals in clinical oncology. They must qualify as 1) members of an ethnic or racial group shown to be underrepresented in health-related sciences on a national basis; 2) individuals with a disability; or 3) individuals from a disadvantaged background, including those from a low-income family and those from a social, cultural, and/or educational environment that have inhibited them from preparation for a research career. At least 2 mentors are required: 1 who is recognized as an accomplished clinical investigator and at least 1 additional mentor or adviser who is recognized as an accomplished independent basic science investigator in the proposed research area.
Financial data The award provides salary up to $75,000 per year plus related fringe benefits. In addition, up to $30,000 per year is provided for the following types of expenses: tuition, fees, and books related to career development; research expenses, such as supplies, equipment, and technical personnel; statistical services, including personnel and computer time; tuition, fees, and books related to career development; and travel to research meetings or for training. Facilities and administrative costs are reimbursed at 8% of modified total direct costs.
Duration Up to 5 years.
Additional information Recipients must devote at least 75% of their full-time professional effort to cancer-related research and training activities.
Number awarded Varies each year.
Deadline February, June, or October of each year.

[1067]
NCI TRANSITION CAREER DEVELOPMENT AWARD TO PROMOTE DIVERSITY

National Cancer Institute
Attn: Comprehensive Minority Biomedical Branch
6116 Executive Boulevard, Suite 7031
Bethesda, MD 20892-8350
(301) 496-7344   Fax: (301) 402-4551
TTY: (301) 451-0088   E-mail: lockeb@mail.nih.gov
Web: www.cancer.gov/researchandfunding/training

Purpose To provide funding to Native American and other underrepresented scientists who are transitioning from a mentored research environment to an independent research and academic career in cancer research.
Eligibility This program is open to U.S. citizens, nationals, and permanent residents who 1) have a research or a health professional doctorate or equivalent; 2) have been in or currently are in a "mentored" research postdoctoral position and have completed 2 years or more of research in that capacity; and 3) intend to conduct a research project highly relevant to cancer biology, etiology, pathogenesis, prevention, diagnosis, and treatment that has the potential for establishing an independent research program. Candidates must be sponsored by a domestic, nonprofit or for-profit organization, public or private (such as a university, college, hospital, laboratory, unit of state or local government, or eligible agency of the federal government) that can demonstrate a commitment to the development of the research careers of junior underrepresented minority research scientists in biomedical cancer research. They must qualify as an underrepresented minority individual, defined as members of a particular ethnic, racial, or other group determined by their institution to be underrepresented in biomedical, behavioral, clinical, or social sciences, e.g., first generation college students or graduates, socio-economically disadvantaged persons, or persons with disabilities.
Financial data The award provides salary up to $75,000 per year plus related fringe benefits. In addition, up to $50,000 per year is provided for the following types of expenses: research expenses, such as supplies, equipment, and technical personnel; statistical services, including personnel and computer time; tuition, fees, and books related to career development; and travel to research meetings or for training. Facilities and administrative costs are reimbursed at 8% of modified total direct costs.
Duration Up to 3 years.
Additional information Recipients must devote at least 75% of their full-time professional effort to cancer-related research and peer review activities. The remaining 25% can be divided among other activities only if they are consistent

with the program goals, i.e., the candidate's development into an independent investigator.
Number awarded Approximately 10 each year.
Deadline January, May, or September of each year.

[1068]
NHLBI MENTORED CAREER DEVELOPMENT AWARD TO PROMOTE FACULTY DIVERSITY IN BIOMEDICAL RESEARCH
National Heart, Lung, and Blood Institute
Attn: Division of Epidemiology and Clinical Applications
6701 Rockledge Drive, Room 8158
Bethesda, MD 20892-7934
(301) 435-0709   Fax: (301) 480-1667
E-mail: silsbeeL@nhlbi.nih.gov
Web: www.nhlbi.nih.gov

Purpose To provide funding to members of underrepresented groups interested in developing into independent biomedical investigators in research areas relevant to the mission of the National Heart, Lung, and Blood Institute (NHLBI).

Eligibility This program is open to full-time faculty members at U.S. domestic institutions (universities, colleges, hospitals, and laboratories) who have a governments, and eligible agencies of the federal government) who have a doctoral degree or equivalent in the biomedical or behavioral sciences. Candidates must be members of a group that is currently underrepresented in biomedical or behavioral research, including African Americans, Hispanic Americans, Alaska Natives, American Indians, Native Hawaiians, non-Asian Pacific Islanders, and individuals with disabilities. They must 1) be U.S. citizens, nationals, or permanent residents; 2) have completed their doctoral degree at least 2 years previously; 3) have documented research experience; and 4) have identified a sponsor who is an accomplished investigator in the proposed research area and has experience in developing independent investigators. The proposed research development plan must enable the candidate to become an independent investigator in cardiovascular, pulmonary, hematologic, and sleep disorders research with either a clinical or basic science emphasis.

Financial data The awardee receives salary support of up to $75,000 per year plus fringe benefits. In addition, up to $30,000 per year may be provided for research project requirements and related support (e.g., technical personnel costs, supplies, equipment, candidate travel, telephone charges, publication costs, and tuition for necessary courses). Facilities and administrative costs may be reimbursed at the rate of 8% of total direct costs.

Duration 3 to 5 years.

Additional information At least 75% of the awardee's effort must be devoted to the research program. The remainder may be devoted to other clinical and teaching pursuits that are consistent with the program goals of developing the awardee into an independent biomedical scientist or the maintenance of the teaching and/or clinical skills needed for an academic research career.

Number awarded Varies each year; recently, 8 to 10 awards were available through this program with total funding of $1,200,000.

Deadline Letters of intent must be submitted by June of each year; completed applications are due in July.

[1069]
NIAAA CAREER TRANSITION AWARD
National Institute on Alcohol Abuse and Alcoholism
Attn: Division of Neuroscience and Behavior
5635 Fishers Lane
Bethesda, MD 20892-9304
(301) 443-9334   Fax: (301) 443-1650
TTY: (301) 451-0088   E-mail: dtwombly@mail.nih.gov
Web: www.niaaa.nih.gov

Purpose To provide funding to minority and other new investigators interested in establishing an independent program in basic or clinical research related to alcohol consumption and alcoholism.

Eligibility This program is open to basic science and clinical investigators with a research or health-professional doctoral degree (e.g., Ph.D., M.D., D.O., D.D.S., D.M.D., O.D., D.C., Pharm.D., or a doctoral degree in nursing research or practice) and from 2 to 6 years of postdoctoral training. Applicants must be interested in a career development program to establish an independent program in basic or clinical research related to the health risks and benefits of alcohol consumption, or the prevention and treatment of alcohol-related problems. They must be sponsored by a domestic, for-profit or nonprofit, public or private institution, such as a university, college, hospital, or laboratory. Members of underrepresented racial and ethnic groups and individuals with disabilities are especially encouraged to apply. Only U.S. citizens, nationals, and permanent residents are eligible.

Financial data Grants provide 1) salary support equal to 75% of their institutional base salary; 2) up to $75,000 per year for research expenses (e.g., supplies, equipment, technical personnel, statistical services (including personnel and computer time), tuition and fee related to career development, and travel to relevant research meetings or for training; and 3) reimbursement of facilities and administrative costs at 8% of modified total direct costs.

Duration Up to 3 years.

Additional information Scholars are expected to devote 75% of full-time professional effort to the funded research career development plan.

Number awarded 2 to 5 each year.

Deadline February, June, or October of each year.

[1070]
NIDA MENTORED CLINICAL SCIENTISTS DEVELOPMENT PROGRAM AWARD IN DRUG ABUSE AND ADDICTION
National Institute on Drug Abuse
Attn: Division of Clinical Neuroscience and Behavioral Research
6001 Executive Boulevard, Room 3153
Bethesda, MD 20892-9551
(301) 443-0107   Fax: (301) 443-6814
TTY: (310) 451-0088   E-mail: dg79a@nih.gov
Web: grants.nih.gov/grants/guide/index.html

Purpose To provide funding to minority and other postdoctorates interested in a program of mentored training for a career as an independent investigator in the area of drug abuse and addiction.

Eligibility This program is open to U.S. citizens, nationals, and permanent residents who have a clinical or research doctorate, including Ph.D., M.D., D.O., D.C., D.D.S., D.M.D., D.N.S., or equivalent. Applicants must be interested in a program of supervised research training and career development experiences leading to research independence in the area of drug abuse and addiction. Areas of interest include epidemiology, health services, prevention, treatment, clinical neurosciences, genetics, and medical consequences of drug abuse, including HIV/AIDS. They must be sponsored by a domestic, for-profit or nonprofit, public or private institution (such as a university, college, hospital, or laboratory). Members of underrepresented ethnic and racial groups and individuals with disabilities are especially encouraged to apply.

Financial data Grants provide salary support to fellows equivalent to their institution's base annual salary, to a maximum of $90,000 per year. An additional $50,000 per year is available for research-related costs, including consultants, supplies, equipment, technical personnel, statistical services, and other program-related expenses. Facilities and administrative costs may be reimbursed at 8% of modified total direct costs.

Duration 3 to 5 years.

Additional information Scholars must devote at least 75% of full-time professional effort conducting clinical research and relevant career development activities related to drug abuse.

Number awarded Varies each year.

Deadline February, June, or October of each year.

[1071]
NIDDK MENTORED CLINICAL SCIENTIST AWARD TO PROMOTE DIVERSITY IN HEALTH-RELATED RESEARCH

National Institute of Diabetes and Digestive and Kidney Diseases
Attn: Office of Minority Health Research Coordination
6707 Democracy Boulevard, Room 648A
Bethesda, MD 20892-5454
(301) 594-9652   Fax: (301) 594-9358
TTY: (301) 451-0088   E-mail: ff54t@nih.gov
Web: www2.niddk.nih.gov

Purpose To provide funding to physicians from Native American and other underrepresented groups who are interested in a program of research training in fields of interest to the National Institute of Diabetes and Digestive and Kidney Diseases (NIDDK) of the National Institutes of Health.

Eligibility This program is open to investigators who have 1) a health professional doctoral degree (e.g., M.D., D.D.S., D.O., D.V.M., O.D., Pharm.D.) and 2) a recently acquired (within the past 3 years) Master of Science in Clinical Research or Master of Public Health in a clinically relevant area. Applicants must be 1) a member of an ethnic or racial group that is underrepresented in health-related sciences on a national basis (e.g., African Americans, Hispanics, Native Americans, Alaska Natives, Hawaiian Natives, and non-Asian Pacific Islanders); or 2) an individual from a disadvantaged background, defined to include those who come from a low-income family and those who come from a social, cultural, and/or educational environment that has inhibited them from obtaining the knowledge, skills, and abilities necessary to develop and participate in a research career. They must be sponsored by a domestic for-profit or nonprofit, public or private institution, such as a university, college, hospital, or laboratory. Their proposed research training must relate to a high-priority interest of NIDDK, including diabetes, obesity, nutrition-related disorders, hepatitis C, gallbladder disease, sickle cell disease, kidney diseases, and complications from infection with HIV. Only U.S. citizens, nationals, and permanent residents are eligible.

Financial data Grants provide salary support up to $75,000 per year; an institutional allowance of up to $25,000 per year for tuition and fees related to career development, research expenses (supplies, equipment and technical personnel), travel to research meetings or training, and statistical services; and facilities and administrative costs at 8% of modified total direct costs.

Duration 3 years.

Additional information This program is also supported by the Office of Dietary Supplements within NIH.

Number awarded 2 each year.

Deadline November of each year.

[1072]
NIH DIRECTOR'S NEW INNOVATOR AWARD PROGRAM

National Institutes of Health
Office of Extramural Research
Attn: Grants Information
6705 Rockledge Drive
Bethesda, MD 20892-7974
(301) 435-0714   Fax: (301) 480-0525
TTY: (301) 451-0088   E-mail: GrantsInfo@nih.gov
Web: grants2.nih.gov/grants/new_investigators

Purpose To provide funding to minority and other new investigators in the biomedical and behavioral sciences who propose especially innovative research programs.

Eligibility This program is open to investigators who have an independent research position at a U.S. institution and received their doctoral degree or completed their medical internship and residency within the past 10 years. Applicants must qualify as a "new investigator," meaning they have not yet been the principal investigator on a prior major grant from the National Institutes of Health (NIH). They must be proposing new and innovative research with potential for exceptionally high impact on biomedical problems. Women and members of groups underrepresented in biomedical or behavioral research are especially encouraged to apply. There are no citizenship or residency requirements.

Financial data Grants provide up to $300,000 per year for direct costs plus applicable facilities and administrative costs.

Duration 5 years.

Additional information This program was established in 2007. Awardees are expected to devote at least 30% of their effort to the project supported by the award.

Number awarded At least 14 each year.

Deadline May of each year.

[1073]
NINDS MENTORED RESEARCH AND CLINICAL SCIENTIST DEVELOPMENT AWARDS IN TRANSLATIONAL RESEARCH

National Institute of Neurological Disorders and Stroke
Attn: Technology Development
6001 Executive Boulevard, Room 2139
Bethesda, MD 20892-9527
(301) 496-1779　　　　　Fax: (301) 402-1501
TTY: (301) 451-0088　　E-mail: millert@ninds.nih.gov
Web: www.ninds.nih.gov

Purpose To provide funding to minority and other postdoctorates interested in establishing an independent career in translational neuroscience research.

Eligibility This program is open to investigators who have 1) a Ph.D. or equivalent research-intensive degree or 2) a clinical doctoral degree or Ph.D. in a clinical discipline. Applicants should have significant postdoctoral or clinical fellowship experience or a junior faculty appointment at a sponsoring institution, which may be a domestic for-profit or nonprofit, public or private organizations, such as a university, college, hospital, laboratory, or unit of state or local tribal government. They must be interested in a program of mentored training and career development in translational research, defined as the process of applying ideas, insights, and discoveries generated through basic scientific inquiry to the treatment or prevention of human disease. The proposed research project should address therapy development for a specific neurological disorder or a group of closely-related disorders. Members of underrepresented racial and ethnic groups and individuals with disabilities are especially encouraged to apply. Only U.S. citizens, nationals, and permanent residents are eligible.

Financial data Grants provide an annual award of up to $85,000 for salary and fringe benefits and an annual research allowance of up to $50,000 for direct research costs. The institution may apply for up to 8% of direct costs for facilities and administrative costs.

Duration 3 to 5 years.

Additional information Grantees must commit at least 75% of full-time professional effort conducting research career development and clinical research activities associated with this award.

Number awarded Varies each year.

Deadline February, June, or October of each year.

[1074]
NINR MENTORED RESEARCH SCIENTIST DEVELOPMENT AWARD FOR UNDERREPRESENTED OR DISADVANTAGED INVESTIGATORS

National Institute of Nursing Research
Attn: Division of Extramural Activities
6701 Democracy Boulevard, Room 710
Bethesda, MD 20892-4870
(301) 594-5970　　　　　Fax: (301) 480-8260
TTY: (301) 451-0088　　E-mail: HussK@mail.nih.gov
Web: www.ninr.nih.gov

Purpose To provide funding for research career development to postdoctoral nursing investigators who are members of underrepresented or disadvantaged groups.

Eligibility This program is open to nurses who are employed full health-professional doctorate or its equivalent and are employed full time at an institution that conducts research. Applicants must qualify as an individual whose participation in scientific research will increase diversity, including 1) individuals from racial and ethnic groups that have been shown to be underrepresented in health-related science on a national basis; 2) individuals with disabilities; and 3) individuals from disadvantaged backgrounds, including those from a family with an annual income below established levels and those from a social, cultural, or educational environment that has demonstrably and recently directly inhibited the individual from obtaining the knowledge, skills, and abilities necessary to develop and participate in a research career. They must have a research or health-professional doctorate (e.g., Ph.D., D.N.Sc.) or its equivalent; have demonstrated the capacity or potential for a productive independent research career; have a Registered Nurse license; and have secured the commitment of an appropriate research mentor actively involved in research relevant to the mission of the National Institute of Nursing Research (NINR). Only U.S. citizens, nationals, and permanent residents are eligible.

Financial data The grant provides up to $50,000 per year for salary and fringe benefits plus an additional $20,000 per year for other expenses, such as tuition, fees, and books related to career development; research expenses, such as supplies, equipment, and technical personnel; travel to research meetings or trainings; and statistical services, including personnel, research, and computer time. Facilities and administrative costs are allowed at 8% of total direct costs.

Duration Up to 3 years.

Additional information These grants have been awarded annually since 1998. Grantees are expected to spend at least 75% of their professional effort time to the program and the other 25% devoted to other research-related and/or teaching or clinical pursuits consistent with the objectives of the award.

Number awarded 3 to 4 new grants are awarded each year.

Deadline February, June, or October of each year.

[1075]
NOAA SMALL BUSINESS INNOVATION RESEARCH GRANTS

National Oceanic and Atmospheric Administration
Office of Research and Technology Applications
Attn: SBIR Program Manager
1335 East-West Highway, SSMC1, Room 106
Silver Spring, MD 20910-3284
(301) 713-3565　　　　　Fax: (301) 713-4100
E-mail: joseph.bishop@noaa.gov
Web: www.oar.noaa.gov/orta

Purpose To support small businesses (especially those owned by minorities and women) that have the technological experience to contribute to the research and development mission of the National Oceanic and Atmospheric Administration (NOAA).

Eligibility For the purposes of this program, a "small business" is defined as a firm that is organized for profit with a location in the United States; is in the legal form of an individual proprietorship, partnership, limited liability company, corporation, joint venture, association, trust, or cooperative; is at least 51% owned and controlled by 1 or more individuals who are citizens or permanent residents of the United States; and has (including its affiliates) fewer than 500 employees. The primary employment of the principal investigator must be with the firm at the time of award and during the conduct of the proposed project. Preference is given to women-owned small business concerns and to socially and economically disadvantaged small business concerns. Women-owned small business concerns are those that are at least 51% owned by a woman or women who also control and operate them. Socially and economically disadvantaged small business concerns are at least 51% owned by an Indian tribe, a Native Hawaiian organization, or 1 or more socially and economically disadvantaged individuals (African Americans, Hispanic Americans, Native Americans, Asian Pacific Americans, or subcontinent Asian Americans). The project must be performed in the United States. Current priority areas of research include: ecosystems, climate, weather and water, and commerce and transportation. Selection is based on the scientific and technical merit of the research plan and its relevance to the objectives, with special emphasis on its innovativeness and originality; importance of the problem or opportunity and anticipated benefits of the proposed research to NOAA; the commercial potential, if successful; how well the research objectives, if achieved, establish the feasibility of the proposed concept; and qualifications of the principal investigator, other key staff, and consultants.

Financial data Grants are offered in 2 phases. In phase 1, awards normally do not exceed $95,000 (for both direct and indirect costs); in phase 2, awards normally do not exceed $400,000 (including both direct and indirect costs).

Duration Phase 1 awards may extend up to 6 months; phase 2 awards may extend up to 2 years.

Number awarded Varies each year; recently, NOAA planned to award 10 Phase 1 contracts. Approximately one third of Phase 1 awardees receive Phase 2 awards.

Deadline January of each year.

[1076]
NSF DIRECTOR'S AWARD FOR DISTINGUISHED TEACHING SCHOLARS

National Science Foundation
Directorate for Education and Human Resources
Attn: Division of Undergraduate Education
4201 Wilson Boulevard, Room 835N
Arlington, VA 22230
(703) 292-4627   Fax: (703) 292-9015
TDD: (800) 281-8749   E-mail: npruitt@nsf.gov
Web: www.nsf.gov

Purpose To recognize and reward, with funding for additional research, minority and other scholars affiliated with institutions of higher education who have contributed to teaching of science, technology, engineering, and mathematics (STEM) at the K-12 and undergraduate level.

Eligibility This program is open to teaching-scholars affiliated with institutions of higher education who are nominated by their president, chief academic officer, or other independent researcher. Nominees should have integrated research and education and approached both education and research in a scholarly manner. They should have demonstrated leadership in their respective fields as well as innovativeness and effectiveness in facilitating K-12 and undergraduate student learning in STEM disciplines. Consideration is given to faculty who have a history of substantial impact on 1) research in a STEM discipline or on STEM educational research; or 2) the STEM education of K-16 students who have diverse interests and aspirations, including future K-12 teachers of science and mathematics, students who plan to pursue STEM careers, and those who need to understand science and mathematics in a society increasingly dependent on science and technology. Based on letters of nomination, selected scholars are invited to submit applications for support of their continuing efforts to integrate education and research. Nominations of women, underrepresented minorities, and persons with disabilities are especially encouraged.

Financial data The maximum grant is $300,000 for the life of the project.

Duration 4 years.

Number awarded Approximately 6 each year.

Deadline Letters of intent are due in September of each year; full applications must be submitted in October.

[1077]
NSF SMALL BUSINESS INNOVATION RESEARCH GRANTS

National Science Foundation
Directorate for Engineering
Attn: Division of Industrial Innovation and Partnerships
4201 Wilson Boulevard, Room 590 N
Arlington, VA 22230
(703) 292-8050   Fax: (703) 292-9057
TDD: (800) 281-8749
Web: www.nsf.gov

Purpose To provide funding to small and creative engineering, science, education, and technology-related firms (especially those owned by minorities) to conduct innovative, high-risk research on scientific and technical problems.

Eligibility For the purposes of this program, a "small business" is defined as a firm that is organized for profit with a location in the United States; is in the legal form of an individual proprietorship, partnership, limited liability company, corporation, joint venture, association, trust, or cooperative; is at least 51% owned and controlled by 1 or more individuals who are citizens or permanent residents of the United States; and has (including its affiliates) fewer than 500 employees. The primary employment of the principal investigator must be with the firm at the time of award and during the conduct of the proposed project. Members of minority racial and ethnic groups, women, and persons with disabilities are particularly encouraged to apply as principal investigators. Preference is given to women-owned small business concerns and to socially and economically disadvantaged small business concerns. Women-owned small business concerns are at least 51% owned by a woman or women who also control and operate them. Socially and economically disadvantaged small business concerns are at least 51% owned by an Indian tribe, Native Hawaiian organization, or 1 or more socially and economically disadvantaged individuals (African Americans, Hispanic Americans, Native Americans, Asian Pacific Americans, or subcontinent Asian Americans). The project must be performed in the United States. Current priorities for critical technology areas of national importance include 1) advanced materials, chemical technology and manufacturing; 2) biotechnology; 3) electronics; 4) information technology; and 5) emerging opportunities (projects with a focus on near-term commercialization).

Financial data Support is offered in 2 phases. In phase 1, awards normally may not exceed $100,000 (for both direct and indirect costs); in phase 2, awards normally may not exceed $500,000 (including both direct and indirect costs).

Duration Phase 1 awards may extend up to 6 months; phase 2 awards may extend up to 2 years.

Number awarded Depends on the availability of funds; the National Science Foundation (NSF) plans to award 125 phase 1 grants each year. Recently, $12.5 million was budgeted for this program.

Deadline June of each year for proposals in advanced materials, chemical technology, manufacturing innovation, biotechnology, electronics, information technology, and emerging opportunities; December of each year for biological and environmental technologies, components and systems, and software and services.

[1078]
NSF SMALL BUSINESS TECHNOLOGY TRANSFER GRANTS

National Science Foundation
Directorate for Engineering
Attn: Division of Industrial Innovation and Partnerships
4201 Wilson Boulevard, Room 590 N
Arlington, VA 22230
(703) 292-8050   Fax: (703) 292-9057
TDD: (800) 281-8749
Web: www.nsf.gov

Purpose To provide financial support to cooperative research and development projects carried out between small business concerns (especially those owned by minorities) and research institutions in areas of concern to the National Science Foundation (NSF).

Eligibility For the purposes of this program, a "small business" is defined as a firm that is organized for profit with a location in the United States; is in the legal form of an individual proprietorship, partnership, limited liability company, corporation, joint venture, association, trust, or cooperative; is at least 51% owned and controlled by 1 or more individuals who are citizens or permanent residents of the United States; and has (including its affiliates) fewer than 500 employees. Unlike the NSF Small Business Innovation Research Grants, the primary employment of the principal investigator does not need to be with the business concern. This program, however, requires that the small business apply in collaboration with a nonprofit research institution for conduct of a project that has potential for commercialization. At least 40% of the work must be performed by the small business and at least 30% of the work must be performed by the research institution. Preference is given to women-owned small business concerns and to socially and economically disadvantaged small business concerns. Women-owned small business concerns are those that are at least 51% owned by a woman or women who also control and operate them. Socially and economically disadvantaged small business concerns are at least 51% owned by an Indian tribe, a native Hawaiian organization, or 1 or more socially and economically disadvantaged individuals (African Americans, Hispanic Americans, Native Americans, Asian Pacific Americans, or subcontinent Asian Americans). The project must be performed in the United States. Current priorities for critical technology areas of national importance include 1) advanced materials, chemical technology and manufacturing; 2) biotechnology; 3) electronics; 4) information technology; and 5) emerging opportunities (projects with a focus on near-term commercialization).

Financial data In the first phase, annual awards may not exceed $150,000 for direct costs, indirect costs, and negotiated fixed fees. In the second phase, awards up to $500,000 are available.

Duration Normally, 12 months for phase 1 and 2 years for phase 2.

Additional information Grants in the first phase are to determine the scientific, technical, and commercial merit and feasibility of the proposed cooperative effort and the quality of performance of the small business concern. In the second phase, the research and development efforts continue, depending on the results of the first phase.

Number awarded 25 phase 1 grants are awarded each year. Approximately one third of phase 1 awardees receive phase 2 grants. Approximately $3,750,000 is budgeted for this program each year.

Deadline June of each year for proposals in advanced materials, chemical technology, manufacturing innovation, biotechnology, electronics, information technology, and emerging opportunities; December of each year for biological and environmental technologies, components and systems, and software and services.

[1079]
NWRI FELLOWSHIPS

National Water Research Institute
Attn: Fellowship Program
18700 Ward Street
P.O. Box 8096
Fountain Valley, CA 92728-8096
(714) 378-3278   Fax: (714) 378-3375
E-mail: fellow@nwri-usa.org
Web: www.nwri-usa.org/fellowship.htm

Purpose To provide funding to minority and other graduate students interested in conducting research in science and technology fields related to water.

Eligibility This program is open to full-time graduate students interested in conducting research in areas of interest to the National Water Research Institute (NWRI): water treatment technologies, water quality, water environmental chemistry, water policy and economics, public health and risk assessment, or water resources management. Research areas include, but are not limited to, engineering, physical and chemical sciences, biological sciences, health sciences, political sciences, economics, and planning and public policy that are related to water and/or water resources. Preference is given to doctoral candidates, but outstanding students in master's programs may be considered. Applicants must submit a letter of inquiry describing the importance of the research to them and the water community, how their research will contribute to water science in general, what they expect to accomplish, and how their research relates to the mission of the NWRI to create new sources of water through research and technology and to protect the freshwater and marine environments. Women and members of minority groups underrepresented in academia are strongly encouraged to apply.

Financial data Grants range from $2,000 to $20,000 per year, but are typically $10,000 per year.

Duration 1 year; may be renewed up to 2 additional years.

Number awarded 3 to 4 each year.

Deadline February of each year.

[1080]
OAK RIDGE NATIONAL LABORATORY/OAK RIDGE ASSOCIATED UNIVERSITIES HBCU/MEI FACULTY SUMMER RESEARCH PROGRAM

Oak Ridge Institute for Science and Education
Attn: Science and Engineering Education
P.O. Box 117
Oak Ridge, TN 37831-0117
(865) 574-7798   Fax: (865) 241-5219
E-mail: Ruth.Keller@orau.gov
Web: see.orau.org

Purpose To provide funding to faculty at minority-serving educational institutions (MEIs) who wish to engage in ongoing research at Oak Ridge National Laboratory (ORNL) in Tennessee.

Eligibility This program is open to full-time faculty members at Hispanic Serving Institutions (HSIs), Historically Black Colleges and Universities (HBCUs), Tribal Colleges and Universities TCUs), Alaska Native Serving Institutions (ANSIs), and Native Hawaiian Serving Institutions (NHSIs). Applicants must be interested in collaborating on specific research projects at ORNL in computer science; earth, environmental, or marine sciences; engineering; life, health, or medical sciences; mathematics; or physical sciences. Selection is based on the strength of the applicant's capabilities and experience; the match between the applicant's qualifications and the research needs of the selected project; and the potential for establishing an ongoing research partnership.

Financial data The stipend is based on the recipient's regular university salary. at least $4,500 per month. Participants also receive limited reimbursement for inbound and outbound transportation and a monthly dislocation allowance of $1,000.

Duration 10 weeks during the summer.

Additional information This program is funded by ORNL and Oak Ridge Associated Universities (ORAU) and administered by Oak Ridge Institute for Science and Education (ORISE). Research projects are currently available in advanced energy systems, advanced materials, national security, neutron sciences, systems biology, and ultrascale computing.

Number awarded Varies each year.

Deadline January of each year.

[1081]
OFFICE OF NAVAL RESEARCH SABBATICAL LEAVE PROGRAM

American Society for Engineering Education
Attn: Projects Department
1818 N Street, N.W., Suite 600
Washington, DC 20036-2479
(202) 331-3558   Fax: (202) 265-8504
E-mail: a.hicks@asee.org
Web: www.asee.org/summer/sabbatical.cfm

Purpose To provide support to minority and other faculty members in engineering and science who wish to conduct research at selected Navy facilities while on sabbatical leave.

Eligibility This program is open to U.S. citizens with teaching or research appointments in engineering and science at U.S. universities or colleges. Applicants must intend to conduct research while in residence at selected facilities of the U.S. Navy. Faculty from Historically Black Colleges and Universities, Hispanic Serving Institutions, and Tribal Colleges and Universities are especially encouraged to apply.

Financial data Fellows receive a stipend equivalent to the difference between their regular salary and the sabbatical leave pay from their home institution. Fellows who must relocate their residence receive a relocation allowance and all fellows receive a travel allowance.

Duration Appointments are for a minimum of 1 semester and a maximum of 1 year.

Additional information Participating facilities include the Naval Air Warfare Center, Aircraft Division (Patuxent River, Maryland); Naval Air Warfare Center, Naval Training Systems Division (Orlando, Florida); Naval Air Warfare Center, Weapons Division (China Lake, California); Space and Naval Warfare Systems Center (San Diego, California); Naval Facilities Engineering Service Center (Port Hueneme, California); Naval Research Laboratories (Washington, D.C.; Stennis Space Center, Mississippi; and Monterey, California); Naval Surface Warfare Centers (Bethesda, Maryland; Indian Head, Maryland; Dahlgren, Virginia; and Panama City, Florida); Naval Undersea Warfare Center (Newport, Rhode Island and New London, Connecticut); Defense Equal Opportunity Management Institute (Cocoa Beach, Florida); Navy Personnel Research, Studies & Technology Department (Millington, Tennessee); Naval Aerospace Medical Research Laboratory (Pensacola, Florida); Naval Health Research Center (San Diego, California); Naval Medical Research Center (Silver Spring, Maryland); and Naval Submarine Medical Research Laboratory (Groton, Connecticut). This program is funded by the U.S. Navy's Office of Naval Research but administered by the American Society for Engineering Education.

Number awarded Varies each year.

Deadline Applications may be submitted at any time, but they must be received at least 6 months prior to the proposed sabbatical leave starting date.

[1082]
OFFICE OF NAVAL RESEARCH SUMMER FACULTY RESEARCH PROGRAM

American Society for Engineering Education
Attn: Projects Department
1818 N Street, N.W., Suite 600
Washington, DC 20036-2479
(202) 331-3558 Fax: (202) 265-8504
E-mail: a.hicks@asee.org
Web: www.asee.org/summer/summer.cfm

Purpose To provide support to minority and other faculty members in engineering and science who wish to conduct summer research at selected Navy facilities.

Eligibility This program is open to U.S. citizens with teaching or research appointments in engineering and science at U.S. universities or colleges. In addition to appointments as Summer Faculty Fellows, positions as Senior Summer Faculty Fellows are available to applicants who have at least 6 years of research experience in their field of expertise since earning a Ph.D. or equivalent degree and a substantial, significant record of research accomplishments and publications. A limited number of appointments are also available as Distinguished Summer Faculty Fellows to faculty members who are preeminent in their field of research, with a senior appointment at a leading research university and international recognition for their research accomplishments. Faculty from Historically Black Colleges and Universities, Hispanic Serving Institutions, and Tribal Colleges and Universities are especially encouraged to apply.

Financial data The weekly stipend is $1,400 at the Summer Faculty Fellow level, $1,650 at the Senior Summer Faculty Fellow level, and $1,900 at the Distinguished Summer Faculty Fellow level. Fellows who must relocate their residence receive a relocation allowance and all fellows receive a travel allowance.

Duration 10 weeks during the summer; fellows may reapply in subsequent years.

Additional information Participating facilities include the Naval Air Warfare Center, Aircraft Division (Patuxent River, Maryland); Naval Air Warfare Center, Naval Training Systems Division (Orlando, Florida); Naval Air Warfare Center, Weapons Division (China Lake, California); Space and Naval Warfare Systems Center (San Diego, California); Naval Facilities Engineering Service Center (Port Hueneme, California); Naval Research Laboratories (Washington, D.C.; Stennis Space Center, Mississippi; and Monterey, California); Naval Surface Warfare Centers (Bethesda, Maryland; Indian Head, Maryland; Dahlgren, Virginia; and Panama City, Florida); Naval Undersea Warfare Center (Newport, Rhode Island and New London, Connecticut); Defense Equal Opportunity Management Institute (Cocoa Beach, Florida); Navy Personnel Research, Studies & Technology Department (Millington, Tennessee); Naval Aerospace Medical Research Laboratory (Pensacola, Florida); Naval Health Research Center (San Diego, California); Naval Medical Research Center (Silver Spring, Maryland); and Naval Submarine Medical Research Laboratory (Groton, Connecticut). This program is funded by the U.S. Navy's Office of Naval Research but administered by the American Society for Engineering Education.

Number awarded Varies each year.

Deadline November of each year.

[1083]
PACIFIC ISLANDERS IN COMMUNICATIONS MEDIA FUND GRANTS

Pacific Islanders in Communications
Attn: Program Associate
1221 Kapi'olani Boulevard, Suite 6A-4
Honolulu, HI 96814-3513
(808) 591-0059, ext. 16 Fax: (808) 591-1114
E-mail: gcobb-adams@piccom.org
Web: www.piccom.org/producers.php

Purpose To provide funding to producers of public television programs that relate to the Hawaiian and other Pacific Islander experience.

Eligibility This program is open to independent producers and public television stations interested in developing programs that originate from the Pacific Islander experience and are intended for national public broadcast audiences. Applicants must have artistic, budgetary, and editorial control and must own the copyright of the proposed project. They must be at least 18 years of age, be citizens or legal residents of the United States or its territories, and have previous film or television experience. Student productions are not eligible. All projects must be delivered in standard public television lengths and meet accepted technical, ethical, and journalistic standards for national public television broadcast. Programs may be of any genre, but they must be intended for broadcast on national public television. For purposes of this program, Pacific Islanders are defined as descendants of the first peoples of American Samoa, Guam, Hawai'i, the Northern Mariana Islands, and other Pacific Islands. Selection is based on the power of the finished product to shed light on the Pacific Islander experience; ability of the program to provoke thoughtful dialogue about the subject; knowledge and understanding of the subject as well as a thoughtful and sensitive approach; potential of the finished project to be shown on national public television; production and fundraising plans; ability of the producer and the production team to complete the project within budget and on schedule; and extent to which Pacific Islanders hold key creative production positions.

Financial data Maximum awards are $15,000 for research and development grants or $50,000 for production and completion grants.

Number awarded Varies each year; recently, 3 research and development grants, 5 production grants, and 1 completion grant were awarded.

Deadline July of each year.

[1084]
PACIFIC ISLANDERS IN COMMUNICATIONS SHORT FILM INITIATIVE

Pacific Islanders in Communications
Attn: Program Associate
1221 Kapi'olani Boulevard, Suite 6A-4
Honolulu, HI 96814-3513
(808) 591-0059, ext. 16 Fax: (808) 591-1114
E-mail: gcobb-adams@piccom.org
Web: www.piccom.org/producers.php

Purpose To provide funding to producers of short films and videos that are intended for national public television and deal with the Pacific Islander experience.

Eligibility This program is open to independent producers or independent entities producing television, film, or video. Applicants must be interested in producing short, personal narrative, digital video works (30 seconds to 2 minutes in length) that bring to light contemporary Pacific Islander issues. They must have artistic, budgetary, and editorial control; own the copyright of the proposed project; be at least 18 years of age; and be citizens or legal residents of the United States or its territories, Student productions are not eligible. Most genres are welcome, including video diary, drama, comedy, animation, and mixed-genre.
Financial data Maximum awards are $10,000 per project.
Number awarded Up to 5 each year.
Deadline February of each year.

[1085]
PATHWAYS TO INDEPENDENCE PROGRAM
National Institutes of Health
Office of Extramural Research
Attn: Grants Information
6705 Rockledge Drive
Bethesda, MD 20892-7974
(301) 435-0714 Fax: (301) 480-0525
TTY: (301) 451-0088 E-mail: GrantsInfo@nih.gov
Web: grants2.nih.gov/grants/new_investigators

Purpose To provide funding to minority and other recent postdoctorates in the biomedical and behavioral sciences who need a period of mentored research training followed by a period as a beginning independent investigator.
Eligibility This program is open to postdoctorates who have a clinical or research doctorate (e.g., Ph.D., M.D., D.O., D.C., D.D.S., D.V.M., Sc.D., D.N.S., Pharm.D.) but less than 5 years of postdoctoral research training. Candidates must be nominated by a domestic, for-profit or nonprofit, public or private institution such as a university, college, hospital, or laboratory. They must be interested in a program of research training in the biomedical and behavioral sciences under the mentorship of an experienced investigator. Following that training period, they must accept a tenure-track full-time assistant professor position at a sponsoring institution, where they begin a career as an independent investigator. Members of underrepresented racial and ethnic groups and individuals with disabilities are especially encouraged to apply. U.S. citizens and non-citizens are eligible.
Financial data Each NIH component establishes its own salary and research allowance for the mentored phase, but most have set $75,000 per year as salary and $25,000 per year for direct support of research. During the independent investigator phase, the total cost per year may be up to $249,000, including salary, fringe benefits, research support, and applicable facilities and administrative costs.
Duration 5 years, including 2 years in the mentored phase and 3 years in the independent investigator phase.
Additional information This program was established in 2006. The National Cancer Institute designates its awards the Howard Temin Pathway to Independence Awards in Cancer Research.
Number awarded Approximately 150 to 200 each year.
Deadline February, June, or October of each year.

[1086]
PAUL B. BEESON CAREER DEVELOPMENT AWARDS IN AGING RESEARCH PROGRAM
American Federation for Aging Research
Attn: Executive Director
55 West 39th Street, 16th Floor
New York, NY 10018
(212) 703-9977 Toll-free: (888) 582-2327
Fax: (212) 997-0330 E-mail: grants@afar.org
Web: afar.org/beeson.html

Purpose To provide funding for additional training to minority and other physicians interested in conducting research on aging.
Eligibility Applicants must have a clinical doctoral degree (e.g., M.D., D.O., D.D.S) or equivalent, a combined M.D. and Ph.D. degree, or a Ph.D. in a clinical field (such as clinical psychology, nursing, or physical therapy). They must be interested in a mentored program of medical, academic, and scientific training relative to caring for older people, to be conducted at a domestic public or private institution, such as a university, college, hospital, or laboratory. The sponsoring institution must have a well-established research and clinical career development program, have faculty experienced in research on aging and geriatrics to serve as mentors, and be able to demonstrate a commitment to the applicant's development and emergence as a productive, independent investigator. U.S. citizenship, national status, or permanent resident status is required. Members of underrepresented racial and ethnic groups and individuals with disabilities are especially encouraged to apply for programs of the National Institutes of Health (NIH).
Financial data The maximum grant is $200,000 per year, or $600,000 for 3 years, $700,000 for 4 years, or $800,000 for 5 years. Salaries are paid according to the established structure at the host institution. Facilities and administrative costs are reimbursed at 8% of modified total direct costs.
Duration 3 to 5 years.
Additional information The program is sponsored by the John A. Hartford Foundation, The Atlantic Philanthropies, the Starr Foundation, the National Institutes of Health (NIH) Office of Dietary Supplements, and an anonymous donor. The program is administered by the NIH's National Institute on Aging, Office of Extramural Affairs, 7201 Wisconsin Avenue, Room 2C218, Bethesda, MD 20892-9205, (301) 496-9322, Fax: (301) 402-2945, E-mail: BarrR@mail.nih.gov. Grantees must devote at least 75% of their full-time professional effort to the goals of this program.
Number awarded 8 to 12 each year.
Deadline Letters of intent must be submitted by the end of September of each year. Complete applications are due in early November.

[1087]
PEACE SCHOLAR DISSERTATION FELLOWSHIPS

United States Institute of Peace
Attn: Jennings Randolph Program for International
  Peace
1200 17th Street, N.W., Suite 200
Washington, DC 20036-3011
(202) 429-3886   Fax: (202) 429-6063
TTY: (202) 457-1719   E-mail: jrprogram@usip.org
Web: www.usip.org/fellows/scholars.html

Purpose To provide financial support to minority and other doctoral candidates working on dissertations that address the nature of international conflict and ways to prevent or end conflict and to sustain peace.

Eligibility This program is open to doctoral candidates, from anywhere in the world, who are enrolled in U.S. universities and conducting dissertation research on international peace and conflict management. Projects from a broad range of disciplines (political science, history, sociology, economics, anthropology, psychology, conflict resolution, and other fields within the humanities and social sciences, including interdisciplinary programs) are welcome. Priority is given to projects that contribute knowledge relevant to the formulation of policy on international peace and conflict issues. Women and members of minority groups are especially encouraged to apply. Selection is based on the candidate's record of achievement and/or leadership potential; the significance and potential of the project for making an important contribution to knowledge, practice, or public understanding; and the quality of the project design and its feasibility within the timetable proposed.

Financial data The stipend is $17,000 per year.

Duration 12 months, beginning in September.

Additional information These fellowships, first awarded in 1988, are tenable at the recipient's university or any other appropriate research site. This program is offered as part of the Jennings Randolph Program for International Peace at the United States Institute of Peace. These awards are not made for projects that constitute policymaking for a government agency or private organization; focus to any substantial degree on conflicts within U.S. domestic society; or adopt a partisan, advocacy, or activist stance.

Number awarded Varies each year; recently, 10 of these fellowships were awarded.

Deadline January of each year.

[1088]
PEMBROKE CENTER POSTDOCTORAL FELLOWSHIPS

Brown University
Attn: Pembroke Center for Teaching and Research on
  Women
172 Meeting Street
Box 1958
Providence, RI 02912
(401) 863-2643   Fax: (401) 863-1298
E-mail: Donna_Goodnow@brown.edu
Web: www.pembrokecenter.org

Purpose To provide funding to minority and other scholars interested in conducting research at Brown University's Pembroke Center for Teaching and Research on Women on the cross-cultural study of gender.

Eligibility Fellowships are open to scholars in the humanities, social sciences, or life sciences who do not have a tenured position at an American college or university. Applicants must be willing to spend a year in residence at the Pembroke Center for Teaching and Research on Women and participate in a research project related to gender. The project focuses on a theme that changes annually (recently: "Markets and Bodies in Transnational Perspective"). The center encourages underrepresented minority scholars to apply.

Financial data The stipend is $50,000. Health insurance is also provided.

Duration 1 academic year.

Additional information Postdoctoral fellows in residence participate in weekly seminars and present at least 2 public papers during the year, as well as conduct an individual research project. Supplementary funds are available for assistance with travel expenses from abroad. This program includes the following named fellowships: the Nancy L. Buc Postdoctoral Fellowship, the Artemis A.W. and Martha Joukowsky Postdoctoral Fellowship, and the Carol G. Lederer Postdoctoral Fellowship.

Number awarded 3 or 4 each year.

Deadline December of each year.

[1089]
PFIZER MINORITY RESEARCH FELLOWSHIP

American Psychiatric Association
Attn: Institute for Research and Education
1000 Wilson Boulevard, Suite 1825
Arlington, VA 22209-3901
(703) 907-8622   Toll-free: (800) 852-1390
Fax: (703) 907-1085   E-mail: eguerra@psych.org
Web: www.psych.org

Purpose To provide funding to Native American and other underrepresented minority members of the American Psychiatric Association (APA) who wish to conduct research.

Eligibility This program is open to underrepresented minority members of the association. Applicants must have an M.D., Ph.D., or D.O. degree and have completed residency training in general psychiatry or child psychiatry. They should demonstrate significant research potential, have not had extensive research training prior to residency, and not already be established investigators. They must be nominated by the chair of their department. Individuals with an interest in conducting research in underserved ethnic and racial populations are particularly encouraged to apply.

Financial data The grant is $45,000. Funds are paid to the institution for disbursement to the fellow.

Duration 1 year.

Additional information This program, established in 2006, is funded by Pfizer and administered by the APA's American Psychiatric Institute for Research and Education. Fellows are expected to devote more than 85% of their time to research.

Number awarded 2 each year.

Deadline October of each year.

[1090]
PHILLIPS FUND GRANTS FOR NATIVE AMERICAN RESEARCH

American Philosophical Society
Attn: Committee on Research
104 South Fifth Street
Philadelphia, PA 19106-3387
(215) 440-3429   Fax: (215) 440-3436
E-mail: LMusumeci@amphilsoc.org
Web: www.amphilsoc.org/grants/phillips.htm

Purpose To provide funding to scholars interested in conducting research on North American Indian anthropological linguistics and ethnohistory.

Eligibility Eligible to apply are scholars, preferably young scholars, working in the fields of Native American linguistics and ethnohistory, and the history of studies of Native Americans, in the continental United States and Canada. Applications are not accepted for projects in archaeology, ethnography, psycholinguistics, or for the preparation of pedagogical materials. Graduate students may apply for support for research on their master's or doctoral dissertations.

Financial data The grants average $2,500 and rarely exceed $3,500. These funds are intended for such extra costs as travel, tapes, films, and informants' fees, but not for general maintenance or the purchase of books or permanent equipment.

Duration 1 year.

Additional information Telephone requests for forms are not accepted.

Number awarded Varies each year; recently, 25 of these grants were awarded.

Deadline February of each year.

[1091]
POSTDOCTORAL FELLOWSHIP IN BEHAVIORAL NEUROSCIENCE

Texas Consortium in Behavioral Neuroscience
c/o University of Texas at Austin
Department of Psychology
1 University Station A8000
Austin, TX 78712
(512) 471-1068   Fax: (512) 471-1073
E-mail: lima@mail.utexas.edu
Web: homepage.psy.utexas.edu

Purpose To provide an opportunity for Native American and other underrepresented minority postdoctorates to obtain research training at selected universities in Texas.

Eligibility This program is open to members of racial and ethnic groups that have been underrepresented in health-related sciences on a national basis (Blacks, Hispanics, and Native Americans). Applicants must have a doctoral degree in neuroscience, psychology, biomedical or natural sciences, or engineering. They must be interested in a program of research training at the University of Texas at Austin, the University of Texas at San Antonio, the University of Texas Health Science Center at San Antonio, Texas A&M University, or Texas A&M University System Health Science Center. U.S. citizenship or permanent resident status is required.

Financial data Stipends are established in conformity with guidelines of the U.S. National Institutes of Health (NIH).

Duration 2 years.

Additional information This program is sponsored by 3 components of the NIH: the National Institute of Mental Health, the National Institute on Drug Abuse, and the National Institute of Neurological Disorders and Stroke. The training program covers brain metabolic mapping of behavioral functions, neuropharmacology, electrophysiology, and molecular neurobiology.

Number awarded 5 each year.

Deadline Applications may be submitted at any time.

[1092]
POSTDOCTORAL FELLOWSHIPS AT FDA

National Science Foundation
Directorate for Engineering
Attn: Division of Bioengineering and Environmental Systems
4201 Wilson Boulevard, Room 565 S
Arlington, VA 22230
(703) 292-7943   Fax: (703) 292-9098
TDD: (800) 281-8749   E-mail: gdevey@nsf.gov
Web: www.nsf.gov

Purpose To provide an opportunity for minority and other recent postdoctorates to conduct research at an intramural laboratory of the U.S. Food and Drug Administration (FDA).

Eligibility Applicants for these fellowships must have held a Ph.D. degree in a science, engineering, or mathematics field of interest to NSF for no more than 3 years. They must be U.S. citizens, nationals, or permanent residents. Along with their application, they must submit a plan for full-time work at an FDA laboratory under the guidance of an FDA mentor. The program encourages applications from women, underrepresented minorities, and persons with disabilities.

Financial data Grants range up to $55,000 per year. Funding includes 85% of the fellow's stipend and fringe benefits, transportation and moving expenses (up to $3,000), up to 10% of the total as allowance to the faculty adviser for research-related expenses, and an allowance of up to 15% of the total direct costs as an administrative allowance for a sponsoring academic institution. Proposals must include a commitment of funds from the applicant's home institution to support the other 15% of the fellow's salary and fringe benefits. FDA provides office space, research facilities, research costs in the form of expendable and minor equipment purchases in the host laboratory, and the time of its research staff.

Duration 1 to 2 years.

Additional information This program is also offered by the NSF Directorate for Computer and Information Science and Engineering; for information, contact its Division of Computer-Communications Research, (703) 292-8910, Fax: (703) 292-9059, E-mail: hgill@nsf.gov. The FDA contact is William A. Herman, Director, Division of Physical Sciences, Center for Devices and Radiological Health, 12725 Twinbrook Parkway, Rockville, MD 20852, (301)827-5599, E-mail: wah@cdrh.fda.gov.

Number awarded A total of 3 to 10 grants for all FDA programs is awarded each year; total funding is approximately $500,000.

Deadline March of each year.

[1093]
POSTDOCTORAL FELLOWSHIPS IN LAW AND SOCIAL SCIENCE

American Bar Foundation
Attn: Assistant Director
750 North Lake Shore Drive
Chicago, IL 60611
(312) 988-6560 Fax: (312) 988-6579
E-mail: fellowships@abfn.org
Web: www.abf-sociolegal.org/abffellow.html

Purpose To provide funding to minority and other postdoctoral scholars who wish to conduct research on law, the legal profession, and legal institutions.

Eligibility Applications are invited from junior scholars who completed all requirements for their Ph.D. within the past 2 years; in exceptional circumstances, candidates with a J.D. who have substantial social science training may also be considered. Proposed research must be in the general area of sociolegal studies or in social scientific approaches to law, the legal profession, or legal institutions and legal processes. Applications must include 1) a sample of written work; 2) 2 letters of recommendation; 3) a curriculum vitae; and 4) a statement describing research interests and achievements to date and plans for the fellowship period. Minority candidates are especially encouraged to apply.

Financial data The stipend is $30,000 per year; fringe benefits are also provided. Fellows may request up to $3,500 each fellowship year for research support. Relocation expenses of up to $1,000 may be reimbursed on application.

Duration 1 year; may be renewed for 1 additional year.

Additional information Fellows are offered access to the computing and word processing facilities of the American Bar Foundation and the libraries of Northwestern University and the University of Chicago. This program was established in 1996. Fellowships must be held in residence at the American Bar Foundation. Appointments to the fellowship are full time; fellows are not permitted to undertake other work.

Number awarded 2 each year.

Deadline January of each year.

[1094]
POSTDOCTORAL FELLOWSHIPS OF THE FORD FOUNDATION DIVERSITY FELLOWSHIP PROGRAM

National Research Council
Attn: Fellowships Office, GR 346A
500 Fifth Street, N.W.
Washington, DC 20001
(202) 334-2860 Fax: (202) 334-3419
E-mail: infofell@nas.edu
Web: www7.nationalacademies.org

Purpose To provide funding for postdoctoral research to scholars whose success will increase the racial and ethnic diversity of U.S. colleges and universities.

Eligibility This program is open to U.S. citizens and nationals who earned a Ph.D. or Sc.D. degree within the past 7 years and are committed to a career in teaching and research at the college or university level. The following are considered as positive factors in the selection process: evidence of superior academic achievement; promise of continuing achievement as scholars and teachers; membership in a group whose underrepresentation in the American professoriate has been severe and longstanding, including Black/African Americans, Puerto Ricans, Mexican Americans/Chicanos/Chicanas, Native American Indians, Alaska Natives (Eskimos or Aleuts), and Native Pacific Islanders (Micronesians or Polynesians); capacity to respond in pedagogically productive ways to the learning needs of students from diverse backgrounds; sustained personal engagement with communities that are underrepresented in the academy and an ability to bring this asset to learning, teaching, and scholarship at the college and university level; and likelihood of using the diversity of human experience as an educational resource in teaching and scholarship. Applicants must have earned their degree in 1 of the following fields: American studies, anthropology, archaeology, art and theater history, astronomy, chemistry, communications, computer science, earth sciences, economics, education, engineering, ethnomusicology, geography, history, international relations, language, life sciences, linguistics, literature, mathematics, performance study, philosophy, physics, political science, psychology, religion, sociology, urban planning, or women's studies. Also eligible are interdisciplinary ethnic studies programs, such as African American studies and Native American studies, and other interdisciplinary programs, such as area studies, peace studies, and social justice. Awards are not made for such practice-oriented areas as administration and management, audiology, business, educational administration and leadership, filmmaking, fine arts, guidance, home economics, library and information science, nursing, occupational health, performing arts, personnel, physical education, social welfare, social work, or speech pathology. Research may be conducted at an appropriate institution of higher education in the United States (normally) or abroad, including universities, museums, libraries, government or national laboratories, privately sponsored nonprofit institutes, government chartered nonprofit research organizations, or centers for advanced study. Applicants should designate a faculty member or other scholar to serve as host at the proposed fellowship institution. They are encouraged to choose a host institution other than that where they are affiliated at the time of application.

Financial data The stipend is $40,000. Funds may be supplemented by sabbatical leave pay or other sources of support that do not carry with them teaching or other responsibilities. The employing institution receives an allowance of $1,500, paid after fellowship tenure is completed; the employing institution is expected to match the grant and to use the allowance and the match to assist with the fellow's continuing research expenditures.

Duration 9 to 12 months.

Additional information Fellows may not accept another major fellowship while they are being supported by this program.

Number awarded Approximately 20 each year.

Deadline November of each year.

[1095]
POSTDOCTORAL INDUSTRIAL FELLOWSHIPS

National Science Foundation
Directorate for Engineering
Attn: Division of Industrial Innovation and Partnerships
4201 Wilson Boulevard, Room 550 S
Arlington, VA 22230
(703) 292-7082   Fax: (703) 292-9056
TDD: (800) 281-8749   E-mail: dsenich@nsf.gov
Web: www.nsf.gov

Purpose To provide an opportunity for minority and other recent postdoctorates to work in industry as part of the Grant Opportunities for Academic Liaison with Industry (GOALI) program of the National Science Foundation (NSF).

Eligibility Applicants for these fellowships must have held a Ph.D. degree in a science, engineering, or mathematics field of interest to NSF for no more than 3 years. They must be U.S. citizens, nationals, or permanent residents. Along with their application, they must submit a plan for full-time work in industry under the guidance of an academic adviser and an industrial mentor. The program encourages applications from women, underrepresented minorities, and persons with disabilities.

Financial data Grants range up to $50,000 per year. Funding, up to $4,000, may also be provided for transportation and moving expenses. Indirect costs are not allowed, but an institutional allowance of $5,000 is provided.

Duration 1 or 2 years.

Additional information This program is also offered by most other NSF directorates. Check the website for a name and e-mail address of the contact person in each directorate.

Number awarded A total of 60 to 80 grants for all GOALI programs is awarded each year; total funding is approximately $5 million.

Deadline Applications may be submitted at any time.

[1096]
POSTDOCTORAL RESEARCH FELLOWSHIPS IN BIOLOGY

National Science Foundation
Directorate for Biological Sciences
Attn: Division of Biological Infrastructure
4201 Wilson Boulevard, Room 615
Arlington, VA 22230
(703) 292-8470   Fax: (703) 292-9063
TDD: (800) 281-8749   E-mail: ckimsey@nsf.gov
Web: www.nsf.gov

Purpose To provide funding for training and research in biology and biological informatics to minority and other junior doctoral-level scientists or students at sites in the United States or abroad.

Eligibility This program is open to citizens, nationals, and permanent residents of the United States who are graduate students completing a Ph.D. or have earned the degree no earlier than 12 months preceding the deadline date. Applicants must be interested in a program of research and training in biological informatics that addresses scientific questions at the intersection of biology and computational, mathematical, or statistical sciences. They may not have been a principal investigator or co-principal investigator on a federal research grant of more than $20,000. Fellowships are available to postdoctorates who are proposing a research and training plan in biological informatics at an appropriate nonprofit U.S. or foreign host institution (colleges and universities, government and national laboratories and facilities, and privately-sponsored nonprofit institutes and museums). The proposed research should be data intensive, computationally intensive, and theoretical. The application must also include a rigorous training program that will significantly advance the candidate's expertise in applying and teaching informatics and computational methods in biology. That training must be under the sponsorship of a scientist at the host institution who will provide mentoring and guidance with the proposed research and training. Applicants are encouraged to gain international experience by selecting foreign hosts for at least part of the tenure of the fellowship. Applications are encouraged from women, underrepresented minorities, and persons with disabilities.

Financial data The fellowship grant is $60,000 for the first year, $63,000 for the second year, and $66,000 for the third year; that includes 1) an annual stipend of $45,000 for the first year, $48,000 for the second year, and $51,000 for the third year; 2) a research allowance of $10,000 per year paid to the fellow for materials and supplies, subscription fees, and recovery costs for databases, travel, and publication expenses; and 3) an institutional allowance of $5,000 per year for fringe benefits and expenses incurred in support of the fellow.

Duration Fellowships are for 2 years; may be renewed for 1 additional year at a U.S. institution if the first 2 years are at a foreign institution.

Number awarded Approximately 15 fellowships are awarded each year. Total available funding is approximately $2.0 million.

Deadline November of each year.

[1097]
POSTDOCTORAL RESEARCH FELLOWSHIPS IN EPILEPSY

Epilepsy Foundation
Attn: Research Department
8301 Professional Place
Landover, MD 20785-2237
(301) 459-3700   Toll-free: (800) EFA-1000
Fax: (301) 577-2684   TDD: (800) 332-2070
E-mail: grants@efa.org
Web: www.epilepsyfoundation.org

Purpose To provide funding for a program of postdoctoral training to minority and other academic physicians and scientists committed to epilepsy research.

Eligibility Applicants must have a doctoral degree (M.D., Ph.D., or equivalent) and be a resident or postdoctoral fellow at a university, medical school, research institution, or medical center. They must be interested in participating in a training experience and research project that has potential significance for understanding the causes, treatment, or consequences of epilepsy. The program is geared toward applicants who will be trained in research in epilepsy rather than those who use epilepsy as a tool for research in other fields. Equal consideration is given to applicants interested in acquiring experience either in basic laboratory research or in the conduct of human clinical studies. Academic faculty holding the rank of instructor or higher are not eligible, nor are graduate or medical students, medical residents, permanent government employees, or employees of private industry. Applications from women, members of minority groups, and people with disabilities are especially encouraged. Selection is based on scientific quality of the proposed research, a statement regarding its relevance to epilepsy, the applicant's qualifications, the preceptor's qualifications, and the adequacy of facility and related epilepsy programs at the institution.

Financial data The grant is $45,000. No indirect costs are covered.

Duration 1 year.

Additional information Support for this program is provided by many individuals, families, and corporations, especially the American Epilepsy Society, Abbott Laboratories, Ortho-McNeil Pharmaceutical, and Pfizer Inc. The fellowship must be carried out at a facility in the United States where there is an ongoing epilepsy research program.

Number awarded Varies each year.

Deadline August of each year.

[1098] PREDOCTORAL RESEARCH TRAINING FELLOWSHIPS IN EPILEPSY

Epilepsy Foundation
Attn: Research Department
8301 Professional Place
Landover, MD 20785-2237
(301) 459-3700   Toll-free: (800) EFA-1000
Fax: (301) 577-2684   TDD: (800) 332-2070
E-mail: grants@efa.org
Web: www.epilepsyfoundation.org

Purpose To provide funding to minority and other doctoral candidates in designated fields for dissertation research on a topic related to epilepsy.

Eligibility This program is open to full-time graduate students working on a Ph.D. in biochemistry, genetics, neuroscience, nursing, pharmacology, pharmacy, physiology, or psychology. Applicants must be conducting dissertation research on a topic relevant to epilepsy under the guidance of a mentor with expertise in the area of epilepsy investigation. Applications from women, members of minority groups, and people with disabilities are especially encouraged. Selection is based on the relevance of the proposed work to epilepsy, the applicant's qualifications, the mentor's qualifications, the scientific quality of the proposed dissertation research, the quality of the training environment for research related to epilepsy, and the adequacy of the facility.

Financial data The grant is $20,000, consisting of $19,000 for a stipend and $1,000 to support travel to attend the annual meeting of the American Epilepsy Society.

Duration 1 year.

Additional information Support for this program, which began in 1998, is provided by many individuals, families, and corporations, especially the American Epilepsy Society, Abbott Laboratories, Ortho-McNeil Pharmaceutical, and Pfizer Inc.

Number awarded Varies each year.

Deadline August of each year.

[1099] PUBLIC HEALTH SERVICE SMALL BUSINESS INNOVATION RESEARCH PROGRAM

Public Health Service
c/o National Institutes of Health
Attn: SBIR/STTR Program Coordinator
6705 Rockledge Drive, Room 3534
Bethesda, MD 20892-7911
(301) 435-2688   Fax: (301) 480-0146
TTY: (301) 451-0088   E-mail: jg128w@nih.gov
Web: grants.nih.gov/grants/guide/index.html

Purpose To support small businesses (especially those owned by minorities and women) that have the technological experience to contribute to the research and development mission of components of the U.S. Public Health Service.

Eligibility For the purposes of this program, a "small business" is defined as a firm that is that is independently owned and operated for profit, not dominant in the field in which it is operating, and meets the size standard of 500 employees or less. The primary employment of the principal investigator must be with the firm at the time of award and during the conduct of the proposed project. Preference is given to women-owned small business concerns and to socially and economically disadvantaged small business concerns. Women-owned small business concerns are at least 51% owned by a woman or women who also control and operate them. Socially and economically disadvantaged small business concerns are at least 51% owned by an Indian tribe, Native Hawaiian organization, or 1 or more socially and economically disadvantaged individuals (African Americans, Hispanic Americans, Native Americans, Asian Pacific Americans, or subcontinent Asian Americans). The project must be performed in the United States. Research is supported in all areas of biomedical and behavioral science that fall within the mission of the agency.

Financial data Support is offered in 2 phases. In phase 1, awards normally do not exceed $100,000 (for both direct and indirect costs); in phase 2, awards normally do not exceed $750,000 (including both direct and indirect costs).

Duration Phase 1 awards may extend up to 6 months; phase 2 awards may extend up to 2 years.

Additional information Grants are offered by 3 components of the Public Health Service (PHS): National Institutes of Health (NIH), Centers for Disease Control and Prevention (CDC), and Food and Drug Administration (FDA). For information on the research interests of each of those components and their various agencies, contact the sponsor. Actual solicitations are available only from that address.

Number awarded Varies each year; recently, this program allocated $571 million for grants by NIH, $8.1 million for grants by CDC, and $533,000 for grants by FDA.

Deadline April, August, or December of each year.

[1100]
READING AWARD PROGRAM

Catching the Dream
8200 Mountain Road, N.E., Suite 203
Albuquerque, NM 87110-7835
(505) 262-2351   Fax: (505) 262-0534
E-mail: NScholarsh@aol.com
Web: www.catchingthedream.org/grants.htm

Purpose To provide funding to teachers and schools for projects that are designed to improve the reading ability of Indian students.

Eligibility This program is open to schools that serve large numbers of Indian students. Applicants must describe the school, the students to be served, the reading habits of those students, how the program will work, how the funds from the grant will be used, the background of the person in charge, and project objectives.

Financial data Grants are $1,000. Some of the previous acceptable uses of funds have included financial rewards to students for reading heavily, student scholarships, student trips at the end of the year, and even pizza parties for students. Funds cannot be used for the purchase of books, the purchase of computers or reading equipment, or staff training or travel.

Duration Grants are awarded annually.

Additional information The sponsor was formerly known as the Native American Scholarship Fund.

Number awarded 10 each year.

Deadline October of each year.

[1101]
RESEARCH AND TRAINING PROGRAM ON POVERTY AND PUBLIC POLICY POSTDOCTORAL FELLOWSHIPS

University of Michigan
Gerald R. Ford School of Public Policy
Attn: Program on Poverty and Public Policy
Joan and Sanford Weill Hall
735 South State, Room 5100
Ann Arbor, MI 48109-3091
(734) 615-4326   Fax: (734) 615-8047
E-mail: fordschoolinfo@umich.edu
Web: www.fordschool.umich.edu

Purpose To provide funding to Native American and other minority postdoctorates interested in conducting research and pursuing intensive training on poverty-related public policy issues at the University of Michigan.

Eligibility This program is open to U.S. citizens who are members of a minority group that is underrepresented in the social sciences. Applicants must have received the Ph.D. degree within the past 5 years and be engaged in research on poverty and public policy. Preference is given to proposals that would benefit from resources available at the University of Michigan and from interactions with affiliated faculty.

Financial data The stipend is $48,000 per calendar year.

Duration 1 or 2 years.

Additional information This program is funded by the Ford Foundation. Fellows spend the year participating in a seminar on poverty and public policy and conducting their own research. Topics currently pursued include economic self-sufficiency and the well-being of vulnerable families and children; the effects of economic conditions and public policies on poverty and family well-being; longitudinal analyses of youth development; family formation and healthy marriages; safety, stability, and healthy development of children; investing in low-income families: the accumulation of financial assets and human capital; qualitative research on barriers to self-sufficiency; and the role of religiosity and non-government organizations in the lives of the poor. Fellows must be in residence at the University of Michigan for the duration of the program.

Deadline January of each year.

[1102]
RESEARCH INITIATION GRANTS AND CAREER ADVANCEMENT AWARDS TO BROADEN PARTICIPATION IN BIOLOGY

National Science Foundation
Directorate for Biological Sciences
Attn: RIG/CAA Coordinator
4201 Wilson Boulevard, Room 805
Arlington, VA 22230
(703) 292-8470   TDD: (800) 281-8749
E-mail: rig-caabp@nsf.gov
Web: www.nsf.gov

Purpose To provide funding for research to scientists in the biological sciences who are from Native American and other ethnic groups underrepresented in the field.

Eligibility This program is open to U.S. citizens, nationals, and permanent residents who have a doctoral degree or equivalent experience in a field of biology supported by the National Science Foundation (NSF). Applicants must be able to show how their proposal will increase the participation of scientists from underrepresented groups (African Americans, Hispanics, American Indians, and Native Americans) in biological research and the numbers of such individuals that serve as role models for the scientific workforce of the future. Research Initiation Grants (RIGs) are available to new investigators in their first academic appointment as a faculty member of research-related position other than a postdoctoral appointment who have not previously served as principal investigator on an independent federal research grant. Career Advancement Awards (CAAs) are available to established investigators who have a faculty or research-related position. Proposers affiliated with Minority-Serving Institutions (MSIs), including Historically Black Colleges and Universities (HBCUs), Hispanic-Serving Institutions (HSIs), and Tribal Colleges and Universities (TCUs), are especially encouraged to apply. Selection is based on the scientific merit of the proposed research and the extent to which the proposed activities will broaden participation of individuals from underrepresented groups in the areas of the biological sciences supported by NSF. For RIG applications, proposals are also judged on the potential of the research initiation activities to produce sufficient preliminary data to serve as the basis for a competitive research proposal to NSF. For CAA applications, proposals are also judged on the degree to which the career advancement activities are specified in the proposal and the potential to advance the career of the investigator in a foreseeable way beyond the obvious benefit of federal support.

Financial data Grants provide up to $150,000 over the life of the award, including both direct and indirect costs. An additional $25,000 may be provided for equipment.

Duration 24 months.
Number awarded Varies each year; a total of $4 million to $7 million is available for this program annually.
Deadline January of each year.

[1103]
RIDGE 2000 POSTDOCTORAL FELLOWSHIP PROGRAM

National Science Foundation
Directorate for Geosciences
Attn: Division of Ocean Sciences
4201 Wilson Boulevard, Room 725 N
Arlington, VA 22230
(703) 292-7597   Fax: (703) 292-9085
TDD: (800) 281-8749   E-mail: aschultz@nsf.gov
Web: www.geo.nsf.gov
Web: www.nsf.gov

Purpose To provide opportunities for minority and other young scientists to conduct geological research on the mid-ocean ridge system as part of the Ridge Inter-Disciplinary Global Experiments (RIDGE) 2000 Initiative.

Eligibility Eligible are U.S. citizens, nationals, or permanent residents who will have earned a doctoral degree within 2 years of taking up the award and who have arranged to conduct research under a senior scientist at an appropriate U.S. nonprofit institution (government laboratory, privately-sponsored nonprofit institution, national laboratory, or institution of higher education). Applicants must be proposing to conduct research that attempts to understand the geological processes of planetary renewal that occur along the mid-oceanic plate boundary and the chemical and biological processes that sustain life, in the absence of sunlight, in the deep ocean. Currently, the program has identified 3 sites as the focus of research: 9-10 degrees North segment of the East Pacific Rise, East or Central Lau Spreading Center, and Endeavor segment of the Juan de Fuca Ridge. Selection is based on ability as evidenced by past research work; suitability and availability of the sponsoring senior scientist and other associated colleagues; suitability of the host institution for the proposed research; likely impact on the future scientific development of the applicant; scientific quality of the research likely to emerge; and the potential impact of the research on the RIDGE 2000 Initiative. The program encourages applications from women, underrepresented minorities, and persons with disabilities.

Financial data Grants range from $100,000 to $150,000. Funding includes a research allowance of $5,000 per year and an institutional allowance (in lieu of indirect costs) of $300 per months.

Duration 2 years; may be renewed for 1 additional year.

Additional information Additional information is available from the RIDGE 2000 office, University of California at San Diego, Scripps Institution of Oceanography, IGPP Revelle Laboratory, Room 4112, 8785 Biological Grade, La Jolla, CA 92037, (858) 534-8588, Fax: (858) 534-9873, E-mail: ridgE2000@ucsd.edu.

Number awarded 10 each year.
Deadline January of each year.

[1104]
ROBERT D. WATKINS GRADUATE RESEARCH FELLOWSHIP

American Society for Microbiology
Attn: Education Board
1752 N Street, N.W.
Washington, DC 20036-2904
(202) 942-9283   Fax: (202) 942-9329
E-mail: fellowships-careerinformation@asmusa.org
Web: www.asm.org/Education/index.asp?bid=6278

Purpose To provide funding for research in microbiology to Native American and other underrepresented minority doctoral students who are members of the American Society for Microbiology (ASM).

Eligibility This program is open to African Americans, Hispanic Americans, Native Americans, Alaskan Native Americans, and Native Pacific Islanders enrolled as full-time graduate students who have completed their first year of doctoral study and who are members of the society. Applicants must propose a joint research plan in collaboration with a society member scientist. They must have completed all graduate course work requirements for the doctoral degree by the date of the activation of the fellowship. U.S. citizenship or permanent resident status is required. Selection is based on academic achievement, evidence of a successful research plan developed in collaboration with a research adviser/mentor, and relevant career goals in the microbiological sciences.

Financial data Students receive $21,000 per year as a stipend; funds may not be used for tuition or fees.

Duration 3 years.
Number awarded Varies each year.
Deadline April of each year.

[1105]
ROBERT WOOD JOHNSON FOUNDATION PHYSICIAN FACULTY SCHOLARS PROGRAM

Robert Wood Johnson Foundation
College Road East and U.S. Route 1
P.O. Box 2316
Princeton, NJ 08543-2316
(609) 932-8701   Toll-free: (877) 843-RWJF
E-mail: mail@rwjf.org
Web: www.rwjf.org

Purpose To provide funding to minority and other junior faculty in medical schools who are interested in developing their careers in academic medicine.

Eligibility This program is open to physicians (M.D. or D.O.) who have had an appointment for 4 years or less as an instructor or assistant professor at a medical school (allopathic or osteopathic) in the United States. Applicants must be committed to a career in academic medicine and have had at least 2 papers published in peer-reviewed journals. They must be able to demonstrate excellence as a teacher, and also care for patients at least 1 half day per week. Physicians who have served as the principal investigator on a grant (research or career development) that carries more than 48 months of funding are not eligible. Applicants must be interested in participating in receiving support to enhance their skills and productivity through institutional and national mentoring, specific research experience, and required protected time. They must be nominated by

their school. Preference is given to applicants interested in the fields of health policy, epidemiology, health services, or community-based research. Selection is based on evidence of the nominee's commitment to an academic career and ability to conduct research; the quality. creativity, and feasibility of the proposed research; the availability of mentors and research resources; evidence that the nominee is an excellent clinical teacher; and evidence that the nominating institution and its senior leadership are committed to supporting the nominee's academic career. U.S. citizenship or permanent resident status is required. The program embraces racial, ethnic, gender, and disciplinary diversity and encourages applications from candidates with diverse backgrounds.
Financial data Grants of $100,000 per year are made annually to the sponsoring institutions. Funds may be used to pay for a portion of the scholar's salary, research assistance, medical student summer stipends, travel, and other direct expenses essential to carrying out the approved plan.
Duration 3 years.
Additional information This program was established in 1993. Further information is available from the national program director, Iris F. Litt, Stanford University, 30 Alta Road, Stanford, CA 94305, (650) 566-2348, Fax: (650) 566-2340, E-mail: rwjfpfsp@stanford.edu.
Number awarded Up to 15 each year.
Deadline August of each year.

[1106]
ROLLIN AND MARY ELLA KING NATIVE AMERICAN ARTIST FELLOWSHIP
School for Advanced Research
Attn: Indian Arts Research Center
660 Garcia Street
P.O. Box 2188
Santa Fe, NM 87504-2188
(505) 954-7205   Fax: (505) 954-7207
E-mail: iarc@sarsf.org
Web: www.sarweb.org/iarc/king/king.htm

Purpose To provide an opportunity for Native American artists to improve their skills through a fall residency at the Indian Arts Research Center in Santa Fe, New Mexico.
Eligibility This program is open to Native Americans who excel in the visual, written, or performing arts. Applicants should be proposing a project in which the spirit of expression, discovery, and personal growth are realized. Along with their application, they must submit a statement describing the project they plan to complete during the residency.
Financial data The fellowships provide financial support, an opportunity to study the collections, and interaction with the staff.
Duration 3 months, beginning in September.
Additional information Fellows work with the staff and research curators at the Indian Arts Research Center, an academic division of the School of American Research that is devoted solely to Native American art scholarship. The center has a significant collection of Pueblo pottery, Navajo and Pueblo Indian textiles, and early 20th-century Indian paintings, as well as holdings of jewelry and silverwork, basketry, clothing, and other ethnological materials. This fellowship was established in 2001.

Number awarded 1 each year.
Deadline April of each year.

[1107]
RONALD B. LINSKY FELLOWSHIP FOR OUTSTANDING WATER RESEARCH
National Water Research Institute
Attn: Fellowship Program
18700 Ward Street
P.O. Box 8096
Fountain Valley, CA 92728-8096
(714) 378-3278   Fax: (714) 378-3375
E-mail: fellow@nwri-usa.org
Web: www.nwri-usa.org/fellowship.htm

Purpose To provide funding to minority and other graduate students interested in conducting research in science and technology fields related to water.
Eligibility This program is open to full-time graduate students interested in conducting research in areas of interest to the National Water Research Institute (NWRI): water treatment technologies, water quality, water environmental chemistry, water policy and economics, public health and risk assessment, or water resources management. Research areas include, but are not limited to, engineering, physical and chemical sciences, biological sciences, health sciences, political sciences, economics, and planning and public policy that are related to water and/or water resources. Preference is given to doctoral candidates, but outstanding students in master's programs may be considered. Applicants must submit a letter of inquiry describing the importance of the research to them and the water community, how their research will contribute to water science in general, what they expect to accomplish, and how their research relates to the mission of the NWRI to create new sources of water through research and technology and to protect the freshwater and marine environments. They must also submit a 1-page essay on their technical capabilities, interest in fields other than what they are studying, career goals, and where they hope to take their technical expertise and vision in the future. Women and members of minority groups underrepresented in academia are strongly encouraged to apply.
Financial data The grant is $20,000 per year.
Duration 2 years.
Additional information This fellowship was first offered in 2007.
Number awarded 1 each even-numbered year.
Deadline February of each even-numbered year.

[1108]
RONALD N. AND SUSAN DUBIN NATIVE AMERICAN ARTIST FELLOWSHIP

School for Advanced Research
Attn: Indian Arts Research Center
660 Garcia Street
P.O. Box 2188
Santa Fe, NM 87504-2188
(505) 954-7205   Fax: (505) 954-7207
E-mail: iarc@sarsf.org
Web: www.sarweb.org/iarc/dubin/dubin.htm

Purpose To provide an opportunity for Native American artists to improve their skills through a summer residency at the Indian Arts Research Center in Santa Fe, New Mexico.

Eligibility This program is open to Native American artists; priority is given to individuals who excel in the visual arts that relate to the center's collecting emphasis, but artists who work in the verbal and performing arts are also considered. Along with their application, they must submit a statement describing the project they plan to complete during the residency.

Financial data The fellowships provide financial support, an opportunity to study the collections, and interaction with the staff.

Duration 2 months, beginning in June.

Additional information Fellows work with the staff and research curators at the Indian Arts Research Center, an academic division of the School of American Research that is devoted solely to Native American art scholarship. The center has a significant collection of Pueblo pottery, Navajo and Pueblo Indian textiles, and early 20th-century Indian paintings, as well as holdings of jewelry and silverwork, basketry, clothing, and other ethnological materials.

Number awarded 1 each year.

Deadline March of each year.

[1109]
SABBATICALS FOR LONG-TIME ACTIVISTS OF COLOR

Alston/Bannerman Fellowship Program
1627 Lancaster Street
Baltimore, MD 21231
(410) 327-6220   Fax: (501) 421-5862
E-mail: info@AlstonBannerman.org
Web: www.AlstonBannerman.org

Purpose To finance a sabbatical for Native Americans and other people of color who have been community activists for at least 10 years.

Eligibility This program is open to persons of color (people of African, Latino, Asian, Pacific Islander, Native American, or Arab descent) who are U.S. residents and have at least 10 years of experience as community activists. Applicants must be committed to continuing to work for social change. Preference is given to applicants whose work attacks root causes of injustice by organizing those affected to take collective action; challenges the systems that perpetrate injustice and effects institutional change; builds their community's capacity for self-determination and develops grassroots leadership; acknowledges the cultural values of the community; creates accountable participatory structures in which community members have decision-making power; and contributes to building a movement for social change by making connections between issues, developing alliances with other constituencies, and collaborating with other organizations. Individuals are ineligible if they only provide services (such as substance abuse counseling, after-school programs, HIV-AIDS outreach, or shelter for the homeless) or if they advocate on behalf of a community without directly involving the members of that community in asserting their own interests and choosing their own leadership. An equal number of men and women are selected.

Financial data The stipend is $25,000.

Duration The sabbaticals are to be 3 months or longer.

Additional information Fellows are encouraged to use their sabbaticals to engage in activities that are substantially different from their normal routine. Activities during the sabbatical must strengthen the recipient's ability to contribute to social change in the future. This program was established in 1987 as the Bannerman Fellowship Program. Its name was changed in 2002. Sabbaticals must be taken within 1 year of receipt of the award. Fellows must submit a report on their sabbatical.

Number awarded At least 10 each year. Since 1988, more than 180 fellowships have been awarded.

[1110]
SCIENCE AND TECHNOLOGY CENTERS SUMMER RESEARCH APPOINTMENTS FOR STEM FACULTY AT MINORITY INSTITUTIONS

Quality Education for Minorities (QEM) Network
1818 N Street, N.W., Suite 350
Washington, DC 20036
(202) 659-1818   Fax: (202) 659-5408
E-mail: qemnetwork@qem.org
Web: qemnetwork.qem.org/stc.htm

Purpose To provide faculty at minority institutions with an opportunity to work during the summer at Science and Technology Centers (STC) supported by the National Science Foundation (NSF) in fields of science, technology, engineering, and mathematics (STEM).

Eligibility This program is open to faculty who are either tenured or in a tenure-track position at Historically Black Colleges and Universities (HBCUs), Hispanic Serving Institutions (HSIs), or Tribal Colleges and Universities (TCUs). The institution must offer at least 1 master's degree in at least 1 STEM field. Applicants must be U.S. citizens, nationals, or permanent residents who have a Ph.D. in a STEM field supported by NSF. They must be interested in collaborating on a summer project with a researcher in their STEM field at a participating STC funded by NSF.

Financial data Fellows receive a stipend of $9,000 plus travel and housing allowances.

Duration 10 weeks during the summer.

Additional information This program is supported by the NSF.

Number awarded Varies each year; recently, 8 of these fellowships were awarded.

Deadline January of each year.

[1111]
SHORT-TERM CAREER DEVELOPMENT AWARD IN THE ENVIRONMENTAL HEALTH SCIENCES FOR ESTABLISHED INVESTIGATORS

National Institute of Environmental Health Sciences
Attn: Division of Extramural Research
Building 4401, Room 3411
P.O. Box 12233
Research Triangle Park, NC 27709
(919) 541-1445 Fax: (919) 541-5064
E-mail: shreffl1@niehs.nih.gov
Web: www.niehs.nih.gov

Purpose To provide funding to minority and other established investigators interested in a program of mentored research training to expand their activities to include the environmental health sciences.

Eligibility This program is open to mid-career and senior investigators who have a research or health professional doctorate and are at the academic rank of associate or full professor. Applicants must be interested in a short-term mentored career development experience that will impact upon their ability to conduct future research in the environmental health sciences. They must identify a mentor at a domestic, for-profit or nonprofit, public or private institution, such as a university, college, hospital, laboratory, unit of state or local government, or eligible agency of the federal government. Members of underrepresented racial and ethnic groups and individuals with disabilities are especially encouraged to apply. Only U.S. citizens, nationals, and permanent residents are eligible.

Financial data The salary is based on the grantee's regular full-time salary and the percentage of effort devoted to program activities. Grants also provide 1) up to $40,000 in direct costs per year (tuition and fees for short-term courses, consultant fees, travel to scientific meetings, and research-related costs, primarily supplies and technical services), and 2) reimbursement of facilities and administrative costs at 8% of modified total direct costs.

Duration From 3 to 12 months.

Additional information Awardees must devote at least 50% effort to the proposed activities, although a full-time commitment is encouraged.

Number awarded Varies each year; approximately $500,000 is available for this program annually.

Deadline February, June, or October of each year.

[1112]
SLOAN SCHOLARSHIP FACULTY GRANTS

Alfred P. Sloan Foundation
630 Fifth Avenue, Suite 2550
New York, NY 10111-0242
(212) 649-1645 Fax: (212) 757-5117
E-mail: greenwood@sloan.org
Web: www.sloan.org

Purpose To provide funding to faculty interested in recruiting underrepresented minority students to pursue a Ph.D. in mathematics, natural science, or engineering.

Eligibility This program is open to mathematics, natural science, and engineering faculty who are interested in recruiting, mentoring, and graduating African Americans, Hispanic Americans, and Native Americans with Ph.D.s. Preference is given to faculty with a record of success in graduating minority students with Ph.D.s, but for faculty who have not had an opportunity to work with minority Ph.D. students, other factors are considered. Young minority faculty are usually preferred. Interested faculty should submit a table with the following data for each African American, Hispanic American, and Native American student who has entered the Ph.D. program during the last 10 years: name, citizenship status, where they earned their undergraduate or master's degree, date of entry into the Ph.D. program, name of the faculty adviser, current status of the student (still enrolled, graduated with Ph.D., left program without Ph.D.), and place of initial employment for those who have graduated. Once faculty are selected to participate in this program, they are encouraged to recruit new Ph.D. students from underrepresented minority groups. For each candidate they recruit who is designated as a Sloan Scholar, they receive this funding.

Financial data Each Sloan Scholarship grant that is awarded triggers a recruiting grant of $2,000 to the faculty or designated university office. Funds may be used for any purpose related to further recruitment of minority Ph.D. students, but not to provide direct benefits to minority students that are not available to other students.

Number awarded Varies each year.

Deadline Proposals may be submitted at any time.

[1113]
SMITHSONIAN MINORITY STUDENT INTERNSHIP

Smithsonian Institution
Attn: Office of Fellowships
Victor Building, Suite 9300, MRC 902
P.O. Box 37012
Washington, DC 20013-7012
(202) 633-7070 Fax: (202) 633-7069
E-mail: siofg@si.edu
Web: www.si.edu/ofg/ofgapp.htm

Purpose To provide Native American and other minority undergraduate or graduate students with the opportunity to work on research or museum procedure projects in specific areas of history, art, or science at the Smithsonian Institution.

Eligibility Internships are offered to minority students who are actively engaged in graduate study at any level or in upper-division undergraduate study. An overall GPA of 3.0 or higher is generally expected. Applicants must be interested in conducting research in specified fields of interest to the Smithsonian.

Financial data The program provides a stipend of $500 per week; travel allowances may also be offered.

Duration 10 weeks during the summer or academic year.

Additional information Eligible fields of study currently available include animal behavior, ecology, and environmental science (including an emphasis on the tropics); anthropology (including archaeology); astrophysics and astronomy; earth sciences and paleobiology; evolutionary and systematic biology; history of science and technology; history of art (especially American, contemporary, African, Asian, and 20th-century art); American crafts and decorative arts; social and cultural history of the United States; folklife; and materials research.

Number awarded Varies each year.

Deadline January of each year for summer or fall; September of each year for spring.

[1114]
SMITHSONIAN NATIVE AMERICAN COMMUNITY SCHOLAR AWARDS

Smithsonian Institution
Attn: Office of Research Training and Services
470 L'Enfant Plaza, Suite 7102
P.O. Box 37012, MRC 902
Washington, DC 20013-7012
(202) 633-7070 Fax: (202) 633-7069
E-mail: siofg@si.edu
Web: www.si.edu/ofg/ofgapp.htm

Purpose To provide opportunities for Native Americans to work on projects related to Native American topics at the Smithsonian Institution.

Eligibility Native Americans who are formally or informally related to a Native American community are eligible to apply. Applicants must be proposing to undertake a project that is related to a Native American topic and requires the use of Native American resources at the Smithsonian Institution.

Financial data Scholars receive a stipend of $150 per day and allowances for travel and research.

Duration Up to 21 days.

Additional information Projects are carried out in association with the Smithsonian's research staff. Fellows are required to be in residence at the Smithsonian for the duration of the fellowship.

Number awarded Varies each year.

Deadline January of each year for summer or fall residency; September of each year for spring residency.

[1115]
SOCIETY FOR THE STUDY OF SOCIAL PROBLEMS RACIAL/ETHNIC MINORITY GRADUATE SCHOLARSHIP

Society for the Study of Social Problems
Attn: Executive Officer
University of Tennessee
901 McClung Tower
Knoxville, TN 37996-0490
(865) 689-1531 Fax: (865) 689-1534
E-mail: sssp@utk.edu
Web: www.sssp1.org/index.cfm/m/261

Purpose To provide funding to Native American and other minority members of the Society for the Study of Social Problems (SSSP) who are interested in conducting research for their doctoral dissertation.

Eligibility This program is open to SSSP members who are Black or African American, Hispanic or Latino, Asian or Asian American, Native Hawaiian or other Pacific Islander, or American Indian or Alaska Native. Applicants must have completed all requirements for a Ph.D. (course work, examinations, and approval of a dissertation prospectus) except the dissertation. They must have a GPA of 3.25 or higher and be able to demonstrate financial need. Their field of study may be any of the social and/or behavioral sciences that will enable them to expand their perspectives in the investigation into social problems. U.S. citizenship or permanent resident status is required.

Financial data The stipend is $12,000. Additional grants provide $500 for the recipient to 1) attend the SSSP annual meeting prior to the year of the work to receive the award, and 2) attend the meeting after the year of the award to present a report on the work completed.

Duration 1 year.

Additional information Information is also available from Joya Misra, Scholarship Committee Chair, (413) 545-5969, Fax: (413) 545-0746, E-mail: misra@soc.umass.edu.

Number awarded 1 each year.

Deadline January of each year.

[1116]
SOUTHERN REGIONAL EDUCATION BOARD DISSERTATION-YEAR FELLOWSHIPS

Southern Regional Education Board
592 10th Street N.W.
Atlanta, GA 30318-5776
(404) 875-9211, ext. 269 Fax: (404) 872-1477
E-mail: doctoral.scholars@sreb.org
Web: www.sreb.org/programs/dsp/dspindex.asp

Purpose To provide funding to Native American and other minority students who wish to complete a doctoral dissertation while in residence at a university in the southern states.

Eligibility This program is open to U.S. citizens who are members of racial/ethnic minority groups (Native Americans, Hispanic Americans, Asian Americans, and African Americans) and have completed all requirements for a Ph.D. except the dissertation. Applicants must be in a position to write full time and must expect to complete their dissertation within the year of the fellowship. Eligibility is limited to individuals who plan to become full-time faculty members at a southern institution upon completion of their doctoral degree. It does not include students working on a professional degree (M.D., D.B.A., D.D.S., J.D., and D.V.M.) or doing graduate work leading to the Ed.D.

Financial data Fellows receive waiver of tuition and fees (in or out of state), a stipend of $15,000, a $500 research allowance, and reimbursement of expenses for attending the Compact for Faculty Diversity's annual Institute on Teaching and Mentoring.

Duration 1 year; nonrenewable.

Additional information This program was established in 1993 as part of the Compact for Faculty Diversity, supported by the Pew Charitable Trusts and the Ford Foundation.

Number awarded Varies each year.

Deadline March of each year.

[1117]
SOUTHWESTERN ASSOCIATION FOR INDIAN ARTS FELLOWSHIPS

Southwestern Association for Indian Arts, Inc.
3600 Cerrillos Road, Suite 712
P.O. Box 969
Santa Fe, NM 87504-0969
(505) 983-5220   Fax: (505) 983-7647
E-mail: info@swaia.org
Web: www.swaia.org/fellowship.php

Purpose To provide funding to American Indian artists interested in advancing their education and careers.

Eligibility This program is open to American Indian artists in the visual arts whose work conforms to the standards and classification definitions of the Southwestern Association for Indian Arts (SWAIA): jewelry; pottery; paintings, graphics, and photography; Pueblo wooden carving; sculpture; textiles and baskets; beadwork and quillwork; and diverse arts. Applicants must be at least 18 years of age and interested in pursuing an opportunity to travel, develop marketing plans, purchase supplies, expand their studies, develop their portfolio, or explore new directions. Funding is not provided to full-time students or for use as a scholarship. Along with their application, they must submit a 250-word essay about their artwork, such as their style, subject matter, materials, techniques, and artistic goals. They must also submit a copy of their tribal documentation from a U.S. federally-recognized tribe or Alaska Native corporation, 4 slides of artwork from the last 2 years, an explanation of how they plan to use the funds, and a formal resume.

Financial data The grant is $5,000. The first $4,000 is paid at the time of awarding the fellowship and the remaining $1,000 after a final report is received from the artist.

Duration The grants are awarded annually.

Additional information This program, established in 1980, is supported by private individuals and Toyota Motor Sales, U.S.A., Inc.

Number awarded 6 to 8 each year.

Deadline January of each year.

[1118]
STANFORD HUMANITIES CENTER EXTERNAL FACULTY FELLOWSHIPS

Stanford Humanities Center
Attn: Fellowship Administrator
424 Santa Teresa Street
Stanford, CA 94305-4015
(650) 723-3054   Fax: (650) 723-1895
E-mail: rbarrick@stanford.edu
Web: shc.stanford.edu

Purpose To offer minority and other scholars in the humanities an opportunity to conduct research and teach at Stanford University.

Eligibility External fellowships at Stanford University fall into 2 categories: 1) senior fellowships for well-established scholars, and 2) junior fellowships for scholars who at the time of application are at least 3 but normally no more than 10 years beyond receipt of the Ph.D. The fields of study should be the humanities as defined in the act that established the National Foundation for the Arts and Humanities. Scholars who are members of traditionally underrepresented groups are encouraged to apply. Applications are judged on 1) the promise of the specific research project being proposed; 2) the originality and intellectual distinction of the candidate's previous work; 3) the research project's potential interest to scholars in different fields of the humanities; and 4) the applicant's ability to engage in collegial interaction and to contribute to the discussion of presentations.

Financial data The annual stipend is up to $55,000. In addition, a housing/travel subsidy of up to $10,000, depending on size of family, is offered.

Duration 1 academic year.

Additional information In addition to these External Fellowships, the Humanities Center offers 6 Internal Fellowships to Stanford faculty each year. All fellows are expected to make an intellectual contribution not only within the center but to humanistic studies in general at Stanford. Normally, this requirement is fulfilled by teaching an undergraduate or graduate course or seminar for 1 quarter within a particular department or program. Fellows should live within the immediate area of Stanford University. Regular attendance at center events is expected and fellows are expected to be present during the fall, winter, and spring quarters and to attend weekday lunches on a regular basis.

Number awarded 6 to 8 each year.

Deadline October of each year.

[1119]
STUDENT ACHIEVEMENT IN RESEARCH AND SCHOLARSHIP (STARS) AWARDS

Ohio Science and Engineering Alliance
c/o Ohio State University
247 University Hall
230 North Oval Mall
Columbus, OH 43210-1366
(614) 247-7267
Web: www.ohiosea.org/research/stars.html

Purpose To provide an opportunity for Native American and other underrepresented minority undergraduate students in Ohio to work on a research project during the academic year.

Eligibility This program is open to African Americans, Native Americans, and Hispanics enrolled at colleges and universities in Ohio. Preference is given to sophomores and juniors, although seniors may be eligible if they are available for a full year of mentoring. Applicants must demonstrate an interest in conducting independent research under the mentorship of a faculty member and continuing on to a doctoral degree and an academic career. They must be U.S. citizens and have a GPA of 3.0 or higher.

Financial data Awards provide payment of $1,200 to fund an original research project.

Duration 1 academic year.

Additional information In addition to conducting the research project, participants gain presentation experience at research conferences, attend a series of STARS workshops to learn about the graduate application process and graduate funding opportunities, work with staff at Ohio State University to prepare graduate applications and identify and compete for sources for graduate funding, and attend the Ohio STARS conference. This program is coordinated by the Ohio State University Office of Graduate Student Recruitment and Diversity Initiatives, (614) 247-6377, E-mail: papio.1@gradsch.ohio-state.edu.

Number awarded Varies each year; recently, 65 students were participating in this program.

[1120]
SUSAN G. KOMEN BREAST CANCER FOUNDATION POSTDOCTORAL FELLOWSHIP

Susan G. Komen Breast Cancer Foundation
Attn: Grants Department
5005 LBJ Freeway, Suite 250
Dallas, TX 75244
(972) 855-1616   Toll-free: (888) 300-5582
Fax: (972) 855-1640   E-mail: grants@komen.org
Web: www.komen.org

Purpose To provide funding to minority and other postdoctoral fellows interested in pursuing research training related to breast cancer.

Eligibility This program is open to postdoctorates who are no more than 5 years past completion of their Ph.D. or, if an M.D., no more than 3 years past completion of clinical fellowship or 5 years past completion of residency. Applicants must be interested in pursuing postdoctoral training in breast cancer research, public health, or epidemiology. A principal investigator from the same institution must sponsor the applicant. The proposed activity must enable the applicant to begin or continue independent investigations in breast health and breast cancer. Priority is given to projects that are innovative, non-duplicative of other efforts, and have the potential to seed continuing study. U.S. citizenship or residency is not required. Women and members of groups historically underrepresented in breast cancer research are especially encouraged to apply.

Financial data The stipend is $45,000 per year.

Duration 2 or 3 years.

Number awarded Varies each year; recently, 41 of these grants were awarded.

Deadline August of each year.

[1121]
SUSAN KELLY POWER AND HELEN HORNBECK TANNER FELLOWSHIP

Newberry Library
Attn: McNickle Center for American Indian History
60 West Walton Street
Chicago, IL 60610-3305
(312) 255-3564   Fax: (312) 255-3513
E-mail: mcnickle@newberry.org
Web: www.newberry.org/mcnickle/frances.html

Purpose To provide funding to American Indian doctoral candidates and postdoctorates who wish to use the resources of the D'Arcy McNickle Center for the History of the American Indian at the Newberry Library.

Eligibility This program is open to Ph.D. candidates and postdoctoral scholars of American Indian heritage. Applicants must be interested in conducting research in the humanities while in residence at the McNickle Center.

Financial data The stipend is $1,600 per month.

Duration 1 week to 2 months.

Additional information This program was established in 2002.

Number awarded 1 each year.

Deadline February of each year.

[1122]
SYLVIA TAYLOR JOHNSON MINORITY FELLOWSHIP IN EDUCATIONAL MEASUREMENT

Educational Testing Service
Attn: Fellowships
Rosedale Road
MS 09-R
Princeton, NJ 08541-0001
(609) 734-5543   Fax: (609) 734-5410
E-mail: internfellowships@ets.org
Web: www.ets.org

Purpose To provide funding to Native American and other minority scholars who are interested in conducting independent research under the mentorship of senior researchers at the Educational Testing Service (ETS).

Eligibility This program is open to minority scholars who have earned a doctorate within the past 10 years and are U.S. citizens or permanent residents. Applicants must be prepared to conduct independent research at ETS under the mentorship of a senior researcher. They should have a commitment to education and an independent body of scholarship that signals the promise of continuing contributions to educational measurement. Projects should relate to issues involved in measurement theory, validity, natural language processing and computational linguistics, cognitive psychology, learning theory, linguistics, speech recognition and processing, teaching and classroom research, or statistics. Studies focused on issues concerning the education of minority students are especially encouraged. Selection is based on the scholar's record of accomplishment, proposed topic of research, commitment to education, and promise of continuing contributions to educational measurement.

Financial data The stipend is set in relation to compensation at the home institution. Scholars and their families also receive reimbursement for relocation expenses.

Duration Up to 2 years.

Number awarded 1 each year.

Deadline January of each year.

[1123]
SYNERGISTIC IDEA DEVELOPMENT AWARDS OF THE PROSTATE CANCER RESEARCH PROGRAM

U.S. Army
Medical Research and Materiel Command
Attn: MCMR-ZB-C
1077 Patchel Street (Building 1077)
Fort Detrick, MD 21702-5024
(301) 619-7079   Fax: (301) 619-7792
E-mail: cdmrp.pa@amedd.army.mil
Web: cdmrp.army.mil/funding/pcrp.htm

Purpose To provide funding to minority and other scientists who are interested in conducting innovative research on prostate cancer in collaboration with colleagues.

Eligibility This program is open to independent investigators at universities, colleges, hospitals, laboratories, companies, and agencies of local, state, and federal governments. Applicants must be at or above the level of assistant professor. The sponsor is especially interested in receiving applications from Historically Black Colleges and Universities and Minority Institutions (HBCU/MI). Proposals must involve 2 or 3 independent, faculty-level investigators using synergistic and complementary perspectives to address a central problem or question in prostate cancer research. Applicants must jointly design a single project, but each partner is recognized as a principal investigator, submits a separate proposal, and receives an individual award. All areas of basic, preclinical, behavioral, and epidemiological research are eligible. Clinical trials are not acceptable.

Financial data Grants range up to $750,000 for direct costs over the term of the award, plus indirect costs as appropriate. Funds must be divided equally among the partners.

Duration 3 years.

Additional information The Prostate Cancer Research Program was established in 1997 as part of the Congressionally Directed Medical Research Programs (CDMRP) of the U.S. Department of Defense. The Synergistic Idea Development Award mechanism was introduced in 2007.

Number awarded Approximately 5 awards, representing 10 to 15 individuals, are granted each year. Approximately $5.6 million is available for this program annually.

Deadline Pre-applications must be submitted by May of each year; full proposals are due in June.

[1124]
TED SCRIPPS FELLOWSHIPS IN ENVIRONMENTAL JOURNALISM

University of Colorado at Boulder
Attn: Center for Environmental Journalism
1511 University Avenue
Campus Box 478
Boulder, CO 80309-0478
(303) 492-4114   E-mail: cej@colorado.edu
Web: www.colorado.edu

Purpose To provide minority and other journalists with an opportunity to gain more knowledge about environmental issues at the University of Colorado at Boulder.

Eligibility This program is open to full-time U.S. print and broadcast journalists who have at least 5 years' professional experience and have completed an undergraduate degree. Applicants may be general assignment reporters, editors, producers, environmental reporters, full-time freelancers, or photojournalists. Prior experience in covering the environment is not required. Professionals in such related fields as teaching, public relations, or advertising are not eligible. Applicants must be interested in a program at the university that includes classes, weekly seminars, and field trips. They also must engage in independent study expected to lead to a significant piece of journalistic work. Applications are especially encouraged from women, ethnic minorities, and disabled persons.

Financial data The program covers tuition and fees and pays a $46,000 stipend. Employers are strongly encouraged to continue benefits, including health insurance.

Duration 9 months.

Additional information This program, established in 1992 at the University of Michigan and transferred to the University of Colorado in 1997, is supported by the Scripps Howard Foundation. This is a non-degree program. Fellows must obtain a leave of absence from their regular employment and must return to their job following the fellowship.

Number awarded 5 each year.

Deadline February of each year.

[1125]
UCSB LIBRARY FELLOWSHIP PROGRAM

University of California at Santa Barbara
Attn: Associate University Librarian, Human Resources
Davidson Library
Santa Barbara, CA 93106-9010
(805) 893-2187   Fax: (805) 893-7010
E-mail: bankhead@library.ucsb.edu
Web: www.library.ucsb.edu/depts/lpo/fellowship.html

Purpose To provide an opportunity for recent library school graduates, especially members of underrepresented groups, to serve in the library system at the University of California at Santa Barbara (UCSB).

Eligibility This program is open to recent graduates of library schools accredited by the American Library Association. Applicants must be interested in a postgraduate appointment at UCSB. They must have a knowledge of and interest in academic librarianship and a strong desire for professional growth. Members of underrepresented groups are encouraged to apply.

Financial data Fellows are regular (but temporary) employees of the university and receive the same salary and benefits as other librarians at the assistant librarian level ($41,292 to $46,164 per year).

Duration 2 years.

Additional information The program began in 1985. Fellows spend time in at least 2 different departments in the library, serve on library committees, attend professional meetings, receive travel support for 2 major conferences, and participate in the Librarians' Association of the University of California.

Number awarded 1 each year.

Deadline January of each year.

[1126]
UNITED STATES INSTITUTE OF PEACE SENIOR FELLOWSHIPS

United States Institute of Peace
Attn: Jennings Randolph Program for International Peace
1200 17th Street, N.W., Suite 200
Washington, DC 20036-3011
(202) 429-3886   Fax: (202) 429-6063
TTY: (202) 457-1719   E-mail: jrprogram@usip.org
Web: www.usip.org/fellows/srfellows.html

Purpose To provide funding to a wide range of professionals (especially minorities) who wish to conduct research at the United States Institute of Peace (USIP) in Washington, D.C.

Eligibility This program is open to candidates from a wide variety of professional backgrounds, including governmental and nongovernmental practitioners in international security, peacemaking, and public affairs; scholars and researchers; and media and communications specialists. Fellows may be at any stage of their careers and have any educational background. They should be proposing a research project related to preventive diplomacy, ethnic and regional conflicts, peacekeeping and peace operations, peace settlements, post-conflict reconstruction and reconciliation, democratization and the rule of law, cross-cultural negotiations, U.S. foreign policy in the 21st century, and related topics. Preference is given to projects that demonstrate relevance to the sources and nature of interstate or civil conflict, with ways to prevent, limit, or end violent conflict, and with post-conflict reconstruction and reconciliation. Candidates must be proposing to produce 1 or more products, such as books or monographs published by USIP Press, reports published by the institute, articles for professional or academic journals, op-eds and articles for newspapers or magazines, radio or TV media projects, demonstrations or simulations, teaching curricula, lectures or other public speaking, or workshops, seminars, or symposia, while at the institute. Applicants may be citizens of any country. Women and members of minority groups are especially encouraged to apply. Selection is based on the candidate's record of achievement and/or leadership potential; the significance and potential of the project for making an important contribution to knowledge, practice, or public understanding; and the quality of the project design and its feasibility within the timetable proposed.

Financial data The stipend is based on the fellow's earned income for the preceding year, up to a maximum of $80,000. In the case of candidates from countries with salaries greatly different from the United States, seniority is the basis for calculation. Also provided are transportation to and from Washington, D.C. for the fellow and eligible family members.

Duration Up to 10 months, beginning in October.

Additional information These fellowships, first awarded in 1988, are tenable at the United States Institute of Peace in Washington, D.C., where fellows interact with other fellows and Institute staff by presenting their work and participating in workshops, conferences, and other events. These awards are not made for projects that constitute policymaking for a government agency or private organization; focus to any substantial degree on conflicts within U.S. domestic society, or adopt a partisan, advocacy, or activist stance.

Number awarded Approximately 12 each year.

Deadline September of each year.

[1127]
UNIVERSITY OF CALIFORNIA PRESIDENT'S POSTDOCTORAL FELLOWSHIP PROGRAM FOR ACADEMIC DIVERSITY

University of California
Attn: Office of the President
1111 Franklin Street, 11th Floor
Oakland, CA 94607-5200
(510) 987-9503   Fax: (510) 587-6077
E-mail: kim.adkinson@ucop.edu
Web: www.ucop.edu/acadadv/ppfp

Purpose To provide minority and other recent postdoctorates who are committed to careers in university teaching and research with an opportunity to conduct research at campuses of the University of California.

Eligibility This program is open to U.S. citizens or permanent residents who have a Ph.D. from an accredited university. Applicants must be proposing to conduct research at a branch of the university under the mentorship of a faculty or laboratory sponsor. Preference is given to applicants 1) with the potential to bring to their academic careers the critical perspective that comes from their nontraditional educational background or their understanding of the experiences of groups historically underrepresented in higher education; 2) who have the communications skill and cross-cultural abilities to maximize effective collaboration with a diverse cross-section of the academic community; 3) who have demonstrated significant academic achievement by overcoming barriers such as economic, social, or educational disadvantage; and 4) who have the potential to contribute to higher education through their understanding of the barriers facing women, domestic minorities, students with disabilities, and other members of groups underrepresented in higher education careers, as evidenced by life experiences and educational background.

Financial data The stipend ranges up to $55,000 for the humanities and social sciences or up to $65,000 for the physical sciences, life sciences, mathematics, and engineering. The program also offers health benefits and up to $4,000 for supplemental and research-related expenses.

Duration Appointments are for 1 academic year, with possible renewal for a second year.

Additional information Research may be conducted on any of the University of California's 10 campuses (Berkeley, Davis, Irvine, Los Angeles, Merced, Riverside, San Diego, San Francisco, Santa Barbara, or Santa Cruz). The program provides mentoring and guidance in preparing for an academic career. This program was established in 1984 to encourage applications from minority and women scholars in fields where they were severely underrepresented; it is now open to all qualified candidates who are committed to university careers in research, teaching, and service that will enhance the diversity of the academic community at the university.

Number awarded Varies each year; recently, 21 of these fellowships were awarded.

Deadline October of each year.

[1128]
UNIVERSITY OF IOWA LIBRARIAN RESIDENCY PROGRAM

University of Iowa
Libraries
Attn: Director for Human Resources and Diversity
   Programs
100 Main Library
Iowa City, IA 52242-1420
(319) 335-5871   Fax: (319) 335-5900
E-mail: susan-marks@uiowa.edu
Web: www.lib.uiowa.edu

Purpose To provide professional experience to recently graduated librarians from underrepresented groups at the University of Iowa in Iowa City.

Eligibility This program is open to members of historically underrepresented groups who are recent graduates or master's degree programs in library and information science. Applicants must be interested in a residency at the University of Iowa as preparation for a professional career in university libraries. They must be able to demonstrate general knowledge of traditional and electronic information

sources; general knowledge of information literacy and instruction principles; demonstrated commitment to diversity in the workplace or community; ability to work in a team environment; excellent written and oral communication skills; and a demonstrated interest in professional development and contribution.
Financial data The appointment is at the Librarian I level with an entry-level salary of $41,000. A full package of benefits is also included.
Duration 2 years.
Number awarded 1 each year.
Deadline February of each year.

[1129]
UNIVERSITY OF WISCONSIN VISITING MINORITY SCHOLAR LECTURE PROGRAM

University of Wisconsin at Madison
Attn: Wisconsin Center for Education Research
1025 West Johnson Street, Suite 785
Madison, WI 53706-1796
(608) 263-4200   Fax: (608) 263-6448
E-mail: uw-wcer@education.wisc.edu
Web: www.wcer.wisc.edu/lectureSeries/index.php

Purpose To enable Native American and other minority scholars in education to present a guest lecture at the University of Wisconsin.
Eligibility Minority scholars on the faculty of other universities are invited to present lectures on topics related to minorities and education at the University of Wisconsin. Candidates are nominated through a solicitation process within the university's school of education.
Financial data Lecturers receive travel expenses and an honorarium.
Duration Each visit lasts 2 days.
Additional information The visiting scholar makes a general presentation open to the University of Wisconsin's community and meets with a group of minority students at the university to discuss the scholar's work. This program is cosponsored by the University of Wisconsin's School of Education and the Wisconsin Center for Education Research.
Number awarded 2 to 6 each year.

[1130]
UNIVERSITY–INDUSTRY COOPERATIVE RESEARCH PROGRAM GRADUATE RESEARCH ASSISTANTSHIPS AND COOPERATIVE FELLOWSHIPS

National Science Foundation
Directorate for Mathematical and Physical Sciences
Attn: Division of Mathematical Sciences
4201 Wilson Boulevard, Room 1025 N
Arlington, VA 22230
(703) 292-4862   Fax: (703) 292-9032
TDD: (800) 281-8749   E-mail: ldouglas@nsf.gov
Web: www.nsf.gov

Purpose To provide funding to minority and other graduate students in mathematics who are interested in conducting research or serving as an intern in an industrial environment.
Eligibility This program is open to graduate students in mathematics who are U.S. citizens, nationals, or permanent residents. Applicants must be interested in conducting research in an industrial setting. For research assistantships, the research must form the basis of a master's thesis or Ph.D. dissertation and must be conducted under the joint supervision of a university faculty member and an industrial scientist; students will alternate their time between the industrial site and the classroom or other campus-based activities. For cooperative fellowships, students work full time as interns in an industrial setting and their research is not necessarily the basis for a thesis or dissertation. Selection is based on the quality of the proposed activity at the industrial site, the qualifications of both the supervising faculty member and the industrial sponsor, the appropriateness of the academic/industrial interaction, and the impact of the proposed training on the professional development of the graduate assistant/fellow. The program encourages applications from women, underrepresented minorities, and persons with disabilities.
Financial data Grants provide 50% of the total annual support for a student (to a maximum of $20,000 per year. The awardee institution must cost share the balance of support. The supervising faculty member is eligible for a research allowance of $6,000.
Duration 1 year.
Number awarded This program awards a total of 10 grants, with a value of $1,000,000, each year.
Deadline May of each year.

[1131]
UNIVERSITY–INDUSTRY COOPERATIVE RESEARCH PROGRAM POSTDOCTORAL RESEARCH FELLOWSHIPS

National Science Foundation
Directorate for Mathematical and Physical Sciences
Attn: Division of Mathematical Sciences
4201 Wilson Boulevard, Room 1025 N
Arlington, VA 22230
(703) 292-4862   Fax: (703) 292-9032
TDD: (800) 281-8749   E-mail: ldouglas@nsf.gov
Web: www.nsf.gov

Purpose To provide financial assistance to minority and other recent doctoral recipients in mathematics who wish to broaden their knowledge, experience, and research perspectives in an industrial environment.
Eligibility This program is open to U.S. citizens, nationals, or permanent residents who are eligible to be appointed as a research associate or assistant professor at the institution submitting the proposal. Applicants must have earned a Ph.D. within the past 7 years in a mathematical science or have had equivalent research training and experience. They may not have held a tenured position at an academic institution and not have previously held any other postdoctoral fellowship from the National Science Foundation (NSF). Approximately half of the proposed research must be conducted in an industrial setting and half in a university environment. Applications must be submitted by a university principal investigator who will serve as scientific mentor to a fellow with an industrial sponsor. The proposal may either identify the prospective postdoctoral fellow or present a plan for recruiting the fellows. Principal investigators are

encouraged to submit nominations of women, underrepresented minorities, and persons with disabilities as postdoctoral fellows. Selection is based on the quality of the proposed research to be conducted at both the academic and industrial sites, the qualifications of and commitment by both the faculty mentor and the industrial sponsor, the appropriateness of the academic/industrial interaction, and the impact of the proposed training on the professional development of the postdoctoral fellow.

Financial data The total award is $111,000, of which $71,000 is provided by the National Science Foundation and $40,000 by the industrial sponsor. The award includes a stipend allowance for the fellow of $80,000 ($40,000 per year) plus a fringe benefit allowance of $16,000 ($8,000 per year), an allowance of $4,500 for the sponsoring institution in lieu of indirect costs, a research allowance of $4,500 for the fellow to be used for travel, publication costs, and other research-related expenses, and an allowance of $6,000 for the faculty mentor for research expenses related to the industrial partnership.

Duration 2 years.

Number awarded This program awards a total of 10 grants, with a value of $1,000,000, each year.

Deadline May of each year.

[1132]
UNIVERSITY–INDUSTRY COOPERATIVE RESEARCH PROGRAM SENIOR RESEARCH FELLOWSHIPS

National Science Foundation
Directorate for Mathematical and Physical Sciences
Attn: Division of Mathematical Sciences
4201 Wilson Boulevard, Room 1025 N
Arlington, VA 22230
(703) 292-4862   Fax: (703) 292-9032
TDD: (800) 281-8749   E-mail: ldouglas@nsf.gov
Web: www.nsf.gov

Purpose To provide funding to minority and other mid-career and senior scholars in mathematics who wish to broaden their knowledge, experience, and research perspectives by exposure to industrial environments, and to industrial researchers who wish to experience and participate in the full range of university research environments.

Eligibility This program is open to faculty members and industrial scientists who are U.S. citizens, nationals, or permanent residents and who have earned a Ph.D. in a mathematical science or have had equivalent research training and experience. Academic applicants must be proposing to conduct research while on sabbatical in an industrial setting; industrial scientists must be proposing to conduct research in a university environment. They must make a commitment to return to the home institution for a minimum of 1 year following the fellowship tenure. Applications are encouraged from women, underrepresented minorities, and persons with disabilities.

Financial data The program provides a salary equivalent to the fellow's regular 6-month full-time salary (to a maximum of $50,000, or $60,000 including fringe benefits), a research allowance of $10,000, and an institutional allowance of $10,000 as partial reimbursement for fringe benefits and other indirect costs. Awardee institutions must cost share salary over and above the 6-month salary amount.

Duration Normally 12 months.

Number awarded This program awards a total of 10 grants, with a value of $1,000,000, each year.

Deadline May of each year.

[1133]
USDA SMALL BUSINESS INNOVATION RESEARCH PROGRAM

Department of Agriculture
Cooperative State Research, Education, and Extension Service
Attn: Director, SBIR Program
1400 Independence Avenue, S.W.
Stop 2201
Washington, DC 20250-2201
(202) 401-4002   Fax: (202) 401-6488
E-mail: sbir@csrees.usda.gov
Web: www.crees.usda.gov/funding/sbir/sbir.html

Purpose To stimulate technological innovation related to agriculture in the private sector by small business firms, especially those owned by women or members of socially and economically disadvantaged groups.

Eligibility For the purposes of this program, a "small business" is defined as a firm that is organized for profit with a location in the United States; is in the legal form of an individual proprietorship, partnership, limited liability company, corporation, joint venture, association, trust, or cooperative; is at least 51% owned and controlled by 1 or more individuals who are citizens or permanent residents of the United States; and has (including its affiliates) fewer than 500 employees. The primary employment of the principal investigator must be with the firm at the time of award and during the conduct of the proposed project. Applications are encouraged from socially and economically disadvantaged small business concerns and from women-owned small business concerns. A socially and economically disadvantaged small business concern is at least 51% owned by either 1) an Indian tribe or a Native Hawaiian organization, or 2) 1 or more socially disadvantaged individuals (African Americans, Hispanic Americans, Native Americans, Asian Pacific Americans, or subcontinent Asian Americans). A woman-owned small business concern is at least 51% owned by a woman or women who also control and operate it. The project must be performed in the United States, its territories, or its possessions. Proposals are accepted in 13 topic areas: forests and related resources; plant production and protection (biology); animal production and protection; soil and water resources; food science and nutrition; rural development; aquaculture; biofuels and biobased products; marketing and trade; animal manure management; small and mid sized farms; and plant production and protection (engineering). Selection is based on scientific and technical feasibility of the project, important of the problem, qualifications of the investigator and research facilities, appropriateness of the budget, and extent of duplication of the project with other ongoing or previous research.

Financial data Support is offered in 2 phases. In phase 1, awards normally do not exceed $80,000 (for both direct and indirect costs); in phase 2, awards normally do not exceed $350,000 (including both direct and indirect costs).

Duration Phase 1 awards may extend up to 8 months; phase 2 awards may extend up to 2 years.

Additional information Phase 1 is to determine the scientific or technical feasibility of ideas submitted by the applicants on research topic areas. Phase 2 awards are made to firms with approaches that appear sufficiently promising as a result of phase 1 studies.
Number awarded Recently, the department granted 80 phase 1 awards and 32 phase 2 awards. Total program funding was approximately $18.9 million.
Deadline September of each year for phase 1 awards; February of each year for phase 2 awards.

[1134]
WASHINGTON STATE UNIVERSITY SUMMER DOCTORAL FELLOWS PROGRAM
Washington State University
Attn: Graduate School
P.O. Box 641030
Pullman, WA 99164-1030
(509) 335-6412   E-mail: gsdean@wsu.edu
Web: gradschool.wsu.edu

Purpose To provide financial assistance to Native American and other students from diverse backgrounds who are completing their doctoral program at any school and are interested in working closely with faculty members at Washington State University (WSU) during the summer to prepare for their academic careers.
Eligibility This program is open to U.S. citizens from diverse backgrounds who have completed all requirements other than the dissertation for their doctorate. Applicants must be interested in a career in higher education and working on their degree in an area relevant to the work of the following WSU colleges: agriculture, human, and natural resources sciences; business; education; engineering and architecture; liberal arts; nursing; pharmacy; sciences; or veterinary medicine. Along with their application, they must submit a curriculum vitae, graduate school transcripts, 3 letters of recommendation, and a 3- to 5-page statement of career goals and research interests.
Financial data The stipend is $3,000; university housing is also provided.
Duration 6 weeks during the summer, beginning in June.
Additional information This program was established in 1993 and initially involved only the College of Education at Washington State University. In 1998, the program was expanded to include additional colleges at the university; it is coordinated by the Graduate School. During the program, fellows are actively engaged in seminars on the changing roles and expectations of faculty, the future of academia, the changing nature of higher education, and issues facing faculty of color and women in higher education. Fellows are expected to design individualized programs for enhancing their ability to teach, conduct research, and other scholarly activities.
Number awarded Varies each year; recently, 9 fellows were selected for this program.
Deadline March of each year.

[1135]
W.E.B. DUBOIS FELLOWSHIP PROGRAM
Department of Justice
National Institute of Justice
Attn: W.E.B. DuBois Fellowship Program
810 Seventh Street, N.W.
Washington, DC 20531
(202) 353-7294
E-mail: Nicole.Gaskin-Laniyan@usdoj.gov
Web: www.ojp.usdoj.gov/nij/funding.htm

Purpose To provide funding to minority and other junior investigators interested in conducting research on the "confluence of crime, justice, and culture in various societal contexts."
Eligibility This program is open to investigators who have a Ph.D. or other doctoral-level degree or a legal degree of J.D. or higher. Applicants should be early in their careers. They must be interested in conducting research that relates to the following high-priority topics: immigration, crime, and victimization; trafficking in human beings; transnational crime; police-community relations; courts, sentencing, and corrections; civil rights; and ethnographic studies. The research should emphasize crime, violence, and the administration of justice in diverse cultural contexts. Because of that focus, the sponsor strongly encourages applications from diverse racial and ethnic backgrounds. Selection is based on quality and technical merit; impact of the proposed project; capabilities, demonstrated productivity, and experience of the applicant; budget; dissemination strategy; and relevant of the project for policy and practice.
Financial data The grant is approximately $75,000. Funds may be used for salary, fringe benefits, reasonable costs of relocation, travel essential to the project, and office expenses not provided by the sponsor. Indirect costs are limited to 20%.
Duration 6 to 12 months; fellows are required to be in residence at the National Institute of Justice (NIJ) for the first 2 months and may elect to spend all or part of the remainder of the fellowship period either in residence at NIJ or at their home institution.
Number awarded 1 each year.
Deadline January of each year.

[1136]
WILDLIFE CONSERVATION SOCIETY RESEARCH FELLOWSHIP PROGRAM
Wildlife Conservation Society
Attn: Global Conservation Program
2300 Southern Boulevard
Bronx, NY 10460
(718) 741-8197   Fax: (718) 364-4275
E-mail: fellowship@wcs.org
Web: www.wcs.org/international/tcbp/rfp

Purpose To provide funding to individual research projects (particularly by Native Americans) that lead directly to the conservation of threatened wildlife and wildlife habitat in selected regions of the world.
Eligibility All individuals are eligible to apply for this funding to conduct marine or terrestrial field research related to wildlife conservation in Africa, Asia, and Latin America (including Mexico). Proposals for research in North America are accepted only from Native Americans and First Nation

People who are recognized members of established native groups and who intend to conduct their work on native lands, on issues of direct relevance to wildlife conservation or management on native lands, or on species governed by treaty or intertribal agreements. Research in Australia, New Zealand, Japan or Europe is not supported. Although any individual may apply, most grantees are professional conservationists from the country of research and/or graduate students working on a higher degree. Applications may be submitted in English, French, or Spanish, but all proposals must be accompanied by an English abstract. Selection is based on applicant's potential as a conservation professional, relevance to wildlife conservation, and scientific merit and value.

Financial data Grants range up to $25,000 and average $10,655. Funds may not be used for conferences, expeditions, travel to scientific meetings, legal actions, construction of permanent field stations, tuition or salaries for the principal investigator, costly laboratory analyses, gene storage, vehicle purchase, computer purchase, captive breeding, or overhead costs. Stipends are not offered, but investigators who have no other source of support may request modest per diem expenses.

Duration Projects are limited to 1 year; preference is given to discrete, short-term projects.

Number awarded Varies each year. Recently, 16 of these grants were awarded: 7 for the winter cycle and 9 for the summer cycle.

Deadline March of each year for the summer cycle; September of each year for the winter cycle.

[1137]
WILLIAM TOWNSEND PORTER FELLOWSHIP FOR MINORITY INVESTIGATORS

Woods Hole Marine Biological Laboratory
Attn: Fellowship Coordinator
7 MBL Street
Woods Hole, MA 02543-1015
(508) 289-7441   Fax: (508) 457-1924
E-mail: skaufman@mbl.edu
Web: www.mbl.edu

Purpose To support Native American and other underrepresented minority physiologists who wish to conduct research during the summer at the Woods Hole Marine Biological Laboratory (MBL).

Eligibility This program is open to young scientists (undergraduates, senior graduate students, and postdoctoral trainees) who are from an underrepresented minority group (African American, Hispanic American, or Native American), are U.S. citizens or permanent residents, and are interested in conducting research in the field of physiology with senior investigators at MBL.

Financial data Participants receive a stipend and a travel allowance. Recently, grants averaged $1,500.

Duration At least 6 weeks during the summer.

Additional information This fellowship was first awarded in 1921. Funding is provided by the Harvard Apparatus Foundation.

Number awarded Varies each year.

Deadline January of each year.

[1138]
W.K. KELLOGG FOUNDATION DOCTORAL FELLOWSHIP IN HEALTH POLICY

National Medical Fellowships, Inc.
Attn: Scholarship Program
5 Hanover Square, 15th Floor
New York, NY 10004
(212) 483-8880   Fax: (212) 483-8897
E-mail: info@nmfonline.org
Web: www.nmfonline.org

Purpose To provide financial assistance to Native Americans and other minorities enrolled in a doctoral program in health policy research who are committed to working with underserved populations.

Eligibility This program is open to members of minority groups (African Americans, Native Americans, Asians, and Hispanics) enrolled in doctoral programs in public health, social policy, or health policy (Ph.D., Dr.P.H., or Sc.D.). Applicants must demonstrate a willingness to complete relevant dissertation research and a commitment to work with underserved populations upon completion of the doctorate. They must include an essay of 500 to 1,000 words discussing their reasons for applying for a fellowship, their qualifications, how it will support their career plans, and which of 4 areas of focus (health policy, men's health, mental health, substance abuse) most interests them and why.

Financial data Fellowships cover tuition, fees, and a partial living stipend.

Duration Up to 5 years: 2 years to do the necessary course work and 3 years to complete the dissertation.

Additional information The program was created in 1998 with grant support from the W.K. Kellogg Foundation. Recently, it operated at 8 institutions: the RAND Graduate School, the Heller Graduate School at Brandeis University, the Joseph L. Mailman School of Public Health at Columbia University, the Harvard School of Public Health, the Johns Hopkins School of Hygiene and Public Health, the UCLA School of Public Health, the University of Michigan School of Public Health, and the University of Pennsylvania. Information is also available from the sponsor's Washington office at 1627 K Street, N.W., Suite 1200, Washington, DC 20006-1702, (202) 296-4431, Fax: (202) 293-1990.

Number awarded 5 each year.

Deadline June of each year.

[1139]
WOMEN OF COLOR DISSERTATION SCHOLARSHIP

Sociologists for Women in Society
Attn: Executive Officer
University of Rhode Island
Department of Sociology
Kingston, RI 02881
(401) 874-9510   Fax: (401) 874-2588
E-mail: sws@etal.uri.edu
Web: www.socwomen.org/page.php?sss=115

Purpose To provide funding to Native Americans and other women of color who are conducting dissertation research in sociology.

Eligibility This program is open to women from a racial/ethnic group that faces racial discrimination in the United States. Applicants must be in the early stages of writing a doctoral dissertation in sociology on a topic relating to the concerns that women of color face domestically and/or internationally. They must be able to demonstrate financial need. Both domestic and international students are eligible to apply. program in sociology in the United States. Applicants must have studied for at least 1 year at a 2-year college before transferring to complete a bachelor's degree. They must submit a 2-page letter of application that describes their decision to study sociology, career goals, research, activism, and service. Selection is based on commitment to teaching, especially at a community college; research and/or activism in social inequality, social justice, or social problems, with a focus on gender and/or gerontology; and service to the academic and/or local community, including mentoring.

Financial data The stipend is $15,000. An additional grant of $500 is provided to enable the recipient to attend the winter meeting of Sociologists for Women in Society (SWS) and travel expenses to attend the summer meeting are reimbursed.

Duration 1 year.

Number awarded 1 each year.

Deadline May of each year.

[1140]
WOODS HOLE OCEANOGRAPHIC INSTITUTION SUMMER STUDENT FELLOWSHIP PROGRAM

Woods Hole Oceanographic Institution
Attn: Education Office
Clark Laboratory 223, MS 31
360 Woods Hole Road
Woods Hole, MA 02543-1541
(508) 289-2219 Fax: (508) 457-2188
E-mail: education@whoi.edu
Web: www.whoi.edu

Purpose To provide funding to minority and other undergraduates interested in conducting research at the Woods Hole Oceanographic Institution (WHOI) during the summer.

Eligibility This program is open to undergraduate students who have completed their junior or senior year at colleges or universities with a major in any science or engineering field, including (but not limited to) biology, chemistry, engineering, geology, geophysics, mathematics, meteorology, physics, oceanography, or marine policy. Applicants must have at least a tentative interest in the ocean sciences, oceanographic engineering, mathematics, or marine policy. They must be interested in conducting an independent research project under the guidance of a member of the WHOI research staff. Along with their application, they must submit a 3-page statement on how a summer of research at WHOI would benefit their education and career plans, the skills they expect to obtain from this research experience, the skills they have that would make them a good researcher, information on previous research projects in which they have been involved, and the areas of marine research in which they are interested and why. Selection is based on previous academic and scientific achievements and promise as future ocean scientists or ocean engineers. Women and members of underrepresented groups are especially encouraged to apply.

Financial data The stipend is $415 per week; housing is also provided. Additional support may be provided for travel.

Duration 10 to 12 weeks during the summer.

Additional information Fellows are not required to take any prescribed courses nor are they required to provide any services to the institution in return for the grant. This program is supported by grants from the National Science Foundation's Research Experiences for Undergraduates Program. Fellows are expected to give an oral report on their research.

Deadline February of each year.

[1141]
YERBY POSTDOCTORAL FELLOWSHIP PROGRAM

Harvard School of Public Health
Attn: Office of Faculty Affairs
677 Huntington Avenue, Room 1010
Boston, MA 02115
(617) 432-1047 Fax: (617) 432-4711
E-mail: facultyaffairs@hsph.harvard.edu
Web: www.hsph.harvard.edu

Purpose To provide Native American and other minority postdoctorates with an opportunity to pursue a program of research training at Harvard School of Public Health.

Eligibility This program is open to 1) members of minority groups underrepresented in public health, and 2) first-generation college graduates. Applicants must have a doctoral degree and be interested in preparing for a career in public health. They must submit 3 letters of recommendation; a curriculum vitae; a proposal for research to be undertaken during the fellowship; a statement of professional objectives in academic public health, including how those objectives would be advanced by research opportunities at HSPH; and a sample publication.

Financial data Fellows receive a competitive salary.

Duration 1 year; may be renewed 1 additional year.

Additional information Fellows are associated with a faculty mentor who assists in the transition to an academic career. With the help of the faculty mentor, fellows develop their research agendas, gain experience in publishing papers in peer-reviewed journals and in obtaining grant support, participate in a variety of professional development workshops, and increase their teaching expertise.

Number awarded Up to 5 each year.

Deadline December of each year.

[1142]
YOUTH PUBLIC ART PROJECT PROGRAM OF THE NATIONAL MUSEUM OF THE AMERICAN INDIAN

National Museum of the American Indian
Attn: Native Arts Program
Cultural Resources Center
4220 Silver Hill Road
Suitland, MD 20746-2863
(301) 238-1540 Fax: (301) 238-3200
E-mail: NAP@si.edu
Web: www.nmai.si.edu

Purpose To provide Native American professional artists with an opportunity to organize and conduct a collaborative art project focused on youth within their local community.

Eligibility This program is open to Native artists from the western Hemisphere and Hawaii who are recognized by their community, have at least 10 years of experience, and can demonstrate significant artistic accomplishments in any media (e.g., visual arts, media arts, performance arts, literature). Students enrolled in a degree program are ineligible. Applicants must be interested in creating an art project within their home community in collaboration with a local youth organization. Along with their application, they must submit a statement that describes the youth group with whom they plan to collaborate, the community in which the project will be created, the need for the project and the purpose it will serve for the youth and the community, potential subject matter to be included in the project design, the size and scope of the project and a location where it will be housed and/or presented, a target completion date, and ideas for the presentation of the completed project. The project should reflect the community's cultural values, ideas, and images.

Financial data The grant is $6,000. Funds are to be disbursed as tasks are completed during the period of work.

Duration Projects must be completed within 3 months.

Additional information Following the completion of the project, the artist and the youth organization must invite community members to a presentation ceremony.

Number awarded 1 each year.

Deadline April of each year.

Awards

Described in this section are 33 competitions, prizes, and honoraria open to Native Americans in recognition or support of creative work, personal accomplishments, professional contributions, or public service. Excluded are prizes received solely as the result of entering contests. If you are looking for a particular program and don't find it in this section, be sure to check the Program Title Index to see if it is covered elsewhere in the directory.

AWARDS

[1143]
AMERICAN INDIAN LAW REVIEW WRITING COMPETITION

American Indian Law Review
Attn: Writing Competition Editor
Andrew M. Coats Hall
300 Timberdell Road
Norman, OK 73019
(405) 325-2840   Fax: (405) 325-6282
E-mail: ailr@ou.edu
Web: adams.law.ou.edu/ailr/competition.cfm

Purpose To recognize and reward outstanding unpublished papers written by law students on American Indian law.
Eligibility This competition is open to students at accredited law schools in the United States or Canada. They may submit an unpublished paper (from 20 to 50 pages in length) on any issue concerning American Indian law (although topics recently published in the *American Indian Law Review* are not encouraged). Selection is based on originality and timeliness of topic, knowledge and use of applicable legal principles, proper and articulate analysis of the issues, use of authorities, extent of research, logic and reasoning in analysis, ingenuity and ability to argue by analogy, clarity and organization, correctness of format and citations, grammar and writing style, and strength and logic of conclusions.
Financial data First prize is $1,000 and publication of the paper in the *American Indian Law Review*. Second prize is $500. Third prize is $250.
Duration The competition is held annually.
Number awarded 3 each year.
Deadline January of each year.

[1144]
ANISFIELD-WOLF BOOK AWARDS

Cleveland Foundation
1422 Euclid Avenue, Suite 1300
Cleveland, OH 44115-2001
(216) 861-3810   Fax: (216) 861-1729
E-mail: awinfo@clevefdn.org
Web: www.anisfield-wolf.org

Purpose To recognize and reward recent books that have contributed to an understanding of racism or appreciation of the rich diversity of human cultures.
Eligibility Works published in English during the preceding year that "contribute to our understanding of racism or our appreciation of the rich diversity of human cultures" are eligible to be considered. Entries may be either scholarly or imaginative (fiction, poetry, memoir). Plays and screenplays are not eligible, nor are works in progress. Manuscripts and self-published works are not eligible, and no grants are made for completing or publishing manuscripts.
Financial data The prize is $10,000. If more than 1 author is chosen in a given year, the prize is divided equally among the winning books.
Duration The award is presented annually.
Additional information These awards were first presented in 1936. Information is also available from Laura Scharf, 700 West St. Clair Avenue, Suite 414, Cleveland, OH 44113.
Number awarded 3 each year: 1 for fiction, 1 for nonfiction, and 1 for lifetime achievement.
Deadline December of each year.

[1145]
ASSE/DUPONT MINORITIES IN ENGINEERING AWARD

American Society for Engineering Education
Attn: Manager, Administrative Services
1818 N Street, N.W., Suite 600
Washington, DC 20036-2479
(202) 331-3500   Fax: (202) 265-8504
Web: www.asee.org/activities/awards/special.cfm

Purpose To recognize and reward outstanding achievements by engineering educators to increase the participation of underrepresented students in engineering curricula.
Eligibility Eligible for nomination are engineering educators who, as part of their education activity, either assume or are charged with the responsibility of motivating underrepresented students to enter and continue in engineering curricula at the college or university level, graduate or undergraduate. Nominees from previous years will be eligible for the award provided they have been renominated in a letter from the original nominator that includes updated material. Renominated candidates will be considered on the same basis as new nominees.
Financial data The award consists of $1,500, a certificate, and a grant of $500 for travel expenses to the ASEE annual conference.
Duration The award is granted annually.
Additional information Funding for this award is provided by Dupont. It was established in 1956 as the Vincent Bendix Minorities in Engineering Award.
Number awarded 1 each year.
Deadline January of each year.

[1146]
BEYOND MARGINS AWARD

PEN American Center
Attn: Beyond Margins Coordinator
588 Broadway, Suite 303
New York, NY 10012
(212) 334-1660, ext. 109   Fax: (212) 334-2181
E-mail: stacyleigh@pen.org
Web: www.pen.org/page.php/prmID/280

Purpose To recognize and reward Native American and other outstanding authors of color from any country.
Eligibility This award is presented to an author of color (African, Arab, Asian, Caribbean, Latino, and Native American) whose book-length writings were published in the United States during the current calendar year. Works of fiction, literary nonfiction, biography/memoir, and other works of literary character are strongly preferred. U.S. citizenship or residency is not required. Nominations must be submitted by publishers or agents.
Financial data The prize is $1,000.
Duration The prizes are awarded annually.
Number awarded 5 each year.
Deadline December of each year.

[1147]
CHAMPIONS OF HEALTH PROFESSIONS DIVERSITY AWARD

The California Wellness Foundation
6320 Canoga Avenue, Suite 1700
Woodland Hills, CA 91367
(818) 702-1900   Fax: (818) 702-1999
Web: www.tcwf.org/leadership_awards/index.htm

Purpose To recognize and reward residents of California who have helped to increase diversity in the health professions.

Eligibility Eligible to be considered for this award are residents of California who have demonstrated a commitment to increasing diversity in the health professions. Nominees must be health professionals who have overcome significant barriers.

Financial data The prize is $25,000.

Duration The prize is awarded annually.

Additional information This prize was first awarded in 2003.

Number awarded Up to 3 each year.

[1148]
CHICKASAW NATION DEGREE COMPLETION INCENTIVE AWARDS

Chickasaw Nation
Attn: Department of Education Services
122 East Main
Ada, OK 74820
(580) 421-7711   Fax: (580) 436-3733
E-mail: education.services@chickasaw.net
Web: www.chickasaweducationservices.com

Purpose To recognize and reward citizens of the Chickasaw Nation who complete an undergraduate or graduate degree at a school in any state.

Eligibility This award is available to members of the Chickasaw Nation who complete a bachelor's degree or higher. Applicants must submit a final official college transcript showing the degree awarded.

Financial data The award is $1.000.

Duration Students are eligible for this award each time they complete a college degree.

Number awarded Varies each year.

Deadline Applications must be submitted within 6 months after graduation.

[1149]
CIRCLE OF HONOR AWARD

Tulsa Library Trust
c/o Tulsa City-County Library System
400 Civic Center
Tulsa, OK 74103-3830
(918) 596-7985   Fax: (918) 596-7990
E-mail: trust@tulsalibrary.org
Web: www.tulsalibrary.org

Purpose To recognize and reward American Indians who have enriched the lives of others.

Eligibility This award is available to American Indians whose achievements and contributions have enriched the lives of others. Recipients are inducted into the Circle of Honor at a ceremony in Tulsa, Oklahoma as recognition for their actions in the face of adversity, commitment to the preservation of American Indian culture, and legacy for future generations.

Financial data The award is $5,000.

Duration The award is presented biennially.

Additional information This award was first presented in 2004.

Number awarded 1 each even-numbered year.

[1150]
COCOPAH ACHIEVEMENT INCENTIVE AWARDS

Cocopah Indian Tribe
Attn: Education Department
County 15th and Avenue G
Somerton, AZ 85350
(928) 627-2101   Fax: (928) 627-3173
E-mail: cocopah@cocopah.com
Web: www.cocopah.com/docs/education.html

Purpose To recognize and reward members of the Cocopah Indian Nation who complete an academic degree.

Eligibility This program is open to enrolled members of the Cocopah Indian Nation who complete an associate, bachelor's, master's or doctoral degree at an accredited college or university in the United States. Applicants must have received financial assistance from the tribal education department during their course of study. They must submit a copy of their diploma.

Financial data Awards are $1,000.

Duration Awards are presented each time an enrolled member completes an academic degree.

Number awarded Varies each year.

[1151]
DDW STUDENT ABSTRACT PRIZES

Foundation for Digestive Health and Nutrition
Attn: Research Awards Program
4930 Del Ray Avenue
Bethesda, MD 20814-2512
(301) 222-4012   Fax: (301) 652-3890
E-mail: awards@fdhn.org
Web: www.fdhn.org/wmspage.cfm?parm1=152

Purpose To recognize and reward minority and other students at any level who submit outstanding abstracts for presentation during Digestive Disease Week (DDW).

Eligibility This program is open to high school, undergraduate, premedical, predoctoral, and medical students and medical residents (up to and including postgraduate year 3) who have performed original research related to gastroenterology and hepatology. Postdoctoral fellows, technicians, visiting scientists, and M.D. research fellows are not eligible. Applicants must submit an abstract on their research and must be the designated presenter or first author of the abstract. They must be sponsored by a member of the American Gastroenterological Association (AGA). Travel awards are presented to authors of outstanding abstracts to enable them to attend DDW. After presentation of the papers at DDW, the most outstanding abstracts receive prizes. Selection is based on novelty, significance of the proposal, clarity of the abstract, and contribution of the student. Women and minority students are strongly encouraged to apply.

Financial data The prizes are $1,000; the travel awards are $500.

Duration Awards and prizes are presented annually.

Additional information This award is administered by the Foundation for Digestive Health and Nutrition (FDHN) and sponsored by the AGA.

Number awarded 10 travel awards are presented each year. Of the 10 awardees, 3 receive additional prizes of $1,000.

Deadline March of each year.

[1152]
EDWARD A. BOUCHET AWARD

American Physical Society
Attn: Honors Program
One Physics Ellipse
College Park, MD 20740-3844
(301) 209-3268   Fax: (301) 209-0865
E-mail: honors@aps.org
Web: www.aps.org

Purpose To recognize and reward outstanding research in physics by Native Americans or members of other under-represented minority groups.

Eligibility Nominees for this award must be African Americans, Hispanic Americans, or Native Americans who have made significant contributions to physics research and are effective communicators.

Financial data The award consists of a grant of $3,500 to the recipient, a travel allowance for the recipient to visit 3 academic institutions to deliver lectures, and an allowance for travel expenses to the meeting of the American Physical Society (APS) at which the prize is presented.

Duration The award is presented annually.

Additional information This award was established in 1994 and is currently funded by a grant from the Research Corporation. As part of the award, the recipient visits 3 academic institutions where the impact of the visit on minority students will be significant. The purpose of those visits is to deliver technical lectures on the recipient's field of specialization, to visit classrooms where appropriate, to assist the institution with precollege outreach efforts where appropriate, and to talk informally with faculty and students about research and teaching careers in physics.

Number awarded 1 each year.

Deadline June of each year.

[1153]
FRANKLIN C. MCLEAN AWARD

National Medical Fellowships, Inc.
Attn: Scholarship Program
5 Hanover Square, 15th Floor
New York, NY 10004
(212) 483-8880   Fax: (212) 483-8897
E-mail: info@nmfonline.org
Web: www.nmfonline.org

Purpose To recognize and reward the outstanding academic achievement, leadership, and community service of medical school seniors who are minorities.

Eligibility This competition is open to African American, Native Hawaiian, Alaska Native, American Indian, Mexican American, and mainland Puerto Rican students enrolled in accredited medical schools or osteopathic colleges. Candidates must be nominated by their schools during the summer preceding their senior year. Selection is based on academic achievement, leadership, and community service. U.S. citizenship is required.

Financial data This honor includes a certificate of merit and a $3,000 award.

Duration 1 year; nonrenewable.

Additional information This award, the first award offered by the National Medical Fellowship, was established in 1968 in memory of the Chicago bone physiologist who founded the organization.

Number awarded 1 each year.

Deadline Nominations must be submitted by July of each year.

[1154]
HO-CHUNK NATION GRADUATION ACHIEVEMENT AWARDS

Ho-Chunk Nation
Attn: Higher Education Division
P.O. Box 667
Black River Falls, WI 54615
(715) 284-4915   Toll-free: (800) 362-4476
Fax: (715) 284-1760
E-mail: higher.education@ho-chunk.com
Web: www.ho-chunknation.com/?PageId=47

Purpose To recognize and reward Ho-Chunk students who received financial assistance from the tribe and are now graduating with an undergraduate or graduate degree.

Eligibility Applicants must be enrolled in the Ho-Chunk Nation and have received financial assistance from the tribe to work on a postsecondary degree. Funds are paid to these students when they complete any of the following degrees: 1-year certificate or diploma, associate degree (2 years), bachelor's degree (4 years), master's or professional degree, J.D. degree, or doctoral degree.

Financial data Awards are $300 for a 1-year certificate or degree, $750 for an associate degree, $1,000 for a bachelor's degree, $3,000 for a master's or professional degree, $4,000 for a J.D. degree, or $5,000 for a doctoral degree.

Duration Students are eligible for only 1 award per degree.

Number awarded Varies each year.

Deadline Applications must be submitted within 1 year of completion of the degree.

[1155]
INCENTIVE AWARDS OF THE SEMINOLE NATION JUDGMENT FUND

Seminole Nation of Oklahoma
Attn: Judgment Fund Office
2007 West Wrangler Boulevard
Seminole, OK 74868
(405) 382-0549   Toll-free: (877) 382-0549
Fax: (405) 382-0571
Web: www.seminolenation.com

Purpose To recognize and reward undergraduate student members of the Seminole Nation of Oklahoma who achieve high grades in college.

Eligibility This program is open to enrolled members of the Seminole Nation who are descended from a member of the Seminole Nation as it existed in Florida on September 18, 1923. Applicants must be attending a college or university as an undergraduate student and complete either 1) 12 units with a GPA of 3.5 or higher, or 2) 15 units with a GPA 3.0 or higher.

Financial data Students who complete 12 credit hours with a GPA of 3.5 or higher receive an award of $300 per semester. Students who complete 15 credit hours with a GPA of 3.0 or higher receive an award of $500 per semester. The total of all incentive awards to an applicant may not exceed $4,000.

Duration 1 semester; may be renewed each semester the student completes the required number of units with the required minimum GPA.

Additional information The General Council of the Seminole Nation of Oklahoma approved a plan for use of the Judgment Fund Award in 1990. This aspect of the program went into effect in September of 1991.

Number awarded Varies each year.

Deadline Applications must be submitted within 60 days of the end of the semester.

[1156]
IOWA TRIBE EDUCATION INCENTIVE AWARDS

Iowa Tribe of Oklahoma
Attn: Human Services
RR 1, Box 721
Perkins, OK 74059
(405) 547-2402   Toll-free: (888) 336-4692
Fax: (405) 547-1090
E-mail: HumanServices@iowanation.org
Web: www.iowanation.org

Purpose To recognize and reward members of the Iowa Tribe of Oklahoma who complete specified levels of education.

Eligibility This program is open to Iowa tribal members who graduate from eighth grade, high school, college, or graduate school, or who complete a GED or 800 hours of vocational training.

Financial data The awards are $100 for eighth-grade graduates, $200 for high school graduates, $200 for completion of a GED, or $200 for completion of 800 hours of vocational training. For college graduates, the award is calculated by multiplying a dollar amount based on GPA by the credit hours passed; the amount is $70 for a GPA of 3.5 or higher, $65 for a GPA of 2.5 to 3.49, or $60 for a GPA of 2.0 to 2.49. For graduate students, the award is $92 times the credit hours passed.

Duration These are 1-time awards.

Number awarded Varies each year.

Deadline Applications must be submitted in the same year as completion of the education.

[1157]
JAMES A. RAWLEY PRIZE

Organization of American Historians
Attn: Award and Prize Coordinator
112 North Bryan Street
P.O. Box 5457
Bloomington, IN 47408-5457
(812) 855-9852   Fax: (812) 855-0696
E-mail: oahawards@oah.org
Web: www.oah.org

Purpose To recognize and reward outstanding books dealing with race relations in the United States.

Eligibility This award is presented to the author of the outstanding book on the history of race relations in America. Entries must have been published during the current calendar year.

Financial data The award is $1,000 and a certificate.

Duration The award is presented annually.

Additional information The award was established in 1990.

Number awarded 1 each year.

Deadline September of each year.

[1158]
LEE & LOW BOOKS NEW VOICES AWARD

Lee & Low Books
95 Madison Avenue, Suite 606
New York, NY 10016
(212) 779-4400   Fax: (212) 683-1894
E-mail: info@leeandlow.com
Web: www.leeandlow.com/editorial/voices.html

Purpose To recognize and reward outstanding unpublished children's picture books by Native Americans and other writers of color.

Eligibility The contest is open to writers of color who are residents of the United States and who have not previously published a children's picture book. Writers who have published in other venues, (e.g., children's magazines, young adult fiction and nonfiction) are eligible. Manuscripts previously submitted to the sponsor are not eligible. Submissions should be no more than 1,500 words and must address the needs of children of color by providing stories with which they can identify and relate and that promote a greater understanding of each other. Submissions may be fiction or nonfiction for children between the ages of 5 and 12. Folklore and animal stories are not considered. Up to 2 submissions may be submitted per entrant.

Financial data The award is a $1,000 cash grant plus the standard publication contract, including the standard advance and royalties. The Honor Award winner receives a cash grant of $500.

Duration The competition is held annually.

Additional information This program was established in 2000. Manuscripts may not be sent to any other publishers while under consideration for this award.
Number awarded 2 each year.
Deadline October of each year.

[1159]
LIFETIME ACHIEVEMENT AWARD FOR LITERATURE

Native Writers Circle of the Americas
c/o University of Oklahoma
633 Elm Avenue
Norman, OK 73019-3119
(405) 325-2312   Fax: (405) 325-0842
E-mail: nas@ou.edu
Web: www.ou.edu/cas/nas/writers.html

Purpose To recognize and reward the lifetime work of outstanding Native American writers.
Eligibility This award is given to Native American writers who have a long history of outstanding literary activities. The winner is selected by fellow Native American writers. There is no application process.
Financial data The prize is $1,000.
Duration The prize is given annually.
Additional information This award was established in 1992.
Number awarded 1 each year.

[1160]
MARIE F. PETERS ETHNIC MINORITIES OUTSTANDING ACHIEVEMENT AWARD

National Council on Family Relations
3989 Central Avenue, N.E., Suite 550
Minneapolis, MN 55421
(763) 781-9331   Toll-free: (888) 781-9331
Fax: (763) 781-9348   E-mail: info@ncfr.com
Web: www.ncfr.org/member/awards.asp

Purpose To recognize and reward Native Americans and other minorities who have made significant contributions to the area of ethnic minority families.
Eligibility Members of the National Council on Family Relations (NCFR) who have demonstrated excellence in the area of ethnic minority families are eligible for this award. Selection is based on leadership and/or mentoring, scholarship and/or service, research, publication, teaching, community service, contribution to the ethnic minorities section, and contribution to the NCFR.
Financial data The award is $1,000 and a plaque.
Duration The award is granted biennially, in odd-numbered years.
Additional information This award, which was established in 1983, is named after a prominent Black researcher and family sociologist who served in many leadership roles in NCFR. It is sponsored by the Ethnic Minorities Section of NCFR.
Number awarded 1 every other year.
Deadline April of odd-numbered years.

[1161]
MILLE LACS BAND ACADEMIC ACHIEVEMENT AWARDS

Mille Lacs Band of Ojibwe
Attn: Higher Education Office
43408 Oodena Avenue
Onamia, MN 56359-2236
(320) 532-7508   Toll-free: (800) 532-9059
Fax: (320) 532-3785
E-mail: mlbsp@MilleLacsOjibwe.nsn.us
Web: www.millelacsojibwe.org/scholarship.asp

Purpose To recognize and reward members of the Mille Lacs Band of Ojibwe who have completed their education.
Eligibility This program is open to enrolled members of the band, their non-enrolled biological children, and legally adopted children of enrolled band members. Applicants must have completed their GED certificate or high school diploma, a vocational/technical diploma or certificate (for a program 9 months or more in length), an associate degree, a bachelor's degree, or a graduate (master's or doctoral) degree.
Financial data Awards are $500 for completion of a GED certificate or high school diploma, $1,000 for a vocational/technical diploma or certificate, $1,250 for an associate degree, $1,500 for a bachelor's degree, or $2,000 for a graduate degree.
Duration Awards are presented whenever a student completes a diploma, certificate, or degree.
Number awarded Varies each year.
Deadline Applications may be submitted at any time.

[1162]
MINORITY AFFAIRS COMMITTEE AWARD FOR OUTSTANDING SCHOLASTIC ACHIEVEMENT

American Institute of Chemical Engineers
Attn: Awards Administrator
Three Park Avenue
New York, NY 10016-5991
(646) 495-1348   Fax: (646) 495-1504
E-mail: awards@aiche.org
Web: www.aiche.org

Purpose To recognize and reward Native American and other underrepresented minority students majoring in chemical engineering who serve as role models for other minority students.
Eligibility Members of the American Institute of Chemical Engineers (AIChE) may nominate any chemical engineering student who serves as a role model for minority students in that field. Nominees must be members of a minority group that is underrepresented in chemical engineering (i.e., African American, Hispanic, Native American, Alaskan Native). They must have a GPA of 3.0 or higher. Along with their application, they must submit a 300-word essay on their immediate plans after graduation, areas of chemical engineering of most interest, and long-range career plans. Selection is based on that essay, academic record, participation in AIChE student chapter and professional or civic activities, and financial need.
Financial data The award consists of a plaque and a $1,500 honorarium.
Duration The award is presented annually.

Additional information This award was first presented in 1996.
Number awarded 1 each year.
Deadline Nominations must be submitted by May of each year.

[1163]
MISS INDIAN USA SCHOLARSHIP PROGRAM
American Indian Heritage Foundation
P.O. Box 750
Pigeon Forge, TN 37868
(703) 819-0979 E-mail: MissIndianUSA@indians.org
Web: www.indians.org/catalog/our_programs.php

Purpose To recognize and reward the most beautiful and talented Indian women.
Eligibility American Indian women between the ages of 18 and 26 are eligible to enter this national contest if they are high school graduates and have never been married, cohabited with the opposite sex, been pregnant, or had children. U.S. citizenship is required. Selection is based on public appearance (20%), a traditional interview (15%), a contemporary interview (15%), beauty of spirit (15%), a cultural presentation (10%), scholastic achievement (10%), a platform question (10%), and a finalist question (5%).
Financial data Awards vary each year. Recently, Miss Indian USA received an academic scholarship of $4,000 plus a cash grant of $6,500, a wardrobe allowance of $2,000, appearance fees of $3,000, a professional photo shoot worth $500, gifts worth more than $4,000, honoring gifts worth more than $2,000, promotional materials worth more than $2,000, and travel to Washington, D.C. with a value of approximately $2,000; the total value of the prize was more than $26,000. Members of her court received scholarships of $2,000 for the first runner-up, $1,500 for the second runner-up, $1,000 for the third runner-up, and $500 for the fourth runner-up.
Duration This competition is held annually.
Additional information The program involves a week-long competition in the Washington, D.C. metropolitan area that includes seminars, interviews, cultural presentations, and many public appearances. The application fee is $100 if submitted prior to mid-April or $200 if submitted later. In addition, a candidate fee of $750 is required.
Number awarded 1 winner and 4 runners-up are selected each year.
Deadline May of each year.

[1164]
NNALSA WRITING COMPETITION
National Native American Law Students Association
c/o Seth Davis, Vice President
601 West 115th Street, Apartment 46
New York, NY 10025
E-mail: rsd2114@columbia.edu
Web: www.nationalnalsa.org

Purpose To recognize and reward members of the National Native American Law Students Association (NNALSA) who submit outstanding articles on Indian law.
Eligibility This competition is open to NNALSA members who submit articles, up to 50 pages in length in standard legal essay format, on a topic of international importance to Indians, tribal government, or indigenous peoples. Recently, the topic was "Native Rights, Human Rights, and America." Selection is based originality, timeliness of topic, quality and creativity of analysis, knowledge and use of relevant law, grammar, punctuation, and citation style.
Financial data The first-place winner receives $2,000 and publication in the *Columbia Human Rights Law Review*. The second-place winner receives $1,000 and the third-place winner receives $500.
Duration The competition is held annually.
Additional information This competition was first held in 2002. Recently, first prize was sponsored by Nordhaus Law Firm LLP and the Columbia University chapter of NNALSA, second prize was sponsored by Kirkland Ellis LLP, and third prize was sponsored by Patton Boggs LLP.
Number awarded 3 each year.
Deadline March of each year.

[1165]
NORTH AMERICAN INDIAN PROSE AWARD
University of Nebraska Press
1111 Lincoln Mall
Lincoln, NE 68588-0630
(402) 472-3581 Toll-free: (800) 755-1105
Fax: (402) 472-6214 E-mail: pressmail@unl.edu
Web: www.nebraskapress.unl.edu

Purpose To recognize and reward outstanding book-length nonfiction manuscripts written by authors of American Indian descent.
Eligibility This program is open to authors of North American Indian descent. They are invited to submit book-length nonfiction manuscripts, including biographies, autobiographies, history, literary criticism, essays, nonfiction works for children, and political commentary. The competition excludes novels, short stories, poetry, drama, collections of interviews, and work previously published in book form. Selection is based on literary merit, originality, and familiarity with North American Indian life.
Financial data The winner receives a cash advance of $1,000 and publication of the award-winning manuscript by the University of Nebraska Press.
Duration The award is presented annually.
Number awarded 1 each year.
Deadline June of each year.

[1166]
NSF DIRECTOR'S AWARD FOR DISTINGUISHED TEACHING SCHOLARS
National Science Foundation
Directorate for Education and Human Resources
Attn: Division of Undergraduate Education
4201 Wilson Boulevard, Room 835N
Arlington, VA 22230
(703) 292-4627 Fax: (703) 292-9015
TDD: (800) 281-8749 E-mail: npruitt@nsf.gov
Web: www.nsf.gov

Purpose To recognize and reward, with funding for additional research, minority and other scholars affiliated with institutions of higher education who have contributed to teaching of science, technology, engineering, and mathematics (STEM) at the K-12 and undergraduate level.

Eligibility This program is open to teaching-scholars affiliated with institutions of higher education who are nominated by their president, chief academic officer, or other independent researcher. Nominees should have integrated research and education and approached both education and research in a scholarly manner. They should have demonstrated leadership in their respective fields as well as innovativeness and effectiveness in facilitating K-12 and undergraduate student learning in STEM disciplines. Consideration is given to faculty who have a history of substantial impact on 1) research in a STEM discipline or on STEM educational research; or 2) the STEM education of K-16 students who have diverse interests and aspirations, including future K-12 teachers of science and mathematics, students who plan to pursue STEM careers, and those who need to understand science and mathematics in a society increasingly dependent on science and technology. Based on letters of nomination, selected scholars are invited to submit applications for support of their continuing efforts to integrate education and research. Nominations of women, underrepresented minorities, and persons with disabilities are especially encouraged.
Financial data The maximum grant is $300,000 for the life of the project.
Duration 4 years.
Number awarded Approximately 6 each year.
Deadline Letters of intent are due in September of each year; full applications must be submitted in October.

[1167]
RALPH J. BUNCHE AWARD
American Political Science Association
1527 New Hampshire Avenue, N.W.
Washington, DC 20036-1206
(202) 483-2512 Fax: (202) 483-2657
E-mail: apsa@apsanet.org
Web: www.apsanet.org/section_278.cfm

Purpose To recognize and reward outstanding scholarly books on ethnic/cultural pluralism.
Eligibility Eligible to be nominated (by publishers or individuals) are scholarly political science books issued the previous year that explore issues of ethnic and/or cultural pluralism.
Financial data The award is $1,000.
Duration The award is presented annually.
Additional information This award was first presented in 1978.
Number awarded 1 each year.
Deadline January of each year for nominations from individuals; February of each year for nominations from publishers.

[1168]
SOUTHWESTERN ASSOCIATION FOR INDIAN ARTS MARKET AWARDS
Southwestern Association for Indian Arts, Inc.
3600 Cerrillos Road, Suite 712
P.O. Box 969
Santa Fe, NM 87504-0969
(505) 983-5220 Fax: (505) 983-7647
E-mail: info@swaia.org
Web: www.swaia.org/awards.php

Purpose To recognize and reward outstanding Indian artists who participate in the Santa Fe Indian Market.
Eligibility This program is open to artists who have a Certificate of Indian Blood as an enrolled member of a U.S. federally-recognized tribe or Alaska Native corporation and a New Mexico Taxation and Revenue CRS Identification Number. Artists must be 18 years of age and older. The 8 divisions are 1) jewelry; 2) pottery; 3) paintings, drawings, graphics, and photography; 4) Pueblo wooden carvings; 5) sculpture; 6) textiles and baskets; 7) diverse art forms; and 8) beadwork and quillwork. Along with their application, artists must submit slides of each medium that they wish to show at the annual Santa Fe Indian Market. The work must comply with standards of the Southwestern Association for Indian Arts (SWAIA) and be representative of the artwork they plan to sell at the Market.
Financial data A total of up to $60,000 in prize money is awarded each year. Awards vary each year, but they have included $1,000 for Best of Show and $500 for first place in each category.
Duration The Market is held on 2 days in August of each year.
Additional information Artists are responsible for payment of a $25 application fee, a $10 city of Santa Fe business license fee, a $10 city of Santa Fe booth permit fee, and a booth fee of $400 to $650.
Number awarded Varies each year.
Deadline Applications must be submitted by January of each year.

[1169]
STEPHEN H. COLTRIN AWARD FOR EXCELLENCE IN COMMUNICATION EDUCATION
International Radio and Television Society Foundation
Attn: Director, Special Projects
420 Lexington Avenue, Suite 1601
New York, NY 10170-0101
(212) 867-6650 Toll-free: (888) 627-1266
Fax: (212) 867-6653 E-mail: apply@irts.org
Web: irts.org/awards/ccsa/ccsa.html

Purpose To recognize and reward minority and other college faculty members who teach electronic communications and participate in a case study competition.
Eligibility Each year, the sponsoring organization conducts a faculty/industry seminar for 75 faculty members who teach in fields relevant to electronic communications at schools nationwide. At the seminar, teams of participants engage in a case study competition on methods of teaching in the field. The winning team receives this award. Minority faculty are given priority.
Financial data The prize is $2,500 to be divided among team members.

Duration The prize is awarded annually.
Additional information The registration fee to attend the seminar is $150. That covers hotel accommodations and most meals, but participants are responsible for their own transportation and incidental expenses.
Number awarded 1 each year.
Deadline December of each year.

[1170]
TRAIL OF TEARS ART SHOW
Cherokee Heritage Center
21192 South Keeler Drive
P.O. Box 515
Tahlequah, OK 74465
(918) 456-6007   Toll-free: (888) 999-6007
Fax: (918) 456-6165
E-mail: info@CherokeeHeritage.org
Web: www.CherokeeHeritage.org

Purpose To recognize and reward artists and craftsmen who submit work to a competition with a Native American flavor.
Eligibility This competition is open to artists 17 years of age and older. All artists and all subject matters are eligible, but the show has always retained a distinctively Native American flavor. Artists may submit entries in 7 categories: paintings, graphics, sculpture, Trail of Tears theme, miniatures, pottery, and basketry. All work must have been completed since January of the competition year, although it may have started before then. It may not have received a cash award in any other show and must be for sale at a reasonable market price. Each artist may submit only 2 works per category and only a total of 3. The Grand Award is presented to the work judged the most significant expression of art that exhibits the best overall quality, composition, technical achievement, and historical accuracy.
Financial data The Grand Award is $1,500. In each category, the first-place award is $600, second-place $400, and third-place $200.
Duration The competition is held annually.
Additional information This competition was first held in 1971.
Number awarded 1 Grand Award and 21 category awards (3 in each category) are presented each year.
Deadline April of each year.

[1171]
UTAH SPORTS HALL OF FAME NATIVE AMERICAN SCHOLARSHIPS
Utah Sports Hall of Fame Foundation
c/o Berdean Jarman, Scholarship Chair
873 West 1200 North
Orem, UT 84057
(801) 225-3352
Web: www.utahsportshalloffame.org/AboutUs.html

Purpose To recognize and reward outstanding Native American high school seniors in Utah who have been involved in athletics and are interested in attending college in the state.
Eligibility Each high school in Utah may nominate 1 Native American high school senior. Nominees must be planning to attend college in the state. Selection is based on academic record, personal character, financial need, leadership qualities, and involvement in athletic activities, including football, basketball, cross country, volleyball, tennis, track and field, soccer, rodeo, baseball, swimming, wrestling, officiating, community recreation, or intramural sports.
Financial data The stipend is $2,000. Funds are paid to the recipient's institution.
Duration 1 year; nonrenewable.
Additional information Formerly, the sponsoring organization was known as the Old Time Athletes Association. Recipients must attend an academic institution in Utah.
Number awarded 2 each year.
Deadline March of each year.

[1172]
WILLIAM A. HINTON RESEARCH TRAINING AWARD
American Academy of Microbiology
Attn: Committee on Awards
1752 N Street, N.W.
Washington, DC 20036-2904
(202) 942-9226   Fax: (202) 942-9353
E-mail: awards@asmusa.org
Web: www.asm.org/Academy/index.asp?bid=2317

Purpose To recognize and reward microbiologists for their involvement in the research training of underrepresented minorities.
Eligibility Nominees for this award must have contributed to the research training of undergraduate students, graduate students, postdoctoral fellows, or health professional students. Their efforts must have led to the increased participation of underrepresented minorities in microbiology. Self-nominations are not accepted.
Financial data The award consists of a $2,000 cash prize, a commemorative piece, and travel expenses to the presentation ceremonies at the general meeting of the American Society for Microbiology (ASM).
Duration The award is presented annually.
Additional information This award, first presented in 1998, honors 1 of the first African Americans to join the ASM.
Number awarded 1 each year.
Deadline September of each year.

[1173]
WILLIAM AND CHARLOTTE CADBURY AWARD
National Medical Fellowships, Inc.
Attn: Scholarship Program
5 Hanover Square, 15th Floor
New York, NY 10004
(212) 483-8880   Fax: (212) 483-8897
E-mail: info@nmfonline.org
Web: www.nmfonline.org

Purpose To recognize and reward underrepresented minority medical school students' outstanding academic achievement, leadership, and community service.
Eligibility This award is open to minority students enrolled in their senior year at an accredited medical school. For the purposes of this program, "minority" is defined as African American, Native Hawaiian, Alaska Native, American

Indian, Mexican American, and mainland Puerto Rican. Candidates must be nominated by their medical school during the summer preceding their senior year. Selection is based on academic achievement, leadership, and community service.
Financial data This honor includes a certificate of merit and a $2,000 stipend.
Duration The award is presented annually.
Additional information This award was established in 1977.
Number awarded 1 each year.
Deadline Nominations must be submitted by July of each year.

[1174]
WYETH-AYERST LABORATORIES PRIZE IN WOMEN'S HEALTH
National Medical Fellowships, Inc.
Attn: Scholarship Program
5 Hanover Square, 15th Floor
New York, NY 10004
(212) 483-8880   Fax: (212) 483-8897
E-mail: info@nmfonline.org
Web: www.nmfonline.org

Purpose To recognize and reward outstanding underrepresented minority women medical students.
Eligibility This program is open to underrepresented minority (African American, Native Hawaiian, Alaska Native, American Indian, Mexican American, and mainland Puerto Rican) women medical students in their fourth year of study. Candidates must demonstrate exceptional academic achievement, leadership, and the potential to make significant contributions in the field of women's health. Direct applications are not accepted; candidates must be nominated by their medical school dean.
Financial data This honor includes a certificate of merit and a $5,000 stipend.
Duration The award is presented annually.
Additional information Funding for this program is provided by Wyeth-Ayerst Laboratories.
Number awarded 2 each year.
Deadline Nominations must be submitted by February of each year.

[1175]
YAKAMA INCENTIVE AWARDS PROGRAM
Yakama Indian Nation
Department of Human Services
Attn: Higher Education Programs
P.O. Box 151
Toppenish, WA 98948
(509) 865-5121, ext. 519   Toll-free: (800) 543-2802
Fax: (509) 865-6994

Purpose To recognize and reward the outstanding academic achievement of Yakama Indians.
Eligibility Yakama Indian college students who maintain excellent academic and attendance performance during the year are eligible to apply. Selection is based on cumulative GPA, course level, and class level.
Financial data Stipends are presented (amount not specified).
Duration The awards are presented annually.
Number awarded Varies each year.

Internships

Described here are 181 work experience programs open to undergraduate, graduate, or postgraduate Native Americans. Only salaried positions are covered. If you are looking for a particular program and don't find it in this section, be sure to check the Program Title Index to see if it is covered elsewhere in the directory.

[1176]
AAAS MINORITY SCIENCE WRITERS INTERNSHIP
American Association for the Advancement of Science
Directorate for Education and Human Resources
Attn: Minority Science Writers Internship
1200 New York Avenue, N.W., Room 608
Washington, DC 20005-3920
(202) 326-6441   Fax: (202) 371-9849
E-mail: spasco@aaas.org
Web: www.aaas.org

Purpose To provide summer work experience at *Science* magazine to Native American and other minority undergraduate students.

Eligibility This program is open to minority undergraduates with a serious interest in science writing. Preference is given to students majoring in journalism. Applicants must be interested in a summer internship at *Science* magazine, the journal of the American Association for the Advancement of Science (AAAS). Along with their application, they must submit an 800-word essay on their commitment to journalism, their career goals, their thoughts about science and science writing, and what they hope to get out of this opportunity. A telephone interview is conducted of semifinalists.

Financial data Interns receive a salary and reimbursement of travel expenses to the work site in Washington, D.C.

Duration 10 weeks during the summer.

Number awarded Varies each year.

Deadline February of each year.

[1177]
ACHE MINORITY INTERNSHIP
American College of Healthcare Executives
Attn: Human Resources Manager
One North Franklin Street, Suite 1700
Chicago, IL 60606-3529
(312) 424-9341   Fax: (312) 424-0023
E-mail: hr-intern-fellow@ache.org
Web: www.ache.org/carsvcs/internship.cfm

Purpose To provide Native American and other minority graduate students who are members of the American College of Healthcare Executives (ACHE) with an opportunity to work at the organization's headquarters.

Eligibility This program is open to ACHE student associates or affiliates who have completed 1 year of graduate study in health care management from an accredited college or university in the United States or Canada. Applicants must be a member of a minority group. They must be interested in working in 1 or more of the major ACHE divisions, including administration, communications and marketing, education, executive office, finance, health administration press, management information systems, membership, regional services, and research and development. Along with their application, they must submit a short statement of interest, a current curriculum vitae, an official undergraduate transcript, and a letter of recommendation.

Financial data The stipend is $17.61 per hour.

Duration 3 months during the summer.

Additional information This program was established in 1991.

Number awarded 1 each year.

Deadline November of each year.

[1178]
ACT SUMMER INTERNSHIP PROGRAM
American College Testing
Attn: Human Resources Department
500 ACT Drive
P.O. Box 168
Iowa City, IA 52243-0168
(319) 337-1763   E-mail: working@act.org
Web: www.act.org/humanresources/jobs/intern.html

Purpose To provide work experience during the summer to doctoral students (particularly women and minorities) interested in careers in assessment and educational studies.

Eligibility This program is open to doctoral students enrolled in such fields as educational psychology, measurement, program evaluation, counseling psychology, educational policy, mathematical and applied statistics, industrial or organizational psychology, and counselor education. Applicants must be interested in working at American College Testing (ACT) in 1 of the following categories: 1) psychometrics and statistics; 2) education and workforce research services; 3) industrial-organizational psychology; or 4) career and vocational psychology. Along with their application, they must submit a description of their interests and experiences. They must be able to demonstrate the ability to function both independently and as a team member in a professional work environment and must possess excellent written and oral communication skills. The program is also intended to assist in increasing the number of women and minority professionals in measurement and related fields.

Financial data Interns receive a stipend of $5,000 and round-trip transportation between their graduate institution and Iowa City. A supplemental living allowance of $400 is provided if a spouse and/or children accompany the intern.

Duration 8 weeks during the summer.

Number awarded Varies each year.

Deadline February of each year.

[1179]
AISES INTERNSHIP PROGRAM
American Indian Science and Engineering Society
Attn: Internship Coordinator
2305 Renard, S.E., Suite 200
P.O. Box 9828
Albuquerque, NM 87119-9828
(505) 765-1052, ext. 105   Fax: (505) 765-5608
E-mail: tina@aises.org
Web: www.aises.org
Web: www.aises.org/highered/internships

Purpose To provide summer work experience with federal agencies in the United States or abroad to American Indian and Alaska Native college students who are members of the American Indian Science and Engineering Society (AISES).

Eligibility This program is open to AISES members who are full-time college or university sophomores, juniors, seniors, or graduate students with a GPA of 3.0 or higher. Applicants must be American Indians or Alaska Natives interested in working at selected sites with a federal agency. They must submit an application that includes an essay on their reasons for participating in the program, how it relates to their academic and career goals, what makes them a strong candidate for the program, what they hope to learn and gain as a result, and their leadership skills and experience. Students in the following fields are particularly encouraged to apply: accounting, business, computer science and technology, economics, engineering, finance, graphic design, health care, health policy, human resources/personnel, international relations, logistics, medicine and pre-med, nursing, political science, psychology, public administration, and science. U.S. citizenship is required for most positions, although permanent residents may be eligible at some agencies.

Financial data Interns receive a weekly stipend, dormitory lodging, round-trip airfare or mileage to the internship site, and an allowance for local transportation.

Duration 10 weeks during the summer.

Additional information Internships are available at the U.S. Department of Commerce (in Washington, D.C.), the Centers for Disease Control and Prevention (in Atlanta, Georgia), the U.S. Department of State (at various domestic and overseas sites), the Central Intelligence Agency (in Washington, D.C.), the Arctic Slope Regional Corporation Federal Holding Company (in Greenbelt, Maryland), NASA Goddard Space Flight Center (in Greenbelt, Maryland), the National Science Foundation (in Arlington, Virginia), the Bonneville Power Administration (in Portland, Oregon), and the U.S. Department of Veterans Affairs (in Washington, D.C.).

Number awarded Varies each year.

Deadline October of each year for the Department of State or the Central Intelligence Agency; February of each year for other agencies.

[1180]
ALASKA NATIVE TRIBAL HEALTH CONSORTIUM SUMMER INTERNSHIPS

Alaska Native Tribal Health Consortium
Attn: Education and Development
4000 Ambassador Drive, Suite 114
Anchorage, AK 99508
(907) 729-1348　　　　Toll-free: (800) 684-8361
Fax: (907) 729-1335　　E-mail: kruesch@anthc.org

Purpose To provide summer work experience at the Alaska Native Tribal Health Consortium (ANTHC) to Native Alaskan and American Indian high school, undergraduate, and graduate students.

Eligibility This program is open to Alaska Natives and American Indians who are high school students, undergraduates, graduate students, and recipients during the past 6 months of a GED, diploma, or degree. Applicants must be residents of Alaska and interested in an internship at ANTHC in such areas as finance, human resources, health records, computer technology, engineering, maintenance, or housekeeping. Along with their application, they must submit a resume, documentation of financial need, and a 1-page personal statement that covers their personal and educational history, accomplishments, educational and career goals, involvement in the Native community, and how this internship corresponds with their career goals.

Financial data These are paid internships.

Duration 9 weeks during the summer.

Number awarded 30 each year: 25 for high school and undergraduate students and 5 for graduate students.

Deadline February of each year.

[1181]
ALASKA SPACE GRANT PROGRAM FELLOWSHIPS

Alaska Space Grant Program
c/o University of Alaska at Fairbanks
Duckering Hall, Room 269
P.O. Box 755919
Fairbanks, AK 99775-5919
(907) 474-6833　　　　Fax: (907) 474-5135
E-mail: fyspace@uaf.edu
Web: www.uaf.edu

Purpose To provide minority and other undergraduate and graduate students at member institutions of the Alaska Space Grant Program (ASGP) with an opportunity to work on aerospace-related projects.

Eligibility This program is open to undergraduate and graduate students at the lead institution and academic affiliates of the ASGP. Applicants must be interested in assisting on projects that provide a professional development opportunity for the student but also develop aerospace capabilities within Alaska. The ASGP is a component of the Space Grant program of the U.S. National Aeronautics and Space Administration (NASA), which encourages participation by women, underrepresented minorities, and persons with disabilities.

Financial data The amount of each award depends on the scope of the project and the level of responsibility assumed by the recipient. Most awards are less than $5,000.

Additional information The ASGP lead institution is the University of Alaska at Fairbanks; academic affiliates include the University of Alaska Southeast, the University of Alaska at Anchorage, and Alaska Pacific University. Funding for this program is provided by NASA.

Number awarded Varies each year.

[1182]
ARENT FOX DIVERSITY SCHOLARSHIPS

Arent Fox LLP
Attn: Senior Attorney Recruitment Coordinator
1050 Connecticut Avenue, N.W.
Washington, DC 20036-5339
(202) 857-6224　　　　Fax: (202) 857-6395
E-mail: salvaterra.jessica@arentfox.com
Web: www.arentfox.com

Purpose To provide financial assistance and work experience to Native American and other minority law students.

Eligibility This program is open to first-year law students who are members of a diverse population that historically has been underrepresented in the legal profession. Applicants must be U.S. citizens or otherwise authorized to work in the United States. They must also be willing to work as a summer intern at the sponsoring law firm's offices in New York City or Washington, D.C. Along with their application, they must submit a resume, an undergraduate transcript and law school grades when available, a 5- to 10-page legal writing sample, 3 letters of recommendation, and an essay on how their background, skills, experience, and interest

equip them to meet the sponsor's goal of commitment to diversity. Selection is based on academic performance during college and law school, oral and writing communication skills, leadership qualities, and community involvement.
Financial data The scholarship stipend is $15,000. The summer salary is $2,500 per week.
Duration 1 year.
Additional information These scholarships were first offered in 2006. Recipients are also offered summer internships with Arent Fox: 1 in New York City and 1 in Washington, D.C. Students interested in the summer program in New York should contact Attorney Recruitment Manager, 1675 Broadway, New York, NY 10019, (212) 484-3913, Fax: (212) 484-3990, E-mail: visconti.lisa@arentfox.com.
Number awarded 2 each year.
Deadline January of each year.

[1183]
ARIZONA SPACE GRANT CONSORTIUM UNDERGRADUATE RESEARCH INTERNSHIPS
Arizona Space Grant Consortium
c/o University of Arizona
Lunar and Planetary Laboratory, Room 349
1629 East University Boulevard
Tucson, AZ 85721-0092
(520) 621-8556   Fax: (520) 621-4933
E-mail: sbrew@lpl.arizona.edu
Web: spacegrant.arizona.edu

Purpose To provide an opportunity for underrepresented minority and other undergraduate students at member and affiliate institutions of the Arizona Space Grant Consortium to participate as interns in scientific research activities on campus.
Eligibility This program is open to full-time undergraduate students at member institutions (University of Arizona, Northern Arizona University, Arizona State University, and Embry-Riddle Aeronautical University) of the consortium. Applicants must be at least sophomores and U.S. citizens, but they do not need to be science or engineering majors. Applications are especially encouraged from members of underrepresented minority groups and women.
Financial data Interns are paid at the rate of $9.50 per hour.
Duration 1 academic year.
Additional information Interns work with faculty members and graduate students on space-related science projects. Funding for this program is provided by the U.S. National Aeronautics and Space Administration (NASA).
Number awarded Varies each year.
Deadline June of each year.

[1184]
ARTTABLE MENTORED INTERNSHIPS FOR DIVERSITY IN THE VISUAL ARTS PROFESSIONS
ArtTable Inc.
116 John Street, Suite 822
New York, NY 10038
(212) 343-1735, ext. 25   Fax: (212) 343-1430
E-mail: programs@arttable.org
Web: www.arttable.org/mentoring.html

Purpose To provide an opportunity for women who are from diverse backgrounds to gain mentored work experience during the summer and to prepare for a career as an art professional.
Eligibility This program is open to women who are juniors, seniors, recent graduates, or graduate students and interested in preparing for a as a visual arts professional (including administrative director, art adviser, art appraiser, art critic, art dealer, art librarian, arts funder, arts lawyer, conservator, curator, editor, educator, fundraiser, management consultant, public relations consultant, writer). Applicants must be a member of an ethnic, racial, cultural, or financial group that is underrepresented in the field. They must be interested in working during the summer with a mentor at an art museum or similar facility in the New York City Tri-State region, Washington D.C. metropolitan area, San Francisco Bay area, or Los Angeles area. U.S. citizenship or permanent resident status is required.
Financial data The stipend is $3,000. The hosting institution or mentor receives $500 for administrative and other costs.
Duration 8 weeks during the summer.
Additional information This program began in 2000.
Number awarded 4 each year: 1 in each of the participating locations.
Deadline March of each year.

[1185]
ASPET INDIVIDUAL SUMMER UNDERGRADUATE RESEARCH FELLOWSHIPS
American Society for Pharmacology and Experimental Therapeutics
9650 Rockville Pike
Bethesda, MD 20814-3995
(301) 634-7060   Fax: (301) 634-7061
E-mail: info@aspet.org
Web: www.aspet.org/public/surf/surf.htm

Purpose To provide funding to underrepresented minority and other undergraduate students who are interested in participating in a summer research project at a laboratory affiliated with the American Society for Pharmacology and Experimental Therapeutics (ASPET).
Eligibility This program is open to undergraduate students interested in working during the summer in the laboratory of a society member who must agree to act as a sponsor. Applications must be submitted jointly by the student and the sponsor, and they must include 1) a letter from the sponsor with a brief description of the proposed research, a statement of the qualifications of the student, the degree of independence the student will have, a description of complementary activities available to the student, and a description of how the student will report on the research results; 2) a letter from the student indicating the

nature of his or her interest in the project and a description of future plans; 3) a copy of the sponsor's updated curriculum vitae; and 4) copies of all the student's undergraduate transcripts. Selection is based on the nature of the research opportunities provided, student and sponsor qualifications, and the likelihood the student will prepare for a career in pharmacology. Applications from underrepresented minorities and women are particularly encouraged.

Financial data The stipend is $2,800. Funds are paid directly to the institution but may be used only for student stipends.

Duration 10 weeks during the summer.

Additional information Some of these awards are funded through the Glenn E. Ullyot Fund; those recipients are designated as the Ullyot Fellows.

Number awarded Varies each year; recently, 4 of these fellowships were awarded.

Deadline February of each year.

[1186]
ATLANTA JOURNAL AND CONSTITUTION MINORITY INTERNSHIPS

Atlanta Journal and Constitution
Attn: Office of Community Affairs
72 Marietta Street, N.W.
Atlanta, GA 30303
(404) 577-5772   E-mail: aeintern@ajc.com
Web: www.ajc.com

Purpose To provide financial assistance and summer newspaper work experience in Atlanta to Native Americans and other students of color at selected Georgia colleges who are interested in preparing for a career in journalism.

Eligibility This program is open to Georgia college students of color (Asian Americans, Hispanics, African Americans, and Native Americans) interested in newspaper careers. Applicants must be interested in working at the *Atlanta Journal-Constitution* in the newsroom, online, advertising, accounting, marketing, or information technology departments. They must be enrolled as a sophomore or junior at a Georgia college or university (seniors may be considered if they plan to continue on to graduate school), have a cumulative GPA of 3.0 or higher, and have demonstrated an interest in the department where they wish to work (campus publication experience and work with daily deadlines are preferable). Along with their application, they must submit a 500-word essay explaining why they want a career in newspapers and how this internship and scholarship will help them with that goal, samples of their work (if applicable), a resume, and references.

Financial data Upon successful completion of the internship, participants receive a $1,000 scholarship.

Duration The internship is 10 weeks during the summer; the scholarship is a 1-year nonrenewable award.

Number awarded 3 each year.

Deadline January of each year.

[1187]
ATLAS SCHOLARS PROGRAM

Johns Hopkins University
Applied Physics Laboratory
Attn: College Recruiting Manager
11100 Johns Hopkins Road
Laurel, MD 20723-6099
(443) 778-4249   Fax: (443) 778-5274
Web: www.jhuapl.edu/employment/diversity/atlas.asp

Purpose To provide an opportunity for undergraduate students from Minority Serving Institutions to obtain research experience during the summer at Johns Hopkins University's Applied Physics Laboratory (APL).

Eligibility This program is open to students at Historically Black Colleges and Universities (HBCUs), Hispanic Serving Institutions (HSIs), and other minority institutions who are completing their junior year. Applicants must be majoring in electrical engineering or computer sciences and have a GPA of 3.5 or higher. They must be interested in working at the laboratory on a research project under the mentorship of a staff scientist or engineer. U.S. citizenship is required.

Financial data Scholars receive a stipend (amount not specified) and round-trip travel expenses.

Duration 12 weeks during the summer.

Additional information This program was established in 1997 as the APL Technology Leaders Summer Internship Program.

Number awarded Varies each year.

Deadline December of each year.

[1188]
AT&T LABORATORIES FELLOWSHIP PROGRAM

AT&T Laboratories
Attn: Fellowship Administrator
180 Park Avenue, Room C103
P.O. Box 971
Florham Park, NJ 07932-0971
(973) 360-8109   Fax: (973) 360-8881
E-mail: recruiting@research.att.com
Web: www.research.att.com/index.cfm?portal=20

Purpose To provide financial assistance and work experience to Native American and other underrepresented minority and women students who are working on a doctoral degree in computer and communications-related fields.

Eligibility This program is open to minorities underrepresented in the sciences (Blacks, Hispanics, and Native Americans) and to women. Applicants must be U.S. citizens or permanent residents who are graduating college seniors or graduate students enrolled in their first or second year. They must be working on or planning to work on a Ph.D. in a field of study relevant to the business of AT&T; currently, those include computer science, electrical engineering, industrial engineering, mathematics, operations research, systems engineering, statistics, and related fields. Along with their application, they must submit a personal statement on why they are enrolled in their present academic program and how they intend to use their technical training, official transcripts, 3 academic references, and GRE scores. Selection is based on potential for success in scientific research.

Financial data This program covers all educational expenses during the school year, including tuition, books, fees, and approved travel expenses; educational expenses for summer study or university research; a stipend for living expenses of $2,380 per month (paid for 10 months of the year); a $500 book allowance; and support for attending approved scientific conferences.

Duration 1 year; may be renewed for up to 2 additional years, as long as the fellow continues making satisfactory progress toward the Ph.D.

Additional information The AT&T Laboratories Fellowship Program (ALFP) provides a mentor who is a staff member at AT&T Labs as well as a summer research internship within AT&T Laboratories during the first summer. The ALFP replaces the Graduate Research Program for Women (GRPW) and the Cooperative Research Fellowship Program (CRFP) run by the former AT&T Bell Laboratories. If recipients accept other support, the tuition payment and stipend received from that fellowship will replace that provided by this program. The other provisions of this fellowship will remain in force and the stipend will be replaced by an annual grant of $2,000.

Number awarded Approximately 8 each year.

Deadline January of each year.

[1189]
AWARDS FOR RESEARCH IN ENGINEERING AND SCIENCE (ARES) PROGRAM

Montana Space Grant Consortium
c/o Montana State University
416 Cobleigh Hall
P.O. Box 173835
Bozeman, MT 59717-3835
(406) 994-4223　　　　　　　　Fax: (406) 994-4452
E-mail: msgc@montana.edu
Web: spacegrant.montana.edu/Text/ARES.html

Purpose To provide funding to minority and other undergraduate students in Montana who are interested in working on a space-related science or engineering research project.

Eligibility This program is open to full-time undergraduate students at selected member institutions of the Montana Space Grant Consortium (MSGC) majoring in fields related to space sciences and engineering. Applicants must be interested in working on a research project as a team with a faculty mentor. Students must submit a 2- to 4-page proposal, including a project title, explanation of the problem to be studied, goals to be achieved, experimental approach, and references. The faculty member must write a supporting letter, describing how the student will contribute to the research project and indicating support for the proposal. U.S. citizenship is required. The MSGC is a component of the U.S. National Aeronautics and Space Administration (NASA) Space Grant program, which encourages participation by women, underrepresented minorities, and persons with disabilities.

Financial data The grant is $500 per semester ($1,000 per year) or $330 per quarter.

Duration 1 semester or quarter; may be renewed.

Additional information The participating MSGC member institutions are Blackfeet Community College, Carroll College, Chief Dull Knife College, Dawson Community College, Flathead Valley Community College, Fort Belknap College, Fort Peck Community College, Little Big Horn College, Miles Community College, Montana State University at Billings, Montana State University Northern, Rocky Mountain College, Salish Kootenai College, Stone Child College, University of Great Falls, and University of Montana Western. Funding for this program is provided by NASA.

Number awarded Varies each year.

[1190]
BAKER & DANIELS DIVERSITY SCHOLARSHIPS

Baker & Daniels LLP
Attn: Assistant Director of Legal Personnel
300 North Meridian Street, Suite 2700
Indianapolis, IN 46204
(317) 237-0300　　　　　　　　Fax: (317) 237-1000
Web: www.bakerdaniels.com

Purpose To provide summer work experience and financial assistance to students from diverse backgrounds entering the second year of law school in Indiana.

Eligibility This program is open to residents of any state who are entering their second year at selected law schools in Indiana. Applicants must reflect diversity, defined to mean that they come from varied ethnic, racial, cultural, and lifestyle backgrounds, as well as those with disabilities or unique viewpoints. They must also be interested in a place in the sponsor's summer associate program. Along with their application, they must submit a personal statement that includes an explanation of how this scholarship would benefit them, an overview of their background and interests, an explanation of what diversity they would bring to the firm, and any other financial assistance they are receiving. Selection is based primarily on academic excellence.

Financial data The stipend is $10,000.

Duration 1 year.

Additional information The eligible law schools are those at Indiana University at Bloomington, Indiana University at Indianapolis, and the University of Notre Dame.

Number awarded 2 each year.

Deadline June of each year.

[1191]
BARBARA JORDAN HEALTH POLICY SCHOLARS PROGRAM

Henry J. Kaiser Family Foundation
c/o Howard University
Center for Preprofessional Education
2225 Georgia Avenue, N.W., Suite 518
Washington, DC 20059
(202) 238-2363　　　　　　　　Fax: (202) 588-9820
E-mail: bjscholarsinfo@kff.org
Web: www.kff.org

Purpose To provide Native American and other minority college seniors and recent graduates with an opportunity to work during the summer in a Congressional office with major health policy responsibilities.

Eligibility This program is open to U.S. citizens who are entering or currently enrolled in their senior year of college or who have graduated within the last 2 years from an accredited college or university. Current law, medical, and graduate students are not eligible. Applicants must 1) be a member of a population that is adversely affected by racial or ethnic disparities in health; and/or 2) have experience working in or with programs that address health issues disproportionately affecting racial and ethnic minorities or underserved communities or have done previous academic work related to health disparities. Along with their application, they must submit 400-word essays on 1) their personal background and how it led them to be interested in health policy (specifically racial or ethnic disparities); and 2) their views on a current health policy issue. Selection is based on the essays, academic performance, letters of recommendation, and extracurricular activities.

Financial data Scholars receive lodging at Howard University in Washington, D.C., round-trip transportation to Washington, D.C., a daily expense allowance for meals and local transportation, and a stipend of $2,000 upon completion of the program.

Duration 9 weeks during the summer.

Additional information Scholars are first provided with an orientation to the program by its sponsors: Howard University and the Henry J. Kaiser Family Foundation. They are then assigned to work for a Congressional office or committee with significant health policy involvement. This program began in 2000.

Number awarded Approximately 15 each year.

Deadline December of each year.

[1192]
BAY AREA COMMUNITY SERVICE SCHOLARSHIPS

National Medical Fellowships, Inc.
Attn: Scholarship Program
5 Hanover Square, 15th Floor
New York, NY 10004
(212) 483-8880   Fax: (212) 483-8897
E-mail: info@nmfonline.org
Web: www.nmfonline.org

Purpose To provide clinical experience and financial assistance to Native American and other underrepresented minority medical students at designated schools in California.

Eligibility This program is open to third- or fourth-year medical students from any state who are African Americans, mainland Puerto Ricans, Mexican Americans, Native Hawaiians, Alaska Natives, or American Indians. Applicants must be enrolled at a California M.D.-granting school and planning to practice in the San Francisco Bay area. They must be interested in either 1) clinical rotation at an approved community health center in the San Francisco Bay area dedicated to medically underserved populations, or 2) a basic science or clinical science research project in an area of critical need (e.g., HIV/AIDS care and research, hypertension, tuberculosis, cardiovascular disease, diabetes, asthma, substance abuse, women's health research). Selection is based on demonstrated commitment to practice in California, interest in community-based primary care or research, academic performance, financial need, and leadership.

Financial data The stipend is $7,500 for 6-week clinical rotations or 8-week research projects, or $15,000 for 12-week clinical rotations or research projects.

Duration Clinical rotations may be either 6 weeks or 12 weeks. Research projects may extend either 8 weeks or 12 weeks.

Additional information This program was established in 2002 with support from the San Francisco Foundation, the McKesson Foundation, and the California Endowment. Information is also available from the administrator's California Regional Office, The Chancery Building, 564 Market Street, Suite 209, San Francisco, CA 94101, (415) 397-2526, Fax: (415) 397-2556. Students who choose a 12-week clinical rotation must plan and implement a clinical project at their site. Projects may involve qualitative or quantitative research, health education, or another area of relevance to the site.

Number awarded 6 each year.

Deadline January of each year.

[1193]
BIOMEDICAL RESEARCH TRAINING PROGRAM FOR UNDERREPRESENTED GROUPS

National Heart, Lung, and Blood Institute
Attn: Office of Minority Health Affairs
6701 Rockledge Drive, Suite 8184
Bethesda, MD 20892-7913
(301) 451-5081   Fax: (301) 480-0862
Toll-free: (301) 451-0088
E-mail: mishoeh@nhlbi.nih.gov
Web: www.nhlbi.nih.gov

Purpose To provide training in fundamental biomedical sciences and clinical research disciplines to undergraduate and graduate students from underrepresented groups.

Eligibility This program is open to underrepresented undergraduate and graduate students (and postbaccalaureate individuals) interested in receiving training in fundamental biomedical sciences and clinical research disciplines of interest to the National Heart, Lung, and Blood Institute (NHLBI) of the National Institutes of Health (NIH). Underrepresented individuals include African Americans, Hispanic Americans, Native Americans, Alaskan Natives, Native Hawaiians and Pacific Islanders, individuals with disabilities, and individuals from disadvantaged backgrounds. Applicants must be U.S. citizens or permanent residents; have completed academic course work relevant to biomedical, behavioral, or statistical research; be enrolled full time or have recently completed baccalaureate work; and have a GPA of 3.3 or higher. Research experiences are available in the NHLBI Division of Intramural Research (in its cardiology, hematology, vascular medicine, or pulmonary critical care medicine branches) and its Division of Prevention and Population Sciences (which provides training in the basic principles of design, implementation, and analysis of epidemiology studies and clinical trials).

Financial data Stipends are paid at the annual rate of $24,300 for sophomores, $25,000 for juniors, $25,800 for seniors, $26,500 for postbaccalaureate individuals, $26,500 for first-year graduate students, $27,200 for second-year graduate students, or $28,000 for third-year graduate students.

Duration 6 to 24 months over a 2-year period; training must be completed in increments during consecutive academic years.

Additional information Training is conducted in the laboratories of the NHLBI in Bethesda, Maryland.

Number awarded Varies each year.

Deadline January of each year for placements beginning in June; March of each year for post-baccalaureate research internships beginning in July, August, or September.

[1194] BROOKHAVEN NATIONAL LABORATORY PROFESSIONAL ASSOCIATES PROGRAM FOR WOMEN AND MINORITIES

Brookhaven National Laboratory
Attn: Diversity Office, Human Resources Division
Building 400B
P.O. Box 5000
Upton, New York 11973-5000
(631) 344-2703   Fax: (631) 344-5305
E-mail: palmore@bnl.gov
Web: www.bnl.gov/diversity/programs.asp

Purpose To provide professional experience in scientific areas at Brookhaven National Laboratory (BNL) to members of underrepresented groups.

Eligibility This program is open to underrepresented minorities (African Americans, Hispanics, Native Americans, or Pacific Islanders), people with disabilities, and women. Applicants must have earned at least a bachelor's degree and be seeking professional experience in such fields as biology, chemistry, computer science, engineering, health physics, medical research, or physics. They must plan to attend a graduate or professional school and express an interest in long-term employment at BNL. U.S. citizenship or permanent resident status is required.

Financial data Participants receive a competitive salary.

Duration 1 year.

Additional information Interns work in a goal-oriented on-the-job training program under the supervision of employees who are experienced in their areas of interest.

Number awarded Varies each year.

Deadline Applications may be submitted at any time.

[1195] BROOKHAVEN NATIONAL LABORATORY SCIENCE AND ENGINEERING PROGRAMS FOR WOMEN AND MINORITIES

Brookhaven National Laboratory
Attn: Diversity Office, Human Resources Division
Building 400B
P.O. Box 5000
Upton, New York 11973-5000
(631) 344-2703   Fax: (631) 344-5305
E-mail: palmore@bnl.gov
Web: www.bnl.gov/diversity/programs.asp

Purpose To provide on-the-job training in scientific areas at Brookhaven National Laboratory (BNL) during the summer to underrepresented minority and women students.

Eligibility This program at BNL is open to women and underrepresented minority (African American/Black, Hispanic, Native American, or Pacific Islander) students who have completed their freshman, sophomore, or junior year of college. Applicants must be U.S. citizens or permanent residents, at least 18 years of age, and majoring in applied mathematics, biology, chemistry, computer science, engineering, high and low energy particle accelerators, nuclear medicine, physics, or scientific writing. Since no transportation or housing allowance is provided, preference is given to students who reside in the BNL area.

Financial data Participants receive a competitive stipend.

Duration 10 to 12 weeks during the summer.

Additional information Students work with members of the scientific, technical, and professional staff of BNL in an educational training program developed to give research experience.

Deadline April of each year.

[1196] BUCKINGHAM, DOOLITTLE & BURROUGHS DIVERSITY SCHOLARSHIP PROGRAM

Buckingham, Doolittle & Burroughs, LLP
Attn: Benefits and Employment Coordinator
3800 Embassy Parkway, Suite 300
Akron, OH 44333
(330) 376-5300   Toll-free: (800) 686-2825
E-mail: bdb@bdblaw.com
Web: www.bdblaw.com/diversity-program.asp

Purpose To provide summer work experience and financial assistance to Native American and other minority students from any state who are enrolled at designated law schools in Ohio and Florida.

Eligibility This program is open to first-year students at law schools in Ohio and Florida who are of minority (African American, Hispanic, Asian, or Native American) descent. Applicants must submit a 1,000-word personal statement about themselves that includes a discussion of the life influences that have contributed to the person they are today. Selection is based on academic excellence, demonstrated leadership skills, service to the community, and commitment to excellence.

Financial data As summer associates, students receive a salary of $1,538.46 per week at offices in Akron and Canton, $1,586.54 per week at offices in Cleveland and Columbus, or $1,730.77 per week at offices in Boca Raton and West Palm Beach. The stipend for the academic year following completion of the associateship is $5,000.

Duration 1 year.

Additional information This program, which began in 2005, is available at the following Ohio law schools: Capital University Law School, Case Western Reserve University School of Law, Ohio Northern University Pettit College of Law, Ohio State University Moritz College of Law, University of Akron School of Law, University of Cincinnati College of Law, University of Dayton School of Law, and University of Toledo College of Law. It is also available to students at the following Florida law schools: University of Florida Levin College of Law, Florida State University College of Law, University of Miami School of Law, Nova Southeastern University Shepard Broad Law Center, Stetson University College of Law, Barry University School of Law, Florida Coastal School of Law, and St. Thomas University School of Law. Summer associateships are available at the firm's offices in Ohio (Akron, Canton, Cleveland, and Columbus) and in Florida (Boca Raton and West Palm Beach).

Number awarded 1 each year.

Deadline January of each year.

[1197]
BULLIVANT HOUSER BAILEY LAW STUDENT DIVERSITY SCHOLARSHIP PROGRAM

Bullivant Houser Bailey PC
Attn: Recruitment and Diversity Manager
888 S.W. Fifth Avenue, Suite 300
Portland, OR 97204-2089
(503) 228-6351   Toll-free: (800) 654-8972
Fax: (503) 295-0915
E-mail: jill.valentine@bullivant.com
Web: www.bullivant.com/shownews.asp?Show=4795

Purpose To provide financial assistance and work experience to law students who come from a minority or disadvantaged background.

Eligibility This program is open to first-year law students who are members of a minority group (including any group underrepresented in the legal profession) and/or students coming from a disadvantaged educational or economic background. Applicants must have 1) a record of academic achievement and leadership in college and law school; 2) a willingness to complete a 12-week summer associateship at a California office of the firm; and 3) a record of contributions to the community that promote diversity within society, the legal community, and/or law school.

Financial data The program provides a salaried associate position at an office of the firm during the summer following the first year of law school and a stipend of $7,500 for the second year.

Duration 1 year.

Number awarded 2 each year: 1 assigned to an associateship in the Sacramento office and 1 assigned to an associateship in the San Francisco office.

Deadline January of each year.

[1198]
BUSINESS REPORTING INTERN PROGRAM FOR MINORITY COLLEGE SOPHOMORES AND JUNIORS

Dow Jones Newspaper Fund
P.O. Box 300
Princeton, NJ 08543-0300
(609) 452-2820   Fax: (609) 520-5804
E-mail: newsfund@wsj.dowjones.com
Web: DJNewspaperFund.dowjones.com

Purpose To provide work experience and financial assistance to Native American and other minority college students who are interested in careers in journalism.

Eligibility This program is open to college sophomores and juniors who are U.S. citizens interested in careers in journalism and participating in a summer internship at a daily newspaper as a business reporter. Applicants must be members of a minority group (African American, Hispanic, Asian American, Pacific Islander, American Indian, or Alaskan Native) and enrolled as full-time students. They must submit a resume, 3 to 5 recently-published clips, a list of courses with grades, and a 500-word essay on why they want to spend the summer writing business news.

Financial data Interns receive a salary of at least $350 per week during the summer and a $1,000 scholarship at the successful completion of the program.

Duration 10 weeks for the summer internship; 1 year for the scholarship.

Additional information Interns attend a 1-week training seminar and then work as business reporters on a daily newspaper. Recently, the seminar was held at New York University.

Number awarded Up to 12 each year.

Deadline October of each year.

[1199]
BUTLER RUBIN DIVERSITY SCHOLARSHIP

Butler Rubin Saltarelli & Boyd LLP
Attn: Director of Marketing
70 West Madison Street, Suite 1800
Chicago, IL 60602
(312) 444-9660   Fax: (312) 444-9287
E-mail: agordon@butlerrubin.com
Web: www.butlerrubin.com

Purpose To provide financial assistance and summer work experience to Native Americans and other diverse law students who are interested in the area of business litigation.

Eligibility This program is open to law students of racial and ethnic backgrounds that will contribute to diversity in the legal profession. Applicants must be interested in the private practice of law in the area of business litigation and in a summer associateship in that field with Butler Rubin Saltarelli & Boyd in Chicago. Selection is based on academic performance and achievement, intention to remain in the Chicago area following graduation, and interpersonal and communication skills.

Financial data The stipend is $10,000 per year; funds are to be used for tuition and other expenses associated with law school. For the summer associateship, a stipend is paid.

Duration 1 year; may be renewed.

Additional information This program was established in 2006.

Number awarded 1 each year.

[1200]
CALIFORNIA COMMUNITY SERVICE SCHOLARSHIPS

National Medical Fellowships, Inc.
Attn: Scholarship Program
5 Hanover Square, 15th Floor
New York, NY 10004
(212) 483-8880   Fax: (212) 483-8897
E-mail: info@nmfonline.org
Web: www.nmfonline.org

Purpose To provide clinical experience to Native American and other underrepresented minority medical students at schools in California.

Eligibility This program is open to third- or fourth-year medical students from any state who are African Americans, mainland Puerto Ricans, Mexican Americans, Native Hawaiians, Alaska Natives, or American Indians. Applicants must be attending an M.D.-granting institution or college of osteopathic medicine in California. They must be interested in a clinical rotation at an approved community health center in California dedicated to medically underserved populations. Selection is based on demonstrated commitment to practice in California, interest in community-based primary care or research, academic performance, financial need, and leadership.

Financial data The stipend is $7,500.

Duration 6 weeks.

Additional information This program was established in 2002 with support from the San Francisco Foundation, the McKesson Foundation, and the California Endowment. Information is also available from the administrator's California Regional Office, The Chancery Building, 564 Market Street, Suite 209, San Francisco, CA 94104, (415) 397-2526, Fax: (415) 397-2556.

Number awarded 10 each year.

Deadline January of each year.

[1201]
CALIFORNIA SPACE GRANT CONSORTIUM STUDENT-MENTOR AEROSPACE WORKFORCE DEVELOPMENT SCHOLARSHIPS

California Space Grant Consortium
c/o University of California at San Diego
Engineering Building Unit II, Room 104
9500 Gilman Drive, Department 0411
La Jolla, CA 92093-0411
(858) 822-1597   Fax: (858) 534-7840
E-mail: spacegrant@ucsd.edu
Web: calspace.ucsd.edu/casgc/sm_scholarships.html

Purpose To provide assistance to minority and other undergraduate and graduate students at affiliate institutions of the California Space Grant Consortium (CaSGC) who are interested in working on space-related projects.

Eligibility This program is open to teams of science, engineering, and management students at K-12, undergraduate, and graduate levels. Applicants must be interested in participating in aerospace workforce student-mentor development efforts at CaSGC affiliates under the guidance of mentors from the industrial, academic, and government sectors. The program is sponsored by the U.S. National Aeronautics and Space Administration (NASA) Space Grant program, which encourages participation by underrepresented minorities, women, and persons with disabilities.

Financial data Scholarships and training grants are provided by each project.

Duration 1 semester, summer, or year.

Additional information CaSGC affiliate members include the University of California campuses at Berkeley, Davis, Irvine, Los Angeles, Riverside, San Diego, Santa Barbara, and Santa Cruz; the California State University campuses at Long Beach, Los Angeles, Sacramento, San Bernardino, San Diego, and San Luis Obispo; Santa Clara University; Stanford University; the University of Southern California; and the Grossmont-Cuyamaca Community College District. Associate members, whose students may participate on a project-by-project basis, include California State Polytechnic University at Pomona, California State University at Fresno, San Jose State University, California Institute of Technology, Pomona College, San Francisco Art Institute, Astronomical Society of the Pacific, the San Diego Supercomputer Center, and the University of San Diego.

Number awarded Varies each year.

Deadline Each of the participating institutions sets its own deadline.

[1202]
CGSM FELLOWSHIPS

Consortium for Graduate Study in Management
5585 Pershing Avenue, Suite 240
St. Louis, MO 63112-4621
(314) 877-5500   Toll-free: (888) 658-6814
Fax: (314) 877-5505   E-mail: recruiting@cgsm.org
Web: www.cgsm.org

Purpose To provide financial assistance and work experience to Native American and other underrepresented racial minorities interested in preparing for a management career in business.

Eligibility This program is open to African Americans, Hispanic Americans (Chicanos, Cubans, Dominicans, and Puerto Ricans), and Native Americans who have graduated from college and are interested in a career in business. Other U.S. citizens and permanent residents who can demonstrate a commitment to the sponsor's mission of enhancing diversity in business education are also eligible. An undergraduate degree in business or economics is not required. Applicants must be planning to work on an M.B.A. degree at 1 of the consortium's 13 schools. Preference is given to applicants under 31 years of age.

Financial data The fellowship pays full tuition and required fees. Summer internships with the consortium's cooperative sponsors, providing paid practical experience, are also offered.

Duration Up to 4 semesters.

Additional information This program was established in 1966. The participating schools are Carnegie Mellon University, Dartmouth College, Emory University, Indiana University, University of Michigan, New York University, University of North Carolina at Chapel Hill, University of Rochester, University of Southern California, University of Texas at Austin, University of Virginia, Washington University, University of Wisconsin at Madison, and Yale. Fellowships are tenable at member schools only. Application fees are $150 for students applying to 1 to 3 schools, $210 for 4 schools, $270 for 5 schools, or $330 for 6 schools.

Number awarded Varies; up to 400 each year.

Deadline March of each year.

[1203]
CHIPS QUINN SCHOLARS PROGRAM

Freedom Forum
Attn: Chips Quinn Scholars Program
555 Pennsylvania Avenue, N.W.
Washington, DC 20001
(202) 292-6271   E-mail: kcatone@freedomforum.org
Web: www.chipsquinn.org

Purpose To provide work experience, career mentoring, and scholarship support to Native American and other minority college students and recent graduates who are majoring in journalism.

Eligibility This program is open to students of color who are college juniors, seniors, or recent graduates with journalism majors or career goals in newspapers. Candidates must be nominated or endorsed by journalism faculty, campus media advisers, editors of newspapers, or leaders of minority journalism associations. Along with their application, they must submit a resume, transcripts, 2 letters of recommendation, and an essay of 200 to 500 words on why they want to be a Chips Quinn Scholar. Reporters must also submit 6 samples of published articles they have written; photographers must submit 6 samples of their work on a CD. Applicants must have a car and be available to work as a full-time intern during the spring or summer. U.S. citizenship or permanent resident status is required. Campus newspaper experience is strongly encouraged.

Financial data Students chosen for this program receive a travel stipend to attend a workshop at the Freedom Forum in Arlington, Virginia prior to reporting for their internship. Upon completion of the internship, they receive a $1,600 scholarship.

Duration Internships are for 10 to 12 weeks; the scholarship is for 1 year.

Additional information This program was established in 1991 in memory of the late John D. Quinn Jr., managing editor of the *Poughkeepsie Journal*. Funding is provided by the Freedom Forum, formerly the Gannett Foundation. After graduating from college and obtaining employment with a newspaper, alumni of this program are eligible to apply for fellowship support to attend professional journalism development activities.

Number awarded Approximately 70 each year. Since the program began, more than 1,000 scholars have been selected.

Deadline October of each year.

[1204]
CIA UNDERGRADUATE INTERNSHIP PROGRAM
Central Intelligence Agency
Attn: Human Resource Management
Recruitment and Retention Center, 4B14-034 DD1
Washington, DC 20505
(703) 371-2107
Web: https:

Purpose To provide work experience at the Central Intelligence Agency (CIA) to undergraduates, especially minorities and people with disabilities.

Eligibility This program is open to undergraduate students, particularly minorities and people with disabilities. Applicants must be U.S. citizens, have a GPA of 3.0 or higher, be available to work in metropolitan Washington, D.C. during the summer or for a semester, and meet the same employment standards as permanent CIA employees. They must be majoring in fields such as accounting, area studies, business administration, computer science, economics, engineering, finance, foreign languages, geography, graphic design, human resources, international relations, logistics, mathematics, military and foreign affairs, national security studies, physical sciences, or political science.

Financial data Student positions offer salaries competitive with the private sector and the same benefits as permanent employees. Student trainees are also eligible to apply for the agency's tuition assistance program.

Duration Interns are required to work either 1) a combination of 1 semester and 1 summer, or 2) 2 90-day summer internships.

Number awarded Varies each year.

Deadline Applications for winter, spring, or fall may be submitted at any time, but they should be completed 6 to 9 months prior to the desired start date. Summer applications are due by October of each year.

[1205]
CIRI FOUNDATION INTERNSHIP PROGRAM
Cook Inlet Region, Inc.
Attn: The CIRI Foundation
3600 San Jeronimo Drive, Suite 256
Anchorage, AK 99508-2870
(907) 793-3575　　　　　　　Toll-free: (800) 764-3382
Fax: (907) 793-3585　E-mail: tcf@thecirifoundation.org
Web: www.thecirifoundation.org/internships.htm

Purpose To provide on-the-job training to Alaska Natives who are original enrollees to the Cook Inlet Region, Inc. (CIRI) and their lineal descendants.

Eligibility This program is open to Alaska Native enrollees to CIRI under the Alaska Native Claims Settlement Act (ANCSA) of 1971 and their lineal descendants. Applicants must 1) be enrolled in a 2-year or 4-year academic or graduate degree program with a GPA of 3.0 or higher; 2) have recently completed an undergraduate or graduate degree program; or 3) be enrolled or have recently completed a technical skills training program at an accredited or otherwise approved postsecondary institution. Preference is given to applicants in the following fields: business, natural resources management, earth sciences, languages, education, social sciences, arts, communications, law, general academic fields, technical skills training programs, and culinary arts.

Financial data The intern's wage is based on a trainee position and is determined by the employer of the intern with the approval of the foundation (which pays one half of the intern's wages).

Duration Internships are approved on a quarterly basis for 480 hours of part-time or full-time employment. Interns may reapply on a quarter-by-quarter basis, not to exceed 12 consecutive months.

Additional information The foundation and the intern applicant work together to identify an appropriate placement experience. The employer hires the intern. Placement may be with Cook Inlet Region, Inc., a firm related to the foundation, or a business or service organization located anywhere in the United States. The intern may be placed with more than 1 company during the internship period. Interns may receive academic credit.

Deadline March, June, September, or November of each year.

[1206]
COLORADO SPACE GRANT RESEARCH SUPPORT
Colorado Space Grant Consortium
c/o University of Colorado at Boulder
Discovery Learning Center, 270
Campus Box 520
Boulder, CO 80309-0520
(303) 492-4750　　　　　　　Fax: (303) 492-5456
E-mail: koehler@colorado.edu
Web: spacegrant.colorado.edu

Purpose To provide an opportunity to participate in space-related research to minority and other undergraduate and graduate students at member institutions of the Colorado Space Grant Consortium (CoSGC).

Eligibility This program is open to undergraduate and graduate students at the 13 colleges and universities affiliated with the consortium. Applicants must be interested in participating in designing, flying, building, operating, and analyzing real space engineering and science experiments. The sponsored research activities are part of the Space Grant program of the U.S. National Aeronautics and Space Administration (NASA), which encourages participation by women, underrepresented minorities, and people with disabilities.

Financial data Stipends are provided.

Additional information The members of CoSGC include the University of Colorado at Boulder, the University of Colorado at Colorado Springs, Colorado State University at Fort Collins, Colorado State University at Pueblo, Pikes Peak Community College, Mesa State College, the University of Northern Colorado, Western State College, Adams State College, Colorado School of Mines, Fort Lewis College, Metro State College, and Front Range Community College. This program is funded by NASA.

Number awarded Varies each year.

[1207]
COMMERCIAL AND FEDERAL LITIGATION SECTION MINORITY FELLOWSHIP

The New York Bar Foundation
One Elk Street
Albany, NY 12207
(518) 487-5651   Fax: (518) 487-5699
E-mail: foundation@tnybf.org
Web: www.tnybf.org/restrictedfunds.htm

Purpose To provide an opportunity for Native American and other minority residents of any state attending law school in New York to gain summer work experience in a litigation position in the public sector in the state.

Eligibility This program is open to minority students from any state who are enrolled in the first year at a law school in New York state. Applicants must have demonstrated an interest in commercial and federal litigation. They must be interested in working in a litigation position during the summer in the public sector in New York.

Financial data The stipend is $5,000.

Duration 10 weeks during the summer.

Additional information This program was established in 2007 by the Commercial and Federal Litigation Section of the New York State Bar Association. It is administered by The New York Bar Foundation.

Number awarded 1 each year.

Deadline December of each year.

[1208]
COMMUNICATIONS INTERNSHIP AWARD FOR STUDENTS OF COLOR

College and Public Relations Association of Pennsylvania
Attn: Administrative Support
Calder Square
P.O. Box 10034
State College, PA 16805-0034
(814) 865-0248   Fax: (814) 863-3428
E-mail: kln1@psu.edu
Web: www.cuprap.org/default.aspx?pageid=16

Purpose To provide funding to students of color from any state at schools that are members of the College and Public Relations Association of Pennsylvania (CUPRAP) who have accepted an unpaid summer internship.

Eligibility This program is open to full-time undergraduate students who are members of a racial minority group (African American, Asian/Pacific Islander, Hispanic/Latino, Native American). Applicants must have completed at least their freshman year at an accredited college or university that is a member of CUPRAP, although they are not required to be residents of Pennsylvania. They must have obtained a internship in a communications-related field (e.g., print media, radio, television, public relations, advertising, graphic/Web design). Selection is based on academic ability, communication skills and creativity as demonstrated through work samples, and financial need.

Financial data The grant is $1,500.

Duration The internship may be at any time of the year, but it must be for at least 150 hours. This grant is nonrenewable.

Number awarded 1 or more each year.

Deadline January of each year.

[1209]
COMTO'S INSIDE TRACK FOR YOUTH (CITY) INTERNSHIP PROGRAM

Conference of Minority Transportation Officials
Attn: Internship Program
818 18th Street, N.W., Suite 850
Washington, DC 20006
(202) 530-0551   Fax: (202) 530-0617
Web: www.comto.org/news-city.php

Purpose To provide summer work experience in transportation-related fields to Native American and other minority upper-division students.

Eligibility This program is open to full-time minority students entering their junior or senior year with a GPA of 2.5 or higher. Applicants must be working on a degree related to public transportation. They must be interested in a summer internship with transit firms or agencies in New York City, Houston, or, Washington, D.C. Along with their application, they must submit a 1-page essay on their transportation interests, including how participation in this internship will enhance their educational plan, their mid- and long-term professional goals, their specific transportation-related goal, issues of interest to them, how they plan to further their education and assist in making future contributions to their field of study, and their expectations of this internship experience. U.S. citizenship is required.

Financial data The stipend is $4,000.

Duration 10 weeks during the summer.

Additional information This program is managed by the Conference of Minority Transportation Officials (COMTO) with funding is provided by the Federal Transit Administration. Interns work at transit agencies, private transit-related consulting firms, transportation service providers, manufacturers, and suppliers.

Number awarded Varies each year. Recently, 9 of these internships were awarded: 4 in New York City, 3 in Houston, and 2 in Washington, D.C.

Deadline April of each year.

[1210]
CONNECTICUT COMMUNITY COLLEGE MINORITY FELLOWSHIP PROGRAM

Connecticut Community College System
Attn: System Officer for Diversity Awareness
61 Woodland Street
Hartford, CT 06105-9949
(860) 244-7606 Fax: (860) 566-6624
E-mail: karmstrong@commnet.edu
Web: www.commnet.edu/minority_fellowship.asp

Purpose To provide work experience and financial assistance to graduate students, especially minorities, in Connecticut who are interested in preparing for a career in community college teaching or administration.

Eligibility This program is open to graduate students who have completed at least 6 credits of graduate work and have indicated an interest in a career in community colleges. Current employees of the Connecticut Community Colleges are also eligible. Applicants must be willing to commit to at least 1 year of employment in the Connecticut Community College System. Although all qualified graduate students are eligible, the program encourages applicants to register who strengthen the racial and cultural diversity of the minority fellow registry. That includes, in particular, making all possible efforts to recruit from historically underrepresented groups.

Financial data Non-employee fellows receive a stipend of $3,500 per semester. Fellows who are current employees are reassigned time from their responsibilities.

Duration 1 year; may be renewed.

Additional information Fellows are expected to dedicate 9 hours per week to the program. They spend 6 hours per week in teaching or administrative activities under the supervision of a mentor. During the second semester, they assist the mentor in teaching a course or engaging in structured administrative activities. The remaining time is spent on program and campus orientation activities, attendance at relevant faculty or staff meetings, and participation in other college meetings or professional development activities.

Number awarded Up to 13 each year: 1 at each of the 12 colleges in the system and 1 in the chancellor's office.

Deadline July of each year.

[1211]
C.T. LANG JOURNALISM MINORITY SCHOLARSHIP AND INTERNSHIP

Albuquerque Journal
Attn: Scholarship Committee
7777 Jefferson Street, N.E.
P.O. Drawer J
Albuquerque, NM 87103
(505) 823-7777

Purpose To provide financial assistance and work experience to Native American and other minority upper-division students in journalism programs at universities in New Mexico.

Eligibility This program is open to minority students from any state who are majoring or minoring in journalism at a New Mexico university in their junior year with a GPA of 2.5 or higher. Applicants must be enrolled full time. They must be planning a career in newswriting, photography, design, copy editing, or online. Selection is based on clips of published stories, a short autobiography that explains the applicant's interest in the field, a grade transcript, and a letter of recommendation.

Financial data The scholarship is $1,000 per semester; the recipient also receives a paid internship and moving expenses.

Duration The scholarship is for 2 semesters (fall and spring). The internship is for 1 semester.

Additional information This program is funded by the *Albuquerque Journal*, where the internship takes place.

Number awarded 1 each year.

Deadline December of each year.

[1212]
CULTURAL RESOURCES DIVERSITY INTERNSHIP PROGRAM

Student Conservation Association, Inc.
Attn: Diversity Internships
1800 North Kent Street, Suite 102
Arlington, VA 22209
(703) 524-2441 Fax: (703) 524-2451
E-mail: diversity@thesca.org
Web: www.thesca.org/ptnrs_other

Purpose To provide work experience to ethnically diverse undergraduate and graduate students and students with disabilities at facilities of the U.S. National Park Service (NPS).

Eligibility This program is open to currently-enrolled students at the sophomore or higher level. Applicants must be U.S. citizens or permanent residents with a GPA of 3.0 or higher. Although all students may apply, the program is designed to give ethnically diverse students and students with disabilities the opportunity to experience the diversity of careers in the federal sector. Applicants are assigned to a position within the NPS. Possible placements include archaeology and anthropology; historic building preservation; journalism and graphic design; civil and environmental engineering; project management and research; costumed interpretation and living history; landscape architecture; museum studies and library relations; web site design; public relations and outreach; and Native American studies.

Financial data The weekly stipend ranges from $60 to $650, depending on the program and the intern's academic

level. Other benefits include reimbursement of travel expenses, no-cost housing, medical insurance for a small fee, and accident insurance.
Duration 10 weeks in the summer (beginning in June), 15 weeks in the fall (beginning in September), or 15 weeks in the spring (beginning in January).
Additional information While participating in the internship, students engage in tri-weekly evening career and professional development events, ongoing career counseling, mentoring, and personal and career development services.
Number awarded Approximately 15 each year.
Deadline February of each year for summer; June of each year for fall; November of each year for spring.

[1213]
DALMAS A. TAYLOR MEMORIAL SUMMER MINORITY POLICY FELLOWSHIP

Society for the Psychological Study of Social Issues
208 I Street, N.E.
Washington, DC 20002-4340
(202) 675-6956   Fax: (202) 675-6902
E-mail: awards@spssi.org
Web: www.spssi.org

Purpose To enable graduate students of color to be involved in the public policy activities of the American Psychological Association (APA) during the summer.
Eligibility This program is open to graduate students who are members of an ethnic minority group (including, but not limited to, African American, Alaskan Native, American Indian, Asian American, Hispanic, and Pacific Islander) and/or have demonstrated a commitment to a career in psychology or a related field with a focus on ethnic minority issues. Applicants must be interested in spending a summer in Washington, D.C. to work on public policy issues in conjunction with the Minority Fellowship Program of the APA. Their application must indicate why they are interested in the fellowship, their previous and current research experiences, their interest and involvement in ethnic minority psychological issues, and how the fellowship would contribute to their career goals.
Financial data The stipend is $3,000. Housing and travel funds are also provided.
Duration Summer months.
Additional information This program was established in 2000. The sponsor is Division 9 of the APA.
Number awarded 1 each year.
Deadline March of each year.

[1214]
DAVIS WRIGHT TREMAINE 1L DIVERSITY SCHOLARSHIP PROGRAM

Davis Wright Tremaine LLP
Attn: Diversity Scholarship Program
1201 Third Avenue, Suite 2200
Seattle, WA 98101-3045
(206) 622-3150   Toll-free: (877) 398-8416
Fax: (206) 757-7700   E-mail: carolyuly@dwt.com
Web: www.dwt.com/recruit/intro/scholarship.htm

Purpose To provide financial assistance and summer work experience to Native Americans and other law students of color.
Eligibility This program is open to first-year law students of color and others of diverse background. Applicants must have a record of academic achievement as an undergraduate and in the first year of law school that demonstrates promise for a successful career in law, a commitment to civic involvement that promotes diversity and will continue after entering the legal profession, and a willingness to become an associate in the sponsor's Seattle or Portland office during the summer between their first and second year of law school. They must submit a current resume, a complete undergraduate transcript, grades from the first semester of law school, a short personal essay indicating their interest in the scholarship, a legal writing sample, and 2 or 3 references. Although demonstrated need may be taken into account, applicants need not disclose their financial circumstances.
Financial data The award consists of a $7,500 stipend for second-year tuition and expenses and a paid summer clerkship.
Duration 1 academic year and summer.
Number awarded 3 each year: 2 in the Seattle office and 1 in the Portland office.
Deadline January of each year.

[1215]
DEPARTMENT OF ENERGY HEALTH, SAFETY AND SECURITY MINORITY SERVING INSTITUTION SUPPORT PROGRAM

Oak Ridge Institute for Science and Education
Attn: Science and Engineering Education
P.O. Box 117
Oak Ridge, TN 37831-0117
(865) 241-6704   Fax: (865) 576-8293
E-mail: MCarl.Wheeler@orau.gov
Web: see.orau.org

Purpose To provide funding to faculty members and students at Minority Serving Institutions who wish to participate in summer internships at facilities of the U.S. Department of Energy across the country.
Eligibility This program is open to full-time faculty members, graduate students, and undergraduates affiliated with Minority Serving Institutions, including Alaska Native Serving Institutions (ANSIs), Hispanic Serving Institutions (HSIs), Historically Black Colleges and Universities (HBCUs), Native Hawaiian Serving Institutions (NHSIs), and Tribal Colleges and Universities (TCUs). Applicants must be teaching or studying nuclear engineering, health physics, environmental engineering, civil engineering, or occupational safety and health. They must be interested in participating in summer internships in Germantown, Maryland or at other DOE facilities around the country. U.S. citizenship is required.
Financial data The stipend is $1,200 per week for faculty, $500 per week for graduate students, or $450 per week for undergraduates; a housing allowance of $200 per week and limited travel reimbursement for round-trip transportation expenses between the facility and home or campus are also provided.
Duration 10 weeks during the summer.
Additional information This program is funded by DOE and administered by Oak Ridge Institute for Science and Education (ORISE).
Number awarded Varies each year.

Deadline February of each year.

[1216]
DEPARTMENT OF THE INTERIOR DIVERSITY INTERN PROGRAM

Department of the Interior
Attn: Office of Educational Partnerships
1849 C Street, N.W., MS 5221 MIB
Washington, DC 20240
(202) 208-6403 Toll-free: (888) 447-4392
Fax: (202) 208-3620 TTY: (202) 208-5069
E-mail: ed_partners@ios.doi.gov
Web: www.doi.gov/hrm/student.html

Purpose To provide work experience to ethnically diverse college and graduate students and students with disabilities at federal agencies involved with natural and cultural resources.

Eligibility This program is open to currently-enrolled students at the sophomore or higher level at Historically Black Colleges and Universities (HBCUs), Hispanic-Serving Institutions (HSIs), Tribal Colleges and Universities (TCUs), and some other major institutions. Applicants must be U.S. citizens or permanent residents with a GPA of 3.0 or higher. Although all students may apply, the program is designed to give ethnically diverse students and students with disabilities the opportunity to experience the diversity of careers in the federal sector. Applicants are assigned to a position within the U.S. Department of the Interior (DOI). Possible placements include archaeology and anthropology; wildlife and fisheries biology; business administration, accounting, and finance; civil and environmental engineering; computer science, especially GIS applications; human resources; mining and petroleum engineering; communications and public relations; web site and database design; environmental and realty law; geology, hydrology, and geography; Native American studies; interpretation and environmental education; natural resource and range management; public policy and administration; and surveying and mapping.

Financial data The weekly stipend is $420 for sophomores and juniors, $450 for seniors, or $520 for law and graduate students. Other benefits include a pre-term orientation, transportation to the orientation and the work site, worker's compensation, and accident insurance.

Duration 10 weeks in the summer (beginning in June) or 15 weeks in the fall (beginning in September) or spring (beginning in January).

Additional information This program, which began in 1994, is administered through 5 nonprofit organizations: Haskell Indian Nations University, Hispanic Association of Colleges and Universities, Minority Access, Inc., Student Conservation Association, and National Association for Equal Opportunity in Higher Education. While participating in the internship, students engage in tri-weekly evening career and professional development events, ongoing career counseling, mentoring, and personal and career development services.

Number awarded Varies each year; since the program began, more than 700 interns have participated.

Deadline February of each year for summer; June of each year for fall; November of each year for spring.

[1217]
DEPARTMENT OF TRANSPORTATION MINORITY-SERVING INSTITUTIONS AND EDUCATIONAL PARTNERSHIPS INTERNSHIPS

ADNET Systems, Inc.
164 Rollins Avenue, Suite 303
Rockville, MD 20852
(301) 770-4850 Fax: (301) 770-4828
E-mail: info@adnet-sys.com
Web: www.adnet-sys.com/internships.html

Purpose To provide summer work experience at offices of the U.S. Department of Transportation (DOT) to minority and disabled students.

Eligibility This program is open to students who are from Historically Black Colleges and Universities (HBCUs), Hispanic Serving Institutions (HSIs), Tribal Colleges and Universities (TCUs), Asian American and Pacific Islander communities, and disability communities. Applicants must be U.S. citizens currently enrolled in a college or university as a sophomore or above (including graduate students) with a GPA of 3.0 or higher. They must be interested in an internship with a DOT agency. Jobs have included, but are not limited to, accounting, business, human resources, international affairs, operations, computer science, mathematics, engineering, journalism, and criminal justice. Along with their application, they must submit 50-word statements on 1) their community activities, hobbies, associations, publications, and other relevant experience; and 2) why they want to participate in this program.

Financial data Interns are paid a stipend and receive housing.

Duration 10 weeks in the summer.

Additional information Information on this program is also available from the U.S. Department of Transportation, Office of Civil Rights, Minority Serving Institutions and Educational Partnerships (S-30.10), 400 Seventh Street, S.W., Room 5414A, Washington, DC, (202) 366-8964, Fax: (202) 366-7717, TTY: (202) 366-9696. Assignments are available with the Bureau of Transportation Statistics, Federal Motor Carrier Safety Administration, Federal Transit Administration, Federal Railroad Administration, Maritime Administration, National Highway Traffic Safety Administration, Research and Special Programs Administration, St. Lawrence Seaway Development Corporation, and Transportation Administrative Services Center.

Number awarded Varies each year.

Deadline Applications are accepted until all positions are filled.

[1218]
DIETETIC INTERNSHIP SCHOLARSHIPS

American Dietetic Association
Attn: Accreditation, Education Programs, and Student Operations
120 South Riverside Plaza, Suite 2000
Chicago, IL 60606-6995
(312) 899-0040 Toll-free: (800) 877-1600, ext. 5400
Fax: (312) 899-4817 E-mail: education@eatright.org
Web: www.eatright.org

Purpose To provide financial assistance to minority and other student members of the American Dietetic Association (ADA) who have applied for a dietetic internship.

Eligibility This program is open to student members who have applied for a CADE-accredited dietetic internship. Applicants must be participating in the computer-matching process, be U.S. citizens or permanent residents, and show promise of being a valuable, contributing member of the profession. Some scholarships require membership in a specific dietetic practice group, residency in a specific state, or underrepresented minority group status. The same application form can be used for all categories. Students who are currently completing the internship component of a combined graduate/dietetic internship should apply for the American Dietetic Association's Graduate Scholarship.
Financial data Stipends range from $500 to $3,000; most are for $1,000.
Duration 1 year.
Number awarded Varies each year, depending upon the funds available. Recently, the sponsoring organization awarded 211 scholarships for all its programs.
Deadline February of each year.

[1219]
DINSMORE & SHOHL LLP DIVERSITY SCHOLARSHIP PROGRAM
Dinsmore & Shohl LLP
Attn: Manager of Legal Recruiting
255 East Fifth Street, Suite 1900
Cincinnati, OH 45202
(513) 977-8488
E-mail: dinsmore.legalrecuiting@dinslaw.com
Web: www.dinslaw.com/careers/diversityscholarship

Purpose To provide financial assistance and summer work experience to Native American and other underrepresented minority law students.
Eligibility This program is open to first- and second-year law students who are members of groups traditionally underrepresented in the legal profession. Applicants must have a demonstrated record of academic or professional achievement and leadership qualities. They must also be interested in a summer associateship with Dinsmore & Shohl LLP.
Financial data The program provides an academic scholarship of $10,000 and a paid associateship at the firm.
Duration The academic scholarship is for 1 year. The summer associateship is for 12 weeks.
Additional information Associateships are available at firm offices in Charleston (West Virginia), Cincinnati (Ohio), Columbus (Ohio), Dayton (Ohio), Lexington (Kentucky), Louisville (Kentucky), Morgantown (West Virginia), Pittsburgh (Pennsylvania), and Wheeling (West Virginia). The program includes 1 associateship in which the student spends 6 weeks as a clerk in the legal department of the Procter & Gamble Company's worldwide headquarters in Cincinnati and 6 weeks at Dinsmore & Shohl's Cincinnati office. All associates are assigned to an attorney with the firm who serves as a mentor.
Number awarded Varies each year.
Deadline August of each year for second-year students; December of each year for first-year students.

[1220]
DONALD W. BANNER DIVERSITY SCHOLARSHIP
Banner & Witcoff, Ltd.
Attn: Christopher Hummel
1100 13th Street, N.W., Suite 1200
Washington, DC 20005-4051
(202) 824-3000   Fax: (202) 824-3001
E-mail: chummel@bannerwitcoff.com
Web: www.bannerwitcoff.com/diversity.cfm

Purpose To provide financial assistance and work experience to law students who come from Native American and other groups historically underrepresented in intellectual property law.
Eligibility This program is open to students enrolled in the first or second year of a J.D. program at an ABA-accredited law school in the United States. Applicants must come from a group historically underrepresented in intellectual property law; that underrepresentation may be the result of race, sex, ethnicity, sexual orientation, or disability. Selection is based on academic merit, commitment to the pursuit of a career in intellectual property law, written communication skills, oral communication skills (determined through an interview), leadership qualities, and community involvement.
Financial data The stipend is $5,000 per year.
Duration 1 year (the second or third year of law school); students who accept and successfully complete the firm's summer associate program may receive an additional $5,000 for a subsequent semester of law school.
Number awarded 1 or more each year.
Deadline September of each year.

[1221]
EATON MULTICULTURAL SCHOLARS PROGRAM
Eaton Corporation
Attn: EMSP
1111 Superior Avenue
Cleveland, OH 44114-2584
(216) 523-4354   E-mail: mildredneumann@eaton.com
Web: www.eaton.com

Purpose To provide financial assistance and work experience to Native American and other minority college students interested in a career in designated fields.
Eligibility This program is open to full-time minority students who are U.S. citizens or permanent residents. Applicants must have completed 1 year in an accredited program and have 3 remaining years of course work before completing a bachelor's degree. They must be majoring in information technology, engineering, supplier resource management, or accounting. Selection is based on academic performance, the student's school recommendation, and an expressed interest in pursuing challenging and rewarding internship assignments.
Financial data Stipends range from $500 to $3,000 per year. Funds are paid directly to the recipient's university to cover the cost of tuition, books, supplies, equipment, and fees.
Duration 3 years.
Additional information In addition to the scholarships, recipients are offered paid summer internships at company headquarters in Cleveland. The target schools participating in this program recently were Cornell, Detroit-Mercy, Florida

A&M, Georgia Tech, Illinois at Chicago, Illinois at Urbana-Champaign, Lawrence Technological, Marquette, Massachusetts Institute of Technology, Michigan at Ann Arbor, Michigan at Dearborn, Michigan State, Milwaukee School of Engineering, Minnesota, Morehouse College, North Carolina A&T State, North Carolina State, Northwestern, Notre Dame, Ohio State, Purdue, Southern, Tennessee, Western Michigan, and Wisconsin at Madison. This program was established in 1994. Until 2002, it was known as the Eaton Minority Engineering Scholars Program.

Number awarded Varies each year; a total of $150,000 is available for this program annually.

Deadline December of each year.

[1222]
EISENHOWER GRANTS FOR RESEARCH AND INTERN FELLOWSHIPS

Department of Transportation
Federal Highway Administration
Attn: Office of Professional and Corporate
   Development, HPC-32
4600 North Fairfax Drive, Suite 800
Arlington, VA 22203-1553
(703) 235-0538   Toll-free: (877) 558-6873
Fax: (703) 235-0593
E-mail: transportationedu@dot.gov
Web: www.fhwa.dot.gov/opd/universitygrants.htm

Purpose To enable minority and other students to participate in transportation-related research activities either at facilities of the U.S. Department of Transportation (DOT) Federal Highway Administration in the Washington, D.C. area or as interns for private or public organizations.

Eligibility This program is open to 1) students in their junior year of a baccalaureate program who will complete their junior year before being awarded a fellowship; 2) students in their senior year of a baccalaureate program; and 3) students who have completed their baccalaureate degree and are enrolled in a program leading to a master's, Ph.D., or equivalent degree. Applicants must be enrolled full time at an accredited U.S institution of higher education and planning to enter the transportation profession after completing their higher education. They must be U.S. citizens or have an I-20 (foreign student) or I-551 (permanent resident) identification card. For research fellowships, they select 1 or more projects from a current list of research activities underway at various DOT facilities; the research is conducted with academic supervision provided by a faculty adviser from their home university (which grants academic credit for the research project) and with technical direction provided by the DOT staff. Intern fellowships provide students with opportunities to perform transportation-related research, development, technology transfer, and other activities at public and private sector organizations. Specific requirements for the target projects vary; most require engineering backgrounds, but others involve transportation planning, information management, public administration, physics, materials science, statistical analysis, operations research, chemistry, economics, technology transfer, urban studies, geography, and urban and regional planning. The DOT encourages students at Historically Black Colleges and Universities (HBCUs), Hispanic Serving Institutions (HSIs), and Tribal Colleges and Universities (TCUs) to apply for these grants. Selection is based on the match of the student's qualifications with the proposed research project (including the student's ability to accomplish the project in the available time), recommendation letters regarding the nominee's qualifications to conduct the research, academic records (including class standing, GPA, and transcripts), and transportation work experience (if any), including the employer's endorsement.

Financial data Fellows receive full tuition and fees that relate to the academic credits for the approved research project (to a maximum of $10,000) and a monthly stipend of $1,450 for undergraduates, $1,700 for master's students, or $2,000 for doctoral students. An allowance for travel to and from the DOT facility where the research is conducted is also provided, but selectees are responsible for their own housing accommodations. Recipients are also provided with a 1-time allowance of up to $1,500 to attend the annual Transportation Research Board (TRB) meeting.

Duration Projects normally range from 3 to 12 months.

Number awarded Varies each year; recently, 9 students participated in this program.

Deadline Applications remain open until each project is filled.

[1223]
EMMA L. BOWEN FOUNDATION INTERNSHIPS

Emma L. Bowen Foundation
Attn: President and CEO
1299 Pennsylvania Avenue, N.W., Ninth Floor
Washington, DC 20004
(202) 637-4494   Fax: (202) 637-4495
E-mail: phyllis.eagle-oldson@corporate.ge.com
Web: www.emmabowenfoundation.com

Purpose To provide Native American and other minority students with an opportunity to gain work experience during the summer at participating media companies.

Eligibility This program is open to minority students who are rising high school seniors, graduating high school seniors, or college freshmen. Applicants must be interested in working at a media company during the summer and school breaks until they graduate from college. They must have a GPA of 3.0 or higher, plans to attend an accredited 4-year college or university, and an interest in the media industry as a career. Along with their application, they must submit an essay of 500 to 1,000 words on how the media industry helps to create the images that influence our decisions and perceptions on a daily basis.

Financial data Interns receive a stipend of approximately $2,500 and matching compensation of $2,500 to help pay for college tuition and other expenses.

Duration 1 summer; may be renewed until the intern graduates from college if he or she maintains a GPA of 3.0 or higher.

Additional information This program was established in 1989. The sponsoring companies have included ABC, Inc., Arbitron, Inc. Broadcast Music Inc., CBS Incorporated, Comcast Foundation, C-SPAN, Fox Television Stations, Inc., Gannett Television, NBC Universal, Turner Entertainment Networks, and the Weather Channel. Students in eastern states should contact the Vice President, Eastern Region. 524 West 57th Street, New York, NY 10019, (212) 975-2545, Fax: (212) 975-5884, E-mail: sdrice@cbs.com. Students in western states should contact the Vice President, Western Region, CBS Studio Center, Editorial 2, Suite 1, 4024 Radford Avenue, Studio City, CA 91604, (818) 655-5708, Fax: (818) 655-8358.

Number awarded Approximately 60 to 70 new interns are selected each year.

Deadline January of each year.

[1224]
ENDOCRINE SOCIETY SUMMER RESEARCH FELLOWSHIPS

Endocrine Society
Attn: Summer Research Fellowships
8401 Connecticut Avenue, Suite 900
Chevy Chase, MD 20815
(301) 951-2616 Toll-free: (888) 363-6274
Fax: (301) 576-7787
E-mail: awards@endo-society.org
Web: www.endo-society.org

Purpose To provide funding to minority and other undergraduate, medical, and graduate students interested in conducting a summer research project in endocrinology.

Eligibility This program is open to full-time students who are undergraduates in the third year of study or higher, medical students beyond their first year of study, and first-year graduate students. Applicants must be interested in participating in a research project under the supervision of a mentor. The mentor must be an active member of the Endocrine Society. Each member may sponsor only 1 student. Projects must be relevant to an aspect of endocrinology and are expected to have clearly defined research goals; students should not function as aides or general research assistants. Applications on behalf of underrepresented minority students are especially encouraged.

Financial data The grant of $4,000 provides funding for a stipend, fringe benefits, and indirect costs.

Duration 10 to 12 weeks during the summer.

Additional information At the conclusion of the fellowship period, students must submit a 1-page summary of their research project explaining how the fellowship affected their consideration of a career in endocrinology.

Number awarded 20 each year.

Deadline January of each year.

[1225]
ENERGY RESOURCE DEVELOPMENT TRIBAL INTERNSHIP PROGRAM

Argonne National Laboratory
Division of Educational Programs
Attn: Tribal Internship Program
9700 South Cass Avenue
Argonne, IL 60439-4845
(630) 252-3366 Fax: (630) 252-3193
E-mail: Lreed@dep.anl.gov
Web: www.dep.anl.gov

Purpose To provide Native American undergraduate students with an opportunity to work on summer research projects at Argonne National Laboratory (ANL).

Eligibility This program is open to undergraduate students who are members of federally-recognized tribes, Alaska villages, and Alaska corporations; members of bands or groups of state-recognized tribes, and first peoples of Guam or Hawaii are not eligible. Applicants must be U.S. citizens who are 18 years of age or older and have a GPA of 2.5 or higher. They must be interested in working at ANL on a summer project related to energy resource development, both renewable and nonrenewable, and environmental evaluation and analysis of potential impacts from energy resource developmental activities. Research projects involve wind energy, solar energy, fuel cells, hydrogen storage, advanced fuels, lithium batteries, environmental and economic systems analysis, production of chemicals from renewable resources, climate change, and environmental impact assessments.

Financial data Interns receive housing allowances, reimbursement of transportation expenses (up to $350), and a stipend of $400 per week.

Duration 10 weeks, beginning at the end of May.

Additional information This program was established in 2009 in cooperation with the Council of Energy Resource Tribes (CERT), which recruits applicants from public, private, and Tribal institutions of higher learning and selects the interns.

Number awarded 10 each year.

Deadline April of each year.

[1226]
EPA GREATER RESEARCH OPPORTUNITIES (GRO) FELLOWSHIPS FOR UNDERGRADUATE ENVIRONMENTAL STUDY

Environmental Protection Agency
Attn: National Center for Environmental Research
Ariel Rios Building
1200 Pennsylvania Avenue, N.W.
Washington, DC 20460
(202) 343-9741 Toll-free: (800) 490-9194
E-mail: boddie.georgette@epa.gov
Web: es.epa.gov/ncer/rfa

Purpose To provide financial assistance and summer internships to minority and other undergraduates who are enrolled at colleges and universities that receive limited federal funding and who are interested in majoring in fields related to the environment.

Eligibility This program is open to U.S. citizens or permanent residents who are enrolled full time at a college or university in this country that receives less than $35 million in federal research and development expenditures. That includes, but is not limited to, Minority Serving Institutions, defined as Historically Black Colleges and Universities (HBCUs), Hispanic Serving Institutions (HSIs), Tribal Colleges and Universities (TCUs), Native Hawaiian Serving Institutions (NHSIs), and Alaska Native Serving Institutions (ANSIs). Applicants must have at least 2 years remaining for completion of a bachelor's degree and must be majoring in environmental science, physical sciences, natural and life sciences, mathematics and computer science, social sciences, economics, or engineering. They must be available to work as interns at an EPA facility during the summer between their junior and senior years. A goal of the program is to meet the need for scientists from diverse cultural backgrounds, so the sponsor strongly encourages women, minorities, and persons with disabilities to apply. A minimum GPA of 3.0 is required.

Financial data The fellowship provides up to $17,000 per year, including up to $10,000 for tuition and academic fees, a stipend of $4,500 ($500 per month for 9 months), and an expense allowance of up to $2,500 for items and activities for the direct benefit of the student's education, such as books, supplies, and travel to professional conferences and workshops. The summer internship grant is $7,500, including a stipend of $6,000, an allowance of $1,000 for travel to and from the site, and an allowance of $500 for travel while at the site.
Duration The final 2 years of baccalaureate study, including 12 weeks during the summer between those years.
Additional information This program began in 1982. It was formerly known as Culturally Diverse Academic Institutions Undergraduate Student Fellowships program and subsequently as Minority Academic Institutions Undergraduate Student Fellowships.
Number awarded Approximately 15 each year.
Deadline November of each year.

[1227]
ETHNIC MINORITY AND WOMEN'S INTERNSHIP GRANT PROGRAM
National Collegiate Athletic Association
Attn: Office for Diversity and Inclusion
700 West Washington Avenue
P.O. Box 6222
Indianapolis, IN 46206-6222
(317) 917-6222   Fax: (317) 917-6888
E-mail: kdavis@ncaa.org
Web: www.ncaa.org/about/scholarships.html
Purpose To provide work experience at Division III institutions of the National Collegiate Athletic Association (NCAA) to women or minority college graduates.
Eligibility This program is open to women and ethnic minorities who have completed the requirements for an undergraduate degree. Applicants must have demonstrated a commitment to prepare for a career in intercollegiate athletics and the ability to succeed in such a career. They must be selected by an NCAA Division III college or university to work full time in athletics administration.
Financial data Grants provide $20,100 per year as a stipend for the intern and $3,000 to cover the cost of attendance at professional development activities.
Duration 2 years.
Number awarded Up to 15 each year.
Deadline February of each year.

[1228]
EXPLORATIONS IN BIOMEDICINE UNDERGRADUATE SUMMER RESEARCH FELLOWSHIPS FOR NATIVE AMERICAN STUDENTS
American Physiological Society
Attn: Education Office
9650 Rockville Pike, Room 3111
Bethesda, MD 20814-3991
(301) 634-7132   Fax: (301) 634-7098
E-mail: education@the-aps.org
Web: www.the-aps.org
Purpose To provide an opportunity for Native American undergraduate students to work in the laboratory of an established physiological investigator during the summer.
Eligibility This program is open to Native American undergraduate students who are interested in learning more about biomedical research. Applicants may have had little or no laboratory or research experience in physiology or the life sciences, but they must be interested in working during the summer in the laboratory of an established investigator who is a member of the American Physiological Society (APS). Along with their application, they must submit a 1-page personal statement that 1) describes their background, achievements, interests, and short-term goals; 2) describes their long-term career goals; and 3) comments on why they are applying for this fellowship. Selection is based on the value of the research experience to the student.
Financial data Awardees receive a stipend of $3,500 to $4,000 and an allowance of up to $3,500 for summer housing and travel costs if they have to move beyond commuting distance. In addition, they are eligible for a travel grant of up to $1,000 to attend the Experimental Biology meeting. The faculty sponsor/adviser receives an unrestricted grant of $1,000.
Duration 8 to 10 weeks during the summer.
Number awarded Varies each year; recently, 14 of these fellowships were awarded.
Deadline January of each year.

[1229]
FACULTY AND STUDENT TEAMS (FAST) PROGRAM
Department of Energy
Attn: Office of Science
1000 Independence Avenue, S.W.
Washington, DC 20585
(202) 586-9742   Toll-free: (800) DIAL-DOE
Fax: (202) 586-0019
E-mail: sc.helpwithapplication@science.doe.gov
Web: www.scied.science.doe.gov
Purpose To provide support to faculty-student teams, especially those from institutions serving women and minorities, interested in working during the summer on research projects at designated laboratories of the Department of Energy.
Eligibility This program is open to teams of faculty and students from 1) colleges, universities with limited research facilities, and 2) those institutions serving populations, women, and minorities underrepresented in the fields of science, engineering, and technology. Faculty applicants must be U.S. citizens or permanent residents. Students must be

currently enrolled as undergraduates, have completed at least 1 semester of college work, be U.S. citizens or permanent residents, and have coverage under a health insurance plan. Preference is given to faculty at community colleges; at universities and colleges that are in the 50th percentile or lower of total federal funding; and those associated with 1 of the following programs supported by the National Science Foundation (NSF): Tribal Colleges and Universities Program (TCUP), Historically Black Colleges and Universities Undergraduate Program (HBCU-UP), Louis Stokes Alliances for Minority Participation (LSAMP), Centers of Research Excellence in Science and Technology (CREST), Advanced Technology Education (ATE), Computer Science, Engineering, and Mathematics Scholarships (CSEMS), Centers for Learning and Teaching (CLT), Gender Diversity in STEM Education (GDSE), Math and Science Partnership (MSP), Collaboratives for Excellence in Teacher Preparation (CETP), Science, Technology, Engineering and Mathematics Teacher Preparation (STEMTP), and Program for Persons with Disabilities (PPD).

Financial data Students receive a stipend of $4,500, allocated as 10 weekly stipends of $400 each and up to $500 for travel. Faculty members receive a stipend equal to 2/9 of their academic year salary, up to $12,000. Both student and faculty team members receive funding assistance with travel and housing. An additional grant of $1,000 is available as support for unusual travel expenses incurred by people with disabilities.

Duration 10 weeks during the summer. Students may participate in only 2 of these projects.

Additional information Teams work on specified projects at the following Department of Energy facilities: Argonne National Laboratory in Argonne, Illinois; Brookhaven National Laboratory in Upton, New York; Lawrence Berkeley National Laboratory in Berkeley, California; Lawrence Livermore National Laboratory in Livermore, California; Oak Ridge National Laboratory in Oak Ridge, Tennessee; or Pacific Northwest National Laboratory in Richland, Washington.

Number awarded Varies each year.
Deadline January of each year.

[1230]
FAEGRE & BENSON DIVERSITY SCHOLARSHIP
Faegre & Benson LLP
Attn: Manager of Legal Personnel Services
2200 Wells Fargo Center
90 South Seventh Street
Minneapolis, MN 55402
(612) 766-7209   Toll-free: (800) 328-4393
Fax: (612) 766-1600   E-mail: dgray@faegre.com
Web: www.faegre.com/diversityscholarship

Purpose To provide financial assistance and work experience to Native American and other law students who will contribute to diversity in the legal profession.

Eligibility This program is open to students enrolled in the first year at an accredited law school in the United States. Applicants must submit a 500-word personal statement explaining their interest in the scholarship program, how diversity has influenced their life, and how it impacts the legal profession. Selection is based on that statement, a resume, undergraduate transcripts, a legal writing sample, and 2 professional recommendations.

Financial data The stipend is $6,000 per year.
Duration 2 years: the second and third year of law school.
Additional information Recipients are also offered an associateship during the summer between the first and second year at an office of the firm in Minneapolis, Denver, Boulder, or Des Moines. An attorney from the firm is assigned as a mentor to help them adjust to the firm and to the legal profession.

Number awarded 2 each year.
Deadline January of each year.

[1231]
FEDERAL AVIATION ADMINISTRATION ASIAN AMERICAN/PACIFIC ISLANDER AND NATIVE AMERICAN/ALASKAN NATIVE INTERNSHIP PROGRAM
Oak Ridge Institute for Science and Education
Attn: Science and Engineering Education
P.O. Box 117
Oak Ridge, TN 37831-0117
(865) 576-3409   Fax: (865) 241-5220
E-mail: PressleP@orau.gov
Web: see.orau.org

Purpose To enable postsecondary students and recent graduates to participate in ongoing research programs of the U.S. Federal Aviation Administration (FAA).

Eligibility This program is open to U.S. citizens who are either currently enrolled in an accredited college or university as an undergraduate or graduate student or a recent graduate. The program is limited to Asian American, Pacific Islander, Native American, and Alaskan Native students and graduates. Applicants must have a GPA of 3.0 or higher and be studying in a field related to the work of the FAA, including aviation research, computer sciences, engineering (aerospace, civil, computer, electrical, electronics, mechanical), law, mathematics, science, and other aviation safety and security studies. disciplines. They must be interested in participating in ongoing FAA research and related technologies at various sites across the United States.

Financial data The stipend is $450 per week. Also provided are a housing allowance of $150 per week, limited travel reimbursement, and accident and medical insurance.

Duration 10 weeks during the summer or 15 weeks during the semester.

Additional information This program is funded by the FAA and administered by Oak Ridge Institute for Science and Education (ORISE).

Number awarded Varies each year.
Deadline February of each year for summer; any time for semester programs.

[1232]
FINNEGAN HENDERSON DIVERSITY SCHOLARSHIP

Finnegan, Henderson, Farabow, Garrett & Dunner, LLP
Attn: Director of Professional Recruitment and Development
901 New York Avenue, N.W.
Washington, D.C. 20001-4413
(202) 408-4034   Fax: (202) 408-4400
E-mail: diversityscholarship@finnegan.com
Web: www.finnegan.com

Purpose To provide financial assistance and work experience to Native American and other underrepresented minority law students interested in a career in intellectual property law.

Eligibility This program is open to law students from underrepresented minority groups who have demonstrated a commitment to a career in intellectual property law and are currently enrolled either as a first-year full-time student or second-year part-time student. The sponsor defines underrepresented minorities to include American Indians/Alaskan Natives, Blacks/African Americans, Asian Americans, Native Hawaiians or other Pacific Islanders, and Hispanics/Latinos. Applicants must have earned an undergraduate degree in life sciences, engineering, or computer science, or have substantial prior trademark experience. Selection is based on academic performance at the undergraduate, graduate (if applicable), and law school level; relevant work experience; community service; leadership skills; and special accomplishments.

Financial data The stipend is $15,000 per year.

Duration 1 year; may be renewed 1 additional year as long as the recipient completes a summer associateship with the sponsor and maintains of GPA of 3.0 or higher.

Additional information The sponsor, the world's largest intellectual property law firm, established this scholarship in 2003. Summer associateships are available at its offices in Washington, D.C.; Atlanta, Georgia; Cambridge, Massachusetts; Palo Alto, California; or Reston, Virginia.

Number awarded 1 each year.

Deadline February of each year.

[1233]
FIRST-YEAR INTERNSHIP PROGRAM OF THE OREGON STATE BAR

Oregon State Bar
Attn: Affirmative Action Program
16037 S.W. Upper Boones Ferry Road
P.O. Box 231935
Tigard, OR 97281-1935
(503) 620-0222, ext. 337
Toll-free: (800) 452-8260, ext. 337 (within OR)
Fax: (503) 684-1366   TTY: (503) 684-7416
E-mail: fgarcia@osbar.org
Web: www.osbar.org/aap

Purpose To provide work experience to minority law students in Oregon.

Eligibility This program is open to Native American and other ethnic minority students from any state who are completing the first year of law school in Oregon. Applicants must be interested in a summer internship at a law firm in the state. Along with their application, they must submit 1) a resume that includes their community activities; 2) up to 10 pages of a first-semester legal writing assignment; and 3) a 2-page personal statement that covers their past and present ties to ethnic minority communities in Oregon and elsewhere, diversity issues that inspired them to become a lawyer, and their expectations of this internship experience. Participating employers receive a catalog with all application packets; they select students whom they wish to interview and make the final hiring decisions.

Financial data Employers who hire interns through this program pay competitive stipends.

Duration Summer months.

Number awarded Varies each year.

Deadline January of each year.

[1234]
FISH & RICHARDSON DIVERSITY FELLOWSHIP PROGRAM

Fish & Richardson P.C.
Attn: Recruiting Department
1717 Main Street, Suite 5000
Dallas, TX 75201
(214) 760-6131   Fax: (214) 747-2091
E-mail: krassy@fr.com
Web: www.fr.com

Purpose To provide financial assistance and work experience to Native Americans and other students who will contribute to diversity in the legal profession.

Eligibility This program is open to students enrolled in the first year at a law school anywhere in the country. Applicants must be African American/Black, American Indian/Alaskan, Hispanic/Latino, Native Hawaiian/Pacific Islander, Asian, 2 or more races, disabled, or openly homosexual, bisexual, and/or transgender. Along with their application, they must submit a 500-word essay describing their background, what led them to the legal field, their interest in the sponsoring law firm, and what they could contribute to its practice and the profession. They must also indicate their first 3 choices of an office of the firm where they are interested in a summer associate clerkship.

Financial data The stipend is $5,000.

Duration 1 year: the second year of law school.

Additional information Recipients are also offered a paid associate clerkship during the summer following their first year of law school at an office of the firm in the location of their choice in Atlanta, Austin, Boston, Dallas, Delaware, New York, San Diego, Silicon Valley, Twin Cities, or Washington, D.C. This program began in 2005.

Number awarded 5 each year.

Deadline January of each year.

INTERNSHIPS

[1235]
FOLK ARTS APPRENTICESHIP AWARDS

State Foundation on Culture and the Arts
Attn: Folk Arts Program
250 South Hotel Street, Second Floor
Honolulu, HI 96813
(808) 586-0736   Fax: (808) 586-0308
TTY: (808) 586-0740   E-mail: sfca@sfca.state.hi.us
Web: www.hawaii.gov/sfca/grants.php?article_id=176

Purpose To enable master folk artists in Hawaii to share their knowledge and skills with experienced individuals.

Eligibility This program is open to practitioners of any traditional art form in any culture in Hawaii. A master artist and an apprentice must apply together as a team for an apprenticeship. It is the responsibility of the applicants to meet and agree to undertake a master-apprentice training relationship with each other prior to submitting the application. Both the master and the apprentice must be residents of Hawaii. Master artists must explain how they learned the traditional art form they wish to teach; how long they have been actively involved in the art form; their community activities, performances, lectures, teaching, and awards; why preserving the art form and their cultural heritage is important to them; why they wish to participate in the apprenticeship; and why they would like to teach the apprentice. Prospective apprentices must explain how they first became interested in the tradition they wish to study; how long they have been actively involved in the tradition; they current skill level; why they wish to participate in the apprenticeship award; why they wish to work with this particular master artist; and how they plan to preserve this tradition and share it with others after their apprenticeship award is completed.

Financial data Grants range from $2,800 to $5,000. Funds are intended to be used to cover fees for the master folk artist and essential material or travel expenses associated with the apprenticeship.

Duration The apprenticeship should involve a minimum of 80 to a maximum of 130 total hours of contact over a period of 6 to 7 months.

Additional information The foundation may wish to document a portion of the apprenticeship with still photographs and/or audio or videotapes. Funding for this program is provided by the State Foundation on Culture and the Arts and the National Endowment for the Arts. Funding is not available for apprenticeships conducted abroad. Similarly, the funds may not be used to cover out-of-state travel expenses. Upon completion of the program, the master folk artist and the apprentice are asked to give a brief community presentation covering what was learned during the course of study.

Number awarded Approximately 17 each year.

Deadline March of each year.

[1236]
FOUR DIRECTIONS SUMMER RESEARCH PROGRAM

Harvard Medical School
Division of Medical Sciences
Attn: Minority Faculty Development Program
260 Longwood Avenue
Boston, MA 02115-5720
(617) 432-4422   Toll-free: (800) 367-9019
Fax: (617) 432-2644   E-mail: info@fdsrp.org
Web: www.fdsrp.org

Purpose To provide an opportunity for Native American undergraduate and graduate students to participate in a summer research project at Harvard Medical School.

Eligibility This program is open to Native American undergraduate and graduate students who are interested in preparing for a career as a physician or in biomedical research. Applicants must have completed at least 1 year of undergraduate study and have taken at least 1 introductory science course (may include biology or chemistry). They must be interested in conducting a research project at Harvard Medical School under the supervision of a scientist engaged in medical or biomedical research, ranging from neurobiology and neuropathology to cell biology and molecular genetics. Selection is based on demonstrated commitment to the health of Native American communities and demonstrated interest in a career in medical sciences. Students from rural state colleges, tribal colleges, and community colleges are especially encouraged to apply.

Financial data The program provides a stipend of at least $2,500, airfare, transportation, and lodging expenses.

Duration 8 weeks during the summer.

Additional information This program began in 1994. Participants may not take the summer MCAT, because the time constraints of this program do not allow time to study for that examination.

Number awarded 6 each year.

Deadline February of each year.

[1237]
FREDRIKSON & BYRON FOUNDATION MINORITY SCHOLARSHIPS

Fredrikson & Byron Foundation
Attn: Attorney Recruiting Administrator
200 South Sixth Street, Suite 4000
Minneapolis, MN 55402-1425
(612) 492-7141   Fax: (612) 492-7077
E-mail: glarson@fredlaw.com
Web: www.fredlaw.com/firm/scholarship.htm

Purpose To provide financial assistance and summer work experience to Native American and other minority law students from any state who are interested in practicing in the Twin Cities area of Minnesota.

Eligibility This program is open to African American, Asian American, Pacific Islander, Hispanic, Native American, and Alaska Native students enrolled in their first year of law school. Applicants must be interested in practicing law in the Minneapolis-St. Paul area. Along with their application, they must submit 2 recommendations, a writing sample from their first-year legal writing course, transcripts from undergraduate and law school, and a resume. Financial need is not considered.

Financial data The fellowship stipend is $10,000. The internship portion of the program provides a $1,000 weekly stipend.
Duration 1 year.
Additional information Fellows are also eligible to participate in an internship at the firm's offices in Minneapolis.
Number awarded 1 each year.
Deadline March of each year.

[1238]
FSNE MULTIMEDIA SCHOLARSHIP

Florida Society of Newspaper Editors
c/o Florida Press Association
2636 Mitcham Drive
Tallahassee, FL 32308
(850) 521-1161   Fax: (850) 577-3611
E-mail: info@fsne.org
Web: www.fsne.org/mmscholar.shtml

Purpose To provide financial assistance to Native American and other minority students from any state who are majoring in journalism or communications at a college or university in Florida and also complete a paid multimedia internship at a newspaper in the state.
Eligibility This program is open to full-time minority students from any state enrolled in accredited journalism or mass communication programs at 4-year colleges and universities in Florida who have a GPA of 2.5 or higher. Preference is given to students between their junior and senior year, but others are welcome to apply. They must first arrange through the normal application process for an internship at a Florida newspaper in the field of multimedia or multiplatform journalism, which includes combinations of print, online, video, and audio journalism. The internship may be at any time during the current calendar year. After their acceptance as an intern, they may apply for this scholarship. Along with their application, they must submit a 300-word autobiographical essay explaining why they want to prepare for a career in journalism and provide a standard resume, references, and clips or examples of relevant classroom work.
Financial data The scholarship stipend is $3,000. Funds are released after the designee successfully completes the internship.
Duration 1 academic year for the scholarship.
Additional information Information is also available from Pat Yack, FSNE Scholarship Committee, The Florida Times-Union, 1 Riverside Avenue, Jacksonville, FL 32202, E-mail: pat.yack@jacksonville.com. This program is sponsored by the John S. and James L. Knight Foundation.
Number awarded 1 each year.
Deadline May of each year.

[1239]
GEM M.S. ENGINEERING FELLOWSHIP PROGRAM

National Consortium for Graduate Degrees for
  Minorities in Engineering and Science (GEM)
Attn: Manager, Fellowships Administration
1800 K Street, N.W., Suite 900
Washington, DC 20006
(202) 457-8688   Fax: (202) 207-3518
E-mail: akee@genfellowship.org
Web: www.gemfellowship.org

Purpose To provide financial assistance and summer work experience to Native American and other underrepresented minority graduate students in engineering.
Eligibility This program is open to U.S. citizens who are members of ethnic groups underrepresented in engineering: Native Americans, African Americans, Latinos, Puerto Ricans, and other Hispanic Americans. Applicants must be enrolled as at least a junior in an ABET-accredited engineering discipline with an academic record that indicates the ability to pursue graduate studies in engineering (including a GPA of 2.8 or higher). Students in computer science and computer engineering may also apply, but engineering technology majors are not eligible. Applicants must be planning to attend 1 of the 100 GEM member universities that offer a master's degree.
Financial data The fellowship pays tuition, fees, and a stipend of $10,000 over its lifetime. In addition, each participant receives a salary during the summer work assignment as a GEM Summer Intern. Employer members reimburse GEM participants for travel expenses to and from the summer work site.
Duration Up to 3 semesters or 4 quarters, plus a summer work internship lasting 10 to 14 weeks for up to 3 summers, depending on whether the student applies as a junior, senior, or college graduate; recipients begin their internship upon acceptance into the program and work each summer until completion of their master's degree.
Additional information During the summer internship, each fellow is assigned an engineering project in a research setting. Each project is based on the fellow's interest and background and is carried out under the supervision of an experienced engineer. At the conclusion of the internship, each fellow writes a project report. Recipients must work on a master's degree in the same engineering discipline as their baccalaureate degree.
Number awarded Varies each year; recently, 327 of these fellowships were awarded.
Deadline October of each year.

[1240]
GEM PH.D. ENGINEERING FELLOWSHIP PROGRAM

National Consortium for Graduate Degrees for
  Minorities in Engineering and Science (GEM)
Attn: Manager, Fellowships Administration
1800 K Street, N.W., Suite 900
Washington, DC 20006
(202) 457-8688   Fax: (202) 207-3518
E-mail: akee@genfellowship.org
Web: www.gemfellowship.org

Purpose To provide financial assistance and summer work experience to Native American and other underrepresented minority students interested in obtaining a Ph.D. degree in engineering.

Eligibility This program is open to U.S. citizens who are members of ethnic groups underrepresented in engineering: American Indians/Native Americans, Blacks/African Americans, and Latinos/Hispanic Americans. Applicants must have completed or be in the process of completing a master's degree in engineering with an academic record that indicates the ability to work on a doctoral degree in engineering (including a GPA of 3.0 or higher).

Financial data The stipend is $14,000 for the first year; in subsequent years, fellows receive full payment of tuition and fees plus a stipend and assistantship from their university that is equivalent to funding received by other doctoral students in their department.

Duration 3 to 5 years for the fellowship; 12 weeks during at least 1 summer for the internship.

Additional information This program is valid only at 1 of 100 participating GEM member universities; write to GEM for a list. The fellowship award is designed to support the student in the first year of the doctoral program without working. Subsequent years are subsidized by the respective universities and will usually include either a teaching or research assistantship. Recipients must participate in the GEM summer internship; failure to agree to accept the internship cancels the fellowship.

Number awarded Varies each year; recently, 49 of these fellowships were awarded.

Deadline October of each year.

[1241]
GEM PH.D. SCIENCE FELLOWSHIP PROGRAM

National Consortium for Graduate Degrees for
    Minorities in Engineering and Science (GEM)
Attn: Manager, Fellowships Administration
1800 K Street, N.W., Suite 900
Washington, DC 20006
(202) 457-8688   Fax: (202) 207-3518
E-mail: akee@genfellowship.org
Web: www.gemfellowship.org

Purpose To provide financial assistance and summer work experience to Native American and other underrepresented minority students interested in working on a Ph.D. degree in the life sciences, mathematics, or physical sciences.

Eligibility This program is open to U.S. citizens who are members of ethnic groups underrepresented in the natural sciences: American Indians/Native Americans, Blacks/African Americans, and Latinos/Hispanic Americans. Applicants must be college juniors, seniors, master's degree students, or recent graduates in the biological sciences, mathematics, or physical sciences (chemistry, computer science, earth sciences, and physics) with an academic record that indicates the ability to pursue doctoral studies (including a GPA of 3.0 or higher).

Financial data The stipend is $14,000 for the first year; in subsequent years, fellows receive full payment of tuition and fees plus a stipend and assistantship from their university that is equivalent to funding received by other doctoral students in their department.

Duration 3 to 5 years for the fellowship; 12 weeks during at least 1 summer for the internship. Fellows selected as juniors or seniors intern each summer until entrance to graduate school; fellows selected after college graduation intern at least 1 summer.

Additional information This program is valid only at 1 of 100 participating GEM member universities; write to GEM for a list. The fellowship award is designed to support the student in the first year of the doctoral program without working. Subsequent years are subsidized by the respective university and will usually include either a teaching or research assistantship. Recipients must participate in the GEM summer internship; failure to agree to accept the internship cancels the fellowship. Recipients must enroll in the same scientific discipline as their undergraduate major.

Number awarded Varies each year; recently, 40 of these fellowships were awarded.

Deadline October of each year.

[1242]
GEOPHYSICAL FLUID DYNAMICS FELLOWSHIPS

Woods Hole Oceanographic Institution
Attn: Education Office
Clark Laboratory 223, MS 31
360 Woods Hole Road
Woods Hole, MA 02543-1541
(508) 289-2219   Fax: (508) 457-2188
E-mail: gfd@whoi.edu
Web: gfd.whoi.edu/index.html

Purpose To provide research and study opportunities at Woods Hole Oceanographic Institution (WHOI) to minority and other pre- and postdoctoral scholars interested in geophysical fluid dynamics.

Eligibility This program is open to pre- and postdoctorates who are interested in pursuing research or study opportunities in a field that involves nonlinear dynamics of rotating, stratified fluids. Fields of specialization include oceanography, meteorology, geophysics, astrophysics, engineering, physics, and applied mathematics. Applications from women and members of underrepresented groups are particularly encouraged.

Financial data Participants receive a stipend of $4,900 and an allowance for travel expenses within the United States.

Duration 10 weeks during the summer.

Additional information Each summer, the program at WHOI revolves around a central theme. A recent theme related to boundary layers. The main components of the summer program are a series of principal lectures, a set of supplementary research seminars, and research projects conducted by the student fellows with the active support of the staff. Funding for this program, which began in 1959, is provided by the National Science Foundation and Office of Naval Research.

Number awarded Up to 10 graduate students are supported each year.

Deadline February of each year.

[1243]
GEORGE V. POWELL DIVERSITY SCHOLARSHIP

Lane Powell Spears Lubersky LLP
Attn: Manager of Attorney Recruiting
1420 Fifth Avenue, Suite 4100
Seattle, WA 98101-2338
(206) 223-6123 Fax: (206) 223-7107
E-mail: rodenl@lanepowell.com
Web: www.lanepowell.com/firm/scholarship.asp

Purpose To provide financial assistance and work experience to Native American and other law students who will contribute to the diversity of the legal community.

Eligibility This program is open to second-year students in good standing at an ABA-accredited law school. Applicants must be able to contribute meaningfully to the diversity of the legal community and have a demonstrated desire to work, live, and eventually practice law in Seattle or Portland. They must submit a cover letter including a statement indicating eligibility to participate in the program, resume, current copy of law school transcript, legal writing sample, and list of 2 or 3 professional or academic references. Selection is based on academic achievement and record of leadership abilities, community service, and involvement in community issues.

Financial data The program provides a stipend of $6,000 for the third year of law school and a paid summer associate clerkship.

Duration 1 year, including the summer.

Additional information This program was established in 2005. Clerkships are provided at the offices of the sponsor in Seattle or Portland.

Number awarded 1 each year.

Deadline September of each year.

[1244]
GLENN-STOKES SUMMER RESEARCH INTERNSHIP PROGRAM

Ohio Science and Engineering Alliance
c/o Ohio State University
247 University Hall
230 North Oval Mall
Columbus, OH 43210-1366
(614) 247-7267
Web: www.ohiosea.org/research/su_prog.html

Purpose To provide an opportunity for Native American and other underrepresented minority students at designated institutions in Ohio to work on a summer research project in a field of science, technology, engineering, or mathematics (STEM).

Eligibility This program is open to students at the 15 member institutions of the Ohio Science and Engineering Alliance (OSEA) who are members of underrepresented minority racial or ethnic groups (African Americans, Hispanics, American Indians, Pacific Islanders, and Puerto Ricans). Applicants must be interested in conducting a summer research project at any OSEA member institution under the mentorship of a faculty member. The proposed research may relate to any approved STEM field.

Financial data Interns receive a stipend of $3,000, a room and board allowance of $500, and payment of summer tuition and fees (if they are required to register).

Duration Summer months.

Additional information The OSEA, funded by the National Science Foundation, consists of the following Ohio institutions: Bowling Green State University, Case Western Reserve University, Central State University, Cleveland State University, Kent State University, Miami University, Ohio State University, Ohio University, University of Akron, University of Cincinnati, University of Dayton, University of Toledo, Wilberforce University, Wright State University, and Youngstown State University. This program is named in honor of John Glenn (Ohio Senator and astronaut) and Louis Stokes (Ohio Congressman).

Number awarded Varies each year.

Deadline February of each year.

[1245]
GOALI UNDERGRADUATE STUDENT INDUSTRIAL FELLOWSHIPS/TRAINEESHIPS

National Science Foundation
Directorate for Engineering
Attn: Division of Industrial Innovation and Partnerships
4201 Wilson Boulevard, Room 550 S
Arlington, VA 22230
(703) 292-7082 Fax: (703) 292-9056
TDD: (800) 281-8749 E-mail: dsenich@nsf.gov
Web: www.nsf.gov

Purpose To provide an opportunity for minority and other undergraduate students to work in industry as part of the Grant Opportunities for Academic Liaison with Industry (GOALI) program of the National Science Foundation (NSF).

Eligibility This program is open to undergraduate students in science, engineering, and mathematics fields of interest to NSF. Applicants must be U.S. citizens, nationals, or permanent residents. They must be proposing a program of full- or part-time work in industry in an area related to their academic program under the guidance of an academic adviser and an industrial mentor. The program encourages applications from women, underrepresented minorities, and persons with disabilities.

Financial data Undergraduate students may receive stipends from $500 to $800 per week; they may also receive some assistance with housing or travel expenses, or both. No indirect costs are allowed. The total award may be up to $10,000 for a fellowship for a single student.

Duration Support may be provided for a summer project, or for 1 or 2 semesters of part- or full-time work.

Additional information This program is also offered by most other NSF directorates. Check the website for a name and e-mail address of the contact person in each directorate.

Number awarded A total of 60 to 80 grants for all GOALI programs is awarded each year; total funding is approximately $5 million.

Deadline Applications may be submitted at any time.

[1246]
GOLDMAN SACHS MBA FELLOWSHIP
Goldman, Sachs & Company
Attn: Human Capital Management
Diversity Recruiting
180 Maiden Lane, 23rd Floor
New York, NY 10038
(212) 855-6184   E-mail: martin.rodriguez@gs.com
Web: www2.goldmansachs.com

Purpose To provide financial assistance and work experience to Native American and other underrepresented minority students interested in working on an M.B.A. degree at designated universities.

Eligibility This program is open to graduate students of Black, Hispanic, and Native American descent. Applicants must be interested in working on an M.B.A. degree at Columbia University Business School, the Fuqua School of Business at Duke University, Harvard Business School, Sloan School of Management at Massachusetts Institute of Technology, the Kellogg School of Management at Northwestern University, Stanford Graduate School of Business, Anderson School of Management at the University of California at Los Angeles, University of Chicago Graduate School of Business, the Ross School of Business at the University of Michigan, or the Wharton School at the University of Pennsylvania. Along with their application, they must submit 2 essays of 500 words or less on the following topics: 1) their interest in preparing for a career in the investment banking industry; and 2) their current involvement with a community-based organization. Selection is based on analytical skills and the ability to identify significant problems, gather facts, and analyze situations in depth; interpersonal skills, including, but not limited to, poise, confidence, and professionalism; academic record; evidence of hard work and commitment; ability to work well with others; and commitment to community involvement.

Financial data Fellows receive tuition for the first year of business school; a summer internship at a domestic office of Goldman Sachs; and (after successful completion of the summer internship and acceptance of an offer to return to the firm after graduation as a full-time regular employee) payment of tuition costs for the second year of business school.

Duration Up to 2 years.

Additional information This program was initiated in 1997.

Number awarded 1 or more each year.

Deadline April of each year.

[1247]
GOLDMAN SACHS SCHOLARSHIP FOR EXCELLENCE
Goldman, Sachs & Company
Attn: Human Capital Management
Diversity Recruiting
180 Maiden Lane, 23rd Floor
New York, NY 10038
(212) 855-6184   E-mail: cindy.joseph@gs.com
Web: www2.goldmansachs.com

Purpose To provide financial assistance and work experience to Native American and other underrepresented minority students preparing for a career in the financial services industry.

Eligibility This program is open to undergraduate students of Black, Hispanic, and Native American heritage. Applicants must be entering their sophomore or junior year with a GPA of 3.4 or higher. Students with all majors and disciplines are encouraged to apply, but they must be able to demonstrate an interest in the financial services industry. Along with their application, they must submit 2 essays of 500 words or fewer on the following topics: 1) why they are interested in the financial services industry; and 2) their current involvement with a campus or community-based organization. Selection is based on academic achievement, interest in the financial services industry, community involvement, and demonstrated leadership and teamwork capabilities.

Financial data Sophomores receive a stipend of $5,000, a summer internship at Goldman Sachs that pays a salary of $7,500, an opportunity to receive a second award upon successful completion of the internship, and an offer to return for a second summer internship. Juniors receive a stipend of $7,500 and a summer internship at Goldman Sachs that pays a salary of $7,500.

Duration Up to 2 years.

Additional information This program was initiated in 1994 when it served only students at 4 designated Historically Black Colleges and Universities: Florida A&M University, Howard University, Morehouse College, and Spelman College. It has since been expanded to serve underrepresented minority students in all states.

Number awarded 1 or more each year.

Deadline December of each year.

[1248]
GRADUATE STUDENT INDUSTRIAL FELLOWSHIPS/TRAINEESHIPS
National Science Foundation
Directorate for Engineering
Attn: Division of Industrial Innovation and Partnerships
4201 Wilson Boulevard, Room 550 S
Arlington, VA 22230
(703) 292-7082   Fax: (703) 292-9056
TDD: (800) 281-8749   E-mail: dsenich@nsf.gov
Web: www.nsf.gov

Purpose To provide an opportunity for minority and other graduate students to work in industry as part of the Grant Opportunities for Academic Liaison with Industry (GOALI) program of the National Science Foundation (NSF).

Eligibility This program is open to graduate students (preferably Ph.D. students) in science, engineering, and mathematics fields of interest to NSF. Applicants must be U.S. citizens, nationals, or permanent residents. They must be proposing a program of full- or part-time work in industry in an area related to their research under the guidance of an academic adviser and an industrial mentor. The program encourages applications from women, underrepresented minorities, and persons with disabilities.

Financial data Graduate students may receive stipends from $1,500 to $1,800 per month, plus transportation expenses. The faculty adviser may receive 10% of the total award for research-related expenses, excluding equipment.

No indirect costs are allowed. The total award may be up to $30,000 for a fellowship for a single student.
Duration Up to 1 year.
Additional information This program is also offered by most other NSF directorates. Check the website for a name and e-mail address of the contact person in each directorate.
Number awarded A total of 60 to 80 grants for all GOALI programs is awarded each year; total funding is approximately $5 million.
Deadline Applications may be submitted at any time.

[1249]
HARTER SECREST & EMERY LLP DIVERSITY SCHOLARSHIP
Harter Secrest & Emery LLP
Attn: Director of Legal Recruiting and Development
1600 Bausch & Lomb Place
Rochester, NY 14604
(585) 231-1292   Fax: (585) 232-2152
E-mail: ehofmeister@hselaw.com
Web: www.hselaw.com/AboutHSE/Diversity

Purpose To provide summer work experience (in Rochester, New York) and financial assistance to Native American and other law students from any state who will contribute to the diversity of the legal profession.
Eligibility This program is open to students who are currently enrolled full time in their first year at an accredited law school. Members of racial, ethnic, and other minority groups are encouraged to apply. They must also be interested in a summer associateship at the sponsoring law firm's main office in Rochester, New York. Along with their application, they must submit a 750-word essay on 1 of the following topics: 1) how their diverse status has influenced their decision to become a lawyer and how it will influence them throughout their professional career; 2) how their personal and professional accomplishments are an indicator of their potential for making a substantial contribution to the legal profession; or 3) a challenge they have faced, how they met the challenge, and how it will influence the role they play in the legal profession. Selection is based on academic record, interest, promise of a successful career during the remainder of law school and in the legal profession, and contribution to the diversity of the student body at law school. A disclosure of financial circumstances is not required, but a demonstrated need for financial assistance may be taken into consideration. The top 2 finalists are invited to an interview.
Financial data The salary for the summer associateship is the same as for all associates of the firm. The stipend for the academic year is $5,000, paid directly to the student's law school.
Duration The summer associateship is for 12 weeks following the first year of law school. The academic stipend is for the second year.
Additional information This program was established in 2005.
Number awarded 1 each year.
Deadline January of each year.

[1250]
HARVARD SCHOOL OF PUBLIC HEALTH UNDERGRADUATE MINORITY SUMMER INTERNSHIP PROGRAM
Harvard School of Public Health
Attn: Division of Biological Sciences
655 Huntington Avenue, Building 1-1312
Boston, MA 02115
(617) 432-4470   Fax: (617) 432-0433
E-mail: dbs@hsph.harvard.edu
Web: apps.sph.harvard.edu/apps/bph/summer.cfm

Purpose To enable Native American and other minority college science students to participate in a summer research internship in biological sciences at Harvard School of Public Health.
Eligibility This program is open to 1) members of ethnic groups underrepresented in graduate education (African Americans, Hispanics/Latinos, American Indians/Alaskan Natives, Pacific Islanders, and biracial/multiracial), and 2) first-generation college students. Applicants must be entering their junior or senior year and interested in preparing for a research career in the biological sciences. They must be interested in participating in a summer research project related to biological science questions that are important to the prevention of disease, especially such public health questions as cancer, infections (malaria, tuberculosis, parasites), lung diseases, common diseases of aging, diabetes, and obesity.
Financial data The program provides a stipend of at least $3,460, a travel allowance of up to $475, and free dormitory housing.
Duration 10 weeks, beginning in mid-June.
Additional information Interns conduct research under the mentorship of Harvard faculty members who are specialists in cancer cell biology, immunology and infectious diseases, molecular and cellular toxicology, environmental health sciences, nutrition, and cardiovascular research. Funding for this program is provided by the National Institutes of Health.
Number awarded Up to 12 each year.
Deadline January of each year.

[1251]
IBM PHD FELLOWSHIP PROGRAM
IBM Corporation
Attn: University Relations
1133 Westchester Avenue
White Plains, NY 10604
Toll-free: (800) IBM-4YOU   TTY: (800) IBM-3383
E-mail: phdfellow@us.ibm.com
Web: www-304.ibm.com

Purpose To provide funding and work experience to Native American and other students working on a Ph.D. in a research area of broad interest to IBM.
Eligibility Students nominated for this fellowship should be enrolled full time at an accredited college or university and should have completed at least 1 year of graduate study in the following fields: business sciences (including financial services, communication, and learning/knowledge); computer science and engineering; electrical and mechanical engineering; management; mathematical sciences (including optimization); physical sciences

(including chemistry, materials sciences, and physics); or service sciences. They should be planning a career in research. Nominations must be made by a faculty member and endorsed by the department head. The program values diversity, and encourages nominations of women, minorities, and others who contribute to that diversity. Selection is based on the applicants' potential for research excellence, the degree to which their technical interests align with those of IBM, and academic progress to date.

Financial data Fellowships pay tuition, fees, and a stipend of $17,500 per year.

Duration 1 year; may be renewed up to 2 additional years, provided the recipient is renominated, interacts with IBM's technical community, and demonstrates continued progress and achievement.

Additional information Recipients are offered an internship at 1 of the IBM Research Division laboratories and are given an IBM computer.

Number awarded Varies each year; recently, 57 of these scholarships were awarded.

Deadline October of each year.

[1252]
ILLINOIS BROADCASTERS ASSOCIATION MULTICULTURAL INTERNSHIPS

Illinois Broadcasters Association
300 North Pershing Street, Suite B
Energy, IL 62933
(618) 942-2139   Fax: (618) 988-9056
E-mail: iba@ilba.org
Web: www.ilba.org

Purpose To provide funding to Native American and other minority college students in Illinois who are majoring in broadcasting and interested in interning at a radio or television station in the state.

Eligibility This program is open to currently-enrolled minority students majoring in broadcasting at a college or university in Illinois. Applicants must be interested in a fall, spring, or summer internship at a radio or television station that is a member of the Illinois Broadcasters Association. Along with their application, they must submit 1) a 250-word essay on how they expect to benefit from a grant through this program, and 2) at least 2 letters of recommendation from a broadcasting faculty member or professional familiar with their career potential and 1 other letter. The president of the sponsoring organization selects those students nominated by their schools who have the best opportunity to make it in the world of broadcasting and matches them with internship opportunities that would otherwise be unpaid.

Financial data This program provides a grant to pay the living expenses for the interns in the Illinois communities where they are assigned. The amount of the grant depends on the length of the internship.

Duration 16 weeks in the fall and spring terms or 12 weeks in the summer.

Number awarded 12 each year: 4 in each of the 3 terms.

[1253]
INROADS NATIONAL COLLEGE INTERNSHIPS

INROADS, Inc.
10 South Broadway, Suite 300
St. Louis, MO 63102
(314) 241-7488   Fax: (314) 241-9325
E-mail: info@inroads.org
Web: www.inroads.org

Purpose To provide an opportunity for Native Americans and other young people of color to gain work experience in business or industry.

Eligibility This program is open to African Americans, Hispanics, and Native Americans who reside in the areas served by INROADS. Applicants must be interested in preparing for a career in business, computer and information sciences, engineering, health, marketing, retail store management, or sales. They must be 1) seniors in high school with a GPA of 3.0 or higher; or 2) freshmen or sophomores in 4-year colleges and universities with a GPA of 2.8 or higher. Citizenship in the country where they are applying to work is required.

Financial data Salaries vary, depending upon the specific internship assigned; recently, the range was from $170 to $750 per week.

Duration Up to 4 years.

Additional information INROADS places interns in Fortune 1000 companies, where training focuses on preparing them for corporate and community leadership. The INROADS organization offers internship opportunities through 45 local affiliates in 29 states, Canada, and Mexico.

Number awarded Approximately 5,000 high school and college students are currently working for more than 600 corporate sponsors nationwide.

Deadline March of each year.

[1254]
INSTITUTE FOR INTERNATIONAL PUBLIC POLICY FELLOWSHIPS

United Negro College Fund Special Programs Corporation
2750 Prosperity Avenue, Suite 600
Fairfax, VA 22031
(703) 677-3400   Toll-free: (800) 530-6232
Fax: (703) 205-7645   E-mail: iippl@uncfsp.org
Web: www.uncfsp.org

Purpose To provide financial assistance and work experience to Native American and other minority students who are interested in preparing for a career in international affairs.

Eligibility This program is open to full-time sophomores at 4-year institutions who have a GPA of 3.2 or higher and are nominated by the president of their institution. Applicants must be African American, Hispanic/Latino American, Asian American, American Indian, Alaskan Native, Native Hawaiian, or Pacific Islander. They must be interested in participating in policy institutes, study abroad, language training, internships, and graduate education that will prepare them for a career in international service. U.S. citizenship or permanent resident status is required. Preference is given to students interested in pursuing advanced language and area studies in targeted world areas who are supported by Title VI fellowships. Targeted languages include Arabic,

Azeri, Armenian, Dari, Hindi, Kazakh, Kyrgyz, Persian, Pashto, Tajik, Turkish, Turkmen, Uzbek, Urdu, and other languages spoken in central and south Asia, the Middle East, and Russia/eastern Europe.
Financial data For the sophomore summer policy institute, fellows receive student housing and meals in a university facility, books and materials, all field trips and excursions, and a $1,050 stipend. For the junior year study abroad component, half the expenses for 1 semester are provided. For the junior summer policy institute, fellows receive student housing and meals in a university facility, books and materials, travel to and from the institute, and a $1,000 stipend. For the summer language institute, fellows receive tuition and fees, books and materials, room and board, travel to and from the institute, and a $1,000 stipend. During the internship, a stipend of up to $3,500 is paid. During the graduate school period, fellowships are funded jointly by this program and the participating graduate school. The program also provides $15,000 toward a master's degree in international affairs with the expectation that the graduate school will provide $15,000 in matching funds.
Duration 2 years of undergraduate work and 2 years of graduate work, as well as the intervening summers.
Additional information This program consists of 6 components: 1) a sophomore year summer policy institute based at Clark Atlanta University's Department of International Affairs and Development, comprised of lectures, discussions, and group assignments, complemented by guest speakers and local site visits to international agencies and organizations in Washington, D.C. and New York; the program of study includes international politics, research methods, U.S. foreign policy, international business, economics, and selected area studies; 2) a junior year study abroad program at an accredited overseas institution; 3) a junior year summer institute of intensive academic preparation for graduate school, with course work in economics, mathematics, communication skills, and policy analysis; 4) for students without established foreign language competency, a summer language institute following the senior year; 5) fellows with previously established foreign language competence participate in a post-baccalaureate internship to provide the practical experience needed for successful graduate studies in international affairs; and 6) a master's degree in international affairs (for students who are admitted to such a program). This program is administered by the United Negro College Fund Special Programs Corporation in partnership with the Hispanic Scholarship Fund Institute and the Association of Professional Schools of International Affairs; funding is provided by a grant from the U.S. Department of Education.
Number awarded 30 each year.
Deadline March of each year.

[1255]
IRTS BROADCAST SALES ASSOCIATE PROGRAM
International Radio and Television Society Foundation
Attn: Director, Special Projects
420 Lexington Avenue, Suite 1601
New York, NY 10170-0101
(212) 867-6650   Toll-free: (888) 627-1266
Fax: (212) 867-6653   E-mail: apply@irts.org
Web: irts.org/programs/sfp/sfp.htm
Purpose To provide work experience to Native American and other minority graduate students interested in working during the summer in broadcast sales in the New York City area.
Eligibility This program is open to graduate students who are attending 4-year colleges and universities. Applicants must be a member of a minority (Black, Hispanic, Asian/Pacific Islander, American Indian/Alaskan Native) group. They must be interested in working during the summer in a sales training program traditionally reserved for actual station group employees. They must be a communications major or have demonstrated a strong interest in the field through extracurricular activities or other practical experience, but they are not required to have experience in broadcast sales.
Financial data Travel, housing, and a living allowance are provided.
Duration 9 weeks during the summer.
Additional information The program consists of a 1-week orientation to the media and entertainment business, followed by an 8-week internship experience in the sales division of a network stations group.
Number awarded Varies each year.
Deadline February of each year.

[1256]
JAMES E. WEBB INTERNSHIPS
Smithsonian Institution
Attn: Office of Research Training and Services
470 L'Enfant Plaza, Suite 7102
P.O. Box 37012, MRC 902
Washington, DC 20013-7012
(202) 633-7070   Fax: (202) 633-7069
E-mail: siofg@si.edu
Web: www.si.edu/ofg/ofgapp.htm
Purpose To provide internship opportunities throughout the Smithsonian Institution to Native American and other minority upper-division and graduate students in business or public administration.
Eligibility This program is open to U.S. minority juniors, seniors, and graduate students majoring in areas of business or public administration (finance, human resource management, accounting, or general business administration). Applicants must have a GPA of 3.0 or higher. They must seek placement in offices, museums, and research institutes within the Smithsonian Institution.
Financial data Interns receive a stipend of $500 per week and a travel allowance.
Duration 10 weeks during the summer, fall, or spring.
Number awarded Varies each year; recently, 8 of these internships were awarded.
Deadline January of each year for summer or fall; September of each year for spring.

[1257]
JEANNE SPURLOCK MINORITY MEDICAL STUDENT CLINICAL FELLOWSHIP IN CHILD AND ADOLESCENT PSYCHIATRY

American Academy of Child and Adolescent Psychiatry
Attn: Department of Research, Training, and Education
3615 Wisconsin Avenue, N.W.
Washington, DC 20016-3007
(202) 966-7300   Fax: (202) 966-2891
E-mail: research@aacap.org
Web: www.aacap.org

Purpose To provide funding to Native American and other minority medical students who are interested in working with a child and adolescent psychiatrist during the summer.

Eligibility This program is open to African American, Asian American, Native American, Alaska Native, Mexican American, Hispanic, and Pacific Islander students in accredited medical schools. Applicants must present a plan for a clinical training experience that involves significant contact between the student and a mentor. The plan should include program planning discussions, instruction in treatment planning and implementation, regular meetings with the mentor and other treatment providers, and assigned readings. Clinical assignments may include responsibility for part of the observation or evaluation, conducting interviews or tests, using rating scales, and psychological or cognitive testing of patients. The training plan should also include discussion of ethical issues in treatment.

Financial data The stipend is $3,500. Fellows also receive reimbursement of travel expenses to attend the annual meeting of the American Academy of Child and Adolescent Psychiatry.

Duration 12 weeks during the summer.

Additional information Upon completion of the training program, the student is required to submit a brief paper summarizing the clinical experience. The fellowship pays expenses for the fellow to attend the academy's annual meeting and present this paper. This program is supported by the Center for Mental Health Services of the Substance Abuse and Mental Health Services Administration.

Number awarded Up to 14 each year.

Deadline February of each year.

[1258]
JEANNE SPURLOCK RESEARCH FELLOWSHIP IN DRUG ABUSE AND ADDICTION FOR MINORITY MEDICAL STUDENTS

American Academy of Child and Adolescent Psychiatry
Attn: Department of Research, Training, and Education
3615 Wisconsin Avenue, N.W.
Washington, DC 20016-3007
(202) 966-7300   Fax: (202) 966-2891
E-mail: research@aacap.org
Web: www.aacap.org

Purpose To provide funding to Native American and other minority medical students who are interested in working with a child and adolescent psychiatrist researcher-mentor during the summer on drug abuse and addiction.

Eligibility This program is open to African American, Asian American, Native American, Alaska Native, Mexican American, Hispanic, and Pacific Islander students in accredited medical schools. Applicants must present a plan for a program of research training in drug abuse and addiction that involves significant contact with a mentor who is an experienced child and adolescent psychiatrist researcher. The plan should include program planning discussions; instruction in research planning and implementation; regular meetings with the mentor, laboratory director, and the research group; and assigned readings. Research assignments may include responsibility for part of the observation or evaluation, developing specific aspects of the research mechanisms, conducting interviews or tests, using rating scales, and psychological or cognitive testing of subjects. The training plan also should include discussion of ethical issues in research, including protocol development, informed consent, collection and storage of raw data, safeguarding data, bias in analyzing data, plagiarism, protection of patients, ethical treatment of animals. etc.

Financial data The stipend is $3,500. Fellows also receive reimbursement of travel expenses to attend the annual meeting of the American Academy of Child and Adolescent Psychiatry.

Duration 12 weeks during the summer.

Additional information Upon completion of the training program, the student is required to submit a brief paper summarizing the research experience. The fellowship pays expenses for the fellow to attend the academy's annual meeting and present this paper. This program is cosponsored by the National Institute on Drug Abuse.

Number awarded Up to 5 each year.

Deadline February of each year.

[1259]
JUDICIAL EXTERNSHIP PROGRAM

Just the Beginning Foundation
c/o Schiff Hardin LLP
233 South Wacker Drive, Suite 6600
Chicago, IL 60606
(312) 701-8965   E-mail: info@jtbf.org
Web: www.jtbf.org

Purpose To provide work experience to minority and economically disadvantaged law students who plan to seek judicial clerkships after graduation.

Eligibility This program is open to students currently enrolled in their second or third year of law school who are members of minority or economically disadvantaged groups. Applicants must intend to work as a clerk in the federal or state judiciary upon graduation or within 5 years of graduation.

Financial data Program externs receive a quarterly or summer stipend in an amount determined by the sponsor.

Duration The academic year externships require a 1- or 2-year commitment, beginning each September and ending in May or June. During the academic year, participants are expected to work a minimum of 10 hours per week on externship assignments. The summer externships require students to perform at least 35 hours per week of work for at least 8 weeks during the summer.

Additional information This program began in 2005. Law students are matched with federal and state judges across the country who provide assignments to the participants that will enhance their legal research, writing, and analytical skills (e.g., drafting memoranda). Students are expected to complete at least 1 memorandum of law or

other key legal document each semester of the externship. Course credit may be offered, but students may not receive academic credit and a stipend simultaneously.
Number awarded Varies each year.
Deadline July of each year.

[1260]
JUDICIAL INTERN OPPORTUNITY PROGRAM
American Bar Association
Attn: Section of Litigation
321 North Clark Street
Chicago, IL 60610
(312) 988-6348 Fax: (312) 988-6234
E-mail: howardg@staff.abanet.org
Web: www.abanet.org/litigation/jiop

Purpose To provide an opportunity for minority and financially disadvantaged law students to gain experience as judicial interns in selected courts during the summer.
Eligibility This program is open to first- and second-year students at ABA-accredited law schools who are members of minority or financially disadvantaged groups. Applicants must be interested in a judicial internship at courts in selected areas and communities. They may indicate a preference for the area in which they wish to work, but they may not specify a court or a judge. Along with their application, they must submit a current resume, a 10-page legal writing sample, and a 2-page statement of interest that outlines their qualifications for the internship. Screening interviews are conducted by staff of the American Bar Association, either in person or by telephone. Final interviews are conducted by the judges with whom the interns will work. Some spots are reserved for students with an interest in intellectual property law.
Financial data The stipend is $1,500.
Duration 6 weeks during the summer.
Additional information Recently, internships were available in the following locations: Chicago and surrounding suburbs; central and southern Illinois; Houston, Dallas, southern, and eastern Texas; Miami, Florida; Phoenix, Arizona; Los Angeles, California; San Francisco, California; and Washington, D.C. Some internships in Chicago, Los Angeles, Texas, and Washington, D.C. are reserved for students with an interest in intellectual property law.
Number awarded Varies each year; recently, 167 of these internships were awarded, including 14 at courts in Arizona, 29 in California, 16 in Florida, 54 in Illinois, 37 in Texas, and 17 in Washington, D.C.
Deadline January of each year.

[1261]
JUDITH L. WEIDMAN RACIAL ETHNIC MINORITY FELLOWSHIP
United Methodist Communications
Attn: Communications Resourcing Team
810 12th Avenue South
P.O. Box 320
Nashville, TN 37202-0320
(615) 742-5481 Toll-free: (888) CRT-4UMC
Fax: (615) 742-5485 E-mail: crt@umcom.org
Web: crt.umc.org/interior.asp?ptid=1&mid=6891

Purpose To provide work experience to Methodists who are Native Americans or members of other minority groups and interested in a communications career.
Eligibility This program is open to United Methodists of racial ethnic minority heritage who are interested in preparing for a career in communications with the United Methodist Church. Applicants must be recent college or seminary graduates who have broad communications training, including work in journalism, mass communications, marketing, public relations, and electronic media. They must be able to understand and speak English proficiently and to relocate for a year. Selection is based on Christian commitment and involvement in the life of the United Methodist Church; achievement as revealed by transcripts, GPA, letters of reference, and work samples; study, experience, and evidence of talent in the field of communications; clarity of purpose and goals for the future; desire to learn how to be a successful United Methodist conference communicator; and potential leadership ability as a professional religion communicator for the United Methodist Church.
Financial data The stipend is $30,000 per year. Benefits and expenses for moving and professional travel are also provided.
Duration 1 year, starting in July.
Additional information This program was established in 1998. Recipients are assigned to 1 of the 63 United Methodist Annual Conferences, the headquarters of local churches within a geographic area. At the Annual Conference, the fellow will be assigned an experienced communicator as a mentor and will work closely with that mentor and with United Methodist Communications in Nashville, Tennessee. Following the successful completion of the fellowship, United Methodist Communications and the participating Annual Conference will assist in a search for permanent employment within the United Methodist Church but cannot guarantee a position.
Number awarded 1 each year.
Deadline March of each year.

[1262]
KAISER MEDIA INTERNSHIPS IN HEALTH REPORTING
Henry J. Kaiser Family Foundation
Attn: Kaiser Media Fellowships Program
2400 Sand Hill Road
Menlo Park, CA 94025
(650) 234-9220 Fax: (650) 854-4800
E-mail: pduckham@kff.org
Web: www.kff.org/mediafellows/mediainternships.cfm

Purpose To provide summer work experience to minority and other new journalists who want to specialize in health reporting, especially in coverage of health issues affecting diverse and immigrant communities.

Eligibility This program is open to journalists graduating from college or journalism school with considerable experience, including previous internships at a newspaper or TV/radio station. Applicants must be able to demonstrate a commitment and ability to report on health issues affecting diverse and immigrant communities. Strong writing skills and previous newsroom reporting experience are essential. Priority is given to journalists who are bilingual or bicultural and to those who have studied or reported on health issues affecting diverse or immigrant communities (e.g., previous reporting experience and/or academic expertise in health, medical, or science-related issues or urban affairs). U.S. citizenship or permanent resident status is required.

Financial data This program provides a stipend of at least $500 per week (matching that of the hosting news organization) and all travel expenses.

Duration 12 weeks in the summer, including a 1-week orientation in Washington, D.C., 10 weeks on the metro or health science desk at a media organization (print, radio, or television), and a 3-day wrap-up in Boston.

Additional information This program, sponsored by the Henry J. Kaiser Family Foundation, began in 1994. Each participating news organization selects its own intern; recently, those were the *Atlanta Journal-Constitution, Baltimore Sun, Boston Globe, Charlotte Observer, Detroit Free Press, Milwaukee Journal Sentinel, Orlando Sentinel,* Reuters, *Sacramento Bee, San Jose Mercury News, Sun-Sentinel* of Fort Lauderdale, *Times-Picayne* of New Orleans, *Washington Post,* BET News, KQED Public Radio of San Francisco, and KTVU/2-TV or San Francisco-Oakland.

Number awarded Generally, 1 intern is selected at each participating news organization.

Deadline Applicants to print organizations should submit their applications in early December; applicants to broadcast organizations should submit their applications in early January.

[1263]
KATTEN MUCHIN ROSENMAN MINORITY SCHOLARSHIPS

Katten Muchin Rosenman LLP
Attn: Director of Attorney Recruiting and Development
525 West Monroe Street
Chicago, IL 60661-3693
(312) 902-5547   Fax: (312) 577-8937
E-mail: elizabeth.cibula@kattenlaw.com
Web: www.kattenlaw.com

Purpose To provide summer work experience (in Chicago or New York City) and financial assistance to Native American and other minority law students from any state.

Eligibility This program is open to minority students from any state who have completed their first year of law school. Applicants must have applied for and been accepted as a summer associate at the sponsoring law firm's Chicago or New York office. Along with their application, they must submit 250-word statements on 1) their strongest qualifications for this award; 2) their reasons for preparing for law as a profession; and 3) their views on diversity and how their personal experience and philosophy will be an asset to the firm. Selection is based on academic achievement, leadership experience, and personal qualities that reflect the potential for outstanding contributions to the firm and the legal profession.

Financial data Participants receive the standard salary for the summer internship and a stipend of $15,000 for the academic year.

Duration 1 year.

Additional information Information on the New York program is available from the Attorney Recruiting and Development Manager, 575 Madison Avenue, New York, NY 10022-2585, (212) 940-6327, Fax: (212) 894-5627, E-mail: janeen.berkowitz@kattenlaw.com.

Number awarded 3 each year: 2 who intern at the Chicago office and 1 who interns at the New York office.

Deadline September of each year.

[1264]
KIRKLAND & ELLIS LLP DIVERSITY FELLOWSHIP PROGRAM

Kirkland & Ellis LLP
Attn: Attorney Recruiting Manager
777 South Figueroa, Suite 3700
Los Angeles, CA 90017
(213) 680-8436   Fax: (213) 680-8500
E-mail: cconrad@kirkland.com
Web: www.kirkland.com

Purpose To provide summer work experience at an office of Kirkland & Ellis to Native American and other minority law students from any state.

Eligibility This program is open to second-year students at ABA-accredited law schools who meet the racial and ethnic categories established by the Equal Employment Opportunity Commission. Applicants must have been accepted as summer associates with the sponsoring law firm. They must indicate an intention to practice in a city in which the firm has an office (Chicago, Hong Kong, London, Los Angeles, Munich, New York, San Francisco, Washington, D.C.) after graduation.

Financial data Fellows receive a salary during their summer associateship and a $15,000 stipend at the conclusion of the summer. Stipend funds are to be used for payment of educational expenses during the third year of law school.

Duration 1 year.

Additional information This program, which replaced the Kirkland & Ellis Minority Fellowship Program, was established at 14 law schools in 2004. In 2006, it began accepting a limited number of applications from students at all ABA-accredited law schools.

Number awarded Varies each year; recently, 16 of these fellowships were awarded.

Deadline September of each year.

[1265]
K&L GATES DIVERSITY FELLOWSHIP
Kirkpatrick & Lockhart Preston Gates Ellis LLP
Attn: Recruiting Coordinator
925 Fourth Avenue, Suite 2900
Seattle, WA 98104
(206) 623-7580
Web: www.klgates.com/lawstudents/studentsdiversity

Purpose To provide financial assistance and summer work experience (in Seattle) to Native American or other minority law students from any state.
Eligibility This program is open to first-year students at ABA-accredited law schools in the United States. Applicants must be Native American or members of other minority racial and ethnic groups.
Financial data Fellows receive a paid associateship with the Seattle office of the sponsoring firm during the summer following their first year of law school and an academic scholarship of $7,500 for their second year of law school.
Duration 1 year.
Number awarded 2 each year: 1 for a law student nationally and 1 for a student at the University of Washington School of Law.
Deadline January of each year.

[1266]
LASPACE UNDERGRADUATE RESEARCH ASSISTANTSHIPS
Louisiana Space Consortium
c/o Louisiana State University
Department of Physics and Astronomy
371 Nicholson Hall
Baton Rouge, LA 70803-4001
(225) 578-8697   Fax: (225) 578-1222
E-mail: laspace@lsu.edu
Web: laspace.lsu.edu/scholarships.html

Purpose To provide minority and other undergraduate science and engineering students in Louisiana with a mentored research experience in the space sciences.
Eligibility This program is open to U.S. citizens who are high school seniors, recent high school graduates, and students currently enrolled at 1 of the Louisiana Space Consortium (LaSPACE) member schools. The consortium is a component of the U.S. National Aeronautics and Space Administration (NASA) Space Grant program, which encourages participation by members of groups underrepresented in mathematics, science, and engineering (women, African Americans, Native Americans, Native Pacific Islanders, Mexican Americans, Puerto Ricans, Alaska Natives, and persons with disabilities). Applicants must be studying or planning to study a space- or aerospace-related field or program at an LaSPACE institution full time. They must coordinate with a faculty member at the institution who will file a joint application with the student and agree to serve as a mentor on a proposed research project. Selection is based on scholastic accomplishments, pertinent science experiences and accomplishments, leadership and recognitions, intellectual abilities, character, and relevance of the proposed research project to a future career in space or aerospace fields.
Financial data Grants are provided in blocks of $6,000. Funding may support 1 or 2 assistants. Funds may be used for wage support for the student(s), travel for a student research presentation, or research supplies.
Duration 12 months.
Additional information The participating LaSPACE member institutions are Dillard University, Grambling State University, Louisiana State University, Louisiana Tech University, Loyola University, McNeese State University, Nicholls State University, Northwestern State University of Louisiana, Southeastern Louisiana University, Southern University and A&M College, Southern University in New Orleans, Tulane University, University of New Orleans, University of Louisiana at Lafayette, University of Louisiana at Monroe, and Xavier University of Louisiana. This program was established in 2000 as a replacement for the LaSPACE Undergraduate Scholars Program. Funding is provided by NASA.
Number awarded 5 to 8 each year.
Deadline March of each year.

[1267]
LAUNCHING LEADERS MBA SCHOLARSHIP
JPMorgan Chase
Campus Recruiting
Attn: Launching Leaders
277 Park Avenue, Second Floor
New York, NY 10172
(212) 270-6000
E-mail: bronwen.x.baumgardner@jpmorgan.com
Web: launchingleaders.jpmorgan.com/02.0.ashx

Purpose To provide financial assistance and work experience to Native American and other underrepresented minority students enrolled in the first year of an M.B.A. program.
Eligibility This program is open to Black, Hispanic, and Native American students enrolled in the first year of an M.B.A. program. Applicants must have a demonstrated commitment to working in financial services. Along with their application, they must submit essays on 1) a hypothetical proposal on how to use $50 million from a donor to their school to benefit all of its students; and 2) the special background and attributes they would contribute to the sponsor's diversity agenda and their motivation for applying to this scholarship program. They must be interested in a summer associate position in the sponsor's investment banking, sales and trading, or research divisions.
Financial data The stipend is $40,000 for the first year of study; a paid summer associate position is also provided.
Duration 1 year; may be renewed 1 additional year if the recipient successfully completes the 10-week summer associate program.
Number awarded Varies each year.
Deadline October of each year.

[1268]
LAUNCHING LEADERS UNDERGRADUATE SCHOLARSHIP

JPMorgan Chase
Campus Recruiting
Attn: Launching Leaders
277 Park Avenue, Second Floor
New York, NY 10172
(212) 270-6000
E-mail: bronwen.x.baumgardner@jpmorgan.com
Web: launchingleaders.jpmorgan.com/01.0.ashx

Purpose To provide financial assistance and work experience to Native Americans and other underrepresented minority undergraduate students interested in a career in financial services.

Eligibility This program is open to Black, Hispanic, and Native American students enrolled as sophomores or juniors and interested in financial services. Applicants must have a GPA of 3.5 or higher. Along with their application, they must submit 500-word essays on 1) why they should be considered potential candidates for CEO of the sponsoring bank in 2020; and 2) the special background and attributes they would contribute to the sponsor's diversity agenda. They must be interested in a summer associate position in the sponsor's investment banking, sales and trading, or research divisions.

Financial data The stipend is $5,000 for recipients accepted as sophomores or $7,500 for recipients accepted as juniors. For students accepted as sophomores and whose scholarship is renewed for a second year, the stipend is $10,000. The summer associateship is a paid position.

Duration 1 year; may be renewed 1 additional year if the recipient successfully completes the 10-week summer associate program and maintains a GPA of 3.5 or higher.

Number awarded Approximately 12 each year.

Deadline November of each year.

[1269]
LENA CHANG INTERNSHIPS

Nuclear Age Peace Foundation
1187 Coast Village Road, Suite 1
PMB 121
Santa Barbara, CA 93108-2794
(805) 965-3443   Fax: (805) 568-0466
E-mail: youth@napf.org
Web: www.wagingpeace.org

Purpose To provide work experience at the Nuclear Age Peace Foundation in Santa Barbara, California to undergraduate and graduate students, especially ethnic minorities.

Eligibility This program is open to students currently enrolled in undergraduate or graduate course work who can demonstrate financial need and academic excellence. Preference is given to students of color. Applicants must submit their transcript; 2 letters of recommendation; a letter of intent describing their work experience, educational background, field of study, plans after graduation, and preference for fall, spring, or summer internship; and a copy of their resume or curriculum vitae.

Financial data The stipend is $2,500 for summer; interns are responsible for their own transportation and housing costs. Academic year interns receive academic credit only.

Duration The summer internship is 10 weeks of full-time work. Academic year interns are expected to work at least 200 hours.

Number awarded 3 each year: 1 for the summer and 2 for the academic year.

Deadline March of each year for the summer internship; September of each year for an academic year internship.

[1270]
LIFCHEZ/STRONACH CURATORIAL INTERNSHIPS

Metropolitan Museum of Art
Attn: Internship Programs
1000 Fifth Avenue
New York, NY 10028-0198
(212) 570-3710   Fax: (212) 570-3782
E-mail: mmainterns@metmuseum.org
Web: www.metmuseum.org

Purpose To provide museum work experience at the Metropolitan Museum of Art to Native American and other disadvantaged graduate students and recent graduates who wish to prepare for a career in art history.

Eligibility This program is open to recent college graduates and students enrolled in master's degree programs in art history. Applicants should come from a background of financial need or other disadvantage that will jeopardize their preparing for a career in art history without the support.

Financial data The honorarium is $16,500.

Duration 9 months, beginning in September.

Additional information Interns are assigned to 1 or more of the Metropolitan Museum of Art's departments, where they work on projects that match their academic background, professional skills, and career goals. This program was reestablished in 1998 with funding from Raymond Lifchez and Judith L. Stronach.

Number awarded 3 each year.

Deadline January of each year.

[1271]
LSAMP UNDERGRADUATE SUMMER RESEARCH PROGRAM

Cornell University
College of Engineering
Attn: Diversity Programs in Engineering
146 Olin Hall
Ithaca, NY 14853-5201
(607) 255-6403   Fax: (607) 255-2834
E-mail: dpeng@cornell.edu
Web: www.engineering.cornell.edu

Purpose To provide an opportunity for Native Americans and other traditionally underrepresented minority groups in the sciences and engineering to participate in a summer research program in engineering at Cornell University.

Eligibility This program is open to members of minority groups traditionally underrepresented in the sciences and engineering who are entering their sophomore, junior, or senior year at a college or university anywhere in the country. Applicants must be interested in working on a research project in engineering under the guidance of a faculty or research mentor at Cornell University. They must have a GPA of 3.0 or higher.

Financial data Participating students receive a stipend of $2,156, a round-trip travel stipend of up to $135, a double room in a campus residential hall, a meal plan valued at approximately $465, and access to laboratories, libraries, computer facilities, and study lounges.

Duration 8 weeks during the summer.

Additional information This program is part of the Louis Stokes Alliance for Minority Participation (LSAMP), supported by the National Science Foundation. Students are encouraged to enter and present their research at their affiliated National Society of Black Engineers (NSBE), Society of Hispanic Professional Engineers (SHPE), or American Indian Science and Engineering Society (AISES) or professional conference.

Deadline February of each year.

[1272]
LUCENT TECHNOLOGIES BELL LABORATORIES SUMMER RESEARCH PROGRAM FOR MINORITIES AND WOMEN

Lucent Technologies
Attn: Special Programs Manager
283 King George Road, Room B1-D32
Warren, NJ 07059
(732) 559-4267   E-mail: summersearch@lucent.com
Web: www.bell-labs.com/employment/srp/info.html

Purpose To provide technical work experience at facilities of Bell Laboratories during the summer to women and underrepresented minority undergraduate students.

Eligibility This program is open to women and members of minority groups (African Americans, Hispanics, and Native American Indians) who are underrepresented in the sciences. Applicants must be interested in pursuing technical employment experience in research and development facilities of Bell Laboratories. The program is primarily directed at undergraduate students who have completed their second or third year of college. Emphasis is placed on the following disciplines: chemistry, communications science, computer science and engineering, data networking, electrical engineering, information science, materials science, mathematics, optics, physics, statistics, and wireless and radio engineering. U.S. citizenship or permanent resident status is required. Selection is based on academic achievement, personal motivation, and compatibility of student interests with current Bell Laboratories activities.

Financial data Salaries are commensurate with those of regular Bell Laboratories employees with comparable education. Interns are reimbursed for travel expenses up to the cost of round-trip economy-class airfare.

Duration 10 weeks during the summer.

Additional information This program is sponsored by Lucent Technologies and Bell Laboratories.

Number awarded Varies each year.

Deadline November of each year.

[1273]
MAINE ARTS COMMISSION TRADITIONAL ARTS APPRENTICESHIP PROGRAM

Maine Arts Commission
193 State Street
25 State House Station
Augusta, ME 04333-0025
(207) 287-2726   Fax: (207) 287-2725
TTY: (877) 887-3878
E-mail: MaineArts.info@maine.gov
Web: mainearts.maine.gov

Purpose To provide an opportunity for traditional artists in Maine to share their skills with and train qualified apprentices.

Eligibility This program is open to master artists who practice a significant and/or endangered traditional art form in Maine. Traditional arts are defined as artistic practices that reflect a community's shared cultural heritage and are learned in an informal way, usually by example rather than through academic or institutional means. Apprentices should be from the same ethnic, religious, occupational, or familial group as the master artist. Both master and apprentice must be legal Maine residents. Masters must be 18 years of age or older, but apprentices may be of any age.

Financial data The maximum grant is $4,000. Funds are available for the master artist's teaching fee, apprentices' supplies and travel costs, and documentation of the apprenticeship.

Duration 8 to 12 months.

Additional information Master artists and apprentices work together on a one-to-one basis. The work may be in crafts, dance, or music.

Number awarded Varies each year; recently, 6 of these grants were awarded.

Deadline June of each year.

[1274]
MARYLAND SEA GRANT RESEARCH EXPERIENCES FOR UNDERGRADUATES

Maryland Sea Grant College
c/o University of Maryland
4321 Hartwick Road, Suite 300
College Park, MD 20740
(301) 405-7500   Fax: (301) 314-5780
E-mail: moser@mdsg.umd.edu
Web: www.mdsg.umd.edu/Education/REU/index.html

Purpose To provide minority and other undergraduate students with an opportunity to conduct marine research during the summer in biology, chemistry, and physical oceanography on Chesapeake Bay.

Eligibility This program is open to undergraduate students who have completed at least 2 years of study towards a bachelor's degree. Applicants must be interested in conducting individual research projects (under the mentorship of scientists from the University of Maryland or the Academy of Natural Science Estuarine Research Center) in such areas as estuarine processes, biochemistry, coastal technologies, modeling and analysis, contaminants, fisheries, physical oceanography, the benthic environment, and submerged aquatic vegetation. U.S. citizenship or permanent resident status is required. Selection is based on a 1-page description of interests, course work and grades, letters of

recommendation, and the potential benefits students will gain from the research experience. Preference is given to rising seniors. Students from underrepresented groups and institutions with limited research opportunities are especially encouraged to apply.
Financial data Fellows receive a stipend of $3,700, payment of dormitory costs, round-trip travel expenses, and funding to assist in publishing or presenting the results of summer research.
Duration 12 weeks during the summer.
Additional information This program is supported by the National Science Foundation as part of the Research Experiences for Undergraduates Program.
Number awarded 13 each year.
Deadline February of each year.

[1275]
MASTER ARTIST AND APPRENTICE GRANTS IN TRADITIONAL NATIVE ARTS
Alaska State Council on the Arts
Attn: Community and Native Arts Program Director
411 West Fourth Avenue, Suite 1E
Anchorage, AK 99501-2343
(907) 269-6603   Toll-free: (888) 278-7424
Fax: (907) 269-6601   TTY: (800) 770-8973
E-mail: saunders.mcneill@alaska.gov
Web: www.eed.state.ak.us/aksca

Purpose To provide funding to masters and apprentices interested in supporting and encouraging the maintenance and development of the traditional arts of Alaska's native people.
Eligibility This program is open to apprentices and masters in a traditional Alaska Native art form, including but not limited to visual arts, crafts, music, dance, storytelling, and singing. The apprentice applicants must be residents of Alaska, have demonstrated experience in the art form in which they are interested, be 18 years of age or older, and have identified and located a master artist willing to accept apprentices. The master applicants must be able to provide evidence of excellence in the art form, agree to take on the applicant as an apprentice, be recognized for their proficiency and skill in an art form by members of their own cultural community, and be 18 years of age or older. Priority is given to apprentices who wish to study an art form within their own cultural tradition. Selection is based on quality of the work of the apprentice (35 points), quality of the work of the master artist (20 points), lesson plan (35 points), and total budget and materials list (10 points).
Financial data The maximum grant is $2,000. The funds are to be used to pay the fees of the master artist and to cover essential expenses of the apprenticeship (primarily materials and, in rare cases, travel).
Number awarded Varies each year.
Deadline February, May, August, or November of each year.

[1276]
MCDERMOTT MINORITY SCHOLARSHIP
McDermott Will & Emery
Attn: Recruiting Committee Chair
227 West Monroe Street
Chicago, IL 60606
(312) 984-6470   Fax: (312) 984-7700
E-mail: mcdermottscholarship@mwe.com
Web: www.mwe.com

Purpose To provide financial assistance and work experience to Native American and other minority law students.
Eligibility This program is open to second-year minority (African American, Asian, Hispanic, Middle Eastern, Native American) law students at ABA-accredited U.S. law schools. Applicants must be able to demonstrate leadership, community involvement, and a commitment to improving diversity in the legal community. They must be interested in participating in the sponsor's summer program and be able to meet its hiring criteria. Along with their application, they must submit an essay of 1 to 2 pages that provides ideas they have on how the number of minority students in law schools can be increased and how they have improved and intend to help improve diversity in the legal profession throughout their law school and legal career.
Financial data The stipend is $15,000.
Duration 1 year.
Additional information Recipients also participate in a summer program at the sponsor's offices in Boston, Chicago, Los Angeles, Miami, New York, Orange County, Silicon Valley, or Washington, D.C.
Number awarded 2 each year.
Deadline October of each year.

[1277]
MENTORSHIP FOR ENVIRONMENTAL SCHOLARS
United Negro College Fund Special Programs
  Corporation
2750 Prosperity Avenue, Suite 600
Fairfax, VA 22031
(703) 677-3400   Toll-free: (800) 530-6232
Fax: (703) 205-7645   E-mail: portal@uncfsp.org
Web: www.uncfsp.org

Purpose To provide an opportunity for upper-division students at Minority Institutions (MIs) to work on a summer research project in a field of interest to the U.S. Department of Energy (DOE).
Eligibility This program is open to rising juniors and seniors at MIs (Historically Black Colleges and Universities, Hispanic Serving Institutions, and Tribal Colleges and Universities) who are members of underrepresented groups, including ethnic minorities and persons with disabilities. Applicants must be working on a degree in a science, technology, engineering, or mathematics (STEM) field of interest to DOE (e.g., biology, chemistry, physics, engineering, environmental science) and have a GPA of 3.0 or higher. They must be interested in working on a research project during the summer at a DOE laboratory or research facility. U.S. citizenship is required.
Financial data A stipend is provided (amount not specified).
Duration 9 weeks during the summer.

Additional information This program is funded by DOE and administered by the United Negro College Fund Special Programs Corporation.
Number awarded Varies each year.
Deadline January of each year.

[1278]
MERCER DIVERSITY SCHOLARSHIP PROGRAM
Mercer Human Resource Consulting LLC
1166 Avenue of the Americas
New York, NY 10036
(212) 345-7000   Fax: (212) 345-7414
Web: www.mercerhr.com/diversityscholarship

Purpose To provide financial assistance and work experience to Native American and other minority undergraduates working on a degree in selected business-related fields.
Eligibility This program is open to students who identify as Hispanic or Latino, Black or African American, Native Hawaiian or other Pacific Islander, American Indian, Alaska Native, or Asian. Applicants must be sophomores or juniors and either have a GPA of at least 3.25 or rank in the top 5% of their class (if their school uses a ranking system). They must be working on a degree in actuarial sciences, mathematics, statistics, business, economics, finance, or liberal arts and sciences. Along with their application, they must submit a 1-page essay on why they are interested in Mercer Human Resource Consulting and the unique skills they can contribute. If a summer internship at Mercer is available, they must be willing to accept it. Selection is based on academic achievement, campus and community involvement, and a writing sample. Finalists are interviewed.
Financial data The stipend is $5,000 per year. A paid summer internship may also be offered.
Duration 1 year; may be renewed, provided the recipients accept a summer internship if offered, maintain a GPA of at least 3.25 or rank in the top 5% of their class, and act as an ambassador for Mercer at their school.
Number awarded Up to 20 each year.
Deadline December of each year.

[1279]
METPRO/EDITING PROGRAM
Newsday
Attn: METPRO/Editing Director
235 Pinelawn Road
Melville, NY 11747-4250
(631) 843-2367   Toll-free: (888) 717-9817, ext. 2367
Fax: (631) 843-4719   E-mail: jobs@newsday.com
Web: www.metpronews.com/editing.html

Purpose To provide an opportunity for Native Americans and other minorities to obtain training for editing positions on daily metropolitan newspapers.
Eligibility Applicants for the Minority Editorial Training Program (METPRO) should be minority (African American, Asian American, Hispanic, American Indian) college graduates with excellent writing skills and an interest in a newspaper career. Selection is based on academic record and potential. Previous professional editing experience is not required.
Financial data Trainees receive a weekly stipend, a monthly housing allowance, and medical benefits for the first year. During the second year, trainees receive compensation and benefits applicable at the newspaper where they are working.
Duration 2 years.
Additional information Participants in this program receive intensive training in editing at *Newsday* during the first year, including a 2-week orientation, 3 weeks of reporting in Queens and on Long Island, 10 weeks of full-time classroom instruction, and 31 weeks of work as editors on *Newsday* copy desks. During the second year, they work for 1 of the 11 Tribune Company newspapers (in Allentown, Pennsylvania; Baltimore, Maryland; Chicago, Illinois; Fort Lauderdale, Florida; Greenwich, Connecticut; Hartford, Connecticut; Los Angeles, California; Melville, New York; Newport News, Virginia; Orlando, Florida; or Stamford, Connecticut).
Number awarded Up to 10 each year.
Deadline January of each year.

[1280]
METPRO/REPORTING PROGRAM
Los Angeles Times
Attn: METPRO/Reporting Director
202 West First Street
Los Angeles, CA 90012
Toll-free: (800) LA-TIMES, ext. 77366
Web: www.metpronews.com

Purpose To provide an opportunity for Native Americans and other minorities to obtain training for reporting positions on daily metropolitan newspapers.
Eligibility Applicants for the Minority Editorial Training Program (METPRO) should be college graduates with excellent writing skills and an interest in a newspaper career. Applications by African Americans, Asian Americans, Latinos, and Native Americans are particularly encouraged. Selection is based on essays, a review of written work, college transcripts, recommendations, writing tests, and personal interviews. Previous professional reporting experience is not required.
Financial data Trainees receive a regular stipend for the first year and are furnished housing, utilities, and medical insurance while in the program. During the second year, trainees receive compensation and benefits applicable at the newspaper where they are working.
Duration 2 years.
Additional information This program was established in 1984. Participants spend the first 12 months at the *Los Angeles Times,* beginning with a full-time classroom instruction phase that includes reporting and writing techniques, interviewing, researching, and beat coverage, then several weeks covering a police beat; concluding with work at 1 of the *Times* regional editions. During the second year, they work for 1 of the 11 Tribune Company newspapers (in Allentown, Pennsylvania; Baltimore, Maryland; Chicago, Illinois; Fort Lauderdale, Florida; Greenwich, Connecticut; Hartford, Connecticut; Los Angeles, California; Melville, New York; Newport News, Virginia; Orlando, Florida; or Stamford, Connecticut).
Number awarded Approximately 10 each year.
Deadline January of each year.

[1281]
METROPOLITAN MUSEUM OF ART MENTORING PROGRAM FOR COLLEGE JUNIORS

Metropolitan Museum of Art
Attn: Internship Programs
1000 Fifth Avenue
New York, NY 10028-0198
(212) 570-3710   Fax: (212) 570-3782
E-mail: mmainterns@metmuseum.org
Web: www.metmuseum.org

Purpose To provide summer work experience at the Metropolitan Museum of Art to college juniors from diverse backgrounds.
Eligibility These internships are available to college juniors who come from diverse backgrounds. Applicants must be interested in preparing for a museum career.
Financial data The honorarium is $3,250.
Duration 10 weeks, beginning in June.
Additional information Interns are assigned to departmental projects (curatorial, administration, or education) at the Metropolitan Museum of Art; the program includes a 2-week orientation at the museum, meetings with museum professionals, a museum mentor, and field trips to other institutions.
Number awarded 1 or more each year.
Deadline January of each year.

[1282]
METROPOLITAN MUSEUM OF ART 6-MONTH INTERNSHIPS

Metropolitan Museum of Art
Attn: Internship Programs
1000 Fifth Avenue
New York, NY 10028-0198
(212) 570-3710   Fax: (212) 570-3782
E-mail: mmainterns@metmuseum.org
Web: www.metmuseum.org

Purpose To provide work experience at the Metropolitan Museum of Art to candidates who can promote diversity in the profession.
Eligibility This program is open to graduating college seniors, recent graduates, and graduate students in art history or related fields. Selection is based on an essay in which applicants indicate how their selection will promote greater diversity in the national pool of future museum professionals and describe their financial need.
Financial data The stipend is $11,000.
Duration 6 months, beginning in June.
Additional information Interns work at the Metropolitan Museum for 35 hours a week.
Number awarded 2 each year.
Deadline January of each year.

[1283]
MICKEY LELAND ENERGY FELLOWSHIPS

Department of Energy
Attn: Office of Fossil Energy
1000 Independence Avenue, S.W.
Washington, DC 20585
(202) 586-7421   E-mail: dorothy.fowlkes@hq.doe.gov
Web: www.fossil.energy.gov

Purpose To provide summer work experience at fossil energy sites of the Department of Energy (DOE) to underrepresented minority and female students.
Eligibility This program is open to U.S. citizens currently enrolled at an accredited institution of higher learning. Applicants must be working on an associate, bachelor's, or master's degree in mathematics, science, geoscience, or engineering and have a GPA of 3.0 or higher. They must be interested in a summer internship at a DOE fossil energy research facility. Along with their application, they must submit a 100-word statement on why they want to participate in this program. A goal of the program is to recruit women and underrepresented minorities into careers related to fossil energy.
Financial data Weekly stipends are $500 for undergraduates or $650 for graduate students. Travel costs for a round trip to and from the site and for a trip to a designated place for technical presentations are also paid.
Duration 10 weeks during the summer.
Additional information This program began as 3 separate activities: the Historically Black Colleges and Universities Internship Program established in 1995, the Hispanic Internship Program established in 1998, and the Tribal Colleges and Universities Internship Program, established in 2000. Those 3 programs were merged into the Fossil Energy Minority Education Initiative, renamed the Mickey Leland Energy Fellowship Program in 2000. Sites to which interns may be assigned include the Albany Research Center (Albany, Oregon), the National Energy Technology Laboratory (Morgantown, West Virginia and Pittsburgh, Pennsylvania), Lawrence Berkeley National Laboratory (Berkeley, California), Argonne National Laboratory (Argonne, Illinois), Pacific Northwest National Laboratory (Richland, Washington), Rocky Mountain Oilfield Testing Center (Casper, Wyoming), or Strategic Petroleum Reserve Project Management Office (New Orleans, Louisiana), Other possible locations include United States Geological Survey (Reston, Virginia), Marathon Oil Corporation (Houston, Texas), Schlumberger (Sugar Land, Texas), or U.S. Department of Energy Headquarters (Washington, D.C.).
Number awarded Varies each year; recently, 30 students participated in this program.
Deadline February of each year.

[1284]
MICROBIOLOGY UNDERGRADUATE RESEARCH FELLOWSHIP

American Society for Microbiology
Attn: Education Board
1752 N Street, N.W.
Washington, DC 20036-2904
(202) 942-9283 Fax: (202) 942-9329
E-mail: fellowships-careerinformation@asmusa.org
Web: www.asm.org/Education/index.asp?bid=4322

Purpose To provide Native American and other underrepresented minority college students with the opportunity to work on a summer research project in microbiology under the mentorship of a member of the American Society for Microbiology (ASM).

Eligibility This program is open to African Americans, Hispanic Americans, Native Americans, Alaskan Native Americans, and Native Pacific Islanders who 1) are enrolled as full-time undergraduate students; 2) have taken introductory courses in biology, chemistry, and (preferably) microbiology prior to applying; 3) have a strong interest in obtaining a Ph.D. or M.D./Ph.D. in the microbiological sciences; 4) have laboratory research experience; and 5) are U.S. citizens or permanent residents. Applicants must be interested in conducting basic science research at a host institution during the summer under an ASM mentor. Selection is based on academic achievement, achievement in previous research experiences or independent projects, career goals as a research scientist, commitment to research, personal motivation to participate in the project, willingness to conduct summer research with an ASM member located at an institution other than their own, and leadership skills.

Financial data Students receive $3,500 as a stipend, up to $850 for student lodging, up to $500 for round-trip travel to the host institution, 2-year student membership in the ASM, and travel support up to $1,000 if they present the results of the research project at the ASM general meeting the following year.

Duration 10 to 12 weeks during the summer.

Additional information Recently, placements were available at Albert Einstein College of Medicine (Bronx, New York) and Tufts University School of Medicine (Boston, Massachusetts). In addition to their research activities, fellows participate in a weekly seminar series, journal club, GRE preparatory course, graduate admission counseling, and career counseling.

Number awarded 5 to 8 students are placed at each institution.

Deadline January of each year.

[1285]
MICROSOFT NATIONAL SCHOLARSHIPS

Microsoft Corporation
Attn: Microsoft Scholarship Program
One Microsoft Way
Redmond, WA 98052-8303
(425) 882-8080 TTY: (800) 892-9811
E-mail: scholars@microsoft.com
Web: www.microsoft.com/college/ss_overview.mspx

Purpose To provide financial assistance and summer work experience to undergraduate students, especially members of underrepresented groups, interested in preparing for a career in computer science or other related technical fields.

Eligibility This program is open to students who are enrolled full time and making satisfactory progress toward an undergraduate degree in computer science, computer engineering, or a related technical discipline (such as electrical engineering, mathematics, or physics) with a demonstrated interest in computer science. Applicants must be enrolled at a 4-year college or university in the United States, Canada, or Mexico. They must have a GPA of 3.0 or higher. Although all students who meet the eligibility criteria may apply, a large majority of scholarships are awarded to women, underrepresented minorities (African Americans, Hispanics, and Native Americans), and students with disabilities. Along with their application, students must submit an essay that describes the following 4 items: 1) how they demonstrate their passion for technology outside the classroom; 2) the toughest technical problem they have worked on, how they addressed the problem, their role in reaching the outcome if it was team-based, and the final outcome; 3) a situation that demonstrates initiative and their willingness to go above and beyond; and 4) how they are currently funding their college education.

Financial data Scholarships cover 100% of the tuition as posted by the financial aid office of the university or college the recipient designates. Scholarships are made through that school and are not transferable to other academic institutions. Funds may be used for tuition only and may not be used for other costs on the recipient's bursar bill, such as room and board.

Duration 1 year.

Additional information Selected recipients are offered a paid summer internship where they will have a chance to develop Microsoft products.

Number awarded Varies each year; a total of $540,000 is available for this program annually.

Deadline January of each year.

[1286]
MINORITY ACCESS INTERNSHIP

Minority Access, Inc.
Attn: Directory of Internship Program
5214 Baltimore Avenue
Hyattsville, MD 20781
(301) 779-7100 Fax: (301) 779-9812
Web: www.minorityaccess.org

Purpose To provide work experience to minority and other undergraduate and graduate students interested in internships at participating entities in Washington, D.C. and throughout the United States.

Eligibility This program is open to full-time undergraduate and graduate students who have a GPA of 3.0 or higher. Applicants must be U.S. citizens for most positions. All academic majors are eligible. Interns are selected by participating federal government and other agencies. Most of these are located in Washington, D.C., but placements may be made anywhere in the United States.

Financial data The weekly stipend ranges from $390 to $420 for sophomores and juniors, from $430 to $450 for seniors, or from $510 to $520 for graduate and professional students. In addition, most internships include paid round-trip travel between home and the internship location.

Duration Spring internships are 5 months, starting in January; summer internships are 3 months, starting in August; fall internships are 4 months, starting in September.

Additional information Minority Access, Inc. is committed to the diversification of institutions, federal agencies and corporations of all kinds and to improving their recruitment, retention, and enhancement of minorities. The majority of interns are placed in the Washington, D.C. metropolitan area. Both full-time and part-time internships are awarded. Students may receive academic credit for full-time internships. Students are expected to pay all housing costs. They are required to attend a pre-employment session in Washington, D.C., all seminars and workshops hosted by Minority Access, and any mandatory activities sponsored by the host agency.

Number awarded Varies each year.

Deadline February of each year for summer internships; July of each year for fall internships; and December of each year for spring internships.

[1287]
MINORITY INSTITUTIONS BIOLOGICAL AND ENVIRONMENTAL STUDENT RESEARCH PARTICIPATION PROGRAM

Oak Ridge Institute for Science and Education
Attn: Science and Engineering Education
P.O. Box 117
Oak Ridge, TN 37831-0117
(865) 576-3937   Fax: (865) 241-5219
E-mail: michael.hubbard@orau.gov
Web: see.orau.org

Purpose To provide opportunities for students at minority institutions to participate in health and environmental research at facilities of the U.S. Department of Energy's Office of Biological and Environmental Research (BER) during the summer.

Eligibility This program is open to graduate students at Historically Black Colleges and Universities (HBCUs), Tribal Colleges and Universities (TCUs), and Hispanic Serving Institutions (HSIs) who are interested in conducting research at BER facilities in the areas of health and the environment. U.S. citizenship or permanent resident status is required. Fields of study include atmospheric science, biochemistry, biology, biophysics, bioremediation, biostatistics, chemistry, ecology, genetics, genomics, marine science, molecular and cellular biology, measurement science, molecular nuclear medicine, nuclear medicine, pathology, physics, physiology, radiation biology, structural biology, terrestrial sciences, toxicology, and other related life, biomedical, and environmental science disciplines.

Financial data The stipend is $650 per week. Participants also receive limited travel reimbursement for round-trip transportation expenses between their home or campus and the research facility.

Duration 10 weeks during the summer.

Additional information Fellows may conduct research at any of the following participating BER facilities: Ames Laboratory (Ames, Iowa); Argonne National Laboratory (Argonne, Illinois); Brookhaven National Laboratory (Upton, New York); Ernest Orlando Lawrence Berkeley National Laboratory (Berkeley, California); Lawrence Livermore National Laboratory (Livermore, California); Los Alamos National Laboratory (Los Alamos, New Mexico); Oak Ridge National Laboratory (Oak Ridge, Tennessee); Pacific Northwest National Laboratory (Richland, Washington); Savannah River Site (Aiken, South Carolina); or Savannah River Ecology Laboratory (Aiken, South Carolina). This program is funded by BER and administered by Oak Ridge Institute for Science and Education (ORISE).

Number awarded Varies each year.

Deadline January of each year.

[1288]
MINORITY MEDICAL STUDENT SUMMER EXTERNSHIP IN ADDICTION PSYCHIATRY

American Psychiatric Association
Attn: Department of Minority and National Affairs
1000 Wilson Boulevard, Suite 1825
Arlington, VA 22209-3901
(703) 907-8653   Toll-free: (888) 35-PSYCH
Fax: (703) 907-7852   E-mail: mking@psych.org
Web: www.psych.org

Purpose To provide funding to Native American and other minority medical students who are interested in working on a research project during the summer with a mentor who specializes in addiction psychiatry.

Eligibility This program is open to minority medical students who have a specific interest in services related to substance abuse treatment and prevention. Minorities include American Indians, Alaska Natives, Native Hawaiians, Asian Americans, Hispanic/Latinos, and African Americans. Applicants must be interested in working with a mentor who specializes in addiction psychiatry. Work settings provide an emphasis on working clinically with or studying underserved minority populations and issues of co-occurring disorders, substance abuse treatment, and mental health disparity. Most of them are in inner-city or rural settings.

Financial data Externships provide $1,500 for travel expenses to go to the work setting of the mentor and up to another $1,500 for out-of-pocket expenses directly related to the conduct of the externship.

Duration 1 month during the summer.

Additional information Funding for this program is provided by the Substance Abuse and Mental Health Services Administration (SAMHSA).

Number awarded 10 each year.

Deadline February of each year.

[1289]
MINORITY MEDICAL STUDENT SUMMER MENTORING PROGRAM

American Psychiatric Association
Attn: Department of Minority and National Affairs
1000 Wilson Boulevard, Suite 1825
Arlington, VA 22209-3901
(703) 907-8653   Toll-free: (888) 35-PSYCH
Fax: (703) 907-7852   E-mail: mking@psych.org
Web: www.psych.org

Purpose To provide funding to Native American and other minority medical students who are interested in working on a summer project with a psychiatrist mentor.

Eligibility This program is open to minority medical students who are interested in psychiatric issues. Minorities include American Indians, Alaska Natives, Native Hawaiians, Asian Americans, Hispanic/Latinos, and African Americans. Applicants must be interested in working with a psychiatrist mentor, primarily on clinical work with underserved minority populations and mental health care disparities. Work settings may be in a research, academic, or clinical environment. Most of them are inner-city or rural, preferably those dealing with psychiatric subspecialties, particularly substance abuse and geriatrics. Selection is based on interest of the medical student and specialty of the mentor, practice setting, and geographic proximity of the mentor to the student.

Financial data Fellowships provide $1,500 for living expenses and up to another $1,500 for out-of-pocket expenses directly related to the conduct of the fellowship.

Duration Summer months.

Number awarded Varies each year.

Deadline February of each year.

[1290]
MINORITY MEDICAL STUDENTS ELECTIVE IN HIV PSYCHIATRY

American Psychiatric Association
Attn: Institute for Research and Education
1000 Wilson Boulevard, Suite 1825
Arlington, VA 22209-3901
(703) 907-8668   Toll-free: (888) 357-7849
Fax: (703) 907-1089   E-mail: dpennessi@psych.org
Web: www.psych.org/aids

Purpose To provide an opportunity for Native American and other minority medical students to spend an elective residency learning about HIV psychiatry.

Eligibility This program is open to minority medical students entering their fourth year at an accredited M.D. or D.O. degree-granting institution. Applicants must be interested in a psychiatry, internal medicine, pediatrics, or research career. They must be interested in participating in a program that includes intense training in HIV mental health (including neuropsychiatry), a clinical and/or research experience working with a mentor, and participation in the Committee on AIDS of the American Psychiatric Association (APA). U.S. citizenship is required.

Financial data A stipend is provided (amount not specified).

Duration 1 year.

Additional information The heart of the program is in establishing a mentor relationship at 1 of 5 sites, becoming involved with a cohort of medical students interested in HIV medicine/psychiatry, participating in an interactive didactic/experimental learning program, and developing expertise in areas related to ethnic minority mental health research or psychiatric services. Students selected for this program who are not APA members automatically receive membership.

Number awarded Varies each year.

Deadline March of each year.

[1291]
MINORITY UNDERGRADUATE RESEARCH FELLOWSHIP PROGRAM

California Institute of Technology
Attn: Minority Undergraduate Research Fellowship Program
Student-Faculty Programs Office
Mail Code 08-31
Pasadena, CA 91125
(626) 395-2885   Fax: (626) 568-9102
E-mail: sfp@caltech.edu
Web: www.murf.caltech.edu

Purpose To provide an opportunity for Native American and other underrepresented college students to work in a research laboratory at California Institute of Technology (Caltech) during the summer.

Eligibility This program is open to African American, Latino, and Native American students who are interested in working in an academic research laboratory at Caltech under the guidance of experienced scientists and engineers. Applicants must be undergraduate sophomores, juniors, or nongraduating seniors who have a GPA of 3.0 or higher and a major in astronomy, biology, chemistry and chemical engineering, engineering and applied science, geological and planetary sciences, mathematics, or physics. U.S. citizenship or permanent resident status is required.

Financial data The stipend is $600 per week. A housing and travel allowance is also provided.

Duration 8 to 10 weeks during the summer, beginning in June.

Additional information Support for this program is provided by the NSF Center for the Science and Engineering of Materials, the Gordon and Betty Moore Foundation, and the Howard Hughes Medical Institute.

Number awarded Varies each year.

Deadline January of each year.

[1292]
MISSOURI SPACE GRANT CONSORTIUM SUMMER HIGH SCHOOL INTERNSHIPS

Missouri Space Grant Consortium
c/o Missouri University of Science and Technology
226 Toomey Hall
400 West 13th Street
Rolla, MO 65409-0050
(573) 341-4887   Fax: (573) 341-4607
E-mail: sbhaug@mst.edu
Web: web.mst.edu/~spaceg/scholarships.html

Purpose To provide work experience during the summer to minority and other high school students in Missouri interested in a career in an aerospace field.

Eligibility This program is open to Missouri high school students who have just completed their junior or senior year. Applicants must be proposing a specific research or education project at a participating affiliate of the Missouri Space Grant Consortium. Selection is based on academic records, letters of recommendation, and reasons for wanting to enter the program. U.S. citizenship is required. The Missouri Space Grant Consortium is a component of the U.S. National Aeronautics and Space Administration

(NASA), which encourages participation by women, underrepresented minorities, and people with disabilities.
Financial data The maximum award is $2,000.
Duration Summer months.
Additional information This program is funded by NASA. The participating affiliates are University of Missouri at Columbia, Missouri University of Science and Technology, Missouri State University, and Washington University.
Number awarded Approximately 5 each year.

[1293]
MISSOURI SPACE GRANT CONSORTIUM UNDERGRADUATE RESEARCH INTERNSHIP PROGRAM

Missouri Space Grant Consortium
c/o Missouri University of Science and Technology
226 Toomey Hall
400 West 13th Street
Rolla, MO 65409-0050
(573) 341-4887   Fax: (573) 341-4607
E-mail: sbhaug@mst.edu
Web: web.mst.edu/~spaceg/scholarships.html

Purpose To provide research experience to minority and other undergraduate students in Missouri working on a degree in an aerospace field.
Eligibility This program is open to undergraduate students studying engineering, physics, astronomy, or planetary sciences at member institutions of the Missouri Space Grant Consortium. Applicants must be proposing a specific research or education project in a research laboratory, a computing facility, or the galleries of the St. Louis Science Center. Selection is based on academic records, letters of recommendation, and reasons for wanting to enter the program. U.S. citizenship is required. The Missouri Space Grant Consortium is a component of the U.S. National Aeronautics and Space Administration (NASA), which encourages participation by women, underrepresented minorities, and people with disabilities.
Financial data Awards are approximately $2,000 for the summer or $3,000 for the academic year.
Duration Both summer and academic year appointments are available.
Additional information The consortium members are Missouri State University, University of Missouri at Columbia, Missouri University of Science and Technology, University of Missouri at St. Louis, and Washington University. This program is funded by NASA.
Number awarded Approximately 30 each year.

[1294]
MORGAN STANLEY MBA FELLOWSHIP

Morgan Stanley
Attn: Diversity Recruiting
750 Seventh Avenue, 31st Floor
New York, NY 10019
(212) 762-0211   Fax: (212) 507-4972
E-mail: diversityrecruiting@morganstanley.com
Web: www.morganstanley.com

Purpose To provide financial assistance and work experience to Native Americans and members of other underrepresented minority groups who are working on an M.B.A. degree.
Eligibility This program is open to M.B.A. students of African American, Hispanic, and Native American descent. Selection is based on assigned essays, academic achievement, recommendations, extracurricular activities, leadership qualities, and on-site interviews.
Financial data The program provides full payment of tuition and fees and a paid summer internship.
Duration 1 year; may be renewed for a second year, providing the student remains enrolled full time in good academic standing and completes the summer internship following the first year.
Additional information The paid summer internship is offered within Morgan Stanley institutional securities (equity research, fixed income, institutional equity, investment banking), investment management, or private wealth management. This program was established in 1999.
Number awarded 1 or more each year.
Deadline April of each year.

[1295]
MORRIS K. UDALL NATIVE AMERICAN CONGRESSIONAL INTERNSHIP PROGRAM

Morris K. Udall Foundation
Attn: Program Manager, Internship Program
130 South Scott Avenue
Tucson, AZ 85701-1922
(520) 901-8568   Fax: (520) 670-5530
E-mail: ben@udall.gov
Web: www.udall.gov/udall.asp?link=300

Purpose To provide an opportunity for Native American upper-division and graduate students to work in a Congressional office during the summer.
Eligibility This program is open to American Indians and Alaska Natives who are enrolled members of recognized tribes and have an interest in tribal government and policy. Applicants must have a GPA of 3.0 or higher as a junior, senior, graduate student, law student, or recent graduate of a tribal or 4-year college. They must be able to participate in an internship in Washington, D.C., where they will gain practical experience in the legislative process, Congressional matters, and governmental proceedings that specifically relate to Native American issues. Fields of study of previous interns have included American Indian studies, political science, law and pre-law, psychology, social work, history, business and public administration, anthropology, community and urban planning, architecture, communications, health sciences, public health, biology, engineering, sociology, environmental studies and natural resources, economics, and justice studies. Applicants must demonstrate strong research and writing skills; organizational abilities and time management skills; maturity and responsibility; interest in learning how the federal government "really works;" commitment to their tribal community; knowledge of Congressman Morris K. Udall's legacy with regard to Native Americans; and awareness of issues and challenges currently facing Indian Country.
Financial data Interns receive round-trip airfare to Washington, D.C.; dormitory lodging at a local university; a daily allowance sufficient for meals, transportation, and inciden-

tals; and an educational stipend of $1,200 to be paid at the conclusion of the internship.
Duration 10 weeks during the summer.
Additional information These internships were first offered in 1996.
Number awarded 12 each year.
Deadline January of each year.

[1296]
MULTICULTURAL ADVERTISING INTERN PROGRAM

American Association of Advertising Agencies
Attn: Manager of Diversity Programs
405 Lexington Avenue, 18th Floor
New York, NY 10174-1801
(212) 850-0732 Toll-free: (800) 676-9333
Fax: (212) 682-2028 E-mail: maip@aaaa.org
Web: www.aaaa-maip.org

Purpose To provide Native Americans and other racial minority students with summer work experience in advertising agencies and to present them with an overview of the agency business.
Eligibility This program is open to college juniors, seniors, graduate students, and students at any academic level attending a portfolio school of the sponsor who are Black/African American, Asian/Asian American, Pacific Islander, Hispanic, North American Indian/Native American, or multiracial. Applicants may be majoring in any field, but they must be able to demonstrate a serious commitment to preparing for a career in advertising. They must have a GPA of 3.0 or higher. Students with a cumulative GPA of 2.7 to 2.9 are encouraged to apply, but they must complete an additional essay question. U.S. citizenship or permanent resident status is required.
Financial data Interns are paid a salary of $350 to $400 per week. If they do not live in the area of their host agencies, they may stay in housing arranged by the sponsor. They are responsible for a percentage of the cost of housing and materials.
Duration 10 weeks during the summer.
Additional information Interns may be assigned duties in the following departments: account management, broadcast production, media buying/planning, creative (art direction or copywriting), digital/interactive technologies, print production, strategic/account planning, or traffic. The portfolio schools are the AdCenter at Virginia Commonwealth University, the Creative Circus and the Portfolio Center in Atlanta, the Miami Ad School, the University of Texas at Austin, Pratt Institute, the Minneapolis College of Art and Design, and the Art Center College of Design in Pasadena, California.
Number awarded Approximately 100 each year.
Deadline December of each year.

[1297]
MULTICULTURAL UNDERGRADUATE INTERNSHIPS AT THE GETTY CENTER

Getty Foundation
Attn: Multicultural Undergraduate Internships
1200 Getty Center Drive, Suite 800
Los Angeles, CA 90049-1685
(310) 440-7320 Fax: (310) 440-7703
E-mail: summerinterns@getty.edu
Web: www.getty.edu

Purpose To provide summer work experience at facilities of the Getty Center to Native American and other minority undergraduates with ties to Los Angeles County, California.
Eligibility This program is open to currently-enrolled undergraduates who either reside or attend college in Los Angeles County, California. Applicants must be members of groups currently underrepresented in museum professions and fields related to the visual arts and humanities: individuals of African American, Asian, Latino/Hispanic, Native American, or Pacific Islander descent. They may be majoring in any field, including the sciences and technology, and are not required to have demonstrated a previous commitment to the visual arts. Along with their application, they must submit a personal statement of up to 500 words on why they are interested in this internship, including what they hope to gain from the program, their interest or involvement in issues of multiculturalism, aspects of their past experience that they feel are most relevant to the application, and any specific career or educational avenues they are interested in exploring.
Financial data The stipend is $3,500.
Duration 10 weeks during the summer.
Additional information Internships provide training and work experience in such areas as conservation, library collections, publications, museum education, curatorship, grants administration, public programs, site operations, and information technology.
Number awarded Varies each year.
Deadline February of each year.

[1298]
MUTUAL OF OMAHA ACTUARIAL SCHOLARSHIP FOR MINORITY STUDENTS

Mutual of Omaha
Attn: Strategic Staffing-Actuarial Recruitment
Mutual of Omaha Plaza
Omaha, NE 68175
(402) 351-3300
Web: www.mutualofomaha.com

Purpose To provide financial assistance and work experience to Native American and other minority undergraduate students who are preparing for an actuarial career.
Eligibility This program is open to members of minority groups (African American, Hispanic, Native American, Asian or Pacific Islander, or Alaskan Eskimo) who have completed at least 24 semester hours of full-time study. Applicants must be working on an actuarial or mathematics-related degree with the goal of preparing for an actuarial career. They must have a GPA of 3.0 or higher and have passed at least 1 actuarial examination. Prior to accepting the award, they must be available to complete a summer internship at the sponsor's home office in Omaha, Nebraska. Along with

their application, they must submit a 1-page personal statement on why they are interested in becoming an actuary and how they are preparing themselves for an actuarial career.

Financial data The scholarship stipend is $2,500 per year. Funds are paid directly to the student. For the internship, students receive an hourly rate of pay, subsidized housing, and financial incentives for successful examination results received during the internship period.

Duration 1 year. Recipients may reapply if they maintain a cumulative GPA of 3.0 or higher.

Number awarded Varies each year.

Deadline January of each year.

[1299] NASA GRADUATE STUDENT RESEARCHERS PROGRAM

National Aeronautics and Space Administration
Attn: Office of Education
500 E Street, S.W., Suite 200
Washington, DC 20024-2760
(202) 358-0402   Fax: (202) 358-3523
E-mail: katie.blanding@nasa.gov
Web: fellowships.hq.nasa.gov/gsrp/program

Purpose To provide funding to minority and other graduate students interested in conducting research in fields of interest to the U.S. National Aeronautics and Space Administration (NASA).

Eligibility This program is open to full-time students enrolled or planning to enroll in an accredited graduate program at a U.S. college or university. Applicants must be citizens of the United States, sponsored by a faculty adviser or department chair, and interested in conducting research in space sciences. They must also be interested in a summer internship at a NASA field center. Selection is based on academic qualifications, quality of the proposed research and its relevance to NASA's program, proposed utilization of center research facilities (except for NASA headquarters), and ability of the student to accomplish the defined research. Individuals from underrepresented groups in science, technology, engineering, and mathematics (STEM) fields (African Americans, Native Americans, Alaskan Natives, Mexican Americans, Puerto Ricans, Native Pacific Islanders, women, and persons with disabilities) are strongly urged to apply. First-time applicants are eligible only for research opportunities offered by NASA field centers or the Aeronautics Research Mission Directorate; renewal awards are available from NASA field centers and all Mission Directorates.

Financial data The program provides a $21,000 student stipend, a $4,000 student travel allowance, up to $1,000 for health insurance, and a $4,000 university allowance. The student stipend may cover tuition, room and board, books, software, meal plans, school and laboratory supplies, and other related expenses. The student travel allowance may be used for national and international conferences and data collection. The university allowance is a discretionary award that typically goes to the research adviser. If the student already has health insurance, that $1,000 grant may be added to the student stipend or student travel allowance. An additional stipend of $10,000 for the first year is available to students approved for the Aeronautics Fellowship.

Duration 1 year; may be renewed for up to 2 additional years.

Additional information This program was established in 1980. Under the current NASA organizational structure, the Aeronautics Research Mission Directorate (ARMD) supports research in aeronautical engineering; the Exploration Systems Mission Directorate (ESMD) supports research in chemical, electrical, materials, mechanical, and metallurgical engineering, chemistry, physics, biological and life science, environmental science, and other sciences; the Science Mission Directorate, Office of Earth Science Division (SMD-ES) supports research in mechanical engineering, chemistry, physics, physical science, mathematics, computer science, biological science, social science, atmospheric science, geological science, oceanography, and environmental science; the Science Mission Directorate-Office of Space Science (SMD-SS) supports research in astronomy, chemistry, physics, physical science, computer science, biological science, and atmospheric science; the Space Operations Mission Directorate (SOMD) supports research in materials, mechanical, and metallurgical engineering, mathematics, and computer science. Other awards are distributed through NASA field centers, each of which has its own research agenda and facilities. These centers include Ames Research Center (Moffett Field, California), Dryden Flight Research Facility (Edwards, California), Goddard Space Flight Center (Greenbelt, Maryland), Jet Propulsion Laboratory (Pasadena, California), Johnson Space Center (Houston, Texas), Kennedy Space Center (Kennedy Space Center, Florida), Langley Research Center (Hampton, Virginia), Glenn Research Center (Cleveland, Ohio), Marshall Space Flight Center (Huntsville, Alabama), and Stennis Space Center (Stennis Space Center, Mississippi). Fellows spend some period of time in residence at the center, taking advantage of the unique research facilities of the installation and working with center personnel. They also conduct an internship there during the summers. Travel outside the United States is allowed if it is essential to the research effort and charged to a grant.

Number awarded This program supports approximately 300 graduate students each year.

Deadline January of each year.

[1300] NASA UNDERGRADUATE STUDENT RESEARCH PROGRAM

Universities Space Research Association
Attn: NASA USRP Project Administrator
2101 NASA Parkway, AE2 Education Office
Houston, TX 77058
(281) 244-6957   E-mail: usrp@epo.usra.edu
Web: www.epo.usra.edu/usrp

Purpose To provide an opportunity for minority and other undergraduate students to participate in a research project at centers of the U.S. National Aeronautics and Space Administration (NASA).

Eligibility This program is open to sophomores, juniors, and seniors enrolled full time at accredited U.S. colleges and universities. Applicants must have a GPA of 3.0 or higher with an academic major or demonstrated course work concentration in engineering, mathematics, computer science, or physical/life sciences. They must be interested in participating in a mentored research experience at a designated NASA center. The program seeks participation from students who represent America's rich and diverse population: female and male students of all races, creeds, colors, national origins, ages, and disabilities. U.S. citizenship is required.

Financial data The stipend is $6,000 for the summer session or $9,000 for the fall or spring semester. Participants also receive round-trip airfare or ground transportation costs to and from the NASA host center.

Duration 10 weeks during the summer or 15 weeks during the fall or spring semester.

Additional information The participating NASA centers include Ames Research Center (Mountain View, California), Dryden Flight Research Center (Edwards, California), Glenn Research Center (Cleveland, Ohio), Goddard Space Flight Center (Greenbelt, Maryland), Jet Propulsion Laboratory (Pasadena, California), Johnson Space Center (Houston, Texas), Kennedy Space Center (Florida), Langley Research Center (Hampton, Virginia), Los Alamos National Laboratory (New Mexico), Marshall Space Flight Center (Huntsville, Alabama), Stennis Space Center (Mississippi), Wallops Flight Facility (Virginia), and White Sands Test Facility (New Mexico).

Number awarded Up to 100 each year.

[1301]
NATIONAL ASSOCIATION OF STUDENT PERSONNEL ADMINISTRATORS UNDERGRADUATE FELLOWSHIP PROGRAM

National Association of Student Personnel
  Administrators
Attn: NUFP
1875 Connecticut Avenue, N.W., Suite 418
Washington, DC 20009-5728
(202) 265-7500, ext. 1163   Fax: (202) 797-1157
E-mail: nvictoria@naspa.org
Web: www.naspa.org/programs/nufp/index.cfm

Purpose To provide summer work experience and leadership training to minorities, students with disabilities, and persons who identify as lesbian, gay, bisexual, or transgender (LGBT) and are completing their second year in college.

Eligibility Eligible to be nominated for this program are 1) ethnic minority students (Indigenous, African, Asian, or Hispanic Americans), 2) students with disabilities; or 3) students who identify as LGBT. Applicants must be completing their sophomore year in a 4-year institution or their second year in a 2-year transfer program. They must have a GPA of 2.2 or higher and be able to demonstrate academic promise and an interest in a future in higher education.

Financial data Participants are offered a paid summer internship, and all expenses are paid to attend the leadership institutes.

Duration The internship lasts 8 weeks during the summer. Leadership institutes last 4 days.

Additional information The program was initiated in the 1989-90 academic year as the Minority Undergraduate Fellows Program (MUFP). In 2000-01 it was broadened to include students with disabilities and in 2005 was renamed and expanded again to include LGBT students. It offers 3 main components: 1) participation in a 1- or 2-year internship or field experience under the guidance of a mentor; 2) participation in a summer leadership institute designed to enhance skill building and career development; and 3) participation in an 8-week paid summer internship designed to encourage the development of future student affairs and higher education administrators.

Number awarded Varies each year; recently, 167 undergraduates were participating in the program.

Deadline April of each year.

[1302]
NATIONAL CENTER FOR COOPERATIVE EDUCATION SCHOLARSHIPS

National Center for Cooperative Education
c/o Haskell Indian Nations University
Natural Resources Liaison Office
155 Indian Avenue, Box 5018
Lawrence, KS 66046
(785) 749-8414   E-mail: daeifler@fs.fed.us
Web: www.haskell.edu

Purpose To provide financial assistance and work experience to American Indian and Alaska Native students interested in preparing for a career in a natural resource field.

Eligibility This program is open to American Indian and Alaska Native students who have finished at least their freshman year at an accredited college or university. Applicants must be working on a bachelor's or higher degree in a natural resources field, including forestry, soil conservation, range management, geographic information systems (GIS), wildlife management, watershed/hydrology, fisheries management, or civil engineering. They must be interested in preparing for a career with tribes, the Bureau of Indian Affairs (BIA), or other natural resources agencies. Along with their application, they must submit a letter that includes their perception of their academic and professional strengths and a description of their academic and career potential. They must also be interested in summer employment related to their academic field of study.

Financial data The scholarship stipend is $5,000 per year. The salary for summer employment ranges from $9 to $11 per hour.

Duration 1 academic year and 1 summer; may be renewed.

Additional information The National Center for Cooperative Education (NCCE) was established in 1997 by the BIA.

Number awarded Varies each year.

Deadline March of each year.

[1303]
NATIONAL CONGRESS OF AMERICAN INDIANS FELLOWSHIPS

National Congress of American Indians
Attn: Internship Program
1301 Connecticut Avenue, N.W., Suite 200
Washington, DC 20036
(202) 466-7767   Fax: (2020 466-7797
E-mail: ncai@ncai.org
Web: www.ncai.org/Internships_Fellowships.13.0.html

Purpose To provide an opportunity for recent college graduates to gain work experience at the offices of the National Congress of American Indians (NCAI).

Eligibility Applicants must have recently completed an undergraduate or graduate degree and be interested in gaining work experience at NCAI. They must describe their previous experience with American Indian and Alaska Native issues; the areas of NCAI's work that are of most interest to them; the relevant work, volunteer experience, or other involvement they have had in the field of Indian affairs or other political, social, or community issues of concern to them; their familiarity with electronic communications, including research and specific software; why they are interested in working with NCAI; what they hope to gain from the fellowship experience; how the fellowship experience relates to their long-range plans; and any special skills or experience they feel they would bring to NCAI. Contact information for 2 references should also be provided; they may be professors, employers, tribal leaders, or personal references.

Financial data The stipend is approximately $16,500. Fellows also receive coverage under NCAI's health insurance plan.

Duration 11 months, beginning in September.

Additional information Work assignments cover 3 areas: advocacy, research, and writing.

Number awarded 2 or 3 each year.

Deadline April of each year.

[1304]
NATIONAL ENERGY TECHNOLOGY LABORATORY MINORITY MENTORING AND INTERNSHIP PROGRAM

Department of Energy
Attn: National Energy Technology Laboratory
626 Cochrans Mill Road
P.O. Box 10940 (MS 921-204)
Pittsburgh, PA 15236-0940
(412) 386-5822 E-mail: MMIT@netl.doe.gov
Web: www.netl.doe.gov

Purpose To provide an opportunity for Native American and other minority students to gain work experience at a National Energy Technology Laboratory (NETL).

Eligibility This program is open to minority students enrolled at least half time in a program leading to a baccalaureate, graduate, or professional degree. Applicants must have demonstrated an aptitude for and interest in science and/or engineering. They must be able to complete at least 640 hours of work while enrolled as a student at an accredited educational program. Along with their application, they must submit a resume that includes a reference to the Minority Mentoring and Internship Program, their address and contact information, citizenship, educational history including month and year of anticipated degree, GPA, field of study, skills, employment history, and other information they wish to have considered. Recently, the program focused on students majoring in chemistry, engineering, and geology.

Financial data Salaries range from the GS-4 to GS-11 level (approximately $11.43 to $23.45 per hour), depending on education and experience.

Duration 1 year. Interns work full or part time throughout the year as their educational commitment allows.

Additional information This program began in 2001. The NETL facilities are located in Pittsburgh, Pennsylvania; Morgantown, West Virginia; and Tulsa, Oklahoma. Interns work under the guidance of an NETL technical expert.

Number awarded Varies each year.

[1305]
NATIONAL MEDICAL FELLOWSHIP PROGRAM IN ACADEMIC MEDICINE FOR MINORITY STUDENTS

National Medical Fellowships, Inc.
Attn: Scholarship Program
5 Hanover Square, 15th Floor
New York, NY 10004
(212) 483-8880 Fax: (212) 483-8897
E-mail: info@nmfonline.org
Web: www.nmfonline.org

Purpose To provide an opportunity for Native American and other underrepresented minority medical school students to gain research experience in biomedical research and academic medicine.

Eligibility This program is open to U.S. citizens who are members of 1 of the following underrepresented minority groups: African American, Alaska Native, American Indian, Native Hawaiian, Mexican American, or mainland Puerto Rican. Applicants must be first- through third-year students attending accredited medical schools or osteopathic colleges in the United States. M.D./Ph.D. candidates are eligible but do not receive first consideration. Applicants must submit a statement discussing their career goals over the next 10 years and how the fellowship would be instrumental in reaching those goals. Selection is based on academic achievement, potential for playing a responsible role in academic medicine, leadership ability, the clarity of the project description, the definition of the project objectives, a clear demonstration of the student's grasp of the project objectives, and evidence of a clear relationship between the student and a mentor.

Financial data The grant is $6,000, up to $2,000 of which is available to the mentor to offset expenses during the research period.

Duration 8 to 12 weeks, either during the summer or as an elective rotation during the academic year.

Additional information Interns work in a major research laboratory under the tutelage of a well-known biomedical scientist. The program was created in 1983 with grant support from The Commonwealth Fund of New York to foster mentor relationships between students and prominent scientists. The Bristol-Myers Squibb Foundation joined as a cosponsor in 1990 and assumed sole sponsorship in 1993.

Number awarded Up to 35 each year.

Deadline November of each year.

[1306]
NATIONAL MUSEUM FELLOWS PROGRAM FOR MINORITY STUDENTS

Atlanta History Center
Attn: Director, National Museum Fellows Program
130 West Paces Ferry Road, N.W.
Atlanta, GA 30305-1366
(404) 814-4024   Fax: (404) 814-2041
E-mail: bgaines@AtlantaHistoryCenter.com
Web: www.atlhist.org/template.cfm?cid=628

Purpose To provide museum training to Native American and other minority students who are attending designated colleges and universities in Georgia.

Eligibility This program is open to undergraduate students at 9 designated colleges and universities in metropolitan Atlanta. Candidates must be interested in preparing for a museum career and must be nominated by their college or university; each participating institution may nominate 3 students. Nominees must be full-time juniors or seniors in the following academic year with a declared major in a liberal arts discipline. Minority students (African American, Asian American, Latino American, Native American, or any other ethnic group underrepresented in the museum profession) are encouraged to seek nomination from their major professors. No minimum GPA is required, but a GPA of 3.0 or higher is generally considered preferable.

Financial data The stipend is $6,000, disbursed at the rate of $750 for the fall semester, $750 for the spring semester, and $4,500 during a summer apprenticeship. There are no restrictions on the stipend, and fellows can use the money in ways that best support their academic and/or financial needs during the year. Their college or university is asked to provide 2 semesters of course credit at no additional tuition expense.

Duration The program is a year-long internship that consists of 2 12-week semesters (fall and spring) and a 12-week summer apprenticeship.

Additional information This program began in 1994. During the academic year, fellows attend a weekly 3-hour seminar taught by the Atlanta History Center staff. During the summer, they are considered full-time employees of the Center. A week of travel to museums in other cities is provided by the program. The participating colleges and universities are Agnes Scott College, Clark Atlanta University, Emory University, Georgia State University, Georgia Institute of Technology, Morehouse College, Morris Brown College, Oglethorpe University, and Spelman College.

Number awarded Varies each year.

Deadline Nominations must be submitted by February of each year.

[1307]
NATIONAL MUSEUM OF THE AMERICAN INDIAN INTERNSHIP PROGRAM

National Museum of the American Indian
Attn: Internship Program
Cultural Resources Center
4220 Silver Hill Road
Suitland, MD 20746-2863
(301) 238-1540   Fax: (301) 238-3200
E-mail: NMAIinterns@si.edu
Web: www.nmai.si.edu

Purpose To provide work and/or research opportunities for Native American students in the area of museum practice and related programming at the Smithsonian Institution's National Museum of the American Indian (NMAI).

Eligibility These internships are intended primarily for American Indian, Native Hawaiian, and Alaska Native students currently enrolled in undergraduate or graduate academic programs with a cumulative GPA of 3.0 or higher. Applicants must be interested in guided work/research experiences using the resources of the NMAI or other Smithsonian Institution facilities. Along with their application, they must submit a personal statement on their interest in the museum field, what they hope to accomplish through an internship, how it would relate to their academic and professional development, and what in particular about the NMAI interests them and leads them to apply for an internship.

Financial data Travel, housing, and stipends are provided on a limited basis.

Duration 4 sessions of 10 weeks each are held annually.

Additional information Intern projects vary by department. Most projects provide the intern with museum practice and program development experience. Some projects may be more research oriented. Most interns work from 20 to 40 hours per week. Positions are available at the Cultural Resources Center in Suitland, Maryland, the George Gustav Heye Center in New York, or the administrative offices in Washington, D.C.

Number awarded Varies each year. More than 100 students have participated in the program since it began in 1994.

Deadline February of each year for summer; July of each year for fall; October of each year for winter; November of each year for spring.

[1308]
NATIONAL OCEANIC AND ATMOSPHERIC ADMINISTRATION EDUCATIONAL PARTNERSHIP PROGRAM WITH MINORITY SERVING INSTITUTIONS GRADUATE SCIENCES PROGRAM

Oak Ridge Institute for Science and Education
Attn: Science and Engineering Education
P.O. Box 117
Oak Ridge, TN 37831-0117
(865) 241-6704   Fax: (865) 576-8293
E-mail: MCarl.Wheeler@orau.gov
Web: see.orau.org

Purpose To provide financial assistance and summer research experience to graduate students at Minority Serving Institutions who are majoring in scientific fields of interest to the National Oceanic and Atmospheric Administration (NOAA).

Eligibility This program is open to graduate students working on master's or doctoral degrees at Minority Serving Institutions, including Alaska Native Serving Institutions (ANSIs), Hispanic Serving Institutions (HSIs), Historically Black Colleges and Universities (HBCUs), Native Hawaiian Serving Institutions (NHSIs), and Tribal Colleges and Universities (TCUs). Applicants must be working on a degree in biology, cartography, chemistry, computer science, economics, engineering, environmental planning, fishery biology, geography, geology, hydrology, mathematics, meteorology, oceanography, physical science, physics, or social science. The program includes a training program during the summer at a NOAA research facility.

Financial data During the school year, the program provides payment of tuition, fees, books, housing, meals, travel expenses, and a 1-time academic allowance. During the summer, students receive a salary and benefits from NOAA.

Duration 2 years of study plus 16 weeks of research training during the summer.

Additional information This program is funded by NOAA and administered by Oak Ridge Institute for Science and Education (ORISE). Summer assignments are available in the following sections of NOAA: National Environmental, Satellite, Data and Information Service; National Weather Service; National Ocean Service; National Marine Fisheries Service; and Office of Oceanic and Atmospheric Research.

Number awarded 5 each year.

Deadline January of each year.

[1309]
NATIONAL OCEANIC AND ATMOSPHERIC ADMINISTRATION EDUCATIONAL PARTNERSHIP PROGRAM WITH MINORITY SERVING INSTITUTIONS UNDERGRADUATE SCHOLARSHIPS

Oak Ridge Institute for Science and Education
Attn: Science and Engineering Education
P.O. Box 117
Oak Ridge, TN 37831-0117
(865) 241-6704   Fax: (865) 576-8293
E-mail: MCarl.Wheeler@orau.gov
Web: see.orau.org

Purpose To provide financial assistance and research experience to undergraduate students at Minority Serving Institutions who are majoring in scientific fields of interest to the National Oceanic and Atmospheric Administration (NOAA).

Eligibility This program is open to juniors at Minority Serving Institutions, including Hispanic Serving Institutions (HSIs), Historically Black Colleges and Universities (HBCUs), and Tribal Colleges and Universities (TCUs). Applicants must be majoring in atmospheric science, biology, cartography, chemistry, computer science, engineering, environmental science, geodesy, geography, marine science, mathematics, meteorology, photogrammetry, physical science, physics, or remote sensing. They must also be interested in participating in a research internship at a NOAA site. U.S. citizenship is required.

Financial data This program provides payment of tuition and fees (to a maximum of $4,000 per year) and a stipend during the internship of $650 per week.

Duration 2 academic years and 2 summer internships.

Additional information This program is funded by NOAA through an interagency agreement with the U.S. Department of Energy and administered by Oak Ridge Institute for Science and Education (ORISE).

Number awarded 15 each year.

Deadline February of each year.

[1310]
NATIVE AMERICAN WOMEN'S HEALTH EDUCATION RESOURCE CENTER INTERNSHIPS

Native American Women's Health Education Resource Center
Attn: Internship Coordinator
P.O. Box 572
Lake Andes, SD 57356-0572
(605) 487-7072   Fax: (605) 487-7964
E-mail: colleenfasthorse@yahoo.com
Web: www.nativeshop.org/internships.html

Purpose To provide work experience to students and recent graduates interested in Native American rights and health issues.

Eligibility This program is open to college students, graduate students, and recent graduates. Applicants must have a background of work in Native American rights and health issues to promote civil rights, women's rights, and a healthy environment. They must be interested in working at the Native American Women's Health Education Resource Center and its Domestic Violence Shelter.

Financial data Interns receive a stipend of $500 per month, free room at the shelter, and partial board from the resource center's food pantry.

Duration 3 months to 1 year; priority is given for internships of 6 months or longer.

Additional information The Native American Women's Health Education Resource Center is a project of the Native American Community Board. It is located in Lake Andes, South Dakota in a rural area of the Yankton Sioux Reservation. The Domestic Violence Shelter is 4 blocks away. Past intern projects have included domestic violence advocacy at the shelter, counseling on the youth crisis hotline, environmental activism, Native women's reproductive health and rights, indigenous people's rights projects, web site development, organizing the annual community health fair, producing a Dakota language CD-ROM, and AIDS education.

Number awarded Varies each year.

[1311]
NEW JERSEY SPACE GRANT CONSORTIUM UNDERGRADUATE SUMMER FELLOWSHIPS

New Jersey Space Grant Consortium
c/o Stevens Institute of Technology
Castle Point on the Hudson
Hoboken, NJ 07030
(201) 216-8964   Fax: (201) 216-8929
E-mail: sthangam@stevens-tech.edu
Web: www.njsgc.org

Purpose To provide financial assistance for summer research experiences in space-related fields to minority and other college students in New Jersey.

Eligibility This program is open to undergraduate students who have completed at least 2 years at member institutions of the New Jersey Space Grant Consortium (NJSGC). Applicants must be proposing a program of space-related research in industry or at universities and their affiliated research laboratories. Their field of study may be aerospace engineering, biological science, chemical engineering, computer science and engineering, electrical engineering, materials science and engineering, mechanical engineering, natural science, or physical science. U.S. citizenship is required. The New Jersey Space Grant Consortium is a component of the U.S. National Aeronautics and Space Administration (NASA) Space Grant program, which encourages participation by women, underrepresented minorities, and people with disabilities. Selection is based on a biographical sketch, a brief statement of what they hope to accomplish as a space grant fellow, a statement of career goals (including their relationship to aerospace engineering and science), and a description of their plan for the immediate future.

Financial data The stipend is $600 per week, with an additional $600 per student available for laboratory supplies.

Duration 10 weeks during the summer.

Additional information Members of the NJSGC include New Jersey Institute of Technology, Princeton University, Rutgers University, Stevens Institute of Technology, and the University of Medicine and Dentistry of New Jersey. This program is funded by NASA.

Number awarded Varies each year. Recently, 8 of these fellowships were awarded. Approximately 60% of the fellows are placed in industries (or industry sponsored programs) and 40% go to universities and their affiliated research laboratories.

Deadline March of each year.

[1312]
NORTH CAROLINA COMMISSION OF INDIAN AFFAIRS WIA SUMMER WORK EXPERIENCE PROGRAM

North Carolina Commission of Indian Affairs
c/o North Carolina Department of Administration
100 East Six Forks Road, Suite 201
1317 Mail Service Center
Raleigh, NC 27699-1317
(919) 733-5900   Fax: (919) 420-1373
E-mail: Elk.Richardson@doa.nc.gov
Web: www.doa.state.nc.us/cia/progr-aiwdp.htm

Purpose To provide work experience during the summer to Indians in North Carolina who are economically disadvantaged.

Eligibility This program is open to Indian youth who live in 59 of the 100 counties in North Carolina. Candidates must be between 14 and 21 years of age; either a high school graduate or enrolled in high school, a 2-year college, or a 4-year college or university; and economically disadvantaged. They must be seeking work experience to develop good work habits and become exposed to various types of employment and opportunities.

Financial data Participants receive a salary that they can use for expenses during the coming school year.

Duration Summer months.

Additional information The North Carolina Commission of Indian Affairs administers this Workforce Investment Act (WIA) program in the 59 designated counties. In the other 41 counties, Indian tribes or other organizations are designated by the U.S. Department of Labor as administrators.

[1313]
NPSC GRADUATE FELLOWSHIPS

National Physical Science Consortium
c/o University of Southern California
3716 South Hope Street, Suite 348
Los Angeles, CA 90007-4344
(213) 743-2409   Toll-free: (800) 854-NPSC
Fax: (213) 743-2407   E-mail: npschq@npsc.org
Web: www.npsc.org/students/info.html

Purpose To provide financial assistance and summer work experience to underrepresented minorities and women interested in working on a Ph.D. in designated science and engineering fields.

Eligibility This program is open to U.S. citizens who are seniors graduating from college with a GPA of 3.0 or higher, enrolled in the first year of a doctoral program, completing a terminal master's degree, or returning from the work force and holding no more than a master's degree. Students currently in the third or subsequent year of a Ph.D. program or who already have a doctoral degree in any field (Ph.D., M.D., J.D., Ed.D.) are ineligible. Applicants must be interested in working on a Ph.D. in the physical sciences or related fields of science or engineering. The program welcomes applications from all qualified students and continues to emphasize the recruitment of underrepresented minority (African American, Hispanic, Native American Indian, Eskimo, Aleut, and Pacific Islander) and women physical science and engineering students. Fellowships are provided to students at the 116 universities that are members of the consortium. Selection is based on academic standing (GPA), course work taken in preparation for graduate school, university and/or industry research experience, letters of recommendation, and GRE scores.

Financial data The fellowship pays tuition and fees plus an annual stipend of $16,000. It also provides on-site paid summer employment to enhance technical experience. The exact value of the fellowship depends on academic standing, summer employment, and graduate school attended; the total amount generally exceeds $200,000.

Duration Support is initially provided for 2 or 3 years, depending on the employer-sponsor. If the fellow makes satisfactory progress and continues to meet the conditions of the award, support may continue for a total of up to 6 years or completion of the Ph.D., whichever comes first.

Additional information This program began in 1989. Tuition and fees are provided by the participating universities. Stipends and summer internships are provided by sponsoring organizations. Students must submit separate applications for internships, which may have additional eligibility requirements. Internships are currently available at Lawrence Livermore National Laboratory in Livermore, California (astronomy, chemistry, computer science, geology, materials science, mathematics, and physics); Los Alamos National Laboratory in Los Alamos, New Mexico (computer science, engineering, mathematics, and physics); National Security Agency in Fort Meade, Maryland (astronomy, chemistry, computer science, geology, materials science,

mathematics, and physics); Sandia National Laboratory in Livermore, California (biology, chemistry, computer science, environmental science, geology, materials science, mathematics, and physics); and Sandia National Laboratory in Albuquerque, New Mexico (chemical engineering, chemistry, computer science, materials science, mathematics, mechanical engineering, and physics). Fellows must submit a separate application for dissertation support in the year prior to the beginning of their dissertation research program, but not until they can describe their intended research in general terms.
Number awarded Varies each year; recently, 11 of these fellowships were awarded.
Deadline November of each year.

[1314]
NSTI SUMMER SCHOLARS PROGRAM
United Negro College Fund Special Programs
 Corporation
2750 Prosperity Avenue, Suite 600
Fairfax, VA 22031
(703) 677-3400   Toll-free: (800) 530-6232
Fax: (703) 205-7645   E-mail: portal@uncfsp.org
Web: www.uncfsp.org

Purpose To provide an opportunity for Native American and other underrepresented undergraduate and graduate students to work on a summer research project at the Ames Research Park (ARC) of the U.S. National Aeronautics and Space Administration (NASA) in Moffett Field, California.
Eligibility This program is open to rising sophomores, juniors, seniors, and graduate students at accredited institutions who are members of underrepresented groups, including women, ethnic minorities, and persons with disabilities. Applicants must be working on a degree in a science, technology, engineering, or mathematics (STEM) field and have a GPA of 3.0 or higher. They must be interested in working on a research project during the summer at ARC. U.S. citizenship is required.
Financial data A stipend is provided (amount not specified).
Duration 10 weeks during the summer.
Additional information This program, which began in 2006, is funded by NASA and administered by the United Negro College Fund Special Programs Corporation.
Number awarded Varies each year. Since the program began, 31 students have participated.
Deadline January of each year.

[1315]
OFFICE OF CIVILIAN RADIOACTIVE WASTE MANAGEMENT MINORITY SERVING INSTITUTIONS UNDERGRADUATE SCHOLARSHIP PROGRAM
Oak Ridge Institute for Science and Education
Attn: Science and Engineering Education
P.O. Box 117
Oak Ridge, TN 37831-0117
(865) 241-6704   Fax: (865) 241-9445
E-mail: MCarl.Wheeler@orau.gov
Web: see.orau.org

Purpose To provide scholarships and internship experience to students at Minority Serving Institutions (MEIs) working on undergraduate degrees in areas related to the Office of Civilian Radioactive Waste Management (OCRWM).
Eligibility This program is open to full time juniors and seniors at Historically Black Colleges and Universities (HBCUs), Hispanic Serving Institutions (HSIs), and Tribal Colleges and Universities (TCUs). Applicants must be working on a degree in science, mathematics, engineering, engineering technology, or social sciences (if their program focuses on public policy development of issues relevant to the OCRWM mission). As part of their program, they must be willing to participate in a summer internship at a U.S. Department of Energy (DOE) site conducting activities for the OCRWM. Along with their application, they must submit a 1- to 2-page statement of their career and academic goals and objectives. Selection is based on that statement, academic honors and awards, extracurricular activities, employment experience, and references.
Financial data The program provides for payment of tuition and fees (to a maximum of $8,000) plus a monthly stipend of $700 during the academic year and $1,400 during the summer internship.
Duration 2 years.
Additional information This program is funded by DOE/OCRWM and administered by Oak Ridge Institute for Science and Education (ORISE).
Number awarded 8 each year.
Deadline January of each year.

[1316]
PACIFIC NORTHWEST NATIONAL LABORATORY STUDENT RESEARCH APPRENTICESHIP PROGRAM
Pacific Northwest National Laboratory
Attn: Science Education Programs
902 Battelle Boulevard
P.O. Box 999, MS K9-83
Richland, WA 99352
(509) 375-2569   Toll-free: (888) 375-PNNL
E-mail: kathy.feaster@pnl.gov
Web: science-ed.pnl.gov

Purpose To provide an opportunity for underrepresented minority high school and college students who live within commuting distance of Pacific Northwest National Laboratory (PNNL) to work on a research project at the laboratory during the summer.
Eligibility This program is open to high school juniors and seniors who live within daily commuting distance of the laboratory. Applicants must be at least 16 years of age and of Hispanic, African American, or Native American ethnic origin. They must have an expressed interest in and potential for educational opportunities and careers in science, engineering, mathematics, or computer technology. Participants who complete at least 1 summer appointment as a high school student and are current freshmen in either community college or a 4-year university are eligible to apply for the Advanced Student Research Apprenticeship Program (SRAP).
Financial data The stipend is $320 per week for high school juniors in the SRAP program, $400 per week for high school seniors in the SRAP program, or $480 per week for college students in the Advanced SRAP program.

Duration 8 weeks, beginning in June.
Additional information This program was established in 1979. Students spend 4 days a week assigned to a scientist-mentor in a specific research area. The other day is devoted to educational, career, and leadership development activities involving laboratory demonstrations, field trips, self-esteem, team building, and communications workshops.
Number awarded Varies each year.
Deadline February of each year.

[1317]
PAUL D. WHITE SCHOLARSHIP
Baker Hostetler LLP
Attn: Attorney Recruitment and Development Manager
3200 National City Center
1900 East Ninth Street
Cleveland, OH 44114-3485
(216) 861-7092   Fax: (216) 696-0740
E-mail: ddriscole@bakerlaw.com
Web: www.bakerlaw.com

Purpose To provide financial assistance and summer work experience to minority law school students.
Eligibility This program is open to first- and second-year law students of African American, Hispanic, Asian American, or American Indian descent. Selection is based on law school performance, demonstrated leadership abilities (as evidenced by community and collegiate involvement), collegiate academic record, extracurricular activities, work experience, and a written personal statement.
Financial data The program provides a stipend of $6,000 for the scholarship and $8,400 per month for a summer clerkship with the sponsoring firm. To date, the firm has paid out more than $1.5 million in scholarships and clerkships.
Duration 1 year, including the following summer.
Additional information This program was established in 1997.
Number awarded 2 each year: 1 in the Cincinnati office and 1 in the Columbus office.
Deadline January of each year.

[1318]
PORTER WRIGHT MORRIS & ARTHUR LLP/RALPH K. FRASIER SCHOLARSHIP
Porter Wright Morris & Arthur LLP
Huntington Center
41 South High Street
Columbus, OH 43215
(614) 227-2000   Toll-free: (800) 533-2794
Fax: (614) 227-2100
Web: www.porterwright.com

Purpose To provide financial assistance and summer work experience to minority students from any state who are enrolled at designated law schools in Ohio.
Eligibility This program is open to minority students enrolled in the first year at the following law schools: Ohio State University Moritz College of Law, Capital University Law School, Case Western Reserve University School of Law, Cleveland-Marshall College of Law, University of Cincinnati College of Law, University of Dayton School of Law, and University of Toledo College of Law. Applicants must submit undergraduate and law school transcripts, a resume, and an essay in the form of a legal memorandum on a hypothetical law case. They must also indicate their choice of the sponsoring firm's offices in Cleveland and Columbus for a summer clerkship.
Financial data The program provides a competitive salary for the summer clerkship and a stipend of $5,000 for the second year of law school.
Duration 1 year.
Additional information This program was established in 2005.
Number awarded 2 each year: 1 for a clerkship in Cleveland and 1 for a clerkship in Columbus.
Deadline January of each year.

[1319]
PRESIDENTIAL MANAGEMENT FELLOWS PROGRAM
Office of Personnel Management
Attn: Presidential Management Fellows Program
1900 E Street, N.W., Room 1425
Washington, DC 20415
(202) 606-1040   TTY: (202) 606-3040
E-mail: pmf@opm.gov
Web: www.pmf.opm.gov

Purpose To provide Native American and other graduate students an opportunity to experience an entry-level career development and training program in Federal public service.
Eligibility Applicants must be U.S. citizens (or expecting to become a citizen prior to appointment) who have received or are scheduled to receive a graduate degree (master's or doctoral) during the current academic year. Nominations are made by participating graduate schools; each degree-granting program may nominate up to 10% of its total number of graduates who will receive master's and doctoral degrees. Preference of 5 points is given to veterans who served on active duty during any war declared by Congress or through July 1, 1955, for more than 180 consecutive days any part of which occurred between January 31, 1955 and October 15, 1976, during the Gulf War period from August 2, 1990 through January 2, 1992, or in a campaign or expedition for which a campaign medal has been authorized (including El Salvador, Grenada, Haiti, Lebanon, Panama, Somalia, Southwest Asia, and Bosnia). Preference of 10 points is given to 1) an honorably separated veteran who served on active duty at any time and has a service-connected disability, or is receiving compensation, disability retirement benefits, or pension from the military or the Department of Veterans Affairs, or is a Purple Heart recipient; 2) the unremarried widow or widower of certain deceased veterans; 3) the spouse of a veteran unable to work because of a service-connected disability; or 4) the mother of a veteran who died in service or who is permanently and totally disabled. A veteran's preference is not available to 1) military retirees at the rank of major, lieutenant commander, or higher, unless they qualify as disabled veterans, or 2) veterans who served in the National Guard or Reserves, unless they were called to active duty. Preference is also given to members of a federally-recognized Indian tribe or Native Alaskan village for positions within the Bureau of Indian Affairs of the Department of the Interior

and the Indian Health Service of the Department of Health and Human Services. Selection is based on breadth and quality of accomplishments, capacity for leadership, and demonstrated commitment to excellence in the leadership and management of public policies and programs.

Financial data Interns begin at the GS-9 level (currently, starting at $38,824 per year) and are eligible for promotion to the GS-12 level (currently, $56,301 per year) after the first year of service. Upon completion of the program, they may be eligible for permanent positions at the GS-13 level (currently, $66,951 per year). Their compensation includes health and life insurance, retirement/investment plans, annual and sick leave, and all other benefits of civil service employees.

Duration 2 years.

Additional information Following nomination by the dean, director, or chairperson of the graduate schools each fall, Presidential Management Fellow (PMF) finalists are selected and notified each spring. Selection as a finalist does not guarantee a job; PMF finalists must still contact federal agencies and compete for available job openings. Each finalist receives a list of agencies wanting to hire PMFs.

Number awarded Varies each year; recently, approximately 750 fellows participated in this program.

Deadline February of each year.

[1320]
PUBLIC HONORS FELLOWSHIPS OF THE OREGON STATE BAR

Oregon State Bar
Attn: Affirmative Action Program
16037 S.W. Upper Boones Ferry Road
P.O. Box 231935
Tigard, OR 97281-1935
(503) 620-0222, ext. 337
Toll-free: (800) 452-8260, ext. 337 (within OR)
Fax: (503) 684-1366   TTY: (503) 684-7416
E-mail: fgarcia@osbar.org
Web: www.osbar.org/aap

Purpose To provide law students in Oregon with summer work experience in public interest law, especially those who will help the Oregon State Bar achieve its Affirmative Action objectives.

Eligibility This program is open to students at Oregon's 3 law schools (Willamette, University of Oregon, and Lewis and Clark) who are not in the first or final year of study. Each school may nominate up to 5 students. Nominees must have demonstrated a career goal in public interest or public sector law. Preference is given to students who will contribute to the Oregon State Bar's Affirmative Action Program and "increase the diversity of the Oregon bench and bar to reflect the diversity of the people of Oregon." They must be interested in working in a law office during the summer; the employment should be in Oregon, although exceptions will be made if the job offers the student special experience not available within the state. Along with their application, they must submit 1) a personal statement on their history of disadvantage or barriers to educational advancement, personal experiences of discrimination, extraordinary financial obligations, composition of immediate family, extraordinary health or medical needs, and languages in which they are fluent as well as barriers they have experienced because English is a second language; and 2) a state bar statement on why they chose to attend an Oregon law school; if they are not committed but are considering practicing in Oregon, what would help them to decide to practice in the state; and how they will improve the quality of legal service or increase access to justice in Oregon. From the nominees of each school, 2 students are selected on the basis of financial need (30%), the personal statement (25%), the state bar statement (25%), and public service (20%). The information on those students is forwarded to prospective employers in Oregon and they arrange to interview the selectees.

Financial data Fellows receive a stipend of $4,800.

Duration 3 months during the summer.

Additional information There is no guarantee that all students selected by the sponsoring organization will receive fellowships at Oregon law firms.

Number awarded 6 each year: 2 from each of the law schools.

Deadline Each law school sets its own deadline.

[1321]
QEM SCIENCE STUDENT INTERNSHIPS

Quality Education for Minorities (QEM) Network
Attn: Internship Program
1818 N Street, N.W., Suite 350
Washington, DC 20036
(202) 659-1818   Fax: (202) 659-5408
E-mail: qemnetwork@qem.org
Web: www.qem.org/internship.htm

Purpose To provide underrepresented undergraduate and graduate minority students with an opportunity to work during the summer at the National Science Foundation (NSF).

Eligibility This program is open to undergraduate and graduate students who are members of underrepresented minority groups. Applicants must have completed at least the sophomore year of a degree program in mathematics, science (life, physical, social, behavioral, or computer science), technology, or engineering. They must be interested in working in Washington, D.C. during the summer at the NSF to increase their understanding of how science policy is made and develop their potential for becoming leaders and proponents of increased participation in science and engineering fields. Students enrolled at Historically Black Colleges and Universities (HBCUs), Hispanic Serving Institutions (HSIs), and Tribal Colleges and Universities (TCUs) are particularly encouraged to apply. U.S. citizenship is required.

Financial data The stipend is $3,000 for undergraduates or $4,000 for graduate students. Other benefits include round-trip airfare between home or school and Washington, D.C. and housing for all interns who are not from the Washington, D.C. metropolitan area.

Duration 10 weeks during the summer.

Additional information This program is supported by the Office of Integrative Activities of the NSF.

Number awarded Varies each year.

Deadline January of each year.

[1322]
REAL PROPERTY LAW SECTION MINORITY FELLOWSHIP

The New York Bar Foundation
One Elk Street
Albany, NY 12207
(518) 487-5651   Fax: (518) 487-5699
E-mail: foundation@tnybf.org
Web: www.tnybf.org/restrictedfunds.htm

Purpose To provide an opportunity for minority residents of any state attending law school in New York to gain summer work experience at a public interest organization that represents tenants in local landlord/tenant cases.

Eligibility This program is open to minority students from any state who are enrolled at a law school in New York state. Students must be interested in working during the summer for a public interest legal organization in the state that represents tenants in local landlord/tenant cases. Applications must be submitted by the organization.

Financial data The stipend is $3,333.

Duration Summer months.

Additional information This program was established in 2007 by the Real Property Law Section of the New York State Bar Association. It is administered by The New York Bar Foundation.

Number awarded 3 each year.

Deadline October of each year.

[1323]
RESEARCH AND ENGINEERING APPRENTICESHIP PROGRAM (REAP) FOR HIGH SCHOOL STUDENTS

Academy of Applied Science
1 Maple Street
Concord, NH 03301
(603) 228-0121   Fax: (603) 228-0210
E-mail: admin@aas-world.org
Web: www.aas-world.org

Purpose To provide an opportunity for Native American and other disadvantaged high school students to engage in a research apprenticeship in science or engineering.

Eligibility This program is open to high school seniors, rising seniors, and rising juniors who have an interest in science or engineering. Applicants must be interested in working as an apprentice on a research project in the laboratory of a mentor scientist at a university near their home. Selection is based on previously demonstrated abilities and interest in science and engineering; potential for a successful career in the field as indicated from overall scholastic achievement, aptitude, and interest areas; recommendations of high school teachers and administrators; and an interview. A deliberate effort is made to identify high school students from socially and economically disadvantaged groups.

Financial data Interns receive a salary in accordance with student minimum wage guidelines.

Duration Summer months.

Additional information The program provides intensive summer training for high school students in the laboratories of scientists. The program, established in 1980, is funded by a grant from the U.S. Army Research Office. Students must live at home while they participate in the program and must live in the area where an approved professor lives. The program does not exist in every state.

Number awarded Varies; recently, approximately 120 students were funded at 52 colleges and universities nationwide.

Deadline February of each year.

[1324]
RETAIL MANAGEMENT INSTITUTE INTERNSHIPS

INROADS, Inc.
10 South Broadway, Suite 300
St. Louis, MO 63102
(314) 241-7488   Fax: (314) 241-9325
E-mail: info@inroads.org
Web: www.inroads.org

Purpose To provide an opportunity for young people of color to gain work experience in retailing.

Eligibility This program is open to African Americans, Hispanics, and Native Americans who reside in the areas served by INROADS. Applicants must be interested in preparing for a career in department stores, mass merchant discount stores, specialty stores, consumer electronic stores, supermarkets, or ready-to-wear specialty stores. They must be high school seniors or freshmen or sophomores in accredited 2- or 4-year colleges or universities with a GPA of 2.5 or higher. Students attending a 2-year college must intend to transfer to a 4-year college or university. Some applicants may be asked to take the Retail Readiness Assessment test and achieve a score within the 40 to 60 point range. All applicants must be permanent residents of the United States. Along with their application, they must submit official transcripts, a resume, SAT or ACT scores (for high school seniors and first-semester college students), and a 250-word essay on why this internship is right for them.

Financial data Salaries vary, depending upon the specific internship assigned.

Duration Up to 4 years.

Additional information INROADS places interns in companies where they receive the necessary pre-professional training and experience to launch a career as a manager of a department, store, district, or chain of stores. The INROADS organization offers internship opportunities through 45 local affiliates in 29 states.

Number awarded Varies each year.

[1325]
RHODE ISLAND SPACE GRANT CONSORTIUM UNDERGRADUATE SUMMER SCHOLAR PROGRAM

Rhode Island Space Grant Consortium
c/o Brown University
Lincoln Field Building
Box 1846
Providence, RI 02912-1846
(401) 863-2889   Fax: (401) 863-3978
E-mail: RISpaceGrant@brown.edu
Web: www.planetary.brown.edu/RI_Space_Grant

Purpose To provide funding for summer research activities to minority and other undergraduate students at institutions that are members of the Rhode Island Space Grant

Consortium (RISGC) who are interested in a career in a space-related field of science, mathematics, or engineering.
Eligibility This program is open to undergraduate students at RISGC-member universities. Applicants must be studying in science, mathematics, or engineering fields of interest to the National Aeronautics and Space Administration (NASA). They must be interested in participating in a research project during the summer with an adviser in their own department. U.S. citizenship is required. The sponsor is a component of NASA's Space Grant program, which encourages participation by women, underrepresented minorities, and persons with disabilities.
Financial data The stipend is $4,000.
Duration 1 summer.
Additional information Members of the RISGC are Bryant College, Community College of Rhode Island, Providence College, Roger Williams University, Rhode Island College, Rhode Island School of Design, Salve Regina University, University of Rhode Island, and Wheaton College. This program is funded by NASA. Scholars are required to devote 75% of their time to their research and 25% of their time to science education outreach activities organized and coordinated by Rhode Island Space Grant.
Number awarded Varies each year; recently, 3 of these scholarships were awarded.
Deadline February of each year.

[1326]
RICHARD B. FISHER SCHOLARSHIP
Morgan Stanley
Attn: Diversity Recruiting
750 Seventh Avenue, 31st Floor
New York, NY 10019
(212) 762-0211   Fax: (212) 507-4972
E-mail: diversityrecruiting@morganstanley.com
Web: www.morganstanley.com

Purpose To provide financial assistance and work experience to Native Americans and other minorities who are preparing for a career in technology within the financial services industry.
Eligibility This program is open to members of minority groups who are enrolled in their sophomore or junior year of college (or the third or fourth year of a 5-year program). Applicants must be enrolled full time and have a GPA of 3.0 or higher. They must be willing to commit to a paid summer internship in the Morgan Stanley Information Technology Division. All majors and disciplines are eligible, but preference is given to students preparing for a career in technology within the financial services industry. Along with their application, they must submit 1-page essays on 1) why they are applying for this scholarship and why they should be selected as a recipient; 2) a technical project on which they worked, either through a university course or previous work experience, their role in the project, and how they contributed to the end result; and 3) a software, hardware, or new innovative application of existing technology that they would create if they could and the impact it would have. Financial need is not considered in the selection process.
Financial data The stipend is $7,500 per year.
Duration 1 year (the junior year); may be renewed for the senior year.
Additional information The program, established in 1993, includes a paid summer internship in the Morgan Stanley Information Technology Division in the summer following the time of application.
Number awarded 1 or more each year.
Deadline January of each year.

[1327]
SCHWABE, WILLIAMSON & WYATT DIVERSITY SCHOLARSHIP PROGRAM
Schwabe, Williamson & Wyatt, Attorneys at Law
Attn: Director of Attorney Recruiting
1211 S.W. Fifth Avenue, Suite 1500-1900
Portland, OR 97204
(503) 796-2858   Fax: (503) 796-2900
E-mail: djohn@schwabe.com
Web: www.schwabe.com/recruiting/sum_jobs.html

Purpose To provide financial assistance and summer work experience in Portland, Oregon to law students who will contribute to the diversity of the legal profession.
Eligibility This program is open to first-year students working on a J.D. degree at an ABA-accredited law school. Applicants must 1) contribute to the diversity of the law school student body and the legal community; 2) possess a record of academic achievement, capacity, and leadership as an undergraduate and in law school that indicates promise for a successful career in the legal profession; and 3) demonstrate a commitment to practice law in the Pacific Northwest upon completion of law school. They must be interested in a paid summer associateship at the sponsoring law firm's office in Portland, Oregon. Along with their application, they must submit a resume, undergraduate and law school transcripts, a legal writing sample, and a 1- to 2-page personal statement explaining their interest in the scholarship and how they will contribute to diversity in the legal community.
Financial data The program provides a paid summer associateship during the summer following completion of the first year of law school and an academic scholarship of $7,500 to help pay tuition and other expenses during the recipient's second year of law school.
Duration 1 year.
Number awarded 1 each year.
Deadline January of each year.

[1328]
SCIENCE AND TECHNOLOGY CENTERS STEM DOCTORAL INTERNSHIP PROGRAM
Quality Education for Minorities (QEM) Network
1818 N Street, N.W., Suite 350
Washington, DC 20036
(202) 659-1818   Fax: (202) 659-5408
E-mail: qemnetwork@qem.org
Web: www.qem.org/stc.htm

Purpose To provide Native American and other underrepresented minority doctoral candidates with the opportunity to work on a research project in a field of science, technology, engineering, or mathematics (STEM) at a Science and Technology Center (STC) funded by the National Science Foundation (NSF).

Eligibility This program is open to doctoral candidates at accredited institutions of higher learning who are working on a degree in a STEM field supported by NSF. Applicants must be U.S. citizens, nationals, or permanent residents who are members of minority groups underrepresented in STEM disciplines (African Americans, Alaska Natives, American Indians, Mexican Americans, and Puerto Ricans). They must be interested in working on a research project at an NSF-funded STC during the summer or academic year.

Financial data Academic-year internships provide a stipend of $30,000 plus a $10,500 cost of education allowance for the host institution. Summer internships provide a stipend of $5,000, round-trip airfare to and from the host STC institution and a housing allowance of $1,600 that can be applied to either on- or off-campus housing.

Duration 1 academic year or 10 weeks during the summer.

Additional information This program is supported by the NSF.

Number awarded 1 or 2 each year.

Deadline January of each year.

[1329]
SCOTTS COMPANY SCHOLARS PROGRAM

Golf Course Superintendents Association of America
Attn: Environmental Institute for Golf
1421 Research Park Drive
Lawrence, KS 66049-3859
(785) 832-4445　　Toll-free: (800) 472-7878, ext. 4445
Fax: (785) 832-3643　　E-mail: mwright@gcsaa.org
Web: www.gcsaa.org

Purpose To provide financial assistance and summer work experience to high school seniors and college students, particularly those from diverse backgrounds, who are preparing for a career in golf management.

Eligibility This program is open to high school seniors and college students (freshmen, sophomores, and juniors) who are interested in preparing for a career in golf management (the "green industry"). Applicants should come from diverse ethnic, cultural, and socioeconomic backgrounds, defined to include women, minorities, and people with disabilities. Selection is based on cultural diversity, academic achievement, extracurricular activities, leadership, employment potential, essay responses, and letters of recommendation. Financial need is not considered. Finalists are selected for summer internships and then compete for scholarships.

Financial data The finalists receive a $500 award to supplement their summer internship income. Scholarship stipends are $2,500.

Duration 1 year.

Additional information The program is funded from a permanent endowment established by Scotts Company. Finalists are responsible for securing their own internships.

Number awarded 5 finalists, of whom 2 receive scholarships, are selected each year.

Deadline February of each year.

[1330]
SEALASKA CORPORATION INTERNSHIPS

Sealaska Corporation
Attn: Intern Program Coordinator
One Sealaska Plaza, Suite 400
Juneau, AK 99801-1276
(907) 586-1512　　Toll-free: (800) 848-5921
Fax: (907) 586-2304
E-mail: ken.southerland@sealaska.com
Web: www.sealaska.com

Purpose To provide work experience during the summer to Native Alaskan college students affiliated with Sealaska Corporation.

Eligibility This program is open to Sealaska Corporation shareholders who are at least 25% Alaskan Native or a direct descendant of an originally-enrolled shareholder. Applicants must have completed at least 2 years of college, have a GPA of 2.5 or higher, and be attending college in the following fall. They must be interested in working with Sealaska Corporation (for students majoring in accounting, administration, communications, finance, legal, marketing, or natural resources); Sealaska Timber Corporation (for students majoring in computer science, forestry, or engineering); Sealaska Heritage Institute (for students majoring in anthropology, business administration, or education); Synergy Systems (for students majoring in business administration); or other Sealaska business associates.

Financial data A competitive salary is paid, along with a housing stipend, transportation, and tuition for summer credit for the internship.

Duration Summer months.

Number awarded Varies each year.

Deadline March of each year.

[1331]
SIGNIFICANT OPPORTUNITIES IN ATMOSPHERIC RESEARCH AND SCIENCE (SOARS) PROGRAM

University Corporation for Atmospheric Research
Attn: SOARS Program Manager
1850 Table Mesa Drive
P.O. Box 3000
Boulder, CO 80307-3000
(303) 497-8622　　Fax: (303) 497-8629
E-mail: soars@ucar.edu
Web: www.soars.ucar.edu

Purpose To provide summer work experience to undergraduate or graduate students, especially those from underrepresented groups, who are interested in preparing for a career in atmospheric or a related science.

Eligibility This program is open to U.S. citizens or permanent residents who have completed their sophomore year of college and are majoring in atmospheric science or a related field (e.g., biology, chemistry, computer science, earth science, engineering, environmental science, the geosciences, mathematics, meteorology, oceanography, physics, or social science). Applicants must have a GPA of 3.0 or higher and be planning to prepare for a career in the field of atmospheric or a related science. The program especially encourages applications from members of groups that are historically underrepresented in the atmospheric and related sciences, including Blacks/African Americans, Hispanics/Latinos, American Indians/Alaskan Natives, women, first-generation college students, and students with disabilities. It also welcomes applications from students who are gay, lesbian, bisexual, or transgender; have experienced, and worked to overcome, educational or economic disadvantage; or have personal or family circumstances that may complicate their continued progress in research careers.

Financial data Participants receive a competitive stipend and a housing allowance. Round-trip travel between Boulder and any 1 location within the continental United States is also provided. Students who are accepted into a graduate program receive full scholarships (with SOARS and the participating universities each sharing the costs).

Duration 10 weeks during the summer. Students are encouraged to continue for 4 subsequent summers.

Additional information This program began in 1996. Students are assigned positions with a research project. They are exposed to the research facilities at the National Center for Atmospheric Research (NCAR), including computers, libraries, laboratories, and aircraft. NCAR is operated by the University Corporation for Atmospheric Research (a consortium of 40 universities) and sponsored by the National Science Foundation, the Department of Energy, the National Aeronautics and Space Administration, and the National Oceanic and Atmospheric Administration. Before completing their senior years, students are encouraged to apply to a master's or doctoral degree program at 1 of the participating universities.

Number awarded At least 12 each year.

Deadline January of each year.

[1332]
SMITHSONIAN MINORITY STUDENT INTERNSHIP

Smithsonian Institution
Attn: Office of Fellowships
Victor Building, Suite 9300, MRC 902
P.O. Box 37012
Washington, DC 20013-7012
(202) 633-7070   Fax: (202) 633-7069
E-mail: siofg@si.edu
Web: www.si.edu/ofg/ofgapp.htm

Purpose To provide Native American and other minority undergraduate or graduate students with the opportunity to work on research or museum procedure projects in specific areas of history, art, or science at the Smithsonian Institution.

Eligibility Internships are offered to minority students who are actively engaged in graduate study at any level or in upper-division undergraduate study. An overall GPA of 3.0 or higher is generally expected. Applicants must be interested in conducting research in specified fields of interest to the Smithsonian.

Financial data The program provides a stipend of $500 per week; travel allowances may also be offered.

Duration 10 weeks during the summer or academic year.

Additional information Eligible fields of study currently available include animal behavior, ecology, and environmental science (including an emphasis on the tropics); anthropology (including archaeology); astrophysics and astronomy; earth sciences and paleobiology; evolutionary and systematic biology; history of science and technology; history of art (especially American, contemporary, African, Asian, and 20th-century art); American crafts and decorative arts; social and cultural history of the United States; folklife; and materials research.

Number awarded Varies each year.

Deadline January of each year for summer or fall; September of each year for spring.

[1333]
SMITHSONIAN NATIVE AMERICAN STUDENT INTERNSHIP AWARDS

Smithsonian Institution
Attn: Office of Research Training and Services
470 L'Enfant Plaza, Suite 7102
P.O. Box 37012, MRC 902
Washington, DC 20013-7012
(202) 633-7070   Fax: (202) 633-7069
E-mail: siofg@si.edu
Web: www.si.edu/ofg/ofgapp.htm

Purpose To support Native American students interested in conducting projects related to Native American topics that require the use of Native American resources at the Smithsonian Institution.

Eligibility Applicants must be Native American students who are actively engaged in graduate or undergraduate study and are interested in working with Native American resources at the Smithsonian Institution. Along with their application, they must submit a 2- to 4-page essay in which they describe their past and present academic history and other experiences which they feel have prepared them for an internship, what they hope to accomplish through an internship and how it would relate to their academic and career goals, and what about the Smithsonian in particular interests them and leads them to apply for the internship.

Financial data Interns receive a stipend of $500 per week and a travel allowance.

Duration 10 weeks.

Additional information Interns pursue directed research projects supervised by Smithsonian staff members. Recipients must be in residence at the Smithsonian Institution for the duration of the program.

Number awarded Varies each year.

Deadline January of each year for summer or fall residency; September of each year for spring residency.

[1334]
STOKES EDUCATIONAL SCHOLARSHIP PROGRAM

National Security Agency
Attn: Office of Recruitment and Hiring
9800 Savage Road, Suite 6779
P.O. Box 1661
Fort Meade, MD 20755-6779
(410) 854-4725   Toll-free: (866) NSA-HIRE
Web: www.nsa.gov

Purpose To provide minority and other high school seniors and college sophomores with financial assistance and work experience at the National Security Agency (NSA).

Eligibility This program is open to 1) graduating high school seniors, particularly minorities, who are planning a college major in electrical or computer engineering or computer science; and 2) college sophomores who are majoring in mathematics, foreign language (currently, Russian or Farsi only), or fields related to intelligence analysis, such as regional studies (Middle East; south, east, or central Asia), topical studies (terrorism, proliferation, or related sciences), international banking and finance, telecommunications and information system networks, intelligence or information analysis, international relations, or security studies. High school seniors must have minimum scores of 1600 on the SAT (1100 on critical reading and mathematics, 500 in writing) or 25 on the ACT. All applicants must have a GPA of 3.0 or higher. Along with their application, they must submit a 1-page essay on why they want to have a career with the NSA. U.S. citizenship and eligibility to obtain a high-level security clearance are required.

Financial data Participants receive college tuition for up to 4 years, reimbursement for books and certain fees, a year-round salary, and a housing allowance and travel reimbursement during summer employment if the distance between the agency and school exceeds 75 miles. Following graduation, participants must work for the agency for 1 and a half times their length of study, usually 5 years. Students who leave agency employment earlier must repay the tuition cost.

Duration Up to 4 years, followed by employment at the agency for 5 years.

Additional information Participants must attend classes full time and work at the agency during the summer in jobs tailored to their course of study. They must maintain at least a 3.0 GPA. This program, established in 1986, was formerly known as the National Security Agency Undergraduate Training Program.

Number awarded Varies each year.

Deadline November of each year.

[1335]
STUDENT CANCER RESEARCH FELLOWSHIP

University of Colorado Cancer Center
Attn: Grants and Education Office
13001 East 17th Place, Sixth Floor
P.O. Box 6508, Mailstop F434
Aurora, CO 80045
(303) 724-3174   Fax: (303) 724-3163
E-mail: jill.penafiel@uchsc.edu
Web: www.uccc.info

Purpose To provide an opportunity for minority and other high school, college, graduate, dental, medical, and nursing students to work during the summer on a cancer research project in Colorado.

Eligibility This program is open to high school juniors and seniors, college undergraduates, graduate students, and health professional (dental, medical, and nursing) students. Applicants must be interested in working on a cancer research project at the University of Colorado Health Sciences Center, the Boulder campus of the University of Colorado, or other institutions in the Denver area. Along with their application, they must submit a 2-page essay explaining why they wish to apply for this fellowship, school transcripts, and 2 letters of recommendation. Underrepresented minority students are particularly encouraged to apply.

Financial data Stipends are $275 per week for high school students, $300 per week for college undergraduate and graduate students, or $325 per week for medical students.

Duration 6 to 8 weeks during the summer.

Additional information Funding for this program is provided by a grant from the National Cancer Institute.

Number awarded Varies each year.

Deadline February of each year.

[1336]
SUMMER HONORS UNDERGRADUATE RESEARCH PROGRAM

Harvard Medical School
Attn: Division of Medical Sciences
T-MEC Room 432
260 Longwood Avenue
Boston, MA 02115-5720
(617) 432-1342   Toll-free: (800) 367-9019
Fax: (617) 432-2644
E-mail: SHURP@hms.harvard.edu
Web: www.hms.harvard.edu

Purpose To provide an opportunity for Native American and other underrepresented minority students to engage in research at Harvard Medical School during the summer.

Eligibility This program at Harvard Medical School is open to undergraduate students belonging to minority groups that are underrepresented in the sciences. Applicants must have had at least 1 summer (or equivalent) of experience in a research laboratory and have taken at least 1 upper-level biology course that includes molecular biology. They should be considering a career in biological or biomedical research.

Financial data The program provides a stipend of $390 per week, dormitory housing, travel costs, a meal card, and health insurance if it is needed.

Duration 10 weeks during the summer.

Number awarded Varies each year.

Deadline January of each year.

[1337]
SUMMER INTERNSHIP PROGRAM IN BIOMEDICAL RESEARCH

National Institutes of Health
Attn: Office of Intramural Training and Education
2 Center Drive, Room 2E06
Bethesda, MD 20892-0240
(301) 496-2427   Toll-free: (888) 695-5343
Fax: (301) 402-0483   E-mail: dc26a@nih.gov
Web: www.training.nih.gov/student/sip/index.asp

Purpose To enable minority and other students to receive training and participate in ongoing research studies in a variety of laboratory and clinically-related disciplines at the National Institutes of Health (NIH) during the summer.

Eligibility This program is open to graduate, health professions, undergraduate, and high school students who have a strong interest in preparing for a career related to biomedical or behavioral research, including the disciplines of biology, chemistry, physical science, psychology, computer science, biostatistics, mathematics, and biomedical engineering. They must be at least 16 years of age and U.S. citizens, nationals, or permanent residents.

Financial data Salaries depend on the academic level of the recipient, ranging from $1,700 per month for high school students to $3,100 per month for graduate students with 3 or more years of experience.

Duration At least 8 weeks, in the summer.
Additional information Most components of the National Institutes of Health participate in this program. Some of them reserve positions for interns who are members of minority groups underrepresented in the biomedical and behavioral sciences (African Americans, Hispanics, Native Americans, and Pacific Islanders). Laboratories are located in Bethesda, Baltimore, Frederick, and Rockville, Maryland; Detroit, Michigan; Research Triangle Park, North Carolina; Phoenix, Arizona; and Hamilton, Montana.
Number awarded Varies each year.
Deadline February of each year.

[1338]
SUMMER INTERNSHIPS FOR STUDENTS FROM TRIBAL COLLEGES AND UNIVERSITIES
Quality Education for Minorities (QEM) Network
Attn: Internship Program
1818 N Street, N.W., Suite 350
Washington, DC 20036
(202) 659-1818   Fax: (202) 659-5408
E-mail: qemnetwork@qem.org
Web: www.qem.org/internship.htm

Purpose To provide students at Tribal Colleges and Universities (TCUS) with an opportunity to learn more about science and health issues during a summer internship at Quality Education for Minorities (QEM).
Eligibility This program is open to students who have completed at least the freshman year at a TCU and are planning to return to school the following year (or, if they will have completed their program at their TCU, to transfer to a 4-year university or to continue on to graduate school). Applicants must be working on a degree in science or engineering. They must be interested in participating in a summer internship at QEM to 1) become familiar with science and science education policies and how they affect the education of American Indians and other Native Americans; 2) to learn about health disparities disproportionately affecting American Indians and other minority groups; and 3) design a community outreach program that will enable them to share their experiences with peers and faculty on campus as well as engage K-12 students in their respective communities.
Financial data The stipend is $3,000. Other benefits include round-trip airfare between home or school and Washington, D.C. and housing for all interns who are not from the Washington, D.C. metropolitan area.
Duration 10 weeks during the summer.
Additional information This program is supported by the Tribal Colleges and Universities Program (TCUP) of the National Science Foundation (NSF). During the internship, students have an opportunity to interact with program officers at NSF and other federal agencies who are involved in making science and education policy; become knowledgeable about issues preventing American Indian and other minority students from receiving a quality education as well as about various health disparities that disproportionately affect American Indian and other minority groups; and become familiar with policies, programs, and strategies being implemented to address those issues.
Number awarded Varies each year.
Deadline April of each year.

[1339]
SUMMER PROGRAM IN QUANTITATIVE SCIENCES FOR PUBLIC HEALTH RESEARCH
Harvard School of Public Health
Department of Biostatistics
Attn: Diversity Program Coordinator
655 Huntington Avenue, SPH2, Fourth Floor
Boston, MA 02115
(617) 432-3175   Fax: (617) 432-5619
E-mail: biostat_diversity@hsph.harvard.edu
Web: biosun1.hsph.harvard.edu

Purpose To enable Native American and other underrepresented minority science undergraduates to participate in a summer research internship at Harvard School of Public Health that focuses on biostatistics, epidemiology, and health and social behavior.
Eligibility This program is open to members of ethnic groups underrepresented in the sciences (Blacks/African Americans, Hispanics, Native American, Pacific Islanders, biracial/multiracial) who are currently college undergraduates interested in public health as a career. Applicants must be interested in participating in a summer program on the use of quantitative methods for biological, environmental, and medical research. They must have some course work in calculus, but prior exposure to statistics is not required. U.S. citizenship or permanent resident status is required.
Financial data Funding covers travel, accommodations, and a modest stipend.
Duration 4 weeks, in June.
Additional information Interns participate in seminars, led by faculty members from various departments at the Harvard School of Public Health and Harvard Medical School, that are designed to broaden a participant's understanding of the relationship of biostatistics to human health. They also attend non-credit classes in biostatistics, epidemiology, and health and social behavior.
Number awarded Varies each year.
Deadline February of each year.

[1340]
SUMMER RESEARCH DIVERSITY FELLOWSHIPS IN LAW AND SOCIAL SCIENCE FOR UNDERGRADUATE STUDENTS
American Bar Foundation
Attn: Assistant Director
750 North Lake Shore Drive
Chicago, IL 60611
(312) 988-6560   Fax: (312) 988-6579
E-mail: fellowships@abfn.org
Web: www.abf-sociolegal.org/sumfel.html

Purpose To provide an opportunity for Native American and other underrepresented minority undergraduates to work on a summer research project in the field of law and social science.
Eligibility This program is open to African Americans, Hispanic/Latinos, Puerto Ricans, and Native Americans who are sophomores or juniors in college, have a GPA of 3.0 or higher, are working on a major in the social sciences or humanities, and are willing to consider a research-oriented career. Applicants must submit a brief essay on their future plans and why this fellowship would contribute to them, another essay on an assigned topic, official transcripts, and

a letter of recommendation from a faculty member familiar with their work.

Financial data Participants receive a stipend of $3,600.

Duration 35 hours per week for 10 weeks during the summer.

Additional information Students are assigned to an American Bar Foundation Research Fellow who involves the student in the design and conduct of the fellow's research project and who acts as mentor during the student's tenure.

Number awarded 4 each year.

Deadline February of each year.

[1341]
SUMMER RESEARCH OPPORTUNITIES PROGRAM (SROP)

Committee on Institutional Cooperation
Attn: Academic and International Programs
1819 South Neil Street, Suite D
Champaign, IL 61820-7271
(217) 333-8475   Fax: (217) 244-7127
E-mail: cic@staff.uiuc.edu
Web: www.cic.uiuc.edu/programs/SROP/index.shtml

Purpose To provide an opportunity for undergraduates from diverse backgrounds to gain research experience at member institutions of the Committee on Institutional Cooperation (CIC) during the summer.

Eligibility This program is open to students currently enrolled in a degree-granting program at a college or university who have a GPA of 3.0 or higher and an interest in continuing on to graduate school. Applicants must be interested in conducting a summer research project under the supervision of a faculty mentor at a CIC member institution. The program is designed to increase educational access for students from diverse backgrounds; members of racial and ethnic minority groups and low-income first-generation students are especially encouraged to apply. U.S. citizenship or permanent resident status is required.

Financial data Participants are paid a stipend of at least $2,500 plus up to $1,100 toward room and board and travel to and from the host institution. Faculty mentors receive a $500 research allowance for the cost of materials.

Duration 8 to 10 weeks during the summer.

Additional information Participants work directly with faculty mentors at the institution of their choice and also engage in other enrichment activities, such as workshops and social gatherings. In July, all participants come together at 1 of the CIC campuses for the annual SROP conference. The CIC member institutions are University of Chicago, University of Illinois at Urbana-Champaign, University of Illinois at Chicago, University of Iowa, University of Michigan, University of Minnesota, University of Wisconsin at Madison, University of Wisconsin at Milwaukee, Indiana University, Michigan State University, Northwestern University, Ohio State University, Indiana University/Purdue University at Indianapolis, Pennsylvania State University, and Purdue University. Students are required to write a paper and an abstract describing their projects and to present the results of their work at a campus symposium.

Number awarded Varies each year; recently, 594 students from 187 universities participated in this program.

Deadline February of each year.

[1342]
SUMMER RESEARCH OPPORTUNITY PROGRAM IN PATHOLOGY

American Society for Investigative Pathology
Attn: Executive Officer
9650 Rockville Pike
Bethesda, MD 20814-3993
(301) 634-7130   Fax: (301) 634-7990
E-mail: asip@asip.org
Web: www.asip.org/awds/sropp/index.htm

Purpose To provide an opportunity for Native Americans and other underrepresented minority groups to participate in a summer research program in pathology.

Eligibility This program is open to students who are members of underrepresented minority groups. Applicants must be interested in visiting prominent research laboratories and institutions during the summer to learn and participate in new research in the mechanisms of disease. To qualify for additional funding, they must select a pathology mentor.

Financial data The program provides 1) a travel and living allowance to cover airfare, ground transportation, meals, housing, and related expenses incurred during the summer research program; 2) a grant up to $1,850 to provide travel support to submit and present an abstract at the Experimental Biology meeting; and 3) for students who select a pathology mentor, a supplemental grant of $2,500 to cover travel and subsistence.

Additional information This program operates as a component of the Minority Access to Research Careers (MARC) program of the Federation of American Societies for Experimental Biology (FASEB), funded by the National Institute of General Medical Sciences of the National Institutes of Health. Additional support is provided by the Intersociety Council for Pathology Information, Inc.

Number awarded Varies each year; recently, 2 of these grants were awarded.

[1343]
SUMMER TRANSPORTATION INTERNSHIP PROGRAM FOR DIVERSE GROUPS

Department of Transportation
Attn: Summer Transportation Internship Program for Diverse Groups
HAHR-40, Room E63-433
1200 New Jersey Avenue, S.E.
Washington, DC 20590
(202) 366-1201
Web: www.fhwa.dot.gov/education/stipdg.htm

Purpose To enable students from diverse groups to gain work experience during the summer at facilities of the U.S. Department of Transportation (DOT).

Eligibility This program is open to all qualified applicants, but is designed to provide women, persons with disabilities, and members of diverse social and ethnic groups with summer opportunities in transportation. Applicants must be U.S. citizens currently enrolled in a degree-granting program of study at an accredited institution of higher learning at the undergraduate (community or junior college, university, college, or Tribal College or University) or graduate level. Undergraduates must be entering their junior or senior year (students attending a Tribal or community college must

have completed their "first year" of school). Law students must be entering their second or third year of school. Students who will graduate during the spring or summer are not eligible unless they have been accepted for enrollment in graduate school. Major fields of study include, but are not limited to, aviation, business, criminal justice, economics, engineering, environmental studies, hazardous materials, law, management information systems, marketing, planning, public administration, or transportation management. Preference is given to students with a GPA of 3.0 or higher. Undergraduates must submit a 1-page essay on their transportation interests and how participation in this program will enhance their educational and career plans and goals. Graduate students must submit a writing sample representing their educational and career plans and goals. Law students must submit a legal writing sample.
Financial data The stipend is $4,000 for undergraduates or $5,000 for graduate and law students. The program also provides housing and reimbursement of travel expenses from interns' homes to their assignment location.
Duration 10 weeks during the summer.
Additional information Assignments are at the DOT headquarters in Washington, D.C., a selected modal administration, or selected field offices around the country.
Number awarded 60 to 100 each year.
Deadline February of each year.

[1344]
TEXAS HISTORICAL COMMISSION PRESERVATION FELLOWS PROGRAM
Texas Historical Commission
1511 Colorado Street
P.O. Box 13497
Austin, TX 78711-3497
(512) 463-6100   Fax: (512) 463-8222
E-mail: thc@thc.state.tx.us
Web: www.thc.state.tx.us/awards/awdfellows.html

Purpose To provide an opportunity for undergraduate and graduate students in Texas, especially those from diverse cultural backgrounds, to learn more about historic preservation through an internship with the Texas Historical Commission (THC).
Eligibility This program is open to residents of Texas enrolled at the sophomore level or higher at a public or private university, junior college, or community college in the state. Applicants must be interested in historical preservation, as evidenced by their study of history, preservation, architecture, archaeology, landscape architecture, downtown revitalization, or heritage tourism. They must have a GPA of 3.0 or higher, a record of community service, life experience as it relates to the field of historic preservation, and completion of projects related to that field. Students from underrepresented ethnic groups are especially encouraged to apply.
Financial data The stipend is $5,000.
Duration 8 weeks.
Additional information Internships are completed at the Austin headquarters of the THC or in the field with an associated preservation organization.
Number awarded 2 or 3 each year.
Deadline February of each year.

[1345]
THOMAS R. PICKERING GRADUATE FOREIGN AFFAIRS FELLOWSHIPS
Woodrow Wilson National Fellowship Foundation
Attn: Foreign Affairs Fellowship Program
5 Vaughn Drive, Suite 300
P.O. Box 2437
Princeton, NJ 08543-2437
(609) 452-7007   Fax: (609) 452-0066
E-mail: pickeringfaf@woodrow.org
Web: www.woodrow.org

Purpose To provide funds for study and work experience to minority and other graduate students interested in preparing for a career with the Department of State's Foreign Service.
Eligibility This program is open to U.S. citizens who are applying to a 2-year full-time master's degree program, including public policy, international affairs, public administration, or such academic fields as business, economics, foreign languages, political science, or sociology. Applicants must have an undergraduate cumulative GPA of 3.2 or higher. They must plan to prepare for a career in the Foreign Service. Selection is based on leadership skills, academic achievement, and financial need. Women, members of minority groups historically underrepresented in the Foreign Service, and students with financial need are encouraged to apply.
Financial data Tuition, room, board, and mandatory fees are paid, along with reimbursement for books and 1 round trip. Fellows also receive stipends for participation in the internships.
Duration 2 years (provided the student maintains a GPA of 3.2 or higher).
Additional information Graduate fellows participate in 1 domestic summer internship between the first and second year of graduate school and 1 summer overseas internship following the second year of graduate school. This program is funded by the State Department and administered by the Woodrow Wilson National Fellowship Foundation. Fellows must commit to a minimum of 3 years of service in an appointment as a Foreign Service Officer following the second year of graduate study. Candidates who do not successfully complete the program and Foreign Service entry requirements may be subject to a reimbursement obligation to the Department of State.
Number awarded Approximately 20 each year.
Deadline February of each year.

[1346]
THOMPSON HINE MINORITY SCHOLARSHIP PROGRAM
Thompson Hine LLP
Attn: Manager of New Lawyer Recruiting
3900 Key Center
127 Public Square
Cleveland, OH 44114-1291
(216) 566-5500   Fax: (216) 566-5800
E-mail: info@thompsonhine.com
Web: www.thompsonhine.com

Purpose To provide financial assistance and work experience to Native American and other minority law students from any state who have been accepted as a summer associate with the law firm of Thompson Hine.

Eligibility This program is open to second-year law students who are members of minority groups as defined by the Equal Employment Opportunity Commission (Native American or Alaskan Native, Asian or Pacific Islander African American or Black, or Hispanic). Applicants must first be offered a summer associateship at an office of Thompson Hine in Atlanta, Cincinnati, Cleveland, Columbus, Dayton, New York, or Washington, D.C. Along with their application, they must submit a writing sample (a legal brief or memorandum prepared for their first-year legal writing course or a prior employer), law school and undergraduate transcripts, a current resume, and a list of at least 2 references.

Financial data The stipend is $10,000. Funds are paid to the student after completing the summer associateship and may be used for tuition and other law school related expenses during the third year.

Duration 1 year.

Number awarded 1 or more each year.

Deadline August of each year.

[1347]
TONKON TORP FIRST-YEAR DIVERSITY FELLOWSHIP PROGRAM

Tonkon Torp LLP
Attn: Manager of Attorney Recruiting
1600 Pioneer Tower
888 S.W. Fifth Avenue
Portland, OR 97204
(503) 221-1440   Fax: (503) 274-8779
E-mail: LoreeD@tonkon.com
Web: www.tonkon.com

Purpose To provide financial assistance and summer work experience (in Portland, Oregon) to Native American and other first-year minority law students from any state.

Eligibility This program is open to members of racial and ethnic minority groups who are currently enrolled in their first year at an ABA-accredited law school. Applicants must be able to demonstrate 1) a record of academic achievement that indicates a strong likelihood of a successful career during the remainder of law school and in the legal profession; 2) a commitment to practice law in Portland, Oregon following graduation from law school; and 3) an ability to contribute meaningfully to the diversity of the law school student body and, after entering the legal profession, the legal community. They are not required to disclose their financial circumstances, but a demonstrated need for financial assistance may be taken into consideration.

Financial data The recipient is offered a paid summer associateship at Tonkon Torp in Portland, Oregon for the summer following the first year of law school and, depending on the outcome of that experience, may be invited for a second summer following the second year of law school. Following the successful completion of that second associateship, the recipient is awarded an academic scholarship of $7,500 for the third year of law school.

Duration The program covers 2 summers and 1 academic year.

Number awarded 1 each year.

Deadline January of each year.

[1348]
TRIBAL PUBLICATIONS INTERNSHIPS

Native American Journalists Association
c/o University of Oklahoma
Gaylord College
395 West Lindsey
Norman, OK 73019-0001
(405) 325-9008   Fax: (405) 325-7565
E-mail: info@naja.com
Web: www.naja.com

Purpose To provide summer work experience at tribal publications to student members of the Native American Journalists Association (NAJA).

Eligibility This program is open to NAJA members who are interested in a summer internship at a tribal publication. Applicants must submit a current resume, 5 to 8 newspaper clips or writing samples, verification of NAJA membership, 2 letters of reference, and a cover letter on how the internship will benefit their career and assist them in their plans to graduate from college. Preference is given to students who have participated in past NAJA training programs, such as workshops held during the annual convention, Project Phoenix, or the college Student Projects. Special consideration is also given to participants in the Freedom Forum's American Indian Journalism Institute.

Financial data The stipend is $500 per week.

Duration 10 to 12 weeks during the summer.

Number awarded 1 or more each year.

Deadline March of each year.

[1349]
UNCF CORPORATE SCHOLARS PROGRAMS

United Negro College Fund
Attn: Corporate Scholars Program
P.O. Box 1435
Alexandria, VA 22313-9998
Toll-free: (866) 671-7237   E-mail: internship@uncf.org
Web: www.uncf.org

Purpose To provide financial assistance and work experience to Native American and other minority students pursuing a degree in designated fields of business, science, and engineering.

Eligibility A number of corporate sponsors provides funding for this program; each establishes its own specifications. All are open to undergraduates; some are also available to graduate students. Some allow students to be enrolled at the college or university of their choice, others are limited to students at Historically Black Colleges and Universities (HBCUs), and others are restricted to UNCF member institutions. Some are open to minority (African American, Alaskan Native, American Indian, Asian Pacific Islander American, Hispanic) students in general, but others are more restrictive. Fields of study vary, but most focus on areas of business, science, and engineering of interest to the corporate sponsor. All include summer internships at the sponsor. GPA requirements vary, but may be as high as 3.0.

Financial data The students selected for this program receive paid internships and need-based scholarships that range up to $15,000 per year.

Duration 8 to 10 weeks for the internships; 1 year for the scholarships, which may be renewed.

Additional information Current corporate sponsors include Booz Allen Hamilton, Dell Inc., Ford Motor Company, HSBC North America, JPMorganChase, Malcolm Pirnie Inc., Marathon Oil Corporation, Oracle Corporation, RR Donnelley, Sprint Nextel, United Parcel Service of America, Inc., and Weyerhaueser.

Number awarded Varies each year.

Deadline Each sponsor sets its own deadline.

[1350]
UNDERGRADUATE STUDENT RESEARCH EXPERIENCES AT FDA

National Science Foundation
Directorate for Engineering
Attn: Division of Bioengineering and Environmental Systems
4201 Wilson Boulevard, Room 565 S
Arlington, VA 22230
(703) 292-7943 Fax: (703) 292-9098
TDD: (800) 281-8749 E-mail: gdevey@nsf.gov
Web: www.nsf.gov

Purpose To provide an opportunity for minority and other undergraduate students to work at an intramural research laboratory of the U.S. Food and Drug Administration (FDA).

Eligibility This program is open to undergraduate students in science, engineering, and mathematics fields of interest to the National Science Foundation (NSF). Applicants must be U.S. citizens, nationals, or permanent residents. They must be proposing a program of full- or part-time work at an FDA laboratory in an area related to their academic program under the guidance of an academic adviser and an FDA mentor. The program encourages applications from women, underrepresented minorities, and persons with disabilities.

Financial data Undergraduate students may receive stipends up to $300 per week; they may also receive some assistance with housing or travel expenses, or both. No indirect costs are allowed. The total award may be up to $6,000 for a fellowship for a single student. FDA provides office space, research facilities, research costs in the form of expendable and minor equipment purchases in the host laboratory, and the time of its research staff.

Duration Support may be provided for a summer project, or for 1 or 2 semesters of part- or full-time work.

Additional information This program is also offered by the NSF Directorate for Computer and Information Science and Engineering; for information, contact its Division of Computer-Communications Research, (703) 292-8910, Fax: (703) 292-9059, E-mail: hgill@nsf.gov. The FDA contact is William A. Herman, Director, Division of Physical Sciences, Center for Devices and Radiological Health, 12725 Twinbrook Parkway, Rockville, MD 20852, (301)827-5599, E-mail: wah@cdrh.fda.gov.

Number awarded A total of 3 to 10 grants for all FDA programs is awarded each year; total funding is approximately $500,000.

Deadline March of each year.

[1351]
UNIVERSITY–INDUSTRY COOPERATIVE RESEARCH PROGRAM GRADUATE RESEARCH ASSISTANTSHIPS AND COOPERATIVE FELLOWSHIPS

National Science Foundation
Directorate for Mathematical and Physical Sciences
Attn: Division of Mathematical Sciences
4201 Wilson Boulevard, Room 1025 N
Arlington, VA 22230
(703) 292-4862 Fax: (703) 292-9032
TDD: (800) 281-8749 E-mail: ldouglas@nsf.gov
Web: www.nsf.gov

Purpose To provide funding to minority and other graduate students in mathematics who are interested in conducting research or serving as an intern in an industrial environment.

Eligibility This program is open to graduate students in mathematics who are U.S. citizens, nationals, or permanent residents. Applicants must be interested in conducting research in an industrial setting. For research assistantships, the research must form the basis of a master's thesis or Ph.D. dissertation and must be conducted under the joint supervision of a university faculty member and an industrial scientist; students will alternate their time between the industrial site and the classroom or other campus-based activities. For cooperative fellowships, students work full time as interns in an industrial setting and their research is not necessarily the basis for a thesis or dissertation. Selection is based on the quality of the proposed activity at the industrial site, the qualifications of both the supervising faculty member and the industrial sponsor, the appropriateness of the academic/industrial interaction, and the impact of the proposed training on the professional development of the graduate assistant/fellow. The program encourages applications from women, underrepresented minorities, and persons with disabilities.

Financial data Grants provide 50% of the total annual support for a student (to a maximum of $20,000 per year. The awardee institution must cost share the balance of support. The supervising faculty member is eligible for a research allowance of $6,000.

Duration 1 year.

Number awarded This program awards a total of 10 grants, with a value of $1,000,000, each year.

Deadline May of each year.

[1352]
U.S. ARMY SUSTAINMENT COMMAND MINORITY INTERNSHIP PROGRAM

ADNET Systems, Inc.
164 Rollins Avenue, Suite 303
Rockville, MD 20852
(301) 770-4850 Fax: (301) 770-4828
E-mail: info@adnet-sys.com
Web: www.adnet-sys.com/internships.html

Purpose To provide work experience at facilities of the U.S. Army Sustainment Command (ASC) to students at minority institutions.

Eligibility This program is open to students who are from Historically Black Colleges and Universities (HBCUs), Hispanic Serving Institutions (HSIs), Tribal Colleges and Univer-

sities (TCUs), Asian American and Pacific Islander communities, and disability communities. Applicants must be U.S. citizens currently enrolled in a college, university, or law school as a sophomore or above (including graduate students) with a GPA of 2.5 or higher; recent (within 6 months) graduates are also eligible. They must be interested in an internship at an ASC facility. Jobs have included mechanical engineering, safety engineering, civil engineering, architectural engineering, environmental sciences, chemistry, computer science, and such business fields as accounting, marketing, human resources, international affairs, contracting, and law. Along with their application, they must submit 50-word statements on 1) their community activities, hobbies, associations, publications, and other relevant experience; and 2) why they want to participate in this program.
Financial data Interns are paid a stipend and receive housing.
Duration 10 weeks in summer or 15 weeks in spring.
Additional information Recently, assignments were available at ASC facilities in Crane, Indiana; Herlong, California; McAlester, Oklahoma; Richmond, Kentucky; Rock Island, Illinois; Tooele, Utah; and Watervliet, New York.
Number awarded Varies each year.
Deadline May of each year for summer; November of each year for spring.

[1353]
WASHINGTON NASA SPACE GRANT CONSORTIUM PRIVATE INDUSTRY INTERNSHIPS
Washington NASA Space Grant Consortium
c/o University of Washington
Johnson Hall, Room 141
P.O. Box 351310
Seattle, WA 98195-1310
(206) 543-1943   Toll-free: (800) 659-1943
Fax: (206) 543-0179   E-mail: nasa@u.washington.edu
Web: www.waspacegrant.org/pvtindinterns.html

Purpose To provide an opportunity for minority and other upper-division and graduate students in Washington to gain summer work experience in a science or engineering field of interest to the U.S. National Aeronautics and Space Administration (NASA).
Eligibility This program is open to full-time juniors, seniors, and graduate students at colleges and universities that are members of the Washington NASA Space Grant Consortium. Applicants must be interested in a summer internship with a private firm or institute in a NASA-related field of science and engineering. U.S. citizenship is required. The program is part of the NASA National Space Grant program, which encourages participation by members of underrepresented groups (women, minorities, and persons with disabilities).
Financial data These are paid internships; salaries depend on the employer.
Duration Summer months.
Additional information Members of the consortium include Heritage University, Northwest Indian College, North Seattle Community College, Seattle Central Community College, Seattle University, University of Washington, University of Puget Sound, Washington State University, Western Washington University, and Whitman College.

Number awarded Varies each year; recently, 7 of these internships were awarded.
Deadline Deadlines are set by participating companies and institutes.

[1354]
WILLIAM RANDOLPH HEARST ENDOWED FELLOWSHIP FOR MINORITY STUDENTS
Aspen Institute
Attn: Director, Nonprofit Sector Research Fund
One Dupont Circle, N.W., Suite 700
Washington, DC 20036
(202) 736-5838   Fax: (202) 293-0525
E-mail: nsrf@aspeninstitute.org
Web: www.nonprofitresearch.org

Purpose To provide an opportunity for Native American and other minority students to learn more about nonprofit activities, including philanthropy and its underlying values, through an internship at the Aspen Institute in Washington, D.C.
Eligibility This program at the Aspen Institute is open to minority graduate and undergraduate students. Applicants must be interested in learning about nonprofit organizations by working at the institute, by assisting in preparations for its annual conference, and by engaging in general research and program support for its grantmaking and outreach efforts. They must be able to demonstrate outstanding research skills, interest or experience in the nonprofit sector, writing and communication skills, financial need, and U.S. citizenship.
Financial data Stipends range from $2,500 to $5,000, depending on the recipient's educational level, financial need, and time commitment.
Duration 10 to 15 weeks, in summer, fall, or spring.
Additional information This program, established in 1991, is funded by the William Randolph Hearst Foundation.
Number awarded Varies each year.
Deadline March, July, or December of each year.

[1355]
WOMBLE CARLYLE SCHOLARS PROGRAM
Womble Carlyle Sandridge & Rice, PLLC
Attn: Director of Diversity and Workplace Initiatives
One West Fourth Street
Winston-Salem, NC 27101
(336) 728-7055   Fax: (336) 733-8306
E-mail: gagard@wcsr.com
Web: www.wcsr.com/?id=149

Purpose To provide financial assistance and summer work experience to Native American and other underrepresented students at designated law schools.
Eligibility This program is open to students at designated law schools who are members of underrepresented groups. Applicants must be able to demonstrate solid academic credentials, personal or professional achievement outside the classroom, and significant participation in community service. Along with their application, they must submit a 300-word essay on either 1) a situation in which they and a person they respect disagreed over values or ideals and what they did, or 2) what idea has most influenced their life and why.

Financial data The stipend is $4,000. Recipients are also offered summer employment at an office of the sponsoring law firm. Salaries are the same as the firm's other summer associates in each office.

Duration 1 year (the second year of law school); may be renewed 1 additional year.

Additional information This program was established in 2004. The eligible law schools are North Carolina Central University School of Law (Durham, North Carolina), University of North Carolina at Chapel Hill School of Law (Chapel Hill, North Carolina), Duke University School of Law (Durham, North Carolina), Wake Forest University School of Law (Winston-Salem, North Carolina), University of South Carolina School of Law (Columbia, South Carolina), Howard University School of Law (Washington, D.C.), University of Virginia School of Law (Charlottesville, Virginia), University of Georgia School of Law (Athens, Georgia), Georgia Washington University Law School (Washington, D.C.), and Emory University School of Law (Atlanta, Georgia). The sponsoring law firm has offices in Atlanta (Georgia), Baltimore (Maryland), Charlotte (North Carolina), Greensboro (North Carolina), Greenville (South Carolina), Raleigh (North Carolina), Research Triangle Park (North Carolina), Tysons Corner (Virginia), Washington (D.C.), Wilmington (Delaware), and Winston-Salem (North Carolina).

Number awarded Varies each year; recently, 9 of these scholarships were awarded.

Deadline May of each year.

[1356]
WOODS HOLE OCEANOGRAPHIC INSTITUTION MINORITY FELLOWSHIPS

Woods Hole Oceanographic Institution
Attn: Education Office
Clark Laboratory 223, MS 31
360 Woods Hole Road
Woods Hole, MA 02543-1541
(508) 289-2219   Fax: (508) 457-2188
E-mail: education@whoi.edu
Web: www.whoi.edu

Purpose To provide work experience to Native Americans and other minorities who are interested in preparing for careers in the marine sciences, oceanographic engineering, or marine policy.

Eligibility This program is open to ethnic minority undergraduates enrolled in U.S. colleges or universities who have completed at least 2 semesters of study and who are interested in the physical or natural sciences, mathematics, engineering, or marine policy. Applicants must be U.S. citizens or permanent residents and African American or Black; Asian American; Chicano, Mexican American, Puerto Rican or other Hispanic; or Native American. They must be interested in a program of study and research at Woods Hole Oceanographic Institution.

Financial data The stipend is $415 per week; trainees may also receive additional support for travel to Woods Hole.

Duration 10 to 12 weeks during the summer or 1 semester during the academic year; renewable.

Additional information Trainees are assigned advisers who supervise their research programs and supplementary study activities. Some traineeships involve field work or research cruises. This program is conducted with support from and in cooperation with the Center for Marine and Coastal Geology of the U.S. Geological Survey.

Number awarded 4 to 5 each year.

Deadline For a summer appointment, applications must be submitted in February of each year. For the remaining portion of the year, applications may be submitted at any time, but they must be received at least 2 months before the anticipated starting date.

Indexes

Program Title Index •
Sponsoring Organization Index •
Residency Index •
Tenability Index •
Subject Index •
Calendar Index •

Program Title Index

If you know the name of a particular funding program and want to find out where it is covered in the directory, use the Program Title Index. Here, program titles are arranged alphabetically, word by word. To assist you in your search, every program is listed by all its known names or abbreviations. In addition, we've used an alphabetical code (within parentheses) to help you determine if the program falls within your scope of interest: S = Scholarships; F = Fellowships; G = Grants; A = Awards; and I = Internships. Here's how the code works: if a program is followed (S) 141, the program is described in entry 141 in the Scholarships section. If the same program title is followed by another entry number—for example, (G) 680—the program is also described in entry 680 in the Grants section. Remember: the numbers cited here refer to program entry numbers, not to page numbers in the book.

AAAE Foundation Scholarships for Native Americans, (S) 1
AAAS Minority Science Writers Internship, (I) 1176
AAUW Postdoctoral Research Leave Fellowships, (G) 909
Academic Research Enhancement Award, (G) 910
Accenture Graduate Fellowships, (F) 540
Accenture Undergraduate Scholarships, (S) 2
ACHE Minority Internship, (I) 1177
Acoustical Society of America Graduate Fellowship for Minorities. See ASA Graduate Fellowship for Minorities, entry (F) 577
ACT Summer Internship Program, (I) 1178
Adolph van Pelt Scholarships, (S) 3
Adrienne M. and Charles Shelby Rooks Fellowship for Racial and Ethnic Theological Students, (F) 541
Adult Vocational Training Program of the Wyandotte Nation, (S) 4
Advanced Degree Scholarship Fund of the Seminole Nation Judgment Fund, (F) 542
Advanced Postdoctoral Fellowships in Diabetes Research, (G) 911
AERA Minority Fellowships in Education Research, (G) 912
Aetna Scholars Program. See NCEMNA Aetna Scholars Program, entries (S) 370, (F) 793
Afognak Career Enhancement Opportunities Program, (S) 5
Afognak Higher Education Program, (S) 6, (F) 543
AGA Student Research Fellowship Awards, (G) 913
Aging Research Dissertation Awards to Increase Diversity, (G) 914
AICPA Fellowships for Minority Doctoral Students, (F) 544
AISES Google Scholarship, (S) 7, (F) 545
AISES Internship Program, (I) 1179
Akaka Scholarship. See Daniel Kahikina and Millie Akaka Scholarship, entries (S) 151, (F) 628
Al Qöyawayma Awards. See A.T. Anderson Memorial Scholarship Program, entries (S) 47, (F) 580

Alan Compton and Bob Stanley Minority and International Scholarship, (S) 8
Alaska Library Association Graduate Library Studies Scholarship, (F) 546
Alaska Native Tribal Health Consortium Scholarships, (S) 9, (F) 547
Alaska Native Tribal Health Consortium Summer Internships, (I) 1180
Alaska Space Grant Program Fellowships, (I) 1181
Albert W. Dent Student Scholarship, (F) 548
Aleut Foundation Graduate Scholarships, (F) 549
Aleut Foundation Part-Time Scholarships, (S) 10, (F) 550
Aleut Foundation Scholarship Program, (S) 11
Aleut Foundation Vocational Scholarships, (S) 12
Aleutian Pribilof Island Community Development Association Higher Education Scholarships. See APICDA Higher Education Scholarships, entries (S) 35, (F) 569
Aleutian Pribilof Island Community Development Association Supplemental Education Grants. See APICDA Supplemental Education Grants, entry (S) 36
Aleutian/Pribilof Islands Association Education and Training Program, (S) 13
Aleutian/Pribilof Islands Association Vocational Rehabilitation Assistance, (S) 14
Alfred J. Duran Sr. Trust Scholarship, (S) 15, (F) 551
Alfred P. Sloan Foundation Research Fellowships, (G) 915
Alice Tonemah Memorial Scholarships. See John C. Rouillard and Alice Tonemah Memorial Scholarships, entries (S) 264, (F) 714
All Native American High School Academic Team Scholarships, (S) 16
Allen Fellowships. See Frances C. Allen Fellowships, entry (G) 991
Allergy/Immunology Fellowship of Excellence Training Award, (G) 916

S–Scholarships F–Fellowships G–Grants A–Awards I–Internships

PROGRAM TITLE INDEX

Allogan Slagle Memorial Scholarship, (S) 17
Allogan Slagle Scholarship, (F) 552
Alyeska Match Scholarships, (S) 18
Alzheimer's Association Investigator–Initiated Research Grants, (G) 917
AMA Foundation Minority Scholars Awards, (F) 553
Amelia Kemp Memorial Scholarship, (S) 19, (F) 554
American Anthropological Association Minority Dissertation Fellowship Program, (G) 918
American Association for the Advancement of Science Minority Science Writers Internship. See AAAS Minority Science Writers Internship, entry (I) 1176
American Association of Airport Executives Foundation Scholarships for Native Americans.. See AAAE Foundation Scholarships for Native Americans, entry (S) 1
American Association of Blacks in Energy National Scholarships, (S) 20
American Association of University Women Postdoctoral Research Leave Fellowships. See AAUW Postdoctoral Research Leave Fellowships, entry (G) 909
American Chemical Society Scholars Program, (S) 21
American College of Healthcare Executives Minority Internship. See ACHE Minority Internship, entry (I) 1177
American College Testing Summer Internship Program. See ACT Summer Internship Program, entry (I) 1178
American Council of Learned Societies Fellowships, (G) 919
American Educational Research Association Minority Fellowships in Education Research. See AERA Minority Fellowships in Education Research, entry (G) 912
American Gastroenterological Association Student Research Fellowship Awards. See AGA Student Research Fellowship Awards, entry (G) 913
American Indian Arts Council Scholarship Program, (S) 22, (F) 555
American Indian Chamber of Commerce of California Scholarship, (S) 23, (F) 556
American Indian Chamber of Commerce of Wisconsin Scholarships, (S) 24, (F) 557
American Indian Community College Scholarship, (S) 25
American Indian Education Foundation Scholarship Program, (S) 26
American Indian Fellowship in Business Scholarship, (S) 27, (F) 558
American Indian Graduate Center Fellowships, (F) 559
American Indian Law Review Writing Competition, (A) 1143
American Indian Program, (G) 920
American Indian Science and Engineering Society Internship Program. See AISES Internship Program, entry (I) 1179
American Indian Services Scholarship Program, (S) 28
American Indian Studies Postdoctoral and Visiting Scholars Fellowship Program, (G) 921
American Institute of Architects Minority/Disadvantaged Scholarship Program, (S) 29
American Institute of Certified Public Accountants Fellowships for Minority Doctoral Students. See AICPA Fellowships for Minority Doctoral Students, entry (F) 544
American Library Association Spectrum Initiative Scholarships, (F) 560
American Medical Association Foundation Minority Scholars Awards. See AMA Foundation Minority Scholars Awards, entry (F) 553

American Membrane Technology Association Fellowship for Membrane Technology. See AMTA Fellowship for Membrane Technology, entry (G) 923
American Meteorological Society Undergraduate Scholarships. See AMS Undergraduate Scholarships, entry (S) 31
American Nurses Association Clinical Research Pre–Doctoral Fellowship Program. See ANA Clinical Research Pre–Doctoral Fellowship Program, entries (F) 566, (G) 924
American Physical Society Scholarships for Minority Undergraduate Physics Majors, (S) 30
American Planning Association Planning Fellowships, (F) 561
American Political Science Association Minority Fellows Program. See APSA Minority Fellows Program, entry (F) 570
American Society for Engineering Education DuPont Minorities in Engineering Award. See ASSE/DuPont Minorities in Engineering Award, entry (A) 1145
American Society for Microbiology Minority Undergraduate Research Fellowship. See Microbiology Undergraduate Research Fellowship, entries (G) 1037, (I) 1284
American Society for Pharmacology and Experimental Therapeutics Individual Summer Undergraduate Research Fellowships. See ASPET Individual Summer Undergraduate Research Fellowships, entry (I) 1185
American Society of Clinical Oncology Medical Student Rotation. See ASCO Medical Student Rotation, entry (G) 928
American Society of Criminology Fellowships for Ethnic Minorities, (F) 562
American Society of Criminology Undergraduate Student Minority/Mentor Research Grant, (G) 922
American Society of Hematology–Amos Medical Faculty Development Program Research Grants. See ASH–AMFDP Research Grants, entry (G) 929
American Society of Neephrology John Merrill Transplant Scholar Grant. See John Merrill Transplant Scholar Grant, entry (G) 1019
American Society of Safety Engineers Diversity Committee Scholarship. See ASSE Diversity Committee Scholarship, entries (S) 43, (F) 579
American Society of Safety Engineers UPS Diversity Scholarships. See ASSE UPS Diversity Scholarships, entry (S) 44
American Sociological Association Minority Fellowship Program, (F) 563
American Sociological Association Minority Fellowship Program General Fellowship. See ASA Minority Fellowship Program General Fellowship, entry (F) 578
American Speech–Language–Hearing Foundation Scholarship for Minority Students, (F) 564
Amos Medical Faculty Development Program. See Harold Amos Medical Faculty Development Program, entry (G) 1005
AMS Undergraduate Scholarships, (S) 31
AMTA Fellowship for Membrane Technology, (G) 923
Amy Louise Hunter–Wilson, M.D. Memorial Scholarship, (S) 32, (F) 565
ANA Clinical Research Pre–Doctoral Fellowship Program, (F) 566, (G) 924
ANAC Student Diversity Mentorship Scholarship, (S) 33, (F) 567
Anderson, D.O. Minority Scholarship. See William G. Anderson, D.O. Minority Scholarship, entry (F) 898

S–Scholarships   F–Fellowships   G–Grants   A–Awards   I–Internships

PROGRAM TITLE INDEX

Anderson Memorial Scholarship Program. See A.T. Anderson Memorial Scholarship Program, entries (S) 47, (F) 580
Anisfield-Wolf Book Awards, (A) 1144
ANL Laboratory-Graduate Research Appointments, (G) 925
Ann Malo Scholarship. See Makia and Ann Malo Scholarship, entry (F) 744
Anne H. Myers Scholarship, (S) 34
Annie Wauneka Visiting Faculty Fellowship, (F) 568
Antarctic Research Program, (G) 926
APICDA Higher Education Scholarships, (S) 35, (F) 569
APICDA Supplemental Education Grants, (S) 36
APL Technology Leaders Summer Internship Program. See ATLAS Scholars Program, entry (I) 1187
Appraisal Institute Minorities and Women Educational Scholarship Program, (S) 37
APSA Minority Fellows Program, (F) 570
Aqqaluk Trust Scholarships, (S) 38
Arapaho Educational Trust Scholarship, (S) 39, (F) 571
Arapaho Ranch Educational Trust Scholarship, (S) 40, (F) 572
Arapaho Ranch Trust Scholarship. See Bill Thunder, Jr./Arapaho Ranch Trust Scholarship, entries (S) 58, (F) 586
Arctic Education Foundation Scholarships, (S) 41, (F) 573
Arctic Research Opportunities, (G) 927
Arent Fox Diversity Scholarships, (F) 574, (I) 1182
Argonne National Laboratory-Graduate Research Appointments. See ANL Laboratory-Graduate Research Appointments, entry (G) 925
Arizona Space Grant Consortium Undergraduate Research Internships, (I) 1183
ARL Initiative to Recruit a Diverse Workforce, (F) 575
Arnstein Minority Student Scholarship. See Sherry R. Arnstein Minority Student Scholarship, entry (F) 856
Arnstein New Student Minority Student Scholarship. See Sherry R. Arnstein New Student Minority Student Scholarship, entry (F) 857
Artemis A.W. and Martha Joukowsky Postdoctoral Fellowship. See Pembroke Center Postdoctoral Fellowships, entry (G) 1088
Arthur C. Parker Scholarships, (S) 42, (F) 576
ArtTable Mentored Internships for Diversity in the Visual Arts Professions, (I) 1184
ASA Graduate Fellowship for Minorities, (F) 577
ASA Minority Fellowship Program General Fellowship, (F) 578
Asche Memorial Scholarship. See Elizabeth and Sherman Asche Memorial Scholarship, entries (S) 175, (F) 650
ASCO Medical Student Rotation, (G) 928
ASH-AMFDP Research Grants, (G) 929
ASPET Individual Summer Undergraduate Research Fellowships, (I) 1185
ASSE Diversity Committee Scholarship, (S) 43, (F) 579
ASSE UPS Diversity Scholarships, (S) 44
ASSE/DuPont Minorities in Engineering Award, (A) 1145
Association for Women Geoscientists Minority Scholarship, (S) 45
Association of Nurses in AIDS Care Student Diversity Mentorship Scholarship. See ANAC Student Diversity Mentorship Scholarship, entries (S) 33, (F) 567
Association of Research Libraries Initiative to Recruit a Diverse Workforce. See ARL Initiative to Recruit a Diverse Workforce, entry (F) 575
Association on American Indian Affairs Displaced Homemaker Scholarships, (S) 46

Astronomy and Astrophysics Postdoctoral Fellowships, (G) 930
A.T. Anderson Memorial Scholarship Program, (S) 47, (F) 580
Atlanta Journal and Constitution Minority Internships, (I) 1186
ATLAS Scholars Program, (I) 1187
AT&T Laboratories Fellowship Program, (F) 581, (I) 1188
Awards for Research in Engineering and Science (ARES) Program, (I) 1189

Baker & Daniels Diversity Scholarships, (I) 1190
Baker Donelson Diversity Scholarships, (F) 582
Baker Hughes Scholarships, (S) 48, (F) 583
Baker Scholarship. See Colbert "Bud" Baker Scholarship, entry (S) 119
Balfour Phi Delta Phi Minority Scholarship Program, (F) 584
Bank2 Banking Scholarship, (S) 49
Bank2 Ta-ossaa-asha' Scholarships, (S) 50
Banner Diversity Scholarship. See Donald W. Banner Diversity Scholarship, entries (F) 636, (I) 1220
Bannerman Memorial Fellowships. See Sabbaticals for Long-Time Activists of Color, entry (G) 1109
Barbara Dobkin Native American Artist Fellowship. See Eric and Barbara Dobkin Native American Artist Fellowship, entry (G) 977
Barbara Jordan Health Policy Scholars Program, (I) 1191
Barrow Minority Doctoral Student Scholarship. See Lionel C. Barrow Minority Doctoral Student Scholarship, entry (F) 740
Bay Area Community Service Scholarships, (G) 931, (I) 1192
Beamer Scholarship. See Edwin Mahiai Copp Beamer Scholarship, entry (S) 172
Beeson Career Development Awards in Aging Research Program. See Paul B. Beeson Career Development Awards in Aging Research Program, entry (G) 1086
Begay III Scholarship Program. See Notay Begay III Scholarship Program, entry (S) 387
Bendix Minorities in Engineering Award. See ASSE/DuPont Minorities in Engineering Award, entry (A) 1145
Bering Straits Foundation Higher Education and Vocational Training Scholarships, (S) 51, (F) 585
Berkeley Foundation Scholarships. See Michael J. Berkeley Foundation Scholarships, entry (S) 324
Bernard Bouschor Honorary Scholarship Program, (S) 52
Bessie Elizabeth Delaney Fellowship. See Dr. Bessie Elizabeth Delaney Fellowship, entry (F) 640
Betty Lea Stone Research Fellowship, (G) 932
Bevins Endowment Scholarship Fund. See Susie Qimmiqsak Bevins Endowment Scholarship Fund, entries (S) 481, (F) 872
Beyond Margins Award, (A) 1146
BHP Billiton Scholarship Program, (S) 53
BIA Higher Education Grant Program, (S) 54
Bienstock Fellowship. See N.S. Bienstock Fellowship, entry (F) 805
Big Goose Memorial Scholarship. See The Rev. Francene Eagle Big Goose Memorial Scholarship, entry (F) 837
Bill Dickey Golf Scholarships, (S) 55
Bill Fryrear Memorial Scholarships, (S) 56
Bill Taylor Scholarship Endowment, (S) 57
Bill Thunder, Jr./Arapaho Ranch Trust Scholarship, (S) 58, (F) 586
Billy L. Cypress Scholarship, (S) 59

S-Scholarships   F-Fellowships   G-Grants   A-Awards   I-Internships

Biomedical Research Training Program for Underrepresented Groups, (I) 1193
Blackfeet Adult Vocational Training Grants, (S) 60
Blackfeet Higher Education Grants, (S) 61
Blitman, P.E. Scholarship to Promote Diversity in Engineering. See Maureen L. and Howard N. Blitman, P.E. Scholarship to Promote Diversity in Engineering, entry (S) 318
Blossom Kalama Evans Memorial Scholarships, (S) 62, (F) 587
Bob Stanley Minority and International Scholarship. See Alan Compton and Bob Stanley Minority and International Scholarship, entry (S) 8
Bois Forte Higher Education Program, (S) 63, (F) 588
Bolin Dissertation Fellowships. See Gaius Charles Bolin Dissertation Fellowships, entry (G) 993
Bonner Scholarship. See Jewell Hilton Bonner Scholarship, entry (S) 261
Booker T. Washington Scholarships, (S) 64
Bouchet Award. See Edward A. Bouchet Award, entry (A) 1152
Bouschor Honorary Scholarship Program. See Bernard Bouschor Honorary Scholarship Program, entry (S) 52
Bowen Foundation Internships. See Emma L. Bowen Foundation Internships, entry (I) 1223
Boyd Scholarship. See Triad Hospitals Corris Boyd Scholarship, entry (F) 879
Brandt Scholarships. See Gladys Kamakakuokalani Ainoa Brandt Scholarships, entries (S) 215, (F) 683
Breakthrough to Nursing Scholarships for Racial/Ethnic Minorities, (S) 65
Breast Cancer Disparities Research Grants, (G) 933
Bristol Bay Native Corporation Education Foundation Higher Education Scholarships, (S) 66
Brocksbank Scholarship. See A.T. Anderson Memorial Scholarship Program, entries (S) 47, (F) 580
Brooker Collegiate Scholarship for Minorities. See George M. Brooker Collegiate Scholarship for Minorities, entries (S) 213, (F) 679
Brookhaven National Laboratory Professional Associates Program for Women and Minorities, (I) 1194
Brookhaven National Laboratory Science and Engineering Programs for Women and Minorities, (I) 1195
Brown and Caldwell Minority Scholarship, (S) 67
Brown COREM Scholarships. See Richard and Helen Brown COREM Scholarships, entry (F) 838
Brown Fellowship. See Howard Mayer Brown Fellowship, entry (F) 701
Brown Foundation Academic Scholarships, (S) 68
Brown Memorial Award. See Nell B. Brown Memorial Award, entry (F) 794
Brown Memorial Scholarship. See Ronald H. Brown Memorial Scholarship, entry (S) 446
Bruce T. and Jackie Mahi Erickson Scholarship, (S) 69, (F) 589, (G) 934
Buc Postdoctoral Fellowship. See Pembroke Center Postdoctoral Fellowships, entry (G) 1088
Buckingham, Doolittle & Burroughs Diversity Scholarship Program, (I) 1196
Bud Baker Scholarship. See Colbert "Bud" Baker Scholarship, entry (S) 119
Buffalo Bandits Native American College Fund, (S) 70
Bullivant Houser Bailey Law Student Diversity Scholarship Program, (F) 590, (I) 1197
Bunche Award. See Ralph J. Bunche Award, entry (A) 1167
Bunche Summer Institute. See Ralph Bunche Summer Institute, entry (S) 439
Bureau of Indian Affairs Higher Education Grant Program. See BIA Higher Education Grant Program, entry (S) 54
Burlington Northern Santa Fe Foundation Scholarship, (S) 71
Business Reporting Intern Program for Minority College Sophomores and Juniors, (S) 72, (I) 1198
Butler Rubin Diversity Scholarship, (F) 591, (I) 1199

CAA Professional Development Fellowships, (F) 592
Cadbury Award. See William and Charlotte Cadbury Award, entry (A) 1173
Calder Summer Undergraduate Research Program, (G) 935
California Community Service Scholarships, (I) 1200
California Library Association Scholarship for Minority Students in Memory of Edna Yelland. See CLA Scholarship for Minority Students in Memory of Edna Yelland, entry (F) 611
California Space Grant Consortium Student–Mentor Aerospace Workforce Development Scholarships, (I) 1201
Calista Scholarship Fund, (S) 73, (F) 593
Campbell Graduate Fellows Program. See Jeffrey Campbell Graduate Fellows Program, entry (G) 1017
Cancer Prevention, Control, Behavioral, and Population Sciences Career Development Award, (G) 936
Cap Lathrop Endowment Scholarship Fund, (S) 74, (F) 594
Cape Fox Scholarships, (S) 75, (F) 595
Career Awards for Medical Scientists, (F) 596, (G) 937
Career Awards in the Biomedical Sciences. See Career Awards for Medical Scientists, entries (F) 596, (G) 937
Career Development Award to Promote Diversity in Neuroscience, (G) 938
Career Transition Awards of the Tuberous Sclerosis Complex Research Program, (G) 939
Career Upgrade Grants, (S) 76
Carl H. Marrs Scholarship Fund, (S) 77, (F) 597
Carol G. Lederer Postdoctoral Fellowship. See Pembroke Center Postdoctoral Fellowships, entry (G) 1088
Carolina Postdoctoral Program for Faculty Diversity, (G) 940
Cartwright Scholarship Program, (S) 78
Cary Institute of Ecosystem Studies Research Experiences for Undergraduates Program, (G) 941
Caterpillar FFA Scholarships, (S) 79
CDC/PRC Minority Fellowships, (G) 942
Cecelia Somday Education Fund, (S) 80
CEDAR, GEM, and SHINE Postdoctoral Research Grants, (G) 943
Centers for Disease Control/Prevention Research Centers Minority Fellowships. See CDC/PRC Minority Fellowships, entry (G) 942
Central Intelligence Agency Undergraduate Internship Program. See CIA Undergraduate Internship Program, entry (I) 1204
Central Intelligence Agency Undergraduate Scholarship Program, (S) 81
CGSM Fellowships, (F) 598, (I) 1202
Champions of Health Professions Diversity Award, (A) 1147
Chancellor's Postdoctoral Fellowships for Academic Diversity, (G) 944
Chang Internships. See Lena Chang Internships, entry (I) 1269

S–Scholarships F–Fellowships G–Grants A–Awards I–Internships

Charles A. Eastman Dissertation Fellowship for Native American Scholars, (G) 945
Charles Cockett 'Ohana Scholarship, (S) 82
Charles Shelby Rooks Fellowship for Racial and Ethnic Theological Students. See Adrienne M. and Charles Shelby Rooks Fellowship for Racial and Ethnic Theological Students, entry (F) 541
Charley Memorial Scholarships. See Walter Charley Memorial Scholarships, entry (S) 514
Charlotte Cadbury Award. See William and Charlotte Cadbury Award, entry (A) 1173
Charlotte DeHorse Scholarship. See First Sergeant Douglas and Charlotte DeHorse Scholarship, entries (S) 185, (F) 660
Cherokee Nation Graduate School Scholarship Program, (F) 599
Cherokee Nation Pell Scholarships, (S) 83
Cherokee Nation Scholarship Program, (S) 84
Cherokee Nation Tribal Council Award, (S) 85
Chester E. Faris Higher Education Fund. See Norman TeCube Sr. Higher Education Fund, entries (S) 379, (F) 800
Cheyenne and Arapaho Higher Education Grants, (S) 86, (F) 600
Chickasaw Foundation Fine Arts Scholarship, (S) 87
Chickasaw Nation Agriculture Scholastic Program, (S) 88
Chickasaw Nation Degree Completion Incentive Awards, (A) 1148
Chickasaw Nation Division on Aging Scholarship, (S) 89
Chickasaw Nation General Scholarships, (S) 90, (F) 601
Chickasaw Nation Higher Education Grants, (S) 91, (F) 602
Chickasaw Nation Life-Time Scholarships, (S) 92, (F) 603
Chickasaw Nation Lighthorse Scholarship, (S) 93
Chief Freeman Johnson Scholarship, (S) 94, (F) 604
Chief Manuelito Scholarship Program, (S) 95
Chief Pushmataha College Scholarship Fund, (S) 96
Chips Quinn Scholars Program, (S) 97, (I) 1203
Choctaw Nation Agriculture Scholastic Program, (S) 98
Choctaw Nation Higher Education Grants, (S) 99
Choctaw Nation Higher Education Scholarships, (S) 100
Choy-Kee 'Ohana Scholarship, (S) 101
Chugach Heritage Foundation Scholarships, (S) 102, (F) 605
Chugach Heritage Foundation Vocational Training Funding, (S) 103
Chugachmiut Higher Education Grants, (S) 104, (F) 606
Chugachmiut Vocational Training Tuition Assistance, (S) 105
CIA Undergraduate Internship Program, (I) 1204
Circle of Honor Award, (A) 1149
CIRI Education Project Grants, (G) 946
CIRI Foundation Achievement Scholarships, (S) 106, (F) 607
CIRI Foundation Excellence Scholarships, (S) 107, (F) 608
CIRI Foundation General Semester Scholarships, (S) 108, (F) 609
CIRI Foundation Internship Program, (I) 1205
CIRI Foundation Special Excellence Scholarships, (S) 109, (F) 610
CIRI Foundation Vocational Training Grants, (S) 110
Citi Foundation Scholarship Program, (S) 111
Citizen Potawatomi Nation Adult Vocational Training, (S) 112
Citizen Potawatomi Nation Higher Education Grants, (S) 113
Citizen Potawatomi Nation Tribal Rolls Scholarships, (S) 114
CITY Internship Program. See COMTO's Inside Track for Youth (CITY) Internship Program, entry (I) 1209

CLA Scholarship for Minority Students in Memory of Edna Yelland, (F) 611
Clara Zimmerman Foundation Education Scholarships. See Dr. Hans and Clara Zimmerman Foundation Education Scholarships, entry (S) 159
Clark Fellowship. See Michele Clark Fellowship, entry (F) 757
Clem Judd, Jr. Memorial Scholarship, (S) 115
Clifton O. Dummett and Lois Doyle Dummett Fellowship. See Dr. Clifton O. Dummett and Lois Doyle Dummett Fellowship, entry (F) 641
Clinical Research Post-Doctoral Fellowship Program, (G) 947
Clinical Science Faculty Development Grant, (G) 948
Coca-Cola First Generation Scholarship, (S) 116
Cocopah Achievement Incentive Awards, (A) 1150
Cocopah Graduate Fellowships, (F) 612
Cocopah Higher Education Grants, (S) 117
Cocopah Summer Tuition Assistance, (S) 118, (F) 613
Colberg Endowment Scholarship Fund. See John N. Colberg Endowment Scholarship Fund, entries (S) 265, (F) 716
Colbert "Bud" Baker Scholarship, (S) 119
Colgate "Bright Smiles, Bright Futures" Minority Scholarships, (S) 120
Collaborative Neurological Sciences Award, (G) 949
Collaborative Research Experience for Undergraduates in Computer Science and Engineering, (G) 950
College Student Pre-Commissioning Initiative, (S) 121
Colorado Indian Education Foundation Scholars Program, (S) 122
Colorado Space Grant Research Support, (I) 1206
Coltrin Award for Excellence in Communication Education. See Stephen H. Coltrin Award for Excellence in Communication Education, entry (A) 1169
Comanche Nation Adult Vocational Training Program, (S) 123
Comanche Nation College Scholarship Program, (S) 124
Commercial and Federal Litigation Section Minority Fellowship, (I) 1207
Communications Internship Award for Students of Color, (I) 1208
Communications Scholarship for Ethnic Minority Students. See Leonard M. Perryman Communications Scholarship for Ethnic Minority Students, entry (S) 303
Community Arts Symposium Program of the National Museum of the American Indian, (G) 951
Community-Based Education Program, (S) 125
Compton and Bob Stanley Minority and International Scholarship. See Alan Compton and Bob Stanley Minority and International Scholarship, entry (S) 8
ComputerCraft Corporation Scholarship, (S) 126
COMTO's Inside Track for Youth (CITY) Internship Program, (I) 1209
ConAgra Foods Foundation Scholarships, (S) 127
Confederated Salish and Kootenai Tribes Higher Education Scholarships, (S) 128, (F) 614
Confederated Tribes of the Umatilla Indian Reservation Higher Education Scholarships, (S) 129, (F) 615
Connecticut Community College Minority Fellowship Program, (I) 1210
Consortium for Graduate Study in Management Fellowships. See CGSM Fellowships, entries (F) 598, (I) 1202
Consuelo W. Gosnell Memorial Scholarships, (F) 616
Continental Society, Daughters of Indian Wars Scholarship, (S) 130

S–Scholarships   F–Fellowships   G–Grants   A–Awards   I–Internships

Cook Inlet Region, Inc. Education Project Grants. See CIRI Education Project Grants, entry (G) 946
Cook Inlet Region, Inc. Heritage Project Grants, (G) 952
Cook Inlet Tribal Council Tribal Higher Education Program, (S) 131, (F) 617
Copper River Native Association Adult Vocational Training Scholarship, (S) 132
Copper River Native Association Higher Education Scholarship, (S) 133, (F) 618
Coquille Indian Tribe Adult Vocational Training Grants, (S) 134
Coquille Indian Tribe Computer Equipment Program, (S) 135, (F) 619
Coquille Indian Tribe Education Scholarship, (S) 136
Coquille Indian Tribe Higher Education Grants, (S) 137, (F) 620
COREM Scholarships. See Richard and Helen Brown COREM Scholarships, entry (F) 838
Cornell Scholarship. See Holly A. Cornell Scholarship, entry (F) 695
Cornell University Library Fellowship Program, (G) 953
Corporate-Sponsored Scholarships for Minority Undergraduate Students Who Major in Physics. See American Physical Society Scholarships for Minority Undergraduate Physics Majors, entry (S) 30
Corris Boyd Scholarship. See Triad Hospitals Corris Boyd Scholarship, entry (F) 879
Corwin Scholarships. See Juanita Corwin Scholarships, entries (S) 270, (F) 721
Council for Racial and Ethnic Ministries Scholarships. See Richard and Helen Brown COREM Scholarships, entry (F) 838
Council of Energy Resource Tribes Scholarships, (S) 138, (F) 621
Cow Creek Band Adult Vocational Training Program, (S) 139
Cow Creek Band Continuing and Distance Education Program, (S) 140, (F) 622
Cow Creek Band Higher Education Program, (S) 141, (F) 623
Cow Creek Band Tribal Education Program, (S) 142
Crane Award, (F) 624
Crazy Horse Memorial Journalism Scholarship, (S) 143
Creek Nation Higher Education Scholarships, (S) 144
Creek Nation Post Graduate Program, (F) 625
Creek Nation Post Graduate Program. See Creek Nation Post Graduate Program, entry (F) 625
Creek Nation Tribal Funds Grant Program, (S) 145
Creek Nation Tribal Incentive Grant Program, (S) 146
Crowe Memorial Scholarship. See Richard (Yogi) Crowe Memorial Scholarship, entry (F) 840
Crumbly Minorities in Energy Grant. See Isaac "Ike" Crumbly Minorities in Energy Grant, entry (G) 1015
C.T. Lang Journalism Minority Scholarship and Internship, (S) 147, (I) 1211
Cultural Anthropology Scholars Awards, (G) 954
Cultural Resources Diversity Internship Program, (I) 1212
Culturally Diverse Academic Institutions Undergraduate Student Fellowships. See EPA Greater Research Opportunities (GRO) Fellowships for Undergraduate Environmental Study, entries (S) 179, (I) 1226
Cummins Scholarships, (S) 148, (F) 626
Cypress Scholarship. See Billy L. Cypress Scholarship, entry (S) 59

Dakota Indian Foundation Scholarship, (S) 149
Dalmas A. Taylor Memorial Summer Minority Policy Fellowship, (I) 1213
Dan and Rachel Mahi Educational Scholarship, (S) 150, (F) 627
Daniel Kahikina and Millie Akaka Scholarship, (S) 151, (F) 628
Daniel Kovach Foundation Minority Student Scholarship, (S) 152, (F) 629
Daniel T. Jenks Scholarship. See Mary K. Moreland and Daniel T. Jenks Scholarship, entry (S) 314
Darlene Dyer Stanhoff Memorial Scholarship. See American Indian Chamber of Commerce of California Scholarship, entries (S) 23, (F) 556
David Oakerhater Merit Fellowship. See ECIM Scholarships, entry (F) 646
David Sankey Minority Scholarship in Meteorology, (S) 153, (F) 630
Davis Scholarship Fund. See Edward Davis Scholarship Fund, entry (S) 171
Davis Wright Tremaine 1L Diversity Scholarship Program, (F) 631, (I) 1214
DDW Student Abstract Prizes, (A) 1151
de Merieux Rheumatology Fellowship Award. See Paula de Merieux Rheumatology Fellowship Award, entry (F) 818
DeHorse Scholarship. See First Sergeant Douglas and Charlotte DeHorse Scholarship, entries (S) 185, (F) 660
Delaney Fellowship. See Dr. Bessie Elizabeth Delaney Fellowship, entry (F) 640
Deloria Jr. Memorial Scholarship. See Vine Deloria Jr. Memorial Scholarship, entry (F) 888
Dennis Wong and Associates Scholarship, (S) 154, (F) 632
Dent Student Scholarship. See Albert W. Dent Student Scholarship, entry (F) 548
Department of Agriculture Small Business Innovation Research Program. See USDA Small Business Innovation Research Program, entry (G) 1133
Department of Defense Experimental Program to Stimulate Competitive Research, (G) 955
Department of Defense Small Business Innovation Research Grants, (G) 956
Department of Defense Small Business Technology Transfer Grants, (G) 957
Department of Education Small Business Innovation Research Grants, (G) 958
Department of Energy Health, Safety and Security Minority Serving Institution Support Program, (I) 1215
Department of Energy Small Business Innovation Research Grants. See DOE Small Business Innovation Research Grants, entry (G) 967
Department of Energy Small Business Technology Transfer Grants. See DOE Small Business Technology Transfer Grants, entry (G) 968
Department of Homeland Security Small Business Innovation Research Grants, (G) 959
Department of Homeland Security Summer Faculty and Student Research Team Program, (G) 960
Department of the Interior Diversity Intern Program, (I) 1216
Department of Transportation Minority-Serving Institutions and Educational Partnerships Internships, (I) 1217
Department of Transportation Small Business Innovation Research Grants, (G) 961
Dibner Math and Science Teaching Program, (G) 962

S–Scholarships   F–Fellowships   G–Grants   A–Awards   I–Internships

PROGRAM TITLE INDEX

Dickey Golf Scholarships. See Bill Dickey Golf Scholarships, entry (S) 55

Dietetic Internship Scholarships, (I) 1218

Digestive Disease Week Student Abstract Prizes. See DDW Student Abstract Prizes, entry (A) 1151

Dinsmore & Shohl LLP Diversity Scholarship Program, (F) 633, (I) 1219

Dissertation Fellowship for Native American Scholars. See Charles A. Eastman Dissertation Fellowship for Native American Scholars, entry (G) 945

Dissertation Year Visiting Diversity Fellowships for Advanced Graduate Students, (G) 963

Distance Delivery Scholarships, (S) 155

Diversity Fellowships in Environmental Reporting, (F) 634

Diversity Program in Neuroscience Postdoctoral Fellowships, (G) 964

Diversity Program in Neuroscience Predoctoral Fellowships, (F) 635

Dobkin Native American Artist Fellowship. See Eric and Barbara Dobkin Native American Artist Fellowship, entry (G) 977

Doctor Memorial Iroquois Indian Emlen Awards. See Peter Doctor Memorial Indian Emlen Awards, entries (S) 411, (F) 821

Doctor Memorial Iroquois Indian Scholarship Grants. See Peter Doctor Memorial Indian Scholarship Grants, entries (S) 412, (F) 822

Doctoral Dissertation Improvement Grants in the Directorate for Biological Sciences, (G) 965

DOE Faculty Sabbatical Program, (G) 966

DOE Small Business Innovation Research Grants, (G) 967

DOE Small Business Technology Transfer Grants, (G) 968

Don Leonard Memorial Academic Scholarship. See National Native American Law Enforcement Association Academic Scholarship Program, entry (S) 354

Donald W. Banner Diversity Scholarship, (F) 636, (I) 1220

Dora Ames Lee Leadership Development Fund, (S) 156, (F) 637

Doris Duke Clinical Scientist Development Awards, (G) 969

Dorothy Miller Native American Vocational Scholarship. See Verl and Dorothy Miller Native American Vocational Scholarship, entry (S) 510

Douglas and Charlotte DeHorse Scholarship. See First Sergeant Douglas and Charlotte DeHorse Scholarship, entries (S) 185, (F) 660

Doyon Foundation Basic Scholarships, (S) 157, (F) 638

Doyon Foundation Competitive Scholarships, (S) 158, (F) 639

Dr. Bessie Elizabeth Delaney Fellowship, (F) 640

Dr. Clifton O. Dummett and Lois Doyle Dummett Fellowship, (F) 641

Dr. Hans and Clara Zimmerman Foundation Education Scholarships, (S) 159

Dr. Joseph L. Henry Scholarships, (F) 642

Dr. Jules M. Rothstein Minority Research Fellowship Award, (G) 970

Dr. Phillip R. Lee Health Careers Scholarship, (S) 160

Dr. Roe B. Lewis Memorial Scholarships, (S) 161, (F) 643

DRI Law Student Diversity Scholarship, (F) 644

Drug Abuse Dissertation Research: Epidemiology, Prevention, Treatment, Services, and Women and Sex/Gender Differences, (G) 971

Dubin Native American Artist Fellowship. See Ronald N. and Susan Dubin Native American Artist Fellowship, entry (G) 1108

DuBois Fellowship Program. See W.E.B. DuBois Fellowship Program, entry (G) 1135

Duke Clinical Scientist Development Awards. See Doris Duke Clinical Scientist Development Awards, entry (G) 969

Dummett Fellowship. See Dr. Clifton O. Dummett and Lois Doyle Dummett Fellowship, entry (F) 641

DuPont Minorities in Engineering Award. See ASSE/DuPont Minorities in Engineering Award, entry (A) 1145

Duran Sr. Trust Scholarship. See Alfred J. Duran Sr. Trust Scholarship, entries (S) 15, (F) 551

Dwayne "Nakila" Steele Scholarship, (S) 162

Dwight David Eisenhower Graduate Transportation Fellowships, (F) 645

Dwight David Eisenhower Tribal Colleges and Universities Transportation Fellowships, (S) 163

Dwight Mosley Scholarships, (S) 164

Earl Frawner Family Scholarship, (S) 165

Eastman Dissertation Fellowship for Native American Scholars. See Charles A. Eastman Dissertation Fellowship for Native American Scholars, entry (G) 945

Eaton Minority Engineering Scholars Program. See Eaton Multicultural Scholars Program, entries (S) 166, (I) 1221

Eaton Multicultural Scholars Program, (S) 166, (I) 1221

ECIM Scholarships, (F) 646

Ecology of Infectious Diseases Initiative, (G) 972

Edith Kanaka'ole Foundation Higher Education Scholarship, (S) 167, (F) 647

Edna P. McCurdy Scholarships, (S) 168

Edna Yelland Memorial Scholarship. See CLA Scholarship for Minority Students in Memory of Edna Yelland, entry (F) 611

EDSA Minority Scholarship, (S) 169

Education Awards for Hopi Tribal Members, (S) 170, (F) 648

Educational Testing Service Visiting Scholar Program. See ETS Visiting Scholar Program, entry (G) 978

Edward A. Bouchet Award, (A) 1152

Edward D. Stone, Jr. and Associates Minority Scholarship. See EDSA Minority Scholarship, entry (S) 169

Edward Davis Scholarship Fund, (S) 171

Edward L. Kruger Memorial *Ittish Aaisha* Scholarship, (F) 649

Edwin Mahiai Copp Beamer Scholarship, (S) 172

Eight Northern Indian Pueblos Council Higher Education Grant Program, (S) 173

Eisenhower Grants for Research and Intern Fellowships, (G) 973, (I) 1222

Eisenhower Tribal Colleges and Universities Transportation Fellowships. See Dwight David Eisenhower Tribal Colleges and Universities Transportation Fellowships, entry (S) 163

Eklutna, Incorporated Scholarship and Grant Program, (S) 174

Elizabeth and Sherman Asche Memorial Scholarship, (S) 175, (F) 650

Ellen Masin Persina Scholarship, (S) 176

Emery Fast Scholarship. See Ethel and Emery Fast Scholarship, entries (S) 180, (F) 651

Emilie Hesemeyer Memorial Scholarship, (S) 177

Emily Shagen Scholarship. See Paul and Emily Shagen Scholarship, entries (S) 402, (F) 816

S–Scholarships F–Fellowships G–Grants A–Awards I–Internships

Emma L. Bowen Foundation Internships, (I) 1223
EMPOWER Scholarship Awards, (S) 178
Encourage Minority Participation in Occupations with Emphasis on Rehabilitation Scholarship Award. *See* EMPOWER Scholarship Awards, entry (S) 178
Endocrine Society Summer Research Fellowships, (G) 974, (I) 1224
Energy Resource Development Tribal Internship Program, (I) 1225
Environmental Protection Agency Greater Research Opportunities (GRO) Fellowships for Undergraduate Environmental Study. *See* EPA Greater Research Opportunities (GRO) Fellowships for Undergraduate Environmental Study, entries (S) 179, (I) 1226
Environmental Protection Agency Small Business Innovation Research Grants. *See* EPA Small Business Innovation Research Grants, entry (G) 975
EPA Greater Research Opportunities (GRO) Fellowships for Undergraduate Environmental Study, (S) 179, (I) 1226
EPA Small Business Innovation Research Grants, (G) 975
Epilepsy Foundation Research Grants Program, (G) 976
Episcopal Council of Indigenous Ministries Scholarships. *See* ECIM Scholarships, entry (F) 646
Eric and Barbara Dobkin Native American Artist Fellowship, (G) 977
Erickson Scholarship. *See* Bruce T. and Jackie Mahi Erickson Scholarship, entries (S) 69, (F) 589, (G) 934
Ethel and Emery Fast Scholarship, (S) 180, (F) 651
Ethel Curry Scholarships, (S) 181, (F) 652
Ethnic In-Service Training Fund, (F) 653
Ethnic Minority and Women's Internship Grant Program, (I) 1227
Ethnic Minority Postgraduate Scholarship for Careers in Athletics, (F) 654
ETS Visiting Scholar Program, (G) 978
Evans Memorial Scholarships. *See* Blossom Kalama Evans Memorial Scholarships, entries (S) 62, (F) 587
Exploration-Hypothesis Development Awards of the Neurofibromatosis Research Program, (G) 979
Explorations in Biomedicine Summer Research Fellowships, (G) 980
Explorations in Biomedicine Undergraduate Summer Research Fellowships for Native American Students, (I) 1228
Extramural Associates Faculty Research Enhancement Support Program. *See* Extramural Associates Research Development Award, entry (G) 981
Extramural Associates Research Development Award, (G) 981
Eyak Foundation Scholarships, (S) 182, (F) 655

Faculty and Student Teams (FAST) Program, (I) 1229
Faculty at FDA Grants, (G) 982
Faculty Early Career Development Program, (G) 983
Faculty Fellowships at the Newberry Library, (G) 984
Faculty Research Awards for Historically Black and Tribal Colleges and Universities and Institutions with High Hispanic Enrollment, (G) 985
Faegre & Benson Diversity Scholarship, (F) 656, (I) 1230
Faris Higher Education Fund. *See* Norman TeCube Sr. Higher Education Fund, entries (S) 379, (F) 800

FAST Program. *See* Faculty and Student Teams (FAST) Program, entry (I) 1229
Fast Scholarship. *See* Ethel and Emery Fast Scholarship, entries (S) 180, (F) 651
Federal Aviation Administration Asian American/Pacific Islander and Native American/Alaskan Native Internship Program, (I) 1231
Fellowships for Human Embryonic Stem Cell Research, (G) 986
Ferebee Endowment Scholarship. *See* Percy B. Ferebee Endowment Scholarship, entry (S) 410
Fermilab Doctoral Fellowship Program for Minority Students in Physics, (F) 657
Finnegan Henderson Diversity Scholarship, (F) 658, (I) 1232
First Americans in the Arts Scholarships, (S) 183
First Book Grant Program for Minority Scholars, (G) 987
First Person Journalism Scholarship Fund, (S) 184, (F) 659
First Sergeant Douglas and Charlotte DeHorse Scholarship, (S) 185, (F) 660
First-Year Internship Program of the Oregon State Bar, (I) 1233
Fish & Richardson Diversity Fellowship Program, (F) 661, (I) 1234
Fisher Scholarship. *See* Richard B. Fisher Scholarship, entries (S) 441, (I) 1326
Five College Fellowship Program, (G) 988
Flandreau Santee Sioux Adult Vocational Training Grants, (S) 186
Flandreau Santee Sioux BIA Higher Education Grants, (S) 187
Flandreau Santee Sioux Student Assistance Scholarships, (S) 188, (F) 662
Flemmie D. Kittrell Fellowship, (F) 663
Flintco Scholarship, (S) 189
Florence Young Memorial Scholarship, (F) 664
Florida Employment and Training Program, (S) 190
Florida Library Association Minority Scholarships, (F) 665
Florida Society of Newspaper Editors Multimedia Scholarship. *See* FSNE Multimedia Scholarship, entries (S) 204, (I) 1238
FMMDA Scholarships, (S) 191
Focus Professions Group Fellowships, (F) 666
Folk Arts Apprenticeship Awards, (I) 1235
Fool Soldier Scholarship, (S) 192
Ford Foundation Diversity Dissertation Fellowship Program, (G) 989
Ford Motor Company Scholarships, (S) 193
Ford Motor Company Tribal College Scholarship, (S) 194
Ford Motor Minority Dealers Association Scholarships. *See* FMMDA Scholarships, entry (S) 191
Fort Peck Tribes Adult Vocational Training Program, (S) 195
Fort Peck Tribes Scholarship Grant Assistance, (S) 196
Forum for Concerns of Minorities Scholarships, (S) 197
Fossil Energy Minority Education Initiative. *See* Mickey Leland Energy Fellowships, entry (I) 1283
Foundation for Digestive Health and Nutrition/AGA Research Scholar Awards, (G) 990
Foundation of Research and Education Diversity Scholarships, (S) 198, (F) 667
Four Corners Power Plant Navajo Scholarships, (S) 199
Four Corners Power Plant Navajo Scholarships. *See* Four Corners Power Plant Navajo Scholarships, entry (S) 199
Four Directions Summer Research Program, (I) 1236

S-Scholarships   F-Fellowships   G-Grants   A-Awards   I-Internships

PROGRAM TITLE INDEX

Francene Eagle Big Goose Memorial Scholarship. See The Rev. Francene Eagle Big Goose Memorial Scholarship, entry (F) 837
Frances C. Allen Fellowships, (G) 991
Frances Crawford Marvin American Indian Scholarship, (S) 200–201
Frances Johnson Memorial Trust Scholarship, (S) 202, (F) 668
Franchise Law Diversity Scholarship Award, (F) 669
Francis Memorial Scholarship. See American Indian Education Foundation Scholarship Program, entry (S) 26
Franklin C. McLean Award, (A) 1153
Franklin Dissertation Fellowship. See John Hope Franklin Dissertation Fellowship, entry (G) 1018
Frasier Scholarship. See Porter Wright Morris & Arthur LLP/Ralph K. Frasier Scholarship, entries (F) 828, (I) 1318
Frawner Family Scholarship. See Earl Frawner Family Scholarship, entry (S) 165
Fred L. Hatch Memorial Teacher Education Scholarship, (S) 203
Fredrikson & Byron Foundation Minority Scholarships, (F) 670, (I) 1237
Freeman Johnson Scholarship. See Chief Freeman Johnson Scholarship, entries (S) 94, (F) 604
Frontiers in Physiology Professional Development Fellowships, (G) 992
Fryrear Memorial Scholarships. See Bill Fryrear Memorial Scholarships, entry (S) 56
FSNE Multimedia Scholarship, (S) 204, (I) 1238

G. Michael McDonald Scholarship. See FMMDA Scholarships, entry (S) 191
Gaius Charles Bolin Dissertation Fellowships, (G) 993
Gaskin Scholarship. See Rosemary Gaskin Scholarship, entry (S) 447
Gates Millennium Graduate Scholars Program, (F) 671
Gates Millennium Undergraduate Scholars Program, (S) 205
Gay Indian Studies Association Berdach Research Grants. See GISA Berdach Research Grants, entry (G) 998
G.C. and Ruth Whitmore Memorial Scholarship, (S) 206
GEM M.S. Engineering Fellowship Program, (F) 672, (I) 1239
GEM Ph.D. Engineering Fellowship Program, (F) 673, (I) 1240
GEM Ph.D. Science Fellowship Program, (F) 674, (I) 1241
General Mills Foundation Tribal College Scholarship Program, (S) 207
General Motors Engineering Scholarship, (S) 208, (F) 675
General Motors Minority Dealers Association Minority Scholarship Program, (S) 209
General Motors Minority Engineering and Science Scholarship Program, (S) 210
Geophysical Fluid Dynamics Fellowships, (G) 994, (I) 1242
George A. Strait Minority Scholarship Endowment, (F) 676
George Geng On Lee Minorities in Leadership Scholarship, (S) 211
George Hi'ilani Mills Perpetual Fellowship Award, (F) 677
George K. Nolan Tribal Judicial Scholarship, (S) 212, (F) 678
George M. Brooker Collegiate Scholarship for Minorities, (S) 213, (F) 679
George Miller Jr. Management Leadership Endowment Fellowship, (F) 680
George V. Powell Diversity Scholarship, (F) 681, (I) 1243

Georgetown University Law Center Library Resident Program, (G) 995
Geoscience Minority Student Scholarships, (S) 214, (F) 682
Gerald Oshita Memorial Fellowship, (G) 996
Gerber Fellowship in Pediatric Nutrition, (G) 997
GISA Berdach Research Grants, (G) 998
Gladden Society Resident Scholarships. See J. Robert Gladden Society Resident Scholarships, entry (F) 709
Gladys Kamakakuokalani Ainoa Brandt Scholarships, (S) 215, (F) 683
Glenn Godfrey Memorial Scholarship, (S) 216
Glenn–Stokes Academic Year Research Internship Program, (G) 999
Glenn–Stokes Summer Research Internship Program, (I) 1244
GOALI Faculty in Industry Awards, (G) 1000
GOALI Undergraduate Student Industrial Fellowships/Traineeships, (I) 1245
Godfrey Memorial Scholarship. See Glenn Godfrey Memorial Scholarship, entry (S) 216
Goldberg Fellowships. See Leo Goldberg Fellowships, entry (G) 1025
Goldman Sachs MBA Fellowship, (F) 684, (I) 1246
Goldman Sachs Scholarship for Excellence, (S) 217, (I) 1247
Goldman Sachs/Matsuo Takabuke Commemorative Scholarships, (F) 685
Goldsmith, M.D. Scholarship. See Oliver Goldsmith, M.D. Scholarship, entry (F) 807
Goodwin MassMutual Diversity Fellowship. See Goodwin Procter Diversity Fellowships, entry (F) 686
Goodwin Procter Diversity Fellowships, (F) 686
Gosnell Memorial Scholarships. See Consuelo W. Gosnell Memorial Scholarships, entry (F) 616
Graduate Fellowship in the History of Science, (G) 1001
Graduate Student Fellowships at FDA, (G) 1002
Graduate Student Fellowships in American Indian Studies, (G) 1003
Graduate Student Industrial Fellowships/Traineeships, (I) 1248
Grand Portage Scholarship Program, (S) 218, (F) 687
Grand Traverse Band Adult Vocational Training Grants, (S) 219
Grand Traverse Band Higher Education Grants, (S) 220, (F) 688
Grant Opportunities for Academic Liaison with Industry Faculty in Industry Awards. See GOALI Faculty in Industry Awards, entry (G) 1000
Grant Opportunities for Academic Liaison with Industry Undergraduate Student Industrial Fellowships/Traineeships. See GOALI Undergraduate Student Industrial Fellowships/Traineeships, entry (I) 1245
Grants for Health Services Research Dissertations, (G) 1004
Greater Research Opportunities (GRO) Fellowships for Undergraduate Environmental Study. See EPA Greater Research Opportunities (GRO) Fellowships for Undergraduate Environmental Study, entries (S) 179, (I) 1226
GRO Fellowships for Undergraduate Environmental Study. See EPA Greater Research Opportunities (GRO) Fellowships for Undergraduate Environmental Study, entries (S) 179, (I) 1226

Hagen–Minerva Harvey Memorial Scholarship. See Richard Hagen–Minerva Harvey Memorial Scholarship, entry (S) 442
Hailey AAJ Law Student Scholarships. See Richard D. Hailey AAJ Law Student Scholarships, entry (F) 839

S–Scholarships   F–Fellowships   G–Grants   A–Awards   I–Internships

HANA Scholarships, (S) 221, (F) 689
Hans and Clara Zimmerman Foundation Education Scholarships. See Dr. Hans and Clara Zimmerman Foundation Education Scholarships, entry (S) 159
Harold Amos Medical Faculty Development Program, (G) 1005
Hart Memorial Scholarship. See Leon C. Hart Memorial Scholarship, entry (S) 302
Harter Secrest & Emery LLP Diversity Scholarship, (I) 1249
Harvard School of Public Health Undergraduate Minority Summer Internship Program, (I) 1250
Harvey Memorial Scholarship. See Richard Hagen–Minerva Harvey Memorial Scholarship, entry (S) 442
Hatch Memorial Teacher Education Scholarship. See Fred L. Hatch Memorial Teacher Education Scholarship, entry (S) 203
Hawaii Hotel Industry Foundation Native Hawaiian Scholarship, (S) 222
Hawaiian Civic Club of Honolulu Scholarship, (S) 223, (F) 690
Hawaiian Homes Commission Scholarships, (S) 224, (F) 691
Haynes/Hetting Award, (S) 225, (F) 692
Hays Memorial Scholarship. See Stacie Lynn Hays Memorial Scholarship, entry (S) 477
Health Disparity Research Awards in Prostate Cancer, (G) 1006
Health Professions Pregraduate Scholarship Program, (S) 226
Health Professions Preparatory Scholarship Program, (S) 227
Hearst Endowed Fellowship for Minority Students. See William Randolph Hearst Endowed Fellowship for Minority Students, entry (I) 1354
Helen Brown COREM Scholarships. See Richard and Helen Brown COREM Scholarships, entry (F) 838
Helen Hornbeck Tanner Fellowship. See Susan Kelly Power and Helen Hornbeck Tanner Fellowship, entry (G) 1121
Henhawk Nursing Scholarship. See Iola M. Henhawk Nursing Scholarship, entry (S) 255
Henry Scholarships. See Dr. Joseph L. Henry Scholarships, entry (F) 642
Herrington Scholarship. See John Bennett Herrington Scholarship, entry (S) 263
Hesemeyer Memorial Scholarship. See Emilie Hesemeyer Memorial Scholarship, entry (S) 177
Hewlett-Packard Scholar Awards. See HP Scholar Awards, entry (S) 241
High Risk Research in Anthropology Grants, (G) 1007
Higher Education Scholarships of the Wyandotte Nation, (S) 228
The Hill Group Scholarship, (S) 229
Hill, Jr. Leadership Award. See A.T. Anderson Memorial Scholarship Program, entries (S) 47, (F) 580
Hilton Tribal College Diversity Scholarship, (S) 230
Hinton Award. See William A. Hinton Research Training Award, entry (A) 1172
Hispanic, Asian, Native American Scholarships. See HANA Scholarships, entries (S) 221, (F) 689
Historically Black Colleges and Universities and Other Minority Institutions Education and Training Program in Fossil Energy, (G) 1008
Ho–Chunk Nation Graduation Achievement Awards, (A) 1154
Ho–Chunk Nation Higher Education Scholarships, (S) 231, (F) 693
Ho–Chunk Nation Summer Tuition Assistance, (S) 232, (F) 694

Ho–Chunk Nation Training and Employment Assistance, (S) 233
Holly A. Cornell Scholarship, (F) 695
Hoopa Tribal Education Association Adult Vocational Training Awards, (S) 234
Hoopa Tribal Education Association Higher Education Awards, (S) 235, (F) 696
Hopi Academic Achievement Awards, (S) 236
Hopi Tribal Members BIA Higher Education Grants, (S) 237, (F) 697
Hopi Tuition/Book Scholarships, (S) 238, (F) 698
Howard Hughes Medical Institute Research Training Fellowships for Medical Students, (F) 699, (G) 1009
Howard Keck/Westmin Endowment Scholarship Fund, (S) 239, (F) 700
Howard Mayer Brown Fellowship, (F) 701
Howard Memorial Scholarships. See Irene C. Howard Memorial Scholarships, entry (S) 257
Howard N. Blitman, P.E. Scholarship to Promote Diversity in Engineering. See Maureen L. and Howard N. Blitman, P.E. Scholarship to Promote Diversity in Engineering, entry (S) 318
Howard Rock Foundation Graduate Scholarship Program, (F) 702
Howard Rock Foundation Undergraduate Scholarship Program, (S) 240
Howard Temin Pathway to Independence Awards in Cancer Research. See Pathways to Independence Program, entry (G) 1085
HP Scholar Awards, (S) 241
Hualapai Employment Assistance Program, (S) 242
Hualapai Graduate Student Grants, (F) 703
Hualapai Higher Education Grants, (S) 243
HUD Urban Scholars Postdoctoral Fellowship Program, (G) 1010
Hughes Medical Institute Research Training Fellowships for Medical Students. See Howard Hughes Medical Institute Research Training Fellowships for Medical Students, entries (F) 699, (G) 1009
Huhndorf Endowment Scholarship Fund. See Roy M. Huhndorf Endowment Scholarship Fund, entries (S) 448, (F) 843
Huna Heritage Foundation Education Assistance Program, (S) 244, (F) 704
Huna Heritage Foundation Vocational Education Assistance Program, (S) 245
Hunter-Wilson, M.D. Memorial Scholarship. See Amy Louise Hunter-Wilson, M.D. Memorial Scholarship, entries (S) 32, (F) 565
Hyatt Hotels Fund for Minority Lodging Management Students, (S) 246

IBM PhD Fellowship Program, (F) 705, (I) 1251
Ida M. Pope Memorial Trust Scholarships, (S) 247, (F) 706
Idaho Grow Your Own Teacher Scholarship Program, (S) 248
Ike Crumbly Minorities in Energy Grant. See Isaac "Ike" Crumbly Minorities in Energy Grant, entry (G) 1015
Illinois Broadcasters Association Multicultural Internships, (I) 1252
Incentive Awards of the Seminole Nation Judgment Fund, (A) 1155

S–Scholarships   F–Fellowships   G–Grants   A–Awards   I–Internships

PROGRAM TITLE INDEX 463

Independent Scientist Awards, (G) 1011
Indian Nurse Scholarship Awards, (S) 249
Indian Summer Criminal Welfare/Social Justice Scholarship, (S) 250
Indian Summer Recent High School Graduate Scholarship, (S) 251
Industry Minority Scholarships, (S) 252
Industry Studies Fellowships, (G) 1012
INROADS National College Internships, (I) 1253
Inspirational Educator Scholarship, (S) 253
Institute for International Public Policy Fellowships, (S) 254, (I) 1254
Institute for Research on Poverty Visiting Scholars Program, (G) 1013
Institutional Research and Academic Career Development Awards, (G) 1014
Intel Scholarship, (F) 707
International Radio and Television Society Foundation Broadcast Sales Associate Program. See IRTS Broadcast Sales Associate Program, entry (I) 1255
Iola M. Henhawk Nursing Scholarship, (S) 255
Iowa Tribe Education Incentive Awards, (A) 1156
Iowa Tribe Higher Education Program, (S) 256
Irene C. Howard Memorial Scholarships, (S) 257
IRTS Broadcast Sales Associate Program, (I) 1255
Isaac "Ike" Crumbly Minorities in Energy Grant, (G) 1015
Iwalani Carpenter Sowa Scholarship, (F) 708

J. Robert Gladden Society Resident Scholarships, (F) 709
Jackie Mahi Erickson Scholarship. See Bruce T. and Jackie Mahi Erickson Scholarship, entries (S) 69, (F) 589, (G) 934
Jackie Robinson Scholarships, (S) 258
Jackson Scholarship Award. See Marilyn A. Jackson Scholarship Award, entry (F) 745
Jalene Kanani Bell 'Ohana Scholarship, (S) 259, (F) 710
James A. Rawley Prize, (A) 1157
James D. Voelker Foundation Native American Scholarship, (S) 260, (F) 711
James E. Webb Internships, (I) 1256
JDRF Faculty Grant, (G) 1016
Jeanne Spurlock Minority Medical Student Clinical Fellowship in Child and Adolescent Psychiatry, (I) 1257
Jeanne Spurlock Research Fellowship in Drug Abuse and Addiction for Minority Medical Students, (I) 1258
Jeffrey Campbell Graduate Fellows Program, (G) 1017
Jenks Scholarship. See Chickasaw Foundation Fine Arts Scholarship, entry (S) 87
Jenks Scholarship. See Mary K. Moreland and Daniel T. Jenks Scholarship, entry (S) 314
Jewell Hilton Bonner Scholarship, (S) 261
Jo Morse Scholarship, (F) 712
John and Muriel Landis Scholarships, (S) 262, (F) 713
John Bennett Herrington Scholarship, (S) 263
John C. Rouillard and Alice Tonemah Memorial Scholarships, (S) 264, (F) 714
John Hope Franklin Dissertation Fellowship, (G) 1018
John McLendon Memorial Minority Postgraduate Scholarship Award, (F) 715
John Merrill Transplant Scholar Grant, (G) 1019

John N. Colberg Endowment Scholarship Fund, (S) 265, (F) 716
John Shurr Journalism Award, (S) 266, (F) 717
John Stanford Memorial Scholarship, (F) 718
Johnny Pineapple Scholarship Fund, (S) 267
Johnson Foundation Physician Faculty Scholars Program. See Robert Wood Johnson Foundation Physician Faculty Scholars Program, entry (G) 1105
Johnson Memorial Trust Scholarship. See Frances Johnson Memorial Trust Scholarship, entries (S) 202, (F) 668
Johnson Minority Fellowship in Educational Measurement. See Sylvia Taylor Johnson Minority Fellowship in Educational Measurement, entry (G) 1122
Johnson Postdoctoral Fellowship. See Lyman T. Johnson Postdoctoral Fellowship, entry (G) 1027
Johnson Scholarship. See Chief Freeman Johnson Scholarship, entries (S) 94, (F) 604
Jordan Health Policy Scholars Program. See Barbara Jordan Health Policy Scholars Program, entry (I) 1191
Joseph A. Sowa Scholarships, (S) 268
Joseph K. Lumsden Memorial Scholarship, (S) 269, (F) 719
Joseph L. Henry Scholarships. See Dr. Joseph L. Henry Scholarships, entry (F) 642
Joseph Nawahi Scholarship, (F) 720
Josephine Nipper Memorial Scholarship. See American Indian Education Foundation Scholarship Program, entry (S) 26
Joukowsky Postdoctoral Fellowship. See Pembroke Center Postdoctoral Fellowships, entry (G) 1088
Juanita Corwin Scholarships, (S) 270, (F) 721
Judd, Jr. Memorial Scholarship. See Clem Judd, Jr. Memorial Scholarship, entry (S) 115
Judd, Jr. Memorial Scholarship. See Hawaii Hotel Industry Foundation Native Hawaiian Scholarship, entry (S) 222
Judicial Externship Program, (I) 1259
Judicial Externship Program. See Judicial Externship Program, entry (I) 1259
Judicial Intern Opportunity Program, (I) 1260
Judith L. Weidman Racial Ethnic Minority Fellowship, (I) 1261
Judith McManus Price Scholarships, (S) 271, (F) 722
Jules M. Rothstein Minority Research Fellowship Award. See Dr. Jules M. Rothstein Minority Research Fellowship Award, entry (G) 970
Jump Start Awards, (S) 272
Junior Diabetes Research Foundation Faculty Grant. See JDRF Faculty Grant, entry (G) 1016
Just the Beginning Foundation Judicial Externship Program. See Judicial Externship Program, entry (I) 1259
Juvenile Diabetes Research Foundation Scholar Awards, (G) 1020

Kaiser Media Internships in Health Reporting, (I) 1262
Kalifornsky Memorial Endowment Scholarship Fund. See Peter Kalifornsky Memorial Endowment Scholarship Fund, entries (S) 413, (F) 823
Kanaka'ole Foundation Higher Education Scholarship. See Edith Kanaka'ole Foundation Higher Education Scholarship, entries (S) 167, (F) 647
Katrin H. Lamon Fellowship, (G) 1021
Katten Muchin Rosenman Minority Scholarships, (I) 1263
Kaw Nation Academic Scholarship Program, (S) 273

S–Scholarships   F–Fellowships   G–Grants   A–Awards   I–Internships

Kaw Nation Adult Education, (S) 274
Kaw Nation Adult Vocational Training Program, (S) 275
Kaw Nation Graduate Program, (F) 723
Kaw Nation Higher Education Grant Program, (S) 276
Kawerak Higher Education Scholarships, (S) 277
Kawerak Vocational Training Scholarships, (S) 278
Keck/Westmin Endowment Scholarship Fund. See Howard Keck/Westmin Endowment Scholarship Fund, entries (S) 239, (F) 700
Kellogg Foundation Fellowship Program in Health Research. See W.K. Kellogg Foundation Doctoral Fellowship in Health Policy, entries (F) 903, (G) 1138
Kemp Memorial Scholarship. See Amelia Kemp Memorial Scholarship, entries (S) 19, (F) 554
Kenai Natives Association Scholarship and Grant Fund, (S) 279, (F) 724
Kenaitze Indian Tribe Higher Education Scholarship Program, (S) 280, (F) 725
Keweenaw Bay Indian Community BIA Higher Education Grants, (S) 281
Keweenaw Bay Indian Community Sovereign Student Fund, (S) 282
Key Diversity Residency Program. See Mary P. Key Diversity Residency Program, entry (G) 1029
Kick Start Awards, (S) 283
Kikiktagruk Inupiat Corporation Scholarships, (S) 284
Kimball Office Scholarship, (S) 285
King Jr. Scholarship Awards. See Martin Luther King Jr. Scholarship Awards, entries (S) 312, (F) 747
King Native American Artist Fellowship. See Rollin and Mary Ella King Native American Artist Fellowship, entry (G) 1106
King–Chavez–Parks Visiting Professors Program, (G) 1022
Kirby McDonald Education Endowment Scholarship Fund, (S) 286, (F) 726
Kirkland & Ellis LLP Diversity Fellowship Program, (I) 1264
Kittrell Fellowship. See Flemmie D. Kittrell Fellowship, entry (F) 663
K&L Gates Diversity Fellowship, (F) 727, (I) 1265
Klumb Business Scholarship. See Kurt Klumb Business Scholarship, entry (S) 293
Komen Breast Cancer Foundation Postdoctoral Fellowships. See Susan G. Komen Breast Cancer Foundation Postdoctoral Fellowship, entry (G) 1120
Koniag Education Foundation Academic Achievement/Graduate Scholarships, (S) 287, (F) 728
Koniag Education Foundation Career Development Grants, (S) 288
Koniag Education Foundation College/University Basic Scholarships, (S) 289
Koniag Education Foundation Vocational Education Grants, (S) 290
Kotzebue I.R.A. Adult Vocational Training Grant, (S) 291
Kotzebue I.R.A. Higher Education Scholarship, (S) 292
Kovach Foundation Minority Student Scholarship. See Daniel Kovach Foundation Minority Student Scholarship, entries (S) 152, (F) 629
Kruger Memorial Ittish Aaisha Scholarship. See Edward L. Kruger Memorial Ittish Aaisha Scholarship, entry (F) 649
Kurt Klumb Business Scholarship, (S) 293
Kuskokwim Educational Foundation General Scholarships, (S) 294, (F) 729

Lagrant Foundation Graduate Scholarships, (F) 730
Lagrant Foundation Undergraduate Scholarships, (S) 295
Laguna Education Foundation Graduate Scholarships, (F) 731
Lamon Fellowship. See Katrin H. Lamon Fellowship, entry (G) 1021
Land O'Lakes Purina Feed Scholarships, (S) 296
Land O'Lakes Purina Feeds Dealer Scholarships. See Land O'Lakes Purina Feed Scholarships, entry (S) 296
Landis Scholarships. See John and Muriel Landis Scholarships, entries (S) 262, (F) 713
Lang Journalism Minority Scholarship and Internship. See C.T. Lang Journalism Minority Scholarship and Internship, entries (S) 147, (I) 1211
Larry Matfay Scholarship, (S) 297, (F) 732
Lasley/Osage Scholarships. See Mae Lasley/Osage Scholarships, entries (S) 308, (F) 743
LaSPACE Research Initiation Grants Program, (G) 1023
LaSPACE Undergraduate Research Assistantships, (I) 1266
Latham & Watkins Diversity Scholars Program, (F) 733
Lathrop Endowment Scholarship Fund. See Cap Lathrop Endowment Scholarship Fund, entries (S) 74, (F) 594
Launching Leaders MBA Scholarship, (F) 734, (I) 1267
Launching Leaders Undergraduate Scholarship, (S) 298, (I) 1268
Laura Thompson Scholarship. See Myron and Laura Thompson Scholarship, entries (S) 346, (F) 771
Law and Social Science Doctoral Dissertation Fellowships, (G) 1024
Lawrence Matson Memorial Endowment Fund Scholarships, (S) 299, (F) 735
Leadership and Career Development Program, (F) 736
Leadership for Diversity Scholarship, (S) 300, (F) 737
Lederer Postdoctoral Fellowship. See Pembroke Center Postdoctoral Fellowships, entry (G) 1088
Lee Health Careers Scholarship. See Dr. Phillip R. Lee Health Careers Scholarship, entry (S) 160
Lee Leadership Development Fund. See Dora Ames Lee Leadership Development Fund, entries (S) 156, (F) 637
Lee & Low Books New Voices Award, (A) 1158
Lee Minorities in Leadership Scholarship. See George Geng On Lee Minorities in Leadership Scholarship, entry (S) 211
Leech Lake Postsecondary Grant Program, (S) 301
Legal Opportunity Scholarship, (F) 738
Leland Energy Fellowships. See Mickey Leland Energy Fellowships, entry (I) 1283
Lena Chang Internships, (I) 1269
Leo Goldberg Fellowships, (G) 1025
Leon C. Hart Memorial Scholarship, (S) 302
Leonard M. Perryman Communications Scholarship for Ethnic Minority Students, (S) 303
Leonard Memorial Academic Scholarship. See National Native American Law Enforcement Association Academic Scholarship Program, entry (S) 354
LeRoy C. Merritt Humanitarian Fund Award, (G) 1026
Lewis Memorial Scholarships. See Dr. Roe B. Lewis Memorial Scholarships, entries (S) 161, (F) 643
Library and Information Technology Association/OCLC Minority Scholarship. See LITA/OCLC Minority Scholarship, entry (F) 741
Library Systems & Services Inc. Minority Scholarship. See LSSI Minority Scholarship, entry (F) 742
Lifchez/Stronach Curatorial Internships, (I) 1270

S–Scholarships   F–Fellowships   G–Grants   A–Awards   I–Internships

PROGRAM TITLE INDEX

Lifetime Achievement Award for Literature, (A) 1159
Liko A'e Scholarships, (S) 304, (F) 739
Linsky Fellowship for Outstanding Water Research. See Ronald B. Linsky Fellowship for Outstanding Water Research, entry (G) 1107
Lionel C. Barrow Minority Doctoral Student Scholarship, (F) 740
LITA/OCLC Minority Scholarship, (F) 741
Lockheed Martin TCU Scholarship, (S) 305
Lois Doyle Dummett Fellowship. See Dr. Clifton O. Dummett and Lois Doyle Dummett Fellowship, entry (F) 641
Lori Piestewa Vocational/Technical or 4-Year Scholarship, (S) 306
Louis Stokes Alliance for Minority Participation Undergraduate Summer Research Program. See LSAMP Undergraduate Summer Research Program, entry (I) 1271
Louisiana Space Consortium Research Initiation Grants Program. See LaSPACE Research Initiation Grants Program, entry (G) 1023
Louisiana Space Consortium Undergraduate Research Assistantships. See LaSPACE Undergraduate Research Assistantships, entry (I) 1266
LSAMP Undergraduate Summer Research Program, (I) 1271
LSSI Minority Scholarship, (F) 742
Luce Trust Scholarships. See Oden Luce Trust Scholarships, entry (S) 388
Lucent Technologies Bell Laboratories Summer Research Program for Minorities and Women, (I) 1272
Lumsden Memorial Scholarship. See Joseph K. Lumsden Memorial Scholarship, entries (S) 269, (F) 719
Lyman T. Johnson Postdoctoral Fellowship, (G) 1027

Madeline Moose Scholarship Fund, (S) 307
Mae Lasley/Osage Scholarships, (S) 308, (F) 743
Maher Memorial Fund. See Doyon Foundation Competitive Scholarships, entries (S) 158, (F) 639
Mahi Educational Scholarship. See Dan and Rachel Mahi Educational Scholarship, entries (S) 150, (F) 627
Maine Arts Commission Traditional Arts Apprenticeship Program, (I) 1273
Major Ridge Award, (S) 309
Makia and Ann Malo Scholarship, (F) 744
Malo Scholarship. See Makia and Ann Malo Scholarship, entry (F) 744
Many Voices Residencies, (G) 1028
Marathon Oil Corporation College Scholarship Program of the Hispanic Scholarship Fund, (S) 310
Marie F. Peters Ethnic Minorities Outstanding Achievement Award, (A) 1160
Marilyn A. Jackson Scholarship Award, (F) 745
Mark Ulmer Native American Scholarship. See Triangle Native American Society Scholarships, entry (S) 489
Marriage and Family Therapy Minority Fellowship Program, (F) 746
Marrs Scholarship Fund. See Carl H. Marrs Scholarship Fund, entries (S) 77, (F) 597
Martha Joukowsky Postdoctoral Fellowship. See Pembroke Center Postdoctoral Fellowships, entry (G) 1088
Martha Miller Tributary Scholarship, (S) 311
Martin Luther King Jr. Scholarship Awards, (S) 312, (F) 747

Martin Olson Memorial Scholarship, (S) 313, (F) 748
Marvin American Indian Scholarship. See Frances Crawford Marvin American Indian Scholarship, entry (S) 200 201
Mary Ella King Native American Artist Fellowship. See Rollin and Mary Ella King Native American Artist Fellowship, entry (G) 1106
Mary K. Moreland and Daniel T. Jenks Scholarship, (S) 314
Mary P. Key Diversity Residency Program, (G) 1029
Mary Tinker Scholarship Fund, (S) 315, (F) 749
Maryland Sea Grant Research Experiences for Undergraduates, (G) 1030, (I) 1274
Massachusetts Indian Association Scholarship Fund, (S) 316, (F) 750
Massachusetts Native American Tuition Waiver Program, (S) 317
Master Artist and Apprentice Grants in Traditional Native Arts, (I) 1275
Matfay Scholarship. See Larry Matfay Scholarship, entries (S) 297, (F) 732
Mathematics, Engineering, Science, Business, Education, Computers Program. See MESBEC Program, entries (S) 322, (F) 754
Mathews Memorial Scholarship for California Indians. See Rodney T. Mathews Memorial Scholarship for California Indians, entries (S) 445, (F) 842
Matson Memorial Endowment Fund Scholarships. See Lawrence Matson Memorial Endowment Fund Scholarships, entries (S) 299, (F) 735
Matsuo Takabuke Commemorative Scholarships. See Goldman Sachs/Matsuo Takabuke Commemorative Scholarships, entry (F) 685
Maureen L. and Howard N. Blitman, P.E. Scholarship to Promote Diversity in Engineering, (S) 318
McAndrews Diversity in Patent Law Fellowship, (F) 751
McCurdy Scholarships. See Edna P. McCurdy Scholarships, entry (S) 168
McDermott Minority Scholarship, (F) 752, (I) 1276
McDonald Education Endowment Scholarship Fund. See Kirby McDonald Education Endowment Scholarship Fund, entries (S) 286, (F) 726
McDonald Scholarship. See FMMDA Scholarships, entry (S) 191
McJulien Minority Graduate Scholarship. See Patrick D. McJulien Minority Graduate Scholarship, entry (F) 815
McLean Award. See Franklin C. McLean Award, entry (A) 1153
McLendon Minority Postgraduate Scholarship Program. See John McLendon Memorial Minority Postgraduate Scholarship Award, entry (F) 715
Medical Library Association Scholarship for Minority Students, (F) 753
Meekins Scholarship. See Phyllis G. Meekins Scholarship, entry (S) 414
Mendenhall Fellowships. See Five College Fellowship Program, entry (G) 988
Menominee Indian Tribal Scholarships, (S) 319
Menominee Indian Tribe Adult Vocational Training Program, (S) 320
Mental Health Dissertation Research Grants to Increase Diversity in the Mental Health Research Arena, (G) 1031
Mentor-Based Minority Postdoctoral Fellowships in Diabetes, (G) 1032

S—Scholarships   F—Fellowships   G—Grants   A—Awards   I—Internships

Mentored Clinical Scientist Research Career Development Awards, (G) 1033
Mentored Research Scientist Development Awards, (G) 1034
Mentorship for Environmental Scholars, (I) 1277
Mercer Diversity Scholarship Program, (S) 321, (I) 1278
Merrill Transplant Scholar Grant. See John Merrill Transplant Scholar Grant, entry (G) 1019
Merritt Humanitarian Fund Award. See LeRoy C. Merritt Humanitarian Fund Award, entry (G) 1026
MESBEC Program, (S) 322, (F) 754
Mescalero Apache Tribal Scholarship, (S) 323, (F) 755
METPRO/Editing Program, (I) 1279
METPRO/Reporting Program, (I) 1280
Metropolitan Life Foundation Awards Program for Academic Excellence in Medicine, (F) 756
Metropolitan Museum of Art Mentoring Program for College Juniors, (I) 1281
Metropolitan Museum of Art 6–Month Internships, (I) 1282
Miami University Resident Librarian, (G) 1035
Michael J. Berkeley Foundation Scholarships, (S) 324
Michele Clark Fellowship, (F) 757
Michigan Indian Elders Association Scholarship, (S) 325
Michigan Indian Tuition Waiver Program, (S) 326, (F) 758
Michigan Space Grant Consortium Undergraduate Underrepresented Minority Fellowships, (G) 1036
Mickey Leland Energy Fellowships, (I) 1283
Mickey Williams Minority Student Scholarships, (S) 327
Mickey Williams Minority Student Scholarships. See Mickey Williams Minority Student Scholarships, entry (S) 327
Microbiology Undergraduate Research Fellowship, (G) 1037, (I) 1284
Microsoft National Scholarships, (S) 328, (I) 1285
Miguel Scholarship. See Pauline Miguel Scholarship, entry (S) 403
Milbank Diversity Scholars Program, (F) 759
Mille Lacs Band Academic Achievement Awards, (A) 1161
Mille Lacs Band Post Graduate Degree Program, (F) 760
Mille Lacs Band Scholarship Program, (S) 329
Millennium Scholarship Program of the Chickasaw Nation, (S) 330
Miller Jr. Management Leadership Endowment Fellowship. See George Miller Jr. Management Leadership Endowment Fellowship, entry (F) 680
Miller Native American Vocational Scholarship. See Verl and Dorothy Miller Native American Vocational Scholarship, entry (S) 510
Miller Tributary Scholarship. See Martha Miller Tributary Scholarship, entry (S) 311
Millie Akaka Scholarship. See Daniel Kahikina and Millie Akaka Scholarship, entries (S) 151, (F) 628
Mills Perpetual Fellowship Award. See George Hi'ilani Mills Perpetual Fellowship Award, entry (F) 677
Minerva Harvey Memorial Scholarship. See Richard Hagen–Minerva Harvey Memorial Scholarship, entry (S) 442
Minnesota Indian Scholarship Program, (S) 331, (F) 761
Minorities in Clinical Oncology Program Grants. See National Cancer Institute Mentored Clinical Scientist Award to Promote Diversity, entry (G) 1051
Minorities in Government Finance Scholarship, (S) 332, (F) 762
Minorities in Leadership Scholarship. See George Geng On Lee Minorities in Leadership Scholarship, entry (S) 211

Minority Academic Institutions Undergraduate Student Fellowships. See EPA Greater Research Opportunities (GRO) Fellowships for Undergraduate Environmental Study, entries (S) 179, (I) 1226
Minority Access Internship, (I) 1286
Minority Affairs Committee Award for Outstanding Scholastic Achievement, (A) 1162
Minority Dental Student Scholarship, (F) 763
Minority Editing Training Program/Editing. See METPRO/Editing Program, entry (I) 1279
Minority Editorial Training Program/Reporting. See METPRO/Reporting Program, entry (I) 1280
Minority Entrepreneurs Scholarship Program, (S) 333
Minority Faculty Development Scholarship Award in Physical Therapy, (F) 764
Minority Institutions Biological and Environmental Student Research Participation Program, (I) 1287
Minority Medical Student Award Program of the American Society of Hematology, (G) 1038
Minority Medical Student Clinical Fellowship in Child and Adolescent Psychiatry. See Jeanne Spurlock Minority Medical Student Clinical Fellowship in Child and Adolescent Psychiatry, entry (I) 1257
Minority Medical Student Summer Externship in Addiction Psychiatry, (I) 1288
Minority Medical Student Summer Mentoring Program, (I) 1289
Minority Medical Students Elective in HIV Psychiatry, (F) 765, (I) 1290
Minority Nurse Magazine Scholarship Program, (S) 334, (F) 766
Minority Opportunities for Research Faculty Development Awards. See MORE Faculty Development Awards, entry (G) 1045
Minority Postdoctoral Research Fellowships, (G) 1039
Minority Research Training in Psychiatry, (F) 767, (G) 1040
Minority Scholar–in–Residence Dissertation Fellowships, (G) 1041
Minority Scholar–in–Residence Program Postdoctoral Fellowships, (G) 1042
Minority Scholarship Award for Academic Excellence in Physical Therapy, (S) 335
Minority Scholarship in Classics and Classical Archaeology, (S) 336
Minority Undergraduate Research Fellowship Program, (I) 1291
Minority Visiting Student Awards Program, (G) 1043
Mishkoswln (Strength) Scholarship Program, (S) 337, (F) 768
Miss Indian USA Scholarship Program, (S) 338, (A) 1163
Missile Defense Agency Historically Black Colleges and Universities and Minority Institutions Broad Agency Announcement, (G) 1044
Missouri Space Grant Consortium Summer High School Internships, (I) 1292
Missouri Space Grant Consortium Undergraduate Research Internship Program, (I) 1293
Mohawk Higher Education Program, (S) 339
Montana American Indian Student Waiver, (S) 340, (F) 769
Moose Scholarship Fund. See Madeline Moose Scholarship Fund, entry (S) 307
MORE Faculty Development Awards, (G) 1045
Moreland and Daniel T. Jenks Scholarship. See Mary K. Moreland and Daniel T. Jenks Scholarship, entry (S) 314
Morgan Stanley MBA Fellowship, (F) 770, (I) 1294
Morgan Stanley Scholars Program, (S) 341

S–Scholarships   F–Fellowships   G–Grants   A–Awards   I–Internships

PROGRAM TITLE INDEX 467

Morgan Stanley Tribal Scholars Program, (S) 342
Morris K. Udall Native American Congressional Internship Program, (I) 1295
Morris K. Udall Scholarships, (S) 343
Morris Thompson Scholarship Fund. See Doyon Foundation Competitive Scholarships, entries (S) 158, (F) 639
Morse Scholarship. See Jo Morse Scholarship, entry (F) 712
Mosley Scholarships. See Dwight Mosley Scholarships, entry (S) 164
Multicultural Advertising Intern Program, (I) 1296
Multicultural Undergraduate Internships at the Getty Center, (I) 1297
Muriel Landis Scholarships. See John and Muriel Landis Scholarships, entries (S) 262, (F) 713
Mutual of Omaha Actuarial Scholarship for Minority Students, (S) 344, (I) 1298
MWH Fellowship for Advanced Water/Wastewater Treatment Technologies, (G) 1046
Myaamia Scholarship, (S) 345
Myron and Laura Thompson Scholarship, (S) 346, (F) 771

NAAJ Scholarships, (S) 347, (F) 772
NACME Pre-Engineering Student Scholarships, (S) 348
NAIEA/NY Scholarship, (S) 349
NAJA Professional Development Fellowships, (F) 773
Nakila Steele Scholarship. See Dwayne "Nakila" Steele Scholarship, entry (S) 162
Nakoa Hawaiian Language Perpetual Scholarship. See Sarah Keli'ilolena Lum Konia Nakoa Hawaiian Language Perpetual Scholarship, entries (S) 454, (F) 848
NALE Program, (S) 350, (F) 774
NAMEPA Beginning Freshmen Award, (S) 351
NAMEPA Transfer Engineering Student Award. See Transfer Engineering Student Award, entry (S) 488
Nancy L. Buc Postdoctoral Fellowship. See Pembroke Center Postdoctoral Fellowships, entry (G) 1088
NASA Administrator's Fellowship Program, (G) 1047
NASA Faculty Fellowship Program, (G) 1048
NASA Graduate Student Researchers Program, (G) 1049, (I) 1299
NASA Motivating Undergraduates in Science and Technology (MUST) Scholarship Program, (S) 352
NASA Science and Technology Institute (NSTI) Summer Scholars Program. See NSTI Summer Scholars Program, entry (I) 1314
NASA Small Business Innovation Research Grants, (G) 1050
NASA Undergraduate Student Research Program, (I) 1300
National Action Council for Minorities in Engineering Pre-Engineering Student Scholarships. See NACME Pre-Engineering Student Scholarships, entry (S) 348
National Aeronautics and Space Administration Administrator's Fellowship Program. See NASA Administrator's Fellowship Program, entry (G) 1047
National Aeronautics and Space Administration Faculty Fellowship Program. See NASA Faculty Fellowship Program, entry (G) 1048
National Aeronautics and Space Administration Graduate Student Researchers Program. See NASA Graduate Student Researchers Program, entries (G) 1049, (I) 1299

National Aeronautics and Space Administration Motivating Undergraduates in Science and Technology (MUST) Scholarship Program. See NASA Motivating Undergraduates in Science and Technology (MUST) Scholarship Program, entry (S) 352
National Aeronautics and Space Administration Small Business Innovation Research Grants. See NASA Small Business Innovation Research Grants, entry (G) 1050
National Aeronautics and Space Administration Undergraduate Student Research Program. See NASA Undergraduate Student Research Program, entry (I) 1300
National Association of Multicultural Engineering Program Advocates Beginning Freshmen Award. See NAMEPA Beginning Freshmen Award, entry (S) 351
National Association of Multicultural Engineering Program Advocates Transfer Engineering Student Award. See Transfer Engineering Student Award, entry (S) 488
National Association of School Psychologists Minority Scholarship, (F) 775
National Association of Student Personnel Administrators Undergraduate Fellowship Program, (I) 1301
National Cancer Institute Mentored Career Development Award to Promote Diversity. See NCI Mentored Career Development Award to Promote Diversity, entry (G) 1065
National Cancer Institute Mentored Clinical Scientist Award to Promote Diversity, (G) 1051
National Cancer Institute Mentored Patient-Oriented Research Award to Promote Diversity. See NCI Mentored Patient-Oriented Research Award to Promote Diversity, entry (G) 1066
National Cancer Institute Transition Career Development Award to Promote Diversity. See NCI Transition Career Development Award to Promote Diversity, entry (G) 1067
National Center for Cooperative Education Scholarships, (S) 353, (F) 776, (I) 1302
National Coalition of Ethnic Minority Nurse Associations Aetna Scholars Program. See NCEMNA Aetna Scholars Program, entries (S) 370, (F) 793
National Collegiate Athletic Association Ethnic Minority Postgraduate Scholarship Program, (F) 777
National Congress of American Indians Fellowships, (I) 1303
National Congress of American Indians Youth Ambassador Leadership Program Scholarships. See NCAI Youth Ambassador Leadership Program Scholarships, entry (S) 369
National Consortium for Graduate Degrees for Minorities in Engineering and Science (GEM) M.S. Engineering Fellowship Program. See GEM M.S. Engineering Fellowship Program, entries (F) 672, (I) 1239
National Consortium for Graduate Degrees for Minorities in Engineering and Science (GEM) Ph.D. Engineering Fellowship Program. See GEM Ph.D. Engineering Fellowship Program, entries (F) 673, (I) 1240
National Consortium for Graduate Degrees for Minorities in Engineering and Science (GEM) Ph.D. Science Fellowship Program. See GEM Ph.D. Science Fellowship Program, entries (F) 674, (I) 1241
National Crusade Scholarship Program, (F) 778
National Dental Association Foundation Memorial Award, (F) 779
National Dental Association Foundation Pre-Doctoral Scholarship Program, (F) 780

National Educational Enrichment Program for Minority Graduate Students Fellowship in Gerontology, (G) 1052

National Energy Technology Laboratory Minority Mentoring and Internship Program, (I) 1304

National Heart, Lung, and Blood Institute Career Transition Award, (G) 1053

National Heart, Lung, and Blood Institute Mentored Career Development Award to Promote Faculty Diversity in Biomedical Research. See NHLBI Mentored Career Development Award to Promote Faculty Diversity in Biomedical Research, entry (G) 1068

National Institute of Nursing Research Mentored Research Scientist Development Award for Minority Investigators. See NINR Mentored Research Scientist Development Award for Underrepresented or Disadvantaged Investigators, entry (G) 1074

National Institute on Alcohol Abuse and Alcoholism Career Transition Award. See NIAAA Career Transition Award, entry (G) 1069

National Institute on Drug Abuse Mentored Clinical Scientists Development Program Award in Drug Abuse and Addiction. See NIDA Mentored Clinical Scientists Development Program Award in Drug Abuse and Addiction, entry (G) 1070

National Institutes of Health Small Business Technology Transfer Grants, (G) 1054

National Institutes of Health Small Research Grant Program, (G) 1055

National Library of Medicine Individual Fellowship for Informationist Training. See NLM Individual Fellowship for Informationist Training, entry (F) 798

National Medical Fellowship Program in Academic Medicine for Minority Students, (I) 1305

National Medical Fellowship Program in AIDS Care, (F) 781

National Medical Fellowships Need-Based Scholarship Program. See NMF Need-Based Scholarship Program, entry (F) 799

National Museum Fellows Program for Minority Students, (I) 1306

National Museum of the American Indian Internship Program, (I) 1307

National Museum of the American Indian Visiting Artist Program, (G) 1056

National Museum of the American Indian Workshops in Museum Training, (F) 782

National Native American Law Enforcement Association Academic Scholarship Program, (S) 354

National Native American Law Students Association Writing Competition. See NNALSA Writing Competition, entry (A) 1164

National Native Creative Development Grant Program, (G) 1057

National Native Master Artist Initiative: Artist Teaching Artists, (G) 1058

National Oceanic and Atmospheric Administration Educational Partnership Program with Minority Serving Institutions Graduate Sciences Program, (F) 783, (I) 1308

National Oceanic and Atmospheric Administration Educational Partnership Program with Minority Serving Institutions Undergraduate Scholarships, (S) 355, (I) 1309

National Oceanic and Atmospheric Administration Small Business Innovation Research Grants. See NOAA Small Business Innovation Research Grants, entry (G) 1075

National Optical Astronomy Observatories 5-Year Science Fellowship. See Leo Goldberg Fellowships, entry (G) 1025

National Physical Science Consortium Dissertation Support Program, (G) 1059

National Physical Science Consortium Graduate Fellowships. See NPSC Graduate Fellowships, entries (F) 804, (I) 1313

National Science Foundation Director's Award for Distinguished Teaching Scholars. See NSF Director's Award for Distinguished Teaching Scholars, entries (G) 1076, (A) 1166

National Science Foundation Graduate Fellowships. See NSF Graduate Research Fellowships, entry (F) 806

National Science Foundation Small Business Innovation Research Grants. See NSF Small Business Innovation Research Grants, entry (G) 1077

National Science Foundation Small Business Technology Transfer Grants. See NSF Small Business Technology Transfer Grants, entry (G) 1078

National Security Agency Undergraduate Training Program. See Stokes Educational Scholarship Program, entries (F) 871, (I) 1334

National Space Grant College and Fellowship Program, (S) 356, (F) 784, (G) 1060

National Strength and Conditioning Association Minority Scholarships, (F) 785

National Urban Fellows Program, (F) 786

National Water Research Institute Fellowships. See NWRI Fellowships, entry (G) 1079

Native American Education Grants, (S) 357

Native American Finance Officers Association Student Scholarship, (S) 358, (F) 787

Native American Health Education Fund Scholarship, (S) 359, (F) 788

Native American Indian Education Association of New York Scholarship. See NAIEA/NY Scholarship, entry (S) 349

Native American Journalists Association Professional Development Fellowships. See NAJA Professional Development Fellowships, entry (F) 773

Native American Journalists Association Scholarships. See NAAJ Scholarships, entries (S) 347, (F) 772

Native American Leadership in Education (NALE) Program. See NALE Program, entries (S) 350, (F) 774

Native American Public Telecommunications Public Television Program Fund, (G) 1061

Native American Scholarships of the Vermont Space Grant Consortium, (S) 360

Native American Summer Congressional Internship Program. See Morris K. Udall Native American Congressional Internship Program, entry (I) 1295

Native American Supplemental Grants, (F) 789

Native American Visiting Student Awards, (G) 1062

Native American Women's Health Education Resource Center Internships, (I) 1310

Native American Women's Health Education Resource Center Scholarships, (S) 361

Native Hawaiian Chamber of Commerce Scholarships, (S) 362, (F) 790

Native Vision Scholarships, (S) 363

Navajo Generating Station Scholarship, (S) 364

Navajo Nation College Developmental Studies Program, (S) 365

Navajo Nation Dissertation Funding, (G) 1063

S–Scholarships F–Fellowships G–Grants A–Awards I–Internships

PROGRAM TITLE INDEX

Navajo Nation Financial Need–Based Assistance Program, (S) 366
Navajo Nation Graduate Trust Fund and Fellowship, (F) 791
Navajo Nation Teacher Education Program, (S) 367, (F) 792
Navajo Nation Vocational Education Program, (S) 368
Naval Research Laboratory Broad Agency Announcement, (G) 1064
Nawahi Scholarship. See Joseph Nawahi Scholarship, entry (F) 720
NCAI Youth Ambassador Leadership Program Scholarships, (S) 369
NCEMNA Aetna Scholars Program, (S) 370, (F) 793
NCI Mentored Career Development Award to Promote Diversity, (G) 1065
NCI Mentored Patient–Oriented Research Award to Promote Diversity, (G) 1066
NCI Transition Career Development Award to Promote Diversity, (G) 1067
Nell B. Brown Memorial Award, (F) 794
New Jersey Library Association Diversity Scholarship. See NJLA Diversity Scholarship, entry (F) 797
New Jersey Space Grant Consortium Undergraduate Summer Fellowships, (I) 1311
New Voices Award. See Lee & Low Books New Voices Award, entry (A) 1158
New York Aid to Native Americans, (S) 371
Nez Perce Higher Education Grants, (S) 372
NHLBI Mentored Career Development Award to Promote Faculty Diversity in Biomedical Research, (G) 1068
NIAAA Career Transition Award, (G) 1069
Nickerson West Shakespeare/Arapaho Trust Graduate Scholarship, (F) 795
Nickerson West Shakespeare/Arapaho Trust Undergraduate Scholarship, (S) 373
NIDA Mentored Clinical Scientists Development Program Award in Drug Abuse and Addiction, (G) 1070
NIDDK Mentored Clinical Scientist Award to Promote Diversity in Health–Related Research, (G) 1071
NIH Director's New Innovator Award Program, (G) 1072
Nihewan Scholarships, (S) 374
NINDS Mentored Research and Clinical Scientist Development Awards in Translational Research, (G) 1073
Ninilchik Higher Education Grant Program, (S) 375, (F) 796
Ninilchik Native Association Scholarship and Vocational Grant, (S) 376
NINR Mentored Research Scientist Development Award for Underrepresented or Disadvantaged Investigators, (G) 1074
Nipper Memorial Scholarship. See American Indian Education Foundation Scholarship Program, entry (S) 26
Nissan North America Scholarship, (S) 377
Nissan North America Tribal College Scholarship Program, (S) 378
NJLA Diversity Scholarship, (F) 797
NLM Individual Fellowship for Informationist Training, (F) 798
NMF Need–Based Scholarship Program, (F) 799
NNALSA Writing Competition, (A) 1164
NOAA Small Business Innovation Research Grants, (G) 1075
NOAO 5–Year Science Fellowship. See Leo Goldberg Fellowships, entry (G) 1025
Nolan Tribal Judicial Scholarship. See George K. Nolan Tribal Judicial Scholarship, entries (S) 212, (F) 678
Norman TeCube Sr. Higher Education Fund, (S) 379, (F) 800

North American Doctoral Fellowships, (F) 801
North American Indian Prose Award, (A) 1165
North Carolina American Indian Fund Scholarships, (S) 380
North Carolina Commission of Indian Affairs WIA Summer Work Experience Program, (I) 1312
North Carolina Incentive Scholarship and Grant Program for Native Americans. See University of North Carolina Campus Scholarships–Part II, entry (S) 507
North Dakota Indian Scholarship Program, (S) 381
Northern Arapaho Adult Vocational Training Grants, (S) 382
Northern Arapaho Tribal Scholarships, (S) 383
Northern Cheyenne Adult Vocational Training Program, (S) 384
Northern Cheyenne Higher Education Scholarship Program, (S) 385, (F) 802
Norton Sound Health Corporation Scholarships, (S) 386, (F) 803
Notay Begay III Scholarship Program, (S) 387
NPSC Graduate Fellowships, (F) 804, (I) 1313
N.S. Bienstock Fellowship, (F) 805
NSF Director's Award for Distinguished Teaching Scholars, (G) 1076, (A) 1166
NSF Graduate Research Fellowships, (F) 806
NSF Scholarships for Archaeological Training for Native Americans and Native Hawaiians. See Arthur C. Parker Scholarships, entries (S) 42, (F) 576
NSF Small Business Innovation Research Grants, (G) 1077
NSF Small Business Technology Transfer Grants, (G) 1078
NSTI Summer Scholars Program, (I) 1314
NWRI Fellowships, (G) 1079

Oak Ridge National Laboratory/Oak Ridge Associated Universities HBCU/MEI Faculty Summer Research Program, (G) 1080
Oakerhater Award. See ECIM Scholarships, entry (F) 646
Oakerhater Merit Fellowship. See ECIM Scholarships, entry (F) 646
OCLC Minority Scholarship. See LITA/OCLC Minority Scholarship, entry (F) 741
Oden Luce Trust Scholarships, (S) 388
Office of Civilian Radioactive Waste Management Minority Serving Institutions Undergraduate Scholarship Program, (S) 389, (I) 1315
Office of Hawaiian Affairs Scholarships, (S) 390
Office of Naval Research Sabbatical Leave Program, (G) 1081
Office of Naval Research Summer Faculty Research Program, (G) 1082
Ohkay Owingeh Scholarships, (S) 391
Olive Whitman Memorial Scholarship, (S) 392
Oliver Goldsmith, M.D. Scholarship, (F) 807
Olson Memorial Scholarship. See Martin Olson Memorial Scholarship, entries (S) 313, (F) 748
Oneida Tribe Higher Education Grant Program, (S) 393, (F) 808
Online Computer Library Center Minority Scholarship. See LITA/OCLC Minority Scholarship, entry (F) 741
Operation Jump Start III Scholarships, (F) 809
Oregon Native American Chamber of Commerce Scholarships, (S) 394
Osage Higher Education Grants, (S) 395, (F) 810
Osage Scholarships. See Mae Lasley/Osage Scholarships, entries (S) 308, (F) 743

S–Scholarships   F–Fellowships   G–Grants   A–Awards   I–Internships

Osage Tribal Education Committee Program, (S) 396, (F) 811
Osborn Minority Student Scholarships. See Royce Osborn Minority Student Scholarships, entry (S) 449
Oshita Memorial Fellowship. See Gerald Oshita Memorial Fellowship, entry (G) 996
Osmann Family Native American Scholarship, (S) 397
Ottawa Tribe Higher Education Grants, (S) 398, (F) 812
OTZ Telephone Cooperative Scholarships, (S) 399

Pacific Islanders in Communications Media Fund Grants, (G) 1083
Pacific Islanders in Communications Scholarships, (S) 400, (F) 813
Pacific Islanders in Communications Short Film Initiative, (G) 1084
Pacific Northwest National Laboratory Student Research Apprenticeship Program, (I) 1316
Parker Scholarships. See Arthur C. Parker Scholarships, entries (S) 42, (F) 576
Pascua Yaqui Higher Education Scholarship, (S) 401, (F) 814
Pathways to Independence Program, (G) 1085
Patrick D. McJulien Minority Graduate Scholarship, (F) 815
Paul and Emily Shagen Scholarship, (S) 402, (F) 816
Paul B. Beeson Career Development Awards in Aging Research Program, (G) 1086
Paul D. White Scholarship, (F) 817, (I) 1317
Paul Francis Memorial Scholarship. See American Indian Education Foundation Scholarship Program, entry (S) 26
Paula de Merieux Rheumatology Fellowship Award, (F) 818
Pauline Miguel Scholarship, (S) 403
Peace Scholar Dissertation Fellowships, (G) 1087
Pearl Carter Scott Aviation Scholarship, (S) 404, (F) 819
Pebble Limited Partnership/BBNC Scholarships, (S) 405
Peggy Vatter Memorial Scholarships, (S) 406
Pembroke Center Postdoctoral Fellowships, (G) 1088
Penobscot Nation Adult Vocational Training, (S) 407
Penobscot Nation Fellowship, (F) 820
Penobscot Nation Higher Education Grant Program, (S) 408
Peoria Tribal Education Program, (S) 409
Percy B. Ferebee Endowment Scholarship, (S) 410
Perryman Communications Scholarship for Ethnic Minority Students. See Leonard M. Perryman Communications Scholarship for Ethnic Minority Students, entry (S) 303
Persina Scholarship. See Ellen Masin Persina Scholarship, entry (S) 176
Peter Doctor Memorial Indian Emlen Awards, (S) 411, (F) 821
Peter Doctor Memorial Indian Scholarship Grants, (S) 412, (F) 822
Peter Kalifornsky Memorial Endowment Scholarship Fund, (S) 413, (F) 823
Peters Ethnic Minorities Outstanding Achievement Award. See Marie F. Peters Ethnic Minorities Outstanding Achievement Award, entry (A) 1160
Pfizer Minority Research Fellowship, (G) 1089
Phillip R. Lee Health Careers Scholarship. See Dr. Phillip R. Lee Health Careers Scholarship, entry (S) 160
Phillips Fund Grants for Native American Research, (G) 1090
Phyllis G. Meekins Scholarship, (S) 414
Pi State Native American Grants-in-Aid, (S) 415, (F) 824

Picard Scholarship Program. See Truman D. Picard Scholarship Program, entry (S) 491
Pickering Graduate Foreign Affairs Fellowships. See Thomas R. Pickering Graduate Foreign Affairs Fellowships, entry (I) 1345
Piestewa Vocational/Technical or 4-Year Scholarship. See Lori Piestewa Vocational/Technical or 4-Year Scholarship, entry (S) 306
Pineapple Scholarship Fund. See Johnny Pineapple Scholarship Fund, entry (S) 267
Pistilli Scholarships. See P.O. Pistilli Scholarships, entry (S) 416
P.O. Pistilli Scholarships, (S) 416
Poarch Band of Creek Indians Tuition Payment Program, (S) 417
Pokagon Band Adult Vocational Scholarship, (S) 418
Pokagon Band Higher Education Scholarship, (S) 419, (F) 825
Polingaysi Qöyawayma Award. See A.T. Anderson Memorial Scholarship Program, entries (S) 47, (F) 580
Ponca Tribe of Nebraska Educational Grants, (S) 420, (F) 826
Po'Pay Scholarships, (S) 421
Porky White Scholarship Fund. See Walter "Porky" White Scholarship Fund, entries (S) 515, (F) 890
Porter Fellowship for Minority Investigators. See William Townsend Porter Fellowship for Minority Investigators, entry (G) 1137
Porter Physiology Development Awards, (F) 827
Porter Wright Morris & Arthur LLP/Ralph K. Frasier Scholarship, (F) 828, (I) 1318
Postdoctoral Fellowship in Behavioral Neuroscience, (G) 1091
Postdoctoral Fellowships at FDA, (G) 1092
Postdoctoral Fellowships in Law and Social Science, (G) 1093
Postdoctoral Fellowships of the Ford Foundation Diversity Fellowship Program, (G) 1094
Postdoctoral Industrial Fellowships, (G) 1095
Postdoctoral Research Fellowships in Biology, (G) 1096
Postdoctoral Research Fellowships in Epilepsy, (G) 1097
Powell Diversity Scholarship. See George V. Powell Diversity Scholarship, entries (F) 681, (I) 1243
Power and Helen Hornbeck Tanner Fellowship. See Susan Kelly Power and Helen Hornbeck Tanner Fellowship, entry (G) 1121
Powless Scholarship. See Purcell Powless Scholarship, entry (S) 435
Prairie Band Potawatomi Nation Adult Education Program, (S) 422
Prairie Band Potawatomi Nation Adult Vocational Training Grant, (S) 423
Prairie Band Potawatomi Nation Higher Education Graduate Program, (F) 829
Prairie Band Potawatomi Nation Higher Education Undergraduate Program, (S) 424
Predoctoral Fellowships of the Ford Foundation Diversity Fellowship Program, (F) 830
Predoctoral Research Training Fellowships in Epilepsy, (G) 1098
Presidential Management Fellows Program, (I) 1319
Price Scholarships. See Judith McManus Price Scholarships, entries (S) 271, (F) 722
Prince Kuhio Hawaiian Civic Club Scholarship, (S) 425, (F) 831
Private Colleges & Universities Community Service Scholarship Program for Multicultural Students, (S) 426

S–Scholarships   F–Fellowships   G–Grants   A–Awards   I–Internships

PROGRAM TITLE INDEX 471

Professional Development and Education Fund Mickey Williams Minority Student Scholarships. See Mickey Williams Minority Student Scholarships, entry (S) 327
Professional Golf Management Diversity Scholarship, (S) 427
Public Health Service Small Business Innovation Research Program, (G) 1099
Public Honors Fellowships of the Oregon State Bar, (I) 1320
Public Policy and International Affairs Fellowships, (F) 832
Public Relations Student Society of America Multicultural Affairs Scholarships, (S) 428
Pueblo of Acoma Higher Education Grant Program, (S) 429
Pueblo of Isleta Higher Education Program, (S) 430, (F) 833
Pueblo of Jemez Scholarship Program, (S) 431
Pueblo of Laguna Higher Education Program, (S) 432
Pueblo of Pojoaque Higher Education Scholarship Program, (S) 433, (F) 834
Pueblo of San Felipe Higher Education Program, (S) 434
Purcell Powless Scholarship, (S) 435
Pyramid Lake Paiute Tribe Adult Vocational Training Program, (S) 436
Pyramid Lake Paiute Tribe Enrichment Scholarship, (S) 437

QEM Science Student Internships, (I) 1321
Qöyawayma Awards. See A.T. Anderson Memorial Scholarship Program, entries (S) 47, (F) 580
Quality Education for Minorities Science Student Internships. See QEM Science Student Internships, entry (I) 1321
Quinn Scholars Program. See Chips Quinn Scholars Program, entries (S) 97, (I) 1203

Race Relations Multiracial Student Scholarship, (S) 438, (F) 835
Rachel Mahi Educational Scholarship. See Dan and Rachel Mahi Educational Scholarship, entries (S) 150, (F) 627
Racial Ethnic Supplemental Grants, (F) 836
Ralph Bunche Summer Institute, (S) 439
Ralph J. Bunche Award, (A) 1167
Ralph K. Frasier Scholarship. See Porter Wright Morris & Arthur LLP/Ralph K. Frasier Scholarship, entries (F) 828, (I) 1318
Rawley Prize. See James A. Rawley Prize, entry (A) 1157
Reading Award Program, (G) 1100
Real Property Law Section Minority Fellowship, (I) 1322
Red Clay Award, (S) 440
Research and Engineering Apprenticeship Program (REAP) for High School Students, (I) 1323
Research and Training Program on Poverty and Public Policy Postdoctoral Fellowships, (G) 1101
Research Initiation Grants and Career Advancement Awards to Broaden Participation in Biology, (G) 1102
Retail Management Institute Internships, (I) 1324
The Rev. Francene Eagle Big Goose Memorial Scholarship, (F) 837
Rhode Island Space Grant Consortium Undergraduate Summer Scholar Program, (I) 1325
Richard and Helen Brown COREM Scholarships, (F) 838
Richard B. Fisher Scholarship, (S) 441, (I) 1326
Richard D. Hailey AAJ Law Student Scholarships, (F) 839

Richard Hagen–Minerva Harvey Memorial Scholarship, (S) 442
Richard S. Smith Scholarship, (S) 443
Richard W. Tanner Scholarship Fund, (S) 444
Richard (Yogi) Crowe Memorial Scholarship, (F) 840
Ridge Award. See Major Ridge Award, entry (S) 309
Ridge Inter–Disciplinary Global Experiments 2000 Initiative Postdoctoral Fellowships. See RIDGE 2000 Postdoctoral Fellowship Program, entry (G) 1103
RIDGE 2000 Postdoctoral Fellowship Program, (G) 1103
Robert D. Watkins Graduate Research Fellowship, (G) 1104
Robert Toigo Foundation Fellowships, (F) 841
Robert W. Brocksbank Scholarship. See A.T. Anderson Memorial Scholarship Program, entries (S) 47, (F) 580
Robert Wood Johnson Foundation Physician Faculty Scholars Program, (G) 1105
Robinson Scholarship. See Jackie Robinson Scholarships, entry (S) 258
Rock Foundation Graduate Scholarship Program. See Howard Rock Foundation Graduate Scholarship Program, entry (F) 702
Rock Foundation Undergraduate Scholarship Program. See Howard Rock Foundation Undergraduate Scholarship Program, entry (S) 240
Rodney T. Mathews Memorial Scholarship for California Indians, (S) 445, (F) 842
Roe B. Lewis Memorial Scholarships. See Dr. Roe B. Lewis Memorial Scholarships, entries (S) 161, (F) 643
Rollin and Mary Ella King Native American Artist Fellowship, (G) 1106
Ronald B. Linsky Fellowship for Outstanding Water Research, (G) 1107
Ronald H. Brown Memorial Scholarship, (S) 446
Ronald N. and Susan Dubin Native American Artist Fellowship, (G) 1108
Rooks Fellowship for Racial and Ethnic Theological Students. See Adrienne M. and Charles Shelby Rooks Fellowship for Racial and Ethnic Theological Students, entry (F) 541
Rosemarie Maher Memorial Fund. See Doyon Foundation Competitive Scholarships, entries (S) 158, (F) 639
Rosemary Gaskin Scholarship, (S) 447
Rothstein Minority Research Fellowship Award. See Dr. Jules M. Rothstein Minority Research Fellowship Award, entry (G) 970
Rouillard and Alice Tonemah Memorial Scholarships. See John C. Rouillard and Alice Tonemah Memorial Scholarships, entries (S) 264, (F) 714
Roy M. Huhndorf Endowment Scholarship Fund, (S) 448, (F) 843
Royce Osborn Minority Student Scholarships, (S) 449
Russell Black College Fund. See United Methodist Higher Education Foundation Native Alaskan Fund, entries (S) 504, (F) 884
Ruth Whitmore Memorial Scholarship. See G.C. and Ruth Whitmore Memorial Scholarship, entry (S) 206

Sabbaticals for Long–Time Activists of Color, (G) 1109
Sac and Fox Nation Higher Education Grants, (S) 450, (F) 844
SACNAS Genome Scholars Program, (F) 845
Salamatof Native Association, Inc. Scholarship Program, (S) 451, (F) 846

S–Scholarships   F–Fellowships   G–Grants   A–Awards   I–Internships

Sandia Master's Fellowship Program, (F) 847
Sankey Minority Scholarship in Meteorology. *See* David Sankey Minority Scholarship in Meteorology, entries (S) 153, (F) 630
Santa Fe Veterans for Peace Scholarships, (S) 452
Santo Domingo Scholarship Program, (S) 453
Sarah Keli'ilolena Lum Konia Nakoa Hawaiian Language Perpetual Scholarship, (S) 454, (F) 848
Sault Higher Education Grant Program, (S) 455
Sault Tribe Higher Education Self Sufficiency Fund, (S) 456
Sault Tribe Higher Education Vocational Training Program, (S) 457
Scholarship Awards for Incoming Minority College Freshmen in Chemical Engineering, (S) 458
Scholarship Awards for Minority College Students in Chemical Engineering, (S) 459
Scholarship for Minority Students in Memory of Edna Yelland. *See* CLA Scholarship for Minority Students in Memory of Edna Yelland, entry (F) 611
Scholarships for Minority Accounting Students, (S) 460, (F) 849
Schwabe, Williamson & Wyatt Diversity Scholarship Program, (I) 1327
Science and Technology Centers STEM Doctoral Internship Program, (I) 1328
Science and Technology Centers Summer Research Appointments for STEM Faculty at Minority Institutions, (G) 1110
Scott Aviation Scholarship. *See* Pearl Carter Scott Aviation Scholarship, entries (S) 404, (F) 819
Scotts Company Scholars Program, (S) 461, (I) 1329
Scripps Fellowships in Environmental Journalism. *See* Ted Scripps Fellowships in Environmental Journalism, entries (F) 874, (G) 1124
Sealaska Corporation Internships, (I) 1330
Sealaska Heritage Institute Scholarships, (S) 462, (F) 850
Sealaska Heritage Institute 7(i) Scholarships, (S) 463, (F) 851
Seldovia Native Association Foundation Scholarships. *See* SNA Foundation Scholarships, entries (S) 470, (F) 862
Semiconductor Research Corporation Master's Scholarship Program, (F) 852
Seneca Nation Higher Education Program, (S) 464, (F) 853
Sequoyah Graduate Fellowships, (F) 854
Shack, Jr. Scholarship. *See* FMMDA Scholarships, entry (S) 191
Shagen Scholarship. *See* Paul and Emily Shagen Scholarship, entries (S) 402, (F) 816
Shee Atiká Academic Scholarships, (S) 465, (F) 855
Sherman Asche Memorial Scholarship. *See* Elizabeth and Sherman Asche Memorial Scholarship, entries (S) 175, (F) 650
Sherry R. Arnstein Minority Student Scholarship, (F) 856
Sherry R. Arnstein New Student Minority Student Scholarship, (F) 857
Short-Term Career Development Award in the Environmental Health Sciences for Established Investigators, (G) 1111
Shoshone Tribal Scholarship Program, (S) 466
Shurr Journalism Award. *See* John Shurr Journalism Award, entries (S) 266, (F) 717
Sidney B. Williams, Jr. Intellectual Property Law School Scholarships, (F) 858
Significant Opportunities in Atmospheric Research and Science (SOARS) Program, (I) 1331

Sitka Tribe Adult Vocational Grant, (S) 467
Sitka Tribe of Alaska Higher Education Program, (S) 468, (F) 859
Sitnasuak Foundation Scholarships, (S) 469, (F) 860
Sky People Graduate Scholarship Program, (F) 861
Slagle Memorial Scholarship. *See* Allogan Slagle Memorial Scholarship, entry (S) 17
Slagle Scholarship. *See* Allogan Slagle Scholarship, entry (F) 552
Sloan Foundation Research Fellowships. *See* Alfred P. Sloan Foundation Research Fellowships, entry (G) 915
Sloan Scholarship Faculty Grants, (G) 1112
Smith Scholarship. *See* Richard S. Smith Scholarship, entry (S) 443
Smithsonian Minority Student Internship, (G) 1113, (I) 1332
Smithsonian Native American Community Scholar Awards, (G) 1114
Smithsonian Native American Student Internship Awards, (I) 1333
SNA Foundation Scholarships, (S) 470, (F) 862
SOARS Program. *See* Significant Opportunities in Atmospheric Research and Science (SOARS) Program, entry (I) 1331
Society for the Study of Social Problems Racial/Ethnic Minority Graduate Scholarship, (G) 1115
Society of American Indian Government Employees Academic Scholarships, (S) 471, (F) 863
Society of American Indian Government Employees Professional Development Scholarships, (F) 864
Somday Education Fund. *See* Cecelia Somday Education Fund, entry (S) 80
Southern Regional Education Board Dissertation-Year Fellowships, (G) 1116
Southern Regional Education Board Doctoral Scholars Program. *See* SREB Doctoral Scholars Program, entry (F) 868
Southwestern Association for Indian Arts Fellowships, (G) 1117
Southwestern Association for Indian Arts Market Awards, (A) 1168
Sovereign Nations Scholarship Fund Graduate Awards, (F) 865
Sovereign Nations Scholarship Fund Undergraduate Awards, (S) 472
Sowa Scholarship. *See* Iwalani Carpenter Sowa Scholarship, entry (F) 708
Sowa Scholarships. *See* Joseph A. Sowa Scholarships, entry (S) 268
Special Libraries Association Affirmative Action Scholarship, (F) 866
SpecPro Scholarships, (S) 473
Spirit of Sovereignty Scholarships, (S) 474, (F) 867
Spurlock Minority Medical Student Clinical Fellowship in Child and Adolescent Psychiatry. *See* Jeanne Spurlock Minority Medical Student Clinical Fellowship in Child and Adolescent Psychiatry, entry (I) 1257
Spurlock Research Fellowship in Drug Abuse and Addiction for Minority Medical Students. *See* Jeanne Spurlock Research Fellowship in Drug Abuse and Addiction for Minority Medical Students, entry (I) 1258
SREB Doctoral Scholars Program, (F) 868
St. Louis Chapter National Graduate Scholarship, (F) 869
St. Louis Chapter National Undergraduate Scholarship, (S) 475
Stables Education Award, (S) 476
Stacie Lynn Hays Memorial Scholarship, (S) 477

PROGRAM TITLE INDEX

Standing Rock Sioux Tribe Higher Education Scholarships, (S) 478

Stanford Humanities Center External Faculty Fellowships, (G) 1118

Stanford Memorial WLMA Scholarship. *See* John Stanford Memorial Scholarship, entry (F) 718

Stanhoff Memorial Scholarship. *See* American Indian Chamber of Commerce of California Scholarship, entries (S) 23, (F) 556

Stanley Minority and International Scholarship. *See* Alan Compton and Bob Stanley Minority and International Scholarship, entry (S) 8

Steele Scholarship. *See* Dwayne "Nakila" Steele Scholarship, entry (S) 162

Stephen H. Coltrin Award for Excellence in Communication Education, (A) 1169

Stockbridge–Munsee College and Vocational Assistance, (S) 479, (F) 870

Stokes Educational Scholarship Program, (F) 871, (I) 1334

Stone Research Fellowship. *See* Betty Lea Stone Research Fellowship, entry (G) 932

Strait Minority Scholarship Endowment. *See* George A. Strait Minority Scholarship Endowment, entry (F) 676

Stronach Curatorial Internships. *See* Lifchez/Stronach Curatorial Internships, entry (I) 1270

Student Achievement in Research and Scholarship (STARS) Awards, (G) 1119

Student Cancer Research Fellowship, (I) 1335

Student Opportunity Scholarships for Ethnic Minority Groups, (S) 480

Summer Honors Undergraduate Research Program, (I) 1336

Summer Internship Program in Biomedical Research, (I) 1337

Summer Internships for Students from Tribal Colleges and Universities, (I) 1338

Summer Program in Quantitative Sciences for Public Health Research, (I) 1339

Summer Research Diversity Fellowships in Law and Social Science for Undergraduate Students, (I) 1340

Summer Research Opportunities Program (SROP), (I) 1341

Summer Research Opportunity Program in Pathology, (I) 1342

Summer Transportation Internship Program for Diverse Groups, (I) 1343

Susan Dubin Native American Artist Fellowship. *See* Ronald N. and Susan Dubin Native American Artist Fellowship, entry (G) 1108

Susan G. Komen Breast Cancer Foundation Postdoctoral Fellowship, (G) 1120

Susan Kelly Power and Helen Hornbeck Tanner Fellowship, (G) 1121

Susie Qimmiqsak Bevins Endowment Scholarship Fund, (S) 481, (F) 872

Suulutaaq Construction Scholarship, (S) 482

Sylvia Taylor Johnson Minority Fellowship in Educational Measurement, (G) 1122

Synergistic Idea Development Awards of the Prostate Cancer Research Program, (G) 1123

Takabuke Commemorative Scholarships. *See* Goldman Sachs/Matsuo Takabuke Commemorative Scholarships, entry (F) 685

Tanana Chiefs Conference Higher Education Grants, (S) 483, (F) 873

Tanner Fellowship. *See* Susan Kelly Power and Helen Hornbeck Tanner Fellowship, entry (G) 1121

Tanner Scholarship Fund. *See* Richard W. Tanner Scholarship Fund, entry (S) 444

Taylor Memorial Summer Minority Policy Fellowship. *See* Dalmas A. Taylor Memorial Summer Minority Policy Fellowship, entry (I) 1213

Taylor Scholarship Endowment. *See* Bill Taylor Scholarship Endowment, entry (S) 57

TeCube Sr. Higher Education Fund. *See* Norman TeCube Sr. Higher Education Fund, entries (S) 379, (F) 800

Ted Scripps Fellowships in Environmental Journalism, (F) 874, (G) 1124

Temin Pathway to Independence Awards in Cancer Research. *See* Pathways to Independence Program, entry (G) 1085

Texas Historical Commission Preservation Fellows Program, (I) 1344

Texas Medical Association Minority Scholarship Program, (F) 875

Thomas R. Pickering Graduate Foreign Affairs Fellowships, (I) 1345

Thompson Hine Minority Scholarship Program, (I) 1346

Thompson Scholarship Fund. *See* Doyon Foundation Competitive Scholarships, entries (S) 158, (F) 639

Thompson Scholarship. *See* Myron and Laura Thompson Scholarship, entries (S) 346, (F) 771

Thunder, Jr./Arapaho Ranch Trust Scholarship. *See* Bill Thunder, Jr./Arapaho Ranch Trust Scholarship, entries (S) 58, (F) 586

Time Warner Tribal Scholars Program, (S) 484

Tinker Scholarship Fund. *See* Mary Tinker Scholarship Fund, entries (S) 315, (F) 749

Tlingit and Haida Indian Tribes of Alaska College Student Assistance Program, (S) 485, (F) 876

TMA Systems Scholarship, (S) 486

Toigo Foundation Fellowships. *See* Robert Toigo Foundation Fellowships, entry (F) 841

Tonemah Memorial Scholarships. *See* John C. Rouillard and Alice Tonemah Memorial Scholarships, entries (S) 264, (F) 714

Tonkawa Tribe Higher Education Program, (S) 487

Tonkon Torp First–Year Diversity Fellowship Program, (F) 877, (I) 1347

Townsend and Townsend and Crew Diversity Scholarship, (F) 878

Trail of Tears Art Show, (A) 1170

Transfer Engineering Student Award, (S) 488

Triad Hospitals Corris Boyd Scholarship, (F) 879

Triangle Native American Society Scholarships, (S) 489

Tribal Business Management (TBM) Program, (S) 490

Tribal Publications Internships, (I) 1348

Truman D. Picard Scholarship Program, (S) 491

Tsay Corporation "Let's Get Started" Scholarship, (S) 492

Tsay Corporation "Many Paths to Success" Scholarship, (S) 493

Tsay Corporation "You're Almost There" Scholarship, (S) 494

Turtle Mountain Band of Chippewa Indians Scholarship Program, (S) 495, (F) 880

Two Feathers Endowment American Indian Scholarships, (S) 496

S–Scholarships   F–Fellowships   G–Grants   A–Awards   I–Internships

Two Feathers Fund Health Initiative Scholarship, (S) 497
Tyonek Native Corporation Scholarship and Grant Program, (S) 498

UCSB Library Fellowship Program, (G) 1125
Udall Native American Summer Congressional Internship Program. See Morris K. Udall Native American Congressional Internship Program, entry (I) 1295
Udall Scholarships. See Morris K. Udall Scholarships, entry (S) 343
Ullyot Fellows. See ASPET Individual Summer Undergraduate Research Fellowships, entry (I) 1185
Ulmer Native American Scholarship. See Triangle Native American Society Scholarships, entry (S) 489
UNCF Corporate Scholars Programs, (S) 499, (F) 881, (I) 1349
Undergraduate Awards of the Seminole Nation Judgment Fund, (S) 500
Undergraduate Student Research Experiences at FDA, (I) 1350
Underrepresented Mental Health Research Fellowship Program, (F) 882
Unitarian Universalist Association Incentive Grants, (F) 883
United Indians of Virginia Scholarship Program, (S) 501
United Methodist Church ONNSFA Scholarships, (S) 502
United Methodist Ethnic Minority Scholarships, (S) 503
United Methodist Higher Education Foundation Native Alaskan Fund, (S) 504, (F) 884
United Methodist Native American Seminary Awards, (F) 885
United Methodist Women of Color Scholars Program, (F) 886
United Parcel Service Scholarship for Minority Students, (S) 505
United States Institute of Peace Senior Fellowships, (G) 1126
United Utilities Scholarships, (S) 506
University of California at Santa Barbara Library Fellowship Program. See UCSB Library Fellowship Program, entry (G) 1125
University of California President's Postdoctoral Fellowship Program for Academic Diversity, (G) 1127
University of Iowa Librarian Residency Program, (G) 1128
University of North Carolina Campus Scholarships–Part II, (S) 507
University of Wisconsin Visiting Minority Scholar Lecture Program, (G) 1129
University–Industry Cooperative Research Program Graduate Research Assistantships and Cooperative Fellowships, (G) 1130, (I) 1351
University–Industry Cooperative Research Program Postdoctoral Research Fellowships, (G) 1131
University–Industry Cooperative Research Program Senior Research Fellowships, (G) 1132
UPS Diversity Scholarships. See ASSE UPS Diversity Scholarships, entry (S) 44
Urban Scholars Postdoctoral Fellowship Program. See HUD Urban Scholars Postdoctoral Fellowship Program, entry (G) 1010
U.S. Army Sustainment Command Minority Internship Program, (I) 1352
U.S. Department of Housing and Urban Development Urban Scholars Postdoctoral Fellowship Program. See HUD Urban Scholars Postdoctoral Fellowship Program, entry (G) 1010
USDA Small Business Innovation Research Program, (G) 1133
Utah Navajo Trust Fund Higher Education Scholarships, (S) 508, (F) 887
Utah Sports Hall of Fame Native American Scholarships, (S) 509, (A) 1171

van Pelt Scholarships. See Adolph van Pelt Scholarships, entry (S) 3
Vatter Memorial Scholarships. See Peggy Vatter Memorial Scholarships, entry (S) 406
Verl and Dorothy Miller Native American Vocational Scholarship, (S) 510
Victor Matson Sr. Tributary Scholarship, (S) 511
Victor Matson Sr. Tributary Scholarship. See Victor Matson Sr. Tributary Scholarship, entry (S) 511
Vincent Bendix Minorities in Engineering Award. See ASSE/DuPont Minorities in Engineering Award, entry (A) 1145
Vine Deloria Jr. Memorial Scholarship, (F) 888
VIP Museum Studies Program of the National Museum of the American Indian. See Visiting Indigenous Professional (VIP) Museum Studies Program of the National Museum of the American Indian, entry (F) 889
Virginia D. Wilson Scholarship, (S) 512
Visiting Indigenous Professional (VIP) Museum Studies Program of the National Museum of the American Indian, (F) 889
Vocational School Awards of the Seminole Nation Judgment Fund, (S) 513
Voelker Foundation Native American Scholarship. See James D. Voelker Foundation Native American Scholarship, entries (S) 260, (F) 711

Walter Charley Memorial Scholarships, (S) 514
Walter "Porky" White Scholarship Fund, (S) 515, (F) 890
Wampanoag Higher Education Scholarship Program, (S) 516, (F) 891
Warner Norcross & Judd Secretarial Studies Scholarship, (S) 517
Washington Indian Gaming Association Scholarships, (S) 518
Washington NASA Space Grant Consortium Private Industry Internships, (I) 1353
Washington Scholarships. See Booker T. Washington Scholarships, entry (S) 64
Washington State American Indian Endowed Scholarship Program, (S) 519, (F) 892
Washington State University Summer Doctoral Fellows Program, (G) 1134
Washoe Tribe Adult Vocational Scholarships, (S) 520
Washoe Tribe Higher Education Grant Program, (S) 521, (F) 893
Washoe Tribe Incentive Scholarships, (S) 522, (F) 894
Watkins Graduate Research Fellowship. See Robert D. Watkins Graduate Research Fellowship, entry (G) 1104
Watson Midwives of Color Scholarship, (S) 523, (F) 895
Wauneka Visiting Faculty Fellowship. See Annie Wauneka Visiting Faculty Fellowship, entry (F) 568
W.E.B. DuBois Fellowship Program, (G) 1135

S–Scholarships   F–Fellowships   G–Grants   A–Awards   I–Internships

PROGRAM TITLE INDEX

Webb Internships. *See* James E. Webb Internships, entry (I) 1256
Weidman Racial Ethnic Minority Fellowship. *See* Judith L. Weidman Racial Ethnic Minority Fellowship, entry (I) 1261
Wells Fargo Graduate Scholarships, (F) 896
Wells Fargo Undergraduate Scholarships, (S) 524
Wells Fargo–BBNC Scholarship Fund, (S) 525
Westmin Endowment Scholarship Fund. *See* Howard Keck/Westmin Endowment Scholarship Fund, entries (S) 239, (F) 700
White Earth Scholarship Program, (S) 526, (F) 897
White Scholarship Fund. *See* Walter "Porky" White Scholarship Fund, entries (S) 515, (F) 890
White Scholarship. *See* Paul D. White Scholarship, entries (F) 817, (I) 1317
Whitman Memorial Scholarship. *See* Olive Whitman Memorial Scholarship, entry (S) 392
Whitmore Memorial Scholarship. *See* G.C. and Ruth Whitmore Memorial Scholarship, entry (S) 206
Wildlife Conservation Society Research Fellowship Program, (G) 1136
William A. Hinton Research Training Award, (A) 1172
William and Charlotte Cadbury Award, (A) 1173
William E. Shack, Jr. Scholarship. *See* FMMDA Scholarships, entry (S) 191
William G. Anderson, D.O. Minority Scholarship, (F) 898
William Randolph Hearst Endowed Fellowship for Minority Students, (I) 1354
William Randolph Hearst Endowed Fellowship for Minority Students. *See* William Randolph Hearst Endowed Fellowship for Minority Students, entry (I) 1354
William Townsend Porter Fellowship for Minority Investigators, (G) 1137
Williams, Jr. Intellectual Property Law School Scholarships. *See* Sidney B. Williams, Jr. Intellectual Property Law School Scholarships, entry (F) 858
Williams Minority Student Scholarships. *See* Mickey Williams Minority Student Scholarships, entry (S) 327
Wilson Scholarship. *See* Virginia D. Wilson Scholarship, entry (S) 512
Winnebago Tribe Higher Education Assistance, (S) 527, (F) 899
Winners for Life Foundation Scholarship, (S) 528
Winston & Strawn Diversity Scholarship Program, (F) 900
Wisconsin Indian Education Association Scholarships, (S) 529, (F) 901
Wisconsin Indian Student Assistance Grants, (S) 530, (F) 902
W.K. Kellogg Foundation Doctoral Fellowship in Health Policy, (F) 903, (G) 1138
Woksape Oyate: "Wisdom of the People" Distinguished Scholar Award, (S) 531
Woksape Oyate: "Wisdom of the People" Keepers of the Next Generation Award, (S) 532
Womble Carlyle Scholars Program, (F) 904, (I) 1355
Women of Color Dissertation Scholarship, (G) 1139
Wong and Associates Scholarship. *See* Dennis Wong and Associates Scholarship, entries (S) 154, (F) 632
Woods Hole Oceanographic Institution Minority Fellowships, (I) 1356
Woods Hole Oceanographic Institution Summer Student Fellowship Program, (G) 1140
Wyeth–Ayerst Laboratories Prize in Women's Health, (A) 1174

Xerox Technical Minority Scholarship Program, (S) 533, (F) 905

Yakama Adult Vocational Training Program, (S) 534
Yakama College Student Assistance Program, (S) 535
Yakama Incentive Awards Program, (A) 1175
Yakama Tribal Scholarship, (S) 536, (F) 906
YDFDA Vocational Training Grants, (S) 537
Yelland Memorial Scholarship. *See* CLA Scholarship for Minority Students in Memory of Edna Yelland, entry (F) 611
Yerby Postdoctoral Fellowship Program, (G) 1141
Yogi Crowe Memorial Scholarship. *See* Richard (Yogi) Crowe Memorial Scholarship, entry (F) 840
Young Memorial Scholarship. *See* Florence Young Memorial Scholarship, entry (F) 664
Youth Public Art Project Program of the National Museum of the American Indian, (G) 1142
Yukon Delta Fisheries Development Association Vocational Training Grants. *See* YDFDA Vocational Training Grants, entry (S) 537

Zimmerman Foundation Education Scholarships. *See* Dr. Hans and Clara Zimmerman Foundation Education Scholarships, entry (S) 159
Zuni Higher Education Scholarships, (S) 538, (F) 907

The 13th Regional Heritage Foundation Scholarships, (S) 539, (F) 908

S–Scholarships   F–Fellowships   G–Grants   A–Awards   I–Internships

Sponsoring Organization Index

The Sponsoring Organization Index makes it easy to identify agencies that offer financial aid primarily or exclusively to minorities. In this index, sponsoring organizations are listed alphabetically, word by word. In addition, we've used an alphabetical code (within parentheses) to help you identify which programs sponsored by these organizations fall within your scope of interest: S = Scholarships; F = Fellowships; G = Grants; A = Awards; and I = Internships. Here's how the code works: if the name of a sponsoring organization is followed by (S) 141, a program sponsored by that organization is described in the Scholarships section in entry 141. If the same sponsoring organization's name is followed by another entry number—for example, (G) 680—the same or a different program sponsored by that organization is described in the Grants chapter in entry 680. Remember: the numbers cited here refer to program entry numbers, not to page numbers in the book.

Abbott Laboratories, (G) 976, 1097–1098
ABC, Inc., (I) 1223
Academy of Applied Science, (I) 1323
Accenture, (S) 2, (F) 540
Acoustical Society of America, (F) 577
ADNET Systems, Inc., (I) 1217, 1352
Advancing Hispanic Excellence in Technology, Engineering, Math, and Science, Inc., (S) 352
Aetna Foundation, Inc., (S) 370, (F) 781, 793
Afognak Native Corporation, (S) 5–6, (F) 543
Ahtna, Incorporated, (S) 514
Alaska Library Association, (F) 546, 712
Alaska Native Tribal Health Consortium, (S) 9, (F) 547, (I) 1180
Alaska Space Grant Program, (I) 1181
Alaska State Council on the Arts, (I) 1275
Alaska Village Initiatives, Inc., (S) 240, (F) 702
Albuquerque Community Foundation, (S) 387
Albuquerque Journal, (S) 147, (I) 1211
ALCOA Foundation, (S) 351, 488
The Aleut Corporation, (S) 10–12, 125, 155, (F) 549–550
Aleutian Pribilof Island Community Development Association, (S) 35–36, (F) 569
Aleutian/Pribilof Islands Association, Inc., (S) 13–14
Alfred P. Sloan Foundation, (G) 915, 1012, 1112
Alpha Kappa Delta, (F) 578
Alston/Bannerman Fellowship Program, (G) 1109
Alyeska Pipeline Service Company, (S) 18
Alzheimer's Association, (G) 917
American Academy of Allergy, Asthma & Immunology, (G) 916
American Academy of Child and Adolescent Psychiatry, (I) 1257–1258
American Academy of Microbiology, (A) 1172
American Anthropological Association, (G) 918
American Architectural Foundation, (S) 29

American Association for Justice, (F) 839
American Association for Marriage and Family Therapy, (F) 746
American Association for the Advancement of Science, (I) 1176
American Association of Advertising Agencies, (F) 809, (I) 1296
American Association of Airport Executives Foundation, (S) 1
American Association of Blacks in Energy, (S) 20
American Association of Colleges of Osteopathic Medicine, (F) 856–857
American Association of Critical–Care Nurses, (S) 65
American Association of Family and Consumer Sciences, (F) 663
American Association of Law Libraries, (F) 676
American Association of Petroleum Geologists Foundation, (G) 1015
American Association of Retired Persons. Andrus Foundation, (G) 1052
American Association of University Women, (F) 666, (G) 909
American Bar Association. Fund for Justice and Education, (F) 738
American Bar Association. Section of Intellectual Property Law, (F) 858
American Bar Association. Section of Litigation, (I) 1260
American Bar Foundation, (G) 1024, 1093, (I) 1340
American Cancer Society. New England Division, (G) 932
American Chemical Society, (S) 21
American College of Healthcare Executives, (F) 548, (I) 1177
American College of Nurse–Midwives, (S) 523, (F) 895
American College of Rheumatology, (F) 818
American College Testing, (I) 1178
American Correctional Association, (S) 312, (F) 747
American Council of Learned Societies, (G) 919
American Dental Association, (F) 763
American Dental Hygienists' Association, (S) 120

S–Scholarships   F–Fellowships   G–Grants   A–Awards   I–Internships

SPONSORING ORGANIZATION INDEX

American Diabetes Association, (G) 1032
American Dietetic Association, (I) 1218
American Educational Research Association, (G) 912
American Epilepsy Society, (G) 976, 1097–1098
American Federation for Aging Research, (G) 1086
American Gastroenterological Association, (G) 913, 990, (A) 1151
American Geological Institute, (S) 214, (F) 682
American Health Information Management Association, (S) 198, (F) 667
American Hotel & Lodging Educational Foundation, (S) 246
American Indian Arts Council, Inc., (S) 22, (F) 555
American Indian Chamber of Commerce of California, (S) 23, (F) 556
American Indian Chamber of Commerce of Wisconsin, Inc., (S) 24, (F) 557
American Indian College Fund, (S) 78, 111, 116, 193–194, 207, 230, 305, 341–342, 377–378, 472, 484, 528, 531–532, (F) 865, 888
American Indian Education Foundation, (S) 26
American Indian Graduate Center, (S) 2, 16, 205, 524, (F) 540, 559, 671, 896
American Indian Heritage Foundation, (S) 338, (A) 1163
American Indian Law Review, (A) 1143
American Indian Science and Engineering Society, (S) 7, 47, 71, 208, (F) 545, 580, 675, (I) 1179
American Indian Services, (S) 28
American Institute of Architects, (S) 29
American Institute of Certified Public Accountants, (S) 460, (F) 544, 849
American Institute of Chemical Engineers, (S) 458–459, (A) 1162
American Intellectual Property Law Association, (F) 858
American Library Association. Library and Information Technology Association, (F) 741–742
American Library Association. Office for Diversity, (F) 560
American Medical Association, (F) 553
American Membrane Technology Association, (G) 923
American Meteorological Society, (S) 31, 252, (G) 1001
American Musicological Society, (F) 701
American Nuclear Society, (S) 262, (F) 713
American Nurses Association, (F) 566, (G) 924, 947
American Osteopathic Foundation, (F) 898
American Philological Association, (S) 336
American Philosophical Society, (G) 1018, 1090
American Physical Society, (S) 30, (A) 1152
American Physical Therapy Association, (S) 335, (F) 764, (G) 970
American Physiological Society, (F) 827, (G) 980, 992, (I) 1228
American Planning Association, (S) 271, (F) 561, 722
American Political Science Association, (S) 439, (F) 570, (A) 1167
American Psychiatric Association, (F) 765, 767, (G) 1040, 1089, (I) 1288–1290
American Psychological Association. Minority Fellowship Program, (F) 635, (G) 964
American Society for Clinical Laboratory Science, (S) 197
American Society for Engineering Education, (G) 1048, 1081–1082, (A) 1145
American Society for Investigative Pathology, (I) 1342
American Society for Microbiology, (G) 1037, 1104, (I) 1284

American Society for Pharmacology and Experimental Therapeutics, (I) 1185
American Society of Clinical Oncology, (G) 928
American Society of Criminology, (F) 562, (G) 922
American Society of Hematology, (G) 929, 1038
American Society of Nephrology, (G) 1019
American Society of Radiologic Technologists, (S) 449
American Society of Safety Engineers, (S) 43–44, (F) 579
American Society of Transplantation, (G) 948, 1016, 1019
American Sociological Association, (F) 563, 578
American Speech–Language–Hearing Foundation, (F) 564
American Water Works Association, (F) 695
Andrew W. Mellon Foundation, (G) 919
Anheuser–Busch Companies, Inc., (S) 55
Appraisal Institute, (S) 37
April, (S) 196
Arbitron, Inc., (I) 1223
Arent Fox LLP, (F) 574, (I) 1182
Argonne National Laboratory, (G) 925
The Arizona Republic, (S) 347, (F) 772
Arizona Space Grant Consortium, (I) 1183
Arthur W. Page Society, (S) 295, (F) 730
Artist Trust, (G) 1057
ArtTable Inc., (I) 1184
Asian & Pacific Islander American Scholarship Fund, (S) 205, (F) 671
Aspen Institute, (I) 1354
Association for Computing Machinery, (S) 416
Association for Education in Journalism and Mass Communication, (F) 740
Association for Educational Communications and Technology, (F) 815
Association for Public Policy Analysis and Management, (F) 832
Association for Women Geoscientists, (S) 45
Association of Black Sociologists, (F) 578
Association of Nurses in AIDS Care, (S) 33, (F) 567
Association of Professional Schools of International Affairs, (S) 254, (F) 832, (I) 1254
Association of Research Libraries, (F) 575, 736
Association of Schools of Public Health, (G) 942
Association of Universities for Research in Astronomy, Inc., (G) 1025
Association of University Programs in Health Administration, (F) 879
Association on American Indian Affairs, Inc., (S) 3, 17, 46, 175, 177, (F) 650, 664, 854
AstraZeneca Pharmaceuticals, L.P., (G) 990
Atlanta History Center, (I) 1306
Atlanta Journal and Constitution, (I) 1186
The Atlantic Philanthropies, (G) 1086
AT&T Laboratories, (F) 581, (I) 1188

Baker & Daniels LLP, (I) 1190
Baker, Donelson, Bearman, Caldwell & Berkowitz, P.C., (F) 582
Baker Hostetler LLP, (F) 817, (I) 1317
Baker Hughes Incorporated, (S) 48, (F) 583
Bank2, (S) 49–50
Banner & Witcoff, Ltd., (F) 636, (I) 1220
Baptist Communicators Association, (S) 8

SPONSORING ORGANIZATION INDEX

Bell Laboratories, (I) 1272
Bering Straits Native Corporation, (S) 51, 313, (F) 585, 748
BHP Billiton–New Mexico Coal, (S) 53
Bill and Melinda Gates Foundation, (S) 205, (F) 671
Black Coaches Association, (F) 654
Blackfeet Nation, (S) 60–61
Bois Forte Band of Chippewa, (S) 63, (F) 588
Booz Allen Hamilton, (S) 499, (F) 881, (I) 1349
Bristol Bay Native Corporation, (S) 66, 405, 473, 525
Bristol–Myers Squibb Foundation, (I) 1305
Broadcast Music Inc., (I) 1223
Brookhaven National Laboratory, (I) 1194–1195
Brown and Caldwell, (S) 67
Brown Foundation for Educational Equity, Excellence and Research, (S) 68
Brown University. Pembroke Center for Teaching and Research on Women, (G) 1088
Buckingham, Doolittle & Burroughs, LLP, (I) 1196
Buffalo Bandits, (S) 70
Bullivant Houser Bailey PC, (F) 590, (I) 1197
Burlington Northern Santa Fe Foundation, (S) 71
Burroughs Wellcome Fund, (F) 596, (G) 937
Butler Rubin Saltarelli & Boyd LLP, (F) 591, (I) 1199

C–SPAN, (I) 1223
California Endowment, (G) 931, (I) 1192, 1200
California HealthCare Foundation, (F) 781
California Indian Law Association, (F) 552
California Institute of Technology, (I) 1291
California Library Association, (F) 611
California Rural Indian Health Board, Inc., (S) 160
California School Library Association, (S) 300, (F) 737
California Space Grant Consortium, (I) 1201
California Wellness Foundation, (S) 160, (A) 1147
Calista Corporation, (S) 73, (F) 593
Capture the Dream, Inc., (S) 211
Catching the Dream, (S) 185, 322, 350, 490, (F) 660, 754, 774, (G) 962, 1100
Caterpillar, Inc., (S) 79
CBS Incorporated, (I) 1223
Center for Scholarship Administration, Inc., (S) 410
Central Council, Tlingit and Haida Indian Tribes of Alaska, (S) 270, 485, (F) 721, 876
Charles and Nancy Oden Luce Trust, (S) 388
Cherokee Heritage Center, (A) 1170
Cherokee Nation, (S) 83–85, 266, 309, 440, (F) 599, 717, 794
ChevronTexaco Corporation, (S) 214, (F) 682
Cheyenne and Arapaho Tribes of Oklahoma, (S) 86, (F) 600
Chickasaw Foundation, (S) 49–50, 56, 87, 89, 93, 119, 126, 229, 257, 263, 314, 404, 477, (F) 649, 819
Chickasaw Nation, (S) 88, 90–92, 330, (F) 601–603, (A) 1148
Chippewa County Community Foundation, (S) 402, 447, (F) 816
Choctaw Nation, (S) 96, 98–100, 189, 486
Christian Reformed Church, (S) 438, (F) 835
Chugach Alaska Corporation, (S) 102–103, (F) 605
Chugachmiut, (S) 104–105, (F) 606
CH2M Hill, (F) 695
Citigroup Foundation, (S) 111
Citizen Potawatomi Nation, (S) 112–114

City University of New York. Bernard M. Baruch College, (F) 786
Cleveland Foundation, (A) 1144
CNN, (S) 347, (F) 772
Coca–Cola Company, (S) 116
Cocopah Indian Tribe, (S) 117–118, (F) 612–613, (A) 1150
Colgate–Palmolive Company, (S) 120, (F) 640–642, 763, 779–780
College and Public Relations Association of Pennsylvania, (I) 1208
College Art Association of America, (F) 592
Colorado Space Grant Consortium, (I) 1206
Comanche Nation, (S) 123–124
Comcast Foundation, (I) 1223
Committee on Institutional Cooperation, (I) 1341
Commonwealth Fund, (I) 1305
Community Foundation for Southern Arizona, (S) 403
ComputerCraft Corporation, (S) 126
Computing Research Association, (G) 950
ConAgra Foods Foundation, (S) 127
Confederated Salish and Kootenai Tribes, (S) 128, (F) 614
Confederated Tribes of the Colville Reservation, (S) 80
Confederated Tribes of the Umatilla Indian Reservation, (S) 129, (F) 615
Conference of Minority Transportation Officials, (I) 1209
Connecticut Community College System, (I) 1210
ConocoPhillips, (S) 214, (F) 682
Consortium for Faculty Diversity at Liberal Arts Colleges, (G) 1041–1042
Consortium for Graduate Study in Management, (F) 598, (I) 1202
Continental Society, Daughters of Indian Wars, (S) 130
Cook Inlet Region, Inc., (S) 74, 76–77, 106–110, 174, 239–240, 265, 272, 279, 283, 286, 299, 376, 413, 448, 451, 481, 498, (F) 594, 597, 607–610, 680, 700, 702, 716, 724, 726, 735, 823, 843, 846, 872, (G) 946, 952, (I) 1205
Cook Inlet Tribal Council, Inc., (S) 18, 131, (F) 617
Copper River Native Association, (S) 132–133, (F) 618
Coquille Indian Tribe, (S) 134–137, (F) 619–620
Cornell University. College of Engineering, (I) 1271
Cornell University. Olin Library, (G) 953
Corporation for Public Broadcasting, (G) 1061
Council of Energy Resource Tribes, (S) 138, (F) 621, (I) 1225
Council on Social Work Education, (F) 882
Courage Center, (S) 178
Cow Creek Band of Umpqua Tribe of Indians, (S) 139–142, (F) 622–623
Crazy Horse Memorial Foundation, (S) 143
Cummins, Inc., (S) 148, (F) 626

Dakota Indian Foundation, (S) 149
Daniel Kovach Scholarship Foundation, (S) 152, (F) 629
Dartmouth College, (G) 945
Daughters of the American Revolution. New York State Organization, (S) 392
Davis Wright Tremaine LLP, (F) 631, (I) 1214
Dell Inc., (S) 499, (F) 881, (I) 1349
Delta Kappa Gamma Society International. Pi State Organization, (S) 415, (F) 824
Design Automation Conference, (S) 416

S–Scholarships   F–Fellowships   G–Grants   A–Awards   I–Internships

Dinsmore & Shohl LLP, (F) 633, (I) 1219
Djerassi Resident Artists Program, (G) 996
DLA Piper US LLP, (F) 669
Doris Duke Charitable Foundation, (G) 969
Dow Jones Newspaper Fund, (S) 72, (I) 1198
Doyon, Limited, (S) 157–158, (F) 638–639
DRI–The Voice of the Defense Bar, (F) 644

Eaton Corporation, (S) 166, (I) 1221
Edith Kanaka'ole Foundation, (S) 167, (F) 647
Educational Testing Service, (G) 978, 1122
Edward Davis Education Foundation, (S) 171
E.I. duPont de Nemours and Company, Inc., (A) 1145
Eight Northern Indian Pueblos Council, Inc., (S) 173
Eklutna, Inc., (S) 174
Eli Lilly and Company Foundation, Inc., (S) 531–532
Endocrine Society, (G) 974, (I) 1224
Epilepsy Foundation, (G) 976, 1097–1098
Episcopal Church Center, (F) 646
Ethel and Emery Fast Scholarship Foundation, Inc., (S) 180, (F) 651
Evergreen State College. Longhouse Education and Cultural Center, (G) 1057–1058
ExxonMobil Corporation, (S) 214, (F) 682
ExxonMobil Foundation, (S) 45
Eyak Corporation, (S) 182, (F) 655

Faegre & Benson LLP, (F) 656, (I) 1230
Federation of American Societies for Experimental Biology, (I) 1342
Fermi National Accelerator Laboratory, (F) 657
Finnegan, Henderson, Farabow, Garrett & Dunner, LLP, (F) 658, (I) 1232
First Americans in the Arts, (S) 183
Fish & Richardson P.C., (F) 661, (I) 1234
Five Colleges, Incorporated, (G) 988
Flandreau Santee Sioux Tribe, (S) 188, (F) 662
Flintco, Inc., (S) 189
Florida Governor's Council on Indian Affairs, (S) 190
Florida Library Association, (F) 665
Florida Society of Newspaper Editors, (S) 204, (I) 1238
Ford Foundation, (F) 830, 868, (G) 919, 989, 1057–1058, 1094, 1101, 1116
Ford Motor Company, (S) 193–194, 499, (F) 881, (I) 1349
Ford Motor Minority Dealers Association, (S) 191
Fordham University. Louis Calder Center Biological Field Station, (G) 935
Fort Peck Assiniboine and Sioux Tribes, (S) 195
Foundation for Child Development, (F) 832
Foundation for Digestive Health and Nutrition, (G) 913, 990, (A) 1151
Fox Television Stations, Inc., (I) 1223
Fredrikson & Byron Foundation, (F) 670, (I) 1237
Freedom Forum, (S) 97, (I) 1203
The Fund for Theological Education, Inc., (F) 801

Gannett Television, (I) 1223

Gay Indian Studies Association, (G) 998
Genentech BioOncology, (G) 1038
General Mills Foundation, (S) 207
General Motors Corporation, (S) 208, 210, (F) 675
General Motors Minority Dealers Association, (S) 209
Georgetown University. Law Center, (G) 995
Geraldine R. Dodge Foundation, (F) 592
Gerber Companies Foundation, (G) 997
Getty Foundation, (I) 1297
GMAC, (S) 347, (F) 772
Goldman Sachs, (F) 685
Goldman, Sachs & Company, (S) 217, (F) 684, (I) 1246–1247
Golf Course Superintendents Association of America, (S) 461, (I) 1329
Goodwin Procter LLP, (F) 686
Google Inc., (S) 7, (F) 545
Gordon and Betty Moore Foundation, (I) 1291
Government Finance Officers Association, (S) 332, (F) 762
Grand Portage Tribal Council, (S) 218, (F) 687
Grand Rapids Community Foundation, (S) 517
Grand Traverse Band of Ottawa and Chippewa Indians, (S) 219–220, (F) 688
Gravure Association of America, (S) 302

Harry J. Bosworth Company, (F) 763
Harter Secrest & Emery LLP, (I) 1249
Harvard Apparatus Foundation, (G) 1137
Harvard University. Medical School, (I) 1236, 1336
Harvard University. School of Public Health, (G) 1141, (I) 1250, 1339
Haskell Indian Nations University, (I) 1216
Hawai'i Community Foundation, (S) 62, 159, 224, 247, 390, (F) 587, 691, 706, 744
Hawaii. Department of Hawaiian Home Lands, (S) 224, (F) 691
Hawai'i Hotel & Lodging Association, (S) 115, 222
Hawaii. State Foundation on Culture and the Arts, (I) 1235
Hawaiian Civic Club of Honolulu, (S) 223, (F) 690
Henry J. Kaiser Family Foundation, (I) 1191, 1262
Hewlett–Packard Development Company, (S) 241
Hilton Hotels Corporation, (S) 230
Hispanic Association of Colleges and Universities, (I) 1216
Hispanic College Fund, (S) 352
Hispanic Scholarship Fund, (S) 205, 310, (F) 671
Hispanic Scholarship Fund Institute, (S) 254, (I) 1254
Ho-Chunk Nation, (S) 231–233, (F) 693–694, (A) 1154
Hoopa Valley Tribe, (S) 234–235, (F) 696
Hopi Tribe, (S) 170, 236–238, (F) 648, 697–698
Howard Hughes Medical Institute, (F) 699, (G) 1009, (I) 1291
Howard University, (I) 1191
HSBC North America, (S) 499, (F) 881, (I) 1349
Hualapai Nation Education Office, (S) 242–243, (F) 703
Huna Heritage Foundation, (S) 244–245, (F) 704
Hyatt Hotels & Resorts, (S) 246

IBM Corporation, (F) 705, (I) 1251
Idaho State Board of Education, (S) 248
Illinois Broadcasters Association, (I) 1252
Indian Summer Festivals, Inc., (S) 250–251, 293, 306, 435

S–Scholarships   F–Fellowships   G–Grants   A–Awards   I–Internships

SPONSORING ORGANIZATION INDEX

Indigenous Early Intervention Alliance, (S) 337, (F) 768
INROADS, Inc., (I) 1253, 1324
Institute for Diversity in Healthcare Management, (F) 879
Institute of Ecosystem Studies, (G) 941
Institute of Electrical and Electronics Engineers. Circuits and Systems Society, (S) 416
Institute of Industrial Engineers, (S) 505
Institute of Real Estate Management Foundation, (S) 213, (F) 679
Inter-Tribal Council of Michigan, Inc., (S) 326, (F) 758
International Franchise Association, (S) 333, (F) 669
International Interior Design Association, (S) 285
International Radio and Television Society Foundation, (A) 1169, (I) 1255
Intersociety Council for Pathology Information, Inc., (I) 1342
Intertribal Timber Council, (S) 491
Iowa Tribe of Oklahoma, (S) 256, (A) 1156

J. Robert Gladden Society, (F) 709
Jackie Robinson Foundation, (S) 55, 258
James D. Voelker Foundation, (S) 260, (F) 711
James M. Cox Foundation, (S) 347, (F) 772
Janssen Pharmaceutica Products, L.P., (G) 990
January, (G) 1048
JCPenney Company, Inc., (F) 663
Jerome Foundation, (G) 1028
Jicarilla Apache Tribe, (S) 379, (F) 800
John A. Hartford Foundation, (G) 1086
John Hopkins University. Applied Physics Laboratory, (I) 1187
John S. and James L. Knight Foundation, (S) 204, (I) 1238
Johns Hopkins University. Center for American Indian Health, (S) 363, (F) 568
Johnson & Johnson/Merck Consumer Pharmaceuticals, (G) 990
JPMorgan Chase, (S) 298, (F) 734, (I) 1267–1268
JPMorganChase, (S) 499, (F) 881, (I) 1349
Just the Beginning Foundation, (I) 1259
Juvenile Diabetes Research Foundation, (G) 911, 1016, 1020

Kaiser Permanente, (F) 781
Kaiser Permanente, Southern California, (F) 807
Katrin H. Lamon Endowment for Native American Art and Education., (G) 1021
Katten Muchin Rosenman LLP, (I) 1263
Kaw Nation, (S) 273–276, (F) 723
Kawerak, Inc., (S) 277–278
Ke Ali'i Pauahi Foundation, (S) 34, 69, 82, 101, 150–151, 154, 162, 172, 215, 223, 253, 259, 267–268, 346, 362, 454, (F) 589, 627–628, 632, 677, 683, 685, 690, 708, 710, 720, 771, 790, 848, (G) 934
Kenai Natives Association, (S) 279, (F) 724
Kenaitze Indian Tribe, (S) 280, (F) 725
Keweenaw Bay Indian Community–Lake Superior Band of Chippewa Indians, (S) 281–282
Kikiktagruk Inupiat Corporation, (S) 284
Kimball International, Inc., (S) 285
Kirkland Ellis LLP, (A) 1164, (I) 1264
Kirkpatrick & Lockhart Preston Gates Ellis LLP, (F) 727, (I) 1265

Koniag Incorporated, (S) 216, 287–290, 297, (F) 728, 732
The Kuskokwim Corporation, (S) 294, 482, (F) 729

Ladies Professional Golf Association, (S) 414
Lagrant Foundation, (S) 295, (F) 730
Laguna Education Foundation, (F) 731
Landscape Architecture Foundation, (S) 169
Lane Powell Spears Lubersky LLP, (F) 681, (I) 1243
Latham & Watkins LLP, (F) 733
Lawrence Livermore National Laboratory, (F) 804, (I) 1313
Lee & Low Books, (A) 1158
Leech Lake Band of Ojibwe, (S) 301
LeRoy C. Merritt Humanitarian Fund, (G) 1026
Library Systems & Services Inc., (F) 742
Lilly Endowment, Inc., (F) 801, (G) 987
Lloyd G. Balfour Foundation, (F) 584
Lockheed Martin Corporation, (S) 305
Los Alamos National Laboratory, (F) 804, (I) 1313
Los Angeles Times, (I) 1280
Louisiana Space Consortium, (G) 1023, (I) 1266
Louisville Institute, (G) 987
Lucent Technologies, (I) 1272

Maine Arts Commission, (I) 1273
Malcolm Pirnie Inc,, (S) 499, (F) 881, (I) 1349
Marathon Corporation, (S) 214, (F) 682
Marathon Oil Corporation, (S) 310, 499, (F) 881, (I) 1349
March, (S) 59
Marriott International, Inc., (S) 333
Maryland Sea Grant Program, (G) 1030, (I) 1274
Massachusetts Indian Association, (S) 316, (F) 750
Massachusetts Mutual Life Insurance Company, (F) 686
Massachusetts Office of Student Financial Assistance, (S) 317
Maui Community College, (S) 304, (F) 739
Mayo Clinic, (S) 65
McAndrews, Held & Malloy, Ltd., (F) 751
McDermott Will & Emery, (F) 752, (I) 1276
McKesson Foundation, (G) 931, (I) 1192, 1200
Medical Library Association, (F) 736, 753
Menominee Indian Tribe of Wisconsin, (S) 319–320
Mercer Human Resource Consulting LLC, (S) 321, (I) 1278
Mescalero Apache Tribe, (S) 323, (F) 755
Metropolitan Life Foundation, (F) 756
Metropolitan Museum of Art, (I) 1270, 1281–1282
Miami Nation, (S) 165, 345, 476, (F) 624
Miami University. Library, (G) 1035
Michael J. Berkeley Foundation, (S) 324
Michigan Indian Elders Association, (S) 325
Michigan Space Grant Consortium, (G) 1036
Microsoft Corporation, (S) 328, (I) 1285
Midwest Sociological Society, (F) 578
MIGIZI Communications, Inc., (S) 184, 307, 515, (F) 659, 890
Milbank, Tweed, Hadley & McCloy LLP, (F) 759
Mille Lacs Band of Ojibwe, (S) 329, (F) 760, (A) 1161
Milwaukee Indian Education Committee, (S) 250–251, 293, 306, 435
Minnesota Department of Education, (S) 181, (F) 652
Minnesota Office of Higher Education, (S) 331, (F) 761

S–Scholarships   F–Fellowships   G–Grants   A–Awards   I–Internships

Minority Access, Inc., (I) 1216, 1286
Minority Corporate Counsel Association, (F) 858
Minority Educational Foundation of the United States of America, (S) 25
Minority Nurse Magazine, (S) 334, (F) 766
Missouri Space Grant Consortium, (I) 1292–1293
Montana Guaranteed Student Loan Program, (S) 340, (F) 769
Montana Space Grant Consortium, (I) 1189
Morgan Stanley, (S) 341–342, 441, (F) 770, (I) 1294, 1326
Morongo Band of Mission Indians, (S) 445, (F) 842
Morris K. Udall Foundation, (S) 343, (I) 1295
Muscogee (Creek) Nation of Oklahoma, (S) 144–146, (F) 625
Mutual of Omaha, (S) 344, (I) 1298
MWH, (G) 1046

NANA Regional Corporation, (S) 38
National Action Council for Minorities in Engineering, (S) 348
National Association for Equal Opportunity in Higher Education, (I) 1216
National Association of Collegiate Directors of Athletics, (F) 715
National Association of Multicultural Engineering Program Advocates, Inc., (S) 351, 488
National Association of School Psychologists, (F) 775
National Association of Schools of Public Affairs and Administration, (F) 832
National Association of Social Workers, (F) 616
National Association of Student Personnel Administrators, (I) 1301
National Black MBA Association. St. Louis Chapter, (S) 475, (F) 869
National Caucus and Center on Black Aged, (G) 1052
National Center for American Indian Enterprise Development, (S) 27, (F) 558
National Center for Atmospheric Research, (I) 1331
National Center for Cooperative Education, (S) 353, (F) 776, (I) 1302
National Coalition of Ethnic Minority Nurse Associations, (S) 370, (F) 793
National Collegiate Athletic Association, (F) 777, (I) 1227
National Congress of American Indians, (S) 369, (I) 1303
National Consortium for Graduate Degrees for Minorities in Engineering and Science (GEM), (F) 672–674, (I) 1239–1241
National Council of Churches, (F) 801
National Council on Family Relations, (A) 1160
National Dental Association, (F) 640–642, 779–780
National FFA Organization, (S) 64, 79, 127, 296
National Football League Players Association, (S) 363
National Hispanic Council on Aging, (G) 1052
National Indian Council on Aging, (G) 1052
National Indian Education Association, (S) 264, (F) 714
National Indian Gaming Association, (S) 474, (F) 867
National Medical Fellowships, Inc., (F) 756, 781, 799, 903, (G) 931, 997, 1138, (A) 1153, 1173–1174, (I) 1192, 1200, 1305
National Minority Junior Golf Scholarship Association, (S) 55
National Native American Law Enforcement Association, (S) 354
National Native American Law Students Association, (A) 1164
National Optical Astronomy Observatories, (G) 1025

National Physical Science Consortium, (F) 804, (G) 1059, (I) 1313
National Press Club, (S) 176
National Research Council, (F) 830, (G) 989, 1010, 1094
National Science Foundation, (S) 42, 439, (F) 576, (G) 941, 994, 998–999, 1025, 1030, 1110, 1140, (I) 1242, 1244, 1271, 1274, 1291, 1321, 1328, 1331, 1338
National Science Foundation. Directorate for Biological Sciences, (G) 965, 972, 1039, 1096, 1102
National Science Foundation. Directorate for Computer and Information Science and Engineering, (G) 982, 1002, 1092, (I) 1350
National Science Foundation. Directorate for Education and Human Resources, (F) 806, (G) 983, 1076, (A) 1166
National Science Foundation. Directorate for Engineering, (G) 982, 1000, 1002, 1077–1078, 1092, 1095, (I) 1245, 1248, 1350
National Science Foundation. Directorate for Geosciences, (F) 634, (G) 943, 972, 1103
National Science Foundation. Directorate for Mathematical and Physical Sciences, (G) 930, 1130–1132, (I) 1351
National Science Foundation. Directorate for Social, Behavioral, and Economic Sciences, (G) 954, 972, 1007, 1039
National Science Foundation. Office of Polar Programs, (G) 926–927
National Society Daughters of the American Revolution, (S) 200–201
National Society of Professional Engineers, (S) 318
National Society of the Colonial Dames of America, (S) 249
National Strength and Conditioning Association, (F) 785
National Student Nurses' Association, (S) 65
National Urban Fellows, Inc., (F) 786
National Water Research Institute, (G) 923, 1046, 1079, 1107
National Weather Association, (S) 153, (F) 630
Native American Community Board. Native American Women's Health Education Resource Center, (S) 361, (I) 1310
Native American Finance Officers Association, (S) 358, (F) 787
Native American Health Education Fund, (S) 359, (F) 788
Native American Indian Education Association of New York, (S) 349
Native American Journalists Association, (S) 347, (F) 772–773, (I) 1348
Native American Public Broadcasting Consortium, Inc., (G) 1061
Native Hawaiian Chamber of Commerce, (S) 362, (F) 790
Native Village of Kotzebue–Kotzebue I.R.A., (S) 291–292
Native Vision, (S) 363
Native Writers Circle of the Americas, (A) 1159
Navajo Nation, (S) 95, 365–368, 502, 512, (F) 791–792, (G) 1063
Navy League of the United States, (S) 261
NBC, (I) 1223
New Jersey Library Association, (F) 797
New Jersey Space Grant Consortium, (I) 1311
The New York Bar Foundation, (I) 1207, 1322
New York State Bar Association. Commercial and Federal Litigation Section, (I) 1207
New York State Bar Association. Real Property Law Section, (I) 1322
New York State Education Department, (S) 371
Newberry Library, (G) 984, 991, 1003, 1121
Newsday, (I) 1279

S–Scholarships   F–Fellowships   G–Grants   A–Awards   I–Internships

SPONSORING ORGANIZATION INDEX

Nez Perce Tribe, (S) 372
Nihewan Foundation for Native American Education, (S) 374
Ninilchik Traditional Council, (S) 375, (F) 796
Nissan North America, Inc., (S) 377–378
Nordhaus Law Firm LLP, (A) 1164
North Carolina American Indian Fund, (S) 380
North Carolina Commission of Indian Affairs, (I) 1312
North Carolina Community Foundation, (S) 57
North Carolina State Education Assistance Authority, (S) 507
North Dakota University System, (S) 381
Northeast Consortium for Faculty Diversity, (G) 963
Northern Arapaho Tribe, (S) 15, 39–40, 58, 202, 373, 382–383, (F) 551, 571–572, 586, 668, 795, 861
Northern Cheyenne Nation, (S) 384–385, (F) 802
Northwest Advisory District Indian Education Office, (S) 360
Norton Sound Health Corporation, (S) 386, (F) 803
November, (S) 41, (F) 573
Nuclear Age Peace Foundation, (I) 1269
Nugget Construction, (S) 482

Oak Ridge Associated Universities, (G) 1080
Oak Ridge Institute for Science and Education, (S) 355, 389, (F) 783, (G) 960, 1080, (I) 1215, 1231, 1287, 1308–1309, 1315
Oak Ridge National Laboratory, (G) 1080
Occaneechi Band of the Saponi Nation, (S) 206
Ohio Science and Engineering Alliance, (G) 999, 1119, (I) 1244
Ohio State University. Libraries, (G) 1029
Oklahoma Youth Expo, (S) 88, 98
Omaha Presbyterian Seminary Foundation, (F) 745
Oneida Nation of Wisconsin, (S) 393, (F) 808
Online Computer Library Center, (F) 741
Oracle Corporation, (S) 499, (F) 881, (I) 1349
Oregon Community Foundation, (S) 510
Oregon Native American Chamber of Commerce, (S) 394
Oregon State Bar, (I) 1233, 1320
Organization of American Historians, (A) 1157
Ortho–McNeil Pharmaceutical Corporation, (G) 976, 1097–1098
Osage Nation Education Department, (S) 315, 395, (F) 749, 810
Osage Scholarship Fund, (S) 308, (F) 743
Osage Tribal Education Committee, (S) 396, (F) 811
Ottawa Tribe of Oklahoma, (S) 398, (F) 812
OTZ Telephone Cooperative, Inc., (S) 399
Ounalashka Corporation, (S) 168

Pacific Islanders in Communications, (S) 400, (F) 813, (G) 1083–1084
Pacific Northwest National Laboratory, (I) 1316
Pascua Yaqui Tribe, (S) 401, (F) 814
Patton Boggs LLP, (A) 1164
Pebble Limited Partnership., (S) 405
PEN American Center, (A) 1146
Penobscot Nation, (S) 407–408, (F) 820
Peoria Tribe of Indians of Oklahoma, (S) 409
Peter Doctor Memorial Indian Scholarship Foundation, Inc., (S) 411–412, (F) 821–822
Pew Charitable Trusts, (F) 868, (G) 1116
Pfizer Inc., (F) 553, (G) 976, 1089, 1097–1098
PGA of America, (S) 55

Phi Delta Phi International Legal Fraternity, (F) 584
Philanthrofund Foundation, (S) 225, (F) 692
Pinnacle West Capital Corporation, (S) 199
Playwrights' Center, (G) 1028
Poarch Band of Creek Indians, (S) 417
Pokagon Band of Potawatomi Indians, (S) 418–419, (F) 825
Ponca Tribe of Nebraska, (S) 420, (F) 826
Porter Wright Morris & Arthur LLP, (F) 828, (I) 1318
Prairie Band Potawatomi Nation, (S) 422–424, (F) 829
Presbyterian Church (USA), (S) 357, 480, (F) 789, 836
Prince Kuhio Hawaiian Civic Club, (S) 425, (F) 831
Private Colleges & Universities, Inc., (S) 426
Procter & Gamble Company, (F) 763
Professional Golfers' Association of America, (S) 427
Public Policy and International Affairs Fellowship Program, (F) 832
Public Relations Student Society of America, (S) 428
Pueblo of Acoma, (S) 429
Pueblo of Isleta, (S) 430, (F) 833
Pueblo of Jemez, (S) 431
Pueblo of Laguna, (S) 432
Pueblo of Ohkay Owingeh, (S) 391, 421, 492–494
Pueblo of Pojoaque, (S) 433, (F) 834
Pueblo of San Felipe, (S) 434
Pueblo of Zuni, (S) 538, (F) 907
Purina Mills, LLC, (S) 296
Pyramid Lake Paiute Tribe, (S) 436–437

Qivliq, LLC, (S) 38
Quality Education for Minorities (QEM) Network, (G) 1110, (I) 1321, 1328, 1338

Radio and Television News Directors Foundation, (F) 757, 805
Research Corporation, (A) 1152
Rhode Island Space Grant Consortium, (I) 1325
Richard (Yogi) Crowe Memorial Scholarship Fund, (F) 840
Robert Aqqaluk Newlin, Sr. Memorial Trust, (S) 38
Robert Toigo Foundation, (F) 841
Robert Wood Johnson Foundation, (G) 929, 1005, 1105
Roche Pharmaceuticals, (G) 990
Rochester City School District, (S) 94, (F) 604
Rockefeller Foundation, (G) 919
Rocky Mountain Indian Chamber of Commerce, (S) 122
RR Donnelley, (S) 499, (F) 881, (I) 1349

Sac and Fox Nation, (S) 450, (F) 844
Saint Paul Foundation, (S) 444, 496–497
Salamatof Native Association, Inc., (S) 451, (F) 846
Salt River Project, (S) 364
Samuel I. Newhouse Foundation, (S) 347, (F) 772
San Francisco Foundation, (G) 931, (I) 1192, 1200
Sandia National Laboratories, (F) 804, 847, (I) 1313
Santo Domingo Tribe, (S) 453
Sault Tribe of Chippewa Indians, (S) 52, 203, 212, 269, 311, 455–457, 511, (F) 678, 719
Scholarship Administrative Services, Inc., (S) 25
School for Advanced Research, (G) 977, 1106, 1108

S–Scholarships   F–Fellowships   G–Grants   A–Awards   I–Internships

SPONSORING ORGANIZATION INDEX

School of American Research, (G) 1021
Schwabe, Williamson & Wyatt, Attorneys at Law, (I) 1327
Scotts Company, (S) 461, (I) 1329
Scripps Howard Foundation, (F) 874, (G) 1124
Sealaska Corporation, (S) 75, 462–463, (F) 595, 850–851, (I) 1330
Seismological Society of America, (S) 214, (F) 682
Seldovia Native Association, Inc., (S) 470, (F) 862
Semiconductor Research Corporation, (F) 852
Seminole Nation of Oklahoma, (S) 500, 513, (F) 542, (A) 1155
Seneca Nation of Indians, (S) 255, 464, (F) 853
Shee Atiká, Incorporated, (S) 465, (F) 855
Shoshone Higher Education Program, (S) 466
Sioux Falls Area Community Foundation, (S) 192, 397
Sitka Tribe of Alaska, (S) 467–468, (F) 859
Sitnasuak Native Corporation, (S) 469, (F) 860
Smithsonian Institution. National Museum of Natural History, (G) 920
Smithsonian Institution. National Museum of the American Indian, (F) 782, 889, (G) 951, 1056, 1142, (I) 1307
Smithsonian Institution. Office of Research Training and Services, (G) 1043, 1062, 1113–1114, (I) 1256, 1332–1333
Society for Advancement of Chicanos and Native Americans in Science, (F) 845
Society for American Archaeology, (S) 42, (F) 576
Society for the Psychological Study of Social Issues, (I) 1213
Society for the Study of Social Problems, (G) 1115
Society of American Indian Government Employees, (S) 471, (F) 863–864
Society of Nuclear Medicine, (S) 327
Society of Women Engineers, (S) 48, 148, (F) 583, 626, 707
Sociologists for Women in Society, (F) 578, (G) 1139
South Dakota Department of Education, (S) 442
South Dakota Newspaper Association, (S) 143
Southern Regional Education Board, (F) 868, (G) 1116
Southwest Indian Agricultural Association, (S) 161, (F) 643
Southwestern Association for Indian Arts, Inc., (G) 1117, (A) 1168
Southwestern Sociological Association, (F) 578
Special Libraries Association, (F) 866
SpecPro Inc., (S) 473
Sprint Nextel, (S) 499, (F) 881, (I) 1349
St. Lawrence University, (G) 1017
St. Regis Mohawk Tribe, (S) 339
Standing Rock Sioux Tribe, (S) 478
Stanford University. Humanities Center, (G) 1118
Starr Foundation, (G) 1086
Student Conservation Association, Inc., (I) 1212, 1216
Sunstar Americas, Inc., (F) 763
Susan G. Komen Breast Cancer Foundation, (G) 933, 1120
Susan G. Komen for the Cure, (G) 928

Tanaina Corporation, (S) 279, (F) 724
Tanana Chiefs Conference, (S) 483, (F) 873
TAP Pharmaceuticals, Inc., (G) 990
Teck Cominco Limited, (S) 38
Texas Consortium in Behavioral Neuroscience, (G) 1091
Texas Historical Commission, (I) 1344
Texas Medical Association, (F) 875
Thompson Hine LLP, (I) 1346

Thomson West, (F) 676
Thurgood Marshall Scholarship Fund, (F) 858
Tiger Woods Foundation, (S) 55
Time Warner, (S) 484
TMA Systems, (S) 486
Tommy Hilfiger Corporate Foundation, (S) 16
Tonkawa Tribe of Oklahoma, (S) 487
Tonkon Torp LLP, (F) 877, (I) 1347
Townsend and Townsend and Crew LLP, (F) 878
Toyota Motor Sales, U.S.A., Inc., (G) 1117
Travel Industry Association of America, (S) 446
Triad Hospitals, Inc., (F) 879
Triangle Community Foundation, (S) 359, (F) 788
Triangle Native American Society, (S) 489
Tribune Corporation, (I) 1279–1280
Tulsa Library Trust, (A) 1149
Turner Entertainment Networks, (I) 1223
Turtle Mountain Band of Chippewa Indians, (S) 495, (F) 880
Tyonek Native Corporation, (S) 498

Unitarian Universalist Association, (F) 883
United Church of Christ, (F) 541, 838
United Indians of Virginia, (S) 501
United Methodist Church. Arkansas Conference, (F) 837
United Methodist Church. General Board of Discipleship, (S) 443
United Methodist Church. General Board of Global Ministries, (S) 156, (F) 637, 778
United Methodist Church. General Board of Higher Education and Ministry, (S) 221, 503, (F) 653, 689, 885–886
United Methodist Communications, (S) 303, (I) 1261
United Methodist Higher Education Foundation, (S) 504, (F) 884
United Negro College Fund, (S) 205, 499, (F) 671, 881, (I) 1349
United Negro College Fund Special Programs Corporation, (S) 254, 352, (G) 1047, (I) 1254, 1277, 1314
United Parcel Service of America, Inc., (S) 499, (F) 881, (I) 1349
United States Institute of Peace, (G) 1087, 1126
United States Tennis Association, (S) 164
United Utilities, Inc., (S) 506
Universities Space Research Association, (G) 1048, (I) 1300
University Corporation for Atmospheric Research, (I) 1331
University of California at Berkeley. Office of the Chancellor, (G) 944
University of California at Los Angeles. American Indian Studies Center, (G) 921
University of California at San Francisco. AIDS Research Institute, (F) 781
University of California at Santa Barbara. Library, (G) 1125
University of California. Office of the President, (G) 1127
University of Colorado at Boulder. Center for Environmental Journalism, (F) 874, (G) 1124
University of Colorado Cancer Center, (I) 1335
University of Iowa. Libraries, (G) 1128
University of Kentucky. Vice President for Research, (G) 1027
University of Michigan. Gerald R. Ford School of Public Policy, (G) 1101
University of Michigan. Office of the Associate Provost—Academic Affairs, (G) 1022

S—Scholarships   F—Fellowships   G—Grants   A—Awards   I—Internships

SPONSORING ORGANIZATION INDEX

University of Nebraska Press, (A) 1165
University of North Carolina at Chapel Hill. Office of the Vice Chancellor for Graduate Studies and Research, (G) 940
University of Rhode Island. Graduate School of Oceanography, (F) 634
University of Wisconsin at Madison. Institute for Research on Poverty, (G) 1013
University of Wisconsin at Madison. School of Education, (G) 1129
UPS Foundation, (S) 44, 505
U.S. Agency for Healthcare Research and Quality, (G) 1004
U.S. Air Force. Office of Scientific Research, (G) 955
U.S. Army. Medical Research and Materiel Command, (G) 939, 979, 1006, 1123
U.S. Army. Research Office, (G) 955, (I) 1323
U.S. Army. Sustainment Command, (I) 1352
U.S. Bureau of Indian Affairs, (S) 54, 99, 186–187, 280, 353, 436, 479, (F) 725, 776, 870, (I) 1302
U.S. Centers for Disease Control and Prevention, (G) 942, 1099
U.S. Central Intelligence Agency, (S) 81, (I) 1204
U.S. Coast Guard, (S) 121
U.S. Department of Agriculture. Cooperative State Research, Education, and Extension Service, (G) 1133
U.S. Department of Commerce. National Oceanic and Atmospheric Administration, (S) 355, (F) 783, (G) 1075, (I) 1308–1309, 1331
U.S. Department of Defense, (G) 956–957
U.S. Department of Defense. Missile Defense Agency, (G) 1044
U.S. Department of Education, (S) 304, (F) 739
U.S. Department of Education. Institute of Education Sciences, (G) 958
U.S. Department of Education. Office of Postsecondary Education, (S) 254, (I) 1254
U.S. Department of Education. Office of Special Education and Rehabilitative Services, (G) 958
U.S. Department of Energy, (S) 355, (F) 657, (I) 1215, 1277, 1309, 1331
U.S. Department of Energy. National Energy Technology Laboratory, (I) 1304
U.S. Department of Energy. Office of Biological and Environmental Research, (I) 1287
U.S. Department of Energy. Office of Civilian Radioactive Waste Management, (S) 389, (I) 1315
U.S. Department of Energy. Office of Fossil Energy, (G) 1008, (I) 1283
U.S. Department of Energy. Office of Science, (G) 925, 966–968, (I) 1229
U.S. Department of Homeland Security, (G) 959–960
U.S. Department of Housing and Urban Development, (G) 1010
U.S. Department of Justice. National Institute of Justice, (G) 1135
U.S. Department of Labor, (I) 1312
U.S. Department of State, (I) 1345
U.S. Department of the Interior, (I) 1216
U.S. Department of Transportation, (I) 1217, 1343
U.S. Department of Transportation. Federal Highway Administration, (S) 163, (F) 645, (G) 973, (I) 1222
U.S. Department of Transportation. Federal Transit Administration, (I) 1209
U.S. Department of Transportation. Research and Special Programs Administration, (G) 961
U.S. Environmental Protection Agency, (S) 179, (G) 975, (I) 1226
U.S. Federal Aviation Administration, (I) 1231
U.S. Food and Drug Administration, (G) 982, 1002, 1092, 1099, (I) 1350
U.S. Geological Survey, (I) 1356
U.S. Indian Health Service, (S) 226–227
U.S. National Aeronautics and Space Administration, (S) 352, 356, 360, (F) 784, (G) 1023, 1036, 1047–1050, 1060, (I) 1181, 1183, 1189, 1201, 1206, 1266, 1292–1293, 1299–1300, 1311, 1314, 1325, 1331, 1353
U.S. National Endowment for the Arts, (F) 592, (I) 1235
U.S. National Endowment for the Humanities, (F) 592, (G) 919, 985
U.S. National Institutes of Health, (G) 910, 1054, 1072, 1085, 1099, (I) 1250, 1337
U.S. National Institutes of Health. Fogarty International Center, (G) 972
U.S. National Institutes of Health. National Cancer Institute, (G) 936, 1033–1034, 1051, 1065–1067, (I) 1335
U.S. National Institutes of Health. National Center for Complementary and Alternative Medicine, (G) 1033–1034
U.S. National Institutes of Health. National Center for Research Resources, (G) 992, 1034
U.S. National Institutes of Health. National Eye Institute, (G) 1033
U.S. National Institutes of Health. National Heart, Lung, and Blood Institute, (G) 986, 1011, 1033, 1053, 1068, (I) 1193
U.S. National Institutes of Health. National Human Genome Research Institute, (G) 1034, 1055
U.S. National Institutes of Health. National Institute for Biomedical Imaging and Bioengineering, (G) 1033–1034, 1055
U.S. National Institutes of Health. National Institute of Allergy and Infectious Diseases, (G) 972, 1011, 1033–1034, 1055
U.S. National Institutes of Health. National Institute of Arthritis and Musculoskeletal and Skin Diseases, (G) 1011, 1033–1034
U.S. National Institutes of Health. National Institute of Biomedical Imaging and Bioengineering, (G) 981
U.S. National Institutes of Health. National Institute of Child Health and Human Development, (G) 981, 986, 1011, 1033–1034, 1055
U.S. National Institutes of Health. National Institute of Dental and Craniofacial Research, (G) 1011, 1033
U.S. National Institutes of Health. National Institute of Diabetes and Digestive and Kidney Diseases, (G) 986, 992, 1033–1034, 1071
U.S. National Institutes of Health. National Institute of Environmental Health Sciences, (G) 972, 986, 1011, 1033–1034, 1055, 1111
U.S. National Institutes of Health. National Institute of General Medical Sciences, (G) 972, 980, 986, 1014, 1033, 1045, (I) 1342
U.S. National Institutes of Health. National Institute of Mental Health, (F) 563, 635, 767, 882, (G) 964, 1011, 1031, 1033–1034, 1040, 1055, 1091
U.S. National Institutes of Health. National Institute of Neurological Disorders and Stroke, (F) 635, (G) 938, 949, 1011, 1033–1034, 1055, 1073, 1091
U.S. National Institutes of Health. National Institute of Nursing Research, (G) 1034, 1055, 1074

U.S. National Institutes of Health. National Institute on Aging, (G) 914, 1011, 1033–1034, 1055, 1086
U.S. National Institutes of Health. National Institute on Alcohol Abuse and Alcoholism, (G) 949, 1011, 1033–1034, 1055, 1069
U.S. National Institutes of Health. National Institute on Deafness and Other Communication Disorders, (G) 986, 1011, 1033–1034
U.S. National Institutes of Health. National Institute on Drug Abuse, (F) 563, 635, (G) 971, 1011, 1033–1034, 1055, 1070, 1091, (I) 1258
U.S. National Institutes of Health. National Library of Medicine, (F) 736, 798, (G) 1055
U.S. National Institutes of Health. Office of Dietary Supplements, (G) 1011, 1033–1034, 1071, 1086
U.S. National Park Service, (I) 1212
U.S. National Security Agency, (F) 804, 871, (I) 1313, 1334
U.S. Navy. Naval Research Laboratory, (G) 1064
U.S. Navy. Office of Naval Research, (G) 955, 994, 1081–1082, (I) 1242
U.S. Office of Personnel Management, (I) 1319
U.S. Substance Abuse and Mental Health Services Administration, (F) 566, (G) 924, 947, (I) 1257, 1288
Utah Navajo Trust Fund, (S) 508, (F) 887
Utah Sports Hall of Fame Foundation, (S) 509, (A) 1171

Vermont Space Grant Consortium, (S) 360
Veterans for Peace. Santa Fe Chapter, (S) 452

Wampanoag Tribe of Gay Head, (S) 516, (F) 891
Warner Norcross & Judd LLP, (S) 517
Washington Higher Education Coordinating Board, (S) 519, (F) 892
Washington Indian Gaming Association, (S) 518
Washington Library Media Association, (F) 718
Washington NASA Space Grant Consortium, (I) 1353
Washington Science Teachers Association, (S) 406
Washington State University. Graduate School, (G) 1134
Washoe Tribe, (S) 520–522, (F) 893–894
Weather Channel, (I) 1223
Wells Fargo Bank, (S) 524–525, (F) 896
Weyerhaueser, (S) 499, (F) 881, (I) 1349
White Earth Indian Reservation Tribal Council, (S) 526, (F) 897
Wildlife Conservation Society, (G) 1136
William and Flora Hewlett Foundation, (G) 919
William Randolph Hearst Foundation, (F) 801, (I) 1354
William T. Grant Foundation, (F) 832
William Townsend Porter Foundation, (F) 827
Williams College. Dean of the Faculty, (G) 993
Winnebago Tribe of Nebraska, (S) 527, (F) 899
Winners for Life Foundation, (S) 528
Winston & Strawn LLP, (F) 900
Wisconsin Center for Education Research, (G) 1129
Wisconsin Higher Educational Aids Board, (S) 530, (F) 902
Wisconsin Indian Education Association, (S) 529, (F) 901
Wisconsin Medical Society, (S) 32, (F) 565
W.K. Kellogg Foundation, (F) 903, (G) 1138
Womble Carlyle Sandridge & Rice, PLLC, (F) 904, (I) 1355

Women of the Evangelical Lutheran Church in America, (S) 19, (F) 554
Woodrow Wilson National Fellowship Foundation, (I) 1345
Woods Hole Marine Biological Laboratory, (G) 1137
Woods Hole Oceanographic Institution, (G) 994, 1140, (I) 1242, 1356
Wyandotte Nation of Oklahoma, (S) 4, 228
Wyeth Foundation for American Art, (F) 592
Wyeth–Ayerst Laboratories, (G) 990, (A) 1174

Xerox Corporation, (S) 533, (F) 905

Yakama Indian Nation, (S) 534–536, (F) 906, (A) 1175
Yukon Delta Fisheries Development Association, (S) 537

The 13th Regional Corporation, (S) 539, (F) 908

S–Scholarships   F–Fellowships   G–Grants   A–Awards   I–Internships

Residency Index

Some programs listed in this book are restricted to residents of a particular state, region, etc. Others are open to applicants wherever they may live. The Residency Index will help you pinpoint programs available only to residents in your area as well as programs that have no residency restrictions at all (these are listed under the term "United States"). To use this index, look up the geographic areas that apply to you (always check the listings under "United States"), jot down the entry numbers listed after the program types that interest you (scholarships, fellowships, etc.), and use those numbers to find the program descriptions in the directory. To help you in your search, we've provided some "see also" references in each index entry. Remember: the numbers cited here refer to program entry numbers, not to page numbers in the book.

Adair County, Oklahoma: **Scholarships,** 84, 440; **Fellowships,** 599. See also Oklahoma

Alameda County, California: **Fellowships,** 756. See also California

Alaska: **Scholarships,** 5–6, 9, 18, 38, 75, 102–103, 105, 158, 168, 244–245, 270, 280, 284, 291–292, 294, 375, 386, 462–463, 465, 467–469, 482–483, 485, 504, 506; **Fellowships,** 543, 546–547, 595, 605, 639, 680, 704, 712, 721, 725, 729, 796, 803, 850–851, 855, 859–860, 873, 876, 884; **Grants,** 946, 952, 955; **Internships,** 1180–1181, 1275, 1330. See also United States; names of specific cities

Alaska, regional: **Scholarships,** 10–14, 35–36, 41, 51, 66, 73, 104, 125, 155, 157, 182, 216, 277–278, 287–290, 297, 313, 399, 405, 473, 514, 525, 537; **Fellowships,** 549–550, 569, 573, 585, 593, 606, 638, 655, 728, 732, 748. See also Alaska

Albany, New York: **Fellowships,** 756. See also New York

American Samoa: **Scholarships,** 400; **Fellowships,** 813; **Grants,** 1083–1084. See also United States

Arizona: **Scholarships,** 71, 95, 170, 199, 236–238, 242–243, 365–368, 452; **Fellowships,** 648, 697–698, 703, 791–792; **Grants,** 1063; **Internships,** 1183. See also United States; names of specific cities and counties

Arizona, southern: **Scholarships,** 403. See also Arizona

Arkansas: **Fellowships,** 837; **Grants,** 955. See also Southern states; United States; names of specific cities and counties

Atlanta, Georgia: **Fellowships,** 756. See also Georgia

Aurora, Illinois: **Fellowships,** 756. See also Illinois

Austin, Texas: **Fellowships,** 756. See also Texas

Baraga County, Michigan: **Scholarships,** 282. See also Michigan

Benton County, Arkansas: **Scholarships,** 84; **Fellowships,** 599. See also Arkansas

Boston, Massachusetts: **Fellowships,** 756. See also Massachusetts

California: **Scholarships,** 23, 71, 160, 300, 445, 520–522; **Fellowships,** 552, 556, 611, 737, 842, 893–894; **Awards,** 1147. See also United States; names of specific cities and counties

Canada: **Scholarships,** 42, 52, 70, 328, 332, 336, 374, 438, 505; **Fellowships,** 541, 548, 560, 576–577, 596, 701, 741–742, 746, 753, 762, 782, 801, 835, 866; **Grants,** 913, 937, 948, 950–951, 987, 990, 1012, 1016, 1019, 1038, 1056, 1142; **Awards,** 1143, 1151; **Internships,** 1177, 1285. See also Foreign countries

Central America: **Grants,** 951, 1056, 1142. See also Foreign countries; names of specific countries

Cherokee County, Kansas: **Scholarships,** 84; **Fellowships,** 599. See also Kansas

Cherokee County, North Carolina: **Scholarships,** 410. See also North Carolina

Cherokee County, Oklahoma: **Scholarships,** 84, 440; **Fellowships,** 599. See also Oklahoma

Chicago, Illinois: **Fellowships,** 756. See also Illinois

Clay County, North Carolina: **Scholarships,** 410. See also North Carolina

Cleveland County, Oklahoma: **Scholarships,** 112–113. See also Oklahoma

Colorado: **Scholarships,** 71, 122, 199; **Internships,** 1206. See also United States; names of specific cities and counties

Connecticut, southern: **Fellowships,** 756. See also United States

Coos County, Oregon: **Scholarships,** 139. See also Oregon

Craig County, Oklahoma: **Scholarships,** 84, 440; **Fellowships,** 599. See also Oklahoma

Crawford County, Arkansas: **Scholarships,** 84; **Fellowships,** 599. See also Arkansas

Curry County, Oregon: **Scholarships,** 139. See also Oregon

Dallas, Texas: **Fellowships,** 756. See also Texas

Dayton, Ohio: **Fellowships,** 756. See also United States

Delaware: **Grants,** 955. *See also* Southern states; United States; names of specific cities and counties
Delaware County, Oklahoma: **Scholarships,** 84, 440; **Fellowships,** 599. *See also* Oklahoma
Denver, Colorado: **Fellowships,** 756. *See also* Colorado
Douglas County, Oregon: **Scholarships,** 139. *See also* Oregon

Ferry County, Washington: **Scholarships,** 80. *See also* Washington
Florida: **Scholarships,** 59, 190; **Fellowships,** 665. *See also* Southern states; United States; names of specific cities and counties
Foreign countries: **Scholarships,** 8; **Fellowships,** 645, 699; **Grants,** 911, 917, 933, 965, 973, 1009, 1020, 1072, 1085, 1087–1088, 1120, 1126, 1136, 1139; **Awards,** 1146; **Internships,** 1222, 1228. *See also* names of specific continents; names of specific countries
Fort Worth, Texas: **Fellowships,** 756. *See also* Texas
Fremont County, Wyoming: **Scholarships,** 382. *See also* Wyoming

Georgia: **Scholarships,** 190; **Internships,** 1186. *See also* Southern states; United States; names of specific cities and counties
Graham County, North Carolina: **Scholarships,** 410. *See also* North Carolina
Greenville, South Carolina: **Fellowships,** 756. *See also* South Carolina
Guam: **Scholarships,** 310, 400; **Fellowships,** 813; **Grants,** 1083–1084. *See also* United States

Harbor City, California. *See* Los Angeles, California
Haskell County, Oklahoma: **Scholarships,** 84; **Fellowships,** 599. *See also* Oklahoma
Hawaii: **Scholarships,** 34, 62, 115, 159, 162, 167, 215, 222–223, 247, 259, 304, 346, 400, 425, 454; **Fellowships,** 587, 647, 683, 685, 690, 706, 708, 710, 720, 739, 744, 771, 813, 831, 848; **Grants,** 955, 1083–1084; **Internships,** 1235. *See also* United States; names of specific cities and counties
Hollywood, California. *See* Los Angeles, California
Hot Springs County, Wyoming: **Scholarships,** 382. *See also* Wyoming
Houghton County, Michigan: **Scholarships,** 282. *See also* Michigan
Houston, Texas: **Fellowships,** 756. *See also* Texas

Idaho: **Scholarships,** 248; **Grants,** 955. *See also* United States; names of specific cities and counties
Illinois: **Internships,** 1252. *See also* United States; names of specific cities and counties

Jackson County, North Carolina: **Scholarships,** 410. *See also* North Carolina
Jackson County, Oregon: **Scholarships,** 139. *See also* Oregon
Josephine County, Oregon: **Scholarships,** 139. *See also* Oregon

Kansas: **Scholarships,** 71; **Grants,** 955. *See also* United States; names of specific cities and counties
Kentucky: **Grants,** 955. *See also* Southern states; United States; names of specific cities and counties
Klamath County, Oregon: **Scholarships,** 139. *See also* Oregon

Labette County, Kansas: **Scholarships,** 84; **Fellowships,** 599. *See also* Kansas
Lane County, Oregon: **Scholarships,** 139. *See also* Oregon
Latin America. *See* Central America; Mexico; South America
Le Flore County, Oklahoma: **Scholarships,** 84; **Fellowships,** 599. *See also* Oklahoma
Lincoln County, Oklahoma: **Scholarships,** 112–113. *See also* Oklahoma
Long Island, New York: **Fellowships,** 756. *See also* New York
Los Angeles, California: **Fellowships,** 756. *See also* California
Los Angeles County, California: **Internships,** 1297. *See also* California
Louisiana: **Grants,** 1023; **Internships,** 1266. *See also* Southern states; United States; names of specific cities and parishes

Macon County, North Carolina: **Scholarships,** 410. *See also* North Carolina
Maine: **Scholarships,** 407–408; **Fellowships,** 820; **Grants,** 955; **Internships,** 1273. *See also* United States; names of specific cities and counties
Marin County, California: **Fellowships,** 756. *See also* California
Marquette County, Michigan: **Scholarships,** 282. *See also* Michigan
Massachusetts: **Scholarships,** 317. *See also* United States; names of specific cities and counties
Mayes County, Oklahoma: **Scholarships,** 84, 440; **Fellowships,** 599. *See also* Oklahoma
McDonald County, Missouri: **Scholarships,** 84; **Fellowships,** 599. *See also* Missouri
McIntosh County, Oklahoma: **Scholarships,** 84, 440; **Fellowships,** 599. *See also* Oklahoma
Mexico: **Scholarships,** 328, 505; **Grants,** 948, 951, 1016, 1019, 1056, 1142; **Internships,** 1285. *See also* Foreign countries
Miami, Florida: **Fellowships,** 756. *See also* Florida
Michigan: **Scholarships,** 203, 212, 260, 269, 281, 311, 326, 455, 511, 517; **Fellowships,** 678, 711, 719, 758; **Grants,** 1036. *See also* United States; names of specific cities and counties
Minnesota: **Scholarships,** 63, 71, 178, 181, 218, 225, 301, 329, 331, 444, 496–497; **Fellowships,** 588, 652, 687, 692, 760–761; **Grants,** 1028; **Awards,** 1161. *See also* United States; names of specific cities and counties
Missouri: **Internships,** 1292–1293. *See also* United States; names of specific cities and counties
Montana: **Scholarships,** 60–61, 71, 128, 195, 340, 384–385, 495; **Fellowships,** 614, 769, 802, 880; **Grants,** 955, 980;

RESIDENCY INDEX

Internships, 1189. *See also* United States; names of specific cities and counties
Montgomery County, Kansas: **Scholarships,** 84; **Fellowships,** 599. *See also* Kansas
Moody County, South Dakota: **Scholarships,** 188; **Fellowships,** 662. *See also* South Dakota
Muskogee County, Oklahoma: **Scholarships,** 84, 440; **Fellowships,** 599. *See also* Oklahoma

Nebraska: **Grants,** 955. *See also* United States; names of specific cities and counties
Nevada: **Scholarships,** 520–522; **Fellowships,** 893–894; **Grants,** 955. *See also* United States; names of specific cities
New Hampshire: **Grants,** 955. *See also* United States; names of specific cities and counties
New Jersey: **Fellowships,** 797; **Internships,** 1311. *See also* United States; names of specific cities and counties
New Jersey, central: **Fellowships,** 756. *See also* New Jersey
New Jersey, northern: **Fellowships,** 756. *See also* New Jersey
New Mexico: **Scholarships,** 71, 95, 173, 199, 323, 365–368, 379, 387, 391, 421, 429–434, 452–453, 492–494, 512, 538; **Fellowships,** 731, 755, 791–792, 800, 833–834, 907; **Grants,** 1063. *See also* United States; names of specific cities and counties
New York: **Scholarships,** 94, 339, 349, 371, 392, 411–412, 415, 464; **Fellowships,** 604, 821–822, 824, 853; **Internships,** 1195. *See also* United States; names of specific cities and counties
New York, New York: **Fellowships,** 756. *See also* New York
New York, southern: **Fellowships,** 756. *See also* New York
New York, western: **Scholarships,** 70. *See also* New York
North Carolina: **Scholarships,** 57, 380, 489, 507; **Fellowships,** 840; **Internships,** 1312. *See also* Southern states; United States; names of specific cities and counties
North Dakota: **Scholarships,** 71, 381, 478, 495; **Fellowships,** 880; **Grants,** 955. *See also* United States; names of specific cities
Northern Marianas: **Scholarships,** 400; **Fellowships,** 813; **Grants,** 1083–1084. *See also* United States
Nowata County, Oklahoma: **Scholarships,** 84, 440; **Fellowships,** 599. *See also* Oklahoma

Okanogan County, Washington: **Scholarships,** 80. *See also* Washington
Oklahoma: **Scholarships,** 71, 86, 88, 96, 98–100, 114, 123–124, 144–146, 165, 189, 256, 273–276, 308, 315, 345, 395–396, 398, 409, 476, 486–487, 500, 513; **Fellowships,** 542, 600, 624–625, 723, 743, 749, 810–812, 837; **Grants,** 955; **Awards,** 1155–1156. *See also* Southern states; United States; names of specific cities and counties
Oklahoma County, Oklahoma: **Scholarships,** 112–113. *See also* Oklahoma
Ontonagon County, Michigan: **Scholarships,** 282. *See also* Michigan
Oregon: **Scholarships,** 71, 510; **Internships,** 1233, 1320. *See also* United States; names of specific cities and counties
Oregon, northeastern: **Scholarships,** 129; **Fellowships,** 615. *See also* Oregon
Osage County, Oklahoma: **Scholarships,** 84; **Fellowships,** 599. *See also* Oklahoma
Ottawa County, Oklahoma: **Scholarships,** 84, 440; **Fellowships,** 599. *See also* Oklahoma

Pacific Islands: **Scholarships,** 400; **Fellowships,** 813; **Grants,** 1083–1084. *See also* Foreign countries; names of specific islands
Payne County, Oklahoma: **Scholarships,** 112–113. *See also* Oklahoma
Philadelphia, Pennsylvania: **Fellowships,** 756. *See also* United States
Phoenix, Arizona: **Fellowships,** 756. *See also* Arizona
Pittsburg County, Oklahoma: **Scholarships,** 84; **Fellowships,** 599. *See also* Oklahoma
Pittsburgh, Pennsylvania: **Fellowships,** 756. *See also* United States
Pottawatomie County, Oklahoma: **Scholarships,** 112–113. *See also* Oklahoma
Providence, Rhode Island: **Fellowships,** 756. *See also* Rhode Island
Puerto Rico: **Scholarships,** 310, 352; **Grants,** 955. *See also* United States

Rensselaer, New York: **Fellowships,** 756. *See also* New York
Rhode Island: **Grants,** 955; **Internships,** 1325. *See also* United States; names of specific cities
Rogers County, Oklahoma: **Scholarships,** 84, 440; **Fellowships,** 599. *See also* Oklahoma

Samoa. *See* American Samoa
San Francisco, California: **Fellowships,** 756. *See also* California
San Juan County, Utah: **Scholarships,** 508; **Fellowships,** 887. *See also* Utah
San Mateo County, California: **Fellowships,** 756. *See also* California
San Pedro, California. *See* Los Angeles, California
Scranton, Pennsylvania: **Fellowships,** 756. *See also* United States
Sequoyah County, Oklahoma: **Scholarships,** 84, 440; **Fellowships,** 599. *See also* Oklahoma
South America: **Grants,** 951, 1056, 1142. *See also* Foreign countries; names of specific countries
South Carolina: **Grants,** 955. *See also* Southern states; United States; names of specific cities and counties
South Dakota: **Scholarships,** 71, 186, 192, 397, 442, 478; **Grants,** 955. *See also* United States; names of specific cities and counties
Southern states: **Fellowships,** 868; **Grants,** 1116. *See also* United States; names of specific states
St. Louis, Missouri: **Scholarships,** 475; **Fellowships,** 756. *See also* Missouri
St. Petersburg, Florida: **Fellowships,** 756. *See also* Florida
Sunland, California. *See* Los Angeles, California
Swain County, North Carolina: **Scholarships,** 410. *See also* North Carolina

Tampa, Florida: **Fellowships,** 756. *See also* Florida

RESIDENCY INDEX

Tennessee: **Grants,** 955. *See also* Southern states; United States; names of specific cities and counties

Texas: **Internships,** 1344. *See also* Southern states; United States; names of specific cities and counties

Tujunga, California. *See* Los Angeles, California

Tulsa County, Oklahoma: **Scholarships,** 84, 440; **Fellowships,** 599. *See also* Oklahoma

Tulsa, Oklahoma: **Fellowships,** 756. *See also* Oklahoma

United States: **Scholarships,** 1–4, 7–8, 15–17, 19–22, 25–33, 37, 39–40, 42–50, 52–56, 58, 60, 63–65, 67–69, 72, 74, 76–79, 81–83, 85, 87, 89–93, 95–97, 99–101, 106–111, 116–121, 124, 126–127, 129–138, 140–154, 156, 161, 163–166, 169–177, 179–180, 183–185, 187, 189, 191, 193–194, 196–198, 200–202, 204–211, 213–215, 217, 219–221, 224, 226–243, 246, 249, 252–255, 257–258, 260–268, 270–273, 276, 279, 283, 285–286, 295–296, 298–299, 302–305, 307–312, 314–316, 318–325, 327–328, 330, 332–338, 341–348, 350–359, 361–370, 372–374, 376–379, 383–385, 388–391, 393–396, 398, 401–402, 404, 406–408, 413–414, 416–428, 430–433, 436–439, 441, 443, 446–451, 453, 456–461, 464, 466–467, 470–472, 474–477, 479–481, 484–486, 488, 490–495, 498–499, 502–505, 511, 515–516, 520–524, 526–528, 531–536, 538–539; **Fellowships,** 540–541, 544–545, 548, 551, 553–555, 558–568, 570–572, 574–584, 586, 588–592, 594, 596–598, 601–603, 607–610, 612–613, 615–637, 640–646, 648–651, 653–654, 656–661, 663–664, 666–677, 679, 681–686, 688–689, 691, 693–703, 705, 707–709, 711, 713–717, 721–724, 726–727, 730–731, 733–736, 738–743, 745–747, 749–755, 757, 759, 762–768, 770–795, 798–802, 804–812, 814–820, 823, 825–836, 838–839, 841, 843–847, 849, 852–854, 856–858, 861–867, 869–872, 874–886, 888–891, 893–900, 903–908; **Grants,** 909–945, 947–951, 953–954, 956–979, 981–1022, 1024–1027, 1029–1035, 1037–1082, 1085–1115, 1117–1142; **Awards,** 1143–1146, 1148–1154, 1157–1160, 1162–1170, 1172–1175; **Internships,** 1176–1179, 1182, 1184–1185, 1187–1188, 1190–1205, 1207–1232, 1234, 1236–1251, 1253–1265, 1267–1272, 1274, 1276–1291, 1294–1310, 1313–1315, 1317–1319, 1321–1324, 1326–1329, 1331–1343, 1345–1352, 1354–1356. *See also* names of specific cities, counties, states, and regions

Utah: **Scholarships,** 199, 509; **Awards,** 1171. *See also* United States; names of specific cities and counties

Utica, New York: **Fellowships,** 756. *See also* New York

Vermont: **Scholarships,** 360; **Grants,** 955. *See also* United States; names of specific cities and counties

Virgin Islands: **Scholarships,** 310; **Grants,** 955. *See also* United States

Virginia: **Scholarships,** 501. *See also* Southern states; United States; names of specific cities and counties

Wagoner County, Oklahoma: **Scholarships,** 84, 440; **Fellowships,** 599. *See also* Oklahoma

Warwick, Rhode Island: **Fellowships,** 756. *See also* Rhode Island

Washington: **Scholarships,** 71, 406, 518–519, 534–536; **Fellowships,** 718, 892, 906; **Awards,** 1175; **Internships,** 1353. *See also* United States; names of specific cities and counties

Washington County, Arkansas: **Scholarships,** 84; **Fellowships,** 599. *See also* Arkansas

Washington County, Oklahoma: **Scholarships,** 84, 440; **Fellowships,** 599. *See also* Oklahoma

Washington, regional: **Internships,** 1316. *See also* Washington

Washington, southeastern: **Scholarships,** 129; **Fellowships,** 615. *See also* Washington

West Virginia: **Grants,** 955. *See also* Southern states; United States; names of specific cities

Wilmington, California. *See* Los Angeles, California

Wisconsin: **Scholarships,** 24, 32, 250–251, 260, 293, 306, 319–320, 393, 435, 529–530; **Fellowships,** 557, 565, 711, 808, 901–902. *See also* United States; names of specific cities and counties

Wyoming: **Scholarships,** 15, 39–40, 58, 202, 373, 383, 466; **Fellowships,** 551, 571–572, 586, 668, 795, 861; **Grants,** 955. *See also* United States; names of specific cities and counties

Tenability Index

Some programs listed in this book can be used only in specific cities, counties, states, or regions. Others may be used anywhere in the United States (or even abroad). The Tenability Index will help you locate funding that is restricted to a specific area as well as funding that has no tenability restrictions (these are listed under the term "United States"). To use this index, look up the geographic areas where you'd like to go (always check the listings under "United States," since those funds can be used anywhere in the country), jot down the entry numbers listed after the program types (scholarships, fellowships, etc.) that interest you, and use those numbers to find the program descriptions in the directory. To help you in your search, we've provided some "see also" references in each index entry. Remember: the numbers cited here refer to program entry numbers, not to page numbers in the book.

Africa: **Grants,** 1136. See also Foreign countries; names of specific countries
Aiken, South Carolina: **Internships,** 1287. See also South Carolina
Alameda County, California: **Fellowships,** 756. See also California
Alaska: **Scholarships,** 10–14, 36, 38, 105, 125, 245, 278, 288, 290–292, 375, 468, 537; **Fellowships,** 550, 680, 796, 859; **Grants,** 946, 952, 955; **Internships,** 1181, 1205, 1275, 1330. See also United States; names of specific cities
Albany, New York: **Fellowships,** 756. See also New York
Albany, Oregon: **Internships,** 1283. See also Oregon
Albuquerque, New Mexico: **Scholarships,** 147; **Fellowships,** 804, 847; **Internships,** 1211, 1313. See also New Mexico
Allentown, Pennsylvania: **Internships,** 1279–1280. See also Pennsylvania
American Samoa: **Grants,** 1083–1084. See also United States
Ames, Iowa: **Scholarships,** 127; **Internships,** 1287. See also United States
Amherst, Massachusetts: **Grants,** 988. See also Massachusetts
Anchorage, Alaska: **Scholarships,** 504; **Fellowships,** 884; **Internships,** 1180. See also Alaska
Ann Arbor, Michigan: **Scholarships,** 166; **Fellowships,** 598, 684, 903; **Grants,** 1022, 1101, 1138; **Internships,** 1202, 1221, 1246, 1341. See also Michigan
Antarctica: **Grants,** 926. See also Foreign countries
Arctic region: **Grants,** 927. See also Foreign countries; names of specific countries
Argonne, Illinois: **Grants,** 925; **Internships,** 1225, 1229, 1283, 1287. See also Illinois
Arizona: **Grants,** 1025; **Internships,** 1183. See also United States; names of specific cities and counties
Arkansas: **Grants,** 955. See also Southern states; United States; names of specific cities and counties
Arlington, Virginia: **Internships,** 1179. See also Virginia
Armonk, New York: **Grants,** 935. See also New York

Asia: **Grants,** 1136. See also Foreign countries; names of specific countries
Athens, Georgia: **Fellowships,** 904; **Internships,** 1355. See also Georgia
Atlanta, Georgia: **Scholarships,** 166; **Fellowships,** 598, 658, 745, 756, 809, 904; **Grants,** 960; **Internships,** 1179, 1186, 1202, 1221, 1232, 1306, 1346, 1355. See also Georgia
Aurora, Illinois: **Fellowships,** 756. See also Illinois
Austin, Texas: **Fellowships,** 598, 745, 756, 809; **Internships,** 1202. See also Texas

Baltimore, Maryland: **Scholarships,** 241; **Fellowships,** 568, 903; **Grants,** 960, 1138; **Internships,** 1279–1280, 1337. See also Maryland
Baton Rouge, Louisiana: **Scholarships,** 166; **Internships,** 1221. See also Louisiana
Berkeley, California: **Grants,** 944, 1127; **Internships,** 1229, 1283, 1287. See also California
Bethesda, Maryland: **Grants,** 981, 1053, 1081–1082; **Internships,** 1193, 1337. See also Maryland
Big Rapids, Michigan: **Scholarships,** 427. See also Michigan
Bloomington, Indiana: **Fellowships,** 598; **Internships,** 1190, 1202, 1341. See also United States
Boston, Massachusetts: **Fellowships,** 752, 756, 903; **Grants,** 1056, 1138, 1141; **Internships,** 1236, 1250, 1276, 1336, 1339. See also Massachusetts
Boulder, Colorado: **Fellowships,** 874; **Grants,** 960, 1124; **Internships,** 1331. See also Colorado
Brunswick, Maine: **Grants,** 1041–1042. See also Maine
Bryn Mawr, Pennsylvania: **Grants,** 1041–1042. See also Pennsylvania
Buies Creek, North Carolina: **Scholarships,** 427. See also North Carolina

Tenability Index

California: **Scholarships,** 23, 160, 241, 300; **Fellowships,** 552, 556, 611, 737; **Grants,** 931; **Awards,** 1147; **Internships,** 1192, 1200–1201. *See also* United States; names of specific cities and counties

California, northern: **Fellowships,** 752; **Internships,** 1276. *See also* California

Cambridge, Massachusetts: **Scholarships,** 166; **Fellowships,** 658, 684; **Internships,** 1221, 1232, 1246. *See also* Massachusetts

Canada: **Scholarships,** 42, 52, 70, 328, 332, 336, 374, 438, 505; **Fellowships,** 541, 548, 560, 576–577, 596, 701, 741–742, 746, 753, 762, 782, 801, 835, 866; **Grants,** 913, 937, 948, 950–951, 987, 990, 1012, 1016, 1019, 1038, 1090, 1142; **Awards,** 1143, 1151; **Internships,** 1285. *See also* Foreign countries

Canton, New York: **Grants,** 1017. *See also* New York

Cape Canaveral, Florida: **Grants,** 1048. *See also* Florida

Carlisle, Pennsylvania: **Grants,** 1041–1042. *See also* Pennsylvania

Casper, Wyoming: **Internships,** 1283. *See also* Wyoming

Cedar Rapids, Iowa: **Grants,** 1041–1042. *See also* United States

Central America: **Grants,** 951, 1136, 1142. *See also* Foreign countries; names of specific countries

Champaign, Illinois: **Scholarships,** 127, 166; **Grants,** 960; **Internships,** 1221, 1341. *See also* Illinois

Chapel Hill, North Carolina: **Fellowships,** 598, 904; **Grants,** 940; **Internships,** 1202, 1355. *See also* North Carolina

Charleston, West Virginia: **Fellowships,** 633; **Internships,** 1219. *See also* West Virginia

Charlotte, North Carolina: **Grants,** 960. *See also* North Carolina

Charlottesville, Virginia: **Fellowships,** 598, 904; **Internships,** 1202, 1355. *See also* Virginia

Chicago, Illinois: **Scholarships,** 166; **Fellowships,** 591, 684, 745, 752, 756; **Grants,** 984, 991, 1003, 1024, 1093, 1121; **Internships,** 1177, 1199, 1221, 1246, 1260, 1263, 1276, 1279–1280, 1340–1341. *See also* Illinois

Chile: **Grants,** 1025. *See also* Foreign countries; South America

China Lake, California: **Grants,** 1081–1082. *See also* California

Cincinnati, Ohio: **Fellowships,** 633; **Internships,** 1219, 1346. *See also* Ohio

Claremont, California: **Grants,** 1041–1042. *See also* California

Clemson, South Carolina: **Scholarships,** 302, 427. *See also* South Carolina

Cleveland, Ohio: **Scholarships,** 166; **Grants,** 1048–1049; **Internships,** 1221, 1299–1300, 1346. *See also* Ohio

Clinton, New York: **Grants,** 1041–1042. *See also* New York

Cocoa Beach, Florida: **Grants,** 1081–1082. *See also* Florida

College Park, Maryland: **Grants,** 960. *See also* Maryland

College Station, Texas: **Grants,** 960. *See also* Texas

Colorado: **Scholarships,** 122, 241; **Internships,** 1206, 1335. *See also* United States; names of specific cities and counties

Colorado Springs, Colorado: **Scholarships,** 427; **Grants,** 1041–1042. *See also* Colorado

Columbia, South Carolina: **Fellowships,** 904; **Internships,** 1355. *See also* South Carolina

Columbus, Ohio: **Scholarships,** 166; **Fellowships,** 633; **Grants,** 1029; **Internships,** 1219, 1221, 1341, 1346. *See also* Ohio

Connecticut: **Internships,** 1210. *See also* New England states; Northeastern states; United States; names of specific cities and counties

Connecticut, regional: **Internships,** 1184. *See also* Connecticut

Conway, South Carolina: **Scholarships,** 427. *See also* South Carolina

Crane, Indiana: **Internships,** 1352. *See also* United States

Dahlgren, Virginia: **Grants,** 1081–1082. *See also* Virginia

Dallas, Texas: **Fellowships,** 756; **Internships,** 1260. *See also* Texas

Danville, Kentucky: **Grants,** 1041–1042. *See also* Kentucky

Davis, California: **Grants,** 960, 1127. *See also* California

Dayton, Ohio: **Fellowships,** 633, 756; **Grants,** 1081–1082; **Internships,** 1219, 1346. *See also* Ohio

Dearborn, Michigan: **Scholarships,** 166; **Internships,** 1221. *See also* Michigan

Decatur, Georgia: **Fellowships,** 745. *See also* Georgia

Decorah, Iowa: **Grants,** 1041–1042. *See also* United States

DeKalb, Illinois: **Scholarships,** 166; **Internships,** 1221. *See also* Illinois

Delaware: **Grants,** 955. *See also* Northeastern states; Southern states; United States; names of specific cities and counties

Denver, Colorado: **Fellowships,** 756. *See also* Colorado

Detroit, Michigan: **Scholarships,** 166; **Internships,** 1221, 1337. *See also* Michigan

District of Columbia. *See* Washington, D.C.

Dubuque, Iowa: **Fellowships,** 745. *See also* United States

Durham, North Carolina: **Scholarships,** 439; **Fellowships,** 684, 904; **Internships,** 1246, 1355. *See also* North Carolina

East Lansing, Michigan: **Scholarships,** 166; **Grants,** 960; **Internships,** 1221, 1341. *See also* Michigan

Edmond, Oklahoma: **Scholarships,** 427. *See also* Oklahoma

Edwards, California: **Grants,** 1048–1049; **Internships,** 1299–1300. *See also* California

Egypt: **Scholarships,** 336. *See also* Africa; Foreign countries

Evanston, Illinois: **Scholarships,** 166; **Fellowships,** 684; **Internships,** 1221, 1246, 1341. *See also* Illinois

Fargo, North Dakota: **Scholarships,** 127; **Grants,** 960. *See also* North Dakota

Fayetteville, North Carolina: **Scholarships,** 427. *See also* North Carolina

Florida: **Scholarships,** 190, 204; **Fellowships,** 665; **Internships,** 1196, 1238. *See also* Southern states; United States; names of specific cities and counties

Foreign countries: **Scholarships,** 254; **Fellowships,** 806; **Grants,** 911, 917, 930, 933, 972, 986, 1020, 1039, 1049, 1094, 1096, 1103, 1120; **Awards,** 1146; **Internships,** 1179, 1254, 1299, 1345. *See also* names of specific continents; names of specific countries

Fort Lauderdale, Florida: **Internships,** 1279–1280. *See also* Florida

Fort Meade, Maryland: **Fellowships,** 804, 871; **Internships,** 1313, 1334. *See also* Maryland

Fort Myers, Florida: **Scholarships,** 427. *See also* Florida

TENABILITY INDEX

Fort Worth, Texas: **Fellowships,** 756. *See also* Texas
Frederick, Maryland: **Internships,** 1337. *See also* Maryland

Geneva, New York: **Grants,** 1041–1042. *See also* New York
Georgetown, Texas: **Grants,** 1041–1042. *See also* Texas
Georgia: **Scholarships,** 190. *See also* Southern states; United States; names of specific cities and counties
Germantown, Maryland: **Internships,** 1215. *See also* Maryland
Gettysburg, Pennsylvania: **Grants,** 1041–1042. *See also* Pennsylvania
Granville, Ohio: **Grants,** 1041–1042. *See also* Ohio
Greece: **Scholarships,** 336. *See also* Foreign countries
Greenbelt, Maryland: **Grants,** 1048–1049; **Internships,** 1179, 1299–1300. *See also* Maryland
Greencastle, Indiana: **Grants,** 1041–1042. *See also* United States
Greensboro, North Carolina: **Scholarships,** 166, 241; **Internships,** 1221. *See also* North Carolina
Greenville, South Carolina: **Fellowships,** 756. *See also* South Carolina
Greenwich, Connecticut: **Internships,** 1279–1280. *See also* Connecticut
Grinnell, Iowa: **Grants,** 1041–1042. *See also* United States
Groton, Connecticut: **Grants,** 1081–1082. *See also* Connecticut
Guam: **Scholarships,** 310; **Grants,** 1083–1084. *See also* United States

Hamilton, Montana: **Internships,** 1337. *See also* Montana
Hampton, Virginia: **Grants,** 1048–1049; **Internships,** 1299–1300. *See also* Virginia
Hanover, New Hampshire: **Fellowships,** 598; **Grants,** 945; **Internships,** 1202. *See also* New Hampshire
Harbor City, California. *See* Los Angeles, California
Hartford, Connecticut: **Internships,** 1279–1280. *See also* Connecticut
Haverford, Pennsylvania: **Grants,** 1041–1042. *See also* Pennsylvania
Hawaii: **Scholarships,** 223, 247, 425, 454; **Fellowships,** 690, 706, 720, 744, 831, 848; **Grants,** 955, 1083–1084; **Internships,** 1235. *See also* United States; names of specific cities and counties
Hawaii, regional: **Scholarships,** 167; **Fellowships,** 647. *See also* Hawaii
Herlong, California: **Internships,** 1352. *See also* California
Holland, Michigan: **Grants,** 1041–1042. *See also* Michigan
Hollywood, California. *See* Los Angeles, California
Houston, Texas: **Fellowships,** 756; **Grants,** 1048–1049; **Internships,** 1209, 1260, 1283, 1299–1300. *See also* Texas
Huntingdon, Pennsylvania: **Grants,** 1041–1042. *See also* Pennsylvania
Huntsville, Alabama: **Grants,** 1048–1049; **Internships,** 1299–1300. *See also* United States
Huntsville, Texas: **Scholarships,** 427. *See also* Texas

Idaho: **Scholarships,** 241, 248; **Grants,** 955. *See also* United States; names of specific cities and counties
Illinois: **Internships,** 1252. *See also* United States; names of specific cities and counties

Illinois, central: **Internships,** 1260. *See also* Illinois
Illinois, southern: **Internships,** 1260. *See also* Illinois
Indian Head, Maryland: **Grants,** 1081–1082. *See also* Maryland
Indianapolis, Indiana: **Internships,** 1190, 1341. *See also* United States
Iowa City, Iowa: **Scholarships,** 127; **Grants,** 1128; **Internships,** 1178, 1341. *See also* United States
Irvine, California: **Grants,** 1127. *See also* California
Italy: **Scholarships,** 336. *See also* Foreign countries
Ithaca, New York: **Scholarships,** 127, 166; **Grants,** 953; **Internships,** 1221, 1271. *See also* New York

Kalamazoo, Michigan: **Scholarships,** 166, 302; **Internships,** 1221. *See also* Michigan
Kansas: **Grants,** 955. *See also* United States; names of specific cities and counties
Kennedy Space Center, Florida: **Grants,** 1049; **Internships,** 1299–1300. *See also* Florida
Kentucky: **Grants,** 955. *See also* Southern states; United States; names of specific cities and counties
Knoxville, Tennessee: **Scholarships,** 166; **Grants,** 960; **Internships,** 1221. *See also* Tennessee

Lake Andes, South Dakota: **Internships,** 1310. *See also* South Dakota
Las Cruces, New Mexico: **Scholarships,** 427; **Grants,** 1048. *See also* New Mexico
Las Vegas, Nevada: **Scholarships,** 427. *See also* Nevada
Latin America. *See* Central America; Mexico; South America
Laurel, Maryland: **Internships,** 1187. *See also* Maryland
Lexington, Kentucky: **Fellowships,** 633; **Grants,** 1027; **Internships,** 1219. *See also* Kentucky
Lincoln, Nebraska: **Scholarships,** 127, 427. *See also* Nebraska
Livermore, California: **Fellowships,** 804, 847; **Internships,** 1229, 1287, 1313. *See also* California
Long Island, New York: **Fellowships,** 756. *See also* New York
Los Alamos, New Mexico: **Fellowships,** 804; **Internships,** 1287, 1300, 1313. *See also* New Mexico
Los Angeles, California: **Scholarships,** 241; **Fellowships,** 598, 684, 752, 756, 903; **Grants,** 921, 960, 1041–1042, 1127, 1138; **Internships,** 1202, 1246, 1260, 1276, 1279–1280, 1297. *See also* California
Los Angeles County, California: **Internships,** 1184. *See also* California
Louisiana: **Grants,** 1023; **Internships,** 1266. *See also* Southern states; United States; names of specific cities and parishes
Louisville, Kentucky: **Fellowships,** 633, 745; **Internships,** 1219. *See also* Kentucky
Lubbock, Texas: **Scholarships,** 127. *See also* Texas

Madison, Wisconsin: **Scholarships,** 166; **Fellowships,** 598; **Grants,** 960, 1013, 1129; **Internships,** 1202, 1221, 1341. *See also* Wisconsin
Maine: **Grants,** 955; **Internships,** 1273. *See also* New England states; Northeastern states; United States; names of specific cities and counties

Marin County, California: **Fellowships,** 756. *See also* California

Maryland: **Grants,** 1030; **Internships,** 1274. *See also* Northeastern states; Southern states; United States; names of specific cities and counties

Maryland, regional: **Internships,** 1184. *See also* Maryland

Massachusetts: **Scholarships,** 317. *See also* New England states; Northeastern states; United States; names of specific cities and counties

McAlester, Oklahoma: **Internships,** 1352. *See also* Oklahoma

Melville, New York: **Internships,** 1279–1280. *See also* New York

Memphis, Tennessee: **Grants,** 1041–1042. *See also* Tennessee

Merced, California: **Grants,** 1127. *See also* California

Mesa, Arizona: **Scholarships,** 427. *See also* Arizona

Mexico: **Scholarships,** 328, 505; **Grants,** 948, 951, 1016, 1019, 1136, 1142; **Internships,** 1285. *See also* Foreign countries

Miami, Florida: **Fellowships,** 752, 756, 809; **Internships,** 1260, 1276. *See also* Florida

Michigan: **Scholarships,** 203, 269, 281, 326, 455, 517; **Fellowships,** 719, 758; **Grants,** 1036. *See also* United States; names of specific cities and counties

Millbrook, New York: **Grants,** 941. *See also* New York

Millington, Tennessee: **Grants,** 1081–1082. *See also* Tennessee

Milwaukee, Wisconsin: **Scholarships,** 166; **Internships,** 1221, 1341. *See also* Wisconsin

Minneapolis, Minnesota: **Scholarships,** 166; **Fellowships,** 670, 809; **Grants,** 960, 1028; **Internships,** 1221, 1237, 1341. *See also* Minnesota

Minnesota: **Scholarships,** 181, 207, 225, 331; **Fellowships,** 652, 692, 761; **Awards,** 1161. *See also* United States; names of specific cities and counties

Mississippi State, Mississippi: **Scholarships,** 427. *See also* United States

Missouri: **Internships,** 1292–1293. *See also* United States; names of specific cities and counties

Moffett Field, California: **Grants,** 1049; **Internships,** 1299. *See also* California

Montana: **Scholarships,** 60, 195, 340, 384–385, 495; **Fellowships,** 769, 802, 880; **Grants,** 955; **Internships,** 1189. *See also* United States; names of specific cities and counties

Monterey, California: **Grants,** 960, 1064, 1081–1082. *See also* California

Morgantown, West Virginia: **Fellowships,** 633; **Internships,** 1219, 1283, 1304. *See also* West Virginia

Moscow, Idaho: **Scholarships,** 427. *See also* Idaho

Mountain View, California: **Internships,** 1300. *See also* California

Murray, Kentucky: **Scholarships,** 302. *See also* Kentucky

Narragansett, Rhode Island: **Fellowships,** 634. *See also* Rhode Island

Nebraska: **Grants,** 955. *See also* United States; names of specific cities and counties

Nevada: **Grants,** 955. *See also* United States; names of specific cities

New Brunswick, New Jersey: **Grants,** 960. *See also* New Jersey

New England states: **Grants,** 932. *See also* Northeastern states; United States; names of specific states

New Hampshire: **Grants,** 955. *See also* New England states; Northeastern states; United States; names of specific cities and counties

New Haven, Connecticut: **Fellowships,** 598; **Internships,** 1202. *See also* Connecticut

New Jersey: **Internships,** 1311. *See also* Northeastern states; United States; names of specific cities and counties

New Jersey, regional: **Internships,** 1184. *See also* New Jersey

New London, Connecticut: **Grants,** 1081–1082. *See also* Connecticut

New Mexico: **Scholarships,** 147, 207, 512; **Internships,** 1211. *See also* United States; names of specific cities and counties

New Orleans, Louisiana: **Internships,** 1283. *See also* Louisiana

New York: **Scholarships,** 371, 392, 415, 464; **Fellowships,** 824, 853; **Internships,** 1207, 1322. *See also* Northeastern states; United States; names of specific cities and counties

New York, New York: **Scholarships,** 72; **Fellowships,** 574, 598, 684, 752, 756, 786, 809, 903; **Grants,** 960, 1048, 1056, 1138; **Internships,** 1182, 1184, 1198, 1202, 1209, 1246, 1255, 1263, 1270, 1276, 1281–1282, 1307, 1346. *See also* New York

Newport News, Virginia: **Internships,** 1279–1280. *See also* Virginia

Newport, Rhode Island: **Grants,** 1081–1082. *See also* Rhode Island

North Carolina: **Scholarships,** 410, 489, 507; **Internships,** 1312. *See also* Southern states; United States; names of specific cities and counties

North Dakota: **Scholarships,** 381, 495; **Fellowships,** 880; **Grants,** 955. *See also* United States; names of specific cities

Northampton, Massachusetts: **Grants,** 988. *See also* Massachusetts

Northeastern states: **Grants,** 963. *See also* United States; names of specific states

Northern Marianas: **Grants,** 1083–1084. *See also* United States

Northfield, Minnesota: **Grants,** 1041–1042. *See also* Minnesota

Norton, Massachusetts: **Grants,** 1041–1042. *See also* Massachusetts

Notre Dame, Indiana: **Scholarships,** 166; **Internships,** 1190, 1221. *See also* United States

Oak Ridge, Tennessee: **Grants,** 1080; **Internships,** 1229, 1287. *See also* Tennessee

Oberlin, Ohio: **Grants,** 1041–1042. *See also* Ohio

Ohio: **Fellowships,** 828; **Grants,** 999, 1119; **Internships,** 1196, 1244, 1318. *See also* United States; names of specific cities and counties

Oklahoma: **Scholarships,** 88, 98, 123, 274–275, 315, 395, 500, 513; **Fellowships,** 542, 749, 810; **Grants,** 955; **Awards,** 1155–1156. *See also* Southern states; United States; names of specific cities and counties

Oklahoma, central: **Scholarships,** 112. *See also* Oklahoma

Omaha, Nebraska: **Scholarships,** 344; **Internships,** 1298. *See also* Nebraska

TENABILITY INDEX

Orange County, California: **Fellowships,** 752; **Internships,** 1276. *See also* California

Oregon: **Scholarships,** 241, 394, 510; **Internships,** 1233, 1320. *See also* United States; names of specific cities and counties

Orlando, Florida: **Grants,** 1081–1082; **Internships,** 1279–1280. *See also* Florida

Oxford, Ohio: **Grants,** 1035. *See also* Ohio

Pacific Islands: **Grants,** 1083–1084. *See also* Foreign countries; names of specific islands

Palo Alto, California: **Fellowships,** 658; **Internships,** 1232. *See also* California

Panama City, Florida: **Grants,** 1081–1082. *See also* Florida

Pasadena, California: **Fellowships,** 809; **Grants,** 1048–1049; **Internships,** 1291, 1299–1300. *See also* California

Patuxent River, Maryland: **Grants,** 1081–1082. *See also* Maryland

Pennsylvania: **Internships,** 1208. *See also* Northeastern states; United States; names of specific cities and counties

Pensacola, Florida: **Grants,** 1081–1082. *See also* Florida

Philadelphia, Pennsylvania: **Fellowships,** 684, 756, 903; **Grants,** 960, 1018, 1056, 1138; **Internships,** 1246. *See also* Pennsylvania

Phoenix, Arizona: **Fellowships,** 756; **Internships,** 1260, 1337. *See also* Arizona

Pittsburgh, Pennsylvania: **Fellowships,** 598, 633, 745, 756; **Grants,** 960; **Internships,** 1202, 1219, 1283, 1304. *See also* Pennsylvania

Port Hueneme, California: **Grants,** 1081–1082. *See also* California

Portland, Oregon: **Fellowships,** 631, 681, 877; **Grants,** 1041–1042; **Internships,** 1179, 1214, 1243, 1327, 1347. *See also* Oregon

Poughkeepsie, New York: **Grants,** 1041–1042. *See also* New York

Princess Anne, Maryland: **Scholarships,** 427. *See also* Maryland

Princeton, New Jersey: **Fellowships,** 745; **Grants,** 978, 1122. *See also* New Jersey

Providence, Rhode Island: **Fellowships,** 756; **Grants,** 1088. *See also* Rhode Island

Puerto Rico: **Scholarships,** 310, 352; **Grants,** 955. *See also* United States

Pullman, Washington: **Grants,** 1134. *See also* Washington

Raleigh, North Carolina: **Scholarships,** 166, 427; **Internships,** 1221. *See also* North Carolina

Rensselaer, New York: **Fellowships,** 756. *See also* New York

Research Triangle Park, North Carolina: **Internships,** 1337. *See also* North Carolina

Reston, Virginia: **Fellowships,** 658; **Internships,** 1232, 1283. *See also* Virginia

Rhode Island: **Grants,** 955; **Internships,** 1325. *See also* New England states; Northeastern states; United States; names of specific cities

Richland, Washington: **Grants,** 960; **Internships,** 1229, 1283, 1287, 1316. *See also* Washington

Richmond, Kentucky: **Scholarships,** 427; **Internships,** 1352. *See also* Kentucky

Richmond, Virginia: **Fellowships,** 745, 809; **Grants,** 1041–1042. *See also* Virginia

Riverside, California: **Grants,** 1127. *See also* California

Rochester, New York: **Scholarships,** 302; **Fellowships,** 598; **Internships,** 1202, 1249. *See also* New York

Rock Island, Illinois: **Internships,** 1352. *See also* Illinois

Rockville, Maryland: **Internships,** 1337. *See also* Maryland

Sacramento, California: **Fellowships,** 590; **Internships,** 1197. *See also* California

Salem, Oregon: **Grants,** 1041–1042. *See also* Oregon

Samoa. *See* American Samoa

San Anselmo, California: **Fellowships,** 745. *See also* California

San Diego, California: **Grants,** 1081–1082, 1127. *See also* California

San Francisco, California: **Fellowships,** 590, 756, 781; **Grants,** 1127; **Internships,** 1184, 1197, 1260. *See also* California

San Jose, California: **Scholarships,** 241. *See also* California

San Luis Obispo, California: **Scholarships,** 302. *See also* California

San Mateo County, California: **Fellowships,** 756. *See also* California

San Pedro, California. *See* Los Angeles, California

Santa Barbara, California: **Grants,** 1125, 1127; **Internships,** 1269. *See also* California

Santa Cruz, California: **Grants,** 1127. *See also* California

Santa Fe, New Mexico: **Grants,** 977, 1021, 1106, 1108; **Awards,** 1168. *See also* New Mexico

Santa Monica, California: **Fellowships,** 903; **Grants,** 1138. *See also* California

Saratoga Springs, New York: **Grants,** 1041–1042. *See also* New York

Scranton, Pennsylvania: **Fellowships,** 756. *See also* Pennsylvania

Seattle, Washington: **Scholarships,** 241; **Fellowships,** 631, 681, 727; **Grants,** 960; **Internships,** 1214, 1243, 1265. *See also* Washington

Sewanee, Tennessee: **Grants,** 1041–1042. *See also* Tennessee

Shawnee, Oklahoma: **Scholarships,** 308; **Fellowships,** 743. *See also* Oklahoma

Silver Spring, Maryland: **Grants,** 1081–1082. *See also* Maryland

South America: **Grants,** 951, 1136, 1142. *See also* Foreign countries; names of specific countries

South Carolina: **Grants,** 955. *See also* Southern states; United States; names of specific cities and counties

South Dakota: **Scholarships,** 111, 186, 192, 397, 442; **Grants,** 955. *See also* United States; names of specific cities and counties

South Hadley, Massachusetts: **Grants,** 988, 1041–1042. *See also* Massachusetts

Southern states: **Fellowships,** 868; **Grants,** 1116. *See also* United States; names of specific states

St. Louis, Missouri: **Fellowships,** 598, 756; **Internships,** 1202. *See also* Missouri

St. Paul, Minnesota: **Grants,** 1041–1042. *See also* Minnesota

St. Petersburg, Florida: **Fellowships,** 756. *See also* Florida

Stamford, Connecticut: **Internships,** 1279–1280. *See also* Connecticut

TENABILITY INDEX

Stanford, California: **Fellowships,** 684; **Grants,** 960, 1118; **Internships,** 1246. See also California

Stennis Space Center, Mississippi: **Grants,** 1048–1049, 1064, 1081–1082; **Internships,** 1299–1300. See also United States

Stout, Wisconsin: **Scholarships,** 302. See also Wisconsin

Sugar Land, Texas: **Internships,** 1283. See also Texas

Suitland, Maryland: **Grants,** 1056; **Internships,** 1307. See also Maryland

Sunland, California. See Los Angeles, California

Swarthmore, Pennsylvania: **Grants,** 1041–1042. See also Pennsylvania

Tallahassee, Florida: **Scholarships,** 166, 427; **Internships,** 1221. See also Florida

Tampa, Florida: **Fellowships,** 756. See also Florida

Tempe, Arizona: **Scholarships,** 302. See also Arizona

Tennessee: **Grants,** 955. See also Southern states; United States; names of specific cities and counties

Texas: **Scholarships,** 241; **Fellowships,** 875; **Grants,** 1091; **Internships,** 1344. See also Southern states; United States; names of specific cities and counties

Texas, eastern: **Internships,** 1260. See also Texas

Texas, southern: **Internships,** 1260. See also Texas

Tooele, Utah: **Internships,** 1352. See also Utah

Tujunga, California. See Los Angeles, California

Tulsa, Oklahoma: **Fellowships,** 756; **Internships,** 1304. See also Oklahoma

United States: **Scholarships,** 1–13, 15–35, 37–87, 89–97, 99–104, 106–110, 113–121, 124, 126, 128–146, 148–159, 161–165, 168–180, 182–185, 187–189, 191, 193–202, 205–206, 208–240, 242–244, 246–247, 249–268, 270–273, 276–277, 279–280, 282–287, 289, 291–299, 301, 303–316, 318–325, 327–330, 332–339, 341–359, 361–370, 372–380, 382–391, 393, 395–396, 398–405, 407–409, 411–414, 416–426, 428–438, 440–441, 443–453, 456–488, 490–500, 502–506, 508, 511–516, 518, 520–529, 531–536, 538–539; **Fellowships,** 540–541, 543–567, 569–597, 599–610, 612–633, 635–646, 648–651, 653–664, 666–679, 681–683, 685–718, 721–736, 738–744, 746–757, 759–760, 762–768, 770–780, 782–808, 810–823, 825–827, 829–847, 849–867, 869–873, 876–891, 893–901, 903, 905–908; **Grants,** 909–920, 922–924, 926–929, 933–934, 936–939, 942–943, 947–951, 954, 956–959, 961–962, 964–976, 979–980, 982–987, 989–992, 997–998, 1000–1012, 1014–1016, 1018–1020, 1026, 1031–1034, 1037–1040, 1044–1047, 1049–1055, 1057–1061, 1063–1079, 1085–1087, 1089–1090, 1092, 1094–1100, 1102–1105, 1107, 1109–1112, 1115, 1117, 1120–1121, 1123, 1130–1133, 1135, 1138–1139, 1142; **Awards,** 1143–1146, 1148–1155, 1157–1160, 1162–1167, 1169–1170, 1172–1175; **Internships,** 1179, 1182, 1185, 1188, 1197–1199, 1203–1205, 1212, 1214–1220, 1222–1224, 1226–1228, 1230–1232, 1234, 1237, 1239–1241, 1243, 1245, 1247–1249, 1251, 1253–1254, 1257–1259, 1261–1265, 1267–1268, 1272, 1276–1278, 1284–1286, 1288–1290, 1294, 1296, 1298–1299, 1301–1302, 1305, 1308–1309, 1313–1315, 1317, 1319, 1323–1324, 1326–1329, 1334, 1342–1343, 1345–1351. See also names of specific cities, counties, states, and regions

University Park, Pennsylvania: **Scholarships,** 427; **Grants,** 960; **Internships,** 1341. See also Pennsylvania

Upton, New York: **Internships,** 1194–1195, 1229, 1287. See also New York

Urbana, Illinois. See Champaign, Illinois

Utah: **Scholarships,** 509; **Awards,** 1171. See also United States; names of specific cities and counties

Utica, New York: **Fellowships,** 756. See also New York

Vermont: **Scholarships,** 360; **Grants,** 955. See also New England states; Northeastern states; United States; names of specific cities and counties

Virgin Islands: **Scholarships,** 310; **Grants,** 955. See also United States

Virginia: **Scholarships,** 501. See also Southern states; United States; names of specific cities and counties

Virginia, regional: **Internships,** 1184. See also Virginia

Walla Walla, Washington: **Grants,** 1041–1042. See also Washington

Wallops Island, Virginia: **Grants,** 1048; **Internships,** 1300. See also Virginia

Waltham, Massachusetts: **Fellowships,** 903; **Grants,** 1138. See also Massachusetts

Warwick, Rhode Island: **Fellowships,** 756. See also Rhode Island

Washington: **Scholarships,** 241, 406, 518–519; **Fellowships,** 892; **Internships,** 1353. See also United States; names of specific cities and counties

Washington, D.C.: **Scholarships,** 81; **Fellowships,** 574, 658, 752, 904; **Grants,** 920, 973, 995, 1043, 1052, 1056, 1062, 1064, 1081–1082, 1113–1114, 1126, 1135; **Internships,** 1176, 1179, 1182, 1184, 1191, 1204, 1209, 1213, 1222, 1232, 1256, 1260, 1276, 1283, 1295, 1303, 1307, 1321, 1332–1333, 1338, 1343, 1345–1346, 1354–1355. See also Northeastern states; Southern states; United States

Watervliet, New York: **Internships,** 1352. See also New York

Wellesley, Massachusetts: **Grants,** 1041–1042. See also Massachusetts

West Lafayette, Indiana: **Scholarships,** 127, 166; **Grants,** 960; **Internships,** 1221, 1341. See also United States

West Virginia: **Grants,** 955. See also Southern states; United States; names of specific cities

Wheeling, West Virginia: **Fellowships,** 633; **Internships,** 1219. See also West Virginia

White Sands, New Mexico: **Internships,** 1300. See also New Mexico

Williamstown, Massachusetts: **Grants,** 993. See also Massachusetts

Wilmington, California. See Los Angeles, California

Winston-Salem, North Carolina: **Fellowships,** 904; **Internships,** 1355. See also North Carolina

Wisconsin: **Scholarships,** 32, 530; **Fellowships,** 565, 902. See also United States; names of specific cities and counties

Woods Hole, Massachusetts: **Fellowships,** 635; **Grants,** 994, 1137, 1140; **Internships,** 1242, 1356. See also Massachusetts

Woodside, California: **Grants,** 996. See also California

Wooster, Ohio: **Grants,** 1041–1042. See also Ohio

Wyoming: **Grants,** 955. See also United States; names of specific cities and counties

Subject Index

There are hundreds of different subject areas covered in this directory. You can use the Subject Index to identify both the subject focus and the type (scholarships, fellowships, etc.) of available funding programs. To help you pinpoint your search, we've included numerous "see" and "see also" references. In addition to looking for terms that represent your specific subject interest, be sure to check the "General programs" entry; hundreds of funding opportunities are listed there that can be used to support study, research, or other activities in *any* subject area (although the programs may be restricted in other ways). Remember: the numbers cited in this index refer to program entry numbers, not to page numbers in the book.

Academic librarianship. *See* Libraries and librarianship, academic
Accounting: **Scholarships,** 49–50, 53, 77, 163, 166, 193, 199, 310, 332, 341–342, 358, 373, 460, 463, 524; **Fellowships,** 544, 597, 762, 787, 849, 851, 896; **Internships,** 1179, 1186, 1204, 1216–1217, 1221, 1256, 1352. *See also* Finance; General programs
Acoustical engineering. *See* Engineering, acoustical
Acoustics: **Fellowships,** 577. *See also* General programs; Physics
Acquired Immunodeficiency Syndrome. *See* AIDS
Acting. *See* Performing arts
Actuarial sciences: **Scholarships,** 321, 344; **Fellowships,** 686; **Internships,** 1278, 1298. *See also* General programs; Statistics
Addiction. *See* Alcohol use and abuse; Drug use and abuse
Administration. *See* Business administration; Education, administration; Management; Personnel administration; Public administration
Adolescents: **Internships,** 1257–1258. *See also* Child development; General programs
Advertising: **Scholarships,** 295; **Fellowships,** 730, 809; **Internships,** 1186, 1208, 1296. *See also* Communications; General programs; Marketing; Public relations
Aeronautical engineering. *See* Engineering, aeronautical
Aeronautics: **Scholarships,** 263; **Grants,** 1036, 1048–1049; **Internships,** 1299. *See also* Aviation; Engineering, aeronautical; General programs; Physical sciences
Aerospace engineering. *See* Engineering, aerospace
Aerospace sciences. *See* Space sciences
African American studies: **Fellowships,** 830; **Grants,** 1094. *See also* General programs; Minority studies
Aged and aging: **Scholarships,** 89; **Grants,** 914, 1052, 1086. *See also* General programs; Social sciences
Agribusiness: **Scholarships,** 58, 127, 373; **Fellowships,** 586. *See also* Agriculture and agricultural sciences; Business administration; General programs
Agricultural communications: **Scholarships,** 127. *See also* Agriculture and agricultural sciences; Communications; General programs

Agricultural economics. *See* Economics, agricultural
Agricultural education. *See* Education, agricultural
Agricultural engineering. *See* Engineering, agricultural
Agriculture and agricultural sciences: **Scholarships,** 58, 64, 161, 296; **Fellowships,** 586, 643; **Grants,** 960, 1133–1134. *See also* Biological sciences; General programs
Agrimarketing and sales. *See* Agribusiness
Agronomy: **Scholarships,** 58, 127; **Fellowships,** 586. *See also* Agriculture and agricultural sciences; General programs
AIDS: **Scholarships,** 33; **Fellowships,** 567, 781; **Grants,** 1070–1071; **Internships,** 1250. *See also* General programs; Immunology; Medical sciences
Alcohol use and abuse: **Fellowships,** 563; **Grants,** 1069. *See also* Drug use and abuse; General programs; Health and health care
Allergies: **Grants,** 916. *See also* General programs; Health and health care; Medical sciences
Alzheimer's Disease: **Grants,** 917. *See also* Aged and aging; General programs; Medical sciences
American history. *See* History, American
American Indian affairs. *See* Native American affairs
American Indian language. *See* Language, Native American
American Indian studies. *See* Native American studies
American studies: **Fellowships,** 830; **Grants,** 919, 989, 1094. *See also* General programs; Humanities
Animal science: **Scholarships,** 40, 58; **Fellowships,** 572, 577, 586; **Grants,** 1043, 1113, 1133; **Internships,** 1332. *See also* General programs; Sciences; names of specific animal sciences
Anthropology: **Scholarships,** 297; **Fellowships,** 732, 794, 830; **Grants,** 918–920, 927, 954, 989, 998, 1007, 1018, 1021, 1043, 1087, 1090, 1094, 1113; **Internships,** 1212, 1216, 1295, 1330, 1332. *See also* General programs; Social sciences
Antitrust and trade regulation: **Fellowships,** 669. *See also* General programs; Law, general
Applied arts. *See* Arts and crafts
Aquatic sciences. *See* Oceanography
Arabic language. *See* Language, Arabic

SUBJECT INDEX

Archaeology: **Scholarships,** 42, 336; **Fellowships,** 576, 794, 830; **Grants,** 919–920, 927, 989, 1007, 1043, 1094, 1113; **Internships,** 1212, 1216, 1332, 1344. See also General programs; History; Social sciences

Architectural engineering. See Engineering, architectural

Architecture: **Scholarships,** 29, 163; **Fellowships,** 577; **Grants,** 1134; **Internships,** 1295, 1344. See also Fine arts; General programs; Historical preservation

Arithmetic. See Mathematics

Armed services. See Military affairs

Armenian language. See Language, Armenian

Art: **Scholarships,** 22, 56, 69, 87; **Fellowships,** 555, 589, 664; **Grants,** 934, 951, 977, 1021, 1056–1058, 1106, 1117, 1142; **Awards,** 1168, 1170; **Internships,** 1235, 1273, 1275. See also Education, art; General programs; names of specific art forms

Art conservation: **Internships,** 1184. See also Art; General programs

Art education. See Education, art

Art history. See History, art

Art law: **Internships,** 1184. See also General programs; Law, general

Arthritis: **Fellowships,** 818. See also General programs; Health and health care; Medical sciences

Arts and crafts: **Scholarships,** 69; **Fellowships,** 589; **Grants,** 934, 1043, 1113; **Awards,** 1170; **Internships,** 1235, 1273, 1275, 1332. See also Art; General programs; names of specific crafts

Asian studies: **Fellowships,** 871; **Internships,** 1334. See also General programs; Humanities

Astronomy: **Fellowships,** 804, 806, 830; **Grants,** 930, 989, 1025, 1043, 1049, 1059, 1094, 1113; **Internships,** 1291, 1293, 1299, 1313, 1332. See also General programs; Physical sciences

Astrophysics: **Grants,** 926, 930, 994, 1043, 1113; **Internships,** 1242, 1332. See also Astronomy; General programs

Athletic training: **Fellowships,** 785. See also Athletics; General programs

Athletics: **Fellowships,** 654, 715, 777; **Internships,** 1227. See also Athletic training; Education, physical; General programs; Sports medicine; names of specific sports

Atmospheric sciences: **Scholarships,** 31, 252, 355; **Grants,** 926–927, 943, 1001, 1049, 1075; **Internships,** 1287, 1299, 1309. See also General programs; Physical sciences

Attorneys. See Law, general

Audiology: **Grants,** 1033, 1066. See also General programs; Health and health care; Medical sciences

Automation. See Computer sciences; Information science; Technology

Automobile industry: **Scholarships,** 171. See also General programs

Automotive engineering. See Engineering, automotive

Aviation: **Scholarships,** 1, 404; **Fellowships,** 819; **Internships,** 1231, 1343. See also General programs; Space sciences; Transportation

Aviation and space law: **Scholarships,** 404; **Fellowships,** 819; **Internships,** 1231. See also General programs; Law, general

Azerbaijani language. See Language, Azeri

Azeri language. See Language, Azeri

Ballet. See Dance

Banking: **Scholarships,** 49–50, 298, 341–342, 490, 524–525; **Fellowships,** 684, 734, 770, 841, 871, 896; **Internships,** 1246, 1267–1268, 1294, 1334. See also Finance; General programs

Basketry: **Grants,** 1117; **Awards,** 1168, 1170. See also Arts and crafts; General programs

Behavioral sciences: **Fellowships,** 563; **Grants,** 914, 933, 936, 960, 965, 971, 979, 993, 1014, 1031, 1039, 1045, 1054–1055, 1072, 1085, 1099, 1115; **Internships,** 1321, 1337. See also General programs; Social sciences; names of special behavioral sciences

Bilingualism: **Scholarships,** 248. See also Education, bilingual; General programs; Language and linguistics

Biochemistry: **Scholarships,** 21, 359; **Fellowships,** 699, 788; **Grants,** 1009, 1030, 1098; **Internships,** 1274, 1287. See also Biological sciences; Chemistry; General programs

Biological sciences: **Scholarships,** 67, 126, 179, 355, 463, 473, 515; **Fellowships,** 674, 699, 783, 804, 806, 830, 851, 890; **Grants,** 920, 923, 925–927, 935, 959–960, 965, 967–968, 972, 989, 1009, 1030, 1037, 1039, 1043, 1046–1047, 1049–1050, 1079–1080, 1088, 1094, 1096, 1102, 1104, 1107, 1113, 1140; **Awards,** 1172; **Internships,** 1194–1195, 1216, 1226, 1241, 1250, 1274, 1277, 1284, 1287, 1291, 1295, 1299–1300, 1308–1309, 1311, 1313, 1321, 1331–1332, 1336, 1339. See also General programs; Sciences; names of specific biological sciences

Biomedical engineering. See Engineering, biomedical

Biomedical sciences: **Fellowships,** 596; **Grants,** 914, 937–938, 971, 981, 986, 1014, 1019, 1031, 1045, 1053–1055, 1068, 1072–1073, 1085, 1091, 1099; **Internships,** 1193, 1236, 1287, 1305, 1336–1337. See also Biological sciences; General programs; Medical sciences

Biophysics: **Fellowships,** 699; **Grants,** 1009; **Internships,** 1287. See also Biological sciences; Chemistry; Computer sciences; Mathematics; Physics

Biotechnology: **Grants,** 1077–1078. See also Biological sciences; Technology

Black American studies. See African American studies

Brain research. See Neuroscience

Broadcast journalism. See Journalism, broadcast

Broadcasting: **Scholarships,** 74; **Fellowships,** 594; **Awards,** 1169; **Internships,** 1223, 1252, 1255. See also Communications; Radio; Television

Business administration: **Scholarships,** 2, 20, 23–24, 27, 49–50, 57, 71, 74, 77, 109, 138, 163, 194, 199, 286, 293, 298, 321–322, 332–333, 342–343, 358, 362, 463, 474–475, 490, 499, 524, 526; **Fellowships,** 540, 556–558, 594, 597–598, 610, 612, 621, 666, 680, 684–685, 705, 726, 734, 754, 762, 770, 787, 790, 841, 851, 867, 869, 881, 896–897; **Grants,** 1134; **Internships,** 1179, 1202, 1204–1205, 1216–1217, 1246, 1251, 1253, 1256, 1267–1268, 1278, 1294–1295, 1330, 1343, 1345, 1349, 1352. See also General programs; Management

Business enterprises. See Entrepreneurship

Business law: **Fellowships,** 591, 686; **Internships,** 1199, 1352. See also General programs; Law, general

Business reporting: **Scholarships,** 72; **Internships,** 1198. See also Broadcasting; Business administration; General programs; Journalism

Canadian history. See History, Canadian

SUBJECT INDEX

Cancer: **Grants,** 928, 932–933, 936, 1006, 1051, 1065–1067, 1120, 1123; **Internships,** 1250, 1335. See also General programs; Health and health care; Medical sciences

Cardiology: **Grants,** 1053, 1068; **Internships,** 1193, 1250. See also General programs; Medical sciences

Cars. See Automobile industry; Engineering, automotive

Cartography: **Scholarships,** 355; **Fellowships,** 783; **Internships,** 1308–1309. See also General programs; Geography

Cattle ranching. See Ranching

Cell biology: **Fellowships,** 699; **Grants,** 964, 1009. See also Biological sciences; General programs

Chemical engineering. See Engineering, chemical

Chemistry: **Scholarships,** 18, 21, 45, 179, 199, 263, 355, 463, 533; **Fellowships,** 674, 705, 783, 804, 806, 830, 851, 905; **Grants,** 915, 923, 926, 959–960, 973, 989, 1030, 1044, 1046–1047, 1049, 1059, 1077–1079, 1094, 1103, 1107, 1140; **Internships,** 1194–1195, 1222, 1226, 1241, 1251, 1272, 1274, 1277, 1287, 1291, 1299, 1304, 1308–1309, 1313, 1331, 1337, 1352. See also Engineering, chemical; General programs; Physical sciences

Child development: **Scholarships,** 367; **Fellowships,** 792; **Internships,** 1257–1258. See also General programs

Children's literature. See Literature, children's

Chiropractic: **Grants,** 910. See also General programs; Medical sciences

Choruses. See Voice

Church music. See Music, church

Cinema: **Grants,** 919. See also Filmmaking; General programs; Literature

City and regional planning: **Scholarships,** 271, 343; **Fellowships,** 561, 722, 786, 830; **Grants,** 973, 989, 1094; **Internships,** 1222, 1295, 1343. See also Community development; General programs; Urban affairs

Civil engineering. See Engineering, civil

Civil rights: **Internships,** 1310. See also General programs; Political science and politics

Classical studies: **Scholarships,** 336; **Grants,** 919. See also General programs; Literature

Clerical skills. See Secretarial sciences

Colleges and universities. See Education, higher; Libraries and librarianship, academic

Commerce. See Business administration

Communications: **Scholarships,** 8, 74, 184, 204, 266, 268, 299, 303, 400, 428; **Fellowships,** 577, 594, 659, 705, 717, 720, 735, 740, 813, 815, 830; **Grants,** 919, 960, 989, 1094; **Awards,** 1169; **Internships,** 1205, 1208, 1216, 1238, 1251, 1255, 1261, 1272, 1295, 1330. See also General programs; Humanities

Communications, agricultural. See Agricultural communications

Community colleges. See Education, higher; Libraries and librarianship, academic

Community development: **Grants,** 1133. See also City and regional planning; General programs; Urban affairs

Community services. See Social services

Composers and compositions: **Grants,** 996. See also General programs; Music

Computer engineering. See Engineering, computer

Computer sciences: **Scholarships,** 7, 48, 138, 148, 179, 199, 205, 241, 305, 322, 328, 355, 416, 463, 474, 533; **Fellowships,** 545, 581, 583, 621, 626, 671–672, 674, 705, 754, 783, 804, 806, 830, 847, 851–852, 867, 871, 905; **Grants,** 915, 925, 950, 960, 967–968, 989, 1018, 1044, 1047, 1049, 1059, 1080, 1094, 1096, 1122; **Internships,** 1179–1180, 1187–1188, 1194–1195, 1204, 1216–1217, 1226, 1231, 1239, 1241, 1251, 1253, 1272, 1285, 1299–1300, 1308–1309, 1311, 1313, 1316, 1321, 1330–1331, 1334, 1337, 1352. See also General programs; Mathematics; Technology

Computers. See Computer sciences

Conflict resolution. See Peace studies

Conservation. See Art conservation; Environmental sciences

Construction. See Housing

Construction engineering. See Engineering, construction

Construction industry: **Scholarships,** 189, 482. See also General programs

Contracts law: **Fellowships,** 669. See also General programs; Law, general

Cooking. See Culinary arts

Copyright law. See Intellectual property law

Corporate law: **Fellowships,** 670; **Internships,** 1237. See also General programs; Law, general

Counseling: **Scholarships,** 477; **Fellowships,** 746; **Internships,** 1178. See also Behavioral sciences; General programs; Psychiatry; Psychology

Counselors and counseling, school: **Scholarships,** 350, 367; **Fellowships,** 774, 792. See also Counseling; General programs

Crafts. See Arts and crafts

Creative writing: **Scholarships,** 22; **Fellowships,** 555. See also Fine arts; General programs; Literature

Criminal justice: **Scholarships,** 93, 212, 250, 312, 354; **Fellowships,** 562, 678, 747; **Grants,** 922, 1135; **Internships,** 1217, 1295, 1343. See also General programs; Law, general

Culinary arts: **Scholarships,** 286; **Fellowships,** 726; **Internships,** 1205. See also Food service industry; General programs

Dance: **Scholarships,** 87; **Grants,** 919; **Internships,** 1273, 1275. See also General programs; Performing arts

Dari language. See Language, Dari

Data entry. See Computer sciences; Secretarial sciences

Deafness. See Hearing impairments

Defense. See Military affairs

Demography. See Population studies

Dental hygiene: **Scholarships,** 120; **Fellowships,** 780. See also Dentistry; General programs

Dentistry: **Scholarships,** 226; **Fellowships,** 640–642, 699, 763, 779–780; **Grants,** 910, 1009, 1011, 1033–1034, 1055; **Internships,** 1335. See also General programs; Health and health care; Medical sciences

Diabetes: **Grants,** 911, 1016, 1020, 1032, 1071. See also General programs; Health and health care; Medical sciences

Dietetics. See Nutrition

Disabilities, hearing. See Hearing impairments

Discrimination, racial: **Grants,** 1026; **Awards,** 1144. See also General programs; Race relations

Discrimination, sex: **Grants,** 1026. See also General programs; Women's studies and programs

Divinity. See Religion and religious activities

Documentaries. See Filmmaking

Drug use and abuse: **Fellowships,** 563; **Grants,** 971, 1070; **Internships,** 1258, 1288. See also Alcohol use and abuse; General programs; Health and health care

Early childhood education. *See* Education, preschool
Earth sciences: **Scholarships,** 45; **Fellowships,** 674, 830; **Grants,** 926–927, 989, 1015, 1043, 1049–1050, 1080, 1094, 1113; **Internships,** 1205, 1241, 1287, 1299, 1331–1332. *See also* General programs; Natural sciences; names of specific earth sciences
Ecology. *See* Environmental sciences
Economic development: **Scholarships,** 343. *See also* Economics; General programs
Economic planning. *See* Economics
Economics: **Scholarships,** 37, 77, 321, 332, 343, 463, 474, 490; **Fellowships,** 597–598, 762, 783, 830, 851, 867; **Grants,** 915, 919, 923, 927, 960, 973, 979, 989, 1012, 1039, 1046, 1079, 1087, 1094, 1107; **Internships,** 1179, 1202, 1204, 1222, 1278, 1295, 1308, 1343, 1345. *See also* General programs; Social sciences
Economics, agricultural: **Scholarships,** 127. *See also* Agriculture and agricultural sciences; Economics; General programs
Education: **Scholarships,** 2, 68, 71, 109, 119, 130, 159, 177, 194, 203, 205, 215, 248, 253, 299, 304, 314, 322, 343, 350, 357, 415, 480, 526; **Fellowships,** 610, 612, 671, 683, 735, 739, 754, 774, 815, 824, 868, 897; **Grants,** 912, 946, 958, 989, 1076, 1094, 1100, 1122, 1129, 1134; **Awards,** 1166; **Internships,** 1178, 1205, 1216, 1330. *See also* General programs; Social sciences; specific types and levels of education
Education, administration: **Scholarships,** 350, 367; **Fellowships,** 774, 792. *See also* Education; General programs; Management
Education, agricultural: **Scholarships,** 127. *See also* Agriculture and agricultural sciences; Education; General programs
Education, art: **Internships,** 1184. *See also* Art; Education; General programs
Education, bilingual: **Scholarships,** 248, 367; **Fellowships,** 792. *See also* Education; General programs
Education, elementary: **Scholarships,** 367, 406; **Fellowships,** 792. *See also* Education; General programs
Education, higher: **Awards,** 1145; **Internships,** 1210, 1301. *See also* Education; General programs
Education, journalism: **Scholarships,** 347; **Fellowships,** 772. *See also* Education; General programs; Journalism
Education, physical: **Fellowships,** 785. *See also* Athletics; Education; General programs
Education, preschool: **Scholarships,** 346, 367; **Fellowships,** 771, 792. *See also* Education; General programs
Education, science and mathematics: **Scholarships,** 45, 214, 367, 406; **Fellowships,** 682, 792; **Grants,** 962. *See also* Education; General programs; Sciences
Education, special: **Scholarships,** 367; **Fellowships,** 792. *See also* Education; General programs
Electrical engineering. *See* Engineering, electrical
Electronic engineering. *See* Engineering, electronic
Electronic journalism. *See* Journalism, broadcast
Electronics: **Fellowships,** 852; **Grants,** 1077–1078. *See also* Engineering, electronic; General programs; Physics
Elementary education. *See* Education, elementary
Elementary school librarians. *See* Libraries and librarianship, school
Eminent domain. *See* Real estate law
Emotional disabilities. *See* Mental health
Endocrinology: **Grants,** 974; **Internships,** 1224. *See also* General programs; Medical sciences

Energy: **Scholarships,** 310, 389; **Grants,** 925, 967–968, 1008, 1015, 1080; **Internships,** 1225, 1283, 1315. *See also* Environmental sciences; General programs; Natural resources
Engineering: **Scholarships,** 20, 39, 47, 71, 74, 79, 109, 138, 166, 179, 194, 199, 205, 208, 210, 227, 263, 286, 318, 322, 348, 351–352, 355, 364, 389, 458, 463, 473, 488, 499; **Fellowships,** 571, 580, 594, 610, 621, 671–673, 675, 695, 726, 754, 783, 804, 806, 830, 851, 868, 881; **Grants,** 923, 925, 955, 960, 966, 973, 982–983, 989, 994, 999–1000, 1002, 1012, 1042, 1046, 1064, 1076–1082, 1092, 1094–1095, 1107, 1110, 1112, 1134; **Awards,** 1145, 1166; **Internships,** 1179–1180, 1194–1195, 1204, 1217, 1221–1222, 1226, 1239–1240, 1242, 1244–1245, 1248, 1253, 1271, 1277, 1283, 1291, 1295, 1300, 1304, 1308–1309, 1313–1316, 1321, 1323, 1325, 1328, 1330–1331, 1338, 1343, 1349–1350. *See also* General programs; Physical sciences; names of specific types of engineering
Engineering, acoustical: **Fellowships,** 577. *See also* Engineering; General programs
Engineering, aeronautical: **Scholarships,** 404; **Fellowships,** 819; **Grants,** 1049; **Internships,** 1299. *See also* Aeronautics; Engineering; General programs
Engineering, aerospace: **Scholarships,** 305, 356, 360, 404; **Fellowships,** 784, 819; **Grants,** 1023, 1036, 1044, 1048, 1050, 1060; **Internships,** 1181, 1183, 1189, 1201, 1206, 1231, 1266, 1292–1293, 1311, 1325, 1353. *See also* Engineering; General programs; Space sciences
Engineering, agricultural: **Scholarships,** 127; **Grants,** 1133. *See also* Agriculture and agricultural sciences; Engineering; General programs
Engineering, architectural: **Internships,** 1352. *See also* Architecture; Engineering; General programs
Engineering, automotive: **Scholarships,** 148; **Fellowships,** 626. *See also* Engineering; General programs
Engineering, biomedical: **Fellowships,** 699, 845; **Grants,** 1009, 1091; **Internships,** 1337. *See also* Biomedical sciences; Engineering; General programs
Engineering, chemical: **Scholarships,** 21, 48, 67, 148, 210, 305, 310, 459, 533; **Fellowships,** 583, 626, 707, 804, 847, 905; **Grants,** 1049, 1059; **Awards,** 1162; **Internships,** 1291, 1299, 1311, 1313. *See also* Chemistry; Engineering; General programs
Engineering, civil: **Scholarships,** 18, 53, 67, 310, 353; **Fellowships,** 776, 847; **Internships,** 1212, 1215–1216, 1231, 1302, 1352. *See also* Engineering; General programs
Engineering, computer: **Scholarships,** 7, 126, 148, 193, 241, 305, 328, 416, 533; **Fellowships,** 545, 626, 705, 707, 806, 871, 905; **Grants,** 950, 1059; **Internships,** 1231, 1251, 1272, 1285, 1311, 1334. *See also* Computer sciences; Engineering; General programs
Engineering, construction: **Scholarships,** 189. *See also* Engineering; General programs
Engineering, electrical: **Scholarships,** 18, 48, 53, 148, 193, 208, 210, 241, 305, 310, 328, 416, 533; **Fellowships,** 581, 583, 626, 675, 705, 707, 847, 871, 905; **Grants,** 1047, 1059; **Internships,** 1187–1188, 1231, 1251, 1272, 1285, 1311, 1334. *See also* Engineering; General programs
Engineering, electronic: **Internships,** 1231. *See also* Electronics; Engineering; General programs
Engineering, environmental: **Scholarships,** 43–44, 53, 67, 343; **Fellowships,** 579; **Grants,** 1059; **Internships,** 1212, 1215–1216. *See also* Engineering; Environmental sciences; General programs

SUBJECT INDEX

Engineering, geological: **Scholarships,** 310. *See also* Engineering; General programs; Geology

Engineering, industrial: **Scholarships,** 43–44, 148, 208, 210, 505; **Fellowships,** 579, 581, 626, 675, 707; **Internships,** 1188. *See also* Engineering; General programs

Engineering, manufacturing: **Scholarships,** 148, 210, 404, 533; **Fellowships,** 626, 707, 819, 905. *See also* Engineering; General programs

Engineering, materials: **Scholarships,** 148, 305; **Fellowships,** 626, 707; **Grants,** 1049; **Internships,** 1299, 1311. *See also* Engineering; General programs; Materials sciences

Engineering, mechanical: **Scholarships,** 18, 48, 53, 148, 193, 208, 210, 305, 310, 533; **Fellowships,** 583, 626, 675, 705, 707, 804, 847, 905; **Grants,** 1044, 1047, 1049, 1059; **Internships,** 1231, 1251, 1299, 1311, 1313, 1352. *See also* Engineering; General programs

Engineering, metallurgical: **Grants,** 1049; **Internships,** 1299. *See also* Engineering; General programs

Engineering, mining: **Scholarships,** 53; **Internships,** 1216. *See also* Engineering; General programs; Mining industry

Engineering, nuclear: **Scholarships,** 262; **Fellowships,** 713, 847; **Internships,** 1215. *See also* Engineering; General programs; Nuclear science

Engineering, ocean: **Grants,** 1140; **Internships,** 1356. *See also* Engineering; General programs; Oceanography

Engineering, optical: **Scholarships,** 533; **Fellowships,** 905. *See also* Engineering; General programs; Optics

Engineering, petroleum: **Scholarships,** 48, 310; **Fellowships,** 583, 847; **Internships,** 1216. *See also* Engineering; General programs

Engineering, plastics: **Scholarships,** 463; **Fellowships,** 851. *See also* Engineering; General programs

Engineering, structural: **Grants,** 1047. *See also* Engineering; General programs

Engineering, systems: **Fellowships,** 581; **Internships,** 1188. *See also* Engineering; General programs

Engineering technology: **Scholarships,** 18, 389; **Internships,** 1315. *See also* Engineering; General programs

Engineering, transportation: **Scholarships,** 163; **Fellowships,** 645; **Grants,** 973; **Internships,** 1222. *See also* Engineering; General programs; Transportation

English as a second language: **Scholarships,** 248. *See also* Education, bilingual; General programs; Language and linguistics

English language. *See* Language, English

Entomology: **Grants,** 972. *See also* General programs; Zoology

Entrepreneurship: **Scholarships,** 333. *See also* Business administration; General programs

Environmental engineering. *See* Engineering, environmental

Environmental health: **Scholarships,** 227, 310; **Grants,** 1111; **Internships,** 1339. *See also* Public health; General programs

Environmental law: **Scholarships,** 463; **Fellowships,** 851. *See also* General programs; Law, general

Environmental sciences: **Scholarships,** 21, 40, 43–44, 58, 67, 163, 179, 194, 343, 353, 355, 364, 463, 473, 515; **Fellowships,** 572, 579, 586, 634, 695, 776, 783, 804, 851, 874, 890; **Grants,** 925–926, 935, 941, 965, 967–968, 972, 975, 979, 1008, 1015, 1030, 1043, 1049, 1080, 1113, 1124, 1136; **Internships,** 1216, 1225–1226, 1274, 1277, 1287, 1295, 1299, 1302, 1308–1310, 1313, 1330–1332, 1343, 1352. *See also* General programs; Sciences

Epidemiology: **Fellowships,** 596, 699; **Grants,** 933, 937, 972, 979, 1009, 1070, 1105, 1120; **Internships,** 1193, 1339. *See also* General programs; Medical sciences

Epilepsy: **Grants,** 976, 1097–1098. *See also* General programs; Health and health care; Medical sciences

Ethics: **Grants,** 979. *See also* General programs; Humanities

Ethnic affairs. *See* Minority affairs

Ethnic studies. *See* Minority studies

Evolution: **Grants,** 915, 935, 965, 1043, 1113; **Internships,** 1332. *See also* Biological sciences; General programs; Sciences

Exercise science. *See* Athletic training

Eye doctors. *See* Optometry

Family and consumer studies: **Fellowships,** 663. *See also* General programs; Social sciences

Family relations: **Fellowships,** 746; **Awards,** 1160. *See also* General programs; Sociology

Farming. *See* Agriculture and agricultural sciences

Farsi language. *See* Language, Farsi

Feminist movement. *See* Women's studies and programs

Fiber. *See* Textiles

Film as a literary art. *See* Cinema

Filmmaking: **Scholarships,** 183; **Grants,** 1061. *See also* General programs; Television

Finance: **Scholarships,** 49–50, 77, 127, 193, 217, 298, 321, 332–333, 341–342, 358, 460, 463, 490, 524; **Fellowships,** 597, 685, 705, 734, 762, 770, 787, 841, 849, 851, 871, 896; **Internships,** 1179–1180, 1216, 1247, 1251, 1256, 1267–1268, 1278, 1294, 1334. *See also* Accounting; Banking; Economics; General programs

Fine arts: **Scholarships,** 22, 87, 299; **Fellowships,** 555, 592, 735; **Grants,** 977, 1106; **Internships,** 1205, 1273. *See also* General programs; Humanities; names of specific fine arts

Fishing industry: **Scholarships,** 353, 463, 511; **Fellowships,** 776, 783, 851; **Internships,** 1216, 1302, 1308, 1330. *See also* General programs

Flight science. *See* Aviation

Floriculture. *See* Horticulture

Flying. *See* Aviation

Folklore: **Grants,** 1043, 1113; **Internships,** 1332. *See also* General programs; Literature

Food. *See* Culinary arts; Nutrition

Food science: **Scholarships,** 127; **Grants,** 960, 1133. *See also* Food service industry; General programs; Nutrition

Food service industry: **Scholarships,** 524; **Fellowships,** 896; **Internships,** 1218. *See also* General programs

Food technology. *See* Food science

Foreign affairs. *See* International affairs

Foreign language. *See* Language and linguistics

Forestry management: **Scholarships,** 40, 353, 463; **Fellowships,** 572, 776, 851; **Grants,** 1133; **Internships,** 1302, 1330. *See also* General programs; Management

Gaming industry: **Scholarships,** 524; **Fellowships,** 896. *See also* General programs

Gardening. *See* Horticulture

Gastroenterology: **Grants,** 913, 990; **Awards,** 1151. *See also* General programs

Gay men and women. *See* Homosexuality

Gender. *See* Women's studies and programs

SUBJECT INDEX

General programs: **Scholarships,** 2–6, 10–17, 19, 23–26, 28, 34–36, 38, 41, 46, 51–52, 54–55, 59–63, 66, 70, 73, 75–76, 78, 80–86, 88, 90–92, 94–96, 98–108, 110–114, 116–118, 121–126, 128–129, 131–137, 139–142, 144–146, 149–152, 154–155, 157–158, 164–165, 167–168, 170, 173–174, 177, 180–182, 185–188, 190–192, 195–196, 200–201, 205–207, 209, 211, 216, 218–221, 223–225, 228–229, 231–240, 242–245, 247, 251, 256–258, 261, 264, 269–270, 272–284, 286–292, 294, 301, 304, 306, 308–309, 313, 315–317, 319–320, 323–326, 329–331, 337–340, 345, 349, 361, 363, 365–366, 368–369, 371–372, 375–385, 387–388, 390–399, 401–403, 407–415, 417–426, 429–434, 436–438, 440, 442, 444–445, 447, 450–453, 455–457, 462, 464–472, 476, 478–479, 483–487, 489, 492–496, 498, 500–504, 506–510, 512–514, 516, 518–522, 526–532, 534–539; **Fellowships,** 540, 542–543, 549–551, 554, 556–557, 559, 569, 573, 585, 587–588, 593, 595, 599–609, 612–615, 617–620, 622–625, 627–629, 632, 638–639, 647–648, 651–652, 655, 660, 662, 687–694, 696–698, 700, 702–704, 706, 714, 719, 721, 723–726, 728–729, 731, 739, 743, 748–750, 755, 758, 760–761, 768–769, 778, 791, 795–796, 800, 802, 808, 810–812, 814, 816, 820–826, 829, 831, 833–835, 840, 842, 844, 846, 850, 853–855, 859–865, 870, 873, 876, 880, 884, 887–888, 891–894, 897, 899, 901–902, 906–908; **Grants,** 909, 940, 944–945, 963, 988, 1017, 1022, 1027–1028, 1041–1042, 1063, 1109, 1116, 1119, 1127; **Awards,** 1146, 1148, 1150, 1154–1156, 1159, 1161, 1163, 1171, 1175; **Internships,** 1269, 1286, 1312, 1319, 1341

Genetics: **Fellowships,** 596, 699; **Grants,** 937, 1009, 1018, 1033, 1066, 1070, 1098; **Internships,** 1287. See also General programs; Medical sciences

Genomics: **Fellowships,** 845; **Internships,** 1287. See also General programs; Genetics

Geography: **Scholarships,** 353, 355; **Fellowships,** 776, 783, 830; **Grants,** 919, 927, 973, 989, 1094; **Internships,** 1204, 1216, 1222, 1302, 1308–1309. See also General programs; Social sciences

Geological engineering. See Engineering, geological

Geology: **Scholarships,** 45, 67, 214, 310, 463; **Fellowships,** 682, 783, 804, 806, 851; **Grants,** 926, 1049, 1059, 1103, 1140; **Internships,** 1216, 1283, 1291, 1299, 1304, 1308, 1313, 1330. See also Earth sciences; General programs; Physical sciences

Geophysics: **Scholarships,** 45, 214, 263, 310; **Fellowships,** 682; **Grants,** 926, 960, 994, 1140; **Internships,** 1242. See also General programs; Meteorology; Oceanography; Physics

Geosciences. See Earth sciences

Geriatrics. See Aged and aging

Gerontology. See Aged and aging

Golf course management. See Turfgrass science

Golf industry: **Scholarships,** 427. See also Athletics; Business administration; General programs

Government. See Political science and politics; Public administration

Grade school. See Education, elementary

Graphic arts: **Scholarships,** 302; **Grants,** 1117; **Awards,** 1168, 1170; **Internships,** 1216. See also Art; Arts and crafts; General programs

Graphic design: **Scholarships,** 18, 126, 147; **Internships,** 1179, 1186, 1204, 1208, 1211–1212. See also General programs; Graphic arts

Guidance. See Counseling

Hawaiian language. See Language, Hawaiian

Hawaiian studies: **Scholarships,** 69, 162, 172, 259, 267, 346, 425, 454; **Fellowships,** 589, 710, 720, 771, 831, 848; **Grants,** 934. See also General programs; Native American studies

Health and health care: **Scholarships,** 9, 32, 71, 109, 156, 160, 179, 202, 343, 357, 359, 386, 448, 480, 497; **Fellowships,** 547, 565, 568, 610, 612, 637, 668, 677, 788, 798, 803, 843; **Grants,** 910, 933, 981, 1004, 1011, 1033–1034, 1046, 1070, 1079–1080, 1105, 1107; **Awards,** 1147; **Internships,** 1179–1180, 1191, 1226, 1253, 1262, 1295, 1310, 1338. See also General programs; Medical sciences

Health and health care, administration: **Fellowships,** 548, 879; **Internships,** 1177. See also Business administration; General programs; Health and health care

Health care informatics: **Scholarships,** 198; **Fellowships,** 667, 699; **Grants,** 1009. See also Health and health care; Information science

Health information. See Health care informatics

Health information administration. See Health care informatics

Health physics: **Internships,** 1194, 1215. See also General programs; Health and health care; Physics

Hearing impairments: **Fellowships,** 564. See also General programs; Rehabilitation

Heart disease. See Cardiology

High school librarians. See Libraries and librarianship, school

Higher education. See Education, higher

Hindi language. See Language, Hindi

Historical preservation: **Internships,** 1212, 1344. See also General programs; History

History: **Scholarships,** 56, 297; **Fellowships,** 732, 830; **Grants,** 919, 927, 989, 1021, 1087, 1094; **Internships,** 1212, 1295, 1344. See also Archaeology; General programs; Humanities; Social sciences; specific types of history

History, American: **Scholarships,** 119; **Fellowships,** 794; **Grants,** 920, 998, 1018, 1043, 1090, 1113; **Awards,** 1157, 1165; **Internships,** 1332. See also American studies; General programs; History

History, art: **Fellowships,** 592, 830; **Grants,** 919, 989, 1043, 1094, 1113; **Internships,** 1270, 1281–1282, 1332. See also Art; General programs; History

History, Canadian: **Grants,** 1090. See also General programs; History

History, natural: **Grants,** 1018. See also Sciences; specific aspects of natural history

History, science: **Grants,** 1001, 1018, 1043, 1113; **Internships,** 1332. See also General programs; History; Sciences

Homeland security. See Security, national

Homosexuality: **Grants,** 998. See also General programs

Horticulture: **Scholarships,** 58; **Fellowships,** 586. See also Agriculture and agricultural sciences; General programs; Landscape architecture; Sciences

Hospitality industry. See Hotel and motel industry

Hospitals. See Health and health care

Hotel and motel industry: **Scholarships,** 115, 222, 230, 246, 333, 474, 490, 524; **Fellowships,** 867, 896. See also General programs

Housing: **Grants,** 1010. See also General programs

Human resources. See Personnel administration

Human rights. See Civil rights

Human services. See Social services

SUBJECT INDEX

Humanities: **Grants,** 919, 985, 991, 993, 1087–1088, 1118, 1121; **Internships,** 1297, 1340. *See also* General programs; names of specific humanities
Hydrology: **Scholarships,** 31, 45, 67, 214, 252, 353; **Fellowships,** 682, 776, 783; **Grants,** 1001, 1075; **Internships,** 1216, 1302, 1308. *See also* Earth sciences; General programs

Immigration: **Grants,** 960. *See also* General programs
Immunology: **Fellowships,** 699; **Grants,** 916, 964, 1009. *See also* General programs; Medical sciences
Indian law: **Scholarships,** 212, 260; **Fellowships,** 678, 711; **Awards,** 1143, 1164; **Internships,** 1205, 1295. *See also* General programs; Law, general
Industrial engineering. *See* Engineering, industrial
Industrial hygiene: **Scholarships,** 18, 43–44, 67; **Fellowships,** 579. *See also* General programs; Health and health care; Safety studies
Industrial relations: **Scholarships,** 53. *See also* General programs
Infectious diseases: **Internships,** 1250. *See also* General programs; Medical sciences
Information science: **Scholarships,** 7, 18, 53, 166, 193, 341–342, 463, 473–474, 524, 533; **Fellowships,** 545, 806, 851, 867, 871, 896, 905; **Grants,** 973, 1077–1078, 1096; **Internships,** 1221–1222, 1253, 1272, 1334. *See also* General programs; Library and information services, general
Insurance. *See* Actuarial sciences
Intellectual property law: **Fellowships,** 636, 658, 669, 751, 858, 878; **Internships,** 1220, 1232, 1260. *See also* General programs; Law, general
Interior design: **Scholarships,** 285. *See also* Architecture; General programs
International affairs: **Scholarships,** 126, 254; **Fellowships,** 830, 832, 871; **Grants,** 989, 1087, 1094, 1126; **Internships,** 1179, 1204, 1217, 1254, 1334, 1345, 1352. *See also* General programs; Political science and politics
International law: **Fellowships,** 733. *See also* General programs; Law, general
International relations. *See* International affairs
Internet design and development: **Internships,** 1212, 1216. *See also* General programs; Graphic arts; Technology
Internet journalism. *See* Journalism, online

Jewelry: **Grants,** 1117; **Awards,** 1168, 1170. *See also* Arts and crafts; General programs
Journalism: **Scholarships,** 8, 72, 74, 97, 143, 147, 176, 184, 204, 266, 303, 347, 425, 428; **Fellowships,** 594, 634, 659, 717, 720, 740, 772–773, 831, 874; **Grants,** 1124; **Internships,** 1186, 1198, 1203, 1208, 1211–1212, 1217, 1238, 1261–1262, 1279–1280, 1348. *See also* Broadcasting; Communications; General programs; names of specific types of journalism
Journalism, agriculture. *See* Agricultural communications
Journalism, broadcast: **Scholarships,** 204, 303, 347; **Fellowships,** 634, 757, 772, 805; **Internships,** 1208, 1238, 1255, 1261–1262. *See also* Communications; General programs; Radio; Television
Journalism, business. *See* Business reporting
Journalism, education. *See* Education, journalism
Journalism, medical. *See* Science reporting

Journalism, online: **Scholarships,** 147, 204, 303, 347; **Fellowships,** 634, 772; **Internships,** 1186, 1211, 1238. *See also* General programs; Journalism
Journalism, religion. *See* Religious reporting
Journalism, science. *See* Science reporting
Junior colleges. *See* Education, higher
Jurisprudence. *See* Law, general

Kazakh language. *See* Language, Kazakh
Kidney disease: **Grants,** 1071. *See also* General programs; Health and health care; Medical sciences
Kyrgyz language. *See* Language, Kyrgyz

Landscape architecture: **Scholarships,** 169; **Internships,** 1212, 1344. *See also* General programs; Horticulture
Language and linguistics: **Scholarships,** 254, 299; **Fellowships,** 735, 830; **Grants,** 919–920, 927, 978, 989, 1094, 1122; **Internships,** 1204–1205, 1254, 1345. *See also* General programs; Humanities; names of specific languages
Language, Arabic: **Scholarships,** 254; **Internships,** 1254. *See also* General programs; Language and linguistics
Language, Armenian: **Scholarships,** 254; **Internships,** 1254. *See also* General programs; Language and linguistics
Language, Azeri: **Scholarships,** 254; **Internships,** 1254. *See also* General programs; Language and linguistics
Language, Dari: **Scholarships,** 254; **Internships,** 1254. *See also* General programs; Language and linguistics
Language, English: **Scholarships,** 8. *See also* English as a second language; General programs; Language and linguistics
Language, Farsi: **Scholarships,** 254; **Fellowships,** 871; **Internships,** 1254, 1334. *See also* General programs; Language and linguistics
Language, Hawaiian: **Scholarships,** 162, 259, 267, 346, 425, 454; **Fellowships,** 710, 771, 831, 848. *See also* General programs; Language and linguistics
Language, Hindi: **Scholarships,** 254; **Internships,** 1254. *See also* General programs; Language and linguistics
Language, Kazakh: **Scholarships,** 254; **Internships,** 1254. *See also* General programs; Language and linguistics
Language, Kyrgyz: **Scholarships,** 254; **Internships,** 1254. *See also* General programs; Language and linguistics
Language, Native American: **Scholarships,** 307, 367; **Fellowships,** 792; **Grants,** 1018, 1090. *See also* General programs; Language and linguistics
Language, Pashto: **Scholarships,** 254; **Internships,** 1254. *See also* General programs; Language and linguistics
Language, Russian: **Fellowships,** 871; **Internships,** 1334. *See also* General programs; Language and linguistics
Language, Tajik: **Scholarships,** 254; **Internships,** 1254. *See also* General programs; Language and linguistics
Language, Turkish: **Scholarships,** 254; **Internships,** 1254. *See also* General programs; Language and linguistics
Language, Turkmen: **Scholarships,** 254; **Internships,** 1254. *See also* General programs; Language and linguistics
Language, Urdu: **Scholarships,** 254; **Internships,** 1254. *See also* General programs; Language and linguistics
Language, Uzbek: **Scholarships,** 254; **Internships,** 1254. *See also* General programs; Language and linguistics

SUBJECT INDEX

Laser science: **Scholarships,** 533; **Fellowships,** 905; **Grants,** 1044. See also General programs; Physical sciences

Law enforcement. See Criminal justice

Law, general: **Scholarships,** 39, 119, 212, 260, 265, 299, 437, 526; **Fellowships,** 552, 571, 574, 582, 584, 590, 612, 631, 633, 644, 656, 661, 664, 666, 676, 678, 681, 686, 711, 716, 720, 727, 733, 735, 738, 744, 752, 759, 817, 828, 877, 897, 900, 904; **Grants,** 919, 995, 1021, 1024, 1093; **Awards,** 1154; **Internships,** 1182, 1190, 1196–1197, 1205, 1214, 1216, 1219, 1230–1231, 1233–1234, 1243, 1249, 1259–1260, 1263–1265, 1276, 1317–1318, 1327, 1340, 1346–1347, 1355. See also Criminal justice; General programs; Social sciences; names of legal specialties

Law librarianship. See Libraries and librarianship, law

Lawyers. See Law, general

Leadership: **Fellowships,** 680. See also General programs; Management

Legal studies and services. See Law, general

Lesbianism. See Homosexuality

Librarians. See Library and information services, general

Libraries and librarianship, academic: **Fellowships,** 575; **Grants,** 953, 1029, 1035, 1125, 1128. See also Education, higher; General programs; Library and information services, general

Libraries and librarianship, art: **Internships,** 1184. See also Libraries and librarianship, special; General programs

Libraries and librarianship, law: **Fellowships,** 676; **Grants,** 995. See also General programs

Libraries and librarianship, medical: **Fellowships,** 736, 753, 798. See also General programs

Libraries and librarianship, school: **Scholarships,** 300, 367; **Fellowships,** 712, 718, 737, 792. See also General programs; Library and information services, general

Libraries and librarianship, special: **Fellowships,** 866. See also General programs; Library and information services, general

Libraries and librarianship, technology: **Fellowships,** 741–742. See also General programs; Information science; Library and information services, general; Technology

Library and information services, general: **Scholarships,** 205; **Fellowships,** 546, 560, 611, 665, 671, 797; **Grants,** 1026; **Internships,** 1212. See also General programs; Information science; Social sciences; Names of specific types of librarianship

Life insurance. See Actuarial sciences

Life sciences. See Biological sciences

Linguistics. See Language and linguistics

Literature: **Scholarships,** 481; **Fellowships,** 830, 872; **Grants,** 919, 951, 989, 1056–1058, 1094, 1142. See also General programs; Humanities; specific types of literature

Literature, children's: **Awards,** 1158. See also General programs; Literature

Litigation: **Fellowships,** 591, 839; **Internships,** 1199, 1207. See also General programs; Law, general

Logistics: **Scholarships,** 310; **Internships,** 1179, 1204. See also General programs; Transportation

Lung disease: **Grants,** 1053, 1068; **Internships,** 1193, 1250. See also General programs; Health and health care; Medical sciences

Machine trades: **Scholarships,** 79. See also General programs

Magazines. See Journalism; Literature

Management: **Scholarships,** 22, 77, 127, 358, 404, 463, 473, 475, 490; **Fellowships,** 555, 597, 680, 705, 715, 777, 786–787, 819, 851, 869; **Grants,** 1012; **Internships,** 1227, 1251, 1253, 1343. See also General programs; Social sciences

Manufacturing engineering. See Engineering, manufacturing

Maps and mapmaking. See Cartography

Marine sciences: **Scholarships,** 463, 515; **Fellowships,** 851, 890; **Grants,** 926, 994, 1030, 1075, 1080, 1140; **Internships,** 1242, 1274, 1287, 1356. See also General programs; Sciences; names of specific marine sciences

Marketing: **Scholarships,** 18, 127, 193, 295, 310, 333, 341–342, 463, 473; **Fellowships,** 730, 851; **Internships,** 1253, 1261, 1343, 1352. See also Advertising; General programs; Public relations; Sales

Marriage. See Family relations

Mass communications. See Communications

Materials engineering. See Engineering, materials

Materials sciences: **Scholarships,** 21, 533; **Fellowships,** 705, 804, 847, 905; **Grants,** 973, 1044, 1059, 1077–1078, 1080; **Internships,** 1222, 1251, 1272, 1311, 1313. See also General programs; Physical sciences

Mathematics: **Scholarships,** 20, 47, 71, 109, 138, 179, 194, 205, 263, 321–322, 328, 344, 352, 355–356, 360, 364, 389, 463; **Fellowships,** 580–581, 610, 621, 671, 674, 705, 754, 783–784, 804, 806, 830, 851, 868, 871; **Grants,** 915, 925, 955, 960, 966, 978, 982, 989, 994, 999–1000, 1002, 1036, 1044–1045, 1047–1049, 1059–1060, 1076, 1080, 1092, 1094–1096, 1110, 1112, 1130–1132, 1140; **Awards,** 1166; **Internships,** 1178, 1188, 1195, 1204, 1217, 1226, 1229, 1231, 1241–1242, 1244–1245, 1248, 1251, 1272, 1277–1278, 1283, 1285, 1291, 1298–1300, 1308–1309, 1313–1316, 1321, 1325, 1328, 1331, 1334, 1337, 1350–1351, 1356. See also Computer sciences; General programs; Physical sciences; Statistics

Measurement. See Testing

Mechanical engineering. See Engineering, mechanical

Media. See Broadcasting; Communications; names of specific media

Media specialists. See Libraries and librarianship, school; Library and information services, general

Medical journalism. See Science reporting

Medical librarianship. See Libraries and librarianship, medical

Medical malpractice. See Personal injury law

Medical sciences: **Scholarships,** 32, 47, 71, 199, 226, 359, 435, 437, 526; **Fellowships,** 553, 565, 580, 666, 677, 699, 756, 765, 788, 799, 807, 875, 897; **Grants,** 910, 919, 926, 929, 931–932, 939, 948, 969, 972, 979, 1005, 1009, 1011, 1016, 1033–1034, 1038, 1080, 1105; **Awards,** 1153, 1173–1174; **Internships,** 1179, 1192, 1194–1195, 1200, 1236, 1287, 1290, 1335, 1339. See also General programs; Health and health care; Sciences; names of specific diseases; names of medical specialties

Medical technology: **Scholarships,** 32, 197, 199, 227, 327, 359; **Fellowships,** 565, 788. See also General programs; Medical sciences; Technology

Mental health: **Fellowships,** 563, 566, 882; **Grants,** 924, 947, 1031. See also General programs; Health and health care; Psychiatry

Mental health nurses and nursing. See Nurses and nursing, psychiatry and mental health

Merchandising. *See* Sales

Metal trades. *See* Machine trades

Metallurgical engineering. *See* Engineering, metallurgical

Meteorology: **Scholarships,** 31, 45, 153, 214, 252, 355, 404; **Fellowships,** 630, 682, 783, 819; **Grants,** 994, 1001, 1140; **Internships,** 1242, 1308–1309, 1331. *See also* Atmospheric sciences; General programs

Microbiology: **Fellowships,** 699; **Grants,** 1009. *See also* Biological sciences; General programs

Microcomputers. *See* Computer sciences

Microscopy. *See* Medical technology

Middle Eastern studies: **Fellowships,** 871; **Internships,** 1334. *See also* General programs; Humanities

Midwifery. *See* Nurses and nursing, midwifery

Military affairs: **Grants,** 956–957, 1044; **Internships,** 1204. *See also* General programs

Mineral law. *See* Environmental law

Mining engineering. *See* Engineering, mining

Mining industry: **Scholarships,** 405, 463; **Fellowships,** 851. *See also* General programs

Minority affairs: **Grants,** 1122, 1129; **Awards,** 1158, 1160, 1167. *See also* General programs; names of specific ethnic minority groups

Minority studies: **Grants,** 1052; **Internships,** 1213. *See also* General programs; names of specific ethnic minority studies

Missionary work. *See* Religion and religious activities

Molecular biology: **Fellowships,** 699; **Grants,** 915, 964, 1009. *See also* Biological sciences; General programs

Motel industry. *See* Hotel and motel industry

Museum studies: **Fellowships,** 782, 889; **Grants,** 1043, 1113; **Internships,** 1212, 1270, 1281–1282, 1297, 1306–1307, 1332. *See also* General programs; Library and information services, general

Music: **Scholarships,** 87; **Fellowships,** 577; **Internships,** 1273, 1275. *See also* Fine arts; General programs; Humanities; Performing arts

Music, church: **Scholarships,** 357, 480. *See also* General programs; Music; Performing arts; Religion and religious activities

Music, piano: **Scholarships,** 172. *See also* General programs; Music

Musicology: **Fellowships,** 701, 830; **Grants,** 919, 989, 1094. *See also* General programs; Music

Narcotics. *See* Drug use and abuse

National security. *See* Security, national

Native American affairs: **Grants,** 1061–1062, 1114; **Awards,** 1143, 1149, 1165; **Internships,** 1295, 1303, 1310, 1333. *See also* General programs; Minority affairs

Native American language. *See* Language, Native American

Native American law. *See* Indian law

Native American studies: **Scholarships,** 119, 297, 307, 343, 367, 374, 413; **Fellowships,** 732, 782, 792, 794, 823, 830, 889; **Grants,** 920–921, 946, 951–952, 977, 984, 991, 998, 1003, 1018, 1056, 1090, 1094, 1106, 1108, 1142; **Awards,** 1170; **Internships,** 1212, 1216, 1295, 1307. *See also* General programs; Minority studies

Natural history. *See* History, natural

Natural resources: **Scholarships,** 47, 58, 343, 353, 463, 491, 515; **Fellowships,** 580, 586, 776, 851, 890; **Internships,** 1205, 1216, 1295, 1302, 1330. *See also* General programs; names of specific resources

Natural resources law. *See* Environmental law

Natural sciences: **Scholarships,** 71, 263; **Fellowships,** 674; **Grants,** 993, 1091, 1112; **Internships,** 1241, 1311, 1356. *See also* General programs; Sciences; names of specific sciences

Naval science: **Grants,** 1064, 1081–1082. *See also* General programs

Nephrology. *See* Kidney disease

Neuroscience: **Fellowships,** 635, 699; **Grants,** 915, 938, 949, 964, 1009, 1070, 1073, 1091, 1098. *See also* General programs; Medical sciences

Neuroscience nurses and nursing. *See* Nurses and nursing, neuroscience

Newspapers. *See* Journalism

Nonprofit sector: **Internships,** 1354. *See also* General programs; Public administration

Nuclear engineering. *See* Engineering, nuclear

Nuclear science: **Scholarships,** 262, 389; **Fellowships,** 713; **Grants,** 967–968; **Internships,** 1315. *See also* General programs; Physical sciences

Nurses and nursing, general: **Scholarships,** 32–33, 65, 160, 199, 202, 227, 249, 255, 334, 359, 370; **Fellowships,** 565, 567, 668, 766, 788, 793; **Grants,** 910, 979, 1011, 1033–1034, 1074, 1134; **Internships,** 1179. *See also* General programs; Health and health care; Medical sciences; names of specific nursing specialties

Nurses and nursing, midwifery: **Scholarships,** 523; **Fellowships,** 895. *See also* General programs; Nurses and nursing, general

Nurses and nursing, neuroscience: **Grants,** 1098. *See also* General programs; Neuroscience; Nurses and nursing, general

Nurses and nursing, occupational health: **Scholarships,** 43–44; **Fellowships,** 579. *See also* General programs; Nurses and nursing, general

Nurses and nursing, oncology: **Grants,** 1051, 1066; **Internships,** 1335. *See also* Cancer; General programs; Nurses and nursing, general

Nurses and nursing, psychiatry and mental health: **Fellowships,** 566; **Grants,** 924, 947. *See also* General programs; Mental health; Nurses and nursing, general; Psychiatry

Nutrition: **Scholarships,** 227, 257, 359; **Fellowships,** 788; **Grants,** 913, 997, 1133; **Internships,** 1218, 1250. *See also* General programs; Medical sciences

Occupational health nurses and nursing. *See* Nurses and nursing, occupational health

Occupational safety: **Scholarships,** 43–44, 53, 463; **Fellowships,** 579, 851; **Internships,** 1215. *See also* General programs; Health and health care

Occupational therapy: **Scholarships,** 227. *See also* Counseling; General programs

Ocean engineering. *See* Engineering, ocean

Oceanography: **Scholarships,** 31, 45, 214, 252; **Fellowships,** 577, 682, 783; **Grants,** 926–927, 994, 1001, 1030, 1049, 1075, 1103, 1140; **Internships,** 1242, 1274, 1299, 1308, 1331. *See also* General programs; Marine sciences

Office skills. *See* Secretarial sciences

Oncology. *See* Cancer

Oncology nurses and nursing. *See* Nurses and nursing, oncology

Online journalism. *See* Journalism, online
Opera. *See* Music; Voice
Operations research: **Scholarships,** 193; **Fellowships,** 581; **Grants,** 973; **Internships,** 1188, 1222. *See also* General programs; Mathematics; Sciences
Optical engineering. *See* Engineering, optical
Optics: **Scholarships,** 533; **Fellowships,** 905; **Internships,** 1272. *See also* General programs; Physics
Optometry: **Grants,** 910. *See also* General programs; Medical sciences
Orthopedics: **Fellowships,** 709. *See also* General programs; Medical sciences
Osteopathy: **Fellowships,** 666, 807, 856–857, 898; **Grants,** 1105; **Internships,** 1200. *See also* General programs; Medical sciences

Painting: **Grants,** 977, 1106, 1117; **Awards,** 1168, 1170. *See also* Art; General programs
Pashto language. *See* Language, Pashto
Patent law. *See* Intellectual property law
Pathology: **Internships,** 1287, 1342. *See also* General programs; Medical sciences
Peace studies: **Fellowships,** 830; **Grants,** 1087, 1094, 1126. *See also* General programs; Political science and politics
Pediatrics: **Fellowships,** 765; **Grants,** 997; **Internships,** 1290. *See also* General programs; Medical sciences
Performing arts: **Scholarships,** 22, 183, 481; **Fellowships,** 555, 872; **Grants,** 919, 951, 977, 1056–1058, 1106, 1108, 1142. *See also* General programs; Humanities; names of specific performing arts
Personal injury law: **Fellowships,** 669. *See also* General programs; Law, general
Personnel administration: **Scholarships,** 53, 199, 321, 463, 524; **Fellowships,** 851, 896; **Internships,** 1179–1180, 1204, 1216–1217, 1256, 1278, 1352. *See also* General programs; Management
Petroleum engineering. *See* Engineering, petroleum
Pharmaceutical sciences: **Scholarships,** 227, 359; **Fellowships,** 596, 649, 699, 788; **Grants,** 910, 937, 1009, 1098, 1134; **Internships,** 1185. *See also* General programs; Medical sciences
Philanthropy: **Internships,** 1354. *See also* General programs
Philology. *See* Language and linguistics
Philosophy: **Fellowships,** 830; **Grants,** 919, 989, 1021, 1094. *See also* General programs; Humanities
Photogrammetry: **Scholarships,** 355; **Internships,** 1309. *See also* Cartography; General programs; Photography
Photography: **Scholarships,** 69; **Fellowships,** 589; **Grants,** 934, 1117; **Awards,** 1168. *See also* Fine arts; General programs
Photojournalism: **Scholarships,** 97, 147, 347; **Fellowships,** 772, 874; **Grants,** 1124; **Internships,** 1186, 1203, 1211. *See also* General programs; Journalism; Photography
Physical education. *See* Education, physical
Physical sciences: **Scholarships,** 47, 71, 179, 355; **Fellowships,** 580, 783, 868; **Grants,** 923, 925, 1046, 1049–1050, 1079–1080, 1107; **Internships,** 1204, 1226, 1299–1300, 1308–1309, 1311, 1321, 1337, 1356. *See also* General programs; Sciences; names of specific physical sciences

Physical therapy: **Scholarships,** 227, 335, 359; **Fellowships,** 764, 785, 788; **Grants,** 970. *See also* General programs; Health and health care; Rehabilitation
Physician assistant: **Scholarships,** 32; **Fellowships,** 565. *See also* General programs; Health and health care; Medical sciences
Physics: **Scholarships,** 30, 263, 328, 355, 360, 463, 533; **Fellowships,** 577, 657, 674, 705, 783, 804, 806, 830, 851, 905; **Grants,** 915, 930, 967–968, 973, 989, 994, 1018, 1044, 1047, 1049, 1059, 1094, 1103; **Awards,** 1152; **Internships,** 1194–1195, 1215, 1222, 1241–1242, 1251, 1272, 1277, 1285, 1287, 1291, 1293, 1299, 1308–1309, 1313, 1331. *See also* General programs; Mathematics; Physical sciences
Physiology: **Fellowships,** 577, 699, 827; **Grants,** 980, 992, 1009, 1047, 1098, 1137; **Internships,** 1228, 1287. *See also* General programs; Medical sciences
Piano. *See* Music, piano
Plastics engineering. *See* Engineering, plastics
Podiatry: **Scholarships,** 226; **Grants,** 910. *See also* General programs; Medical sciences
Poisons. *See* Toxicology
Police science. *See* Criminal justice
Political science and politics: **Scholarships,** 212, 332, 343, 439; **Fellowships,** 570, 678, 720, 762, 830; **Grants,** 919, 923, 927, 989, 1012, 1046, 1079, 1094, 1107; **Awards,** 1167; **Internships,** 1179, 1204, 1295, 1345. *See also* General programs; Public administration; Social sciences
Pollution: **Grants,** 975. *See also* Environmental sciences; General programs
Population studies: **Grants,** 936. *See also* General programs; Social sciences
Posters. *See* Graphic arts
Pottery: **Grants,** 1117; **Awards,** 1168, 1170. *See also* Arts and crafts; General programs
Poverty: **Grants,** 1013, 1101. *See also* General programs; Social services; Social welfare
Preschool education. *See* Education, preschool
Preservation, historical. *See* Historical preservation
Presidents, U.S. *See* History, American
Press. *See* Journalism
Print journalism. *See* Journalism
Printing industry: **Scholarships,** 302. *See also* General programs
Prints. *See* Art; Graphic arts
Products liability. *See* Personal injury law
Psychiatric nurses and nursing. *See* Nurses and nursing, psychiatry and mental health
Psychiatry: **Fellowships,** 566, 765, 767; **Grants,** 924, 947, 1040, 1089; **Internships,** 1257–1258, 1288–1290. *See also* Behavioral sciences; Counseling; General programs; Medical sciences; Psychology
Psychology: **Scholarships,** 227; **Fellowships,** 577, 775, 806, 830; **Grants,** 919, 927, 979, 989, 1033, 1066, 1087, 1091, 1094, 1098, 1122; **Internships,** 1178–1179, 1213, 1295, 1337. *See also* Behavioral sciences; Counseling; General programs; Psychiatry; Social sciences
Public administration: **Scholarships,** 212, 254, 332; **Fellowships,** 678, 762, 786, 832, 841, 903; **Grants,** 923, 973, 979, 1046, 1079, 1101, 1107, 1138; **Internships,** 1179, 1191, 1213, 1216, 1222, 1254, 1256, 1295, 1343, 1345. *See also* General programs; Management; Political science and politics; Social sciences
Public affairs. *See* Public administration

SUBJECT INDEX

Public health: **Scholarships,** 175, 205, 343; **Fellowships,** 568, 640–641, 650, 664, 671, 779, 903; **Grants,** 910, 942, 979, 1079, 1099, 1107, 1120, 1138, 1141; **Internships,** 1250, 1262, 1295, 1339. See also General programs; Health and health care

Public interest law: **Internships,** 1320, 1322. See also General programs; Law, general

Public policy. See Public administration

Public relations: **Scholarships,** 8, 295, 428; **Fellowships,** 730; **Internships,** 1208, 1212, 1216, 1261. See also General programs; Marketing

Public sector. See Public administration

Public service: **Scholarships,** 343; **Internships,** 1319. See also General programs; Public administration; Social services

Publicity. See Public relations

Race relations: **Awards,** 1144, 1157. See also Discrimination, racial; General programs; Minority affairs

Racial discrimination. See Discrimination, racial

Racism. See Discrimination, racial

Radio: **Scholarships,** 400; **Fellowships,** 813; **Internships,** 1208. See also Communications; General programs

Radiology: **Scholarships,** 449. See also General programs; Medical sciences

Ranching: **Scholarships,** 40, 127; **Fellowships,** 572. See also Agriculture and agricultural sciences; General programs

Reading: **Grants,** 1100. See also Education; General programs

Real estate: **Scholarships,** 37, 213; **Fellowships,** 679, 841; **Internships,** 1216. See also General programs

Real estate law: **Internships,** 1322. See also General programs; Law, general

Regional planning. See City and regional planning

Rehabilitation: **Scholarships,** 178; **Grants,** 1033, 1066. See also General programs; Health and health care; specific types of therapy

Religion and religious activities: **Scholarships,** 357, 438, 443, 480; **Fellowships,** 541, 646, 653, 708, 745, 789, 801, 830, 835–838, 883, 885–886; **Grants,** 919, 987, 989, 1094; **Internships,** 1261. See also General programs; Humanities; Philosophy

Religious reporting: **Scholarships,** 303. See also Broadcasting; General programs; Journalism; Religion and religious activities

Resource management: **Scholarships,** 343, 515; **Fellowships,** 890. See also Environmental sciences; General programs; Management

Restaurants. See Food service industry

Retailing. See Sales

Risk management: **Grants,** 960. See also Actuarial sciences; Business administration; Finance; General programs

Rural affairs: **Grants,** 1133. See also Agriculture and agricultural sciences; General programs; Sociology

Russian language. See Language, Russian

Safety studies: **Scholarships,** 18, 43–44, 199, 463; **Fellowships,** 579, 851; **Internships,** 1352. See also Engineering; General programs

Sales: **Scholarships,** 127; **Internships,** 1253, 1255, 1324. See also General programs; Marketing

School counselors. See Counselors and counseling, school

School libraries and librarians. See Libraries and librarianship, school

Schools. See Education

Science education. See Education, science and mathematics

Science, history. See History, science

Science reporting: **Internships,** 1176, 1195, 1262. See also Broadcasting; General programs; Journalism; Sciences

Sciences: **Scholarships,** 20, 39, 47, 109, 138, 194, 205, 210, 257, 322, 352, 389, 458, 499; **Fellowships,** 571, 580, 610, 612, 621, 671, 754, 881; **Grants,** 910, 919, 955, 966, 978, 982–983, 999–1000, 1002, 1048, 1064, 1076, 1081–1082, 1092, 1095, 1110, 1134; **Awards,** 1166; **Internships,** 1179, 1229, 1231, 1244–1245, 1248, 1283, 1314–1316, 1323, 1325, 1328, 1338, 1349–1350. See also General programs; names of specific sciences

Sculpture: **Grants,** 1117; **Awards,** 1168, 1170. See also Fine arts; General programs

Secretarial sciences: **Scholarships,** 517. See also General programs

Securities law: **Fellowships,** 669. See also General programs; Law, general

Security, national: **Fellowships,** 871; **Grants,** 959, 1080; **Internships,** 1334. See also General programs; Military affairs

Sex discrimination. See Discrimination, sex

Singing. See Voice

Social sciences: **Scholarships,** 179, 299, 357, 389, 480; **Fellowships,** 735, 783, 806; **Grants,** 914, 919, 960, 971, 978, 991, 993, 1024, 1039, 1049, 1087–1088, 1093, 1115; **Internships,** 1205, 1226, 1299, 1308, 1315, 1321, 1331, 1340. See also General programs; names of specific social sciences

Social services: **Scholarships,** 2, 130, 311, 357, 480, 526; **Fellowships,** 897. See also General programs; Public service; Social welfare; Social work

Social welfare: **Scholarships,** 250. See also General programs; Social services

Social work: **Scholarships,** 227, 311, 359; **Fellowships,** 612, 616, 788, 882; **Internships,** 1295. See also General programs; Social sciences

Sociology: **Fellowships,** 563, 578, 830; **Grants,** 919, 927, 989, 1012, 1021, 1087, 1094, 1139; **Awards,** 1160; **Internships,** 1295, 1345. See also General programs; Social sciences

Soils science: **Scholarships,** 353; **Fellowships,** 776; **Grants,** 1133; **Internships,** 1302. See also Agriculture and agricultural sciences; General programs; Horticulture

Songs. See Music

South Asian studies: **Fellowships,** 871; **Internships,** 1334. See also General programs; Humanities

Space law. See Aviation and space law

Space sciences: **Scholarships,** 263, 356, 360; **Fellowships,** 784; **Grants,** 1023, 1036, 1047–1050, 1060; **Internships,** 1181, 1183, 1189, 1201, 1206, 1266, 1292–1293, 1299, 1311, 1325, 1353. See also General programs; Physical sciences

Special education. See Education, special

Special librarianship. See Libraries and librarianship, special

Speech impairments: **Fellowships,** 564. See also General programs

Speech pathology: **Grants,** 1033, 1066. See also General programs; Medical sciences; Speech impairments; Speech therapy

Speech therapy: **Fellowships,** 564. See also General programs; Health and health care

SUBJECT INDEX

Sports. *See* Athletics
Sports medicine: **Fellowships,** 785. *See also* General programs; Medical sciences
Stage design. *See* Performing arts
Statistics: **Scholarships,** 321; **Fellowships,** 581; **Grants,** 973, 978, 1096, 1122; **Internships,** 1178, 1188, 1222, 1272, 1278, 1337, 1339. *See also* General programs; Mathematics
Storytelling: **Internships,** 1275. *See also* Folklore; General programs; Literature; Literature, children's
Structural engineering. *See* Engineering, structural
Substance abuse. *See* Alcohol use and abuse; Drug use and abuse
Surveying: **Internships,** 1216. *See also* General programs
Systems engineering. *See* Engineering, systems

Tajik language. *See* Language, Tajik
Taxation: **Scholarships,** 460; **Fellowships,** 849. *See also* Economics; General programs; Public administration
Teaching. *See* Education
Technology: **Scholarships,** 2, 47, 71, 328, 352, 356, 441; **Fellowships,** 540, 580, 784, 815; **Grants,** 919, 925, 960, 966, 973, 999, 1036, 1044, 1060, 1064, 1076, 1110; **Awards,** 1166; **Internships,** 1222, 1229, 1244, 1285, 1314, 1321, 1326, 1328. *See also* Computer sciences; General programs; Sciences
Teenagers. *See* Adolescents
Telecommunications: **Scholarships,** 74; **Fellowships,** 594, 871; **Internships,** 1334. *See also* Communications; General programs; Radio; Television
Television: **Scholarships,** 400; **Fellowships,** 813; **Grants,** 1061, 1083–1084; **Internships,** 1208. *See also* Communications; Filmmaking; General programs
Testing: **Grants,** 978, 1122; **Internships,** 1178. *See also* General programs; Psychology
Textiles: **Grants,** 1117; **Awards,** 1168, 1170. *See also* Arts and crafts; General programs
Theater. *See* Performing arts
Theology. *See* Religion and religious activities
Tourism: **Scholarships,** 230, 446, 524; **Fellowships,** 896. *See also* General programs
Toxic torts. *See* Personal injury law
Toxicology: **Scholarships,** 21, 67; **Internships,** 1287. *See also* General programs; Medical sciences
Trademarks law. *See* Intellectual property law
Transportation: **Scholarships,** 163, 310; **Fellowships,** 645; **Grants,** 960–961, 973, 1075; **Internships,** 1209, 1222, 1343. *See also* Automobile industry; Aviation; General programs; Space sciences
Transportation engineering. *See* Engineering, transportation
Transportation law: **Internships,** 1343. *See also* General programs; Law, general
Travel and tourism. *See* Tourism
Tribal law. *See* Indian law
Tropical studies: **Grants,** 1043, 1113; **Internships,** 1332. *See also* General programs
Tuberculosis. *See* Lung disease
Turfgrass science: **Scholarships,** 461; **Internships,** 1329. *See also* Biological sciences; General programs; Management
Turkish language. *See* Language, Turkish
Turkmen language. *See* Language, Turkmen
TV. *See* Television

Typing. *See* Secretarial sciences

Unions and unionization. *See* Industrial relations
Universities. *See* Education, higher; Libraries and librarianship, academic
Unrestricted programs. *See* General programs
Urban affairs: **Fellowships,** 786; **Grants,** 1010; **Internships,** 1262. *See also* City and regional planning; Community development; General programs
Urban development. *See* Community development
Urban planning. *See* City and regional planning
Urdu language. *See* Language, Urdu
Uzbek language. *See* Language, Uzbek

Veterans. *See* Military affairs
Veterinary sciences: **Scholarships,** 58; **Fellowships,** 586, 699; **Grants,** 910, 972, 1009, 1134. *See also* Animal science; General programs; Sciences
Veterinary technology: **Scholarships,** 58; **Fellowships,** 586. *See also* Animal science; General programs; Sciences
Video. *See* Filmmaking; Television
Violence: **Scholarships,** 477. *See also* General programs
Virology: **Fellowships,** 699; **Grants,** 1009. *See also* General programs; Medical sciences
Visual arts: **Scholarships,** 22, 481; **Fellowships,** 555, 592, 872; **Grants,** 951, 1056–1058, 1108, 1117, 1142; **Internships,** 1184, 1297. *See also* General programs; Humanities; names of specific visual arts
Voice: **Scholarships,** 172. *See also* General programs; Music; Performing arts

Water resources: **Scholarships,** 199; **Fellowships,** 695; **Grants,** 923, 975, 1046, 1079, 1107. *See also* Environmental sciences; General programs; Natural resources
Weaving: **Grants,** 1117; **Awards,** 1168. *See also* Arts and crafts; General programs
Web design. *See* Internet design and development
Web journalism. *See* Journalism, online
Welding: **Scholarships,** 79. *See also* General programs
Welfare. *See* Social services; Social welfare
Wildlife management: **Scholarships,** 353, 463; **Fellowships,** 776, 851; **Grants,** 1136; **Internships,** 1216, 1302, 1330. *See also* Environmental sciences; General programs
Women's studies and programs: **Fellowships,** 830; **Grants,** 989, 1094; **Awards,** 1174; **Internships,** 1310. *See also* Discrimination, sex; General programs
World literature. *See* Literature

Youth. *See* Adolescents; Child development

Zoning, planning, and land use. *See* Real estate law
Zoology: **Internships,** 1216. *See also* General programs; Sciences; names of specific zoological subfields

Calendar Index

Since most funding programs have specific deadline dates, some may have already closed by the time you begin to look for money. You can use the Calendar Index to identify which programs are still open. To do that, go to the type of program (scholarships, fellowships, etc.) that interests you, think about when you'll be able to complete your application forms, go to the appropriate months, jot down the entry numbers listed there, and use those numbers to find the program descriptions in the directory. Keep in mind that the numbers cited here refer to program entry numbers, not to page numbers in the book. Note: not all sponsoring organizations supplied deadline information to us, so not all programs are listed in this index.

Scholarships:
January: 32, 38, 65, 70, 90–91, 129, 149, 163, 180, 186–188, 195, 200–201, 205, 225, 244–245, 262, 328, 344, 372, 389, 392, 410, 416, 434, 441, 449, 464–465, 491, 508, 519, 522, 535–536
February: 9, 19, 22, 28, 30–31, 38, 41, 60–62, 64, 67, 75, 79, 121, 127, 138–139, 141–142, 159, 164, 169, 176, 214, 224, 247, 252, 261, 277, 296, 304, 318, 320, 332, 355, 379, 384–385, 390, 434, 439, 453, 455, 461–463, 474, 483, 510, 539
March: 20–21, 61, 68, 76, 80, 85–86, 90–91, 99–100, 110, 118, 124, 143, 157, 170, 174, 192, 197, 206, 213, 221, 235, 237–238, 240–241, 243, 254, 258, 272, 283, 287, 289–290, 295, 297, 303, 309, 319, 322, 330, 343, 347, 350, 353, 361, 384–385, 387, 397, 400, 425–426, 430, 438, 440, 445, 469, 490, 498, 509, 517, 523, 529
April: 2, 6, 16, 24–26, 34, 37, 54–55, 66, 69, 71, 82, 95, 101, 117, 120, 128–129, 150–151, 153–154, 157–158, 162, 165, 172–173, 185, 198, 215, 226–227, 231–233, 246, 253, 259, 267–268, 271, 277, 281, 292, 300, 308, 315, 317, 322, 324, 345–346, 350, 360, 362, 364–368, 370, 382–383, 386, 391, 393, 395, 405–406, 428–429, 431–433, 442, 454, 464–466, 468, 473, 476, 478, 483, 490, 500, 503, 506, 508, 524–525, 527, 535–536, 538
May: 1, 28, 33, 38, 41, 48, 52, 57, 74, 77–78, 86, 104, 106–109, 111, 113–114, 116, 124, 139, 141–142, 144–146, 148, 174, 178, 181, 184, 186–188, 193–194, 203–204, 207, 210, 212, 223, 230, 235, 239, 265, 269, 276, 279–280, 286–287, 289–290, 297, 299, 302, 304–305, 307, 311–312, 323, 338, 341–342, 351–352, 363, 371, 375–378, 380, 401, 411–414, 420, 432, 443, 448, 451, 458–460, 466, 471–472, 475, 478–479, 481–482, 484–485, 488, 498, 504, 511, 515, 518, 526, 528, 531–532
June: 3, 7, 10–12, 15, 18, 35, 39–40, 45–47, 49–51, 53–54, 56, 58–59, 73, 76, 83–84, 87, 89–93, 110, 115, 119, 126, 129–131, 136, 155–156, 170, 173–175, 177, 182, 199, 202, 208, 222, 229, 235–238, 243, 255, 257, 263, 272–273, 283, 294, 301, 313–315, 325, 329, 331, 334, 357, 359, 365–368, 372–373, 382–383, 391, 395–396, 399, 401–402, 407–408, 421, 424, 430, 436–437, 444, 450, 464, 469–470, 477, 480, 489, 492–494, 496–498, 508, 516, 535–536, 538–539
July: 17, 27, 38, 41, 94, 113–114, 139, 141–142, 149, 171, 186–188, 196, 211, 250–251, 277, 292–293, 306, 339, 371, 381, 398, 404, 409, 433, 435, 447, 464–465, 514
August: 28, 90–91, 112, 160, 180, 216, 304, 337, 375, 420, 495, 501, 521
September: 22, 76, 99–100, 110, 117, 124, 138, 157, 174, 185, 264, 270, 272, 283, 316, 322, 349–350, 379, 384–385, 393, 429, 468, 479, 490, 498, 522, 533
October: 23, 38, 54, 59, 72, 81, 86, 97, 122, 129, 243–245, 276, 310, 323, 327, 339, 358, 372, 424, 430–432, 434, 436, 453, 456, 464–465, 471, 508, 527, 535–536, 538
November: 10–12, 18, 28, 35, 43–44, 76, 108, 110, 114, 131, 139, 141–142, 152, 155, 157, 161, 170, 174, 179, 191, 209, 235, 237–239, 265, 272, 279–280, 283, 286, 294, 298–299, 304, 335, 354, 365–368, 376, 382–383, 386, 401–402, 413, 420, 437, 448, 450, 452, 464, 466, 469, 478, 481, 483, 498, 500, 505
December: 8, 29, 42, 51, 88, 98, 112–113, 144–147, 160, 166, 173, 183, 186–188, 217, 235, 277, 292, 315, 321, 336, 371, 375, 391, 394–396, 409, 420–421, 433, 514, 521
Any time: 5, 36, 38, 63, 102–103, 105, 140, 242, 266, 278, 288, 291, 417, 457, 467, 520, 530, 534, 537

Fellowships:
January: 546, 563, 565, 574, 578, 581, 590, 601–602, 615, 631, 635, 651, 656, 661–663, 665–666, 671, 692, 695, 699, 701, 704, 712–713, 727, 746, 751, 783, 817, 827–828, 841, 853, 855, 877, 886–887, 892, 894, 906
February: 541, 547, 554–555, 560, 562, 566, 573, 587, 595, 621, 623, 645, 658, 669, 682, 691, 706, 738–739, 741–742, 744, 756, 762, 786, 797, 800–802, 807, 845, 850–852, 858, 867, 873–874, 882, 908
March: 544, 548, 598, 600–602, 613, 616, 638, 648, 670, 676, 679, 689, 696–698, 702, 709, 728, 730, 732, 754, 760, 765, 767, 772, 774, 776, 785, 794, 802, 813, 831, 833, 835, 840, 842, 856–857, 860, 868, 879, 889, 895, 898, 901
April: 542–543, 553, 557, 561, 577, 589, 612, 614–615, 624, 627–628, 630, 632, 634, 638–639, 654, 660, 667, 677,

510 CALENDAR INDEX

683–685, 693–694, 708, 710, 718, 720, 722, 737, 743, 745, 749, 754, 770–771, 774, 790–793, 798, 803, 808, 810, 834, 839, 841, 848, 853, 855, 859, 873, 875, 883, 885, 887, 899, 906–907
May: 540, 559, 567, 573, 583, 594, 597, 600, 606–611, 623, 626, 640–642, 646, 652, 659, 662, 678, 690, 696, 700, 707, 716, 719, 723–726, 728, 731–732, 735, 739–740, 747, 755, 757, 773, 779–780, 796, 805, 814, 821–823, 826, 843, 846, 849, 863–865, 869–870, 872, 876, 884, 888, 890, 896–897, 904
June: 545, 549–551, 564, 569, 571–572, 580, 582, 585–586, 593, 599, 601–603, 615, 617, 625, 637, 648–650, 655, 664, 668, 675, 696–698, 703, 715, 729, 748–749, 761, 766, 788–789, 792, 795, 799, 810–811, 814, 816, 820, 833, 836, 840, 844, 853–854, 860, 862, 887, 891, 903, 906–908
July: 558, 573, 604, 623, 644, 657, 662, 812, 815, 818–819, 834, 837, 853, 855
August: 575, 601–602, 633, 651, 653, 739, 759, 768, 796, 798, 826, 878, 880, 893
September: 555, 592, 596, 612, 621, 636, 638, 660, 681, 714, 721, 736, 750, 754, 774, 800, 802, 808, 859, 866, 870, 889, 894, 905
October: 552, 556, 570, 584, 600, 615, 625, 646, 672–674, 686, 704–705, 723, 734, 752, 755, 763, 775, 787, 806, 833, 840, 853, 855, 863–864, 887, 899–900, 906–907
November: 542, 549–550, 569, 579, 609, 617, 623, 629, 638, 643, 648, 696–698, 700, 703, 716, 724–726, 729, 733, 735, 739, 753, 764, 767, 778, 781, 792, 803–804, 814, 816, 823, 826, 830, 843–844, 853, 860, 871–873
December: 576, 585, 633, 662, 696, 749, 773, 777, 796, 798, 810–811, 826, 834, 837, 893
Any time: 588, 605, 622, 680, 717, 767, 902

Grants:
January: 911, 921, 928, 931, 940, 943, 945, 949, 954, 956, 958, 960, 963–964, 968–969, 974, 980, 984, 988, 992, 1003, 1008–1009, 1015, 1017, 1019, 1022, 1024, 1032, 1037, 1043, 1045, 1047, 1049, 1062, 1067, 1075, 1080, 1087, 1093, 1101–1103, 1110, 1113–1115, 1117, 1122, 1125, 1135, 1137
February: 910, 914, 918, 923–924, 932, 935–936, 938, 941–942, 946–947, 952, 959, 981, 987, 991, 994–996, 1001, 1004, 1011, 1030, 1033–1034, 1046, 1051, 1053, 1055, 1065–1066, 1069–1070, 1073–1074, 1079, 1084–1085, 1090, 1107, 1111, 1121, 1124, 1128, 1133, 1140
March: 913, 916, 956, 979, 982, 1002, 1005, 1018, 1022, 1038, 1040, 1092, 1108, 1116, 1134, 1136
April: 922, 934, 951, 957, 961, 971, 985–986, 1031, 1054, 1056, 1063, 1099, 1104, 1106, 1142
May: 939, 946, 949–950, 952, 975, 1045, 1057–1058, 1067, 1072, 1123, 1130–1132, 1139
June: 910, 926, 936, 938, 956, 1004, 1006, 1011, 1013, 1033–1034, 1044, 1051, 1053, 1055, 1065–1066, 1068–1070, 1073–1074, 1077–1078, 1085, 1111, 1138
July: 911, 983, 1061, 1083
August: 933, 946, 952, 954, 970–971, 976, 986, 1020, 1022, 1028, 1031, 1054, 1097–1099, 1105, 1120
September: 915, 919, 937, 949, 956, 990, 1014, 1043, 1045, 1050, 1062, 1067, 1076, 1113–1114, 1126, 1133, 1136
October: 910, 914, 930, 936, 938, 944, 946, 952, 955, 962, 997, 1004, 1011–1012, 1021, 1027, 1033–1034, 1051, 1053, 1055, 1065–1066, 1069–1070, 1073–1074, 1085, 1089, 1100, 1111, 1118, 1127

November: 909, 917, 927, 953, 965, 967, 977, 989, 993, 1022, 1025, 1036, 1039–1042, 1059, 1071, 1082, 1086, 1094, 1096
December: 912, 948, 971–972, 978, 986, 998, 1010, 1016, 1029, 1031, 1035, 1054, 1077–1078, 1088, 1099, 1141
Any time: 920, 925, 999–1000, 1007, 1023, 1026, 1040, 1081, 1091, 1095, 1112

Awards:
January: 1143, 1145, 1167–1168
February: 1167, 1174
March: 1151, 1164, 1171
April: 1160, 1170
May: 1162–1163
June: 1152, 1165
July: 1153, 1173
September: 1157, 1166, 1172
October: 1158
December: 1144, 1146, 1169
Any time: 1148, 1154, 1161

Internships:
January: 1182, 1186, 1188, 1192, 1196–1197, 1200, 1208, 1214, 1223–1224, 1228–1230, 1233–1234, 1249–1250, 1256, 1260, 1262, 1265, 1270, 1277, 1279–1282, 1284–1285, 1287, 1291, 1295, 1298–1299, 1308, 1314–1315, 1317–1318, 1321, 1326–1328, 1331–1333, 1336, 1347
February: 1176, 1178–1180, 1185, 1193, 1212, 1215–1216, 1218, 1227, 1231–1232, 1236, 1242, 1244, 1255, 1257–1258, 1271, 1274–1275, 1283, 1286, 1288–1289, 1297, 1306–1307, 1309, 1316, 1319, 1323, 1325, 1329, 1335, 1337, 1339–1341, 1343–1345, 1356
March: 1184, 1202, 1205, 1213, 1235, 1237, 1253–1254, 1261, 1266, 1269, 1290, 1302, 1311, 1330, 1348, 1350, 1354
April: 1195, 1209, 1225, 1246, 1294, 1301, 1303, 1338
May: 1238, 1275, 1351–1352, 1355
June: 1183, 1190, 1205, 1212, 1216, 1273
July: 1210, 1259, 1286, 1307, 1354
August: 1219, 1275, 1346
September: 1205, 1220, 1243, 1256, 1263–1264, 1269, 1332–1333
October: 1179, 1198, 1203–1204, 1239–1241, 1251, 1267, 1276, 1307, 1322
November: 1177, 1205, 1212, 1216, 1226, 1268, 1272, 1275, 1305, 1307, 1313, 1334, 1352
December: 1187, 1191, 1207, 1211, 1219, 1221, 1247, 1262, 1278, 1286, 1296, 1354
Any time: 1194, 1204, 1217, 1231, 1245, 1248, 1356